CW00543007

IMAGE WARS

IMAGE WARS
PROMOTING KINGS AND COMMONWEALTHS IN ENGLAND, 1603–1660

KEVIN SHARPE

YALE UNIVERSITY PRESS
NEW HAVEN AND LONDON

For information about this and other Yale University Press publications, please contact:
U.S. Office: sales.press@yale.edu   www.yalebooks.com
Europe Office:sales@yaleup.co.uk   www.yaleup.co.uk

Set in Minion by IDSUK (DataConnection) Ltd
Printed in Great Britain by TJ International Ltd, Padstow, Cornwall

Library of Congress Cataloging-in-Publication Data

Sharpe, Kevin (Kevin M.)
  Image wars: promoting kings and commonwealths in England, 1603–1660/Kevin Sharpe.
    p. cm.
  ISBN 978-0-300-16200-4 (cl: alk. paper)
  I. Great Britain–History–Stuarts, 1603–1714. 2. Great Britain—Politics and government—1603–1714. 3. Political culture—Great Britain—History—17th century. 4. Politics and culture—Great Britain—History—17th century. 5. Monarchy—Great Britain—Public opinion—History—17th century. 6. Great Britain—Kings and rulers—Public opinion. 7. Great Britain—Civilization—17th century. I. Title.
  DA375.S54 2010
  942.062—dc22
                                                                                    2009040150

A catalogue record for this book is available from the British Library.

10 9 8 7 6 5 4 3 2 1

Published with the support of The Paul Mellon Centre for Studies in British Art.

For Family and Friends

CONTENTS

ILLUSTRATIONS

PREFACE AND ACKNOWLEDGEMENTS

It has often been – rightly – remarked that, because early modern English governments had no standing army or paid civil service, effective rule depended on securing co-operation and compliance. That is to say – and it is at the core of my study – that authority was culturally constructed and communicated, that politics was inseparable from culture. In *Selling the Tudor Monarchy: Authority and Image in Sixteenth-Century England*, I have shown how it was through a new emphasis on writing, depicting and performing their rule that the Tudors not only survived the challenges thrown up by religious divisions and opposition but managed, in the main, to get their way and even to enhance their power. By the end of the sixteenth century, the monarchy was more than ever at the centre of the national imagination and Queen Elizabeth, for all the discontents, was widely regarded as a sacred ruler.

Tudor authority was constructed and enhanced by the representation of rule in words, portraits and artefacts, and in rituals and performances. Though the new dynasty that succeeded faced many problems, not least (as we shall see) the very success of Elizabeth in personalizing her authority, the opening of England, after peace with Spain, to greater continental influences presented myriad opportunities. Travel to Catholic countries introduced Englishmen, the English court and the monarchy to the great continental artists, such as Titian, who had brilliantly fashioned the images – and hence the authority – of the greatest dynasties of early modern Europe. In the seventeenth century, as we have learned, the baroque arts in portraiture and the classicism long fashionable on the continent, and with them the stage sets, architecture and ceremonies of the European royal courts, at last came to England; and in canvas and stone, in stage designs and *mises-en-scène*, transformed the representation of English kingship.

And yet the story of seventeenth-century England is not – at least apparently – one of the greatest triumph of the arts of representation. James I's classical Banqueting House designed by Inigo Jones after Palladio, the architect's masques, and Van Dyck's illusionist portraits of Charles I gave way to violent rebellion and bloody civil war which ruptured the domestic peace more or less secured since Henry VII's succession in 1485. Indeed, we might think that the civil war and revolution make the seventeenth century a singularly inappropriate period for a study that wishes to emphasize the power of cultural forms as well as the culture of authority. During the 1640s and 1650s, English regimes for the first time were supported by large armies; major events were determined by the sword; and during Cromwell's Protectorate even local government was overseen by Major-Generals whose questionable constitutional authority was supported by battalions. Though a battle of words had preceded conflict, after 1642, it seems, and Hobbes famously argued, that raw force was the principal means of effecting outcomes.

This book returns me to a period and set of problems with which I have been engaged for a scholarly lifetime: the seventeenth century and the story, causes and consequences of the civil wars. But this study approaches that period and those problems from a very different perspective. Since the 1970s, historians have been divided over whether the civil war was the result of long-term structural causes or shorter-term contingencies; whether pre-civil-war England was a political culture characterized by conflict or consensus; and whether the civil war had profound and enduring consequences for the nature of English society and the state.

Many of the disputes between historians have been centred on the types of sources scholars have privileged. In turn, disagreements have arisen because of the different perspectives of those who prefer to relate what happened and those who are as interested in what contemporaries perceived (or sometimes feared) was happening. The historical emphasis on perceptions of the monarchs and governments of early modern England is relatively new. Surprisingly, for all the valuable works that have been published on aspects of the subject, even more neglected has been systematic study of the images they projected of themselves: in words, in portraits, and in rituals and processions.[1] As I have explained in an earlier volume, not least in a methodological introduction which sets out my approaches to this subject, such images or representations of rule cannot be seen (as they once were) as official, if by that is meant devised by and under the control of the sovereign. Many councillors, panegyrists and impresarios at court, in the capital and in provincial cities at times represented the king or queen, advanced their own agendas and proffered counsel as well as praise to their monarchs. Moreover, in the early modern period, as today, governments had to project images which subjects found appealing in order to secure support for their authority and policies. Representations of monarchy, that is, were inseparable from perceptions of monarchy: the image of the ruler was forged in and out of dialogue with subjects and, in an increasingly contestatory political culture, such representations were fashioned amid debate, animadversion and opposition.[2]

There have been thousands of history books on the English (or now British) civil war – or wars – or revolution. And literary scholars especially have studied extensively the pamphlet wars between Royalists and Parliamentarians and latterly the newspapers and newsbooks which were so carefully collected and preserved for posterity by George Thomason. But there has been no systematic address of the cultural forms of authority for the period 1640–60; no study of the impact of violent division and war on traditional modes of representing authority; and curiously little attention paid to the new forms of representation to which the civil war gave rise: battle reports, military rewards and medals, portraits of generals and military processions and parades.

This study therefore examines the attempts by a series of regimes in seventeenth-century England to represent themselves in the most favourable light: to win support for particular courses and to secure and enhance their authority. It studies the image of rule in words, visuals and performances and briefly looks at other and counter-representations as a means of evaluating the measure of success rulers had in projecting their authority. As will be seen, though I argue that the crisis of the mid-seventeenth century was related to effective and ineffective modes of representing rule, the nature and chronology of the relationship between politics and image were complicated and at times surprising. Not least, I will suggest that the moment of regicide served to effect a re-sacralization of kingship which robbed the military and political victors of the civil war of a long-term stability or triumph. My story is one of a struggle to appropriate and control the traditional scripts and signs of authority, of the efforts to forge new representations which might validate new polities and constitutions, and of contest between old and new in the modes and methods of representing governments to their subjects or citizens. A concentration on images and representations throws a different light not only on the monarchs and rulers of seventeenth-century England but on its conflicts and struggles, on the course of its civil wars and revolutions, and on the failure of republic and return to monarchy.

Indeed, it will be the argument of this study that, far from rendering them secondary, the civil war made the arts of representation and the cultural foundation of legitimacy more important than ever. Parliament, after all, won the military conflict but was in 1647 in grave danger of losing the peace to a king who brilliantly fashioned a new image and skilfully performed a part to secure widespread public support. And because the army leaders who ousted two parliaments struggled to secure a legitimacy which they never attained, their rule, like that of so many modern military regimes, ultimately collapsed because it had no foundation other than force and fear. Civil war and revolution in England underlined the centrality of a legitimacy founded on texts, images and performances that conveyed authority. Civil war and revolution also transformed some of those texts of representation and so, in the end, the nature of monarchical government too. But since the legacy of revolution was a passionate insistence on 'no standing armies', post-revolutionary governments, like pre-civil-war monarchies, had also to construct and sustain their authority by arts of securing compliance.

If the arts of representation were then central across the period, we must ask both why and how certain rulers or regimes succeeded in establishing legitimacy and why and how others failed. Was it because of the skill or ineptitude of individual rulers or their advisers and impresarios? Or did circumstances and new problems make securing support nearly impossible? Why did James I fail to form an affective bond with his people? Why did Charles I, who later showed he could brilliantly perform on the stage of majesty, see his authority collapse in the face of challenges from first his Scottish, then his English, subjects? How did the Rump succeed in forming a government after a thousand years of monarchy but fail to win support of the people sufficient to sustain it? And why did even the charismatic Cromwell not succeed in attaining the settlement he so desperately sought? The answers to such questions have led to hundreds of studies of economy, society, church and politics; and I would not pretend that the images of these rulers and regimes provide the only answer. But image and representation were central to the legitimacy they all sought and so played a large part in their success or failure. It is because image has been a relatively neglected part, because the discourses, signs and performances of successive seventeenth-century sovereigns, regimes and protectors have not been fully studied and compared that I undertook this volume.

Image Wars: Promoting Kings and Commonwealths in England, 1603–1660 studies the arts of representing rule in a century not only increasingly divided but one in which, ever more, the business of government ceased to be *arcana imperii.* Though princes may, while publicizing themselves, still have wished to police and control subjects' discussions and speculations on their policies and personal lives, increasingly during this period the exercise of rule was conducted and the life of the ruler was lived in the full glare of publicity: reported in newspapers, news pamphlets and gossip, and publicized in ballads, engravings and woodcuts. In a new media world, princes and protectors found it ever more vital to make their words and images the dominant ones, and found it ever harder to do so. The art of politics was becoming what we would call the art of spin: of representing government in the best light in a culture in which many were increasingly invested in undermining its image as well as authority.

There were many revolutions in seventeenth-century England and many scholars have studied them. My purpose is to turn attention to the changes in the modes and media of representing rule and of the relationship of such representations to perceptions of rule: to politics and political change and crisis, to new forms of governing, and new notions of subjectivity and citizenship.

I have acknowledged the help of several individuals and institutions in the preface to my *Selling the Tudor Monarchy*, the first of three books which I am writing on representations of early modern rule. Here I would like to reiterate my thanks to the Leverhulme Trust, for the whole of this volume was researched and written while I held a Leverhulme Major Fellowship and could not have been completed without it. I would also like to thank Queen Mary, University of London and my colleagues in English and History who provided the stimulating environment in which it was written. As I return here, albeit from a different perspective, to the seventeenth century, I would also like to acknowledge all the stimulus I have derived from those many scholars of this century with whom I have discussed, exchanged references, or quarrelled. Though, since my own early forays into the period in the 1970s, debates have remained heated, I have learned from, and been led to think again by, many of those with whom I most disagreed and I hope that they will discern how my thinking has changed – even if not in the ways they would have wished. Though to single out names when what follows emerged from (often silent) debates with the works of most scholars of seventeenth-century England may seem invidious, I must in particular thank John Adamson, Julia Alexander, Alastair Bellany, George Bernard, Tom Corns, Richard Cust, Tim Harris, Karen Hearn, Ann Hughes, Ronald Hutton, Mark Kishlansky, Mark Knights, Laura Knoppers, Peter Lake, Annabel Patterson, Steve Pincus, Joad Raymond, Mark Stoyle, Greg Walker and Steven Zwicker whom I have subjected to innumerable questions and discussions.

As with *Selling the Tudor Monarchy*, for the work of turning a manuscript into a typescript I thank Liz Cameron. For transforming a typescript into a publishable book, I must thank both the readers for the press, especially Malcolm Smuts who, as well as writing a 30-page report of detailed comment and criticism, generously broke anonymity to conduct a discussion with me which greatly improved my book. I wish to express my thanks to Robert Baldock who, as always, showed unfailing support and encouragement, to Rachael Lonsdale who helpfully secured the illustrations and permissions and to Beth Humphries, Meg Davies and especially Candida Brazil who so carefully oversaw the passage to publication. My agent Peter Robinson was, as always, supportive. I am most grateful also to the Paul Mellon Centre for Studies in British Art for a grant that assisted with the costs of illustrations and permissions.

This volume is dedicated to family and friends who sometimes indulged me in discussing it but more often and more valuably distracted me over many a walk, meal, glass and evening of good cheer, good company and warm friendship.

INTRODUCTION

Henry VIII had encountered an age-old problem, but one which had destroyed a number of kings for over a century: that of siring an adult male heir who would secure an undisputed succession. The course he embarked upon to solve it led to a revolution in church and state which he had clearly not originally desired and which, if anything, presented him and the monarchy with greater challenges and dangers still: religious division, the threat of invasion from abroad, and rebellions at home. Henry accomplished his first priority: his son, albeit only nine, succeeded without challenge and outlived his protectorate to assume power and become a third Tudor king. And Henry responded ingeniously as well as ruthlessly to the dangers which he had made for himself. He assumed supremacy over spiritual as well as secular affairs; he fostered and appropriated for the monarchy and Tudor dynasty an emerging national sentiment; and he relentlessly publicized himself as the embodiment of the nation and as the head of an English Commonwealth. Whatever the many reservations and discontents, or the extent of criticism and opposition, Henry enacted his will, secured his family, and established himself as a charismatic, even popular, ruler.

For all the quite proper historical emphasis on his tyrannical courses, Henry also assiduously cultivated the people and the new media (of print – sermons and plays – and portraiture) for reaching out to them; and he forged new affective languages and strategies in order to create what his PR supremo Richard Morison called 'lovely bonds' with them.[1]

Henry's heirs, as well as sharing his concern to secure dynastic succession, had different beliefs and agendas. But in many respects Henry had created a new style of monarchy which (to some degree necessarily) became a model for his successors. He had, that is, made his representation an essential aspect of his authority and himself the focus of the nation's and people's attention. Though the leading historian of Tudor England, Geoffrey Elton, described sixteenth-century government as becoming more bureaucratic, in reality Henry and his heirs made the person and personality of the monarch more important than ever and affective relations with subjects more important than administrative procedures in establishing royal authority. Indeed, the cult of personality which he had initiated was in some ways to complicate, if not override, the Tudor dynasty and brand he had been so desperate to establish.[2]

Henry's will secured, even against dynastic challenges, the succession of all three of his children. But his first two successors used the Tudor brand to advance beliefs and courses very different from their father's. It is not just that Edward was a convinced Protestant and Mary a devout Catholic; it was that, in attaching the Tudor brand to a confession, or party, they to some extent undermined the identity of dynasty and monarchy with the whole nation, an association which had been vital to Henry's survival, let alone success. It would be to exaggerate to argue that there was a mid-Tudor crisis in the representation of monarchy, not least because for Edward and Mary their personal belief was inseparable from their authority. But, in representation as in religious policy, under Henry's immediate successors Tudor monarchy became confessional monarchy and so contributed to the widening divisions in the realm that Henry had laboured to prevent.

Elizabeth I, through temperament and policy, sought to reconnect the Tudor brand with the whole nation and with a church which was, and which might be accepted as, synonymous with the nation: the church of (as opposed to the old Catholic church in) England. Her efforts, as I have shown, were often compromised or undermined by the many agents who fashioned representations and images of the queen from strong evangelical sympathies and political values quite different to hers. But, though she was only one actor in the making of her image, the queen interestingly, in reverting to what she (not without good reason) believed to be her father's programme, also revived his strategies and styles of representation. Far more than her brother or sister, indeed even more than Henry, Elizabeth used languages and images to represent the sanctity of her majesty and deployed a discourse of love and affect and a common touch to bond with her subjects. Most of all, far more than her predecessors, Elizabeth made her personal (female) body the synecdoche of the public body, the body of the commonweal and nation. While publicizing herself, Elizabeth, unlike her immediate predecessors, subordinated her private beliefs and desires (whatever – and it is significant that we remain uncertain – they were) in order to identify herself with the whole, the public.

Yet, while in so many ways she revived the representational tropes of her father, in one vital respect she departed from them. For where Henry had acted primarily to secure his dynasty and had then been led to forge a new style of kingship in the wake of the divorce and break from Rome, Elizabeth not only oversaw the end of the Tudor dynasty but made a virtue of her heirlessness, her virginity. More than Henry, Elizabeth publicized not her dynasty but herself: we speak of a cult of Elizabeth not of Elizabeth Tudor. More than her father, she made her image the centre of her authority; more than any ruler before her, and many after, she made monarchy inseparable from her person and personal brand. After nearly a half-century of Elizabethan rule, England in 1603 was Elizabeth.

Historians have, especially recently, recognized the difficult legacy that the Tudor century bequeathed to the Stuarts.[3] Economic problems and social dislocations, the rise of a market economy, the poverty of the crown and the mounting importance of parliaments, most importantly permanent religious divisions, made the exercise of royal authority ever more difficult. But what has been less often noticed is that the very success of the Tudors and particularly of Elizabeth in representing themselves, in establishing their dynastic and personal authority, was to present very real problems to any successor. To state the obvious, any successor faced the difficulty of acceding to a monarchy which had been so relentlessly branded Tudor and then Elizabethan: a difficulty which anyone involved in modern campaigns of commercial – or political – re-branding will not be inclined to understate.

But there were other problematic legacies of Tudor representation. For one, Henry and his heirs had forged and fostered a new political culture which was unique to England. Given that the successor to a childless Elizabeth was, even before James VI of Scotland was accepted as likely to accede, probably to be a foreigner, this posed problems of adapting to an English style of rule which had become as important as royal policies and programmes. For the Tudors, and especially Elizabeth, had mystified and sacralized monarchy in ways which no other Protestant realm emulated, or perhaps sought to emulate. Like the Church of England which retained so much of Catholic ritual within a loosely Protestant doctrine, the monarchy bequeathed by the Tudors was a monarchy of devotional rites and ceremonies, of veneration and worship, far removed from the experiences of the Stuart who inherited the throne. Monarchical rituals and devotions, like Catholic worship, had also increasingly emphasized the body of the sovereign as both sacred and public and made the representation of the royal body an essential art of rule. Holbein's, Hilliard's and other artists' depictions of Henry and his successors had been vital to the establishment and enhancement of Tudor authority; but the display of the royal body in processions, ceremonies, daily rituals of the court and public progresses had been important too. To rule effectively, any successor to the Tudors would need to fulfil expectations that had been fostered about the royal body and the representation of the royal body as a site of sacred kingship. It was an expectation which the first Stuart was ill-equipped to satisfy.

Related to the representation of the royal body, another legacy of Tudor representation was an emphasis on style; and on feelings, desires and anxieties, as well as arguments and explanations, in exercising rule. Henry and his heirs had ubiquitously written, declaimed, argued and justified; but the bond they had forged with subjects had been strengthened by emotional and psychological ties as well as rational connections and considerations. Henry and Elizabeth, in particular, as memory to this day testifies, became the objects of the nation's affection, despite discontent with aspects of their government. As a consequence, they made emotional ties and affective relationships as important as powerful intellectual arguments for the foundations for monarchy. Again, this was a cultural legacy, if not peculiar to England, then certainly not typical of other, perhaps especially Protestant, polities; and it was to be a problematic inheritance for a successor whose intellect and argument had been the principal weapons in his struggle for authority.

Not least because, like the church, it combined elements of a humanist and Protestant emphasis on words, exegesis and argument with an (appropriated) Catholic devotion to visuals and symbols, rituals and ceremonies, the peculiar style of Tudor monarchy, in this respect different to its continental counterparts, made it a difficult crown for anyone not English to inherit.[4] To make that point, of course, is to return, from a different perspective, to a familiar observation: that the style of monarchy as it had emerged by the end of Elizabeth's reign was inseparable from a Church of England which resisted a clear identity with Geneva or with Rome: both remained a hybrid of liturgical and devotional forms which were essential to them both.

Fully aware that everywhere in Europe religious division had resulted in civil wars, Henry VIII endeavoured to play down differences and to use languages and symbols of unity. If the English Reformation was something of a compromise, even a fudge, that was not least because anything else would have compromised royal authority. Henry, whether he was aware of it or not (and it is difficult to believe that he was not), indulged a fiction that his people were united in love and obedience to their sovereign; and it was a fiction maintained even by Edward and Mary for their more partisan supremacies. The representation of Tudor monarchy, that is, was always something different, as all representations are, from the harsh realities of division and contest, and became more so as religious differences sharpened over the following decades, with acrimonious polemical battles for hearts and minds in cheap print.

Indeed, the medium which Henry had used, in several forms, to present his own case was becoming, as government proclamations testified, a major threat to monarchy. Under Edward, and particularly during Mary's reign, opponents of royal religious policy and persecution, often denied access to the pulpit, used the printing press not only to argue for a different church but also to denounce royal policy and supremacy. Distributed in the streets, sometimes posted where proclamations were displayed and read, and discussed in alehouses, attacks on the church and crown became commonplace, for all the efforts to stop them. In a London in which the population was expanding rapidly in numbers and in literacy, there emerged a civic and citizen consciousness, which we might identify as a public sphere. As well as the religious divisions that resulted from Henry's divorce, his strategies of representation had themselves encouraged others to enter a debate about religion and state and to publicize their views through rumour and print.[5]

Not only, then, Henry VIII's policies and actions, but his very style of king-ship, his assiduous self-representation and self-publicization, had fostered developments which meant that his successors encountered new problems in exercising authority, principally challenges from confessional opponents who learned to use the instruments of publicity to counter official scripts and to question the sanctity of sovereignty itself. Just as Elizabeth I not only revived but in some ways brought to fulfilment courses on which her father had embarked, so her reign, as well as witnessing the elevation of sovereignty to its most sacred heights, was also one in which a number of developments signif-icantly compromised royal authority. First, to an extent even greater than her father, Elizabeth made sustaining a fiction of unity a higher priority than tackling division. While such a comprehensible course may have saved her from bitter disputes, it exposed the Church of England to threats from outside and – more dangerously in the long term – from within. By at times not making a stand, Elizabeth bequeathed to her successor a church and state which embraced occasionally conforming Catholics who hoped for a change in the future and puritans, most of whom wanted godly reformation and many of whom favoured a different, Presbyterian church government – that is to say a different state. Fictions of unity and harmony may have spared England a civil war in the sixteenth century but, arguably, they contributed to one in the seventeenth.

Compromise, fudge and studied inaction were the hallmarks of Elizabeth's reign. Indeed, it was (and is) a reign remembered and noted more for the image of the monarchy and the person of the queen than for policies or actions. To a far greater extent than her father, Elizabeth privileged her image over actions and events, as the unchanging facial mask of her portraits from the 1580s defied the facts of time, loss of fertility, and decay. As well as the Deborah, the Judith and the Virgin, Elizabeth figured herself as the mother of all her subjects and as the body of the commonweal and nation. She, more than the Tudor dynasty, came to personify England, as I have suggested.[6] It was her image which was distributed on thousands of engravings and woodcuts, souvenir plates and playing cards and she who, by the time of her death, was more recognized (in both senses) than her father as the embodiment of the nation.

This intense personalization of monarchy had important consequences. As I have argued, in so relentlessly publicizing herself and in making herself an object of desire and the focus of the popular imagination, Elizabeth became the people's princess, in part owned by the subjects who purchased her image or saw, or read accounts of, her progresses. In focusing attention on herself and in prioritizing image and performance over policy, she also risked making the success or failure of monarchy a matter of personality, image and performance. While during the 1590s her future successor was arguing for the divinity of *monarchy*, in England it was *Elizabeth* who was heralded as a goddess. Indeed, at the same time as she was being worshipped as a person, theoretical challenges to monarchy and arguments for different polities, even quasi-republics, were being published and publicized. Among her own councillors, we have learned, schemes were in place for a constitutional Commonwealth government in the event of her assassination or death. The force of Elizabeth's presence and representation veiled a whole number of developments (the growing assertiveness of parliaments, civic and citizen self-consciousness and popular political participation, as well as religious controversies) which were challenging monarchical sovereignty.

To use one of her favourite metaphors, Elizabeth held the audience enraptured (more or less) to the end. But by privileging her image, by personalizing, and indeed gendering, royal authority, and by theatricalizing regality, she also made the part of a monarch harder for any successor to perform. Let alone the successor whose whole upbringing, education and inclination were so contrary to hers, for all his sympathy with many of her courses.

The image of Tudor monarchy and of Elizabeth presented the Stuarts with more problems than benefits. As a new dynasty they had, like Henry VII, to create a new brand (and brand loyalty) in a culture everywhere marked with the signs of the Tudors. As a king from a distinctly Calvinist Scotland, which had experienced religious war, James VI had to work out a style of royal supremacy which alienated neither Catholic nor puritan subjects. Whilst as a published author and polemicist, he was well qualified to, and confident of his ability to, argue his case, the first Stuart would not have experienced in Edinburgh the flurry of print or the public sphere of news and gossip that London had become.[7] Most importantly, the political culture of Scotland could hardly have been more different from that of late Elizabethan England. In the rough and tumble of Scottish aristocratic politics, the monarch was not an object of veneration and worship but more a first among equals. The Presbyterian kirk recognized no royal supremacy in matters spiritual, and any readiness to believe in the sanctity of kings was conditional on godly rule – as defined by them. James's Scottish upbringing instructed him in the need to intervene in debate to make his case and argue his authority.

James VI was quickly attracted to an England in which not only was the monarchy wealthy by comparison with his native country but the church preached that the sovereign was sacred, and the monarch was reverenced by nobles and subjects. With his forensic intelligence, James quickly familiarized himself with the English constitution and the institutions and personnel of government. But, because it was literally foreign to him, he did not grasp the importance of the image and style of English monarchy as it had developed over the previous seventy years. And he never really did. As well as his upbringing and experience, James's personality was fundamentally different to that of his predecessor (and perhaps predecessors). Where Elizabeth preferred to prevaricate and fudge, James favoured proclamation, action and intervention. Where in many speeches she preferred to conceal disagreements with a

rhetoric of harmony, James preferred to cut to the chase: to be direct, unequiv-
ocal, even confrontational in order to tackle problems. Where she subordinated action to image, James entered England as a new broom, eager to act,
and paid less attention to his appearance. Where Henry and Elizabeth had so
successfully embodied the growing sense of nation, James sought to dissolve
England into a larger union of Britain. Perhaps most damaging, if we can judge
by contemporary report, where the Tudors had sanctified the body of the
sovereign and mystified regality, James was plain, indecorous and (even
allowing for the exaggerations of disgruntled critics) often uncouth.

James VI and I, then, had either to adapt to an English style and royal image
quite other than his experience or inclination, or to create and establish a new
Stuart style. The story of this book is the story of how the first two Stuarts, in
very different ways, attempted to present and represent themselves, in order to
sustain and enhance their authority in increasingly difficult circumstances. As
we shall see, it is not the story often told. It is far too simple to argue that James
paid no attention to his image; or that Charles I developed a royal image
without any regard to his people. It was in quite different ways, however, that
James I and Charles I endeavoured to establish their dynasty, connect with
their people, sustain at least a sense of unity, and tackle the mounting problems
presented by opponents – in and out of parliaments – who seized on the
opportunities presented by new media (corantos, the first newspapers and
libels) to criticize royal policies and question royal prerogatives. James, true to
his Scottish past, entered the polemical fray willingly. Not least as a consequence of seeing his father bloodied, Charles preferred a return to more
removed mystery, only to find critics seizing the polemical initiative.
Subsequently, against his inclinations, Charles too was forced into a discursive
struggle for support.

Contemporaries later talked of the paper bullets that preceded lead shot in
the political struggles which led to civil war. And the civil war itself was a
consequence of the fact that neither Charles I nor his opponents decisively
won the battle for hearts and minds, the contest for public support for their
desired forms of church and state. Ironically, the civil war in many respects
proved no more decisive in resolving the conflict over representation. Even
after he was defeated on the battlefield, the king exercised considerable
authority. And Charles cleverly deployed words, images and performances to
underpin that authority, indeed to make himself, his person, the centre of any
settlement which could claim legitimacy. It may seem perverse to argue that,
in 1647, Charles had returned the monarchy to a position of strength and
authority. But there is no better testament to that than the perception and
consequent action of the army radicals who first seized, then hastened the king
to trial and execution because they knew that they were losing the argument
and the contest for representation and support. Violence, as it turned out,
served them no better. At his trial and on the scaffold, Charles uttered his

finest lines and delivered his most brilliant performances – and in doing so fashioned his own image as martyr for the people and re-endowed monarchy with the sanctity the Tudors had claimed for it.

The year 1649 is a pivotal point in my long study of representations of rule and images of power in early modern England. For, on the one hand, a king was publicly tried and executed as a king – the ultimate and final act, we might think, of the desacralization of authority. On the other hand, 1649 re-sacralized kingship and the person of Charles Stuart. Even in the act of decapitation, regicide once again reunited (as James I had failed to do) the body of the man, Charles, with the public body of the realm: reunited, that is, monarchy, the king and people in an affective bond.

From 1649 to 1660 no republican regime was able to forge a new bond with subjects or to invest naked power with the legitimacy of the sacred or public support. Some radical thinkers even abandoned the attempt, favouring a different, more rational and utilitarian language of politics over fictions of unity and discourses of love. Events were to show, however, that, whatever the harsh new realities of violent division, the discourses and symbols of unity and affect forged by successive Tudor monarchs retained a powerful hold on the national psyche and state. Even, that is, after civil war and revolution, the contest for representation and support still involved a struggle to claim and appropriate, as well as contest, the vocabularies and signs of authority that had underpinned monarchy and successions of kings. The contest over image was central to the origins, course and consequences of the English civil war.

PART I

A New Dynasty and a New Style
Representations of James I

CHAPTER 1

WRITING DIVINE RIGHT

I

After a century of rule, the Tudor dynasty had effected – if not (as scholars now agree) a revolution in government – a revolution in the style and image of monarchy. Indeed, they had made the representation of their rule as vital as institutions, policies and practices to the stability and success of regal government. Some concern with image, of course, long pre-dated the Tudors. But, as I have argued, the Reformation necessitated a greater personalization of monarchy in England, an emphasis on the sovereign as the embodiment of the nation, and on the image of the ruler as the unifying symbol of the commonweal.[1] From Henry VIII on, each of the Tudors sought, with varying success, to represent both their families and themselves not as mere feudal overlords, but as the focus of the nation, the object and site of popular adoration as well as esteem. With a realm increasingly divided over religion, and critics and opponents as ready as themselves to deploy the new media of print and pamphlet to make a case, each ruler faced a contest for representation that became inseparable from the political struggles of the century. Even Elizabeth, as I have shown, was worsted in several such encounters.[2] Yet, by the time of the death of the Virgin Queen, not only the monarchy but the person of the sovereign dominated the public imagination as well as the political constitution and culture of England. Whatever the criticisms or counter-presentations of her, Elizabeth had made herself a national icon, a quasi-mystical object of veneration. Rather than succumbing to the weaknesses of her sex, Elizabeth had skilfully deployed the ambiguities of gender in order to represent herself as both remote and available, sacred yet familiar, as a site both of worship and desire. After her half-century on the throne, the English regal style was enshrined as the Tudor style – the queen endlessly invoked her father – and, still more, as the Elizabethan style: a style of government as much as of self-representation.

As revisionist historians have begun to point out, the powerful image of Elizabeth glossed a series of fundamental weaknesses and problems of rule which she had signally failed to address – chief among them the succession. But, as well as these failings, it is the image of Elizabeth itself that we need to consider as a problematic legacy of her reign and a perhaps impossible challenge for any successor – let alone a new dynasty. In the first place, even more than her father, Elizabeth had personalized regal authority. For all the vital roles and importance of her ministers and councillors, Elizabethan government was seen to be government by Elizabeth. Not only would any successor not be Elizabeth – and so need to refashion the scripts of royal representation; he would, on account of the queen's childlessness, also lose the advantage of being a Tudor, the family with both an established image and the longest tenure of the throne since the Plantagenets. For any male successor, the problem of image was compounded by half a century of female governance during which discourses of love, games of flirtation and gestures of amorous intimacy had been central to the exercise of rule. Moreover, the very success of Elizabeth's self-representation had given rise to problems which she encountered and that threatened any successor. That is, by making herself popular Elizabeth had made herself, and the monarchy, the site of attention and discussion. And by rendering herself a precious icon, she made herself an object that, as the market for images and souvenirs of the queen evidences, the (consuming) public desired to own. Elizabeth brilliantly made sacred rule popular; but in doing so she furthered the demystification of monarchy, and, with hindsight we might even say, the democratization of government. The representation of royal power and personality on the Elizabethan stage dramatized the queen's achievement and her ambiguous legacy: a public fascination with, and voyeuristic interrogation of, the character of rulers and the art of government. On the stage of state as well as theatre, such dramatization of rule made Elizabeth's performance, in every sense, a hard act to follow.[3]

If the very success of Elizabeth's representation and image bequeathed enormous problems to her successor, it may be that it was her failings which offered opportunities to a new ruler. Scholars have identified the last decade of her reign as one of difficulties and disappointments: economic problems, mounting religious tensions, bitter faction and rivalry at court, threats from abroad, and revolt at home.[4] Though the magic of Elizabeth still cast its spell in her old age, some perception of the need to tackle pressing issues, and discontent at the government's failure to do so was mounting. The biggest issue, of course, was the succession itself. Though the clamour for the queen to marry and produce an heir had faded with the onset of menopause, and though ministers were working behind the scenes to secure a peaceful succession, the fear of a foreign claimant supported by invasion or of baronial civil war for the crown stalked the nation.[5] Any successor, then, who ascended the throne in peace was assured of a gratitude that stemmed from the nation's relief that England would not, as Francis Bacon had feared, be submerged in chaos and conflict. Beyond that, a readiness to recognize and address religious and political problems and what was perceived as mounting corruption presented Elizabeth's successor with the possibility of fashioning his own image and script.[6]

If we pose the question of what England wanted on the death of the last Tudor, in 1603, it is tempting to answer that it sought in a new ruler both more of the same and something quite different and better. The poet Samuel Daniel neatly summed up that ambiguous expectation in a panegyric to the new ruler:

> He hath a mightie burthen to sustaine
> Whose fortune doth succeed a gracious Prince
> Or where men's expectations intertaine
> Hopes of more good, and more beneficence.[7]

A ruler who, as Robert Fletcher, a former servant to Elizabeth, hoped, would 'look into the ruins of our church and commonweal' was like to be of another style than the Gloriana whose dazzle had left such problems in the shadows.[8] Moreover, the action and reforms that many sought were likely to expose difficulties and divisions which, for much of the reign, had been veiled, if not hidden, by a rhetoric of harmony. As another panegyrist advised the new sovereign:

> Leave off thy hope to please
> both Court and countrie too;
> Or else thou tak'st in hand a worke,
> that Christ could never doe.[9]

Corruption, after all, was an extreme manifestation of the fact that men were governed by their own interest; and, for all the discourse of unity and common good, interests pitted subjects against each other, and rendered government not as the application of natural law, but as the art of politics – as *realpolitik*. If a rational, sceptical view of politics had co-existed, as it had, with the mystical cult of Elizabeth during the later years of the queen's reign, that was not least a consequence of a national loyalty to the Tudor dynasty and to Elizabeth herself.[10] For any successor, the squaring of the circle, and the fulfilment of a multiplicity of contrary desires and expectations, was going to be 'a mighty burden' indeed.

Perhaps for twenty years, since the end of Elizabeth's courtship with the duc d'Anjou, the identity of the likely successor to the queen had been known. James VI of Scotland was, through the line of Margaret Tudor, the great-great-nephew of Henry VIII. Born in the midst of religious war in Scotland and France in 1566, James became king aged one, when his mother Mary, Catholic widow of Francis II of France, was ousted by the Protestant nobility and kirk. From the time of attaining his majority and actual, as opposed to nominal, rule in Scotland, James set his eyes on succession to the throne of England. To secure Elizabeth's support, he abstained from public protest at the execution of his mother, the focus and source of plots against the queen, and in 1586 was rewarded with a treaty which provided him with an English pension and, richer booty, Elizabeth's promise to accept him as her successor.[11] Though the agreement was qualified and never publicized, it was not only James who placed hope in its promise. With other claimants foreign, Catholic (through Philip II) Habsburg, or among the English all but certain to revive the Wars of the Roses, a cabal of leading councillors supported Scottish succession.[12] Whether or not there is truth in the story that on her deathbed Elizabeth voicelessly signalled her approval of James VI, Cecil had set in motion the mechanisms to bring him to the throne.[13]

As he set off from his native kingdom southwards, without any sign of a challenge, James symbolized what was to be a principal motif of his representation – peace – and received the universal gratitude of a people whose relief that England was spared destructive war was now audibly expressed. 'O welcome Prince of Peace and quietnesse,' sang the author of an epitaph on Elizabeth, whose words were echoed widely.[14] 'Without thee,' Samuel Daniel put it more frankly, 'we had beene now undone.'[15] The Scottish king had saved England from bloodshed. As the sense grew of real dangers that loomed on the death of the queen, not least that James himself 'mightst have falne to some seditious hand', the eventuality that 'never any prince entered more quietly in this land' made our 'now sovereign lord' appear as remarkable as he was welcome.[16] God had given England peace and a new monarch – and it was marvellous in the people's eyes.

Even before he arrived in his new kingdom there were other things that his subjects knew about James and other things and values which he represented. For some he symbolized rightful and national succession. Lately, historians have properly drawn attention to James's Scottishness.[17] But in 1603, perhaps not least because the alternatives had been foreign, it was the British, even the English, descent of the new monarch that panegyrists highlighted. The author of *England's Welcome* celebrated James's 'title' and 'true descent'; Fletcher gave thanks for a new prince 'of our English tribe'.[18] And while George Owen Harry plotted the king's descent from Noah, via Brutus and Cadwallader,[19] the author of a new song emphasized James's Henrician lineage, and several authors depicted the king as Elizabeth's appointed 'cousin and next heir', her 'deare succeeding brother'.[20] Though some writers mentioned his Spanish and French descent or the 'double right/from double title' (to England and Scotland) James brought, it was as rightful king of England and descendant of Henry VII that he was first celebrated.[21]

The second thing, however, that James's new subjects knew of him was that he was king of Scotland and had ruled there, albeit at first in name only, for thirty-six years. In 1603, it was not only the Scottish author of *Northern Poems* who enthused about a new king who might conjoin nations already united by geography, law and faith. John Savile, chronicler of the king's entertainment at Theobalds, heralded the reuniting of a British kingdom divided since the time of Brutus, while a volume of welcoming panegyrics published by Oxford

University praised three kingdoms made one in the succession of James.[22] In Scotland, as Arthur Williamson has shown, news of the Stuart succession to the British throne raised in some circles apocalyptic visions of a Protestant empire which might crush the Beast: as one northern poem put it, 'the three crowne King shall give on Pope his doome'.[23] Though in southern panegyrics, as well as in James's own self-presentation, such apocalyptic strains were muted, several saw in the king's uniting of his two kingdoms the fulfilment of a destiny. For example, in a speech delivered to James at the Tower of London, William Hubbock described the Lord as having 'made Israel and Iuda one in you, no more two kingdoms . . . nor two regions, nor two religions'.[24] And where some 'panegyrics of congratulation' presented James as a second Constantine, or Lucius (the first Christian emperor and king of Britain), a genealogy figured James as 'uniting and knitting together all the scattered members of the British monarchy . . . as one sent of God to fulfil his divine, predestinate will revealed to Cadwallader'.[25] What such language and representations also underline is that James succeeded as a known Protestant king whose reign in Scotland had coincided with the defeat of the Catholic party. Though later his plans for a full union of England and Scotland were to spark the first bitter dispute of his reign, in 1603 the succession of a Scottish king to the English throne only appeared to promise greater security and strength to a new island empire spanning Culloden to Cornwall.[26]

What was also obvious about England's new ruler, and more welcome than historians obsessed with Elizabeth have allowed, was his sex.[27] James literally embodied the return to masculine rule after fifty years of what John Knox had called 'monstrous' female regiment in England. For all the adulation Elizabeth had received, the sheer benefit of being a male ruler, a king, could hardly be exaggerated. 'I must confess that in Elizae's prime,' wrote John Fenton, 'We never did enjoy a happier time.' 'But now,' he continued, '(O blessed now) we have a King.'[28] At the very name of a king, the verse continued, 'we feare no threatning of our forraine foes'; 'the name of a king', the author of *England's Caesar* concurred, 'make forward Insurrection . . . die'.[29] Adult male rule – the author of *England's Welcome* drew attention to James's age pitched perfectly between childhood and later life – represented strength and security.[30] 'O happy English,' a naturalized French author was to reflect from the experience of the civil war engendered by minority and female regency in his native country, 'that have no more women and children for your king but a king full of strength.'[31] The oration for James at the Tower flattered him in the same terms: since the king's succession, men saw no alteration from the glorious days of Queen Elizabeth, except 'the superior degree of your sex above her doth promise both greater and more notable attempts', that is actions.[32]

Nor was James's sex his only improvement on his predecessor. Where, as the author of a welcome verse put it, summing the regrets of a nation, Elizabeth was never a wife, in James God had given England 'a husband and a king'.[33]

James had married Anne of Denmark in 1589 after a romantic journey through storm-tossed seas to bring his bride to Scotland. Whatever was known of his inclination to male favourites in Scotland, the king (who had written amorous verses to his queen) stood as a happily married man and as head of a household.[34] In an early modern England in which the household was a common analogue of the state, James's status as a husband added strength to his rule and enabled the deployment of a powerful language which Elizabeth had only been able to use metaphorically. Whatever the old queen's rhetorical claims, James *was* a husband – to a wife and to his nation. More fruitful still, he was the father of what was already a family, and, still more important, of male heirs.

James VI was the first king to succeed to the English throne with a male heir since Henry IV and the first with two sons in over a hundred years. Given the memory of failed lines and disputed successions, and more recently Henry VIII's struggle to beget a male heir and Mary's barrenness, the importance of the single fact of James's fatherhood cannot be overstated. That England had instantly a king with two heirs promised an end to a century-old problem for the monarchy and security for the realm. As Fenton wrote in 1603:

> Now may we proudly boast we neede not feare,
> We have a King, and this same King an heire.[35]

By the very fact of his paternity, some even dared to say that James eclipsed Elizabeth. 'Our Princesse barren from the world is gone', wrote the author of one of the *Northern Poems*, in harsh terms seldom used of Elizabeth in her life-time and added:

> A happier change we could have never none,
> Then King with issue store by lawfull wife.[36]

Both the quasi-military metaphor ('store') and the emphasis on 'lawfull' are telling. Even the great Elizabeth was of disputed legitimacy as the product of Henry's marriage to Anne Boleyn, the legality of which Catholics denied. And that marriage, then Elizabeth's own failure to marry and produce an heir, had exposed England to foreign, Catholic invasion. No wonder that in a welcoming speech to James in 1603, the Recorder of Southampton, a port on the vulnerable south coast, praised 'the most noble progeny of your royal children', or that the author of *The Soldier's Wish* mentioned how his fellows in arms 'rejoyce to see each princely bud'.[37] Descended from Henry's line, and with two sons and a daughter, James promised the security of indefinite Stuart rule.

As a man, king, legitimate heir and successor, husband and father, James, from the moment of his proclamation, represented a nation's hopes of stable, good government. Indeed, though his family relations were not to remain the best advertisement of his rule, and the marriages of his children were to excite controversy and opposition, James's positions as husband and father were to remain central to his representation and for long to the nation's perception of the king.

In 1603, James's new subjects knew something more about the new king than the facts about his wife and children: they knew of him through the medium that James as king of Scotland had preferred in representing himself: his writings. More than any other ruler of Scotland – or England, for that matter – James VI and I regarded his words, in letters, speech, treatise or verse, as the expression and mainstay of his authority. The author of two treatises on kingship and government, the translator of some of the Psalms, a poet of amorous and epic verse and compiler of a manual of rules for Scottish poetry, James was by 1603 an established author with a European reputation who won the respect of renowned poets such as Guillaume de Salluste Du Bartas. Though many of his works were published in Scots rather than English, James (as we shall see) authorized an English edition of his book of instruction for his son, the *Basilikon Doron*. And it is clear that as his succession became likely, many of his future subjects of England had been acquainting themselves with his writings as the testimonies of his beliefs and as indicators of his style of rule. Accordingly, at the Tower of London, the oration to James referred to 'such worthy golden books out of the circle of sacred sciences', that the king had penned.[38] The mayor of Middlesex, very much in the spirit of James's own beliefs, told his sovereign that the English were fed with hopes, not only by the king's actions but 'by some books now fresh in every man's hands being (to use your majesty's own words) the vive ideas or representations of the mind'.[39] The author of a verse panegyric, who was to be a prominent poet in the new reign, not only made the same point about writing as representation, but, going to the heart of James's philosophy of rule, identified the connection between royal texts and regal authority:

> We know thee more, then by reporte we had,
> We have an everlasting evidence
> Under thy hand, that now we need not dread.[40]

'Thy all commanding sov'raintie', he flattered James, 'stands subject to thy Pen . . .' and the power of the pen might change kingdoms without a sword having been drawn.[41]

II

James VI's writings – poems, biblical translations and exegeses as much as treatises on kingship – were inseparable from the political culture and struggles of his Scottish kingdom and the larger European religious conflict, in which not least through the 'auld alliance' and marriage with the crown of France, Scotland was embroiled. As Catholics and the Lords of the Congregation battled to control kirk and crown, James wrote to assert his own interpretations of Scripture and to appropriate biblical texts as support for his royal authority.[42] Against papal claims to supremacy, against Presbyterian claims for the power of the kirk over the king, and against the arguments of his tutor, George Buchanan, for limited monarchy accountable to the people, James posited a theory of the divine right of kings and of the ruler as head of the church as well as the state.[43] James's writings before 1603 direct us to the very different monarchies and political cultures of the two kingdoms. Where in England the break from Rome led by the king had resulted in a 'monarchical church' with the monarch as Supreme Head, the radical course of the Reformation in Scotland had emphasized the supremacy of the presbytery and people.[44] And where in late Tudor England the ruler was increasingly sacralized, in Scotland kingship was the subject of unfettered rational interrogation and even republican critique. Where Elizabeth had presented herself as an icon, a goddess elevated above political faction and fray, James necessarily pitched into the political contests – and not least with his pen. In Scotland, that is, monarchy was less a site of mystery; rather it was itself part of the discursive rhetorical contests which produced those other sharp exchanges known as flytyngs.

Much has been made of the difference between James's two kingdoms, yet one of the most important has received little attention.[45] James came to his English throne with a belief that he needed not simply to *be* sacred authority but to *argue for it*, and with a conviction that his learning and skill with words would be the means to win the argument and so establish his authority. Such convictions, as we shall see, led to a very different style of rule to that of Elizabeth Tudor, and to some neglect of other media which Henry VIII and his successors had so artfully deployed. In England, as he had in Scotland, James chose to represent himself to his people through his words. In 1616 he was to gather his prose writings into a large folio volume, the first by an English monarch, and he evidently planned to follow it with a similar collection of his poetry. But two decades before then, James clearly believed that the translation of some of his works from Scottish into English might effect his own translation to the English throne. The *Basilikon Doron or his Majesties Instructions To His Dearest Sonne Henry the Prince* was written in Scots at a time when James believed himself to be dying, in 1598. It was originally published in an anglicized version, in 1599, in just seven printed copies, distributed to trusted servants.[46] In 1603, James licensed the re-publication of the book, purportedly to correct false impressions of his text that had spread abroad; however, in this English version, with new references and notes, and a new preface to the reader, James set out to advertise and represent himself to his new subjects.[47]

The new edition, though sent to press by October 1602, while Elizabeth was still alive, appeared about the time of her death in March 1603. On the 28th of that month, six stationers entered the book in the Stationers Company register and no fewer than eight editions have survived, some with royal arms, one with an engraving of James, Anne and Henry based on the 1603 Edinburgh text authorized by James and printed by the royal printer Robert Waldegrave.[48] The editions testify both to obvious interest in the new ruler and to a recognition that, in the Edinburgh edition, James had intended to speak to his English as much as his Scottish subjects.

The marginal notes to the new edition announced the shift from the private to public and from intimate to broad readership. James provided extensive biblical and many classical references to advertise his learning and to display the authorities of Scripture and antiquity that lay behind his text. In addition to sources, marginalia also highlighted sections of books or drew attention to particular points: 'conscience the conserver of religion', 'A king's life must be exemplare' or against an injunction: peace 'a special good rule in government'.[49] A sense that some of these flags were specifically directed at English readers is supported by James's highlighting a 'laudable custom of England', 'a good policy of England' at various points.[50] Most importantly, in the 1603 edition, inserted after the epistle to Henry, James added an address 'To the Reader', which was intended to direct the interpretation of the text – and of the king – by his new subjects.[51] James explained the private origins of his book, its circulation in false copies and its misinterpretation. In issuing a new, revised, authorized edition, he also took the opportunity to clarify misinterpretations that might especially alienate the English: the view, for instance, that he had made a 'vindictive resolution against England' for the murder of his mother, and the claim that his criticisms of 'puritans' raised questions about the sincerity of his Protestant faith.[52] Addressing the subtle denominational differences of the English rather than the Scottish ecclesiastical scene, the king explained that, while he roundly condemned any sect, whether called puritans or no, which disobeyed princes, he was not glued to those ceremonies or ornaments that alienated some godly men from the church. Appealing to all parties at a time when his succession still depended upon it, James protested, 'I do equally love and honour the learned and grave men of either of these opinions'.[53] Though, then, protocol demanded that with 'a lawful queen there presently reigning', James could, at least directly, 'speak nothing of the state of England', the revised *Basilikon Doron* was written for 'the greatest part of the people of this whole isle' who had 'been very curious for a sight' of it.[54] It was the king's 'testament' and to be 'taken to all men for the true image of my very mind and form of rule which I have presented to myself'.[55] Or, as we might say, it was James VI's manifesto to be king of England.

Basilikon Doron is often described as a familiar text because it belongs to a familiar genre: the advice to princes. While counsel to Prince Henry would seem to have been James's motive in writing, it has also been suggested that the king wrote for himself, as a meditation on his position.[56] Yet, though the context was Scottish, in 1603 James chose to publish such meditation as a representation of himself to England, as a work that would demonstrate his authority and suitability for rule. As befitting a king who was also known as a poet, James opens *Basilikon Doron* with a sonnet that sums the argument. The opening two lines have often been quoted by those who have identified James's succession as marking the onset of a constitutional crisis, sparked by claims for divine right kingship:

> God gives not Kings the stile of *Gods* in vaine,
> For on his Throne his Scepter doe they swey.[57]

The lines, however, are metrically and in rhyme scheme inseparable from those that follow:

> And as their subjects ought them to obey,
> So Kings should feare and serve their God againe.

Rather than a simple apologia for divine right, the *Basilikon Doron* was concerned with the obligations and duties of kingship. By instructing his son – now publicly – in those duties, James, as he had in his scriptural exegeses (to which we will return), demonstrated that he was God's lieutenant. It is duties that shape the structure of *Basilikon Doron*, and a king's duty towards God is the subject of the first book. In effect, that book is, like other of James's writings, a gloss of Scripture, the diligent reading of which is stated as a ruler's first duty.[58] James asserted that his own conduct had been always 'grounded upon the plain words of scripture' and commanded his son to 'frame all your affections to follow precisely the rule there set down'.[59] As with his biblical exegeses, James instructed his son (and his readers) in the right interpretation and meaning of Scripture, so figuring himself as a mediator of God's word. As an instruction in prayer, for example, he recommended the Psalms, whereof 'the composer was a King' – David; and, not coincidentally, the translator was another king – himself.[60] 'The conserver of Religion', James instructed his son, was that 'light of knowledge' which he was to invoke so often in his writings and speeches: conscience.[61] Though many 'prattled' of it, few acted on a true conscience which, rightly followed, alone ensured a godly virtue and the eschewing of 'deceitful dissimulation'.[62]

The second book, 'Of a King's Duty in Office', followed almost inevitably from the first. For a good Christian, true to conscience, made a good king. That is, he understood his duty not to rule like a tyrant pursuing his own ends, but to carry out his responsibility to God to make and execute good laws with justice for the common interest. For when a king sat in justice, he sat on God's throne. Before proceeding to the second principle of good kingship – teaching by example – James reviewed the difficulties presented by the three estates of

Scotland: the churches, the nobility and the people, whose pursuit of their own interests and power a just king needed to check. To allure them to 'the love of virtue', the king's own life, he told his son, had to be 'a law book and a mirror to your people', just as the *Basilikon Doron* itself was a mirror of James's virtues.[63] In this second book, though conscience and Scripture underlie James's injunctions, the prescription of the moral virtues of the good ruler is taken from myriad classical sources noted in the margins. In citing Plato, Aristotle, Xenophon, Cicero, Quintilian and Seneca, to name a few, James was advertising his humanist learning, as he had his knowledge of Scripture, and was representing himself not only as God's lieutenant but as Plato's philosopher king. Accordingly, James urged that a royal court be 'a pattern of godliness and all honest virtues', that his son choose honest servants, that in his own person he be chaste until marriage, and faithful as a husband, that in all things he be temperate, merciful and magnanimous.[64] And to those ends, he – mirroring himself – recommended study: of 'all arts and sciences', in particular histories.[65]

While the whole of the text of James's instructions to his son is, I would argue, a representation of his own qualities, in the third and final book he turned, revealingly, to the subject of representation itself. 'It is a true old saying,' he opened, 'that a king is as one set on a stage, whose smallest actions and gestures, all the people gazingly do behold.'[66] It was not sufficient, he advised Henry, for a prince to be virtuous; he must *appear to be* virtuous, especially to the people who 'seeth but the outward part'.[67] All actions and attributes of a king – eating and sleeping, dress, and especially speaking and writing – were viewed as significations of virtue and vice. James therefore gave advice to his son on public behaviour, suitable appearance and appropriate recreations – not all of it advice he was to follow himself. Referring directly to future rule of 'more kingdoms than this', he instructed his son that 'these outward and indifferent things will serve greatly for the people, to embrace and follow virtue'.[68] In particular, he insisted, a king's words disclosed his quality and authority; therefore, 'it best becometh a king to purify and make famous his own tongue; wherein he may go before all his subjects; as it setteth him well to do in all honest and lawful things'.[69]

The *Basilikon Doron*, though familiar, has yet to be studied as a rhetorical and polemical text. Normally discussed as political theory, it should be considered as representational performance. In the 1603 edition, authorized at Edinburgh and printed in London, James, who declined to act in court theatricals, brought himself on to the English stage. Similarly, the king who was reluctant to sit for his portrait described royal writings as 'true pictures' of the mind.[70] Even before he came among his people, his word was James's preferred mode of self-representation, which is to say his style of government.

In 1603, James also reissued and licensed for publication his other teaching on kingship, *The True Law of Free Monarchies*.[71] If the first compilation and printing of *Basilikon Doron* was semi-private, the *True Law* was published anonymously, as the work of Philopatris (lover of his country) in 1598. When re-published after *Basilikon Doron*, the text, at least in two of the three print-ings, bore the king's name; and James evidently intended that it complement the other work as a testament of his values and an image of his kingship.[72] Like the *Basilikon Doron*, the *True Law* arose from specific Scottish, as well as inter-national, circumstances. Though he eschewed engagement with them by name, James's treatise is a counter to the contract theorists, like Knox and Buchanan, and 'seditious preachers' who defended resistance to kings.[73] Affirming, in a preface to the reader, that he will 'only lay down herein the true grounds, to teach you the right way, without wasting time upon refuting the adversaries', James, in what was to be the hallmark of all his writings, re-read Scripture and interpreted and selected from it to make an argument that, he hoped, was incontestable.[74] As monarchy was 'the true pattern of divinity', so Scripture prescribed the roles and duties of monarchs and subjects.[75] James focused on the account in the first book of Samuel, chapter 8, verses 8–20, where the prophet responds to the Jewish people's request for a king.[76] As well as granting the request, Samuel forewarned them of the worst sort of king and 'putteth them out of hope, that weary as they will, they shall not have leave to shake off that yoke, which God hath laid upon them'.[77] From this first estab-lishment of kingship in Israel, James moved through Scripture, citing the cases of David and Elias to demonstrate that 'we never read that ever the prophets persuaded the people to rebel against the prince, how wicked so ever he was'.[78] Rather, 'the practice through *the whole Scripture* [sic] proveth the people's obedience given to that sentence in the law of God: "Thou shalt not rayle upon the Judges, neither speak evil of the ruler of thy people" '.[79] Having selected a passage – though claiming 'the whole Scripture' – which made the case against disobedience even to the very worst king, James easily moved to argue the necessity of the 'allegiance of the people to their lawful king', one who was 'a natural father', ever anxious in 'procuring his children's welfare'.[80]

Only after establishing principle from Scripture did James turn to (Scottish) history and law. Here, to counter the seditious argument that laws preceded kings, James described feudal monarchy, in which 'the king is over-lord of the whole land', and found it to agree with 'the laws and constitutions of God'.[81] Though princes had an obligation to God to reign as a tender father, no subjects could hold them accountable. James did not posit a theory of absolute unac-countable kingship. The subtitle of *The True Law* is 'The Reciprock and Mutual Dutie Betwixt A Free King, and His Naturall Subjects'. He did not even avoid the word contract. Rather, just as he selectively reinterpreted Scripture, so he rewrote the meaning of 'contract', as a counter to those who used it to justify resistance. 'Now in this contract (I say) betwixt the king and his people, God is doubtless the only judge, both because to him only the king must make count of his administration . . . as likewise by the oath in the coronation, God is made judge . . .'[82] To posit that, he argued, was not to free monarchs from control but to remit them to the 'sharpest school master' – to God, who punished transgression of obligations by rulers more sharply than any other.[83] As he had at length in *Basilikon Doron*, James described the attributes of the good king as prescribed by the law of nature and the coronation oath: the maintenance of good laws and liberties, of the safety, wealth and weal of the people, of a constant vigilance for their good. His hope was for caring kings ruling over loving and obedient subjects. The purpose of the *True Law* was again to enunciate the ideal, and James's own commitment to it, and to persuade subjects of their duty to 'keep their hearts and hands free from . . . monstrous and unnatural rebellions'.[84]

If, as it does, the *True Law* resonates with Scottish debates and circumstances, why did James revise it for publication at the point of his succession to the English throne? In part, of course, the description of the monarch as nurturing father and head of the body again advertised James's own virtues. And the now familiar argument that kings were God's lieutenants is nicely pointed by description of the monarch, like God, as a 'great school master of the whole land'.[85] It would seem, however, that James regarded the argument and purpose of the *True Law* as having wider applicability than its original Scottish context; and it may not be hard to see why. Though in England a radical Presbyterian advocacy of limited monarchy had not been voiced as forcefully as in Scotland, James had identified Robert Browne, John Penry and 'such brain-sick and heady preachers their disciples and followers' as men who challenged the authority of the magistrate, even to the point of resistance.[86] Though he had qualified its remit, he had used the English form of opprobrium ('puritans') to characterize those who 'contemn the law and sovereign authority', and may (as his outburst at the Hampton Court conference was to suggest) have harboured doubts about radical English, as well as Scots, Calvinists.[87] Further, the king's address to the debates over law and kingship evoked English as well as Scottish circumstances. In referring to the Scottish dispute over whether laws preceded kings or kings laws, James also, whether by design or not, alluded to a debate already being conducted by English antiquaries on the nature of the ancient constitution and the feudal law.[88] That he knew something of those debates may be suggested by his reference to England as a monarchy by conquest where William of Normandy 'gave the law', and 'in his language' to his subjects.[89] But a few years after his arrival in England such debates were to become part of the king's difficulties with parliaments, difficulties which the controversy over monopolies had begun to signal in the last years of Elizabeth's reign. The *True Law* is not an apologia for absolute rule, but it may be that, as reissued in 1603, it was an attempt to marginalize those whom, in England as well as in Scotland, James feared as potential menaces to his rule, as contemners of royal authority and obstacles to that reciprocal love which he believed to be, and publicized as, the foundation of good governance.

These two treatises on kingship, especially the *Basilikon Doron*, were widely circulated and well known. And they were read and favourably received by

James's new subjects very much as testaments of the new monarch whose injunctions and words were quoted, paraphrased and echoed in several contemporary writings. A sonnet of 1603, for example, told young Prince Henry that his father had written the perfect guide, 'How to become a perfit King indeede'.[90] Samuel Daniel, in his welcoming panegyric verse, parsed *Basilikon Doron*, at every point arguing its demonstration of a good king's beliefs.[91] Henry Peacham drew on the *Basilikon Doron* for one of the emblems (directed against the puritans) gathered in his popular *Minerva Britanna or A Garden of Heroical Devises* published in 1612, a year which, with Henry's death, was to see the publication of many elegies and obsequies that recalled the advice book written for a prince who had, until his sad early death, fulfilled all hopes of him.[92] The text had a vibrant life beyond the son, and outside the circles of the court. Preaching at an assize sermon in Hertford in 1619, William Pemberton, minister at Ongar in Essex, quoted extensively from the *Basilikon Doron*.[93] The book doubtless enjoyed its broadest readership when it was plagiarized and paraphrased into a courtesy book, *The Fathers Blessing or Counsaile to His Sonne*, which, published in 1616, went into five editions by 1624, and a further two by the early 1630s.[94] What had been first a manuscript, personal communication between King James VI and Prince Henry, then a household text printed for a few confidants at court, became a courtesy manual 'directing all men to a virtuous and honest life', the ultimate publicization of the virtuous example of King James VI.[95] Not least in recognition of its popularity, James re-dedicated the work to his second son, Prince Charles, on whom it was to exercise a powerful influence.[96]

Since James's views on kingship have traditionally been presented as one of the major problems of his reign, it is important to note that in 1603 these royal texts outlining his position met only with applause. They were not the sole writings of the Scottish king which were re-published in London on James's accession; and it may be that their commercial success prompted printers as well as the king to reissue other royal treatises. None was directly a 'political work' and as a consequence none was re-published in James McIlwain's edition of James's political writings. But, as scholars have recently begun to appreciate, all of James's writings were engaged with his authority and the representation of that authority; and, as the writings of a king, all were read as discourses of authority and as presenting an image of the king.[97] James's treatise on *Daemonologie*, first published by the king's printer at Edinburgh in 1597, might at first sight seem far removed from the business of representation of kingship.[98] However, as Stuart Clark has persuasively argued, there was a close relationship between mystical politics and the claims made by authors about witchcraft.[99] The prince's role as God's lieutenant carried primarily the responsibility to eradicate heresy, and demonic manifestations were the antithesis of Christian politics.[100] James founded his authority on the texts of Scripture and 'any discussion of rulership grounded on biblical models encouraged the view that princes . . . should confront demonism'.[101] No less than the *Basilikon Doron*, James's *Daemonologie* was a display of Christian kingship.

In the form of a dialogue (between Philomathes and Epistemon), James made clear why the subject of magic and necromancy so concerned him. That concern was not limited to a king's duty to oppose a practice which was 'an horrible defection from God'.[102] Not least as a biblical exegete, he seemed determined to oppose any who claimed knowledge of 'heavenly mysteries' beyond what was revealed in Scripture.[103] More broadly, what emerges clearly is that James viewed the debate about demons and witches as inseparable from questions of authority and power. 'Doubtless', he asserted, 'who denyeth the power of the Devil would likewise deny the power of God', and with that, of course, the authority of his lieutenant on earth.[104] Necromancers and witches represented the forces that underpinned the need for strong Christian kingship. Because for James that was Protestant kingship, he associated the false claims of witches to transformative power with the Catholic mass and questioned the capacity of papists to counter magic and demons. Moreover, as the enemies of God, demons also stood for opponents of, and rebels against, kingship.[105] Perhaps revealingly in the light of Queen Elizabeth's translation of Plutarch's essay *De curiositate*, James described curiosity as 'only the incitement of magicians and necromancers'.[106] Citing at the opening of the treatise the first book of Samuel chapter 15 on the prophet's contemnation of Saul, he paraphrased the passage: 'disobedience is as the sin of witchcraft'.[107] The figuring of rebellion, to use the term in the King James Bible, as witchcraft was to be a commonplace of seventeenth-century political argument. Here, James, in politicizing witchcraft, demonizes 'disobedience' and reasserts his claim to be not a false, deceitful ruler like Saul, but God's voice and agent. Accordingly, on the title page of *Daemonologie*, along with the imprimatur 'cum privilegio regis', the crowned lion of Truth is etched inside an oval that bears the motto 'In my defence, God me defend'.

James's concern with witchcraft had unquestionably arisen from the particular circumstance of the Berwick witches during the winter of 1590–1.[108] One, Agnes Thompson, confessed under examination to plotting the king's death, while another even claimed responsibility for the storms which had nearly taken his life on his voyage to Denmark.[109] Yet, if a distinctly Scottish context inspired the writing, the publication of *Daemonologie* was clearly directed at English readers. Waldegrave's printed text of 1597 'systematically anglicised' the spelling of James's original manuscript, and did so with the king's knowledge and approval.[110] The entry of *Daemonologie* in the registers of the Stationers' Company of London on 16 March adds further strength to a suggestion that James even then revised the text 'as part of his campaign to prepare the people of England to receive him as their monarch whenever Elizabeth should die'.[111] The two 1603 editions saw further anglicization and, of these, at least one and perhaps both had royal approval. The one 'printed by

Arnold Hatfield for Robert Waldegrave' bore a large royal coat of arms oppo-site the preface to the reader; while the edition printed for William Aspley became the text used by Barker and Bill for their 1616 folio of James's works.[112] James's *Daemonologie* was certainly well known in England. Dorset Justices cited it in the trial of a local witch and the king's work was praised in the pros-ecution speech of 1612 arraigning one of the Lancashire witches.[113] In his *Guide to Grand Jury Men* (1627), Richard Bernard drew attention to James's book.[114] If James's purpose in writing and publishing was the advancement of 'particular political interests' and 'a commitment to mystical politics', if, as has been argued for the case of Jean Bodin, his writing on demonology was part and parcel of his theory of absolutism, it is not possible to conclude from such citations that his subjects discerned it.[115] But *Daemonologie* could have kept no reader in doubt that in James England had a monarch devoted to doing God's work and battling against the forces of darkness, be they witches, necro-mancers or papists.

The accession of James to the throne of England also saw the re-publication of two very early works by the king of Scotland: his *Fruitfull Meditation Containing a Plaine and Easy Exposition . . . of the 20 Chapter of the Revelation* published in 1588, and the *Meditation upon the . . . XV Chapter of the First Book of the Chronicles of the Kings*, printed the next year.[116] Both works belong to a genre that, though it has not been regarded by historians or biographers as political discourse, James, throughout his reigns in both kingdoms, regarded as inextricable from his kingship: biblical exegesis. In early modern Scotland and England, as Europe, stability and authority often depended upon the interpretation of Scripture. As well as believing it his duty to act as God's vicar on earth, leading his subjects to salvation, James needed and determined to ensure that Scriptural texts supported rather than undermined his authority in a culture of reformed Protestantism.[117] In the case of the Book of Chronicles, Scripture directly addressed the nature of kingship and, as 'sincere professor of the truth', James purposed to gloss it to demonstrate the trust he had from God.[118] A prefatory address directed as well as informed the 'Christian Reader' of the book.[119] God raised kings to be nursing fathers and, like another Solomon, James was committed to protect and nourish his church. A prefatory epigram to a most Christian king of the tree of David connected James with a biblical ruler – and writer – and voiced the thanks of the people that, through their own David, they had come to know God's truth.[120] The commentary begins with the 25th verse of chapter 15. More accu-rately, it opens with reference to the Armada (that 'foreign and godless fleet') and the circumstance that led James to write, in 1589, 'that these meditations of mine' may be 'a testimony of my upright . . . meaning in this so great and weighty a cause'.[121] Thereafter, in the form of a sermon, James 'opens up' his text.[122] The first lesson, he posits, is that the chief virtue in a prince is zeal to promote the glory of God who supports such a ruler in his endeavours. But

Scripture also describes the support David enjoyed from the estates, the clergy and the soldiers, from which, James interprets, 'we may learn first that a godly king finds as his heart wisheth, godly estates concurring with him'.[123] Finally, having invoked unity and compassion, James glossed the rejoicing of David and dancing before the ark in thanks to God for giving victory to his chosen. As he rejoiced, his hypocritical wife 'interprets . . . this indifferent action . . . as only proceeding of a lascivious wantonness' by which, James wrote, 'we may note the nature of the hypocrits and inferior enemies of the church'.[124] 'The application of all' brought the text squarely back to contemporary circumstances.[125] A new Philistine (Spain) attacked Israel (Scotland and England) but God put him to flight, a cause of legitimate rejoicing, whatever the objections, the 'deceit and treason of hypocrites that go about to trap us'.[126] The depiction of all united in the service of a godly prince made this meditation very much a representation of the polity James wished to rule. While the denigration of hypocrites undoubtedly speaks to his experience of the kirk, reissued in 1603 these passages point also to James's determination to check the extreme demands of the puritans, especially their assault on the indifferent, or legitimate, church ceremonies, festivals and games. James presented himself, as biblical exegete and head of the church, as another David who, as God's protected, would safeguard his people and direct them in the rightful worship of the Lord. In 1603, no less than in 1589, no argument mattered more to the authority of the king or monarchy.

In the meditation on Chronicles, James refers to an earlier commentary, his *Fruitfull Meditation . . . and Exposition of . . . the 20 Chapter of the Revelation*, published by the royal printer at Edinburgh in 1588 and 'newly reprinted' in 1603.[127] The *Meditation* was one of two discourses on Revelation written in 1588, underlining the importance of that scriptural text to James at a critical point in his reign.[128] Revelation, as I have argued elsewhere, was of all scriptural books that most at the centre of hermeneutic controversy and the struggles of Christendom, and had been read and appropriated to defend both the authority of princes and armed insurrection against them.[129] It was a text which James appreciated that he needed to make his own. Another preface by Patrick Galloway, who had become a loyal supporter of James in Scotland, pointed up the importance and purpose of the commentary. Identifying James with John himself, Galloway described the meditation as 'a work . . . which God his spirit did utter by our Sovereign, as a witness of his grace's knowledge in the high mysteries of God and a testimony of his highness's most unfeigned love towards true religion'.[130] James's writings, Galloway advertised, manifested him 'worthy of the style or title of the most gracious and Christian king above all the kings on the earth': the victor in spiritual armour, as prefatory verses praised, over popish Rome and Spain.[131]

From the start, James cut through controversy with the pen of authority – 'the apostle his meaning in this place . . . then is this'.[132] Glossing the prophecy of the rise of the Antichrist to afflict the saints before their final victory, James asserted that the application to the papacy 'expounds itself'.[133] And, warning against the force of Antichrist and his agents in the world – in France, in Flanders, and 'against this Isle' – he appealed for common purpose against Gog and Magog.[134] Together with his *Paraphrase* of Revelation, to which Galloway alludes but which was not then published, the *Meditation* was to be placed at the forefront of the 1616 edition of James's works.[135] In 1603, the claim to be God's exegete and champion of the war against popery was the central platform of James's representation of his kingship.

On the eve of his succession in 1603, James evidently authorized the re-publication of one other work, the only example of his poetic *oeuvre* he then so privileged: his 'heroical song' on the Battle of Lepanto, written in 1585 and first published with the royal privilege at Edinburgh in 1591.[136] The poem had celebrated the unity of Christian forces against the Turk, and even praised the leadership of Don John of Austria who had helped secure victory. Addressing, in the 1603 edition, an English audience, James conveyed his concern that, a 'stolen copy' having been published, the poem had been misconstrued – not least as in part praise of Don John whom he now vitriolically termed 'a foreign popish bastard'.[137] Rather, he protested, he had been stirred to write by the cruel persecutions of Protestants. Parsing the structure of his verse, he then read it for the reader as 'invocation to the true God onely' and as epic history, the business of a king.[138] Just as the meditation on Revelations claimed divine utterance, so James here implores God 'To make thy holy Spirit my Muse', to enable the royal poet to 'magnify Thy name'.[139] Like several of the king's writings, *Lepanto* paints an ordered community, fashioned by their leader, to advance virtuous ends.[140] For all the 'misunderstanding', in the closing lines James presented God as behind the saints, rather than 'Antichrist the whore'.[141] Though he was happy to publicize in poetry as well as prose his godly rule, he took no risk that it be read as anything other than Protestant rule.

Lepanto was one of the two works which established James's reputation as a poet; and, as James had outlined in his treatise on the writing of verse, the arts of poetry and kingship had affinities.[142] Because more than any of his predecessors or successors James believed wholeheartedly in the power of words not only to represent authority but to enhance and enact authority, he authorized, and in some cases orchestrated, the reprinting of his writings to be heralds of his new title of king of England and France as well as Scotland. Even after he had ascended his throne, his word – published, spoken or proclaimed – was to remain, and to be perceived to be, James's favoured medium of representing himself: to his people, as also to a European audience that his new circumstances led him increasingly to address. Amidst the busy, not to say turbulent, early years of his reign, James wrote several treatises – some of them lengthy: *An Apologie for the Oath of Allegiance, A Premonition to All Christian Monarchs, A Defence of the Right of Kings,* and the *Counterblaste to Tobacco,* published as early as 1604. Though each deserves close study, as an example of James's rhetorical and discursive strategies as a polemicist, space prevents that here.[143] What we must note, however, is that, even when prompted by European events or interventions (letters of Pope Paul V or an oration by Cardinal du Perron), James's writings were published, as well as in Latin and French, for, and to, his English subjects who would have welcomed his standing as a Protestant polemicist against European popery. And, as well as their particular purposes, they proclaimed and argued in general James's authority and his words as its principal medium. 'One of the means for which God hath advanced me upon the lofty stage of the Supreme Throne,' the royal preface to *A Remonstrance* proclaims, 'is that my words uttered from so eminent a place for God's honour . . . might with greater facility be conceived.'[144] Perhaps even as he wrote, he had begun to render his words into a monument as well as testament to his kingship: the folio volume of his *Works* published in 1616.

The Works of the Most High and Mighty Prince James is a unique event in the history of royal publishing.[145] The form of the text, as well as its folio format, the royal privilege, royal arms and elaborately engraved additional title page by Renold Elstrack, immediately proclaim authority – both literary and political. To better appreciate their performance in 1616, I would suggest, we might first turn to another royal folio by now widely known to almost all of James's subjects: *The Holy Bible . . . Newly Translated . . . By His Majesty's Special Commandment; Appointed to be Read in Churches.*[146] What has remained commonly known as the Authorized King James Version is the most enduring and best-known image of the king; and it is evident that James intended it should be.[147] Though the request and suggestion for a new translation of the Bible were made to James by John Reynolds at the Hampton Court conference, it was the king who quickly became 'the motive force behind the new translation', even though the bishops were not immediately favourable.[148] The programme of translation, involving six teams of professors and divines, was a vast scholarly project that doubtless attracted James as a monument to his own learning and patronage of learning. But James's interest – in both senses of that word – went further. He hoped and believed that a definitive translation, based on the Bishops' Bible but drawing on Tyndale's, Coverdale's, the Great Bible and the Geneva Bible, might establish an English Bible on which all would agree.[149] His rule that no marginal notes be provided reflected not only the king's distaste for certain Geneva notes equivocal about kingship, but also a desire that a clear, agreed text might convey the plain message of Scripture as the king and church saw it rather than 'a shew of uncertainty' and 'diversity of signification and sense in the margin'.[150] If, as the translators' preface to the reader put it, it belonged to kings most to take care of religion, what better demonstration of a king's care could there be than his 'opening and clearing of the word of God'? 'We have a prince', they continued, 'that seeketh the increase of the spiritual wealth of Israel' and nowhere was that demonstrated more than in his Bible.[151]

In all its forms and paratexts, the Bible served both as a representation and an image of King James I. Though Geneva bibles continued to be printed – some by the royal printer – and popular, the 1611 Bible was the only text of Scripture that bore the king's name on the title page, alongside 'The Holy Bible'; the only Bible that was prepared and published 'by his Majesty's special commandment'; and the only Bible after 1611 produced in folio.[152] As well as instituted and authorized by him, the Bible was also dedicated to James, in terms that echo the accession panegyrics of 1603. On the death of Elizabeth, that dedication recalled, 'thick and palpable clouds of darkness . . . overshadowed the land'; but 'the appearance of your Majesty, as of the sun in his strength, instantly dispelled those . . . mists.'[153] Most of all, James had manifested his zeal towards God, both by his 'writing in defence of the Truth', and by having been 'the principal Mover and *Author*' of the Bible.[154] In early modern England, the word 'author' could often mean one who authorized; but, more often it was, and here it may be, used to mean 'originator, promoter'. Holy Scripture itself had become the king's writ.

The elaborate engraved title page, though it bore the king's name, did not reproduce his image.[155] The title tablet is flanked by Moses, with the Ten Commandments, and Aaron in the vestments of a high priest, with a cup and knife. Above them, beneath the tetragrammaton and the Holy Ghost, are Peter and Paul with the other apostles facing the Saviour. Borrowed from other bibles, the figures of the engraved title page represent tradition and authority in a tableau that suggests God was the word, and this edition of the word, the king's. Though James is here powerfully represented, he was – as was his trademark – represented in, *and as*, words, not visuals.

When James's own words were published five years later in his collected *Works*, the book cannot but have appeared as a complement to the Bible. The folio format is not the only immediate connection. The title page carries a verse of Scripture from the King James translation: 'Lo, I have given thee a wise and an understanding heart.' Below, in an oval a folio book with clasps opened is bathed in light from the heavenly source above. The architecture of the additional engraved title page by Renold Elstrack also evokes the Bible.[156] Each side of the 'tabernacle-like structure' in which the title panel is placed, two figures stand in niches, as had Moses and Aaron, in the 1611 Bible. On the left Religion, crushing death beneath her feet, holds a book – the Book of Life; on the right, Peace is figured in Roman leather armour. Above, on the column supports of an arcaded base, stand the royal devices: the lion and unicorn with the king's arms and the rose and thistle. Between them, and exactly above the name of the king, an obelisk reaches heavenwards, with four crowns of diminishing size representing James's four kingdoms. Above, two angels bear that celestial crown to which James, not least by his works, reaches: a crown of glory for the righteous under which, on a ribbon, is written 'Superest' – he overcomes. The strong vertical line at the centre of the architecture, then, directly connects publication, the king's

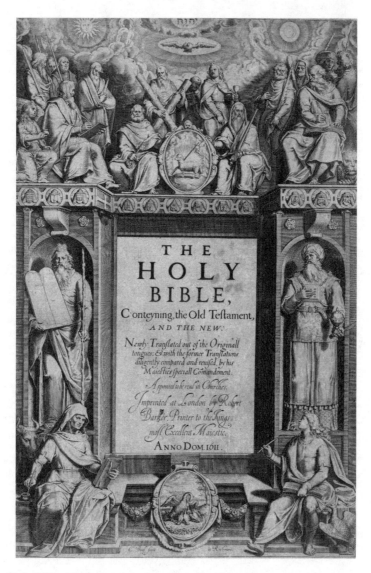

1 The Holy Bible, title page engraved by Cornelius Bol, 1611.

works, the crown, the sun (a symbol of both the deity and the monarch) and the heavenly crown, the victory over death. James's works sustain Religion and Peace, but they lead the king, and others, to God.[157]

Where the Bible opens with a dedication to James, the *Works* is dedicated to Prince Charles, now 'the only son of our sovereign lord the King'. To Charles, James's 'WORKS of his Royal virtues' were presented 'as to the true heir and inheritor of them'.[158] As with the Bible, the dedication is followed by a lengthy preface to the reader by the 'publisher' of the works, James Montagu, bishop of

2 Frontispiece to *The Workes of the Most High and Mighty Prince, Iames, by the Grace of God Kinge of Great Brittaine France & Ireland*, 1616.

Winchester and Dean of the Chapel Royal. In a revealing preface, never properly analysed, Montagu contrasted most writings with 'the different manner of God his setting forth of his own works', from which he proceeds to those of the king.[159] Montagu reminds us of the strikingly novel nature of a folio volume of royal writings by acknowledging that some protest that 'little it befits the majesty of a king to turn clerk', rather than stand as military leader.[160] Against such critics he asserts the power of James's royal words: 'for we have seen with our eyes the operation of His Majesty's works in the consciences . . . of men so far as there have been [those] that have been converted by them'.[161] On the European stage, Montagu claimed, kings and princes had been led by James to assert their rights over false papal claims; just as in Scotland and England, subjects had taken from the royal books 'divine truth and light'.[162] Though the writings that have proved of least interest to historians, James's works opened with a *Paraphrase upon the Revelation* and the meditation on Revelation chapter 20. Royal words melded with divine words to make the king's *Works* in the spirit of the Lord's.

Although in 1616 there was already a recognition that even royal words could not escape contemporary and sharp rebuttal (with good reason, as we shall see), James placed faith in his *Works* as both authoritative and a support to his authority. A Latin edition of the *Works* was published, with royal privilege and with some revision, in 1619, followed in 1620 by a reissue, with additional material.[163] This year also saw the publication of a second edition, now titled *A Collection of His Majesty's Works*, with an engraved portrait of the king and two additional works, written since 1616.[164] Together with the strong suggestion that James may have planned to prepare a volume of his translations and poetry, these editions manifest a king who, to the last, remained convinced that writing was the best medium for sustaining his authority.[165]

The two additional texts included in the 1620 *Works* were both published that year, although evidently written in 1618 and 1619.[166] The *Meditation upon the Lord's Prayer* returned James to the genre of scriptural exegesis which he had not essayed since coming to the English throne. Though the preface denied controversy, the dedication to James's favourite and minister, the Duke of Buckingham, as well as the address to courtiers, rendered the meditation a political statement in new circumstances.[167] Where in the 1580s, and even in 1603, the principal threat to his authority identified in James's exegesis of Scripture was the Catholics, in 1619 the meditation on the Lord's Prayer opens with an attack on puritans who challenged the church and, by extension, the monarchy.[168] Indeed, James's gloss on the Lord's Prayer becomes a restatement of his authority as head of the church and realm against those challenges and a re-presentation of himself as a ruler and writer with privileged understanding of God's will.

The title of the second of James's later prose works echoed once more his first writings on Scripture, and explicitly announced its political intent. *A Meditation upon the 27, 28, 29 Verses of the XXVII Chapter of St Matthew* is subtitled 'A Pattern for a King's Inauguration'.[169] Published in 1620, the meditation (according to another edition not written before 1619) was dedicated to Prince Charles.[170] Following his discourse on the Lord's Prayer, and meditating on Scripture, James told his son, he lighted on a passage that would 'put inheritors to kingdoms in mind of their calling'.[171] As well as scriptural exegesis, then, the meditation, though different in genre, was, like *Basilikon Doron* (to which he refers), an advice manual on kingship and, as such, a representation of kingship.[172]

More than ever after recent struggles, he emphasized the cares of the crown but, as an epistle to the reader explained, James, who was planning a fuller treatment of the duties of kings, both knew and taught the duties and obligations of a monarch and had publicized them as a pattern of his own godly rule. Subtly against puritans, James confirmed the unity and authority of the church; against any – and perhaps he felt he had begun to hear their voices in England – who argued for the king's appointment by the people, he emphasised the divine institution of monarchy.[173] Throughout the meditation he moved between the heavenly and earthly kings, stressing Christ's actual regal status as king of the Jews.[174] Most of all, he underlined the care and love of kings for their people and the 'happy and willing acclamation of his people' that a godly king merits.[175] As the frequent reference to *Basilikon Doron* suggests, few of these utterances were new. But, newly stated to English readers after recent criticism of his rule, James's prescriptions were written to buttress ideals, sustained belief in which was essential to monarchy.

James never managed to publish a collected volume of his poems, and though the cares and 'knotty difficulties' of English kingship stole time from the composition of verse, James did not entirely cease to be a poet or abandon his clear belief that poetry was an instrument of kingship.[176] Even as he completed his prose *Works*, he was preparing the manuscript of a third volume of his verse, including early amatoria and sonnets.[177] Moreover, James returned to poetry about the time when he wrote his last prose works in 1618–19 and deployed verse with and for specific and topical political commentary. Since these poems remained unpublished in James's lifetime, it might be thought inappropriate to consider them as representations of the king. On the contrary, the survival of these royal verses in several separates, miscellanies and commonplace books confirms both the public circulation of scribal publications and the role of these texts in political as well as literary exchange. The manuscript of the first of the late poems, on the comet that appeared in October 1618, is signed 'Jacobus rex' and a copy in state papers places it firmly amidst the business rather than leisure of kingship.[178] We soon see why. James attacks the widespread speculation – 'rash imagination' – about the meaning of the comet as illicit prying into state affairs; and in lines that apply to kings as much as comets, instructs:

And misinterpret not with vayne conceyte
The character you see on heavens heighte.[179]

News and the gossip of St Paul's Walk about the marriage of the prince and the future of religion had grown to challenge authorized royal discourse: that is had almost amounted to 'Treason'.[180] James rejected the capacity of those without reason to comprehend God's meaning, while, signing with his royal title, he implicitly advanced his own.

The other poems explicitly engaged with controversy. In verses to the Duke of Buckingham, whose promotion to the post of Lord Admiral in January 1619 stirred popular and factional discontent, James compared the grant of royal favour to divine favour and celebrated in panegyric on a visit to his favourite's house he 'whose virtues pure no pen can duly blaze'.[181] In 1622, the king resorted to a witty poem ordering the gentry and their wives to leave London, in the hope that verse might command obedience from those 'whom scarce a Proclamation can expell'.[182] If it is tempting to suggest that James, in the new climate of critical news pamphlets and libels, was led back to the Scottish culture of vituperative poetic contests, a poem that has only lately drawn historical attention makes the case. Surviving in voluminous copies, it is variously titled an 'answer to' or 'verses made upon a libel', signalling the poem as a response to counter-presentation of the king and court.[183] In this, 'the wiper of the people's Tears', James addressed a popular audience in plain language and a simple couplet rhyme scheme. In some respects, the repeated conceits are familiar: 'Kings walke the heavenly . . . way'; 'God and Kings doe pace together'; 'God above all men Kings enspires'.[184] But the mantra-like repetition, as well as the popular form, betray the radical differences of this poetic representation. For, rather than arguing lofty principles, James descended to the defence of particular policies and powers: those of choosing favourites, calling parliaments and conducting diplomacy.[185] And, though it reiterated a king's love for his subjects, it uncharacteristically and unregally threatened. Moreover, the poem responded to and opened up the dilemma of representation and James's favoured medium of representation, the word. For the king still held to that mystery that placed sovereigns above 'common' comprehension; yet in writing he had stimulated discussion and exchange, even the sharp criticisms of, and 'railing rhymes' against, his rule.[186] Here, in responding to them, he validated them and so reduced representation, supposedly the sovereign word, to verbal and political contest.

It may be no coincidence that the reign of the king who of all monarchs wrote most was, as we shall see, that in which the newspaper was born and the verse satire, libel and political pamphlet came of age.[187] For all his hopes and expectations, for all his unusual rhetorical skill, James's royal words did not protect royal authority from criticism and challenge. However, though by the 1620s the folio grandeur of the *Works* was giving way to doggerel rant, James never gave up on his conviction that his writings and words were essential representations of his majesty. Accordingly, no less than with his poems and meditations, he paid careful attention to those discursive modes of early modern monarchy: royal prayers, proclamations and speeches.

From the beginning of his reign, James identified his own authority with the established forms of the Church of England, not least of which were the official prayers periodically prescribed, with the king's authority as head of the church, to mark particular, often royal, occasions. On 5 March 1604, frustrating any hope the puritans might have held, he reissued the Book of Common Prayer by proclamation as a form of worship of his own personal authorization.[188] In the first year of his English rule, James also authorized a form of prayer which very much reminded his subjects of his regal experience and divine protection. A Form of Prayer with Thanksgiving to be used every 5 August, the day of James's deliverance from the Gowrie conspiracy, was printed cum privilegio with a large crowned royal arms.[189] From the script for this day of worship, the parish congregations throughout the realm recited the psalm 'The king putteth his trust in the lord', heard of David's deliverance and gave thanks that God had protected by his providence 'godly kings and governors', especially his Jacob for whom all prayed for a long and happy reign.[190] Thanksgiving for the king's preservation was soon followed by an official service of annual worship to commemorate 24 March, the day of James's arrival in England.[191]

Lessons of the day, as well as being taken from the general injunction to obedience to higher powers (chiefly Romans 13), compared James to Solomon, the king of legendary wisdom. Like Israel's godly rulers, James, the service ran, was 'a man chosen after thine [God's] own heart that he might lead us into green pastures'.[192] Placed by God, James represented the nation's 'joyful delivery from great dread and fear, to the happy continuance of our peace and welfare, and to the blessed maintenance of thy gospel and true religion amongst us'.[193] In return for these blessings, the people delivered up prayers of thanks to their Lord and made the promise of allegiance and obedience to a king favoured by divine providence.[194] Historians might question how long the nation's gratitude lasted. But, though few copies of those prayers survive, a Bodleian edition, with added prayers for Princess Elizabeth and Frederick the Elector, indicates that the service was still being held a decade later – and probably beyond.[195]

After the succession itself, subsequent events, happy and menacing in turn, provided occasion for official prayers. The first was the pregnancy in 1605 of a queen who was already more fruitful than any could remember. The Prayers Appointed to be Read . . . by Every Minister for the Queen's Safe Deliverance, printed by the royal printer and 'Set forth and Enjoined by Authority', took advantage of the opportunity to re-present the royal family.[196] On the title page, a phoenix surrounded by books and an angel with books and writing implements, flanking the royal arms, gestured to James the custodian and mediator of the word. To the left and right of the title tablet, figures of Faith and Humility advertised the royal virtues that had merited God's blessing. The service led the people in prayer for God's 'handmaid' Queen Anne who, unlike the last queen who had so described herself in her published prayers, had 'become a joyful mother of many children'.[197] Increase of the royal issue, the prayers reminded the congregation of every parish in the land, not only

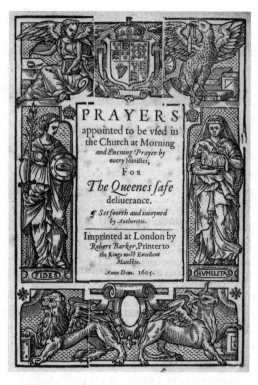

PRAYERS
appointed to be vfed in
the Church at Morning
and Euening Prayer by
euery Minifter,
FOR
The Queenes fafe
deliuerance.
¶ Set foorth and inioyned
by Authoritie.

Imprinted at London by
Robert Barker, Printer to
the Kings moſt Excellent
Maieſtie.
Anno Dom. 1605.

FIDES · HVMILITAS

3 Title page of *Prayers Appointed to be Used . . . for the Queenes Safe Deliverance*, 1605.

promised succession through generations and the peace that followed secure lineage but 'the good of this thy church'.[198]

The year of the queen's safe delivery, however, was also one which delivered from destruction the whole royal family and the nation, as, at the eleventh hour, Guido Fawkes and his co-conspirators were discovered in their plot to blow up the king, his family and the houses of parliament. The official thanksgiving opened with prayers of gratitude for kings and all in authority and with a psalm which spoke in the voice of King James as well as King David in praying: 'Lead thou my cause, O Lord, . . . and fight thou against them that fight against me'.[199] After a passage from the second book of Samuel describing David's deliverance by God from Saul, the people prayed for their own David who put his trust in the Lord and asked for Christ's protection for 'thy servant James, our most gracious king and governor'.[200] Following a reading from Romans 13 ('let every soul be subject unto the higher powers'), and a reading from St Matthew's gospel, chapter 27, on the betrayal of Christ, the service ended with prayers for godly and peaceful government under the king and royal family.[201] Assembled together for such a service, each congregation was presented with a vision of godly community and a holy prince, protected by divine providence against the nation's (and the Lord's) enemies; published by authority, such prayers represented, as they also sustained, royal authority.

Whilst he authorized these services and prayers, and though it seems likely that a monarch who placed such value in words might have helped devise them, we cannot know what, if any, role James had in scripting them. No such question arises with those traditional media of royal communication and representation: letters, proclamations and declarations. Though they did not all circulate in a public sphere,[202] James attached great importance to letters: the correspondence he sustained with Queen Elizabeth and her ministers he believed, not inaccurately, brought him to the English throne; after 1603, he boasted, again with good reason, that he governed his Scottish kingdom with his pen.[203] The editor of James's voluminous letters points out that many were neither written nor dictated by the king, yet a large number of surviving holographs and drafts testify to the time he gave to his correspondence, even in late years when arthritis made writing painful.[204] Moreover, though this output has not been fully studied, the letters reveal a king adept at combining cajoling with gratitude and at manipulating tones and terms of formal distance and familiarity.[205] Space prevents us analysing James's letters here. But since such deftness is not usually associated with James's public addresses, we must turn to examine James's declarations and speeches in the light of what we have learned from his writings.

Speaking to his parliament of 1621 of royal proclamations, James informed them: 'Most of them myself doth dictate every word.'[206] Given an average of one a month over the years, this also, as well as qualifying James's reputation for laziness, indicates the importance he attached to the texts as public distribution of his royal thoughts and commands and as publicization of his kingship. Printed and published but also read at the market cross and so heard by illiterate auditors, early modern proclamations were both pronouncements and performances of royal authority and opportunities for rulers not only to command but to explain and even justify policies in order to support their authority. Proclamations, not least at the beginning of a new reign, were often a response to a specific occasion or need. However, even from the first in which we hear the king's own voice (some after his accession were written by councillors pending his arrival), James also used them to rehearse large ideas about and to project images of his own kingship. He knew, he assured his subjects in July 1603, he owed account to God for his governance of his kingdoms; he had 'manifold proof of God ... protecting ... us'; he therefore insisted that the people trust to his conscience the matter of religious grievances.[207] He gave thanks for the people's demonstrations of love and promised, as Elizabeth had, 'to show our self careful in all things to preserve their greatest affection and to answer their expectation'.[208] 'The Christian care which all kings are bound by the law of God ... to take over all their people', he assured them, led him to help and redress their complaints.[209] Against early puritan critics, he skilfully explained his care for the uniformity of the church and the 'furtherance of religion' as opposed to 'semblance of zeal'.[210] Opponents of his project of union he presented as 'endeavour[ing] to separate that which God hath put together'.[211]

But, as James, like his predecessors, increasingly discovered, though the prescriptive word of the king, proclamations not only met with non-compliance but entered a veritable Babel of contesting texts and voices. As the royal proclamation banning Dr Cowell's law dictionary *The Interpreter* lamented, 'men in these our days do not spare to wade in all the deepest mysteries that belong to the persons or state of kings or princes'.[212] His response, in proclamations as his other writings, was to reiterate the ideals of good king-ship and to re-present himself as virtuous ruler: the protector of 'the true catholic and Christian religion', the merciful king, the shepherd who kept 'continual watch' and took 'tender care' to 'nourish and maintain the happy estate of our loving subjects'.[213] Indeed, James advertised that he was not for turning when, in a proclamation of 1614, he announced that there was 'nothing that doth more adorn the true majesty and greatness of sovereign princes than to be constant in their well-grounded resolutions . . . and by their policy and lawful power, to scatter and beat down all difficulties and undue oppositions, until they have conducted their actions to a good and happy end'.[214] However, with repeated injunctions and proclamations 'not . . . duly obeyed and observed', James's tone became more exasperated and even authoritarian, and the king 'straitly' charged on pain of high displeasure rather than explaining and persuading.[215] Royal proclamations of the later Jacobean period evidence his wider disappointment that royal orders for the public good, even when explained and powerfully argued, as for example in the treatise against tobacco, were being ignored.[216] In 1620, James freely admitted a shift in his attitude to 'freedom of speech', in a proclamation outlawing censures of the government that was a recognition that his own words were being swamped by those of others.[217] The meeting of a parliament in 1621 was accompanied initially by proclamations in which, as early in the reign, James presented himself as ever ready to listen to and redress the people's grievances.[218] But the parliament only serving, it seemed, to increase 'bold discourse' and 'unreverend speech', James shifted from his natural 'mildness and clemency' to threats of 'severity' against the culprits.[219] While attempting to regulate public curiosity and discussion, however, James more than ever felt the need to justify himself to the public as the longed-for parliament was dissolved in acrimony. In his *Proclamation Declaring His Majesty's Displeasure Concerning the Dissolving of the Parliament*, issued in January 1622, James endeavoured to paint a picture of harmony disrupted by a few, of his own sincerity and patience in the face of unreasonable obstruction, and of his desire for good laws not least attested to by the 'comforts given . . . by proclamation'.[220] In defending his actions, James skil-fully cast his parliamentary critics as extremists ('We found our crown actually possessed') and invoked 'renowned Queen Elizabeth' as one of those princes whose 'best government' he took as his pattern.[221] The proclamation with its appeal to the 'hearty love and affection of our subjects' was a skilful rhetorical performance; but it tacitly acknowledged a new world in which, as we shall see, European affairs and the first newspapers or corantos were sharpening as well as publicizing divisions in England.[222]

James's sterling effort to sustain a rhetoric of harmony and order was being undermined not only by events but by other discourses and voices that did not blanch at openly countering the king. In consequence, the James who had always been confident that he would, by his learning and wit, win the argument was reduced to (vain) attempts at silencing critics.[223] As has been observed, however, proclamations did not suppress libels.[224] No less a comment on the force of his word, one of James's last proclamations, his seventh commanding nobles and gentry to reside in the country – though it insisted that 'our said proclamations be in all points dutifully obeyed' – acknowledged (as had his poem on the same subject) that there were many who did 'contemn our royal commandments', even though they had been 'so often iterated'.[225] For all their rhetoric of authority, royal proclamations had always been devices of persuasion as well as command. The number and form of Jacobean proclamations testify to the king's clear grasp of their importance in publicizing his kingship. As a man who believed so passionately in the authority of words, perhaps nothing brought him more disillusionment than that his royal words directed to the public weal failed to meet with acquiescence or even, towards the end of his reign, with reverence.

As well as the large number of his proclamations, James made use of that form of address to the people opened by print: the royal declaration. In 1611, already beset with financial problems that were to plague his entire reign, the king had published by Robert Barker, the royal printer, *A Declaration of His Majesty's Royal Pleasure . . . in Matter of Bounty*.[226] Bearing a large royal arms, the declaration was candid about the problems of balancing the royal books and promised to curtail expenditure. Most important, in what was a direct address to subjects outside the narrow circle of the court, James gave assurance that he would take no course 'which may drive us to lay burdens on our people, to whom we desire to endear ourselves by all the princely offices of favour and protection which any earthly king can afford unto his subjects'.[227] As well as announcing that care, the royal declaration presented a ruler with scrupulous regard for the law as a reforming king who was as ready to get his own house in order as to redress the abuses in the realm.[228] Unfortunately for James's image as well as purse, the problems were not resolved and eight years later the declaration was re-published in exactly the same words. Two better known royal declarations were, against James's wishes, to plunge the king into controversy. James's *Declaration of Sports* was a – typical – discursive intervention by the king directed at resolving a controversy.[229] During the late sixteenth and early seventeenth centuries, puritan magistrates in various parts of England had issued orders suppressing Sunday games. As he made his way back from Scotland through Lancashire, James received a petition against the local magistrates' blanket ban on amusements even after evening prayers and promised to consider it. After consulting Bishop Morton of Chester, who then drew up a draft, which James changed 'from the words of a bishop to those of a king', he issued in 1617 a declaration to the people of Lancashire.[230] In May of the next year, it was published to the nation and ordered to be read in every parish church. The *Declaration*, like others of James's writings, was prompted in part by his fear of being misinterpreted and misrepresented, and by his desire to protect the church from extremists, papist or puritan; it was published 'to strike equally on both hands against the contemners of our authority'.[231] Defending 'old custom' as well as lawful recreation for all who partook of Anglican service, and frequently speaking of 'our good people', James sought to shore up the community of the church that was also the community of the state, urging nonconformists 'to leave the country' if they could not comply.[232] Though puritan critics were later to condemn it, and its reissue in the same words in 1633 under a very different archbishop undoubtedly caused a furore, James's declaration appears to have settled the immediate dispute and to have furthered his reputation as a conciliator.[233]

Three years later, his long *Declaration* touching his proceedings in the late parliament was published into a changed world.[234] As we have seen, the king's proclamation concerning the dissolution had been marked by an uncharacteristic tone of self-justification and appeal.[235] Even though it was long for the genre, the proclamation evidently did not meet the need James perceived to present his case to his people, especially at a time when critical representations of his foreign policy were circulating widely in pamphlets such as Thomas Scott's *Vox Populi* and *Tom Tell Troth*.[236] The 63-page declaration mixed affirmation of royal authority – 'that forbidden ark of our absolute and indisputable prerogative concerning the calling and dissolving of parliament' – with the announcement of concessions.[237] For, on the one hand, James condemned the House of Commons which meddled with the prerogative and 'things far above your reach', insisting on *arcana imperii* which were the business of kings alone.[238] On the other, as he told the house, and as he did again in the declaration in print, the sovereign showed himself willing 'to descend from our royal dignity by explaining at this time our meaning'.[239] The ambiguity, always present in royal representation, had been exacerbated by the broader publicization of politics, even former state secrets such as details of diplomacy and of royal marriage. Worse, by 1621 James feared that his favourite medium of representation, his word, was being deployed by Scott and others to misrepresent him. He had, he here declared, in letters to parliament, tried to 'interpret or restrain our former words'; but efforts to control the reception of his discourse were undermined by 'carping wits that were more inclinable to pervert and wrest our words'.[240] Interestingly and revealingly, James's response to a 'crisis of discursive authority' was an address to the wider public whose intrusion into the mysteries of power he deplored.[241] Castigating extremists in the Commons (as he had extremists in the church) as 'captious and curious heads', or 'tribunal orators', he endeavoured to isolate his principal opponents and to silence their voice.[242] Yet the declaration published the exchange between king and Commons, opening these texts to public debate and interpretation; even to misinterpretation. Like the later manuscript verse and proclamations, James's declaration nicely points up the difficulties faced by a king who rested his authority on the word in new circumstances where even royal words jostled for predominance in a market-place of news and gossip and a climate of criticism and contestation. To say the least, the king's hope that 'enlarging himself', or that 'plainness and freedom will most advantage us' was to remain unfulfilled.[243]

For all his formidable output of published writings, in *Basilikon Doron* James had told his son that writing was 'nothing else but a form of en-registrate speech' – an implication that speech was the primary mode of discourse.[244] Certainly, as his advice to Henry on style and his prescriptions about language indicate, James attached the greatest importance to oratory as an act of kingship. Indeed, in 1616 he chose to 'en-registrate' – that is place on permanent record – five of his speeches in the volume that was to be his monument. Historians have tended to make that look like an act of folly. In Whig historiography, and even much of current scholarship, James's speeches, perhaps even more than his writings, are taken as evidence either of absolutist views and/or of a tactlessness in addressing his subjects in parliament that accelerated constitutional tensions.[245] Since James, by contrast, described his speeches as the windows to his heart, the best advertisement of his sincerity and virtue, we must re-examine them briefly not only as political statement but as advocacy and representation. Certainly, James could impress as an orator. On a visit to Oxford in 1605, the king joined in, as well as heard, university disputations.[246] At one moot, 'his Majesty . . . did speak some six or seven times in very good Latin'; during a philosophy debate at St Mary's, 'he made a long discourse in Latin, which did so fill the audience with wonder and admiration that they generally concluded and pronounced our country to be that Commonwealth which Plato affirmed to be happy . . . under the governance . . . of a king so learned, wise and virtuous'.[247] Nor were James's oratorical skills purely academic. Praising Britain's Solomon in a funeral sermon, Bishop John Williams recalled the 'massive conception' and 'flowing and princely kind of elocution' of James's discourse and singled out his speeches to parliament as proving him 'to be the most powerful speaker that ever swayed the sceptre of this kingdom'.[248] Thomas Heywood concurred: in parliament, he claimed, MPs attended to his words as if he were an oracle.[249]

History has lost sight of such admiration.[250] As soon, however, as we turn to James's very first speech to his first parliament, on 19 March 1604, we imme-diately encounter an orator whose skills matched, and even surpassed, those of Queen Elizabeth. James subtly reminded his auditors of the benefits he had brought by his succession: legitimacy by descent from Henry VII, issue, the Protestant faith in which he had been nurtured, God's blessing, and peace and freedom from invasion or conflict.[251] His emphasis, however, was on his parliament and the people it represented. As in *Basilikon Doron*, James declared that the righteous king 'acknowledge[d] himself to be ordained for the procuring of the wealth and prosperity of his people'; and, in turn, he thanked them for their dutiful expressions of love, the 'harmony of your hearts in . . . embracing me as your undoubted and lawful king'.[252] The evocation of his welcome to his capital rose, for all the insistence on plainness, to poetic strains: 'shall it ever be blotted out of my mind, how at my first entry into this kingdom, the people of all sorts rid and ran, nay rather flew to meet me? Their eyes flaming, nothing but sparkles of affection, their mouths and tongues uttering nothing but sounds of joy'.[253]

Having reconstructed a scene of harmony and love, James turned to policy. From descanting on peace and love, he moved to the benefits of a union of his two kingdoms, deploying a marital discourse which Elizabeth had used to her parliaments: 'what God hath conjoined then, let no man separate'.[254] Having spoken of his faith, he outlined his position with regard to Catholics and puritans who questioned authority; having distinguished a lawful king from a tyrant, he urged the making of a few good laws and the impartial execution of all statutes.[255] Most of all, James insisted, that his subjects might know him, he spoke from the heart. In this most rhetorical of performances, he expressed his 'mislike' of 'a tongue too smooth'; he flattered the learning of an assembly that contrasted with his own lack of oratorical skill; he offered 'no other eloquence than plainness' – 'to discover . . . the secrets of my heart'.[256] Using, with freshness, the metaphors of marriage, of the head and body, of the king as shepherd of the flock, scriptural and classical references, logical arguments with homely images, and a repeated first person pronoun, the speech was a skilful self-presentation of James to his people crafted, he hoped, to occlude 'contrary senses' of his meaning.[257] Though it was not published *cum privilegio*, this first speech to parliament was published by the royal printer, with the king's arms – that is with royal approval and for an audience outside the House of Lords where the Commons had joined the peers to attend the monarch.

James did not authorize for publication at the time the speech he delivered on proroguing parliament in November 1605. The title in the 1616 *Works*, 'A Speech . . . as Near the Very Words as Could Be Gathered at the Instant' suggests that there was no official version at the time, and that it was later that the king attributed enough importance to it to include it with other texts of his kingship in his *Works*.[258] Already by 1605 there had arisen some of the misunderstanding James had hoped to prevent: disputes over elections, the *Apology*, and – most important to the king – the Union, had not exactly followed the script of harmony he had outlined.[259] But the attempt to blow up the king, the royal family and his parliament in the Gunpowder Plot presented an opportunity to reaffirm unity which James was quick to take. Giving thanks on behalf of the nation for his and their deliverance, James connected his private family and person to 'the whole body of the state in general'.[260] In an inspired line, he flattered the house, and at the same time underlined his commitment to parliament, by assuring them that, had he been murdered, he would not have died ingloriously: 'mine end should have been with the most honourable and best company, and in the most honourable and fittest place for a king to be in'.[261] Here, however, flattery was accompanied by a reminder of royal authority and parliament's subordinate place. 'Kings,' he repeated his famous axiom, 'are in the word of God called Gods, as being his lieutenants and vice-gerents on earth'.[262] And discoursing on an approved sentence of divinity ('the mercy of God is above all his works'), James spoke as a mediator of God's word, or, as he put it, 'more like a divine'.[263] Speaking with the voice of authority, he declared his purpose to outline 'the true nature and definition of a parliament', which was, he asserted, 'nothing else but the King's great Council which the king doth assemble'.[264] It was for parliament to proffer advice 'in the matters proposed by him unto you', and no other, and to act for the good of king and realm 'whose weals cannot be separated'.[265] Parliament, he advised, was no place for shows of eloquence or 'long studied . . . orations'.[266] If, however, in 1605 he hoped that his own delivered oration might restore co-operation, evidently by 1616, when he included a text in his *Works*, he had come to see the importance of the views he had expressed as part of his political testament.

James I for at least a decade persisted in his belief that his speeches to parliament were the principal means of securing its co-operation. In an address of March 1607, responding to concerns about union with Scotland, he adopted the device of the rhetorical question so as to lead MPs to the answer he advocated.[267] In a speech in which every other sentence posed such a question, James asked, while flattering the Commons, 'when I have two nations under my government, can you imagine I will respect the lesser, and neglect the greater?' and concluded, 'who is so ignorant that doth not know how the gain will be great?'[268] In 1610, faced with wider problems and anxieties, he once again restated his beliefs about monarchy, the laws, parliaments, and the grievances of the subject.[269] Though he sought to argue a case and persuade, this was not spin – the packaging or slanting of argument. Where he had always insisted on the sincerity of his words, the king now used a metaphor for his speech to manifest how he took words as not merely the representation of himself but *as* himself. To the Lords and Commons on 21 March 1610 he offered 'a great and a rare present, which is a fair and crystal mirror . . . through the transparentness thereof, you may see the heart of your king'.[270] Having spoken for well over an hour, ranging over principles and particular policies, he returned to the image. The king asked that the mirror be not viewed in a false light – that none misunderstand his words; he urged that none soil the glass or, that is, pervert his words; he cautioned that they handle it with care, not lightly esteem it or 'conform not . . . to my persuasions'.[271] Rhetoric, he insisted, was for the university; the king's speech was 'animam meam' – his very soul.[272] Already by 1610, there is more than a hint that James feared what he proscribed: that his words, that is his kingship, would be misinterpreted. In collecting and publishing those words in 1616, he shifted his appeal from parliament to a wider readership – and perhaps, beyond that, to history.

In speeches to parliament, James knew that he was addressing, too, the wider political nation: that, to use Geoffrey Elton's phrase, parliament was a 'point of contact' between the crown, local gentry and people.[273] After the acrimonious so-called Addled Parliament of 1614 commenced what was to be a seven-year 'personal rule' without parliament, James did not abandon speech as the principal medium of his representation to the political nation.[274] In 1616 he addressed, for the first time, the judges and other auditors in the court of Star Chamber.[275] As befitted the place and occasion, the speech was dominated by the king's injunctions to uphold justice and observe the law. More broadly, however, by positing a descending theory of justice from God through the king to the judges and via them to the people, James constructed an alternative line of communication to the nation to that of a parliament.[276] Speaking in Star Chamber, he claimed, was 'equal to a proclamation'; and James used the occasion, like a proclamation, to explain himself as well as to enact an order.[277] Against the criticism aired against him, that he misunderstood the constitution and laws of England, James explained that he had abstained from addressing Star Chamber until he had served a long apprenticeship learning these laws.[278] Since some had seemed to hold this view, the king spoke 'to root out the . . . misapprehension . . . that I would change, damnify and vilify or suppress the law of this land'.[279] Answering the fears of those who had opposed a union which they perceived as a threat to England, he explained, with the project now in tatters, 'my intention was always to effect union by uniting Scotland to England and not England to Scotland'.[280] More generally, James used the speech, the gist of which would be repeated around the country, to re-present himself as a Christian king with a strong sense of his duty and accountability to God, a lover and protector of the Church of England (the 'most pure of any church in Christendom') and as a prince quick to listen to grievances and reform the ills of the commonweal: alehouses and rogues, excessive buildings and the decay of hospitality.[281] James asked the judges and JPs to uphold his prerogative as well as the law; especially against those who 'give a snatch against a monarchy through their puritanical itching after popularity'.[282] But, most of all, through this direct address, as well as the judges' charges to the assizes, he sought once more 'an open declaration of my meaning'.[283] As he closed his address, he requested that his auditors 'inform my people truly of me, how zealous I am for religion, how I desire law may be maintained and flourish' and that all may 'live a happy people under a just king enjoying the fruit of peace and justice'.[284]

If this, the last speech he published and James's direct address to the nation, was motivated by the desire, by broad publication, to preserve his word from misunderstanding and misrepresentation, it was the same impulse that led to the publication of the 1616 *Works*, in which the royal speeches form the final section. No less, however, than his writings, James's words delivered in his person were not to be free from controversy or riposte. Even as he spoke in parliament, James bemoaned the pasquils that had begun to circulate criticizing government; and as he addressed the audience in Star Chamber, vicious libels and invectives against his favourite and lover were not stopping short of attacking the king.[285]

III

Far more than any of his early modern predecessors, James was his own spokesman in print – both in prose and poetry. Far, however, from this overshadowing panegyrical works celebrating the new dynasty and monarch, the king's literary reputation and writings, well known before his succession, stimulated others to laud a sovereign who they expected might especially value – and reward – literary support. James's poor historical and later contemporary reputation has led to scholarly neglect of the accession panegyrics which welcomed the new king and of the help he continued to enjoy from the authors of histories, sermons and other works, at key episodes (his entry into London, the inauguration and funeral of Prince Henry, the wedding of Princess Elizabeth) and, in some measure, virtually to the end of his reign.[286] Not least because they often echoed the king's language as well as his favourite adages and conceits, they complemented royal writings in representing the first Stuart to his subjects.

> Never did King set foote on English ground
> With more applaw'd than our renowned *Iames!*[287]

If such a claim rings to us with poetic hyperbole, it may not have seemed so to contemporaries, as the presses produced an outpouring of verse welcoming the new king. Poems lamenting the death of Elizabeth moved swiftly to praise of her successor – and not only from obvious relief at peaceful succession. James Stuart succeeded, poets sang, with Elizabeth's blessing; still more he was, as the author of an Oxford University panegyric wrote, worthy of the great queen's crown.[288] Some, as we have seen, even dared to think that James, the husband and father, might have more to bring to the country than his predecessor; and a sense that golden days might be in the future not the past leaks through even some pious elegies on the queen.

> Confesse with shame, *Elizae*'s happy raigne
> Will never over-matched be againe.[289]

wrote the author of *King James His Welcome to London*, before adding:

> But yet farre be it from my erred scooling
> To make compare with high King *James* his ruling.[290]

James, he continued, brought peace and promised to be a scourge of popery, 'Our golden-age', the author of *England's Wedding Garment* concurred, 'is not yet out of date'.[291] Both the time of year (James made his entry on 24 March) and the fertility of the royal patriarch turned many versifiers to images of spring and a new birth after the dark barren winter of the last days of old Elizabeth. The elegist who shed the tears on behalf of England for the queen was nevertheless quick to greet James as a rising sun bringing new warmth and life.[292] 'Thou art the Sunne', another similarly welcomed the new king, 'that melts our winter showers'; 'with thy beginning', the poet Michael Drayton told James, 'doth the spring begin'.[293] As university poets and popular ballads alike rehearsed the same joy at rebirth, a verse heralding James's coronation figured orphans smiling and widows breaking into song and prophesied:

> What doth the springing yeare presage,
> But that our Spring proclaimed King:
> With store of sommer-fruites, to us
> Of blissful peace and plentie bring.[294]

The month James entered London was not only the dawn of spring but the month, Drayton reminded his sovereign, dedicated to wisdom; and England had a wise Solomon to succeed her Deborah.[295] Not only 'a man to sit on David's throne', a 'Gideon', James was welcomed as that philosopher king whom Plato had described as the ideal ruler: 'most prudent, wise and iust in everything'.[296] Nor was James lauded only for his learning and his poetry. The author of an elegy, describing his escutcheon, reflected that 'The name of Lyon-heart becomes him best,/Witness the Lyon on his Lordly brest'.[297] Though welcomed as a prince of peace and goodness, he was, too, the fulfilment of a 'soldier's wish': a man, William Alexander wrote in *A Paranaesis to the Prince*, of 'heroicke parts'.[298] As the glorious bonfires lit up the night sky like the sun, the poets lauded the warmth and light of the new king, 'Saint James', from the north.[299]

After the flood of verse panegyrics which accompanied James's entry and coronation, vatic celebration began to fall silent. Yet James did not want for praise or gratitude in verse and particular events brought panegyrists back to sing the virtues of the Stuarts. The outpouring of praise for, as well as grief over, Prince Henry on his early death in 1612 is well known; less noted was that the death of the son was also the occasion for (by no means unfavourable) consideration of the father.[300] In, for example *The Laudable Life and Deplorable*

Death of our Late Peerless Prince Henry, James Maxwell paused to celebrate the living – 'our king of hearts', King James whom he compared to St James:

> O happy *Britaines* thus have in One
> A iust, wise Prince, a prompt Philosopher,
> A pregnant Poet, a Phisition,
> A deepe Divine, a sweet-tongued Orator.[301]

'Long live, King James,' the author prayed at this moment of reflection on the mortality of princes, 'our Salver and our Saint.'[302] Consoling his sovereign as well as the nation, John Davies praised a St James who was 'a King of Kings' who 'plai'st God's part' and from whom the people drew their strength and solace.[303]

If the chronology of panegyrical verse is the barometer of the king's image, it would seem to be the mid-teens of the century when verse paeans fell quiet. Whether (and we will return to it) it was the Overbury scandal or the outbreak of the Thirty Years War which changed the mood, by 1619 there was a feeling, as one preacher starkly put it, that 'panegyrics are not fit for this age'.[304] One genre of panegyric, however, came of age during and survived the course of the Jacobean era: the court masque. Though masque-like entertainments were certainly held at the Tudor court, it was the reign of James I which saw the development of the masque form as a leading vehicle of royal representation.[305] Quite simply, whether he performed in it or not, the monarch was the hinge of the masque as it evolved during the early seventeenth century. After a series of anti- or antic masques, representing disorder and chaos, the arrival of the king, queen or prince marked the change of scene from darkness to light and from anarchy to harmony, before the revels sang the virtues of regality. A form which was a fitting complement (and indeed compliment) to the divine right of kings, the masque represented a Platonic monarch with transformative powers to regulate nature and transmute vices into virtues: to make ideals real. In some ways, a logical development from the Tudor elevation of monarchy to its greatest heights, the masque marked the apogee of the extolment of sovereignty: the representation of royal as natural, divine power. During the reign of James I, the tense but creative partnership of the poet who became a virtual laureate and the king's surveyor-general combined verse, scenery and spectacle to enact before the audience of courtiers, ambassadors and others who gained entrance the ideology of absolute and perfect rule. Masque was, in Roy Strong's famous phrase, a 'liturgy of state', a service of worship of the sovereign and his divine wisdom.[306]

Unlike his wife and his sons, James I did not perform in masques. At times, the extravagant praise of the queen or prince who appeared on the stage to transform the action intruded uncomfortably into the masque's ultimate purpose: the apotheosis of the king. However, as critics have reminded us, the most important action of the masque took place not on the stage or behind the proscenium but in the dancing space before the king. Moreover, the most important actor, whether he 'performed' or not, was the king who sat on the perfect perspective line which represented his divine vision and who was the object of the spectators' gaze, as much as the action on the stage.[307] Accordingly, whatever the different agendas at times of members of the royal family, masques written for Anne of Denmark or for princes Henry and Charles also sounded the praises of King James. Even, for example, on the occasion of the nuptials of the Princess Elizabeth to Frederick Elector Palatine, the masque written by George Chapman for the Middle Temple and Lincoln's Inn praised James, the author of all who 'A learned King, is, as in skies/To poore dimme stars, the flaming day'.[308]

Once (and still often) read as unqualified praise of the monarch, masques could and did articulate counsel for, even criticism of, the sovereign.[309] Some of the tensions critics have identified in Jacobean masques may not be explained simply by the king's not performing but by the difficulties in making the ideal real; by, that is, the disjunctures between James's actual behaviour and masque eulogy. Towards the end of his reign, such strains appear to have led to the abandonment of a masque celebrating the Prince of Wales and the king. Masques, however, remained a genre of panegyric representation. Whatever his occasional reservations, Ben Jonson, as much as Inigo Jones, continued to portray a virtuous philosopher king. And, whatever criticism of the court he ventured in his plays, when he prepared *A Courtly Masque* for the entertainment of James at Denmark House in 1620, Thomas Middleton had all the characters of the antimasque deliver up the world to the king. As a scholar praised the glorious peace the land enjoyed (almost uniquely in a Europe again plunged into war), final songs, flattering James, presented England as a realm 'where the Head/Of him that rules to Learnings faire renowne,/Is doubly deckt with Lawrell, and a Crowne'.[310]

Though they expressed widely- as well as deeply-held beliefs about principles of order, harmony and hierarchy, masques were for too long dismissed – and by historians still often are – as escapist fantasies detached from the realities of politics and power, rather than seen as documents and representations of kingship in early modern England.[311] Yet, while they undoubtedly, to echo Ben Jonson, engaged with 'present occasions', the purpose of masques was 'to lay hold on more removed mysteries', to effect transcendence and to portray the king as above dispute and contest, not part of it.[312] During his reign, in which differences and disputes over policies increasingly sparked controversies about authority and power, James, perhaps even more than his predecessors, depended upon advocates who, in championing royal programmes and the royal prerogative, argued for that which poets idealized and simply lauded: James's kingship. From the beginning of his reign, James did not lack such supporters even for controversial royal policies.

For all that the project ran into trouble and floundered, the plan for a union of England and Scotland drew powerful supporters who presented the king who devised the plan as a ruler of rare historical greatness. In *England and Scotland's Happiness*, for example, John Gordon moved from congratulation on the unity of the island under one king to a representation of James as a second Constantine, as the perfecter of the work of reformation and as a God-like figure ruling a trinity of three realms.[313] William Cornwallis similarly took the occasion of *The Miraculous and Happy Union* to celebrate a unique prince 'whose virtues give lustre to his authority' and to publicize 'the testimonies given to the whole world of his abilities of government'.[314] Heralding another King Arthur, John Thornborough felt confident that under 'our golden head . . . we may live a blessed life in the golden age of this our happy time'.[315] As the union project began to get bogged down, the Gunpowder Plot once again focused writers' attention on the blessing England had in 'such a godly religious king' who had followed a good queen.[316] For the author of *Lucta Jacobi*, James Stuart was no less than his name: a second Jacob who 'outhunted those Romish Esaus' and secured peace for his people.[317] Following the Powder Plot, the assassination of the French king, Henri IV, in 1610 reminded England both of how close it had come to losing its own good king and of how thankful it should be for his survival. The naturalized Frenchman George Marcelline translated in 1610 his *Triumphs of King James* to portray the king to his own subjects as one who surpassed Pompey and Scipio.[318] Presenting him as one protected by God who 'adorned him with a simpler and supereminent quality of a king', Marcelline described James as 'great in virtue and faithfulness, great in wisdom and experience . . . the lively image of Great Hercules', adding that 'all his actions, all his words and cogitations are nothing but great'.[319] Support for and celebration of the virtues of King James were not, as is sometimes supposed, completely overshadowed by the encomiums that accompanied Henry's creation as Prince of Wales and emergence as an adult on the public stage. Henry Peacham's popular book of 'heroical devises', *Minerva Britanna*, may have been presented to Prince Henry, but Peacham, who also translated *Basilikon Doron* into an emblem book, making the king a fount of all wisdom, lavishly flattered and praised James.[320] No less, William Leigh paused in his lauding of Princess Elizabeth's virtues, which he compared with those of Joshua and Hezekiah, to praise 'the thrice happy government of our liege lord and king . . . in whom the flowers flourish and the kingdoms are united'.[321]

Even as troubles mounted at court, with parliament and in his relationship with his favourite, there was no absence of writers who, taking a wider and longer perspective, could discern and praise much to be glad of in Stuart rule. The author, for example, of a dialogue defending the oath of allegiance, as well as upholding regal authority generally, singled out 'our gracious, and religious sovereign' as amongst the best of rulers.[322] Richard Eburne concurred: 'we do live (God be praised),' he reminded readers of his treatise on equity, 'under so happy a government that we may boldly compare with any else.'[323] In 1618,

4 Emblem from Henry Peacham's *Minerva Britanna*, 1612

Thomas Gainsford, trumpeting *The Glory of England* as comparable to biblical Canaan's happiness, felt certain that the wealth and blessings of his country owed most to 'the best manner of government' under a monarch wise, learned and judicious, the fitting successor to a race of great kings: 'Oh happy England,' under such a ruler, he observed; 'Oh happy people'.[324]

The outbreak of the Thirty Years War, in the year that Gainsford published his work, while it underlined the benefits of peace also undermined some of England's – and James I's – glory. Though admiration for James continued, the plight of his daughter, evicted from the Palatinate in 1620, further tarnished the king's image; and we clearly detect a defensive tone in some of the treatises on the sovereign and his court. One author, praising 'the most illustrious and most magnificent James the first', 'our most religious, gracious, potent and most prudent king', openly acknowledged carpers and critics – and incidentally felt the need to defend James's hunting.[325] The next year, Thomas Procter's 'Defence' of *The Right of Kings* and their authority over clergy and church appears to reflect the mounting challenges to the king, as, in the wake of war in Europe, religious issues and divisions sharpened and discontent increased at home.[326] Still, towards the end of two decades of his rule, James, as well as representing himself in verse, speeches and meditations, did not lack supporters who, with or without official encouragement, praised his virtues and policies and publicized the benefits of Stuart rule to readers and subjects.

Ever since the break from Rome, representations of the past and histories had been important to the presentation and authority of the monarch. Henry VIII had justified his Reformation from a reading of history, and the struggle for supremacy of contending denominations – in Europe and England – was inseparable from interpretations of ecclesiastical history. In the later years of Elizabeth's reign, the foundation of the Society of Antiquaries and the publication of Camden's *Britannia* were part of a mounting nationalism. The past, however, was a contentious place; and it may be that growing interest by the government in archives reflected an appreciation of the importance of history in winning an argument. Under the early Stuarts, as questions and disputes arose over matters of law and royal prerogative, precedents became central to political discourse and to claims to authority.[327] Though some scholars were once tempted to write of a conflict over the interpretation and use of the past that mirrored a constitutional conflict, few would now endorse such a simple characterization. Yet a sense remains that the past favoured the critics of James I and Charles I and that history was a predominantly oppositionist discourse in early Stuart England. Indeed, such it could be; but we should not lose sight of the powerful endorsement James I received from historians and their representation of him, until late in his reign, as a monarch of historical destiny.

The uniting of the two kingdoms in the Stuart succession led many, as we have seen, to regard James VI and I as only the second British king in a long genealogical descent from Brutus.[328] Indeed, Stuart succession revived a cult of Brutus which (for long popular after the printing of Geoffrey of Monmouth's *History of the Kings of Britain*) had increasingly been treated with scepticism, along with the prophecies of Cadwallader, last king of the Britons, of a British imperium revived under a king who brought peace and concord.[329] Reflection on such prophecy led William Herbert to compare the new Stuart king with Caesar Augustus and Henry V and to conclude that 'the golden age begins with Iacob's raigne', and with 'a new found Troy'.[330] The hope James symbolized of a new age of British empire by no means faded with the obstacles to the royal project for full union. As theatre and art historians have shown, the revived vision of a Jacobean British empire, a new Troy, is evident in plays and in architectural plans and designs.[331] Thomas Heywood's 1619 poem *Troia Britanica*, for example, begins with the history of the world (James's descent was elsewhere traced from Noah) before sketching British history and the course that had now brought to the throne a king 'unrival'd yet, by such as raignd before him'.[332] In Heywood's verse chronicle, James almost marks the end, that is the fulfilment, of history:

His praise is for my pen a straine too hye,
Therefore where he begins I make my pause,
and onely pray that he may still supply
Great *Brittaines* Empire, with the Lands applause.[333]

The next year, in a prose history, Thomas Gainsford posited James as the fulfilment of the vision of Henry VII for Britain, and as the 'true champion in this Christian weale' who might topple Rome.[334] Praising the king, in whom the Britons, Saxons and Normans all lived, as a second Constantine, Gainsford presented James as

A matchlesse champion in this monarchie,
Who with firme constancie and zeale unfain'd
Doth labour to confirme an Vnitie.[335]

Similarly, Thomas Milles, in a prefatory address to the reader of his influential *Catalogue of Honour*, explained his decision to compile a treasury of nobility, 'seeing that now by the Providence of God, both England, Scotland and Ireland concur in one happiness under one true God, one true religion, one true king and monarch of Great Britain'.[336] Such representations of James as destined to revive British imperial greatness seem to have survived disenchantment and scandal. The verse accompanying the image of James in John Taylor's popular *Brief Remembrance of All the English Monarchs* (1618) describes him as a uniter of kingdoms into an empire, the first true monarch of Britain.[337] In his *Catalogue* of kings, the herald Ralph Brooke closed with 'this potent and magnificent monarch of Great Britain'.[338] Again, after 1618 historical eulogies tailed off – perhaps as both Britain and James failed to fulfil the historical destiny as scourge of Rome and founder of a new empire: the dedication to and description of James as 'the fort royal' of princes in Forset's *Defence of the Right of Kings* against Rome sounded a warning against the papacy which may have been a call to arms.[339] But, as this suggests, the expectations and hopes of a Jacobean imperium lived on from the first apocalyptic celebrations of his succession to the appeals for championship of the Protestant cause from 1618 to the end of the reign. Though the king did not always fulfil those expectations, contemporary historians, in singling him out as a specially chosen figure in the large scheme of history, represented James Stuart not only as God's lieutenant but as the agent of his providence, the champion of godly rule.

In his advocacy of his views on kingship and in his disputes with common lawyers and parliaments over prerogative, privileges and rights, James found more support from the writers of histories and political treatises than has been recognized. Appropriately, however, James's theory of the divine right of kings brought to prominence the clergy and the sermon as privileged authors and texts of royal representation: as the champions of both monarchy and of the person of the king. The tone was set by the Bishop of Winchester, Thomas Bilson's sermon at Westminster on the coronation on 28 July.[340] Preaching on Romans 13, and taking his cue from James's writings, Bilson glossed his text to argue that princes were not only 'gods by office' but also 'in the sanctity of their person which may not be violated, in the sovereignty of their power which must not be resisted'.[341] Kings, Bilson continued, should be free not only from violent resistance, but from 'all offence in speech and thought'; they were to be 'honoured and served as his [God's] lieutenants and vice-regents here on earth'.[342] The 'reverence due to princes', he asserted, encompassed 'the love of our hearts, the prayer of our lips, and the submission of our bodies'.[343] Because no price would match the benefit of monarchy, subjects were told that they must hold all their lands and goods, their bodies and their lives as the king's, should he require them.[344] In James, the sermon assured the assembled, England had a king both chosen by God and cognizant of the duties his godly office imposed upon him. Though he owed no account to subjects for his actions, James knew of the reckoning he must make to the Lord, that his sovereignty over men 'must be a service unto God'.[345] Like James's own writings, there was nothing especially novel in the argument of the coronation sermon, but the insistent rehearsal of these conceits, the language and the tone, signalled a church establishment ready to promote absolutist ideas of rule.

This, together with the sheer number of published sermons in the early seventeenth century, made the printed texts of sermons, as well as the pulpit, invaluable media of royal representation. Doubtless, the clergy were encouraged into the arena of politics by James's own spiritual exegeses and a desire to secure royal support for the protection and maintenance of the church. But, whatever the motives and interests of the preachers, the pulpit became a weekly stage for the advertisement of the sanctity of kings on a scale not witnessed before. Several of the published sermons were either presented before James or directly tackled a matter of royal policy. The Bishop of St David's' sermon at Whitehall on 13 May 1604, for example, flattered James as a David and Solomon, as did the Dean of Christ Church's sermons at Hampton Court giving thanks for 'our Jacob, our Solomon'.[346] The Dean of Salisbury's sermon on the union, also preached in the royal presence, presented James's rule and policy as heaven's course and urged compliance with Britain's Constantine who ruled by enacting God's will.[347] Richard Meredith, a royal chaplain, repeating the adage of the *Basilikon Doron* that 'the king is a God upon earth', told his congregation that 'God hath given us a good Moses' and a Solomon, a patron of a learned clergy and faithful ministry; another royal chaplain, William Hubbock, asked all to thank God for a sovereign and royal family protected by Providence and for 'the most evangelical monarchy in the world'.[348] As with verse panegyrics, crises spurred loyal preachers. Where Guy Fawkes's attempt on the king's life prompted a flood of sermons underlining James's chosen status, divine right and the evil of resistance, in the wake of enclosure riots in the Midlands, sermons against the rebels, such as that preached by Dr Robert Wilkinson at Northampton, took the occasion to praise a 'king . . . so earnest in hand to unite two kingdoms' for the good of all.[349]

Sermons on state and official occasions, often by royal chaplains, became regular paeans to kingship and to James which placed the monarch at the centre of worship.[350] A sermon preached at Westminster on the eve of the coronation of Henry as Prince of Wales, for instance, celebrated both the glories of Christian kingship in general and 'our most religious, gracious, zealous and miraculously preserved sovereign' in particular.[351] Sebastian Benefield's sermon at Oxford the same year, commemorating James's inauguration, proclaimed it as 'the word of truth' that kings had their authority immediately from God and led all in thanks to God for James who had delivered the nation.[352] The rise of nonconformity and criticism of prescribed church ceremonies and the episcopal hierarchy if anything led to greater emphasis on the power of the king as head of the church and protector of bishops and clergy. In *A Sermon of Obedience*, published in 1613 and specifically directed against the 'preciser sort', Francis Holyoake, preaching on Hebrews 13: 17 ('Obey them that have the oversight of you') taught that it was not for subordinates to question rulers.[353] 'Magistrates,' he admonished, '(especially of estate) do and must do many things whereof we cannot tell the reasons . . . it is not fit for us to take accompt of them but to look to our own duties and know they were more wise than we.'[354] In a sermon preached to the king the next year at Woodstock, the Vice-Chancellor of Oxford specifically outlined the duties of clerics to the crown at a time when, from Catholics as well as puritans, there were mounting challenges to authority. 'We are now forced to spend our time and studies,' he told James in a reminder of the clergy's service, 'in upholding the throne, in sustaining the sceptre.'[355] And demonstrating this by countering arguments that the people might resist an ungodly prince, Goodwin affirmed that 'the very name of a lawful and anointed king is sacred, his authority sovereign, his person inviolable'; there was, he added, 'no tribunal to which he may be cited; no law by which he may be punished', for 'God hath directly commanded obedience and subjection'.[356]

While the outbreak of war in Europe, and the consequent religious tensions in England, also gave further impetus to more loyal sermons on princely authority in matters spiritual and civil, the king's recovery from a near-fatal illness shortly after the death of the queen, in March 1619, provided a perfect occasion for clerical thanksgiving.[357] Bishop John King of London went to Paul's Cross to preach his sermon of public thanksgiving on 11 April; here, patterning James's life, sickness and deliverance from danger from the story of Hezekiah, he led all in prayers for a good and a holy king, preserved by God.[358] As, over the next years, not least to counter the puritans, James and the Duke of Buckingham advanced a clericist party, the pulpit oratory sounded ever louder with praise of the Supreme Head.[359] Preaching before James on his birthday, on 19 June 1621, William Laud, Dean of Gloucester and a champion of the high church party who was eager for a bishopric (which he secured only weeks later), urged the mutual dependence of church and state, prayed for kings and gave thanks for 'our Solomon . . . the Peace-Maker'.[360] In a sermon delivered to the king on progress at Beaulieu, the royal chaplain Christopher Hampton turned his scriptural text (Luke 22: 24–5) into what he described as a 'treatise of sovereignty'.[361] 'Kings,' he told his readers as well as the congregation, 'are . . . invested with supreme authority by the sentence and censure of the Son of God.'[362] Never subject to papal authority, they were also free of state censure: the Holy Ghost, he admonished, ordered there be no calumny against kings.[363] Urging the obligation in conscience of obedience, Hampton praised the learning, clemency, justice and piety of James to whom all reverence was due as the protector of the church and people.[364] In a sermon published by command in 1622, Walter Curll, warning against 'private murmuring and mutterings', damned those who 'spit their poison in the face of princes' and lauded the king for his 'care of the common peace' of the church.[365] A few months later, preaching at Theobalds, another royal chaplain bravely faced down the mounting noise to the contrary to reassert that 'the power of a king is from God', announcing it as a doctrine 'without all controversy'.[366] Christian subjects, he continued, should not think, let alone utter, ill of the king.[367]

Insistence, in the face of criticism and challenges, on the divine authority of the king was a frequent refrain of sermons by royal chaplains. It was a message that the clergy also endeavoured to communicate broadly. In his 5 November sermon to the Westminster judges, for example, Robert Willan took the opportunity to remind the judges, who in their courts and circuits were charged with suppressing 'the furious clamour of . . . unbridled . . . spirits', of their duty to the king.[368] Religion was, with the law, the strongest pillar in upholding obedience, he maintained, and by way of demonstration presented a king who was 'the Nestor of the times', the Noah of his age, a gracious ruler protected by God.[369]

Indeed, though many of the published sermons had been delivered to the king or were 'official', at Beaulieu, Theobalds and other progress residences they were probably heard by local congregations as well as the court and, once published, were read by a wider audience evidently hungry for sermons.[370] Moreover, similar sermons extolling the powers of monarchs and the blessing of James Stuart were delivered, we know, in the counties at assizes and doubtless also in hundreds of parish churches where local clergy took their cue from royal chaplains and bishops. To take just a couple of examples, in a sermon before those gathered in 1616 at the Somerset assizes at Taunton, William Sclater, minister for Pitmester, preaching on Psalm 82, discoursed on the divine ordinance of government.[371] Because 'Kings and Princes are God's vicegerents on earth, by whom . . . he governs the world', he explained in a hint to the judge and juries not to punish lightly their detractors, he 'could wish Moses law revived: who blasphemes the ruler . . . shall be put to death'.[372] 'Fear the Lord and the king', he cautioned all, 'and meddle not . . . with them that are seditious' – be they papists or 'of the brotherly separation'.[373] In 1619, other assize sermons pressed home the same message. At Reading in June, William Dickinson, a fellow of Merton College, Oxford, preaching on the 'sacred prerogative and right of the higher powers', reminded auditors that English kings bore the title *Dei gratia*, that they were the fathers of the realm, 'fundamenta, foundations and pillars' of the commonweal.[374] And countering any case for resistance even to tyrants and usurpers, he decreed that 'the person and power of the king is always sacred and inviolable'.[375] At Hertford, William Pemberton, minister for Ongar, Essex reminded the assembled company that kings were stamped with God's image and were instituted by God as 'nursing fathers', 'for the common good of all'.[376] Quoting from the *Basilikon Doron*, Pemberton told the magistrates, who had their charge from the king, that England's monarch, King James, knew that his office was one of *onus* more than *honos*, and that he owed account to God.[377] The next year at Warwick, the Archdeacon of Gloucester, Samuel Burton, preached at the General Assizes from a less familiar passage of Romans 13.[378] Since the monarch was the representative of God, he declaimed, 'we ought not to reproach him or revile him'.[379] Yet, on the one hand Jesuits rejected the duty of obedience; while on the other, opponents of church ceremonies ignored the prescriptions of authority. Worse, pasquils and libels lampooned governors when what was due to them, especially to a godly prince, was reverence and respect. Appealing for the maintenance of obedience and reverence at a time when they were little in evidence, Burton pleaded: 'If this affection, this revered conceit of the magistrate's person, were (as it ought to be) truly imprinted in the hearts of men, who sees not what good it would do and what a singular hope and furtherance it would be for all order and government?'[380]

Since, over the last year of James's reign, criticism and libels against the state and the king's favourite did not abate, we might ask how effective the clergy were in upholding the sanctity of kingship and promoting the godly image of the first Stuart. We will endeavour to find some answers to that question having reviewed not only other official representations of the king, but also the nature and forms of the opposition to his government. For now, however, it is worthy of note that, to the end, none of his subjects questioned James's faith nor undermined his supremacy. For all the tensions, bishops and king maintained the mutual partnership on which James believed the authority of both was founded and the Church of England clergy were often ardent apologists for kingship. Later events would prove that he was right and indicate how vital the church, its bishops and clergy, and the loyalist sermons they had preached, had been in sustaining divine right rule.

CHAPTER 2

FIGURING STUART DYNASTY

I

For all the queen's skill as an orator, for all the importance of her prayers and poems, Elizabeth is probably better remembered for her portraits, which were a principal representation of her monarchy. Figuring the queen as legitimate Tudor successor, classical goddess, virgin and sacred icon, portraits of Elizabeth, on canvas, medals and engravings, represented the queen as a mystical sacred object of worship, a godly ruler rather than an unmarried childless woman whose body was increasingly manifesting old age and mortality. While portraits had always been a vital medium for disseminating the royal image – abroad and at home – in the later sixteenth century English nobles, gentry and even civic communities appear to have taken a far greater interest in the visual arts, especially paintings on canvas. Doubtless that rise in interest was related to the vogue for prodigy houses in which nobles and aspirants to noble favour displayed their powerful connections as well as their family in long galleries which became the must-have architectural fashion of the age. The vogue for the portrait also related to the booming interest in heraldry in an age of social mobility and the quest for honour and place; more broadly it evidenced the heightened sense of self, perhaps even a desire for self-fashioning, which, we have learned, influenced vital developments on the stage, and in literature, drama, faith and civic life. Even at levels below the elite, there was a growing market for engraved and woodcut images, especially of Elizabeth and her courtiers, and for other souvenirs of the queen. By the end of the Tudor century, the image of the monarch was inextricably part of the exercise and perception of government: visual representation was essential to rule.

James VI had not been brought up in, or reigned in, that culture. Though we should not underestimate the importance of religious decorative painting and should be cautious about easy identifications between Protestantism and iconophobia, the kirk was an environment less supportive of the visual arts than the Church of England.[1] Moreover, Scotland was poor and, for much of the latter half of the sixteenth century, in political turmoil as factions vied to control the king. With an ever larger deficit in the royal treasury and endemic strife, the arts could hardly flourish. In fact, 'painters of any degree of sophistication were rare and inevitably foreign, and such were the rewards and such the limited demand that they were hardly likely to be of the greatest accomplishment'.[2] As he came to full authority on the death of his mother, though he did not neglect architecture or spectacle (especially for the christening of Prince Henry), James's chosen medium of representation – we recall the treatises on Revelation – appeared to be literary rather than visual. That said, the king cannot have been unaware of the dynastic significance of his image. After the (perhaps revealing) dispatch of the Dutch painter Arnold Bronchorst to London in 1583, his compatriot Adrian Vanson became principal court artist in Scotland. The city of Edinburgh's attempt to encourage him to train apprentices suggests that slowly there may have been growing interest in the arts in Scotland; if so, greater stability in the 1590s, perhaps too the influence of James's wife Anne of Denmark, encouraged those developments.[3] Yet, by English let alone continental standards, when it came to the visual arts Scotland remained a backwater.

Vanson painted two known portraits of James VI, the second of which, although our focus will not be on Scotland, merits attention. The 1595 portrait of the king appears to have been cut down, making him look less authoritative and probably obscuring a hand that appears to be grasping a sword hilt.[4] But what remains striking about this portrait of the king in ermine and embroidered doublet is that on his black sugar-loaf hat he wears a prominent jewel, an A, representing his marriage to Anne of Denmark. The repetitions of this on a miniature of the same date – one of a pair – and on coin very much suggest James's own commission and decision to represent himself as a husband and future sire.[5] Other than this, we know of no portrait of the king before his succession to an England in which the image of his predecessor hung in almost every noble house.

Evidently the James who authorized the English publication of his *Basilikon Doron* and *True Law* on the eve of his succession did not commission an official portrait for his new kingdom or title as king of Britain. And though peace with Spain in 1604 was to open England to travel, continental influences and artists, who were to be patronized by members of the royal family and leading nobles, James himself did not follow Henry VIII or precede his son in attracting to his service a continental portraitist to create a style, or a new mode of representation, for his dynasty. In his later, critical account of *The Court and Character of King James*, Anthony Weldon reported that James 'would never be brought to sit for the taking of that' (his portrait); which, he added, 'is the reason of so few good pieces of him'.[6] The less hostile Henry Peacham similarly lamented that he could 'never find any true picture of his majesty' and he was unimpressed by those he did find.[7] Indeed, it was not until two years after his accession (in May 1605) that James appointed a Sergeant Painter to the king, John de Critz the Elder, who had resided in England since 1568, to hold office jointly with Leonard Fryer who had executed decorative work on the queen's palaces.[8] The next year de Critz painted the first officially commissioned portrait of James, the queen and prince to be sent to the Archduke of Austria. That this became the template for the official royal portrait seems confirmed by another commission by Robert Cecil and by other versions that followed it.[9] The portrait very much suggests the royal agenda. In this first full-length of the king, James sports no royal regalia. In white doublet and embroidered costume with a cloak, the Garter and the Garter Jewel, James stands by a chair on a turkey carpet. Again, it is his hat that appears the most interesting feature. For on it James wears a jewel described as the 'Mirror of

5 *James I* attributed to John de Critz the Elder, *c.* 1606.

Great Britain' which had been made in 1604 to mark the union of Scotland and England. As with the earlier Vanson portrait, James advertises lineage and succession, but here identifies himself with the project most dear to him: the union of England and Scotland. It is ironic that, though he failed to achieve that, the many versions of the de Critz canvas, in three-quarter-length and head and shoulder as well as full-length, testify to 'the immense demand for the king's portrait both in Britain and as diplomatic gifts to be sent abroad'.[10]

The large number of later copies also suggests the scarcity of available royal images and the need to draw on this model, possibly some time after the meaning the canvas had first conveyed had faded or been tarnished by events. For it was evidently more than another decade before James again sat for a portrait that, like the de Critz, may very much have been determined by circumstances. Though de Critz was still working, the artist chosen for the new royal sitting was Paul van Somer, who had come to London in 1616 and soon entered the employ of Anne of Denmark whose artistic tastes and knowledge may have begun to influence her husband.[11] In this full-length portrait dated 1618, James stands wearing the gorget of a suit of Greenwich armour which bears his initials and lies on the floor to his right.[12] In his right hand, the king holds the George suspended from his neck, while with his left he leans on a table on which are laid the crown, orb and sceptre. Roy Strong has suggested that the canvas was connected with 'the reorientation of the arts at court effected by the desire for the Spanish match', and there can be little doubt of that in general.[13] The regalia advertise the attractions of an English marriage, as does the Garter, the complement to the Habsburg Order of the Golden Fleece. The armour laid on the floor signifies the blessings of peace which a match might bring to a Europe on the brink of, if not already embroiled in, war. But James, who stands between the emblem of war and the fruits of the English match, wears, as well as the gorget, his sword, perhaps as a hint that England's neutrality should not be taken for granted. An accomplished piece, the portrait was not only commissioned by the king and hung at Whitehall for public display, it was evidently regarded as the new authorized royal image. A second version may have been painted for Princess Elizabeth; numerous full-lengths were produced by Van Somer's studio; and Van Dyck was to take it as his model for a portrait of James commissioned later for Charles I; after, that is, the failure of the match which may have been the occasion of the original.[14]

As part of his preparation for the Anglo-Spanish marriage, James had commissioned Inigo Jones to build a new classical Banqueting House at Whitehall as a fit stage for the state festivities and entertainments planned to celebrate the match. Significantly, even before it was completed James sat for Van Somer again, with a rendering of his new building as a backdrop. Here, on a canvas dated to c. 1620, James stands in robes of state, wearing his crown and greater George.[15] Dominating the canvas, the king spreads his arms and holds in his hands the sceptre and orb. The viewer is drawn in, to the body of the

6 *James VI and I* by Paul van Somer, 1618.

king, and through the window that bears the legend ('Dieu et mon droit') to the Banqueting House, the new symbol of Stuart majesty and power. It may be significant that this most regal of the portraits of James belongs not to the time of his succession but to nearly two decades later. Together with the king's stance, the classical façade suggests imperium, perhaps the prospect of a Habsburg–Stuart empire which might secure peace for Christendom.

Whether Van Somer had already died or a new artist was preferred, the last full-length portrait of James during his reign was by the Delft painter Daniel Mytens who had come to England in 1618 and worked for Thomas Howard, Earl of Arundel before receiving commissions from Prince Charles and the

7 *James I* by Paul van Somer, *c.* 1620.

king. Here, in the version at the National Portrait Gallery, we see James – for the first time – seated, in a suit of white satin and Garter robes with, on a table on his left, a black hat with a jewel and ostrich plumes.[16] Above the king's head is a tapestry background with a large Tudor rose and a scroll inscribed 'Beati pacifici'. Roy Strong describes the king as having 'black eyes'; and it is not fanciful to discern a tired, anxious look. In 1621, James's self-presentation as a Christian king of peace (the ostrich feathers sometimes symbolized faith, hope and charity) was strained not only by war in Europe but by the defeat of his son-in-law at the Battle of the White Mountain and the eviction by Habsburg armies of Frederick and Elizabeth from the Palatinate.[17] Within months, the careful diplomacy directed towards a Spanish match, on which James believed the hope of Christendom rested, gave way to Charles's foolhardy journey to Spain, then pressure for war against the Habsburg.[18] James's last official portrait, copied as a present for an ambassador, epitomized a foreign policy that, having prompted three successive portraits, had failed.[19] Though he was granted a royal pension in 1627, Mytens executed no more portraits for James, not least perhaps because new policies were supplanting the image of the *rex pacificus*.[20]

Though, then, there is evidence that James sat for his portrait on a couple of occasions, the canvases appear to be related to, and perhaps limited by, specific policy objectives: first the union, then the match. Moreover, with the exception of the Van Somer of James in robes of state, the portraits do not obviously convey regality, let alone the mysteries of rule that characterized Elizabeth's image or the easy naturalizing of authority that Van Dyck was to bring to the representation of Charles I. Where Elizabeth's advancing years were obscured by an iconic mask, James appears in 1621 as evidently aged, indeed old. Most important, there are relatively few portraits of the first Stuart, and still fewer are remembered. Of all the early modern kings and queens, James I is the ruler least recognized or visually imagined. The obvious explanation lies in the relatively low priority he gave to portraiture in his representation of his kingship. But no less important was the fact that on canvas (as in some other respects) the image of James was overshadowed by those of his wife and children who not only patronized the best continental artists, but more obviously manifested an appreciation of the role of the arts in the struggles for publicity and power.

The artistic patronage both of Anne of Denmark and of Prince Henry is a large subject which is not our focus here.[21] But a recent biography has argued persuasively that the queen gathered an entourage of noblewomen through whom she was connected to the circles of artists, and that her cultural patronage was vital to her regal identity – perhaps an identity and image strategically different from that of her husband.[22] A glance at a couple of her portraits, even by the same artist, suggests significant differences in commission and taste to that of James. After what have been described as the 'curiously characterless pendants' to the portraits of her husband by de Critz, Anne

8 *King James I of England and VI of Scotland* by Daniel Mytens, 1621.

patronized and sat for Marcus Gheeraerts the Younger.[23] His portrait of Anne, executed c. 1611–14, resonates far more with Elizabethan than contemporary Jacobean royal paintings. Indeed, Anne exploits Elizabeth's visual legacy in a stance reminiscent of the Ditchley Portrait and, in her placement within a classical archway, the canvas recalls the Rainbow Portrait of Elizabeth at Hatfield. The echoes of Elizabethan representation do not stop there: Anne wears over an Elizabethan farthingale a dress embroidered with flowers and peacock feathers sacred to Juno, wife of Jupiter. She also, like her husband, wears identifiable jewellery – a crowned S (symbol of her mother Sophie of Mecklenburg) and a C4, given by Christian IV of Denmark. These displays of earthly majesty are complemented by a large double cross, most likely that in her inventory.[24] The canvas is inscribed with the queen's motto: 'La mia grandezze del excelsio' ('my greatness comes from God'), a reference back to the Virgin and the Virgin Queen, and with 'Fundamentum meum' (presumably meaning God my foundation). In this complex iconographical text, there can be little doubt that Anne was drawing attention to her descent from kings, her place as successor to Queen Elizabeth's legacy, and her divine election, all markers and signifiers of her independent authority.

One other portrait of the queen is worth attention, not least because it was a companion piece to Van Somer's of James.[25] Echoing the portrait of James, Anne rests her left hand on a table, but not (as in the portrait of the king) one on which lay the regalia. Her signifiers of regality she again wears as jewels in her ruff. And her farthingaled dress and stance, like that in the Gheeraerts, dominate the canvas more than the figure of James does. Behind Anne's left shoulder rises an elaborate architectural scene, which was evidently not painted by Van Somer. The building has not been persuasively identified and Millar describes it as a 'fantasy'.[26] But it evidently represents the queen's patronage of architecture and her identification with the greatest claims made for that art by Inigo Jones as the application of divine wisdom and order. In another portrait of her by Van Somer, painted about the same time, Anne stands in hunting costume in a park, with, in the background, the palace of Oatlands, alterations to which Inigo Jones had just completed.[27] In this painting, an owl (of Minerva) perches in a tree above the queen and a scroll displays her motto. Divine guidance and wisdom are claimed in relation to the queen's patronage of building and, through Jones, the arts.[28] Not least as a consequence of James's indifference, Anne of Denmark found a space for her independent representation and a medium in which she could vie with, and even eclipse, the king.

Anne bequeathed her passion for and appreciation of the power of the arts to her elder son. Though Henry sat for James's official painter in 1606, like the queen he preferred other artists to de Critz's pedestrian work, and in particular favoured Robert Peake.[29] Peake was hardly avant-garde, but his experience of the tradition of Elizabeth's reign may have been part of his appeal to the prince.

9 *Anne of Denmark* by Marcus Gheeraerts the Younger, *c.* 1611–14.

Indeed, in an early portrait of the nine-year-old Henry at the hunt with Sir John Harington, Peake figured the boy, on the eve of his creation as Prince of Wales, in the pose of Henry VIII's Holbein mural and William Scrots' version of it for Edward VI.[30] The depiction of Henry about to deliver the *coup de grâce* to the hunted stag adds a military dimension to the climactic scene in which the kneeling Harington pays homage to a future king and victor. Evidently Henry was pleased with the work, and a later copy (with the young Earl of Essex) now at Hampton Court may have been made for him.[31] Certainly from 1608 Peake was receiving payments listed in Henry's accounts, and became a member of the prince's household when it was established in

10 *Henry, Prince of Wales, with Sir John Harington* by Robert Peake the Elder, 1603.

1610.[32] Indeed, that year and probably to mark the occasion, Peake reprised the outdoor action scene, but this time not of a hunt. Against a background of a moat and castle, which may be Richmond Palace, Henry stands, poised but captured in motion, as he is about to draw a military (as opposed to ceremonial) sword.[33] As his right foot suggests his readiness to strike, his left stands firmly on a tournament shield bearing the Prince of Wales's feathers and motto, 'Ich Dien'. Roy Strong identified a source of the unusual pose in an engraving from Hendrik Goltzius's *The Roman Heroes* (*c.* 1586) of Manlius Torquatus, Livy's model of Roman discipline and greatness.[34] Though it has

11 *Henry, Prince of Wales* by Robert Peake, *c.* 1610.

not been so interpreted, the portrait appears to represent Henry rejecting the pasteboard shield of the tilt for actual military heroics and intervention, and so presenting himself as a different model of kingship to the pacific rule of his father and perhaps even to the inactivity of Elizabeth's reign. Such an interpretation gains strength from another Peake of Henry, this time an equestrian portrait figuring the prince in armour, leading the figure of Time or Opportunity who bears Henry's lance and helmet.[35] We shall return to Henry's martial representation and the difficulties the royal family presented to James I's image. For now, what is striking is the use by Anne and her son of different artists and conceits, and of elaborate symbolic visual vocabularies, which the poet-king James showed little interest in deploying for his own portraits.

Like many large-scale portraits, Peake's painting of Henry as Roman hero was a gift to a foreign prince and was not displayed for an English audience. However, as we have seen, many portraits survive in studio copies and it seems that copies became the models for forms of visual representation that were yet more widely disseminated. One, and very much a genre of the Elizabethan and early Stuart years, was the miniature. James continued in his employ the miniaturist responsible for Elizabeth's image for thirty years, Nicholas Hilliard. Unfortunately Hilliard was past his best and 'could never respond to the Stuarts as he had to Elizabeth'.[36] Though quite a number of workmanlike, or worse, miniatures were produced, James gave Hilliard little patronage (the artist was impoverished by 1613) and sat for him only twice.[37] Perhaps significantly again, Anne abandoned the appointed royal miniaturist to patronize Isaac Oliver who in 1602 had married the sister of Gheeraerts, painter of the queen in oil. Each of the dozen miniatures Oliver executed for her from 1605 was the result of a sitting, and Anne's strong interest in the genre as a form of representation is evidenced by her commissioning miniatures visualizing themes from her masques in which she performed as Divine Beauty and as a British empress.[38] Henry too gave Oliver 'abundant patronage' as the artist figured him armoured, à l'antique, with scenes of the camp, as the martial prince.[39] Despite the quality, even brilliance of his work, Oliver appears to have painted no miniatures of James, who stuck with Hilliard until his death in 1619, aged seventy-two, and then abandoned the genre. Reviewing his early Stuart work, a critic concluded: 'To judge by the results he achieved, Nicholas Hilliard did not find the portrayal of James I a congenial task.'[40] It would seem that the king concurred.

II

As James succeeded to the throne, a new form of royal representation was becoming a commercial and even popular object: the engraved or wood block portrait. During the last years of Elizabeth's reign, a volume of pictures of all the monarchs since the Conquest had been published, and in James's reign,

Henry Holland's *Braziliologia* consisted of plates of monarchs engraved by Renold Elstrack, which was successful enough to merit a second edition.[41] There are few examples of engraved or woodcut images of James as king of Scotland. One woodcut of about 1580 displays the young king in armour, holding a thistle in his left hand while grasping a sword in his right, above the legend 'in utrumque paratus' – prepared for all eventualities.[42] Although better executed images of the king of Scotland survive, by Elstrack and others, it is likely these were English productions, or engraved after Stuart succession.[43]

After 1603 – a testament to the popularity at this time of both the genre and the monarchy – large numbers of engraved images of the new king were produced. Among the earliest, as with the verse and prose panegyric, were engraved representations of James with Anne of Denmark on genealogical tables displaying and again underlining their lineage, their right to the throne of England, and the dynastic marriage of the northern and southern kingdoms. In 1603, for example, William Kip and Benjamin Wright both published genealogies with engraved portraits, Kip's dedicated to James – though there is no evidence of an official commission.[44] Renold Elstrack's *The Most Happy Unions Contracted betwixt . . . These Two Famous Kingdoms*, published by John Speed without date, is likely to belong to the same period. Placing James and his wife on a genealogical tree that traces their descent from Robert II, the sheet may have been intended for pasting on a wall or similar public display.[45]

Given the paucity of paintings of the king, especially in the early years, there were quite a few anonymous and authored engravings of James published and sold to an English public which, whatever the king's disinclination, was evidently anxious to see and own an image of their new sovereign. Though the head and shoulders portrait, with plumed hat and ruff, was archetypical, verses on various versions of this type singled out and publicized royal qualities and virtues. In one, sold by John Overton at the White Horse, verses flattered James's learning and godliness by proclaiming 'knowledge makes the King most like his maker'; another sold by John Boswell in Pope's Head Alley celebrated the people's happiness in a king who brings peace and prosperity.[46] Yet another, a small image of James wearing the George, draws attention to his words 'so deeply wise' and prudent.[47] More than paintings, some of the earliest engravings of James depict the king of three realms with the regalia. Laurence Johnson's 1603 plate very much emphasized costume, the embroidered doublet and cloak, and the sceptre and orb the king holds, in presenting James as 'the high and mighty prince . . . by the grace of God King of England, Scotland, France and Ireland, defender of the faith'.[48] Whether or not he came to England to execute it, in 1604 the engraver Crispin van de Passe, who engraved a full-length portrait of Elizabeth after Isaac Oliver and who in 1598 had engraved a portrait of James VI in armour, etched another plate, this time an oval of the king in ermine, part of a set of the royal family, that heralded the new ruler who by God's will succeeded to three kingdoms.[49] Though Van de Passe's work

12 *The Royal Progeny* by William Kip, in *Description of the Kingdoms of England, Scotland and Ireland*, 1603.

seems to have been produced for a Dutch publication, the image evidently circulated in England and was simplified and copied for broader, popular consumption.[50]

Van de Passe continued to engrave images of James. For one, a portrait of James is placed beneath a laurel and the motto 'Beati pacifici', while, around the oval, a verse presents the James who has united kingdoms as the true heir of a Henry VII who had united warring families.[51] Under the image of the king, the biblical injunction 'Touch not mine anointed' echoed James's own views on kingship.[52] In 1613, Van de Passe returned to his royal subject, this time in larger format.[53] Here on a plate measuring nearly 12″ × 9″, James is depicted under an arched niche with laurel and holding the sceptre, above Latin verses praising his imperial sway, his learning, the peace he had brought to the church and his justice: praise very much reprising James's own boasts of his achievements, whether or not there was official patronage of Van de Passe's work. Some connection between the royal family and the Van de Passes may

13 *The Roial Progenei of Our Most Sacred King Iames*, print by Benjamin Wright, published by Hans Woutneel, 1603.

lie behind the remove of Crispin's younger brother Simon in about 1612 to London, where he produced numerous images of English nobles, royal favourites, Queen Anne and Prince Charles, and of James I himself.[54] As well as contributing the plate of the first Stuart to Holland's *Braziliologia*, Simon etched James in regal posture, seated on his throne and wearing royal robes and with crown, sceptre and orb.[55] To the right of the king's throne, on a table, a sword inscribed 'Iustitia' and a book, 'Verbum Dei', announce James's patronage of a new bible as well as the chief virtue of a king, the care of justice, while, beneath, an official commission is confirmed by the name on a plate with Van de Passe's: that of John Bill, the king's printer, and indeed printer of the king's own *Works*.

We shall return to Van de Passe in considering later group portraits of the Stuart royal family. Two other engravers of James's solo portrait command our attention: Renold Elstack and Francis Delaram. Elstrack, a Dutch immigrant to London and son of a glazier, began his career as an engraver about the turn of the century, and his portrait of James VI may have been one of his earliest works.[56] In 1604, he executed a plate important in the representation of the new king, depicting him in the opening of his first parliament on 19 March of that year.[57] Surrounded by the armorial shields of Scottish, Irish and English nobles, James is shown enthroned beneath a large royal arms and between his Lord Chancellor (Thomas Egerton, Baron Ellesmere) and Lord Treasurer (the Earl of Dorset) in front of whom is seated Prince Henry. On each side stand bishops and peers, the Earl Marshal and Lord Chamberlain. Published by John Speed, who was to provide genealogies for the King James Bible and whose *History of Great Britain* was published with royal privilege, the sheet (reissued in 1621 and 1624) advertised the new monarch with his English officers in the White Chamber (or Parliament Chamber), to which the Commons also would have been summoned to hear the first speech James delivered the same day; indeed, it may have been published as a complement to the printed speech in which James presented himself to the representatives of his people.[58] Certainly, it was to Elstrack that James turned for the engraved title page of his most important representation, his *Works*, a little over a decade later.[59]

The life of Francis Delaram is shadowy before his first dated work of 1615, but it has been conjectured that he worked closely with Van de Passe and early on was involved in etching royal portraits.[60] Delaram engraved four portraits of the first Stuart, of which three were almost certainly contemporary, and two remarkable. The larger bust of the king, at 22″ × 16″, is obviously striking – not to say unique – for its size and form. Not only is James figured here larger than life, as Antony Griffiths has observed, but his shoulders appear to burst out of the frame, as if the king were about to spring into action.[61] The second engraving very much departs from the traditional image of the *rex pacificus*. One of only two (the other anonymous) of James mounted, Delaram's plate

Behind BEATI PACIFICI

Crownes have their compasse, length of dayes their date,
Triumphes their tombes; felicitie thee fate :
Of more then earth, can earth make none partakers,
But knowledge makes the KING most-like his maker.

Simon Passæus sculp:Lond.   Ioh: Bill excudit.

14 James I by Simon van der Passe, frontispiece to *Workes*, 1619.

shows the king with a sword on a prancing horse, the model for which may have been taken from portraits of Henri IV or even the Earl of Essex.[62] Behind and below lies London, with ships on the Thames. The imperial image is underpinned by the verse placed next to Delaram's signature:

Behold the shadow of great Britains King
Whose Fame throughout the World the Muses sing
Heavens graunt thy happy days may never end
Since on Thy life millions of lives depend.

15 Engraving of James I on horseback by Francis Delaram, 1616.

The plate has been assigned to 1616 when Compton Holland, the publisher, issued similar equestrian portraits of Anne and Prince Charles. If, as seems likely, they had at least official approval, we must conclude that James's reputation as peacemaker did not preclude representation as an imperial figure and a king of action.[63] Whatever his own intentions, the equestrian portrait was reissued, this time with the king in armour, in 1621 – in circumstances where many were calling for a martial prince and militant foreign policy.[64] If in 1616 Delaram's equestrian image of the king related to the desired union of two empires, after the outbreak of the Thirty Years War the anonymous engraver may have had another agenda. But in either event, these were representations of James which were very different from his traditional image as peacemaker, equestrian images that would influence the design of Oliver Cromwell's seal.

One of the central representations of James in verse panegyrics was as a husband and father and the novel blessing of a paterfamilias and family to an England which had seen three childless monarchs. Though, as David Bergeron has observed, 'no paintings exist of the Stuart royal family during its first decade in England', there were several engraved images.[65] Elstrack's large engraving of the royal couple, standing with their armorial bearings and sumptuously dressed, with their titles and birth dates, sold by John Sudbury in

16 *James I and Anne of Denmark* by Renold Elstrack.

Pope's Head Alley, was probably an early visual introduction of the royal couple to their new subjects as well as another assertion of their dynastic claim.[66] In another likely early work, James and Anne are etched under two arches beneath their armorial bearings in poses that evoke Henry VIII and Elizabeth I.[67] Before them, at the top of a genealogical tree decorated with Tudor roses, in an oval the small figure of Prince Henry advertises the royal progeny. James was represented with his son in an anonymous engraving early in the reign and, after Henry's creation as Prince of Wales, in a double equestrian portrait with a battle scene in the background, an image which may owe more to the patronage of the prince's circle than the king's.[68]

As panegyrists hoped he would step into Henry's shoes, after the death of the prince Charles rapidly took his brother's place in engravings which continued to publicize Stuart fecundity and secure succession. Indeed, two versions of one engraving of James with the prince depict, respectively, Charles and Henry.[69] The king may also have sat for William Van de Passe's double portrait of James and Charles, published by Thomas Jenner in 1621.[70] If so, it is an important text which commands more attention than it has received. James is shown seated, in state robes and crowned, with (in his left hand) an orb, and (in his right) not a sceptre but a sword, inscribed *Fidei Defensor*. Charles stands to his father's left wearing, like his father, his George and Garter. Beneath each figure, verses single out their praises: James's wisdom

17 *Triumphus Jacobi Regis Augustaeque Ipsius Prolis*, by William van der Passe, 1622.

and majesty, the peace he has brought, his renown and his defence of the faith and word of God, not least by means of his own works denouncing heresy; Charles as a Solomon who, it is hoped, might even surpass David. Van de Passe's *Triumph of King James and of his August Progeny*, issued the next year, is an even more obvious state dynastic portrait.[71] The print is dedicated to James and Charles by John Bill, who indicates that he has royal privilege to produce it, again to be sold by Thomas Jenner. In this complex family group, which echoes William Rogers's engraving of Henry VIII and his successors issued shortly before 1603, James, crowned and enthroned with the regalia, is placed at the centre, with Charles and his dead mother and brother (holding skulls to signify their deaths) and the twin girls Maria and Sophia. By a window opening on to a peaceful pastoral scene and beneath an angel hovering with crowns, Charles stands with his left hand on his hip (in a gesture imitating his father) and with his right touching a large open bible which lies on a table with other books. Beside the bible, almost certainly the King James Version, the only other book bearing a title is the *Opera regis*, the Latin works of James published in 1619. On the king's left, by a window opening on to a church and beneath an angel holding crowns, stand the king's daughter Elizabeth of Bohemia and her husband Frederick, hands joined, with their children. The engraving exists in several states, with children added as they were born, and indeed in a version posthumous to James, in which Charles appears crowned and with his wife Henrietta Maria.[72] The adaptations emphasize the perceived importance of the image in its first creation in 1622. Charles is figured as heir to his father's peaceful and beneficial rule, to his virtues and values as expressed in his works and his bible. But King James's other relations are not forgotten, least of all his daughter, whose large family also claim the dynastic rights of which they have recently been deprived and who stand as the hope of the Protestant cause in Europe. One of the few critics to have considered the image analyses it as a portrait of a Christian saint (James is modelled on figures from Flemish and Italian religious paintings) as well as the imperial *rex pacificus*.[73] But it appears, too, as dynastic assertion as well as display, as a statement that the Stuart family is at one, and that, despite the voiced criticisms of inactive pacifism, neither James nor Charles will ignore what the accompanying verse describes as the 'imperial offspring' of the Palatine. In licensing, possibly even commissioning the *Triumph*, at a moment when the royal policy of a Habsburg marriage was being countered by those calling for the king to join in a Protestant crusade, James still looked for an empire that might 'Ore all the forms, ore all the Mains extend'. And, again proclaiming his steadfast faith, he promised his grandchildren: 'God by your means will mighty things atchive'.[74]

Though we can by no means know the extent to which engraved images of James and his family were published with official licence or approval, in instances where we do know, there is a clear suggestion that, however small his interest in portraiture, the king may have given more attention to engravings which, often accompanied with verses, had close association with the words and books that remained his favourite medium of representation. As importantly, the large number and range of engraved portraits meant that the image of James was broadly distributed and known at a time when (as well as *Braziliologia*) the popular poet John Taylor's *Brief Remembrance of All the English Monarchs*, issued in two editions, indicates a market eager to acquire images of regality.[75] With James and his son the last of twenty-five plates of the monarchs since the Conquest, books like Taylor's did much to make the Stuarts part of an English pantheon of kings.

A feature of many, perhaps most, of the engravings was the royal arms, which is also published and displayed without the royal portrait in a multitude of books, as on proclamations and declarations. As John Wickham Legg observed, 'it must not be forgotten that the coming of the Scottish king to our country as its ruler brought with it a great change in the royal coat of arms'; and the advertisement of that change was vital to James's project of union and to his representation as monarch of all his kingdoms.[76] John Jonston published a large royal Scottish arms as part of his description of the house of Stuart in 1603; and in 1613 John Speed included in his *Theatre of the Empire of Great Britain* a plate displaying the arms of the British king.[77] James added to the royal coat of arms the Scottish lion in the second quarter; and he replaced the red dragon of Cadwallader, which was an emblem of the Tudors, with the white unicorn of Scotland.[78] The new arms which marked the change of dynasty also endeavoured to bring about what they and the king symbolized. The king's proposal to change by legislation the name of his kingdom to Great Britain having run into opposition, James assumed the new style by his own declaration.[79] His arms were the visual statement of that declaration. Certainly the new royal arms drew attention and analysis in the early Stuart years. Early accession poems identified the lion as a symbol of fortitude, and protection;[80] the clergyman William Fennor went further, boasting that 'the lion rampant keeps the rest in feare'; noting the removal of the dragon, he adds:

> And in the place you have put the *Unicorne*,
> To expell the poyson with his precious *Horne*.

– a reference perhaps to the unicorn as a symbol of purity.[81] George Marcelline endeavoured a full explication of the emblems and symbols of the new royal arms. Reading the royal lion – he claimed James had one on his left breast as well as on his arms – as a signifier of generosity, he went on to decipher flowers and beasts as mystical expressions of that 'sweet harmony . . . which entertaineth and preserveth the whole kingdom in good peace and quietness'.[82] Whatever the frustrations he felt at the failure of union, James's armorial achievement, carefully constructed and ubiquitously reproduced, displayed the fact of nations joined under one sovereign and into one powerful empire.

Although the royal arms were swiftly altered, James lived for some months with his predecessor's seal before he had his own.[83] James's Great Seal, in use by the end of 1603, figured the king enthroned, wearing the collar of St George and bearing a sceptre and orb with a cross; on the throne, fleurs-de-lis and roses represent the crowns of England and France.[84] On the right side of the dais, the Scottish lion supports a standard of the arms of Cadwallader, last king of the Britons; on the left the unicorn introduced by the king supports a similar pennon with the arms of Edward the Confessor. Above those supporters, the royal arms (quartered for France, England, Scotland and Ireland) are encircled with the Garter and motto of the order: Honi soit qui mal y pense. The seal bears the king's legend 'Iacobus dei gratia angliae scotiae franciae et hiberniae rex fidei defensor'. On the reverse, the king is depicted on horseback galloping to the right, in armour with a crested helmet and very heavy sword. Restoring a gesture to Cadwallader, and incorporating for the first time the Irish harp along with the lion and unicorn, James ensured that every document that bore his seal reminded subjects of a new ruler, a new kingdom and the possibilities for a new empire.[85]

The imperial pretension is even more apparent on James's early medals. For his accession medal, James – the first time a monarch did so in English history – assumed the dress of a Roman emperor, a laureate bust that was repeated (this time in profile) for his coronation medal of 25 July that year.[86] As well as imperium, in these early medals James proclaimed his piety: for his accession he ordered a die for a bezant expressing his gratitude to God for his peaceful succession.[87] In an image which appears to be taken directly from the frontispiece to Queen Elizabeth's prayer book, the king kneels (to the left) in prayer before a large volume – perhaps the Bible or a Book of Common Prayer. At the king's side, four crowns signify the earthly kingdoms he has inherited by the grace of God and which he now lays aside to give thanks to his heavenly king; the inscription explains that he gives a little back to God for all that the Lord has bestowed on him.

James continued to commission medals throughout his reign to commemorate – or perhaps even to promote – policies which he felt the need to sell. That, for example, struck in 1604 to celebrate the peace with Spain, a policy less than popular with the militant Protestants, was apparently cast to be worn as a badge.[88] On the reverse of the bust of the king, Religion and Peace stand each side of a cornucopia, signifying the fruits of peace. The peace medal was issued in three states, on one of which the bust of James follows the coronation type with the title now king of Great Britain that he took by proclamation in October of that year. As part of his campaign for union, the king also issued a special medal in silver and copper with two sceptres united in one crown and the legend, 'They are made stronger under one [sovereign]'.[89]

Though a medal was struck in Holland to commemorate the discovery of the Gunpowder Plot, none was issued by the king.[90] Nor, though he had ordered the peace with Spain medal, did James mark the alliance of 1609 with France and the United Provinces, as did the Dutch. It was the creation of Henry as Prince of Wales and the marriage of Elizabeth in 1613 that provided the next occasion for medals, though whether these were of James's or his children's devising is uncertain. Two surviving medals, in gold and silver, depict Henry in Roman armour and with his motto 'Fax mentis honestae gloria' (the

18 The Great Seal of James I.

19 Medal of James I at prayer.

fire of an honest mind is glory); while Elizabeth is represented in a style not unlike the images of her namesake, the last queen.[91]

Perhaps following his sitting for a portrait, in 1616 James authorized medals of himself, Queen Anne, Prince Charles, Frederick and Elizabeth as a family group and one of the Infanta of Spain with whom, after the death of his elder son, he hoped to effect a marriage for Prince Charles.[92] All the medals were the work of Simon van de Passe, who, since his arrival in London in 1612, had been executing engravings for the king. The medals, of high quality, presented more detailed likenesses of the king in ermine and with his Garter collar, with, on the reverse, a large royal arms above the motto 'Beati pacifici'.[93] Engraved and published the same year, these medals reminded subjects of the peace and blessings which the Stuarts had brought and of the future security their dynastic union with the house of Habsburg might provide. Though numerous medals were struck abroad celebrating the coronation of Frederick and Elizabeth as king and queen of Bohemia, it is unlikely that any were officially commissioned by James, who doubted the legality as well as the wisdom of his son-in-law's usurping a throne.[94] After the death of Queen Anne in 1619, we encounter no medals of James that we can date and it would appear that none was issued. After the collapse of peace, the death of two members of his family and the disaster that beset his daughter, then the frustrations of the Spanish match, the policies which had inspired a medallic programme had ended in failure. However, the medals, especially those engraved by Van de Passe, again suggest a greater interest by James in his visual representation than has been allowed. Moreover, the execution of cheap copper and lead badges and counters, as well as gold and silver medals, indicates an intention to see the royal image in this form distributed widely. Badges of the king as *Defensor Fidei* with a reverse depicting the ark safe from the flood, or with a verse from Psalm 72, 'Unto the king give thy judgement, O God', state visually and briefly that claim to be God's lieutenant and

20 *Defensor Fidei* medal.

exegete that James Stuart argued at length in his prose treatises and biblical commentaries.[95]

As did his seal, James's coins announced and effected important changes in the royal image as represented in this the most public medium of its distribution. Several Jacobean coins carried on the reverse the new arms, quartered for the first time with the Scottish lion and the Irish harp; and James was the first English king to be depicted on coin with a bust laureate and in Roman costume, that is as an emperor. Early coins (which pre-date the Gunpowder Plot), with a profile of James in armour, crowned, carried the legend 'exurgat deus dissipentur inimici' from the opening line of Psalm 68: 'Let God arise, let his enemies be scattered: let them also that hate him flee before him'.[96] Here, as in his writings, the king figured himself both as protected by God and as the agent of God: one coin bearing the inscription has an equestrian image of James with a sword which, we have seen, was depicted with the bible in other images of Stuart rule. Other early coins related to, and again seem intended to promote, the union of the two kingdoms. On gold coins known as 'the unite', the obverse and reverse depicted, respectively, the English rose and Scottish thistle crowned between the king's initials I.R.[97] Other union coins reprised the boast we have encountered in the legend which announced that Henry (VII) joined the roses, James the nations, while another claims, somewhat optimistically as events proved, 'Faciam eos in gentem unam' – I will forge them into one people.[98] Arguments in royal speeches extolling union are summarized in inscriptions such as 'Deus tueatur unita', may God protect the united nations.[99] And one of James's favourite metaphors (from Matthew 19: 6) appears on several coins:

21 Gold coin of James I.

'what God has joined together let no man separate'.[100] Most Jacobean coins figured the king as a bust, crowned, or mounted and (later) laureate.[101] Some, however, represented James enthroned with the regalia between two pillars – probably a gesture to the pillars of Hercules, the emblem of Charles V and of imperial sway.[102] If so, the legend (from Psalm 118) 'This is the Lord's doing; it is marvellous in our eyes' suggests that James may be the cornerstone of God's own foundation, of the empire of Christ. The same inscription appeared on the reverse of the only Jacobean coin I have seen representing James with the new arms of British monarchy on a ship, and on a coin on the obverse of which St Michael slays a dragon, a common representation of the triumph of faith over evil and, of course, the conceit behind the cult of St George.[103]

The repetition of images and themes in the different genres of medals, coins and engravings, all executed by different artists, suggests that, for all his famous disinclination to sit for his portrait, James appreciated the value of visual representation in advancing arguments and policies of importance to him. The best as well as most enduring demonstration of that, of course, is that monument both to a specific foreign policy and to an ideology of kingship which is still too often passed over in biographies and histories of the king: the Banqueting House at Whitehall. The later Tudor decades had been unremarkable in the history of royal architecture. Elizabeth I had ordered a new banqueting house to be built for the entertainment of the duc d'Alençon on his second visit in 1581; but it was essentially a temporary structure designed for an occasion rather than as a permanent statement.[104] The succession of a king with a wife and family necessitated more fundamental changes in palace architecture; and James's bibliophilia probably explains the construction of a new library early in his reign.[105] As early as 1604, James determined to replace Elizabeth's temporary Banqueting House, and evidently took a close interest in the progress of the building which was completed by 1609.[106] In January 1619, the room (which served often as the venue for the masques that had become fashionable on state occasions) was destroyed in a fire at Whitehall. For all his non-participation in, and supposed indifference to, the masques, James moved quickly to establish a commission to rebuild it – 'expeditiously', and with grandeur.[107] As Per Palme long ago argued persuasively, the impetus for rebuilding at a time of economic difficulty appears to have been prompted by dynastic and diplomatic policy: in particular, after the outbreak of the Thirty Years War by James's hopes for peace in Europe and an Anglo-Habsburg marriage alliance which might help effect it. The Banqueting House, that is, was to be the stage for a marriage, the scene of dynastic triumph, and a monument to the *rex pacificus*. Whatever the genius of the architect, Inigo Jones, the *raison d'être* of the Banqueting House lay in a policy dear to the king and in his representation and as (he hoped) commemoration of that policy: 'The rebuilding of the Banqueting House should be seen not just as an unparalleled event in the history of English architecture, but as the most important part of a comprehensive programme for the augmentation and reshaping of the representative aspects of the Court milieu.'[108]

That programme included improvements to, and redecoration of, other state apartments, most sumptuous of the refurbishments being improvements to the chapel. In August 1619, as the commission for the Banqueting House began its work, the king established a board to investigate the creation of an English tapestry workshop, at Mortlake, to produce suitable hangings for the new building and to mark the occasion of the Habsburg marriage.[109] About the same time, James (as we have seen) sat to Van Somer for a state portrait, in one version of which he is placed in front of the building that was the depiction of his self and his rule.[110] In a sermon at Reading in June 1619, the preacher William Dickenson used appropriately elaborate architectural metaphors to describe monarchy. 'The King,' he told his congregation at the assizes, 'is a foundation; others are but part of the frame raised upon this foundation; some are main cross beams, some polished pilasters.'[111] Indeed, as well as the architect and artisans, the principal officers of the royal household were involved in the plans for the building from the start; and Sir John Digby, the agent of the Spanish match negotiations, joined them.[112] By St George's Day 1621, the Banqueting House was sufficiently advanced to receive the Garter knights at the end of their grand procession; the next year the building was ready for other ceremonies, and an inauguration masque in anticipation of the match: Ben Jonson's *The Masque of Augurs*.[113] In his masque, Jonson, as so often, captured the king's purposes as expressed in stone:

It is enough your people learne
The reverence of your peace,
As well as strangers doe discerne

The Glories, by th'increase:

And that the princely Augur here, your Sonne,

Doe by his father's lights his courses run.[114]

If, then, the Banqueting House was conceived and designed to glorify the Stuart dynasty and to advance and celebrate a dynastic union, how did it do so? The revolution in architectural style that the Banqueting House signalled cannot be separated from the novel statements about Stuart royal magnificence it was intended to make.[115] In his departure from a native English style, to favour the classicism of Palladio, Jones from the outset designed a building which was for a European audience and occasion, as much as English ones. Echoing Roman imperial architecture as interpreted in the late Italian Renaissance, James was inventing a palace for that new British imperium prophesied in accession pane-gyrics on the king.[116] Jones based his plans for a double cube both on Palladio's for the basilica at Vicenza, where judges had sat at the end of a colonnaded hall, and on the Egyptian hall, a place for entertainment, and adjusted them for James's wish to make the Banqueting House a grand Presence Chamber for state ceremonies.[117] The design of the building, imagined as the nave of a basilica, the architectural form adopted by the early Christian churches, gave the interior the semblance of a church; originally a great niche was constructed at the south end of the hall to provide a space for the throne.[118] Both the classical proportions and the religious appropriations make allusion to James as God's lieutenant, the object of worship and the source of harmony who might, like the perfect geometric design, bring all into beautiful reconciliation. As scholars have demonstrated, the organization of space and light from a double row of square windows each side and directional lines figured the king as the focus, the centre of the room.[119] In what was to be a space used for masques, banquets, royal audi-ences and ceremonies (such as the sacred touching for the king's evil), the archi-tecture 'provided a folium [as well as] a symbol for this all-pervading power of the king's command'.[120] In a building based on a basilica, Jones provided a hall in which the king sat as sacerdotal Christian ruler, as both Jupiter and Solomonic judge, delivering his most solemn decrees.[121]

Recently it has been suggested that, as well as following Roman, Egyptian and Christian models, Jones's Banqueting House alluded to Platonic and hermetic philosophy. In a study of *Art and Magic in the Court of the Stuarts*, Vaughan Hart reminds us that the cube was the fundamental form in Platonic cosmology: it was a perfect shape that symbolized perfect harmony and proportion. Harmony and proportion also depended upon numerical ratios; and, Hart demonstrates, Jones in his plans for the Banqueting House embodied Pythagorean proportions, based on a scheme of perfect numbers he had read and annotated in Alberti's *De re aedificatoria*.[122] Through the deploy-ment of Platonic forms, and what Henry Wotton called the 'mysteries of proportion', Jones re-created the 'cubic New Jerusalem of biblical prophecy' and a building the ratios of which expressed 'Solomon's comprehension of God's ordering the world through number'.[123] The Banqueting House therefore articulated in stone James's verbal self-presentation: as a Solomon and as the source of harmony in the world. As a space not only for masques but for state functions and a royal marriage (as was hoped), the Banqueting House was intended to elevate to Platonic ideals all the court ceremonies and enactments within its walls: to, like masques, make the king's ideals real.

However persuasive we may find such suggestions, the argument for the Banqueting House as a temple to a British vision gains strength from considerations of the ceiling. It was in 1635 that a series of paintings by Rubens was sent to Charles I for placement on the ceiling panels of the Banqueting House. The theme of the canvases was James I's recreation of the empire of Great Britain, a composition based on the Judgment of Solomon.[124] In the series of panels, James is figured with Minerva, the goddess of wisdom, and as the father of concord, peace and plenty – all the fruits of union. In one panel, the Virtues bear the king to heaven assisted by Religion and Faith clasping the Bible, leaving on earth the divine gift of peace. Placed in 1636, these canvases may seem more a tribute by Charles to his father than a text of the contemporary representation of King James. However, Per Palme and Roy Strong have traced the debt the scheme owed to James's writings and suggest that the programme for the paintings may have been devised by Jones at the time of the building of the Banqueting House in the early 1620s.[125] Evidently some commission to Rubens for the painting was mooted, for in a postscript to a letter in 1621 the artist, 'regarding the hall in the new palace', boasts of his skill in 'very large works'.[126] And, as has recently been argued, the scheme based on the happy effects of union 'is entirely understandable in the circumstances of c.1620 when James was in full and dominant control'.[127] Though what Rubens executed more than ten years later was necessarily adjusted to different circumstances, not least the death of the first Stuart, it appears that the project had been devised earlier. Moreover, while Strong is right to posit Jones as designer, the visual narrative so closely follows James I's own project of union and his speeches and writings, that we must suppose that, as with the building itself, the king had a directorial hand in it. If such a suggestion carries conviction, it may indicate too, as we have begun to see, that, whatever his reluctance to sit for his portrait, James was by no means indifferent to the proclamation in visuals of his projects and principles.

Before we leave the Banqueting House, we should note Rubens's reference to 'the hall in the new palace'. A single building, of course, was not a palace; unless Rubens was using the term unusually loosely, it would seem that he had something else in mind. Some of the architectural features of the Banqueting House – the absence of a formal stair to the first floor, for example – have puzzled scholars; and more than one has suggested that unfinished features (such as the undecorated north and south entrances) point to the possibility that 'from the first, the Banqueting House was envisaged as part of a longer range of build-ings'.[128] Certainly contemporaries noted the effects of its radical refusal to follow the design of the Tudor structure all around it: the letter writer John Chamberlain described the new building in 1621 as 'too fair and nothing suitable to the rest of the house', that is Whitehall.[129] During his personal rule, Charles I was to commission plans for a rebuilding of Whitehall in its entirety after the neo-Palladian style of the Banqueting House. No plans for such have been found by Jones, and none earlier than 1637–8 – shortly after the Rubens canvases were put in place.[130] However, speculative though it remains, Strong's hypothesis that the ceiling and building were from the beginning only part of a larger scheme of royal palace architecture which Charles later endeavoured to honour and that Rubens may have understood is worthy of serious reflection.[131] If, along with his Surveyor, King James from 1619 entertained 'a vast scheme for a new palace centring on the Solomonic ideal', then the political aesthetics of the first Stuart also demonstrated the imperialist ambitions to which, as well as his own writings, panegyrical verses and masques gestured.[132]

CHAPTER 3

STAGING STUART DYNASTY

I

The attention James gave to the Banqueting House, the *raison d'être* of which was to provide a ceremonial space, must lead us to question the assertion that, unlike his Tudor predecessors, the first Stuart had little regard for state ceremonial or public display.[1] James's royal entry and coronation were among the most magnificent of those of the early modern monarchs; and while, after a second civic entry in 1606, there was some decline in the king's participation in public civil ceremonies, public pageants for, and visits by, members of the extended royal family ensured the Stuarts remained very much in the public eye.[2]

The proclamation of James as king, as we have seen, met with a national relief that was expressed in an outpouring of public attention and affection.[3] Indeed, well before his civic entry into his new capital, James's journey from Edinburgh to London had all the marks of a triumphal progress. Riding northwards hard, immediately after Elizabeth's death, Sir Robert Carey stopped at Berwick on 26 March 1603 to proclaim James king of England, before proceeding to Holyrood to make obeisance to his new master. As the ceremonies began in Scotland as in England to recognize the new sovereign (the Governor at Holyrood surrendered his staff), James made his preparation for his journey and for the presentation of himself to his subjects.[4] Far from shunning the public, one of his first acts after the proclamation of his succession was to attend a public sermon at Edinburgh, as a display of godliness and humility. The sermon over, he addressed the burgesses and people in 'a most learned but more loving oration', exhorting them to obedience, love and charity, expressing his sorrow at leaving them and promising to return and to keep the bond of affection he had with them.[5] The speech – James was clearly a powerful public orator – moved the crowd: 'such an universal sorrow was amongst them that some of the meaner sort spoke even distractedly', or were lost for words.[6] At his proclamation at the market cross on 31 March sorrow turned to joy, as hundreds of bonfires, 'with great feasting and merriment' all night, provided a send-off for the royal progress the next morning.[7] Moved by emotion at the cries of his people, James departed on 1 April, reaching English soil at Berwick on the 6th. As the narrator of the triumph observed, the welcome there was to mark a revolution – a 'happy day when peaceably so many warlike English gentlemen went to bring in an English and Scottish king both included in one person, into that town that many a hundred years hath been a town of the enemy'.[8] As James approached, a gun salute – louder, it was said, than that heard even by 'old king Harry's lads' – announced a welcome.[9] As he passed through the guard of honour to the market cross, the symbol of worship and civic community, 'the common people seemed so over-wrapt with his presence that they omitted nothing their power and capacities could attain unto to express loyal duty and hearty affection'.[10]

Significantly, as he had in Scotland, James's first act was to go to church, to hear a sermon by Tobie Matthew. After showing that sense of his duty to God he had so clearly outlined in *Basilikon Doron*, the next day James – in a display which reminds us that he did not present himself only as *rex pacificus* – surveyed the fortifications of the town, fired a cannon to show his love of the military arts, commended the soldiers, and bestowed gifts and rewards.[11] As he perambulated the town, the first English subjects to meet him rose early from sleep 'that they might be comforted with the sight of their beloved sovereign'.[12] Journeying south, James, in a gesture which shows him fully alive to the power of the common touch so seldom associated with him, took a detour to Witherington to visit an old soldier, Sir William Reed. He, or so the narrator reports, 'being blind with age was so comforted with the presence and gracious speeches of the king . . . as he boasted himself to feel the warmth of youth stir in his frost-nipped blood'.[13] At Newcastle a few days later, in a feudal display of service and reward, the mayor presented James with his sword and the keys of the city; the new king returned these, granting the magistrates and citizens all the privileges they had held under his predecessor.[14] Here, again after church on the Sunday, James viewed the city and, in a display of royal mercy and charity as well as Protestant faith, released all prisoners, with the exception of murderers and papists, even paying money to free debtors who 'praised God and blessed his majesty for their unexpected liberty'.[15]

And so the journey south continued. At Durham, as well as his generous gift to the bishop of the diocese of Durham House in London, a symbol by the Scottish king of his support and patronage of the episcopacy, James's visit was remembered for joyous times and witty jests which circulated long after he had left.[16] By the time he reached York, the northern capital, in mid-April his train had been increased by more nobles and gentry who had travelled from the south and 'an abundance of other people' who came to meet them.[17] Demonstrating a remarkable tact, for which history has not remembered him, James smoothed over a dispute about precedency between the mayor and the Lord President of the Council of the North which might have marred the celebrations. And in a spectacular recognition of the importance of this city and his performance on the public stage of it, on the Sunday he declined an offer of a coach to take him to service in the Minster, saying: 'I will have no coach, for the people are desirous to see a king, and so they shall, for they shall as well see his body as his face.'[18] Receiving a petition at Kingston upon Hull for relief from Dunkirkers who picked off local merchantmen, James vowed that no pirates would be allowed to do his subjects harm.[19] Lodged in Doncaster at an ordinary inn, The Bear, James had the grace to thank his common host for his good entertainment with the present of a reversion to a lease of a manor house 'of good value'.[20] At Newark, the king freed the prisoners, while sending a cutpurse to the gallows to demonstrate his reconciling of justice with mercy.[21]

As the royal procession moved southwards through Lincolnshire, near Stamford they were met by around a hundred more men, apparently over twelve feet tall. These turned out to be petitioners on stilts who, by their ingenious masque-like device, drew the attention of the king, who promised to hear them at London.[22] *En route* from Burleigh, to dinner at Sir Anthony Mildmay's before a visit to Oliver Cromwell's house, yet more petitioners approached, this time requesting an end to encroachment on a common 'which his Highness most graciously promised should be performed according to their hearts desire'.[23] After sumptuous entertainment at Cromwell's, where the poor were invited to toast the monarch in free beer, James journeyed via Royston to Theobalds, the grand retreat of Elizabeth's minister William Cecil. Thither were drawn not only more of the southern nobility and gentry, but the poet John Savile, who provides us with a full account of the occasion. So infinite, he tells us, were the numbers that were arriving that he and others borrowed an hourglass to try to count them, both those on horse and those on foot; but 'before it was half run out, we could not possibly truly number them, they came so exceedingly fast'.[24] As Cecil conducted his sovereign into his house, the people threw up their hats and cried for joy. Hearing them, though he had rested only an hour, James went to his window to show himself before walking in the garden. As the royal train went for supper, others enjoyed food, wine and beer, down to the poor and maimed soldiers who had come to see their king.[25]

After four days at Theobalds, where he appointed his Privy Council on 7 May, James embarked on the final stage of his journey to London.[26] At Stamford Hill he was met by the Lord Mayor, the aldermen in scarlet, and 500 citizens. The crowds were so great that an enterprising cartman let his cart for eight groats every quarter-hour – an astonishing 50 pence an hour at a time when a week's wages for a skilled journeyman was much less.[27] According to one observer, 'the multitudes of people in highways, fields, meadows, closes and on trees were such that they covered the beauty of the fields and so greedy were they to behold the countenance of the king that with much unruliness they injured and hurt one another'.[28] But 'as uncivil as they were among themselves', all along the route they welcomed the king with shouts and cries as he made his way into the city, which he reached on 11 May.[29]

The relation of James's six-week progress from his Scottish to his English capital has far more than antiquarian interest. Not least, it suggests that England's new king had excellent skills in presenting himself to his subjects. As well as his display of the traditional virtues of good kingship – piety, justice, mercy, charity and accessibility – James had, with gentlemen and common folk alike, exhibited the charisma and a common touch for which his predecessor is better known. To a degree not simply explained by relief at a peaceful succession, James had made a real impression on his subjects and had acted with tact, grace and charm. As important, the reverse was also true. The warmth of his welcome, from all classes of society, left its mark on a king who was later to recall the numbers who had flocked joyfully to see him.[30] The journey, as the petitions and royal answers underlined, had demonstrated the reciprocal love of ruler and subjects which was essential to royal representations and to rule. If, as critics were later to note, James disappointed his people by his impatience with crowds and ceremonies, there was little sign of that as he entered London.[31] In the name of the sheriffs of London and Middlesex, Richard Martin delivered a speech of welcome, full of eulogy of the 'bright star of the north' whose virtues of justice, openness and goodness had shone before him.[32] Subtly counselling the monarch away from 'oppression' and towards reform of 'unjust monopolies' and abuse of powers, he welcomed a philosopher king whose action and writings promised that felicity which Plato had described as ideal government.[33] It was not the full welcome which London had planned. Traditionally, the city provided, as a prelude to the coronation, a public entry and entertainment which symbolized the union of king, city and people. London had immediately embarked on planning for an elaborate entertainment for St James's Day, 25 July, which had been appointed for the coronation.[34] Even as the new king was approaching, however, plague broke out in the southern counties and plans for a state entry were reluctantly suspended.[35] After some hesitation, perhaps because there was residual anxiety, it was decided that the royal coronation should go ahead.

On account of the plague and associated risks, there were significant differences in the ceremonies. There was, for example, no preliminary election in Westminster Hall which meant that the ancient custom of lifting the king into his stone seat was omitted; instead, James and Anne proceeded directly from Westminster Bridge to the abbey.[36] Inside the abbey, the audience witnessed not only the first coronation in half a century but the first of a king and consort since Henry IV. On a raised stage with rails, open to the altar and choir, two thrones awaited James and Anne as they processed, with their train, to the choir. As he was invested with the regalia, prayers were said for a King James who was 'strengthened with the faith of Abraham, indued with the mildness of Moses, armed with the fortitude of Joshua, exalted with the humility of David, beautified with the wisdom of Solomon'.[37] The rituals of investiture performed, the earls and barons approached to kiss the king's hand. The Earl of Pembroke kissed his face and 'the king, laughing, gave him a slap; but it was in joke'.[38] If the joke was inappropriate on such a solemn occasion, it evidently drew no criticism. The Roman envoy Effeti described the king as 'most familiar' with all.[39] Indeed, as if to make up for the absence of a civic entry, on their barge journey back to the palace James and Anne 'showed themselves on the river to the people'.[40]

Though in some respects the *raison d'être* of the civic entry – the presentation of the monarch to the people on the eve of coronation – had passed, James, unlike his son (who also faced a plague on his succession) revived the planned celebrations. His decision to ride through his capital ceremonially before the opening of parliament on 15 March 1604 was an important one which suggests the king had a grasp of the symbolic significance of the coronation entry. As his speeches confirm, James was hoping for much from his first assembly and a state entry promised that manifestation of reciprocal love which was the theme of his early addresses to his Lords and Commons. Moreover, the theme and motif of the devices – which, though prepared by the city, almost certainly followed consultation with the court – were very pertinent to James's purposes in meeting parliament: the promotion of a union of his two kingdoms.

Quite unlike Elizabeth's, James I's entry was a classical triumph in the high Roman style.[41] It commenced with the king's arrival at the Tower where the clergyman William Hubbock delivered a Latin address (later by 'his highness's special command' published in English).[42] The Tower, Hubbock told James, was the first entrance into the land of promise and into a 'kingdom determined unto you by divine decree'.[43] At this point of entry, on the king's ceremonial journey, Hubbock promised the adoration of people of all sorts who had come from every 'county, borough, precinct, city, hamlet' as if 'some great and festival day of the ever-loving God were now celebrated'.[44] England, he continued, was bringing home its David. The nation had mourned on the death of Elizabeth. But now, Hubbock counselled as well as praised the king, they expected all the good things of her age and more. The people had come to worship 'the anointed of the Lord' – 'wherefore', he urged, in a gesture to James's self-representation, 'take unto you the triumphs of peace'.[45] Turning to the theme of several pageants, Hubbock called on James to unite his realms, for God 'hath made Israel and Juda one in you . . . one king, one people, one law and, as it was in the beginning, one land of Albion'.[46] Concluding with counsel to the king to plant the gospel, promote justice, protect the poor and advance the arts, Hubbock introduced to the stage of the theatre of spectacle 'James of England and Scotland, or, to speak also one word, King of whole Britain'.[47]

We are fortunate to have several descriptions (themselves a testament to the popularity of the occasion) of the procession of the king and queen and the royal household from the Tower to Whitehall. Ben Jonson and Thomas Dekker (who uneasily co-operated) each wrote an account of their contribution to the entertainment; Stephen Harrison, who constructed the triumphal arches, published an illustrated account of them; and in *The Time Triumphant*, Gilbert Dugdale offered a brief narrative of the coronation and entry – perhaps to reconnect the two.[48] The seven triumphal arches erected along the processional route each provided the stage for a symbolic pageant, two of which were devised by the Italian and Dutch merchants. The theme of the first one was the presentation of London as the seat of a new British monarchy. Beneath an elaborate model of the city, two crowns hung over the figure of Monarchia Britannica, at whose feet sat Divine Wisdom (Theosophia).[49] Beneath her, figures representing the genius and counsel of the city, the warlike force of the

22 Pageant arch at Fenchurch from Stephen Harrison's *The Arch's of Triumph*, 1604.

city, and the River Thames expressed joy at the king's approach, while the figure of Agape with a flaming heart stood for loving affection to the monarch.[50] As the king drew up, Genius gave thanks for the sight the city had longed for since Brutus's days and welcomed James to 'his empire's seat', with his consort, the mother of Stuart progeny.[51] Though those assembled there had wished the royal procession might tarry longer, the train moved on to Gracious Street where the Italian merchants had erected a triumphal arch with four Corinthian columns, on which, beneath the royal arms, was written 'Tu regere imperio populus Iacobe memento', a passage adapted from the *Aeneid* (VI, 851–3) which James had quoted at the end of *Basilikon Doron*.[52] In a large square above, between columns reminiscent of imperial pillars, Henry VII seated in imperial robes hands to a mounted figure of King James a sceptre – an allusion to James's descent and his uniting kingdoms where Henry had joined once warring families.[53] On the right side of the arch, Peace holds the olive branch, while on the left a woman with a shield and motto announces James as the 'surest hope of all things'.[54] As James passed under the arch, the figures of two naked women seemed to place a laurel over his head. On the back, the four kingdoms held hands with the motto 'United in the firm will of the Fates'.[55] With inscriptions alluding to royal writings, the arch praised a king of the Muses as well as of empire; and the only speech proclaimed James the fulfilment of the ideal of the philosopher king whom he had 'pencilled down' in his own words.[56]

The Dutch arch at the Royal Exchange took Religion and Peace as its conceit. Above the arch, on the frieze of which was written 'I arise by divine will', a tablet bore a dedication by the seventeen United Provinces 'To the restorer of the world, securer of peace, defender of the faith, our lord King James . . . father of the country'.[57] On the upper level, as it were protecting the seventeen damsels each one bearing the escutcheon of her province, the figure of James was drawn, seated in imperial robes, crowned, with the orb and sceptre, and flanked by attendants. On the left and right, respectively, the figures of Justice and Fortitude stood between pyramids, while, above the king and atop the crown, crossed with sceptres (which we have seen on the reverse of coins) figuring two kingdoms made one, stood Divine Providence, the enactor of all. On the other side of the arch, inscriptions heralded James as a second Solomon and as heir of Lucius, mythical king of Britain who was reputed to have introduced Christianity to the island. All over the arch, inscriptions and figures of Dutch men, women and children at their crafts advertised the benefits of mutual trade, commerce and industry – a gesture to continuing Anglo-Dutch alliance. A boy addressed the king as he passed: God, he told him, 'teaches thee the art of ruling; because none but he made thee a king'.[58] Chief of the king's royal virtues, he continued, was Religion with whom Justice always kept company. Accordingly, the Dutch, who had loved their mother Eliza, now vowed that love to a father whose protection they entreated and in whose reign and progeny they saw future glory.[59]

23 Dutch pageant arch by the Royal Exchange.

The royal train advanced to the Poultry where, close to St Mildred's Church, musicians played Danish music in honour of the queen, then on to Cheapside where another arch had been erected at Soper Lane, inscribed 'Nova Faelix Arabia' (New happy Arabia).[60] On the pinnacle, the figure of Arabia Britannica wore an imperial crown and beneath it a veil, with, below her, Fame. Below her, in a concave niche, the five senses sat around the fount of virtue at the foot of which lay, sleeping, Detraction and Oblivion. To the right were figured three

Graces, on the left Love, Justice and Peace. As the king approached, Fame called the scene to life, explaining its meaning. For with the arrival of the king, the fount of virtue flows with wine and the milk of new life, while an address to the phoenix and 'Great Monarch of the West' announces the new spring his 'imperial name' brings to 'England's new Arabia'.[61]

At the Cheapside cross (where a year before he had proclaimed the succession), the Recorder delivered an oration to his 'high imperial majesty'.[62] Now, he said, the king came as a bridegroom, as a 'conqueror of hearts'; and in token of the love of the city he presented the king, queen and prince with cups of gold. By the cross, too, on a device called Hortus Emporiae (garden of plenty) a pastoral pageant celebrated the fruits of Peace and Plenty, the reanimation of the arts and Muses. James, Dekker reported, 'dwelt here a reasonable long time', to grace the spectacle, before moving forward to St Paul's (where a Latin oration was delivered by one of the scholars) and the Conduit at Fleet Street.[63] There the entourage beheld a device 90 feet high by 50 feet wide, representing the New World.[64] Over the entrance, a globe was seen to move, filled with all the estates and turned by the four elements. The figure of Fortune treading on the globe; above her Virtue enthroned beneath Astraea; and, atop the device, a Roman figure holding a small globe in his hand. On the two 'ascensions', topped with the royal devices and banners, were the virtues of Justice, Fortitude, Temperance and Prudence and, on the opposite side, the four kingdoms. As Dekker informs us, the intimation was that 'His Majesty's fortune was above the world, but his virtues above his fortune.'[65] At the approach of the king, the globe was set in motion, as Zeal praised him for all the virtues he embodied and the empire his succession created:

> Whose fruitful glories shine so far and even,
> They touch not only earth, but they kiss heaven.[66]

James, in other words, by his virtue masters the world and, 'as great' as Jove, ranks with the gods.[67]

The final device (the second created by Ben Jonson), erected at Temple Bar, was a simulacrum of the Temple of Janus, topped with a huge royal arms.[68] In the temple, the figure of Mars, with his weapons broken around him, submits to Peace and Wealth, as Tumult lies at the feet of Quiet who, significantly given James's interest in the Banqueting House, holds a perpendicular or level, associating architectural properties with stability in the state. In a series of such binaries, Liberty triumphs over Servitude, Safety over Danger and Felicity over Unhappiness – all signifying the restoration of a Virgilian golden age.[69] Jonson glosses the inscription on the top of the arch ('Jano quadrifonti sacrum') by reference to Ovid: 'the custody of the whole great world is mine alone, and the authority for turning its axis is all mine'.[70] After he passed the last arch, closing Janus's gates, the king came into the Strand where, before a rainbow and stars and a pyramid displaying his pedigrees, Electra, daughter of Atlas (and mother of Harmonia) anticipates 'lasting glory to Augustus state'.[71]

Even a brief sketch of this still largely unstudied royal entry indicates not only the extraordinary praise of the new monarch but complex allusions to themes that dominated James's self-representation in writings and speeches. In Jonson's and Dekker's entertainments (for all their differences), James was figured as the champion of Peace and Plenty, of Faith and Justice, as the embodiment of virtues, as the herald of a new spring and golden age, as the heir to ancient kingdoms, as emperor of a new Troy, a new Britain, as commander of the globe – and as a god. As Jonson's annotations to his account of the more classical parts he devised indicate, the classical as well as biblical allusions that explicated the arches and pageants were both more, and more complex, than for any former English royal entry. If such were a gesture to the king's own learning, it raises the question of how many of the spectators, unable to emulate it, followed the iconographic narrative plotted along the processional routes. Jonson himself implied that his devices were 'presented as upon the view they might without cloud or obscurity declare themselves to the sharp and learned'. As for 'the multitude', he added, 'no doubt but their grounded judgements gazed, said it was fine, and were satisfied'.[72] Not least because of his own anxiety to distinguish his devices from 'pageantry', Jonson's dismissal of the people should not be taken straightforwardly.[73] Though few had the formidable learning he paraded, and that Dekker mocked, and for all that the subject of who understood exactly what is an elusive one, we should not leap to the assumption that the symbolism of the arches and pageants passed over all but elite and educated spectators.[74] Jonson himself notes that in such pageants, 'the garments and ensigns deliver the nature of the person'; Dekker, describing the Arabian arch, addressed his readers familiarly, assuming their acquaintance with some symbols: that having mentioned the figure of Justice, 'I hope you will not put me to describe what properties she held in her hands, since every painted cloth can inform you'.[75] Harrison, the joiner who not only built the arches but invented them, included 'many thousand of worthy citizens' among those who made the entertainment; and evidently he, and others who published descriptions of the day, anticipated that consumers would buy their books.[76] Moreover, legends or myths, such as that of Brutus, even some acquaintance with the classics, were part of a metropolitan popular culture less distanced from the elite than was once assumed. In particular, the emphasis on visual effects enabled even the illiterate to read some of the signs of majesty.

What then did the spectators make of the principal performer, of James himself? It has been suggested that, for all the flattery that greeted him, James endured his civic entry with thinly disguised impatience; and that his behaviour on the day disappointed his subjects.[77] Some of the sources used to support this argument were either vague and unspecific or tainted by bitterness. Sir John

Oglander's remark about James's dislike of crowds concerned his irritation at
the hordes that came to observe him hunting, while Arthur Wilson's *History*,
published in 1653, was, understandably in the circumstances, highly critical of
the king.[78] It has been suggested that the speech by the St Paul's scholar
imploring James's patience, indicates royal weariness; but as the speech was
almost certainly prepared ahead, and appears to voice the usual humble
gestures to sovereignty, it cannot be taken as a critical comment on James's
behaviour.[79] Doubtless the long day was tiring.[80] But James, as we have seen,
went to lengths at his coronation to show himself; and it would seem that on
his entry into the city he at least endeavoured to respond with attention and
grace. At the end of a speech at the Arabian arch, for example, James was about
to move on but waited to hear a song; at the Garden of Plenty, 'His majesty
dwelt . . . a reasonable long time, giving good allowance for the song and music
and liberally bestowing his eye on the workmanship of the place'.[81] Though,
when he tried to preview incognito the preparation for his entry, James
evidently 'discommended the rudeness of the multitude', on the day of his
procession, referring to the fireworks on the Thames, he told his citizens 'that
their love was like the wild-fire unquenchable'.[82] James admired the Cornhill
pageant, smiled as he passed by the Exchange, and gave a gracious farewell at
Temple Bar.[83] The royal family may have exceeded the king in graciousness.
Gilbert Dugdale reports that Queen Anne 'did all the way so humbly and with
mildness salute her subjects, never leaving to bend her body to them . . . that
women and men . . . wept with joy'; while Prince Henry, 'smiling . . ., saluted
them with many a bend [bow]'.[84] Certainly James's memory was that the day
had been a spectacular success – which is also how it appears in contemporary
accounts. Untold multitudes came to watch the show and see their king and
express that love in their persons that was the theme of so many speeches and
devices. Michael Drayton, in a paean congratulating the king on the entry, was
sure that any witness of the occasion could only ask:

> Whether of two did take the more delight,
> They that in triumph rode or they that stand,
> To view the pompe and glorie of the land,
> Each unto other such reflection sent.[85]

Indeed, James was to process again through his capital two years later, on the
occasion of entertaining his wife's brother. In the textbook histories of James's
reign, what we know of the entertainment of Christian IV is the drunken
affray which spoiled a banquet at court.[86] Accounts of the public reception of
the king of Denmark, however, both present a very different perspective and
suggest a people far from disenchanted with their king. Christian arrived at
Gravesend on 17 July, whither the next day James rode to escort him, by a state
barge, to Greenwich. There, though little notice had been given of the plans,

'multitudes of people . . . came to see them'.[87] The two kings spent the Saturday hunting in Eltham Park but their return was eagerly awaited by the large numbers of 'vaingazers' who waited to see them. On the Saturday, as they rode to chapel with 'sumptuous attendance', they 'gave great and honourable regard to the multitude of people there present'.[88] The citizens who gathered, H.R. reported, were 'innumerable' and the sight of them caused admiration.[89] After their return from chapel, James feasted his brother-in-law 'in most sumptuous manner'.[90] The two remained at Greenwich a few days, hunting bucks in the park there and at Eltham, whence 'they returned themselves to the court, all the way pacing easily that the people might the better obtain their desires in beholding of them'.[91] A week after Christian had arrived, as James escorted him to Blackwall and Theobalds, they 'all the way met with great company of people which saluted them and prayed for their happiness . . . such is the love of this nation for the king and his lovers and friends'.[92] Despite the distance from London, while the two sovereigns stayed at Theobalds 'great abundance of people' came out to see them.[93] A few days later, on the last day of the month, they moved to London to prepare a formal entry into the city. Mounted on horses of the same colour, the kings ('regarding more the true love of their nation than gorgeous apparel') rode in plain suits rich in jewels at the head of their guard and household attendants.[94] All along the two-mile route to Whitehall, for the second time, the people cheered their king from windows, balconies and the streets, where wine ran freely from the conduits, so that it was not until seven in the evening that James and Christian reached the palace.[95]

There were few such public spectacles after 1606, but whether this was due to James's growing disenchantment with his subjects, or simply the absence of another such occasion, we cannot say. It was his family rather than James himself who provided the occasions of state ceremony for much of the rest of the reign: the inauguration, then the funeral, of Prince Henry; the marriage of Princess Elizabeth; the creation of Charles as Prince of Wales in 1616; the funeral of Queen Anne three years later. Yet, whatever the tensions within the royal family, these events and festivities should not be omitted from an account of the ceremonial representation of the king. James's image and appeal were as a husband and father: and the occasions on which his wife or children made an entry or ceremonial appearance were publicizations of the king too. For example, the pageant performed at Chester on St George's Day in 1610, to inaugurate Henry as Prince of Wales, was replete with references to and orations on the king and his 'imperial majesty', as well as the principal themes of royal representation – Peace, Justice and Plenty.[96] Chester's Triumph was presented in honour of the prince, but Britain praised her 'royall, clement, chaste and bounteous King' who 'such radiant luster to the Earth doth bring'.[97] James, the audience was reminded in words that echoed his own, was 'next the high'st, great King of Kings'.[98] At Henry's funeral, the magnificent procession of 2,000 people was a display of the king's majesty, as indeed 'the great embroidered banner of the union' represented James's proud achievement as much as Henry's descent.[99] As George Chapman's epicede (or funeral ode) sang, Great Britain's Henry made his end at a time 'when his great father did so far transcend/All other kings'.[100] When Queen Anne made her entry to a 'sumptuous entertainment' at Bristol in 1613, she heard, as well as compliments to herself, more praise of her husband 'our Albion Thesius true' who had curbed Rome, and who 'rules us with most gentle love, from all oppression free', a 'valiant Caesar', 'another Cicero' whose 'learned fame and Pietie, throughout the world doth ring'.[101] Similarly, Thomas Middleton, in devising entertainment for Prince Charles at Whitehall in 1616, described the whole occasion as a bounty of the king and 'a lively impression of his kingly care for continuance of the happy and peaceable government of his land in his issue'.[102] And, most of all, like Henry's, the entertainment for Charles lauded the king's peace, that had 'Enricht our homes, extinguish't forraine feares'.[103]

Royal processions, entries and pageants were the most important performances on what James I was fond of calling the stage of the theatre of state. In the words of one narrator, 'Nothing can better set forth the greatness of princes, together with the duty, love and applause of subjects than these solemn and sumptuous entertainments . . . the outward face of cost and disbursement being the true and lovely picture of that hearty love which is locked up in the bosoms of the givers'.[104] Magnificence not only displayed majesty, it publicized the people's love for their king as the foundation of his authority.

Though royal entries were occasional, in some sense an annual civic feast celebrated the monarchy as it presented to the citizens of London the magistrate who held office as the king's deputy – that is, the mayor. Since relations with the crown and court were vital to the interests of the city, the Lord Mayor's shows were, and increasingly, connected with courtly concerns. In some cases written by the poets and playwrights who also worked for the court, they adopted regal conceits and symbols for civic festival. The annual mayoral feasts of course were very much a display of the city's wealth and power; but, except at times of the greatest political tension (on the eve of civil war, or at the time of the Popish Plot), that wealth and power were displayed by proximity to the king and court and by representation of regal as well as civic achievements.

A brief sample of these entertainments suggests they should be read, as they were seen, as paeans to royal as well as mayoral virtues.[105] Indeed, the title of Anthony Munday's entertainment for the inauguration of Sir Leonard Holliday in 1605 spoke very much to James's preoccupations. The *Triumphs of Reunited Britannia* told the story of Brute as well as of New Troy, and so figured London as an ally in his purpose of union to 'our second Brute (Royal King James)'.[106] As well as greeting the new mayor, Fame welcomes 'bright Britain's king': 'I bring thee Monarch now into the field/With peace and gaiety in his sacred band'.[107] The British throne was also the motif of the 1612 mayoral entertainment for Sir John Swinerton by Thomas Dekker who, of course, had scripted the pageants for the 1604 entry. In his preface to *Troia Nova Triumphans*, Dekker outlined the purpose of such occasions as 'to dazzle and amaze the common eye' with the spectacle of magistracy 'that thereby the gazer may be drawn to more obedience and admiration'.[108] In this entertainment, in which the iconographic scheme closely followed the royal entry, the throne of Virtue and the house of Fame are flanked by kings and a representation of Prince Henry in particular. Munday's 1615 pageant *Metropolis Coronata* proudly compared the time of Jason and the golden fleece to a 'royal masque', as indeed the mayor was reminded that it was 'An oath of Faith and Fealtie/Unto his sacred Majestie/That makes you his Great Deputie/Or Image of Authoritie'.[109] Whatever disenchantment with the king may have existed, the mayoral entertainments continued to praise James in representations to the people. Middleton may have been offering counsel as well as compliment when in *The Triumphs of Love and Antiquity*, the entertainment for William Cockayne in 1619, he proclaimed that kings were at their greatest when they rode (as James had not for many years) in parliament robes – 'the richest robes of their loves'.[110] But he was keen, too, to demonstrate that 'herein honours to his Majestie/Are not forgotten'.[111] Two years later, in *The Sun in Aries*, the 'solemnity' for the new mayor, he presented James, 'the joy of honest hearts', uniting the kingdoms and clasping all in the arms of love.[112] In the final mayoral pageant of his reign, John Webster's *Monuments of Honour*, the pillars of the Temple of Honour are bound with roses 'which shoot up to the adorning of the King's Majesty's arms on the top of the Temple'.[113] Webster traced Stuart descent through Edward III to Henry VII 'from whence his Royal majesty . . . took his motto for one piece of coin, Henricus Rosas Regni Jacobus'.[114] At the close of the pageant, a monument of gratitude is festooned with the prince's arms, and verses laud both Charles and the memory of Henry, James's progeny.[115] Though it was not always to do so, during the reign of the first Stuart the city represented the monarch in many of the discursive and symbolic forms of the king's own image, bringing royal virtue annually to the stage of the London streets.

Another annual festival had become increasingly important in the politics of monarchical display. As I have argued, the revival of the ceremonies of the Garter was inseparable from the growth in authority of the Tudor monarchy, and by the 1590s the annual St George's Day ceremonies at court had been transformed into great public spectacles.[116] In his portraits, James nearly always appears with – and in some cases is depicted drawing attention to – his George and Garter. The first Stuart evidently attached great importance to the Order which he may have seen as the badge of a British imperial order to emulate that of the Habsburg Order of the Golden Fleece. Certainly James showed concern to uphold the magnificence of the Order.[117] In a chapter during his reign, it was decreed that all knights, current and future, should 'give £20 to the use and ornament of the altar and chapel of St George in

Windsor'.[118] Thomas Rowe estimated the 'donations' at £800 and confirms the impression given by the Venetian ambassador that the altar and chapel at Windsor were richly adorned.[119] The Jacobean age 'also marked the heyday of the cavalcade'.[120] At least one envoy thought that a Garter procession could surpass even the magnificence of the coronation, and the annual festival made a dramatic impact on English as well as foreign observers. In 1603, for example, Lady Anne Clifford reported on the deferred Garter feast at which Prince Henry was installed, along with the Duke of Lennox and Earls of Pembroke and Southampton. At the dinner at Windsor, when the king and queen received the ambassador from the archduke, she reported, 'there was such an infinite company of Lords and Ladies and so great a court as I think I shall never see the like'.[121] On St George's Day 1615, Gondomar, the Spanish envoy, was taken for a view of the Garter procession at Whitehall and the splendid procession to Windsor; in 1618 John Chamberlain informed his correspondent Dudley Carleton that 'St George's day passed with much solemnity, the lords and their followers being very gay and gallant', especially the king's favourite, the Duke of Buckingham.[122] So accustomed had observers become to splendour that in 1623, perhaps on account of the subdued mood arising from Prince Charles's absence in Spain, as well as James's weakness through bad health, it was said that there was 'no great show . . . the knights and procession went not out their ordinary circuit'.[123]

For much of his reign, James had sustained the magnificence of the chivalric Order that, like his predecessor, he recognized as the display of royal honour. In 1610, in his *Catalogue of Honour*, Thomas Milles summed up what he saw as the importance of the Garter to monarchy: 'here', he claimed, 'our king with his prince, our prince with his peers, and our peers with their worthies, meet and march together in one bond of love . . . for mutual defence both of church and commonwealth, amazing the beholders of the stately sight and view of one personal majesty, in one fellowship of honour'.[124] At the feast for 1616, William Fennor, in a poem sketching 'The original and continuance of the Most Noble Order of The Garter' delivered before the king, praised James for the vitality and strength the Order enjoyed under him: it, he rhymed, 'In this age present hath as many friends . . . As any ages ever had before' and he prayed 'God keepe our King . . . let all that love the Garter says Amen'.[125]

Though parts of the Garter festival, of course, were open only to the knights themselves and a privileged audience of ambassadors (who went to considerable lengths to see the ceremony), household officers and nobles, the outdoor procession was in a real sense public. Crowds evidently gathered to see the knights file through the Whitehall courtyard to the chapel royal, on one occasion holding up the arrival of knights who could not pass through the throng.[126] As well as at Whitehall and Windsor, in James's reign Garter festivals were also held at Greenwich, providing another public with a sight of resplendent majesty as Henry Howard, Earl of Northampton was, on that occasion, installed alongside the queen's brother.[127] The Garter was a popular as well as elite spectacle and one which presented the king, as virtuous, chivalrous knight, annually to his subjects.

During Elizabeth's reign, the sight of the queen had come to be fairly common as, famously, she moved around and between the houses of her ministers and aristocrats, living off their hospitality and, in some cases, keeping a watchful eye on their behaviour. James is seldom discussed in similar terms, as an itinerant monarch. But an early description of him as 'living in the saddle', far from hyperbole, scarcely begins to characterize his movements.[128] James seems to have been almost in perpetual motion, between royal palaces and lodges, hunting and visiting; and on frequent longer progresses to the various corners of England, and in 1617 Scotland. Within weeks of arriving at Whitehall in 1603, James was visiting the principal houses in Surrey and Middlesex – Bedington, the residence of Sir Francis Carew, Sir John Fortescue's house at Hendon, and Sion House, to name but three.[129] At the end of June, he met the queen, who had travelled south, at Easton Neston whence he departed on progress for Muresley, Buckinghamshire, then Aylesbury and Great Missenden, the seat of Sir William Fleetwood, before presiding over the Garter feast at Windsor on 2 July.[130] On 1 August, the king and queen commenced a formal progress together scheduled for over forty days and nearly 200 miles.[131] Starting in Surrey, their route took them through Hampshire, Wiltshire and Oxfordshire, where the king stayed hunting at Woodstock for some time. The next year, still before his coronation, James left Whitehall for his sports at Royston and Newmarket for much of February.[132] He was back there shortly after the coronation service, for on 1 April he conferred knighthoods on five gentlemen at his beloved Royston.[133] The summer season of 1604 saw little business executed during what Sir Thomas Edmondes told Sir Ralph Winwood was 'the king's hunting progress'.[134] And so the pattern was set. James disappeared back to Royston immediately after Twelfth Night formally closed the Christmas festivities, and spent much of the winter there, at Thetford and at Newmarket.[135] The year of the Gunpowder Plot, the royal entourage departed for nearly seven weeks, taking in the parks of Houghton and Ampthill where the sport was good, as well as visiting the houses of nobles and an Old Armada veteran, William Harvey, and the city of Oxford.[136]

While many of the royal journeys involved returns to favourite hosts and hunting lodges, the king did plan visits to different parts of his realm. In 1608, for example, the progress took in Northamptonshire and Bedfordshire; in 1612, leaving Theobalds on 20 July, the royal entourage journeyed to Newark in Lincolnshire, Nottingham, Loughborough and Leicester, before returning, after a month, via Holmby and Grafton to Woodstock.[137] At each town and city, as much as every noble house, elaborate preparations were made to provide a welcome that included 'the commonalty, such as can furnish themselves fit for the purpose', as well as grandees.[138] Chamberlain may have complained that 'the progress hath been so far off and we so far out of the way' – out of the 'loop', we would say – but for thousands this summer offered an experience of the best representation of majesty: a sight of the king himself.[139]

The sudden death of Prince Henry and the marriage of his daughter kept James in, or close to, London for a couple of years. But James, and Anne, soon resumed their long summer progresses – that of 1616 involving a circuit into the midlands of nearly 250 miles.[140] The next year, of course, saw the king fulfil – ten years after he made it – an old promise and embark on the longest journey of any early modern English monarch: his progress into Scotland. From an early departure on 15 March, James was 'on the road' for effectively six months before his return to Whitehall, the journey north itself taking sixty days.[141] On the Scottish progress, the king made entries to, and sojourns at, some of the principal cities of the north of England. And these were very much public occasions and representations. At Lincoln, after a sermon at the Minster, he touched fifty people to cure the king's evil, as well as attending a horse race, and a cockfight in the town.[142] At York, similarly, he touched about seventy ordinary folk as well as dining with the mayor, the archbishop and the Lord President of the North.[143] For all the exertions, James, it was reported, 'goes on cheerfully', and he displayed again a charm for which he has been given little credit.[144] 'If God lent him life', he told the people of Lincoln, 'he would see them oftener'; the cathedral at York and the Chapter House 'he much commended'.[145] Durham and Newcastle were the next stops, at the first of which the mayor was invited by a court usher to ride before the king to the sermon. James was, his closest confidant Buckingham wrote, in very good spirits – 'I never saw him better, nor merrier' – and obviously enjoying the encounter with his subjects.[146] It was 10 May – eight weeks since he had left London – when the king finally reached his border palace at Berwick; but, whatever the recent storms in London, the journey had provided plentiful demonstrations of the reciprocal love between king and subjects and James had, it would seem, shown his best face to the people.

On 16 May, James made a long-delayed formal state entry into the capital of his northern kingdom. The contrast between the culture of the two realms is nowhere better seen than in this reception where, in contrast to the finery of London, the Council and 'one hundred honest men . . . were all assembled in black gowns', as the procession passed to the kirk for a sermon.[147] The Deputy Recorder's speech praised the 'sacred person' of the king, 'the bright star of our northern firmament', and the virtues of his government; but here were no elaborate allegorical arches or pageants.[148] From Edinburgh, James began a perambulation of Scotland (Falkland, Dundee, Stirling, Perth, St Andrews and Glasgow), but evidently little news of the visit reached England: 'we have little out of Scotland since the king being there,' Chamberlain reported, and moving swiftly to other news, he sounded as though he did not much care; only the activities of the English in the royal party captured his attention.[149] Though

Dudley Carleton acknowledged they had been well entertained, he and his fellows could hardly wait to leave.[150] The return progress, through Lancashire and Cheshire, took the whole of August and the first half of September, with civic entries at Preston and Chester, days of sojourn for hunting, and visits to noble and gentry houses, at all of which ordinary people as well as courtiers and magnates took the opportunity to see their new sovereign.[151] Indeed, at Townsend, a suburb of Nantwich, James went to see brine drawers at work, asked them about their labours and 'rewarded them with his own hand' – a remarkable grace to mere commoners.[152] It was a grace he exhibited the whole journey south, commending sermons, helping to resolve disputes (over games), knighting hosts, and giving gracious thanks.[153] Though the rhetorics of compliment should not be read uncritically, at every station speeches lauded James and the beneficence of his rule. At Houghton Tower, near Preston, for example, the speech praised an Augustus the 'splendour and . . . glorious ray' of whose majesty struck the attender dumb; the Recorder of Coventry recalled 'the blessed beams of a new sun rising' and 'the full brightness and strength wherefrom we have enjoyed ever since . . . a concurrence of so many festivities proportioned to your incomparable wisdom, justice, mercy and other princely virtues'; at Warwick the speech welcoming James celebrated a monarch 'whose felicity hath opened an easy passage to the remotest corners of Great Britain, which could never be accomplished by the Roman armies'.[154] Far from the libels and squibs circulating in the capital in the aftermath of the Overbury affair, those who attended on James as he returned from his northern kingdom saw and heard a king of Britain, an emperor, heralded as one near unto a god.

James travelled less during the last years of his reign and his progresses were confined to journeys between royal palaces and lodges. At the beginning of June 1619 he made a solemn entry into London, after staying at Greenwich and Theobalds, and his progress later that summer took in Belvoir Castle, Welbeck, and the towns of Nottingham, Derby and Tamworth, before he returned to give audience to the French ambassador.[155] But, after 1620 – whether from failing health or the need to be close to Whitehall during the tense diplomacy that followed the resurgence of war in Europe – the New Forest, Beaulieu and Newmarket typically marked the bounds of the royal summer progresses. Until then, however, James had travelled literally the length (if not breadth) of his realm. Moreover, as has recently been demonstrated, the king made careful preparations for progresses and took pains to ensure good communications with his councillors in London.[156] For James, no less than Elizabeth, progresses were not distractions from the business of government; as displays of majesty, they were the business of government.

As befitted a monarch who, like his predecessor, cultivated his reputation for learning, visits to the two universities were especially important to James's self-representation. Both Oxford and Cambridge benefited from the king's love of hunting in the vicinity of the universities. But the royal visits were about serious business, as well as entertainment: about the representation of the Platonic king, the Solomon, to the capitals of learning in the kingdom. James visited Oxford in August 1605, with his queen and Prince Henry. The visit was evidently planned some months ahead and the preparations were elaborate.[157] Though their workmanship did not please all, the fellows of Christ Church built a throne of state for the king and an elaborate stage with turning pillars for entertainments.[158] After a ceremonial entry on the 27th, when the university paid the scholar king the compliment of a gift of a Greek bible, the full three-day programme of sermons, plays, acts and disputations began.[159] At the divinity acts, James intervened, immediately finding the scriptural passage in dispute; while at the moots, as well as 'talk[ing] much to diverse about him', he displayed the royal virtue of good justice by resolving a question of whether a judge should strictly follow the laws, even against his private knowledge of the truth – to the cry from the students of 'Vivat Rex!'[160] As well as his learning, James displayed a gracious readiness to listen attentively, accept compliments and put his hosts at ease, joking about his dislike of tobacco in a quip 'which moved great delight'; only a comedy at St John's tried his patience.[161] Looking back on the visit, Chamberlain, by no means an uncritical observer, thought that news of it had spread wide and that the king had impressed. In several disputations, he 'spake often and to the purpose', and interrupted entertainments and exercises only 'with applauding'; and he had endowed the university divinity lecture with the gift of a canonry and parsonage.[162] More even than Elizabeth, the first Stuart had taken pains to present himself as a scholar and patron of learning, as well as the royal judge and Defender of the Faith.

Though Cambridge came second to its ancient rival in the timetable of royal progresses, it enjoyed no fewer than three royal visitations in the last decade of James's rule. On the first, with Prince Charles in March 1615, Chamberlain, an Oxford man, gave the impression that the success of the occasion had been mixed; but 'the king was exceedingly pleased many times both at the plays and disputations', and the university hailed, as had Oxford, the 'Rex Platonicus'.[163] James enjoyed himself sufficiently to return in May the same year, and to grant the university 'the third most happy aspect of their Jove' in the spring of 1623, on which occasion the scholars delivered paeans to his 'imperial abundance' as well as learning.[164] For a monarch who envied the scholar's life and told his Oxford hosts of his desire to be a don, who once asked why a king should not be 'the best clerk in his own country', who made his own learning the principal representation of his regality, these occasions were royal representations indeed.[165]

II

On his visits to the universities, as on several of his progresses, James was often accompanied by his wife and children. The appearance of the king with Queen Anne or one of the princes was not simply evidence of domestic affection.

Accompanied by a fertile queen and young, virile princes, or a nubile princess, James, especially after seventy years of childless rule in England, displayed the longevity and power of Stuart dynasty. As we have seen, from the moment of his succession, the first Stuart was hailed as a husband and father as well as king.[166] Although the early panegyrics faded, the importance of James's paternal status did not: rather, as he, then his sons and daughter, advanced in age, died or were married, the royal progeny were inseparable from the representation and perceptions of the king himself. As William Leigh observed in 1612, James was 'no less blessed in his three children than in his three kingdoms'.[167]

The royal family, as several scholars have suggested, was by no means a simple reflection of the king's majesty. Anne of Denmark, Prince Henry and Prince Charles all challenged the preferences and policies of James at particular points, and the courts of the first two became semi-independent power bases which drew critics of the king. Such differences and tensions, however, had benefits as well as disadvantages, in enabling the Stuart dynasty simultaneously to stand for quite contrary values, to represent the aims and ambitions of different factions, and to embody the differing hopes of subjects.[168] But whether for worse or better, it was the royal family, in all its complex relations, as well as the monarch that captured the attention and imagination of contemporaries; and James's image was not easily separated from that of his wife and children.

'And those sweet streames her mate and she combined/In love.'[169] The words of Patrick Hannay's elegy on Queen Anne do not read as a very accurate portrait of the royal marriage. James, as is infamous, was homosexual and given to infatuations with male favourites, which meant, according to Edward Peyton, that though he stayed married to Queen Anne, he 'never lodged with her a night for many years'.[170] Such testimonies, however, though they cannot be discounted, do not present the whole picture. James's youthful infatuations with boys, after all, did not preclude a romantic journey to pursue his bride, nor experiments in amorous verse inspired by her.[171] Anne's seven pregnancies also attest to physical, as well as literary passion, at least up to the birth of Sophia in June 1606, by which time she suffered from illness, and in her thirties was close to the end of her child-bearing years. Moreover, other seventeenth-century biographies depict an affectionate relationship, with James taking leave of her on one occasion 'by kissing her sufficiently to the middle of the shoulders'.[172] Francis Osborne reports that the king did so 'to show himself more uxorious before the people'; and, if it can be trusted, the observation is important to our story.[173] For, whatever the secrets of the bedroom, James clearly wished to continue to be *seen* as a husband and to regard his marriage as central to his representation. Anne, as recent revisionist biographers have shown, was strong-willed and independent; it has emerged that she manoeuvred to assist the downfall of Somerset, to promote Villiers, and to encourage James to pursue Habsburg marriage alliances for her children.[174] But it is far from clear that at any point she directly – let alone successfully – opposed royal policy; and in so far as her court provided support for factions hostile to James's lover, Robert Carr, she helped to earth critics of the favourite to the royal court. And, importantly, Anne brought glamour, as well as progeny, to the Stuart dynasty. As Leeds Barroll and others have demonstrated incontrovertibly, the queen was the principal patron of the arts, literary, visual and architectural, at the court. Not least she played a vital role in the development of Tudor masque into a panegyrical form for the representation of Stuart absolutism, while her penchant for expensive dress and jewels meant that she dazzled on ceremonial occasions. When Anne went on progress or on visits, she was greeted as 'our Goddesse', 'that [jem] most excellent'.[175] Engraved, her portrait was published as that of 'the EMPRESSE of true MAJESTIE'. As references to her as 'our Cynthia' suggest, Anne represented and enabled continuities from the female court of Elizabeth to the masculine court of James.[176] Whatever her quest for independence or the sexual estrangement between the royal couple, Queen Anne, in her extravagant display, complemented James's bookishness and charmed envoys and subjects alike. In penning one of his last (like his earliest) sonnets to his wife, James may even have expressed his own recognition of the importance of 'our Queene' to his representation and reign.[177]

From the moment of James's succession, the presence of his nine-year-old son was a powerful component of the royal image; from the outset, too, the image of the prince complicated as well as complemented that of the king. For all James's reputation and self-representation as *rex pacificus*, and of Henry as his father's heir, the prince immediately became the focus of other aspirations. There is a hint of this in verses presented to Henry on his entry to Althorpe with the queen as early as June 1603 when he is told:

And when slow Time hath made you fit for war,
Looke over the strict Ocean, and thinke where
You may leade us forth . . .[178]

In a *Paraenesis* to the prince the next year, William Alexander of Menstrie boldly claimed that, though a king at peace, James had fashioned his son to arms.[179] The image of a military Henry preceded the prince's own self-representation, and followed him from Scotland to England.[180] In the southern kingdom, Henry was immediately invested with the Garter and, as we have seen, an early portrait by Peake figured the prince with sword unsheathed as Protestant champion.[181] Henry the Protestant hero stood alongside his father who had made peace with Spain. As he matured towards adulthood, Henry avidly took up the image of martial, Protestant prince already prepared for him. The theme of the triumphs and entertainments of his investiture as Prince of Wales in 1610 was chivalric and warlike, as Henry was heralded as a prince of heroical parts and virtues.[182] As scholars have observed, the happy occasion of the first investiture of a Prince of Wales since 1504 did not pass without tensions. James I was uneasy about the *Barriers* to be performed on Twelfth Night, not least because the entertainment 'presented the Prince as the exponent of a policy diametrically opposed to the royal one', as, effectively, the new leader of the Elizabethan war party championed by the Earl of Essex.[183] The text of the *Barriers* indeed resonates with the tensions involved in serving the prince and the king.[184] But, in any consideration of Prince Henry's image-making, the latter should not be forgotten. For in James's own early represen-tation, the image of the *rex pacificus* had incorporated imperial visions and hopes, as his ecumenical policies had also accommodated apocalyptic prophecies of the king as conqueror of the Antichrist. The sermon preached before the prince the day before his inauguration similarly spoke of both a young Alexander – a martial hero – and a young Josiah and Ptolemy, who stood for piety and learning.[185] George Marcelline's treatise, dedicated to Henry at his investiture, was entitled *The Triumph of King James* and presented Henry not as an alternative but as heir to his father's policies and victories.[186]

Tensions there undoubtedly were in relations between father and son; James, realistic about England's relative military weakness, was sceptical about the wilder proclamations of Protestant militancy of some around the prince; had he lived longer, Henry might have made difficulties for James's diplomacy. In his short life, however, he may have benefited the king (whose poets and architects after all helped devise the entertainments for the prince) by enabling James, who was, we are coming to appreciate, less firmly committed to peace and appeasement than has been argued, to keep his options open. By acting as the focus and symbol for one policy, while James himself more represented another, Henry enabled the Stuart family, indeed the king himself, to represent both peace and war, a pacific diplomacy with the prospect of militant action; as one elegist put it, 'halfe love, halfe warre'.[187] The reactions to the premature death of the prince may serve to underline his contribution to James's representation and perhaps his subtle diplo-macy. In 1612, a veritable flood of histories, Lives and elegies mourned the loss of a prince skilled at the tilt and all 'warre-like feats', a terror to foreign foes, who 'would have thundred lowd in war'.[188] While some such sentiments undoubtedly implied criticism of the king, many texts still praised 'the zealous King/His God-like Syre'.[189] The ever-popular John Taylor, perhaps answering critics, asked in his *Great Britain All in Black*: 'Then in thy [James's] Glory how can men be mute/That knows such Glorious Branches sprung from thee'.[190] The death of Henry focused more attention on the pacific aspect of the king and was, in time, to expose James's diplomacy as pusillanimous and too friendly to papists. In terms both of his foreign diplomacy and his personal image, 'James's lofty notion of the calm ordering of chaos necessarily required . . . the implication of bravery and courage and superior strength held in check' which Henry had provided.[191] In 1612, however, as Henry lay dying, a happier event in the royal family served in part to protect the king from the consequences of the death of his son – if only for a while.

By her very naming, Princess Elizabeth Stuart brought to Stuart succession the memory and fame of the last Tudor. She was, too, close to her brother Henry and shared the 'idealistic militant Protestantism' of the prince.[192] Henry had opposed a Catholic marriage for his sister, whose betrothal to Frederick V, Count Palatine of the Rhine and Elector of the empire, led many to perceive her as the heir to her brother's cause. Frederick arrived for the marriage ceremonies in October 1612, as Henry entered his last days. Immediately, he was represented as another royal brother and son, as, after the prince's death, a replacement for Prince Henry; and the new couple were heralded by the militants as a shining light that would 'dim th'adulterate light of Spanish Rome'.[193] James, who had in 1612 concluded an alliance with an association of German princes led by the Palatinate, intended that the marriage be part of a balanced dynastic policy to advance his ideal of European peace but also to keep his options open. But Elizabeth and Frederick did more. They kept alive, and associated with the Stuart royal family, the policies of (and hopes embodied by) the prince: as George Webbe, pastor of Steeple Aston, put it in his congratulations on the marriage, 'Though Henry be gone, yet Frederick is left behind' and the cause of true religion was secure.[194] Recounting the investiture of Frederick into the Order of the Garter in February, Anthony Nixon conjured up a vision of Henry, too, in his Garter, dead, but 'alive in fame's records' and reborn in his brother-in-law, as the 'perfect comfort' to 'Brutes new Troy'.[195] The birth of a prince (Frederick Henry) to the couple in January 1614, named after Henry as well as Frederick, further strengthened the connection. Indeed, Henry Peacham's congratulatory poem on the birth, dedicated to Elizabeth, was titled *Prince Henry Revived* and his verses greeted the infant as 'faire morning bud of England's white-red Rose'.[196] In the new Henry, Peacham saw both the hopes of peace and triumphal conquests, which James I and his son had together represented. George Weckherlin's account of the prince's christening and triumphal shows set forth at Stuttgart, with tilts and the entry of the Palatine as Scipio, was translated into English as a relation of Stuart dynasty and power, just as the description of Elizabeth as 'England's faire Phoenix, Europe's admiration' evoked the last Tudor's might and majesty.[197] Even if they symbolized hopes of war sometimes in ways that were at odds with James's avowed preference for peace, Henry, Elizabeth and her husband were still powerful representations of the Stuarts – and on the English as well as the continental stage enabled the dynasty to be seen as a champion of European Protestantism. Only when Frederick's ambitions led him to accept the offer of the throne of Bohemia – and then to suffer defeat and eviction from his ancestral electorate – did James's daughter and her husband become, in the eyes of the king, a liability. After 1620, their court in exile symbolized no longer the imperial reach of Stuart diplomacy but the weakness of a *rex pacificus* bereft of the 'superior strength held in check'.

As they departed from England in April 1613, Elizabeth and Frederick could not fill the gap left by the tragic death of Prince Henry. Naturally the person looked to to perform that role was James's second son, Charles who, the year of his brother's death, had reached the age of twelve. In his *Great Britain All in Black*, Taylor expressed the hopes of a nation when he assured the prince, 'Thou maiest atchive thy famous Brothers praise'.[198] In *Prince Henrie's Obsequies*, the poet George Wither summoned Charles to take Henry's place; while Maxwell ended his sketch of the life and death of Prince Henry with a 'congratulations of Prince Charles', his skills in riding, shooting and the exercise of arms very much akin to his brother's.[199] 'His forward prowesse', Maxwell proclaimed, 'spreads his name right farre', and the author imagines him in future leading an army against the Turk.[200] These early presentations of Charles, though the expression of hopes, question the usual portrayal of the young prince as timorous and frail. Charles did enjoy running at the ring and tournaments, which were very much a part of the entertainments staged for his creation as Prince of Wales in November 1616.[201] As early portraits reveal, Charles lacked his older brother's confidence and charisma. His very presence, however, enabled the transference to him of the hopes placed in Prince Henry, which in declaring war on Spain, he was later to fulfil. In 1616, such hopes had looked remote. Taylor and others may still in 1618 have looked to 'our happy hope, our Royall CHARLES the great' as the champion of Britain, but, like his father, after 1618 the prince seemed more interested in peace and a Habsburg marriage than in war as a solution to his beloved sister's plight.[202] Charles's association with his brother and early support for Elizabeth and Frederick, however, may have sustained hopes that he could be won over to an anti-Habsburg party, as indeed he was after his abortive journey to Madrid. On his return in 1623, he was greeted with exaltations that had not been witnessed since Stuart succession; and for the rest of the reign the prince brought more support to the crown than it had enjoyed since his investiture.[203] In 1624, John Webster's city entertainment placed Charles alongside his revered brother. As verses praised the memory of Henry in a pageant entitled 'The Monument of Gratitude', the poet was sure 'a new Phoenix springs up in his stead'.[204]

From his succession, James's family, not least on account of the novel longevity and security it promised, had been inseparable from the presentation and perception of the king; and it remained so. Whatever the differences among them, the royal family enhanced the image of the king and, I have suggested, enabled James to contain within a discourse of Stuart representation different values, programmes, policies and options. It may be no coincidence that, along with other unfavourable circumstances, it was in the period when no member of his family was prominent on the public stage that James's monarchy faced its sharpest criticism. With Henry dead, Elizabeth on the continent and Charles not yet sure of his identity, it was the royal favourite who became the focus of attention and a royal policy of peace no longer tempered by princely ambitions to arms that drew opposition. When Charles was won over, it seemed, to a Spanish marriage, the hope of the Protestants for what a later century was to call the 'reversionary' interest faded; and with it, parliament emerged as the focus of militant Protestant hopes – and of a broader opposition to the king and much of what he stood for.

III

In the *Basilikon Doron*, James had counselled Henry on the importance of the royal court to the reputation of his rule. 'In the person' of his court and company', he advised, the king displayed 'good example, alluring his subjects to the love of virtue and hatred of vice'.[205] 'Take good heed anent your court and household,' he admonished, and 'make your court . . . to be a pattern of godliness and all honest virtues.' Partly because the text was so well known, James's English subjects, somewhat disillusioned with the corruption and factionalism of Elizabeth's last years, had high expectations of the new reign. Samuel Daniel's lines in a 1603 panegyric may stand for many:

What a great checke wil this chaste Court be now
To wanton Courts debaucht with Luxurie.[206]

To say this is hardly the image of the Jacobean court that has transferred to history is an understatement. James's court has been criticized as a place of extravagance, disorder, drunkenness and homosexual favourites; and Sir Anthony Weldon's account of it has recently been compared to the salacious reports of the modern tabloid press.[207] Clearly contemporaries complained about the costs of court entertainments and 'vanities' as they always had, and – those who had heard of them – castigated the drunken scenes such as accompanied the visit of the king of Denmark, which led Chamberlain for one to make an unfavourable contrast between the household of James I and his predecessor.[208] Such denunciations, however, are not the whole picture. In July 1604, James himself, being informed of the 'great . . . expense', signed ordinances for the governing of the royal household, its costs, diet and personnel, many of them based on the practices of Elizabeth.[209] It seems unlikely that such an attempt at reform produced results – few in early modern England did. But several ambassadors to the court of James I convey a very different image to that of the first Stuart's (mainly later) detractors. The chaplain to the Venetian ambassador, for example, seemed in 1618 almost overawed by the handsome dress and splendid gowns of the court ladies, the 'most graceful masques', and the majesty of the king's entry.[210]

English observers and attendants could be no less impressed. Thomas Gainsford, for example, in *The Glory of England*, argued that 'for state, good order, expenses, entertainment and continual attendancy', the English court could more than hold its own with 'other places [that] come far short'.[211] 'If you come to our court,' he invited, 'I hope you will not find such another for stately attendants, dutiful service, plenty of fare, resort of nobles, comeliness of ladies, gallantry of gentles, concourse of people, princely pastimes, noble entertainment, and all things befitting the majesty of a king or glory of a nation.'[212] Whether his vaunts were accurate, Gainsford's *Glory of England*, published in 1618 and running to four editions by 1622, was popular.[213] In 1619, *The Court of the Most Illustrious and Most Magnificent King James*, a courtesy guide, specifically contrasted the few whose vice stained the court with the majority of courtiers who were 'instruments both of church and commonwealth'.[214] In his own Jacobean moment, he asked, 'may we not most apparently behold . . . a lively, real and royal pattern of majesty, grace, wisdom, learning . . . in that most renowned courtier, our most sacred sovereign KING James?'[215] James was, as we shall see, often less decorous than his precursor or successor; his son came to regard his father's court as imperfectly ordered and in need of reform.[216] But, if James's court was, as he had advised his son, a display of his kingship, it did not meet with universal condemnation. What tainted the image of the court and the reign was not the institution itself, nor even the royal extravagance, but the king's sexual dalliances and especially the sexual scandal in which his favourite Robert Carr was implicated. And it is these scandals more than anything that have overshadowed the person of James himself and the image of himself he had laboured to project.

As well as advising his son that his court stood as a symbol of his kingship, James, in the *Basilikon Doron*, had counselled on the importance of justice to the exercise of monarchy. It was when the king sat in judgment that he sat on the throne of God and, like God, it was a king's duty to mix severity with mildness, so as to win the love and praise of subjects.[217] On his journey south from Scotland, as we have seen, James took care both to display mercy, in releasing prisoners, and on occasion to set an example by sending a felon to the gallows.[218] The king regarded himself as a staunch protector of the law, which he viewed as the prop of his sovereign authority, and informed his son that it was the due making and executing of the law that differentiated a good king from a tyrant. In the older Whig histories of the reign, James was presented in very different colours: as a Scottish king who little understood the common law of England and as an absolutist whose ideas on kingship threatened the liberties and properties guaranteed by the common law. It was in the reign of the first Stuart, after all, that Sir Edward Coke felt the need to assert the special nature, antiquity and status of the English common law and in some noisy parliamentary debates James was reminded of the authority of the law. However, as revisionist scholarship, notably the work of Glenn Burgess, has persuasively argued, there was more agreement than disagreement about the relationship of the royal prerogative to the law and little in James's writings (or practice) that deserves the label absolutist.[219] Many of those who had greeted the new monarch with enthusiasm in 1603 were familiar with his ideas on kingship and law and evidently discerned nothing to cause concern in them.[220]

Indeed, though there was some nervousness about the implications of union for two realms with different legal systems, the reign of James I gave rise to no major legal controversies or notorious trials of the sort that blighted the reputation of Charles I and even, in some eyes, that of Queen Elizabeth. That is, no Stubbes or Prynne, Burton and Bastwick drew the sympathy of the people as the victims of harsh royal justice. The judicial blood-letting that followed the Gunpowder Plot was far from severe by early modern standards and, other than some papists who condemned the 'bloody executions' of eight conspirators in Paul's Churchyard and the Old Palace of Westminster, the traitors were dispatched 'to the great joy of the beholders'.[221] Before the plot, James had treated his Catholic subjects with mildness and was still inclined to do so even afterwards.[222] Certainly there was no large-scale pursuit of Catholics in the wake of the plot, nor even a grisly succession of executions of missionary priests, for all the tightening of security. Indeed, whatever his subjects may have feared, James reigned as a stalwart defender of the common law, which he once claimed he preferred even to the law of Moses.[223] Indeed, he suggested to parliament that the common law be codified and clarified as 'every subject ought to understand the law under which he lives'.[224] In 1618, Thomas Gainsford was to list as one of the 'remarkable blessings' of England its courts of justice (where one might 'view the sun in most perspicuous splendour') under the protection of the king.[225] It was not empty flattery. For all his run-ins with Sir Edward Coke, in which, in the words of J. P. Kenyon, the king 'showed remarkable tolerance . . . under the most intense provocation', James had taken a keen interest in the law and in law reforms that were only realized much later.[226] Preaching his funeral sermon on James, Bishop Williams described the balance of justice and mercy so evenly poised under a king renowned for upholding justice.[227] When on his death, reviewing his reign, Hugh Holland concluded of James, 'You should not find a [king] gentler nor a Juster', there is no reason to doubt that he expressed the views of many.[228] Even as civil war broke out in England, not least over issues of law and royal authority, a treatise by a clergyman who had by no means been uncritical of James nevertheless praised a reign in which 'the courts of justice were not interrupted, but the laws and seats of judgement were open for every man'.[229] To Andrew Willet, James had shown himself what he had urged his son to be: 'the guardian of both the 2 tables of the law'.[230] After his tense relations with Coke, despite the internal professional battles among the lawyers, James went to the grave with his reputation as another Solomon intact.

For James the law was inseparable from God's law, and the king's duty to uphold the law was part of his larger duty to God and his duty to sustain the true faith and church. James very much regarded the state of the church as the most important test of his kingship and clearly entertained large ambitions not only for the peace of the church in England but for its role in effecting an ecumenical settlement to the fissures and conflicts of Christendom.[231] The challenge to the head of the church as he succeeded to his throne was considerable. All religious groups from Catholics to Presbyterians had hopes and expectations of James; and many individuals looked to him for 'the full delivery and restoring of Israel' to the realm.[232] Amid the flurry of lobbying and advice, the University of Oxford came closest to James's own hopes when, on his visit in 1605, its spokesman urged that the king must 'put to flight all Romish superstitions and to remove, forsake and abolish all schismatical and new opinions.'[233] Though his own upbringing had been within the bosom of a Presbyterian kirk, James was suspicious of its claims to authority and its ambiguous loyalty to the crown; and early on he seems to have determined to support and strengthen the Church of England against its enemies and critics, of the left and the right. That church itself, however, was of recent creation and had been, too, a site of struggle for its identity and direction throughout Elizabeth's reign. In typical style, James began his English supremacy willing to listen. In a move quite uncharacteristic of Elizabeth, he met the puritans to hear their grievances against the church in a conference at Hampton Court, in January 1604. At the meeting, James offered reform of long-standing abuses such as pluralism and the law of excommuni-cation; he promised a new translation of the Bible and a strengthened preaching ministry, but he rigorously defended church ceremonies such as the use of the cross in baptism and insisted, against the claims made for such matters to be left to private conscience, on conformity to ecclesiastical and royal authority.[234] Such was the course – some have called it a *via media* – that James sought to pursue throughout his reign, but it was a course often disturbed not only by intrinsic differences and divisions, but also by shifting circumstances at home and abroad.

Early in his reign, the Gunpowder Plot radically disturbed the appeal to unity and moderation which characterized James's policy. The king, unlike many of his subjects, was prepared to take the Church of Rome, though corrupted by error, as a true church and, importantly, was ready to treat English Catholics as loyal subjects and to treat them leniently.[235] Amid the hysteria, even a loyal author, dedicating his treatise to the king, urged James not to endeavour to reform Catholics but to cast them out, as traitors outside the bonds of Nature and God. 'Away then,' he concluded, 'with all popery.'[236] Though, in the wake of the plot, Catholics suffered greater fines for recusancy, James never indulged those who advocated outright persecution. As well as his temperamental moderation, the king harboured hopes of a Catholic match for first Henry, then Charles; and indeed that match, balanced with a Protestant marriage for his daughter, was part of James's grander scheme to restore reli-gious unity and peace to Europe. As much as the Powder Plot, it was the failure of his attempts to persuade the Pope to call a Council that undermined royal ambitions during the years of uneasy peace in Europe.[237] Meanwhile, at home various groups within the church vied (as they had under Elizabeth) to draw the king to their party. Where Andrew Willet urged that it was time to rein in the recusants, John King, Dean of Christ Church, lambasted the Presbyterians, and Anthony Maxey, a royal chaplain, criticized the undue emphasis placed on the doctrine of predestination, along with puritans who 'never cease to be clamorous to the Christian prince'.[238]

If the hope harboured by the author of *Ecclesia Triumphans* in 1603, that the new king would 'bring us to one uniform doctrine', proved excessively optimistic, James did at least manage the theological controversies to an extent that more or less enabled him to govern the church in peace.[239] For the most part, Catholics remained loyal to the crown at a time when the French king fell to a Guise assassin's knife. As for the Presbyterians, their 'pretensions among the clergy largely disappeared and reluctant conformists were won round to the Jacobean establishment'.[240] Quite literally James championed a broad church: his archbishops ranged from the high church Richard Bancroft to the successor to Grindal, George Abbot; and the committees appointed to translate the Bible incorporated a wide range of clerics, as did the episcopal bench. Moreover, as a grateful Richard Meredith observed in a sermon before the king, unlike his predecessor, James sustained not only the authority but the wealth of the episcopacy by checking sacrilege and alienations.[241] Under James too, he noted, the church was strengthened by a learned clergy and faithful ministry which helped to temper puritan criticisms that it had not been easy for the Elizabethan establishment to deny.[242] So while he did not succeed in heading a church at home, let alone in Europe, forged under his supremacy into unity, under James's headship for long the church sustained a balance of positions in peace – in securing which, Richard Meredith not unreasonably argued, 'he hath done more than any of his noble progenitors'.[243]

Had James died younger that verdict would surely have been the judgement of history. What, however, all but destroyed his policy – and with it his image as the champion of a moderate religious settlement – was the resurgence of war in Europe in 1618. Though the causes of the Thirty Years War were by no means simply religious, the outbreak of hostilities polarized Europe into broad Catholic and Protestant camps. Moreover, when James's son-in-law accepted the throne of Bohemia, then lost it, along with his imperial electorate and homeland, the equilibrium of Jacobean policy came under incredible pressure. James had been able to balance a Habsburg match with anti-papal rhetoric, but the war, viewed by some as an apocalyptic struggle, called for action. James endeavoured to sustain his hopes and strategies in the radically new circumstances: indeed, he had to trust in Spain and hope that it would come to the aid of his daughter. While at home religious and political rhetoric became noisily polarized, the king issued directions to preachers, requiring them to eschew contentious matters of church and state.[244] The tensions, however, could not be contained. Preaching before the judges at Westminster Abbey on 5 November 1622, Dr Robert Willan acknowledged: 'Never could any king or governor contain all their people under the yoke of one and the same religion.'[245] Preaching at Whitehall the same year on Hebrews 12: 14 ('follow peace with all men'), Bishop Walter Curll, Dean of Lichfield, lamented that few were following his scriptural injunction: for all the king's care, there was strife and contention within the church.[246]

During James's last years, a party of anti-Calvinists took advantage of the king's mounting anger with the puritans to try to win him to a more ceremonialist position, and so brought to the fore divisions that had been quiescent. Worse, James's foreign policy and the necessary tempering of anti-Catholic rhetoric it entailed led some, even outside the circles of the godly, to fear the influence of Roman sympathizers close to the throne.[247] These concerns are audible in sermons such as that delivered in February 1627 at the assizes at Winchester by Abraham Browne, a prebend of the cathedral there. Browne delivered a sermon against the mass and its 'pretended sacrifice' and underlined the doctrinal differences which separated London from Rome.[248] Other sermons – again deploying the language of 'harlot' to describe the papacy and Rome – praised the Church of England as the custodian of the true faith, and figured its bishops, as well as head, as gods lent power by God himself.[249] But if a few had – dangerously – begun to doubt James's commitment to that church, death prevented an increase in their number. In his funeral sermon for Great Britain's Solomon preached in Westminster Abbey, Bishop John Williams singled out James I's headship of the church. James, he affirmed, was a 'constant, resolute and settled Protestant' who 'defended this doctrine of ours with his pen, his laws and his sword the whole progress of his life'.[250] As well as doctrine, Williams continued, the king sustained the discipline of the church, and its hierarchy of bishops, chapters and cathedral churches, all of which he maintained with his patronage as well as authority.[251] More than any of his predecessors, Williams claimed, James was a founder of churches, in many ways of the Church of England which he had built up on the foundations of doctrine and discipline.[252] If that was not the only portrait of James I as Supreme Head of the church in 1625, it was one that came nearest to the king's own self-image as a second Solomon – and not without justice.

If, not least on account of his writings, the image of James was inseparable from the church and the law, the person and perception of the king were also interwoven with policies and values that, from 1603, he had made his blazon. As we have seen, James's ambition for a full union of his two kingdoms was itself bound up with his sense of his role as Chief Justice of the commonweal and Supreme Head of the church. As a genealogist of the first Stuart put it, 'by uniting and knitting together all the scattered members of the British monarchy', James stood 'as one sent of God to fulfil his divine predestinate will.'[253] 'An empire of many kingdoms thus reduced into one,' an advocate of the *Necessity of . . . Union* argued in 1607, 'is not unlike the firmament of heaven.'[254] James's image, his identity, was bound up with union; and there can be no doubt that, after all his promotion of the project and of himself as a king of a united Britain, the rejection of both hastened the king's disenchantment with his new subjects, as it threatened to reduce to mere empty symbols what had been powerful representations of British rule. What the collapse of the union project exposed even more as a vain pretence was the portrayal and self-presentation of James VI and I as an imperial figure. From his own writings, panegyrics, medals and coins, we have pursued an imperial representation that figured James, not merely as emperor of a Britain that stretched from Culloden to Cornwall, but as one whose sun-like beams would spread throughout Europe and who might be a conqueror further afield. As the poet and courtier Ludovick Lloyd put it in a triumph dedicated to James:

Sit on Romane *Scipios* seate,
seeke out some *Carthage* new:
Let *India* be the up-shot marke,
claime *Affricke* for thy due.[255]

If the imperial dream faded with union, the creation and ambition of Prince Henry concealed it for the short duration of his adult life. And after 1618, rather than the head of a Protestant *imperium* to replace Rome with a new Troy, James appeared to many pusillanimous and subordinated. For the king himself, the imperial dream lived on, manifested in the stone of the Banqueting House and nurtured by the prospect of marriage into Europe's imperial dynasty. But with his own daughter in exile, any vision of Stuart empire was overridden by defeat abroad and denunciations at home.

The representation of himself that James cherished was also seriously tarnished by these developments: the image of the *rex pacificus*. Though there had been a militant strain to James's anti-Catholic writings in Scotland, and while for much of the first part of his reign he did not rule out other options, from 1603 he was greeted, and evidently chose to be welcomed, in panegyrics and pageants as a king who brought peace: to England, between England and Scotland, and with Spain. 'O welcome Prince of Peace and quietness,' the author of *Ave Caesar* sang in 1603; 'Adore your Solomon of Peace' enjoined another poet, while Andrew Willet in prose expressed 'a great hope that our own peaceable Solomon and princely Ecclesiastes will bring unto this land a general peace and quietness both at home and abroad.'[256] The king's peace was not opposite to, but part of, his imperial vision of a united Europe. As Thomas Gainsford put it in a treatise imagining James as champion of Christendom, 'In peace this virtue most triumphant is/Her victories no drop of bloode do spill.'[257] It was the ideal and option of peace that James was anxious to protect during the ascendancy of his son Prince Henry and his militant counsellors. Indeed, in the midst of *Chester's Triumph*, the city's entertainment for the martial prince, Peace speaks to persuade as well assert that 'No massacre or bloody stratageme/Shall stirre in Peaces new Jerusalem.'[258] Whatever his subtle diplomacy, James stood as the embodiment of Peace (and its accompanying virtue Plenty) while Henry pursued a quite contrary iconographical programme. The theme of peace not only outlived the first Stuart Prince of Wales, it formed the subject of the entertainment of the second. In Thomas Middleton's entertainment for Prince Charles at Chelsea and Whitehall, Peace, astride a dolphin, welcomes a 'spring of joy and peace', as London proclaims:

> What a Faire Glorious Peace for many yeares,
> Has sung her sweet calmes to the hearts of men?
> Enricht our homes, extinguish't forraine feares,
> And at this houre beginnes her Hymns agen.[259]

For all the hopes some placed in Charles as champion of more martial courses, James, as he advanced a Spanish match for his second son, proclaimed himself ever louder a prince of peace. As he arrived in his native kingdom of Scotland in 1617, the poet William Drummond welcomed him as a king who had sustained halcyon days to the benefit of his people.[260] In his sermon preached before the king at Wanstead in June 1621, the aspirant William Laud, then still Dean of Gloucester, took the prayers for peace in Psalm 122 (verses 6–7) as his text. In a sermon, published by royal command and delivered on James's birthday, Laud celebrated the 'very birthday of both Peace and the Peacemaker', England's Solomon.[261]

Even as Laud preached, however, Habsburg troops were storming the Rhenish Palatinate lands of Frederick and Elizabeth: peace appeared a distant prospect and to many an unwise course. During the last years of his reign, as he struggled to remain the *rex pacificus* amid mounting opposition from parliament, the press, and ultimately his son and favourite, James did not entirely want for support. In a sermon preached at Whitehall in the spring of 1622, Walter Curll, Dean of Lichfield, censured the Protestant hawks who were clamouring for a holy war, prayed for peace in Europe, and praised James as the blessed peacemaker among kings.[262] The image of *rex pacificus*, which had accompanied James's succession to the English throne, remained central to the representation of the first Stuart – throughout his reign and in historical memory. By his later years, however, that image and representation were being overtaken by other presentations of the king and by men antagonistic to both Jacobean policies and the king's personal style.

In the traditional Whig historiography, the phrase 'Jacobean style' appears only as an oxymoron. The king has been portrayed as physically ungainly and unkempt; his academic ability has been contrasted with the political astuteness he lacked; his penchant for favourites has been taken, when it has not been treated with prurient disgust, as the sign of a psychological flaw, or the legacy of a disturbed childhood. Recent evaluations have been kinder: James's policies on union and his preferences for peace have been judged visionary and sensible. Yet his style, when it has been discussed, has been more excused than defended. Whatever revisions have offered more favourable assessments of the first Stuart, James as a Scot, we are still told, simply did not appeal to his subjects or present himself to them in ways that made him attractive. Was the reign of James Stuart a classic example of a failure of image? Certainly James was a very different style of ruler to his predecessor. Whereas Elizabeth often left problems alone, James acted and intervened; where she at times stayed silent, he endlessly spoke and wrote; where she clothed her majesty in the raiment of mystery, James was ever ready to argue and debate even the *arcana imperii*. Such differences should not disguise the values and policies they had in common: a distaste for religious persecution, caution about intervening in European struggles, commitment to conscience and the church, and a conviction of their divine right. Nor should it be assumed that where they differed it was always to James's detriment. As we have seen, many heralded the new king not just as a father, but as a reformer, ready to tackle the corruption of the late Elizabethan age. Even in matters of style, James could manifest a charm for which he has not been credited. He was informal, witty, funny and, as his progresses evidence, had an understanding of the importance of public display, as well as, on occasions, the gift of a common touch. Some contemporaries at least considered him a good judge of character ('he beholdes all men's faces with steadfastness'), which he was when his affections were not engaged.[263]

Where he most differed from Queen Elizabeth was not in remoteness, as was once argued, but in his endless interventions, with his pen and in person, in the discourse and turmoil of politics. Except in the case of masques, James was reluctant to remain a spectator. When he went to Denmark to bring back his bride, he attended at the courts of justice; at Oxford, he participated in all the disputations.[264] There, as he did in affairs of state, the king 'many times urged contraries to find out the certainty'.[265] And when he intervened, as well as witty, the king could be blunt and sharp: 'I love not one that will never be angry,' he once opined, for 'he that is without anger is without love'.[266] Though he has been criticized for it, James did not lack Elizabeth's humanity; he lacked her numinosity. For all his proclamations of the sanctity of kingship, James eschewed mystery: in writings, speeches and in person he exposed himself, even his 'crystal' heart and conscience, to public scrutiny. In doing so, he invited public scrutiny of the mysteries of majesty itself. Though he did not favour the formal portrait, James certainly did not fail to cultivate public support. Where he failed – or misjudged – was in his belief (though perhaps it was always more a hope) that he would win the argument by the force of his learning and forensic skill. No English monarch came better equipped with those attributes. But the Tudors, and especially Elizabeth, had combined involvement and advocacy with distance and reverence of their sanctity and mystery. In attending little to the sacred ceremonies and symbols of majesty, James rendered himself a disputant in a burgeoning public sphere.

In the case of the last Tudor, the mystery of rule was dependent upon and symbolized by the inviolability of the virgin royal body. Though Elizabeth did not escape rumours about her sexual life, her represented body remained a sacred national symbol of England's impenetrability and purity. While her sex both dictated and enabled that representation, Charles I would also discern the power of the mysterious royal body to signify virtuous rule and appropriated Elizabethan somatic conceits for his own representation of chaste marriage.[267] In the case of James I, the royal body sexual served far more to undermine than underpin authority. It was not so, as we have seen, from the beginning. Images of fertility, procreation and virility abounded in the succession panegyrics and for some years after. A change in language and perception appears to have coincided with the rise of James's first English favourite, Robert Carr.[268] James had had his attractive male favourites, perhaps lovers, in Scotland – notably Lennox – but in England, whatever was known of them was probably put down to youth before marriage: after all, even the relentlessly virile Henry VIII had had his minions and boon companions. Carr was different: from early on, James treated him in public with an explicit affection that drew attention to what was evidently a sexual relationship, one that coincided with the end of royal issue and perhaps the king's sexual marriage.[269] And the relationship with Carr transformed the image of the king. The histories and stories of emperors and kings and their male lovers – Tiberius and Sejanus, Edward II and Gaveston – had connected homosexual relations with tyrannical, corrupt and effeminate government. If the rapid promotion of an unknown to an earldom did not itself signal corruption, the trading of sexual favours for advancement, Carr's later involvement in the death of Overbury and humiliation of Essex immersed James as well as his favourite in sexual and political scandal.[270] Perhaps during the hegemony of Somerset, Jacobean peace began to be re-read as womanish timorousness, just as the reforming king appeared all too embroiled in corruption and sin.[271] The favourites, that is, transformed the perception of James: his policies and his person. When Somerset fell, and was replaced by Villiers in the royal favour, the new favourite initially promised a more positive image for the king. Villiers was active, courageous and interested in reform. But he, too, was beautiful in an androgynous way, delicately slender and effeminate; and joined the king not only in his bed but in the advocacy of peace.[272] As well as drawing envy as an upstart raised above his station through corrupt affections, Buckingham (his title as a duke) became a figure of popular calumny – which also tarnished the image of the king. As the recent historian of James's homosexual relations has stated, sodomy and effeminacy were inseparable in the public mind from weakness, sin and Catholicism; the king's relationships with his favourites and the stories which freely circulated involving their sexual activities undermined his reputation. Significantly, only after the collapse of the royal marriage and the rise of Carr did Englishmen look back nostalgically to Elizabeth, whose womanly but uncorrupted body became a symbol of a manly valour so lacking in the court and the king.

CHAPTER 4

CONTESTING THE KING

The reign of James I was once characterized as the period that witnessed the rise of the opposition to monarchy. The first Stuart indeed faced not only more turbulent parliaments, but new genres and forms of criticism which circulated in print and in the public sphere: the satire, verse libel, newsletter and the coranto, or first newspaper. Traditionally it has been assumed that the virulent opposition to King James was a reaction to his attitudes and behaviour: to his absolutist views, his homosexuality, his pacifism; latterly we would add his Scottishness. A longer view complicates any such simple picture. As we have learned, during the last years of Elizabeth's reign, disenchantment spilled out in criticism of the court and the queen, in histories, plays and satires.[1] While such disillusionment explains the warm welcome that greeted James, it placed him in, to say the least, a difficult position. Daniel's panegyric of 1603 warned:

> He hath a mightie burthen to sustaine
> Whose fortune doth succeed a gracious Prince,
> Or where mens expectations intertaine
> Hopes of more good, and more beneficence.[2]

Though the task was great, Daniel promised the new monarch 'A people tractable, obsequious/Apt to be fashion'd by thy glorious hand'.[3] Others more realistically did not regard manifestations of joy at the succession as the suspension of all criticism. 'Leave off thy hope to please/both Court and Countrie too,' one well-wisher counselled.[4] For the rhetoric of harmony masked debates and discussions about policy and government that would not go away. James himself appears to have recognized what the vogue for Tacitean histories, the drama and verse satire also suggests: that politics was a subject of public discussion and that some regarded government not as godly rule but Machiavellian artfulness. In his insistence on his conscience, integrity and transparency James, I have argued elsewhere, endeavoured to reaffirm the Christian foundations of governance.[5] But even loyal observers saw that in the world around them:

> Such pride, disdaine and envie rules the hart,
> That now the world must be maintain'd by Art.[6]

The perception of a world of 'politicking', of artfulness and intrigue, emerging already in the sixteenth century, grew during the reign of the first Stuart. As well as the king, royal chaplains and preachers like Francis Mason denounced Machiavels and 'politicians' who undermined godly rule.[7] But, not least, the theatre testifies not only to a preoccupation, but to a popular preoccupation, with 'politics', and with the arts of rule as much as the divinity of kings. Whatever James's mantras about a king being God's lieutenant on earth, on the stage of the Jacobean theatre audiences saw tyrants, Machiavels, and simply fallible men occupying, and sometimes losing, thrones.[8]

The Tudors, especially Henry VIII and Elizabeth, had succeeded spectacularly in making themselves the focus of the nation. Yet, in publicizing themselves, they had, unwittingly, rendered monarchy itself a public text and site; they had demystified its sanctity. Along with the engravings, medals and souvenirs of Elizabeth eagerly garnered by loyal subjects came endless gossip about monarchy and the person of the monarch – gossip which circulated in newsletters, manuscript verse and other forms of 'scribal publication', which commercially minded publishers then turned into print. As Andrew McRae has recently shown, the satires with moral lessons which emerged at the end of the sixteenth century appear almost ubiquitously in Jacobean commonplace books, as vituperative libels of courtiers and favourites.[9] Such libels, McRae argues, in parodying an authorized discourse of virtue and conscience, helped readers to imagine a polity corrupt and divided. Satiric literature, that is, fundamentally questioned and challenged sovereign representation – and encouraged, perhaps compelled, a broad public involvement in the process of government. So much had verse libels become a medium of politics that, as we have seen, James I himself felt driven to write one in a (failed) attempt to stem debate and criticism.[10] Loyal supporters of the king such as Bishop Richard Corbett, abandoning any pretence of a realm of *arcana imperii* beyond critical scrutiny, felt the need to embrace criticism in a series of 'anti-libels' in support of the crown.[11]

Like verse libels, newsletters and early newspapers emerged in, and contributed to, a culture of the demystification of authority. Private newsletters relaying information, gossip, scandal and judgement about the court or figures in authority are doubtless as old as writing itself. In the early Stuart period, however, the newsletter became a genre, and the writing of news probably a profession, as correspondents like John Chamberlain or John Pory, Joseph Mede or John Flower, took it on themselves to provide a regular and detailed report on state affairs and personalities.[12] Such letters, often drawing on common sources and sent to more than one recipient, circulated among the provincial as well as metropolitan gentry and have been credited with contributing to 'a process of political polarisation', and to the growth of opposition by the 1620s.[13] Printed news pamphlets were almost unknown in England before the end of the sixteenth century and newspapers were very much a Jacobean invention. Though the 1580s saw pamphlets reporting on the French wars, it was from 1600 onwards that domestic as well as foreign news became common and it was in the 1620s that the 'coranto' or current, the first real newspaper, emerged specifically to convey news from abroad during the Thirty Years' War, but with it, of course, editorial and political comment.[14] By the end of James's reign, news was not only an established business but part of the political culture of ordinary English men and women, a powerful medium of the representation of affairs of state in ways that did not always compliment authority.

While popular print distributed accounts of James's journey from Edinburgh or entry into London, it also relayed in songs and sonnets the 'Strange Histories of . . . Kings', including the brutal murder of Edward II and Wat Tyler's rebellion against Richard II.[15] And in a hint that the theatrical metaphor of state might as much demystify as publicize kingship, Thomas Deloney quoted graffiti allegedly seen at Cheapside: 'This world's a stage, whereon to day/Kings and meane-men, parts do play.'[16] Though news and popular print were not intrinsically media of opposition, contemporaries themselves discerned what we would argue: that they complicated natural deference to royal authority. 'Time was,' William Leigh recalled at the celebration of Princess Elizabeth's nuptials, 'when none might touch the Lord's anointed.'[17] 'Time was', he continued 'when rulers were regarded and kings had their majesties'; but now the world had changed.[18]

A sense that discontent and criticism were facts of life seeps through even the loud acclamations that greeted James in 1603. Michael Drayton, congratulating his new sovereign, invoked the Muse that 'thy glory sings/(What ere detraction snarle)' and warned that the multitude were 'unsteady'.[19] By 1605, when the wrangles over union and the Powder Plot signalled that the honeymoon period of the new reign was over, Anthony Maxey, preaching before the king at Greenwich on the theme of contention, urged: 'let all slanderous mouths be stopped and all the factious schismatics in the land [be] ashamed'.[20] Whatever the proclamations of James's virtues, however, wrangles at court and in parliament spilled over into public criticism of the king. In the entertainment staged for Prince Henry at Chester, for example, Love urged the figure of Envy to depart 'and not to interrupt with her detractions' the day, while Peace (who may stand for the *rex pacificus* himself) denounces 'rash dissensions . . . civil mutinies', 'discord', 'domestic strife' and 'damn'd Malice' that threaten mutual concord.[21] Prince Henry, we have seen, both became a focus for opposition to James and yet contained criticism by offering alternative policies within the Stuart dynasty. His death in 1612, then, appears to have furthered the disillusionment with James which had been mounting before 1610. Mourning the prince, Thomas Rogers also remembered the joys of the nation a decade earlier when God had answered their prayers and sent a dazzling sun to rescue Elizabeth and asked:

Where are the eyes that dazeled with the lustre?
Where are the hearts that praises then did yeeld?
Where are the flocking troups that then did muster
With ravish'd soules, into that peacefull field?
They are decayde . . .[22]

The hope that a second prince might, by replacing Henry as a champion of honour and chivalry, restore lustre to the Stuarts was soon dashed by events which marked a turning point in James's reign and did damage to the reputation and image of the king, from which he probably never recovered. Whatever the new difficulties the king faced in representing himself in a changed political climate and developed public sphere, it was James's ill-judged – and widely publicized – personal relationships and the events that unfolded as a consequence of them after 1614 which meant that the pens and voices of James's critics have for so long overridden the king's self-representation.

The marriage of Somerset to the Countess of Essex and the murder of Sir Thomas Overbury were, quite simply, the greatest court scandal in living memory and perhaps in the entire early modern period.[23] The scandal involved the humiliation of a nobleman by an upstart, illicit sex, and murder by poison; worst of all, it implicated the king who had so publicly announced his affection for Somerset and who did not move swiftly enough (as Charles I was to do in the case of the Earl of Castlehaven) to condemn Carr.[24] The whiff of scandal began to circulate well before the revelations of poisoning. The Elizabethan Earl of Essex had been a popular figure and the association of the Devereux family name with honour and daring raised suspicions about the claim that his son, Robert the third earl, had been unable to consummate his marriage with Frances Howard. Though a celebratory form, the masque written by Thomas Campion for the marriage of Howard and Somerset hints at this in the figures of Rumour and Error that try to subvert the occasion.[25] Indeed, an oblique reference to another sexual relationship may even be discerned in the lines of the song that ran: 'Some friendship between man, and man prefer,/But I th'affection betweene man and wife'.[26] Whatever underlay the 'rumours' or whispered scandals, as Chapman called them in *Andromeda liberata*, it was some time before accusations of foul play against Sir Thomas Overbury, who had opposed the marriage, got into print – and quickly opened a floodgate of virulent libels and pornographic squibs which struck to the core of the court and monarchy.[27] As a major recent study has demonstrated, salacious stories of sorcery, the transgressions of gender, popery, sex and poisoning led to widespread public perception of a court corrupted by excess, deviance and sin rather than being the symbol of moral and political virtue.[28] Though, when the accusations were made, James, who was already tiring of his lover, ordered a judicial investigation, the stench of scandal reached the king himself, who had favoured the marriage and who, even in 1616, spared his

favourite the ultimate punishment for his crime. More importantly, the vituperative pamphlets and ballads the Overbury affair unleashed transformed
popular politics and, in drawing attention to James's own sexual proclivities,
the perception of the king.

Historians have long appreciated the damage done by the Overbury scandal
to the reputation of James's court and government. By concentrating, however,
not on the case itself but on the stories, separates, ballads and libels that broadly
circulated it, Alastair Bellany has demonstrated how the damage done both
outlived the events of 1613–16 and stuck to the monarchy and to James himself.
For our purposes, what was most significant was how the public texts and representations of the Overbury affair negated and reversed key elements of James I's
self-presentation in his own writings and in the panegyrics of others. Where the
king had written against witchcraft, his court and favourites were depicted as
involved in demonic activities; where James had written in his best known work
on the need for the court to be a model of virtue, his court was now widely
portrayed as a place of waste, excess and luxury; where the king had advised his
son to remain chaste, the court was shown to be a den of sexual licence and
corruption and, it was hinted, of sodomitical practices – all of which, in an early
modern England in which sex was an analogue for politics, signalled broader
governmental decadence and decay. As news and reports of the trials of Anne
Turner and the Countess of Somerset regaled an eager public with stories of
female lusts and plots, James's image as the patriarch, the husband, was indelibly
tarnished. Most dangerously, and, it is suggested, permanently, the rumours of
popish infiltration and plots (never far in the public imagination from tales of
illicit sex), compromised James's strenuous self-representation as the champion
of the Protestant faith. Moreover, though the king's quick action in bringing the
accused to a hearing initially won him plaudits, his ultimate mercy in sparing
the Somersets from the death which most believed they merited undermined
the king's reputation for justice, his image as a Solomon, and raised further speculation about his political judgement in the choice of his favourites and inti-
mates. 'James's behaviour in the Somerset case', Bellany concludes, 'disrupted the
legitimating power' of a variety of discourses and symbols central to the representation of the first Stuart, many of which James had with some success claimed
in his representations of his kingship.[29] Though the furore died down, the
memories of the events lived on: to determine perceptions of the new royal
favourite, George Villiers, and the king's relations with him, to disturb James's
relationship with parliament, and to figure his treasured policy of peace as
effeminate impotence. The Overbury affair publicized the fact that, in every
sense, the honeymoon was over – and not only the marriage between James and
his wife, or between his two kingdoms, but the loving union, the motif of accession panegyrics, the bond between the king and his people.

After the Overbury affair, contemporaries spoke of panegyric overridden by
calumny. 'I know', the author of a new play, *The Ghost of Richard III*, told his

readers, that 'in a play or poem thou lik'st best of satire stuff'; and in a sermon before the assizes at Taunton in 1616, the preacher felt so concerned about the seditious libels circulating that he ventured to say: 'I would wish Moses law revived, who blasphemes the ruler of the people shall be put to death.'[30] Two years later, the loyal chronicler of the court of 'the most illustrious and most significant James the first' wrote, he told Buckingham, to counter the aspersions cast on the court and, by implication, the king.[31] He undertook the work, too, he explained, as a semi-official commission – 'having been urgently solicited thereunto by the vehement persuasions of some worthy personages who themselves have observed divers pamphlets touching the court to have been . . . published, which seemed rather to have been composed in the disgrace of princes, and derision of their followers, than soundly or sincerely to instruct . . . them what is to be followed, what to be avoided'.[32]

By the time the author was writing, however, the dedicatee, now Marquis of Buckingham, was again reminding many of the ill consequence of the king's sexual intimacy, as well as attracting the ire of his rivals and displaced noblemen. Villiers owed his rise to favour to the patronage of those who had engineered the downfall of Somerset; and he, for a time, represented the hopes of the enemies of the Howards for a more militant foreign policy. However, in his rapid rise to favour and endeavour to monopolize the king, Villiers became a hated figure and drew opposition to his master as well as himself.[33] Though the deluge of libels against him did not appear until his assassination in 1628, libels and squibs against Buckingham circulated from his first rise to high title.[34] The charge of 'effeminacy' (a coded term for homosexuality) against Buckingham could not but again involve the king, especially after 1618 when, as we have seen, James's policy of peace, supported by his favourite, was critiqued as unmanly.[35] After 1618, opposition to peace, to the favourite and to the king became interrelated, and escalated. Court sermons affirming the sanctity of kingship read as nervous endeavours to stem the tide of what, in an address to the Warwick assizes in 1619, the Archdeacon of Gloucester, Samuel Burton, called an assault upon divine kingship.[36] 'Panegyrics', he lamented 'are not for this age'; 'therefore you see pasquils and infamous libels, scurrilous invectives and bitter satires are the only things that are now esteemed'.[37] 'Such books,' he added woefully, 'never hang long upon the printer's hand.'[38] In what was essentially a plea for old-style deference, Burton urged, perhaps with a hint of criticism, that princes needed to be 'careful of their own credit and reputation'.[39] As Buckingham survived attempts to supplant him and rose to greater heights, however, opposition grew at court, leaked into parliament and ran out into a public sphere fully fed by the Overbury affair on a diet of bitter invective. James's effort by a proclamation of December 1621 to check discussion of state matters had little effect.[40] By 1622, libels against not only the king's policies but his 'frantic passions' were again freely alluding to illicit sex as the sign of political corruption.[41] In a sermon on 5 November that year, Robert Willan came to the conclusion that no prince was so happy as to 'eschew the furious clamour of some unbridled and impetuous spirits'; but he warned that kings could be endangered as much by their own people at home as by foreign enemies.[42] In a sermon at Whitehall, published by command, Walter Curll denounced as seditious the 'private murmurings and muttering' of critics of the court who 'spare not to spit their poison in the face of princes'.[43] The French ambassador, Tillières, was even more direct: 'Audacious language, offensive pictures, calumnious pamphlets, those usual forerunners of civil war, are common here'.[44]

Historians engaged in the endless pursuit of 'forerunners of civil war' have traditionally focused on the opposition to James that was demonstrated in the parliament of 1621.[45] In that session, concern over monopolies and corruption at home, over the Palatinate and the king's pro-Spanish policies, blew up into a direct confrontation with the monarch that led to a radical claim to new power by the Commons in the Protestation which James with his own hands tore from the journals of the house. More recently, scholars have analysed the virulent pamphlet attacks on James's policy and government by the radical puritan Thomas Scott, author of *Vox populi*, and by the author of *Tom Tell Truth*, or *A Free Discourse Touching the Manners of the Time*.[46] During the 1620s, as well as pamphlets and printed newsbooks, numerous libels against Villiers and the court, returning to the theme of royal sexual sins, link sexual transgression with inappropriate influence, popery and political disorder at home and abroad. Squibs, such as the widely circulating 'The King's Five Senses' which now drove the attack on corruption to the very body of the king, show how broadly prose and verse – the king's own medium – were performing publicly to discredit the king and undermine the crown.[47]

Tillières's observation alerts us to another form of opposition until recently almost entirely neglected: 'offensive pictures'. During the 1620s, we have recently learned, a series of graphic cartoons critiqued royal domestic and foreign policies, implying that the court and perhaps the monarchy were infected by popery. Like the pamphlets and satires, such images were disseminated swiftly and broadly, were described and discussed in newsletters, and even sketched into commonplace books. Though in one case, that of Samuel Ward, the author was examined, for the most part cartoons appear to have met with the indifference or tolerance of the censor. Their role in undermining the reputation and official representation of the king awaits a thorough study.[48]

Having tried to check opposition by the voice of authority – in proclamations, directions to preachers and in tearing the Protestation from the Commons journals – James, as we have seen, resorted to joining the fray with bitter lines against the libellers and the public who strayed from their station to pry into the business of kings.[49] Though his literary intervention was typical, in penning his answer to 'the wiper of the people's tears' James not only acknowledged, he all but validated, the new forms of opposition which had grown up during his reign – the 'raylinge rhymes and vaunting verse[s]' which denigrated his rule. Even, that is, in his favoured medium of representation, the word, the agenda was now being set not by the king but by his critics. And the monarch who had written so much to represent himself was being represented by opponents – opponents whose bequest to history was, until recently, an almost entirely negative image of the king.

Historiography has left us with the impression that James won little respect or admiration from his subjects: in textbook accounts of the king, the damning judgements of Sir Anthony Weldon and Arthur Wilson are endlessly quoted; not least, perhaps, because they are so quotable.[50] However, Wilson and Weldon published their critiques during the Commonwealth and both had personal reasons for hostility to the Stuarts.[51] That they aimed their attacks at James's image and style, however, suggests that his reputation was especially vulnerable in this respect. Perhaps not surprisingly, the contemporary judgements on the king which were most favourable were those that emphasized what James had made the priorities of his own self-representation. In his funeral sermon, Williams, comparing James with Solomon, laid stress on his learning, his piety and the peace he brought to all his realms; and praised his rare eloquence.[52] The public orator of Oxford, similarly lauding the *rex pacificus*, praised a truly Platonic king.[53] In a sermon at Denmark House, in which he compared James to Moses, the royal chaplain Phineas Hodson, again hymning the fruits of peace, described the king as 'a walking library, an abstract of knowledge, an oracle to resolve questions and mysteries'.[54]

The poets followed the preachers in the same vein. Thomas Heywood and Hugh Holland in their elegies remembered James's rare combination of the virtues of king and poet, as well as his 'present' to his people of peace.[55] In Scotland, Francis Hamilton of Silvertown Hill, in a poem 'in memory and commendation of the high and mighty monarch James' listed the *Basilikon Doron* and the Psalms as well as the king's treatises against Conrad Vorstius and Cardinal Bellarmine as the testaments of 'a learned and religious lord'.[56] Some extolled the broader benefit of the reign and virtues of the sovereign: his mild and just manner, his affability, the texts that made him 'the perfect pattern and model of a most excellent King'.[57] Some, however, even amidst their mourning, acknowledged different, less eulogistic perceptions. In his *Cyprus Garland*, Holland hinted that the late distractions of Christendom had tainted the last years of the reign; Heywood writes of the 'great ingratitude' that led too many to undervalue the great blessings of the Jacobean rule.[58] Francis Hamilton determined to pass over 'what some perverse people say' and the carpings of the 'mumbling Momuses': he hoped 'King James, thy blames are buried and forgot'; they were not.[59] The ever popular John Taylor, in *A Living Sadness* addressed to the new king, assured Charles I (wrongly, as it transpired) that, whatever the unthankful or the carpers, James's place in heaven and men's hearts was secure: 'His government both God and Men did please.'[60] Most interestingly, especially if in this he were a spokesman for his popular audiences, Taylor depicted James as having conquered with those weapons he had always relied upon – his words:

> His pen restrain'd the strong, reliev'd the weake,
> And graciously he could write, doe and speake.
> He had more force and vigour in his wordes,
> Then neigh'bring Princes could have in their swordes.[61]

But in 1625, just as James's prized peace was overrun with the preparations for war, so his words, it seemed, could not overpower critics at home, let alone 'neigh'bring Princes'. Yet both James's martial son and the nation soon came to appreciate the benefits of the king's peace; and Charles, whatever his distaste for aspects of his father's style, took his writings almost as a blueprint for his government.[62] And while few shared Hamilton's conviction that James's 'faith, fame, Name, claime Crowne without a spot', the posthumous reputation in the nation of the first Stuart was at first by no means entirely negative.[63] Even in 1642, a pamphleteer who raised *The Ghost of King James* damned Buckingham but praised 'a good king' whom he had, it was charged, poisoned.[64] The same year Dr Willet compiled extracts from James's speeches as models of 'politique government' and contrasted them with the 'great fears and distempers' that afflicted the kingdom, the peace and happiness the nation enjoyed under 'so godly, pious and religious a prince'.[65] The next year, an edition of James's *Apothegmes or Table-Talke* was offered 'to public view' with a preface that reinvoked the comparison with Solomon that 'incomparable . . . sovereign'.[66] Willet had no doubt that in speaking from the grave, James would only further enhance his reputation.[67]

Though critics of Charles tended to invoke Queen Elizabeth as the model of good monarchical practice, the recognition, even in the 1640s, that James had secured peace and plenty, upheld the law and maintained the gospel enabled positive memories of the king which could be used to criticize his son.[68] But the spots and stains of the past did not wash away. When in the changed circumstances of regicide and republic, apologists for the new regime sought to discredit *all* rulers, they found in James an easy target.[69] The year 1651 saw the publication of *A True and Historical Relation of the Poysoning of Sir Thomas Overbury* [and] *Passages Concerning the Divorce between Robert, Later Earl of Essex and the Lady Frances Howard*.[70] The same year, a time in which the reputation of Queen Elizabeth rose to its greatest height, *Truth Brought to Light*, a narration of the first thirteen years of James's reign, dwelt on the favourite Carr, the Essex divorce and the murder of Overbury, whose portrait faced the title page.[71] Published by the radical printer Michael Sparke, the history, sold 'at the sign of the Bible in Green Arbour', began the assault on James's memory that Weldon, Wilson and Francis Osborne joined over the next few years.[72]

After 1649, James suffered in some ways no less at the hands of Royalists than republicans, as the sanctification of the martyr Charles eclipsed all other re-habilitations.[73] It was to be long before James emerged from the moral criticism, and then homophobia, that damned him; and it is only recently that his skills and virtues have again been credited, as they were by many of his subjects.

Though by no means uninterested in visual culture, James paid too little attention to his image; still more did he eschew the numinosity and mystifica-tion of his person which had characterized Elizabeth's rule. But, at least until the libels that followed scandal all but drowned them out, James's words – in speech, proclamation and printed works – were forceful and often skilful writ-ings and representations of royal authority.

In 1622, in a sermon delivered before the king at Theobalds, William Loe, a royal chaplain, perhaps trying to assure James of his place in history, had proclaimed:

> writings are monuments, and memorials, words reach to them that are near, writings to them that are far off. Words to them that are alive, writings to them that are yet unborn. Speech profiteth the auditory to whom we speak, but writing profiteth all, and he that preacheth profiteth for an houre, but he that writeth profiteth for ever.[74]

James's failings, not least of image, saw his writings for long buried under others' lurid tales of moral decadence and sexual corruption. It is, then, by no means coincidence that James's image and reputation have risen, as only now his writings have again begun to draw the attention they once did. Whatever his other failings, of character and style as well as policy, it is a return to James's chosen medium of representation that is revising the histories of the king. In the words of one of his earliest apologists, let us then abandon Weldon's 'beastly bawdry' and 'leave . . . so great a king to his continued memory by his own excellent impressions in print that fame him to posterity'.[75]

PART II

REMYSTIFYING MONARCHY: REPRESENTATIONS OF CHARLES I 1625–40

Prologue: A Failure of Image?

As we come to the middle of the long historical period of this study, we confront a conundrum that goes to the centre of our subject. Perhaps no early modern monarch paid as much attention to image as King Charles I, who is instantly identifiable to most; yet the king's reign ended in political failure, civil war and military defeat; and his death came not after advanced age or illness but by axe on the executioner's block. The obvious conclusion to be drawn is that, since he took care over his representation, Charles I either projected the wrong image or failed to reach or persuade subjects on whose co-operation and loyalty early modern governments depended. Such conclusions, however, may not be quite as obvious as they at first appear and anyway themselves pose further questions: if Charles got his image or message wrong, *why* – and *how* – did he do so? And, we might further ask, since he reigned a quarter of a century before his execution and nearly twenty years before civil conflict, *when* did he do so?

Such questions, of course, cannot be separated from the unending historiographical controversy over the causes of the English or, latterly it has become fashionable to say, British civil wars. Ever since 1649, if not 1642, parties and scholars have contended over who or what caused England's only violent revolution. In recent times, after the vogue for Marxist and other structural explanations, historians have returned to human agency; and the scholarly consensus has coalesced around attributing to Charles I himself much of the blame for the fate that befell him as well as the nation. Notably, the late Conrad Russell and John Morrill have posited that, unlike his canny father, Charles I was no politician, and that his failure in the political arts destroyed the monarchy.[1] Several scholars have argued that through his policies and actions Charles threatened the law and constitution and the Calvinist consensus of the Church of England.[2] But even those who deny that the king pursued tyranny or popery concur that he evidently excited fears that he did so. The consensus is, then, that Charles not only failed in the political arts of compromise and manoeuvre but also in the principal art of politics: in explaining himself, and securing compliance through the communication of his values and the representation of his rule.[3]

If we accept, as in some measure ultimately we must, that Charles I failed to win the loyalty of his subjects, we shall need to consider whether the failure lay in the image or message, in the media, or the audiences targeted – or ignored. Did the second Stuart depart from the unifying rhetoric which his Tudor predecessors had deployed to temper the bitterness of division and court only a party in church and state, so fostering further division and conflict? Did the policies and values which Charles promoted and communicated alienate his subjects or did he fail to explain or communicate effectively – our modern parlance would be 'sell' – programmes that were unobjectionable or even potentially attractive? Did his antipathy, at least at times, to pamphlet polemic and verbal exchange deprive monarchy of what had become a vital medium of representation and, more importantly, surrender that medium to critics and opponents of the king?

This last question points to other factors in the erosion of faith in the king. As I have shown, the publicization of regality was accompanied (as well as enabled) by a print revolution that also provided a platform for critics of royal policies, personalities and even monarchy itself.[4] Religious and political tensions and divisions fostered by the fall-out from the Reformation in Europe and break from Rome in England added to political difference ideological fervour that fed, and was fed by, print polemic. Increasingly over the course of the sixteenth and the early seventeenth centuries, kings and queens had not only to represent themselves, but to defend themselves against the arguments and representations of others. Where Henry VIII and Elizabeth had been troubled by scurrilous and seditious rumours, James I encountered a torrent of pamphlets, satires, squibs and libels that excoriated his court and kingship. If the contest for representation was sharpening, did Charles fail because he was less adept than his predecessors or because, increasingly, the advantage lay more with the critics of monarchy than with the monarch? One of James's last gestures, after all, his response to his critics in the medium they had made their own – the libel – may evidence as much desperation as skilful endeavour to appropriate a form.

That, however, the high temperature of the later period of James's reign gave way to widespread celebration of Prince Charles and, later, to (at least apparent) political calm suggests that a narrative of the mounting and inevitable failure of royal representation, as indeed the old story of escalating opposition to monarchy, is too simple. Like most monarchs, Charles began his reign with a large measure of popularity. Perhaps more importantly, he also, as his enemies were nervously aware, ended his reign and life with a large measure of popular as well as aristocratic and gentry support. As we will argue, the act of military force needed to bring the king to trial recognized that, at least in 1648, the king had not lost the competition for support, had not entirely failed in the arts of representation and communication.[5] By contrast, the events of 1640–1 suggest a different situation: the near isolation of Charles and the success of his parliamentary critics rather than the king in securing the trust of the nation. The complications which discredit a simple chronology of an escalating failure of royal image impel us to pay careful attention to different periods and moments, and in particular not to take the crisis of 1640–2 as emblematic of the whole reign. Beyond that, the fluctuation in Charles I's popularity and appeal may suggest, as well as altered conditions, different images and messages, or different modes and media of communication and representation, over the period 1625–49. Arising from mounting opposition and division, the political crisis of 1640 established permanently a political culture of contest in which royal representation became, and remained, a partisan programme orchestrated by those now called Royalists against perceived opponents of monarchy. Such radically changed circumstances merit separate discussion. In this chapter, our focus is on the period 1625 to 1640 and on how, why and when, and on the extent to which, Charles's representation of his kingship, for all his attention to image, had alienated his subjects and undermined royal authority.

As we have begun to see, though each ruler succeeded in, and to, particular and personal circumstances – not least of age, sex and marital status – all early modern rulers from the Reformation onwards drew on common texts, discourses, tropes and figures in representing their authority to their subjects. The Bible and the classics, the myths and memories of the English or British past, humanist learning and the emblems of justice, faith and virtue were all deployed by each ruler to validate his or her authority. As well as the rehearsal of these texts and figures, state rituals underlined continuities which rulers themselves highlighted in invoking illustrious predecessors, as Elizabeth I did her father, and as James did Elizabeth I. As the last case reminds us, it was especially important for a new dynasty to claim continuity (as well as new vigour); and there can be little doubt that, on the English throne, James adjusted his rhetoric to accord with, even at times to echo, Elizabethan strains, whatever his marked difference in personal style. Moreover, from the late 1590s, when he wrote his *Basilikon Doron*, to 1620, when he published the treatise on St Matthew's gospel, James endeavoured to ensure some continuity of royal behaviour and reputation by means of prescriptive advice to his sons – not least on the example they set and image they presented as actors upon a stage. Though his 'opposition' to his father may be exaggerated, James's first son, Prince Henry, fostered a very different image to his father while claiming to be a true heir of Elizabeth Tudor, and so complicated – some would say destabilized and discredited – the image of the king. What then of Charles I? Did Charles as king depart from the scripts which had underwritten the monarchy for a century? Did he deploy new languages or images that signalled revolutionary (and unwelcome) changes in royal government?

In many ways, though they have not often been highlighted, it is the continuities in the representational motifs of Jacobean and Caroline rule that are striking. Though his liturgical preferences may have been different, Charles, like his father, next to whose statue he placed his own on the portico of St Paul's, expressed his desire for Christian unity and befriended Catholics as well as Protestants of different beliefs and temperaments; like his father and earlier predecessors, he laid emphasis on order and obedience to authority and on the interdependence of the church and crown in securing them, leaving men's personal beliefs to themselves.[6] Though his position as second genera-tion heir to multiple kingdoms may have led him to emphasize it less, Charles, like his father, presented himself as a British king – or rather emperor. While devoid of Jacobean apocalypticism (which was, as we saw, always evident in others more than in James himself), Caroline representations, in panegyrics and masques, paintings and medals presented a British past and imperium in the Stuart dynastic inheritance and progeny. Thirdly, though as prince – and for the first three years of his reign, Charles, like his elder brother, stood as the public champion of Protestant crusade and military intervention in Europe – the king came to assume the image of James as *rex pacificus*, bringing the bene-fits of halcyon peace and prosperity to Britain, uniquely in Europe. Most of all, Charles continued – and strengthened – his father's royal image as a husband and a father: of both a newly fecund dynasty and of the nation. Nothing had contributed more to James's welcome in 1603 than his sex, marriage and pater-nity, and the king made marital and patriarchal discourses the foundation of arguments for monarchy. After a decade on the throne, however, the tensions between the king and prince, most of all the distance from his wife and the rise of a homosexual favourite, tarnished the discourses and images which had been rooted in marriage and family. By contrast, Charles, as we shall see, made marriage and paternity the dominant themes of his representation and the language of love a discourse of rule. With the queen regularly pregnant from 1629 to 1640, and five children surviving infancy, the representation of Charles as loving husband and father had even more powerful support than James had gained as the first fertile sovereign in over half a century. Like those of James, Charles's children symbolized continuities: continuities of blood, dynasty and divine right rule.

As his predecessors had done, Charles prudently drew attention in many ways to these continuities. In Scotland and in England, he often claimed to take his father's policies as the pattern for his own: the Caroline *Book of Sports* of 1633, for example, re-published that issued by James in 1617.[7] In proclamations and speeches, time after time Charles echoed the words of his father. And in remark-able engravings which belong to the last years of Jacobean and the first of Caroline rule, Charles is figured with the King James Bible and James's *Works*, or as the royal word become flesh: the heir of James's representations as well as his body.[8] As I have argued elsewhere, in his support of the church, his acute sense of his duty as king, in the organization and direction of his court and in his personal habits, Charles I closely followed his father's scripts – not his practice.[9] And, of course, in naming his second son after his father, as he had baptized his first after himself, he honoured both James's memory and his father's patriarchal status as founder of a Stuart race of British kings.

However, these important continuities – of image as well as policy – were accompanied by a radically different style that was as evident to contemporaries as it has been to historians. In part, those differences were the normal consequences of a different personality, upbringing and circumstances. Charles, twenty-five when he succeeded to the throne in 1625, had not lived through the turmoil of the Scottish Reformation and indeed, having left his native kingdom aged four, was little formed by Scottish culture or its rough and tumble politics. His childhood and early adolescence in an English court marked him out not only from his father but perhaps even from a brother who, by the standards of the age, was grown up when he left Edinburgh for London. More importantly, Charles was one of the few kings on the English throne to experience travel on the continent. Though, as was the case with his father, the impetus was the quest for a bride, Charles's sojourn in Spain was to be profoundly more formative than James's voyage to Denmark to bring back Anne as his queen to Scotland. At the court of the Habsburgs and at the Escorial, Charles experienced a very different style of monarchy to that of his father. And he preferred what he saw. Where Whitehall was an antiquated warren of rooms and corridors, milling with ministers, courtiers and servants, at the heart of a city bursting with an ever-expanding population, the Escorial, a few miles distant from Madrid, a quasi-monastic retreat as well as a palace, symbolized dignity, order and calm. Where the Jacobean court and its daily life were characterized by informality and at times coarse familiarity, Habsburg court ritual and ceremony were marked by rigid protocol and exact codes of decorum. The Escorial 'reflected a conception of monarchy as a mysterious, private institution, hidden away from the public eye through its layers of ritual and etiquette'.[10] In Spain, too, Charles came face to face not only with the dominant dynasty of Europe, but with its ubiquitous representation on canvas and in stone. In 1619, Charles inherited his mother's art collection, including some of that of his brother Henry; and he was as prince surrounded by a new generation of noblemen interested in art and architecture. But it was in Spain that his taste in painting, as well as his love of baroque architecture, were formed; in Spain that his collection, which hitherto primarily contained the works of northern European artists – Holbein and Van Somer, for example – was transformed by the sight of Raphaels, and the works of Velázquez, Rubens and, especially, Titian.

Charles was twenty-three when he went to Madrid and, although immature, his personality was largely formed. But what he found in Madrid was a style which suited his personality and that he determined to make his model. As much as a style of governing, of kingship, it was a style of representing kingship, and one that was, in various respects, in marked contrast to that of his father. Contemporaries remarked within days of Charles's succession a change in the nature of the court, which, James had taught in the *Basilikon Doron*, was the mirror of kingship.[11] As we shall see, the new king ordered the restoration of Elizabethan rules and a decorum lacking in the court of his father whose 'light and familiar way', if Bishop Burnet is to be trusted, repelled him.[12] Where James had shown little interest in sitting for his portrait or collecting art, Charles was to amass the greatest collection of paintings and sculptures of any occupant of the English throne and was to find in Van Dyck the perfect depicter of his political style, as well as taste. Where James had declined to perform in masques and at times displayed impatience even as a spectator at the theatricals of his wife and children, Charles took a leading part in court masques and devoted time to careful rehearsal of them.[13] And where James had retained a belief in the power of his word as the principal medium of his representation, and had ubiquitously written and spoken, Charles, for much of his reign, appeared to favour silence.

These preferences for ceremonial decorum and visual representation over discourse and debate doubtless go to the core of Charles's personality: much (too much in my view) has been made of his childhood speech impediment in explaining his distaste for verbal exchange.[14] But they were preferences that were also strategic, that is, deployed for calculated reasons and practised (or not) in different circumstances. Charles, for example, spoke and wrote more in the 1620s and 1640s than during the 1630s, a decade when he also stressed formal protocol more rigidly than in the war years. In harking back to Henry VIII and Elizabeth, as well as looking to Spain, for a model for his court, Charles implied that his father's style, his 'familiar way', had presented an improper image of kingship. Similarly, in his willingness to perform the silent role of leading masquer, as well as his reluctance to emulate James's loquacity, Charles may have intended a shift in political as well as personal style.

Indeed, given Charles's respect for and invocation of his father's policies, we are led to suggest that the new king regarded the former as having made mistakes in representing and communicating those policies, and that he consciously set out to change royal representation. In emphasizing the visual and ritual, he not only emulated the court of the Habsburgs which had so impressed him, but (at least in this) reverted to media which James had somewhat neglected but which had been central to Tudor royal representation. And *relative* silence, too, appears to have been chosen out of Charles's belief that, by speaking and writing too much and in popular forms, James had surrendered some of the mystery of majesty which he again found enshrined in the Escorial and Spanish court etiquette.

If that were the case, Charles's preference for fewer words was by no means inherently foolish or unique. By the early 1620s it was far from clear that, by involving himself in the public discourse about policy and government, James had, as he always hoped to do, won the argument. Though famous for parliamentary oratory and a well-chosen phrase on occasions, Elizabeth had played down her rhetorical skills, limited her public speaking, and had never sparred on paper with writers or opponents.[15] Circumstances, however, had been changing during her reign and were further altered by events during that of James I. Libels, newsletters and newspapers, as we saw, were widely circulating accounts of events in ways beyond the control of, and often in ways unfavourable to, authority. It was these changes, as much as his own experience of Scottish political debate, that led James to judge it necessary to enter the fray of public print to put the royal case. In doing so, he further encouraged pamphlet exchange in which the royal voice risked being drowned in the cacophony of contending utterances. Charles soon decided upon the opposite course: he endeavoured by his own silence to reduce the noise of debate and so to figure the monarchy as above, not part of, the polemical fray. He preferred, he was to say, action to words.

We might sum up the change of style that Charles's succession effected as a shift from *arguments for* royal policies to the (*silent*) *representation of* majesty.[16] The arguments James had made relentlessly for dynasty, divine right and regal authority, for unity, peace and obedience, Charles displayed as given, as natural and intrinsic to his person and his family. The differences between the representational styles of father and son were not only ones of preferred media; they involved different audiences and different modes of securing the support and love of subjects. Historians have suggested that, in the shift in a style of representation, it was Charles rather than his father who made the greater, and costly, misjudgement: Charles who neglected the need to make a case, appeal to his subjects, and earn their love and support. But, before we concur, we must turn to a full examination of all Charles's modes of representation – in words, in visuals, and in rituals and ceremonial performances – and to how others, by no means under royal control, figured and perceived the king and the image of his kingship which he carefully superintended.

CHAPTER 5

THE WORDS AND SILENCES OF A KING

I

On the day of the regicide Charles's political testament, the *Eikon Basilike,* was published – and went into thirty-six editions the same year.[1] Two years later, in 1651, the first collected works of the king, the *Reliquiae sacrae Carolinae* published not only the *Eikon Basilike* but Charles's papers and discussions about Presbyterianism with Alexander Henderson, his papers regarding the Treaty of Newport, his prayers for blessings on the treaty at Uxbridge, and, as well as the speech he delivered on the scaffold, speeches and letters to parliament.[2] On the one hand, this substantial volume discredits any statement that Charles I did not present his case in words. On the other hand, nearly all the royal words collected in it were uttered or presented after 1640: the first speech included, for example, is that to the Long Parliament, delivered on 3 November 1640. The selection of royal words chosen may have been, as most selections are, strategic and polemical. The works gathered dated from the onset of the king's troubles, which, it is implied, had no long-term causes, but rather followed from the Scots' invasion and the treasonable acts of a caucus of MPs after 1640. Interestingly, after the Restoration, a five-volume collection of royal words and works, *Basilika: The Works of King Charles the Martyr* (published in 1662 and reissued in 1687), added letters, speeches and declarations going back to the beginning of the reign.[3] Indeed, the section of speeches opens with Charles's address to his first parliament on 18 June 1625.[4]

If the *Reliquiae sacrae Carolinae* and *Basilika* invite comparison with James I's folio *Works* of 1616, they also point up the contrast between a father keen to publicize and publish his words in his lifetime, and a son who, as he said, favoured few words, and who was drawn more by necessity than inclination to speak and write.[5] Indeed, the force of circumstances driving Charles I to public address is graphically illustrated by the chronology of the king's published speeches: *The English Short Title Catalogue* lists no speech of Charles printed before 1640, but well over seventy between 1641 and his execution in 1649. The inference must be that conflict and civil war compelled the king to articulate a case, where earlier he had felt no need to justify his position or to garner support for obedience, which he held to be the natural duty of subjects. While such an inference is broadly correct, however, it is not the whole truth. Charles did not over the first fifteen years of his reign write treatises or scriptural exegeses like his father. But he made more extensive and careful use of those by now established genres of verbal representation – official prayers and proclamations; and, interestingly, far more even than James I, he deployed royal declarations as direct addresses and appeals to his people. As we turn to study them, not as statements of royal policy but as strategies of representation, along with the speeches Charles delivered to his parliaments, we will see a need to refine assertions about the second Stuart's indifference to words and to reconsider the role of these largely unstudied texts in the dissemination and perception of the royal image.

Facing the title page of the 1651 *Reliquiae sacrae Carolinae*, an engraving depicts Charles I as *Fidei Defensor*. One of the roles of the post-Reformation rulers as head of the Church of England was in leading the nation in official prayers on particular and special occasions such as accessions, royal births, or visitations of the plague. These official prayers, ordered to be used in all the churches of the realm, were almost always devised by bishops. But issued by royal authority and often with a royal proclamation, as well as printed by the royal printer, they represented the king or queen as godly ruler and publicized a style of headship and governance in the occasions and texts chosen and the services prescribed.[6] Most of all, in the ways in which they mingled official words with God's own word, prayers issued in the sovereign's name were important texts of that royal faith and piety which announced the ruler as God's lieutenant.

Several events early in Charles I's reign prompted an official service of common prayer: plague, war and royal births, as well as the king's and queen's succession. But it would also appear that, more than his father, Charles attributed importance to these official services as occasions that expressed his greatest wish for the church and realm, times when, as a 1625 proclamation puts it, 'Prince and people together through the whole land shall join in one common and solemn devotion.'[7] The role of public services of worship in the king's larger religious and political aims is evident from the beginning, when a form of common prayer was ordered to be read every Wednesday in 1625 for 'the averting of God's heavy visitation . . . and for the drawing down of his blessings upon us and our armies by sea and land.'[8] Set forth 'by his Majesty's authority', the service opened with a prayer for the first parliament of a new reign and a kingdom at war. Recalling the example of David, who prayed in such time of trouble, the service figured Charles as another head of a chosen people, leading his flock by example and in prayers of repentance and humiliation.[9] Asking for God's mercy, not only for relief from plague but especially for their 'gracious' king 'thy chosen servant' Charles and his Queen Mary, the congregation were led to pray for deliverance 'from all sedition and privy conspiracy' as well as for victory over foreign enemies.[10] The services the same year of thanksgiving for the end of the contagion similarly figured Charles as the holy patriarch who had saved the nation from the consequences of their sins.[11] The woodcut border to the title page depicts the figures of Faith and Humility flanking the royal arms, which are repeated facing the first page of the printed service book.[12] 'Enlarge', the people prayed, 'thy favours to thy church, our king and state', in a service that was a 'thanksgiving' as much to the king on earth as in heaven.[13]

The connection of official prayers to specific royal policies, hinted at in the first official service of the reign, became explicit in the prayers ordered 'in these dangerous times of war and pestilence for the safety and preservation of his Majesty and his realms'.[14] Printed (again) with a large royal arms on the title page, the book of service not only offered prayers for the king, it implicitly presented him as leading the service and imploring God to 'watch over thy Sion when it is most encompassed with danger'.[15] Indeed, as well as asking absolution from God, the congregation, in the collect for the king, prayed that 'we his subjects, duly considering whose authority he hath, may faithfully serve, honour and humbly obey him' and that his enemies might be scattered

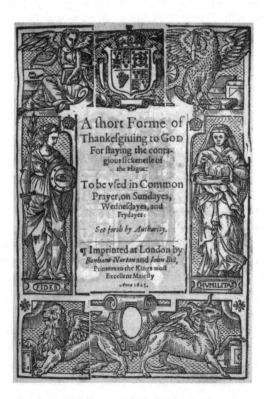

24 *A shorte Forme of Thanksgiving to God for Staying the Contagious Sicknesse of the Plague*, 1625.

by the Lord.[16] Significantly, too, at a time when Charles's religious preferences had begun to stir suspicions, the service included thanks for the Church of England which 'under a most gracious and religious king is for truth of doctrine and purity of worship as truly Catholic and orthodox as ever any church of Christ hath been'.[17] The scriptural patriarchs had, the congregation read, prepared for warfare by spiritual amendment; and 'our gracious sovereign followeth the example of those religious kings by his royal command of a fast'.[18] As well as spiritual preparation, therefore, the Lord was called upon to inflame all subjects 'to employ their bodies, strength and means for the preservation of God's anointed, their gracious sovereign', that second Moses who fought a war 'in which God's cause and true religion is . . . assaulted'.[19] England, the service assured all, having experience of God's deliverances, could place trust in his providence – but also in his chosen prince and champion of his church and people.[20]

Several volumes of official prayers published in the early years of Charles's reign represented the campaigns against Spain and France as holy wars and Protestant crusades. The form of service devised 'at the going forth of the fleet' in 1628 explained the king's motive for war in terms which echoed the language of the old champions of the Protestant cause: 'for the relief of some of our distressed brethren,' the service announced, 'our gracious sovereign, thy beloved servant, is moved, out of zeal to thy house, and compassion to the members of thy spiritual body, to send forth a fleet to sea for their relief.'[21] In another service of prayers the same year, the lesson from 2 Chronicles 13, on Abijah's war against Jeroboam, sacralized Charles's (and Buckingham's) war, and called upon God 'to be his defender and keeper' as he fought God's as well as England's enemies.[22] Here, as prayers for the reformed churches painted Charles as their Protestant champion, other prayers for parliament implicitly also instructed them in their duties to support 'true religion, justice and union of hearts', most of all 'the person of our gracious sovereign'.[23]

At a time, then, of mounting religious division, anxieties excited by the arrival of Queen Henrietta Maria with her Catholic entourage, tensions in relationships with parliament, and the unpopularity of the king's chief minister and government, official services, some explicitly published by His Majesty's special command, represented Charles as pious Christian, biblical patriarch, Protestant champion and arm of God's battle against the enemies of true religion. Though as yet we do not have the evidence to judge the reception or impact of these services, read weekly and sometimes twice weekly in every parish church (as well as the Sunday services), these services disseminated an image of the king far different from that of noisy exchanges in the metropolis and should at least be remembered when we attempt to assess the perceptions of the new monarch in the early years of his reign.

The prayers and services are also a clear barometer of the dramatic shifts in the representation of Charles which we will trace through other genres and media. For, after 1629, prayers celebrating the king as Protestant champion ended with the peace which, not least on account of the failure of his efforts to secure parliamentary subsidies, Charles was compelled to make with France and Spain.[24] During the period of the Caroline peace and personal rule, from 1629 to 1640, Charles authorized fewer services of public worship and the theme of those ordered, in keeping with royal withdrawal from European affairs, was domestic and pacific. However, the image of the king as God's chosen disciple and agent was no less rehearsed, not least from 1629 in an annual service of thanksgiving appointed for 27 March, to commemorate the day of Charles's entry into his kingdom. Published with authority and bearing the royal arms, the service took passages of Scripture, such as 1 Timothy 2 : 1, to lead the people in thanks for princes by whose means they led quiet, peaceful lives.[25] Peace, the service proclaimed, did not mean weakness: 'the king,' the recital of Psalm 21 reminded the congregations, 'shall rejoice in thy strength, O Lord.'[26] As the second lesson from Romans 13 rehearsed the familiar obligation of obedience, prayers commemorated the 'unspeakable goodness' of God in giving the people 'his chosen and anointed to rule over us', 'thereby assuring us of the continuance of the gospel.'[27] Giving thanks to the Lord, the people prayed for the king's glorious reign long to continue and swore allegiance to Charles and his heirs.[28]

If, in early modern England, the birth of any heir was seen as a sign of God's providence and blessing, that was all the more so on the birth of a royal heir, especially in an England which, before the reign of Charles I's father, had seen the sad consequences of too few royal births. Though James I sired three children who lived to adulthood, all were born before his succession to the English throne, soon after which he was estranged from his wife who was not even to conceive again after 1606. By contrast, Henrietta Maria had five children (as well as several miscarriages) by 1640, and was pregnant virtually every other year of the decade of personal rule.[29] The queen's pregnancies and deliveries became occasions when official prayers and services were prescribed, for Henrietta Maria's health and safety and that of the expected royal child. In these services, prayers for 'Mary', as her name was usually anglicized, connected the royal to the holy family and rendered the queen (like Elizabeth but now literally) a blessed mother as well as heir of the Virgin.[30] Moreover, in the service of thanksgiving, the people, knowing that 'lineal succession is under thee the great security of kingdoms and the very life of peace', prayed that God make the queen the happy mother of many children: 'to the increase of thy glory, the comfort of his majesty ... the safety of the state, and the preservation of church and true religion amongst us'. As well as the guarantee of dynastic succession and national security, that is, royal fertility was represented as the sign of God's special favour bestowed on the king and queen and as their furtherance of his divine plan. As a prince was followed by a second son, as well as three princesses, prayers for the queen's safe delivery and of thanks for the royal progeny publicly announced Charles and Henrietta Maria as blessed and the royal children as pledges of peace and (whatever the concerns aired elsewhere) of 'true religion'.[31]

Other than the annual service commemorating Charles's succession and these prayers for the safe deliveries of the queen, no official prayers were ordered during the early years of personal rule, a period when, it has been observed, Charles I stepped back from public addresses to his people. In the later 1630s, however, as in the later 1620s, crises, once again in the form of plague and war, prompted Charles to order services of prayer which very specifically voiced his circumstances and concerns. In 1636, the form of prayer 'for the averting of God's heavy visitation' by a renewed outbreak of the plague, began conventionally enough.[32] Following the example of Kings David and Daniel, the people heard, Charles had thought it 'meet to excite and stir up all godly people within this realm to pray earnestly'.[33] Though the language repeated that of earlier services, the use of the term 'godly', rather than 'innocent', in this official text may have been a move to ostracize the puritans who were escalating their attacks on the church and king. Certainly as pamphlets such as Burton's and Prynne's directly attacked the hierarchies in church and state, there was an obviously topical reading of a passage in the service that ran: 'The people of Israel murmured and rebelled against Moses and Aaron, their leaders; and there have been also among us in England not only such as have despised government and spoken evil of those that are in authority but ... traitors ... murmurers, malcontents, faultfinders'.[34] In including such among the sinners whom the plague was sent to punish, the service of 1636 powerfully aligned the king's authority with God's and countered the puritan appropriation of Scripture as a critique of Charles's church and monarchy. The service of prayers for averting the plague, in fact, again gave Charles an occasion to re-present himself as the pious preacher leading his flock in penitent imprecations to God and to castigate his critics as traitors, not just to him but to the Lord.

Later events, however, were to challenge that representation along with the king's authority. From 1638, as we shall see, Charles I's Scottish subjects directly questioned Charles's claim to act as God's lieutenant and asserted the authority of the kirk and people over his claims to be head of the church. The so-called Bishops' Wars which resulted were as much clashes on paper as on the battlefield; and in the propaganda war, in which the Scots deluged England with pamphlets arguing their case and urging them as co-religionists to join their resistance, the competition to claim godly validation was as bitter as it was vital.[35] Along with other genres of argument and self-presentation, Charles ordered prayers to be read on behalf of his expedition to suppress the rebellion in the north. In 1639, in all churches at the time of divine service, it was mandated that, after the prayer for the queen and the royal progeny (a nice reminder of the king's role as loving father), the congregation was led in prayers for the king's victory.[36] But, in accordance with Charles's claim that he went to compose not destroy his native kingdom, the people were enjoined to pray: 'Give him, blessed father, so to settle his subjects in peace and the true fear of thy divine majesty that he may return with joy and honour and proceed long to govern his kingdoms in peace and plenty and in the happiness of true religion and piety all his days.' The prayer, published as a one-page separate as well as inserted in the service, again figured Charles as pious and as peace-maker and so implicitly represented the Scots not as brethren but as disturbers of God's holy land. Though the mounting clamour against the regime in England, as well as Scotland, suggested that he was not winning the contest to claim a godly cause, Charles issued another official prayer for his armed expe-dition against Scotland the next year.[37] Now, as well as commending a gracious king to the Lord, the prayer denounced as damned by God 'traitorous subjects who having cast off all obedience to their anointed sovereign do . . . seek to invade this kingdom'. If the recurrence of plague in 1640 led many to fear God's disapproval, Charles was determined to use prayers to assert that it was the Covenanters, not he, who had called down divine wrath.[38]

These volumes of official prayers evidence a king as ready as his father to support and publicize his Supreme Headship and image as godly ruler. More surprisingly, perhaps, Charles's proclamations also reveal a king deeply concerned with royal self-presentation in words, and qualify generalizations concerning Charles's preference for silence. In the first place, the modern edition of the proclamations of Charles I dwarfs the volume of his father's, even if, ending in 1646, they cover a slightly shorter period. James I issued on average one proclamation a month; Charles's 519 over twenty-one years is twice that average.[39] However, the average disguises some important differ-ences and changes. During the period of the personal rule, Charles, like his father, issued one proclamation a month. It may not be surprising that with the troubles in Scotland and in England after 1640 that number rose to an average of two after 1640, then to four after the outbreak of civil war in 1642. What is less obvious, and important, is that during the first four years of his reign the new king issued twice as many proclamations as his father had. A perusal indi-cates that, though circumstances (plague for one) cannot be discounted, war in itself does not explain the increased number. Charles I began his reign wishing to address his people. Moreover, his capacities in doing so, though little respected by most historians, made a mark on the editor of Caroline procla-mations, for James Larkin writes: 'Charles was a literary artist of intense conviction and deep feeling, whose most poignant messages were written in his heart's blood'.[40]

The early proclamations reveal a new king very concerned to present himself as his father's son. There are numerous references to 'King James of blessed memory', 'our most dearest Royal father', and in several proclamations Charles specifically expressed his wish to 'observe the acts of so wise and just a father', or to 'renew the course formerly begun by his dear father of blessed memory'.[41] However, Charles's own personality and priorities were also manifested in a new stress on the need for order and uniformity. Rather than the 'undecent manner' of alms-seekers flocking to him on progress, Charles instructed his almoner to make contributions to the overseers of the poor in each town;[42] in his father's court and household the new king saw 'much disorder' which he determined to amend;[43] in making arrangements for subjects to come to be cured of the king's evil in 1625, he expressed a determination that 'in this as in all things order is to be observed';[44] in an early proclamation for Virginia, he articulated his resolution that 'there may be one uniform course of government in and through all our whole monarchy'.[45] If the new tone sounds determined, and insistent on 'quick and due execution' of orders and laws, Charles's early proclamations were not starkly authoritarian.[46] At least as much as his predecessors, the new monarch used language to express repeatedly his care for, and love of, his subjects as the principal motive of his enactments and as the first principle of his rule. Regulating the disorders perpetrated by pressed soldiers, the king announced his 'tender care to secure his loving subjects', even from the consequences of war; prohibiting the unlawful export of leather in 1626, he declared his 'princely care and providence for the general good of his people'.[47] Indeed, he claimed in 1628, he had 'nothing more in his princely desire than the general good of his subjects, preferring their peace and quiet before his own benefit'.[48] Like his predecessors, Charles took pains in these early proclamations to present himself as an example of, as well as the custodian of, the common good. Where, several proclamations acknowledge, 'in all states there will be some ill-disposed persons with whom private and particular gain and advantage will more prevail than any public respects', the king protected the public good and weal of all.[49] No less, Charles took trouble to publicize his care for the church and faith. In a proclamation intended (whatever its consequences) to temper the heat of recent controversies, the king in 1626 swore that he 'by God's assistance will so guide the sceptre of these his kingdoms, and dominions by the divine providence put into his hand'.[50] Advertising his personal faith, how he 'in his private devotions daily lifteth up his heart and hands to God', Charles, in several proclamations, explained his desire for moderation, and 'our care to conserve and maintain the church committed to our charge, in the unity of true religion and the bond of peace'.[51]

During these early years of his reign Charles perhaps felt not only the need so to present himself to his subjects, but also, in the highly charged atmosphere of religious and political tensions at home and war with Spain and France, to win their support. Whatever his supposedly authoritarian instincts, it cannot be doubted that Charles set out to gain that support, and was even ready to make concessions, and to show himself conciliatory, to secure it. When, for example, the benevolence he had requested to finance the war met with a poor response and with resistance, Charles not only discharged the privy seals; he diplomatically declared that the failure of the loan 'we impute not to any disaffection in our people' but vaguely 'to some miscarriage in the business'.[52] Moreover, the king, in a manner that we have been led to suppose not typical of him, went to some lengths during these years to explain his actions to a public beyond the political nation. On 7 October 1628, for example, he outlined his intentions in requesting a loan from his people. The course, he related, had been taken by the advice of Council, 'for the public cause both of religion and state' and 'the common defence', not his own ends.[53] And, in an attempt to deflect charges of unusual courses, the proclamation declared: 'we have thought fit to publish and declare unto all our loving subjects' that the action was 'enforced upon us . . . by necessity' and would not be 'drawn into example, nor made a precedent'.[54] The king acknowledged that, in the heated pamphlet debate, some were 'scattering' speeches stating that the loan was intended to avoid a parliament and responded unequivocally: 'it is far from our heart to make any such use of the love of our people,' he said, and that, as soon as he could he 'purposed to call a parliament'.[55] The explanation and conciliatory language were evidently deployed to try to win the argument, and to prepare the ground for a parliament which might support the war as Charles needed it to do.

As parliament was called in February 1628, Charles continued, in proclamations, to use conciliatory and flattering language to prepare for a co-operative meeting. A proclamation for a fast in March described the parliament as 'that Great Council which is the representative body . . . to consult, debate and conclude' the weightiest matters of the realm; another suppressing two controversial sermons extolling the prerogative, by Roger Mainwaring, described him as 'trenching' upon the right of parliament and as justly censured by them.[56] If, as seems probable, Charles was, in the spirit of his father, labouring to win the contest for public as well as parliamentary support, the experiences of 1628 provided devastating evidence of his failure. Though five subsidies were voted, the House of Commons did little to support the war and, worse, prepared a Remonstrance of grievances that named the king's minister and friend, the Duke of Buckingham, as 'the principal cause' of the 'evils and dangers' that faced the realm.[57] The effect on Charles of the Remonstrance and his thinking about how to respond to it need not be guessed at. Charles prepared a full response to the charges (which deeply offended him) that he countenanced papists and Arminians, contemplated the use of force to secure his will, and was led by the duke.[58] 'Let us,' he concluded in what was an appeal to his subjects as well as moderate backbenchers, 'see moderation and the usual parliamentary way and we shall love nothing more than parliaments.'[59] Charles's response, drafted with Laud's help and with 'a purpose to publish it in print', continued James's and his own early policy of participating in public discourse. But – significantly – the king did not publish his reply. If his decision not to publish suggests a shift in his attitude to self-representation, the public applause at the assassination of Buckingham in August must surely have confirmed an instinct to withdraw. When, on 1 October, the king issued a proclamation proroguing the parliament that was due to reassemble, with unusual brevity and vagueness he cited only 'divers weighty reasons us especially moving'.[60] The failure to explain was perhaps a sign that Charles had come to believe that silence was a better course than self-justification.

Amid the debates in Council about the wisdom and timing of re-summoning parliament, it is not clear how far Charles was persuaded by advice or necessity to meet with one again. Having decided, however, he not only continued with conciliatory proclamations (such as that suppressing Montagu's *Appello Caesarem*), but again used language that underlined the importance of the representative assembly and echoed, as we shall see, the 'honied words' of his speeches to them.[61] The session, however, ended again in failure. But this time it was not only a failure that contemporaries were quick to see as decisive (the 'funeral' of parliament, Sir Thomas Roe predicted): it was one that fundamentally transformed the royal style – and the genres, modes and languages of Charles I's representation.[62] The change is apparent in the proclamation of 2 March dissolving the parliament. Here the king moved from emollient words and invocation of unity to attack and, instead of an appeal to unity, to a tactic of divide and rule. Though many, he informed the public, had been 'sober and grave', the 'malevolent disposition of some ill affected persons of the House of Commons' had undermined their good intentions.[63] The king, in an early move to command sympathy through self-portrayal as long-suffering victim, had been patient with them; but his patience had been repaid only with 'seditious' assaults on his authority which threatened the peace and order of the realm. A contest for representation, for an image as custodian of the public good, was being waged. As the departing MPs, especially the radicals, circulated and publicized their Protestation and a different version of events, Charles felt compelled to issue another publication that outlined the royal version of events.[64] Answering circulating rumours that the Protestation was not the work of a few but voted by the whole house, the king repeated that the blame lay on a few, in particular 'an outlawed man desperate in mind and fortune' – an outsider, that is, from the commonweal.[65] Claiming that he was supported by 'the wisest and best affected' who, no less than he, disavowed such actions, Charles sought to persuade the people that he had not broken with parliaments, but had been 'unwillingly' driven 'for the present' from them by the sedition of the few.[66] The proclamation was set out to 'manifest the truth' of what had happened and 'to make known our royal pleasure'.[67] Rather than being a point of contact with his people, Charles had come to regard parliament as the cause of his misrepresentation to his people, and of suspicions and rumours. Revealingly, in dispensing with parliament, Charles expressed his hope that 'our people shall see more clearly into our intents and actions'.[68] The libel pinned to Paul's Cross claiming that he had lost the people's love indicated that in the fulfilment of that aim, in repairing his image, the king had much to do.[69]

It would seem, however, that as a vehicle for representing him Charles accorded less importance to proclamations after 1629: he issued only ten in 1631, eleven in 1632 and nine in 1633, compared to twenty-five in 1628. Numbers alone do not tell the whole story. During the 1630s, Charles continued to invoke tradition, the name of his father, and indeed Elizabeth I and Henry VIII, to suggest continuity and dispel charges of innovation.[70] His declarations of his care for the public good became a mantra: 'it is a great part of our royal care . . . to maintain and increase the trade of our merchants'; the king had 'a great desire . . . to advance the wealth of our people . . . to cherish and comfort their labours'; the king's 'watchful eye of providence for the public good of his loving subjects is always kept open'.[71] Royal projects, devised to enhance revenue, were carefully represented as devised for the public weal: accordingly the new soap manufacture provided work 'so beneficial for our people'; the incorporation of beaver hat makers was devised for the common good, by a monarch who was always 'graciously inclining to further all worthy inventions, especially such as tend to the general good of our subjects'.[72] Critics of royal policy and projects were again cast as privately motivated enemies of the public good. So opponents of the new soap (there were many) were castigated as 'factious and refractory persons'; critics of the saltpetremen were demonized as threats to public safety; and those who otherwise questioned royal measures were implicitly figured as opposed to noble 'arts and good endeavours'.[73] By such language, Charles sought to represent himself as the embodiment of the public good, and the sole custodian of the safety and welfare of the realm, now frequent parliaments had ceased to meet. Indeed, in a proclamation of 1630 Charles literally connected the royal body with the public weal: announcing the birth of his son not primarily as his own comfort but as 'a principal means for establishing the peace and prosperous estate of this and other kingdoms, whose welfare we will ever preserve before any other blessing that can be for us'.[74]

In his self-representation in proclamations as the guardian of the public good, however, Charles in several ways used rhetorical devices which implied a dialogue with subjects rather than autocratic command. Of course, his proclamations were firm regarding the duties of subjects. But the king frequently cited the advice of his Council which had prompted a proclamation and so advertised that important virtue of early modern monarchy: an openness to counsel.[75] Secondly, he often announced proclamations as a response to public complaints and concerns by a king who was always ready to listen as well as instruct. So, the 1637 proclamation concerning the packing of butter was in response to a petition of 'our loving subjects'; the incorporation of the tradesmen of the suburbs of London was prompted by 'the earnest and frequent complaints of our loving subjects'; and a proclamation regulating the transport of horns even took up a complaint made to parliament in 1610.[76] Towards the end of the decade, proclamations were expressing the king's readiness to entertain and respond to complaints about his own initiatives. Finding that, though they had been granted 'upon pretences that the same would tend to the public good', in April of that year, Charles, more than ever in need of popular support, revoked dozens of licences found to be prejudicial or inconvenient to the people.[77] The comparison is usually made in his disfavour, but this was action and rhetoric very much akin to Elizabeth I's in response to complaints about monopolies.

If he issued fewer proclamations during the 1630s, and the tone of some bordered on the authoritarian, Charles still recognized the need to promote himself as the custodian of the public interest, as open to advice and petition, and as responsive to his subjects. On the odd occasion, he even continued to use proclamations to counter impressions damaging to his objectives or reputation. In March 1635, for example, responding to false reports that he intended to abandon the regulation of tobacco, a royal proclamation announced: 'we have thought meet hereby to declare and publish to all our people that we will not leave unfinished so great a work begun with such advice and care and so much tending to their health and welfare'.[78] In the main, however, the decade of the 1630s, in contrast to the earlier years, was not one of explanation or argument. In proclamations, Charles I announced his good intentions and expected that they would be taken on trust. If the relative calm of the decade encouraged him in the view that withdrawing from the public debate about affairs to a simple self-representation as a loving ruler had proved astute, it was a confidence and strategy that collapsed with the verbal onslaught against the king fired by the opponents of the new Prayer Book in Scotland.

As well as a flood of words in explanatory declarations and speeches, the Scots war prompted a large increase in royal proclamations and, as importantly, a shift in their style. In February 1639, a hybrid 'proclamation and declaration' (to which we will return) was issued 'to inform our loving subjects of . . . England of the seditious practices of some in Scotland seeking to overthrow our royal power under false pretences of religion'.[79] Weeks later, a proclamation declaring the king's intention towards the Scots outlined the king's 'good meaning' and sought to counter the impression, widely circulated by Scottish pamphlets distributed throughout England, that he was going to invade Scotland.[80] Charles was forced to abandon the silence of majesty – to disclose the *arcana imperii* of his affairs in another kingdom, in order to win support, to argue his case, and to limit the damage being done by Scottish propaganda which skilfully hinted at the dangers faced by English subjects and the common cause to be made in resisting a (popishly affected) king.[81] After a decade of proclamations written in moderate prose from a stance of sure authority, Charles had to take up the attack; and in doing so join the discursive battle. By August 1639, his proclamation ordering the burning of 'a scandalous paper lately dispersed' by the Scots attacked the document as 'falsehood, dishonour and scandal'.[82] Now, however, Charles felt the need not only to relate the details of a treaty of peace (traditionally a prerogative of the crown) but to appeal to the witness of peers such as the Earls of Salisbury and Holland to substantiate his words. In the bitter exchange with the Covenanters in 1639, royal words were becoming pitched against other locutions and texts, becoming, that is, contested and contemned. And royal proclamations against them were, though necessary, serving further to render the king's voice merely one of many contesting (and contested) voices. By the spring of 1640, and not least because he had by then resolved on another parliament, Charles tried by proclamation to suppress the 'libellous and seditious pamphlets', and the 'manuscripts' and 'discourses' sent from Scotland and circulating freely among his English subjects.[83] Dangerously, he admitted that such were 'alienat[ing] the hearts of his well affected subjects' to the point where – we note his drawing attention to advice – his Council had, 'with one consent' (that is unanimously) advised action.[84] Recognizing it to be 'necessary, that some . . . public demonstration should be made of so great an insolency', it was agreed that 'An Information from the Estates of . . . Scotland' should be burned by the hangman and its possession made a capital offence.[85] Charles was struggling to retain or reclaim the voice of single authority in this proclamation which called in 'any other relations or discourses . . . other than such . . . as shall be published by his Majesty's special licence or authority'.[86]

If an empty attempt at censorship suggested that royal proclamations had lost the verbal contest with the Scots, riotous assemblies in Lambeth, Faringdon and Wellington, Somerset, then the Covenanters' invasion of Northumberland, graphically revealed the impotence of royal words. In his proclamation of August 1640, disowning the invaders as rebels who used 'pretences of religion' to mask their true design of overturning regal government, Charles was forced very much on the verbal as well as military defensive.[87] For now the king, though he had already given assurances, had to 'profess before God' that he harboured no design against religion and liberties and that he would govern 'as a just and religious prince'.[88] During the 1630s, Charles, for the most part, had assumed that such things need not be uttered, that they were best not said but assumed. The question of whether, for all the repetitions of his care for the public weal, his downplaying of proclamations as a site of self-presentation during the 1630s was a costly error, or whether an unexpected verbal onslaught from Scotland undermined the pose of silent majesty, is one to which we must return. For now we must turn to that other verbal form to which Charles made reference in proclamations and of which he certainly made full use: the royal declaration through which the monarch addressed the nation.

Royal declarations were rare and extraordinary in the sixteenth century. Henry VIII used one to answer the rebels in the Pilgrimage of Grace and even the loquacious James I issued only four.[89] We may, then, be surprised to find that the supposedly taciturn Charles I published no fewer than nine declarations during the first fifteen years of his reign – and scores thereafter. Moreover, Charles's declarations were far longer on average than his father's, and the aptly named *Large Declaration* of 1639 ran to over 400 pages. The inference must be that Charles attributed great importance to this medium of communication to his people: to the royal declaration as a mode of self-presentation. Though his declarations often complement royal proclamations, they take the space and the occasional nature of the genre to make a statement and appeal in particular circumstances and manifest a monarch far from indifferent to the need to argue a case. Again, however, the chronology tells an important story: of the nine declarations issued between 1625 and 1640, only two belong to the decade 1629–39, one of which was a reissue of James I's *Book of Sports*. Charles's declarations were, even more than his proclamations, texts issued in times of parliament and times of crisis: times, that is, when he evidently felt the greatest need to address his subjects directly. Though lack of space prevents the full analysis these neglected texts of royal representation deserve, we must examine some briefly for the strategies and rhetoric of Charles's addresses to his people.

The king's first declaration justifying the loan of 1626 combined an acknowledgement of the unusual course with an appeal for trust and support which was, whatever its success, carefully couched.[90] The loan, Charles explained, was 'forced upon us by that necessity to which no ordinary course can give the law'. It was necessary to maintain religion and defend his people, as his obligation to God bound him to do. But, Charles reassured his subjects, this extraordinary course was 'not in any wise to be drawn into example nor made a precedent for aftertimes'. The king was attempting to dispel the fear and suspicion that the loan signalled a reign of new, extra-legal exactions and the end of parliaments. Those, he endeavoured to persuade his subjects, who stoked those fears were 'malevolous persons' who, for all their 'pretence' to procure liberty, sought nothing but the ruin of the commonweal. For the king's part, he gave his word that 'it is far from our heart to make any such use of the love of our people or to make this any annual or usual course of raising monies'. Urgency had necessitated an extraordinary action; as soon as possible, the king promised a parliament, and parliaments 'as often as the commonwealth and state occasions shall require it'.

Where, interestingly, this first declaration had the form of, and may have been issued despite its title as, a proclamation, the second royal declaration of 1626 is clearly a different genre of document and much longer than a proclamation. *A Declaration of the True Causes Which Moved His Majesty to Assemble and After Enforced him to Dissolve the Two Last Meetings of Parliament* was written both in the third person and as an intensely personal narrative of events, skilfully composed to include the people, while underpinning royal authority and right.[91] The recent dissolution of the parliament, the declaration opened, was 'to the unspeakable grief of [the king] himself and . . . of all his good and well affected subjects'.[92] Reasserting the royal prerogative of calling and dissolving parliament, Charles reminded his subjects (at a time when newsletters and pamphlets were questioning it) that 'he is not bound to give account to any but to God only whose immediate lieutenant . . . he is'.[93] This, however, was a king ready to justify himself not only to his God and conscience but before 'his own people' and 'to the whole world'.[94] Like his father he decided to give an explanation, to 'make a true and plain declaration' 'that . . . the mouth of malice may be stopped'.[95] The declaration took readers back to the (happy) beginning of his reign and the war which several MPs had urged Charles I to champion. In his first parliament, however, they had not, despite promises, supported it and had left him to scrape by, using some of his own money even to keep the navy at sea.[96] Charles, however, did not give up on his parliaments; he recalled them, confident that they could not be oblivious to his honour, and to the nation's (and Christendom's) safety. Yet, even as Spain planned a design against Ireland, the Commons, misled by the violent passions of a few, ignored the urgency abroad to concentrate on attacks on a royal minister at home, finally proceeding to a Remonstrance that contained 'dishonourable aspersions' against the king himself.[97] But, whatever the failure of others to do their duty, Charles assured his subjects that he would proceed against the 'common incendiaries of Christendom' and, as a good father and protector, defend them from Spain and Rome.[98] 'His Majesty,' the 30-page declaration concluded, 'doth publish this to all his loving subjects that they may know what to think with truth and speak with duty of His Majesty's actions.'[99] In other words, this was not only not the last narrative drawn up from the king's point of view yet issued as a neutral relation, but also a deliberate intervention into a public sphere awash with gossip and rumour as the MPs returned to their constituencies. Unlike his father, Charles did not rant or harangue; his tone is one of patient frustration and regret that some have failed in their duty together with a quiet confidence that the people will support him. If the closing lines and the acknowledgement of 'malice' showed an underlying anxiety about the force of others' accounts, Charles's *Declaration* did its best not to contend with them but to take the higher ground.[100] It was the tactic of self-presentation that, for better or worse, Charles was to favour through most of his reign.

One other declaration from the 1620s worthy of our attention is that which the king issued explaining his reasons for dissolving his last parliament, in March 1629. The relationship of, and differences between, the king's use of proclamation and declaration is well illustrated here. For the declaration, with a large royal arms on the title page, reprinted the 2 March proclamation dissolving the parliament, together with the king's last speech to the Lords and Commons (to which we will return).[101] The proclamation, as we saw, blamed the 'malevolent disposition of some ill affected persons' but in brief; in 1629 Charles evidently felt the need for a fuller account of his actions, especially as it was widely believed that parliament would not soon be recalled. As in 1626, the royal declaration protested that kings were not bound to account for their actions, but recognized the need to do so: to present the royal case, 'not in those colours in which we know some turbulent . . . spirits . . . would represent us'.[102] Again the declaration was a narrative which presented the king as the true patriot standing against Rome, Spain and France. Rather than as supporting him, the king presented parliament as obstructing, then 'blasting our government'.[103] For all his patience and concessions, the declaration continued, the Commons grew ever more heated: 'seldom', he wrote using a word that powerfully evoked an unruliness that contrasted with his own calm reason, 'hath greater passion been seen in that house'.[104] Even after Charles had agreed to a Petition of Right, he protested, the radicals were not content and endeavoured to deprive him of tonnage and poundage revenues enjoyed by the crown for centuries – and this in wartime.[105] Though most moderate men were content, those malevolents stirred concerns 'in such as were not well acquainted with the sincerity' of the king's answers.[106] As well as the alleged threat to liberties and property, they complained of the dangers that faced the church. 'This wicked practice,' Charles declared in calm words which almost certainly repressed deep anger on this count, 'hath been to make us seem to walk before our people as if we were halted before God.'[107] Detailing his concessions, even regarding tonnage and poundage, the king made his parliamentary critics appear what he claimed: unreasonable, fiery, even (in their attempts to examine the judges) unconstitutional. Indeed, the narrative of the mounting encroachment on the authority of the king, the courts and the law reached a kind of logical crescendo in Charles's relation of the violent restraint of the Speaker who appears as a victim no less than the ruler.[108] Skilfully citing Scripture, Charles compared speeches against him to that of the wicked Shimei who cast stones at the holy King David.[109] Not only, the inevitable conclusion is drawn, were these men neglectful of their duty, they sought 'anarchy and confusion'.[110] However, as his enemies sank to extremes that threatened all, the king promised that their unforgivable behaviour had not diminished his care or love of his people. In assuring them of his concern for their liberties, rights and religion, his expectation of their reciprocal respect for his prerogative sounded, as he believed it was, only natural. Though it reads as artfully constructed, as well as doubtless a sincere statement of the king's views, the effect of the declaration is hard to gauge. We might note, however, that Esther Cope found few calls for a parliament in the 1630s and that Simonds D'Ewes, no sycophant of king or court, blamed the dissolution on 'fiery spirits' in the House of Commons who 'were very faulty and cannot be excused', while Sir Thomas Roe directly echoed royal language in denouncing a zeal vented 'with more passion than wisdom'.[111] If Charles's capacity to govern and secure co-operation after 1629 suggests that at this stage he had not lost the hearts of his people, in some part that was due to his appeal and self-representation in words.

During the 1630s, Charles abandoned address to his people. At a time when unusual (if not illegal) levies – the revival of knighthood and forest fines or ship money, for example – might have drawn less criticism had they been justified by declarations, Charles issued commands. True, the preambles to ship money writs made brief reference to the state of European affairs that necessitated a strong navy, but the people were left largely in the dark; or rather were left to non-official accounts of government actions and intentions.[112] In the case of ship money, it was a legal challenge which forced the government into a fully argued defence and by then also forced it on to the defensive. Similarly, when he did issue a declaration, in 1633, concerning lawful sports, Charles I simply repeated his father's text with no attempt to argue the importance of its reissue fifteen years after the events which had first led to it being published.[113] In his only other declaration before the Scottish troubles, the king did explain his purposes. Announcing in 1633 his commissions for the repair of St Paul's Cathedral, Charles expressed not only his own but (he hoped) a national sense of scandal that, at a time 'in which God hath been pleased to guide the Church of England in the true ways of his worship', its most beautiful cathedral had been allowed to fall into ruin.[114] The king published his own generosity as an example to all and commended the commissions. Revealingly, he felt the need to assure subjects that all money contributed would go to advance the refurbishment of St Paul's and that 'all rumours or imaginations of diverting the said monies to any other purpose are but the fancies of men either grossly malevolent, or causelessly jealous and mistrustful'.[115] The admission that royal measures were being represented in the darkest hues is striking in the context of the king's silence during the 1630s. Did Charles (naïvely) believe that the fears stirred about his misuse of money were confined to contributions to St Paul's? If not, if, that is, the king intuited that the malevolent men who had wrecked his parliaments were quick to misrepresent him in the localities, why did he not the next year issue a large explanatory declaration before the writs for ship money which was soon suspected as being headed not for the navy but for the royal coffers? The extent of the co-operation with, and opposition to, Charles I's policies and measures during the 1630s remains controversial and disputed.[116] What is certain is that some of those measures did attract support and that opponents of the government played on uncertainties about royal intentions. The Earl of Clarendon famously wrote of Archbishop Laud that he drew opposition not least because he failed 'to make his designs and purposes appear as candid as they were'.[117] It may be that that judgement may stand as a verdict on Charles's government during the personal rule. For all that, after the troubles James I had experienced, Charles's decision to retreat from noisy debate was understandable, it may nevertheless have been a miscalculation, especially when his critics and opponents did not emulate his silence.

When Charles resumed direct address to his people in 1639, he was led to do so not only by crisis, but also on a massive scale. With his effort to appease, then contain, the Covenanters in shambles, and war inevitable, Charles knew that he would need the support of his people. As, therefore, he mobilized an army to march to Berwick in May 1639, he issued in February a proclamation and declaration to inform his loving subjects 'of the seditious practices of some in Scotland seeking to overthrow our regal power'.[118] With war imminent, Charles used words to demonize Scots (who had been represented for three decades as fellow Britons) as enemies to England, religion and government. And, all too aware that, with 'the multitude of their printed pamphlets, or rather indeed infamous libels', the Scots had beaten him to the starting post, he appreciated the need to counter the misrepresentations of him that were circulating so as to convince the English of the right of his cause.[119] The proclamation used contrasting nouns and adjectives to paint a white and black picture: of the king's 'gentleness' and the Covenanters' 'fury'; his 'sincerity' and their 'pretences'; the 'truth' of his position compared to 'their odious cause'. Cleverly, he depicted them both as ambitious for power, and, in a move bound to fire latent xenophobia, as greedy for English lands and goods. The king, the text explained, was arming to save English properties as well as royal prerogative, against those whose design, cloaked in the false language of religion, was to seize both. The proclamation and declaration revealed the king's desperation before the barrage of Scottish pamphlets that were aimed at 'seducing' the English 'to the like rebellious courses'. Recognizing the relationship of his loss of authority to his loss of control of the word, Charles singled out the Covenanters' dismissal of the royal printer. 'Whereas the print is the king's in all kingdoms, these seditious men have taken upon them to print what they please, though we forbid it, and to prohibit what they dislike though we command it.' To try to regain the initiative, Charles ordered that any subjects who received the 'mutinous libels' surrender them to a JP. More importantly, he announced that a fuller statement of his case was forthcoming which would reveal the Covenanters' falsehoods.

A Large Declaration Concerning the Late Tumults in Scotland was penned by Walter Balcanquall, Dean of Durham, but issued by the king's printer as 'By the King'.[120] Rather than a declaration, this massive work was a history of the troubles 'from their first originals' that was written to demonstrate the sedition and treason of the rebels from their own pronouncements. Using the first person plural pronoun, Balcanquall, almost certainly under Charles's direction and supervision, followed the tactic of contrasting representations in 'this our unquestionable narration'.[121] Where the king's proclamations and declarations were figured as 'gracious and clement', 'sincere and real', Scottish writings were examined to show a 'froward comportment' and vilified as 'an abortion of their own brain'.[122] In a new move, Balcanquall branded the Covenanters, who hinted at royal sympathies with papists, as 'Jesuitical' heirs of Cardinal

Bellarmine, against whom James I had written.[123] And he used narrative to disclose a Covenanter conspiracy forged as soon as Charles had ascended the throne, rather than out of hostility to the recent Prayer Book which they claimed as the beginning of their grievances. Charles was presented as his father's son in Scotland, as the heir of his piety, care for religion and policies, even in pursuing a new prayer book which James had authorized just before he died.[124] The declaration discredited Covenanter opposition to the book not only as pretence and hypocrisy, but as a slur on the 'glorious martyrs of the church' who had devised the English book on which it was based.[125]

In the immensely detailed narrative that unfolds from the outbreak of violence in Edinburgh in 1637, the text exploited several devices of polemical print to undermine the Covenanter case. Though Balcanquall included pages of Covenanter texts, petitions and protestations, they were glossed in marginal notes with sarcastic asides and direct denials that render this far from a neutral review of the debate.[126] The 'king' who 'desire[d] the reader to observe these two things' becomes the exegete of the rebels' true meaning and so finds in their own words the treasonous designs he claimed.[127] Charles expressed his unwillingness 'to dispute against this Covenant'.[128] But as he prints more of the Covenanters' writings, the king poses rhetorical questions which (though retaining a stance of impartiality) serve to denounce their premises and claims. Citing his own proclamation, with a favourable gloss, he 'appeals to the judgement of the world whether there was anything in this . . . which deserved such a . . . rebellious protestation'.[129] Despite frequent invitations to independent arbitration ('we shall leave it to the reader to judge'), the story unfolds as one of a king who followed his father's example and the advice of his Council, who made concessions and had the support of all good men, but was opposed by unholy blasphemers who responded to royal grace with bitter invective and violence and plotted to undermine the crown.[130]

To hold the readers' attention as well as to support a narrative of mounting extremism, Balcanquall paused as he closed an account of these violent courses to warn and titillate with anticipation – 'But these were nothing to their other violences.'[131] Continuing the strategy of condemning the Covenanters in their own (glossed and edited) words, the declaration printed the Scots libel against the bishops, despite a stated reluctance to offer it as ammunition to pagans or papists. 'Now', the reader is warned, almost in the manner of the modern television programme caution, 'the very reading of this libel cannot choose but work a detestation of it in the heart of every religious and just man'; and for those who did not so immediately respond Balcanquall adds: 'the reader shall do well to take a more special notice of these particular passages of injustice and impiety in it'.[132]

As the declaration turned to a detailed account of the assembly, Balcanquall used the narrative to reveal the lawfulness and grace of the king's proceedings and the illegality and extremism of the Covenanters. The rebels were accused of Machiavellian manoeuvres to rig the elections and fix the outcome, so that when they protested against dissolution, 'the reader shall not need to look after much reason in this protestation'.[133] The declaration answered the Covenanters' objectives by a mixture of flat assertion ('in their sixth reason there is no reason to be found'), the charge of illegality, and scorn.[134] The Covenanters' text is now not merely glossed but invaded by notes that intrude from the margin into the lines, almost as a typographical demonstration of the royal authority Charles was struggling to reassert.[135] Though the king retained the pose of dignified refusal to engage or answer, the Protestation was printed with 'falsities and impertinences . . . observed on the margent, being assured that the reader will easily find that there is nothing in it worthy of any larger answer'.[136] Notes declaring their claims 'most false' or inspired by 'the devil', as well as witty turns (their 'cloud of weighty reasons' becomes 'reasons . . . wrapped up in a cloud') subvert the Covenanters' words and render them 'absurdities'.[137]

Finally, as well as turning against his enemies the charge of being Jesuitical, Charles stirred fear of sectarian anarchy that lay only just below the surface of post-Reformation Europe. 'Those furious frenziers,' the declaration notes, 'have not been heard of in the world since the Anabaptists' madness reigned in Germany.'[138] In contrast, Charles, in supporting the bishops' lawful assembly and established Acts of parliament, stood as the custodian of traditional order on which the very life of the church and state depended. As the long declaration reached its close, then, Charles's military expedition was pacified, and described as a 'journey' – undertaken by a king who, like Christ, was slow to anger and quick to forgive, and who (unlike the rebels) sought, as he had, he claimed, since his succession, peace and accommodation.[139]

Balcanquall's *Declaration* is a remarkable document in its deployment of rhetorical tricks and typographical tactics, its language of black and white contrasts, the manipulation of emotion and fear, the pose of impartial moderation to veil vitriolic polemic, all serving to write, or rewrite, the king's authority in Scotland and England.[140] The *Large Declaration* also marked a number of important changes in the story of Charles's representation. Not only did it announce the king's return to self-representation in words, it did so on a massive scale: even James had never taken over 400 pages to make a case. Secondly, the *Declaration* marks the first occasion of Charles using another's hand to ghost what was unequivocally published as the king's words. Though doubtless several proclamations and prayers were drafted by others, this employment of another in a direct political exchange and struggle was new and looked forward to the (successful) use the king was to make of Edward Hyde and others to write for him in the 1640s.[141] Thirdly, the *Large Declaration* emerged from, and in the midst of, armed conflict. While discursive struggles were endemic to politics, Balcanquall's treatise was a weapon in a battle for authority in two kingdoms which were both divided, as well as at war with each other. In some ways, the *Large Declaration* signals the dawn of a new era in which bitter ideological division would revolutionize all acts of speaking and writing and the end of an age in which the word was still associated with authorities in church and state. In the *Large Declaration*, Charles claimed as natural an authority that he had to struggle to retain. Though the struggle was ostensibly with Scottish rebels, as he issued Balcanquall's *Declaration* the king had no doubt that it was translating to his English kingdom also.

Indeed, as the collapse of the Peace of Berwick and the resumption of hostilities necessitated the recall of parliament, after a hiatus of eleven years, Charles acutely appreciated the need to win the war of words before asking his Commons for assistance and supply. As well as his proclamation of March 1640 outlawing the reading or possession of pamphlets sent from Scotland, therefore, Charles published another declaration of his proceedings with the Scots since the Pacification.[142] Though, at over 60 pages, by no means short, the declaration eschewed the detailed narrative and full reproduction of documents of the *Large Declaration*.[143] Charles's text was targeted primarily at an English audience and confined itself to the breaches of the Pacification which, it argued, had led him back to war. This was the first royal declaration illustrated not with the royal arms but a portrait bust of the king in ermine – an image of Charles and regal authority that was to reappear frequently over the 1640s. The image faces a text which opens with another image, now in words: of a king who loved peace and who had been willing to make concessions to secure it. If it were then not secured, 'all those that are not partial may judge who they are that have been the disturbers and infractors of the peace'.[144] In a highly selective account, the declaration depicted the Covenanters as bent on subverting government from the outset, and as now undermining the agreed peace and the established constitution as a means of seizing power.[145] By contrast, the declaration claimed, throughout all Charles left no avenue to peace unexplored until, he is careful to point out, his Privy Council resolved that action was required against Scottish treasons.[146] For, the declaration revealed, evoking patriotism and horror, the Covenanters had not stopped short of entering into intelligence with foreign (Catholic) powers and so threatening all the British kingdoms.[147] So that 'the world shall see that we charge them not but upon very good and sure grounds', Charles copied (in French and English) the letter the Covenanters had addressed 'au roi', that is to Louis XIII, which, it was hoped, served to clinch the king's case and confirm claims that the Scots were guilty of treason.[148]

Charles had hoped by means of these careful justifications of his own position and systematic condemnation of the rebels to win over public opinion and to secure the co-operation of parliament. However, the parliament which he assembled in April to grant supply for a second campaign broke up within three weeks without subsidies, leaving Charles to press ahead with a campaign without funding.[149] As importantly, the precipitous failure of the first

CHARLES BY THE GRACE OF GOD
Kinge of England, Scotland France and
Ireland, defendor of the faith, etc.

25 Frontispiece to *His Majesties Declaration, Concerning His Proceedings with His Subjects of Scotland*, 1640.

parliament in more than a decade risked undercutting the king's pose as 'the father of our people' and his strategy of isolating the Covenanters as enemies to England as well as to monarchy.[150] Charles therefore acted swiftly to issue a declaration of the causes that moved him to dissolve the parliament, in the hope that his version of events might be disseminated before the accounts of the more disgruntled and radical MPs spread through their counties and boroughs.[151] Echoing his father's favourite metaphor, Charles announced that he published so 'that the clearness and candour of his royal heart may appear to all his subjects'.[152] Signalling his respect and affection for parliaments, 'those ancient and accustomed ways' and the traditional ways of government of his 'noble progenitors', he related how this parliament had not responded with the similarly traditional vote of supply in time of war.[153] Charles reported, and now published to his subjects, how he had invited the Commons to think of alternatives to ship money to finance the navy and how he had made other concessions, but that, under the leadership of the disaffected, 'they entertained themselves with discourses tending to render odious to his people that gracious government of his under which all his people have, during his happy reign, lived in such peace and felicity'.[154] Printing his speech dissolving the house, Charles appealed to the wider public on whom his military fortunes were to depend. The blame for the break-up of the parliament, he asserted, was not his: 'nothing was wanted that could be expected from a king'; it was a few MPs who had 'vitiated and abused the ancient and noble way of parliament'.[155] Charles appealed – was it as risky a strategy as hindsight might suggest? – to the record of his government, under which the nation had never enjoyed more blessings.[156] It was, he claimed, the Commons that had broken (the language is noteworthy) the bargain and contract with the king and which threatened ruin for the nation.[157] Though Charles had been forced to dissolve it, his care and 'tender affection' for his people was unabated and he invited any with grievances to petition him for redress.[158] This, the last of the declarations which concern us for now, clearly echoes those of the 1620s. Now, however, the stakes were higher and, beneath the rhetoric of patient conciliation, the criticism was sharper. Charles I was representing himself, not unskilfully, as the embodiment of constitutional and traditional courses. If such representations did not secure his authority over a nation, they were to lay the foundations on which a Royalist party was formed and fought and argued for the king.[159] As we review such declarations, we cannot but return to wondering whether, had he taken such pains throughout the 1630s, no such party would have been needed.

Contemporaries, even those not naturally disposed to praise him, often admired Charles's written style. Christopher Dow praised in 1637 the style of the king's prefatory declaration before the reissued Thirty-Nine Articles.[160] After the king's death, William Lily recalled how Charles 'would write his mind singularly well and in good language and style'.[161] Historians, who have paid almost no attention to Charles's early writings, have had little to say about this. When it comes to speech, however, the common verdict is clear: the king, afflicted by a stutter from childhood, was a poor speaker and one understandably reluctant to speak. Support for such a view appears to come from the best source of all: Charles himself. Charles told his first parliament that it did not 'stand with my nature to spend much time in words'; and he repeated the statement in 1640: 'I shall not trouble you long with words; it is not my fashion'.[162] Such disclaimers should not be taken at face value. A protestation of verbal incapacity was (and is) itself a common rhetorical trope: Elizabeth I, a brilliant orator, had often excused herself for her inadequacies.[163] Contemporary observations are ambiguous: while the Venetian envoy characterized Charles as 'usually a prince of few words', there were reports of his enjoying philosophical discussion at dinner and of him speaking succinctly and effectively in Council.[164] Lilly recalled after the king's death that, though sometimes he had trouble, sometimes 'he would speak freely and articulately'.[165] Sir Thomas Wentworth described a master who spoke with brevity but clearness.[166] Whatever Charles's inclinations and preferences, which appear to be towards silence and brevity, during the late 1620s and again in the 1640s Charles did speak to his parliaments. And though, unlike some of his father's, his speeches were not officially published at the time, they circulated in scribal copies and were later gathered and printed by supporters of the king in editions of his works.[167] Moreover, whatever the king's repeated protestations about his oratory, and his leaving to the Lord Keeper the task of addressing the house, Charles's speeches read as the carefully worded statements of a ruler who knew that such texts represented him not only to his MPs but to the nation.

Charles's opening speech to his first parliament immediately dispels any impression we might have that he was a poor speaker. In a style that recalls Elizabeth I, the new king told the assembly on 18 June: 'Thank God that the business to be treated of at this time is of such a nature that it needs no eloquence to set it forth.'[168] The 'business', the war with Spain, 'needeth', Charles added, 'no narrative', revealingly a synonym here for justification, because it had been commenced under James at the instigation of parliament – 'by your interest, your engagement'.[169] Charles was, in modern management jargon, leading the MPs to take ownership of their actions and advice and reminding them that his willing advocacy of their cause before his father carried the reciprocal obligation that they support him now. Cleverly he denied the need to make the point (while making it): 'knowing the constancy of your love both to me and this business, I need not have said this'.[170] For, he again pressed whilst claiming to take it as a given, the honour of his auditors was as much concerned as his own. Alluding only obliquely to the concerns some were airing about his religion, Charles invoked his father, making the kind of scriptural reference that was typical of James, assuring the MPs that he trained at Gamaliel's feet and would walk in his footsteps.[171] After these words, Charles announced his intention 'to bring up the fashion of my predecessors, to have my Lord Keeper speak for me in most things', 'because I am unfit for much speaking'.[172] It may be that Charles had stumbled over his words; but the easy flow of the sentences and personal tone do not suggest awkwardness. In a handful of sentences, the king had done what was needed: both given assurances of continuities and reminded them of the new circumstances which they faced, emulated his father's policies, yet announced a different personal style.

Charles did not get the war funding he needed and the parliament was dissolved after a second session at Oxford, away from the plague-infested capital.[173] Charles rapidly called another – and not solely out of necessity, but in order, he hoped, to continue the co-operation that he had forged with the Commons in 1624.[174] The king spoke to his second parliament on several occasions, clearly intending thereby to make a personal appeal for support. Responding to the Speaker's traditional request for liberty to air grievances, Charles granted the request and endeavoured to put the best gloss on it: 'I take that but for a parenthesis in your speech and not a condition'.[175] Yet from the outset in this parliament, not least because the attack on the Duke of Buckingham struck him personally, Charles's irritation came through. 'I would you would hasten for my supply', he threatened as much as advised, or else 'it will be worse for yourselves'.[176] As, however, instead of supplies, the Commons that met in February turned to grievances and prepared to impeach the king's minister, Charles was forced to summon them to hear him at the end of May in a bid to rescue the situation. The king then informed the Commons, diplomatically, that 'though at the beginning it hath had some rubs', he believed that the session could still end happily.[177] Parliament, he declared, was 'so great and worthy a body' of the realm.[178] But having soothed and flattered them, Charles, frustrated, again resorted to threats: he warned the members that 'parliaments are altogether in my power for their calling . . . therefore as I find the fruits of them good or evil, they are to continue or not to be'.[179] Though understandable in the circumstances, it was not the best course. In contrast to his early proclamations and declarations and his first speech of 1625, Charles came across as short-tempered and autocratic. As the parliament broke up without supply, Charles (as we saw) adopted a more emollient tone in an address to his people for a loan.[180] At least in some measure, despite all his reservations about the wisdom of summoning another parliament, it was a less confrontational stance that Charles decided upon as he convened his third assembly on 17 March 1628.[181]

As he met his third parliament, Charles spoke from a sense of the need to persuade rather than simply instruct. Referring familiarly to his tendency to few words, he urged that MPs might follow him as 'the times are now for action'.[182] Yet though he spoke briefly, the king appealed to a 'common danger', reminded them that he was at war having followed their advice, and reassured them that he was committed to the ancient way of parliament.[183] As for recent 'distractions', Charles expressed his willingness to forgive and forget them, provided – and here he cited Scripture – the house would maintain the unity of the spirit in the bond of peace.[184] A hint of frustration came through ('I scorn to threaten any but my equals'), but the speech promoted an idea of reciprocal duties in language that might have calmed fears in the country about extraordinary levies and actions. Even after nearly three weeks with little progress, Charles continued to gently push the parliament while not hectoring. 'My Lords and gentlemen', he told them on 4 April, 'I do very well approve the method of your proceedings in this parliament, a Jove principium.'[185] Along with this reminder of his own Godlike authority, Charles praised their actions, and applauded their position on religion, which he promised to take as a basis of his own course. But, as he skilfully moved to bring them back to circumstances, he insisted that prayers to God were not enough to preserve the faith: 'as we pray to God to help us, so we must help ourselves', not 'lie in bed and only pray without using other means'.[186] As, however, the Commons' proceedings were dominated by grievances and concerns about liberties, Charles's tone became sharper and his discourse briefer. Evoking again the image of reciprocity and exchange, he asked for his parliament to trust in his care for their liberties, as he did in their affection for his prerogative. Trust, as we know, proved insufficient and the Commons presented a Petition of Right to secure their liberties in a legal form. To get the supply he desperately needed, Charles not only accepted it; in giving his answer on 2 June, he told the house, in words which might have re-established trust, that he came to 'perform my duty' in accepting the petition.[187] Even now, when his answer – that he wished all might be done according to law and custom – did not satisfy and he was forced to reply in the terms used to enact a bill, Charles managed to restrain any anger he felt. Surprised that his first answer had not contented them, he nevertheless announced on 7 June that 'to avoid all ambiguous interpretations . . . I am willing to please you in words as well as in substance'.[188] Endeavouring to further please them with words, the king rehearsed a familiar axiom that expressed the bonds between subject and sovereign: 'My maxim is, the people's liberty strengthens the king's prerogative'.[189] Only – and this is neither the first nor the last time in Charles's speeches – a final warning tarnished the picture of harmony: if now the parliament did not end happily, Charles warned, 'the sin is yours, I am free of it'.[190]

By the end of the month, events had led to a prorogation of the parliament. Dismissing the MPs on the 26th, Charles reminded them he owed no explanation of his actions but explained that the false constructions made of his answer to the petition, and particularly the questioning of his right to tonnage and poundage, had led him to end it. In new, more authoritarian language, he 'commanded' that what he had spoken be received as 'the true intent and meaning of what I granted'.[191] In other words, even as he spoke, Charles intuited that the issue of his authority was bound up with his words and, as important, with the interpretation of his words – an interpretation that he had (like his predecessors) proved unable to control.

That the final session of Charles I's last parliament for a decade ended in violent scenes may tempt us to assume its failure was inevitable.[192] In fact, in elevating enemies of Buckingham, recalling Archbishop Abbot, and restoring judges who had opposed the loan, Charles took action to reassure MPs of his commitment to traditional courses in church and state; and the Venetian envoy reports Privy Councillors 'preparing for a good harmony'.[193] The king's opening speech on 24 January 1629 reads as part of the same strategy. Charles pointed to his care to remove all obstacles to a good correspondency with them and even conceded that he took tonnage and poundage to be a gift rather than a right.[194] Interestingly, his tone was one of charitable *interpretation*. Observing that he might have taken a recent order of the house as an offensive encroachment on his rights, he reiterated his reluctance ever to interpret them harshly. The message was again a none too subtle plea for reciprocity, for the king desperately desired what he claimed not to 'doubt': that 'according to mine example, you will be deaf to ill reports concerning me'.[195] 'Let us not be jealous of one another's actions,' Charles urged; instead they should proceed with 'confidence one towards the other'.[196] With no mention of supply, hardly a reference to the war or foreign policy, the king was trying through speech to reconstitute the mutual trust on which he saw all depended, and to secure a bill for tonnage and poundage that would put his taking of it back on a legal footing. Once again, however, the Commons swung from one bill to another, leaving the king's business unattended. Charles gently reminded them, as they petitioned for a fast, that fighting would do more to aid the reformed churches than fasting, while nevertheless agreeing to their request.[197] But in March, he dissolved the assembly after an extraordinary scene in which the Speaker was forcefully held in his chair while resolutions were read. It was the dashing of his hopes for a new beginning that had convinced the king to bring parliament to an end. And with them ended the speeches to parliament which the MPs were meant to communicate to the country. [198]

Was, then, the failure of his parliament also a failure of the king's oratory, a failure to argue his case, to reassure about his intentions, and to represent his needs and values in speech? That the speeches were not officially published in his lifetime (as James's were in 1616) may suggest that, unlike his direct addresses to the people in proclamations and declarations, Charles doubted the wisdom of publicizing what had resulted in failure. As I have suggested, some of the speeches, intended to foster co-operation and mutual understanding, were inflected with an authoritarian tone – though perhaps no more so than Elizabeth's or James I's. In 1629, Bishop Davenant and the Venetian envoy judged that Charles had spoken well and to the point: 'His Majesty', Contarini reported, 'spoke very mildly' and his 'honied words' won applause.[199] If, as the reports of other contemporaries confirm, he was right, it may have been a misjudgement of Charles's not to print his speeches to the house. Though his declaration of 1629 contained his speech at the dissolution, outlining his sadness at the outcome, other royal speeches remained unprinted, circulating in variant scribal copies rather than as official royal words.[200] A king who fully comprehended the importance of the representation and interpretation of his words might have been expected to take a different course – and a wiser one.

Parliaments were, in the incisive phrase of Sir Geoffrey Elton, a vital 'point of contact' in early modern England.[201] They conveyed not only royal commands, but the king's love, an image of his virtuous rule, to the whole realm, just as (ideally) MPs came to Westminster as ambassadors communicating the people's care of their sovereign. Frequent parliaments enabled dialogues between the ruler and the people; even when they quarrelled, the dialogue itself demonstrated as well as rehearsed the reciprocity and exchange between them. Whatever the difficulties he had faced with his parliaments, Charles's speeches endeavoured to sustain and reinforce that ideal, on which, for all his occasional threats, he knew his authority rested. In 1629, there was evidently sympathy for the king, a sense that he had been badly used by some – and Charles in 1629 (as earlier) had gone to lengths to stress it was only a few – who had not responded in kind to Charles's 'honied words'. It may be that Charles's words had begun to make an impact. But the king himself saw things differently. In 1629 he decided to follow his own counsel and give priority to actions over words. If, as he had experienced, his words were not trusted, or were interpreted differently than he had intended, then it was for the king not just to articulate but to demonstrate his good intentions. As parliament was dissolved, Attorney Heath, expressing the king's own mind, told the Earl of Carlisle: 'now is the time to put . . . noble resolutions into acts', to show the people the evidence of his Majesty's 'just government'.[202] The personal rule signalled in part a drift from explanation to action – a significant change in the royal strategy of representation as well as a change in a style of rule. Though the intention was better to demonstrate the king's virtues, in reality it left the interpretation of royal programmes and intentions to others, some of whom had an interest in unfavourable representations of them.

When, after eleven years, the Scottish crisis forced him to recall a parliament, Charles did little to make amends for the long decade of silence. Here, where there was an opportunity as well as a need to speak to many MPs, especially the many who had never before sat in the house, to explain the course of events in Scotland and the European situation, as well as to pre-empt criticisms by emollient words and promises, Charles's speech was, in the words of the news-writer Edward Rossingham, 'very short'.[203] It was Lord Keeper Finch who was given the task of addressing the parliament in a long speech that praised the king and flattered the Commons.[204] At its close, Charles – in what looks like a planned *coup de théâtre* – rose again to read aloud the letter the Covenanters had sent to Louis XIII, the proof of their treason. If, as seems almost certain, Charles was confident that this dramatic revelation spoke much more than any other words could to plead his cause, he was mistaken. Rossingham reported to Viscount Conway that the king's and Finch's speeches 'gave little hope of a continuing parliament'; the silence on several subjects concerned him as it had the auditors.[205] Silence, however, continued to characterize Charles's dealings with the Short Parliament. When he next spoke to the parliament, it was not to both houses, but to the Lords whom he asked to quicken the Commons to vote supply. In this speech of 24 April, the king gave to the peers assurances about religion, ship money and liberties of persons and goods that would have been better aired to those who (as Finch had acknowledged) were representatives of 'the whole nation'.[206] When the pressure from the Lords failed of its purpose and even provoked greater discontent, Charles still did not address the Commons but, on 2 May, sent a message read by Sir Henry Vane.[207] Three days later he finally spoke – only now to dissolve the parliament. Though he summoned the House of Commons to the Lords for the dissolution, Charles spoke as though they were not there and addressed his remarks to the Lords. Them he thanked for the measures they had taken, them he assured of his trustworthiness; of the lower house he spoke in the third person – 'They'.[208] In so addressing the Lords, the king signalled that dialogue with the Commons was all but over, just days after it had been reopened.

Indeed, the full logic of the king's preference to communicate with his peers but not his Commons was manifested in his decision, as the crisis deepened in the autumn, to assemble the Great Council of the aristocracy at York.[209] Addressing them by an inclusive pronoun, Charles explained that he had revived the ancient practice 'that . . . we might jointly proceed to . . . the securing of our good subjects'.[210] Though the king articulated 'that I desire nothing more than to be rightly understood of my people', it was clear that he was not being rightly understood by the representatives of the people.[211] Whether as a consequence of pressure or his own inclination, Charles accepted as the Council met that he must call another parliament; the site of the Council, the Dean of York's Hall, was 'put into the posture of a house of parliament'.[212] If there were any thought still in the king's mind that it might substitute for a parliament, the advice the Council gave, along with a helpful loan, kept him in no doubt that 'nothing [was] to be done without a parliament for uniting the affections of the people'.[213]

By November 1640, while Charles had been long silent, the 'affections of the people' had been influenced by a barrage of pamphlets and rumours, not least those circulated by the Scots and their supporters in England. Charles, as we saw, belatedly authorized a massive response to Covenanter propaganda and a detailed narrative of, and apology for, his actions.[214] Yet when he convened the parliament that he was never to dissolve, he offered the returning and new MPs little justification for his courses. Rather, he admonished them that had he been believed and trusted before, the threat from the Scots would not have developed as it now had.[215] The king, as before, handed over to the Lord Keeper to update the assembly. This time, however, there was a hint that he had a half-sense that he might better have spoken himself: 'if his account be not satisfactory as it ought to be, I shall, whenever you desire it, give you a full and perfect account of every particular'.[216] It was as though the giving of his own account was a special favour rather than a political necessity. Charles was, he told the MPs, 'so confident of your love . . . that I shall freely and willingly leave to you where to begin'.[217] As the house 'began' its deliberations, it all too rapidly became apparent that Charles had needed to do far more to make his case. By the time, in the new year, when he came to do so, he not only had to seek support for his campaign but had to defend the fundamentals of his prerogative, the church and constitution.

The story of Charles's speeches to the Long Parliament from the winter of 1640–1 is the story of how the king in a crisis learned a different vocabulary of self-representation, how he hired assistants to script his addresses, constructed himself as the champion of tradition – and so won a sizeable party in parliament and the nation to support him.[218] Ironically, the king proved at his oratorical best at a time of greatest division and conflict. His successes from 1641 offer unquestionable evidence that he did not lack the skill to represent himself in words. Rather, the earlier years suggest that, confirming his temperamental aversion to loquacity, the parliaments of the 1620s had revealed the risks (risks, he believed, his father's experience had also highlighted) of speaking: risks of being misinterpreted, mistrusted and misrepresented. From 1629, Charles had chosen to represent himself to his people not in words, and not only by actions, but through other, primarily visual, genres and media. Before we turn to them, we must at least glance at how others, as it were, spoke and wrote for the king: at how verse panegyrists and preachers, the authors of histories and treatises, represented Charles to a public ever more eager to know more of their monarch.

II

Most monarchs in early modern England were welcomed to their thrones by verse panegyrics which typically expressed the relief of the nation at peaceful succession. Though later events have tended to overshadow it, contemporary celebration of the accession of Charles I was noisy and heartfelt – and not without good reason. The succession of Charles (after the tragic, early death of Prince Henry) was the first of the new Stuart dynasty. Moreover, the new king was, whatever his frail infancy, healthy, robust, aged twenty-five, and – most importantly – married. Charles had also proved a popular prince with parliaments and the nation, not least for advocating war with Spain.[219] In 1625, the nation had much to celebrate in its new ruler and panegyrists were quick to their pens to present him to the people. As usual, accession verses emphasized continuity. David Primrose consoled Scottish subjects that, though great James had died, he had left a 'blest and Royall Plant' who was 'sprung of his sacred sire'.[220] The bestselling writer John Taylor, observing a son (a pun on sun) to arise to dry the people's tears, assured readers: 'a pious father leaves a godly son'.[221] James, Francis Hamilton reminded subjects, had through several works trained his second son for kingship, so that the nation could be sure that, having been 'in Christian Schooles uptrained', the new monarch had 'true virtue and Religion gained'.[222] King Charles, his verses proclaimed, was 'magnanimous, and mightie for defence/Of all true Christians'.[223] Though very much his father's heir ('*Elisha* like in good *Eliah's* place'), he represented a new militant defiance of papists and Jesuits in Europe.[224] Divining the new king's virtues by the common practice of making anagrams from his name, John Pyne found, via a Latin formulation of the king's name, a ruler who was heir to Queen Elizabeth as well as King James, a Sun, a protector, a sacred virtuous prince, a Caesar.[225] Describing Charles as the 'people's delight', Pyne also celebrated the nuptials of a prince whose marriage united the rose and the lily and who, he hoped, would father many heirs.[226]

Oxford University greeted the new king with a volume of verse, the first of several during the reign, which focused on the royal marriage. Taking the theme of sadness turned to joy and death to renewal, the scholars penned verses on spring and flowers, and on fertility.[227] The marriage was also represented as having more immediate political import. Where, Thomas Clayton observed, Henry VII had united the roses, and James the discordant British nations, Charles and Mary (the common English form of the queen's name) joined the rose and lily, that is England and France.[228] And their marriage, poems claimed, a union of Mars and Venus, strengthened religion as well as the state.[229]

After the welcoming panegyrics, poetic praise for the new king and queen was muted, perhaps by the plague, and the misfortunes of failed campaigns abroad and disputatious, broken parliaments at home. Moreover, Charles's marriage underwent severe strain during the early years, as the deeply unpopular Buckingham damaged Charles's relations with his bride as well as his subjects. From 1629, however, panegyrics were published regularly to mark occasions, especially the birth of more royal children than any ruler of England in living memory. Henrietta Maria was pregnant soon after Buckingham's death and gave birth in May 1629 to a baby, Charles, who died almost immediately. It may be that this tragedy resulted in a surprisingly restrained response to the birth of Prince Charles the next year. The prince's survival, followed by the birth of Princess Mary a year later, however, prompted another celebratory university volume, this time from Cambridge, that acted as a double congratulation. Playing on the echoes in the children's of the parents' names, Cambridge University poets praised the royal couple as phoenixes who reproduced themselves and so assured the safety and good of the commonweal.[230]

From the beginning of the personal rule, poetry, both old and new, served to represent the virtues of the king. Dedicating an edition of John Beaumont's poems to Charles, the poet's son heralded 'the virtuousest and most untouched of princes, the delight of Britain and the wonder of Europe' – praise that no doubt rang all the louder as readers were reminded of bloody civil conflicts, as they turned to Beaumont's *Bosworth Field* at the opening of the collection.[231] Presenting his continuation of Lucan's poem to the king in 1630, Thomas May also flattered 'Your Majesty's renowned worth and heroical virtues' that, he indicated, 'may make you securely delighted in the reading of great actions'.[232] May's move, from what has been interpreted as earlier criticism, to praise of the monarch may have signalled the larger shift in panegyric that followed the close of the 1620s.[233] As poets began, with the retreat from war, to praise what Thomas Carew called the 'calm securitie' of peace, so the dominant voice was increasingly that of paeans to the 'good prince' who secured it.[234]

In 1632–3, three events prompted heightened panegyrics on the king. Charles's recovery from a sickness which had threatened his life led several poets to voice the relief and gratitude of the nation at its deliverance. The birth of a second son, James, correspondingly promised to secure the Stuarts from such accidents of fortune.[235] And the apparently triumphal progress Charles made to his coronation in Scotland appeared to cement the unity not only of the two nations but also of the king and his people.[236] In its anthology of verses on Charles's recovery, Cambridge University thanked God for preserving a loved king who preserved a people who, under his beneficent rule, enjoyed peace and prosperity.[237] As he embarked on his journey to his coronation, Scottish universities and presses poured out welcoming paeans and panegyrics. As the universities of Edinburgh and Glasgow emulated the practice of Oxford and Cambridge with official volumes of verses written by the scholars in Latin, Greek and Hebrew, the printing press at Aberdeen published the Latin poem *Vivat rex*, on the triumph of Charles's peace by David Wedderburn, the poet and Latin grammarian.[238] Outside the universities and in the vernacular, a variety of Scottish poets published the virtues of their monarch to his subjects of both Scotland and England. William Lithgow, for example, welcomed his country's 'native son', husband and father as well as sovereign, descended of over one hundred kings.[239] As he foresaw the people's faces illuminated by 'thy chearefull face', Lithgow thanked God for 'this sacred work, and happy union/Twixt Prince and people', and prayed for Charles and his frequent return.[240] While Walter Forbes, hoping to see action in Europe, claimed to 'reape more joy' at Charles's coming than Penelope at Ulysses's return from Troy, the author of *Grampius Gratulatius* saw another 'great Apollo coming North': another Charlemagne, 'great CHARLES our native King'.[241] And as David Primrose sounded 'ten thousand welcomes' at 'the neare approach of some blest Deitie', Andrew Ramsay 'offered' to Charles, a prince beyond compare, a volume of sacred poems on the creation, fall and redemption, associating with God's divine plan and sacred history a king who, he hymned, embodied the justice and piety of God.[242] Writing in Latin and paraphrasing his panegyrical song for a wider audience in English, the Bishop of Argyll, Andrew Boyd, lauded Charles's protection of justice and religion and compared him with Anchises who (on Venus) sired Aeneas, the ancestor of the Romans and father of empire.[243] Finally, the poem *King Charles His Birthright*, published at Edinburgh in 1633, greeted 'A mortall God, a Prince divyne,/By lyne, law, lot, the Heavens propyne'.[244] Praising a monarch who defended the faith, secured peace and as 'father to the Commonweal' ruled by virtuous example, the poem hinted at great triumphs yet to come and warned any that might 'Presume to raile . . . Against the Godhead of their earth'.[245]

The outpouring of loyal sentiments and extravagant praise from Scotland stimulated vatic emulation and production in England. A Cambridge University volume of 1633 gathered sad laments at Charles's absence and songs of joy at the anticipation of his happy return, one in the style of a Horatian ode.[246] Standing for several others in the same genre, John Russell's poem on the royal progress and 'much desired return' of the king figured the monarch in his travels as a Sun 'quarter(ing) the Hemisphere'.[247] Forecasting a rush to see the king as he returned, Russell prayed that God conduct him back safely and that 'His sacred head all happiness attend'.[248]

God manifested his blessing the year of Charles's Scottish coronation with the gift of a third child, and a son, James, Duke of York (and future James II). Celebrating this 'wonder' and the happiness of the court and country at this royal birth, the Oxford University poets assured Charles: 'Thou no way couldst be in a better state'.[249] The royal children, the poets told the king, 'are your emblems', symbolic representations of him who led the scholars to 'exercise our loyalties' in verse representations of the royal virtues.[250] Not to be outdone, Cambridge University also published, to supplement its volume celebrating the Scottish coronation, a congratulatory collection on the birth of another prince.[251]

As we shall see with other forms of representation, the royal marriage and the royal births were indeed presented and represented as emblems of Charles I's rule. In an early modern society when the birth of any child was regarded as a sign of God's favour, the survival of all the children born after the death of the first Charles in 1629 appeared to manifest a divine blessing which called forth earthly thanks and praise. No sooner had Prince James been born than Henrietta Maria was pregnant again with Elizabeth, born in 1635, and then Anna the next year. Oxford University's volume *Coronae Carolinae quadratura* directly connected the birth of princesses with the peace which Charles had brought to England, and praised the royal Deucalion and his wife, the 'common parents' who not only sired offspring but 'gave the world its life'.[252] Rising to sacred tones, Thomas Crosfield saw 'gloria in excelsis' resounding as praise for Charles.[253] Again, not to be outdone, the next year Cambridge University praised the sacred royal couple in celebrating the birth of their fifth child.[254]

Though the occasions of these verses were joyous and their function the representation of virtuous majesty, beneath the surface of 1630s' panegyrics the political difficulties of the decade can be discerned. One verse, as we saw, admonished those who reproached kings; an Oxford volume of 1633 condemned busy enquirers into majesty; that of 1636 hits out at the resistance to taxes.[255] When after 1637, then, outright opposition was published in verse as well as prose, loyal poets – and popular balladeers – came forward to counter criticism and to represent Charles's case. *The Complaint of Time Against the Scots*, for example, not only rehearsed the traditional injunctions to obey sovereign authority, it reminded readers that their country '(God be thanked) is blest in the happy government of a most gracious king' – a king who was, the author claimed, like a god on earth.[256] As opposition mounted and crisis loomed for Charles, several poets announced it as their intent:

> Unto the world to say and sing
> The praises of our royall King.[257]

Several of the many, neglected loyal ballads of 1640 were inspired by a jingoistic English hatred of the Scots. Yet, continuing the themes of earlier poems, they presented Charles as 'so mild and gracious' and as fighting God's cause.[258] Whether it was praising the 'peace and happiness' he had brought, or his care for the church, or his justice and mercy, ballads and popular verse echoed with the refrain 'Now God preserve our Gracious King', or 'The Lord Preserve Our gracious King'.[259]

Amid the crisis, on 8 July 1640, there was born to a 'sovereign blessed' his sixth child of the decade and third son, Henry, Duke of Gloucester.[260] On this

26 *An Exact Description of the Manner how his Maiestie and his Nobles Went to the Parliament*, 1640.

final occasion of a royal birth, the university poets entered the now noisy arena of print with congratulatory volumes. In part, the gestures of praise were familiar: Cambridge represented Charles as an imperial Caesar, as 'divorum soboles', an offspring of the gods who defended true religion and ruled in peace; Oxford University panegyric became militant and partisan.[261] The new prince was now represented as a symbol not of all Britain's joy, but of the king's victory – over his own Scottish subjects and his English critics:

> When a new Sonne doth his blest stock adorn,
> Then to great Charles is a new Armie born.[262]

Verses contributed to *Horti Carolini rosa altera* figured the new prince as a conqueror and his birth as a symbol of the preciousness of royal majesty. Still representing Charles as godly ruler of England's Eden, and praising his virtues as constant amid the rage, the Oxford poets now prophetically offered their services as fighters as well as writers and directed 'unto such as doe oppose your throne' their 'every letter' as 'a killing one'.[263] As events transpired, Oxford's pikes were in the end no more effective than the poets' pens in securing victory for Charles against his enemies who also fought with battalions of pamphlets as well as weapons. Right through the 1630s, however, Charles did not want for the support of poets who regularly rehearsed in verse the virtues of the prince and the benefits of his rule.

Unlike his father, during his lifetime Charles I did not write lengthy treatises either on kingship in general or as advocacy of particular policies or actions. There were, however, many writers ready to go into print both in support of particular royal institutions and to advertise the blessings of Caroline government and virtues of the king. Even just before Charles ascended the throne, George Marcelline, in a treatise celebrating the match with France, presented Charles to readers as a 'masterpiece of nature', 'replete with all graces'.[264] Cataloguing his virtues, Marcelline drew attention to the learning, the moderation, the wisdom of 'this Solomon of Kings' in whose virtues and actions one might 'read whole lectures of ethics and morality'.[265] Though the son of his father and as such 'the pledge of our succeeding peace and the propagation of religion', Charles was, as his father had not been, 'a pattern of virtues' for his subjects who, he hoped, would be drawn to the life according to his portraiture'.[266]

Whatever the difficulties that beset the new king's early years, there were many even of the old Jacobean establishment who saw new hope in Charles's succession. His survival after the risky journey to Spain suggested divine favour, while the chastity and austerity of the new monarch were attractive qualities to those who had lived through years of Jacobean scandal and excess.[267] While loyally lamenting 'the inestimable loss of our late sovereign',

Daniel Featley rose to lyrical strains as he wrote of 'the orient beams and bright lustre of your Majesty's imperial crown and most happy reign over us'.[268] Under a king chosen by God, Featley felt sure that church and commonwealth would flourish. During the period of personal rule, several writers who went into print in support of royal actions echoed the language of public good that, as we have seen, Charles deployed in proclamations and declarations introducing new measures. So, the author of *Cambium Regis*, arguing for the exchange of bullion as a prerogative of the crown, supported Charles's resumption of his right as bringing 'good likelihood of advantage to the . . . commonwealth'.[269] Similarly, in his discourse on colonies, William Alexander, Earl of Stirling virtually echoed royal words in representing the king as having 'ever been disposed for the furthering of all good works more for the benefit of his subjects than for his own particular'.[270] And, later in the decade, in his description of the flagship of Charles's ship money fleet, *The Sovereign of the Seas*, Thomas Heywood took the occasion to present Charles not only as heir of Jason, heroic leader of the Argonauts, or of King Edgar, but as 'an inimitable president [*sic*] for all the kings and potentates of the Christian world or elsewhere'.[271]

While prose support for specific royal initiatives is far too large a subject for detailed documentation here, what we must note is the representation, especially during the 1630s, of Charles (and Henrietta Maria) as examples of virtue to the people. Such a commonplace conceit was clearly given new force by Charles's upright character and chaste marriage; but the presentation of the king as the embodiment of moral ideals suggests both dutiful echoes of royal self-presentation and a broad perception of the new king as a model of virtue. In an address to Charles in his book of emblems, for example, Francis Quarles found in the letters of the king's name and title evidence of his virtues which ranked him with Plato and Augustus as the best of rulers ever known.[272] The same year, 1635, George Wither, who had earlier offered loyal criticism of the government, dedicated his bestselling *Collection of Emblems* to 'the most illustrious King Charles and his Excellent Beloved'.[273] Depicting the king and the queen as the sum of the virtues all the emblems signified, Wither told them (and his many readers) 'Your *Lives* are *Patternes* and faire EMBLEMS' 'of all the Vertues OECONOMICAL,/Of Duties MORAL and POLITICALL'.[274] In Wither's text, as in Charles's own philosophy, personal morality had effects on the commonweal, so that the ruler's 'princely virtues' secured the '*Peace* and *Plenty*' that thrived and 'A Chast, a Pious and a Prosperous Age' in the present and future.[275] 'A King, that prudently Commands', an emblem in Book II runs, 'Becomes the glory of his land'; an example of prudence and morality, Charles stood as a glorious 'living emblem to this nation'.[276]

In the midst of the decade in which Charles appears happiest and most at ease, he met with an accident that supporters quickly took advantage of to represent the beneficence of the king. While he was out hunting at Newmarket, a hare startled the king's horse, which threw him. Though it did not prove serious, in a 'discourse' upon the accident Francesco Cevoli glossed the minor event as a providential protection of a glorious ruler.[277] In Charles's hunting, therefore, he saw a king who, though he loved peace, 'yet . . . hath a portion of David's spirit, and is not afraid of wars'.[278] As for the hare that hid under the belly of the king's horse, 'perhaps', he ventured, 'she signified the affability and natural courtesy of the king', as the hare's quick hearing betokened Charles's readiness to give his people audiences.[279] Praising a monarch who never rested in his care for his subjects, Cevoli proclaimed: 'he is so frequent in the exercise of his virtues that after ages will truly judge the bare history of his acts to be no other than a continued panegyric'.[280] For his own part, the king's 'innocency and the love of his people is a double guard which he most relies upon'; but God had saved him from an assassination attempt, Cevoli related, as well as the accident.[281] Subjects were therefore urged to pray for him: 'for the general growth of the Commonwealth, I conceive no prayer either more compendious or complete than trust . . . for the sole safety of the king', for whom 'the public votes of the people' wished a long life and reign.[282]

Though there are occasional hints that some did not value Charles's kingship as they should, few loyal works published in the first half of the 1630s supported Charles by directly countering critical or oppositionist voices. From about 1636–7, however, this noticeably changed, as mounting puritan opposition joined with legal resistance to ship money to strike at the foundations of Charles's government.[283] In *The New English Canaan*, for example, Thomas Morton, having announced his 'allegiance to do his Majesty service', launched an attack on the separatists of New England and their 'fanatical inventions'.[284] Though his treatise offered 'an abstract of New England', the mockery of the falsely zealous, the parody of their preaching and their subversion of authority clearly also applied to old England, as did Morton's fear that 'the vulgar people are so taken with [them] there is no persuading them that [they are] ridiculous'.[285]

Whatever the lack of opposition to the regime before, it was in the later part of the decade that it burst forth into print, directly challenged official and loyal panegyrics and so, in turn, transformed the representation of Charles I and his government by loyal authors. Though a French account of the visit of the Queen Mother, Marie de Medici, in 1639, still spoke of a just king whose glorious example bound all subjects in obedience to him, the reality was palpably different.[286] Indeed, the same year, as well as representing the virtues of his sovereign, Henry Peacham felt the need to argue again the duty of obedience. Significantly now feeling the need to reiterate the divinity of sovereign power ('kings and princes have the gift of the spirit, and . . . their subjects have it not'), Peacham reminded readers of the best kingdoms in which the people were devoted to their ruler, as the Israelites to David.[287] Coming closer to the recent English past, he asked rhetorically: 'what greater love and affection

could be shown or exacted from subjects than that Queen Elizabeth...
received from the hearty votes of her people?'[288] Against any who suggested
otherwise, he affirmed: 'Blessed be God, we now live under a most gracious,
mild and merciful prince as ever reigned in England'; and he prayed to God
for 'constancy in our loves and loyalty to our most dread sovereign, King
Charles'.[289]

From the later 1630s, those writing to publicize the virtues of King Charles
felt the need to oppose counter-representations, and adopted popular styles
and different genres (of mockery and satire, for instance) as modes of loyal
support suited to a new world where every praise of the royal virtues was being
contested.[290] In discursive terms, a revolution occurred before the civil war
and made it possible.[291] That is to say, in the face of a mounting tide of puritan
and Scottish Presbyterian pamphlet attacks on royal policy, the king's
supporters, and ultimately Charles I, discerned the need not only to respond
but to adopt different genres and forms to counter opposition and to represent
authority. Interestingly, as supporters of Charles joined in pamphlet battles
with the Covenanters and their allies, one loyal author, perhaps in an attempt
to save majesty from the pamphlet fray, turned to allegory to remind the
English of their good fortune in a virtuous king. James Howell's *Dendrologia:
Dodona's Grove*, under the transparent veil of allegory, told of a lucky land
of England (Druina) 'in a rare conjunction of Peace, Security, Honour and
Plenty under the brambles of the stately Caledonian Oak' (i.e. Charles I).[292]
Tracing the history of England, and the reign of a king free of vice, 'wonderful
active', of 'excelling judgement', pious and 'most virtuous', Howell called
upon the people to disown the poplars (said aloud, of course, the pun with
populace is obvious) with their 'fantastic forms of ruling' and give allegiance
to their king.[293] Allegory was a recognized mode of disclosing truths hidden
beneath surface meanings. But, as we reflect on its use by defeated Royalists in
exile in the 1640s and 1650s, and the shift it signalled from the representation
of Charles as the emblem of virtue, we cannot but sense that Howell was
uncertain of the outcome, and even fearful that the goats might overrun the
forest.[294]

One form of (what in this context we might consider as) allegorical writing
had long served to represent early modern monarchs in the guise of writing
about something else. Histories could, and did, encode criticism of, but often
performed as celebrations of, kings by comparing them to previous reigns and
rulers. During the later 1620s, Charles himself seemed readier to read into
them criticism than compliment: he identified himself as Tiberius in 1626; and
there can be little doubt that the histories of Sejanus and Edward II published
in 1628 were meant as attacks on Buckingham and the king.[295] After 1630,
however, Charles favoured and patronized historical writing, and historians
appeared in part to represent the king as one of the great historical figures.
In some cases histories did no more than represent Charles as legitimate heir

to a long succession of kings – though one should not underestimate the importance of that. For example, John Taylor's popular *Memorial of All the English Monarchs from Brute to King Charles*, having catalogued 146 kings, 'some bad, some good', closed with praise of 'our gracious Charles' and prayers for his long reign, beneath a small woodcut of his portrait in royal robes.[296] Francis Godwin, Bishop of Hereford, dedicated the 1630 English translation of his *Annals of England* to Charles, who 'inherit as well your father's virtues as his kingdoms'.[297] The next year, in the preface to his magisterial survey *Ancient Funeral Monuments within the United Monarchy of Great Britain*, John Weever, who understandably applauded Charles's efforts to advance the repair of St Paul's, also dedicated his labours to 'the most magnificent, illustrious and puissant monarch Charles . . . the most powerful protector of the faith, the most powerful patron, preserver and fosterer of the undoubted religion of Jesus Christ, the pattern of true piety and justice and the president of all princely virtues'.[298] In what reads like a monument inscription ('books', he observed, 'are all monuments'), Weever enshrined the new king in history and memory and, he hoped, secured his reputation for posterity.[299]

Other histories made explicit comparisons between Charles I and his regal predecessors, to the manifest flattery of the former. Writing from within establishment circles, and as a confidant of Bishop William Laud, Peter Heylyn published a history of the emperor Augustus which was very much intended to speak to the author's own times and in his sovereign's praise.[300] Narrating how Augustus led Rome back from the republic to the natural condition of monarchy, his praise of an emperor who beautified churches and took care to preserve religion gestured to Charles, as much as his outlining of the obligations of subjects to support their rulers in wars alluded to recent circumstances.[301] In the early 1630s, Thomas May embarked on the histories of two medieval kings, evidently at the command of the king. His history of *The Reign of King Henry the Second*, as well as being dedicated to Charles, posited that the reign of that medieval king of great renown was but a prologue to Charles's rule; while his later *Victorious Reign of King Edward the Third*, comparing 'greatest Edward's reign' with that of the 'most high and mighty Charles' told the monarch in the dedication: 'I had the actions of a great king to require my skill, and the commands of a greater king to oblige my care.'[302]

If those favourable comparisons with two of the greatest medieval kings, the pacific lawmaker Henry and the warrior Edward, owed something to official patronage, and possibly ambition for favour, there is no reason to suspect such prompts or motives in Robert Powell's *Life of Alfred . . . with a Parallel of our Sovereign Lord King Charles*, published in 1634.[303] His legal training, Powell informed his readers, had taught him that monarchs were God's vicegerents and therefore he considered it 'most expedient that the lives of good and gracious princes, being gods on earth, should be set forth unto their people as specula, a super eminent watch-tower whom their subjects might behold afar off and learn to obey their supreme power; and as a speculum, a mirror wherein they might gaze on and strive to imitate their sovereign in virtue and goodness'.[304] Alfred was one early example. Chaste, pious, learned and charitable, Alfred carefully protected and increased the law and maintained and nurtured the church; he was 'a precedent for all princes'.[305] Turning, in the second part, from a dead to a living prince, Powell represented Charles I as raised, phoenix-like, out of the ashes of Alfred. Like Alfred, Charles, 'the Constantine and Carolus Magnus of our Age', maintained the faith, ceremonies and fabric of the church, piously attended to his own devotions, and was just, merciful and charitable to his people, whom he protected from all oppression.[306] If the two kings were in their piety, government, justice and mercy equals, Powell yet reminded readers that there was more to expect of Charles, who had reigned a mere nine years![307] Commending England's second Alfred as a ruler of 'exemplary goodness and virtue', and his 'numerous issue', Powell urged the people to be 'gracious subjects' of a king who stood as a precedent 'of imitation to all princes and people'.[308]

No other such exact historical parallels advertised Charles's virtues before the outbreak of civil war. But histories became embroiled in the troubles which began to overtake Charles. In 1640 we encounter that clear politicization of historical writing that we have seen transform other genres in what was becoming a deeply divided public sphere. In 1640, for example, an edition of William Habington's *The Historie of Edward the Fourth* was published with a dedication to the king that was also a clear message to the people.[309] Introducing the life of a king who lost his throne in a coup, then regained it in battle, Habington, an intimate in the queen's household, wrote by way of dedication to Charles: 'His life presents your eye with rugged times, yet smooth'd by a prevailing fortune and a just cause. Faction begot many tempests; but sovereignty found a happy calm in the destruction (since no gentler way had authority) of mighty opposers'.[310] Turning explicitly from the past to the present, Habington praised the peace the nation had enjoyed 'by the excellent wisdom of your Majesty's government'.[311] Then he concluded with a preview of the message that he wished readers to take away: 'The Almighty grant all your people knowledge of their own felicity and their minds so disposed that their blessings may feel no interruption. May your Majesty long continue in peace, the comfort and honour of these times, and the best example for the future'.[312] Finally, he wished and warned that 'if you shall be forced to draw your sword may your enemies submit and taste part of your mercy; if not perish in your victories'.[313]

Histories and precedents had always been open to more than one reading and had been appropriated to support more than one cause. But, for much of the early modern age, histories had been published to underpin the continuity of the nation and the monarchy and to emphasize unity. By 1640, loyal histories, while still holding on to a rhetoric of commonweal, were representing

Charles as a king of nations divided by conflict – initially between each other, but, it was also now being reluctantly acknowledged, within themselves.

From the late sixteenth century, as the Church of England became established, one of the most valuable media for the representation and exaltation of the monarch and Supreme Head was the sermon. Whether official sermons delivered at court that manifested the sovereign's piety, or sermons in the provinces stressing obedience to a victorious and sacred prince, sermons publicized the ruler to the widest public and the farthest corners of the land. The alliance between church and crown, though forged in the Reformation, was not always unproblematic: as well as different factions within the church, the tendency of some rulers to take advantage of the wealth of the episcopacy had strained relations. From the middle years of James I's reign, however, scholars have noted the rise of a high church party committed to the elevation of royal authority and clerical status and to a new representation of puritans as threats to both. In his last years James, frustrated by puritan opposition, leaned towards the high church party; but it was with Charles's succession that they came to prominence.[314] Finding in Charles I a king committed to the maintenance and increase of the clerical estate, in sermons and treatises they extolled regal authority and prerogative as divinely instituted and supported.[315]

Two very early examples of such sermons can be taken from those usually seen as the leaders of the high church party which Charles advanced. Preaching at Whitehall before the king on 19 June 1625, at the opening of the first parliament, Bishop William Laud glossed Psalm 75: 2-3 to point up the connections between David and Christ, God and the king. 'The power that resides in the king,' he told the assembled, 'is not any assuming to himself, nor any gift from the people, but God's power.'[316] Introducing the new king as another Hezekiah, 'a wise and religious king', Laud described Charles as the Sun, as a god ('no less').[317] As he thus reminded the king of the interdependence of church and monarchy, Laud simultaneously instructed the people on the need to honour and obey the king. The second sermon published by command was preached before the king by Matthew Wren, now Clerk of the Closet, and Master of Peterhouse, who had been chaplain to Charles as prince. Preaching on Proverbs 24, verse 21 (Fear God, My Son, and the King), Wren did not only associate God and the king, he emphasized the fear that good Christians felt towards both.[318] 'God is not feared if the king be not,' he asserted; 'No King's fear, no God's fear; God himself of purpose hath here joined them together', both needing to be approached with awe and reverence.[319] Wren, looking over his shoulder at his enemies, admitted that some would spurn his message as court flattery, just as they questioned the divinity of the king. To them his retort was sharp and clear: contempt of majesty was profanation and 'every step of disloyalty is a high degree to atheism'.[320]

Allegiance and faith were, Wren preached, proofs of each other, and the duty of preachers was to be spokesmen for sacred kingship.[321]

Wren's sermon was printed in 1627–8, the year that Charles was raising a forced loan to finance his wars after the failure of his second parliament. Though to any who were familiar with Machiavelli (as well as Scripture), Wren's emphasis on the fear subjects should feel towards a king struck a sinister note, his sermon avoided specific advocacy of royal policy.[322] Laud, however, had encouraged the clergy to support the loan from the pulpit and two preachers, Robert Sibthorpe and Roger Mainwaring, infamously followed his injunctions to extremes, supporting a royal prerogative to raise taxes and obliging subjects to obey any royal command, Mainwaring even denying the subject any recourse to justice in a case in which the king was concerned.[323] These sermons resulted in parliamentary censure in 1628; and Charles himself, though he pardoned the preachers, suppressed the sermons as 'trenching upon the laws'.[324] Extreme as their views were, however, Mainwaring's *Religion and Allegiance* emerged from a climate in which a clerical faction was extolling Charles's authority at a time when war was necessitating extraordinary, some thought illegal, courses – was, that is, re-presenting from the pulpit the king as beyond question or reproach.

Indeed, though he called in Mainwaring's book, Charles commanded the publication of a sermon preached before him by Isaac Bargrave, a royal chaplain and Dean of Canterbury. Bargrave, in his exposition of 1 Samuel 15, not only rehearsed the duty of obedience to kings as appointed by God and lauded Charles as a devout prince whose piety stood as an example to all; he branded rebellion, and by extension any opposition to obedience, even the 'wilfulness' he saw around him, as witchcraft and idolatry.[325] Though injunctions to obedience were commonplaces regularly uttered from the early modern pulpit, Bargrave appeared to threaten even loyal critics of royal actions with the wrath of God.[326] Moreover, in an explicitly partisan move, he condemned 'a generation who think themselves bound by their holy profession to quit subjects from their obedience'.[327] This tendency of a high church party, by extolling the prerogative and presenting other clergy as threats to regality, to forge an alliance with, and act as spokesmen for, the new king is graphically demonstrated in a sermon, the full context of which has only recently been explicated. Stephen Denison's sermon, preached at Paul's Cross in February 1627, did not emerge from court circles. But Denison's blistering attack on the wolves who menaced the church and state was, when published, dedicated to the king, whom he described as defender of the true faith 'in which respect you are highly honoured and sincerely beloved of all your true hearted and truly religious subjects', who 'esteem you the breath of their nostrils'.[328] Denison, though it may have suited him to appear so at times, was no pillar of orthodoxy, let alone a member of the high church party. But, as he appreciated, already by 1628 an alliance had been forged whereby, in recognition of and return for

Charles's patronage and favour, a group of clergy with their own partisan agenda undertook to be apologists for all royal authority and actions. In the pulpit, that is, the representation and publicization of the monarch was – dangerously, as it was to prove – in the control of a party.

During the decade of personal rule, whatever the clandestine meetings of puritans or the grumblings of subjects at government measures, the pulpits of the Church of England loyally proclaimed the divinity of kings and the godly virtues of Charles Stuart. At the assizes at Reading in 1629, for example, Theophilus Taylor, before an audience of judges, jurors and freemen, preaching that 'the ruler is the minister of God for our good', laid stress on the necessity of obedience and branded as Anabaptists any who railed against authority.[329] In two sermons preached before Charles, the now famous Dr John Donne compared the worship of, and obeisance to, the king and God.[330] At Whitehall, Thomas Turner, a royal chaplain, commanded authority and scorned the factious teachers of the private conventicles who spoke ill of governors.[331] In Scotland, in a thanksgiving sermon for the birth of Prince Charles, William Struther preached that princes were God's lieutenants and, refuting others of Anabaptistical error, affirmed that 'preeminency in princes and subjection in people stand well with grace'.[332] Though he also outlined the duties of kings, Struther assured his readers that, in Charles no less than in David, the people could see the portrait of a perfect king: 'God has set over us a king who loves the faith, professeth it with us, and in the exercise of it is exemplar to subjects', who owed him love as well as obedience.[333]

As opposition mounted, especially from 1636–7, against both the high church policies they defended and the authority that supported them, the clerical establishment ever more vociferously spoke up for church and king and presented the monarchy and Charles himself in the most favourable terms. In 1636, for example, Thomas Laurence, who had earlier criticized predestinarian teachings and denounced schismatics, in what became an infamous sermon that earned him the mastership of Balliol, linked the disrespect shown to the church and to the regal chair of state.[334] The next year, the royal chaplain Thomas Hurste, preaching at Lincoln assizes on 'the magistrates patent from heaven', launched a direct attack on the critics of church and crown, accusing rebels (it was to become a familiar charge) of concealing rebellion under the pretence of religion.[335] Those in authority, Hurste instructed, 'have a more special resemblance of the deity', and the king, he continued using a metaphor that connected regal with divine prerogative, 'hath the very current stamp of God's power'.[336] Hurste admonished those inclined to find fault with God's appointed magistrates that they should 'only act in their own spheres and circuits' and cautioned all people not to heed them but to honour and pray for their public father, the king.[337] Importantly, as he did just that, Hurste outlined what he saw as (and what had been) the role of the clergy: 'Even our poor tribe helpeth to carry the canopy over authority, else what need our declarations sometimes at St Paul's cross, or other solemn places, to justify the proceedings of state in matters of conscience?'[338]

Even as Hurste made his claim, the authority of the king in church and state was facing the onslaught, first from Scotland but rapidly too from England, that was to bring about its destruction. What then should we make of the role of clergy as advocates of Charles I? Were they invaluable props to sacred majesty, or did they draw down upon the crown and king the hostility of the godly to the enforcement of orthodoxy in the church? Any attempt to answer such questions plunges us into the historical controversy over the nature of the early modern church and the character of puritanism.[339] But in this study of the representation and image of royal authority, we might observe that in his later years James had come to associate the godly with opposition to his government. It was not least because he was convinced of the connection between opposition in church and in state and obsessed with the interdepend-ence of church and crown that Charles promoted to high clerical office the men he did. Later, at a point of crisis, he championed a broader church and raised to positions some who did not share his preferences in ceremonial conformity and other matters; and it has been suggested that, had he done so earlier, he might have defused opposition. In response, we might note that the strategy had hardly worked for James; and that, in patronizing those clergy who extolled rather than carped at his authority, Charles made an understand-able decision. As to the effect of the clergy's support, at Paul's Cross and in pulpits throughout the country, the verdict must remain open. True, when the Scots rose in rebellion, they found willing supporters in England. Yet for much of the 1630s, and again from 1641, the church enjoyed widespread support, as did the king.[340] Though from 1625 Charles took the risk of being supported by a clerical party, it is not clear, given the divided state of the church, that there was any choice.

Certainly, when the trouble multiplied in the last months of personal rule, the loyal clergy did not shrink from the challenge or cool in their zeal to support the king. Preaching before the king at Durham Cathedral in May 1639, Bishop Thomas Morton turned the familiar passages from Romans 13 to a polemical comment on the times. A seditious faction, he told his congrega-tion, assaulted sacred authority and the Scots were, like the papists, falsely claiming religious justification for rebellion.[341] God, however, and Calvin too required subjection – even to the most tyrannical governors; all the more so to Charles, the 'most religious of kings'.[342] Praising the monarch for his wisdom, charity, justice, temperance and fidelity, Morton presented Charles as 'the mirror of moral virtuousness, the lamp of religiousness, and miracle of clemency and patience'.[343] Praying for remorse in the rebels or, if not, victory over them, Morton placed the church firmly behind the monarch as he prepared for battle. In London, Dr Henry Valentine chose the occasion of the king's inauguration anniversary, the day he left for his northern expedition

against the Covenanters, to deliver his sermon at St Paul's.[344] Taking as his text
1 Samuel 10: 24 ('and people shouted God save the King'), Valentine sought to
strengthen English popular support by denigrating the Scots and illuminating
the virtues of Charles. In the loftiest language, he reminded his auditors and
readers: 'a king is imago dei, the bright image of God and the most magnificent . . . representation of Divine Majesty'; 'the king is our visible God'.[345] The
king, too, he continued, was as well as the soul, the sun of the commonweal
who 'animates the whole collective body of the people and every particular
man of it'.[346] Having reaffirmed the vision of the godly commonwealth with the
king as natural, divine, 'nursing father', Valentine conjured the opposite: the
evil doctrine of Buchanan, of popular sovereignty and the desecration of
majesty that breached 'all common tranquillity'.[347] Against such evils, the
Church of England stood as the defender of sacred authority: 'our church uses
this suffrage in her liturgy: O Lord save the king'.[348] And God, Valentine
preached, had blessed them with 'such a [king] as the like is not among the
kings of the earth'.[349] Recalling the happy inauguration of Charles I, Valentine
emphasized his legitimate and noble descent, his piety and his clemency, even
in the face of outrageous provocation.[350] 'Such a king as this', he challenged:
'show me a better among the people'.[351] And, re-presenting him in the words of
Scripture, Valentine led closing prayers for Charles's victory and prosperity.[352]

For all the church's prayers, the Lord did not give Charles victory, and the
king's inauguration day the next year fell on the eve of the first parliament to
be called for eleven years and amid a crisis that had spread from Scotland to
England. Bishop Henry King's sermon preached at St Paul's on 27 March was
addressed to parliament and people as the king himself was about to ask for
assistance. As opposition pamphlets circulated attacks on the monarch freely,
King's text was chosen as a retort: 'Behold I have this day set thee over the
nations'.[353] Because God had appointed and established the king, the bishop
delivered a caution the force of which can hardly be overstated: 'they that lift
up their heads against him in public rebellion, or their tongues in murmur
against his commands, or their hearts in disobedience and discontented
thoughts are as ill subjects to God as to the King'.[354] Descending from the celestial to the earthly plain, King rehearsed the full list of analogues which had
underpinned monarchy: the king was the shepherd, 'the king is the head', 'the
king is the state's pilot' and, with a slightly different take on the corporeal
metaphor, 'so necessary is a king even as air to our breath'.[355] The reiterations
were necessary now in circumstances in which Covenanter literature directly
questioned monarchy. King branded the Presbyterians as a threat as great
as the hated papists – a threat not only to the monarch but to every head of a
household who was a little king in his own domain.[356] And, countering their
propaganda, he endeavoured to reassure all of Charles's good faith – in
every sense of that word. Charles had protected and re-edified the church; a
good father of prudence, judgement, patience, humility and integrity, he was

'so religious and just a king' for whose preservation the bishop prayed.[357] One senses that it was a plea to the people as well as to God. Henry King knew that the tide of opposition was rising not only against the monarch but against the church establishment which had supported him. From the pulpits of Caroline England, bishops like King had regularly publicized Charles I as godly prince, and cemented the alliance that James I had rendered in an axiom: 'no bishop, no king'. But in ways the first Stuart had never intended, the support of a party in the church had led those who attacked episcopal authority to assault royal authority also, and ultimately to question whether the monarch really was the image of God.

CHAPTER 6

DEPICTING VIRTUE AND MAJESTY

I

Though we may need to qualify the view that Charles I took little trouble over his representation in words, it remains the case that, by the standards of his father, he was a reluctant speaker and writer. Quite unlike James I, the image of Charles has passed into history as a visual representation – of a king powerfully present on the canvases of Anthony van Dyck. Since Henry VIII's patronage of Hans Holbein and importation of a new style of portraiture, no early modern English ruler had shown as much interest in continental artists and styles.[1] Through much of the sixteenth century, England remained outside the artistic revolution taking place on the continent, the later years of Elizabeth seeing, if anything, a regression to older native traditions and styles, as well as a shift from realistic to iconic representation of the queen in portraiture. James, as we have seen, appeared little interested in patronizing artists, especially in the first half of his reign. Thanks, however, to his Danish queen, and then to his son Prince Henry, the reign of James I sowed the seeds of a spectacular aesthetic revolution that was to bring England into the mainstream of the baroque age and also to effect long-lasting changes in the relationship between art and power and in the representation of the monarchy. Anna of Denmark and Prince Henry not only fostered the work of artists like Marcus de Gheeraerts, they gathered within their entourage noblemen and women who emulated their cultural patronage, a group that was slowly to transform English artistic taste.[2]

There is little evidence of the passion for art which characterized his adulthood in the young Charles, who rather emulated his brother's interests in exercises and inventions. His 'sudden interest', as Jerry Brotton described it, appears to have been triggered by his inheritance in 1619 of Anna of Denmark's collection, which included the paintings from Henry's galleries.[3] The conjuncture of dynastic succession and artistic bequest may be more significant than has been noted. For Charles, the arts (and especially portraiture) and family were inseparable and his aesthetic interests were always allied to his dynastic ambitions and beliefs. However, even after his inheritance of Anna's collection, Charles, a recent study argues, was very much a minor figure in what had emerged as the first group of English connoisseurs – a 'naïve but enthusiastic collector', in Brotton's words.[4] What formed (and transformed) Charles's taste, in the arts as in other spheres of life, was his journey to Spain with the Duke of Buckingham to complete a marriage with the Infanta Maria, daughter of Philip IV of Spain. The first English monarch to set foot on the continent since Henry VIII's expedition to the Field of the Cloth of Gold, Charles was dazzled by what he saw in the Spanish capital. Madrid was a 'thriving public art market' and within days of arriving, Buckingham was buying pictures.[5] Seeing the grand tapestries in the Spanish royal residences, Charles immediately ordered the purchase of the Raphael cartoons of the Acts of the Apostles to provide a design for tapestries in England and became a patron of the Mortlake tapestry works established by James I. More importantly, what he saw in the Escorial was significantly to reorient his collecting from predominantly unfashionable northern artists to the schools of Italy – and especially to instil a passion for Titian. As well as receiving gifts of Titians granted by the king of Spain in the hope of advancing Charles's conversion to Catholicism, the prince attempted many, and secured several, purchases through dealers – with, as well as Titians, works by Rubens, Velázquez and Leonardo prominent on his shopping list.[6] Though we cannot list all he acquired, Charles, for all the failure of his diplomatic mission, 'returned with a clutch of superb paintings that formed the cornerstone of his . . . collection'.[7] The appetite whetted and tastes formed by his journey to Spain led Charles, soon after he became king, to make his (successfully) audacious bid to acquire the Gonzaga art collection from Mantua; and it drove him to attract to England artists who might represent and immortalize his dynasty and authority, as he knew they had immortalized the Habsburgs. Though the collections of leading noblemen, like Arundel and Pembroke, were, even more than the royal collection, embracing continental artists, the arrival of first Rubens in 1629, then Van Dyck in 1632, was to bring to England a radically new European style, and a new style not only of portraiture but of politics. For Rubens came to England as an envoy to negotiate an Anglo-Spanish peace and arrived only weeks after Charles, having dissolved a stormy parliament, embarked on what was to be eleven years of rule without one: a period in which the king also shifted his focus from collecting to the commissioning of portraits, especially of himself and the growing royal family.[8]

Where, in the first half of the sixteenth century in England, authority and social status had become associated with the new humanist learning, with the patronage of scholars and the building of libraries, in the first half of the seventeenth century, collecting and connoisseurship became all but necessary attributes of the true nobleman and especially the courtier.[9] Courtesy literature of the reign of James I plots a change from hesitant apology for, to celebration of, aristocratic involvement with the visual arts; and, as John Peacock, Edward Chaney and Pauline Croft have shown, Jacobean noble families collected and arranged portraits to manifest and enhance their standing and proximity to the centres of power.[10] The full impact of these developments, however, required a sympathetic figure on the throne. While those around Queen Anne and Prince Henry had forged aesthetic as well as political affinities, under Charles I collecting, exchanging and commissioning portraits were clearly – and were clearly perceived to be – aspects of influence. In the 1634 edition of *The Gentleman's Exercise*, Henry Peacham noted, following the royal example, the trend towards noble patronage of foreign portraitists and proceeded to instruct amateur artists on the pictorial representation of traditional aristocratic virtues.[11] At court, during the 1620s, the astute Buckingham quickly grasped the need to acquire a good art collection, to rival that of his enemy Thomas Howard, Earl of Arundel; and both, along with the Earl of Pembroke, Marquis of Hamilton and others, saw the benefits and advantages they might derive from gifts of paintings to, or generous exchanges with, the king.[12] Even simply as objects, works of art became political currency in Caroline England. But as appreciation and knowledge of painting developed, the relationship of visual to political culture surpassed the mere politics of gift and exchange. Books such as Peacham's and other courtesy literature responded to, and fuelled, desire for knowledge with increasing discussion of art and aesthetics; works like *The Gentleman's Exercise* or *The Mysteries of Nature and Art* were devoted to painting and drawing; and popular emblem books, like those of George Wither or Francis Quarles, educated readers in symbolism – 'the hieroglyphics of authority', as Wither revealingly called emblems.[13] Most important, the innovative treatise of Arundel's librarian on *The Painting of the Ancients* argued at length the relationship between art and morality, visual and political representation.[14]

While the nobility and gentry were, more than ever, being schooled in the aesthetics and politics of paintings and collecting, in the meaning of symbols and the arts of representation, a still wider public was increasingly eager to possess some token, image or symbol of the ruler – be it a woodcut, a medal, a plate adorned with the royal visage, or even playing cards.[15] By the early seventeenth century, in other words, there was not only a broad market for visual artefacts, but a privileged and, to a growing extent, popular audience for images. A new monarch, therefore, who was himself inclined more to visual than verbal representation, was by no means necessarily out of step with the times. Indeed, in focusing on his image, Charles I entered into possibilities of self-representation too little exploited by his predecessor.

In several ways, his experience of Madrid shaped Charles's appreciation and deployment of the politics of art. Like the Habsburgs, Charles collected and commissioned for his palaces portraits of his children, relatives and royal predecessors: Edward VI, Mary and Henry VIII, Catherine of Aragon and Anne Boleyn. A catalogue entry – 'there are kept two places empty for two more pictures . . . being as yet unfinished, of his Majesty's progenitors' – confirms that these were as carefully arranged as commissioned.[16] Certainly,

Charles recognized the importance to their performance as propaganda of the arrangement and display of such paintings; and references to pictures 'by the king's appointment placed' leaves little doubt that location and placement were often determined by Charles himself.[17] Inventories such as Abraham van der Doort's showing the state rooms adorned with portraits evidently chosen more for the sitters than the renown of the artists, indicates that, for all his refined aesthetic taste, Charles never lost sight of the politics of the *subjects* of representation.[18] The king, too, was learned in the interpretation of the works he collected. Both Quarles and Wither dedicated their books of emblems to a king who, they believed, fully appreciated the symbolics of the genre, as well as to a monarch who was 'a living emblem to this nation'.[19] Certainly Charles owned emblem books, while Van der Doort also records as 'bought by the king' a book 'containing in writing the interpretation of the poetical inventions being in the borders' of royal tapestries.[20]

If in his collecting, arranging and understanding of paintings and other objects, such as medals and coins, Charles manifested his appreciation of their political as well as aesthetic significance, he found a perfect mirror in the person of Van Dyck, who rather as Ben Jonson had done with James I, shared as well as lauded the king's values. Van Dyck wrote to Franciscus Junius, author of *The Painting of the Ancients*, to express his admiration for a work that, he rightly judged, expressed the royal as well as the writer's values.[21] In a fitting gesture of flattery to the king, the artist wore a portrait of Charles I on a chain around his neck.[22] And in self-portraits, as well as royal portraits, he flattered Charles's understanding of symbols, while advertising the close affinity of the artist to the king.[23] Van Dyck is by no means the only artist we need to consider in studying the visual representation of Charles I's monarchy. But, knighted by the king, who persuaded him to sojourn at Whitehall, Van Dyck himself represents the primacy of the artist in representing and (through images derived from him) publicizing monarchy during the 1630s, as much as, literally spectacularly, he re-presented the personal monarch to his subjects.

II

For all the extent and depth of scholarship, the full history of the portraits of Charles I remains uncharted. Our brief sketch here must begin not with Van Dyck, but with artists who preceded him in working for Charles and whose output provides a context for understanding the revolution he effected in the art of representing regality. The early history of Charles's performance is, in several senses, one of continuity. Daniel Mytens, a Dutch painter from Delft, had worked in England since 1618 and 'in consideration of the good service done unto us' had received a pension from James I in July 1624.[24] Soon after his succession, Charles continued him in royal service, appointing him as a 'picture drawer of our chamber' and offering him denization.[25] Mytens's early work for

Charles, paintings of his Scottish ancestors, Margaret Tudor and Mary, Queen of Scots, suggests a new monarch seeking, and seeking to advertise, the continuity of the Stuart family, which, as another commissioned portrait reminded, included the exiled Elizabeth of Bohemia, the sister Charles was determined to restore to her lands.[26] Mytens had already painted portraits of Charles as prince, one most likely after Charles's return from Spain, and was employed soon after the succession for portraits of the new king to be sent abroad or displayed by courtiers and aristocrats in England.[27] A version in the royal collection (dated 1628) shows Mytens reprising the pose of his portrait of the prince but this time depicting Charles with his right hand firmly on a long cane and with a sword at his left, both suggestive of action and authority.[28] Mytens was a distinguished portrait painter and his full-lengths of the Dukes of Buckingham and Hamilton have been described as having 'a swagger which no conventional Dutch portrait painter surpassed' – a confidence still not as evident in the portrait of Charles, despite his newly acquired beard and majesty.[29]

For all the continuity of artist and style, however, Charles early commissioned Mytens to execute what was new to England: double portraits of the new king with his wife, Henrietta Maria. The composition of *Charles I and Henrietta Maria* advertises the centrality of both the marriage and the symbolism of marriage in the representation of the reign.[30] Charles and Henrietta Maria look not outwards to the viewer but at each other and their hands cross their bodies towards each other, marking their union and shared identity. At the centre of the canvas, held between the king's and queen's right hands, is a laurel wreath, the symbol of victory and an attribute of Apollo and Daphne, as well as the Muses. In one, probably an early, version of the portrait, Henrietta with her left hand proffers to Charles an olive branch, a symbol of concord, of wisdom, of peace and specifically of the Virgin Mary, with whom Henrietta Maria was often associated. A contemporary work by Mytens also depicts the royal couple, beneath an angel strewing them with flowers, hand in hand on a terrace as though about to step out into the world, as represented by their horses and an attendant Negro page.[31] In both, the royal marriage is figured as public as well as private, as the union that could (it is implied) bring concord and peace to the country. If, however, in these early canvases we discern symbols and an iconography that were to become central to Charles's representation, there is a suggestion that the king was dissatisfied with Mytens's execution. For the double portrait with the wreath was apparently taken down soon after it was placed and put in store; and Charles later commissioned Van Dyck to paint a more sophisticated and (especially of the queen) more flattering interpretation of the same conceit.[32] If Charles was already clear about an iconographic programme, he had not in Mytens found the artist to enact it.

As well as Mytens, Charles early employed other artists of the Dutch school. Jacob van der Doort, brother of Abraham, Keeper of the Cabinet Room, who

27 *Charles I* by Daniel Mytens, 1628.

28 *Charles I and Henrietta Maria* by Daniel Mytens, *c.* 1630–2.

had come to London in 1624, painted a full-length of Charles, with his right hand on a cane and with a sword, and may have executed other work for the king.[33] Perhaps on the recommendation of his sister, to whose children he was tutor in drawing, Charles invited Gerrit van Honthorst to London in 1628.[34] During his sojourn from April to December, Honthorst painted a little-discussed portrait of Charles seated and reading a letter or paper from which he looks up to the viewer in the manner of Van Dyck's later double portrait of Wentworth with his secretary.[35] How, in the year of the Petition of Right, we would love to know the subject of the document, a little crumpled with perhaps more than one reading, that the king grasps between his hands! What we can suggest is that Charles, who almost certainly sat for this, evidently desired to publicize himself (possibly after the assassination of his favourite, Buckingham) as a working ruler, actively involved in the business of government. Honthorst's other execution for the king was the large allegorical canvas, now at Hampton Court, of Apollo and Diana. As we have seen, Charles was symbolically figured as Apollo in Mytens's double portrait and here, in an image derived from his other portrait, Honthorst has the king appear as Apollo and the queen as Diana: as, that is, the sun and moon (Diana also being the goddess of chastity and of the hunt).[36] In this allegory, the king and queen seated in the clouds receive the Duke of Buckingham, figured as Mercury presenting the seven liberal arts and as guardian of the king and queen of Bohemia's children.

Honthorst's huge *Apollo and Diana* may have been set up in the Banqueting House, the location of the masques that the canvas seems to evoke.[37] As Honthorst returned to Utrecht, where he continued to execute work for the king, the artist who was to paint the nine large ceiling canvases, long planned for the new building, was on his way to England. As Prince of Wales, Charles had long admired Peter Paul Rubens and had asked the artist for his self-portrait.[38] Rubens came to London as a diplomatic envoy, but he brought, as well as credentials for a peace, a style quite different to that of the northern Dutch school Charles had hitherto patronized. In his limited time in London, Rubens painted some portraits, principally for Thomas Howard, Earl of Arundel, and it is sometimes asked why he never portrayed the king.[39] The question is only half appropriate, for the artist's *St George and the Dragon* clearly depicted the protagonists as likenesses of Charles and Henrietta Maria who were represented as embodying the religious, moral and chivalric ideals symbolized by the Order. Though it was painted 'in honour' of England and the sovereign, the work was evidently not an official commission, as Rubens sent it home; but, as Endymion Porter, who later acquired it for Charles, recognized, the canvas mirrored Charles's self-representation as godly Christian knight, just as the allegorical *Peace and War*, which Rubens presented to Charles as part of his diplomatic mission to settle a peace, flattered him as victorious peacemaker at the moment the king was withdrawing from European conflict.[40] Rubens may not have painted portraits of Charles (or Henrietta Maria), but he had represented them, and, having knighted him in March 1630, Charles commissioned him for the grandest exultation of Stuart kingship: the canvases for the Banqueting House ceiling.

By the time he embarked on his period of rule without parliaments, Charles appears to have determined the themes of the visual representation of his kingship: his descent and dynasty, his marriage, his learning and patronage of the arts, his position as virtuous conqueror and victorious peacemaker. What he had not found was an artist who, like the Titians which had awed him in Madrid, might figure him as the literal embodiment of the values which underpinned his kingship: an artist who, that is, might by the brilliance of his brush, erase the tensions between the king's two bodies, private and public, so that the person of the king stood – in the literal as well as metaphoric sense – for the commonweal. For all their skill, Mytens and Honthorst never quite effected the connection between the king and queen and the public weal. As there remains a hint of diffident insecurity in Mytens's portrait of the king, so the *Charles I and Henrietta Maria* exhibits an awkwardness in melding the royal couple with their kingdom, and the movement between them appears (we note the spaniel arrested in mid-bound in the picture of the king and queen departing for the chase) suspended, frozen. In Mytens's work, too, the background landscapes appear somewhat flat and disconnected from the figures, particularly when we view them alongside Rubens's *Landscape with St George* in which the king and queen are positioned in the centre, with the vista of the (poetically evoked) Thames valley opening up behind them.[41] It was Anthony van Dyck who triumphantly rose above these deficiencies and limitations and who revolutionized not only the art of portraiture but, in his transference of a royal philosophy on to canvas, the art of politics, too.

Van Dyck was uniquely equipped to be Charles I's court artist and muse. A pupil of Rubens in his late teens, from 1620 to 1627 he had travelled in Italy where a love of Veronese and especially Titian influenced his portrait style towards a more understated elegance and authority. Charles would have encountered him when Arundel brought the artist to England briefly in 1620; and his instruction in March 1630 to purchase Van Dyck's *Rinaldo and Armida* suggests that the king had continued to follow his career.[42] Though the detail of Van Dyck's move to London remains unknown, Arundel and perhaps Rubens may have been movers behind the scenes, while to a monarch obsessed with Titian, the *Rinaldo* alone provided powerful testimony of an artist working in his tradition.[43] In March 1632, Van Dyck left Brussels for London – to a court and king radically different from that he had seen more than a decade earlier. Almost immediately he was knighted by Charles, given lodging and an annual pension, and set to work repairing and replacing the king's Titians – an equal to Titian, one contemporary called him.[44] And immediately, too, the artist embarked on a series of portraits that were to revolutionize the image of the king.

The partnership between Van Dyck and Charles I was one that drew on the style of the artist's earlier work and the subjects and themes of Charles's visual representation, but one that developed and transformed each and both. As Van Dyck experimented with the challenges of British military and ceremonial costumes and responded vibrantly to the new possibilities presented for varieties of dress and colour in his English portraits, Charles's iconographic themes were overlaid with new forms and genres as well as new techniques of portrait art.[45] Most obviously, Van Dyck's two equestrian portraits of the king are 'almost unprecedented in English royal iconography', though familiar on the continent.[46] The significance of the pose surpasses aesthetic innovation. Mastery of the horse was, in much contemporary courtesy literature, a symbol for mastery of the passions: a virtue essential to nobility, still more to princes.[47] In his account of the entertainment given to Prince Charles in Spain, Mendoza had flattered Charles's virtue by observing that the horses he rode, though 'their mouths were curbed with no bits', tamely obeyed the rider: 'in this they signified that in a high degree they laid down all their natural and brutish fierceness' before him.[48] In his panegyric to the king, written in 1633, Henry Wotton praised Charles's 'use of the great horse . . . which no man doth more skilfully manage . . . or tame the furious'.[49] It is this natural authority of the self-regulated ruler that Van Dyck conveys in his two equestrian portraits. In the painting *Charles I on Horseback*, the king's left hand only lightly touches the reins, while – making the connection to the larger authority his effortless control symbolizes – his right hand grasps a baton of command.[50] Charles rides the dun charger at the trot with relaxed ease.[51] Though he wears armour and a rapier, the atmosphere is calm and the landscape and sky tranquil. Behind the king is a tablet, suspended on a tree. Inscribed 'Charles King of Great Britain', it evokes the genealogical trees of descent, as it also renders Stuart rule of Albion (we note the horse is white) natural and timeless. A servant stands behind with his master's helmet, but he is less prominent than in Rubens's portrait of Philip IV on which Van Dyck draws; and the king looks in the other direction as he surveys a land pacified by his beneficent rule. While recent scholarship has tempered Roy Strong's interpretation of the portraits as, derived from Dürer, that of the Christian knight, the Greenwich armour recalls Rubens's figuring of Charles as St George and the values of a chivalric past.[52] Though the king wears his sword (without a knuckle guard), his mightiest weapon is his faith and virtue.

Charles I on Horseback owes a debt to two equestrian portraits, one by Titian, of the emperor Charles V. But it is in his earlier portrait of the king mounted that Van Dyck most obviously presents Charles as British *imperator*.[53] The famous image of Charles with Monsieur de St Antoine gestures again to the association of equestrian skill with authority. St Antoine was equerry and riding master to Charles, as he had been to Henry; but, in this canvas, the riding master, holding the king's helmet, can only raise his eyes in wondrous awe as Charles – again effortlessly – turns his white horse through a classical arch festooned with drapery. The arch, of course, was a monument to triumph and, executed in 1633, this painting may well have commemorated Charles's coronation in Scotland that year.[54] On the left, at the foot of a column, a shield, quartered with the arms of Charles's kingdoms and surmounted with an imperial crown, draws attention to the British empire over which he rules in peace. The triumph, however, though topical, should not be read as that of a moment. The arch, as Charles's minister Thomas Wentworth eloquently restated, was a metaphor of government and the monarchy its keystone that 'contains each part in due relation to the whole'.[55] The triumph Charles here represents is what a masque of the same year called the 'triumph of peace': the victory over unruly passions in himself and all his kingdoms.[56] *Charles on Horseback* was hung, and probably designed for, the end of the gallery at St James's. There, not only did Charles join the emperors whose equestrian portraits by Giulio Romano and Titian lined the room; the arch, functioning as an illusionistic setting akin to Inigo Jones's masque scenery, almost served as an entrance through which Charles rode into the gallery.[57] That this suggestion of vital realism is not the fancy of the modern

29 *Charles I on Horseback* by Anthony van Dyck, *c.* 1635–6.

30 *Charles I with M. de St Antoine* by Anthony van Dyck, 1633.

observer is confirmed by a visitor to England in the queen mother's entourage in 1639, who described Charles as 'alive in this portrait'.[58] Indeed, as artist and monarch had intended, the king was vibrantly represented as heir to empire and king of a new age and monarchy. We might note, too, that though the theme is classical, in the theme of triumph, in the white horse and the adoration of St Antoine we may discern gestures to the sacred and Christic foundations of kingship, in which James I had tutored his son. If we discern such gestures by a Van Dyck who had spent his years in Antwerp (prior to moving to London) painting altarpieces and other religious art, the triumph suggested is also that of a saviour come to redeem his people.[59]

Though it is not an equestrian portrait, it is in the context of them that we should view a perhaps even more innovatory portrayal of Charles I in the hunting field. The subject was hardly new. Sir Oliver Millar described the canvas as 'an almost deliberate sequel' to Van Somer's portraits of Anne of Denmark and notes the debt to Peake's pictures of Prince Henry in the hunting field.[60] But the differences are as striking. For, though he is painted in hunting

31 *Le Roi à la Chasse* by Anthony van Dyck, *c.* 1635.

costume, nothing in Charles's pose suggests the strenuous activity of the hunt captured by Peake. The king in fact turns away from the attendants and horse behind him that represent the hunt; and his tranquillity contrasts with their busy activity. While his grooms work to settle the beast, the horse bows in obeisance to Charles, who effortlessly commands the natural world – the world of nature. The cane on which he rests his right hand (as he had in the Mytens portrait) here disappears into the foliage, symbolizing that natural authority. The figure of the king is placed to the left, yet the composition of the portrait highlights his position and power. Charles stands elevated on a grassy ledge and in light that falls on his silver jacket; his left elbow, in foreshortening and facing directly to the viewer, draws our line of sight to the king but also seems to secure his command of his mystical distance and space. Again there is a suggestion of a sacred dimension. Van Dyck probably took the horse with its lowered head and the groom from Titian's *Adoration of the Kings*, an appropriation which gestures to Charles as the Christ come to restore paradise.[61] But what is most remarkable in this image is absence. Here are no regalia, tablets or escutcheons signifying regality or dynasty. Charles the man *is* the king because he literally embodies authority and instinctively commands his environment. Pared of the robes of state and trappings of majesty, the king's body and natural person themselves exude divine, regal authority. We are witnessing a personalization of power in paint.

The dramatic effects of this revolutionary new mode reach even to Van Dyck's handling of the conventional royal portrait. Van Dyck's *Charles I in Robes of State*, on a canvas over nine feet high, was executed in 1636 as the official template that he knew would be copied for other rulers, courts and favoured courtiers.[62] It has been suggested that for the artist 'this form of state portraiture, necessarily constrained, can hardly have been as stimulating as the portraits of Charles to which he had already brought all his inventiveness of pose'.[63] The interior setting, single subject and need to follow convention do make this a more traditional image. Again, however, Van Dyck subtly imports echoes and innovations that revise traditional representation, even in this traditional genre. In the 1636 portrait Charles stands full length in robes of state, wearing the collar of the Garter and greater George. Beside him, on his left, the imperial crown and orb are placed on a table before a large column which rises up behind the king. Like the regalia, the pillar symbolizes authority, imperial sway, but is also a symbol of spiritual strength.[64] And it is – even here – the relation between inner personal strength and majesty and outward symbols that Van Dyck brings to the state portrait. For though formal, the canvas departs from the iconic tradition of earlier official regal portraits and is as concerned to present the (ideally virtuous) man as the monarch. Indeed, despite the formality, Charles's pose is not entirely conventional: his right hand on his hip recalls *Le Roi à la Chasse* and displays Charles's arm, emerging from the formality of the robes, clad in white silk and bathed in light. With the king's face

32 *Charles I* by Anthony van Dyck, 1636.

a carefully modelled study in composed self-control, and his slender left hand delicately painted and illuminated, Van Dyck renders Charles (even in this portrait) as a man and monarch rather than an as an icon of majesty. The portrait melds the king's bodies, personal and public, personal composure and public office.

As well as the royal equestrian portrait, Van Dyck virtually introduced the family portrait to English royal iconography. Of course, in the Privy Chamber mural of Henry VIII, *The Family of Henry VIII* and *An Allegory of the Tudor*

Succession we have earlier examples of dynastic portraits.[65] But the stiff arrangement of forms in these is far removed from the domestic intimacy which is the subject and theme of Van Dyck's work. Nowhere else in Europe were there paintings of royalty of the informality of the canvases of Charles's family; indeed, even though he had executed family portraits – of Genoese merchants, for example – before coming to England, Van Dyck himself captured in his English royal family portraits an intimacy and affect more sensitive and convincing than in his earlier works. As we have seen, Charles's marriage was central to his philosophy of kingship and to his representation of his regality; and he had commissioned Mytens to paint a double portrait with his queen. That portrait had evidently not satisfied the king; and, after an attempt to repaint the figure of Henrietta Maria, Van Dyck, soon after his arrival, was appointed to rework the canvas.[66] Though he retained, and even returned to, the original design, Van Dyck's reinterpretation significantly altered the portrait in ways that, since his version pleased the king and replaced Mytens's, are worthy of attention. Where in the Mytens version Charles and Henrietta Maria are placed, somewhat stiffly, in an interior beneath a red curtain, Van Dyck positions them each side of green curtains drawn to open on to a vista of landscape and sky. The change of setting and colours throws the light on to the king's (silver-lined) carnation suit and the queen's silver dress decorated with carnation. The matching colours (Henrietta also wears a carnation ribbon in her hair) subtly point to the harmony of their marriage, as in this version do their hands which, circled like the laurel they exchange, draw and bind the figures together in an image of tender affection. More importantly, Van Dyck points up the wider symbolism that was, if masques may be our guide, always Charles's intention. In his version, the regalia placed behind Charles connect personal intimacy to sovereignty, and the king's happy personal union with the larger union with his people which was the subject of entertainments and panegyrics. The exterior setting similarly opens domestic to public space. Van Dyck's canvas, that is, not only satisfied Charles's aesthetic sensibilities but captured in oils a vital theme of his political ideology.[67]

When Van Dyck arrived in England, Henrietta Maria had already given birth to a prince and a princess and, given her young age and fertility, seemed to have secured Stuart dynasty. The publicization of family and dynasty was perhaps the first priority of early modern rulers and, not least, in James I's dedication of advice manuals and other works to his sons. The family, as every student of Aristotle knew, was the origin of the state, a little commonweal; and courtesy literature, as much as political writing, freely discussed kings as fathers. For all his success in siring offspring, however, James's family, like his marriage, had been marked by tension and conflict; significantly, perhaps, we have, other than engravings, no family portraits of the first Stuart. Charles I, by contrast, made his family itself a dominant representation of his rule and therefore the representation of his family was for him vital to the communication of his authority.[68] Indeed, the instruction to paint a family portrait for his Long Gallery was one of the first the king issued to Van Dyck, within weeks of the artist's arrival.[69] The 'great piece of our royal self, consort and children', authorized on 8 August 1632, should be considered as one of the most important texts of early modern kingship, and offers an eloquent expression of the values of Charles I.[70] Once again Van Dyck transformed a genre to represent the king not as dynastic patriarch but as loving paterfamilias. Quite unlike the conventional

33 *Charles I and Henrietta Maria with their two eldest children, Prince Charles and Princess Mary* by Anthony van Dyck, 1632.

dynastic portrait, the composition emphasized the communications, the affective relations, between the subjects. Henrietta Maria, holding the infant
princess Mary, looks not to the viewer but adoringly towards her husband as a
loving but subordinate wife. On her right, Charles is seated with, between them,
two Italian greyhounds, one turned to each person, the dogs symbolizing
fidelity. The king's right arm reaches behind the small figure of his son, Prince
Charles, who rests both his hands on his father's leg. Touch, rarely depicted in
royal family portraits, and gaze unite the group in domestic intimacy and affection. Other objects and symbols, however, connect the affective family to a
public world. Immediately behind the king's head rises a pillar – a familiar
symbol of sovereignty; and Charles's right hand behind the prince rests, holding
a paper, on a table on which are placed the imperial crown, sceptre and orb.
Where the queen and princess are situated in a draped interior, behind the king
and the prince his heir a vista opens up in which are discernible Westminster
Hall and the Parliament House – the domains of a ruler and a future ruler who
alone look straight out to the viewer. Here the love and unity of the domestic
family represent the love and affection the king feels for his people, and the
well-ordered household the perfectly ordered commonweal.

It may seem surprising that Charles commissioned no more such portraits
as his family grew. However, further portraits of the children which gesture to
the 'great piece' may suggest that the royal progeny themselves represented
Caroline rule. In the portrait of the king's eldest three children, for example,
the composition again tenderly connects the group (the two princes hold
hands); and Prince Charles now leans against a large column inscribed with
the birth dates of the royal offspring of the king of Great Britain.[71] As well as
again symbolizing fidelity, the spaniel dogs had royal associations before
Charles II gave the breed a name.[72] A final group of the royal children, painted
in 1637, was carefully composed to focus attention on the king's heir.[73] In this
canvas, Prince Charles stands square to the viewer with his siblings placed two
and two each side of him, with the clothes of the infant James (second in line
to the throne) decorated with a crimson sleeve which echoes his elder brother's
silk suit. At the centre, the young prince, composed, rests his left hand lightly
on the head of a large mastiff – a symbol, like the horse, of wild nature
governed by the reason and innate authority which a virtuous prince, even one
so young, possesses. Though the father and monarch is not here figured, he is
the subject of this canvas: the sire of progeny and the father of the commonweal who has schooled his son through virtue and self-regulation for good
government.

It may be significant that after 1637 Van Dyck's portraits of the king and
prince were few and depicted them in armour. In one of 1638, for which
Charles almost certainly sat, the portrait is dominated by light that falls across
the black armour, a sword hilt and the baton of command grasped firmly
between Charles's hands.[74] Van Dyck's last portraits of the prince similarly

34 *The Three Eldest Children of Charles I* by Anthony van Dyck, 1635.

portray him in armour with his hand grasping a helmet and his finger on a
pistol, at the ready.[75] As we view these martial images, executed during the
Prayer Book rebellion, we are bound to ask whether the collapse of Charles's
personal government does not evidence a failure of Van Dyck's representation,
despite the critical consensus regarding his technical genius. And indeed
historians, when they have noticed him at all, have tended to regard Charles's
principal painter as one of his problems: as a symbol of the king's detachment
from his people. It has often been asserted that Van Dyck's work was regarded
as popish and contributed to that mounting suspicion of the influence
of popery at court that fatally undermined trust in the king.[76] There is,
however, almost no evidence of direct contemporary comment on these lines;
rather, what is remarkable is that leading puritan noblemen – the Earls of
Warwick and Northumberland, Pembroke and Bedford, Lord Wharton and
Arthur Goodwin – some future Parliamentarian and regicide gentlemen sat

as readily as any Catholic or Anglican for portraits which are characterized by no less flamboyant a style or by any muting of palette.[77] Van Dyck was not only the king's painter; he was the court's painter, the painter of the aristocracy.

If the assertion that Van Dyck fuelled fears of popish influence must be dismissed, what of the (somewhat contradictory) charge that, while his innovative foreign style delighted the king, it isolated Charles I and his court from a country with more conservative and native tastes? Again, as far as the lesser nobles and even gentry are concerned, it seems likely that Van Dyck's portraits reached far beyond the confines of the court in the many copies painted by his studio and assistants for which there was evidently a strong demand.[78] Though the subject of copies has understandably not attracted art critics (especially in the connoisseur tradition) and is not an exact science (because dating of copies is often a matter of critical judgement), we know that Van Dyck ran a studio of copyists and there remain, from what were probably many more, early copies of Charles in state robes and of 'the great piece', several of Charles and Henrietta Maria, and several of the late martial portrait of the king, along with reduced and variant copies of them all.[79] Far from confined to the court (and those with recourse to court were by no means a small community), if surviving examples are an indication it seems likely that – through copies and replicas – Van Dycks reached into provincial noble and gentry houses, where they were seen by visitors, attendants and servants. That they were not only an elite taste is suggested by the rush to purchase them by ordinary army officers, even plain russet-coated captains, when the royal collection was sold after 1649.[80] Moreover, Van Dyck's royal portraits evidently fostered a market for engravings and woodcuts drawn from them, as their conceits and themes were also reproduced in statues and artefacts, medals and badges.

III

During the reign of Charles I, the demand for engraved portraits increased and the Dutch émigré Peter Stent established in London what was probably the first commercial shop dedicated to the sale of prints.[81] Book publishers supplemented the demand and there appear to have been the beginnings of amateur interest in making woodcuts and engravings, which is reflected in the growing number of instruction manuals published for gentry readers. In *The Mysteries of Art and Nature* (1635), for example, John Bate included a book on 'drawing . . . painting and engraving'; as well as giving practical instruction on 'the manner of engraving', he warned readers against exposing work to 'the view of every Stationer', for stationers were, he claimed, quick to publish them in their books.[82] Charles I may have been the first ruler to offer direct patronage and employment to engravers. Lucas Vorsteman the Elder, who had engraved for Rubens and perhaps Van Dyck, worked copying pictures for the king, as well as for the Earl of Arundel and others; Robert van Voerst, who came to England in 1628, was commissioned by Van Dyck as exclusive engraver of his portraits and was appointed engraver to Charles.[83] Royal patronage of, and the market for, engravings were by no means distinct developments. Charles granted his royal privilege to certain portraits which were publicly sold, the royal imprimatur being displayed evidently as a selling point, as it was on Van Voerst's double portrait of the king and queen or on Hollar's of Charles I in armour.[84]

For all the importance of these developments and images, their history remains unstudied. We have no reliable catalogue of the engraved portraits of Charles I. Though it is pioneering, the third volume of Arthur Hind's descriptive catalogue of engravings of the sixteenth and seventeenth centuries is by no means complete and does not reach beyond 1642.[85] Many surviving engravings of the king remain unattributed or dated in uncatalogued collections, and doubtless many have not survived at all.[86] However, those we can identify confidently are sufficient to demonstrate the broad visual publicization of and market for representational themes beyond the medium of elite canvases or even copies of paintings. In the engravings of Charles I which were published, sold and bought, we see again the emphasis placed on dynasty, marriage and family, and begin to appreciate the broader performance of a representation that was to be vital in the popular perception and memory of the king.

Perhaps the earliest engraving of Charles as monarch acted, as did so many of the accession panegyrics, to present the new king to his people as heir to his father and as a Stuart. The broadside *Maiesties Sacred Monument* depicts James I recumbent on a tomb which supports pillars, on top of which is a pyramid structure of five ascending levels.[87] Above the first level of the royal lion, unicorn and arms, on the upper levels female figures represent the virtues of Glory, Magnificence, Science, Religion, Providence and Clemency. Aloft, Faith and Hope stand together with, above them, Charity, while in the sky above, beneath a tetragrammaton, clouds are inscribed with the names of nobles who died between the death of Queen Anne in 1619 and James in 1625. The broadside was, it appears, designed 'in memory of King James, Queen Anne and the nobility'; but at the foot of the tomb are the figures of the royal children. On the right, Elizabeth of Bohemia sits surrounded by her children – a reminder again of the exiled Stuarts; on the left crowned and in robes of state, Charles I bears a sword inscribed, after Virgil's *Aeneid*, DEBELLARE SVPERBOS (to vanquish the proud, or over-mighty). While the verses each side of the monument rehearse the virtues of James, a quatrain points to the depicted figure of Charles I, James's 'succeeding son':

> Perfecting what a father left undone;
> And what his wisdome thought to prosecute
> Ready with a drawne sword to Execute.

35 *Maiesties Sacred Monument* by Robert Vaughan, *c.* 1625–30.

If the representation of dynastic succession is graphically proclaimed on this
broadside, the king's marriage is the theme of a contemporary engraving found in
a copy of George Marcelline's *Epithalamium Gallo Britannicum*, a celebration of
the union of Charles and Henrietta Maria, a broadside sold by Thomas Archer at
the Horse Shoe in Pope's Head Alley.[88] Here, in an anticipation of the Mytens and
Van Dyck double portraits, Charles and Henrietta, beneath an arch decorated
with a large royal arms, hold hands, with, between them, a Cupid bearing a
crowned heart. Scrolls proclaim the love between king and queen. On pedestals

36 *Betrothal of Charles I and Henrietta Maria*, fold-out engraving in *Epithalamium Gallo-Britannicum*, George Marcelline, 1625.

each side of them stand the figures (that on the left with helmet and shield, that on the right with lyre, bow and quiver) of Minerva, goddess of war and wisdom and Apollo, god of music and poetry, with beneath them emblems of war and peace. Around the royal couple, escutcheons of the past French and English kings remind observers of the two great ancient royal houses now united in one and of the power their union represents. As well as celebrating marriage and dynasty, the figures of Minerva and Apollo and the emblems suggest both the ready capacity for war and the love of peace and the arts, Apollo often standing for order, harmony and civilization.[89] Here, in a very early image, almost certainly published with official approval, the royal marriage expresses, as it did on Van Dyck's canvases, a philosophy and represents a triumph – of love and virtue. At the foot of the broadside, verses represent the marriage as a union of Pallas and Ceres, War and Wealth, Peace and Policy – as, that is, the reconciliation of opposites to create the perfect harmony of virtues – and of 'armes and art'.

Charles's desire to publicize his marriage and family as the best representation of his rule is well documented by engravings. Satisfied with Van Dyck's reworking of his portrait with Henrietta Maria, Charles evidently authorized Van Voerst to engrave and publish the image in 1634. Issued 'Cum privil[egio] reg[is]', the engraving bore a Latin inscription, presenting the royal couple as unmatched descendants of the great James and Henry.[90] Similarly an anonymous mezzotint (now in the National Portrait Gallery), depicting the royal couple with their two oldest children, appears to be drawn from Van Dyck's 'great piece' and was probably executed with the artist's and king's approval.[91] Two engravings of the royal family, rather different in style to Van Dyck's, were executed, apparently as a pair, about 1636 by George Glover, a Dutchman who worked in England from 1634.[92] That of Henrietta Maria with Princess Mary and Prince James points to Charles in the accompanying verse that celebrates a king who crowns the isle with his offspring; while the engraving (to which this is pendant) of Charles with Prince Charles, also sold by Robert Peake, carries a verse that relates the royal progeny to the peace and prosperity of the realm:

> Gaze on (Fond world) nor wide enough to be
> Sway'd by so great and pure a Maiestee
> Whose crowne all blisse incircles that can bring
> Health to a Land or Glory to a King.[93]

Late in the decade, a family portrait of the king and queen with their five children was issued for sale at the White Horse near Newgate by an engraver who was, perhaps more than any, to shape the image of the king.[94] William Marshall's engraving places Charles and Henrietta Maria, each between two pillars, on a terrace that opens on to a formal garden, beneath a sun and angels who bear, in a winding sheet, a deceased child to heaven. As the king's heir stands on his father's right, next to the baton of command in his hand, verses remind viewers that, where before it had been eighty years since the birth of a prince, England now had two. Along with dynasty, the verses proclaim the children as God's blessings on the king and on the realm:

> For God gives progeny where true love conioynes
> And happy is the Realme, which for its good,
> Enioyes successive hopes from proper Blood.

It has been said that Marshall's greatest ability was his capacity to 'convey a message in as simple and literal a fashion as possible'.[95] Though his engraving of the royal family lacks Van Dyck's refinement and elegance, it broadly advertised the divinity of sacred kingship and Stuart rule.

As well as publicizing themes of marriage, succession and dynasty, engravings marked particular events and moments important to the image and representation of Charles. It would seem to be more than coincidental that, shortly after Rubens painted *St George and the Dragon*, with the saint depicted with Charles's features, Peter Heylyn dedicated to the king a history of St George, with a title page engraved by Marshall with Charles's portrait.[96] Facing a head and shoulders of Edward III, the founder of the Order of the Garter, a crowned portrait of Charles depicts him as the ruler who has revived and embellished it – just as the king was doing.[97] Though we know little of the artist or engraving, it also seems likely that Cornelius van Dalen's equestrian portrait of Charles crowned and in state robes, bearing a sceptre in his right hand and with Edinburgh in the background, commemorated the king's progress to his coronation in Scotland in 1633, the year Van Dalen came to England.[98]

In addition to official or semi-official productions, portraits of the monarch were becoming more important for the commerce of print and at least qualify easy assumptions about the unpopularity of the king. Engravings of the state opening of parliament and of the upper house, both issued in 1628 as broadsides, feature Charles enthroned in the Lords in a manner that frames the ideal harmony of king and commonweal.[99] Anonymous engravings of Charles in armour, or in robes of state, were sold by Peake and at the Royal Exchange from soon after the accession; and the market for the royal image remained undiminished throughout the 1630s.[100] The 1635 edition of the popular writer Thomas Heywood's *Hierarchie of the Blessed Angels* was illustrated with a Glover engraving that placed Charles and Henrietta Maria in the clouds behind the Principat (the order of angel above the archangels who also took care of princes).[101] In 1640, a Lincoln blacksmith James Yorke figured – as well as a royal coat of arms – a portrait of the king in the engraved architectural title page to his *Union of Honour*; the next year the engraved figure of Charles by Marshall joined those of Elizabeth and James I to decorate a treatise on the benefits of Anglo-Scottish union.[102]

From the fine work of engravers after Van Dyck, some produced with official approval, to the more pedestrian images produced for sale as separates or as illustrations to books, the portrait of Charles I was broadly disseminated and with it, in many cases, the themes and conceits of the king's own representations. Though to us the iconography of some visual texts may appear complex and not easily understandable, the messages of many of these visual documents was clear: England was blessed with a divinely favoured king whose marriage and family secured the love and peace of the kingdom and represented the harmony between king and people. The union (not only of the kingdoms but of king and subjects) which James I had so often proclaimed in words was in Charles's reign no less publicized on canvas, in prints and broadsides, and in the illustrations to books.

While his patronage of the arts and preoccupation with portraiture are famous, relatively little attention has been paid to the king's passion for medals and badges. Yet this interest began early – as a prince Charles acquired a book on the antiquity of medals – and was sustained throughout his life.[103] Francis Cottington, a confidant of Charles from the journey to Spain who was made Chancellor of the Exchequer, knew his sovereign intimately enough to be certain that a gift of medals would endear him further.[104] Indeed, they added to a growing collection of medals which Charles built up: medals of Roman emperors, of modern kings (Francis I and Philip II, for example), and of his own family.[105] Nor were the king's medals, as collections often are, merely hoarded to gather dust. Charles arranged his collection in books, and evidently not infrequently reviewed them; Van der Doort, the keeper, on one occasion found twenty-seven of them out on the table.[106] A monarch with such an interest and knowledge could not but develop a keen sense of the potential of medals as images of kingship. What again is striking is that the royal appreciation of that potential extended far beyond elites to make medals a popular medium of royal representation during the reign. A historian of badges remarked that, during Charles's reign, 'badges were so freely distributed that they might almost be said to be within the reach of all who cared to possess such a portrait of the king'.[107] The claim may apply more to the years of civil war than to the period before; but from early on, official and commemorative medals were struck on many occasions, and in rough and base states for popular distribution as well as in fine examples and precious metals for nobles and courtiers.

We will not be surprised that, whether at James's or his son's instruction, several medals were struck to commemorate Charles's marriage to Henrietta Maria. Small medals with a double portrait of the king and queen under rays from heaven, with, on the reverse, Cupid scattering roses and lilies, were 'distributed in great profusion', as the first visual impression of their soon-to-be king which the ordinary populace received.[108] Whoever commissioned those, Charles's coronation medal illustrates his deployment of medals from the outset to underpin particular policies as well as his regality and authority in general. Nicholas Briot produced gold and silver medals with the king in profile right, crowned and with the collar of the Garter on the obverse.[109] On the reverse, a hand protruding from a cloud holds a raised sword with, around it, the legend: 'Until peace is restored to the earth', an allusion to Charles I's position as godly warrior on behalf of his brother-in-law and the cause of Protestantism. As we have seen in panegyrics and portraits, here in medals the marriage is represented as a harmony of peace and war, and the king as both pacifist and militant in the right cause.

37 Medals struck to commemorate Charles's marriage to Henrietta Maria.

From the coronation onwards, medals were commissioned virtually every year to commemorate key events abroad and at home. Though the prayer inscribed on it was to be dashed by failure at La Rochelle, a medal with Charles mounted and with a sword, and the legend 'Grant, O King, a prosperous course', struck for the expedition, reminds us that Charles was as concerned as anyone to present his war as godly.[110] Together with his other medals of 1628, which feature a sceptre and a trident and were probably issued to support

Charles's plea to parliament for funding of his navy, the Rochelle medal reveals a king utilizing a popular visual medium to make a public case for a (much-criticized) policy.[111] From 1629, the occasions for the minting of medals were happier, domestic events. Interestingly, Charles commissioned a cheap copper as well as a silver medal to publicize his addition to the Garter badge of the stars of the French Order of the Holy Spirit, which we see the king wearing in Van Dyck's portrait now at Dresden – an indication that he intended the elite order should more broadly publicize his kingship.[112]

The birth of Prince Charles was proclaimed by a profusion of medals and medalets in some six versions. The prince was the first to be entitled to bear the arms of four nations and the shields in some versions were arranged with radiations, alluding to the star observed as Charles I was proceeding to St Paul's to give thanks for the birth of his son.[113] In another version, which figures Charles I on the obverse, on the reverse the figures of Mars and Mercury hold wreaths of laurel and olive branches over the infant's cradle, alluding again to the delicate reconciliation of peace and war effected by the Stuart ruler and his marriage.[114] Despite the peace which followed the dissolution of parliament in 1629, the medallic representation of Caroline rule was by no means dominated by pacifism. The year of the prince's birth, in which a medal legend ran 'May he revive the glory of his ancestry', Charles also commissioned Briot to cast a medal asserting British and royal sovereignty of the seas, a claim that lay behind the arguments for the ship money fleets and which had its full exposition a few years later in John Selden's *Mare clausum*.[115] Circulated in a bronze version, as well as gold and silver, the medal pairs on its two sides an armoured bust of Charles with a large ship and the inscription: 'Nor is that a limit to me which is a boundary to the world'. In the year of the birth of a prince, Charles alluded in this medal to the large imperial claims that had followed the Stuart dynasty to the throne of Britain and published them to the people.

38 Medal depicting Charles I, with Mars and Mercury on reverse.

39 Medal depicting Charles I with ship signifying Charles's claim to sovereignty of the seas.

The medallic representation of Stuart British imperium reached its height in 1633, the year of Charles I's coronation in Scotland and of the birth of a second son (James) who secured the dynastic succession. The king himself attributed great importance to his Scottish coronation medal, which was 'much worn in his majesty's pocket'.[116] In several versions struck in large numbers (several pairs of dies were used), the medal depicted, as well as the monarch wearing the collars of the thistle and Garter, the thistle and the rose tree combined.[117] On the silver version, an inscription runs 'Hinc nostrae crevere rosae' ('Hence have our roses grown'), as an advertisement of what Charles, as well as his father, had added to Stuart rule since the union.[118] While the gold version struck from gold found in Clydesdale complimented Scottish recipients, a specifically English audience was targeted by medals celebrating Charles's return. On these, an equestrian portrait of Charles in armour, with his helmet lying amidst flowers on the ground, announces to England the peaceful triumph of 'the most invincible Charles, Monarch of Great Britain'.[119] And the reverse depicts the capital of the British imperium, in a view of the Thames and St Paul's beneath a radiant sun, signifying, as the legend explains, 'As the sun illuminates the world, so does the king's return gladden the city'.

Even as the summer sun faded, there was good news to gladden the city. Prince James was born on 14 October and immediately proclaimed Duke of York. Three medals were issued to announce his birth and baptism; still more to further display the magnificence of a Charles who must, in 1633, have felt at the height of happiness and confidence.[120] The simple medals bore the same inscription in all versions: 'Not so a thousand cohorts' – a vaunt that nothing would so much strengthen Stuart dynasty and authority as the birth of a second son. In the wake of Van Dyck's family portraits and engravings after

40 Medal depicting Charles I on horseback.

them, following James's baptism, a medal represented the royal family as 'The safety of the king, the kingdoms, and the people'.[121] Though it has not been noticed, the double portrait of Charles and Henrietta Maria holding hands is clearly based on Van Dyck's reworking of Mytens; on the reverse, beneath a crown supported by angels or attendant spirits, Princes Charles and James and Princess Mary symbolize the blessings of God on the king, queen, their marriage and the people.[122] Three years after the family medal, Prince Charles was, on 22 May 1638, installed as Knight of the Garter, then formally styled Prince of Wales, the official recognition of his position as heir. Medals publicized both crucial moments, which somewhat surprisingly were not commemorated by paintings. One medal of the young Charles in the plumed hat, robes and collar of the Order has an obverse on which the prince's plume, within a Garter, is surrounded by the inscription 'The great hope of a great parent'.[123] Underlining how the representation of the prince represented the king, a second installation medal depicted not Charles but his coronet, beneath which sheep graze in the shelter of the tall trees of the forest with, in the distance, ships at sea.[124] Inscriptions describe the prince as his father's son and a shelter to his people. But the image may have more topical resonance. For in 1637, Charles had launched *The Sovereign of the Seas*, the flagship of the ship money fleets, which was engraved by John Payne and (as we have seen) the subject of a panegyric by Thomas Heywood.[125] In this second Garter medal for the prince, Briot surely intended to connect the protection of the people not only with Stuart dynasty but with policies and levies which were attracting increasing opposition. And, with the first medal depicting the prince mounted, in imitation of earlier images of his father (whose crowned bust is on the obverse), also announcing his new title as Prince of Wales, there is a gesture to the continuity of policy as well as dynasty.[126]

Though the fleet financed by ship money had no official commemoration, Charles had commissioned in 1636, in base metals for the broadest distribution, medals to celebrate what was, in effect, a Dutch capitulation to England's claim to be the master of the seas. The king reaffirmed his claim, inappropriately as events turned out, in 1639 by instructing Briot to reissue the earlier Dominion of the Sea medal with his revised bust image in armour.[127] As before, on the 1639 medal Charles is figured in armour, making claim to unbounded empire. It was issued, however, as the king was embroiled in domestic warfare with the Scots. The first expedition to suppress them hardly proved a resounding success; but the Covenanters were as anxious to settle without a battle as Charles and an uneasy peace was agreed at Berwick on 11 June 1639. The English government tried to spin the news of the pacification to render it a victory; and as part of that process issued four medals which have hitherto received no attention. The medals, the first work of Thomas Simon, a pupil of Briot, all depict, on the obverse, Charles crowned, mounted on a charging horse, and with a baton in his right hand.[128] Though the pose is one of action, even martial, the king tramples on armour and on other emblems of war. The image, which clearly recalled the medal celebrating the king's return from Edinburgh in 1633, asserts military strength while celebrating peace. On the reverse, a hand reaches down from a cloud holding a cord which unites a rose and a thistle, signifying the holy union of England and Scotland. The inscription recalls James's famous appropriation of the marriage service 'Quos deus' – short for what God has joined let no man separate.[129] In this simple medal, as well as claiming a triumph of peace, Charles reasserted his divine rule over an empire of the kingdom of Great Britain united by God, and so cast the Covenanters and their supporters as sinners as well as traitors.

41 Medal of Charles I with reverse depicting hand uniting rose and thistle.

It was the last medal commissioned by the king before civil conflict broke out in Britain. But, significantly, before then medals were issued marking the execution of the Earl of Strafford (the point at which Charles surrendered his authority to his parliamentary opponents) and the declaration of parliament published on 19 May 1642.[130] In the latter case, variants of the medal engraved by Thomas Rawlins and ordered by parliament depicted Charles I, crowned and with his Garter, but now inside the legend 'Should hear both houses of Parliament [which] for true religion and subjects freedom stand'. On the reverse, an image of the two houses, one presided over by the king, the other by the Speaker, audaciously manifested the authority now shared between king and parliament. In another version the royal bust is replaced by a ship of state – an image which, with the same obverse, now signified that the two houses of parliament had secured the commonweal. In those neglected medals, a whole story unfolds. Parliament, we begin to see, was appropriating royal authority by seizing and redeploying the media of royal representation. Yet in doing so it not only recognized the power of these forms and representations in sustaining and publicizing authority; it also accepted the need to use traditional, therefore often regal, symbols and tropes in its own quest to attain and secure authority. As we shall see, the seeds of the Commonwealth's collapse were sowed in the first moments parliament contested for power.[131] For now, we note that, though largely ignored by historians, medals were seen by contemporaries as vital markers, and makers, of key moments in the representation of, and increasingly in the contest for, authority, validation and public support.

Soon after his succession, Charles also turned his attention to his coins. Early in 1625, probably in May, the king, having 'misliked' the coin 'especially for the effigies which hath been interpreted for want of a better pattern', appointed to make new patterns Abraham van der Doort, who was already embossing medals and who had worked for Prince Charles for sixteen years.[132] The Mint quickly set to work on Van der Doort's patterns for £1, £3 and £5 pieces and the royal pleasure at his work doubtless explains his appointment as Groom of the Privy Chamber in 1630.[133] In 1628 Charles recruited another distinguished artist for this service when he took on Nicholas Briot. Though the royal grant of denizenship and appointment was couched so as not to infringe Van der Doort's rights, it does mention that the 'king found by experience that the graver of his monies was not at all times and places provided with such good and proportionable forms and patterns of his effigy as were necessary' and commissioned Briot to assist.[134]

For all this care over his portrait image, however, which resulted in greatly improved work, Charles's coins exhibit less variety, in image and inscription, than his father's.[135] Briot's pattern for gold coins and silver shillings, sixpences and half-groats featured a crowned bust of Charles facing left with, on the reverse, the arms of the four kingdoms quartered inside the inscription 'Regno auspice Christi' – I reign under the auspices of Christ, or with Christ's favour: that is by divine right and with divine protection.[136] Another pattern type for silver crowns and half-crowns, with the same reverse, represented Charles on the obverse, mounted left, in armour, brandishing a drawn sword, crowned and with his plumed helmet behind him.[137] We find other examples of early coins, notably half-groats and pennies, with a crowned rose and the legend 'Justice strengthens the crown' and a gold coin (the angel) depicting St Michael slaying the beast and a large ship with the royal ensign newly inscribed 'The love of the people is the greatest protection of the king'.[138] Another gold coin, like the angel in the Jacobean tradition, with the quartered arms of the kingdoms crowned, has the inscription 'May the realms flourish in harmony'.[139] Pattern pieces for other gold and silver coins and for farthing tokens offer evidence of variations and designs – including inscriptions 'Fidei defensor' and 'Regit unus utroque' (one king rules all); but without surviving examples we cannot be sure that all these coins were minted.[140] So, apart from the new inscription on the otherwise traditional angel, suggestive of a royal appeal to the people during the war years of the early reign, the simple bust with arms of the four kingdoms remained the pattern throughout much of the reign.[141]

After 1642 the need to represent the king on coins faced new challenges, and crisis gave a new urgency that produced, as we shall see, coins of more variety and inscriptions of polemical topicality.[142] For the earlier period, Charles appears, with the exception of the refinements he ordered to his portrait image, to have rested content with the replication and circulation in coin of the simple message of his divinity. Hindsight might suggest that, as with other media of royal representation, with his coins Charles did not soon enough seize the opportunity they presented, especially as a medium totally in his control, for explaining, justifying and winning support for his actions.

42 Silver coin depicting Charles I on horseback with arms on reverse.

As Charles succeeded to his throne in 1625, the greatest public monument to Stuart rule was unquestionably the Banqueting House at Whitehall, the building which James I had commissioned as the site for the celebration of his son's marriage into the imperial dynasty of the Habsburgs. If, as seems likely, James I, like his architect, had envisioned the building that became a Presence Chamber for the new Stuart dynasty as but the first stage in the rebuilding of the old Tudor palace, his ambitions were unfulfilled. Though he also was to have them frustrated, Charles undoubtedly inherited those ambitions and dreamed of building in London the kind of ordered royal palace he had so much admired in the Escorial outside Madrid.[143] His marriage to a French bride would have added to that ambition, for Henrietta Maria was daughter of a French queen who had planned the Champs-Elysées and built the Palais du Luxembourg and herself took an avid interest in architecture. Within a month of Charles's accession, it was reported that Whitehall was to be rebuilt 'with much beauty and state and that suddenly'.[144] The distractions and expenses of the wars with Spain and France, however, scuppered any such plans; and it was not until after the peace of 1629 that Charles, as he embarked on his personal rule, returned to thoughts of the public edifice which would represent the majesty of the Stuarts to his subjects and the world. Two drawings attributed to Isaac de Caus, who had worked with Inigo Jones on the Banqueting House, have been dated to the early 1630s and suggest that the rebuilding was an early priority of the years of peace.[145] Financial exigencies offer the likeliest explanation for the plans not being translated into action. Still, in 1638 Charles's ambitions remained; and a group of drawings in the name of Jones's assistant John Webb attest to their scale and reach.[146] Webb designed a nearly square building to be entered by a new road from the riverside and new royal lodgings overlooking the park. If Webb's drawings signalled a renewed plan of action, the outbreak of rebellion in Scotland, followed by civil war, put paid to that. But even in captivity at Carisbrooke in 1647, Charles discussed rebuilding Whitehall with Jones and Webb; as well as the insight it offers into his view of his political position, this reveals how far for Charles the project of a Stuart palace was related to the projection of Stuart kingship.[147]

Lacking the resources to rebuild, Charles was confined to making minor alterations to his own and the queen's lodgings in Whitehall.[148] What he did complete, of course, was his father's project of 1621 – by commissioning Rubens to paint canvases for the Banqueting House ceiling. Though the famous series of paintings, figuring the apotheosis of James, glorified his predecessor, it was Charles I, seated under them, who was presented as the heir to Great Britain's Solomon and to Stuart divine kingship; and it was Charles I, enthroned under a panel depicting the benefits of James I's government, whose beneficence was represented.[149] The series of canvases that culminates artistically in 'The Depiction of Benefits of James I's Government' leads the viewer also to the continuation of those benefits (not least of peace and plenty) in the person of Charles enthroned – the image and memory of James made flesh.

Though his grandiose plans for a new royal palace were thwarted, contemporaries did not fail to remark the architectural innovations and enhancements of the reign or Charles's representation of his rule in brick and in stone. In his comparison of the king with King Alfred, for example, Robert Powell wrote of 'the magnificent decoration of his structures and edifices in all symmetrical proportions . . . [that] do far surpass all former times; they are . . . so patterned by the most glorious architectures of all Europe that a man would think Italy translated into England'.[150] While panegyric led Powell to some exaggeration, the architectural manifestations of the second Stuart's rule were evident to all. After he presented it to Henrietta Maria in 1626, Somerset House was extensively enhanced and improved, with the building of a chapel and closet, a cabinet room, a theatre and water stairs.[151] Similarly, extensions and improvements were made to Oatlands.[152] Most importantly, Jones from 1630 to 1640 worked on completing the Queen's House at Greenwich, initiated by Anne of Denmark in 1616 and largely abandoned on her death three years later.[153] Influenced by Scammozi, the palace was Jones's most significant royal commission for Charles I and was fashioned as an antechamber to Stuart kingship, Greenwich often serving as the arrival point to London for dignitaries who had disembarked at Dover.[154]

Perhaps, however, the most significant representation of Charles's architectural patronage was the work the king financed, as well as encouraged, on the rebuilding of St Paul's Cathedral. The king not only held strong beliefs about the importance of maintaining and beautifying the fabric of churches, he considered the cathedral to be God's palace and so regarded its maintenance as a principal duty of his lieutenant on earth, as well as a means of publicizing his divinity and piety.[155] St Paul's had fallen into near ruin by the end of the sixteenth century and in 1620 James appointed a commission, with Inigo Jones as a member, to raise money for its refurbishment.[156] Little was realized, however, until Charles and William Laud pressed contributions from the city, then in 1633 the nation at large, and ordered full records to be kept of contributors – and non-contributors. By September 1634, such contributions had brought in over £30,000 for the work; and Charles himself promised to meet the cost of a new west front. Work began the next year and continued until the civil war, by which time over £80,000 had been spent on restorations that took in all but the repair of the central tower, and which gave the cathedral, as Hollar's engravings reveal, a classical west portico as well as a handsome refurbishment of the Gothic structure.[157] That Charles regarded the project as self-representation as well as the glorification of God is evident from the court masque of 1637 *Britannia Triumphans*, for one of the scenes of which Inigo Jones made St Paul's a centrepiece of the back shutter.[158] In the case of St Paul's,

43 'English Houses with London and the Thames afar off', shutter scene by Inigo Jones from *Britannia Triumphans*, 1637.

Charles evidently also enjoyed a favourable popular response. Despite some grumbling, money for the work came in, and in 1638 a tract had St Paul sing lines that clearly identify the renovation of the cathedral with the public image of the king:

As famous as I ever have bin,
I now shall receive my high renown
And all my honours return'd me agen
I am old Paul of London Town
Now God preserve our Gracious King,
Lord Mayor and the Aldermen
which have bin pleas'd in this noble thing
to give old Paul a new Trimming agen.[159]

One of the trimmings given to St Paul's was a bust of King Charles that was probably set up on the cornice of the new portico on the eve of the troubles that led to civil war.[160] During Charles's reign, for the first time, public statuary and sculptures became important media for displaying the royal image to a broad public. From his youth, Charles had taken an interest in sculpture and part of the attraction for him of the Mantuan collection he anxiously pursued and secured was the sculpture as well as the paintings.[161] As with all his aesthetic interests, this love was not simply that of a connoisseur. Sculptures and statues, standing not just in the interiors of palaces to which elites had access but outside in gardens, displayed the king's collection and taste to all. More significantly, classical sculptures, like the paintings of the emperors which lined the walls leading to Van Dyck's portrait of Charles I on horseback, associated the monarch with past imperial greatness and figured him, as it were, in an imperial succession from antiquity. The observation is well made in the 1634 edition of Henry Peacham's *The Complete Gentleman*. Remarking that 'ever since his coming to the crown' Charles had 'testified a royal liking' for ancient statues, he considered that truly he had 'caus[ed] a whole army of old foreign emperors, captains and senators all at once to land on his coasts to come and do him homage and attend him in his palaces of St James and Somerset House'.[162] In the light of such comment, we can appreciate how the copies of classical statues which Charles ordered from the French sculptor Hubert Le Sueur represented the king as well as their ancient subjects.[163]

But, in the most literal sense, statues powerfully represented the king and, standing in public places, almost served as viceroys of royal authority. From early in his reign, busts of Charles were evidently strategically placed to provide a symbolic presence of the king and the importance the regime attached to them is nowhere better illustrated than in the case of the royal bust placed on the Square Tower at Portsmouth – the major garrison town, port of embarkation of the La Rochelle and Isle de Rhe fleets, and site of the assassination of the royal favourite, the Duke of Buckingham. On 22 October 1635, the Governor of Portsmouth, Viscount Wimbledon, wrote to the city authorities to protest about the treatment of the statue. Reminding them of the honour the king had done them in placing his statue there, he upbraided them that

> Those signs of your inns do not only obscure his Majesty's figure but outface it, as [presently] you yourselves may well perceive. Therefore I desire you all that you will see that such an inconveniency be not suffered . . . for that any disgrace offered his Majesty's figure is as much as to himself. To which end I will and command all the officers and soldiers not to pass it without putting off their hats.[164]

To Wimbledon, that is, a statue of the king performed in a similar way to the chair of state in the Presence: as the representation of the ruler to which homage was paid, as if to himself. Seen in this light, statues of Charles in the provinces as well as the capital should be considered not only representations of – but representatives of – the king.

Charles sustained a circle of sculptors, of whom Le Sueur was the most notable, to execute his bust, of which several of what must have been many more variants survive. From survivals, David Howarth identified five types, in marble and bronze, of busts of the king in classical dress, in armour with a helmet, and crowned with an ermine cape and wearing the Order of the Garter. As well as at Portsmouth, examples of these were placed at Bristol in 1633–4 and at the market cross at Chichester, perhaps about 1637, where (it has been suggested) the bust served to add royal support to the cathedral and close in their struggle with the mayor and corporation.[165] It is likely that Wentworth, who was the king's viceroy in Ireland, displayed a bust of Charles at his official residence at Dublin Castle; and Archbishop Laud, in his capacity as Vice-Chancellor of the university, donated statues of the king to the Bodleian Library and his college, St John's, at Oxford, at a time when his reforms of the university were very much part of the wider programme of social reform he and Wentworth called 'Thorough'.[166] To celebrate the completion of the project and the installation of Rubens's ceiling canvases,

44 Bronze statue of Charles I, St John's College, Oxford.

Charles commissioned Le Sueur to make sculptures of himself and his father for the Banqueting House in 1635. Thenceforth, visitors to Whitehall passed beneath the bronze image of Charles I as they entered to face the royal throne.[167]

Following the Earl of Portland, who commissioned an equestrian statue of the king for his garden at Roehampton, and Laud, whose Le Sueurs of Charles and Henrietta Maria greeted the royal couple on their visit to Oxford, full-length statues of the king were placed at prominent positions in London and Westminster, at Greenwich and outside the capital.[168] As well as the statue in the niche of his portico at St Paul's, a statue of the king joined a series of English monarchs at the Royal Exchange, the commercial hub of the city, and statues of the king and queen facing each other were put up in Queen Street.[169] Another of the king was set up at St Paul's, Covent Garden in the new piazza developed, with royal approval, by the Earl of Bedford and before the church designed by Inigo Jones, the king's architect, in 1631. 'Thus the king stood before what to some was the only true [because post-Reformation] church in London, and in front of the most elegant and commodious square in the kingdom.'[170] In 1638, Charles also commissioned and paid for full-length statues of himself and his father for the new choir screen at Winchester Cathedral, which Jones designed and with which the king was evidently involved.[171] It is tempting to suggest that his decision to stand in effigy alongside his father in 1638, at a time when (in England as well as Scotland) some were accusing Charles of radical innovations in ecclesiastical policy, was more than an act of piety. That the king was still concerned with the erection of his statue at St Paul's in September 1641, as the members of the Long Parliament returned to their second (revolutionary) session, only underlines the importance Charles attached to these most public representations of his regality in bronze and in stone.[172]

It has been suggested that, for all the use he made of him, Charles recognized the deficiencies of Le Sueur, and the royal couple went to great lengths to secure the services of Bernini for the bust of Charles which he considered a treasure of his collection.[173] The importance of most of the public statues for the king was political rather than aesthetic. And it was their all too effective political performance that Charles I's opponents quickly grasped, especially after regicide in 1649. While Royalists tried to secure them, bury them, and preserve them as sacred relics, republicans smashed statues of Charles I; and in the case of that at the Exchange they ceremonially decapitated it.[174] In such actions, we are returned to Viscount Wimbledon's orders to Portsmouth. Like the governor of his garrison, Charles's enemies recognized that public statues did more than represent royal authority: they stood as symbols, attendants (to use Peacham's word) and agents of majesty, the very sight of which awed subjects into obedience. Charles I has been accused of paying too little attention to the arts of public communication. In the first programme of statues of early modern monarchy, he did the next best thing to presenting himself throughout the land: he erected the sign of his kingship and of himself at the sites of holy worship and public congress.

CHAPTER 7

PERFORMING SACRED KINGSHIP

I

As well as the dazzling collection of paintings, on his visit to Madrid Prince Charles was undoubtedly attracted to the formality and decorum of the Habsburg court which contrasted with the easy familiarity of his father's. As we shall see, one of his earliest acts on succeeding as king was a reformation of court ceremony and of the rituals of kingship. In his court, as in his church, Charles placed the greatest importance on rituals and public performances as the outward signs of divine power and presence, and as the means by which reverence for authority was sustained and enhanced. Arguably, no early modern English sovereign devoted more attention to rituals great and small – to coronations, funerals and state entries but also to the daily performance of majesty, be it dining or processing to chapel.

Central, of course, to the function and efficacy of any rituals is audience, and over the last two decades or so a historiographical consensus has argued that, for all his attention to ritual performances, Charles enacted them not on a public stage but behind the closed doors of his palaces and before the circumscribed communities of courtly elites. 'That between 1625 and 1640 Charles I systematically distanced himself from his subjects is common knowledge' – at least to Dr Judith Richards, who posited in an influential article that the king's 'withdrawal from public ceremonials, public displays, public spectacles of various kinds' undermined his kingship.[1] Indeed, she concluded, Charles I 'withdrew in . . . many fields from the practice of kingship' until, after 1640, circumstances compelled him to take action to win support.[2] Though Richards draws useful attention to the subject of early Stuart ritual and display, her argument, which passes over a wealth of evidence that counters it, has misled a generation of scholars. Charles was not only temperamentally inclined to elaborate ritual; as his insistence on conformity to Anglican rites suggests, he was fully aware of its larger public purpose in binding communities and supporting beliefs. Nor was the second Stuart distanced from his people. Rather, from the eve of his succession, Charles used a variety of state occasions to present and re-present himself to the people, both in his capital and through the length and breadth of his kingdom.

Certainly, Charles's early experience of his people could only have encouraged a positive attitude to public presentation and display. When he returned from Spain in October 1623, making his way from Portsmouth he met in London with 'such unlimitable and violent inundations of joy that the people . . . seemed to lose their own being and forget that they were themselves; men, women and children made but one consort and the music of that consort sounded nothing but the prince is come, our Charles is come.'[3] Along with the bells that vied with the shouts to welcome the prince, 'so infinite were the bonfires, so costly and high flaming' that night seemed like daylight.[4] A reporter felt sure that the memory of the day would be imprinted on the spectators for ever and urged 'let one red letter day be added to our calendar and an anniversary held with thanksgiving to God'.[5] Though the people's joy owed much to the failure of the prince's mission to bring home a Spanish bride, the relief at Charles's safety and public expression of love for him were genuine enough and cannot have been lost on him. As we have seen, Charles, during the years of difficulties with parliaments, appealed in declarations to a wider public which, he felt, was loyal and loving. Far from retreating from the public, during his early months as a monarch he took up a prominent place on the public stage.

The first public ritual of a new reign was the funeral of the royal predecessor. Though, traditionally, the new monarch did not present himself at the obsequies for his predecessor, the funeral represented the new as much as the old ruler: it was an occasion to mark dynastic continuity but also the first occasion on which to publicize a personal style.[6] The funeral Charles I staged for his father was very much a homage to the representational vocabularies and signs of the first Stuart. The sermon was rhetorically skilful and long as a fitting tribute to James I's faith in words; a statue of James as Solomon stood in the abbey as a representation of James's personal image; the hearse designed by Inigo Jones, who had built the Jacobean Banqueting House, evoked imperial precedents.[7] But, as much as a tribute to James, this funeral was very much a presentation of Charles I to his subjects. Quite unusually, Charles followed James's hearse as chief mourner.[8] Bishop Williams in his sermon moved from the effigy of the deceased king to another living, not 'artificial representation': 'I mean that statue . . . that walked on foot this day after the hearse . . . a breathing statue of all his virtues . . . a like representation of the virtues of king James in the person of King Charles our gracious sovereign'.[9] As Jennifer Woodward has demonstrated, Charles's role in the offering ceremony in the funeral service underlined the first succession of an adult male heir for more than a century and announced the establishment of the Stuart dynasty. It also, of course, placed Charles at the centre of the spectacle: as divine successor and as a person. And indeed the ritual forms and style of the funeral appear to have been determined by Charles's own preference. For the first time, the effigy of a monarch (one who had taken little interest in visual representation) was laid in state and attended as though the king were still living, in the French style.[10] Moreover, candlesticks and tapers placed by the bed of state added a novel ceremonialism, what some might have considered a Catholic dimension, to the trappings.[11] Charles, however, was not just indulging his personal preferences and taste for ceremony. He planned a funeral procession on a grand scale that would, he hoped, display the ideal social order that he came to the throne with the ambition to re-establish. For all the depleted state of the royal coffers, the funeral cost £50,000.[12] A cavalcade of over 5,000 (Chamberlain estimated it at 9,000), several times as many as the attendance at Elizabeth's funeral, processed at night, the way lit by over 3,000 torches. Special provision was made for spectators: the Earl of Arundel, as Earl Marshal, arranged the erection of a scaffold in the tiltyard; and, as well as the guard, fifty men were employed to keep the passage clear.[13] As the cavalcade made its way, officers of arms uncovered their heads in each town and village. 'The procession was expected to attract attention'.[14] And, it has been suggested, Charles endeavoured to use that public audience to signal that there would be no increased favour to Catholics under his rule. Charles banned Catholic nobles from attending in order, the Venetian envoy believed, to 'show rigour about religion, to the satisfaction of the general' (that is of most people).[15] Bad weather, and some unseemly vying for precedence, meant that not all went according to plan. However, the cost, scale, attention to detail and ritual forms of James's funeral should be seen, as contemporaries viewed them, as a major public self-presentation by a new ruler who certainly did not on this occasion keep a distance from his subjects. Even while the preparations for the funeral of his father were under way, Charles was awaiting the arrival on English soil of his bride, who set out before James's interment.

On 13 May, Secretary Conway reported musicians being sent to Kent for the queen's reception at Dover, while the news-writer John Chamberlain informed Sir Dudley Carleton of the 'great preparations for shows and pageants' to welcome Henrietta Maria.[16] As contemporaries appear to have recognized, in 1625 Charles's marriage was as central to his self-presentation as king as was his advertisement of his Stuart succession. On 13 June, he sped for Dover where, after delays, his bride had landed and been received at the castle. Though the first meeting was in the Privy Chamber, the 'beholders' saw how the king, in response to Henrietta Maria's kneeling before him, 'took her up in his arms, kissed her again and gave her those dear expressions of a never changing love'.[17] As they left Dover for the Downs, noblemen and women attended; as they travelled to Canterbury, all the way was strewn with green rushes and roses, as well as with many spectators who had come to see the first royal bride to arrive in a century. At Canterbury, John Finch recalled the recent loss of a glorious and good king, before hailing Charles as the heir to all his father's virtues.[18] Comparing him to a legendary ruler who also had a French queen, Henry V, Finch praised Charles's connection with his people. Though from their thrones princes enjoyed a perspective view, he argued, it was 'when they descend from themselves and grow acquainted with the hearts and affections of their subjects' that they saw 'at hand and not at distance'.[19] Finch lauded the son of a king who had, in the last parliament, 'become the son of his kingdom'.[20] In Charles, he continued, the people had a king whose 'glory and grace ... so filled our souls with joy'.[21] In joining with France, he doubled the joy as 'the two royal branches of Charlemagne and Hugh Capell are now grown into one tree'.[22] Leaving Canterbury, the royal couple progressed to Rochester where, in the time allowed, the mayor, magistrates and citizens gave them a noble welcome before they left for Gravesend to embark for London.

Their arrival in the capital brought out a 'throng of spectators', some of whom, in their eagerness to get a privileged view, overturned a ship in dry dock, on to which they had clambered.[23] Far from distancing themselves from the crowd, Charles and Henrietta Maria responded to the welcome with grace. 'To every lady that came to kiss her hand', the queen 'bowed herself down and kissed their cheeks'.[24] And 'by the way, during all their long passage, both the king and queen stood publicly in the open barge and not only discovered themselves to every honest and cheerful beholder, but also with all royal affability and grace distributed their favours to all those which came to admire them'.[25] There was 'not a living soul', a reporter related, who did not conclude that majesty and love, the king and his people, were conjoined in happiness.[26] The formal celebration of the marriage itself also involved public spectacle. Though only the few were admitted to the Banqueting House, which was sumptuously adorned for the ceremony of reading the articles, the splendour and the dress and jewels of the French ambassadors and English nobles were 'such like as never before hath been seen in England'.[27] Most importantly, fulfilling a seemingly timeless wish of the English, 'the king kissed the queen in presence of the whole people'.[28] As he was to do on canvas, Charles, from the moment his wife landed on English soil, made his marriage a very public expression of his rule.

Many must have hoped and expected that a formal state entry and coronation would soon follow; and Judith Richards and others have made much of Charles's decision not to undertake the usual public procession to Westminster.[29] Evidence suggests, however, that, far from being opposed to the idea, Charles himself entertained it. On 18 December 1625, Sir Benjamin Rudyard informed Francis Nethersole that 'the king intends his entry and coronation to be at the beginning of the next term', adding 'and presently upon that a parliament'.[30] In January William, Earl of Exeter, asking to be excused on grounds of health, assured Conway that he and his wife 'had all things ready, both for the entry and the coronation'.[31] It may be that the plague which caused parliament to be moved to Oxford led Charles to avoid the formal entry and choose to go by water to Westminster; but plague had not prevented James from making his civic entry a year after his coronation, and the city made preparations for triumphal arches in the expectation that they would be needed.[32] Why did the entry not take place? Ambassadors' references to 'the scarcity of money' may provide a clue.[33] Given that Henrietta Maria allegedly sat in darkness to conceal the shabbiness of her quarters in 1626, the grand display which the royal couple would have been expected to make may not have been supportable by the royal coffers.[34] A third explanation is war. In the early months of 1626, Charles, as well as being at war with Spain, was, not least as a consequence of his resolution to aid the Huguenots at La Rochelle, on the brink of hostilities with France.[35] Such a situation made a triumphant state entry inappropriate and complicated Charles's relationship with his wife and the arrangements for his coronation. Whatever the explanation, it does not appear likely that the king and queen had suddenly taken against the public. Indeed, on 19 January, only days before the appointed coronation, the queen 'went publicly through this town', Chamberlain reported, 'in a rich embroidered carosse . . . from Westminster to the Tower where she had a banquet and so with a peal of ordnance came back the same way'.[36] Significantly he then added: 'This passage was thought might excuse the solemn entry but that is put off till May when the king meant to go into Scotland and to be crowned.'[37] Far from eschewing public procession, then, Charles was planning a double ceremony to accompany his coronation in two kingdoms. It was not to be.

One problem was Henrietta Maria herself. The queen's bishop had wanted to preside at her coronation, but George Abbot, Archbishop of Canterbury denied permission.[38] As a consequence, Henrietta Maria refused to take part in a Protestant ceremony, leaving Charles to be crowned alone.[39] It may be that for this reason, too, the coronation on Candlemas Day went ahead without a show which would have drawn attention to the queen's absence. Though it lacked the element of public procession, the coronation of Charles was an important ritual occasion. The king was crowned on the day of the Purification of the Virgin, and attired not in the usual imperial purple but in white – the colour of purity and innocence.[40] In a service devised by Bishop William Laud, which later became the subject of controversy, Charles was instituted with ceremonies and prayers that, Peter Heylyn was later to suggest, ascribed to him great ecclesiastical power.[41] There is no evidence that in 1626 Charles's coronation caused discontent. Yet, whatever his reasons for forgoing it, the absence of a formal state entry, an occasion for king and people to advertise their love for each other, may have been a miscalculation. In later, different circumstances Charles finally made a triumphal entry into London.[42] Long before then, he fulfilled his plan to be crowned in Scotland – a progress and a spectacular public occasion that must surely discredit arguments that by 1626 Charles had resolved to distance himself or to prefer privacy to public display. For, as well as the long progress to reach Edinburgh, to which we will return, Charles, in 1633, made the formal entry into his Scottish capital that he had not made into London. Travelling without his queen, Charles was greeted as he entered the city as a 'prince so much longed for', as 'Monarch of all hearts'.[43] In Edinburgh, triumphal arches, like those through which James had processed in London in 1604, staged pageants of Mars and Minerva, Mercury and Apollo, of Saturn and Jove. As entertainment and tableaux figured Charles as the protector of Justice and Religion trampling Superstition, as emperor, as a Sun and herald of a golden age, verses praised the 'heroic mind' of a prince 'gracious, affable, divine . . . wise, just [and] valiant', who subjected himself to his own laws.[44] As the people shouted their acclamations for 'Great Jove's Vice-gerent', panegyrists prophesied that 'thy people's love thy greatness shall up-reare'.[45]

Civic pageants were not unqualified panegyric and in placing a figure of Buchanan among the worthies of Scotland the burghers recalled a Presbyterian republican whose views James I had spent a lifetime countering.[46] Similarly, the injunction to remember Elizabeth of Bohemia and 'her children young' was at least implicit criticism of the pacifist policies of the personal rule.[47] Yet the welcome and love shown to a Charles whose presence had been long awaited were real enough: when Walter Forbes told his king 'I will reape more joy from this thy comming here, / Then e'er *Penelope* of *Ulisses* deare', he spoke for many.[48] The people delighted in seeing their sovereign, and Charles evidently took no less pleasure in the expressions of love he received. As the Venetian envoy reported, 'His Majesty was highly delighted with the affection which, he himself writes, surpassed all belief and extended to all ranks'.[49] His return to Greenwich might have offered an opportunity to carry out his earlier plan of state entries to both capitals in the same procession. Indeed, on 6 August, Gussoni, the Venetian envoy, seems to have been expecting some such event. But, he reported, 'His Majesty's entry into this city will be delayed for some months still. An idea is current that as the crowned king of Scotland, he will have to make a public state entry here also, to be celebrated by arrangements and functions which the people are here devising'.[50] For whatever reason, perhaps the time of year, Charles entertained no such plan and, shortly after his return from Scotland, hurried off on his summer progress.

It was to be several years before Gussoni's prediction of a state entry was fulfilled; and during those years there were other opportunities for public ceremony that were not taken. Though, about 1638, an establishment was provided for Charles as Prince of Wales, he was not, perhaps because he was still deemed too young, formally invested as prince before the civil war.[51] The later 1630s, however, were not years devoid of public spectacle. In 1637, for example, a crowd gathered for the reception of Alkand Javror Ben Abdella, the ambassador from Morocco.[52] Importantly, Charles used the occasion of the visit (which was to cement a trading agreement) to show off his new flagship, *The Sovereign of the Seas*, the pride of the ship money fleet, which George Glover described as 'the eighth wonder of the world'.[53] It was probably at this time, too, that Charles authorized a *True Description of the Sovereign* by Thomas Heywood, who not only ranked Charles with the great naval commanders of England but claimed that 'in this last incomparable structure, he hath made an inimitable precedent for all the kings and potentates of the Christian world'.[54] The public launch and display of *The Sovereign of the Seas* in 1637 lent powerful support to the Caroline regime. The figurehead of Edgar, the first absolute monarch of the island according to Heywood, pointed to Charles as 'his true and undoubted successor'.[55] Other carved figures of Counsel, Care and Industry, Strength, Virtue and Victory advertised the royal virtues, while the sheer massive presence of this vessel, unprecedented in its size, stood as a symbol of England's revived naval strength and of the fruits of ship money, the legal right of the king to which had just been confirmed in Hampden's case.[56] The thousands that gathered to see *The Sovereign* with the Moroccan ambassador on the eve of 5 November were probably no less struck than the Venetian envoy by the size and 'marvellous ingenuity' of the vessel, which was launched as Charles was considering a more militant foreign policy in support of his sister.[57]

The occasion of the grandest ceremonial of the 1630s was one not entirely welcome to the king. In October 1638, Marie de Medicis, a semi-exile from her native France, came to England to visit her daughter and to garner her support for her opposition to Louis XIII's chief minister, Richelieu. When he was still in treaty with France, the arrival of the queen mother constituted something of an embarrassment, which was compounded by the suspicion that she represented popish counsels at a time when Charles needed support for the campaign against the Scots.[58] Despite these difficulties, the arrival of a French queen necessitated a grand public reception and Charles, whatever his misgivings, ensured that she was received with magnificence. Moreover, though the main account of her entertainment seems too favourable, it appears that many came out to view Marie de Medicis's train, from her landing at Harwich to her conduct to Whitehall.[59] As her open coach travelled from Harwich, crowds lined the streets; at Colchester, the bonfires and acclamations of public joy caused, it was said, even the most melancholy to lift their spirits.[60] On 8 November, Charles rode from London to meet her and escort her back to the capital where, along with 6,000 troops, the London livery companies lined her route.[61] According to our reporter, the balconies were filled with 'an infinity of people' and those celebrating on the streets were too numerous to count.[62] As a formal procession of trumpets, Gentlemen Pensioners and Sergeants at Arms led the king and queen mother, the reporter praised 'la pompe et la magnificence de cette entrée si belle'; and, seeing the royal pair in their open coach was led to think of Sybilla visiting her son Neptune and their promenade in an open chariot.[63] While many harboured misgivings about the arrival of the queen at a sensitive time, several references to the public joy at her entry ('le concert de l'allegresse publique') suggest that ordinary Londoners appreciated the magnificent show as Charles and Henrietta Maria escorted Marie de Medici to St James's Palace before riding back to Whitehall.[64] That night, as

45 *Histoire de L'entrée de la Reyne Mere du Roy Tres-Chrestien, dans la Grande-Bretaigne* by Jean Puget de la Serre, 1639.

fireworks lit the sky, the crowd, which then, as today, loved these entertainments, sang and danced in the streets and drank healths to the royal family till the sun rose.[65] It may be that, while the thought of the queen and her mother celebrating mass at Somerset House led some to panic and prayer, to ordinary folk her arrival provided occasion for the public display of regal magnificence which was expected of sovereigns, and which had not been as much in evidence in recent years.[66]

In 1637, at a sermon at the assizes in Lincoln, a preacher spoke of the ceremonies that made authority 'have the more due valuation from the people'.[67] If (and this is more open to debate than has been assumed) Charles had not sufficiently appreciated the support that ceremony gave to sovereignty, it would seem that the events of 1639 and 1640 rapidly enlightened him. For, from 1639, a barrage of Scottish propaganda pamphlets circulated criticism of the king and of monarchical government generally to the people of England. As we have seen, Charles, whatever his preference for silence, felt compelled to respond: to counter Scots opposition and put his case to the people.[68] With the same intent, from 1640 the king took the theatre of regality on to the streets, both to display his authority and to 'have the more due valuation from the people' which was vital to maintaining it. The meeting of the first parliament in eleven years, in April 1640, seems to have been preceded by a formal procession which brought 'comfort' to all loyal subjects. Indeed, illustrated with a woodcut of Charles on horseback, crowned and in full state robes in procession, a loyalist broadside described the order of the cavalcade almost as a symbol of the unity of the king with his nobles and subjects. The author, M.P., described the heralds and trumpets, the councillors and judges, the nobles and barons, 'everyone in order', 'in fit accoutrement', processing 'with stately pace', finally coming to King Charles – 'who made the show compleat'. Charles, riding 'in state to open sight' and accompanied by his Gentlemen Pensioners, spared 'no cost . . . to grace the parliament' which the author enjoined similarly to grace and support the king. Here, in a ballad sung to the tune of 'Triumph and Joy', royal ritual is presented as symbolizing the unity of the commonweal and the ceremony is represented in order to gain popular support for Charles.[69] Though the Short Parliament, far from fulfilling the author's expectations, was rapidly to end in failure, we should not conclude that royal display had been ineffective in winning public support. Indeed, increasingly after 1640, Charles was appealing, with some success, directly to his people – in ritual forms no less than in words.

In the autumn of 1641, Charles finally realized his early plan to combine a royal visit to Scotland with a state entry into his English capital. Both were doubtless driven by the king's desperate need to win support, but Judith Richards's implication that they were too little, too late may again need to be challenged. The leaders of the opposition to Charles in the Long Parliament were certainly nervous about the support the king's presence in Scotland might bring him; and the evidence suggests that, even at this late stage, there was an abundance of popular loyalty which the king could yet draw upon both there and in England. Sensing a turn in the mood of the people, the Venetian envoy paid close attention to the king's grand entry into London, observing that 'the pomp and circumstance . . . give rise to hopes that the aspect of affairs here may yet change . . .'.[70] The account of the 'magnificence and honourable triumph' by the mayor, Richard Gurney, related how a party of aldermen and sheriffs, with seventy-two men in scarlet, rode to Theobalds to conduct Charles to Moorfields.[71] Thence, 500 members of livery companies in crimson velvet with attendants assembled with the mayor to escort Charles into the city.[72] At Kingsland, the city dignitaries joined with the dukes, earls, viscounts and barons who had ridden to attend on Charles, Henrietta Maria, the prince, the Duke of York, the other royal children and the Elector Palatine to begin the entry procession. All along the route, the magistrates and guild officers lined the way to greet the king. 'The spectators', Taylor reports, 'of all degrees, sexes, ages and sizes were innumerable'; and, he added, with pardonable exaggeration, 'the banks, hedges, highways, streets, stalls, and windows were al embroidered with millions of people'.[73] As he had in 1625, and in Scotland in 1633, Charles responded to popular expressions of love. 'A short distance out' of the capital, Giustinian reports, 'the king left his coach and mounted a horse . . . in order to show himself better in his passage through the city. When he entered, he was received everywhere with universal acclamations, while he was careful to thank the people by gesture and speech, thus causing a renewal of the shouts of welcome.'[74]

Coming to Cheapside, Charles broke with tradition in a carefully orchestrated gesture of compliment to the city. 'He alighted first at the Guildhall, a thing never done by any of his predecessors, where he had a brave reception.'[75] While the king and queen dined, the 500 horsemen attended in St Paul's churchyard, whence, after dinner, they led the royal party in a torchlit procession back to Whitehall. As the bells of over 120 churches pealed an accompaniment to this second stage of the state entry, there were 'no failings of expression of love and loyalty by the people as appeared by their shouts and acclamations, as also . . . with drinking of innumerable healths to his Majesty' – for which the king (who also restored Londonderry as a gift of thanks to the city) gave his warm thanks and embraced the mayor.[76] Though it had come late, the royal presence yet made a powerful impact on the capital. The mayor, adding this magnificent occasion to the catalogue of civic entertainments given to rulers in former times, recalled James I's entry on his return from Scotland.[77] Nor were the political sentiments so different. Verses presented to Charles at his reception praised God for him and urged 'Let's love and serve him, with our Prayers and Powers.'[78] Pointing to the people lifted from dejection to joy by his presence, the poet asserted:

Hee's come to salve this Kingdoms discontents,
To cure all wrenches, fractures, spraines and rents,
. . .
God's Great Lieutenant, foure great Kingdomes King
No doubt but he those mischifes downe shall ding.

It is hardly surprising that some MPs were 'alarmed by these demonstrations . . . being especially fearful that the support of the people may fail them.'[79] Indeed, Giustinian believed that the popular support Charles had attracted was leading some desperate MPs to draw up a paper of 'all the disorders which have taken place in the government' – that is, the document we know as the Grand Remonstrance.[80] In what had become a fierce contest to win popular support, the Grand Remonstrance was a desperate gamble which – *just* – won for the opponents of Charles a vital round.[81] But to suggest that Charles had lost through a failure of royal ceremony and display is surely mistaken. It may be that, during the 1630s, the king could have taken more opportunities to affirm popular support through ritual and display. Still, however, in 1641, Charles was, as the entertainment described him, the sun of the commonweal, the vigorous life of his kingdom, and 'the show', to which all others were 'spectators.'[82]

II

Soon after his succession, Charles, as we shall see, set about reforming the daily protocols and ceremonies of court life, such as dining and processing to chapel, so as to emphasize the sanctity of kingship. The most obvious occasion on which that sanctity was ritually displayed and performed before subjects was in the ceremony of conferring the royal touch to cure the king's evil – scrofula. Given his religious preferences and his emphasis on the sacred status of kingship, one would expect the ceremonies of touching to be of the greatest importance to Charles I, as the historian of *The Royal Touch*, Marc Bloch, believed it was.[83] More recently, however, Judith Richards has identified a score of royal proclamations restricting and postponing the times when subjects might obtain access to the king to be healed; and has argued that the royal favour in this respect was extended to only a few of the greatest and that ordinary subjects were denied the regal cure.[84] Richards is right to draw attention to the proclamations that Charles issued twice a year compared to the one on the king's evil published by James during his reign; but from their number draws conclusions that are too simple. In the first place, the fact that Charles so often addressed this subject suggests that, rather than indifferent, he was concerned about the royal touch and all it signified. And what Richards reads as restrictions and limitations in those texts should rather be interpreted as another manifestation of Charles's obsession with order and regulations, especially of matters he regarded as central to the dignity of kingship. Thirdly, the experience at the beginning of the reign of plague, and subsequent recurrent outbreaks and endemic scares and fears of it, led the king to favour a fixed timetable for touching that avoided the riskiest seasons of infection. On 17 May 1625, only days after his father's funeral, Charles, amid plague, ordered that none report to court to be touched before Michaelmas; the next month he issued an explanatory proclamation to regulate the ceremony.[85] Reminding the people that, as the new king, he had enjoyed as much success as his predecessors in healing, and underlining that he was 'as ready and willing as any king or queen of this realm ever was . . . to relieve the distresses . . . of his good subjects', Charles also insisted, as he was to do so often, that 'in this as in all other things, order is to be observed and fit times . . . to be appointed'.[86] Whereas traditionally the times for healing had been Easter and Whitsun, the king ordered that henceforth they should be Easter and Michaelmas, 'as times more convenient both for the temperature of the season and in respect of any contagion which may happen in the new access to his Majesty's sacred person'.[87] As well as ensuring safety, this order more equally spaced the times between touchings. In a further typically bureaucratic move, Charles also ordered that any coming to court should obtain a certificate from their local minister or JP testifying that they had not been touched before. While later evidence indicates that some attempting multiple visits may have been hoping fraudulently to acquire the 'nobles' (coins or tokens worth 6s. 8d.), in 1625 the prescription was probably intended to ensure that all the newly inspected obtained access.[88] If the proclamation of 18 June outlined the king's intentions to regularize and regulate, not to downplay, the ceremony of touching, it is true that subsequent events and orders disrupted it. Though on 18 June 1626 the proclamation was reissued, evidence suggests that the sick were seeking and perhaps obtaining access at other times.[89] In 1629, the proclamation was again re-published, this time with an order that it be publicly posted in market towns with a command for its observance.[90] That it failed of its purpose is suggested by its reissue the next spring.[91] A probability that, in breach of proclamation, subjects were flocking to the court when the king was on progress is reinforced by the early re-publication of orders in March 1631, repeated in October the same year, at a time of danger of infection.[92] The winter of 1631 and summer of 1632 saw outbreaks of plague in several parts of the country that resulted in royal proclamations now ordering magistrates to restrain 'as many as they shall find travelling . . . to his majesty' before Lent.[93] Though a respite of contagion led Charles to receive those who attended to be touched after Lent, the return of plague in summer led to a reimposition of restrictions.[94]

What the royal orders suggest, then, was a real concern for the traditional royal ceremonial within the context of a necessary regard for safety in time of contagion. Proclamations annually repeated the king's willingness to touch; and when, in the summer of 1632, an impostor named Boisgaudre claimed to cure the king's evil, he was quickly imprisoned for his contempt and affront to royal authority.[95] In 1634, smallpox again caused three postponements of the times of access to be cured – from All Saints, to Christmas, then to Easter – before the summer of 1635 when a proclamation restored the established times and protocols for the rituals of healing.[96] From the mid-1630s, as before, a regular pattern was periodically disrupted by bouts of plague which, despite Richards's suggestion that it was but an excuse, was reason enough to postpone the touchings, as it also led to the postponing of the famous fairs of St Bartholomew and Stourbridge.[97] In 1638, Charles unusually ordered that those coming to be cured first be screened by a local physician, a decree which may have been motivated by the king's personal concern to counter the 'great abuse . . . committed by people who, to gain gold, have counterfeited the Sergeant Surgeon's tokens'; or was perhaps intended to create another level of health precautions, to ensure that they were free of other sickness.[98] However, as much as his precautionary regulation, what needs reaffirming is Charles's continued commitment to touching amidst the Scottish troubles and the preparations for war.

It has been asserted that Charles I touched far more after 1641 when his circumstances necessitated the courting of popular support.[99] While that assertion has yet to be properly explored, the claim that before 1640 Charles neglected this public ritual of sacred kingship must be dismissed. Except when plague interrupted, as it did more in the 1620s and 1630s than in the following decade, the king established two periods of fourteen days each year when his sick subjects were invited to attend for cure.[100] Accounts of the issues of the Tower Mint for the period 1629 to 1636 reveal over £2,400 dispensed from the Exchequer for the gold used for touch tokens.[101] As importantly, the evidence suggests that Charles's subjects continued to flock to be cured, outside as well as within the prescribed times. As well as the evidence of repeated injunctions against this, a proclamation of 1 July 1638 specifically referred to 'the resort of poor people to his court for cure at other times of the year'.[102] The reference to the poor should not pass without comment; for, though it has been suggested that the powerful and well connected alone bypassed the restrictions on times, it appears that even ordinary subjects, who did present a greater risk of infection, got to the king.[103] In 1643, having left his capital, Charles I received a petition 'of divers hundreds of the king's subjects afflicted with . . . the King's evil of which . . . they have no possibility of being cured . . . by reason of his abode at Oxford'.[104] While we should always be cautious of the evidence of silence, no such petition was presented before the civil war. Moreover, the petitioners claim that until the king's remove, 'we poor wretches used to repair at the feast of Easter to receive redress for our infirmities' and that Charles 'never denied to any of [his] suppliant subjects'; they also pleaded for access to be reopened to the king that was before 'freely enjoyed at London'.[105] In touching for the king's evil, Charles had evidently not appeared deficient to his subjects before his forced departure prevented him from sustaining his practice.

No doubts have been raised about Charles's devotion to another ritual of early modern kingship that displayed the sacred as well as the martial facets of regality: the festival of the Garter. Charles was brought up with a devotion to the Order of the Garter which expressed his own values and attachment to the symbols of divine kingship. His mother, Queen Anne, presented him with books on the Garter, to which he doubtless added to make the collection of forty volumes on the order found in Van der Doort's inventory of Charles's goods.[106] When he made his formal entry into Madrid in 1623, Charles dressed in the Spanish fashion but also wore an enamelled Garter badge that exceeded in brightness the watchet ribbon from which it hung, so displaying an English order that could vie for antiquity with the renowned Habsburg Order of the Golden Fleece.[107] The Garter was as important to Charles's public representation as king as it was to his person. A gentleman of the bedchamber informs us that the king put on his George first thing in the morning and never failed to wear it.[108] On the reverse, significantly, was a picture of his wife.[109] Rubens's painting of *St George and the Dragon*, with Charles depicted as the saint, gestures to the chivalric and religious significations the Garter represented.[110] In this canvas, as in masques, Charles stands, with Henrietta Maria, as the champion of innocence over sin. The king's emphasis on the sacred signification was evidenced in the new Garter badge that he ordered, with silver rays copied from the French Order of the Holy Spirit.[111] Charles commissioned several books and paintings of St George, one after Raphael, and one story has it that he offered Van Dyck the colossal sum of £80,000 to adorn the walls of the Banqueting House with scenes of the ceremonies of the Order.[112]

Charles enhanced and publicized the ceremonies of the Garter festival. In 1634, he ordered the knights to donate plate and himself gave a new set for the altar; at the installation of Prince Charles, he gifted two silver flagons.[113] Importantly, in embarking on what the historian of the order, Elias Ashmole, judged to be 'the most complete and absolute reformation of any of his predecessors', Charles placed emphasis on the public rituals of the Garter.[114] In 1629, he revived the custom of the sovereign processing to Windsor on the eve of St George's Day.[115] And during the 1630s, the public procession became ever more extravagant, as, in Ashmole's words, 'the gallantry of attendants began to increase and augment'.[116] *A Brief Description of the Triumphant Show Made by the Rt. Hon. Algernon Percy*, Earl of Northumberland, at his inauguration in 1635, gives some confirmation of the sumptuous magnificence that led a corre-spondent to tell Wentworth, the king's deputy in Ireland, 'The Garter is grown a dear honour; few subjects will be able to follow this pattern.'[117] But this popular ballad account also illustrates the broad interest in this spectacle that 'dazzled' 'common eyes' with the 'lustre of apparel rich/all Silver, Pearle and Gold' which 'did glister through the Strand'.[118] Moreover, as well as the show of the rich procession with stately mounts, the author of the *Description* understood that the Garter festival, even this time when it celebrated Northumberland, was a royal occasion. Though the people 'all did [con]grat-ulate' the solemnity, it was the king who drew the gaze of the crowd who came to see the public cavalcade and the procession to Windsor:

> King Charles our Royall soveraigne
> and his renowned Mary,
> With (Britaines hope) their progeny,
> all lovingly did tarry.

The royal display was enhanced by Charles dining publicly, still more when 'Britaines hope', his eldest son, was elected to the order.[119] For the installation of Prince Charles in 1638, Charles planned a major public cavalcade from Somerset House in the Strand all the way to Windsor.[120] It seems likely that it was the outbreak of rebellion in Scotland that, in two senses, scotched the plan; but, if a sketch by Van Dyck of a grand feast day procession in preparation for a larger canvas was prepared to commemorate this occasion, what was intended was clearly a procession on the grand scale of the type that Charles is said not to have favoured.[121] In 1630, Soranzo, the Venetian ambassador, described the large crowds that usually attended Garter festivals.[122] During the rest of the decade, his successors reported a festival ever more 'splendid' and 'richly adorned'.[123] Far from withdrawing from his subjects, Charles, as Sovereign of the Order, made the Garter ceremonies the most public manifes-tation of his majesty.

London during Charles's reign saw no diminution of public ritual and display. A prefatory poem to *A Treatise of Artificial Fireworks*, published in 1629, referred to the 'courtly sports' accompanied by firework displays on the Thames that amazed the spectators; and other treatises on fireworks, published during the 1630s, suggest the popularity of those pyrotechnic entertainments.[124] The London mayors' shows of Charles's reign, as before, also represented the king as much as they greeted the new mayor and celebrated the symbiosis of city and court. London was, as Thomas Middleton observed in the first show of the reign, echoing regal language, the 'chamber royal' of the kingdom; the mayor, as Thomas Dekker presented him in the festival of 1628, was 'your Soveraignes Gardner' for one year.[125] The purpose of the show, John Taylor announced, in devising that for 1634, was to display the king's greatness, whence the mayor derived his reflected glory.[126] Accordingly, London festivals celebrated royal as well as civic virtues – peace, religion, justice – and praised the benefits of a reign of peace and plenty in which all had flourished. In Taylor's *Triumph of Fame and Honour*, London ventriloquizes loyalist ideology, declaring:

> For I one God, one King, one Law obey;
> Ther's my security, and my state doth stand.[127]

Similarly, in Heywood's pageant of 1632, a speech hymned the harmony of Power and Obedience and presented honouring the king as the best safeguard of prosperity.[128] Increasingly masque-like in their structure and complexity, the Lord Mayor's shows brought sophisticated representations of authority regularly to the streets of London. First and foremost civic occasions, they staged rulers and figured the king as the ultimate source of authority, and of peace and abundance.

Though, to the dismay of the Stuarts, in early seventeenth-century England more and more subjects, commoners as well as gentry, flocked to the capital, London was not the nation. A royal recognition of this sustained into the early modern age the royal progresses that annually presented the person of the king to the people not privileged with the sight of royal display in the capital. Though royal progresses changed and became processions between royal lodges as well as to rural aristocratic houses, James was often on the move and seen, traversing on his visit to Scotland more of England than even the legendarily itinerant Elizabeth had done.[129] In this respect, Charles I has been presented as the contrast to his father: his progresses, it is said, though they still bore that name, were little more than hunting trips; confined to a small corner of the country, they were arranged to spare a reluctant king any engagement with his people, and were undertaken to secure not his publicization but his privacy.[130] These assertions, though they have become orthodoxy, are inversions of the evidence, which rather indicates that Charles I may have been one of the most itinerant of early modern monarchs.[131]

Of course, the king did indulge a love of hunting that often took him to the New Forest and Salisbury or to Chesterford, near Royston. And he sojourned during progresses at various royal palaces – at Woodstock, Theobalds and Oatlands. But from the beginning of the reign, progresses took Charles far beyond the environs of Whitehall and were often of long duration. As we have seen, Charles in 1625 travelled to meet Henrietta Maria at Dover and visited Canterbury and Rochester.[132] Though the war years may have curtailed some progresses, in the summer of 1625 the Venetian envoy reported the 'incessant journeys' of the king that delayed business in Whitehall, and in September Charles visited both Plymouth and, evidently, Lincoln.[133] In the spring of 1627, the king moved to Newmarket where he resolved to stay for some weeks unless urgent business recalled him, which apparently it did not; in June he rode to Portsmouth to inspect the fleet.[134] Preparations for the La Rochelle expedition kept Charles longer in London than usual the next summer, but in August he again visited Portsmouth, whence he moved to Beaulieu for some hunting before the crisis occasioned by Buckingham's death brought him early to London.[135]

The cessation of hostilities in 1629 released Charles to spend a decade of more and longer progresses. On 13 June 1629 Soranzo reported that 'his Majesty remained the whole of this summer in the country, and keeps going farther off'; in September Charles was 'still away', as he was, to the envoy's frustration, in October.[136] Only in November was he optimistic that 'his Majesty will terminate his progress tomorrow' – a progress, we should note, which had lasted over four months.[137] After a ten-day hunting trip in March the next year, Charles planned a progress in May that was postponed by plague and uncertainties concerning which parts of the country were dangerous.[138] But in July, the progress began for the summer.[139] During the summer of 1631, Charles travelled to inspect the docks at Chatham and Portsmouth, before in July finally embarking at Greenwich on a progress that lasted until the end of August.[140]

Charles for long planned a more ambitious journey north to be crowned in his Scottish kingdom and at last fulfilled his plan in the late spring of 1633. Charles's journey to Scotland took him on a progress longer even than that of his father in 1617. Leaving Whitehall on 8 May, he did not return until late in July.[141] His route north took in Stanford, Worksop, Grantham, York, Durham, Newcastle and Berwick, before he crossed on to Scottish soil. Nor was the journey in any sense private. Charles was splendidly feasted on the way and at York, Durham and Newcastle made formal entries, with crowds in attendance. At Richmond the king displayed a common touch not usually associated with him when he gave £4 to a woman who had given birth to quadruplet boys.[142] Leaving Berwick on 9 June, the royal party reached Edinburgh on the 15th, where the king lodged at Holyrood Palace. At Edinburgh, a state entry and elaborate spectacles were prepared before the service of coronation. Charles stayed to attend a parliament for two weeks; then, after visits to Stirling and Falkland, began his return, which took little less than a month.[143]

After such a trip one might be surprised to learn that less than a fortnight after reaching London, Charles set out on the summer progress he had planned before his Scottish coronation.[144] The next May (1634) Charles left early for Greenwich to begin a progress which, though it commenced in the environs of London, took him and Henrietta Maria to Hinchinbroke, Apethorpe,

Grimthorpe, Belvoir, Welbeck, Nottingham, Holdenby and Castle Ashby, by no means a local perambulation.[145] The failure of the Anglo-Spanish treaty in 1635 signalled a possible reorientation of England's position in Europe that kept Charles either close to London or visiting his ship money fleets in the Downs.[146] The Venetian envoy Anzolo Correr reported that, while the queen's pregnancy was given as a reason for the progress being cancelled, 'the king is glad to seize upon this pretext for not going far away, so that he may be at hand for emergencies that may arise at any moment'.[147] Plague in the spring of 1636 added an extra impetus to the usual decision to begin a progress.[148] Though it began as a sojourn at nearby palaces, Oatlands and Theobalds, Charles travelled to Southampton and to Oxford, where he made a public entry into the city and the university, followed by days of plays, entertainments and feasts.[149] Interestingly, Charles made his progress of 1636 very much a public political statement. The king instructed Secretary John Coke to summon all the ship money sheriffs of the counties through which the court passed, to *quicken* the payment.[150] And Charles travelled with the Elector Palatine, who was visiting his uncle, so manifesting his commitment to his cause at a time when England was considering an alliance with France to restore him.[151] His travelling with Elector Charles Lewis, whose cause was popular in England, also suggests a shrewd sense of public relations for which Charles is rarely credited.

It may be that the marriage of the Duke of Lennox, the king's cousin, in August 1637, kept Charles in the vicinity of London through that summer.[152] But the next year, as well as hunting trips in the winter and sojourns at Greenwich and Windsor (for the installation of the prince into the Garter), Charles, despite the Scottish troubles, planned a progress to begin on 21 July that was followed in November by his visit to receive the queen mother at Harwich, whither he journeyed via Chelmsford and Moulsham.[153] The failure to secure obedience and the decision to lead an army into Scotland led Charles in 1639 to make a second major march to the northern capital of his kingdom. The 'gists of his Majesty's journey', interestingly the language used of a normal progress, set out in March, plotted an itinerary of eleven nights and decided on the towns at which Charles would rest on the way to York, then Warkworth, the furthest point of the journey into Northumberland.[154] As events transpired, he went as far as Berwick and did not return until August.[155] The failure of the Peace of Berwick and of the parliament called to finance another campaign forced Charles back to York with his army the next summer. In 1641, as we have seen, he was in Scotland again, negotiating with the rebels before his triumphant return entry into London.

The details of these progresses are themselves enough to dispel the erroneous view that Charles confined himself to mere hunting trips. No other early modern English monarch made two trips as far as Scotland or travelled as far or for as long as Charles did on these journeys. Moreover, the sheer size and scale of the entourage on the king's progresses seem to have been greater than ever before. For though the number of carriages normally allowed for such progresses was 257, 'the service according to the present practice', a statement of January 1638 reports, 'numbered 406', the king himself paying for over a hundred of the surplus.[156] Progresses of 406 carriages, with attendants and servants, must have made a spectacular impression on the counties and villages through which they passed, not to mention the formal entries prepared at cities and towns, or the ceremonial occasions attended by the people, like the entertainment at Oxford or the launching of *The Sovereign of the Seas*.[157] Though we do not have for Charles (or James) the contemporary printed accounts of progresses which historians of Elizabeth have so often drawn on and we cannot know in most cases how they reacted, it is clear that Charles's subjects crowded to see the king, and his extensive progresses provided many far from the capital with an opportunity to see him.[158] Rather than agree with Richards, we must conclude with Sir Henry Wotton: 'Your Majesty doth not fly the eyes and access of your subjects, you do not joy to be hid, you do not withdraw yourself from those that are yours.'[159]

III

While the words, the images, the ritual performances and most of all the sight of a ruler were the principal modes of royal representation, the image of the monarch in early modern England was inseparable from his (or her) actions and roles, especially as overlord, protector of justice and head of the church. Not only was Charles I sensitive to his performance of these public roles of the office of monarch, but in representing as well as performing them he emphasized (as all early monarchs needed to do) the symbiosis of the personal and the public. Perhaps more than many rulers, and in his own distinct ways, Charles formed policies and programmes out of deeply personal traits and values, while also rendering his intimate life the most public manifestation of his ideology of rule.

This connection between personal values and public image is nowhere better illustrated than in the Caroline court. From at least the later sixteenth century, news media had conveyed more and more details of the royal court to subjects who viewed it as a glass which reflected and revealed the sovereign. During James's reign, however, especially from the time of the Overbury scandal, its reputation as a place of corruption, excess and immorality undoubtedly tarnished the monarchy. Charles, who was allegedly offended by his father's legacy in this regard, moved immediately on his succession to reform the court so as to make it the beacon of his virtues of order and self-regulation.[160] Where ambassadors and other visitors quickly discerned this change to a new morality, regulation and civility, a variety of writers soon intuited Charles's intention to make his reformed court the representation of his kingship.[161] In the significantly titled *A Looking Glass for Princes and People*, published in 1632, William Struther stated Charles's own belief: 'The court of kings is an abridgement of their kingdoms. . . . It is a proof of the government of their persons and an image of the ruling of their estates.'[162] 'People cannot always see the person of their kings,' Struther added, 'but they may guess at their disposition by the manners of their court.'[163] Charles had witnessed in the Escorial the sort of court which, in complete contrast to that of his father, expressed the sobriety, virtue and piety of Philip IV. It may, then, be more than coincidence that in 1632 it was a translation of the Spaniard Juan de Santa Maria's *Christian Policy* which argued that by the nature of his court the king set an example 'to teach and instruct the people by his virtues.'[164] If courts were 'godly and righteous', Struther maintained, 'they win the hearts of people to the king; but if they be profane and godless they procure his contempt.'[165]

Charles issued new orders to govern the behaviour of courtiers: he banished drunkards, swearers and railers; he punished breaches of morality and decorum. The king strictly regulated entry to the royal bedchamber and replaced the casual familiarity of Jacobean arrangements with a rigid hierarchy of rooms. Greater formality was accompanied by renewed emphasis on ceremonies and rituals in the daily round that highlighted the mystery of, and reverence due to, the sovereign.[166] As important as the royal decrees and actions was how they and the reformed court advertised Charles's kingship and were received and perceived. Here, we have plentiful evidence that contemporaries were quickly informed of the changes at court and as quick to read them (as was intended) as signs of a new style of kingship. As early as 1625, George Marcelline praised the court of a prince that, banishing licentiousness, stood as an example to the people.[167] In 1635, Francesco Cevoli, praising Charles, felt that courtiers had been led to emulate his virtuous example.[168] In his popular edition of emblems, George Wither doubted the capacity of courtiers to copy the moral virtues of the king but believed all admired them.[169] In 1640 a poem in a volume of panegyrical verse presented to Charles by an Oxford University poet observed how:

Tis from the greatnesse of your Majesty
That we a Kingdome in your Court may see.[170]

Those who saw, or heard reports of, the court saw not only the kingdom in microcosm but the person of the king. Though some of the praise came from admirers of Charles, as even the wife of one of the king's enemies, Lucy Hutchinson, famously testified, there could be no denying the morality and propriety of the court or the king.[171]

No less important to Charles's presentation of himself was his image as a just king. Though a Whig historiography that has labelled him a tyrant has obscured its significance, it remains the case that no early modern monarch as often invoked the law or appealed to the judges, both to resolve issues and to advertise his rights. The law and the courts were for Charles publicizations of his just and legal courses and he for long believed that his recourse to the law and courts underpinned his reputation as a good king. A later historiography has emphasized how Charles dismissed or suspended judges or pressured them in other ways.[172] But such practices, not entirely absent from modern democracies, were far from unusual in an early modern culture where Francis Bacon, the Lord Chancellor, described judges as 'lions under the throne'.[173] Charles's judges were by no means sycophants and there are not many contemporary accusations – even from hostile critics of the regime – that they were. At least for the first decade or so of his reign, Charles's reputation as a just king appears not to have been controversial. After the king's death, William Lilly recalled the comments of Sir Robert Holborne, a critic of Charles I's fiscal policies and counsel for John Hampden in the ship money case. 'I have heard Sir Robert Holborne oft say', he wrote, that Charles I 'had a quicker conception and would sooner understand a case in law . . . than any of his privy council'.[174] If anyone proposed a monopoly, Lilly added, Charles consulted the judges to ascertain the legality of the proposal. Such retrospective testimonies have contemporary support. In 1633, the diplomat Sir Henry Wotton praised Charles for maintaining justice in her seat.[175] The next year, the lawyer and legal writer Robert Powell compared Charles with the great champion of Anglo-Saxon law, King Alfred. Invoking readers to 'behold him in the chair of Moses', Powell praised Charles for the instruction he gave to his judges, the care he took to protect subjects from the possible oppressions of the laws and courts, his proceedings in Star Chamber, and his exercise of impartiality and mercy.[176] Only his confidence in such a reputation explains Charles's very public recourse to trials in some of the *causes célèbres* of the 1630s. And though the ship money trial was once seen as a miscarriage of justice, there was a widespread appreciation of the king's willingness to have the case heard and even a critic such as Bulstrode Whitelocke, future Chief Justice to the Commonwealth, praised the judgments as 'full of rare and excellent learning'.[177] Whatever concerns it raised, Hampden's case did not destroy the king's reputation as just.

What did taint it was the trial – or perhaps rather the punishment – of the puritans Prynne, Burton and Bastwick. Once again the trial was conducted with normal procedure in the court; but the victims publicly alleged that they had not been given a fair hearing; and their self-representation as martyrs at the scene of their punishment not only won them sympathy but stained royal justice with opprobrium.[178] By no means all, of course, took the puritan view. In his sermon preached at St Paul's in March 1640, Bishop Henry King, a moderate Calvinist not part of Laud's inner circle, praised Charles's sense of justice: 'He will not know the use of his authority,' he preached, 'but where religion and right make his commands legitimate.'[179] England, he closed, was blessed with 'so . . . just a king'.[180] The same year others came forward to commend Charles's sense of justice and concern for the law. In his complex allegorical work *Dodonna's Grove*, James Howell defended the king and the 'sages of the law' in the case of ship money.[181] More interestingly, even a moderate constitutionalist critic such as Henry Parker accepted Charles's own claim to partly balance prerogative with liberty and considered him 'one of the mildest . . . of our kings'.[182] There can be no doubt that in 1640–1 the accusation by his critics in and out of parliament that he was not a just king nor one who could be trusted to uphold the common laws was undermining Charles's image and authority. Even then, however, we should not read such attacks as straightforward evidence of Charles's being widely perceived as a king who had abused justice: the opponents of the king had to wage a long campaign to blacken him as unjust. And, even in 1649, fearing that he would triumphantly re-emerge as a champion of justice, Charles's enemies were forced from legal procedures to arbitrary courses to convict him. The victory of his enemies and later Whig historiography fundamentally undermined Charles's image as a just as well as pious ruler.

Since the Reformation, perhaps the most important public role of the monarch was as Supreme Head of the church. After the reduced significance of that position during the rule of Mary (who favoured restored papal supremacy) and Elizabeth (who, as a woman, could not exercise priestly functions), James I had asserted his full authority as Supreme Head in theory and practice. James's own writings and decrees (such as *The Book of Sports*), as well as his convening of the Hampton Court Conference and patronage of the new Bible, had not only fashioned an ecclesiastical style; they had also powerfully represented a regal style.[183] As with his reform of the court, Charles acted quickly following his succession to stamp his own style on the church and clearly desired the church to be an image of his kingship. Indeed, where Elizabeth and James had privately practised some liturgical preferences without making them public policy – the queen infamously had her crucifixes in her private chapel – Charles, with his church as with his court, refashioned the liturgical style to institutionalize as public worship his private devotions and faith. Even more than his father, whose famous adage 'No bishop, no king' expressed the interdependence of church and monarchy, Charles conceived of his place in his court and household and God's place in his house, the church, as analogous – and so regarded the liturgies of church and state *both* as sacred ceremonies of worship.[184] In a sermon preached before the king at Whitehall, Thomas Laurence, a royal chaplain, nicely captured Charles's own belief: 'as a disrespect to the chair of state reflects upon the king because he is represented there, so doth a disrespect to the church reflect upon God because he is there'.[185]

The subject of Charles I's personal faith, his attitude to a Calvinist theology of predestination, his policy of enforcing ceremonies and his elevation of the bishops and clergy have been the subjects of a considerable historiographical controversy that, in some measure, has mirrored the denominational and factional disputes within the early Stuart church.[186] These controversies, though important, cannot be – and are not – our subject here. In a study of royal representations and images, our focus is rather on how Charles presented himself as Supreme Head of the church and how those self-presentations were publicized and disseminated, received and perceived and, as we shall see, contested. Charles's reign as Supreme Head was quickly characterized by three (some would say inconsistent) priorities, publicized by proclamations, patronage and programmes: a desire for peace and unity, insistence on conformity to Anglican rites and greater emphasis on ritual, and the improvement of the fabric of the church and the status of the clergy. To Charles, the maintenance of 'true religion' depended upon these principles and 'the chief honour and safety of the crown' was inseparable from 'the maintenance of true religion'.[187]

Though his understanding of them and promotion of them were different from his father's, Charles actively presented himself, as any monarch had to, as the protector of peace and unity in the church. Where in James's case these ends had been advanced by extensive publication and polemic, Charles endeavoured to advance them by published declarations urging retreat from controversy and injunctions to silence on disputed points.

Early in his reign, he moved to quieten controversies inherited from James's last years and the tense circumstances of his own first months. So, in 1628–9, the king called in the sermons of Roger Mainwaring that had caused offence, and suppressed a work of self-defence by Richard Montagu, who had instigated the furore over Arminianism.[188] Importantly too, as head of the church, Charles ordered in 1628 a re-publication of the Thirty-Nine Articles, now subtitled 'for the avoiding of diversities of opinions' and with a large royal arms and a royal declaration prefixed.[189] In His Majesty's declaration which prefaced the articles, Charles announced it as his principal duty as Supreme Head to maintain unity and peace and to suppress faction and ordered that differences be referred to Convocation under his authority and that none other should 'either print or preach to draw the article[s] aside anyway' or 'affix any new sense' to them.[190] The king held to this public policy throughout the years before civil war; and, though there were unquestionably opponents who interpreted the injunctions to silence as a sinister plot, many supporters represented Charles, as he had presented himself, as a champion of religious unity and peace. In 1627, for example, the Irish preacher and author of *A Treatise Tending to Unity* praised the royal injunctions to eschew 'curious disputations'.[191] Henry Wotton specifically lauded Charles's edict against the 'itch of disputing' – 'let others think what they list'.[192] And Robert Powell, writing in 1634, thought the king's moves to check new and unorthodox opinions and re-establish unity had rescued the church from schisms.[193] As, in the later 1630s, controversies again became heated, loyal clergy re-presented the king as the protector of peace and unity.

Where, in his 1639 treatise on *The Duty of All True Subjects to Their King*, Henry Peacham proclaimed the Church of England under Charles as 'as well settled and governed as any in the Christian world', preaching on the anniversary that year of Charles's inauguration, Henry Valentine rhetorically asked his audience: 'hath he [Charles] desired or endeavoured anything more than a conformity and uniformity in God's service that there might be but via una?'[194] On the next year's anniversary, preaching at St Paul's, Bishop Henry King similarly asked the assembled: 'under what king's sceptre hath been greater care taken to prevent divisions and weed faction out of the church?'[195] While such praise often came from panegyrists or those like King who were (by 1639) part of the clerical establishment, Charles's reputation as defender of religious peace and unity was not sustained by only a high clerical party. Advice to gentlemen in courtesy books to 'weary not your self with controversies and needless niceties in divinity' suggests that, away from the quarrels of university men and divines, Charles's orders and his stand on peace and unity had an appeal.[196] Peace, as we know, was not settled in the church. But after the outbreak of a civil war caused in large part by religious differences, Charles's success in standing as the champion of the Church of England affirms our sense that his self-presentation in these terms had not been in vain.[197]

Even if the terms meant different things to different people, support for the defence of peace and unity was not hard to secure. Charles's commitment to ritual and ceremony was inevitably more divisive, not least because it exposed divisions that a less public stance on conformity by Elizabeth and James had (if at times thinly) veiled. Such a commitment, however, went to the core of Charles's character and kingship. His personal piety was manifested not in print but in devotion and practices and performances, from his conspicuous wearing of white on the Candlemas Day of his coronation onwards.[198] Unlike his father, Charles joined in prayers every Sunday at the royal chapel, attended confession and in a myriad other ways publicly manifested an attachment to the set forms, rites and ceremonies of the church, as he did to state rituals. The king supported his archbishop, William Laud, and may have been the driving influence in his campaign to enforce ceremonies prescribed by the Elizabethan injunctions and canons: set prayers, bowing, kneeling, standing at the Apostles' Creed, crucifixes, the altar at the east end, candles and so on.[199] The church services, like the kingship, of Charles's reign were less a verbal, more a visual and performative experience which the king regarded as just as important to his regality as to his supremacy. As much as the liturgy in the royal chapel or the silver flagons, basins, candlesticks and decorated prayer books he ordered for Windsor, the altars and rituals in hundreds of parish churches represented Charles to the people. The dominant historical opinion insists that Charles's ceremonialism was an unpopular innovation that undermined the monarchy as well as the church. As I have argued elsewhere, far from being universally unpopular, a fondness for ceremony can be found across the whole spectrum of theological positions and evidence from churchwardens' accounts suggests considerable attachment to the rituals and ceremonial artefacts of the church.[200] As a staunch supporter of Laud, Bishop Robert Skinner was *parti pris*; but his claim in a 1634 sermon, published by royal command, sounds confident: 'I cannot but congratulate the present times wherein the beauty of holiness, in city and country, seems to revive and flourish as never more'; echoing Charles's own belief, he added: 'it argues religion hath life in it'.[201] In his sermon before the king at Whitehall in 1637, the royal chaplain Thomas Laurence, preaching on the sanctity of places and spaces, celebrated a Caroline Church of England which followed in the steps of the church of God where 'the house of God was honoured for God, the throne for the king, the altar for the sacrifice'.[202] In 1640, a popular ballad which praised the 'old fashion' of organs, choristers and music once again revived may have expressed the broader appeal of a more ceremonial piety which certainly had its advocates in the 1640s and again in 1660.[203] In the eyes both of critics and of supporters, Charles I stood for, and embodied, a style of worship as much as of kingship and, for better or worse, rendered the church inseparable from the crown.

A traditionalist in so many respects, in the third principle of his programme for the church Charles broke ranks with his predecessors. Since the Reformation, the authority of the crown had, in some ways, developed out of the plundering of the church and subordination of the clergy.[204] Elizabeth had kept episcopal sees vacant to save money; and even James's belief in the interdependent authority of bishop and king was tempered by a distrust of excessive clerical power, learned in Scotland. Charles came to the throne determined to improve the fabric of the churches and the wealth and status of the clergy because he believed that holiness, and the majesty of God, like that of the monarchy, depended upon the beauty of sacred spaces and the authority of God's servants. From 1629, Charles issued a series of orders 'for preventing the decay of churches' and for enforcing rates for repairs and improvements.[205] His own donations towards the repair of St Paul's were intended as a public example and impetus to a larger national project.[206] The king appointed more bishops to his Privy Council than had been seen since the Reformation and supported bishops and clergy in reasserting their authority in the localities.[207] As he highlighted the sanctity of kingship, so by corollary he endowed the priesthood with greater power. Though the enhancement of the church fabric and the clergy were for Charles interdependent, support for the former was far greater than for the latter, which excited a reactive anticlericalism never far below the surface of early modern English society. Indeed, in some parishes and dioceses, churchwardens' accounts suggest ready compliance with orders to repair churches and church furniture, or to buy plate; in some cases parish initiative preceded directions.[208] The Earl of Huntingdon may have been guilty of exaggeration when, in 1634, he wrote to Sir John Lambe, Dean of the Arches, that 'the beautifying and decoring of the church all that are of impartial judgement must needs consent unto for the fittingness and decency thereof'; but Clarendon's assessment that the work of improvement 'sure was very grateful to all men of devotion' was sound.[209] In his *Life of Alfred*, Powell praised Charles's support for the restoration of churches and his maintenance of the position of the clergy.[210] *The Jews High Commendation* of the newly restored St Paul's similarly celebrated, along with the beautification of the cathedral, that 'the clergy flourish shall again /And heretics will go down'.[211] But in many parts of the kingdom, Charles's support for the appointment of clergy to the Commission of the Peace and other actions enhancing clerical power, such as contesting the authority of mayors or removing the laity's pews from churches, drew widespread lay discontent – both with the episcopacy and the crown.[212] Charles's public self-presentation as the upholder of a powerful clergy undoubtedly added to his difficulties in 1641–2.[213] Ironically, however, as an assault on the episcopacy opened the way first to an ever more clericist Presbyterianism, then to sectarian anarchy, the king's cause gained from his stand for the bishops.[214] Ultimately, the Church of England hierarchies returned the favour of royal support for the clergy's enhanced authority by sanctifying the king as martyr and saint. Though the response to Charles's image as an un-Erastian king shifted, his style of church government (and much of his appointed liturgy) was seen to be inseparable from his kingship and reputation at large.

As well as custodian of justice and head of the church, monarchs were expected to be defenders of their subjects and the realm. The representation of the prince as warrior was the dominant image of medieval kings during periods of incessant wars. In England, the end of the Wars of the Roses brought domestic peace; and, though Henry's rejection of his wife and the papacy exposed England to constant threats, the Tudors met (and survived) them with occasional displays of force, like the Field of the Cloth of Gold; more often by careful diplomacy, strategic alliances and sheer good fortune. In part because, after Henry, the Tudor monarchs were a boy and two women, the depiction of the monarch armoured and ready for battle became a less common mode of representation. Even in Henry VIII's case, Holbein figured the sovereign's authority as much in terms of innate personal strength as in the guise of a warrior, while the spread of humanism to England led to an emphasis on rulers and nobles as learned disputants as much as military combatants.[215] Though he stands as the extreme case, James VI and I took up the pen rather than the sword against his Catholic enemies and actively promoted his image as the *rex pacificus* who might, by skilful diplomacy, restore peace to Europe. James's reputation for pacifism (let alone cowardice) has, as we saw, been exaggerated; moreover critics of his foreign policy remind us that the expectations of the ruler as military leader remained alongside other more civilized images. In the difficult circumstances of early Stuart

England, that is to say, the monarch needed to be represented as a champion of peace and as one equipped and ready for war – for a just war, in case of necessity, to defend his faith, his subjects and his kingdom.

For all the tensions their relationship caused, James's son, Prince Henry, helped to balance his father's peaceful image with a programme of self-representation as chivalric knight, martial hero and Protestant champion.[216] Like his elder brother, Charles, as prince, took pleasure in vigorous physical exercise and in the tilt and was figured as heir to his brother's role.[217] In travelling to Spain incognito, though he excited fears for his safety, Charles displayed chivalric daring and bravery. On his return, he became the principal spokesman for a war party that had long lobbied for a campaign against the Habsburgs to restore the Palatinate to Charles's sister and brother-in-law.[218] When he succeeded his father, Charles I came to the throne of a nation at war and with the reputation as a military king – the first since Henry VIII. From the very moment of Charles's accession, panegyrists, some writing with official support or approval, sensed the new climate. John Taylor, for example, in his verses on the immortal memory of King James, praised 'just arms' as well as peace, while George Marcelline, celebrating the marriage of Charles and Henrietta Maria, maintained that regard of peace should not lead the prince to 'neglect a just occasion of war', and praised Charles for his warlike skills on horse or foot.[219] During the war years, as we might expect, poets and prose panegyrists publicized Charles as a warrior prince. In 1626, Francis Hamilton presented Charles to the readers of his *Encomium* as 'Magnanimous, and mightie for defence/Of all true Christians'; the same year Abraham Holland claimed that Germany and Spain were stunned by Charles's succession and fearful of what was to follow from it.[220] After the peace with Spain and France in 1629–30, it is usually agreed, the image of Charles as warrior was refashioned into that of the Augustan ruler of a halcyon peace hymned in Cavalier poems and masques. Those texts, however, were more complex and ambivalent than has been recognized and, anyway, tell only half the story.[221] During the earliest years of the personal rule, Charles was represented as both a king of peace and of arms. The doubleness may be discerned, I would suggest, in Rubens's allegory of *Peace and War*, painted for the king in 1629 and which Van der Doort described in an inventory of the king's pictures as an 'emblem', or visual moral lesson.[222] In his sermon on the birth of Prince Charles, published in 1632, Struther, who dedicated the text to the king, may have ventriloquized Charles's own beliefs when he followed his statement that 'a good king ruleth his people in peace' with the caveat 'but sometimes security will draw him to war'.[223] Struther repeated the point later in his sermon: 'this is the task of a good king, in peace to be furnished for war and in war to aim at peace'.[224]

The death of the Elector Palatine in 1632 and the succession of his son, Charles's nephew, to the title, as well as the death of Gustavus Adolphus the same year, focused attention on Charles's responsibility to his sister and his role in a Europe increasingly dominated by Catholic victories.[225] Though he remained at peace, Charles was concerned to communicate to Europe and his subjects at home the possibility of war, for which the reform of the militia and the decision to levy ship money for a new fleet were public acts of preparation.[226] Writing very much from within court circles, Henry Wotton in 1633 emphasized Charles's passion for chivalry, the care he had taken over the musters and the navy, and his love of hunting 'in which image of war you do so exercise your vigorous spirits'.[227] Similarly, Robert Powell in his comparison of the king with Alfred pointed to feats of chivalry and the vigilant maintaining of defences that Charles pursued during the peace.[228] When Charles went to be crowned in Scotland, Lithgow was only one of the poets ready to remind him of the Scottish troops in service throughout Europe which he might, if need be, call upon to fight for him.[229] Charles instead concentrated on the fleet, which by 1635 was emerging as a serious counter in the European diplomatic poker game. In a volume of poems dedicated to Charles by Oxford University the year of his visit in 1636, Edward Bathurst's verse urged: 'SEE how our navy does with ease /Our land defend'.[230] Others hinted at a potentially more aggressive role for the fleet. In 1635, the author of a tract on a royal accident, in which Charles was mercifully spared, warned that though the king loved peace 'yet he hath a portion of David's spirit and is not afraid of wars'.[231] Perhaps recalling a portrait of Charles and Henrietta Maria, he added: 'the most invincible Charles hath in the one hand an olive branch, the emblem of peace; in the other a palm, the prognostic of victory'.[232] Though masques, to which we will return, ubiquitously celebrated the triumph of peace, antimasques typically showed battles and wars, ever-present alternative policies.[233] And in the entertainment staged for the royal couple at Richmond in 1636, a captain prayed that the prince might, like Alexander, extend his arms abroad to forge a British empire.[234] Placed on a triumphal arch, Prince Charles, as Prince Britomart, was presented as 'The springing hopes of Armes and Arts' – an order of words that may well be significant.[235]

The next year, diplomacy (not least the Earl of Arundel's mission to the emperor) on his behalf having failed, the Prince Palatine published a manifesto calling on all to support his just rights.[236] As if in response, Charles I publicly launched, as we have seen, *The Sovereign of the Seas* to advertise his capacity as well as readiness to come to his nephew's aid. Albeit with some exaggeration, Thomas Heywood wrote of Spain and France 'cringing and congeeing', before this new symbol of English might.[237] Conjuring up the memory of Drake and Hawkins, in a work 'published with authority' he drew out the full implications of the ship and the launch: 'I must ingeniously confess,' Heywood wrote, 'that for many years together there hath been a long cessation of arms, neither hath just occasion been ministered wherein our noble nation might give any full expression of the hereditary valour and virtue of their ancestors – *till of late*.'[238] On *The Sovereign*, the figure of King Edgar on horseback trampling on seven kings represented the same shift of policy and perception in wood carving: peace, it suggested, would give way to war.[239]

The war that embroiled Charles, however, was not one of intervention in Europe but engagement with his own subjects in Scotland. What is noteworthy is how, during the campaign of propaganda and counter-propaganda between the Covenanters and the king, Charles continued to publicize himself both as a lover of peace and as a strong ruler equipped, should it be necessary, to suppress rebellion with terrible force and war. Though it has been rightly argued that the re-presentation of Charles I, after the outbreak of civil war, required some reconstitution of the royal image, it by no means involved a complete re-branding.[240] More often than his predecessors, Charles was painted in armour and on horseback with the commander's baton, images circulated on engravings, medals and coins. Those of his subjects who lobbied from 1625 for the king to lead a Protestant campaign in Europe were undoubtedly disappointed in Charles. However, the image of the king promulgated abroad and at home was by no means a simply pacific image. Within the (very real) limitations of European circumstances and his resources, Charles succeeded in making the great powers at times nervous of his intentions for his ship money fleet and far from assured of his neutrality. In that sense, his spokesmen were right to represent him as a king of peace and war who, though desirous to keep his subjects safe in their halcyon calm from the ravages of the Thirty Years War, was also ready to take up the sword.

Charles's need to sustain some reputation as a potential military leader was inextricably bound up with the primary duty of an early modern sovereign: the protection and prolongation of dynasty and family. A simple fact about Charles, of which the significance has been too little remarked, is that, like Henry VIII, he was the heir of a new dynasty and had a powerful sense of his position and duty to advance it. For all that he was uncomfortable with the style and some of the actions of his father, Charles was represented and presented himself as his father's son, as a Stuart. As well as several portraits of his father, Charles collected paintings of his Stuart ancestors.[241] In his bedchamber, he hung pictures of Prince Henry, Princess Elizabeth, the Elector and their children and the Duke of Buckingham, part of the extended Stuart family.[242] One object daily presented Charles to himself as his parents' son, for next to a portrait of James in a white hat with a feather, 'a looking glass' hung 'wherein is shining the reflection of King James's picture which makes a representation of Queen Anne in the glass.'[243] In countless pronouncements, Charles invoked his father's sacred memory. And as his own family increased to secure, as it seemed, perpetual Stuart rule, he named his first son for himself and his second after his father, while his daughters were given the names of his mother and sister and, in the cases of Princesses Elizabeth and Mary, those of two Tudor queens.[244] His position as heir and patriarch of the Stuart dynasty was as important to Charles's policy and publicity as it was for his person. His marriage into the Bourbon family was widely represented as a triumph of Stuart dynasty and from 1630 the births of royal children were heralded as 'emblems' of Stuart as well as Caroline kingship.[245] From 1630 to 1640, pregnancies, miscarriages, births and deaths of offspring were annual royal events which were celebrated and publicized in verses and ballads, on coins and woodcuts, as well as in official prayers and baptismal ceremonies. The universities, in particular, took the occasions of royal births to advertise the virtues of Stuart and Caroline rule, not least of the benefits of which was secure succession. In 1633, after the birth of a second prince, the Oxford poets expressed joy that 'The State is now past feare, and all that wee/Need wish besides in perpetuitie'.[246] And, reminding subjects that 'annual happy offspring' were royal gifts to them too, they urged that all should unite with the king in joy and that 'the enquiring busie Common eye' should obediently gaze on majesty.[247] Charles, Thomas Lockey noted, had by 1633 more children than Henry VIII had sired on six wives; another verse looked to perhaps one offspring in future ruling France.[248] By the early 1630s, Charles I's children *were* his images and representations, even as they were themselves represented. 'Whilst the sun and moon do indure,' Powell proclaimed in 1634, 'there never may one be wanting of their thrice royal line to sway the sceptre of Great Britain.'[249]

As still more children followed, the royal offspring were depicted as the blessed fruits not only of a fertile couple but of the union between the king and the commonweal, as, that is, signs of mutual love. Commemorating the birth of a fourth (surviving) child in 1636, the Oxford poets figuratively shared in the intimate processes of the queen's parturition – 'we feel her pangs' – as indeed through the birth they participated in regality itself: 'under many Princes we/Doe live the more/Monarchicall'.[250] Representing, it was said, Nature's four first principles as well as the four corners of the earth, the royal children naturalized royal authority and promised a progeny 'peopling Nations with a Princes blood'.[251] The political role of the children as protagonists of Caroline policies as well as of Stuart dynasty was graphically illustrated in 1640. Prince Henry, Duke of Gloucester, was born at Oatlands on 8 July that year, as Charles, after the collapse of the Short Parliament, endeavoured to lead a second army against the Scots. Commemorative volumes published by both Oxford and Cambridge universities made starkly clear the role of the royal children now in supporting as well as representing the king. Directly acknowledging the adverse political circumstances, the Oxford poets lauded a royal couple that

... midst the brandished swords, and Trumpets voice,
Brings forth a Prince, a Conquest to that noise.[252]

Prince Henry was sent, the verse announced, 'to calme the Tempest' and, the poet urged, the people should take comfort from the omen, the 'pretty mystery' of the royal birth.[253] The Cambridge bards welcomed Henry in similarly loyalist strains: 'Rebellion stand thou by; Mischief make room . . . we have another bright-ey'd Boy'.[254] Both metaphorically and, they hoped, literally, the university wits viewed the royal birth as strengthening Charles against his opponents and rebels:

> When a new Sonne doth his blest stock adorn,
> Then to great Charles is a new Armie born.[255]

On canvas and in masques throughout the 1630s, Charles I had figured his children as the representation as well as successors of his rule. In part, the images and discourse of dynasty were familiar, but in the representation of his progeny Charles made a radically new political as well as aesthetic move. More than that of any other monarch in living memory, Charles's family was an extension of himself and the powerful public image of the king as father struck a chord with later historians and artists as much as with contemporaries.[256] In 1640, the Oxford poets, in a dedication to Charles, claimed that the royal family itself now constituted a court, parliament and nation.[257] After 1642, still more after 1649, Parliamentarians and Commonwealthsmen forgot to represent the republic as a family. That they failed, leaving many subjects feel orphaned, suggests that Charles's representation as dynast and patriarch of an affective family had proved hard to undermine.[258]

The force of Charles's representation as dynast and patriarch cannot be separated from what was unusual and prominent in his self-presentation: his publicization of himself as a husband and the representation of his rule as a marriage. To describe this as unusual may appear a contentious claim. Elizabeth I after all, and James I after her, frequently spoke of being wedded to the people and deployed a language of love and affect as a political discourse and polemic.[259] Yet the case of Charles is different – and not only because, unlike his father or the Virgin Queen, he enjoyed a happy marriage. Charles's case is different because, as with other areas of his representation, Charles made his most intimate relationship, his most intimate emotions, his most *public* statement. Where Elizabeth's *amours* were, at least as far as the queen was able, kept private and distinct from the public discourse of love and succession, and James's actual marriage featured little in contemporary representations or perceptions of the king, which were dominated by other sexual relations, for Charles and Henrietta Maria their love and their union fashioned the public discourses, images and performances of government. The royal marriage, it is not too much to say, became a synecdoche for all social relationships and the model for government. Only once we recognize this can we appreciate that, far from distractions from government, the court masques that enacted a loving dialogue between the king and queen, as indeed the portraits which depicted them with novel intimacy as loving husband and wife, were representations of Caroline government – that is to say they were acts of government.

As well as royal representation, Charles's marriage was publicly received and read as a signification of his kingship. At Dover, before the crowds, Henrietta Maria, having disembarked, threw herself into Charles's arms to manifest her love, then knelt before him to symbolize the obedience a wife owed her husband.[260] By corollary, when the king and queen, only months into their marriage, quarrelled over her household servants who had accompanied her from France, the Earl of Carlisle warned Charles that if he failed to master his wife, he would not govern his realm; Charles responded to the advice by publicly dismissing Henrietta Maria's French attendants and replacing them with those of his appointment.[261] Thereafter, and especially after the assassination of the Duke of Buckingham and the healing of the breach with France, the personal relationship of the king and queen not only replicated the idealized public discourse of love and marriage, but reaffirmed it and made love – monogamous love – and marriage prominent in the public discussion and conception, the imagining, of politics and state. In early modern England marriage and family were, more than mere metaphors, analogues of the state. Charles and Henrietta Maria made that analogue flesh: as they embodied that analogy, so too their own marriage became a political performance – one that was staged and represented by themselves and others.

From the moment of their betrothal, the union of Charles and Henrietta Maria was interpreted as more than a dynastic union; as in fact a fusion of virtuous qualities and a reconciliation of tensions and contradictions. As well as being figured as Hero and Leander, as Pallas, god of wisdom, and Ceres, goddess of fertility, Charles and Henrietta Maria were represented as uniting 'Peace and Policie', bringing protection to Europe through their marriage.[262] George Marcelline described the couple in corporeal language that in early modern England signified also a political statement: 'she is the heart and he is the head', a uniting of affection and reason that implied an ideal form of rule.[263] The public affection of the king and queen for each other, the expression of the only royal love that living English subjects would have seen, clearly made its impression on such ordinary subjects as well as courtiers. Raymond Anselment suggests that 'this marriage may have been as meaningful for the 1630s as Elizabeth's virginity had been in the 1580s' – and, we might add, as political.[264] Treatises such as John Wing's *The Crown Conjugal or the Spouse Royal, A Discovery of the True Honour and Happiness of Christian Matrimony* (1632) hinted even in its title at the influence of the king and queen and at the ready connections contemporaries made between marriage and politics.[265] George Wither made the royal marriage an emblem of virtue and a model of government by example when, dedicating his volume to the royal couple, he told them:

The glorious *Vertues* of your NUPTIALL-state,
Your *Courtiers*, find so hard to imitate,
That, they admire them, rather.[266]

The Oxford poets described the royal marriage as heralding the return of a golden age:

CHARLES and divinest MARY: these are they
That strike an influence through this age of Clay.[267]

The 'influence' reached out into popular culture. Thomas Heywood's play *The Royal King and the Loyal Subject* (written around 1600 but published in 1637) may have been revised to stage a king whose tender address to his queen is both striking and perhaps symbolic of other political relationships – 'the choice jewell/That I weare next my heart'.[268]

The language of love, part of the discourse of chivalry, was intrinsically a political language in early modern England.[269] And the subjects of Charles and Henrietta Maria were quick to make connections between the love manifested between the royal couple and the style of royal government that was signified by it. The new monarch, George Marcelline observed, ruled not with the rod of law but the adamant of love – that is the loadstone or magnet that drew affections after their influence; 'he takes nothing by force', he added, 'yet he hath all by love'.[270] William Struther made a similar observation in even more directly political language: 'when princes exercise their power in love . . . they are loved of all'.[271] As well as, then, celebrating the fertility of the royal couple, the marriage of Charles and Henrietta Maria, and their love, were viewed as not merely a language or symbol of, but as a mode and form of, government. The representations of the royal marriage were, in the fullest sense, political acts, the communication of an ideology with the intention of effecting change.

Love and marriage, as I have argued at length elsewhere, became the dominant theme of Caroline poetry and drama which also debated how authority and kingship were conducted in terms of both compliment and criticism. Plays and verse were often a response to, and in dialogue with, the form of representation which Charles I, unlike his father, favoured: the court masque. Masques were not new in seventeenth-century England. Under James, however, Anne of Denmark and Prince Henry had used and developed masques to advertise values and policies, sometimes at odds with those of the king.[272] James himself never performed in masques and on some occasions appears to have been bored with the hours these entertainments involved. Charles took an active part in masques, was often described as busy rehearsing them, and transformed their nature and form.[273] Under the influence of the queen, the court masques took up the philosophy of Neoplatonism which had been a fashion in Italy and France and were dominated by the subjects of love and beauty as political forces and authorities.[274] In these entertainments, which Charles and Henrietta Maria presented to and performed for each other, love was the force which governed the unruly passions and transformed wild nature into order and calm. The love represented was that not of carnal pleasure but of a Platonic union of souls that represented the victory of higher reason over appetite. Platonic love was an ideal form of government because it led not to forceful regimen but to self-regulation. In the masques, then, the king and queen represented that love which had the best claim to rule; their mutual love, it was suggested, influenced subjects towards an ordering of themselves.

The representation of the marriage and love of the king and queen in the masques was not merely abstract. Though they performed in costume or disguise, Charles and Henrietta's own marriage was often specifically referred to in the texts. At the end of *The Temple of Love*, for example, a valedictory is sung:

> To Charles the mightiest and the best,
> And to the darling of his breast,
> Who rule b'example . . .[275]

In *Coelum Britannicum*, the king and queen, melded into one hermaphrodite 'CarloMaria', effected the reformation of the court, not least by expelling illicit passions.[276] Moreover, the royal love reached out to influence the country, as well as the court:

> And as their own pure souls entwined,
> So are their subjects' hearts combined.[277]

Throughout the 1630s, the masques of Thomas Carew, William Davenant and Aurelian Townshend represented the marriage of the king and queen as the pivotal axis on which appetites and passions were transformed into reason and understanding.[278] The force of the belief in their philosophy is nowhere better illustrated than in the last masque of Charles's reign when, as the Scots rose in rebellion against the order masque represented, Charles and Henrietta Maria, visibly pregnant with the future Prince Henry, danced together on the stage – to, as it were, perform their marriage in order to influence others to reason and, consequently, lead them to obedience. When they were seated, the deities assured them:

> All that are harsh, all that are rude,
> Are by your harmony subdued;
> Yet so into obedience wrought,
> As if not forced to it, but taught.[279]

Still in the 1640s, the example and influence of the royal marriage were considered the antidote to rebellious passions, indeed to political crisis. There can be no better testament to Charles's belief in the power of representation.

That neither the king's Scottish nor his English subjects were 'taught' or 'wrought' into obedience might be taken as evidence of the isolation of the king and court. Masques, it was once agreed, far from representing the king to his people, were an elite medium through which the king spoke only to his supporters. In fact, in many ways even masques reveal an engagement with a wider world beyond Whitehall. Masques often attended (and even responded) to other voices and other representations; some were staged not by courtiers but members of the Inns of Court, or aristocratic patrons; the authors of court masques were themselves also poets and popular dramatists with one foot in the marketplace; and several participated in the literary tavern circles of Caroline London.[280] Though they were performed usually before an elite audience of courtiers and ambassadors, masques were on occasions seen by ordinary visitors to court and in the case of those, like *The Triumph of Peace*, that contained an element of procession and spectacle, by thousands of ordinary citizens.[281] Moreover, in published form, several masques were sold by Thomas Walkley at his shop near York House, or by Richard Meighen next to the Middle Temple, both of whom were presumably in the book trade for profit and expected sales.[282] If the 3,000 copies of *The Triumph of Peace* printed were anywhere near typical, masques as a form of representation reached well beyond the narrow audience of the elite. As well as other literary texts, plays, poems and emblem books, the evidence of entertainments suggests that the ideology of masque reached far beyond Whitehall and indeed far beyond the capital. In York in 1639, as in Edinburgh in 1633, welcoming addresses to Charles resounded with the language and conceits of masque.[283] If the masques failed to communicate the royal marriage as the model of government, it was not necessarily because such representations were narrowly or inadequately portrayed.[284] Indeed, in the 1640s the image of Charles as loving husband was a powerful facet of the king's popular appeal.

One of the obvious difficulties in representing and publicizing the royal marriage was Henrietta Maria herself. Though infinitely preferable to a Spanish bride in a realm where memories of the Armada had never faded, Henrietta Maria was a Catholic who took seriously her duty to advance her faith, of which she had been firmly reminded by the papacy before her departure for England.[285] Once in her new country, she publicized her religion by abstaining from the coronation service and by attending Catholic services at her chapel at Somerset House, to which English Catholics as well as her French attendants were drawn. The queen became a patron of her religion and encouraged a number of conversions which aroused scandal and anxiety – not least in Charles's archbishop, William Laud.[286] The hysteria about an alleged popish plot that sparked the fires of revolution in the late 1630s grew from the suspicions and fears about the influence of the queen and her circle.[287]

Yet, though the presence of Henrietta Maria ultimately contributed considerably to the erosion of trust in Charles's government, it would be wrong to assume that from 1625 the image of the queen was predominantly negative or that her presence inevitably undermined Charles. It may not be surprising that the naturalized Frenchman George Marcelline was extravagant in praise of the new queen, but, writing for an English audience, he evidently anticipated no dissent from his views. Marcelline described Henrietta Maria as like 'an angel sent from heaven' who would be 'a happy mother of kings'.[288] Interestingly, he also sought to allay English concerns about her religion. Marcelline hinted that the queen's Catholicism was by no means dogmatic and suggested that a 'princess of such ripeness of wit and incomparable understanding' might easily be educated to renounce the worship of images, prayers to saints, belief in purgatory, and even papal authority.[289] Reassuring those who already feared her potential influence on the king – that Solomon would be seduced – Marcelline predicted that she would obey Charles and possibly even convert; already, he claimed, there were encouraging signs 'that she will open her breast to entertain the truth, and unfold her arms to embrace affectionately this our own ancient, Catholic, Apostolic and reformed religion'.[290] Hope that Henrietta Maria might convert did not fade quickly. In 1632, William Struther was still praying that the queen might 'forget her people and her father's house' and 'prove new born in Israel'.[291] From her arrival, university poets, addressing her as 'Virgo Maria', had represented the queen as a benefit to the church; still in 1636 an Oxford University volume hailed her as 'divinest Mary'.[292] As the hopes of conversion faded, praise of the queen passed over her faith to focus upon her fertility and her important position as mother of a growing family of Stuart heirs – her being 'with childe as oft as we can pray'.[293] The children, indeed, perhaps to calm anxieties about their upbringing, were presented as counterweights to Catholic influences and threats, as an Oxford poem on the birth of Prince James makes clear:

> . . . But our lab'ring Queene
> Hath now a thousand bullwarkes beene,
> And hath by this proclaim'd to all
> She's Anti-Iesueticall.[294]

Thereafter, the nearly annual representation of the queen's fertility served as well as praise to temper her cult of virginity. And, as opposition and fears of Catholic influence mounted, her fertility and progeny were presented both as signs of her own fidelity and loyalty to both king and nation and as inducements to rebellious or recalcitrant subjects to emulate her:

> But now (as if your wise fertility
> An extract were of all State Policie)
> You give example unto Men, and teach
> Loyalty more then our Divines can preach.[295]

By her children, the Oxford poets argued, Henrietta Maria paid tribute to the nation and so set an example to subjects to similarly contribute to the safety of the king and commonweal.[296] The queen continued to attract supporters and admirers: in *Dodonna's Grove*, an allegory on the troubles in 1640, James Howell figured the royal consort as a heavenly goddess.[297]

Such representations did not quell the fears excited by the arrival in England of papal agents, the proselytizations and conversions within the queen's circle, or her efforts to rally Catholic support against the Scots in 1639. By 1640, she was openly talked of as the principal evil counsellor to the king. As Caroline Hibbard writes, 'The vicious and sustained parliamentary attacks on the queen in the 1640s had a lasting effect on her reputation.'[298] But, before the mid-1630s, such denunciations were heard mostly in puritan circles and were offset by more positive representations and probably even some popular support of the queen who had blessed the land with so many children.

Any study of the image and representation of Charles I must in the end bring us back to the king himself. We know quite a lot about the character, beliefs and manners of the king, but how much did contemporaries know of their austere sovereign and how were his personality and character represented to his subjects? And how was he perceived? As with Henrietta Maria, earlier contemporary impressions of the king were blotted out by the civil war and by both partisan vituperation and hagiography. In the 1620s and 1630s, however, a number of authors summed up the virtues of Charles to his people. The first to do so was George Marcelline who, as well as books on the triumphs of James I and on European war, published a souvenir account of Charles's marriage, sold at the Horseshoe in Pope's Head Alley. Marcelline, who appears to have written for a market, provided the sort of small details which were intended to satisfy readers curious about their new monarch. 'His stature of body,' he wrote beginning with physical appearance, 'is neither a giant or a pigmy but placed in the golden mean.'[299] Charles was moderate in his eating and drinking, well read in Scripture and divinity, and a man of fixed principles and loyalties who 'as he doth not lightly settle affection, so he will not easily remove it'.[300] Interestingly, Marcelline had much to say about the ethical and moral traits of the king's character, his 'spotless chastity', and, most of all, the mastery of passions and self-regulation of a prince whose motto was 'Si vis omnia subiicare, subjice te ratione': if you wish to govern all things, first subject yourself to reason.[301] As if preparing a sketch for the later Van Dyck portraits, Marcelline described Charles as 'a rider and ruler of his affec-tions' who 'reineth in his lusts with the bridle of wisdom'.[302] And the king, he observed, almost incidentally summing the philosophy of future masques, as he loved his queen, so he would rule his people with love.[303] Blessed with a king of so many virtues and 'endowments of mind', he did not doubt that all nobles desired to be 'drawn to the life according to his portraiture'.[304]

In their respective panegyrics, Henry Wotton and Robert Powell singled out similar personal royal qualities – temperance and chastity, learning and affection for the people – that should be examples to subjects. Indeed, concluding his parallel lives of Kings Alfred and Charles, Powell compared two 'who for their religion, piety, devotion, . . . justice, mercy, truth, meekness, temperance, patience, abstinence, conjugal castimony [sic] and all other virtues may be precedents of imitation to all princes and people'.[305] It may be significant that comparable panegyrics appear not to have been published in the second half of the 1630s, when ship money, the trial of Prynne, Burton and Bastwick and other mounting concerns might have rendered Charles an unpopular ruler. However, we should note that in 1639 several sermons still praised the virtues and qualities of the king as one of the best arguments for loyal support, and recall that Charles himself was far from despairing of the affection of his subjects.[306] As we have seen, the events of 1640–1 involved a competition for popular support, at the end of which it appeared, as he retuned triumphantly from Scotland, that Charles had emerged the winner. Indeed, Pym's Grand Remonstrance, that catalogue of the king's failings and attempt to blacken him in the eyes of the people, might be read not merely as a clever move in the parliamentary politics of the autumn of 1641 but as a major turning point in the representation and reputation of Charles. That Pym felt the need not only to address the people but to stir popular fears of popish and unconstitutional counsels, and to offer a critical retrospect of the reign, suggests that he also sensed the need to undermine more favourable percep-tions of the king. Certainly the nervousness in the Remonstrance about the popular hostility to the parliamentary leadership hints at a corresponding anxiety about popular support for the king and church which perhaps forced Pym to give assurances of parliament's commitment to the 'honour and happi-ness [of] his Majesty'.[307] The Grand Remonstrance shows that in 1641 the popular image and perception of Charles I were far from entirely negative and that the positive representations of the king had not fallen on deaf ears. On the other hand, Pym's (albeit narrow) success in getting the Remonstrance passed and its reception, at least in London, also indicate that, well before 1641, other portrayals of Charles had laid fertile ground for opposition.

CHAPTER 8

DEMYSTIFYING MAJESTY

I

A narrative of the opposition to Charles I cannot be attempted here and is anyway familiar enough as the stuff of countless Whig histories, some of them recently revived. However, after a review of the representation of the king in a variety of media and modes, one must briefly examine other more critical portrayals and counter-presentations, not least to begin to gauge how official and other favourable representations performed and were received in the broader political culture. As we have already seen, praise and panegyrics of the king by no means all emerged from court circles; those published by commercial printers and booksellers were evidently produced to sell to subjects who were, one therefore presumes, thought to be disposed to receive favourable notices of the monarch. On the other hand, many of the authors writing in praise of the king acknowledged, either explicitly or indirectly, discontents, criticism and even outright opposition and, in some cases, indicated that they were led to publish to answer them.

Given the legacy of the last years of James's reign and the theological quarrels which spilled over to the succession, we will not be surprised that some of the earliest opposition was perceived to come from a puritan caucus that apologists for the king, as much as Charles himself, began to conceive as a conspiracy. In 1627, for example, both Matthew Wren and Isaac Bargrave, in sermons preached before the king and published by command, identified a puritan threat to divine right kingship. Where Wren referred to some who 'dispute it . . . fiercely whether [the king] can of right be invested with so divine a privilege', Bargrave warned: 'know there is a generation who think themselves bound by their holy profession to quit subjects from their obedience'.[1] Though, after 1629, overt puritan attacks on royal authority are hard to find, opposition to episcopal authority and assertions of individual conscience, as well as the practice of nonconformity, constituted direct challenges to royal authority that persisted and grew, as Charles supported his archbishop in enforcing orthodoxy and ceremonies. In 1630, for example, a treatise on *The Practice of Princes*, allegedly published in Amsterdam but possibly clandestinely in England, in a critique of royal policy affirmed that not all princes ruled with God's blessing.[2] Alluding to Rehoboam who, seeking to be more absolute than his father, lost the hearts of his people, the author described a land full of 'murmurs and groans'.[3] Attacking the wicked counsellors who led Charles to persecute puritans, the author claimed to express the views of some of the godly that 'if God should take away the king issueless and . . . the injured king and queen of Bohemia should come to the crown, things must needs mend'.[4] *The Practice of Princes* suggested that, because the head of the commonweal was corrupted, 'the reciprocal passages between the head and the members are stopped'.[5] The next year, an extended edition of Thomas Beard's *The Theatre of God's Judgements* argued for the subordination of princes to the law and outlined a contractual theory of kingship that evoked the writings of Buchanan.[6] Condemning princes who exercised too much rigour, or levied excessive taxes, as violators of the law of God, Beard concluded that, besides a multitude of 'proud, cruel and vicious princes . . . tyrants and oppressors', the number of the virtuous was small – and, one might suspect, he did not number Charles I among them.[7]

It was just such works and, as much, the radical readings they invited that led the supporters of the king to reaffirm divine right theory and to denounce any who 'in a thought abhord/Curse this Anoynted of the LORD'.[8] Indeed, loyal supporters of the king recognized the intensifying puritan opposition to the monarchy and urged action. In *The King and Queen's Entertainment at Richmond*, in 1636, a Druid, opposing a more absolute rule backed up by a guard, urges: 'inspire thy *Priests* that they may restraine this people'.[9] The next year, as Prynne was brought to trial and puritan opposition reached a crescendo, the clergy raised their voices louder in support of the king and crown. Heeding warnings from new as well as old England about the 'fanatical inventions' of the puritans and the growing influence they had over 'the vulgar people', sermon after sermon, in the provinces as well as the capital, reasserted the divinity of kings.[10] At the Lincoln assizes in 1637, for example, Thomas Hurste preached on *The Descent of Authority: or The Magistrates Patent from Heaven* and, denouncing those who 'pretended religion' to justify insurrection, reminded auditors that those in authority had 'the very stamp of God's power'.[11] In his defence of divine rule, Hurste cited Alexander Leighton's *Sion's Plea*, a vicious attack on the episcopacy printed in 1629, 'and the like' as the means by which the puritans had laboured 'to make the people disaffected to their governors and government'.[12] By 1639, when the Prayer Book rebellion was followed by a flood of Presbyterian tracts from Scotland, and their worst fears come to pass, the loyalist clergy did not doubt that the puritans were reviving Buchanan's theory of popular sovereignty, preaching that the king was an infidel, and justifying resistance. Laud's warning to the king in 1637 that 'Your honour, your safety, your religion is impeached' by godly libels had become reality.[13] Throughout Charles's reign, the king's self-representation and representation by others as a pious monarch ruling by divine right was countered by a body of puritan pamphlets which figured him as a persecutor of the godly and presented monarchy as subordinate to the godly conscience. The contest for God's imprimatur was part of a longer struggle that went back to the Reformation. In Charles's reign, it was a struggle for the representation of the king and for the hearts and souls of his subjects – a struggle that was an essential precondition of England's wars of religion.

Puritanism and Presbyterianism provided the ideological fervour for the most bitter opposition to the king and monarchy. But there was published, too, a stream of writings expressing concern about the legality of Charles's exactions, actions and style of government that tainted the image of the king as a just, merciful and loving prince to his people. The tensions between Charles and his parliaments which emerged from wartime and culminated in the Petition of Right in 1628 doubtless fostered, as well as reflected, discontents in the country, as MPs returned from Westminster; and further levies and exactions during the 1630s fuelled a dissatisfaction which was manifested in legal challenges, most famously John Hampden's appeal to the courts against ship money.[14] Beard in 1631 included a chapter in his account of God's judgments on princes on those who excessively bothered their subjects with 'unnecessary exactions' and admonished that 'the law of God, it is clear that by it authority is not committed unto them to surcharge and . . . trample down their poor subjects by unnumerable and insupportable impositions'.[15] Oxford University's panegyrical volume for 1636, *Coronae Carolinae quadratura* endeavoured to counter continuing concerns about payments and voiced hopes that the birth of a fourth child might encourage the recalcitrant to pay taxes as tributes.[16] It may be that, in permitting a legal trial of ship money, Charles checked a mounting tide of opposition to the legality of his imposts. But the judgment did not quell the discontent, especially of those who had long believed that, rather than being put to the judges, the case of ship money should have been heard in parliament. Henry Parker's 1640 pamphlet, though moderate in language, expounded the case of the supremacy of parliament that the re-publication of Walter Ralegh's *Prerogative of Parliaments* supported.[17] Interestingly, Parker's strategy involved taking Charles's own proclamations of the harmony of liberty and prerogative to argue the subordination of the latter and turning the king's avowed commitment to law into a critique of the judges. The tone and temper of Parker's tract suggest that the constitutional opposition to Caroline governance had not come close to boiling point. But Parker almost certainly voiced concerns that were current and that, like his treatise, presented a very different portrait of the king to that of official representations.

Grumblings about ungodly rule and unconstitutional courses, although they were mounting, were by no means new. While the same is true of criticisms of royal foreign policy, especially by those who since Elizabeth's reign had advocated that England champion the Protestant cause, Charles's personal situation and events in Europe exposed him to opposition to his policy that spread beyond the godly. Charles, we recall, had succeeded to the throne as a king of war and had fostered an image of himself as a warrior prince which remained part of his official representation, even after the settlement of peace.[18] However, though here royal self-presentation was never entirely detached from the reality of political engagement in Europe, the king's pacific policy and his image as protector of England's 'halcyon days' and 'secure Quietus' met with a counter-presentation that hinted at royal pusillanimity and disregard for his family, faith and nation.[19] In the earliest years of the personal rule, criticism of Charles's pacific foreign policy was often expressed by means of extravagant praise of Gustavus Adolphus, king of Sweden, who had led victorious armies against the Habsburgs.[20] Andreas Hildebrandt's praise of 'this heroical and religious prince', descended from 'a race of deliverers and himself the greatest' was but one of the works translated into English that implicitly contrasted Gustavus's glorious deeds with Charles's shameful inaction.[21] George Hakewill's sermon, preached at Barnstaple in 1632, lauding kings who adventured their crowns to save the church from persecution, was a thinly veiled criticism of Charles who, reading the coranto accounts of Gustavus's triumphs as an attack upon himself, moved to outlaw them as damaging to his reputation.[22] While it removed a problem in the longer term, the death of Gustavus on the battlefield prompted a flurry of elegies on 'This Heaven sent furie' who had fought God's cause.[23] An anonymous relation of the Swedish king's funeral, published in England, as well as representing him as a providential figure, lauded a 'great hero' who ranked, it was claimed, as 'great Alexander's parallel'.[24] In a not very subtle rebuke to England's monarch, and a counter to representations of Charles as triumphant conqueror, the author wrote his memorial inscription for Gustavus:

> Without a Rivall, great GUSTAVUS dwell;
> Enioy thy fame without a Parallell.[25]

As well as the fall of Gustavus Adolphus, the death of Frederick, the Elector of the Palatinate focused even more critical attention on Charles I's pacifism. On his triumphant reception into Scotland, verses reminded Charles of his duty to his sister and now especially his nephew and urged action against the Habsburgs and papacy.[26] Recalling Elizabeth's 'victory' over the Armada, the Edinburgh University poets asked by way of a challenge:

> What can not then my Soveragne doe, whoes hand
> Doeth hold the helme of whole Great Britane land.[27]

Here, the Stuarts' claim to British imperial sway is turned into criticism of impotent inaction. That such a form of criticism by inversion of royal self-representation was not only Scottish is suggested by a play presented by the students of Magdalen College, Oxford and published and sold at the Bear in Paul's Yard in 1633. Jasper Fisher's *The True Trojans Being a Story of the Britaines Valour at the Romanes First Invasion* described Mars fighting for his nephews and the British emperor Cassibellaunus (uncle of Cymbeline) driving the Roman Caesar from his kingdom.[28] It may be that the launch of the ship money fleet, cooler relations with Spain and the presence of the young Elector by his uncle's side in 1636 raised hopes of action and so muted criticism. But Charles was acutely conscious of the need to persuade his subjects of his commitment to the Palatine cause and ever aware of opponents who countered his self-representation of peace with vigilance and strength with the accusation of cowardly weakness.

Perhaps even more dangerous than puritan opposition, constitutional challenge or criticism of peace were those seemingly more innocent histories and biographies of other emperors, kings and queens that, more or less coded, constituted a devastating portrait of Charles and criticism of his reign and government. As a staunch supporter of Charles wrote acutely in 1634, 'some write the lives of dead princes to eclipse the glory of the living'.[29] Other critics favoured an implicit comparison of the present ruler with the worst examples of rulers in the past. Countering the favourable parallels drawn between Charles and Augustus, or Charles and kings Alfred, Henry II and Edward III, opponents of the king from early in the reign both compared and contrasted Charles with infamous and renowned predecessors to represent his rule and person in the worst light. The years in which Villiers, Duke of Buckingham dominated the king's counsels saw the publication of some (unexplored) histories that were unquestionably meant to be read as vicious attacks on the duke and the king. Pierre Matthieu's *The Powerful Favourite or The Life of Aelius Sejanus* announced on its title page that it was printed at Paris in 1628, but it may well have been published in London.[30] Matthieu's *Life* narrated the excessive favours Tiberius, the tyrannical Roman emperor, bestowed on Sejanus. Of Tiberius, Matthieu wrote, 'he would not brook that any should bustle [*sic*] with the sovereign authority which was so delicate and tender that it would take hurt by the least touch'.[31] The figure of Tiberius had long been a signifier for tyranny and in 1626, we recall, Charles I had interpreted the mention of the emperor in a parliamentary speech as an attack upon himself.[32] Significantly, a contemporary reader of Matthieu has underlined the above quotation, as well as a few other such passages in the book.[33] From the story of Tiberius and Sejanus, Matthieu pondered the general problem of how to deal with such a situation. Arguing that 'in free cities men's tongues should not be captive' (his 'place' of publication, if it was London, he evidently deemed not free), Matthieu asserted the need to inform princes of their faults and the duty of rulers to heed advice and admonition.[34] 'It is', he advised in a passage also underlined, 'for princes to make themselves to be beloved'; and he warned the king: 'the sovereign authority is a strong causey which is not so soon destroyed by the violence of the current . . . as by some small rift or opening which makes way for the torrent to overthrow it'.[35] Charles here was surely being warned to ditch his favourite and win back the hearts of the people without which his crown would be in jeopardy. Francis Hubert's *The Deplorable Life and Death of Edward the Second*, a verse history of the downfall of two favourites, Gaveston and Spencer, was published the same year. Hubert had composed it in the late 1590s, but because it dealt with the deposition of a monarch, the work was suppressed, though manuscript copies circulated.[36] In 1628, an anonymous version, perhaps from one of them, was printed, prompting Hubert, just before he died, to publish, from the 'original copy', an authentic version that removed passages offensive to Buckingham and Charles I. It is not difficult to see why Hubert felt the need to rush out his own text. The anonymous version identified the scandals caused by favourites, especially such as advised the ruler to break the law. The message for kings was menacing. The sovereign drew the love or hate of the people according to his government, not his position or title. Pointing to a shift that had occurred after the death of James I, a verse noted:

A *King* may leave his name unto his *Sonne*,
But to his *Sonne*, no *King* can leave his Nature.[37]

Each ruler, he continued, had to earn the affection and loyalty of the people. Though '*Some* say that kings are Gods upon the earth', there were others who preached 'that subjects might a King their head remove'.[38] The safest way for a ruler, therefore, was not to assume his right and the public's obedience but to follow 'a just and rightfull course', and to choose the best counsellors.[39]

Charles I, who not only identified himself as Tiberius, but blamed attacks on his favourite for Buckingham's assassination cannot have failed, as Hubert intuited, to read such works as thinly veiled allegories of his own rule. Recently scholars have identified a similar historical allegory in Thomas May's editions of Lucan's *Pharsalia*, published from 1626 to 1631. As David Norbrook has observed, Lucan's poem was a hostile critique of Roman tyranny and May's dedication to leading opponents of Charles I's forced loan pointed up the parallels between Roman and Stuart circumstances.[40] Though May, later a republican, softened his tone during the 1630s and even wrote (as we saw) commissioned histories for the king, still his *Continuation of Lucan's Historical Poem*, dedicated to Charles in 1630, included the complaint of Calliope, the muse of epic poetry, that 'againe am I/Enforc'd to weepe, and tax your tyranny'.[41]

It may be significant that, along with May's move to greater sympathy with those exercising imperial or regal sway, after 1630 there were fewer historical parallels implicitly condemning Charles's kingship. Giovanni Manzini's *Political Observations upon the Fall of Sejanus* was translated into English in 1634, but contains no obvious address to English circumstances. Criticism by means of historical comparison did not come to an end. However, rather than an attack on Charles by way of the portrayal of cruel tyrants or evil kings, writers took models of the best rulers as measures by which readers might gauge the virtues and qualities of their own sovereign. Already in James I's reign, the name and memory of Queen Elizabeth had become a code for a nostalgic evocation of English naval prowess and victory. In the reign of his son, she was to become the focus of a politics of nostalgia as well as a pattern of good Protestant rule and moderate government who was contrasted, to his disfavour, with Charles I. The title of Diana Primrose's *A Chain of Pearl: or A Memorial of the Peerless Graces and Heroic Virtues of Queen Elizabeth* might suggest, if not a feminist, then a feminine appreciation of the queen; but to read the poem is also to detect a possible address to immediate Stuart circumstances.[42] Elizabeth, Primrose posited in a gesture that was not flattering to the present ruler, 'Admits not here the least Comparison'.[43] For in religion, 'Shee bang'd the Pope, and tooke the Gospell's part'; she delighted her parliament with her addresses, she deemed her people's love her greatest treasure; she 'did animate the Army' at Tilbury and made all Europe admire her, and Spain's monarch fear her.[44] Though there is no overt criticism in such lines, the contemporary reader might well have made connections between the catalogue of Elizabeth's virtues and the praise of her prudence and the discontents and failures of Charles's early years. The same may be true of Thomas Heywood's *England's Elizabeth*, published the next year with (opposite to the title page) an engraving of the queen holding a bible open at Psalm 16 and with the words on a scroll from her mouth: 'If the Lord had not been on my side'.[45] For even if criticism were not implied, the detailed account of Elizabeth's triumphal entry into London, her kissing the bible and pausing to speak graciously to the people, certainly pointed up Charles's decision not to so display himself to his people on a similar occasion.[46]

It may, too, be no coincidence that, as Charles retreated from European engagement, a number of historical works were published celebrating great moments of victory. Charles Aleyn's verse history of *The Battles of Cressy and Poitiers* under Edward III celebrated the triumphs of a warrior king whom a Latin commendatory verse by Thomas May described as 'Invictissime princeps'.[47] And the year of Gustavus's death saw a new edition of the satirist Samuel Rowlands's history of Guy, earl of Warwick, whose valour, a dedication to the earl of Montgomery observed, 'hath been the world's wonder'.[48] Rowlands's description of 'the admired champion of Christendom' and his wish that 'all the knights we have, were such as he' was at least a lament for lost glory – a lament that in 1632 the reader would hardly have failed to associate with King Charles.[49] A 1634 *True Picture and Relation of Prince Henry*, dedicated to Elizabeth of Bohemia, was nothing short of an encomium on Charles's deceased elder brother: a prince pious, stately and brave whose representation cowed foreign potentates and powers. 'Sic transit Gloria mundi', the author closed the account of his death, with at least the implication that glory had died with the first of James's sons, and was not to be reborn in the reign of the second.[50]

It may be a perception of history and Lives as criticism and opposition that led loyalists to counter these texts with works such as Powell's parallel lives of King Alfred and King Charles to which we have referred. As the quarrelsome precedents in James's reign (not to mention denominational controversies) had shown, there was in early modern England a struggle to interpret and claim the past. Given the authority of histories as tradition and moral exempla, the past was essential to royal representation and so also as important to the critics and opponents of royal policies and personalities. Comparing Charles as he did with the great Alfred, Powell could not but wonder why the people did not match his virtues by acting as dutiful and thankful subjects.[51] Others, however, who saw the king differently, called different rulers to mind to warn of the fates that awaited bad kings. In 1639, an anonymous verse narrative of the life of 'the all-beloved, admired and renowned Queen Elizabeth', again praising her steadfastness to true religion, her loving relationship with parliaments, and her reputation as 'the glory of the whole world's Commonwealth', acknowledged that her reign and his account would be read differently by readers of different sympathies:

I know that my presumption hath offended,
And that I shall be justly reprehended:
But yet I doubt not, but that some there be,
That in good part will take this work of me.[52]

As they reflected divisions, so histories contributed to mounting polarization. The battle to represent the past (and its relationship to the present) was – as it always is – part of the contest for representation. And that contest, of course, was inseparable from political engagement – indeed increasingly inseparable from an outright struggle for authority and power.

II

We began this section with a paradox: no ruler devoted more attention to the cultivation of an image than Charles I, who was, nevertheless, England's only king to end his life, after a trial, on the scaffold. Did such a paradox, we pondered, question our thesis that representation and regality were interdependent and mutually reinforcing? Or was it the case, as was traditionally maintained, that Charles took care over his image but either misjudged which were the right messages to communicate, or failed to communicate them to any but a narrow circle of already loyal courtiers and 'cavaliers'? This study cannot hope to settle disputes not only about the judgement of Charles I but about whether conflict was likely whoever was on the throne. But one inadequate answer to the question with which we began is that Charles succeeded in representing himself in ways that appealed at particular moments and that he was not always the best judge of the circumstances in which he most needed to explain himself and court support. We have seen that Charles, especially in the 1620s, and again in the later 1630s, wrote and spoke extensively to present his case to the people; that the visual images of the king were not confined to elite portraits but disseminated in engraving, woodcut, medal and coin; that, far from private or reclusive, Charles was often on public show and on progresses further and longer than his predecessors. As myriad verse panegyrics, loyal sermons and other writings (many if not most not produced under official direction) evidence, Charles did not want for advocates; nor did most fail to understand the king's own self-representations or the values and priorities he sought to uphold. Texts critical of the king are plentiful. Yet far from simply documenting his failure to reach out to his subjects, these counter-representations implicitly recognized the pervasive force of royal proclamations and images and the need to deconstruct and oppose them. As for the king's reputation among the ordinary people, some recent assertions have spread more obfuscation than enlightenment. It is unquestionably the case that by the end of the personal rule criticisms of the king were mounting – both within the court and in the country. Yet if Charles was irredeemably unpopular, why did his subjects flock to see him – as late as 1641 – in their thousands? There can be no doubt that, especially from 1638, fear of popish counsels close to the king as well as of Catholic threats to the realm tainted Charles in the eyes of many ordinary people, as well as the hotter sort of Protestants. But it is important to remember too that the zealous godly, far from popular, were laughing-stock figures of the early modern stage and that the Stuart king's support for popular festivity, as well as for the rites of the Church of England, made him and them popular with many common folk. Similar divisions are found in perceptions of royal policies. Though there was widespread popular support for Elizabeth of Bohemia and her children and some vague attachment to the Protestant cause, many who also heard the horrific stories of ravaged peoples and lands in Germany appreciated the peace and prosperity they enjoyed.[53] Though taxes and imposts were an irritant to many more than the legally minded who questioned their constitutional propriety, there was also pride in the fleet that ship money built – as the crowds who witnessed the launch of *The Sovereign of the Seas* indicate. Not only was the realm increasingly divided over a number of issues and policies, people were divided within themselves and perceived things differently as events and circumstances changed.

As to perceptions of Charles himself, a key event was the assassination of Buckingham. This removed the evil counsellor and paved the way for the end of wars that had considerably exacerbated religious tensions and relations with parliament. The death of Villiers was a precondition for the full blossoming of love between Charles and Henrietta Maria which became the central motif of royal representation. Henrietta Maria's public exercise and patronage of her faith did pose a public relations difficulty. But, whatever her practice or the icons in her chapels, the queen did not overtly proselytize in published words or on canvas. Until late in the 1630s, the predominant public representation of Henrietta Maria was as wife and mother, as that of Charles was as husband and father. Souvenir accounts of the marriage ceremony, public rejoicings at royal births, copies of portraits of the king, queen and children, all suggest that the image of the royal family was one that appealed to the people and forged an affective connection between Charles and his subjects.

For all the discontents and doubts, Charles had not, as his opponents warned, irrevocably lost the love of his people. The propaganda campaign waged by Prynne, Burton and Bastwick and their supporters, and by the Covenanters, was an assault on what they recognized was still a considerable bastion of popular support for the monarchy and the king. These campaigns were effective in undermining trust in the king, and the government failed to respond quickly enough to counter them; yet at the end of the 1630s ballads still evidenced a fund of traditional loyalty that was not, even in 1640–1, easily undermined. Though perhaps not as soon as would have been wise, before 1640 Charles had become more acutely aware of the need to nurture and foster that loyalty. So, as his leading parliamentary opponents, who had dabbled with treason, were driven to more radical measures, a life and death (literally for Pym and others) struggle began to secure the trust and support of the people. Events were to make starkly clear that Charles I had failed to secure the love and loyalty of the whole nation; perhaps no monarch had or could in a divided and increasingly polarizing religious and political culture. But the image, reputation and person of the king still forged a loyal following which enabled Charles to raise an army to fight a civil war from strength and, even after defeat, constituted an afterlife, memory and myth that, it is not too much to say, destroyed the English Commonwealth. The outbreak of the civil war itself has much to tell us about representation and counter-representation. Charles raised his standard because he could not command obedience to monarchy; his enemies fought because they could not sufficiently undermine it. We must turn to the struggles of civil war, but here not primarily to military battles but to battles of words and signs that contemporaries rightly judged no less mighty or destructive than pikes and swords.

PART III

THE CONTEST FOR LEGITIMACY

PROLOGUE: THE CIVIL WAR AND THE CONTEST FOR REPRESENTATION

In any polity, the exercise of authority is inseparable from the forms and media through which that authority is represented. While changed circumstances and the developments of new media and technologies might alter the predominant forms of representation, at any time there were, and were perceived to be, texts, words, signs and performances which conveyed, as well as communicated, authority. Those therefore who challenged authority were usually led to deploy (at least initially) the same forms and languages rather than to announce a radical rejection of them. The political process, we might say, was – and remains – a series of negotiations over, and contests for, the media and forms which were seen to convey authority and in turn to validate it.

In early modern England, especially after the break from Rome, Tudor, then Stuart monarchs, clearly discerning the dependence of their authority on forms of representation, tried to control the media of representation, and to make the forms of their representation monarchical. Henry VIII and his successors, through a variety of means, sought to make words, and especially print, a principal medium of royal government. As well as issuing printed statutes, proclamations and declarations, successive rulers publicized and endeavoured to enhance their authority through (often printed) forms of speaking and writing – not least, as we have seen, the authorized volumes of prayers which advertised divine rule and right. And they patronized, or recruited and enjoyed the support of, other writers who in sermons, treatises and panegyrical verses lauded the person and policies of the ruler. As well as harnessing the new opportunities of print, English monarchs, appreciating the public impression made by magnificence and display, attracted to their service the artists, architects and impresarios who gave visual expression to their claims to divine and natural authority – on canvas, paper and stone, in masque, procession and progress.

As we have seen, despite royal efforts to secure control, the media of representation were never monopolized by the crown. Even within the circles of government, the many involved in devising or designing the themes and tropes of publications or entertainments had different values and agendas which they sought to advance under the royal name. More importantly, in a Tudor and

Stuart polity increasingly sharply divided by religious change, the printing press was used by opponents of the establishment in church and state – perhaps most notoriously in the Martin Marprelate treatises which were published from the late 1580s.[1] And popular woodcuts and rituals, as well as following, sometimes (implicitly or explicitly) criticized official images and performances. As, during the later years of Elizabeth's reign and that of the first Stuart, critics of the court or monarch deployed new forms – of verse satire, newsletters, cheap print, engravings and early cartoons – to counter official representations, it became clear that the success of the Tudors in publicizing their authority had resulted in a very public contest for subjects' support. To add to the ruler's difficulties, as they became more conscious of, and concerned about, their liberties and privileges, parliaments and individual MPs took pains to address themselves to an emerging public sphere and, for their own purposes, to claim the public as the arbiter of disputes over prerogative and law.[2] Though the rhetoric of authority – and not just of royal authority – still denounced the intrusion into state affairs of the 'vulgar', both king and parliament, along with Catholics, Protestants and puritans, found it necessary to compete for popular support. When, towards the end of his reign, James I deployed a popular doggerel verse form to denounce popular political participation, he nicely captured what had become the dilemma, the inherent contradiction, of monarchical government: the need for distance and popularity.[3]

Charles I, after encountering similar frustrations, seems to have tried to put the clock back – or, we might say, put the genie of publicity back in the bottle. His decision to govern for a time without parliaments arose as much from a wish to curtail public debate as from his difficulties with the House of Commons.[4] During the 1630s, by not calling parliaments and by attempts to strengthen press licensing on the one hand, and by careful attention to his own image on the other, Charles attempted to re-establish control of his representation, that is to regain authority.[5] The extent of his success remains a subject of controversy.[6] But, even if opposition was only driven underground, at least for several years the noise of public print controversy was tempered and the king himself felt able (whether he was wise to do so or not) to retreat from the discursive fray.[7] As had been the case with his predecessors, however, war not only necessitated the recall of parliament, it reopened the floodgates of public debate and dispute. Scottish propaganda launched an assault on Charles's religious policies and English puritans and critics took the opportunity to print attacks on the government in church and state and increasingly on the queen and king themselves. With the Scots Covenanters and English critics freely charging him with advancing popery and favouring absolutism, Charles was forced back on different forms of representation: to participate in a contest to win trust and support. Where the court masques and canvases of Van Dyck had simply *presented* his authority, Charles and his supporters now had to *argue* for it and to answer other representations and accusations.[8] If he had been able quickly to suppress the rebellious Covenanters in battle, Charles might have been able to return to the style of government and representation he preferred. When, not least on account of the efficacy of Scots propaganda, he could not defeat them, and was forced to recall parliament, it was more than the political balance that was changed. From November 1640, the politics of representation was transformed as the contest to secure public support became not only vital to the nature and being of monarchy and parliament, but, to some of the key players in the emerging struggle, quite literally a matter of life and death.

The struggle to secure public support changed and intensified from the first session of the Long Parliament during which Charles I agreed to a series of statutes reforming abuses and limiting his powers, to the second session and the battle for control of the militia. The drift to arms in 1642 evidenced not only the failure to find a compromise but, we should recognize, the failure of either side decisively to win the argument. That, a century after Henry VIII had taken the headship of church as well as the commonweal, armies were levied against the king clearly indicates the extent to which the monarch (perhaps, too, the monarchy) had suffered a loss of mystique, a loss of the numinous. But that Charles – not unreasonably – felt confident of military supremacy and victory evidences not just what historians have argued was a recovery of political support by 1642 but, in large measure, his belief in the intrinsic loyalty of subjects, secured and sustained (not least) by the languages and texts of early modern royal representation.[9]

Loyalists may have provided the leaders of his armies; but Charles knew that without broader support he would not win the battle or recapture his capital and regain his authority. From 1641, therefore, Charles I, as well as speaking and writing extensively himself, recruited hired pens, most famously Edward Hyde, to present him to his people as a moderate ruler and good king.[10] Though in some cases the tone was different, and the pen not his own, Charles reverted to careful use of traditional forms of communication and representation: he spoke more frequently and published long explanatory speeches and declarations. He wrote and authorized prayers and promoted loyalist sermons and treatises which asserted his rights and prerogatives. The authority of traditional forms is nowhere better manifested than in the need Parliamentarian protagonists felt to claim that they were fighting for, not against, the king. Whatever the extent to which they had been challenged, most of the verbal forms of authority – declarations, proclamations, prayers – were predominantly regal forms. As, therefore, the parliamentary leaders were led to outright opposition to Charles, then to war, they were compelled to appropriate and ape these genres of representation in order to secure some legitimacy. Increasingly after 1642, when in the absence of the king, and at war, parliament began to govern, sermons delivered before the king were matched with sermons before parliament, prayers authorized by the king with services authorized by parliament. With statutes (which of course required royal assent) being no longer practicable, the houses issued by their own authority orders and ordinances which copied royal proclamations in language and visual form. And, as the king recruited penmen such as Hyde and Sir John Culpepper, parliament also hired and patronized lawyers and polemicists who argued their case to the people, and historians who garnered precedents to lend the legitimacy of (a sometimes fictional) antiquity to novel courses.

The civil war years witnessed a battle of representation as much as of arms – indeed a battle of representation that was vital to the outcome of the military conflict. As a consequence, all the traditional forms and genres of representation, the function of which (ideally) was to unite the commonweal, were rendered partisan. On both sides, texts were increasingly directed as much at counter-representation, at discrediting the honesty and claims of opponents, as at a positive presentation of a case or cause. As political division rendered all writing partisan, so in turn decidedly partisan representations hardened divisions and formed parties – Royalist and Roundhead, Presbyterian and Independent.

As well as rendering traditional forms of representation and communication the texts of party warfare, civil war witnessed not only the radical transformation of genres but new modes of writing and print. Satires had a long classical history as well as a more recent Elizabethan and early Stuart revival, but the satires issued by Royalists and Parliamentarians castigating each other deserve to be considered a new development of the form as well as unprecedented in their use of personal abuse.[11] Though they emerged from the corantos of the 1620s, the civil war newsbooks and serials, with their anthropomorphized identities (e.g. Mercurius), continuous publication and weekly dialogues with each other, constituted a new genre that depended upon, as they also fostered, sharp division and mutual hatred. Importantly (and surprisingly neglected), civil war also saw the frequent publication of battle reports which (as remains the case with this genre) were often concerned less with accurate record than with affirming the confidence of one's own side and demoralizing the enemy.

As contemporaries were quick to observe, the contest for support in print heralded and sustained the military conflict.[12] And this in turn irredeemably altered the place of print in representing authority – any authority. Revisionist scholars, rightly arguing that print neither was, nor was perceived to be, stable, truthful and authoritative might insist that what happened during the 1640s was a difference only of degree.[13] But the change was more fundamental. The ubiquitous charges of lying and misrepresentation, the systematic deconstruction and countering of words issued by authority, the relentless deployment of insult, abuse and scatological and sexual invective, demystified not only authority but the status of print itself. Ironically, just as publicity in print had served to desacralize early modern monarchy, so the sheer scale of print publication and the uses to which it was put tarnished the medium itself.

Though it has attracted most attention, the bitter contest for public support was not confined to words or print. The image of authority was central to the exercise of authority at the level of elites educated in emblem literature and heraldry, still more at the level of the illiterate who, in large part, made sense of the world through symbols and signs. Contemporary perception of the power of visual symbols is obviously demonstrated in the many acts of iconoclasm – against royal as well as liturgical images – which were perpetrated on the eve of, and during, the civil war. But simple destruction was not the only, or predominant, mode of the battle for visual authority. With the departure of the king from London, parliament, in order to govern, had to devise a number of new seals, and was acutely conscious of the importance of their image in endowing their fragile new position with authority. Parliamentary coins, needed with the closure of the Royal Mint, increasingly provided an opportunity in image and words to distribute parliamentary propaganda and slowly to counter the prevalent royal – and now *Royalist* – currency. In war, leaders of the Parliamentary armies were no less aware than their Royalist counterparts of the importance of the flags and banners which proclaimed their faith and cause. Like banners and flags, medals, issued to mark victories and given as rewards, were widely used by both sides as visual statements of values and as propaganda.

Interestingly, too, if the inventory of the London printseller Peter Stent may be taken as a guide, the civil war stimulated the public appetite for, and evidenced something of a contest played out in, engravings. In a culture dominated by the image of the ruler, the increased number of engravings of parliament in session advertised the authority of the assembly and hinted at equality with the crown. [14] During the war, the circulation in engraved and woodcut form of portraits of hitherto little-known Parliamentarian generals as well as Royalist commanders served to fashion a visual pantheon of military heroes to complement the accounts of miraculous victories on the battlefield.[15] And, as parliament began to govern, images of leading figures – Essex and Pym, as well as Fairfax and Cromwell – helped to convey the validity of parliamentary government.[16] No less than was the case with words, the visual contest for support involved negative as well as positive propaganda. Recalling earlier Reformation cartoons, Royalists and Parliamentarians illustrated books with, and published as separates, woodcuts and engravings that caricatured in effectively simple ways the vices of their opponents.[17] The king himself was spared, but the leading protagonists on both sides were represented in grotesque forms which were intended to symbolize the corruption of their party and cause. Though they have been little noticed, the etchers and engravers fought the civil war alongside the printers and pikemen.

Combining words and images, rituals – funerals and coronations, weddings and state entries – had been essential to the exercise as well as display of royal authority. From the moment of his triumphal entry into London in 1641, however, Charles endeavoured to deploy ritual not now to unify the nation but to build a party and to isolate his opponents. After he left London, the king made a series of entries into garrison towns and, even in defeat, made his journeys between places of virtual confinement akin to a royal progress. In a culture in which it was the monarch who gave meaning to state ritual, the Parliamentarians were at a distinct disadvantage, yet they did not neglect the significance of display. As John Adamson has recently powerfully demonstrated, the funeral of the Earl of Essex in 1646 provided an opportunity for civic display on a regal scale and for the cultural authority that ritual bestowed as well as displayed and which remained a problem for the parliamentary cause.[18] Ultimately, however, parliament could never vie with a king who retained a court and the power to cure the king's evil. In the area of ritual display (at which he excelled), Charles triumphed on the eve of civil war, forcing his enemies to military action without the cultural authority that sustained government. Most of all, whatever our judgement on the king's earlier representation of his rule as Chief Justice or head of the church or dynasty, in defeat and adversity Charles brilliantly made his own person, and his roles as husband, father and king – and finally martyr – his greatest asset: in the game of rival representations, his trump card.

The volume of writing on the civil wars is all but unmasterable. As well as the history of battles, political manoeuvres and parties, latterly scholars (especially literary scholars) have valuably explored the conflict conducted in pamphlets, languages and discourses. Hitherto, however, little attention has been paid to the representational contest for legitimacy and support and to the texts, rhetorics and strategies through which that contest was waged. The history of the civil wars as a conflict over representation must be the subject of a larger book – or indeed several books. In this chapter, I will sketch the outlines for such a study and endeavour to show how, while traditional representational forms and modes retained force and so had to be contested for, in the act of being contested they were also indelibly changed. In this, and the next two chapters, that is, we will explore the place of representation in the revolution and how revolution while underlining the importance of representation and image, also transformed them and their relationship to authority and power.

CHAPTER 9

WARS OF WORDS AND PAPER BULLETS

I

When Charles I recalled parliament in November 1640, he was led back from the silence of the 1630s to a principal mode of royal representation: speech. Interestingly, even after relations with parliament broke down, the king continued to make carefully crafted speeches – to committees of the Long Parliament, to parliaments called to Oxford, and to assemblies of the gentry in several counties and towns. Whatever his earlier reluctance, or alleged disability of speech, during the 1640s Charles discovered an eloquence along with an evident new appreciation of the power of the royal word uttered in person. His speeches at his trial and on the scaffold, rather than the last words of a desperate man, conveyed a confidence in the power of his word to be effective well beyond the grave. As we have remarked, after 1641 Charles also began to print his speeches – over seventy before his execution. In the new circumstances in which he found himself, Charles clearly determined that his personal 'voice' should be heard throughout the land.

Though the course of the Long Parliament, and especially the second session which convened in October, saw Charles and the leaders of the Commons desperately competing in speech for public support, after the king left London in January and the Militia Bill passed both houses, the rhetorical as well as polemical temperature was raised as it became apparent that the end of persuasion now was recruitment of men for war rather than reconciliation. When he published his speech to the delegates from parliament who went to Newmarket on 9 March to urge him to pass the Militia Bill, Charles's response was a resounding denunciation of those who had brought about the crisis, a proclamation of his right and the rallying slogan of a king preparing for war.[1] Referring overtly to a conspiracy plotted by the leaders of parliament (who had earlier implicated the king in a plot to seize the initiative by arms), Charles appealed to the ultimate arbiter of truth: 'God in his good time will, I hope, discover the secrets and bottoms of all plots and treasons; and then I shall stand right in the eyes of all my people.'[2] Pointing to the seditious pamphlets and sermons, the distributors of which parliament had left unpunished, he answered them with a single claim: his fears and concerns, he maintained, 'are greater for the true Protestant profession, my people and laws, than for my own rights or safety'.[3] In this speech, printed before he was denied entry to Hull, Charles's repeated personal pronouns effectively underlined his royal authority, even the dependence of the laws upon it, and, in subordinating his person to the duties of his office, nicely undercut parliament's claims to be loyal to the monarch while they were at odds with the man.

Over the spring and summer before he raised his standard in August, Charles went on what was virtually a speaking tour to raise support. At York in May, to counter persistent parliamentary charges that he favoured Catholics and even gave passes to Irish papist rebels, Charles issued resolutions announcing the disarming of all Catholics, his commitment to true religion and his openness to the discussion of disputed matters.[4] In June, with the assistance of Culpepper and Falkland, he effectively countered a parliamentary attempt to halt his progress by peace proposals that may have been 'merely . . . a propaganda exercise' with even more skilful propaganda that cast his enemies as destroyers of all social order.[5] The next month, at Leicester, warning his auditors against misinformation, Charles contrasted his own traditional and legal courses with the novelties and illegalities of parliament. 'Your religion, your liberties, your laws', he told them, connecting his interest and theirs with possessive pronouns, 'I will defend with my life'; then, in a definition that exposed a weakness in parliament's position, he continued: 'I mean the good known laws of the land, not ordinances without my consent, which till within these twelve months was never heard of from the foundation of this kingdom'.[6] In that contrast – of lawful royal and unlawful parliamentary acts – Charles predicted, 'will be the quarrel'. And in the quarrel, he assured them, even his enemies' audacity in seizing towns, ships and arms would not dishearten him. 'The concurrence and affection of my people . . . will supply and recover all'.

Returning to York in early August after a second rebuff from Hull, Charles, addressing the gentry, whom (he cleverly noted in passing) parliament had slurred with scandal, spoke in similar vein to identify himself with his people: 'I am', he affirmed in words that combined confidence with humility, 'wholly cast upon the affections of my people and have no hope but in the blessing and assistance of God, the justness of my cause and the love of my subjects . . . for', he added, 'I may justly say they are equal losers with me'.[7] If it was Charles's own belief in the efficacy of his oratory that led him to raise his standard and formally commence war, it may be that his judgement was right. Having for long left the rhetorical initiative to his critics and opponents, with the help of his new advisers Charles discovered a style and formulated a number of messages that he determined to communicate in order to strengthen his position. After his sojourn in the north, he took his message to the Marches and into Wales, to rally troops to his banner. At Shrewsbury on Michaelmas Eve, the king flattered the assembled by claiming that his misfortune had come with the benefit of bringing him to such a good part of his dominion.[8] Deploying a more personal, human tone, he admitted that difficulties faced them all: 'I fear I cannot prevent all disorders, I will do my best,' he promised, and gave force to his words by expressing his willingness to melt his own plate to raise money. Pressing subtly for similar sacrifice from his auditors, he appealed to their interest as well as duty, warning them of the need to labour hard to preserve the commonwealth, and assuring them that their assistance would be remembered and, in better times, rewarded. At Denbigh towards the end of September, observing that along with his own departure the greatest number of MPs had also left London, he identified and warned against a malignant party which threatened the rights of its members no less than his own.[9] In a new language appropriated from the rhetoric of the common law, Charles warned: 'By their power [a term that itself implied illegitimacy], the law of the land (your birthright) is trampled upon and instead thereof they govern my people [the pronouns again isolate the enemy] by votes and arbitrary orders.'[10] On this occasion, too, Charles overtly identified his parliamentary opponents as sectarians, Brownists bent on the destruction of the church.[11] Finally, he called upon the local sheriffs to distribute copies of his recent protestation, 'having no other way to make it public, these men having restrained the use of my presses.'[12] Though his departure from London had presented difficulties, the claim was itself rhetorical: Charles was getting his speeches and declarations into print; that to the gentry of Denbigh and Flint was printed at London. But in claiming parliamentary censorship of his voice, the king conveyed the powerful truth of his own words, the fears vicious, sinful traitors had of them, and the need for his audience to spread the message.

By no means decisive, the first battles of the civil war nevertheless buoyed Charles's confidence in his cause. With a plan to march on London and regain control of his realm, Charles left from Shrewsbury in October, bypassed the parliamentary army under the command of Essex and got between him and the capital. When the two armies met at Edgehill, the Royalist horse carved through their inferior opponents, leaving Essex's foot to hold the royal forces to a stalemate.[13] Undaunted, the next month Charles pressed on towards London, and was checked only at Turnham Green, whence, seeing the defences and citizen bands gathered, he withdrew to make headquarters at Oxford.[14] The absence of a decisive outcome to early battles pointed to a longer campaign than had been anticipated – and one in which, since men and money would be needed, the art of persuasion would be ever more vital to the fortunes of war.

After disappointing military campaigns, parliament sent commissioners to Oxford to negotiate with Charles; but, since the terms were essentially those he had rejected before, it is quite probable that the approach was made to display a willingness to end the war rather than with a serious expectation of the terms being acceptable.[15] For his part, though the military balance was in his favour,

Charles also could not be seen to be an obstacle to peace. Accordingly, in a published speech to his Privy Council, which gave readers a sense of eavesdropping on the king's private counsels, Charles affirmed his desire for peace and the quiet of the realm.[16] Cleverly exonerating most citizens from blame, and so opening the way to their defection with impunity to his cause, he attributed the treason of London to a handful of 'malicious spirits': 'And for the madness of those idle and inconsiderate outcasts of the people, can any man of judgement think it fit the noble, wealthy and moderate inhabitants of the city should suffer?'[17] Playing along for strategic reasons with the parliamentary fiction that they fought for the king not against him, Charles promised to listen to proposals with fatherly love, 'forgetting all things past and imputing them rather to misunderstanding than malice'.[18] Meanwhile, as negotiations continued, after a sermon at Christ Church Cathedral the king issued from Oxford a protestation answering the charge of malignants that the queen had tried to convert him and that he was inclined to popery; and, denouncing those who had driven him from his capital and his parliament, he called on the mayor and aldermen of Oxford to champion his cause, as London had his opponents'.[19]

From his base in Oxford, Charles saw military successes during the spring of 1643 in the north and west, culminating in the taking of Bristol in July.[20] But the defeats brought to the fore in parliament a group committed to the more forceful prosecution of the war and led to an alliance with the Scots, whose entry with 20,000 men turned the balance against the king.[21] As well as military resistance, Charles appreciated the need to counter the new Scottish forces entering on parliament's side with argument. Days after the Scottish troops crossed the border, the king addressed his parliament at Oxford. In a speech cleverly cast to paint his opponents as enemies of *all* English men, he contrasted his own love of peace and the nation with parliament's invitation to a foreign power to invade.[22] The Scots were long hated by the English and even in 1639 there is plenty of evidence of popular jingoistic abuse against them.[23] Charles tried to stir it and to forge a bond of 'trust and confidence' with English subjects to protect liberties, properties and privileges against the foreigner.[24] At King's Moor, in the summer, Charles again warned those assembled that the Scots threatened nothing less than the conquest of the English nation and subjugation of the English people.[25] Urging them to fight for their country, religion and law, as well as for a king who alone protected them, he rose to lofty rhetorical strains that evoked the heroic kings of English history, in particular Henry V: 'He that will not venture his life for these,' he told them, 'I had rather have his room than his company.'[26]

The rhetoric was powerful. Perhaps not least because they felt they were not winning the argument, the war party in the Commons concentrated on an escalation of fire power and a new modelling of the army.[27] Over the next two years, a series of Parliamentary victories overturned Royalist gains and effectively ended the civil war. Interestingly, during these years, though there are reports of his rallying of troops, we have no published speeches from Charles. Even during the complex negotiations that followed the war – with the Scots, the English Presbyterians and the army – for all his formal responses to terms, Charles did not authorize the publication of any speeches. His silence is puzzling; but it may be that, as well as being forced to devote himself to the field, Charles too felt that now the battle was not for hearts and minds but for military victory and survival. After his defeat, it would seem that, as he had in 1629, the king chose silence as a *strategy*. While the Scots and English, Presbyterians and Independents, parliament and the army, wrangled over the future settlement, Charles, while professing openness to all, resolved, it would seem, to position himself above the politicking so as to underline his indispensability and centrality to any peaceful outcome.

Charles did not speak again, or authorize the publication of his speeches, until 1648. By then, his attempts to play off the various interests not having worked as he had anticipated, he was in confinement on the Isle of Wight and parliament had voted to make no further addresses to the king.[28] When the resolution was repealed and another round of negotiation began at Newport, Charles issued the first royal speeches in print that had been published since 1644. Published with a huge royal arms and engraving of the king enthroned with commissioners kneeling before him, the speeches, outlining his support for settlement, also visually asserted Charles's authority.[29] While politely flattering the eloquence of the parliamentary commissions and emphasizing his moderation (his opinions, he said, were 'not . . . like the laws of the Medes and Persians, unalterable or infallible'), Charles also took a stand on his conscience.[30] One senses that, while responding to the proposals, Charles's speeches – indeed his decision to return to speech – served another purpose. By 1648, if not earlier, the king was not speaking only to the moment but to posterity and was – through his personal voice – constructing a new representation of himself: that of a godly martyr for his people. In a message in which he denounced any who 'think it reasonable . . . to offer any violence to the conscience of their sovereign', he took a stand above the politics of negotiation and compromise.[31] If, as he knew they probably would, parliament insisted on its terms, the king would, he made clear, 'with more comfort cast himself upon his saviour's goodness to support him . . . than for any politic consideration which may seem to be a means to restore him deprive himself of the inward tranquillity of a quiet mind'.[32] In a last farewell speech to the commissioners he was yet more explicit: 'I believe,' he told them in language already evocative of the Passion, 'we shall scarce ever see each other again: but God's will be done. I thank God I have made my peace with him, and shall without fear undergo what he shall be pleased to suffer men to do unto me.'[33] That the message, rather than one of resignation, was a seizure of rhetorical victory out of military defeat was soon apparent. For, Charles continued, he knew there had been

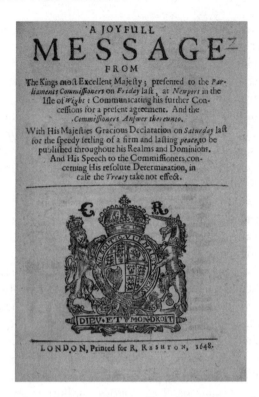

46 *A Joyfull Message from* The Kings Most Excellent Majesty, Presented to the Parliaments Commissioners, *1648.*

a plot and that men violently pursuing their own ends under pretences of public good had sought not only his own ruin, but – and he added 'nothing so much affects me as . . . the sufferings of my subjects' – that of his people. Far from abandoning polemic, Charles's self-scripting as martyr to his own conscience and for the good of his subjects deprived those who had won the military victory of the spiritual and moral authority to rule. 'In my fall and ruin', he prophesied, 'you see your own.' If the report can be trusted, Charles delivered his speech 'with much alacrity and cheerfulness' and with a 'serene countenance'. And it left those who heard it with 'many tender impressions'.[34] If Charles had preferred silence out of a concern that speaking excessively, as had his father, had reduced majesty to a matter of mere debate, by 1648 he had at last found a voice to which there was no easy retort: in the voice of the martyr, he reconciled sacred mystery and popular polemic.

Charles I, as we have seen, made use of often long declarations outlining his position, especially during the late 1630s as a counter to Scots propaganda.[35] As the country drifted into civil war, Charles published by special command the first of a series of declarations that were issued during the 1640s. In 1642, the king's declaration suggests still a royal hope that the royal word, delivered in this form, might be heard above the noisy exchange of charge and counter-charge. Charles wrote to counter dangerous accusations that he was popishly inclined; he vowed to protect the Protestant religion against both papists and schismatics.[36] But beyond his reputation for orthodoxy, the declaration sought, revealingly, to establish the true status of royal utterances. The king expressed his dismay 'that we so just, so pious and merciful in our words and intentions should not be believed in all our declarations and protestations'.[37] In language that identified his divine authority with trust in his sovereign word, he added: 'certainly it is *impiety* to be so full of infidelity to the words of a king'.[38] Where parliament, under the pretence of law and religion, exercised arbitrary power, the king's word, Charles insisted, was a guarantee in which subjects could place their faith.[39]

If the king still harboured serious hope that he might thus re-establish discursive control – that is, his authority – he was immediately disillusioned. His dilemma, however, was that, even though, rather than trusted, his declarations were picked over, disputed and contemned, he still needed to use them. In 1644, Charles reissued to all subjects a declaration of his commitment to the Church of England against the persistent calumnies that, he believed, more than anything had caused the war.[40] To reinforce words, he pointed to his actions – the Protestant education of his children, his practice of his faith at the head of his army; but the declaration was discredited as the work of Digby 'or whoever it was' and as evidence of the corrupt influence of friars.[41] It may well be that the attribution of his sovereign words to a 'contriver' (though it suggests a parliamentary nervousness about the power of royal authorship) dissuaded Charles from further use of declarations for some time.[42]

Whatever the reason, the bookseller George Thomason's collection of civil war writings contains no royal declarations from 1644–7, the same years, we noted, when speeches ceased to be printed, and military fortunes turned from Royalist supremacy to defeat. As was the case with speeches, Charles returned to addressing his subjects through royal declarations only after defeat was followed by negotiations. As tensions mounted between the army and parliament, not least over proposals for disbandment of troops, Charles, in August 1647, took the opportunity of the citizens' petition for a treaty to publicize his own position.[43] The king assured readers he wanted nothing more than peace.[44] To strengthen the peace party, he dismissed resoundingly the rumour that he would not listen to overtures or would seek revenge.[45] Again, indulging a convenient fiction, he exonerated most citizens from blame and repeated the words of an earlier speech in which he promised to attribute their disloyalty to misunderstanding.[46] Recognizing a new world of *realpolitik* fostered by years of claim and counter-claim, rather than simply giving an assurance, Charles observed that it was hardly in his interest to refuse to listen to peace proposals.[47] In June, however, the army intervened in politics and seized the king from parliamentary control.[48] Though a captive, Charles keenly sensed the greater possibilities now presented to him of playing off the army against the parliament. In a declaration issued from Hampton Court, supposedly found on a table after his escape to Carisbrooke, Charles reiterated his commitment to peace, but warned that it depended upon himself.[49] Denouncing Leveller doctrines, yet appealing to the soldiery with intimations of his backing for arrears of pay and religious toleration, Charles implicitly (and not unskilfully) put himself, the 'Pater Patriae' as he reminded them, out to the best offer.[50]

When, after he rejected parliament's preconditions, the houses passed their vote of no addresses in January 1648, Charles issued one of the few declarations published by royal command 'to all his subjects'.[51] Far more adept at adapting to circumstances than he had been – or is credited with having been – the king changed his tone and style of address. With factions in both the parliament and army struggling for the mastery, the king, stealing a trick from his opponents, invoked the people as arbiter: 'who but you', he asked in a new direct and familiar mode, 'can be judge of the differences betwixt me and my two houses? I know none else.'[52] Abandoning the lofty style of a monarch, Charles presented himself to his subjects now as 'a man', and as a husband and father denied the common pleasures and comforts of wife and children, which he shared with ordinary subjects.[53] Having established an affective bond (one the king was henceforth to invoke time and again), the declaration moved on to underline the political bond between king and subjects. Charles explained that, though keen for peace, he had not been able to grant all that parliament demanded 'without deeply wounding my conscience' or – and the coupling is skilful – 'abandoning [his] people to . . . arbitrary and unlimited power'.[54] Cleverly, Charles presented his conscience not as the obstacle to settlement, but as the protector of what his people most desired. Alluding to parliamentary votes to suspend negotiations, he asked: 'if I may not be heard, let any one judge who it is that obstructs the good'.[55] And, cataloguing the misrepresentations and afflictions he had suffered (and had borne with Christian patience and equanimity), he swiftly moved from the personal to the public, warning: 'It may be easily gathered how those men intend to govern who have used me thus.'[56] Charles, offering to stand or fall with and for the liberty of the kingdom, re-presented himself, indeed reconstituted himself, as the *pater patriae* on whom all depended. Connecting his body personal with the body politic of the realm, he made his own condition and fate those of the nation.

It is not easy to evaluate the exact relationship between a royal declaration such as this and the mounting pressure from the constituencies which virtually forced parliament to reopen negotiations. However, petitions sent to parliament in some cases echoed the language of royal addresses; and the discontents that burst out into the second civil war were characterized as Royalist as much as localist – a testament, perhaps, to the extent that Charles had succeeded in identifying his own condition with the grievances of the nation.[57] By early December 1648, parliament reopened peace negotiations on the basis of royal concessions they had earlier deemed unsatisfactory. A sense of the likelihood that Charles might have secured peace on his terms, or at least terms that preserved what was fundamental to him, is strengthened by the purge of parliament led by Colonel Pride, on Ireton's and (almost certainly) Cromwell's authority on 6 December. The coup, of course, terminated negotiations and paved the way for the trial of the king. From another perspective, however, it played into the king's hands. The arbitrary power he had warned of now overrode not only his conscience and rights, but what he had been coupling with them – the sacred liberties of parliament. The military putsch which ended negotiations was needed because popular support, and with it cultural authority, had turned back to the king.[58]

In 1644, a treatise entitled *Vindex anglicus* connected the authority of the English language, the bond of the nation, with that of the monarchy. The anonymous author asked, rhetorically, 'what matchless and incomparable pieces of eloquence hath this time of Civil War afforded?'[59] Specifically, he continued, 'Came there ever from a Prince's pen such exact pictures as are his Majesty's Declarations?'[60] The word 'exact' suggests writings not only precise and true but demanding, forceful (as in *exacting*). It may seem perverse to argue the force of royal declarations that led Charles not back to his throne but to the scaffold. Paradoxically, however, it was their very force, their influence and persuasiveness that compelled the Independents to move to silence him – and to sow the seeds of their own destruction as they did so.

The royal declaration had emerged in early modern England as a new genre for explanation, justification and exhortation, but royal proclamations were traditionally brief, formulaic texts that reinforced statutes or issued a specific instruction to magistrates or subjects in particular circumstances. As we have seen, however, proclamations were not devoid of rhetoric and, in some cases, were issued with preambles which were intended to explain orders in order to secure co-operation with, and more vigorous enactment of, them. During the 1640s the flood of texts, including royal speeches, declarations and loyalist treatises, might lead us to attribute little importance to proclamations as a genre of royal representation and they have largely been neglected by civil war historians. The statistics, however, might lead us to reconsider. Where during the personal rule the king issued on average one proclamation a month, rising to twice that from 1640 to 1642, during the civil war years, 1642 to 1646, Charles I issued nearly two hundred proclamations, about four a month on average – more than any of his predecessors.[61] Obviously, both the impossibility of passing statutes and the need for executive action in war go some way to explain the increased number. During the war, Charles governed by proclamation; and in deploying proclamations, as well as using a practical device he underlined the identity of monarchy with traditional forms. Parliament, by contrast, had to invent a new genre of executive order. But the story of civil war proclamations is not just that of executive orders. As Jerome de Groot has observed, with a print run of over a thousand, proclamations vied with newsbooks in the audience they reached.[62] Not least on that account, Charles was acutely aware that their importance lay as much 'in cultural and representational terms' as in their function as executive decree.[63] Proclamations not only announced, they also displayed and performed majesty. Read aloud after a fanfare of trumpets, or posted on court gates and market crosses, with the royal arms, they represented regality in multi-media ways. During the civil war, they were also reprinted in newsbooks such as *Mercurius Aulicus* and so debated in other serials and pamphlets.[64] In the political and print circumstances of the 1640s, royal proclamations deployed a different language and style. Faced with divided authority, conflicting ordinances and multiple voices, the civil war proclamations 'deploy[ed] the rhetoric of polemical propaganda disguised as authoritative instruction and monarchical truth'.[65]

Other than a few recent pages, royal proclamations of the 1640s have not been studied as polemic or as a (traditionally authoritative) genre of royal representation which was adapted to new circumstances. Where proclamations had often been justificatory, during the second session of the Long Parliament they began to sound distinctly partisan. In the proclamation he issued ordering the arrest of the five MPs on 6 January 1642, Charles identified, as he was often to do, the offences against himself with assaults on 'our laws and the liberties of our subjects'; and he publicized the disobedience of the Commons in neglecting his order to arrest them.[66] Thenceforth, proclamations became the organ of a party, especially (as we shall see) after parliament issued its own ordinances from March 1642. Still, in May 1642 Charles may have hoped that a proclamation carried an authority parliament could not emulate: in forbidding subjects to muster or train under any parliamentary order, his proclamation not only cited the statutes which placed the militia under his command, but also dismissed the new ordinances as having only the 'colour and pretence' of legality.[67] A further proclamation the next month detailed the statutes and legal precedents and answered head on the arguments being made by parliament to justify its militia ordinance which effectively distinguished between the person and the authority of the king.[68] The polemic of this proclamation was emphasized too by Charles's referring to his Answer to the Nineteen Propositions and in his repeated insistence that the subjects' 'interest is involved with ours'.[69] 'Our subjects,' Charles insisted in a denunciation of the parliamentary commission that skilfully evoked early modern fears of novelty, 'cannot be well pleased with any new ways, how specious soever.'[70]

When the refusal to admit the king to Hull heralded the first military encounter of the war, Charles issued a series of proclamations to publicize the illegality of parliamentary orders and the crime of high treason committed by any who followed them, while offering pardon to subjects misled by the malignant party which had hijacked the Commons.[71] Endeavouring to isolate the radical leaders from moderate MPs, the king repeated his earlier promises to honour the statutes to which he had consented and his assurance that he opposed not parliament but those who subverted it: those like Sir John Hotham whose 'unheard of insolence and barbarism' threatened 'cruel oppression' of the king's subjects.[72]

As the fighting proper began and contest for support intensified, the polemic – or rather, the vitriol – of royal proclamations sharpened. In August, proclamations denounced the Earl of Essex, recently appointed Parliamentarian commander, as a man who had long had traitorous designs and the other leaders of parliament as figures 'bearing an inward hatred and malice against our person and government and ambitious of rule and places' – characterizing them, that is, not as the patriots they claimed to be, but as nakedly ambitious men who overturned the peace and order of the commonweal for their selfish ends.[73] Describing himself as liege lord and his opponents as ambitious rebels, Charles presented Essex and others as leaders of the kinds of baronial uprising which had torn England apart in the (still very much remembered) past but which had been succeeded by the Tudor peace. And the constant repetition of words such as 'rebel', along with his coupling of 'our person and government' exposed as blatant illegality the parliamentary claim of loyalty to the crown, if not to Charles.[74] At a moment when men were forced to make difficult decisions, the importance of such argument, the deployment of a feudal language of allegiance, and allusions to past rebellions and memories of the Wars of the Roses, can hardly be overstated. Though such arguments were being expounded more fully in treatises, the very form of the proclamation favoured the king's case. In the summer of 1642, before the full realization of the fact of civil war had gripped the nation, proclamations were not naturally read as polemic and so had the potential to be the most powerful genre of polemic.

During the early months of war, while sharpening his attacks on the parliamentary leaders and calling for recruits, the king wisely kept the door open to those who might have second thoughts now the reality of civil war was upon them. In a series of proclamations published in October and November, Charles held out the promise of pardon to the inhabitants of several counties 'seduced by the cunning and falsehood of the authors of this rebellion'.[75] By the end of the year, however, though his armies had early successes, Charles was expressing evident frustration that he had been less than successful in representing himself as the sole custodian of the law and his opponents as 'an unlimited arbitrary power'.[76] 'We have made so many declarations of our royal intentions concerning the preserving of the religion and laws of the land', a proclamation of 16 December ran, yet 'whilst . . . our just and legal commands are not obeyed, other orders and ordinances (for which there is no legal foundation) which . . . overthrow the laws of the land . . . are submitted unto and obeyed'.[77] As a consequence, the king issued orders forbidding payments to parliament and threatened those who continued in disobedience that their heirs would be subject to wardship fines.[78] Proclamations, too, were used as sharp reminders of the power that resided in the king, those ordering the removal of the Courts of Requests, Chancery and Wards to Oxford emphasizing the dependence of the processes of justice on the person of the king.[79]

With military stalemate, however, and the need to raise manpower and money for what was increasingly looking as if it would be a long war, the rhetoric of proclamations had to be targeted to winning support. Whatever his frustration at the need for repetition, Charles's proclamations repeated his commitment to Protestantism, law and liberty and his 'tender commiserations for the sufferings of our people'.[80] To demonstrate that concern, he ordered a proclamation against plunder to be read in all churches and, perhaps to win over moderate puritan support, published proclamations against swearing and profanity in the army and requiring the soldiers' attendance at catechizing and sermons.[81] As concern mounted at the disorder which began to disrupt the parishes, he appealed to social and religious conservatives by reference in proclamations to the 'Great Charter of the liberties of England' that secured the church and clergy and to the factious schismatics who infringed on them.[82]

In one of the longest proclamations of the war, published in June 1643, Charles transformed the genre into a full-scale polemic that combined a number of strategies and charges.[83] In a text of well over three thousand words, Charles struck at the very name of the parliament at Westminster. Observing that many MPs had departed the house out of conscience, and more had been driven from it by intimidation, he characterized the seditious persons who remained as a rabble of 'mutinous and desperate Brownists, Anabaptists and other ill affected persons' who had no legitimacy beyond the arbitrary power they assumed and the arms that sustained them.[84] Where, it continued, the king conferred with his Great Council to settle the distemper of the kingdom, in London affairs were 'concluded by a private committee . . . contrary to the laws and rules of parliament'.[85] Led by sectaries, this committee, Charles continued, vilified the Prayer Book, seized subjects' estates and, instead of seeking peace, 'invited foreign forces to invade this kingdom' – 'all which for the matter of fact we are ready to make proof of'.[86] Announcing his own plans for a free parliament, the king's proclamation, ordered to be read in all churches and chapels, invited all the expelled, excluded and discontented members to Oxford, where he would willingly heed their counsel.[87] The mention (and later meeting) of a parliament at Oxford was itself a move to shift the geography of constitutional legitimacy entirely from London to the royal headquarters where the court, and the lawcourts, were already re-established. The next month, Charles outlawed all trade with the capital in an attempt to undermine its role as the economic as well as political centre of the realm, and to transfer traffic to Royalist ports.[88] At the same time, in order to undermine London as a headquarters of religious affairs, a royal proclamation declared illegal the Assembly of Divines summoned by parliament to Westminster to forge a new religious settlement, along with the oath or covenant that the Commons had devised to bind men to allegiance.[89]

It was only a few weeks before Charles had to respond to a far more dangerous covenant – that Solemn League and Covenant which formed the basis of a parliamentary alliance with the Presbyterian Scots that would add a formidable army to his opponents' forces. In a proclamation of 9 October, the king exposed the 'specious expressions' of loyalty, piety and religion and re-presented the Covenant as 'in truth nothing else but a traitorous and seditious combination against us and against the established religion and laws ... and endeavour to bring in foreign force to invade this kingdom'; but his words, whatever effect they may have had on some, could not halt the logic of the alliance.[90] When the Scots enemy entered England, Charles's immediate response was a proclamation calling a parliament at Oxford. The proclamation made a bid for the patriotic vote in denouncing the Scots' 'insolent act of ingratitude and disloyalty' to England and their clear 'design of conquest'.[91] In a renewed appeal to the moderates for whom an invitation to the Scots had been a step too far, Charles repeated, and acted on, his earlier summons of MPs to Oxford to advise him on re-establishing peace.[92] Even if the Scots were about to change his fortunes, Charles, alluding to recent successes, was concerned to show that he was acting from a position of strength. It was not out of desperation that he called parliament: 'the condition we are now in [is] improved by God's wonderful blessing to a better degree than we have enjoyed at any time since these distractions'.[93] Rather, it was 'the princely and fatherly care' of his people that prompted him to call an assembly where all true subjects might assist in resisting the 'desperate and malicious enemies of the kingdom' – both Scots and rebellious English.[94]

The new military circumstances required a series of executive proclamations on recruiting men, seizing arms, providing victuals and levying an excise.[95] To continue to uphold the king's claim to be the protector of legal courses, the proclamation for the levy of men emphasized the advice of the parliament – even though the Royalist Council of War had advised it the previous year.[96] The new parliament itself was a casualty of the changed military situation which made free access to Oxford difficult and in September 1644 the king prorogued it. The importance Charles attached to his image, however, especially after the military setbacks of the year, is clear from the proclamation of prorogation. Though he was led, for members' own safety, he claimed, to prorogue the parliament, the king assured all of his 'earnest desiring as soon as with conveniency may be to be assisted with the council and advice of the said members' and, he added revealingly, 'to have them witnesses of all our actions and proceedings in order to the peace of this our kingdom'.[97] When they again met, he promised, they would by 'concurrent counsels', 'with piety towards God and justice' take action to prevent the 'desolation' of war. The contrast of a peace-loving king, wedded to free parliaments, piety, justice and the good of the kingdom, with an illegitimate body bent on destruction of church, state and nation was obvious to all. Lest a proclamation proroguing parliament did not adequately communicate it, Charles followed it with another 'invitation to all his loyal subjects' to assist him in finding the way to peace.[98] Cleverly reminding a war-weary nation of the best times of Queen Elizabeth and King James, he affirmed his own genuine love of peace. 'We have always preferred in the sincerity of our heart,' he wrote, in a familiar, personal tone, 'that no success should ever make us averse to peace.'[99] Silent on some recent defeats, Charles told the people that, after each of his victories, he had solicited peace, only to be rebuffed. To obtain it, therefore he explained, he had resolved to march on London, to free 'our poor subjects oppressed by power' and war, and to re-establish a free parliament that would disband the armies and settle peace, religion, liberties and properties according to the law. The king called upon all good subjects to join him in arms as he approached the capital to 'free themselves from the tyranny of their fellow subjects' and to establish a free parliament to reclaim the nation.[100]

Charles's public protestations of his commitment to peace undoubtedly helped to strengthen the peace party in the parliament and to open the discussions at Uxbridge in January 1645.[101] Appropriating one of parliament's own favoured practices, he issued a proclamation for a Wednesday public fast to implore the blessing of God on the negotiations – and, of course, to publicize his own godliness and sincerity, lest (as transpired) the discussions failed.[102] Charles authorized a form of service and prayer 'that both prince and people may then join together in a true humiliation' before God.[103] The negotiations indeed ended in a failure that gave the political initiative to those in the Commons who pressed for the more vigorous prosecution of the war. In mid-February, they passed the Self Denying Ordinance and created the New Model Army to co-ordinate and escalate the war effort.[104] Faced with the prospect of a new military force he could not equal, Charles used some of his last proclamations to try once more to win back waverers (with the offer of a pardon to all who returned to obedience) and to raise auxiliaries. The arguments he used were not new, but the rhetorical pitch was raised. 'In the prosecution and for the upholding of the rebellion,' he asserted, 'there hath been more profanation and scorn for the Protestant religion ... more oppression of the subject ... more usurpation upon the rights of our crown and violation of laws and of acts of parliament and of privileges of parliament ... than can be paralleled by any former example in this kingdom.'[105] Referring to the 'new armies now moulded' at a time when the king had sought peace, Charles levelled an explicit charge against the new men rising to prominence that, prophetic as events transpired, was at the time a rhetorical device to paint them in the darkest hue. 'It is evident', the proclamation declared, that their 'design tends to the destruction not only of our person and posterity but even of monarchy itself'.[106] A realization of this, he hoped, might at last lead subjects to see the error of their ways. In time, Charles proved right – many MPs as well as ordinary subjects came to suspect and detest those who led the war on towards revolution, as many came to hate the Directory of Worship and rally to the Prayer Book which, Charles persuaded them in November, had been confirmed by martyrs and used in the best times of peace and plenty.[107]

If proclamations were helping the king to win the argument, albeit not the war, their role in representing and publicizing Charles to his people was to come to an abrupt end. The last royal proclamation was issued in February 1646, shortly before Charles's capture and confinement.[108] From 1646 to his execution, the royal argument had to be made in other media and forms. That proclamations terminated with the end of the king's personal freedom and the collapse of his political authority underlines their importance both as evidence of that authority and as a potential mode of representing and sustaining it. Proclamations had served the royal cause in a number of ways: their very form announced that Charles *was* king and so pointed up the illegitimacy of parliamentary ordinances; they 'constructed a loyal populace of Royalist sympathisers'; their language played on the deep-rooted fears of anarchy; and they countered parliamentary propaganda in a genre not associated with partisanship.[109] Read by loyal clergy in churches, they reached large congregations, who, whatever else was happening, heard the royal words in sacred places.

Perhaps the most important royal utterances were not only heard in sacred spaces but were official scripts for services of worship. Whether they were in all cases the actual words of the monarch, or those he or she approved for official dissemination, published volumes of prayers, printed with the royal imprimatur, both manifested the Supreme Headship in action and presented the sovereign as God's lieutenant on earth, almost as a mediator between the deity and the nation.[110] Indeed, the purpose of official prayers was to advertise the sovereign as pious and holy, to present monarchy as sacred rule, and to endeavour to bind the commonweal together, in subjugation to it. The rhetoric of unity used in prayers was, of course, a fiction in an England divided between Catholic and Protestant and by varieties of doctrinal and liturgical differences among Protestants. Royal prayers, however, strengthened the connection between crown and church. And crucially, before 1642 the monarch had the great benefit of a monopoly of these authorized prayers which were most often published at times of plague, threat or trouble, when the ruler especially needed to rally public support.

Though, in the spring of 1642, the removal of the ecclesiastical courts and bishops and anticlerical demonstrations effectively overthrew the Anglican church, the cult and authority of the Church of England, the commitment to it and affection for it, remained, as events were to reveal, powerful.[111] As the church party was to be a vital source of support for the Royalists, the reverse was also true. After the outbreak of civil war, then, it was vital to Charles I to represent himself as head of the church and as a godly prince, all the more so to counter persistent parliamentary charges that he was popishly affected. In the radically charged circumstances of civil conflict, official prayers were used, as they had been before to represent the king; but they now became increasingly polemical and partisan. Still more than proclamations, prayers offered the king a genre of polemical address which reached a wide audience and one that itself carried an authority which was not quickly eroded and which, as we shall see, parliament had to appropriate,

In 1643 (Thomason dates it to 27 September) *A Collection of Prayers Used in His Majesty's Chapel and Armies* was published by royal command.[112] Though the structure of the volume was familiar, more than before the prayers themselves were artful texts designed to strengthen the king's position. In a simple opening prayer which repeated earlier ones for the preservation of the monarch, the minister uttered 'Lord guard the person of thy servant the king'; and the congregation responded 'who putteth his trust in thee'.[113] The simple lines spoken by the community reaffirmed Charles as God's chosen and dispelled the charge that he might be guilty of any straying from the true faith. Though, together with prayers for the king, the assembled were urged to pray for peace (which was then identified with the royal cause), the collection continued with a series of prayers of thanks for royal victories – at Edgehill, in the north and the west – that manifested, it was said, both the king's godliness and divine support for Charles's cause.[114] The minister delivered a prayer of thanks to 'thou God of hosts who goeth forth with our armies and pleadest the cause of thine anointed against them that strive with him'; and, calling on prince and people to join in praise, he led all to pray that the Lord might (as he already had) instil fear in the rebels and lead them to know that they fought not just the king but against heaven.[115] Lamenting God's church invaded by sacrilege and his people deceived by lies, prayers for victories thanked God for championing his own David who, the congregations prayed, may return in peace to Jerusalem.[116] Boldly, the 1643 collection included a prayer of thanks for the safe return of the queen who was figured, against the tide of parliamentary polemic, as an instrument of God.[117] A closing prayer, conjuring the recent happiness of an England that had been as another Garden of Eden, cleverly appropriated parliamentary language by denouncing the 'tyranny' of the rebels and, recalling those who murmured against their appointed liberator Moses, asked God to 'put a stop at last to the madness of the people' – and to return them to reason and allegiance.[118]

The polemical value of such prayers to the Royalists is manifested not only by their official publication but by their dissemination in other, new and more popular forms of print. The 1643 *Mercurius Davidicus* included prayers used in the royal armies to publicize the godliness of the king and his supporters and to expose the evil of the 'tyrants and traitors' who blasphemed and defiled God's temple.[119] In this work too, those in rebellion against God's appointed

David were derided as 'kinglings' and 'princelings' – that is, as petty men ambitious for power; and the 'loyal subjects' prayer' asked that, along with his anointed, God deliver parliament and the people from their ungodly hands.[120] If the many editions and their broad dissemination suggest a Royalist belief in the value of these prayers as representation, parliament's response bore out their judgement. As well (as we shall see) as publishing their own prayers, fast sermons and thanksgivings, parliamentary polemicists moved swiftly to attack the royal collections. *The Cavaliers New Common Prayer Book Unclasp't* appeared in 1644 with crowns on the title page and a (supposed) royal imprimatur.[121] Though the subtitle announced the work as a collection of prayers used in royal chapels and armies, the title more accurately reveals what it in fact was: a parody of an official royal text, published so as to undermine it. Before the body of the book, a preface to 'the benevolent reader' described published royal prayers as in reality 'a hotch potch of episcopal and cavalier mock prayers' for 'their non victories'.[122] Endeavouring to deprive the Royalists of the authority of God and king which their prayers claimed, the *Cavaliers Prayer Book* denounced their 'simulated sanctity' and posited parliament as the 'sole upholder' of Protestantism, liberty and property.[123] The royal prayers were then reprinted with a gloss that overturned them, the prayer to God to preserve Charles, for example, becoming one to save him from Jesuits, papists and Irish rebels.[124] Where the official royal prayers had given thanks for victories, this parody claimed that, God deserting them, the Royalists ran from the battlefield at Edgehill.[125] Where the official prayers spoke of rebels as tyrants, the charge was now turned back against the king's supporters.[126] As the author announced his purpose to vindicate parliament from the slanders the Cavalier prayers had perpetrated, he warned them that 'dare bring out such sordid trash before the presence of Almighty God' of the wrath of Him who 'heareth no dissemblers'.[127] The heated language and systematic contestation of royal prayers line-by-line bore witness to the severe discomfort of the rebels with the impression made by the king's prayers. As the early battles looked likely to extend into a long war, the battle for support was to be fought in volumes of prayers as well as pamphlets.

Over the next two years, several volumes were published with royal approval or imprimatur. Prayers for the king, composed by Brian Duppa, both solicited protection for God's anointed and called for the destruction of 'the sons of violence' who obstructed peace.[128] Further volumes of prayers ordered to be used in the royal armies depicted a king always mindful of his God ('The Lord is our light') and praying him to 'pity a despised church and distracted state'.[129] Moreover, while giving thanks for victories, royal prayers never ceased to emphasize the king's desire for peace – but, it was made clear, peace could only be secured by a return to obedience.[130] 'Unite O Lord,' the armies prayed in 1645, 'the hearts of the people of this land to their king.'[131] Though the title of another Oxford volume, *Private Forms of Prayer*, suggests sincere personal devotions in retirement from the polemical fray, the mention of those who under the guise of religion had advanced profanity makes clear that this too was deeply partisan.[132] As they recited from the Psalms the invocation 'Give the king thy judgement, O God', potential waverers were warned of 'that damnation thou hast threatened to all those that resist the higher powers'.[133]

The year 1645, when the downturn in Royalist military fortunes began, saw the publication of collections of all Royalist prayers printed since the troubles started, directed perhaps to winning public support at a critical time.[134] Not least important in representing Charles as the key to peace and order, the collections contained prayers for peace and the ending of the troubles and 'a prayer drawn by his Majesty's special directions and dictate for a blessing on the treaty at Uxbridge'.[135] Whatever the charge and counter-charge of pamphlets, Charles was here figured as a king sincerely devoted to his people and praying for their peace and safety. If the treaty 'break off in vain', a prayer ordered to be used at a fast implored, 'Lord let the truth clearly appear who these men are which, under pretence of the public good, do pursue their own private ends'.[136]

When the treaty did break off and the fighting escalated, royal collections of prayers, like other texts of royal representation, appear to have given way to arms. It was three years before the publication of another volume of prayers by royal command; and by 1648 Charles's circumstances could hardly have been more different. Lest successive defeats in the spiritual accounting of early modern England might have led to despair at God's desertion of the Royalist cause, the prayers published in 1648 with a large royal arms announced 'God is our hope and strength' and 'the Lord of Hosts is with us'.[137] As the odds against them hardened, the Royalist soldiers were led to pray: 'O be . . . our God, our shield and our strong salvation; so shall five of us chase an hundred and an hundred of us shall put ten thousand to flight'.[138] Prayers said at parade and before battle reminded troops (and readers) of the laws and liberties the king's men fought to preserve along with the crown, and promised victory either on the battlefield or as martyrs in the next life.[139] As always, the audience for the prayers was not just the Royalist armies, or party. In 1648, prayers for the preservation of the civil and ecclesiastical state depicted the victorious rebels as ready to pull down the monarchy with the church and implored fellow subjects as well as God to restore the ancient order.[140] Charles I himself devised a prayer for God's blessing on the treaty negotiations at Newport, in which he urged readers to see through parliament's pretences.[141] And, in a new departure, another 1648 volume printed Prince Charles's litany and prayers for his father.[142] In part, the volume was clearly intended to add further support to the king. Yet there is a sense, too, that the collection, in presenting the prince as 'the pattern of piety', was also preparing him for the inevitable death of his father and the succession.[143] The prince prayed that all enterprises be crowned with good success, and for the peace, 'common good and comfort of the weal public'.[144] But the enemy's design, he knew, 'is to imbrue their hands in blood' and, in the words of Psalm 55, the ungodly 'are minded to do me some mischief'.[145] By 1648, royal prayers were no longer rallying the troops or seeking to garner military support; they were preparing to ensure for Charles I the crown that they had promised the Royalist soldiers: the martyr's crown and the heavenly victory that would surpass all others. And within weeks, royal prayer was to attain its greatest power in a work that drew on earlier collections of the king's prayers: the *Eikon Basilike*.[146]

II

As a succession of monarchs had appreciated, the sovereign's own words carried an unrivalled authority, but the favourable representation of the ruler also depended upon an army of panegyrists, poets, lawyers, historians and preachers, who were advocates of the monarchy and of the policies and persons of the king or queen. In peace, Charles had not wanted for such support; during his period of preferred silence he had depended upon it. The king's departure from Whitehall and London, the removal of the court, and (of course) the disruption of war itself undoubtedly posed challenges to poets and writers who had enjoyed royal favour or patronage. But, during the 1640s – though (until recently and perhaps still) inadequate attention has been paid to them – loyalist poets and pamphleteers wrote both to support the traditional authority of the king and to refigure and re-present Charles, the halcyon prince of the 1630s, to the people successively as a moderate ruler, as a warrior, as a champion of peace, and finally as martyr.

Poetry and poets had, as Ben Jonson most famously versed it, a natural affinity with monarchy.[147] Though there was no absence of verse critical of courts and rulers, poets had heralded each Stuart, just as they had hymned the Tudors. Usually circulated in manuscript, poems (often even when they were critical) very much belonged to, and in, the elite circles of the court, or the Inns of Court and universities, where there were many who hoped to be raised to royal place or patronage. During the 1630s, poems and masques by those like Herrick, Carew, Lovelace and others once (too simply) known as Cavalier poets had idealized Charles as the embodiment of divine action, nature and reason, as the powerful source of virtue in the commonweal, and as the custodian of England's Edenic peace and plenty.[148] It has been shown that several of the court poets had strong connections with popular culture, but it is significant that during the 1640s most of the Caroline poets were published in print for the first time – Thomas Carew and John Suckling posthumously, Edmund Waller, John Cleveland, Robert Herrick, Richard Fanshawe and Richard Lovelace successively from 1645.[149] Though their publisher Humphrey Moseley was doubtless partly motivated by commercial opportunity and a market, the existence of that market, as well as the speed with which they were put in print, suggests their polemical potential and purpose.[150] As James Loxley, Robert Wilcher and others have argued, these collections helped to forge a Royalist identity, to appropriate memory for the Royalist cause, and to identify verses and letters as naturally loyal and royal.[151] Indeed, printed during the 1640s, often with a dedication to the king, poems, whatever their original intention – and perhaps poetry itself – appeared intrinsically Royalist as well as royal. Print and the circumstances and moments of print production made, we might say, Caroline poets into Cavalier poets, into the voices of a party rather than a nation.

Thomas Corns argues the point well for Robert Herrick's *Hesperides*, published in early 1648.[152] Many of the poems on traditional games, customs and festivals pre-date the civil war. But, published in the context of the 1640s, they articulated a political allegiance and voiced a defiant protest against a regime which was rendered in these verses as unnatural, un-English and outside the continuities of history. Published the year in which maypoles were re-erected in defiance of parliament and riots broke out as the authorities suppressed attempts to revive Christmas, Herrick's published poems both evoked a past and polemically addressed an immediate and changed present.[153] As Corns has demonstrated, *Hesperides* encoded religious and political values and implicitly encouraged action to preserve them. Similarly, Lovelace's *Lucasta*, for all its evocation of an earlier chivalric code and culture, when published in 1649 celebrated and commemorated 'people and incidents associated with the royalist cause' and spoke to Royalists – and perhaps to other readers – 'within a royalist value system'.[154]

Important though it was, the printing of earlier courtly verse was not the only way that poetry was summoned to the service of a king at war. From the onset of the conflict, loyal poets and versifiers stood forward to support Charles I and to answer his detractors; and they continued to do so throughout the changing military and political circumstances of the decade. At the height of the struggle for control of the militia, for example, James Howell, author of the allegorical poem *Dodonna's Grove*, presented to the king as a New Year's gift for 1642 a poem entitled *The Vote*.[155] Listing the gifts he might have offered – paintings, sculpture, medals, ermines, Toledo blades or pistols – Howell conjured from the outset the king's cultural authority and hinted at his military strength.[156] But it was verse that he elected to offer and verse that asserted royal authority in every line. Howell's very muse, he tells readers, is given life by the king, and 'the vigor of his beames and heats'.[157] Reminding readers that in his earlier work he had 'made the oke' – the national symbol of England – 'to stand for Charles my King', he announced a plan to write annals 'To vindicate the truth of CHARLES his raigne/From scribling Pamphletors'.[158] But now it was poetry that conveyed Howell's clear message and wish:

> May the Great Senat with the subjects right
> Put in the Counter-scale, the Regall might[159]

Urging parliament to vote for peace, in references to 'the flours of th' crown' as well as 'regall might', he warned them of the force of tradition as well as the arms which the king could call upon.[160]

This strain of verse supporting the king has received less attention than the so-called poetry of retreat, which itself is now being re-read as less innocent and more engaged than earlier critics had allowed.[161] As James Loxley has argued, the challenge that faced Royalist poets in 1642 was that of re-presenting a king of peace as a martial hero and arming the Royalist cause with military support.[162] It is clear that some rose directly to the challenge. A poem circulating in March 1642, and transcribed in one copy as 'Kent's invitation to take Armes', calls for military service to the king and the killing of 'traitors blood'.[163] And, in the universities, especially Oxford after it became the king's headquarters, 'poetic forms were not simply marked by conflict but were themselves mobilised in the active pursuit of the king's cause'.[164]

Throughout the 1640s, Royalist poets served the king's cause in a variety of ways. As well as summoning Cavaliers to arms, in evoking the halcyon plenty of Charles's government they re-presented the king to the people as the only source of peace and order and, by corollary, his enemies as the cause of disruption. Through a series of elegies on fallen Royalist generals and ministers, such as Strafford and Laud, they created a Royalist pantheon, and presented recent parliamentary assaults on them as ambitious conspiracy.[165] In evoking festival days and festivities, they also rendered the national calendar Royalist and condemned a parliament that attacked them as unpatriotic.[166] Most of all, through the association of all language with the king and through the deployment of epic forms (as in Cowley's unfinished poem on the civil war and Davenant's *Gondibert*), the poets endeavoured to sustain the linguistic and cultural authority of the monarch as the means to the restoration of his political supremacy.[167] No less, in poems such as Denham's *Cooper's Hill* or Henry Glapthorne's *Whitehall*, they attempted a control of topography, of place and space that paralleled the armed battle to secure regions.[168] Glapthorne's *Whitehall*, published in 1643, cleverly links the long course of history, legitimate revelry ('the harmless genii of the court'), and the space and fabric of Whitehall to King Charles, without whose presence as 'the Sun' that gave all life, 'death now inhabits here'.[169] If critics are right in identifying the tensions in post-war Royalist verse between (on the one hand) the necessity of partisanship and (on the other) the sustenance of a royal authority that rose above party, we should note that both were essential strategies for securing the military and cultural supremacy of the king and Royalist cause.

It was perhaps in the more popular political poetry that both strategies were managed. The very title of the 1644 poem *Ad populum*, attributed by Thomason to John Taylor but probably by Peter Hausted, suggested a unity which the king (who was said to have had a hand in its composition) alone represented.[170] Hausted deployed the traditional conceits of representation – 'th' blessed influence of a Monarch's Crowne'.[171] But the verse becomes an overtly populist quest for support and an attack on puritans and Parliamentarians, as the cleric mocks the long sermons that now (he is sure) weary the people and paints the parliamentary soldiers as envious plunderers of the people's goods.[172] When they blessed their king, the people, the verse runs, 'were not enslaved, but free-borne Englishmen'.[173] With Charles denied his palaces, and the churches pulled down, the poem argues, the people lost their livelihoods too.[174] In bitter language that reversed parliamentary critiques of royal popery, Hausted urged readers to reject the 'painted whore/Who sits at Westminster', to give allegiance to the Oxford parliament and to 'Returne, returne unto your God and King'.[175] Critics have questioned the success of the cleric and playwright Hausted's experiment with popular verse.[176] But his attempt, by connecting the king's interests with those of *all* the people, to figure (the London) parliament as an illegitimate obstruction should not be discounted. When in 1643 he joined the king's entourage at Oxford, the satirist and self-styled 'water poet' John Taylor published, along with polemical prose pamphlets, sharp satirical squibs against the sectaries and verses that, answering charges levelled against him, elevated Charles as a paragon of virtue, piety and good kingship. Full of literary allusions yet crudely populist and coarse, Taylor's verses combined traditional royal panegyric with the polemical populism necessitated by the war.[177] Perhaps more than any, while castigating the intrusion of the vulgar into politics, he represented the king to the people in the conservative, nostalgic images which appealed beyond the narrowly partisan. And in his poem, *The King's Most Excellent Majesty's Welcome to His Own House . . . Hampton Court*, Taylor, as well as reminding all of the king's authority, depicted Charles I as a Christ-like king whose love and 'bleeding wounds' alone might redeem the nation from its sins and restore the people to a 'blessed peace'.[178]

As much as the fact of the war, the military and political setbacks of 1645 posed difficulties to the loyalist poets. Defeats at Marston Moor and Naseby drastically reduced royal power, while the capture of the king's private letters threatened to undermine what was vital to his representation as authorizing monarch.[179] As parliament seized avidly on the priceless opportunity presented by captured royal letters to condemn the king by his own words (itself a testament to the authority they still held), loyalist poets rose to answer the rebels and, as far as possible, to limit the damage. To take one example, Martin Lluellyn's *Satyr, Occasioned by the Author's Survey of a Scandalous Pamphlet Intitled The King's Cabinet Opened* (published in London as well as Oxford) struggled to reassert royal hegemony over discourse.[180] Deriding the rebels because they resorted 'To *Packet Warre*, to *Paper-Treacherie*', the *Satyr* contrasted them with a prince whose 'public decrees' ought to be inviolate.[181] In prying into the king's papers, Lluellyn argued, parliament had exposed its own illegitimacy and the rebellious intentions that lay behind its duplicitous pose of serving the king and the public good. Indeed, by breaching the authority of royal words, the Parliamentarians had announced their treason.[182] By contrast, Lluellyn predicted, through royal control of language and interpretation, parliament's 'scandals' about him would turn to the king's 'gloryes'.[183] Unlike the slippery words of parliamentary deceivers, the poet depicted royal words as 'diamonds'; that is, as precious crystals in their clarity, openness and hard imperviousness to the false interpretations the rebels endeavoured to impose on them.[184] As the fighting ended and the negotiations began, loyalist verse fought the battle to sustain royal authority as discursive authority: to sustain the king as the determinant of meaning and interpretation. Re-published in a collection of Lluellyn's verse that was dedicated to the Duke of York and contained poems of love and friendship, elegies on Royalists slain or executed, and carols sung to the king on festive days through the 1640s, the *Satyr* folds into an assertion of royal values, resolutely held amid the flux of fortune.[185]

As Charles surrendered to the Scots, then the army, royal poets struggled to uphold through verse the mysteries of majesty that were manifestly no longer Charles's daily experience. Repeating images of the sun, for example, poets such as Cleveland and Vaughan sought to figure Charles as 'our Hieroglyphic King' – as himself a system of signification, a sacred language.[186] The success of Royalist poetic representation may perhaps be seen in the majesty that Charles was still able to wield in adversity and in the strength he was still able to bring to the negotiating table. But the increasing representation of the king as a sacred sign, of course, also tended to place him out of negotiation. And, ultimately, it was this course that Charles himself decided to take, not least in order to preserve the control of interpretation and discourse that, with Thomas Hobbes, he regarded as inseparable from sovereignty.[187] In January 1649, Charles I became his own poet, reinscribing the authority of royal utterance. As Loxley astutely observed, the *Eikon Basilike* was the apotheosis of Royalist poetics.[188] If *Eikon Basilike* again legitimized the representations the poets had fashioned, it also drew on them, honouring in its verses the forms of loyalist poetry which had made its own poetics and politics possible. It may not have saved Charles's life, but what Milton nervously called a 'piece of poetry' was to preserve the crown.[189]

Where poetry typically attempted to elevate Charles above political argument, the events of 1638–42, then the outbreak of war itself, produced easily the biggest increase ever seen in printed prose – much of it concerned with debating, before a new and broader audience, the issues that had led to conflict. Because they proposed novel, revolutionary, and often deceptively modern arguments, it is the Parliamentarian pamphleteers who for long received most historical attention.[190] Latterly, however, scholars have at least begun to appreciate that loyalist writers were by no means worsted in the pamphlet wars; and that, in bringing new arguments and strategies as well as restating conventional axioms, they powerfully presented and re-presented both the monarchy and Charles as the right and rational cause to follow. The history of Royalist prose polemics from 1640 to 1649 still needs to be written.[191] Here we can only sample the modes of Royalist representation in prose to give some sense of how the king's supporters responded to violent division and the changing fortunes of the 1640s.

As the war dawned, then broke out, loyalist writers leapt to the defence of Charles. Pamphlets in 1642 recalled the lives of Jack Straw and Wat Tyler to show 'the just reward of rebels' and to brand rebellion as the sin of witchcraft.[192] According to *A Medicine for the Times*, one of several works associating political disorder with disease, parliament claimed too great a power, and myriad treatises rehearsed the divine authority of monarchy and the obligation of conscience to obedience.[193] Though several, sincerely or strategically, adopted a moderate stance and sought peace and settlement, it was settlement in which, in the words of *Albania*, 'God [was] glorified, the king satisfied, the good subject pleased'.[194] Other treatises pulled no punches. John Taylor launched vitriolic early attacks on the rebels, branding them as schismatics and, in *A Plea for Prerogative or Give Caesar his Due*, identified disloyalty and malice as the faces that had overturned peace and religion.[195] After Charles's departure from

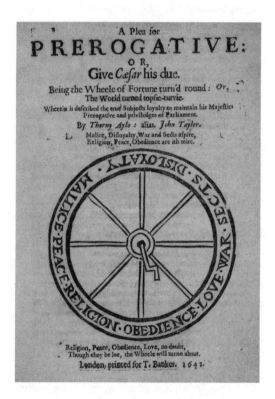

47   *Title page of A Plea for Prerogative: Or, Give Caesar His Due*, John Taylor, 1642.

London, *A Deep Sigh Breathed Through the Lodgings at Whitehall* made the former royal palace the synecdoche of a nation that had lost the person who gave it meaning.[196] Instead of a king providing light 'with more awful brightness than the great luminaries in the firmament', all was dark and deserted, just as, now there was no king or Privy Council, 'a bare vote of the House of Commons is of validity'.[197] 'He that provoketh a king to anger', the author of *A Plea for the King* warned those wavering as the shock of what was unfolding hit them, 'sins against his own soul'.[198] To dishonour a king, especially a good king who tendered his subjects' welfare as his own, was to defy God.[199]

As the hopes of a quick return to normality faded and justifications of parliamentary resistance poured (as we shall see) from the printing presses, loyalist pamphleteers confronted them head on. Though announcing himself as 'a well wisher both to the king and parliament', the author of *Certain Considerations* upon the duties of prince and people poured scorn on the argument that government derived from the people.[200] Kings, he reminded readers, by their anointing, were sacredly ordained with the spirit of God, who elected them to be nursing fathers. Those who thought such authority might be resisted were condemned by Scripture.[201] A similar argument was pitched more personally in *An Appeal to Thy Conscience* which proved from Scripture that it was not the people but God who made kings and that it was only to God they owed account.[202] Praising the tender-hearted David whom God had appointed to rule over them, the *Appeal* also cut the ground from under the parliamentary argument – one which was vital to retaining conservative support – that they opposed not Charles but his evil advisers.[203] Exposing the claim as a false distinction, the author admonished that any resistance would meet with God's wrath on the Day of Judgment.[204] Similarly, attempts to use Sir John Fortescue's writings to justify their claim to render the king accountable were countered by assertions that the law strengthened the king and that parliaments derived what authority they had from him.[205] As both sides were recruiting for what was emerging as most probably a prolonged civil war, the *Appeal* instructed the people not to be misled from Christian duty by false prophets: fear the Lord and the king, Scripture taught, and meddle not with those who are given to change.[206] 'Fear God and Honour the King', the author of *A Rational Discourse* concurred in his instruction, was both the command of Scripture and the only 'fair pattern for a good peace'.[207]

Evidently the hope and strategy of early Royalist polemics were directed at undermining parliament's support and re-establishing royal authority by more or less strident assertions of traditional homilies on obedience and by repeated warnings against the sin of disobedience. Popular petitions to Charles, after he had left the capital, to cure subjects of the king's evil – 'no other sovereign of any kingdom else having the miraculous medicinal virtue infused upon them' – suggest that it was by no means a failed strategy and that belief in the divinity of kings was far from outmoded.[208] However, with the war a year or more long, and parliament effectively governing in London, it became apparent that traditional injunctions to obedience alone were unlikely to restore Charles to Whitehall. In one of the earlier Royalist dialogues, *A Discourse . . . betwixt Patricius and Peregrine . . . Touching the Civil Wars,* Patricius (the patriot) admits as much: 'I fear,' the character landed in France tells his collocutor, 'it will be long before they return to their old English temper, to that rare loyalty and love which they were used to show to their sovereign.'[209] Peregrine (the foreigner) concurs, observing that the parliament had become an idol to some of the people.[210] As the two debate the situation and ponder a solution, Patricius affirming his commitment to good parliaments, Peregrine employs a less moderate stance. Blaming England's troubles on some 'upstart politicians', a term of opprobrium in the seventeenth century, he delivers a damning indictment of them: 'I have heard of some things they have done that if Machiavel himself were alive, he would be reputed a saint in comparison of them.'[211] A giddy-headed faction, he maintained with a (fictional) outsider's supposedly objective perspective, had been allowed to take over the sober and decisive king and people and to 'put division twixt all sorts.'[212] But, he opined, such insurrection had been seen in England before; and, though the king was temporarily eclipsed, he 'will shine afterwards, with a stronger lustre', just as the sun after an eclipse.[213]

During 1643, Charles himself authorized works arguing his divine right and citing Scripture against the rebels. *Christus dei,* announced as a theological discourse, was in fact a loyal gloss on Charles's own response to the Nineteen Propositions which had infamously endeavoured to separate his regality from his person and to argue his subordination to the people.[214] Combining traditional with new proto-Hobbesian arguments that, once the people had resigned power to one person, it was his and his heirs' for perpetuity, the treatise, published at the royal command, asserted that, whatever its origin, 'regal power is divine power and the ordinance of God', with all other subordinate to it.[215] Also published by royal command, with, on the title page, a large C.R. flanked by angels, *Mercurius Davidicus,* paralleling Charles with the biblical David, gathered psalms that damned the rebels who 'have defiled thy temple' and 'risen against thine anointed'.[216] Moving seamlessly from biblical to contemporary imprecations, this highly polemicized psalter (not the last time Charles would use the genre) gave thanks for the victory at Edgehill and prayed: 'with thine own hand . . . give thy servant Charles the victory'.[217]

While the king's own 'words' appropriated Scripture, other loyalist polemicists engaged with parliamentary propaganda more directly. The author of *The King's Cause Rationally, Briefly and Plainly Debated* announced that he wrote against 'the irrational, groundless misprisions' of the rebels who had deceived the people.[218] Parliament's claim to be at war against evil councillors, a rhetoric that eased the minds of many waverers, he (like others) exposed as a pretence; their insistence on their stand for faith he dismissed as bogus – 'religion is pretended but certainly malice acts the business'; their charge that Charles was

popish he called 'a fiction'.[219] Painfully reminding readers that parliament's so-
called remedies had proved far worse than the alleged ills they had risen to
counter, the writer drew the vital distinction between reformation and the
transformation that had left the country at the mercy of the sword and 'pulpit
barraters'.[220] Only in obedience to God and the king lay the preservation of the
nation, it was argued.[221] Rationally debated 'de facto', the king's cause was that
of the people and the nation.

The Shepherd's Oracle issued the same year made the same powerful argument in a very different form. Published with an engraving showing Charles
stepping forward to save the church and nation from tub preachers, the text
took the form of a Virgilian pastoral.[222] Though a prose preface presented the
meaning of the eclogue as 'covered with a veil' and, somewhat disingenuously,
offered the reader freedom of interpretation, the veil was thin and all but
transparent.[223] Shepherds, once bound together 'in looks of love', were now
brought to 'bow to new commands'. As a consequence, their kingdom was
'turned a chaos of confusion', as anarchists destroyed the clerical and social
order, leaving the shepherds to lament the destruction of their idyll.[224] If the
claim can be trusted, the speech of Anarchus, who boasted of pulling down the
clergy, making carts out of pulpits and overthrowing all order, was 'nosed by
the ballad singers about the streets of London' and embellished 'with some
additions . . . to make up a full pennyworth'.[225] Certainly the Royalists
attempted in 1644 to exploit the widespread disenchantment with the course
of affairs and the fear of the disintegration of all order and to separate
old moderate Parliamentarians (represented in The Shepherd's Oracle by
Philorthus) from the radicals who were driving on the war.[226] England's Tears
for the Present Wars, for example, printed with a large royal arms on the title
page and dedicated to the 'imperial chamber of the city of London', had
'England' (associated by the royal arms with the king's own voice) lament 'this
unnatural, self-destroying war' that had been so mistaken.[227] Though in
appealing for peace the pamphlet asked king and parliament to work together,
along with the prominent royal arms the description of parliament as the
king's Great Council (bound in duty to support the crown) and the disparaging
of 'mechanics' who sought to rule all rendered the peace very much one on the
king's terms.[228]

As the war party negotiated a Scots alliance to raise more troops and escalate the conflict, while the people grew ever more weary of it, Royalist apologists, as well as penning laments on England's distracted condition and
proffering the king as the only hope of peace, laid the blame for the disaster
firmly on parliament. An Orderly and Plain Narration of the Beginnings and
Causes of this War (1644) disclosed its partisanship in its title-page epigraph
from Proverbs 24: 'Fear thou the Lord and the King'.[229] Pre-empting
Clarendon's famous History, the author of the narration plotted the rise of a
faction (of 'disciplinarians') that seized control of the Commons and sought to

take control of government.[230] Though Charles made all reasonable concessions, it was said, by pretending dangers they claimed control of the militia,
excluded the king from his own city of Hull, and planned to depose him.[231]
Having shown how the war began and demonstrated the justness of the royal
cause, the author urged 'from thence must thy conscience be directed'.[232] To
assist the reader's conscience, the narrator contrasted the royal assurances to
protect Protestantism and liberties with the acts of an (illegitimate) faction
that first overthrew the king and then overturned the constitution of a true
parliament.[233] Warning that 'whosoever go about to overthrow policies long
since established are enemies to mankind and fight against God's express will',
the author sought to exploit the growing divisions within parliament and to
persuade the moderates to repent.[234]

Probably as part of that effort to divide the moderate from more radical
MPs, a vindication of Charles I, published in 1644, was devoted to countering
the suspicion (one which united MPs of very different religious inclinations)
that Charles was sympathetic to Catholicism. Specifically *Vindiciae Caroli
Regis* was a response to William Prynne's *The Popish Royal Favourite*,
published in 1643.[235] Dedicated to the king and with a large royal arms, the
Vindiciae systematically examined Prynne's charges and answered them, often
with supporting documents, some of which were Charles's own words. Having
re-established the royal word, the author enjoined readers, 'please you now to
wipe the eyes of your mind for the glass is clear'; and urged that they 'may
believe our sacred, gracious sovereign' over those who 'cast aspersions on
God's anointed'.[236]

With Royalist defeats and the creation of the New Model Army, loyalist
polemicists were led to reassert that, whatever the fortunes in the battlefield,
rebellion could have no sanction and was always damned by God. Depicting
the rebels as traitors bent on deposing the king, one writer warned that
'treason doth ever produce fatal and final destruction to the offender'.[237] And
reassuring the king's supporters that they still followed a good and godly cause,
loyalist pamphlets rallied men to the royal banner. Faced with successive
Parliamentarian victories, *The Persuasion of Certain Grave Divines* countered
with a new defiance. 'If our enemies will be inexorable, our patience shall be
invincible,' they vaunted; and assured all who might be despairing at defeat
that 'the weakness of the king's party doth not much weaken our courage: it is
the goodness of the cause not the greatness of his power which doth encourage
us to adhere to his Majesty'.[238] With their church, liberties and estates at risk,
the Royalists were called upon to stand for 'a good cause, a good king and a
good God'.[239] If they suffered for their king and in God's cause, they were
promised, they would have 'heavenly retribution'.[240] As the military odds were
bringing the fighting in the first civil war towards an end, we begin to sense
that loyalist pamphleteers were already preparing to deny their enemies the
moral victory or the claims that God was on their side.

The effective collapse of the Royalist military cause with the surrender of Oxford in July 1646 was followed by more than a year of negotiations that led all parties back to the fundamental religious and political issues. Having lost the war, Royalist writers, like Charles I himself, endeavoured to win the peace; and, given how much peace was desired by nearly all, it did not appear a completely futile pursuit. In 1647, Royalist pamphleteers wrote to underline the need for settlement, to reassert the divine nature of kingship, to praise the character of Charles I, and to discredit opponents who sought harsh terms or, they claimed, the virtual destruction of monarchy. *The Balance Put into the Hand of Every Rational Englishman* cleverly ventriloquized what many in a war-weary nation were thinking.[241] In 1639, the anonymous pamphleteer recalled, some had claimed that the kingdom needed reform. Yet, in that year, church and state were quietly established and a happy people enjoyed peace and plenty.[242] Now, the king was reduced, sects proliferated like 'the wild boars of the forest, rooting up the established religion', and the land was ravaged.[243] 'Where,' the author asked simply, 'lies the improvement?'[244] The clear implication was – and it was a widespread sentiment – that the happiness of the nation depended upon the re-establishment of Charles I. 'England is weary of them [the Roundheads],' wrote the author of *The Cavaliers Diurnal*, (with some accuracy despite his partisanship) and 'heartily desires as they have one God so one good religion and one good king, Charles'.[245] A supposed letter from a 'moderate cavalier' to a 'moderate Independent', appealing to a concern across the political spectrum that order and discipline had collapsed into 'rudeness and indistinction', advised: 'You have a great work to-do to restore religion and law upon which depends the king's re-enthronement and re-investiture with his just rights'.[246] The nature of those 'just rights' was a matter of controversy, but the Royalists, of course, sought the restoration to Charles of all his former powers. Indeed, to quash any thinking that negotiations for peace might involve a radical reduction in royal powers, the author of *Royalty and Loyalty* offered to readers 'a short survey of the power of kings over their subjects and the duty of subjects to their kings', to which a frontispiece of a king attended by angels and loyal subjects provided the entry.[247] The pamphlet restated the natural and divine rights of magistracy and the accountability of monarchs only to God. Citing Jean Bodin, the treatise insisted on the absolute and perpetual power of kings and the duty of subjects to obey and love them.[248] Only the restoration to the king of these rights would bring 'a happy pacification between the king and his people'; 'he ruling as a royal prince and they staying as loyal subjects may be both happy' – 'reciprocally happy in the king their head'.[249] Monarchy, the pamphlet reasserted, was natural government and all other regimens led to a 'beastly life'.[250] Others reiterated what had been urged by a century of apologists for regality. From his prison in the Tower, Michael Hudson charted the divine right of government from the rule of angels, through Adam to kings, in a treatise dedicated to Charles.[251]

48 *Title page of Royalty and Loyalty, Robert Grosse, 1647.*

As well as elaborate restatements of the theory of divine kingship, Royalist polemicists wrote in 1647 to reinscribe the historical and legal bonds of fealty and allegiance. In *The Mirror of Allegiance*, for example, a Reader at the Inns of Court responded to a judge appointed by parliament to explain how allegiance was due from every subject to the king.[252] The government of kings, he insisted, was as ancient as history itself – 'for those who deny the story of Brutus to be true do find out a more ancient plantation here under kings, namely under Samothes, grandchild to Japhet[h], the son of Noah from whom the ancient Britons ... are ... descended'.[253] Since that time, the treatise continued, the law had secured the hereditary rights of the crown to which obedience was due from subjects and parliament alike.[254]

This renewed Royalist appeal to Scripture, history and law was also skilfully contrasted by pamphleteers with the less legitimate foundations, as they saw them, of parliamentary claims. *Anti Machiavell or, Honesty against Policy* cleverly tainted parliamentary arguments with the name of the figure who was still associated with immorality and evil.[255] In what was in part a response to *The Case of the Kingdom Stated*, the author of *Anti-Machiavell* roundly condemned Independent pamphlets which placed interest before conscience or the law.

'For a man to look at interest without consideration of right,' he reminded them, invoking still powerful norms, 'is directly contrary to that self denial which is the cognisance of Christ's disciples.'[256] Though 'for some men what's policy [another pejorative term] and serves interest is honest enough', 'let it be whose interest it will, it is the duty of all to seek to reconcile the king upon honourable terms.'[257]

As well as associating the re-establishment of the king with religion, law and morality and branding his opponents as ungodly Machiavels, Royalist polemicists used humour to good effect to present the king as the only means to the restoration of social – and sexual – order.[258] Throughout the war, as we shall see, both sides represented each other as promiscuous and debauched, and as overturning the hierarchies of family, sex and gender which were, in early modern discourse, common analogues for political order.[259] The actual experience of civil war had also seen the entry of women into the political sphere, as preachers, protesters and petitioners, and with it widespread anxiety about female insubordination, often expressed through pornographic squibs on female sexual appetites.[260] In promising a restoration of order with the king, therefore, Royalist propaganda even figured lusty girls abandoning promiscuity for chaste order. *The Maids Petition to the Honourable Members of Both Houses*, published in 1647, is full of double entendre hinting at their promiscuous copulation with apprentices and tailors, Anabaptists and Adamites – who are mocked for their sexual inadequacies.[261] With the prospect of the king's return to Whitehall, they express their allegiance to vow 'a maiden magnanimity in opposition to all conventicling conjugation' and, in phrases freighted with the language of domestic as well as political order, to vote for the king 'his coming home and residence with his parliament . . . as the only conclusive means against fictions and factions.'[262] As other Royalist pamphlets maintained, kings were 'truly termed Pater Patriae', fathers and heads of the ordered household of the realm, and only kings could restore the natural order of men and women prescribed in hundreds of early modern courtesy manuals.[263]

The case for the re-establishment of the king in 1647 could not be, and was not, made only by these traditional arguments for monarchy or in the general terms of an urgent need for the restoration of social order. The king in question was Charles Stuart, during the war against whom a barrage of personal criticism had been fired. In 1647, as Royalist writers appreciated, it was as essential to vindicate the man as much as the office – and not least in order to dispel doubts about Charles's trustworthiness in negotiating. One text may here give the flavour of several apologias. The title of Edward Symmons's *A Vindication . . . of King Charles or, A Loyal Subjects' Duty Manifested* made the connection between the personal and constitutional issues clear.[264] Probably honestly, Symmons claimed to have written a defence of Charles two years earlier but, the people not being ready to give him a hearing then, he had delayed until now when he 'hath beamed forth in his dark condition' of defeat and confinement.[265] Symmons wrote against the 'ill-disposed libellers' (whom he compared with Martin Marprelate) who had slandered Charles.[266] More particularly since, he sensed, 'vulgar hearts wanted satisfaction in nothing concerning the king's integrity but only in the matter of those letters which did still scruple many of them', he set out to deal with the damaging attack on Charles's integrity that followed the capture of royal letters at Naseby.[267] Arguing that, rather than the letters themselves, it was the interpretation of them that had presented Charles in such a bad light, Symmons countered parliament's glosses and re-presented the letters to give the reader of 1643 entire satisfaction 'of his Majesty's longing desire to see peace restored to his poor subjects'.[268] And comparing parliament's perverting the king's words with Julian the Apostate's treatment of the Bible, he implicitly endorsed and endowed the royal letters with the status and veracity of Scripture.[269] As the petitions to Charles and welcomes he received suggested that Symmons had judged correctly that the moment was right for the king's rehabilitation, other Royalists pressed Charles's honesty and sincere readiness to settle. *The Royal and the Royalist's Plea* contrasted Charles's reasonable propositions with the behaviour of opponents led by factious lecturers who, under the pretence of public safety, had sought to overthrow monarchy; and urged the people to petition parliament to disband the army and come to an accommodation with the king that alone might re-establish peace, liberty and order.[270]

Once again in 1647 the monarchy and Charles were represented in the old metaphors of father, husband, head and sun.[271] Some loyalist writers even saw royal words again rising above the clamour of pamphlet exchange and Charles's conversation confounding his enemies and converting all to his cause.[272] 'It is a brave and gallant way to peace', wrote a Royalist pamphleteer giving a 'character of the times', 'to extinguish the names of parties'.[273] While there was little likelihood of extinguishing either the name or fact of parties, in returning the king to the centre, in arguing for divine right monarchy and the personal virtues of Charles I, and in persuading the people to send welcoming addresses to him, Royalist pamphleteers had, in some measure, succeeded in plucking political victory from military defeat. Indeed, one measure of their success was the radical Independents' abandonment of the arts of persuasion and resort to the power of violence. If, in 1648, Charles enjoyed more support than he had since the outbreak of war, he owed much to the loyal pamphlet-eers and polemicists who, through shifting times and now after defeat, represented and re-presented him to the people.

III

Royal speeches, declarations, proclamations and prayers, and the verse pane-gyrics and prose support of loyal writers were the traditional discursive modes of royal representation in the age of print. As well as driving the rhetorical strategies and sharpening the polemics of these traditional genres, civil war gave birth to new forms and genres of what we might call propaganda. Later we will turn to the military reports, the newsbooks and the satires which Royalist and Parliamentarian writers published to promote themselves and to discredit and dishearten their opponents.[274] First, however, in this chapter's story of the civil war as a contest of representation, we must turn to the greatest new challenge to Charles I's self-representation in print: the appropriation by parliament of what had become authorized forms of discourse, forms which had been hitherto officially, and all but in reality, a royal monopoly.

To make this assertion is not to begin to suggest that royal words had been immune from criticism: we have abundant evidence from Henry VIII's reign onwards of royal words being criticized and contested. But what was different about the 1640s was that the king's critics (if at first unwillingly) had to govern; and, in order to do so, they had necessarily to appropriate the discursive media of early modern government. The most obvious case, of course, is parliament's use from 1642 of new orders and ordinances. With the breakdown of co-operation with the king and his remove from London, conventional statutes could no longer be passed, and proclamations (which of course Charles published in abundance) were a royal genre and form. In order to issue executive instructions, therefore, parliament needed to ape the form of proclamations. And, as importantly, in order to secure credibility and support as a government, it had to establish the authority of its orders and ordinances as equal to proclamations. The difficulties this presented may be glimpsed in the near exact emulation by parliament of royal proclamations, including the appropriation of Gothic script, decorated initial letters and (in the earliest) the royal arms.[275] Yet, gradually, parliament's ordinances gained acceptance as distinct instruments of authority. As they did so, like proclamations, they presented parliament with a medium for more than executive orders: for representation, for polemic, and for propaganda.

Early ordinances, for example, for assessing contributions to parliament and sequestering the estates of recalcitrants, seized the opportunity of the form to argue the rights of their actions, and the errors of the king who had 'withdraw[n] himself from the advice of parliament'.[276] Despite, the texts claimed, all their endeavours to preserve the king from false popish counsels, they had prevailed with him and were responsible for 'this unnatural war raised against the parliaments', parliaments which, rightly perceived, were 'the chief support of his royal dignity'.[277] From the outset, as well as issuing individual ordinances, parliament ordered several of them to be reprinted together. Moreover, whether as a gesture of confidence or in a bid to secure more authority through print and another aping of regal practice, the houses also ordered in March 1643 *An Exact Collection* of all their remonstrances, declarations and ordinances since 1641.[278] Published with a woodcut image of the kings, Lords and

Commons on the title page, this 900-page volume claimed authority by its very size and appearance. Though it included the exchanges on both sides, and the declarations of the king as well as parliament, the illusion of even-handed equality was itself a contentious polemic. Parliament was printing and controlling an early narrative of the textual conflict which led to civil war; at the back, an order of the Clerk of the Parliament forbade the printing of those texts by any other than their designated stationer, Edward Husbands.[279]

Ordinances, one they had become established, helped to endow parliament with discursive forms of authority and so to provide it with a medium of polemic that could appear as an a-polemical instrument of government. The order, for example, that any who assisted Charles with plate, money or arms should be deemed a traitor to the king nicely made a controversial distinction between man and monarch that was vital to parliament's early legitimacy in a brief executive order.[280] In 1643, ordinances for a weekly assessment declared both houses 'fully satisfied and resolved in their consciences that they have lawfully taken up arms' to defend the kingdom; orders for relief of maimed soldiers described them as fighting 'for the defence of the parliament, religion, laws and liberties of the subject'; and several decrees tainted the Royalist cause as 'the advancement of popery by a popish army'.[281] The next year, an ordinance

49 Frontispiece to *An Exact Collection of All Remonstrances*, 1643.

for creating an association of the counties of Pembrokeshire, Carmarthen and Cardigan explained the need to deliver them 'from the tyranny and intolerable oppression of the forces raised against the parliament and kingdom'.[282] And as the war effort escalated, a parliamentary ordinance for pressing men explained that 'the free Protestant religion, the laws and liberties of the subject, and the Parliament are in danger to be subverted, idolatry and tyranny like to be introduced by the force and power of several armies raised by pretence of the king's authority, consisting of papists and other dangerous and ill affected persons'.[283]

Though they tended to be briefer than royal proclamations, parliament clearly attached importance to its proclamations as texts of rhetoric as well as executive decrees. Periodically the houses ordered the publication of full collections of all their declarations and ordinances, with an engraved illustration of the parliament in session; and the 1647 collection of 'forgotten votes' and ordinances of the MPs declared that it was reprinted 'to refresh their memories and prevent all dishonourable and unjust actions, repugnant to all or any of them'.[284] Moreover, in order to attempt to establish control, several ordinances of parliament sought to regulate print and proscribe any pamphlet not licensed by them.[285] Increasingly harsh punishments were ordered for those who printed without licence and against hawkers or ballad singers who spread illicit works.[286] No less than the king and Royalists, Parliamentarians were acutely aware that in the battle to win hearts and minds, control of texts, of words, was vital. By establishing ordinances as a recognized alternative to proclamations, parliament deprived the king of the monopoly of a form of communication he had controlled and vied with him as an equal voice of authority.

In similar fashion, parliament, from March 1642, moved quickly to use declarations as a medium that enabled them to answer royal pronouncements and to represent their own case at greater length than was possible in the ordinances. Indeed, parliament issued over three hundred of these declarations between 1642 and 1648, on matters pertaining to specific individuals, local issues and the affairs of all three kingdoms. Once again, though these texts have never been studied as polemics in the battle for public support, we can here only offer a small sample of a genre new to parliamentary discourse but essential in enabling parliament to conduct the war. The two hundred-plus records of parliamentary declarations issued in 1642 found in Early English Books Online witnesses a nervous parliament's sense of its need to make a case against a king who had the best of law and tradition on his side. But those same declarations also evidence the devices and languages parliament used and the mixture of positive and negative propaganda it deployed to level the polemical as well as military playing field. Declarations of 1642 published lengthy defences of the militia ordinance that skilfully (if disingenuously) argued that, even in going against his person, parliament was acting with the king's consent as well as for his good.[287] In a declaration justifying their taking up arms, parliament's emphasis was on their *defence* against – and the appropriation of royal language should be noted – a 'malignant party' whose violent ways threatened the safety of the king's person, the oppression of true religion and the laws and liberties of the kingdom; 'all which', they insisted in a manner that it was hard to question, 'every honest man is bound to defend'.[288] Again, appropriating Charles's own charge against them, the Commons identified a long design to subvert the government and followed a narrative of that design from the introduction of a popish Prayer Book into Scotland in 1637.[289] Those who led the design had put service to the court before the country and, the declaration asserted, would see the ruin of the parliament even if that meant, as it did, the destruction of the country.[290] If parliament failed, the declaration continued, trying to replace the king as the embodiment of the nation, all were ruined; if it prevailed, then the king, religion and the subjects' rights might yet be preserved.[291]

This turning against Charles and the Royalists the charges of malignancy, novelty and conspiracy was a vital move in endowing parliament's cause with legitimacy. And, in 1642, while it was politic (whatever their sincerity) not to attack Charles directly, declarations repeated how those evil advisers who misled him, 'all kind of delinquents' and papists pretending his service, were traitors who sought to establish 'arbitrary and tyrannous government'.[292] Whether responding to royal declarations, to the raising of the royal standard, or to early Royalist victories, parliamentary declarations audaciously, but in large measure successfully, represented parliament as the protector of church and state and the king's party as the oppressors ready to subject the people with the help of foreign aid. Still more audaciously, in one declaration of 6 July 1642, they prohibited the publication of any royal proclamations 'issued out in his Majesty's name' that contradicted any parliamentary ordinance and forbade sheriffs, mayors or vicars to distribute or read them out.[293]

The progress of the war and the establishment of the royal government as well as garrison at Oxford presented new challenges to parliament which it quickly deployed explanatory and polemical declarations to address. Countering, for example, a royal proclamation ordering the courts of Chancery, Exchequer and Wards to be removed to Oxford – a move that would, of course, have deprived Parliamentarians of access to justice – a declaration argued the danger of moving records and insisted that the courts, and with them the processes of justice, remained in the parliament's stronghold, the capital.[294] Importantly, too, as conflict emphasized the need for men, money and plate, parliamentary declarations became important media for persuading the people to make sacrifices. Yet again, turning one of Charles's strategies against him, a declaration of January 1643, acknowledging that they might have been misled, offered an amnesty to Royalist soldiers who would come over to parliament.[295] To stir men to open purses for the cause, parliamentary declarations also raised the rhetorical level of denigration of their enemies in order to add the argument of self-interest to that of duty as reasons for contributing funds. After some early successes, a declaration warned, Royalist armies that had murdered and raped the innocent subjects in the north planned a march on London 'to pillage and sack their city, cut the throats of all men of estates, and ravish their wives and daughters'.[296] In some cases, the declaration claimed, where they took prisoners the king's men had demanded £1,000 (even, it was said, £3,000!) for their lives, beside which the small contributions an honest parliament sought were easily a price worth paying for security.[297] Other declarations, demonizing the king's followers, stressed the growing strength of papists in Royalist armies and their hunger for 'shedding the blood of all Protestants'.[298] The religious dimension to polemic sharpened with the alliance with the Scots which an 'exhortation' pressed as the best course for the securing of English liberties and religion.[299] During 1643 and 1644 – during, that is, periods of Royalist successes – as well as using declarations to sustain its recruiting and resources, parliament turned them against royal texts. Printing a proclamation of the king which threatened to destroy crops in the area around Oxford, and promising to do all to aid the oppressed, parliament reproduced Charles's proclamation in Roman type, while printing its own in Gothic script, the normal authorized typography of proclamations.[300] In their form as well as content, that is, declarations were helping to fight parliament's war against the Royalists. Moreover, in seemingly casual phrases

50 *A Declaration of the Lords and Commons Assembled in Parliament*, 1644.

describing 'pernicious and desperate' men – 'still about the king and *protected by him*' – they were subtly and slowly taking the war to the king himself.[301]

Given our argument about their role in securing support, it may be signifi-cant that the fewest parliamentary declarations are found during the period when military fortunes had turned in parliament's favour.[302] It was in the period of negotiations after military victory that parliament again deployed declara-tions to explain its purposes and to secure support. And, in the new conditions that unfolded from 1646, it was not only the Royalists against whom the polemics of these declarations was directed. On 13 April 1646, the Commons ordered the printing of 1,000 copies of its declaration of intentions concerning 'the ancient and fundamental government of the kingdom', which MPs were also instructed to distribute in their constituencies.[303] The declaration opened with the self-justification that success had permitted: at the beginning of the war, it stated, royal declarations had misrepresented the parliament, and Royalists had charged it with raising false fears; but events had proved them right and God had blessed their designs by aiding them in defeating the enemy. Now the moment had come for peace, yet still some endeavoured to claim falsely that parliament sought to alter the government in church and state.[304] The declaration assured all that it had no such intent, but was bent on a peace that would uphold religion and law; a statement, we might say, with a coded warning that, with the war won, parliament was determined not to lose the peace. The rub was that, while references to the Covenant suggest that this was a Presbyterian document, there were other elements, within and outside the Commons, with different interests and agendas; and it was as much against these as against Charles I and his supporters that further declarations were aimed. During the early months of 1647, for instance, parliament issued declarations against any preaching by those not ordained.[305] In March, they proclaimed against dangerous petitions sent to stir the army and, seeking to divide the Independents, praised those officers and soldiers in the army who refused to countenance them.[306] It was parliament, the declaration affirmed, that was 'so careful to perform all things appertaining to honour and justice' and unauthorized petitioners (with different agendas) would be treated as enemies of the state.

Indeed, as the differences between the Presbyterians in parliament and the Independents in the army widened, far from representing Charles I as an enemy, parliamentary declarations often appropriated his authority now to strengthen the Presbyterian position. A declaration regarding the king's messages sent from the Isle of Wight in November 1647, for example, was printed with a large royal arms on the title page next to parliament's name – surely a typographic advertisement of the re-establishment of the old order which the Commons sensed had popular support.[307] Though the declaration (again) warned Royalists that, at least for the time being, the king would have to assent to what the parliament judged best for the kingdom, it opened up an invitation to Charles to come to treat in London and expressed regret at 'his Majesty's hard usage, when we call to mind how he was violently carried away from Holmby by a party of the army'.[308] The next year, while a similar declaration, published with a widely circulating woodcut frontispiece portrait of Charles, announced the opening of peace negotiations, other declarations proscribed tumultuous petitioning and assembly – not only by Royalists but by all 'malignants and delinquents' endangering religion, law and parliament.[309] Ironically, as with royal declarations, the rhetorical and polemical effectiveness of parliament's declarations in garnering popular support is evidenced by the resort to violence which radical Independents judged necessary in order to check the drift back to the re-establishing of the old regime.[310] By late 1648, the parliamentary declarations which (from 1642) had done so much to challenge, even destroy, the king's authority and support were becoming the instruments of his rehabilitation. One of the last declarations published before the regicide, a declaration of no further addresses to the king, though issued in the name of parliament, was (as answers to it charged) the text of a faction that had only 'power . . . to beat . . . us into an argument'.[311]

Even more audacious than its appropriating the royal forms of proclamation and declaration was parliament's vying with the king as the interpreter of God

51 *A Declaration of the Lords and Commons in Parliament, 1648.*

to the people and leader of the nation's prayers. Hugh Trevor-Roper demon-strated how, from early in the Long Parliament, services of humiliation accom-panied with 'fast sermons' were, as Clarendon had argued, used as political propaganda that lasted for seven years.[312] As well as these, of course, in 1644 parliament, in defiance of the royal supremacy, authorized the printing of *The New Book of Common Prayer According to the Form of the Kirk of Scotland*.[313] And the next March, the Lords and Commons ordered the printing of *A Directory for Public Worship*, with parliament's imprimatur on the title page.[314] Prefaced to it, in the Gothic script of authority, a parliamentary ordinance required the suspension of all other services and the implementation of the *Directory* in every parish and at all services.[315] In a further preface, as well as declaring its role as the custodian of the nation's conscience, parliament briefly narrated the circumstances that had led to its religious reform, including allu-sions to royal popery and superstition.[316] Banning the celebration of festival days and denying the sanctity of consecrated places, the *Directory* was itself a parliamentary appropriation of the supreme headship and royal authority as much as it was a re-scripting of the forms of worship.

Parliament underlined its claim to exercise authority in matters of worship in subsequent volumes of prayers. To take a case, *A Supply of Prayer for the Ships of this Kingdom* announced that, published by authority, the prayers were 'agreeable to the Directory established by parliament'.[317] Here specific prayers for the churches and kingdoms of England, Scotland and Ireland 'now more strictly and religiously united' in the Solemn League and Covenant and of thanks for 'freeing the land from Antichristian darkness' rendered worship a partisan endorsement of parliamentary policy, and made parliament's official prayers now as much a weapon for the king's opponents as they had been for Charles himself.[318] Similarly, the *Soldier's Catechism* assured parliamentary troops that they fought God's cause against his enemies.[319] As parliament acknowledged in further ordinances prescribing punishments for those who adhered to the Book of Common Prayer, or did not acquire and use the *Directory*, prayer was power.[320]

It will, then, not surprise us to learn that the competition for support as the negotiations for peace were conducted spilled over into published prayers as well as pamphlets. Prayers for the king that followed older forms were printed anonymously in 1647, along with satires on the *Directory*, as part of a Royalist counter-offensive designed to bring 'confusion' on the rebels.[321] On its side, in an illustrated popular work, an apologist for parliament attributed its many victories to the prayers and fasts it had instituted since 1640.[322] The contest for the control of public prayers was to rage through the Commonwealth, the Restoration and, beyond, to our own days; but essentially it had its origins in the English civil war. Whatever their success or failure in securing orthodoxy, Charles I and his predecessors had enjoyed the sole right of prescribing prayers for the Church of England and the nation, and most had regarded that right as inseparable from their sovereignty. From 1640, prayer and prerogative were both disputed.

As well as directly appropriating regal genres of discursive representation, parliament took pains from the onset of conflict to counter royal representations in the forms of sermons and histories. The loyalist sermons delivered often before the king and published by Oxford University during the civil war have yet to be seriously studied as a form of political polemic; but those by the likes of Thomas Barton and Nathaniel Bernard, as well as more familiar figures such as James Ussher, leave little doubt that they belong alongside the newsbooks in the history of partisan advocacy. Barton, a loyalist minister from Sussex, assured Thomas Covert, a Royalist cavalry officer, in a dedication, that he was 'engaged before the world' to the Royalist cause, and his sermon, delivered before the king at Christ Church in 1643, bore out his promise.[323] Preaching at St Mary's in Oxford the next year, Bernard damned rebellion as witchcraft, while Ussher, reminding his congregation of readers as well as his auditors of the sovereign's power and the subject's duty, greatly anticipated the anxieties articulated by the Earl of Manchester in enjoining 'remember that he is still thy prince'.[324] What is perhaps more important here is the ways in which sermons delivered before the Lords and Commons after Charles's departure from London, and published by parliament's authority, echoed and answered the loyalist Oxford texts. To cite a few examples, the Independent Joseph Caryl's 1643 sermon at Christ Church, London, *David's Prayer for Solomon*, though delivered on the day of commemoration of Charles I's inauguration, became a plea to kings to humble themselves and an argument for limited monarchy.[325] John Strickland, a member of the Westminster Assembly, preaching to the Commons in December of the same year, rallied the members by reassuring them – and the wider public addressed in print – that they were the Lord's workmen to carry out his work.[326] As setbacks gave way to advances, victory sermons preached before parliament and printed by authority unequivocally claimed God for the parliamentary cause, asserting that, though both armies appealed to him, 'the Lord himself in that day of our battle seemed to decide the grave doubt . . . whose cause was his'.[327] And in language not only freighted with politics but suggestive of a radical claim to power, Thomas Goodwin told the Commons in 1645 that they were 'Privy Councillors to the great King of Kings' and therefore accountable to none else.[328] Like the rituals prepared for his interment, the funeral sermon for parliament's champion, the Earl of Essex, figured him as a prince in Israel and they who followed him as agents of God's work.[329] Sermons lauding puritan champions of course had long been a thorn in the side of successive heads of the church. What was different after 1642 was that, with parliament established as a government in London (legitimized, as we have seen, by its appropriation of regal forms), sermons delivered to the houses and published by their authority became official representations of the church as much as, and in opposition to, those published by loyalist clergy at Oxford.

The competition for validity and cultural authority, in an age that so much venerated the past and precedent, could not but be manifested also in rival histories. Chroniclers, antiquaries and historians, we have seen, had been advocates of Tudor monarchy, but increasingly from the early Stuart period, the past had become a bitterly disputed territory, not only between rival denominations, but between the king, parliaments and critics of the Stuarts.[330] On the eve of conflict, the debates about the nature and extent of sovereignty, the power of parliaments, and the common law were, necessarily, conducted in the language of precedent. Even after the outbreak of war, both sides, and especially a parliament that was conscious of the charge of novelty, took pains to support their actions with the authority of the past. If a 'historical revolution', as one scholar has argued, took place in England over the century before 1640, civil war made history a key text of revolution.[331]

Thomas Fannant's history, published on the eve of the war, gives some indication of how parliament acted swiftly to use the past to support its position. His *A True Relation of That Memorable Parliament Which Wrought Wonders . . . in the Tenth Year of the Reign of King Richard* was published with 'an abstract of those memorable matters before and since the said king's reign, done by parliament'.[332] Certainly, as parliament began to govern and Royalists denounced its ordinances as illegal innovations, we find anonymously published *Records of Things Done in Parliament (Without the King's Consent)*, with a somewhat defensive addition concerning matters 'of higher consequence than have yet been done by this parliament'.[333] An almost bare list of precedents, principally from the reign of Edward III, Richard II, Henry IV and Henry VI, the *Records* noted past parliaments' appointments of Privy Councillors and archbishops to reassure many who had doubts about the legitimacy of its courses. As well as validating its own authority, apologists for parliament turned historical arguments against the king, whether by invoking Magna Carta to argue the subordination of the monarch to the law, or in narrations of the troubles that laid the blame for civil war squarely on Charles.[334] There is, however, a defensive tone to these partisan histories which suggests a concern that the king, as he himself was quick to tell his subjects, had – and crucially in this war for support might be perceived to have – the precedents on his side.[335] Though contemporary civil war histories await their historian, it would seem that, whatever *de facto* support it was able to secure, parliament lost the contest for the validation of history. Indeed, in 1647, a new spate of Royalist histories reminded those negotiating with Charles I where the authority, if not the power, in the nation lay. For kings, we recall the author of *The Mirror of Allegiance* posited, were as ancient as the land of Britain itself and descended from Noah.[336] The author of *The Present War Paralleled* (with those of Henry III) invoked history as a warning and threat.[337] Stating an acknowledged truism, that 'the most probable way to know what will be is to observe what hath been', the history narrated how a medieval king, at first excluded from his own forts (as Charles had been from Hull), took harsh revenge on the rebels: 'And here was an end', he closed, 'of this wasting, groundless, unnatural war wherein the subject[s] struggled and wrestled with sovereignty till they had wasted the kingdom and wearied themselves, at last are content to . . . let the king have his own right again and some of theirs, according to the usual . . . issue of such embroilments'.[338] History, in other words, taught that rebels always failed and that 'England (like old Rome) cannot long endure more kings than one'.[339] Though the historical battle continued to – and beyond – regicide, the author's (and Edward Hyde's) conviction that the past favoured Royalism and that history would in the end serve the king was borne out by events. Apologists for parliament may have salved some consciences by historical defences of its courses – certainly, and importantly, they denied the Royalists a monopoly on the argument from history; but it was other discourses and other and new forms of argument that more effectively made parliament's case.

From the onset of conflict through to 1649, parliament did not want for advocates who argued that it was the Commons who had right, religion and the public good on their side. Famously, in 1642 the jurist Henry Parker, in a series of pamphlets, argued for a form of parliamentary sovereignty and moved towards acceptance of arguments from necessity and reason of state that he appropriated from apologists for absolutism.[340] While he exemplifies the moderate parliamentary constitutional position as argued to elite audiences, other protagonists for the Commons were deploying more starkly simple polemics to win over a confused people. *The Game at Chess*, for example, took a very familiar cultural practice – and an infamous recent play – to, quite literally, represent the war in black – and white – terms.[341] For, the author told readers of this 1643 tract, the black army 'signifies justly and aptly his Majesty's which hath produced so many black and bloody effects', while 'the white army, which is the ensign and badge of conscience, betokens the parliament's army'.[342] Developing the metaphor to show the queen separating the king from his white knights, and to figure the Cavaliers as black rooks invading subjects' estates, the *Game* urged the king to surrender.[343] The claim that, as opposed to black bishops who corrupted Scripture, parliament championed the cause of conscience was, as we know, a claim most rehearsed in defences of the parliamentary cause. It was popery, idolatry and profanity, *The Burden of England* argued in 1646, that had caused civil conflict; and a host of pamphlets characterized the Royalists as the enemies of godliness.[344] As war gave way to peace negotiations, *England's Petition* to Charles represented parliament as the authority which had protected the laws and religion and, admonishing the king that there was a heavenly judge, 'before whom you must very shortly . . . give account', advised that only his accord with parliament might enable 'God and man [to] forget your mistakings'.[345] It was the king and his atheistical instruments, the readers of *A Sight of the Transactions of These Latter Years* were informed, who had been responsible for the troubles; whereas, as the author of *England's Troubles Anatomized* concurred, it was parliament's armies 'that fight the battle of your God'.[346] Having established itself, not least through argument, as a government and a fighting force, parliament continued throughout the 1640s, and especially again after 1646, to advertise its legitimacy and authority, appropriating all the genres of writing and all the languages which had traditionally represented and sustained royal authority. Though, like Charles himself, the Long Parliament fell to the sword, parliament's successful self-representation across a variety of texts effected changes that were to be enduring.

IV

Along with a bitter struggle for the ownership and control of traditional genres of representation, the civil war gave birth to new forms of political script, devised and utilized by both sides as ammunition in the war for public support. The most obvious, albeit the most neglected, are the battle reports, published by Royalists and Parliamentarians alike, putting the best spin on victories and defeats so as to encourage their own supporters, dishearten the enemy and advertise to the readers the successes achieved in battle and, vitally, the divine approval that success was seen to manifest. A few examples from each side will adequately convey how, for all their pose of factual reportage, these battle reports, as is well known to us today, were vital media of propaganda. In the Royalist account of the battle fought at Hopton Heath in Staffordshire on 19 March 1643, the victory, as it was represented, was not simply military but moral.[347] Contrasting the bravery of the Royalist commander, the Earl of Northampton, with the cowardice of the Parliamentarian generals Sir William Brereton and Sir John Gell, the report argued that the 'greatness of his example cannot but make all that are desirous of honour to follow in his steps'.[348] To underline the difference of breeding and civility which separated the king's followers from parliament's, the author also set against Northampton's nobility the barbarity of his enemies who refused even to honour (by embalming) his corpse – a failing, it was claimed, typical of 'those rebellious forces . . . made up of all religions and trades'.[349] The decisive Royalist victory at Hopton Heath, as it was reported, was a triumph not of superior numbers but superior men. Though they are (wrongly) less well known for it than parliament, Royalist reporters were also ever quick to attribute their victories to God: to publicize both their own godliness and the Lord's blessings upon their cause. *A True Relation* of the victory of royal forces at St Johnston in Scotland in 1645, somewhat incredibly claiming that for the hundreds of enemy killed and taken only one fell on the king's side, announced that 'God by it did manifestly declare his favour towards the justice of his Majesty's cause and his detestation of . . . the rebels'.[350] When, afterwards, such (allegedly) spectacular victories came seldom, Royalist writers were not averse, while acknowledging that the king could not be spared the knowledge of every setback, to prognosticating that 'the several positions of the heavens . . . do generally render his Majesty and his whole army unexpectedly victorious'.[351]

For parliament, at least initially, victories – and, as important, the publicization and public perception of victories – were even more vital to dispelling doubts about their actions; and from early on they employed battle reports for the larger polemical purpose of validating their cause. Accordingly, a report of two victories by the Earl of Essex and Colonel Chomley at Twyford and Reading narrated that they were attained with the loss of only 'about twenty men' 'through the assistance of Almighty God'.[352] *A True Relation of a Late Skirmish at Henley* carried on its title page the scriptural tag 'if God is for us, who can be against us?' and, this time claiming even fewer losses, provided an account of the battle 'God fought on our side'.[353] Similarly narrating Waller's triumph, an author claimed 'the mighty providence of God was seen in this, as in many other mercies towards us; for in this fight, for a certain truth, there were not above five of our men slain'.[354] With victories coming increasingly their way from 1645, parliament not only authorized individual reports of battle successes, like that obtained by Waller at Alton 'through God's providence', they began to list their victories to express the resurgence of parliamentary arms and the inevitable defeat of their opponents. *A Perfect List of the Many Victories Obtained (through the Blessing of God) by the Parliament's Forces* under Essex, Lesley and Manchester, in a broadside topped with a portrait of Essex armed and mounted, listed 175 successes from the 'defeat' of the king at Coventry in July 1642 to the capture of Evesham by Massey in May 1645.[355] At the end of a simple numerical list, evidently deemed eloquent enough to need no comment, the broadside closed: 'these mercies . . . hath God bestowed upon England's lovers and Covenant-helping friends' against 'enemies to truth and Reformation'. In the same vein, *The Jubilee of England. From Naseby to the Mount in Cornwall* listed all the battles won, and prisoners, arms and colours taken in its account 'of a great enemy subdued'.[356] Praising the generals raised by God to be instruments of parliament's cause, the reporter urged: 'consider Christians, we need now a crown to be set upon the great works already done for us'.[357] As each side measured divine and moral support in victories won, numbers slain and few home casualties, parliament was gradually winning this particularly textual battle, as well as the war.

If it did not create the genre, civil war developed and sharpened forms of satire and personal abuse as modes of political discourse. Classical satires, long known and read, which had re-emerged as a political form in late Elizabethan and early Stuart England, had in the main been an 'oppositionist' mode, or one

52 *A Perfect List of the Many Victories Obtained . . . by the Parliaments Forces*, 1645.

used within court circles to settle personal scores.[358] In the unprecedented circumstances of civil war, however, satires became officially sponsored ways of discrediting the authority of the other side – what we now recognize and describe as the all-important political strategy of negative campaigning. From the beginning of the conflict, satirical mockery of parliament's supporters was a Royalist strategy. *A Seasonable Lecture*, for example, published in 1642, mocked the preachers who supported parliament as holding that all property should be held in common, and all 'equally rule alike'.[359] Satirizing the style as well as beliefs of Henry Walker, the pamphlet caricatured the normally moderate and conciliatory Walker as an ignorant ironmonger and advocate of communist anarchy. The author of this assault was none other than the popular John Taylor who was able skilfully to target satirical political forms at popular audiences. In *Mad Fashions*, for example, Taylor (or his printer) used woodcuts of a man walking on his hands and familiar ballad refrains to satirize 'all things . . . turn'd the clean contrary way' by opponents of the king, to whom he avowed his loyalty.[360] Where Taylor evoked former oppositionist ballads critical of upstarts (such as the Duke of Buckingham) who had subverted the natural order, other loyalist satirists deployed tropes of, and anxieties about, gender to discredit parliament.[361] Mocking – it was a familiar trope from the Jacobean stage – the sects as 'feminine', the author of *The Diseases of the Times* associated religious and political radicalism with an

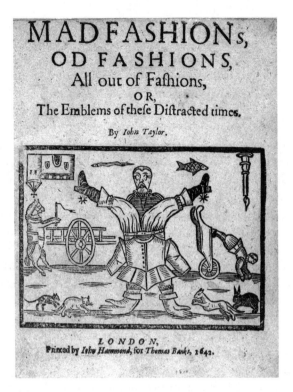

53 *Title page of* Mad Fashions, Od Fashions, *John Taylor, 1642.*

upturned world 'where women shall wear the breeches'; and numerous other satires pushed home the connection between political and sexual disorder.[362] *A Medicine for the Times*, offering cures for factious spirits and shrewish women, insisted that only enforcing a wife's natural obedience to her husband 'will keep her from pulling off the sacred chain that is about the neck of authority' – a language that more than hints at the interrelations of domestic and public order.[363] Similarly, the anthropomorphized Cheapside Cross in its *Lamentation* on the 'staggers' that plagued England, as well as the battering it received, bemoaned that women were claiming positions as divines.[364] Bringing together these attacks, with the first moves to name-calling, *The Resolution of the Roundheads* was a mocking satire that appropriated the first person to present parliament's men as low-life cobblers and cuckolds who had plotted the war from their conventicles.[365] In yet another take on the metaphor of politics as a card game, *The Bloody Game at Cards*, figuring the 'king of hearts' as the defender of the pack, mocked the 'city clubs' who chose as their leader a knave of broken fortunes.[366]

Throughout the war, Royalist satirists continued to mock not only parliaments and puritans but the forms and bodies associated with them. *The Rebels'*

Catechism by Peter Heylyn, for instance, reclaimed the dominant form of religious instruction to satirize parliament's hypocritical protestations of loyalty and to cast its supporters as revolutionaries bent on the murder of the king.[367] Again raising the fears about gender inversion, the notorious *Parliament of Women*, published in 1646, lampooned the name of parliament by again associating it with newly dominant women who, with their lusts unbridled by the collapse of paternal authority, now voted for two husbands and ordered as much 'thumping', 'twanging', or sex, as they desired.[368] Another satire of the same year repeated the charge of whoredom, but added a further catalogue of Roundhead and sectarian outrages that were paraded to shock readers. *Mercurius Rusticus*, published at Oxford, presented 'The Courtier's complaint of the sacrileges, profanations and plunderings committed by the schismatics'.[369] Along with detailed accounts of the destruction of monuments and profanation of altars, the pamphlet related the ravishing of maids, the torturing of servants, and the wounding of an old man, as well as instances of cruelty to Royalist soldiers.[370] During the peace negotiations, Royalist satirists continued to mock parliament as the cause of the inversion of all order, *Grand Pluto's Progress through Great Britain*, for example, revealing an England ruined by greed, ignorance, irreligion and promiscuity.[371]

That parliamentary satirists not only responded in kind but often levelled the same charges at the Royalists as had been directed at them, indicates how satire participated in the contest for the normative vocabularies and discourses of social order which characterized the war years. Mirroring, for example, the mockery of the promiscuous sectarian, parliamentary writers conjured the debauched Cavalier. So, *The Resolution of the Women of London to the Parliament*, illustrated with a woodcut of a wife urging her husband to go to the wars, depicted frustrated women and widows seeking out Cavaliers; while *Nocturnal Occurrences or Deeds of Darkness Committed by the Cavaliers*, as well as a satire on the Royalists' long hair, represented them performing military exercises to instructions delivered in the language of their preferred pastime of debauchery: 'prime your whore'; 'ram your whore'.[372] In *The Debauched Cavalier or the English Midianite*, Cavalier debauchery – including the story of the rape of a virgin while others watched – elided into other charges of blasphemy, dishonesty, banditry and plunder (not least of the properties and liberties of the nation) for which the Old Testament tribe of Midianites was a byword.[373] As the biblical comparison suggested, parliamentarian satirists connected charges of sexual with religious debauchery. We have noted the discrediting of Royalist piety in the mock *Cavaliers New Common Prayer Book Unclasp't*; in similar vein, *The Soldiers Language*, as well as repeating the familiar charges of popery, represented Royalists cursing and profaning freely: 'if a man can but swear and swagger and cry God damn me but I am for the king, he is in the road-way to be knighted'; and in *A Charm for Canterburian Spirits*, published the year of Laud's execution, the 'viperous brood of Hydra-headed Cavaliers' were shown as drunken and blasphemous, as well as men addicted to superstition.[374] Along with such pamphlets, various 'characters', such as *The Character of A Right Malignant* or *The Character of a Cavalier*, deployed a form made popular by John Earle and others, to caricature, parody and satirize a type that loved Irish papists and absolute rulers, hated parliaments and engaged in Machiavellian plots against peace and unity.[375]

On both sides satirical caricatures gave way to a new strain of personal abuse. Royalists focused this on key figures such as Pym, the Earl of Essex and Henry Marten. Pym, the leader of the House of Commons, was routinely figured as an ambitious Machiavel; Essex, who after the Overbury affair presented all too easy a target, was, despite his military successes, mocked as an impotent cuckold; and Marten became the epitome of promiscuous debauchery in myriad squibs.[376] Such personal abuse often took the form of mockery of physical attributes. The large nose of the (hypocritical) puritan was a stock-in-trade of the stage, but in royalist satires the nose 'able to try [that is, equal] a young eagle' became a sign of political corruption, too, and was a trope ubiquitously deployed against Oliver Cromwell.[377] On the Parliamentarian side, the satirists' favourite personal target – perhaps the closest they could get to the king – was the flamboyant Prince Rupert, the feared and brilliant cavalry officer. As well as being condemned as cruel and popish, Rupert, a ladies' man, was routinely represented as a darling of 'the parliament of ladies' – that is as debauched; and pornographic verses did not stop short of accusing the prince of having sex with his dog, Boy, as 'they lie perpetually in one bed, sometimes the prince upon the dog, and sometimes the dog upon the prince and what this may in time produce, none but the close committee can tell'.[378] In a mock *Last Will and Testament of Prince Rupert*, the prince describes himself as a plunderer, a swearer and a drunkard, and a friend of bawds and pimps.[379] Just as Augustan satire owes a debt to the satires of the 1640s, we may discern in the mockery and abuse of individuals in civil war satires and squibs the beginning of that intense personalizing of political verse that so characterized Restoration culture and gave rise to the poems on affairs of state. Rival governments and armies, like the parties of Restoration England, threw up rival leaders who were seen to epitomize, indeed to embody, their cause; and so became the butt of a polemic that cartooned and figured them as the personification of evil. Caricature, sexual slander and political propaganda came together in civil war satire and bequeathed to us an enduring popular form of political comment.

The best-known genre of writing and representation that emerged from conflict, division and civil war was the newsbook. Newsbooks, news pamphlets and serials combined older styles and forms with the satirized, the abusive and the entertaining. The modern authority on them traces their origins to the newsletters and corantos of the 1620s and 1630s, but, recognizing the difference between these and the outright propaganda of their successors, suggests late

1641, when conflict already loomed, as a date for their birth.[380] Though news-books varied in the relationship of reportage to polemic, from the outset they were rhetorical texts and progressively became the clearly identifiable organs of the two sides and warriors in the battle for hearts and minds. On the Royalist side, *Mercurius Aulicus*, produced in Oxford from January 1643 by John Berkenhead, 'played a provocative role in changing the presentation of news' and its overt partisanship prompted parliament to respond with *Mercurius Britannicus*, produced by Marchamont Nedham.[381] Capturing the vitriolic fervour that set in as the war looked likely to be a long one, *Aulicus* and *Britannicus* were themselves anthropomorphized as 'characters' who entered into contact and traded barbs and abuse, becoming, we might say, the official representers, as well as representations, of their parties. More than other discursive representational forms, it was newsbooks contemporaries had in mind when they spoke of the 'paper bullets' that preceded and joined the military engagements of civil war.[382] With substantial sales (sometimes about two thousand) and a broad, popular audience, one probably hooked on the serial rather like the modern viewer of a TV soap, newsbooks were the principal medium of both positive and (even more frequent) negative campaigning throughout the wars.[383]

While scholars, most recently and authoritatively Joad Raymond, have analysed as well as charted the history of civil war newsbooks, to appreciate the efficacy of their rhetorical and stylistic strategies there can be no substitute for the scholar's or student's own reading of the originals – and certainly we cannot substitute for that here. But a few examples may offer an indication of how newsbooks performed as propaganda and how they represented events and positions over the course of the civil war. For parliament, perhaps the very reporting of its activities in the *Diurnal Occurrences* performed the important, and indeed contentious, act of publicizing (and so, as we have seen, authorizing) proceedings – proceedings which, especially after the king's departure, were strictly unconstitutional. Moreover, in a simple phrase, such as that recorded for the *Diurnal* of 3–10 January 1642 – 'The House of Commons on their meeting entered upon the scanning of the liberty of the subject' – which then gives way to polemic, parliament is not only reported but represented as the custodian of the people's freedoms.[384] Similarly, the repeated reports that the king, 'seduced by wicked counsel, intends to make war against the parliament' attributed blame in a seemingly neutral statement.[385] Once hostilities broke out, parliament's *Diurnals* helped to create heroes, like John Hotham (who barred Charles from Hull) and villains and so forge party identities.[386]

Where the *Diurnals*, for all their gloss, were largely restricted by the genre of report, *Aulicus* initiated a mode that permitted more comment, wit and vitriol – more negative representations of the enemy, in an entertaining way. Reports of soldiers in Gloucester, filled with drink 'for the *Cause* as they call it', played on the image of stage puritans, like Ben Jonson's Zeal-of-the-Land Busy, to show the rebels as hypocritical and senseless.[387] In early 1643, *Aulicus* reported how a group of 'zealous young maids' of Norwich, a centre of puritanism, had become pregnant by the brethren, whom, the editor hoped, none would now 'scarce think . . . honest'.[388] Presented with such challenges, parliament's new organ *Britannicus* quickly responded, forging supposed letters of Cavaliers boasting that they would fornicate with all nations (Catholic Irish and French especially) to sate their lusts and not cease even from 'sinning with the very beasts of the field'.[389] Indeed, anticipating the techniques and titillations of modern tabloids, as well as identifying lewd acts by Cavaliers, and even naming figures like the Earl of Dorset and Littleton who (allegedly) sported with concubines, *Britannicus* hints at still worse sodomitical and paedophilic practices ('I would tell you a strange story' . . . 'you would little imagine' . . . 'I leave his transgression') not actually narrated.[390]

Though the newsbooks yield up the funniest passages, negative campaigning was by no means the only strategy of their writers. In reporting speeches – in parliament or in the field – of their leaders and protagonists, in publicizing their courage, moral as well as military, in advertising their own reasonableness and moderation (as opposed to the enemy's extremism and madness), insisting on their own godliness and right, and claiming widespread support, the newsbooks also sold a positive image of their party to a public whose allegiance was increasingly determined by pamphlet information. Accordingly, the elegy on Pym in *Britannicus* (for 7–14 December 1643) represented him and the cause he fought for as the patriotic cause; while *Aulicus*, along with the spleen it vented against the Roundheads, began the process of representing Charles himself in affective terms, as a put-upon but devoted father of his people.[391]

The effect of newsbooks on readers and the political fortunes of the combatants is hard to document precisely but is indisputable.[392] Moreover, as the dialogue between them, and evidence of collecting them indicates, protagonists on either side were, and were perceived to be, reading the polemic of both parties. That is to say, and it is the story of this chapter, that representation – and the processes and media of representation – had become indelibly politicized and part of a dialectic that would henceforth irrevocably characterize the business of politics and the representation of authority.

Civil war news and news pamphlets secured another development that we have traced throughout this study: the increasing involvement of those outside the elites in the debates about government. Rumour and the new medium of print had circulated information about what were still regarded as *arcana imperii* from the early Tudors onwards, but periods of repressive censorship, though seldom fully effective, checked the full flowering of a public sphere. It took the existence of two distinct and rival governments from 1642 (as earlier the existence of two churches) to add the political condition, even official legitimation and encouragement, to the pressures of the marketplace and the appetite of the populace for an unrestrained public sphere. Even those who had lived through the Jacobean age of scandal and libel felt that they were living in a new, more open era of publicity.[393] 'Each City and each Towne, yea every village,' the *Heads of All Fashions* marvelled, 'can fill us now with news.'[394] Commenting on the House of Commons' (failed) order to suppress pamphlets, the author of *The Poets Knavery* observed that, since Strafford's execution a year before, over three hundred – 'lying' – pamphlets had appeared: not much short of the entire annual output of print before 1600.[395] By 1643, it was only slight exaggeration to affirm, as did *A Rational Discourse*, that 'books are as common as is common opinion.'[396] The irrepressible flood of print evidently provided many ordinary folk with a good living: in London seamstresses were allegedly observed selling cheap print.[397] Ironically, however, most who them-selves took full advantage of cheap pamphlets and newsbooks to argue their case reacted negatively to the explosion of print and endeavoured to contain it. From the beginning of the civil war, both sides blamed the press for fomenting the troubles. The author of *The Vote*, for example, believed that 'scribbling pamphleteers' had undermined Charles I; *Britannicus* was accused – 'thou taught'st the people better to rebel'; another loyalist wrote of 'paper Treacherie'; *The Cavaliers Diurnal* denounced 'a swarm of Mercuries with as many heads as Hydras.'[398] For their part, the Lords and Commons issued severe ordinances against the production, or reading, of any pamphlet which they had not licensed and imposed increasingly harsh punishment on offenders.[399]

In part, the entry into print publicity and yet the desire to control it expressed a fundamental tension in attitudes to the representation of authority throughout our period – and to this day. What was disturbingly new about the revolution was the complete absence of any authoritative voice; the sheer number and variety of papers; the relentless animadversion, one tract scarcely off the press before it was answered by another; and, in consequence, the sheer confusion about where truth lay and, more importantly, how a reader might know – or judge – it. In the denominational wars of early modern Europe, Catholic and Protestant polemicists had routinely accused each other of false-hood and lying.[400] But it was the civil war which in England exposed virtually every utterance in print to the charge of falsehood. *The Poets Knavery*, we recall, had discovered 300 'lying pamphlets' in a year, and even before war broke out *The Liar* promised 'a contradiction to those who in the titles of their books affirmed them to be true when they were false.'[401] Though satirical, the point was well made: hundreds of pamphlets appeared boasting in their titles 'A true and exact' account, a 'true description', the 'love of truth and peace' a 'plain narration', and suchlike.[402] And this claim became ever more common – even necessary – as truth claims were undermined, falsehood was exposed, or opposite cases were more powerfully argued. The stark facts of division, then civil war, not only subverted claims to truth; contemporaries *perceived* them to do so. As early pamphleteers observed, adherence to the Protestant faith and the laws was 'pretended on both sides'; both used the word 'loyalty' and protested their allegiance to the king; both claimed 'victories' they did not win.[403] As a consequence, *The Great Assizes Holden in Parnassus* incontrovertibly observed in 1645, 'Truth, and Morall Vertues injur'd are.'[404]

The coupling is interesting. Trust in the truth status of print and the upholding of social and political bonds had been, and they were, closely related; or, as the anonymous author of *The Great Assizes* versed it, 'Typographie doth concerne your state.'[405] While neither governmental nor print authority had ever been spared challenge, they possessed authority and they had become interdependent. As, therefore, the authority of each and both was eroded, the question posed by a lover of truth and peace in 1640 became ever more pressing: 'in this variety of opinions and distractions of sides, everyone challenging truth to be on their party, how shall we know what is that truth which we ought to love and adhere unto?'[406] The numerous remonstrances and declarations, another observed, 'raise such a dust and clouds of scruples.'[407] Some, predominantly – but not only – Royalists, saw the only solution to the anarchy of uncertainty as the re-establishment of the king as sovereign signifier, as determinant of truth. *The Maids Petition* of 1647, we may remember, called for King Charles 'his coming home and residence with his parliament . . . as the only conclusive means against fictions and factions'; others, with more or less regret, recognized that intrinsic faith in authorial truth had been destroyed for all time and replaced by something less fixed and certain.[408] Already in 1641, the broadside *The World is Ruled and Governed by Opinion* was illustrated with blind Opinion in a tree from the branches of which hung a variety of pamphlets.[409] Though the title of the satire was almost a self-contradiction in an early modern England that would have denied that Opinion could govern, it expressed a new reality. The authority of script and utterance had been fractured into multiple contrary claims – that is, had become politicized and democratized; and the only judge of opinion was the individual: the reader and the citizen. In an address to the reader, the author of the 1644 *Shepherd's Oracle* wrote: 'whose soever those lines were, readers they are now yours.'[410] Though, often lamenting the case, authors had made similar statements before, it was never more true.[411] Multiple and contesting claims and cases made in print had transformed the verbal representation of authority from an art of government to a political free-for-all.

Few, even in the 1640s, were ready to accept, or in some cases fully acknowledge, that revolutionary change. Paradoxically, as the capacity of print to command or support authority diminished with relentless animadversion, other forms of authority were deployed to reinforce the status and force of print. The interdependence of forms of publication with other signifiers of authority, and indeed with monarchy, is evidenced in the early ordinances issued by the Commons and Lords that bore the royal arms.[412] Though with

THE WORLD IS RVLED & GOVERNED by OPINION.

54 *The World is Ruled & Governed by Opinion*, print by Wenceslaus Hollar, 1642.

some ordinances, parliament developed an independent visual stamp (an ordinance for accounts, for example, depicted a book crossed with a sword and a
motto), royal symbols – roses, thistles and harps, as well crowns – were used,
even as late as 1647, to add authority; perhaps at that point to suggest parliament and king reunited.[413] As orders issued by both sides claimed the
authority of the royal arms, so Parliamentarian as well as Royalist pamphlets
were illustrated with crowns and portraits of Charles I, along with woodcuts of
the Houses of Parliament in session. Attention (still needed) to the materiality
of civil war publications reminds us that print, and what *The Great Assizes* had
called 'Typography', consisted of form as well as content, and that it signified
visually as well as verbally. Those protagonists for parliament who appropriated traditional regal forms – Gothic script, arms, and decorated initial letters
– did so because they appreciated that authority resided in those forms, as well
as in polemical arguments or decrees. They sensed, that is, that the contest for
representation was a contest not just for the words but for the signs, the
images, of power. It is to that contest, and the story of the civil war as a struggle
for authorizing signs, that we now turn.

CHAPTER 10

VISUAL CONFLICTS AND
WARS OF SIGNS

I

More than any English monarch before him, Charles I had given his attention to the visual representation of his kingship. Van Dyck rendered on canvas a philosophy of government, in fulfilment of the king's passionate belief that artistic forms and representations did not only advertise his own personal and divine authority but might lead viewers to reason and self-regulation. Copied, engraved, reproduced on seals, medals and coins, images of Charles I disseminated the king's representation as ruler, just as James I's folio *Works* had represented the king in print; and it is on canvas that Charles is today best remembered.

Van Dyck died in London on 9 December 1641, as letters arrived announcing the spread of the rebellion in Ireland and as the London mob crowded around the Parliament building braying for the removal of the bishops.[1] Though coincidental to Charles's troubles, Van Dyck's death was almost auspicious: the next month, after his failure to arrest the five MPs guilty of treason, the king removed from London. During the following years of civil war, no artist succeeded to Van Dyck's place of privilege and royal patronage. Some artists in former court employ – Peter Lely for one – worked for courtiers such as the Earl of Northumberland or the Earl of Pembroke, both of whom defected to parliament and became members of the Committee for Safety.[2] The royal court at Oxford, in Oliver Millar's words, 'must, by contrast, have been a much less settled and congenial place' for artists to work in.[3] Indeed, one of the important artists who did work there, William Dobson, a Groom of the Privy Chamber and Sergeant Painter to the king, is said to have died in poverty in London, after he returned there in 1646.[4]

Ironically, it was the civil war that gave Dobson his opportunity. Though little is known of his earlier career, Dobson was evidently at work in Oxford immediately after Charles's arrival there in October 1642; over the next four years he painted portraits of the king, the royal family and Royalist officers in intervals between military campaigns.[5] Dobson's only portrait of the king was unfinished.[6] However, the head and shoulders of Charles I in armour was clearly designed at Oxford and seems to have become the model of a civil war type of portrait of the king, some of them on a smaller scale. The figuring of Charles in armour, like the verse representation of the formerly pacific monarch as a warrior prince, was of obvious import in 1642, and it is puzzling that the canvas at Windsor was not finished. What was completed was a portrait of the king's son. A three-quarter-length of the prince in a richly gilded suit of armour depicts the fourteen-year-old heir to the throne with his right hand on his helmet and his left on a baton.[7] Behind him, the draped pillar, symbolizing authority, recalls Van Dyck's portraits of the royal family, as does the pose and baton. But, here in the background, there is no peaceful

55 *Charles I* by William Dobson, 1642–6.

landscape or Westminster but a cavalry action, indicating that the monarchy is embroiled in war and that the heir to the throne is fighting alongside his father for his rights. Other versions of the portrait, and copies, suggest that this was an important image of a prince who came of age just as civil war erupted. One, now in the National Portrait Gallery of Scotland, depicts the prince, again beside a large column, with his left hand on a helmet proffered by his page and his right holding a commander's baton over colours and weapons piled on a Medusa's head – perhaps symbolizing the prince's (eventual) victory over the horrors of rebellion.[8] Though it has been rightly observed that the figure of Prince Charles is 'thrust forward at the viewer in a very un-Van Dyckian way' – perhaps a change reflecting the new conditions of the just-fought battle of Edgehill – the page with helmet certainly evokes Van Dycks of the king, not least *Charles I with Monsieur St Antoine*.[9] Interestingly, a half-length of James, Duke of York was evidently begun about the same time; while unfinished, it appears not to have been intended as a martial portrait.[10] Similarly, the only surviving Dobson of Prince Rupert, Charles's nephew, remained unfinished – perhaps on account of his departure from Oxford, or the surrender of his commission after the fall of Bristol in 1645; an earlier completed portrait, now lost, is only known from the Faithorne engraving.[11]

These unfinished canvases are, no less than the military portrait of Prince Charles, texts of war. One scholar has recently suggested that, in absences even in completed paintings, Dobson signalled 'the crisis in representation' which the parliamentary challenge to Charles's authority had precipitated.[12] In several canvases, Dobson depicted individuals – an unknown naval commander, Sir Edward Walker, secretary of the Council of War, and the poet Sir Richard Fanshawe – seated in front of blank papers.[13] If these signify the absence of the king as sovereign signifier, it may be, Jerome de Groot suggests, that the sometimes intentionally thin paint and uneven images point to ruptured processes of visual representation: to the absence of the king as the source of symbolic, as much as of textual, meaning.[14] Such must remain suggestion. But what is clear is that, in practice, other than on copies of Van Dycks which were probably made during the 1640s, Charles was no longer newly represented in the large on canvas. The urgency of the times required other regal acts and other forms of royal representation.

It may be significant that, after the outbreak of civil war, Charles evidently authorized several miniature portraits. The king had been, during his peaceful reign, one of the first to collect miniatures, and he patronized miniaturists such as Peter Oliver to copy paintings; but in terms of the royal portrait, though John Hoskins and Jean Petitot painted Charles and Henrietta Maria on vellum and enamel, these were not the prominent visual representations of kingship.[15] The conditions of war were different. Not only was a miniature more quickly executed, it was more easily copied, more portable, and (like Elizabethan miniatures given as love tokens) could be carried, or worn, as a token of a code of honour vital to Royalist values and as a badge of allegiance in divided times. From 1642, there were miniatures of Charles painted by Petitot and Hoskins showing Charles armoured and wearing, on a light blue sash or chain, the emblem of chivalric kingship, the Garter.[16] The likelihood that there were many of these now lost is reinforced by the fact that, by 1660, Hoskins, who had entered royal employ in 1640, was owed over £4,000 by the crown.[17] David Des Granges also produced miniatures of Charles I and Prince Charles after Hoskins, both most probably before the regicide; and went on to work for Charles II after 1649, producing for him official images of his coronation for distribution among followers.[18] In the two miniatures in the National Portrait Gallery, the succession of father and son is underlined by the repetition of the blue Garter sash, and perhaps by some playing down of the very different physical characteristics of father and son.

Compared, however, with the small number of portraits of Charles I or his family in large, or even with miniatures, during the civil war years there were numerous prints, engravings and woodcuts of the king and his wife and children.[19] As we have seen, continental engravers like Robert van Voerst, William Faithorne and Wenceslaus Hollar received royal patronage and etched copies of Van Dyck's images of the king.[20] After Van Dyck's death and the outbreak of war, others followed: probably about 1643, for example, Jonas Suyderhoff, or Suyderhoef, from Haarlem, issued a large printed portrait of Charles, based on the 'Great Piece' by Van Dyck.[21] The dating of undated engravings is not an exact science, and few of the engravings of Charles I during the years 1642–6 are published with dates. Hollar, we know, made in 1644 an engraving of the king in armour with a baton and mounted on a horse, which bore the royal arms. In the background we see pikemen with, in the far distance, a city – an unquestionable image of a warrior king fighting a civil war to regain his capital and kingdom.[22] Though this is one of the only few dated examples, engravings of Charles in armour abound during the 1640s. Some probably pre-date the civil war: Van Dyck had painted Charles in armour in 1638 and engraved copies of the portrait were made at the time and later.[23] But most appear to belong to the 1640s. Hollar evidently executed 'cum privilegio regis' an engraving of Charles in armour, wearing his George in an oval, beneath which cannons, drums and ensigns symbolize the war.[24] The inscription, giving Charles his title Defender of the Faith, announces this as a defiant Royalist image, depicting a king fighting for what was legally his right. An engraving of Charles, in armour and mounted, with a baton, on a rearing horse, as if about to lead a charge (battle is being fought in the background), also clearly belongs to those years, and was sold by the London printseller Peter Stent, who had a considerable stock of civil war generals.[25]

While portraits of the king in armour were numerous and important, and circulated abroad and at home to manifest a prince fighting for his rights, they were not the only engraved representation of Charles during the war years. As well as commander-in-chief, Charles was, and needed to be portrayed as, still king and in various ways engravings were executed to publicize his regal authority. At the simplest level, this involved multiple depictions of the king as monarch, or with the regalia. Some of the engravings of Charles in armour, after Van Dyck, such as that by Johannes Meyssens, depict Charles with his hand on his crown, or with a crowned royal arms beneath his portrait.[26] Several line engravings figure a head and shoulders of Charles crowned and wearing coronation robes, with a George – a simple, but effective reminder of regal authority.[27] One elaborate image shows the king being crowned by Fame and other figures with laurels of victory.[28] In several instances, the polemics of the image is made explicit by brief accompanying text. While this is often simply a rehearsal of Charles's titles as 'The Most High and Mighty Prince Charles by the Grace of God King of Scotland, France and Ireland', the subtle reference to divine appointment should be noted, especially when it was re-inforced with a description of the king as Defender of the Faith, or by angels holding a crown in the border of the portrait, as in Bouttat's engraving after Van Dyck.[29] In some cases, moreover, the inscription serves a specific and topical polemical purpose. An anonymous engraving of Charles, head and shoulders with an elaborate lace collar and Garter collar, bears the inscription 'Per ecclesiam peror'.[30] Presumably a contraction of the phrase 'I labour or toil on behalf of the church', the inscription, repeated on a William Marshall engraving of Charles crouched over a globe with the churches of England and Scotland, proclaims Charles, against his enemies, as the protector of the true church and as fulfilling his duty as Supreme Head.[31] This conceit had its best-known statement in the engraving of *The Shepherd's Oracle* which depicts Charles coming with his sword to the aid of the tree of religion, while crop heads lop at its branches or take pickaxes to its roots, or in the frontispiece to *The Troubles of England*, in which Charles stretches out his hand to raise a fainting figure of Ecclesia.[32] Another inscription, on an engraving by Cornelis Galle, makes yet greater claims for the king, describing him as a miracle of the age who deserved to rank with the gods.[33]

Judging by survivals, however, the most common engraved images of Charles were not as overt, but were no less polemical. Two images, both prob-ably drawn after Van Dyck, formed the most common 'types' of engravings of the king in the 1640s. One (dated to 1649 but possibly earlier), a representa-tion of Charles dressed in black, with a white lace collar, the Garter and some-times the large Garter star on his sleeve, occurs in several versions, in profile left and right.[34] This image, though lacking any obvious signifiers of regality, evokes the Van Dycks that affirm Charles's personal authority – that of a calm, self-controlled gentleman whose personal virtues, and spiritual values, reflected in the chivalric and holy Order of the Garter, qualified him to rule. The other, still more popular, is an anonymous woodcut of Charles, head and shoulders, with a fine lace collar over an ermine robe, printed in 1647, which, as well as circulating as a separate, illustrated many books and pamphlets in the later 1640s.[35]

Though few of those engravings (like the Hollar of Charles) carry an official imprimatur, it is likely that many of the images of Charles that circulated during the war emerged from Royalist circles and that the increase in the more popular representations was part of the campaign to argue the king's case.[36] As with written texts, the campaign was waged as intensely after the military engagements as during them and images of the king circulated as separates or in publications were very much part of the quest for public support during the negotiations for peace. As early as 1645, albeit illustrated with royal arms rather than a portrait, *The Scourge of Civil War* identified the king with the blessings of Peace, herself described in royal terms as a queen.[37] In 1647, with negotiations in full swing, almost every declaration and proposition sent from the king bore his portrait image. Charles's *Declaration and Protestation* for a settlement of religion and his message concerning his departure from Hampton Court both bore portraits, the latter the most popular anonymous woodcut we have discussed above.[38] Similarly, the next year, all the royal propositions sent from the Isle of Wight, the declarations of proceedings at Carisbrooke, the king's declaration from Newport to parliament's commissioners and his remonstrance to his 'loyal subjects' on episcopacy were all

56 Title page of *The Kings Majesties Most Gratious Message in Foure Letters*, 1647.

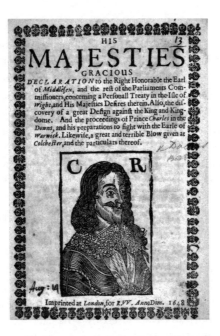

57 *His Majesties Gracious Declaration to the Right Honorable the Earl of Middlesex*, 1648.

58 *A New Remonstrance from The Kings Majesty to All His Loyall Subjects*, 1648.

adorned with the royal portrait.[39] The king's *Last Message and Declaration to*
... Sir Thomas Fairfax shows Fairfax standing dutifully with his hat off before
the figure of Charles, crowned and in full coronation robes.[40] Similarly
stressing the persistent force and rights of majesty, the title page to the
published version of *The Kings Majesty's Speech* to the commission from
parliament depicts Charles enthroned, crowned and with the royal sceptre,
surrounded by officers and counsellors, while small figures kneel some
distance away at a bar.[41] And, advertising Charles's sincere wishes for the
stability of his kingdom and the good of his people, a crude woodcut on *A*
Declaration of the Treaty at Newport seats the king beneath the royal arms and
before a table, below which is written the word Peace.[42] In images such as
these, the centring of the royal person and the spatial arrangements and relationships represent and assert royal hopes and claims, just as had the perspective theatres and rituals of the early Stuart court. Charles may have been in
captivity, but the images reminded readers of what he relied upon in setting his
enemies against each other: that he was still king.

As well as appearing on his own official papers and proposals, some of
the same woodcut portraits were used by advocates of the royal cause. For
example, John Harvey's 1647 attack on *London's Lawless Liberty* and the 'prodi-
gious knaves' of the city, who had robbed men of their goods and liberties,
bore a woodcut portrait of Charles I, implying that only the king might restore

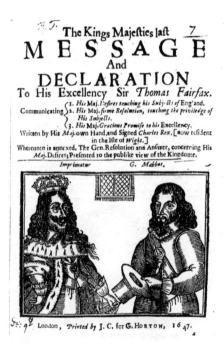

59 *The Kings Majesties Last Message And Declaration To His Excellency Sir Thomas*
Fairfax, 1647.

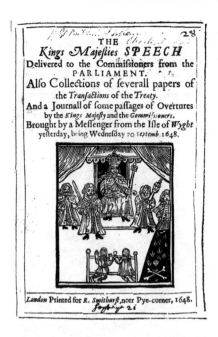

60 *The Kings Majesties Speech Delivered to the Commissioners from the Parliament*, 1648.

those liberties.[43] Published the same year, Michael Hudson's *The Divine Right of Government, Natural and Politique* was illustrated with a portrait of Charles published by Peter Stent, while Michael Symmons's *Vindication of King Charles I, or A Loyal Subjects Duty* had as a frontispiece a small woodcut of Charles I crowned.[44] In myriad works such as these, for all the minor variations, it is the repetition of a few stock portraits that is more striking. Repetition, however, was the point. In 1643–8, Charles and the Royalists still believed, as well as hoped, that the royal person was central to any settlement; and the ubiquitous circulation of the royal image, with or without the regalia, endlessly restated the point. In some instances, illustrations in pamphlets, as on separates, were glossed with texts which spelled out the argument. In *Royalty and Loyalty*, for example, a treatise of 1647, beneath an angel hovering over the figure of Royalty a Latin tag rendered Scripture: 'Per me reges regnant', while on the left is written 'By God's command we rule this land'.[45] The Royalist pamphlet, *King Charles His Royal Welcome to Holmby*, as well as a reproduction of the most common portrait of 1647, also, in an early gesture to a heavenly rather than earthly triumph, depicts Charles in a crude woodcut, with a long staff and a scroll with 'My reward is from above'.[46]

Whether with the aid of explanatory text or not, engraved and woodcut images of Charles I, with others or alone, quite literally *re-presented* to the people the man who, after years of war and military defeat, was yet their sacred, sovereign monarch. If, in adversity in 1647–8, Charles still believed, as

61 *King Charles His Royal Welcome, at His Happy and Gracious Return Towards His Parliament*, 1646.

he always had in happier times, that image was power, events surely proved him to be right. For in 1647, remarkably, those negotiating with Charles, the army no less than parliament, felt the need to appropriate and deploy images of the king on their own papers and remonstrances.[47] Indeed, images of kingship and of Charles I carried an iconic force that not only survived military defeat but outlived his imprisonment and death. As Milton was to discern, the power of Charles's image – engraved no less than painted – drew the affections of the people and ultimately brought about the downfall of the Commonwealth and the restoration of monarchy.

II

As part of the same political class as their Royalist counterparts, most MPs, if they did not share the king's passions for the arts, were certainly aware of the authority of images and visual signs. During the war years, however, parliament did not commission any canvases of itself in session or as a government, nor indeed any pictorial memorials of its battle victories at Marston Moor or Naseby. Old arguments about a puritan distaste for the arts offer little explanation, not least because by no means all Parliamentarians were puritan, and

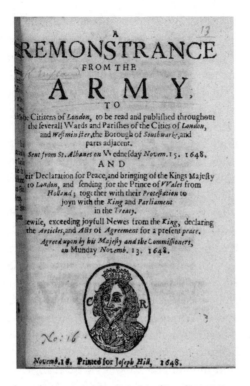

62 *A Remonstrance from the Army to The Citizens of London,* 1648.

anyway the idea of blanket puritan hostility to images is too crude. Parliament, we must recall, was throughout claiming to fight for the monarchy; and, while the demands of government led them to devise ordinances and their own imprimaturs, it was more through appropriating rather than displacing regal forms that they established a cultural authority. Interestingly, when at some point after the war – and perhaps as Maija Jansson suggests (in the absence of firm evidence) after regicide – three Dutch artists approached parliament with a proposal for canvases celebrating their victory, the proposal came to naught.[48] While the reasons remain uncertain, the absence of a tradition of battle paintings in England seems a likely factor: 'still shattered by the recent devastation of war, and with no prior artistic traditions of military themes, England was not ready for images of battle scenes either as memorials or as artworks' – especially when those battle scenes were not those of patriotic triumphs, like the Armada victory, but of the bloody and shameful internecine strife of brother against brother.[49]

If, however, there was no official parliamentary commission during the war, several artists formerly in court employ found patrons in nobles who declared for parliament, such as Pembroke and Northumberland. Sir Peter Lely painted for Northumberland the royal children, while they were under his effective guard in

1647; but he also executed portraits of the earl's family, his daughter Elizabeth, the wife of Arthur Capel, and radical Parliamentarians such as Henry Marten.[50] Interestingly, too, a host of parliamentary leaders and generals commissioned miniatures of themselves and the miniaturist Samuel Cooper became almost a parliamentary rival to Hoskins, painting miniatures of the Speaker of the Commons, William Lenthall, George Fleetwood, the Parliamentarian commander and future regicide, Henry Ireton and Oliver Cromwell.[51] Apparently – and, as we shall see, engravings reinforce the point – there was more than rhetorical disdain to Lovelace's observation that there were several on the parliamentary side eager to find artists to paint 'their own dull counterfeits': to record, as it were, their powerful presence on the public stage.[52]

More infamous than these gestures towards an artistic pantheon of parliamentary figures are the violent acts of destruction of images carried out under the orders or in the name of parliament during the 1640s. Parliamentary ordinances were directed primarily at superstitious religious art; but Charles's close personal identification with some of the objects and paintings that gave offence, and the October 1643 order for the removal of 'scandalous . . . pictures' from the royal chapel at Windsor, made the dividing line between religious and regal far from clear.[53] An attack on the symbols of the Caroline church was, and was intended to be, an attack on Charles I's royal supremacy, even though images of and monuments to kings were themselves exempted from iconoclasm by the ordinance of August 1643.[54] Certainly, in the provinces those who had responsibility for executing the ordinance, if they were anything like the Suffolk puritan William Dowsing, whose journals survive, often displayed more iconoclastic zeal than capacity for subtle discrimination.[55] Moreover, there were plenty of unauthorized actors, especially common soldiers, ready to use the excuse of the parliamentary ordinances for indiscriminate and deliberate destruction of secular and regal images and monuments, as well as 'superstitious' artefacts. *Mercurius Rusticus*, though hardly an unbiased source, reports widespread and deliberate destruction not only of regal images, but of virtually any representations of the Stuarts. At Chelmsford, the pamphlet claims, 'the first thing on which they [the sectaries and soldiers acting in parliament's name] express their rage is the king's picture which with their swords they most traitorously pierce through in divers places'.[56] In Chichester Cathedral, they stabbed out the eyes of a portrait of King Edward VI, while at Winchester they turned on the bronze statues of James I and Charles I cast by Le Sueur.[57] Connecting the earlier assault on royal authority with these acts of iconoclasm, *Rusticus* observes that 'these atheistical rebels, as they would not have so much of the militia to remain with the king . . . [so] they break off the sword from the sides of both the statues, they break the cross from off the globe in the hand of the statue of our gracious sovereign . . . and with their swords hacked and hewed the crown on the head of it'.[58] When, his account continues, 'the heads of this damnable rebellion . . . by their rebellious votes and illegal ordinances daily strike at the substance of that power' of the crown, 'small wonder is it that [they] should offer such scornful indignities to the representation of his royal person and the emblems of his sacred power.'[59] In order to weaken the king, he explained in terms that almost describe our subject, they 'wound him in that representation.'[60] By such acts of symbolic and targeted destruction, the iconoclasts acknowledged and fought against the iconic power that had become vested in images of kings, and in particular, of King Charles Stuart.

But, if the actions of many who preserved religious as well as secular artefacts offer any guide, wanton iconoclasm was far from popular in an England in which increasingly subjects were acquiring and cherishing mementoes of rulers. Whatever was done in the name, or even with the connivance, of individual MPs, parliament never officially condoned such destruction. Indeed, where engravings and woodcuts were concerned, parliament responded to royal images in kind, with a flood of portraits of its leaders, as well as some satirical anti-royal prints. To take some examples, in 1645 one W. Bressie published, to be sold by Peter Stent from his shop at Newgate, an engraving of Thomas Fairfax, Captain General of the parliamentary army.[61] The equestrian portrait of Fairfax in armour and with a long baton, on a rearing horse, echoed earlier royal portraits, perhaps most importantly that of Gustavus Adolphus.[62] Beneath his horse's front legs, a lance, shield and drum signify the warrior, and the plaque bearing his name and title is supported by two cannon. Behind Fairfax, the view of an army and castle may gesture specifically to his victory at York. A depiction of its general's military prowess and triumph, the engraving still describes parliament's army as 'for the defence of the King, Parliament and Kingdom', in accordance with parliament's claims in declarations and ordinances. A similar equestrian portrait of the Earl of Essex was engraved on the centre of a broadside list of 'the many victories obtained (through the blessing of God) by the Parliamentary forces', up to June 1645.[63] Essex, like Fairfax, is presented armoured, on a rearing horse, with his escutcheon and a battle scene in the background, above an inscription 'Robert Earl of Essex, His Excellency, general of ye army raised for the preservation of religion, defence of the king, parliament and kingdom'. Other engravings of Essex depict him with an army and the battles of Edgehill and Newbury in the background, while a further 'Perfect list' of parliamentary victories, published as a broadside in 1646, the year of his death, figures Essex in armour as the first of ten small portraits of English and Scottish generals of the parliament's forces that, along with the earl and Fairfax, include Alexander Lesley, Manchester and Oliver Cromwell.[64] On Essex's death, as well as the magnificent quasi-regal funeral, to which we shall return, various tributes carried engraved frontispieces of the earl as commander. That facing the title page of *The Hearse of the Renowned . . . Robert Earl of Essex*, featured him in armour with a baton gesturing to a little scene inside an oval, the inscription to which describes him

63 *The Most Excellent Sr Thomas Fairfax.* Engraving by W. Bressie, 1645.

as a hero and protector of the realm.[65] The accompanying verse amplified the
Marshall engraving for those

> That seeing first, this Haero's in the face,
> They then might read, but in the second place,
> Englands brave Gen'rall, in its just defence.

During the 1640s, Peter Stent evidently sold numerous engravings of
Parliamentarian heroes, generals and luminaries, such as Viscount Saye and

64 *A Perfect List of All the Victories Obtained . . . by the Parliaments Forces*, 1646.

65 Robert, Earl of Essex. Engraved frontispiece to *The Hearse of the Renowned . . . Robert Earle of Essex* by Richard Vines, 1646.

Sele, Lord Brooke and Algernon Percy, Earl of Northumberland, Sir William Brereton and Edmund Waller.[66] The existence of those portraits, not only in number but in various formats, suggests that parliament, or its supporters, disseminated to a broad public representations of its leaders who had come to the fore during the wars, as part of the vital process of establishing the legitimacy of its war and the authority of its leaders and government.

Illustrations were also used to underpin narratives of the conflict written, as nearly all were, to validate the cause. To take one late case, *A Sight of Ye Transactions of these Latter Years* was published on the eve of the peace negotiations that followed the battles, to explain 'who hath been the cause of all the late and lamentable distractions'.[67] The explanation was, the reader was promised, 'emblemized with ingraven plates, which men may read without spectacles', making it clear that the images were central to the polemics of what was no less than a narrative of civil war from the Prayer Book rebellion in Scotland. Scattered through the text, engravings and woodcuts illustrate the riots in Edinburgh and at Lambeth, the triumphal return of Burton and Prynne, the execution of Strafford and the defence of London.[68] Closing with Loudon's warning to Charles at Newcastle in July 1646 that, if he did not accept parliament's propositions, he would be ruined, the pamphlet with its illustrations rendered parliament the saviour of the nation.[69]

The visual validation of parliament's war and its new authority in 1646 involved, as well as positive images of parliamentary triumphs and heroes, sharply negative representations of the Royalists. Throughout the conflict, woodcuts and engraved illustrations to Roundhead broadsides had lampooned Cavaliers as debauched and *The Sussex Picture* (1644) had carried a title-page image of the king and queen with (at least some said) a Catholic priest.[70] But in 1646 the broadsheet satire, *Englands Miraculous Preservation Emblematically Described* literally drew black-and-white contrasts between those who had protected and those who had endangered the realm.[71] In the image, in an ark which represents the nation, the Houses of Lords and Commons and 'Assembly' (Probably the Westminster Assembly) sit in session. In the choppy sea beneath, we see the heads of Laud, Strafford, Montrose and other Royalists, notably Prince Rupert and – remarkably – Charles and Henrietta Maria, who are thus cast far away from God's saving mercy. Around the scene, oval portraits of Essex and Warwick, Manchester and Lesley, Fairfax and Cromwell, associate the generals of parliament's forces with the godly preservation of the kingdom. Beneath, a verse explicates further: despite the violent efforts of prelates and malignants, the church and Covenant have been secured by a parliament to whom God has given victory as the sign of his blessing. As for the 'cursed crew' that menaced it (the floating Rupert still endeavours to strike at the ark with his sword):

See all their warlike Engines, and their Forces,
Now as feeble as their liveless Corses

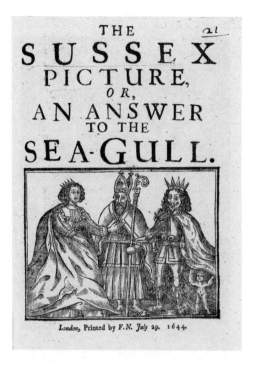

66 *The Sussex Picture, Or, An Answer to the Sea-gull*, 1644.

As for the six 'noble champions', the 'English Admirals of Reformation', the verses foretell that 'Their brave atchievements Chronicles shal speak'. As the poem closes with a prayer that, having escaped perdition, the ark might now be led into 'the key [*sic*] of peace', and that 'our wars may cease', the text makes manifest what the terms of the peace must be – the triumph of both parliament and the gospel.[72] Issued 'for a perpetual MONUMENT to Posterity', *England's Miraculous Preservation*, sold at John Hancock's shop at the entrance to Pope's Head Alley (a district known for prints as well as books), was a powerful visual propaganda statement at a critical political moment.

III

Engravings such as these make starkly clear the fact that in 1646 the competition for public support was a visual as well as verbal contest. It had been so before and throughout the war; once parliament assumed the authority of government, no less than the discourse, it needed to appropriate and fashion signs of authority. The principal sign of regal authority for centuries had been the royal seal. When Charles I departed from London (as famously his son, James, was to do in 1688), he took the seal with him, leaving parliament without the visual signifier that authorized documents, orders and legal grants.

67 *The Sucklington Faction: Or (Sucklings) Roaring Boyes*, 1641.

The Lords and Commons had no alternative but to devise a new one. Accordingly, on 10 November 1643, claiming that the royal seal was being misused by papists, 'to the ruin of the parliament and kingdom', parliament annulled all Acts passed under it since May 1642, and ordered that a new Great Seal made for parliament be used in its place.[73] As was the case with parliament's ordinances, the parliamentary seal aped the forms of the royal seal removed to Oxford and was, as Charles I complained, 'to the similitude and likeness of our Great Seal'.[74] The king responded immediately to the symbolic challenge to his authority with a proclamation reasserting the legality only of his own seal and forbidding any to use 'the said new counterfeit Great Seal'.[75]

The controversy over, and vying for, the legal authority which the Great Seal bestowed was played out in similar disputes over other seals, such as those of the Court of Wards and the County Palatine of Lancaster. In the case of the Wards, it was Charles who found himself with the difficulty, as the seal remained at Westminster and was used, or misused in the king's view, by parliament. On 15 January 1644, therefore, Charles commissioned a new seal for the use of Lord Cottington (Master of the Wards since 1635) and ordered that three feathers and a coronet of the Prince of Wales be added between the royal supporters, 'for the better and notable differencing of the same from the

68 *Englands Miraculous Preservation Emblematically Described,* 1646.

old seal of the court kept and withheld from us'.[76] The seal of the Duchy of Lancaster was seized by Royalist forces from Christopher Banister in 1644, leaving the Palatine with no legal authority to appoint officers or administer justice.[77] Parliament in December ordered a new seal, the use of which they later entrusted to the Speaker of the Commons, along with the authority of any former Chancellor of the Duchy.[78]

In the case of seals, the contest was for ownership of a symbol that authorized action: as Charles complained, the 'new' seals were identical or remarkably similar in appearance to his own royal seals. Where other visual media were concerned, the battle for representation was fought out in overtly different images and forms. Medals and coins, flags and banners had always been important signifiers of, and media for the communication of, values. In the civil wars, in new circumstances, through images and inscriptions they served, like all texts, to shape allegiances and identities, to advertise the virtues of one 'side' and to vilify the other.

Charles I, as we saw earlier, had regularly authorized the issue of medals, to mark the birth of his children, his coronation in Scotland or the launch of his flagship.[79] His ministers, Richard Weston, Earl of Portland, Endymion Porter and Bishop Juxon also had medals and counters struck to commemorate key events; and what we might call 'opposition medals' were struck, often on the continent, such as that celebrating an event embarrassing to the Caroline regime: the destruction of the Spanish fleet by the Dutch off Dover in 1639.[80] Some hint of the way medals could become a site of domestic political contest may be seen in a medal probably commemorating the execution of Strafford, produced in 1641.[81] Shortly thereafter royal medals were certainly issued as part of the propaganda war between king and parliament in the run up to civil war. A bronze medal of Charles in armour, issued in 1642, may pre-date the fighting, but the reverse – though taken from a sixteenth-century medal by Trezzo, with an inscription stating that he was the harbinger of virtue and beauty – seems obviously partisan.[82] In August, Charles issued two copper medals intended for broad distribution as he erected his standard at Nottingham. The legend on the reverse of one, from the sixty-eighth psalm, 'Let God arise and scatter my enemies', reminds us, should we need reminding, of the king's claim to have God on his side; while the other, bearing in English the words 'Honour and victory', was evidently intended to appeal to gentry notions of loyalty and duty, as its reverse ('Fixt on a Rock') announced a constancy that others should emulate.[83]

The early successes in the first stages of conflict were all vaunted in medals issued in silver (perhaps as a reward or memento) and copper (for broader circulation). After the Battle of Edgehill, for example, Thomas Rawlins, who moved to Oxford with the king, struck badges of the king that represented him as both peaceful ruler and military commander, the reverse equestrian figure, beneath an angel with palm and wreath, signifying victory and peace.[84] On 27 July 1643 a medal was struck to celebrate Prince Rupert's taking Bristol with, on the reverse (of an obverse of Charles) a view of the city, intended, perhaps, as a warning to other rebellious towns as well as an advertisement of Royalist strength.[85] A second medal of 1643 indicates how, even enjoying victory, Charles was concerned to temper triumphalism with the (necessary) image of a peacemaker. Issued in various forms, these medalets depicted the king prepared for all outcomes ('paratus in utrumque') – that is, as desirous of peace as of war; as, even in victory a monarch ready to negotiate a peace.[86] Other medals and badges of 1643 now associated the royal family, the essence of Charles's representation in peace, with victories and his cause. A badge, probably issued as a reward for military service, carries on both sides a double portrait of Charles, crowned, with his son, Prince Charles; while a medal issued to commemorate Charles's reunion with Henrietta Maria the very day Sir William Waller was defeated at Roundway Down powerfully associated the royal marriage with a victory also won by virtue.[87] On this medal, inside an inscription 'Iuncti certius pythonem' – united they are more certain of defeating the monster of rebellion – Charles and his queen, crowned and enthroned beneath a sun and moon, appear as Apollo and Diana, with a pierced dragon, the symbol of rebellion, dead at their feet.

69 Badge of Charles I by Thomas Rawlins.

70 Medal with inscription 'Iuncti Certius Pythonem'.

The course of the war, however, gave Charles few more triumphs to celebrate. Perhaps as a consequence, although the king and his nephew and
cavalry commander Prince Rupert, continued to issue numerous military
badges (such as the so-called 'Military Reward' and the 'Forlorn Hope' medal
given to all who had done faithful service), between 1644 and 1648 there are

no other extant civil war medals of the king.[88] During the second civil war, when the old Royalists hoped to rescue and restore the king by means of an uprising in England and a foreign fleet under the command of the prince, the engraver to the University of Oxford cast a medal to promote this last attempt, as the inscription ran, of a king of 'invincible virtue' to 'put to flight the rebels'.[89] With Charles enthroned on one side, the medal's reverse depicts, beneath beneficent rays from heaven, a godly battle to re-establish a king who was Defender of the Faith. After the attempt ended in failure, no more Royalist medals were cast before the many cast to commemorate his death.

Before 1642, medals had been the preserve of the monarch, his family, royal ministers and commanders, and of favoured noblemen who commissioned medals or counters to commemorate an honour bestowed, as Richard Weston, Earl of Portland had, on being invested with the Garter in 1633.[90] From 1642, however, medals were a medium as vital to parliament as to the crown. Medals not only distributed images and words that promoted a cause in various precious and base metals to recipients, elite and common; they were enduring, portable and, in war, vital tokens of allegiance and solidarity as much as military rewards. Parliament lost no time in issuing medals as soon as the king left London. There are three variants of a medal that we can date to May 1642, when the houses called upon Charles to be advised by his parliament. In keeping with the claim, vital to its support, that parliament was at odds not with the king but his evil counsellors, the medal bore on the obverse the portrait of Charles crowned inside an inscription (revealing in its order) 'For religion, the people and the king'.[91] On the reverse are depicted the Lords and Commons in session. Variants carry an English inscription and a ring, suggesting that the medal was worn.[92] In one form, in place of the royal head, a large ship (which may be *The Sovereign of the Seas*) more radically associated parliament with the ship of state – the nation – and so not only appropriated a royal emblem but claimed to represent the nation in place of the king.[93] It would appear, too, that as soon as the fighting broke out, parliament's commander-in-chief, Robert Devereux, Earl of Essex, issued badges that figured him, on the obverse of a medal, with the same reverse of the houses in session with the king on his throne.[94] As with engravings, this representation of the parliamentary commander suggests a need to publicize the leaders of the parliament and to – literally – put a face to the cause. Other Essex badges were issued, with the earl placed beneath a heavenly sword and inside the inscription 'The sword of the Lord and of Gydeon' (Judges 7: 20); and Essex directly appropriated the Royalist equestrian image for a badge distributed as a reward to parliamentary troops that fought at Edgehill.[95] Following Essex's lead, other generals issued badges: Fairfax, commander in the north, Edward Montagu, Earl of Manchester, and Sir William Waller, for example, were depicted, in some cases with legends affirming their championship of religion and law, king and parliament.[96]

Along with military commanders, parliament authorized medals to honour those who were already beginning to be acclaimed as its heroes and champions. A medal of Sir John Hotham, who famously excluded Charles from his garrison at Hull, probably pre-dates Hotham's defection from parliament and beheading in 1645.[97] Like the Royalist medallic memorials of Archbishop Laud, the commemoration of its champions and protagonists, off as well as on the battlefield, was vital to the promotion of the Parliamentarian cause to the people. When Essex died in 1646, along with his magnificent funeral, medals, medalets and badges were struck and distributed to be worn by friends, soldiers and mourners.[98] On some, the figure of Grief sitting beside a column inscribed 'F.E.R.T.' ('Fortitudo eius rem publicam tenuit' – his courage sustained the Commonwealth) presented Essex, and by implication parliament, as the saviour of the nation.[99]

Where Charles I at Oxford could command the service of the Warden of the Mint and the medallist Thomas Rawlins, who executed the best Royalist medals and badges, parliament employed the Huguenot and (later republican) Thomas Simon and sometimes his brother Abraham for executions that needed to rival the king's medals in quality as well as number and effect. In the medallic competition for representation that these figures led, we may discern in a vital visual medium some of the developments now familiar to us from written texts: a parliament that began by appropriating and claiming the image of the king went on, more confidently, to devise its own image and to claim its own authority and that of its leaders to be the best safeguard of the people. It is not easy to gauge how far, beyond rewarding and rallying the faithful, medals, circulated or displayed, won converts or gained supporters. What is certain is the damage either side, and especially parliament, would have suffered had it not projected its case in this medium, which had become an established form of representation. Living in a universe of logos, badges and charity bracelets, we know that, even if we do not always know how, such signifiers forge identities and communities, and advertise ideologies and commitments. No less, the civil war medals, and badges, forged and shaped as well as expressed allegiances and commitments through visual markers that endured long beyond the conflict.

While medals, especially those cast in bronze or copper, were distributed to ordinary soldiers, coins were disseminated still more broadly and, importantly, to many not signed up to one or other party. The survival rate of civil war coins is unusually high – about ten times the average for the seventeenth century; and it has been suggested that many subjects may have hidden their money either when they went off to fight or when they fled from both armies, leaving many coins as relics for the historian.[100] Since over a hundred hoards of coins can be dated, for the civil war we can study Royalist and Parliamentarian coins as rival responses to events and as rival propaganda that reached all. The prerogative of minting coin was the king's, but when Charles left London he also left his Mint and had to take swift steps to establish mints in the provinces. The king summoned his engraver Nicholas Briot to York and arranged for equipment to be sent from the Tower Mint to the northern capital and to Shrewsbury, where campaign mints were designed to pay the armies.[101] A longer campaign than anticipated led in 1643 to the establishment of further mints at Bristol and Exeter.[102] Though much currency in circulation was still that of Tower Mint coins from before 1642, the provincial mints were important in local transactions and for the war effort in the provinces.

Importantly, the new mints, although they had some old dies, quickly issued new coins to promote Charles's cause. The Shrewsbury Mint, for example, produced a coin that stated the king's aims as he had set them out in his declaration of 19 September 1642.[103] With an equestrian portrait on the obverse, silver coins on the reverse bore, dated, the legend 'The Protestant religion, the laws of England, the liberty of parliament' inside the familiar verse from Psalm 68: 'Let God arise, let his enemies be scattered.'[104] We do not have to guess at the impact of this coin, for weeks after its issue the Venetian ambassador reported on it to the Doge as having been issued 'to make it more and more patent to his people that his intentions are directed solely to the preservation of religion and the privileges of the country and remote from those ambitious designs which . . . are put abroad.'[105] As Edward Besly rightly commented, 'the message of the new coins was clearly understood.'[106]

From early 1643, with the establishment of his military headquarters there, Charles moved his principal mint to Oxford, to which the colleges donated plate, with more or less good will, for coining. At Oxford, a former pupil of Briot, Thomas Rawlins was appointed to design coins as well as seals and medals, and became the effective Master of the Mint for the king throughout

71 Silver twenty shillings, Shrewsbury 1642.

the rest of the war, often producing coins of fine quality.[107] While the basic pattern of the coins minted at Shrewsbury was continued, Rawlins's equestrian figure bore a more exact likeness to Charles I and the view of Oxford and its fortifications in the background advertised the Royalist stronghold in the middle of the country.[108] It may have been a similar desire to publicize a second, strategic Royalist stronghold that led to the establishment of a subsidiary mint at Bristol after the capture of England's second city in July 1643, for the coins minted there were marked with BR on the reverse.[109] The equestrian 'Exurgat deus' coins remained the most common but Charles I also authorized civil war coins with, on the obverse, his crowned bust and, on the reverse, the royal arms inside 'Christo auspice regno' that, though found on pre-civil-war coins, now reaffirmed the king as a godly ruler: 'I reign by Christ's favour'.[110]

Along with all the other advantages it gained with the king's decision to leave London, parliament secured control of the Tower Mint, on 10 August 1642. Initially, 'the parliament, anxious to maintain the fiction that it was fighting on behalf of the king, was reluctant to usurp the royal prerogative of coining'.[111] When they began minting, parliament's early coins retained the same appearance and were made from dies of the same design as pre-conflict coins. Not until May 1643 did parliament appoint a new Master of the Mint or issue a new privy mark 'P' – moves that signalled its control of what had been a prerogative intrinsic to royal sovereignty.[112] What is both striking and revealing is that, having taken control of the Tower Mint, parliament ordered no new coins to counter the increasingly polemical messages on royal coins. Thomas Simon's coins for parliament not only continued to be struck in the king's name, like royal money, they represented him on horseback and head and shoulders in profile, with the royal arms and, importantly, the same legend proclaiming his divine right.[113] It may be that to have minted a new design would have exposed parliament to the (still then dangerous) charge of claiming sovereignty; it may be that the privy mark was held to signify parliament's authority over the old regal forms that it appropriated as well as reproduced. But, together with the dominance of the old currency, the presence of the royal image on all coins meant that all subjects were daily reminded of the monarch, of a Charles I who claimed divine right and providential protection, and daily saw images drawn from portraits that had proclaimed regal majesty. Only after the regicide did a rump of the old parliament determine on a new coinage, causing the Master of the Mint appointed in 1647, Sir Robert Harley, to resign.[114] Even in 1648, after his defeat and imprisonment, the king's head on currency was the most widely circulating image of authority. As we shall see, it remained so even during the decade when England had no monarch.

As with other forms of representation we have examined, the novel circumstances of civil war also highlighted and publicized a form of representation endemic to the chivalric culture and humanistic education of the gentry. The emblem or its personalized form, the impresa, combined an image and words that conveyed a moral axiom, a religious commitment or a personal value. As well as being painted on wainscots or etched into furniture, tapestries and coverings, impresas were displayed on shields at tilts and tournaments, and on the banners of corporations and military companies. In 1642, the commissioned officers of both the king's and parliament's armies were evidently given freedom to devise the banners behind which their troops would go into the fight. The designs, with image and motto do, as a historian has recently commented, 'provide important clues to the reasons why men on either side ... took up arms'.[115] But, more interesting than that, they illustrate how both those in high command and more lowly officers chose to represent and justify their cause and how they sought by such means both to sustain the morale of their own men and to garner support more broadly from people as used to reading such signs as we are the corporate logo or advertising billboard. As Ian Gentles claims, without exaggeration, 'in the 1640s, the aristocratic, gentlemanly hobbies of heraldry and emblematics were enlisted in a deadly struggle for the hearts and minds of the English, Scottish and Irish people'.[116]

Though ensigns and colours appear to have been designed by individual officers, they also belonged to, and became the signifier of, the head of the army – whether this was the king, or the Earl of Essex, or parliament. As Edmond Verney, who legendarily refused to surrender his in return for his life at Edgehill, told his enemies, the standard belonged to his sovereign; indeed, it stood for him and the capturing or loss of standards was discussed with as much seriousness as victories and defeats in a war still conducted by the code of honour.[117] Because banners or colours were held synecdochically to stand for the larger cause they pronounced, they met with the same fate as other validating images: they were copied, appropriated, mocked, derided and discredited. Colours and banners became not just symbols, but talismans of the Royalist and Parliamentarian armies and parties in their struggle for victory.

A recent brief essay, one of the few addresses to this neglected subject, makes a number of generalizations about the banners. Both sides, it is argued, drew on well-known emblems, borrowed Latin mottoes in almost equal measure, and quoted Scripture. But, Gentles argues, banners provide 'visual evidence that the Bible loomed much larger in parliamentary than in royalist minds', and the passages of Scripture chosen by Parliamentarians were the more 'militant' texts.[118] Though suggestive, such generalizations may need to be tested by closer study of more Royalist banners, to redress the skewing of the balance more than two to one against them in Gentles's sample. Such cannot be our objective here; but, since there can be no substitute for viewing and reading individual examples, I have sampled about a hundred (fifty on each side) to offer a complementary sketch.[119]

To begin with the Royalists. The king's own standard figured on a banner above a royal lion and the motto 'Dieu et mon droit' (familiar on royal arms) another banner of the crowned royal arms, with the legend above: 'Give Caesar his due'.[120] Such a banner within a banner is unique to the king and may, along with the heraldic beasts on both, have been intended to conjoin his personal and public authority which early parliamentary propaganda was attempting to separate. The hand from heaven that, on the armorial banner, gestures to the crown reminds all that the injunction to give Caesar his due is a divine as well as regal command. On his own banner, Charles delivered a polemical message by displaying what simply was: his regal and divine right. Several banners of senior Royalist commanders reaffirmed feudal loyalties (the Marquis of Winchester, for example) or martial prowess (Montrose). But, interestingly, several re-presented the armorial beasts of the royal arms or the regalia to proclaim, as had Charles, divine kingship. One colour of the Earl of Carnarvon, for example, depicts, beside a bras armé, a large imperial crown (with from beneath hands thrusting to grasp it) and the legend 'Reditte Caesar'.[121] Lord Lucas's banner presents simply the imperial crown beneath 'Dei gratia', while Lord Capel has the crown and sceptre symbolize 'the most perfect form of government'.[122] Negative images and caricatures of the enemy are as evident in my sample as are positive: the Earl of Carnarvon had a banner figuring the five MPs as mad dogs, all named Pym,

72 King's Standard.

attacking the royal lion; Captain Peter Pudsey's colour depicts rebels as a many-headed monster; and several – those of Sir John Berkeley and Sir William Compton, for instance – imply that parliament's opposition had opened a barbarian assault on the social order: an image unquestionably targeted at social conservatives on both sides.[123] Banners from this sample, some not identified, certainly alluded not only to divine right (like that with a crown and laurel and the legend 'Dona dei utraque regi' – Both gifts from God are for the king) and the Scripture injunctions to obedience (one simply has on a scroll 'Romans XIII' in reference to the best-known passage), but also to the king as upholder of the church.[124] On one colour, a mitre and crown are shown beneath the motto 'If we clash, we are ruined'.[125] Correspondingly, those who destroyed the bishops were satirized on a banner displaying a gun firing at a mitre crossed with a crown and sceptre, with the mocking motto 'So great evil can religion lead men to'.[126] Captain Hatton's colour (one of the few here with a motto in English) derides the tyranny of England's new rulers, by reference to Psalm 57: 'In the shadows of thy wings will I make my refuge till these calamities be over past'.[127] Besides these, we find homely images of bees amassing 'Pro rege exacuunt' (they sharpen their stings for the king – with the king bee large in the centre) and of a spinning wheel gathering yarn – claims no doubt of the mounting and popular support for the king's cause and recruitment to his armies.[128]

On the parliamentary side, our sample yields banners that encapsulated parliament's early claim to be for, not against, the king.[129] As well as the Earl of Stamford's banner displaying in English 'For religion, king and country', Captain Neal's and Captain Wither's proclaimed a similar allegiance to the king.[130] In a similar spirit, Lord Grey's colour, featuring an army beside a building (Parliament) beneath a banner inscribed 'Per bellum ad pacem' (Through war to peace) presents parliament as desirous of settlement and the re-establishment of order.[131] But by no means all follow in this vein. On Captain Gold's banner, an armoured soldier with a sword stands, in a daring image, before an enthroned monarch; and, in a nicely subtle rendering of the implied realignment of power, the motto reads 'Ut rex noster sit noster rex' (literally 'As is our king, so be he our king' but with a hint perhaps of a desire that a king who claims to be ours might become indeed our king).[132] Others were even less subtle: the banner of Captain Harvey of the City Trained Bands proclaimed the sovereignty of law as the only security for the nation; while Captain Lifcott's colour, captured at Edgehill, asserted that justice could only be assured by removing evil counsellors from the king's entourage.[133] Such variations in tone, from the moderate to the more radical, give an interesting new perspective on the differences within the parliamentary ranks from the beginning and perhaps some flavour of the very disparate images and messages disseminated in particular regions and communities.

A significant number of the banners in my parliamentary sample proclaim a religious commitment as a motivation to arms. Several depict a bible and sword (symbols used by Queen Elizabeth to signify godly rule), with mottoes,

73 Parliament's banner, 'Per bellum ad pacem', 1642.

such as that of Major Skippon indicating that God orders and aids both praying and fighting for his cause.[134] Parliament's claim to be fighting a holy battle is regularly repeated in their devices and several banners inscribed 'If God be with us who shall be against Us?'; Captain Aylworth's colour represented the victorious parliament's army as fighting with 'the sword of the Lord and Gideon'.[135] Though (as Gentles observes) there are surprisingly few anti-papal images or legends, Parliamentarian banners show the mitre and crosier overthrown by the book, the word of God, as Ludlow's banner presents it; and the various banners proclaiming the battle for 'Reformation' (Captain Copley) or 'Protestantism' (Captain Graves) are obviously meant to claim these for parliament.[136] If it is not clear what room is left for the king's claims to be God's lieutenant on Captain Geste's banner, which asserts his fight 'for God and country', Colonel Ridgeley's, with a mitre overthrown by the sword, appropriated Charles's own favourite psalm 'Exurgat deus' for quite a different proclamation of faith.[137] Colonel Doding's colour, with a ship coming to the rescue beneath an inscription that God appeared in desperate times, at least hinted at divine intervention against not only (what on Captain Noke's banner appear as) unspecified 'evil ones', but even an ungodly ruler.[138]

74 Parliament's banner, 'Ut rex noster sit noster rex', 1642.

There can be no doubt that contemporaries, not least in the act of preserving them, attributed importance to banners and appreciated their value as propaganda. The Royalist *Mercurius Aulicus* felt the need to condemn banners used in Essex's army that 'were set out gloriously with three fair bibles to make poor simple folk believe they fought in defence of the word of God'.[139] *Aulicus's* reference to simple folk documents the reach of emblems from elite into popular culture and so their broad performance as propaganda. Though new in this form in the 1640s, banners circulated in, and were seen and read by, interpretative communities fully cognizant of their symbols. Indeed, it would seem that colours and banners provided the impetus for a work that, despite its apparently elite subject, was popular enough to merit at least four editions over a decade. In 1646, Thomas Blount published a translation of Henri Estienne's treatise under the title, *The Art of Making Devices: Treating of Hieroglyphics, Symbols, Emblems*.[140] In a preface to the nobility and gentry of England, Blount sketched the history of emblems, and especially royal *impresas* in his own country, including that of Charles I, with a motto highly charged in 1646: 'Christo auspice regno'.[141] Having sketched their past use, Blount observed how 'an earnest though much to be lamented war . . . renders them more useful than ever . . . for cornets and ensigns'.[142] And he goes on to give examples of civil war banners from both the Royalist and Parliamentarian armies, before pointing up the deficiencies of several and the need for readers to be educated in the art of their devising. Though what follows is a translation of Estienne, Blount's preface ensures that it will be read as a treatise for the times, and, throughout the text, the translation points up contemporary circumstances: as he writes on page 10: 'We may call a devise the philosophy of Cavaliers.'[143] In Estienne's treatise, chapter IX offers 'Rules of Devises' to which Blount has already directed the reader. As well as insisting on the need to satisfy the eye and the soul, and make the motto 'be concise or brief but not doubtful', Estienne prescribes: 'that it be not so obscure, as to need a Sybill to interpret it; nor yet so plain as the common people may comprehend it'.[144] However, the Paris of Henri Estienne was rather different from the London (or England) of 1646, where a popular involvement in politics and political culture could not be denied. As Blount responded to the desire for further editions of his translation, he added more and more information about English civil war banners to his work. For the 1648 edition, Blount added 'a catalogue of Coronet-devises both on the king's and the parliament's side in the late war'; and this appendix grew in the editions of 1650 and 1655.[145] In this last edition, though lamenting that no record had survived of many, especially Royalist, ensigns devised in provincial towns, Blount announced that he had gathered as many 'as I could with greatest diligence meet with' – over three hundred on parliament's side.[146] As he listed and briefly described them, Blount felt confident in the capacity of his audience to understand the symbolism: he was content simply to describe the banners for the most part without any further explanation; 'the rest needs no interpretation,' he writes of Carnarvon's banner.[147] As media of communication and propaganda that had 'currency within popular culture', banners and colours were, in the symbolic as much as the physical sense, at the centre of civil war conflict and must be returned to it.[148]

CHAPTER 11

RIVAL RITUALS AND PERFORMANCES

I

Perhaps the most conspicuous visual monument of Stuart rule in times of peace had been the Banqueting House at Whitehall, which, commissioned by James as a theatre for the Anglo-Habsburg marriage he sought, became under his son the stage of the masques that enacted Charles I's philosophy of king-ship.[1] The Banqueting House and Stuart majesty were inseparable. In 1642, however, they were separated, when Charles left London; and, though there is little to say of new developments before the palace became the scene of his execution, the absence of the king from Whitehall was seen to be a signifier of bigger changes – in the relationship of architecture to authority, and in the very nature of cultural and regal authority. James Barlow's *A Deep Sigh Breathed through the Lodgings at Whitehall*, a Royalist treatise, deplored, as the title page states, 'the absence of the court' and 'the miseries of the palace'.[2] The identity of the two runs through the tract as Barlow writes (with exclamations of dis-belief) of 'A Palace without a Presence!' 'A Court without a Court!'[3] For it was the king's person that had bestowed 'awful brightness', that had literally animated a building now bereft of ladies, gallants or attendants, in which remained nothing but 'the bare walls and a cold hearth'.[4] In Barlow's eyes, this unpeopling of the court and the removal of tapestries and carpets and the like expressed a major political shift. For now none practised their legal arguments outside the Council chamber: indeed, the Privy Council itself had removed and, in consequence, 'a bare vote of the House of Commons is of validity'.[5] Those who supposedly safeguarded the palace, he protested, crept out with stolen coal and faggots, just as the Parliamentarians robbed the king of his rights.[6] And not only had the masquing rooms gone silent and dark, the symbols of majesty had been contemned: 'You may', Barlow claimed, 'walk into the Presence Chamber with your hat, spurs and sword on' – a serious symbolic affront to the crown – 'and, if you will presume to be so unmannerly, you may sit down in the chair of state and nobody say blacks your eye'; because the reality was that 'nowadays common men do sit in the chair of state'.[7] The symbols and fictions, as well as the buildings and spaces, that had sustained the mysteries of majesty had been laid bare: a man might walk into the masquing theatres and 'view the pullies, the engines . . . or contrivances of every several scene.'[8] Now some even 'imagine the king and queen's favour to be no perpetual inheritance'.[9] Had, Barlow closed, he printed his treatise at York, he might have explicated what he now did not dare: the reasons for the changes he describes.[10] But his intimations are clear. If Whitehall was the monarchy, and vice versa, there was (as Royalist writers claimed of the effect of the royal absence on discourse) an absence of meaning at the centre: a palace indeed without a presence.

Barlow's treatise was, of course, a polemic. The historical reality was that, as the accounts of Edward Carter (who was put in charge of the Works from 1643) indicate, parliament maintained Whitehall and the king's houses, ejecting any held to be papists or delinquents.[11] Parliamentarian nobles, many of them former royal servants, such as Pembroke, Mildmay and Wharton, lodged there; the Council of State met there. In 1643 parliament placed a gun between Holbein Gate and the Banqueting House to protect the approach to Westminster from Royalist attack.[12] In 1645, in a vital symbolic gesture, it pulled down the masquing house which Charles had erected to stage entertainments.[13] Three years later, barracks were built for soldiers garrisoned in Whitehall Palace.[14] These small shifts perhaps indicate a parliament growing in confidence in its own authority and gradually daring to invade royal spaces, as it directly appropriated royal powers. But in the story of the architecture of authority in civil war England, it is less the actions of parliament that transformed these symbols of power in stone, more the absence, the exclusion, of the king from what had been the focus of his court.

Little is yet known – and until very recently virtually nothing was known – about Charles's court at Oxford.[15] Later recollections of the penurious circumstances there are often vivid but should perhaps be read with caution as, at the Restoration, former Royalists often exaggerated the sacrifices they had made for the cause. But that it was poorer, smaller, more cramped and very different cannot be denied; and to accept that is to recognize that the court at Oxford could not represent Charles's kingship as had his magnificent, ordered court at Whitehall. After keeping temporary courts at York and Nottingham during the first months of the war, Charles determined to settle a court at Oxford, not only as an administrative and cultural centre but as a 'symbolic locus' of regality and Royalism.[16] For all the overcrowding, disease and business of a garrison town, a court was established where ambassadors were received and a royal household was reconstituted. As Jerome de Groot has demonstrated, royal dining remained lavish; music and possibly masques provided entertainment; and traditional ceremonies 'were mapped onto the new city'.[17] Charles publicly processed to worship at St Mary's or Christ Church Cathedral and held the Maundy service there in July 1643. Ceremonial walkways were even laid out between the colleges to replicate the palace geographies and processional routes of Whitehall.[18]

But the symbolism, as well as the opulence, was truncated. The newswriter who gibed that there would be fewer masques 'because Inigo Jones cannot conveniently make such heavens and paradise at Oxford as he did at Whitehall' was making a serious point – possibly more serious than he intended.[19] Caroline kingship had been founded on fictions and symbols of power exemplified in masque. The change in the location and nature of the court 'enforced a profound conceptual change in the understanding of form, trope and structure': a change in the representation and performance of monarchy.[20] Charles reconstituted his Presence and Privy Chambers in his college quarters and ordered regulation of access to them and his person; but the arrangements could not be so strictly policed in the new physical circumstances and the realities of wartime administration.[21] Over the period 1642 to 1646, the court became 'no longer the focus of power politics'. In some measure, we will not be surprised to learn, the same was true of the king.[22]

The court, though we might say it was the main theatre, had never been the only stage of the ritual performance of kingship. State occasions and annual progresses had performed a vital role in representing majesty to the people, elite and common. While the circumstances of war curtailed progresses, battles, campaigns and manoeuvres involved Charles frequently leaving his Oxford base and being seen at the head of an army or entourage. Because of the contemporary interest, and at times parliamentary anxiety, they excited, we should not underestimate the significance of the presence and sight of the king amid the conflict. Even in war, Charles I and his supporters milked the propaganda value of royal ritual entries and appearances to advance their cause and to undermine their enemies. It is worth recalling the attention Charles paid to such displays and occasions on the eve of the conflict. The king's entry into York in March 1641 had been followed by entertainment and panegyrics that lauded royal power in the loftiest strains.[23] His return to the capital later the same year had taken on the colours of a triumph, as London at last had the occasion to celebrate its brave Charlemagne and 'His glorious rayes of Maiestie'.[24] Perhaps buoyed by the welcome he received, not least from ordinary citizens, Charles continued to make such spectacular official entries to towns and cities, even as the country drifted to war. In July 1642, for example, the king was received at Lincoln by a crowd that desperately hoped that his reception and visit might yet stave off a civil war. 'How those clouds of our fears lessen,' the loyalist author of *A True Relation* reported, 'and what transcendent expression of justice, protection and mercy he gave to us.'[25] If the king did his part with gracious expressions, the city responded. Though, the author observed, the sudden notice might have excused a thin turnout of spectators, in fact some sixty thousand attended Charles's entry from four miles out, all the way into Lincoln.[26] If the pamphlet were propaganda as much as report, the entry itself was clearly intended to display the popularity of the monarch. The appearance of the trained bands, it was said, made many predict 'the funeral of the new militia', over which king and parliament were quarrelling; and 'doubtless the good example of [the city's] loyalty to his Majesty and affection to the public good will draw on a general concurrence'.[27]

When the hoped for 'concurrence' – or capitulation of parliament – did not materialize, Charles raised his standard at Nottingham on 22 August. As a *Relation*, illustrated by a woodcut, shows, Charles made great preparation for the setting up of the standard that day.[28] The banner was taken out of the castle, and carried into a field by twenty supporters who raised the flag with the motto 'Give God his due', attended by three troops of horse, 500 foot and a company of some two thousand who came to watch. Once it was set up, a herald proclaimed the cause of the king taking up arms (in words Charles personally revised at the last minute) and the multitude responded by throwing their hats in the air and shouting 'God Save the King.'[29] The ritual was repeated over two more days. Though a critical account claimed that 'not yet a hundred persons' joined the king after these occasions, the power of the ritual – of the sight of a feudal king proclaiming war and requiring fealty – was not lost on parliament, which hastily issued a declaration condemning the act and promising protection to those who suffered damage at the Royalists' hands.[30] As events were to show, the ritual and symbolic force of majesty proved more enduring than the military.

Throughout the war, a central plank of Royalist propaganda was the association of the monarch with all national rituals, and especially with popular ceremonies and festivities. As the increasing dominance of the puritans in parliament led to ordinances against festivals and holidays they had long abhorred as pagan and profane, Royalist pamphleteers represented the king as the protector of festivity. The satirical *Arraignment, Conviction and Imprisoning of Christmas* (1646), for example, paralleled the fate of Christmas, who had broken out of confinement, with that of the king and mocked the 'malignant' and 'profane' who force-fed the people with 'wholesome doctrine' instead of Christmas pies.[31] In this pamphlet, for all its advertisement of witty jests, the evocation of earlier happy days and prosperous tradesmen was clearly intended to facilitate a return to the old order – of state, as well as festival. Similarly, John Taylor's *The Complaint of Christmas* anthropomorphized the holiday to make Christmas a spokesman for monarchy. 'Is this England or Turkey that I am in?' Christmas asks, associating the end of festivity and monarchy with tyranny.[32] Those who had banished Christmas had sought, Taylor argued more seriously – and more damagingly – 'to make the people forget that ever they had a saviour', and had similarly injured and sought to marginalize the king.[33] 'Thus,' the tract concluded, 'are the merry lords of misrule suppressed by the mad lords of bad rule at Westminster.'[34] Madness ruled in the place of reason, the parliament instead of the king and, along with Christmas, the church, clergy and all religion were proscribed. Those mercers, grocers, drapers, tailors, cooks and apprentices who told Christmas they despaired 'except I were restored to my ancient right and dignity' clearly advocated another restoration – of Christmas's principal patron and *alter ego*, the king.[35]

If Taylor's imagined petitioners of Christmas hoped 'that he may come again the next year and find better entertainment', the same was true of the Royalists and an increasing number of the war-weary who desired the re-establishing of Charles by parliament and the army.[36] Petitions to parliament from the London apprentices called for the restoration of lawful recreation in language that clearly recalled *The Book of Sports* and hence the royal supremacy.[37] Importantly, the movements of the king from one place of confinement to another also appear to have become the occasion for popular displays of loyalty and affection that probably strengthened – and were certainly represented as reinforcing – Charles's position. When, for example, Charles was delivered by the Scots into the custody of Pembroke and Denbigh at Newcastle, it was reported that 'at the reception of his majesty, all the town were filled with acclamations of joy' and there was 'much triumph throughout all the adjacent parts'.[38] As the king set off for York, the gentry made elaborate preparations to receive him. When he came to Holmby in Northamptonshire, a pamphleteer welcomed the king's happy return and saw many riding to meet their sovereign with 'expressions of extraordinary joy'.[39] Another, announcing the news of the re-establishment of a royal court at Holmby and confirming that thousands had come to greet him with cries of 'God Bless Your Majesty' on the road from Harborough to Holmby, reported how it had touched the king 'who little thought that the joy of his subjects would be so great'.[40] The king had 'entered the house in great triumph' and, the author obviously hoped that he would soon re-enter his capital as undisputed sovereign.[41] In the summer, it was reported that there was 'much resorting to the court both from city, town and country and many desire to kiss the king's hand'; and that Charles once again had 'touched abundance for the king's evil and cured many'.[42] Despite the defeats he had sustained and the difficulties he was in, Charles's sheer presence, his ritual entries, processions and performances were, it seemed, reviving his fortunes. It appeared that what the Royalist poet Cleveland had versed was only partly true:

A Prince most seene, is least; what Scriptures call
The Revelation, is most mysticall.[43]

Certainly in 1647 the revealed Charles was again being fêted as sacred ruler.

II

Whatever its success in establishing an alternative *de facto* government in London, parliament could not compete with Charles I in such symbolic demonstrations of authority. However, the importance of public display and manifestations of support was not lost either on MPs or on adherents to the parliamentary cause. And parliament entered the war with the great advantage of the support of the city of London, which had long experience in staging official entries and processions and of using such occasions to offer advice or to make powerful political statements. From the very earliest days of the conflict, London added to its national support of parliament the validation of civic entertainment as a public manifestation of the legitimacy of the parliamentary cause. The aptly titled pamphlet *London's Love* published a 'true description' of the 'great and generous welcome, given to the houses of Lords and Commons . . . by divers citizens of good quality' at Grocers Hall on 19 January 1642 – just two weeks after Charles's failed attempt to arrest the five members and his departure from the capital.[44] Recounting the splendid feast to which the citizens had invited the Lords and Commons, the pamphlet underlined the point of its lavish hospitality: 'such is the love of the City of London to those worthy heroes of our times'.[45] Emphasizing how the entertainment manifested London's loyalty to the cause, the author closed by urging 'all true subjects to follow their example'.[46]

The war rendered such occasions unsuited to the time, but even amidst the fighting, supporters of parliament naturally celebrated key victories or moments, to boost morale or gain support. On 2 May 1643, for example, a large crowd pulled down Cheapside Cross, which, with its statues of saints, kings and a Madonna, had come to symbolize superstition.[47] On that occasion, the Presbyterian John Vicars claimed the bands of soldiers sounded trumpets and the people gave 'joyful acclamations at the happy downfall of Antichrist in England'.[48] If a 1646 illustration may be trusted, the act of iconoclasm was carefully orchestrated (rather like the toppling of the statues of later twentieth-century dictators) and stage-managed: at the sound of trumpets, 'multitudes of caps were thrown in the air' and statues were burned.[49] A week later (on the 10th) an equally large crowd gathered at the spot where the cross had stood to witness the burning by the public hangman of *The Book of Sports*, long seen as the work of a popish archbishop and king.[50] Other acts of iconoclasm, sanctioned and often reported by parliamentary authority, not only involved what we might call counter-rituals, but also aped and mocked well-known royal ceremonies. At Chelmsford, for instance, soldiers who plundered Sir Richard Mynshall's wine cellar played out a parody of royal dining and 'in a saucy imitation of greatness [would] not drink without a taster'.[51] At Thame, in a fascinating and literal inversion of authorized signs, a troop staged the hanging upside down of a Royalist, taunting him that he and the king would both be brought down together.[52] Though by no means all can be trusted, there are numerous accounts of rampaging soldiers riding in priests' vestments, with organ-pipes borne almost as batons, to signify their triumph over the clerisy.[53] Though many in parliament and many puritans deplored such acts, this parodying of royal ritual forms, no less than the ceremonial endorsement of parliament by the city, reflected a perceived need to strip both the authorities of church and king of the mystical aura with which ritual endowed them.[54] Accordingly, when in 1645 Charles was royally entertained at Huntington, parliamentary propaganda endeavoured to undermine the occasion by observing that local people had been shocked to see the Cavaliers' true natures – 'like devils that come out of hell'.[55]

At the centre of royal ritual, and perhaps any successful ritual, lies a single person. And, just as in engravings, woodcuts and medals, it had elevated its successive leaders, especially the Earl of Essex, so parliament made Essex the focus of state rituals that mirrored, and were even meant to outface, those of Charles Stuart.[56] The ritualistic as well as discursive endorsement of Essex began early, when a 1642 pamphlet, illustrated with his image, narrated the earl's triumphant passage through the city, attended by all the trained bands and 'an infinite number of people'.[57] During the 1640s, as well as news of his victories, parliament authorized panegyrics on the earl, representing him as a charismatic figure who drew men after him.[58] But it was Essex's death that provided parliament with the occasion for a full state ritual that evoked royal rites yet eclipsed anything Charles I was able to do in 1646. Parliament seized the opportunity for a full display of its authority as well as a commemoration of its military leader. Those who planned Essex's funeral ordered that the earl's body with the effigy be drawn in an open chariot, with a full procession of mourners led by the two houses, the prolocutor of the Assembly of Divines, the Lord Mayor and city companies.[59] As John Adamson has demonstrated, modelled on royal funerals and in particular on that of Prince Henry, the spectacle or rituals of Essex's funeral, with the earl's helm, crest and armour carried beside the hearse, 'explicitly linked the now victorious parliamentarian cause with the chivalric past', and, in so doing, represented and legitimized the Parliamentarian cause as 'the proper continuation of this godly, martial, chivalric tradition'.[60] As it was about to enter negotiations with the monarch, parliament orchestrated a state ritual that vied with any that Stuart rulers had staged. Though forces with less sympathy for such trappings were soon to appear on the public stage, members of parliament knew that the power of ritual and ceremony could not be surrendered to the Royalists without yielding to them authority itself.

III

The protection of the church and true religion had been a first duty of medieval kingship, but after Henry VIII's assumption of the Supreme Headship, authority and hierarchy in state and church had become, inseparable: as James I put it neatly, 'No bishop, no king'. The assault on Charles I's authority had come first, both in Scotland and England, from an attack on his exercise of the supremacy, on the episcopacy and on the king's own orthodoxy. As scholars have long recognized, the contest between king and parliament, between Royalists and Roundheads, was – in large part – a war over religion.[61]

That conflict is not our subject; what concern us here are the strategies adopted by king and parliament to represent themselves as custodians of the true church and faith and to undermine each other's claims to ecclesiastical orthodoxy and authority.

Despite the difficulties he had faced in the 1620s and 1630s, as he embarked on civil war Charles made much of his claim to be the Defender of the Faith of the Church of England and castigated his opponents as schismatics bent on undermining it. Though the first round in the war of religious propaganda had been won by his opponents who charged him with being popishly affected, Charles quickly enjoyed the support of popular polemicists ready to defend the church and crown. While the king himself publicized his godliness in proclamations of fasts and prayers, pamphleteers upheld the hierarchy of the church, the author of *A Rational Discourse* (1643) arguing that 'who saith that bishops are not lawful is a wretch'.[62] Invoking James I, Royalist writers identified the opposition to the monarchy with that to the church and, in that spirit, *A Plain Narration of the Beginnings and Causes of this War* traced the auguries of civil war in the rise of a sect of 'disciplinarians' who attacked the church before they turned against the crown.[63] Many sought to rally support for Charles by appeals to defend the church and in the 1640s and 1650s, as recent scholarship has shown, popular affection for the Anglican faith and rituals made this by no means a foolish tactic.[64]

But perhaps the most effective Royalist polemic on behalf of the church and its Supreme Head took the form of funny and bitter characterizations of the puritans (and by implication the Parliamentarians). During the 1640s, the figure of the stage puritan was used by Royalist pamphleteers to caricature their opponents as rebels and hypocrites, as vulgar and debauched. As in other cases, John Taylor, early on in 1642, set the tone of this attack, lampooning the weird preachings of uneducated tinkers and regaling readers with titillating stories of puritan widows impregnated by the lusty brethren in a gravel pit.[65] Though it invoked the loftier arguments of James I's *Basilikon Doron* against the Presbyterians, the pamphlet *A Puritan Set Forth* soon moved to a similar abuse of puritan hypocrisy, to pornographic tales of 'the debauched sisters', and to sexual puns about their following all who 'stand stiff' for the faith.[66] As we have remarked, though funny, these satires of sexual debauchery involved an attack on social inversion and disorder, and countless pamphlets represented puritan preachers as tub preachers, ignorant commoners, and their churches as ones in which 'almost every mechanic calls for what religion he lists'.[67] Worse, according to *The Countries Complaint of the Barbarous Outrages Committed by the Sectaries*, Brownists and other sectaries beat, tortured and murdered orthodox ministers, pissed on prayer books, and called for nobles to be made servants and for the overthrow of all social hierarchy.[68] The rise of the Independents gave further fuel to this satirical invective. As Presbyterians and Independents quarrelled and the latter's leaders in the parliament and army pushed for toleration and the disestablishment of a state church, supporters of Charles proffered the king as the only hope not just for the Church of England, but for any religious order.[69] In the negotiations of 1647, the Royalist argument for the re-establishment of Charles in his rights and powers was very much an argument for a settlement of religion. As the author of *The Balance Put into the Hand of Every Rational English Man* argued, without the Supreme Head to protect the church, there was no preventing 'the wild boars of the forest rooting up the established religion'.[70] Though he never descended to this kind of popular invective, Charles to the last identified the royal cause with that of the church, and ultimately, to safeguard their relationship, went to his death.

In contesting the king's claim to be the determinant and protector of faith and worship, parliament had the advantage of a long tradition of puritan questioning of the royal supremacy, as well as the experience of the recent assault on royal ecclesiastical authority by the Scots. In 1641, a majority in the Commons had supported the popular call in London for the removal of the bishops and had succeeded in presenting itself as the defender of Protestantism from corrupt popish counsellors and Irish Catholics. However, the question of the royal supremacy, not least because it had been (in sixteenth-century England) the instrument of the removal of papal jurisdiction and of Protestant reform, remained an issue: the removal of the bishops had been divisive; a necessary military alliance with the Scots had involved an adherence to Presbyterianism which was unpopular in many quarters; and the leaders of parliament were themselves sensitive to the dangers presented by the behaviour of the more extreme sectarians. We might helpfully see the establishment of the Westminster Assembly of Divines on 1 July 1643 not only as a body to revise worship but as one that, rather like church councils in the Middle Ages, was intended to be an alternative authority to the royal supremacy.[71] The members swore to preserve the rights of parliament, were subordinate to it, and served the interests of the predominant Presbyterian faction within it, cementing the reform of worship to a governing political party.[72] As with the Royalists, however, vital to parliament's self-representation as Defender of the Faith was negative as well as positive campaigning. As well as continuing the relentless depiction of Royalists as papists, parliamentary propaganda turned against their opponents the charge that they were fractured into myriad sects and factions, including, according to the *Cavaliers Bible*, thirty-six religions maintained only by them.[73] Having catalogued such exotic Cavalier beliefs as that of Minanders, Ebonites and Marcions (who believed in two gods), the author rhetorically asked readers: 'why then should we (who lay claim to the true Protestant religion) . . . submit to what discipline they will give us?'[74] In fact, during the 1640s, parliament revived older (anti-Catholic) arguments that it was the church hierarchy that had usurped the ecclesiastical authority of the monarch and that the 'old English puritan' had, by contrast, revered authority.[75]

Parliament's attempts at maintaining, and in representing themselves as, an authority over the church were undermined as much from within their own ranks as by the Royalists. Well before the rise of the Independents in the Commons or the army, there had been calls for toleration which, implicitly or explicitly, questioned the legitimacy of any authority over the domains of worship and conscience. Indeed, in 1643, Henry Robinson, advocating liberty of conscience as 'the sole means to obtain peace and truth', doubted whether law or authority would be good enough reasons to follow any faith.[76] Though he defended obedience to civil powers, the author asked: 'wherefore such labouring in vain . . . to obtain a . . . false lustre of a national church?'; and, by way of answer, advocated the freedom 'for every particular man to understand his own estate betwixt God and himself and [to] manage his own business'.[77] In 1643, Robinson, a merchant and law reformer, was in the minority; but by 1646 toleration was effectively secured and was soon guaranteed by the rising power of the army. Despite the support it attracted to its programme of religious reformation, parliament mounted only a short-lived challenge to the monarchy as the authority over a national church. Not least because of that failure, those who increasingly believed that a national church was the only guarantee of law and order had no recourse but to the monarchy. It was, as we know, the Presbyterians as much as old Royalists who championed the restoration of a king and national church – although it turned out to be quite other than the church they had hoped for.[78]

We have seen how the exercise of justice was a duty of a king and the reputation for justice a vital quality in any monarch deemed to be a good prince. Justice expressed the bonds that tied all to the commonwealth and the king; and ideally the performance of justice reaffirmed the ties between sovereign and subjects, and manifested the unity of the commonweal. Such ideas were often more contested in practice and, as we saw, on occasions such as the trial and mutilation of Prynne, Burton and Bastwick the performance of justice could undermine the image and authority of the king.[79] The ideal of Justice, however, survived and was one that every ruler sought to represent himself as upholding. Not surprisingly, therefore, from the eve of civil war to regicide, claims to embody justice were made by both the king and parliament, as they contended for support. The trial and execution of Thomas Wentworth, Earl of Strafford, in the spring of 1641, partly because it was perceived by many to be a sham in which legal proof of treason was not shown, did not (as much as had been hoped) advance parliament's image as the protector of justice.[80]

During the early 1640s, parliament – to publicize both its authority and its Protestant purity – tried and executed a number of Jesuit priests. Though he 'died very obstinately', Father Bell was presented by the sheriff as representative of those evil priests who had perpetrated the atrocities of the Irish rebellion.[81] The Commons also ordered the publication of the scaffold confessions of Nathaniel Tompkins and Richard Challenor, who were charged with plotting against parliament.[82] 'By special command', an account was also published of the trial by the Council of War and the execution at Smithfield in October 1644 of Francis Pitt, who had planned to betray the garrison at Rushal Hall in Staffordshire to the Royalists – not least because Pitt helpfully made due confession, expressed penitence and blessed parliament and its just cause as he went to his death.[83] The next year, the execution of Strafford's closest ally in Charles I's counsels, Archbishop William Laud (who had also conducted a vigorous defence against the charges), became the occasion of bitter contention over both justice and the legitimacy of Charles's personal rule and parliament's *de facto* government.

Laud made full use of the theatre of the scaffold to defend his own and the king's actions and to denounce the injustice of a parliament which had manufactured false charges of treason against him.[84] Taking as his text Hebrews 12:1–2, Laud compared himself implicitly to a Christ who had been found guilty not by due process but by false witness and injustice and explicitly to St Paul and St Stephen who had been sent to violent deaths not by justice but by 'a persecuting sword'.[85] Having cleared himself of any crime 'now deserving death by any known law of this kingdom' and thus, despite his formal obeisance to the judges, charged his accusers as unjust, Laud went on to proclaim himself and the king as free of popery and as champions of the true religion of the Church of England.[86] Skilfully using the prospect of his imminent death to support his claim that he spoke the truth of his conscience, Laud totally subverted the ritual of execution as one of penitential remorse which acknowledged the right and justice of those in authority.[87] Moreover, the damage Laud did spread wide. As even an unsympathetic commentator noted, Laud's sermon (the frequent reference to his scaffold speech as a sermon itself testifies to his appropriation of authority) quickly travelled abroad, and was translated into French and Dutch.[88] As an indication of its force, parliamentary propagandists moved swiftly to counter Laud's last words. In *A Brief Exposition ... upon the Lord of Canterbury's Sermon*, William Starbuck, accepting that many felt that Laud had died 'like to a martyr', denounced Laud's defence and tried to assure readers that parliament had done no wrong.[89] 'Citizens', he addressed them, 'clear yourselves'; though Laud had represented himself as innocent and his accusers as guilty, they should admire a just parliament that, unlike the archbishop, slit no noses (a reference to Prynne) but followed due judicial courses and punishments.[90] Another defence of parliament, again acknowledging that many had been 'insnared' by Laud's protestations of sincerity and innocence, appealed to the reader not to trust the dragon who concealed himself in the clothes of the lamb, though the author admitted, 'his prayer at the foot of his sermon takes with a world of people, as his sermon did'.[91] So concerned was Laud's old adversary, Henry Burton, that he published (with authority) a line-by-line rebuttal of Laud's scaffold discourse in an attempt to turn back against him the accusation of injustice.[92] 'All things',

Burton insisted, 'were clearly and fully proved in court against him'; indeed, Laud himself had imprisoned, whipped and fined men 'against all justice'.[93] In 1645, Laud became the focus of a battle for justice that parliament's supporters, no less than the king's, knew it dare not lose.

The contest to be perceived as the focus and custodian of justice reached its apogee after the war itself, in the trial of King Charles I. As several MPs, uneasy about the proceedings, discerned, the stakes could hardly be higher: if the king could be brought to trial, the parliament could indeed claim control and represent justice. But traditionally justice was the king's and to try a king for treason, when treason laws were concerned with actions or plots against the king, was, to say the least, novel and problematic.[94] As we know, it took a purge of the Commons and the intervention of the military to bring Charles to trial. And, even of those MPs who remained, many probably hoped that rather than leading to the king's conviction, let alone execution, the judicial proceedings would put pressure on Charles to agree to a settlement.[95] The radicals, however, in army and parliament, were not only determined on the trial and death of the king, they intended that, for the first time, the proceedings against a monarch should be public, to demonstrate the legitimacy of their claims and to represent themselves as the champions of justice and of the people.

A public trial, especially in the novel circumstances and with the Lords refusing any part in it, required the full rituals of justice, and the records reveal careful attention to protocol and advertisements of propriety. Having passed an ordinance for the trial on 6 January, the Commons appointed the presiding Sergeant at Law, John Bradshaw, as Lord President of the court and assigned him the honours due to the title, including the same number of dishes at his meals as the king, and a household in the dean's house at Westminster Abbey.[96] After considering other venues – St James's Palace, the Guildhall and Windsor – the Commons chose the great Hall at Westminster 'because it is a place of public resort . . . the place of the public courts of justice for the kingdom'.[97] As Sean Kelsey has shown, the commissioners for the trial carefully prepared a stage for what they saw as the demonstration of the supremacy of the Commons: they dismantled the public courts at the south end of Westminster Hall; they ordered the removal of tradesmen's stalls; and they set up a stage and richly upholstered crimson and gold chairs for the judges and Lord President, and built extra galleries around the walls for spectators.[98] Here justice was clearly meant to be seen – as well as done. Having authorized the payment of £1,000 'for defraying some incident charges concerning the trial of the king', the Commons ordered the committee to 'consider what habits the officers of the court shall have', taking the advice of the heralds, and appointed that a sword and 'mace or maces' be carried before the Lord President as he entered and left the court.[99] Once again, through aping and appropriating regal ritual forms, the Commons sought to secure the authority which went with them and that they symbolized. Though it contains some errors, a later engraving of the trial captures a President who is virtually enthroned on a raised dais, while separated from him by a table on which, in front of the clerks, lie a sword and mace, the king sits in a plain chair looking up to Bradshaw's and the Commons' authority.[100] Behind the President, the royal arms that vividly hung in Westminster Hall were replaced by the cross of St George – another appropriation of a symbol important to Charles and perhaps a proclamation of the 'supremacy of the national interest over the regal'.[101]

Despite the elaborate attention to ceremony, the symbols themselves – especially the mace with the royal arms – revealed the difficulties at the core of the proceedings.[102] From the first day of the hearings, far from being a showcase for parliamentary justice and supremacy, the trial was taken over by the king, who made Westminster Hall his (penultimate) platform for a remarkable performance of majesty. Quite simply, Charles subverted the very premise of the trial and the jurisdiction of the court. When, at the close of the reading of the charge on 20 January, the clerk impeached him as 'tyrant [and] traitor', the king 'laughed as he sat in the face of the court' – and so destabilized all the formalities of the first day.[103] Being required to give answer, Charles asked 'I would know by what authority' he was brought to trial and, pausing for effect, added, 'I mean lawful – there are many unlawful authorities in the world – thieves and robbers by the highways'.[104] Where the, apparently casual, reference to thieves both delegitimized the proceedings and played on the growing fears of social conservatives about the army, Charles simply reasserted his own authority as not only legal but sacred. 'Remember,' he insisted, 'I am your King – your lawful King – and what sins you bring upon your heads and the judgement of God upon this land . . . I have a trust committed to me by God, by old and lawful descent. I will not betray it to answer to a new unlawful authority.'[105] For the commissioners, the king's refusal even to enter a defence that would enable them to proceed to full prosecution was the worst-case scenario. Still worse, when Bradshaw invoked the people as the authority, Charles retorted that, in rejecting the authority of the court, 'I do stand more for the liberty of my people than any here that come to be my pretended judges'. For there, he observed, were no Lords and no parliament, in which anyway the king himself 'should have been', and so no authority to try him 'warranted by the word of God – the Scriptures – or warranted by the constitutions of the kingdom'.[106]

Bradshaw warned the king of the dangers of not responding but was forced to adjourn the court to take advice. Perhaps encouraged by Charles's stand, Lady Fairfax interrupted the reading of the names of commissioners to insist that her husband, a leading parliamentary general, would not sit amongst them.[107] Meanwhile, over the weekend of 20–21 January, a 'great concourse of people' went from London to Westminster hoping to see their king; and on Monday the 22nd commissioners from Scotland denounced the proceedings.[108] At a private meeting in the Painted Chamber that day, the commissioners debated their difficulty and the king's plan, in denying the authority of the court, 'to wound . . . the supreme authority of the . . . Commons assembled in Parliament'.[109] When the court reconvened, therefore, the Solicitor asked that the Lord President direct the king to give answer. Appropriating the typologies of the trials of Christ and the martyrs (he read Foxe in confinement), and repeating his protestation against the legality of the court, Charles reasserted his stand for God and 'the freedom and liberty of the people of England'.[110] Though he was prevented from delivering a written objection to the jurisdiction of the Commons, the damage was done.[111]

On Tuesday the 23rd, the king was brought back for a third time and ordered not 'to dispute the jurisdiction of the supreme and highest authority of England' but to answer the charge.[112] In response, while he seemed to flatter the President ('You spoke very well the first day. . . .'), Charles was determined and dismissive: 'for the charge', he replied, 'I value it not a rush'.[113] 'It is the liberty of the people of England that I stand for. For me to acknowledge a new court that I have never heard of before . . . I do not know how to do it.' Since it was out of the question to subject him to the torture by pressing that was used on prisoners who refused to plead, Charles had 'caught his adversaries flat footed'.[114] It may be that, as well as Fairfax and Vane, other commissioners were beginning to have serious reservations about the proceedings, for it was ordered that none depart from the court without special leave. On the 24th, having determined (arbitrarily) that standing mute amounted to 'tacit confession of the charge', the court resolved to hear witnesses 'for the further and clearer satisfaction of their own judgements and consciences'.[115] The phrase is revealing: the king's actions had not only thrown his accusers on the defensive; they had led some to question themselves. It may therefore be significant that only forty-seven commissioners were present when the court took depositions in private session, a number reduced by a third the next day. Though the number grew to forty-six by the time the hearings were complete, and the court passed votes condemning and sentencing the king, still they may have hoped beyond hope for a last-minute release from the impasse, for they ordered that the votes 'should not be binding finally to conclude the court'.[116] On the 27th, at a preliminary meeting in the Painted Chamber, the commissioners present briefed Bradshaw on what to do 'in case the king shall still persist in excepting against the court's jurisdiction'.[117]

At the full court in Westminster Hall, trouble was evidently expected for the Captain of the Guard was instructed to arrest any who raised a disturbance.[118] Charles again asked to be heard before the Lords and Commons but the court refused and, nervously reiterating several times its (alleged) authority, it proceeded to a judgment it announced as its 'unanimous resolution'.[119] When the charge was read 'in the behalf of the people of England', according to one account Lady Fairfax interrupted, protesting that not half the people supported it.[120] On this last occasion, however, Charles declined a defence. Rather, in an explicit imitation of Christ, he offered himself for his people and country, bowing to the 'power', but still denying the 'authority', of his judges.[121] As he moved to sentence, Bradshaw summoned Scripture (Proverbs 17:15) to justify the court, the charge and the judgment, and most of all the parliament in whose name it had met.[122] In a long indictment that, in its sweep over the classical past, English and Scottish history and Charles's reign recalled the tactics of the Grand Remonstrance, Bradshaw argued the accountability of kings to parliament and people – to which Charles simply retorted: 'Ha!'[123] From the first day to the last a week later, what parliament had devised as a show trial before a large public to validate its authority had turned into an unanswerable challenge to the legitimacy of the court and the Commons. Sean Kelsey, underlining the king's powerful performance, notes how 'he faced down his accusers, whose callow pragmatism crumbled before the imperturbable moral certitude of a man with principles'.[124] But Charles's victory was greater than that. What he did was no less than reverse the onus of guilt, so that it was the court, rather than he, that appeared on trial and on the defensive. In investing his own case with 'moral and theological power', he 'deepened the political legitimacy of the Royalist cause'.[125] Moreover, in his quiet manner and delivery, as well as in what he said, Charles prepared himself for the role that death secured: that of a martyr for the laws and liberties of the people, a Christ who would rise again.

If the trial itself wrong-footed parliament before an audience of the people, the reporting proved an even greater public relations disaster. As Jason Peacey has shown, the High Court appointed two journalists – Henry Walker and Gilbert Mabbott – to write up official reports of the proceedings. Their differing accounts described the different sympathies and positions behind the claim of 'unanimity', and Royalists who had not been present made use of this information; even the undoctored official accounts backfired, winning more sympathy for Charles than his enemies.[126] Not only was the trial itself proving counter-productive in the battle for support, 'the decision to report the revolution had been a mistake'.[127] The Commonwealth began its life not with a reputation for justice but – probably among a majority – a reputation for murder. By his clear reiteration of simple sentences, Charles had ensured that the trial had delivered a message the reverse of that intended. Far from being the passive subject of others' words and actions, he had dominated the proceedings. Even from his plain defendant's chair he had denied – robbed – the Lord President and parliament of their painted grandeur and the cultural 'authority' they desperately needed. During those days in January he had led many to, as he asked, 'remember, I am your king' and that to oppose a lawful king was to sin.[128] In the paper of objections to the court that he was forbidden to read Charles had, in rehearsing his divine warrant, quoted the Book of Ecclesiastes: 'where the word of a king is, there is power'.[129] Power sent the king to his death; but his words at his trial, on the scaffold, and in print on the day of his execution, were indeed to wield a force – a force that destroyed the republic as it was born and represented monarchy as the only polity for England.

PART IV

REPRESENTING REPUBLIC

PROLOGUE: REPRESENTING REPUBLIC

Though parliament had closed the theatres in 1642 there can be no doubt that the army leaders and radical Rumpers staged the trial and execution of Charles I as a dramatic public spectacle, the first act that presented as well as represented the new Commonwealth born on 30 January 1649. The regicides boasted that, where earlier English kings had been deposed or assassinated by underhand means, Charles Stuart was arraigned, convicted, sentenced and executed in the public eye. Moreover, the sites of the trial and execution were both regal sites. Hitherto, Westminster Hall had been the locus of royal justice, while the Banqueting House, outside which the scaffold for Charles's execution was erected, had been the proud symbol of Stuart dynasty as well as the theatre for the representation of that dynasty in masques and rituals. The trial and execution of the king, we might say, were multi-media events which through words, engraved images and carefully orchestrated performances were intended to end and erase monarchical representations and to publicize and display a new republican regime and polity.

Such a revolution, as opposed to a coup, depended upon depriving the monarchy of the forms and media of representation that had endowed kingship with authority; and, as important, on appropriating or reconstituting the texts, images and performances that bequeathed authority to a new Commonwealth. I have argued elsewhere that the leaders of the Commonwealth failed to cement the revolution, failed to establish a republic, because they paid too little address to the need to erase the representations of regality and to construct a republican literary and aesthetic culture.[1] Since then, scholars have rightly and helpfully drawn attention to efforts made by advocates and leaders of the Commonwealth government to invent a republican culture by new modes of writing, new symbols and reconstituted ceremonial forms.[2] The subject of this chapter, therefore, is a review of the representations of the Commonwealth government and a re-evaluation of the success of the new regime in securing validation and authority, in the eyes of the political nation and the people.

While acknowledging a recognition, at least among some protagonists of republic, of the need not only to argue the Commonwealth cause but to constitute a republican culture, I shall yet maintain that the republican project was so short lived principally because the regime failed to secure its own cultural authority or even significantly to undermine the culture of kingship: the authority of royal words, images and performances. It is fair to observe (as some have) that the situation the regicides faced was entirely novel and presented a nigh impossible challenge. England had had a thousand years of history as a monarchy; and despite a parallel history of baronial revolts, even talk in the late sixteenth century of justified resistance or (as modern scholars insist) of a 'monarchical republic', critics of kingship had been more concerned with limited monarchy than republic.[3] In contemporary Europe, the models of republic, Venice and the Netherlands, were mixed polities with powerful single heads in the Doge and the Stadtholder who, whatever the limitations on their autonomous actions, represented those states to citizens at home as well as polities abroad. As we shall see, models for republic were found in ancient history and Scripture; but, while the interpretation of them was disputed, those same texts had been read and glossed, not least by monarchs themselves, as powerful arguments for kingship, even for divine right absolutism. For a different, or opposed interpretation to become dominant required a cultural shift – one that Milton brilliantly intuited – that in turn depended upon fundamental changes in education as well as in the cultural imagination, in habits of reading and perception.[4]

If, however, the challenge of establishing a republic was formidable, it would be wrong to assume that such a revolution was impossible. Though by the mid-seventeenth century it almost seemed like a natural development, Henry VIII's break from Rome and establishment of a national church and Caesaro-papist monarchy had in the 1530s presented, perhaps, as great a challenge; and more recently the opponents of Charles I had undermined his authority, raised armies and a significant proportion of his subjects against him, and secured his trial and execution. We cannot draw exact parallels between the 1530s and 1640s, but what is striking is the lengths Henry VIII went to – not only to justify his revolutionary changes, but to represent them and his new position as truly historic, as national destiny as well as divine direction. Though he faced formidable and dangerous opposition to his reformation, Henry orchestrated a programme that enabled him to survive it and to secure the changes he sought. On the other side, especially during the later 1630s, the opponents of the Caroline regime in Scotland and England had undermined the king far more by relentless propaganda than by force; and by these means at least hampered the king's chances of bringing them to obedience by force. The very different fate of the monarchy in those two moments of crisis rested, of course, on myriad different circumstances. But if Henry VIII retained, and even enhanced, royal authority in the crisis of reformation where Charles I lost his by 1640, a vital part of the answer lay in the representation and perception of the rulers.

As I have suggested, as if acknowledging such a failing, Charles I after 1640 refashioned his representation, abandoning silence for argument, recruiting (as Henry VIII had) penmen and enacting spectacular civic entries into his metropolitan and northern capitals, as well as other towns.[5] Even before the outbreak of civil war, he began to replace the image of the *rex pacificus* with that of the warrior prince; while during the conflict and especially after military defeat, he retained the pose of a willing peacemaker ever ready to restore calm and order to his people. During the negotiations which followed the battles, the fiercest opponents of the king were frustrated to find that, though they had won the war, Charles looked likely to secure enough support to win the peace, and to re-establish his authority with disquietingly few concessions to the victors. Where they had failed in 1641, from 1646, the king and his supporters began to have the better of the argument – and not only because his opponents were divided, but because, after the war, most had no clear course or proposition to publicize. Those few radicals who had begun to ponder a revolutionary alternative either despaired of making or, for some other reason, did not make their case. It was ultimately military force and a purge, more than any parliamentary political process, that led to the trial of the king.[6] In consequence, even in a legal court which was meant to be the stage for the representation of a new regime, Charles I was able to discredit the whole process and those who instituted it. In the words he uttered and those, including some not spoken, that were published, by his sober dress, regal demeanour and composure, by his brilliant deployment of theatrical timing and gestures in the courtroom, Charles regained the authority of a king and made his judges appear illegitimate. Where, during the 1630s, he had allowed a public trial (of Prynne, Burton and Bastwick) to be hijacked by the accused to damage his authority, in 1648 he publicly claimed and took the authority from the about-to-be-born republic. As Jason Peacey has argued, the official accounts of the trial did not merely fail as republican propaganda; they provided, unrevised, the material of Royalist propaganda.[7]

The theatre of the scaffold, rather than a scene of atonement and retribution, was similarly appropriated by the king as a stage for his own final representation as martyr of the people. Charles, wishing to be 'as trim today as may be', took care over his dress, his dark clothes illuminating his George and Garter Star that had become emblems of his kingship as well as symbols of his faith.[8] While the king was calmly preparing himself, his enemies were agitated by their failure to find an executioner, as well as by rumours that there might be an attempt to free the prisoner.[9] By 1.30 p.m., when Colonel Hacker led Charles through Whitehall to the scaffold, a substantial crowd had gathered – a public audience either for the new Commonwealth or for a final royal performance contesting it. Though the common people were kept at a distance beyond barrier fences, Charles – remarking that he could be 'very little heard' – addressed them. In his written speech, the king protested his innocence and blamed others – 'ill instruments' rather than parliament – for instigating civil war, before taking on a Christic tone of forgiveness to them all.[10] Having disarmed his auditors with words of charity, Charles proceeded to devastating polemic. The people, he implied, were not now free but the subjects of a conquest. Only a king guaranteed their laws and liberties and, in dying rather than surrendering to the arbitrary way of the sword, he claimed, 'I am the martyr of the people'. And, he warned prophetically, 'God will never prosper you until you give God his due, the king his due, that is my successors, and the people their due'.[11] Disdaining the stays that had been constructed to restrain him, Charles then lay down, instructing the executioner to await his sign before wielding the axe. By acting, even now, as the orchestrator of proceedings, by again connecting his own case and language with God's, and his right with the rights of his people, Charles made the occasion not that of the public dispatch of a traitor but that of the creation of an English martyr.

We must allow for Royalist embellishments and bias, but the reported reaction fully manifested the effect on the crowd. Even the soldiers on the scaffold joined others in dipping handkerchiefs in the king's blood or in taking locks of his hair as sacred relics of majesty. The feared disturbance did not occur; but among the crowd spectators groaned, fainted and, it was said, pregnant women miscarried.[12] Two troops of horse were swiftly delegated to disperse an angry people. By his performance Charles had brought about what he had claimed: the people were subjected to force; and it was the king rather than his enemies who was perceived as the guarantor of liberty and law. In Thomas Herbert's account, meeting with Fairfax (who had opposed regicide), the General asked 'how the King did'.[13] Herbert was puzzled at Fairfax's ignorance of Charles's death, but looked at from another perspective the question seems anything but puzzling. For this his last stage, Charles had carefully prepared his dress and his lines and crafted his performance to preserve royal authority in death. How carefully he had rehearsed the part was rapidly made apparent when the long version of his script hit the streets – even as the crowds were dispersing.[14]

CHAPTER 12

WRITING REPUBLIC

I

It may seem strange, even perverse, to open a chapter on the representation of the new Commonwealth and republic with an examination of the book published within days of Charles's death as the king's own authorship. The *Eikon Basilike*, however, was synonymous with the birth of the republic and set the agenda for constructing images of authority even before the new regime had found its own voice. Though there was a bitter and enduring controversy about who had actually authored it, the *Eikon* was often described as the 'King's book' and was broadly received as Charles I's own last words and meditations.[1] Whoever actually authored it, it was, with thirty-five editions in one year, the publishing sensation of the century, yet it is only recently that scholars have paid attention to the artful composition and rhetorical strategies of a text which contributed much to the failure of the republic and the eventual restoration of the monarchy.[2] While there is much more still to be said, our brief discussion here is focused on the place of the book in the representation of both the former royal and the new republican regimes and in the contest for cultural authority and validation that continued to be waged between Royalists and Parliamentarians long after the military outcome had been decided.

The first thing we should note about the *Eikon Basilike* is that it embraced all three principal modes of representation that have been our subject: words, images and performances. Though it is a skilful rhetorical performance, it may be significant that the title, *The Royal Image*, directs attention to visual representation; and, as has been remarked, William Marshall's famous frontispiece virtually makes the argument of the text in a richly complex but readable emblem. Figuring Charles kneeling at his devotions, that frontispiece highlights action, ceremony and ritual. And throughout the book, the prayers at the end of each section render it a series of devout performances by the king who prays in the first person. It was by means of all three modes of representation, and (as Milton knew) perhaps more by the visual and performative, that the *Eikon Basilike* achieved its polemical effect and inflicted such wounds on the fledgling republic, so we must briefly consider them in turn.

To begin with words, it may be helpful to recall the dilemma of royal speaking and writing that has been a recurrent theme of our study from the time of Henry VIII to the outbreak of civil war. By speaking and writing, a ruler might publicize and argue his or her authority; but, in so doing, especially with an expanding marketplace of print and gossip, the ruler opened himself to public scrutiny and retort. Charles I, we have seen, unlike his father, preferred the mystery of silence, at least until events forced him to justify his position; and even then he sought to avoid the polemical fray. What is remarkable about the *Eikon Basilike* is how it successfully resolved the dilemma inherent in public writing and enshrined regal mystery in an act of publication. Above all, this most polemical of seventeenth-century texts muted the force and hid the marks of its polemic, so that its contentions appear, at least on the surface, natural and incontestable positions.

The *Eikon Basilike* is by no means free of overt polemic – that is, of the justification of the king's own courses and the condemnation of his enemies. Throughout the text, Charles explains and justifies controversial actions, such as his attempted arrest of the five MPs in December 1641, or his acceptance of the aid of Catholics; and he asserts his innocence of any involvement in the Irish Rebellion, or of any design to commence a civil war when he left London.[3] Indeed, he blames parliament for instigating conflict, and decries the 'exquisite malice' of the sects who advocated 'popular, specious and deceitful reformations'.[4] Presenting himself throughout as a lover of peace, Charles blames his opponents for the failure of the negotiations at Uxbridge that might have ended conflict and criticizes many who concealed their ambitions in the language of (a false) piety.[5] However, it is not in these self-justifications and recriminations that the polemical force of the *Eikon Basilike* lies. Indeed, for all that he revisits key moments in the history of the conflict – from Strafford's death, through his repulse at Hull to the formation of the Solemn League and the seizure of his letters at Naseby – it is not even the argument that makes the text such powerful advocacy for the king.

More than arguing a case, the *Eikon*, by various devices, re-establishes the natural and divine authority of both the monarch and the man. One device is the unobtrusive, almost silent, redeployment of a series of similes and metaphors long associated with kings. Without directly applying them to himself, Charles recalls and evokes the representation of the king as the father, the Sun, the pilot of the ship, and the good physician who heals the fevered sickness of the body politic; and so re-situates monarchy in a divine order and reconnects the regal head to the members.[6] Pronouns are artfully used, so that though chapter headings refer to 'the king' in the third person, the narrative is in the first person and in some passages (especially the opening lines) a plethora of 'I's underline the authorial, regal control.[7] The narrative form itself, for the most part, suggests simple statement rather than polemic; but here the sequence of events is not straightforwardly chronological and the relation is highly selective: the history and representation of what has happened are subject to royal control.

What immediately strikes a reader who comes to the *Eikon* after immersion in civil war pamphlets is its extraordinarily unstrident tone. The words 'moderate', 'moderation' and 'civility' are used freely throughout a text that is also characterized by these qualities.[8] The author frequently insists on his preference for patience over anger, and on his belief in charity, and appears to act according to those preferences and beliefs in several passages. Charles, for example, writes that he sought the best for his enemies as well as supporters; and he resists any display of satisfaction at the ill fortune that came to opponents such as Sir John Hotham, or those members of the Long Parliament expelled by the army in Pride's Purge.[9] Though it was divine justice, the king informs us that he would not observe it but 'with sorrow and pity'.[10] Even in his worst adversity, Charles commends the 'valour and gallantry' of many in the army.[11] In part, this pose of civility and fairness constitutes a re-validation, as well as a re-presentation, of the qualities of the perfect gentleman or the prince who rises above petty vengeance and partisanship. Here, of course, the pose of civility amidst conflict and the stance of fairness to both sides in war serves to raise the king himself above the contest, rather than representing him as what he had been – one of the combatants. Willing to criticize his own failings and those of his supporters as well as being gracious to opponents, the author/king stands above the discursive as well as military battle in which Charles Stuart has been embroiled. This elevation of the author/king is strengthened by the frequent repetition of another key word in the *Eikon Basilike*: 'reason'.[12] In medical and political theory, the reason was situated in the head (an analogue for the monarch) and the appetite or passions in the members of the body or body politic. A recurring theme of the Caroline masques and royal portraits had been the representation of Charles as a monarch and man who, by regulating his own appetites by reason, stood both as a virtuous ruler and as an example to others of self-regulation and self-rule.[13] In the pages of the *Eikon*, Charles claims to embody and always to act according to reason, and describes those who resort to force as men 'conscious of their defects of reason'.[14] As Milton was to observe, 'the book which I have to answer pretends reason, not authorities'.[15]

In Charles's usage, however, reason is not simply self-regulation or the command of the passions. In what virtually becomes the mantra or soundbite of the *Eikon*, the term is coupled with religion, and with conscience. Early in the text, Charles refers to God directing him 'by reason or religion' and couples his freedom as a king with the use of 'reason and conscience'; explaining his commitment to episcopacy, he writes that he found it confirmed by 'reason and religion'.[16] In chapter XXII, on his leaving Oxford, Charles wrote succinctly: 'Reason is the divinest power: I shall never think myself weakened while I may make full and free use of that.'[17] Reason, in other words, 'the divinest power', is what Charles I as king and man shared with, and was given by, God. Though, in the main, the text of the *Eikon Basilike* does not *argue* the divinity of kings, in the mantra of 'reason and religion' Charles claimed the ultimate authority for his undertaking and direction of affairs – the authority of God.

Before we turn to the relation in the text between the king and God, we must briefly consider that other term coupled with reason on which Charles takes a stand throughout the *Eikon*: the word 'conscience'. Today, we associate the word with deeply personal and private belief, perhaps even with the private self. In early modern England, as the word itself suggests, conscience represented a shared or common understanding. As head of the church, therefore, the monarch stood as the conscience of the commonweal, and correspondingly obedience to the king was prescribed by the dictates of conscience as well as duty. As I have argued elsewhere, James I resisted any puritan claims to personal conscience and insisted that the king's conscience was the conscience of the realm; that he, in other words, mediated God's will for his subjects.[18] Because he regarded it as fundamental not only to his person but to the office of the king, James instructed his heir on the importance of a sound conscience, of which he urged him to take account before God at the end of each day. Heeding his father, Charles I believed that the royal conscience should instruct subjects in what was right and be the conscience for all. He adhered to that concept of a shared national conscience even after the realm divided in civil war; and he attributed opposition to the absence of, or to a false, conscience. Though during the 1640s, often under pressure, Charles was led to compromise what his conscience taught him was right, increasingly from about 1646 he insisted on his conscience as the best determinant of the right course: that is, he stood on his authority to be the conscience of the nation.[19] During the civil war, many sects arose which claimed the interpretation of God's holy will, and Cromwell and other army leaders claimed their personal understanding of Providence as justification of their actions.[20] The *Eikon Basilike* defiantly counters those claims and, in asserting the king's conscience as the conscience of all, underpins his divine authority. Just as God was 'the only king of men's consciences', so Charles regarded acting on his conscience as 'the faithful discharge of my trust as a king'.[21] Those who went against the king's conscience, he wrote, sinned against God. Only in 'penitent consciences' lay the hope for 'the tranquillity of a united kingdom'.[22]

As with the claim to be the reason, the claim to be the conscience of the kingdom again elevated the king above the political contest. Indeed, one of the refrains of the *Eikon Basilike* is a denial, and a condemnation, of politics. Using language familiar to any who were acquainted with Machiavelli, the king accused his enemies of 'stratagems', 'deceitful darknesses', 'specious' acts and 'pretensions'.[23] When he uses the terms 'politics' and 'policy' it is always in a pejorative sense and in contrast with the dictates of religion and his own behaviour. It is, the *Eikon* claims, only 'pretensions of religion in which politicians wrap up their designs'.[24] For his part, the king asked God to direct him in 'pious simplicity, which is the best policy'.[25] In several passages, Charles affirms that he acted not out of policy and interest – in supporting the bishops, for instance – but according to the dictates of conscience that instructed him in the right course.[26] The denial of politic action may sound archaic in 1649, after a decade of political discourse and manoeuvre that often bore out the teachings of Machiavelli. But the writings of the Florentine were still anathema, whatever the practice of politics, in early modern England. By claiming to reject *realpolitik*, therefore, Charles I not only commanded the higher moral ground that he had always regarded as essential to kingship, he positioned the monarchy and himself on a superior plane: as a moral arbiter, rather than participator in political contest. The king's stand on conscience and his rejection of policy figured his opponents as ungodly Machiavels and presented him as the sole custodian of the Christian commonweal.

In chapter XVII, in which he discusses the dispute over church government, in a revealing passage Charles acknowledges: 'This I write rather like a divine than a prince.'[27] In a later chapter, he reiterated the relationship in different words: 'I think both offices, regal and sacerdotal, might well become the same person.'[28] The author of *Eikon Basilike* indeed performs both offices. For whilst in prose and plain font, Charles as prince reviews the events of civil war and the negotiations for peace, at the end of each chapter Charles as priest prays, in italics, to God for aid, guidance and resolution. These prayers need to be read – as they have not been – in the context of the many volumes of official prayers published in the name of kings and queens, especially those of Elizabeth I and Charles I himself. During the 1620s and 1630s, in services (ordered under the royal name) for averting the plague or for the success of armies and fleets, Charles had led the nation as Supreme Head of the church, as a priest king.[29] During the 1640s, others had claimed Providence and, as we saw, parliamentary fast sermons vied with the king's prayers as liturgies of state.[30] By re-presenting the king as a priest conducting prayer, the *Eikon* restored to Charles that spiritual charge over the people which he had often declared to be the first duty of a king. As he or she proceeds through the *Eikon*, the reader participates in a service as well as a text – a service led by an author who, as he moves from prayers to his heavenly father to address the reader, mediates God's word and will to readers. To read the *Eikon Basilike*, that is to say, is to join in worship with a godly prince.

Beyond that, to read the *Eikon* as it was intended was also to join in worship *of* a godly prince. After the break from Rome, Tudor monarchs had needed, and always endeavoured, to present themselves as the heirs of godly patriarchs: a Josiah in the case of Edward VI, a Deborah or Judith in Elizabeth's case. Charles had himself been heralded as a David who followed Solomon, the biblical patriarch with whom James I (like Henry VIII) was frequently compared. In the *Eikon Basilike*, the king again cites Solomon and David as the biblical kings he should follow.[31] But, as has often been noted, the self-representation of this text is not only biblically patriarchal but Christic. In passages scattered throughout the text, the author – almost innocently – compares his circumstances to Christ's: in chapter V he makes a parallel with the temptation of Jesus, whom Satan led to the top of the temple; narrating how he was delivered by the Scots to the English he compares himself to Christ sold.[32] The *Eikon* insistently represents Charles as a martyr and it has rightly been observed that the text owes a rhetorical debt to Foxe's famous *Book of Martyrs*.[33] But the martyrdom the king claims here is not that simply of a witness to the gospel, but that of Christ. Along with his Saviour, Charles writes (as the frontispiece depicts) that he will wear a crown of thorns and be – the use of the word is remarkable – 'crucified'.[34] Where, in his historical exegeses, James had melded his own words with Scripture in order to underpin his claim to be God's mediator as well as vicegerent, Charles I writes his own last performance as a re-enactment of the Passion. In his final meditations, Charles prayed, as had Christ, that the bitter cup of a cruel death be taken from him.[35] But, he promised his heavenly father and his readers, 'If I must suffer a violent death, with my Saviour, it is but mortality crowned with martyrdom.'[36]

The appropriation of the Christic in the *Eikon* marks the ultimate height of the mystification of monarchy in early modern England. While since Henry VIII all rulers had claimed divine approval to sanctify their rule, Charles represented himself, on the eve of death, as the son of God. That this most audacious appropriation was made, and secured widespread support, is remarkable enough. What is all but incredible is that Charles I claimed the most sacred, mystical heights on the eve of his enemies' perpetration of what we might expect to be the ultimate desacralization of regality: regicide on a public scaffold. On the day that in the name of Providence, law and reason of state (or necessity), his opponents ended his life, Charles, appropriating the Christic, all but guaranteed an afterlife for himself, the hope of a resurrection of monarchy and the succession of a monarch who would save the people.

Jesus Christ was both son of God and a man; only as man was he able to reconnect fallen mankind to a God who had made men in his image; Christ was mystical and human. And it is its representation of the humanity as well as the sacred mystery of monarchy that explains the brilliant polemical success of the *Eikon*. For all the negative historiography characterizing Charles I as distant and remote, the king had, at least from 1630, gone to lengths to represent himself in human as well as sacred guise: notably as a loving husband and tender father whose affective familial relationships symbolized his loving union with his people.[37] It may be that during the 1630s that image was not communicated widely enough or through media more popular than masques, portraits or even engravings, while the mounting hysteria over popery complicated the image of uxorious fidelity. By the late 1640s circumstances were different. The sects were seen to pose more of a threat to the social order than the Catholics, the queen was abroad and Charles himself was powerless in confinement. But, even more importantly, in the *Eikon* Charles, as never before, revealed, even bared, himself before his people.

We have remarked the 'I' of authorized control in the *Eikon*, and the proliferation of the first person pronoun also renders this text a very personal one in which Charles the man as much as the mystical monarch is presented to readers and subjects. Similarly, the prayers at the end of each section reveal to us, as well as a godly prince, a Christian in the most private and intimate conversation with God, as they deploy a language of plain and humble piety rather than the formal discourse of state. Charles, in these prayers, confesses his sins, takes the blame for his failings, and implores God's forgiveness: in doing so, he connects himself with every Christian who experiences the anguish of failing his Lord. Moreover, his readiness to express sin and remorse makes his stand on conscience less the assertion of a public sovereignty and more the spiritual fruit of experience of God's ways, learned through error and prayer. In a manner that disarms all hostile interpretations of his actions, Charles, having bared himself to God – and in these pages to readers – can claim that he harbours no secrets or 'evasions' and that his account is therefore the one to be trusted.[38]

As much as a Christian, an imperfect Christian at that, Charles appeals to readers as a man of human love and tenderness. It was, he tells readers, the personal safety of his wife and children above all else that led him to leave London.[39] As well as the traditional language of chivalry, he makes an appeal to every husband when, repeating references to 'my wife' rather than describing Henrietta Maria as the queen, he writes: 'I can perish but half if she be preserved.'[40] Contesting two decades of negative portrayal of his wife, Charles predicts that 'her sympathy with me in my afflictions will make her virtues shine with greater lustre . . . and assure the envious world that she loves me, not my fortunes'.[41] The evocation here of a love that is beyond fortune, and quite opposite to a politics of interest, both elevates the royal marriage, as had masques, to the highest Platonic plane *and* renders the royal union (as marriage was for ordinary men and women) a solace in time of difficulty. Charles's love for, his constancy to, his wife becomes through the pages of the *Eikon* an affective bond that connects him with its readers and subjects.[42] And the opening word of the address to the prince – 'Son' – renders this most political of all sections so personal and affectionate that to contest it as a polemic appears almost unnatural.[43]

The reference to 'afflictions' shared adds the bond of readerly sympathy to the personal, intimate and affective portrayal of the king. In the *Eikon* Charles presents his personal body as weak, vulnerable and threatened, while asserting his spiritual strength. In several sections of the text, playing down what at the outset was probably a Royalist military superiority, Charles presents himself as a ruler with little strength other than that of God in his soul. 'What I want in the hands of force and power, he writes, 'I have in the wings of faith and prayer.'[44] As the narrative progresses to his defeat and confinement, the author more insistently (and now more accurately) represents himself as powerless victim – at least before the secular might of his enemies who seek his destruction. In the letter to the prince, again claiming the Christic, Charles points to the pathos of his fear, his suffering and imminent death as well as the strength of his religious conviction and the glory of dying as a martyr, for his people. As readers, we are empathetically attracted to the suffering man as much as we joy in the triumphant martyr king.

In an obvious sense, the ever-present tensions between the king's two bodies, personal and politic, were only ever resolved by death. But what the *Eikon Basilike* effects is a larger resolution, a reconnection of the personal and public that made it requisite for any subsequent authority to effect the same if it was to claim legitimacy and gain support. More than that, this text reconnected the monarchy with the people and even achieved what all rulers had struggled to attain: making regality both mystical and popular. Unquestionably that achievement was related to, possibly dependent upon, the circumstances of Charles's execution. Yet the brilliance of the work lies in the art with which it represents Charles while seeming not to argue his case. At last, it would seem, in 1649, in the *Eikon Basilike* Charles reconciled for himself, and for the monarchy, the need for utterance in a public sphere with the mystery of silence.

The power of its silent argument is nowhere better illustrated than in the famous Marshall frontispiece which also circulated separately from the book and became the template for scores of images and artefacts enshrining Charles I's memory.[45] In an image divided by a large column (often a symbol of regal authority), Charles, in regal robes, kneels in a chapel in prayer and contemplation. On a table before him lies an open book, inscribed 'In your words my hope', that symbolizes Scripture. In his right hand the king holds a crown of thorns, an object painful but easily supported by a Christian about to emulate his Saviour. Beside the king's feet lies an earthly crown, inscribed 'Vanitas', which is described as a splendid but heavy burden (*gravem* as opposed to the *levem* of the crown of thorns). Charles gazes upwards to heaven where a crown of glory, blessed and eternal, awaits. Behind him lie the world and the adversity from which he has been saved by martyrdom. But even here the symbols and messages are those of defiance and victory. Albeit battered by stormy seas, a rock (is it the monarchy as well as Charles's faith?) stands, secure, *immota triumphans*, unmoved and victorious over assault. Similarly, in a calm landscape a palm tree stands erect, though heavy weights hang from its branches, and bears, like an emblem, the legend 'Virtue increases in adversity'. Though he looks to Scripture and God, Charles, like Christ, is not detached from the world; his triumph is in it and for it. And the *Eikon Basilike* ensured that Charles I remained at the centre of the earthly polity just as the new republic began,

75 Frontispiece by William Marshall to *Eikon Basilike*, 1649.

as its leaders hoped and believed, to build up the first Commonwealth without a king.

There can be absolutely no doubt that the *Eikon Basilike* rocked the newborn regime, nor that moves were made to counter it, or at least temper the damage it inflicted. Evidently several republican apologists took it upon themselves to endeavour a response, but whether because they were caught by surprise or because it was felt that a quick and brief pamphlet retort would not be effective, no direct reply was published until August – seven months after the king's book hit the streets. On 16 August the anonymous *Eikon Alethine* was published with a dedication to the new Council of State.[46] In a frank address, the author acknowledged that the new regime had suffered as a result of the *Eikon* and other works which had (as we shall see) spun off from it.[47] Specifically, it was admitted that 'multitudes biased by attention to the late king . . . readily and very credulously take for current anything stamped with his effigies'.[48] The author urged readers to reject both the words and the worshipping of the images: 'Will you,' he asked rhetorically, but nervously, 'be frighted with his image whose person could neither frown nor flatter you from your fidelity to your country?'[49] Then, recognizing that 'silence might appear guilty in this talkative age', the author turned to answer the text, principally by asserting that the words written were not the king's but forged by some of the 'prelatical tribe'.[50] Lest any remained committed to belief that the *Eikon* was royal writ, *Alethine* advised 'it is not saying but doing, not writing but acting well that adorns a king'.[51] Though *Eikon Alethine* rightly identified the polemical force of the *Eikon Basilike*, it constituted a weak and in some ways contradictory response that failed to undermine it. The new republic, however, had commissioned a brilliant pen and a fuller reply. When John Milton's *Eikonoklastes* appeared on 6 October, it was well over twice the length of the king's book and had been eight – crucial – months in the making.[52]

As its title indicates, *Eikonoklastes* was Milton's attempt not merely to counter the words of a king but to smash the idol of monarchy and to discredit the man, Charles Stuart. Like the author of *Alethine*, Milton acknowledged a history in which royal writing had been closely related (he cites Henry VIII as an example) to royal authority and the fact that in the people's eyes the name of a king endowed a text with authority.[53] Accordingly, Milton makes a closely argued case against Charles being the author. Beyond that he identifies in the text passages lifted – 'quilted out of Scripture phrase' – and often borrowed from Shakespeare and Sidney as well – to render the *Eikon* a patchwork of plagiarized fragments rather than the creation of a royal pen.[54] In accusing Charles of literary theft, *Eikonoklastes* sought both to undermine royal authorship and also to figure the king as the plunderer of the property and rights of subjects, no less than of authors who possessed (Milton argued) 'the property of [their] own work'.[55] As well as undermining royal authorship, Milton dissects the narrative, words and

language of the king's book. At all the crucial points – the seizure of the magazine at Hull is a good example – Milton rewrites the narrative of the *Eikon* to take
back the control of history, events, from the king.[56] And by italicizing, frag-
menting and then responding line by line to passages of the *Eikon*, he endeavours to subordinate the regal text to republican commentary. Part of that process
involves an empowering of the reader and directions on how to re-read and to
deconstruct Charles's words.[57] Inviting readers to enact their freedom both as
citizens and exegetes against a monarch who sought to rob them of it,
Eikonoklastes asserts: 'in words that admit of various sense[s] the liberty is *ours*
to choose that interpretation which may best remind us of what our restless
enemies endeavour.'[58] By returning the royal words of the *Eikon* to pamphlet
controversy and to the reader's interpretation, then, Milton hoped to demystify
the text and open it to rational critical scrutiny.

Milton knew, however, that the appeal of the *Eikon* was not simply a matter
of claimed authorship or argument. 'The book which I have to answer,' he
observes, 'pretends reason, not authorities'; it claimed, that is, to be above
evidence and argument.[59] Most of all, as we have seen, the *Eikon* was a document of the royal conscience and of Charles's claim to be God's exegete and the
nation's conscience. The *Eikonoklastes* directly contests 'the specious plea of his
conscience' and, denying Charles's capacity now as a reader rather than author,
rejects the monarch's role as interpreter of God's will.[60] Comparing the royal
claim – one made throughout our period – to mediate between God and the
people with textual hermeneutics, Milton mocks Charles's pretensions 'as if the
very manuscript of God's judgement had been delivered to his custody and
exposition'; and adds bluntly: 'his reading declares it well to be a false copy
which he uses.'[61] Presenting the royal conscience as personal and fallible and
wrong, Milton again seeks to render Charles but one voice, a mistaken voice,
in the debate about Providence.

I have argued that it is in the humanity as well as divinity of its portrayal of
Charles I that the appeal of the *Eikon* lies; and Milton struggled to refigure
Charles the man as well as the monarch. Where the king represented himself
as loving husband and tender father, *Eikonoklastes* drew on traditional tropes
of gender to present him as unmanly, emasculated, and ruled by his wife.[62] In
doing so Milton intended to depict the king's marriage as not the model for,
but the inverse of, good government and to rewrite tender care as weak subjection. As he puts it in rewriting the *Eikon*'s account of the queen's departure, in
which Charles had staged his marriage and defended his queen, those 'govern'd
and overswayed at home under a feminine usurpation, cannot but be far short
of spirit and authority without doors to govern a whole nation.'[63] And mocking
Charles's evocation of his love for his wife as 'sonnetting', in a curious move, he
seeks to discredit the whole *Eikon* as 'intended [as] a piece of poetry'.[64]

In *Eikonoklastes*, Milton carefully identified the rhetorical strategies of the
Eikon and set out to destroy it as the necessary step towards establishing the

republic. 'It were my happiness,' he tells readers, 'to set free the minds of English men from longing to return . . . under that captivity of kings.'[65] Yet, for all his strenuous efforts, and in part because of them, Milton's response failed to effect its ends. Though he sought to resume control of history and narration, the organization of Milton's *Eikonoklastes* followed the chapter order set out in the *Eikon*. While at the beginning of chapter IX, he condemns 'the verbosity of this chapter', here, as throughout, Milton writes and argues at much greater length, and so with less authority.[66] Even when he promises that a royal assertion is 'soon answered', the retort runs to pages – to the point where even Milton fears 'more repetitions than now can be excusable'.[67] The effort to demystify the *Eikon*, to open it to scrutiny, required a length and detail that risked both boring the reader and appearing defensive. Moreover, it failed to tackle the emotive appeal of a text that Milton himself acknowledged, was 'so feelingly . . . composed'.[68] Interestingly, other than accusing Charles of plagiarizing prayers, *Eikonoklastes* does not respond to the royal prayers at the end of each section: 'with his orisons I meddle not'.[69] Yet it was precisely by means of these prayers that the king represented himself both as God's lieutenant and as a humble sinner before him. While Milton may retort that 'to pray and not to govern is for a monk and not a king', by not addressing Charles's prayers, he failed to undermine all the royal words which precede and follow the king's private conversations with God.[70]

More damaging than Milton's failure finally to discredit royal words was the nearly unanswerable difficulty presented by the *Eikon*'s representation of royal performance and a royal image. As one who had been on the fringes of the Caroline court, and indeed authored a masque, Milton understood, but here could not find a way to contest, the theatricalities of Caroline power. Along with the charge of poetry, he condemns the *Eikon* as ineffective 'stage work', but knows that it is by his acting the role as well as writing it that Charles made himself martyr.[71] Because the *Eikon Basilike* was a performance as well as a text, the failure to answer it on its own terms left the representation of the last (as well as all) regal performance to the Royalists. If Milton sensed and feared that it was this aspect that beguiled the 'simple reader', still more was he anxious about the visual evocations of, as well as the Marshall frontispiece to, the king's book.[72] Early in the preface to *Eikonoklastes*, Milton points to 'the conceited portraiture before his book, drawn out to the full measure of a masking scene, and set there to catch fools and silly gazers'.[73] Though he dismisses it as 'a Romish gilded portraiture', Milton fears not only that it draws the silly, that is the ignorant, common and illiterate, but also, as Marshall intended, that it 'canonizes' Charles.[74] He instructs readers to deride it, yet the frontispiece and the image of Charles it figures haunt *Eikonoklastes* from beginning to end. And in his closing lines, Milton vents his anger as well as frustration at the 'new device of the king's picture at his prayers' which, as he knows, gains 'the worthless approbation of an inconstant, irrational and image-doting rabble'.[75] The frustration is with himself as well as with the common people. Even after a work so long, and long in the making, Milton half sensed that he had lost the competition with the king's book. In closing with the hope that those less bewitched than the 'credulous and hapless herd' might be persuaded to his argument, and to republic, he abandons the common readers and subjects to their servility to kingship.[76]

These closing lines remind us that *Eikonoklastes* was reacting: not only to the text of the *Eikon*, and all the spin-offs, images, engravings and artefacts that drew on it, but to its reception – its popularity.[77] Unsurprisingly, given its length and tone, Milton's book was not at all popular; beside the thirty-five editions of the *Eikon* published in 1649, we note that only two editions of *Eikonoklastes* were printed over the ensuing forty years.[78] By the time Milton completed his official refutation, a popular cult of Charles the martyr was already established and any hope of an immediate popular base for the new regime undermined. The regicide had been the action of a minority, and unpopular. But, as successive episodes from Henry VIII's break from Rome evidence, unpopular measures could be presented and represented, packaged and communicated, to win support. If that was the first task of the new republican government, it was one made much more difficult by the Royalists' seizure of the initiative and setting of the agenda in the *Eikon Basilike*.

Throughout this study, we have examined official scripts, images and performances before turning to critiques and counter-representations. If in this chapter we commence, as we have, with an opposition text and the regime's reaction to it, that is not because we seek to privilege the regal over the republican. It is because the story of the first days of the English Commonwealth is one in which the modes of discourse and representation were monarchical. In the measure to which they remained so lies the failure not only of the new republic as a government, but of the idea of republic or a republican culture, to capture the imagination of Englishmen and women.

II

The latest historian of the Rump and first scholar to study the image and representation of the English Commonwealth points to the 'verbal discursive strategies' through which a republic was invented.[79] Unfortunately, Sean Kelsey's study contains no chapter analysing those discursive and rhetorical strategies or discussing how the Commonwealthsmen proclaimed the new regime through published acts, ordinances or (especially) declarations. In the revolutionary moment of January 1649, it was never more important for the regime to seize the initiative and advertise and publicize its legitimacy, its programme and its virtues: to reassure doubters, to gain support and to announce itself as the new authority. This the new government failed to do – or at least failed to do quickly enough. During January, the Rumpers had issued declarations justifying the trial of Charles I and their resolution to remove the king and the House of Lords and establish a new polity; but the early days of the republic saw no explanatory proclamations or declarations of the revolutionary change that had taken place.[80] As we have seen, the official accounts of the king's trial appear to have been a PR failure, and it may well be that the new governors, aware of the opposition the regicide had excited, considered it politic to avoid public announcements, or felt it more important to cement the shift to republic through action rather than words. Whatever the reason for early silence, faced with the huge impact made by the *Eikon Basilike* the new republic found itself in the position of reacting to discourses rather than setting the discursive agenda.

While the government proceeded to issue ordinances settling proceedings in courts and constituting a Council of State as its executive, Charles II began to publish a series of declarations denouncing the new regime as illegal and illegitimate.[81] On 9 February, parliament issued a declaration of its resolution to maintain the fundamental laws of the nation and to preserve the properties and liberties they guaranteed; but this itself testified to anxieties and fears that were mounting in the early days of the government and which needed to be addressed.[82] In its proclamation, parliament promised a larger explanation of its proceedings; but it was not until fully six weeks after regicide – more than a long time in the fevered politics of 1649 – that any pronouncement was made. On 17 March, parliament published, in the Gothic script of royal proclamation, an Act for the abolition of the office of king.[83] As well as simply abolishing the monarchy so as to establish the republic as more than a temporary expedient, the ordinance used language to justify its actions and to celebrate the possibilities opened by the change effected. Charles Stuart, the ordinance asserted against doubters as well as ubiquitous Royalist polemicists, was 'justly condemned . . . and put to death' and his sons were rightly disabled; for experience had demonstrated that the office of king in England 'is unnecessary, burdensome and dangerous to the liberty, safety and public interest of the people', since those who had exercised regal power had used it 'to oppress and impoverish and enslave the subject' by setting up their will above the laws.[84] The Act declared the office of king in a single person abolished and any who sought to revive it a traitor. But importantly, the declaration closed with a promise and a vision of a positive future. By the abolition of monarchy, it claimed, 'a most happy way is made for this nation . . . to return to its just and ancient right of being governed by its own representatives'; and, to facilitate that, parliament promised its own dissolution, as soon as might conveniently be, to make way for the free election of a new assembly.[85]

On the same day as the Act was passed, parliament ordered the printing of a declaration detailing 'the grounds of their late proceedings' and 'settling the present government in the way of a Free State'.[86] Printed for Edward Husband, printer to the Commons, and sold at his shop in Fleet Street near the Inner Temple, the declaration appeared on the 22nd and was probably acquired by George Thomason soon after.[87] At 27 pages and bearing the Clerk of the

Parliament's imprimatur (though not yet the arms of the new Commonwealth), the declaration offered both the first full explanation of recent events and the first rhetorically crafted representation of the republic. The parliament, it began, that had long contended against a tyrannical power opposed to peace and freedom, had been led by necessity to the change of government which had been effected for 'the honour of God and the good of the nation' which were 'the only end and duty of all their labours'.[88] Cutting briskly through years of contentious discussion, the authors 'suppose[d] it will not be denied' that the office of king was originally instituted by agreement of the people and was appointed for their protection.[89] However, the text continued, 'very few have performed the trust of that office with righteousness and due care of the subjects' good', preferring to advance their own interests and ambitions; 'and in the whole line of them, how far hath the late king exceeded all his predecessors in the destruction of those they were bound to preserve', it trusted, was apparent to all.[90] To remind readers lamenting the death of Charles of his faults and the 'violence of his fury', the declaration hinted at his involvement in James I's death and catalogued his assaults on the liberties of the people by loans and taxes, imprisonments, threats to judges, oppressions of courts such as Star Chamber and, it was alleged, plots to bring in German troops to awe the people.[91] After myriad illegal acts, Charles, the declaration announced, 'prosecuted a fierce and bloody war against the body of all his own subjects', and refused to heed his people's overtures for peace.[92] Even when God declared against him on the battlefield, Charles continued to plot war and so prolonged the bloody misery of the nation.[93] 'Let all the world of indifferent men judge,' the declaration invited, 'whether the parliament had not sufficient cause to bring the king to justice.'[94] Tacitly acknowledging that some indifferent men still harboured concerns, the declaration addressed objections that were widely circulating. The doctrine that the king was not accountable it dismissed as 'a strange monster' and defensively asserted that there 'requireth the less to be said in confrontation of it, [it] being enough to confute itself'.[95] As for the objection that the trial and execution of a monarch were without precedent, the declaration retorted – 'so were the crimes of the late king'; and repeated the parliament's boast that all had been conducted publicly in 'a fair and open trial'.[96] Against those – not only Royalists – who pointed to the king's sons' right of succession, the declaration argued, 'the elder right is the people's'.[97]

Though, perhaps necessarily, several pages were taken up by a rehearsal of past events and a response to apologias for monarchy and for Charles I, the declaration did also attempt to argue the legitimacy and virtue of the new constitution and government. 'The same power and authority which first erected a king', it proclaimed, endeavouring to emphasize continuity, could also pull monarchy down and 'change the government for the better, and instead of restoring tyranny, to resolve it into a free state'.[98] Pointing to God's blessings bestowed on other free states – Rome and Venice, Switzerland and the United Provinces – the declaration posited the benefits such might bring to England.[99] 'In commonwealths they find justice duly administered, the great ones not able to oppress the poorer . . . the poor sufficiently provided for', and freedom of person and conscience, in contrast to the shackles of kingship.[100] Making an overt and clever appeal to the people as well as elites, the authors emotively evoked the wooden shoes of suppressed French peasants, which, it alleged, were 'intended for the fate of England had our monarch prevailed over us'.[101] In contrast to the huge costs and burdens of a profligate king and court which drained hundreds of thousands of pounds from the people's purses, the declaration promised that 'in a free state, these and multitudes of the like grievances and mischiefs will be prevented' and manufactures and trade advanced.[102] The economic welfare of the nation, as well as other reasons, the declaration explained, had impelled the people to their recent change of government which removed, along with the monarch, the Lords who were dependent on him and who threatened to obstruct the people's will.[103]

If the declaration deftly recast a deeply unpopular change as the act of the people and deployed simple statement to bypass contentious argument, its authors yet felt the need to answer specific objections to the new constitution that were being freely printed and discussed. Not least, the declaration of both houses of parliament in April 1646 had expressed a commitment to government by king, Lords and Commons and in a society still used to the sanctity of such pronouncements, it presented an embarrassment to those in government who had been party to it.[104] With some evident awkwardness, the July 1649 declaration attempted to claim that the commitment to the king had been contingent on his co-operation before more boldly justifying rather than denying changes: 'change being for the good of the Commonwealth, no commoner of England can justly repine at it'.[105] A second objection, widely held by excluded MPs as well as Royalists, was that the revolution had been effected by a mere faction under the control of an army rather than by the votes of a free parliament. Since such was the reality, the charge was not easy to answer and the declaration could only weakly observe that the MPs who survived Pride's Purge were more than quorate, that the army was a friend to parliament, and that even statutes enacted under force had in the past held sway and proved beneficial.[106] Though such arguments were unlikely to convert the unconverted, they at least clothed naked force with the garment of pragmatism, if not law. As for the law, one of the greatest concerns was where the regicide had left it and whether it was secure under a changed constitution without a king. As we have seen, one of parliament's earliest ordinances had promised to maintain the laws and courts, and the liberties, properties and peace they preserved. Here the declaration repeated the assurance with an assertion of the republic's clear sense that the common laws were essential to the sustenance of the common interest and the government.[107]

Having negotiated some difficult obstacles to the legality or validity of what had been done, the declaration closed with a summary of reasons for change that also read as a positive agenda for government.[108] The purpose of parliament's design in changing the government, it announced, was to end tyranny and establish a free state that would prevent the recurrence of war, advance the true worship of God by permitting freedom of conscience, encourage trade and manufacture, ease the burden of taxes and maintain the poor. If the promises held out sound all too familiar to those of us wearied by modern party manifestos and election speeches, we might recall that, despite the very different circumstances of 1649, the republic's declaration was the document of a party – a minority party – struggling to secure recognition as a government. Though the authors closed by claiming God's support and in confident expectation of the cheerful concurrence of the people, they knew that, as a revolutionary regime, the contest for support and legitimacy favoured their opponents.[109]

Among the most vocal and dangerous opponents from the outset were the Scots, who had fiercely opposed the regicide and proclaimed Prince Charles as king in the northern kingdom on his father's death.[110] As former allies and co-religionists, the Scots could not easily be represented as papists, or malignants, and their denunciation of the republic, distributed in London, posed a serious threat to the very survival of the new regime. Significantly given its tardiness in proclaiming the new republic, the parliament published an answer to letters from Scotland as early as 17 February, recognizing the urgent need to check the scandalous aspersions cast upon them.[111] In an attempt to revive old anti-Scottish prejudice, a parliamentary declaration, as well as asserting the power of the people, rejected any right of the Scots to order affairs in England.[112] Against the devastating charges made by Scots in their published letters, especially the second, the parliament asserted 'our own intrinsical power and trust' and 'the providence of God' who, they claimed, approved the course of justice they had taken against a tyrannical king 'and mean to follow towards others, the capital enemies of our peace'.[113] The Scots, however, were not easily silenced. As well as resolving on an action against the republic, they issued from 22 February a series of declarations and resolutions, published in England and abroad, expressing their 'detesting against the late proceedings' against both father and son, Charles I and II.[114]

In the face of mounting preparations for invasions, but also a barrage of verbal attacks, the English republic felt the need to respond with pen as well as pike. A *Declaration of the Parliament concerning their Late Endeavours . . . to Remove All Misunderstandings and Differences between the Commonwealth of England and the Kingdom of Scotland*, published on 14 July, was directed more at English than Scottish readers.[115] For, as it argued, the Scottish parliament and commissioners had denied the authority and very name of the Commonwealth and so challenged 'the natural right and inherent power to take up or lay down what form of government we think fit'.[116] Providing discursive ammunition to those in England who wrote against the new regime, Scots propaganda cited the Solemn League as evidence of the republic's illegality and breach of trust and vilified its leaders as sectaries.[117] By way of response, therefore, the parliamentary declaration defended the republic's adherence to the cause and accused the Scots of ignoring the threat to religious and public liberty from the popish and malignant factions.[118] The emotive appeal to a common Protestantism menaced by popery had been the most powerful summons to arms, but it was less effective in 1649 than in 1642.[119] As for the Scots' objections to the legality of proceedings against the king, which were echoed widely throughout England, the declaration could only answer in terms of pragmatism and necessity thinly veiled by questionable historical claims: 'whenever the people's welfare is preferred before the particular interests of them that govern, it hath not been unusual in these nations to lay aside precedent forms of government and introduce others'.[120] As had become customary during the civil war, the declaration printed the exchange between the English and Scottish parliaments, hoping to persuade readers that right was on the republic's side. But the danger remained, as the regime was fully aware, of a domestic uprising coinciding with the invasion of a Scottish army to re-establish the Stuarts.

The precariousness of the republic's position and image was highlighted by an event in another land to which the English republic was looking for support: the United Provinces. International acceptance and recognition of the new republic were as vital to the establishment of its legitimacy – at home as well as abroad – as they were to its security. Recognition was unlikely to come from France, where Henrietta Maria was still campaigning for aid for her son, but the republic had hopes of the Dutch who had themselves, in the previous century, broken free of the tyranny of Habsburg rule. In the spring of 1649, parliament sent as resident envoy to the Hague the native Hollander and civil lawyer Isaac Dorislaus, who had been one of the prosecutors at the trial of Charles I. On 12 May, Dorislaus was murdered by a group of Royalists who may have found shelter in a Holland where the Stadtholder William of Orange was married to the king's daughter.[121] The assassins were never brought to justice and the affront to the English republic was palpable. Again, not least for consumption by readers at home, parliament published a declaration of their 'Just Resentment of the Horrid Murder . . . of Isaac Dorislaus' in which they blatantly acknowledged 'the affront and dishonour that is thereby done to this Commonwealth'.[122] The document, published with the new arms (a George cross and a harp) called for justice on the perpetrators who, 'proceeded from that party from whom all the troubles of this nation have formerly sprung . . . being slaves to that tyranny from which this Commonwealth hath happily (through the blessing of God) vindicated themselves'.[123] Fearing that such events might encourage enemy action, parliament warned that it would resist any who made 'attempt upon the peace and liberty of this Commonwealth' and threatened recriminations against Royalists at home.[124] Yet, whatever the threats to its opponents, the stability of the new republic remained fragile, if only because the legitimacy of the regime had not been established either abroad or at home. Moreover, like the Scots' constant appeal to the Solemn League and protests about the treatment of Charles I, Dorislaus's murder directed attention again to regicide – and to a king whose shadow loomed over the new regime, which never entirely emerged from it into its own light.

During its first months, the verbal representations of the English Commonwealth were reactive and defensive. But, if only because of its large army, the Commonwealth survived; and not only survived, it enacted measures to settle the militia, raise an assessment of a vast £90,000 per month, and appoint Treasurers for War.[125] In addition, the regime organized the sale of the late king's and queen's goods and, more significant as a source of revenue, sold off the lands of bishops, deans and chapters.[126] To quell the still strong tide of opposition, on 17 July the parliament passed an Act redefining treason as any action of 'writing, printing or openly declaring that the . . . government is tyrannical, usurped or unlawful; or that the Commons in parliament assembled are not the supreme authority of this nation'.[127] When even that failed to check the torrent of opposition, they followed it with an Act, published on 20 September, 'against unlicensed and scandalous books and pamphlets and for better regulation of printing'.[128] With all its detailed provisions for licensing, search, bonds from printers, the control of imports, the regulation of carriers and hawkers, for forfeitures and condign punishments for buyers as well as sellers, the Act announced a working government, eight months in being, that was determined to display its authority. The preamble, however, also reveals a regime that sensed it was still losing the struggle for legitimacy, for the hearts and minds of English men and women. For, it acknowledged uneasily, 'scandalous, seditious, and libellous pamphlets, papers and books' were still 'openly . . . printed, vended and dispensed, by malignants' who sought 'the subversion of the Parliament and present government'.[129] Such enemies (and the word 'malignants' appeared not to be restricted to old Royalists), it claimed, knew that their ends 'cannot with more ease be attempted than by lies and false suggestions, cunningly spread amongst the people, and by malicious *misrepresentation* of things acted . . . to take off . . . their affections from that just authority which is set over them'.[130] It was indeed 'malicious misrepresentation', more than force, that had inflicted the greatest damage on the republic – and as was not mentioned here, because such misrepresentations had not been effectively countered by a positive propaganda campaign conducted with that 'officious care and industry' which opponents had brought to their attacks.[131] But, within days of their Act, parliament attempted at last to seize control of its own representation and image, so as to secure its future. On 27 September, it ordered to be printed a declaration that was 'in vindication of their proceedings' as well as a warning of the 'dangerous practices of several interests against the present government and peace of the Commonwealth'.[132]

Opening by celebrating what in some ways had been its greatest achievement – its survival – the declaration noted the wonderful deliverances of a

God who had enabled the republic to withstand the storms and waves which had threatened to topple it. But the purpose of the vindication was more positive. The MPs had, they claimed, worked together 'discharging the high trust of our places' 'in carrying on this great and glorious work of religion and public liberty', as 'true patriots and good Christians'.[133] If the claim was familiar, the rhetoric was now more positive and confident, the language loftier. Moreover, in this September declaration parliament foregrounded religion, both as the end it most kept in view and as a rhetoric for the justification of all its actions. The vindication acknowledged that many discontented had fallen off and were advocating the return of monarchy.[134] This time, however, the MPs did not argue against them in defence of republic, but presented what they had done as God's work. Instead of looking backwards, as they had hitherto, they proudly pointed up what they had achieved as an indication of what they might go on to do. 'We shall briefly lay before them the happy progress that through God's goodness hath been made in procuring the blessings of pure religion and just liberty unto this nation' – and these 'notwithstanding all the reproaches and unthankful murmurings of ill-minded men'.[135] Damning opponents now as obstacles to God's work, parliament called for support against the 'hellish designs' on foot against the regime in order to secure parliament's work and enable it to advance the republic.[136] First, parliament claimed, the republic had recovered religion from confusion and danger. Despite the obstacles to its godly efforts, it had pressed ahead with reforms of doctrine, worship and discipline, and fought off the threats of popery, superstition and blasphemy.[137] As the reference to blasphemy suggests, parliament was conscious of an audience as worried about the disintegration of organized worship as about Catholicism; and the declaration reassured such readers that the liberty of conscience it supported did not mean universal toleration: not least, it would not permit liberty to be abused.[138] Turning secondly to the public liberty of the nation, the declaration boasted that, through MPs hazarding their lives and estates, what had looked to have been swallowed up by tyranny was now in a thriving condition.[139] Dismissing those who criticized the republic on this score, and naming the Levellers as men acting out of private rather than public interest, the declaration listed the oppressions of the subject that had been removed and promised more for the future.[140]

The declaration now represented positively the pragmatic measures it had taken and so redefined what others had depicted as corrupt or self-interested as action taken as part of 'the great trust that is upon us from the people'.[141] While after nearly a year it may have appeared late to many, the regime at least now explained that 'the great work we have first to do is to establish the being and safety of the Commonwealth upon sure foundations . . .' for, the declaration explained, new enemies to religion and liberty threatened, as Levellers joined Royalists to seek the ruin of the Commonwealth and the enslaving of the people.[142] Printing correspondence that showed the connections between the Levellers and Charles II's court, the declaration warned that they sought to undermine and divide parliament and the army 'that this Commonwealth might run into tumultary confusions in the infancy'.[143] Cleverly, the declaration re-presented widespread grievances as the machinations of a party that was the cause of, rather than solution to, them. The army, after all, it claimed, was needed as an antidote to the malignants.[144] Yet, importantly, while rejecting inflated claims that millions of pounds were exacted from the people in taxes, the parliament held out the hope of easier times, assuring them 'there is nothing that is more in our desires and endeavours than that we may be able to abate the taxes and in time to take them off, that the people might come to enjoy entirely the fruit of that which hath cost them so dear'.[145] Finally, skilfully turning what others saw as the ills into part of the cure of the body politic, the parliament (quietly appropriating the royal role of physician of the commonweal) urged the people's patience during a time when the process of healing was itself accompanied by some pain.[146] And promising now to reward good patriots who supported the state as well as punish those who manoeuvred against it, they vowed: 'as our duty is in respect of our great trust, we shall endeavour to make the people happy and promote their good; and shall not give over that good work for any discouragements'.[147]

Parliament's 30-page vindication marked a new stage in the re-presentation of the republic. If it reflected the growing sense of security born of surviving the precarious early months, it also strengthened the regime by manifesting confidence and outlining a clear agenda for action and improvement. That greater confidence in some measure lay behind the Act for the public subscribing of an engagement to the Commonwealth passed in early January 1650.[148] For, though the engagement, as the preamble to the Act explained, was prompted by the continued endeavours of opponents to undermine the government, and though (as several scholars have shown) the oath of fidelity to the regime troubled consciences and was divisive, it forced those not committed to Royalism to declare for the regime or risk renewed war.[149] In so doing, it forced subjects to endow the republic with what it hitherto lacked: if not the love and support, at least the sworn – and recorded – allegiance, of the bulk of its citizens. If, then, the engagement failed in its announced purpose of 'better uniting the nation' (was that ever seriously entertained?), it, and its apologists, did advance a new and very different, more secular and pragmatic basis for obedience to a *de facto* government that made it easier for some publicly to reconcile with the regime, whatever their private beliefs.[150]

Blair Worden perhaps exaggerates when he asserts that 'the engagement was imposed on the nation chiefly out of panic'.[151] But there can be no doubt that the backdrop to it was the threat presented by an alliance of Scots and English Presbyterians with other discontents.[152] If the second year of the republic was dominated by the military threat from the Scots, the public pronouncements of the Commonwealth were similarly focused on responding to Scottish propaganda, and on trying to undermine or prevent English support for the Scots. Though several Cavaliers had taken the engagement, Bradshaw was of the view in April that 'not any one Cavalier is heartily converted to us'; and in the provinces the engagement appears not to have been pressed after the initial enthusiastic subscription drive of the winter.[153] Parliament, however, had grasped the importance of countering negative misrepresentations and of putting a positive spin on its own actions. As it ordered an army under Cromwell to Scotland, parliament also published the first of several declarations against the Scots. The *Declaration of the Parliament of England upon the Marching of the Army into Scotland* was printed by appointment of the Council of State on 26 June, about a fortnight after parliament resolved on the expedition.[154] From the opening lines, it seems that parliament felt the need to explain and justify a war, especially one against co-religionists and former allies. Claiming their reluctance and desire to avoid conflict, the MPs argued the necessity of defending the Commonwealth against those whose declarations denied their legitimacy and rightful existence and who now sought to reimpose tyranny on the nation.[155] Not content with declaring their hostility to the republic, the Scots had audaciously proclaimed Charles Stuart king of England (and Ireland), and had misrepresented the members of parliament as licentious sectarians undermining church and faith.[156] While explaining that there could be 'no other ways of . . . vindication, saving . . . the sword', the declaration rejected (as it had to) Presbyterian calumnies and affirmed the republic's commitment to 'the advancement of God's glory' and the 'furthering of a just freedom' for all.[157]

Not long after its own declaration, the parliament approved, and on 19 July ordered printed, a similar declaration of the army, signed by Cromwell and the officers as they began their march north.[158] Referring to the earlier document as one that 'may satisfy all impartial and uninterested men in all the nations', the army publicized its partnership with parliament that opponents had sought to undermine.[159] And perhaps to enhance its own legitimacy, in arguing for the constitutional propriety of all that had been done in England, the army referred doubters to those parliamentary declarations that were now perceived to be a vital complement to arms.[160] The principles enshrined in the Covenant, the officers argued in an attempt to remove what remained an embarrassing difficulty, had to be upheld even when they were not in the king's interest: 'we therefore reckon it no breach but a religious keeping of the Covenant . . . when our parliament for religion and liberty's sake and the interests of the people, did remove the king and kingship'.[161] Answering Scottish calumnies on their religion, the officers protested that, while they did not hold that faith was tied to one form, in no way did they condone licence and they prosecuted blasphemy.[162] Where few in Scotland were likely to be won over by such defences, the repetition by the army of parliament's vindication of its actions was surely intended to reassure those at home that it was the parliament's army and ultimately the people's protector and servant, rather than their master, as Levellers and others had complained.[163]

The propaganda campaign remained of the first importance even as the armies prepared to engage. In August, Charles, desperate for support, signed a declaration denouncing his father and supporting the Covenant and so forestalled Cromwell's hopes of gaining a party among the Scots.[164] Published to all three kingdoms, Charles's declaration, not least because it was his own words, posed other threats which parliament moved swiftly to check. As its counter-declaration of 28 August warned, Charles's 'pretence of humiliation for his own and his father's opposition to the work of Reformation' was intended to 'seduce the people of *this* nation [in England] from their due obedience and to excite them to war'.[165] Since the end of peace and the prospect of the return of tyranny and slavery were, parliament claimed, all that was offered, it asserted its confidence that 'no pious or judicious person can possibly be deluded under such gross deceits to constitute such an assistance' that would destroy two nations. 'Nevertheless,' the declaration ran, 'they have resolved for the better information and satisfaction of the people . . . more largely and particularly to unmask . . . the wicked hypocrisy and wicked design lodged under the specious pretences in that declaration.' Caught on the back foot again, the republic could for now only announce it treason to print, abet or countenance Charles's declaration. Before the promised fuller response to Charles had been made ready for publication, the immediate crisis had passed, with Cromwell's crushing victory over Leslie at Dunbar on 3 September.

It may be testimony to the importance the English government had come to attach to its public representation that, even after its victory, parliament ordered the printing by Husband of a full, 40-page, *Answer* to the declaration by Charles, which was evidently intended to add discredit to the defeat of the Royalist cause in three nations.[166] The tone of the 20 September declaration is more combative than before. Parliament warned that the unnatural war that the king had waged against the people's liberties would not soon be forgotten and, with now no hint of defensiveness, lauded the justice executed upon a tyrannical king, and the new government 'restored to a Commonwealth and free state'.[167] The declaration scorned Charles's attempt to dress himself in the new garb of the Covenant, presenting it as a cynical new device to enslave two nations with the support of the kirk.[168] The document then proceeded to 'take in pieces' the king's declaration and to demonstrate, paragraph by paragraph, the 'gross hypocrisy of this whole transaction' of (apparently) shifting from popery to Presbyterianism.[169] In an attempt to turn the accusation of cynical pragmatism from themselves against the Royalists, parliament accused Charles of dissimulation and politicking and dismissed his promises of clemency as empty while hinting at its own intentions to pass an Act of Pardon.[170] At the close of what was an effective response to a dangerous move, the declaration called upon 'all true Englishmen' to resist the design rather than risk subjecting themselves to a foreign nation against which, they noted, God had given powerful testimony of his disfavour in Cromwell's recent victory at Dunbar.[171] Parliament was learning the art of effectively countering Royalist propaganda and – to some extent – of presenting its own case; but after two years the new regime had established neither security abroad nor a firm base of popular support at home. For all its unquestionable improvements in representing itself from late 1650, much of the public discourse of the republic continued to be reactive and defensive.

The summer and autumn of 1650 saw the regime turn to long-awaited domestic measures: acts for maintaining the ministry, against incest and adultery, and for conducting legal proceedings in English.[172] But, even after Dunbar, the threat from Scotland did not recede and further reforms lost priority to military measures needed to ensure security. In January 1651, Charles was formally crowned as king of Scotland at Scone. Shortly after, the king issued a declaration to his subjects of Scotland, Ireland and England that was a call for military aid to restore him.[173] From their own intelligence of Royalist plots and recent experience of an insurrection in Norfolk, parliament knew the extent of the danger, but, while it made preparations to counter an invasion and probably authorized the re-publication of the (1542) Declaration of Causes of a war against Scotland, it did not issue a response.[174] Indeed, not until 1 September did a parliamentary Act order the burning of Charles's declaration by the public hangman and condign punishment for any who dispersed it.[175] Otherwise, as a proclamation of August announced, no other response was felt necessary.[176]

Only after Cromwell's (by no means certain) victory at Worcester did the republic, saved from the Scottish threat, issue new declarations for the settlement of Scotland.[177] Here, announcing its sense of an obligation to God to advance his glory as well as the welfare of the people, parliament outlined its plan to incorporate Scotland into one Commonwealth with England, without a monarchy or House of Lords, and to make all tenants subject to the English government.[178] Scotland was effectively a conquered and subject colony; but Ireland remained a problem and the Dutch attack on English ships redirected attention to naval preparations.[179] Moreover, the army that had raised and sustained the government was beginning to voice its discontent at what looked like a self-serving regime that had failed to deliver the promised reformation of church and state.[180] From the winter of 1652, Cromwell was manoeuvring for a dissolution of parliament and for new elections, while other officers were ready to expedite its end by force.[181] As months passed and patience was exhausted, Cromwell threw in his lot with them and expelled the parliament. That it was forcibly dissolved with little popular protest points up not only the unanswerable power of military force, but the failure of the Commonwealth to win support, to persuade either old Royalists, Presbyterians, soldiers or the people, of its fitness as a government. Unpopular from the outset, the Commonwealth did too little, and the little too late, to proclaim its mission or set out its stall. In consequence, it left its enemies and critics to represent it in those negative shades which still colour historical writing on the Rump.

Despite deficiencies in representing itself, the Commonwealth did not entirely neglect genres of propaganda that had emerged during the war, notably the accounts of military victories published to strengthen morale and to display God's blessings on the cause. Soon after the regicide, for example (Thomason received his copy on 10 February), an account of a sea fight between a parliamentary squadron and an Irish fleet was published with 'imprimatur'.[182] The brief relation of the usual victory ('by divine providence and the assistance of the Almighty') over a far superior enemy was here also made a sign of the triumph of the parliament over all its enemies and the report closed with parliament's declaration concerning the new government.[183] The next year, the printer to parliament published with authority Cromwell's letter narrating the proceedings of the army in Scotland, with his defiant challenge to the Scots, followed later by a relation of the victory at Dunbar.[184] *A True Relation of the Routing [of] the Scottish Army*, licensed by Rushworth, was published days after Dunbar, on 9 September.[185] The relation announced four thousand enemy slain, over ten thousand prisoners captured, and colours and ordnance taken, all for the loss of fewer than forty men 'in a happy deliverance' of God.[186] Two months later, in a letter from Cromwell to the parliament, this 'high act of the Lord's Providence to us' received a further relation.[187] In this carefully crafted narrative, a sick army, with the disadvantage of ground, was described as triumphing over a confident enemy through 'support from the Lord himself', who clouded over the moon, enabling the army to unite, and gave victory that was one of 'the most signal mercies God had done for England'.[188] 'God puts it . . . into your hands', Cromwell assured parliament and all readers, 'to give glory to Him, to improve your power . . . [and to] own his people . . . for they are the chariots and horsemen of Israel'.[189] Significantly deploying a passion absent from parliament's own declarations, Cromwell urged them: 'own your authority and improve it, to curb the proud . . . relieve the oppressed . . . [and] . . . to reform the abuses of all professions . . . Set upon these things in order to his glory and the glory of your Commonwealth'.[190] After 1650, there were further publications of parliamentary victories, some like that over the Earl of Derby, printed with parliamentary imprimatur.[191] But, not least on account of the power of the Lord General's rhetoric, none rivalled Cromwell's own accounts which, for all their studied deference to parliament, highlighted the man and through him the army that were to bring about parliament's end. As we shall see, Oliver Cromwell had a highly tuned sense of audience and of the need for any in authority (or aspiring to secure it) to present themselves to the people. Rather than parliament advertising its military triumphs, to improve its power it helped, by printing his letters, to make a hero of Oliver Cromwell and so, unwittingly, assisted in its own dissolution and demise.

To be fair, parliament did make victories the occasion of what had become important events in the politics of representation – the official services of thanksgiving.[192] Parliament began to publish ordinances for days of worship from the summer of 1649. That of 1 June, for example, recalled how 'Almighty God hath been graciously pleased to appear in the cause of the parliament and people of England', against insurrections at home and enemies abroad.[193] To 'transmit the memory' of those providences to posterity, and as much to demonstrate to present citizens 'that some hopeful progress hath been made in settling the government of this Commonwealth', parliament enjoined a day of thanksgiving, to knit the hearts of the people in unity and, presumably it was hoped, obedience.[194] Though, unlike similar royal proclamations, no official text for the service was prescribed, the purpose of the event was clearly political, indeed partisan. As the declaration of the reasons for another day of thanksgiving in August (1649) proclaimed, God had not 'by more evident demonstrations declared to the world, his approbation . . . of any cause than he hath done that in which this parliament hath been engaged' against the 'enemies of religion and liberty'.[195] Specifying those, the ordinance lists 'the old professed malignants and Royalists . . . the pretended Covenanters' and renegade Irish and Scots as those whom the Lord had defeated and drew attention especially to the late miraculous advances in Ireland, where, with 'but a handful of men', 'the Lord defeated an enemy'.[196] As well as prescribing a day of worship, parliament ordered this declaration, with its detailed account of victories, to be read to spread the news of providential successes and deliberation.[197] Despite those many who, by its own admission, did 'shut their eyes or murmur against' those providences, parliament continued to proclaim them and order their commemoration in services of thanksgiving throughout the land.[198] Orders prohibiting fairs and markets on such days underline the importance parliament attached to them as opportunities to reach the people in the parishes, though it was not easy to know what happened on the ground.[199] Certainly, in early ordinances for services of worship, parliament invoked the blessings of God on their courses far more than they did in other official discourses and so represented, as any early modern government had to, their expedient courses as God's work. And to that end the succession of victories in Ireland and Scotland served as powerful testimony to the claim. In fact, several proclamations for days of thanksgiving rehearsed at length the details of battles won against the odds – evidently to discourage and discredit other insurgents.[200] After Dunbar, for example, parliament ordered a day of thanksgiving for a victory which was 'given in a seal and confirmation from heaven of the justice of our cause' and through which (and on this occasion it was hardly exaggeration) 'God hath renewed Being and Life itself for this Commonwealth'.[201] Those who had endeavoured to undermine the rebellion had 'found . . . the mighty hand of God drawn out against them', and as the 'narrative' of the battle illustrated, were vanquished by a smaller army, but one with right on its side.[202]

It may be a sign of growing confidence that in January 1651 parliament ordained a service of thanksgiving for 30 January, the second anniversary of the regicide. On this occasion, countering the unease of many who considered the government to have no authority but the sword, parliament vaunted 'that it hath not been by might nor by power but by the spirit of the Lord that England's safety and deliverances have been obtained'.[203] 'The better to stir up' the people, to obedience to them as well as thanks to God, parliament then narrated a list of recent providential deliverances and victories in Scotland, at sea and at home which showed that 'God hath been with the parliament of the Commonwealth', not with its detractors or opponents.[204] The following March, the declaration prescribing another service specifically praised the 'alterations' God had effected and promised that those were but 'the first fruits' of greater things yet to come.[205] At a time of contagion, all were urged to pray for pardon of their sins and for the perfection of God's work by the parliament's forces by land and sea and by its actions at home.[206] Though we do not have the text of the service, parliament's Act prescribing a day of thanksgiving in October 1651 opened in the language of prayer: 'The works of providence, by which the Lord hath pleaded the cause of this parliament and Commonwealth in the sight of the nations roundabout, are glorious.'[207] Reviewing victories over Scottish foes, from Dunbar to the recent triumph at Worcester, the Act this time praised the support of county militias and so advertised the growing support for the regime whose enemies counted on internal discontent.[208] The day of rejoicing for October 1651 was ordered in all three kingdoms by a government that was not only gradually securing itself, but was more actively representing itself as secure, legitimate and godly.

If, either because it considered there were no suitable occasions, or through simple neglect, parliament ordered no more services of thanksgiving, that may have been a misjudgement. For, as the army's criticisms of the Rump were increasingly justified by scriptural references, the failure of parliament to continue to advertise its own providential mandate proved costly. In 1653, Cromwell and fellow officers dispatched the house in the name of God and replaced it with an assembly drawn from nominations sent in by the gathered churches. Finally, God did not favour the Commonwealth, as it had so often vaunted, with victory over its enemies. It may be that the services of thanksgiving it enjoined were not held, or were held in parishes with communities less than sympathetic to the regime and conducted in terms less celebratory of parliament's achievements. But at least in the regular ordering of services of thanksgiving, the Commonwealth did display the piety which in early modern England carried with it authority, and in its insistent and increasingly confident claim to divine approval, it at least endowed itself with the highest legitimacy. Many – especially Royalists and Presbyterians – remained unpersuaded by official services, discourses and scripts. But, whatever the extent of remaining popular dissatisfaction, the Rump was brought down not by popular insurrection, or even widespread non-co-operation, but by a violent coup.

During the 1640s, as well as officially prescribed services of worship, parliament had deployed a series of fast sermons as political opportunities to publicize its cause.[209] Though those ceased to be regular occurrences from 1649, sermons delivered before parliament continued to be published with official imprimatur and to represent the regime, in circumstances of increasing religious confusion and opposition, as a godly rule.[210] One preacher popular with the parliamentary authorities after regicide was John Owen, whose sermon the day after Charles's execution was ordered to the press by the authorities. [211] Owen described his fellows and leaders as a people returning to God. And whilst, in a series of sermons in 1649 and 1650, he admonished and called the assembly to its duties, Owen's sermons all represented the parliament as carrying out God's work.[212] In, for example, *The Steadfastness of the Promises*, preached on 28 February 1649, a day of humiliation, he exhorted MPs to stand firm against all enemies that threatened their godly mission and progress and promised that, if they continued to embrace God's cause, their enemies would be disappointed.[213] Other preachers given an imprimatur freely preached on the difficulties that the Commonwealth faced in the early years. Thomas Watson, for instance, in his sermon *God's Anatomy*, delivered in December 1649, acknowledged that 'our condition is low'; while John Warren, lecturer, then vicar of Hatfield, warned of 'the blistering storms that rage amongst us at these present alterations.'[214] But the acknowledgement of difficulties and trials came with praise of parliament as God's agent – 'you whom all disposing Providence hath set at the stern of this realm' – and preachers to the house left their auditors with the clear message that, whatever the obstacles, they were 'upon the settling of the nation in a posture of peace and safety' and advancing God's will and work.[215] Preaching to the 'worthy senators' in October 1650, the minister of St Thomas the Apostle, Queen Street, reviewed 'the glorious appearances of God for you' and exhorted them: 'hold on in well doing for his glory'.[216]

As time and the failure of its enemies to destroy it gave the new Commonwealth some stability, supportive preachers began to trumpet the achievements of, and still more the possibilities for, full reformation presented to the government. Vavasour Powell, for example, in his sermon before the Commons praised them for what they had secured and, assuring them that 'God will carry on the work of your hands', urged them to set up Christ and the saints in England.[217] Owen, who also preached the sermon at the funeral of Henry Ireton in 1651, was the same year appointed to preach an official sermon of thanksgiving after the victory over Charles II and the Scots at Worcester.[218] In his prefatory address, 'To the Supreme Authority of the Nation, the Commons assembled in Parliament', Owen praised his audience, saying that the Lord 'hath made you a spectacle unto men and angels, being the instrument in his hand to perform all his pleasures'.[219] Recollecting 'such things that have been brought to pass as have filled the world with amazement', and listing justice against a tyrannical monarch as the principal among them, Owen, as he celebrated them, called upon the parliament to do Charles's work.[220] As Owen's own later collaboration with the officers who ousted the Rumpers indicates, some of those Independent ministers appointed to preach by parliament had different, more radical, visions of reformation than the MPs themselves.[221] However, the official sermons on days of fast, humiliation and thanksgiving continued to represent the Commonwealth as a godly and reforming regime. In doing so, they helped to legitimize a regime that in January 1649 had appeared bereft of legitimacy.

During the civil war the news media become increasingly important to the representation and reputation of governments. After 1649, parliament not only appreciated the importance of exercising a measure of control over news, it licensed official organs as attempts to direct public opinion and gain support. From June 1650, under the editorship of Milton's friend Marchamont Nedham, 'the greatest journalist of his day', *Mercurius Politicus* was published weekly 'as the mouthpiece of the Commonwealth'.[222] In some ways the *Politicus* was the forerunner of the best tabloid journalism of today. Nedham used humour and wit and wrote in a jocular way towards the serious ends of promoting a republic, often delivering complicated theoretical argument in plain, comprehensible terms, even 'sippets' – or sound bites, we might say.[223] In David Norbrook's words '*Mercurius Politics* . . . put its readers through a crash course in republican education', by familiarizing them with the republics of antiquity and contemporary Europe in an accessible and entertaining prose.[224] To grasp the brilliance of Nedham's journalism, there can be no substitute for reading through the issues of *Politicus* that built a republican programme. Here, a few extracts offer a small hint of a style that owed much to the pamphlet and the street and that transformed the nature of news. Issue 5 of *Politicus*, for 4–11 July 1650, opens: 'How sweet the air of a Commonwealth is beyond that of a monarchy' and asks rhetorically: 'is it not much better then to breathe freely, and be lively, upon a new score of allegiance than pine and fret and fume, on behalf of the old *Non-entity*?'[225] Thousands of sentences arguing for rejection of monarchy and acceptance of the new regime were published after 1649; but few were more eloquent than that. Nedham's dismissal of the monarch as a 'non-entity', his portrayal of Charles II as a 'young Tarquin', his mockery of Presbyterians only ambitious for offices and baubles ('golden sausages about their necks'), rendered the Royalists and their supporters ridiculous and insignificant.[226] In more serious mode, but still with a deft touch, Nedham rewrote the familiar arguments ('worn out in the mouths of many') about the popular basis of magistracy to argue that obedience had seldom rested on consent and need not now.[227] Accepting the 'necessity of some coercive power' was enough and constituted tacit consent – and, he clearly hoped, formed a basis of obedience to the new regime.[228] Indeed, during 1651, Nedham's *Politicus*, it is not too much to claim, popularized the Hobbesian argument for the pragmatic basis of obedience: urging in January 'since there is no other possible way to preserve the well-being of this nation, but by a submission to the present powers, we may, and must pay a subjection to them, in order to our own security'.[229] Developing Hobbes's revolutionary case in simple terms, he led readers to the conclusion that 'it is a very unreasonable course in any man to put himself out of the protection of this power, by opposing it, and reserving his obedience to the King of Scots'.[230] Yet beyond the negative and pragmatic arguments, Nedham also powerfully evoked the concepts of liberty and freedom as reborn after a period of darkness, as those gifts that 'inflamed [men] ... to the love of glory and virtue'; and, in religious rather than secular terms, he posited free status as 'more pleasing to God than any other form'.[231] In contrast to the 'yoke' of tyranny, republican rule held out the prospect of both personal and public sublimity.[232]

Though it is almost impossible to assess accurately the impact of Nedham's apologia for republic, he must rank among the most important impresarios of the representation of the new Commonwealth. Royalists called him 'the Goliath of the Philistines' whose mighty pen wielded great influence.[233] If Nedham's journalism helped persuade many to even reluctant obedience, one is kept wondering what his longer-term impact was – or might have been, had the republic lived on. A time-server in some measure, Nedham continued to serve the Protectorate, but it has rightly been noted that his style flattened after 1653; and it may be that he had less sympathy with the new regime.[234] However, it was on account of his pragmatism as well as his self-interest that Nedham's pen followed the course of events and changes of regime. Though he served no party for long, the fact that the parliament, Royalists, Commonwealthsmen, Protectorians, Rumpers and, in the 1670s even Charles II, all used him, testifies to the impact he was believed to make on readers. Thanks to Nedham, though a republic was short-lived in the English state, republican ideas entered the wider culture and imagination of the English.

III

As well as its own official scripts, the new republic was represented and supported by writers who, either out of conviction or pursuit of favour (or both), defended the trial and execution of the king and hailed the birth of a new polity. Among them, the best known is John Milton whose *Tenure of Kings and Magistrates*, defending regicide, earned him the post of Secretary of Foreign Tongues and propagandist for the Commonwealth.[235] More recently, in the first full study of those who wrote the English republic, David Norbrook has elucidated the contribution of other literary figures, notably John Hall and Thomas May, to the defence of the Commonwealth.[236] Hall's 'experiments with sublime rhetoric helped to give the republic a rationale beyond mere expediency'; and he was rewarded for his pro-republican treatise, *The Advancement of Learning*, with a pension and payments in exchange for answering pamphlets published against the state.[237] Thomas May, in an important counter to the Royalist claim to poetry, rendered verse as republican apologia in his *Continuation of Lucan's Historical Poems, Pharsalia*, revised in 1650, just before May's death.[238]

These literary figures, whom recent historical scholarship has returned to their circumstances, were part of an outpouring of defences of regicide and apologias for republic by authors (named and anonymous) in prose and (though rarer) in verse. In response to the flood of laments for Charles I, pamphleteers wrote to counter the saint-like image of the king and to justify his trial. As well as early responses to the *Eikon Basilike*, tracts like *The Privileges of the People* denounced kings and argued that their destruction was God's work, while R. Wharton's *Declaration to Great Britain*, approved by the influential preacher Hugh Peters, outlined how the Lord had brought to justice a tyrant who had preferred his own designs to following the word of God.[239] The simple assertions of God's will, however, were, as was recognized, not enough to win over others to the regime. The author of *King Charles Trial Justified* began by acknowledging that the recent events had 'given occasion to the raising of many regretful objections in the minds of the people'; and he proceeded to attempt to dispel them by answering the objections about the king's death and the supposed inviolability of monarchs and arguing for the rightful authority of the people and parliament.[240] John Goodwin's 'defence of the honourable sentence passed upon the late king', dedicated to the Commons, encouraged them to 'be not troubled that the nation is departed from you'.[241] Promising that time, experience and a better explanation of the 'reasons and causes' of 'things new and strange' would win over the people, Goodwin wrote to persuade readers that Scripture and law placed the people above monarchs, that kings might be deposed and that Charles had deserved to die.[242]

The justification of Charles I's execution was essential because it was inextricable from the issue of obedience to, and hence the survival of, the Commonwealth. The authors of *A Short Discourse . . . or A Sober Persuasive of All True Hearted Englishmen to a Willing Conjunction with the Parliament* believed it more important to look at what had been achieved than the means by which it had been effected, yet still felt the need to 'repeat the miseries of the old' government by recounting why Charles had to be removed.[243] 'There is no such supernatural stamp or ius divinum set on monarchical government,' the pamphlet continued, 'which should engage men's hearts unto it . . . more than any other', so the people were free to 'consider [their] consciences' and by so doing to see the sense in obeying the new regime.[244] 'It is easy,' the author closed with more bravado than confidence, 'to frame an idea of a new government'; and it was, he held, as easy to live under it in peace, 'had we all one mind'.[245] As he knew, however, this was the rub: it had been 'hard to make the people think the king could offend' and harder to persuade them that they were not bound by conscience to monarchy; therefore it was difficult to bring them to that 'willing conjunction' with the Commonwealth he advocated.[246] Other tracts addressed the central problem even more directly. Taking the epigraph from St John's gospel 7: 24 ('Judge not according to the appearance'), the author of *The Lawfulness of Obeying the Present Government* switched tactics by insisting that, far from succeeding by inheritance, most rulers had entered into power by force – yet once in power had willingly been obeyed, as the present government should now be.[247] Such proto-Hobbesian arguments were rehearsed in several other treatises of 1649. *The Bounds and Bonds of Publique Obedience*, for example, asserted both that necessity had dictated a change of government and that 'we ought to submit in obedience to those who plenarily possess, protect and command us', adding that 'so soon as one supreme power is expelled by another, law, life, and estates fall all into the hands of the succeeding power'.[248] By the end of the year, a treatise directed at winning over Royalists and other gentry advised them to go with the flow of events, and acquiesce in what had happened, for 'a year or two more will habituate the present government'.[249]

If the last prophecy proved excessively optimistic, the government's policy of enjoining an oath of obedience, known as the engagement, was accompanied by, as well as fierce opposition, another wave of justifications.[250] The anonymous author of *A Logical Demonstration of the Lawfulness of Subscribing the New Engagement*, who published his tract symbolically on the anniversary of regicide, pressed the case for submission by appeal to Scripture and the obligation to any existing power.[251] 'If any usurp government,' he insisted, 'and confirm their usurpation by conquest, their ... acts of government ... are God's ordinance and to be obeyed.'[252] Those who have read the newspapers we briefly examined will not be surprised that a more powerful case for the engagement was made by Marchamont Nedham in *The Case of the Commonwealth of England Stated*.[253] Taking a disarmingly personal approach in an epistle to the reader, Nedham wrote, 'Perhaps thou art of an opinion contrary to what is here written: I confess that ... I myself was so too'; then embarked on an explanation of what had changed his, and should change the reader's, mind.[254] Types of governments, he argued, had their times and, as events across Europe were demonstrating, the time of monarchy was passing.[255] Echoing others who preempted Hobbes, he observed that the power of the sword and conquest had ever been the foundation of governments and that none should cavil at submitting to such regimes, especially when not submitting robbed men of the protection that was the purpose of entering society.[256] By corollary, to accept the protection of the new government involved acknowledging its right and discountenancing any claims for the king.[257] For, he argued, the sword had created a new title and 'when such an alteration of affairs shall happen as extinguishes his [the king's] title, I conceive we are not obliged in this case to pay him that submission which by oath we promised, but ought rather to swear a new one to those that succeed him in the government'.[258] More succinctly, he repeated: 'the old allegiance is cancelled and we are bound to admit a new'.[259] Astutely, Nedham added incentives to arguments of obligation and utilitarianism. The sooner, he promised, men settled in obedience under the new government, the sooner the burdens of taxes, needed for the army, might be lifted.[260] 'Let the Commonwealth hath leave to take breath a little in the possession of a firm peace', he urged the people, and 'then they would soon find the rivulets of a free state much more pleasing than the troubled ocean of kingly tyranny'.[261] As Nedham used *Mercurius Politicus* to render the arguments from *The Case* in more popular form, others took to verse to argue for the oath to the republic. A poem, for example, titled *A Word of Council to the Disaffected*, referring to the engagement, instructed: 'To present Rule His [God's] word commands ye Bow' and, dismissing those who pleaded the Covenant, continued: 'Shall God's Command be crossed by your Vow?'[262] 'God', readers were told, 'bids yield unto the powers that are' and the poem closed with the only choice any sensible man would make:

Who swears to future powers, doth strife increase;
Who swears to present, is a friend of peace.

Other writers endeavoured to encourage engagement to the Commonwealth by suggesting that, since power had always resided in the people, the government now established, rather than novel, was as it had – or rather should always have – been.[263] *The True Portraiture of the Kings of England*, published in August 1650, reminding readers of the ills of self-interested monarchs, presented the new regime as redeeming liberties and acting in the public faith, 'reducing affairs to their first natural and right principle'.[264] In similar vein, Nathaniel Bacon, having traced in *The Continuation of a Historical Discourse* rule by the Commons acting alone, closed with the words: 'as I found this nation a Commonwealth, so I leave it and so may it be for ever; and so will it be if we may attain the happiness of our forefathers the ancient Saxons'.[265]

The author of *Anglia Liberata*, combining most of the defences of the engagement into one, insisted that parliament could reasonably claim God's word, the dictates of nature, and the laws as support; and, adding these validations to the argument from conquest, stated: 'England established in this new form stands fully possessed [of authority] not only by right of war but also according to the right of nature and the ancient laws and customs of the nation'.[266] *Anglia Liberata*, however, was written in the aftermath of the engagement and in the context of mounting preparations for a Royalist invasion from Scotland. Though the author rejected Prince Charles as 'the young Pretender', and defended the death of his father, the threat of resurgent monarchy overshadows the claim for parliament.[267] Two years after the end of kingship, apologists for the Commonwealth were still confronting the menace of both a dead and a living king.

Indeed, even after victory over the Scots, much of the polemic in support of the Commonwealth still felt the need to engage with monarchy. The author of a tract, *Monarchy or No Monarchy*, the title of which betrayed the uncertainties that still stalked the republic, countered an old prophecy that suggested a restoration of kingship in 1663 and made it 'evident this prophecy, and all others, are against monarchy'.[268] Dedicated to 'the supreme authority of the three nations, the Parliament of the Commonwealth of England', the treatise *Monarchy No Creature of God's Making*, went back over old arguments concerning God's reluctance to give the Israelites a king and claimed divine approval for the rule of the people.[269] Clearly, Charles II's declarations and Scottish propaganda revived uncomfortable issues that parliament had been struggling to lay to rest.

But it was not only the person of the 'young Pretender' who threatened the stability of the government.[270] From 1651, Commonwealth propagandists felt it necessary to return to the figure of Charles I whose memory continued to galvanize support for the prince and the Royalists, even from some who had not fought for him in the civil war. Revealingly, the author of *Monarchy or No Monarchy* included a section of observations on the life and death of Charles I.[271] Here, as well as attacking him personally as a tyrant, the author went to some lengths to discredit the *Eikon Basilike*, claiming that 'it maintains so many contradictions ... that I conceive the most part of it apocrypha'.[272] With its huge sales and popular reach, the *Eikon* kept the figure of Charles I alive and so forced Commonwealth apologists to continue to repeat the case against him. The author of the *Non-Such Charles his Character* even reopened the charges levelled against the king in the Grand Remonstrance; and, cataloguing his failure to support the Palatine and alleged apostasy in Madrid, gave thanks for his execution which, it was asserted, Charles brought upon himself.[273] If the intention of this work was once more to rebury the king, it clearly failed of its purpose. Indeed, the author of a companion work, *The Life and Reign of King Charles or the Pseudo Martyr Discovered*, stated in his preface that the late Scottish threat had given frequent occasion to 'rake over his ashes'.[274] Once again, in this work the discrediting of Charles I involved an attack on the *Eikon*. For, the author recognized, 'by presenting this book with his picture praying in the frontispiece to purposefully catch ... the people', Royalists had succeeded in 'canonising him for a saint and idolising his memory for an innocent martyr'.[275] To explode that myth, the *Life* depicted a reign of blood and oppression and penned a narrative of idolatrous practices, arbitrary rule and duplicitous dealings. But the task, as its author confessed, was a hard one. Together with the *Eikon* the publication of the *Reliquiae Sacrae Carolinae* had 'much taken in the opinion of the vulgar', leading many, even after three years, to maintain that 'his innocency [was] not assaultable'.[276]

A sense that the government itself feared it was losing the contest for validity and legitimacy seems to be confirmed by proposals for a strict regulation of printing that prescribed draconian punishments for offenders.[277] Royalist propaganda had been relentless and evidently effective but the Commonwealth had also paid too little attention to the arts of explanation and presentation. As the author of *Rules of Civil Government* protested in 1653, 'I have of late heard much of a Commonwealth but know not what it meaneth'.[278] And, he added, unless all united behind it, the Commonwealth would be devoured by its enemies.[279] Enemies were indeed plotting the downfall of the regime; in the spring, siding with the army officers who had concluded that the parliament had failed, Cromwell, as we noted, evicted the MPs and called in an assembly of men nominated by the gathered churches to sit under the direction of a Council of State.

From the outset, the fate and image of the Barebones Assembly lay in the hands of Oliver Cromwell, who had called it into being. The assembly did not convene in the parliament houses but in the Council Chamber where, in a two-hour speech, Cromwell set the agenda of reform towards a new Jerusalem.[280] Subsequently, Barebones decided to meet in St Stephen's Chapel and, in other respects, to follow parliamentary traditions. Importantly, on 12 July, in a public declaration, it publicized itself as a parliament responsible for the 'supreme government of England, Scotland and Ireland'.[281] In a deliberate reach for support, the parliament promised to have tender care of the lives, estates and liberties of the people.[282] Reminding subjects of the great works God had effected, the MPs yet admitted that not enough had been done 'to satisfy the thoughts of men for that vast expense of blood and treasure'; and expressed their hopes that they might be the Lord's 'instruments' to bring about his ends.[283] In a declaration written in the language of godliness, the Barebones Parliament represented themselves as 'meek and humble spirits' dedicated to advancing the gospel and the good of God's people.[284] Having established its identity and authority, the new parliament, responsive to the criticisms that had brought down the Rump, then got down to work, meeting long hours, six days a week.[285] In addition to establishing commissions for the army and navy, the parliament appointed committees to look into issues 'already marked out by public opinion as being ripe for consideration'.[286] As well as Acts for the relief of debtors, prisoners and lunatics, Barebones entered into reform of the law and of the tithes that maintained the clergy.[287] What they did not do was continue to explain their actions or convey their plans to the people.

Not least as a consequence, those fearful of radical godly reform, or disdainful of the assembly from its inception, were able to circulate negative images of Barebones virtually unchallenged. As the most authoritative historian of the assembly has demonstrated, the MPs were (largely unfairly) ridiculed and represented as Cromwell's poodles.[288] If they thought that their acts might speak louder than words in countering these negative images, they were mistaken. Barebones never established its constitutional legitimacy, let alone its authority, in the eyes of either the political nation or the public. Not until after its dissolution did members of Barebones appeal for support; and by then it was too late.[289] Even more unpopular than the Rump, Barebones's dissolution was greeted with rejoicing and bonfires in London.[290] And the words that represented the government for the rest of the decade and resonated throughout history were not those of another parliament but of the man who again resurrected government by a single person – Oliver Cromwell.

CHAPTER 13

A REPUBLICAN BRAND?

I

From Henry VIII on, the visual representation of the monarch, on canvas or copperplate, on seals, medals and coins, was vital to the dissemination of the authority of the person of the ruler and often to the promotion of specific values or programmes of rule. Though, especially in Elizabeth's case, portrayals might be allegorical, the principal medium of representation was the portrait – of the ruler him- or herself or of the royal marriage or family. Figures of singular rule and of dynasty shaped visual representations of authority as much as those visual representations served to promote dynasty and regality. The execution of Charles I, then, and still more the abolition of monarchy, necessitated not only a new constitution and government but a different style and image, an entirely new form of visual representation and, beyond that, a new aesthetic. Where royal words and verbal forms, such as proclamations and declarations, might be – and, as we have seen, were – readily appropriated and recast as texts of republic, the visual images of authority, focusing as they had on the dynastic portrait, offered no obvious model for Commonwealth.

One of the Commonwealth's early acts was that passed on 4 July 1649 for the 'sale of the goods and personal estates of the late King, Queen and Prince'.[1] Though the main motive was undoubtedly financial – the Act referred to the 'considerable value' of the collection – it should also be placed in the context of Milton's *Eikonoklastes* and other efforts to smash the idol of monarchy, especially by the destruction of its images and icons.[2] Just as the Rump smashed the image of Charles I set up in the Exchange and replaced it with the words 'Exit tyrannus regum ultimus anno libertate Angliae restituo primo AD 1648 Jan 30', so the sale of the royal portraits, jewels, clothes and furniture was intended to assist in the erasing of monarchy from the state. But even the financial motive was presented in the ordinance in ideological terms. Pressing the distinction that Charles had fought so hard to resist between the office and person of monarchy, parliament declared that 'most of the goods . . . having been of old belonging to the crown and not to the persons of King, Queen or

Prince', now belonged 'to the Commonwealth' and so 'might justly be disposed of for public uses'.[3] That many of the canvases and artefacts were perceived to be 'popish' or 'superstitious' added further to the case for selling them – probably abroad.[4] Under the Act, designated commissioners were appointed to organize the sale of the goods, in line with the valuations assigned to them by the trustees, at the best price they could secure. The literal sale of the century began in October and actively continued over more than two years, with some items not disposed of until the end of the parliament's own life.[5] By the end of the sale, the riches of Charles's collection of paintings, especially, had been dispersed.

If part of the intention was to smash the symbols of Stuart majesty, the success of the sale was limited, and indeed compromised by the Act's own injunctions. In the first place, the Commonwealth regime reserved for itself royal residences, goods and artefacts – 'for the uses of the state' – and in consequence lived in the shadow of royalty at Whitehall, Somerset House, Hampton Court and Windsor Castle.[6] Secondly, many of the royal goods listed as sold were in fact passed to those to whom the government was in debt, in lieu of full monetary settlements. Since some of these were fairly ordinary soldiers, as well as army officers and gentlemen, the sale resulted in (in the late Francis Haskell's words) 'a large range of great artistic masterpieces [being] widely distributed among the ordinary citizens of England'.[7] And not only artistic masterpieces, but images and emblems of Stuart rule. Understandably, many of these reluctant recipients were to sell the goods on, but by no means all did; Colonel Hutchinson for one appears to have begun to collect.[8] Far from fracturing the iconicity or erasing the memory of monarchy, the sale dispersed both valuable goods and very personal possessions of the late king – bedclothes and chamber pots, as well as portraits – to members of the Council of State, to former royal servants and beyond to a large body of subjects who possessed them for a time or, in some cases, kept them.[9] It is one of the many ironies of 1649 that the sale and distribution of Charles's goods may have served to remystify (as well as demystify) monarchy and to make the deceased king, by means of artefacts, a very real presence in the homes and lives of many English men and women.

Interestingly, while engaged in inventorying, valuing and selling royal portraits (that is, we should recall, portraits *of* the royal family as well as those owned by them), parliament showed no interest in commissioning canvases of the Commonwealth to supplant the images of monarchy created by Hilliard and Van Somer, Mytens and, especially, Van Dyck. Though there was of course no English precedent, it was not that the idea of doing so never occurred to them. As we have seen, at some point, and more likely before 1651 than after, when tensions between the two countries mounted, several Dutch painters 'proposed to the Commonwealth a massive artistic tribute to the victors of the civil war'.[10] The scheme was to decorate the walls of the Banqueting House with a memorial, devised 'unto the people's view', representing 'all the memorable achievements since parliament's first sitting'.[11] The proposal to portray a narrative of conflict that went back to 1640 nicely chimed with parliament's desire to underscore continuity and with its own prose catalogues of the providences which had blessed its actions from the outset of the troubles. Moreover, the Dutch announced that a precedent image might be the memorial tapestries commissioned to celebrate the Armada victory, and so promised a connection between the Commonwealth and the great day of England's deliverance, annually commemorated on the nation's ritual calendar.[12] Parliament had, in 1644, moved those Armada tapestries from the Tower to the Palace of Westminster and they were among the goods 'reserved for the use of the state' in 1649.[13] Importantly, too, the Dutch artists Balthasar Gerbier, Peter Lely and George Geldorp offered to commemorate parliament by a genre of painting new to England. For, as well as portraits of commanders, they proposed murals of the major battles and sieges of the war, and so offered a mode of visual representation that did not depend upon a (regal) cult of personality. Indeed, the proposal specifically included, to be placed at the upper end of the Banqueting House, a 'representation of the whole assembly of the parliament by whose directions the said great achievements have been wrought'.[14]

If the proposal echoed parliament's verbal polemics, reprised the language of godly, providential rule, and offered a new mode of representation, it came with added attractions. The artists who proposed it had gone to some lengths to demonstrate their service and loyalty to the new English Commonwealth. Gerbier, who had served Charles I for two decades, offered to hand over to the new republic information he had gleaned as envoy to Brussels and had authored *The Non-Such Charles*, an attack on the character and memory of the late king.[15] Lely had painted the portraits of staunch Parliamentarians since 1647, as well as, under Northumberland's patronage, the royal children, and Cromwell was to sit for him more than once.[16] Evidently a Catholic, Geldorp nevertheless helped to broker the sales of Charles's goods for parliament.[17] Even more enticing to a cash-strapped government, the artists held out the prospect of the commemorative mural being self-financing. The plan was that each person represented, whether member of the Council of State, MP or army officer, pay for his own portrait and so spare the state the 'greatest part of the charges'.[18]

From all considerations, then, the artists' proposition appeared to present the new government with a golden opportunity to make its visual mark, and we are left wondering why it did not happen. An explanation based on Protestant iconophobia is tempting but too simplistic. The proposal was for something far removed from religious or superstitious images, which northern Dutch artists disdained as much as did English puritans; in fact, it offered a counter to the monuments to kings and princes which were officially spared from the iconoclasm initiated by the parliamentary ordinance of 1643. Maija Jansson's suggestion that, after the recent devastation of civil war, 'England was not ready for images of battle scenes' does not fully convince when we recall the detailed accounts of bloody engagements, atrocities and casualties regularly printed, with official approval, throughout the 1640s, or the medals that commemorated victories.[19] More persuasively, she also posits that in 1645 the Commonwealthsmen were not only 'unsure of how to lead the country from monarchy to republicanism', but uncertain, in a still divided country, whether a triumphant image of victory over fellow Englishmen was appropriate.[20]

Whatever the reason, the republic's failure to pursue the Dutch artists' proposal or to take some other course to mark visually the birth of a new republic was more than a missed opportunity: it was a failure to represent the new regime to the people's view, at least in the medium of paint. As the portraits of Charles I, his family and his royal predecessors were distributed around the country, and as members of the Commonwealth Council and parliament met in (former) royal palaces, not least in a Banqueting House still decorated with Rubens's apotheosis of James I, no contrary image of God's deliverance of the nation from monarchical tyranny was displayed to counter countless images of divine Stuart kingship. In some ways, the story of the failed Dutch proposal – part of a wider story of failure to represent the new regime – was the story of the failure of the English Commonwealth.[21]

II

Even more surprising and probably more damaging was the Commonwealth's decision not to make systematic use of engraved or woodcut images to represent its new authority or to promote its policies. Given the long history of these images, either as free-standing engravings, as broadsheets or as illustrations to books, the recent growth in the commercial consumption of engravings exemplified by Peter Stent's London print shop, and the use of such images by both sides in the civil war, the republic's failure to deploy visuals in cheap print seems almost unbelievable. Yet a survey of major print collections and of all the illustrations in Thomason tracts for 1649–53 yields little or nothing that could confidently be described as a positive representation of the Commonwealth.[22] By contrast, even a perusal of collections of engravings or illustrations to books reveals scores, if not hundreds, of images of Charles I, Charles II and Royalist supporters and sympathizers. The first Commonwealth illustration that I have found is the title page to John Parker's *The Government of the People of England*, published in March 1650.[23] In a block beneath the title, two hands join above the motto 'Ut uniamur' and a tied bundle of arrows. Around, lie single, broken arrows. The image, based on a popular emblem, is explained by the tag 'Vis unita fortior' – a united body is stronger; and the message to the subjects of the fledgling new republic is clear: by unity, small things grow to

76 *The Governement of the People of England Precedent and Present the Same,* 1650.

strength. *The Government of the People* opens by asserting that 'the subscription now made or required is just and lawful', and calls for all to act for the public good.[24]

I have found no similar representations of the Commonwealth after 1650. The *Articles of Agreement* for the surrender of Edinburgh Castle vaunted the godliness of the Commonwealth cause by displaying on the title page at the entrance to a castle the words of Psalm 118, verse 20: 'This is the gate of the Lord, the righteous shall enter into it.'[25] The victories over the Scots were also commemorated not only by a list of those killed and taken prisoner, but also by a negative image of monarchy. On one broadsheet, a crowned skeleton, holding in its right hand a sword, displays with its left a tablet inscribed 'The woeful mirror of monarchy'.[26] If this negative image was intended to publicize the final death of the monarchy, it remains surprising that no more positive image proclaimed the vigorous life of the republic. The 1651 *Narration of the Most Material Parliamentary Proceedings of this Present Parliament* illustrated the course of key events with woodcuts from the Scottish Prayer Book rebellion, to the Scots invasion of 1648 and the Act of Indemnity of 1651.[27] But there is no evidence to suggest that this narrative had any official origin or approval, and an illustration of Charles II (so titled) being crowned is included along with the texts of parliamentary declarations.[28] Interestingly, for the

Whilst on this Figure,
thou shalt fixe thine Eye,
Learne thence two Lessons
Howe to live, to Dye

THE
WOEFVLL
MIRROVR
of
MONARCHY

77 'The Woefull Mirrour of Monarchy', engraving from *A List of the Princes, Dukes, Earls,
. . . of the Scots Kings Party Slaine and Taken Prisoners*, 1652.

Barebones assembly, we find an image of the type that one might have
expected to find for 1649. In July or early August (Thomason's copy reached
him in the first of these months) Peter Stent printed and sold, whether with
official encouragement or not we do not know, a broadsheet of *The Maner of
the Sitting of the Parliament of the Commonwealth of England*.[29] Above a list
of the names of the Council of State, the 'Parliament men' and members of
various committees (for Ireland, the law, for the poor and prisoners, for
example) an engraved image represented an orderly assembly of men (not officially MPs) seated with hats and cloaks, with, beneath the arms of the state, a
Speaker presiding, two clerks and a mace bearer. It hardly needs pointing out
that this visual representation of Barebones *as a parliament*, as well as the use
of the term, underpinned the actions and claims of what was a nominated
assembly; rather than representing the regime, it may have been critical of a
Cromwell and army which had not given the assembly the full title of a parliament. Continuity and order, legitimacy and authority, are here displayed, and,
in the act of being displayed, enhanced. And the crowded chamber with only
the Speaker, the servant of the Commons, singled out effaced any authority
other than that of the equal MPs whose names are significantly positioned
above those of the Council of State.

78 *The Maner of Siting of the Parlament of the Commonwealth of England*, 1653.

Rather than promulgating similar images immediately in 1649, the Commonwealth more often gave place to portraits of its great commanders and especially of Oliver Cromwell. As we saw, engravings of army generals were popular in the 1640s and Stent kept a stock of Parliamentarian (as of Royalist) commanders in his print shop.[30] While by no means all carry a date, we can reasonably assign several portraits of figures such as Fleetwood, Desborough, Ireton and Hugh Peter to the early 1650s; and an image of Ireton's effigy and tomb illustrates an elegy on Ireton, Cromwell's son-in-law, who died in 1651.[31] It was, however, Cromwell whose portrait, in various forms, proliferated during the short life of the Commonwealth. Once again, not all of the scores of portraits can be dated. But we know that, following the canvases of Cromwell executed by Robert Walker and Samuel Cooper in 1649, numerous engravings and etchings were issued promptly.[32] More particularly, Cromwell's portrait images adorned a series of popular broadsides announcing triumphs and victories of parliament's forces. *A Perfect Table of One Hundred and Forty Five Victories Obtained by the Lord Lieutenant of Ireland* (1651) figures, in the midst of a list, Cromwell, mounted on a rearing horse, armoured, with a scarf flying behind and with a baton of command in his right hand.[33] The swirling clouds and battle scene behind, not to mention the echoes of images of Gustavus Adolphus, make this the portrait of a warrior and, as I shall argue, of a prince.[34] The *Perfect List of All the Victories Obtained by the Lord General Cromwell*, published the same year, displays Cromwell, after Walker, three-quarter-length in armour, with a baton, and behind him a page tying a fine silk sash.[35] Here the image of the gentleman as well as soldier, evocative of Van Dyck (especially his portrait of Strafford as Lord Deputy of Ireland), along with the crest of Cromwell's arms, suggests a presence and role beyond that of a mere military commander.[36] The impression of a shift in Cromwell's image is confirmed by the reference to him as 'His Excellency' in the title to the sheet.[37] Finally, the next year, an engraving after the same Walker portrait formed a frontispiece to Payne Fisher's English panegyric, *Veni, Vidi, Vici: The Triumphs of the Most Excellent and Illustrious Oliver Cromwell*.[38] In this

79 Engraving of Cromwell, *A Perfect Table of the One Hundred Forty and Five Victories Obtained by the Lord Lieutenant of Ireland*, 1650.

80 Engraving of Cromwell, frontispiece to *Veni; Vidi; Vici*, Payne Fisher, 1652.

version, a sea battle scene in the right background perhaps points to the recent conflict with the Dutch and, beside Cromwell, the inscription (in Latin) reads: 'What age has produced a man of such counsel or military brilliance?' In a Latin version of the panegyric, the image of Cromwell on a rearing horse with the words 'With Christ his leader and under his religious authority' points up Cromwell as the instrument of Providence.[39] In such images, whatever the text's references to his being born for the public, it is Oliver rather than the parliament who is the face of godly republic.

As we shall see, Cromwell once advised parliament against the use of his, rather than its, image in a representation of victory.[40] His famous request to be painted 'warts and all' is often quoted to support a portrait of modest self-effacement; and recently Laura Knoppers has argued that images of Cromwell were quite different to Royalist portraits, even when they aped them, and broadcast a new, plain style, indeed a republican mode of representation.[41] While I would contest or qualify such arguments, this is not the point here.[42] For, even if we allow that the aesthetic was not Royalist, the fact remains that the most prominent image of the republic during the early 1650s was not that of the parliament or of a people made stronger by a union of equals, but that of a military commander. If the continued emphasis on the military (and national divisions and high taxes that went with it) were itself not unfortunate enough, the developing personal elevation of Cromwell suggested the failure of the republic to free itself – as verbal propaganda had boasted it would – of the cult of a single person. Those Royalists and other critics who from early on began to satirize Cromwell as a man ambitious for the crown might easily have gained credence from such visual representations of 'his excellency'; and it seems likely that, as much as they reflected the special position he held in the eyes of army and parliament, these images of Cromwell served also to propel him to authority – to political as well as military dominance.[43] It may be yet another irony of the revolution that unwittingly the Commonwealth helped to create the figure who destroyed it and seized its authority for an entirely new mode of single-person rule. If so, the republic, in not devising and publishing visual images of the new republican polity, bears much of the blame.

The Commonwealth may not have authorized or encouraged official paintings or engravings but a case has been made recently that it by no means lacked 'an iconic aspect'. In Sean Kelsey's words, 'a variety of signs and symbols were invented and deployed by the Rump to replace the outmoded artefacts and images of regality', among which he singles out the seals and maces and the arms of the Commonwealth.[44] Along with the destruction of statues of Charles I, the Rump moved quite quickly to remove the royal arms from public sites, starting with that over the Speaker's chair.[45] By August, legislation was prepared for removing royal arms from 'all public places', including London churches where they would have been displayed since the Reformation.[46] Though the need for subsequent instructions in December 1650 and February 1651 suggests that progress in removing royal insignia was not swift, the Council of State and parliament grasped the importance of new positive heraldic representations as well as the removal of the old. A new Commonwealth arms, with the escutcheons of England and Ireland, was devised and ordered to be displayed on state coaches and barges, ships' flags and the plate used at state banquets, as well as in the courts of Westminster and other public buildings.[47] Surprisingly, they were not set up in the Parliament House for over two years, yet the Commonwealth's arms were adopted not only in the metropolis but by a number of provincial corporations either sympathetic to the new regime or anxious to ingratiate themselves with it.[48]

On the day of the passing of the Act for Abolishing the Kingly Office (17 March 1649), the Commons appointed a committee to design a new mace and replace a potent symbol of regal authority with one that bore the new arms of the Commonwealth.[49] On the new mace the old coronet, orb and cross (which may have disturbed puritans as well as republicans) and the Stuart floral emblems were replaced with oak leaves and an acorn, symbols of Englishness and of rebirth.[50] Further maces, based on the same pattern, were ordered for the Council of State and for use in Ireland, and the design, with variant details, became the basis for new maces for civic authorities across

England.[51] Through such symbols the Commonwealth gestured towards representing a new style as well as form of government.

Most important was the provision of a new Great Seal. As we saw, Charles's ordering of the Great Seal to York had threatened to prevent parliament functioning as an executive in London and eventually the Commons ordered Thomas Simon to devise a new one.[52] In 1643, however, not least to underpin their claim that they fought loyally for the king not against him, parliament's seal was identical to the royal seal and carried Charles's portrait and arms. After regicide, it was recognized that an entirely new design was necessary and a committee ordered Thomas Simon to make one with, on the reverse, the arms of England and Ireland (and the Channel Islands) and, on the obverse, importantly, a depiction of the Commons in session, inside a motto 'In the first year of freedom by God's blessing restored 1648'.[53] It has been suggested that the speed with which parliament moved to commission this may have led to less than good workmanship, which caused the seal to wear out, and in 1651 the Rump ordered a replacement, surviving images of which, with the motto 'In the third year of freedom . . .' are far more common.[54] The seal constituted a vital representation of the new regime that drew attention back to its absence in other visual media. We should be in no doubt that the Commonwealth seal was propaganda for the new regime. For the representation of Ireland as a territory of the Commonwealth expressed more of hope than the reality of a land yet to be conquered. And the crowded Commons depicted on the reverse was more an image of legitimate parliamentary rule than an accurate reflection of the diminished numbers attending an aptly named Rump reduced by civil war, Pride's Purge and regicide. The seal was designed, it would seem, to claim patriotism and continuity while at the same time symbolically removing the

81 Great Seal of England, 1651.

single person whose image had dominated the reverse and replacing it with an image of a collective authority, a representative of the people.

The recent study of republican icons has surprisingly little to say about medals which, as we have seen, had the potential to distribute official images and messages widely. Their importance for the new Commonwealth in 1649 can hardly be overstated. For almost immediately following the regicide, memorial medals commemorating Charles I and Henrietta Maria were struck abroad and in England in gold, silver and – we note – in lead (cheap enough for broad distribution), along with huge numbers of badges and ornaments for book covers, tobacco boxes and counters.[55] Not only were those royal medals embarrassing portrayals of the martyr king; they powerfully denounced the new republic using familiar visual symbols and forms. The seven-headed monster, for example, had been a familiar symbol of rebellion, but in 1649 was used to figure a monstrous mob trampling on a divine sovereign.[56] Other 1649 medals, with a phoenix rising from the ashes, appropriated the favourite emblem of the popular Queen Elizabeth to proclaim Charles II, while Charles's own 1649 succession medal, showing a young tree growing from a stump, bore inscriptions announcing his succession and determination to uphold his royal position and prerogative.[57]

Vital though it was to counter these popular Royalist images, once again the response of the Commonwealth was faltering and inadequate. The only official medal cast by Thomas Simon in 1649 was one of Henry Scobell who was Clerk of the Parliament; and, if that were intended to advertise the authority of the new government, it were overshadowed by the only other two medals of 1649: those issued by John Lilburne to embarrass the regime by celebrating his acquittal that year from a charge of high treason for libelling Cromwell and

82 Medal depicting Medusa, a symbol of rebellion, on reverse, 1649.

Ireton.[58] If a kind of medallic competition for popular support characterized the early years of the republic, it appears that the Commonwealth was worsted and, moreover, uncertain of its own strategy. Where, for example, Royalist supporters of Montrose, who had championed Charles II in Scotland in 1649, issued a medal marking his execution as the death of a true patriot, a medal prototype cast by Thomas Simon for Henry Ireton seems to apologize for his cruelty and bloodshed in Ireland and was evidently not struck.[59] The official medals struck in 1650 represented Oliver Cromwell in armour, probably at the time of his appointment on 26 June as successor to Fairfax as Captain-General and commander-in-chief, and these were promptly answered by satirical medals representing Cromwell as a Machiavellian devil.[60]

The first Commonwealth medals to depart from the Royalist-type representation of a single person were not cast until the summer of 1650. The so-called 'naval reward' medals, commemorating an English fight in July against six Irish frigates, were awarded to the captain and crew and to 'several other mariners who had done good service'.[61] Both these figure on the obverse, with an anchor, the new republican arms of England and Ireland, the George Cross and harp and one (rather like the seal) depicts a busy Commons in session.

83 Cromwell medals, official and satirical.

Given their purpose as both reward and military decoration, the circulation was not likely to have been large. More widely distributed, and struck in copper and lead as well as gold and silver, were the medals parliament ordered to be issued to mark the victory of its forces over the Scots at Dunbar on 3 September.[62] Like the naval rewards, these feature, on the reverse, a crowded House of Commons. This design was suggested, or at least approved, by Cromwell himself.[63] For the obverse, the parliament, to express their 'special thanks' to him, determined on a new bust of Cromwell and ordered Thomas Simon to travel from London to Edinburgh to execute it.[64] Cromwell wrote to express his disapproval. Questioning the wisdom of sending Simon on so long a journey, he suggested that, rather than his image, 'I think the most noble end, to wit the commemoration of that great mercy at Dunbar, and the gratuity to the army . . . might better be expressed upon the medal by engraving as on the one side the parliament which I hear was intended . . . so on the other side an army with this inscription over the head of it, The Lord of Hosts, which was our word that day.'[65] While such a design was one he left to parliament to 'alter . . . as you see cause', Cromwell repeated his request, even begged it as a favour, that they 'spare the having my effigies in it'.[66] Those cynical about Cromwell's protestations may suspect that in this act of modesty, as in other gestures of self-effacement, the Lord-General protested too much. We should not leap to that conclusion, however, before considering what may have been honest advice given by a man with a shrewd understanding of the symbols of power. For in suggesting representation of the parliament and the army, Cromwell was outlining both a vision of partnership to offset the fears of those who felt the army ruled, and *two* images of collective endeavour befitting the

84 Cromwell Lord of Hosts medal.

Commonwealth. Parliament rejected his advice. A bust of the Lord-General in armour with a falling collar and scarf, and his title with a battle in the background, formed the obverse: above him the inscription 'The word at Dunbar the Lord of Hosts' literally followed the letter of his suggestion, but now read as the sign of Cromwell's singular providential victory rather than that of an army or parliament.[67]

The dawn of 1651 saw the republic left behind in the deployment of medals as propaganda. The death of William II of Orange, son-in-law to Charles I, in November 1650 was commemorated by a portrait medal, presumably authorized by Orange supporters, depicting William and his widow, Mary.[68] On the obverse, William prominently wears the George, the badge of the Garter to which Charles had elected him in 1645 and a symbol of royalty, while the reverse of a Mary who was then pregnant with the future William III advertised Stuart as well as Orange dynastic succession. Worse for the republic, in January Charles II was crowned in Scotland and a medal was struck to mark the event.[69] Though it was said the ceremony was without much state, the medal was an effective piece of propaganda. On the obverse, Charles appears crowned and wearing his Garter collar, inside a legend presenting him as 'By the grace of God king of Scotland, England, France and Ireland'. Here, that is, monarchy stands as truly more imperial and unifying than the fractured British kingdoms over only a part of which the Commonwealth claimed sovereignty. Interestingly, too, Charles's bust faces right, in the reverse direction to Cromwell's on the Dunbar medal – perhaps as a deliberate gesture of contrast. On the reverse, a lion rampant, the royal beast, holds a thistle of Scotland in its paw. Around the edge a defiant legend reads 'Nemo me impune lacesset' – no one shall provoke me with impunity, or without repercussions. Charles II was laying down a symbolical gauntlet and a defiant challenge to which the government responded with force. After invading Scotland, parliamentary forces defeated Royalist troops from both kingdoms at Worcester in September 1651 and narrowly missed capturing Charles himself, who was forced to hide in an oak tree, disguise himself as a servant, and finally escape to France.[70] What appeared a decisive victory surely demanded, and presented the republic with a perfect opportunity for, triumphant public celebration. If so, at least where medals are concerned, parliament did not take it. Ironically, however, Charles II did. Shortly after Worcester, royal supporters issued and evidently intended (since it was cast in lead) for wide distribution a medal commemorating the king's escape.[71] On the obverse, Charles on horseback is attended by those who assisted his escape, three of whom are commended to God's blessing in the inscription for service to their divine sovereign. On the reverse, between the initials C R – a reminder that Charles was king, whatsoever the event of one battle – a sword and olive branch are crossed and the legend reads 'In utrumque paratus' – prepared for both, that is for peace or war. Charles's cause had received a major setback; but on medals, at least, he strove to pull defiance, if not victory, from the jaws of defeat. Publicizing himself as king, and a lover of peace as much as war, Charles also reassured followers that the military was not the only means of effecting his restoration. The Rump, by contrast, in not authorizing any medal, foolishly surrendered the claim to providential protection to the king whose miraculous escape became the stuff of story and legend, images and artefacts, memories and popular fictions.

During its short life, the Barebones assembly appears to have commissioned medals only as rewards for naval victories over the Dutch in June and July 1653. While the distribution of these was probably confined to the officers who served in the fleet (they became known as 'Blake medals' after the admiral), they did at last advertise parliament's victory at home as well as at sea.[72] For, on the obverse, the medals depicted – along with the St George Cross and harp of Erin – the St Andrew's Cross of a Scotland now incorporated, after defeat, as part of the Commonwealth.[73] Prophetically, however, the sinking ship on the reverse became symbolic not of the republic's victory at sea but of its own capsizal and with it, significantly, the shift to a Protectorate that paid far more attention to its image on medals.

During the civil war both Royalist and Parliamentarian coins were freely used as propaganda and counter-propaganda that was presumably effective in reaching a wide audience. Undoubtedly, those who formed the new republican government had not forgotten the importance of this medium, nor the use enemies had made, and might again make, of it. As the author of *The Life and Reign of King Charles* recalled in 1652, Charles I, to deceive the people, had designed 'silly devices and quaint impresses [for] his money coined at Oxford pretending that he took up arms in defence of the Protestant religion, the laws and liberties of the people, and the privileges of parliament, when the direct contrary appeared by all his actions'.[74] Accordingly, the Commonwealth took early measures to assert its authority to coin money, one of the essential prerogatives of monarchy, to 'change and alter the former stamps, arms, pictures, with the mottos, words, styles and inscriptions . . . and to cause new coins of gold and silver to be made'.[75] With unusual attention to specific detail, parliament ordered a 20s. piece, with (on one side) a cross, palm and laurel and for the first time the inscription 'The Commonwealth of England', and (on the other) the George Cross and harp of Erin, with the legend, 'God with us'.[76] The same design was appointed for 10s. and 5s. pieces and also for coins of lower denomination, 12d. and 6d. Those of tuppence and a penny bore the same images without the inscriptions, only the halfpenny differing slightly. Other than these, we find milled pattern pieces by Peter Blondeau, with on the obverse, in place of 'God with us', the inscription 'Guarded with angels' and a half-crown bearing the legend 'Truth and Peace'; but it seems that these were not in circulation.[77] Not only did the Commonwealth prescribe an unusually consistent image across all the denominations of its currency, it required that these moneys 'be used and received by all the people of this nation, in all receipts and payments and in all manner of trafficking'.[78]

Most regimes in early modern England lived several years with the predominantly circulating coin that bore the image of their predecessor. In that the Commonwealth was no exception: as Sean Kelsey observed, 'it is ironic that most of the huge sums paid to the regime in taxation . . . bore the dead king's stamp' and it is likely that, given its short life, the new Commonwealth currency never outfaced royal coins.[79] Yet, if the success here did not equal the intention, parliament's care should not pass unremarked. The design for the coin was not only new in including an English inscription but the legend 'The Commonwealth of England' is one of the few instances of the promulgation of the new brand in a visual (and popular) medium. The representation of the St George Cross with a palm and laurel also suggests victory, godliness, honour and achievement as the attributes of the nation and republic; the choice of the palm may even have been intended to contest Marshall's frontispiece to the *Eikon* and its deployment of this Christic symbol for Charles I. Certainly, as well as removing the king's image, the inscription on the reverse – 'God with us' – claimed divine approval for the new polity that was not only a republic but a godly Commonwealth. It may be significant that 'during the whole of the Protectorates of Oliver and Richard Cromwell . . . the Mint continued to coin and issue money with the Commonwealth's type'.[80] Though the quality of the coins was not of the best (it is believed that they are not Thomas Simon's), Cromwell retained the pattern right up to the 1657 issue.[81] That this astute master of the politics of symbols continued to authorize them may support an impression that, with coin at least, the republic got its image right.

Most new rulers in early modern England endeavoured to mark their dynasty and reign by some notable architectural statement. Henry VIII had built, 'acquired', and transformed residences into grand palaces; and, though his successors often lacked the means to build on the grand scale, the Stuarts had the grandest designs for a new classical monument to dynastic kingship, of which the Banqueting House was the most magnificent to be realized.[82] How then did the new republic deal with these representations of divine right kingship in stone? During the civil war, it had been necessary, given the expectation or at least the rhetoric of the king's return, to preserve royal palaces, houses and lodges more or less as Charles I had left them. In 1649, perhaps for financial and symbolic reasons, many were sold off under the Act of 16 July.[83] However, the Commonwealth retained Whitehall, St James's Palace, Somerset House, Hampton Court and Greenwich, along with the Tower of London and Windsor Castle – the primary sites and stages of regal display.

In 1650 and 1651, as we have noted, the Surveyor Edward Carter was ordered to remove the king's arms and all other representations of him throughout Whitehall – no small task. Other changes to accommodate puritan sensibilities included the conversion of the queen's chapel at St James's into a library; while pragmatism dictated the preparing of quarters for soldiers at the palaces.[84] Instructions to Carter to keep the Mortlake tapestry factory going may evidence not only the desire for its profits but a possible future commission from parliament; if so, it was not undertaken.[85] In the main, however, the new government continued to use Whitehall, albeit, in Simon Thurley's words, 'as a vast complex of parliamentary offices' rather than as a symbol of authority.[86] That said, any entering the palace in the 1650s would have seen the Queen's Presence Chamber turned into the chamber of the Council of State, the Committee of Trade sitting in the old royal Council Room, and most other state rooms occupied by committees and Council members. In that sense, the change of regime was obvious and pragmatic. Apart from using it for business, however, the republic made no use of Whitehall to mark the change of regime or to represent the new government. In 1651, a visitor wrote of the Banqueting House which had been the showcase of Stuart majesty: 'there was nothing in the world [there] now except three long dead tables'.[87] Evidently, parliament had planned after 'the final victory' a celebratory meal that did not take place. In 1649 the financial hardship, the tense situation, the uncertain loyalty of the people, perhaps a sense that it might not be appropriate, may have made the Commonwealth understandably reluctant to embark on any grand buildings, refurbishments or decorative schemes which, as well as costly, might have smacked of triumphalism.[88] But, as with their rejection of the mural, parliament's inaction served to undermine the regime in several ways. As they stood, Whitehall and St James's, Hampton Court and Windsor remained in appearance and memory royal palaces, making their new residents appear (temporary?) usurpers: not godly men who had waged a noble struggle for freedom but ambitious parvenus who had sought only spoils. Secondly, with no concrete or visible changes effected, Whitehall, Greenwich and the other residences remained palaces fit for a king – almost waiting for another king to grace them with his presence. On his return from the Irish campaigns in 1650, parliament granted Cromwell and his family rooms on the park side of Whitehall Palace. Three years later, along with a number of other royal houses, Whitehall was vested in him 'for the maintenance of his . . . state and dignity'.[89] The Protector, as he became, lost no time in fitting out Whitehall to advertise his dignity. One cannot help but wonder whether, had the Commonwealth either destroyed or refashioned royal palaces, the history of its own 'state' – in both senses – might have been different.[90]

CHAPTER 14

STAGING REPUBLIC

I

Throughout the early modern period, public spectacles had presented and represented to the people new rulers, their spouses and their offspring. More than words, ritual performances – state entries, coronation processions, funerals and the like – involved subjects in the process of representing and legitimizing the sovereign.[1] The mere presence of the audience signified acquiescence and allegiance; and the shouts of welcome or 'God save the King' echoed to the monarch and back to the spectators the accord between ruler and ruled that it was the purpose of ritual and ceremony to cement – and to represent. Public display and a public audience expressed authority, but they also endowed it.[2] As we have seen, during the civil war, Charles I, even in straitened circumstances, attracted a following as he was moved between prisons.[3] Because regality had long been inseparable from public spectacle, the reverse was also true. Large public occasions were regal occasions and the new Commonwealth faced a major challenge to devise new forms of state ceremony that might rupture the connection between monarchy and display and reconstitute ceremonies as ritual validations of republican rule. Until recently the consensus has been that, far from rising to that challenge, the Commonwealth government paid little attention to rituals; indeed, some contemporaries argued that 'all costly pomp and state [should] hereafter be suspended until the desolations and spoils of the poor people be repaired'.[4] Other voices, however, recognized, even if reluctantly, the politics of ceremonial and the need to refigure ritual forms. In *The Case of the Commonwealth*, the astute Marchamont Nedham lamented that 'our former education under a monarchy' had 'rendered [the people] admirers of the pomp of tyranny' and thus 'enemies to that freedom which hath been so dearly purchased'.[5] Henry Parker similarly expressed regret that 'the temper of this nation [was] apt to be pleased with anything that is stately and costly, though never so dangerous and miserable'.[6]

Recently it has been argued that the Commonwealth, acting on such perceptions, devised a 'number of set piece spectacles, including banquets, state funerals and the public celebration of Cromwell's victories', along with regular military parades or military reviews, to stage and dignify the new regime.[7] One of the urgent priorities for the new government in 1649 was attaining the recognition of other sovereign states (no easy task as the heads of many were related to the Stuarts) and, as was recognized, successful diplomacy required careful attention to protocol. In this regard, the Council of State was fortunate in that Charles I's Master of Ceremonies, Sir Oliver Fleming, was Cromwell's cousin and proved as willing to advise the Commonwealth as he had parliament in the 1640s. As well as contributing his knowledge of royal receptions, Fleming reviewed the diplomatic protocol of Venice and Switzerland, presumably to help fashion a new identity through ritual forms.[8] He urged the provision of barges and coaches with the Commonwealth arms and liveried attendants to receive envoys, and advised on seating arrangements, access, and in general the politics of space and place. Whilst it would seem that Fleming gestured towards a different ritual style, his long experience under monarchy still shaped his thinking and it is revealing that he requested that items from the royal wardrobe be reserved for Commonwealth ceremonials.[9] Such a request may have been pragmatic in the tight financial circumstances, but, as often with the new regime, one is left with a sense of its failure to escape from regal forms.

For the first two years of its life, the English Commonwealth was not recognized by any foreign powers sending an ambassador to establish diplomatic relations. By the time the first envoy was sent, both the occasion and the experience the government had gained in representing itself ensured a fittingly ceremonious reception. When, therefore, Don Alonso de Cardenas, ambassador from Philip IV of Spain, made his entry to parliament in December 1650, he was collected from Sir Abraham Williams's house in Westminster and conveyed to the Parliament House in a state coach, with 'thirty or forty' other coaches attending.[10] With a guard of horse 'in complete arms', displaying the republic's military strength, Cardenas was escorted to the Court of Wards whence the Sergeant of Arms with the mace conducted him to the house.[11] Uncovering himself at the bar of the house, Cardenas 'performed the usual ceremony and compliment', though now to a republican and unicameral parliament, and was seated in a chair 'on a rich carpet' with a cushion and footstool as he presented his letters of credential.[12] Their address 'Parlamento Republica Anglia' (sic) was revolutionary but, as the reference to 'the usual ceremony' implies, much else was – and was perceived as – familiar.[13] The next year Dutch and Swedish envoys were entertained with similar ceremony. As they landed at Gravesend, Fleming went with a flotilla of barges to meet them and conduct them to the Tower.[14] Thence, the Master of Ceremonies 'accompanied them through the city to Sir Abraham Williams his house in the Old Palace Yard where they were in great honour and triumph entertained'.[15] One newspaper reports that the Dutch ambassadors were 'received in very great honour' and that at their audience, 'the Parliament House was beautified with extraordinary rich hangings and very rich chairs and footcloths'.[16] Ceremonial splendour appears to have reached its height with the reception of the Portuguese ambassador Menezes in September 1652. *A Perfect Diurnall* reported his arrival at the Tower 'where he was met by the Master of Ceremonies, with about 40 or 50 of the States and other coaches' and his conduct through the city 'in great state', though it was 'the ambassador and his retinue very gallant' that made the greatest impression.[17] Perhaps because Menezes and his entourage 'went in greater state than any ambassador that came yet to Parliament' and 'his deportment . . . was honourable and magnificent', the Venetian envoy considered this the first full state entry made to, and observed by, the Commonwealth.[18] In other words, though, as Kelsey rightly argued, the republic did not neglect the rituals of audience, seasoned observers with experience of such occasions evidently considered that most of the receptions did not equal those they had witnessed under monarchy.

Perhaps more importantly, such spectacles did not receive, even in official organs of news, the press coverage that communicated them beyond the citizens who watched in the capital to readers in the suburbs and provinces. As the snippets we have quoted illustrate, reports offered few details of the magnificence often lavishly conveyed in accounts of Tudor festivals of state and the *Weekly Intelligencer* for one believed that 'that which wise men do look upon was not the show but the business of his [the Portuguese] embassy'.[19] Though reports mention carriages and military escorts, there are few references to the crowds. We are left with the impression that, where ambassadorial receptions were concerned, the Commonwealth was more interested in making an impression on foreign than on domestic audiences. Kelsey's suggestion that 'the formulaic manner' in which reporters described state audiences may be explained by external events and campaigns in Scotland, or in the Downs, confirms this, but also misses the point.[20] For the allegiance of the people at home was as important as external recognition and, in securing that support, ritual – and the representation of ritual – had a central part to play.

Interestingly, more publicity was given to the reception of the Commonwealth's embassy to the United Provinces in the spring of 1651. Given the importance of Dutch support, and the recent blow to its honour inflicted by the murder of Isaac Dorislaus, the Commonwealth recognized the need to present itself as a powerful and legitimate government. Large sums of money were advanced to equip the ambassadors who sailed with their own state coach and evidently all the trappings needed to make an impression.[21] Coaches gathered at The Hague to see the procession and the States of Holland were caught by surprise, the English retinue being far too large for the accommodation usually provided. News of the grandeur and reception of the English mission was well reported. Nedham gave space in more than one issue (numbers 43 and 45) of *Mercurius Politicus* to the embassy and concluded from the civil and gallant entertainment the envoys received that it would be a success.[22] A pamphlet titled *Joyful News from Holland* published a further narrative of the reception, especially of the three days of feasting and the magnificence of the English ambassadors 'whose habit glittered like the glorious sun', amazing the Dutch.[23] Clearly the author sought to convey to English readers that the republic was well respected abroad. But, like *Mercurius*, *Joyful News* acknowledged the opposition in Holland from Cavaliers who called out 'traitors, rebels' as the state coach passed and spat in the faces of the retinue.[24] Royalist opposition to the republic, abroad as well as at home, was undermining the republic's representation of itself. Its struggle to find its own legitimate image is nowhere better seen than in the language used by the author of *Joyful News* about 'the royal entertainment' the envoys had received.[25] In the English imagination, ceremony and ritual were royal and that association never quite went away.

At home, the Commonwealth introduced a different form of public display in a series of launches of ships and military musters. Charles I, as we have seen, made the launch of *The Sovereign of the Seas* an occasion of celebration and it may be that this was the precedent and model for the republic's feasts at the launching of ships, though now with the very non-regal names of *Speaker* and *President*.[26] As well as ship launches, military parades, with the soldiers of the New Model Army in their distinctive red uniforms, certainly represented the power of the new regime. Shortly after Dunbar, troops of 8,000 men marched from the city to Hyde Park to give the salute to parliament. Other parades were staged as part of Cromwell's triumphal entries into Bristol and London after victories in Ireland and at Worcester, the last occasion mimicking a royal entry as the city corporation rode to meet the Lord General and led him in a procession witnessed by thousands of citizens.[27] Those parades should not be discounted and were important displays of brute strength; they may have instilled – and may have been intended to instil in potential opponents – awe and fear. Given, however, the unpopularity of the army, one questions how far they served to endow the republic with the cultural authority it was the purpose of such ceremonies to impart as well as express, let alone fostered the love that most still advocated over fear as the basis of legitimate and good government. Even after a robust attempt to document their efforts, Sean Kelsey concluded that 'although intended to re-affirm unity in times of both crisis and celebration, the spectacles orchestrated by the Commonwealth regime did not . . . always work', not least because they did not allow sufficient place for public participation in celebrations of the republic's achievements.[28] That the most magnificent *and* popular occasions were Oliver Cromwell's triumphal entries may also throw light on the problem. Ceremony and spectacle were inextricably connected with the cult of a single person; and, though many (including, if his protestations were honest, Cromwell himself) felt uncomfortable about his elevation above his peers, it was not clear how otherwise the Commonwealth could naturally be presented. If a customary association between ceremony and a single head of state compromised republican representations, that was only one of the ways in which custom ultimately destroyed the Commonwealth.

II

The various forms of discourse, visual display and ritual represented early modern governments to their subjects and citizens, but their daily business, their conduct of affairs, their supervision of justice and law, their protection of the church and faith were all crucial to their image. Action and policy were (and are) not identical with representation but the public image of a regime depended, of course, on what it did, or was seen to do, as well as how it publicized itself. We have seen not only how the courts of monarchs were the outward face of their rule, but also how the workings of, and perception of, the court did much to influence the standing of the king or queen.

What then of the Commonwealth? The republic born on 31 January 1649 did not have the financial means to erect a new building or to do much more than repair and maintain the Whitehall which it inherited in succession to six monarchs. Yet the court of the Commonwealth was different and, for better and worse, was seen to be different, to the courts of kings and is therefore important to our assessment of the image of the regime. Whitehall remained, of course, a place both of ceremony and bureaucracy, a warren of personal residences, and a suite of offices; but after 1649, with the demise of the royal household, the emphasis seems to have been less on the ceremonial and more on the function of the building as a headquarters of bureaucracy. As Gerald Aylmer has demonstrated, the parliamentary introduction of committees during the 1640s became the central mode of governing under the Commonwealth and numerous rooms at Whitehall were given over to – and, crucially, were even named after – committees that met in them.[29] Instead of the names of great courtiers, their factional intrigues and manoeuvres for place, the 1650s were marked more by the deliberations of the Council of State, the new executive organ, and of the committees and commissions that served under it. However, 'the biggest difference between the apparatus of government in the 1650s and that in the 1630s was due to the existence of large regular armed forces' which required an administrative infrastructure to fund and manage them.[30] Not least on account of the tasks the new government faced, a more modern professional civil service began to emerge in the 1650s and the evidence suggests that sinecures, deputations and absenteeism were reduced, as a series of acts and ordinances specified working hours and responsibilities.[31] Moreover, whatever Royalist polemics might allege concerning the sexual peccadilloes of the Commonwealth leaders, especially Henry Marten, the court and administration of the republic produced none of the scandals, such as the Overbury murder, that had tainted monarchical courts.[32] It would appear that, even though they fell short of them, the Commonwealth governors saw the need for probity and sought standards of fitness for office that might display the civic virtues of a republic as superior to the debauchery and corruption of royal courts.[33] If such is more an impression than certainty, it is at least one that even those later servants of restored monarchy, such as Samuel Pepys, confirmed by holding up the practices and standards of the Commonwealth administration as models for government.[34]

In light of this, perhaps the greatest problem of the Commonwealth government was that, in the main, it failed to persuade almost anyone at the time of its honesty or probity. As Aylmer remarked, a multitude of pamphlets published grievances and charges against the regime, and Leveller (and other) programmes of reform (of office holding, for example) implied rampant corruption; and whatever the truth, the charge stuck – both with the people and with many in the army.[35] The irony here is that the *perception* of Commonwealth corruption owed much to the high levels of taxation and the enhanced bureaucracy that were necessitated by the army – that is by the dependence of the Commonwealth on military protection from enemies overseas and at home.[36]

More generally, the charges of corruption emerged as much from the disappointment of those who had looked to the Commonwealth for wide-scale reform and the opposition of those who were never reconciled to it as from the reality of favouritism or backhanders. As the expectations of the new republic were always part of the image of the government, so the failure to satisfy expectations tarnished its image and reputation. Embroiled in the daily business of governing, the Rump never progressed far even with the legal, social and religious reforms that it countenanced, let alone with those desired by the radicals. In its declarations and ordinances, as we have seen, the regime took trouble to counter resurgent Royalism. By contrast it paid little attention to army discontents until it was too late. As a consequence, increasingly after 1651, though the immediate dangers had passed, critical voices from among the soldiery were representing the Commonwealth as a failure – and the Rump as a body that had no other end than the cynical retention of power for personal gain. Such a characterization was at best harsh and in some respects mendacious; but that Cromwell rehearsed the charges when dismissing the Rump in 1653 evidences how popular such a negative image had become.

The story of the Rump's failure to satisfy the expectations of reform is inseparable from the larger political history of 1649 to 1653 which has been well recounted elsewhere and cannot be retold here. We should, however, remark that, among the many grievances, it was the Rump's failure with regard to what we have seen were those two primary arenas of royal responsibility – the law and the church – that attracted most discontent. In both cases, the Rump was not entirely inactive. On 22 October 1650, it set up a committee to review expenses and delays in the courts and, after Worcester, it returned to law reform, appointing twenty-one commissioners (none of them MPs) to investigate thoroughly.[37] The expectations raised, however, were not fulfilled and almost none of the commissioners' recommendations passed into law. As for the church, the challenge to find a settlement between draconian order and spiritual anarchy proved too great, not least because divisions remained sharp about what constituted religious order or chaos. The Commonwealth passed the Blasphemy Act to check the extremists and (in February 1652) appointed a Committee for the Propagation of the Gospel, mainly in response to pressure from Independent ministers, like John Owen, who were close to Cromwell.[38] Even more perhaps than divisions within the parliament, campaigns in Ireland and Scotland and a war against the Dutch stymied any further progress.

In terms of public justice, the celebrated state trials of the Commonwealth era hardly contributed to a positive representation of the regime or to unifying the republic. John Lilburne and his followers in the Leveller movement attacked the Commonwealth government from its inception as unrepresentative and subordinate to military power. When, on 28 March, he was called before the Council of State, Lilburne refused (an echo of Charles I's earlier refusal) to recognize its jurisdiction and was committed to the Tower.[39] From there, he continued to publish attacks on the government, while mass petitions to parliament (one was said to contain over eighty thousand signatures) demanded his trial or release.[40] In August, John Lilburne raised the stakes by publishing a pamphlet entitled *An Impeachment of High Treason against Oliver Cromwell* and a special commission was appointed to try him.[41] On 26 October, a jury of Londoners, many as hostile to the military regime as he was, returned a verdict of Not Guilty, leading a crowded hall of Guildhall spectators to shout triumphant cries of joy.[42] As Lilburne was (temporarily) returned to the Tower, 'loud rejoicing' followed him through the streets and 'for joy the people caused that night abundance of bonfires to be made all up and down the streets'.[43] Meanwhile the terrified judges were 'scoffed, mocked and derided' as they made their way home.[44] If the damage done that day to the credibility of Commonwealth justice was inestimable, it was increased by the after-trial publicity (much of it by Lilburne) which systematically undermined all the legal procedures and legitimacy of the Council which, it was charged, had betrayed the liberty and trust of the people. As a short polemical pamphlet claimed, with hardly any exaggeration: 'so odious are the now present junto sitting at Westminster that all the tyrants that ever exercised power here were not half so hateful to the people'.[45]

Where Lilburne's trial tainted the new Commonwealth's legal and constitutional authority, the trial of the preacher Christopher Love exposed the bitter religious divisions within, and religious opposition to, the government. Advertising himself in 1649 as 'a friend to a regulated monarchy, a free parliament, an obedient army' and an 'enemy to tyranny, anarchy and heresy', the leading Presbyterian minister opposed the oath of loyalty to the Commonwealth and preached against the republican saints.[46] On 6 September he was charged with seditious preaching, but when he attended to answer the charge, 'the witnesses not appearing . . . he was dismissed', to the 'loud cries' of joy of 'a great company of people' who had gone to support him.[47] It was not to be his last brush with the government. Love continued a staunch Presbyterian, became involved in a plot to aid the Scottish Covenanters to restore Charles II and was tried for treason in the summer of 1651.[48] Love was undoubtedly guilty, but neither the witnesses nor other evidence proved treason beyond reasonable doubt. Nevertheless, he was convicted and sentenced to death. For nearly two months his fate hung in the balance as Presbyterians petitioned Cromwell for mercy and Independents urged that justice take its course. As the threat from Scotland revived, Love was executed on 22 August.[49] Love's case did not excite the general anxieties about rough justice that Lilburne's had raised; the preacher himself, while denying any 'single fact proved against me which made me guilty of treason', admitted his involvement with Covenanters.[50] But, as he awaited death, Love published petitions and vindications that raised questions about parliament's title, the legality of the court that tried him; worst of all, the godliness of the proceedings and of the government. 'I desire the reader to observe', Love appealed in a treatise shortly before his death, 'that since the days of Queen Mary there hath been no Protestant minister so unchristianly dealt withal.'[51] On the scaffold, comparing himself to Christian martyrs and assuming a Christic tone, Love protested his innocence of the precise charge, reasserted his principles, including commitment to 'a regulated monarchy', and condemned the regicide.[52] As reference to Charles I revived old political divisions, Love turned to condemn religious dissensions and to hold up a Presbyterian church government as the only way to unity and order 'throughout the churches of the saints'.[53] Pamphlets condemning Love, including a detailed animadversion on his scaffold speech, probably evidence the government's nervousness about his trial but in the end only added (since it included his petitions and speech) to the publicization of disunity and contention.[54] Christopher Love was not the Commonwealth's Prynne, Burton and Bastwick. Those, however, who feared that 'Mr Love's reputation should glare in the weak eyes of men to make them blind', rightly judged that the extensive publicity his case had generated had left 'dangerous impressions'.[55] Two years after the public relations disaster of the regicide, public justice and the scaffold were undermining, rather than underpinning, the republic.

CHAPTER 15

SUBVERTING THE
COMMONWEALTH

Recent scholarship, though it has exaggerated their effectiveness, has helpfully brought to light the modes and media through which the Rumpers sought not only to represent but to 'invent' a republic. But any final re-evaluation of the success of these representations must involve a brief examination of the many voices (and signs) of opposition that so often seemed to overpower official scripts. Curiously, a full study of Royalist polemic and propaganda during the Commonwealth (and Protectorate) has yet to be written. But such studies as we have and a sample of the pamphlet literature make immediately obvious how everything the republic did, or said, was enacted and uttered in the shadow of the deceased Charles I. We began this section with the most powerful text of the royal image in early modern England published on the day of regicide. As well as its thirty-fifth edition in 1649, *Eikon Basilike* stimulated a vast Royalist literature of gloss, comment and emulation that dominated the literature of the year. Besides works such as *Eikon e Piste* that directly defended the *Eikon* and Charles's authorship of it, or *The Subject's Sorrow* that referred to the frontispiece image, there were innumerable paeans to the text as writing 'next to hallowed writ and sacred page', and myriad poems on a 'rare, incomparable Booke' that revealed Charles I as priest and prophet as much as king.[1]

While it was inseparable from him, the *Eikon Basilike* was by no means the only memorialization of the late king. Elegies went back over the trial by 'a mock tribunal' of rebels who did 'intombe the Nation in their Soveraigne's grave'; texts of Charles's prayers recalled his piety and stand on conscience; panegyrics praised his 'David-like' faith, religion and wisdom.[2] Where *A Deep Groan* lamented the butchering of 'the best of Monarchs' who had been the 'Bulwarke of law, the Churches Citadell', *Jeremias Redevivus* deplored a crime that had 'widdowed our whole nation'.[3] Woodcuts of Charles – crowned, in armour, or on the scaffold – and of his monument illustrated elegies and laments and disseminated them to the illiterate.[4] In no case should we doubt that lament was also polemic. To invoke the martyr king, his virtues and his love for his people was to deny legitimacy to the republic. In his sufferings, the author of *The Royal Legacies* rightly argued, Charles I had 'wonderfully convinced and subdued all our adversaries'; 'as we have sufficient cause to deplore the absence of his person', another wrote, 'so we have an undeniable reason to rejoice for the presence of his perfections which will build everlasting pyramids in the hearts of those which were his loyal subjects'.[5] Charles's death, it was suggested, had robbed England of honour, along with law and religion. Accounts of miracles performed by relics, such as handkerchiefs soaked in his blood, circulated alongside stories of the nightmares suffered by his executioner before his early death.[6] And, in treatise after treatise, a king who was 'like the sun in the firmament' was contrasted with a Machiavellian, diabolic Cromwell who had schemed to bring him down.[7] Against the figure-head of an illegitimate republic, a Royalist treatise, ventriloquizing scores of others, has Charles I utter: 'Know Caatiffe, in my sonne I live'.[8]

As he plotted, raised armies and sought out foreign aid, the Commonwealth did not need reminding of the presence of Prince Charles. Propagandists for the prince argued from the very moment of regicide the allegiance now due to Charles I's son. The Scots were quick to publish his 'royal name, portrait and seal' and proclaim his right to English readers as well as at every market cross in the northern kingdom.[9] Royalists were quick to present him as 'as hopeful a king as ever swayed the royal crown'; and, after his coronation at Scone in 1651, the question of Charles II's right to the English throne was starkly posed.[10] Though Commonwealth defenders tried to describe him as 'the young Pretender', on his large engraved portrait, mounted in armour, with troops behind him, Charles appeared to many every inch the king coming to reclaim his English, as he had latterly his Scottish, throne.[11] The account of *The True Manner of the Crowning of Charles II, King of Scotland* describes, as the minister presented their new king to them and Charles vowed to give his life for them, the people shouting joyously: 'God Save the King'.[12] As old prophecies circulated about a king of Scotland who would triumph over adversity, government officials knew that in England too 'the vulgar sort of people do cry him up exceedingly and say they must and will have a king'.[13] Marchamont Nedham, in making *The Case of the Commonwealth* in 1650, knew that it was a case that would be hard to make to a people addicted to monarchy.

Nedham's fears were well placed. The opposition to the Commonwealth was not just a matter of recent regicide and the person of King Charles II, it was about the constitution, a belief in monarchy, and serious doubt about the legal foundation of the new government. For all the recent events, the success of early modern monarchs in instilling belief in the divinity of kings is massively demonstrated in treatises affirming the sanctity of monarchy. 'We cannot but observe,' the author of *A Religious Demurrer* writes, 'that the whole universe is governed by God, angels and man . . . all human bodies by a head.'[14] *The Royal Charter Granted unto Kings by God Himself* expanded on its title by asserting: 'Kings are lively representations . . . or pictures drawn to the life of the great deity'.[15] 'God himself,' the author added, 'who is the God of Nature affects

85 Engraving of Charles II, from *The True Manner of the Crowning of Charles the Second King of Scotland*, 1650.

monarchy.'[16] If monarchy was God's ordinance, others argued that the opponents of kings were damned sinners. Making the familiar connection between rebellion and the diabolic arts of witchcraft, *The Rebels Looking-Glass* cited scriptural examples of God's judgments on Corah, Absalom and Shimei who had opposed kings and warned: 'God will not suffer . . . royal blood to go unavenged'.[17] 'Who can stretch forth his hands against the Lords anointed and be guiltless?' *The Royal Charter* asked; and many believers in divine right echoed it with warnings of what might befall a people guilty of spilling sacred blood.[18] In the eyes of many – and not just active Royalists – a non-monarchical government was a defiance of God which promised only divine vengeance: 'we much fear,' one author wrote, 'that God is not well pleased that the sons of men should peremptorily decree that this realm, always governed by royalty, should henceforth never be governed by a king.'[19]

Those who held monarchy to be natural, part of God's creation, could only view the Commonwealth as an artifice against nature, as a monstrous, deformed invention. The title in Latin of a popular satire referred to *Monarchy Transformed into a Deformed Republic*, while Francis Quarles in *Regale Lectum*

Miseriae specifically referred to the debauched monster that had succeeded to the place of a king.[20] The author of *A Religious Demurrer* predicted that the change could not 'bring forth anything but mules and monsters, storms and tempests, unsettledness and madness throughout the kingdom'.[21] As that reference to 'kingdom' discloses, many could not think of any ordered state without a monarch. The reference to monsters and the monstrous emblematized the fear of anarchy that haunted the early modern imagination. As an apologist for Charles I put it, those who 'have overthrown the order of God and Nature [have] dissolved the bonds of humane society, bringing a mere confusion . . . of all things'.[22]

Because in early modern England the law was idealized as fallen man's attempts to recover natural, divine law, the religious arguments against the Commonwealth were connected with, not simply parallel to, the legal objections to the republic. As the author of *The Subjects Sorrow* put it, 'England in her best and loudest language, the law, hath largely declared the sacred sovereignty of her kings, spoke them God's vicars, assigned unto them the fullness of regal power'.[23] In English law, of course, there could be no interregnum nor republic. 'The king's person, never dies, says the law', *A Second Part of the Religious Demurrer* reminded, adding 'such a king we are bound to preserve'.[24] The author of *Majestas Intemerata* cited Plowden to the same effect: 'The king is a name which shall endure for ever, as the head and government of the people, as the law presumes, so long as the people shall remain'.[25] In a staged debate between a judge and a commander of the army, the judge asserts the divine origin and supremacy of monarchy, denies any popular basis for sovereign power and, citing Bracton, argues for the allegiance due to kings.[26] Indeed, pamphleteers starkly contrasted the security of laws under kings with the arbitrary rule of other constitutions. As a defender of Charles I put it, there was 'as big a difference as a mountain betwixt our good old laws and liberties enjoyed under a gracious king . . . and the most slavish of all the governments were ever yet put upon a nation'.[27] The title of another tract simply described the Rump as *The English Tyrants*.[28]

The arguments from law and history were made specifically against the case of necessity advanced by Nedham and other apologists for Commonwealth. Just before the regicide, a representation from ministers in London had warned that the plea of necessity was overridden by a powerful sense of the binding nature of oaths of allegiance.[29] 'No necessity can justify perjury,' they insisted, and it would seem that, at least initially, the argument from necessity was indeed overridden by reminders of the sanctity of oaths of allegiance.[30] MPs were reminded that they themselves had taken an oath of allegiance that effectively rendered the king's trial a nonsense, while *A Religious Demurrer* instructed readers: 'the divine bond of our covenant and oaths . . . chain us by our consciences . . . to preserve that kind of government' – that is, monarchy.[31] As the author of *An Exercitation* put it, 'an unjust action cannot produce or create a right'.[32] In *The Vindication of Abraham Reinaldson*, a freeman of London explained his personal difficulties in subscribing to the new Commonwealth. He had, he explained, taken the oath of supremacy and allegiance which bound him to obey no other 'usurped' or 'pretended' power.[33]

His language illustrates the reasons behind the refusal of many to recognize the title of the new government or to honour it with any name. The pamphleteer who made his address to 'the present visible supreme power at Westminster' perhaps sought thereby to expose the naked military force that alone secured the new republic.[34] *A Curse against Parliament Ale*, a popular tract, referred to widespread tavern talk of a 'usurped power'; the author of *The Royal Legacies* referred to the Rumpers as 'your bastard assembly' and as 'a mongrel parliament'.[35] Such terms of abuse exposed the bitter reality that the parliament, which claimed to represent and act on behalf of the people, was still not a true parliament, but one purged and overawed. *The Rebels Looking Glass* refused its members even the name of parliament, addressing them as 'that junto that sit in the Commons House at Westminster'.[36] The revolution, *The Religious Demurrer* reminded readers, had been a coup effected by a small minority.[37] Though, like many tyrannical regimes, parliament claimed to act with the consent of the people, opponents, probably accurately, retorted that regicide had been effected with two-thirds of MPs excluded and against the wishes of as great a proportion of the people. The government of the Commonwealth, they charged, was not true parliamentary government of king, Lords and a full Commons but that by 'the selected parliament of a faction'.[38]

Attacks on the Rump as unrepresentative, as a junto or faction, easily spilled over into accusations that the new governors had not acted out of principle – a desire to protect liberties – but from ambition and greed. Several Royalists depicted those who 'levell'd at a Princes fall' as plotting to succeed Charles or to gain the spoils of monarchy.[39] High taxes, especially the relatively new burden of the excise, fuelled the suspicion that the army and a junto – men of 'broken fortunes' – were feathering their own nests.[40] *A Curse against Parliament Ale*, describing the Commonwealth governors as 'thieves', urged citizens to withhold their taxes.[41] Charges of greed and ambition, naturally enough, focused on Oliver Cromwell, who in this, as in many other respects, was represented as personifying the new government. Along with personal abuse about his appearance – his poxed nose symbolizing corruption and debauchery – Cromwell was charged with spurning oaths, denouncing God and Scripture, and pursuing high office so as to become an Egyptian taskmaster, squeezing the people's purses and stealing their goods.[42] That so many of these attacks seem to have been intended for a popular audience only underscores the likely effectiveness of opposition to the new republic and its difficulty in securing support.

Time and survival, as we have seen, strengthened the new Commonwealth and in 1650, led by Nedham, pro-government spokesmen wrote to persuade doubting citizens to swear allegiance to it. Opposition, however, did not abate and many directly attacked the Engagements and defence of it. The author of *Two Treatises* concerning the Engagement, for example, dissected the bogus logic used to try to reconcile it with the Covenant and oath of allegiance and, in a clever move, turned the argument back against the Commonwealthsmen. 'If former oaths of allegiance and supremacy,' he posited, 'bound not at all to monarchy there expressed but to the public good abstracted from all particular forms, so that our consciences are still free to subscribe to any platform, then entering this engagement, it doth no more bind to a republic but leaves us free for monarchy as formerly settled.'[43] Others were less subtle but more blunt in denouncing the legitimacy of the Commonwealth in 1650. 'There is now,' the self-styled *Voice of Truth* told readers, 'no lawful power over you.'[44]

Contestation of the legitimacy of the republic sustained momentum throughout its brief life. In 1652, *Observations upon Aristotle's Politics*, reasserting the divine and natural foundations of monarchy, observed that there never had been such a thing as a true republic, Venice and the United Provinces borrowing the best of their constitutions from kingdoms.[45] Taking a different tack against the probably increasing number of pragmatists who were falling in with the regime, the author of *Modern Policies Taken from Machiavel* stated the principle that 'necessity of state is a very competent apology [only] for the worst of actions.'[46] On the very eve of the Commonwealth's demise, pamphleteers still recalled the 'barbarous' dealings of 1649 and dismissed the parliament as 'a base arbitrary power'. Robert Spry, arguing for monarchy, dismissed the four-year-old government with a derisory put-down: 'I have late heard much of a Commonwealth but know not what it meaneth.'[47]

Most dangerously, while it failed to win over former Royalists and many of the uncommitted, the Rump progressively lost the support of its creators. In March 1653, Cromwell held back a move by army officers to dissolve the parliament; but, as the clamour in the army for a new representative increased and parliament proved slow to proceed with a bill for its dissolution, his position became increasingly untenable.[48] On 20 April, convinced that, despite its promises, parliament had no intention of making way for a new representative, Cromwell rose in the house to denounce and dissolve the assembly.[49] It is emblematic of the failure of the Commonwealth to represent itself that Cromwell's speech excoriating many of the leaders is the most remembered statement about the parliament and shorter-lived republican government. In the best account of it we have, Cromwell, rising and removing his hat, opened with formal compliment to the parliament before bitterly criticizing their 'injustice, delays of justice, self-interest and other faults.'[50] Then, denying them the respect due to a parliament by replacing his hat, Cromwell 'chid them soundly', 'with the vilest reproaches', before announcing he had 'done with them.'[51] When Sir Peter Wentworth rose to protest at 'such unbecoming language' from one who was the servant of the parliament, Cromwell became angry, replying 'I say you are no parliament.'[52] Then commanding the mace – one of the few new symbols of a new republic – to be removed, Cromwell uttered the famous line 'What shall we do with this bauble? Here, take it away' – as the soldiers entered the Chamber, seizing MPs and the records of the parliament.[53]

As Blair Worden has persuasively argued, the Rump may not have been guilty of the charge that the bill it was about to pass was intended to recruit MPs to perpetuate the existing parliament.[54] But such a revision more forcefully makes our point. The account of 20 April that has prevailed for over three hundred and fifty years is that of the Rump's critics and enemies. Immediately after the dissolution, army propaganda spread the story that 'a corrupt party' had 'the desire of perpetuating themselves'; and subsequent explanations of events repeated the general charge of a corrupt oligarchy's desire for perpetual office and its spoils.[55] Some members of parliament did attempt public protest; and Lenthall continued to describe himself as Speaker. But, whether on account of army control of news, or, given the difficulties of censorship, a failure once again by the Rump to explain or publicize itself, such protests were overwhelmed by army propaganda and the ringing rhetoric of Cromwell's speech.[56] The English Commonwealth began its life with a powerful text of opposition (*Eikon Basilike*) undermining its legitimacy and authority; it ended its life with some of its leading supporters refusing it even the name of parliament and deriding the most potent visual symbol of its authority. For all the claim bravely advanced that a republic was constructed through discourses and symbols, the all-important image of the only English Commonwealth, both at the time and for most of the historical record, was in fact constructed by others; worse, by others of quite different sympathies who were hostile to it. As a failure of representation, the Rump's failure may have been greater than any early modern monarch's; for – with the possible exception of Queen Mary and King James II – few kings or queens have lacked advocates or sympathetic historians. The Rump may no longer, as was once argued, be charged with 'moral weakness'; but it must remain guilty of ineptitude (a remarkable ineptitude after a decade of pamphlet war) in making its own case.[57]

By contrast, those who ruled from late April to July, as well as disseminating negative propaganda about the Rump, took measures to make a military coup look like a seamless continuity of parliamentary government and forms.[58] The style of language, the proclamations and coins retained Commonwealth forms. Most significantly, when those nominated to meet in a new assembly met on 4 July, though neither Cromwell nor the Council had summoned them as one, they acted as, and assumed the name of, a parliament, resolving to meet in St Stephen's Chapel, according Francis Rous the title of Speaker, appointing the Clerk of the Rump Parliament as their clerk – and retrieving the mace.[59] Moreover, the Barebones assembly publicized itself in a declaration as a parliament. In an eight-page document printed with the seal of the Commonwealth and in the Gothic script of official pronouncement, and ordered to be dispersed by all sheriffs, the assembly quietly claimed authority 'to take upon us the supreme government of England, Scotland and Ireland'.[60] Though tactfully acknowledging the great trust placed upon them, and their human frailty, the MPs described themselves as 'set by God for the good of all' and as his instruments for 'great changes'.[61] Not least, in its promises to secure laws and liberties and to do God's work, the Barebones endeavoured to create a support base as the means to a legitimacy and authority independent of the sword.[62]

The declaration appears to have been the assembly's attempt to represent itself and to deal with an image problem it faced from the outset. The relatively low social status of those summoned was the subject of gossip and news as they began to meet and the French ambassador was not alone in his belief that Cromwell and the army leaders had called them to be puppets while the real power rested with themselves.[63] Barebones resolved on 6 August to suppress unlicensed publishing of its proceedings in newsbooks, so as to prevent hostile reports, but, as with previous attempts, this move to control the press failed.[64] As divisions within the parliament mounted, it may be that various groups sought support outside or even actively briefed against fellow members. From mid-November, news-writers widely reported rumours of an impending dissolution.[65] Most dangerously, radicals began to attack Cromwell as a man of sin, leading moderates in turn to denounce them as fanatics. As well, that is, as the important divisions within the assembly, it was the *perception* of division, and the fears evoked by charges levelled, that undermined a parliament whose declaration had trumpeted the importance of unity. Ultimately, division led the moderate majority to renounce their own authority, to report to Cromwell that 'the sitting of this parliament any longer . . . will not be for the good of the Commonwealth', and to deliver to him the powers it had months earlier claimed.[66] So as to prevent the radical caucus remaining, army officers went to evict them from the house.

Even if the surrender of authority was, at least in part, the work of a probable majority of MPs, the dissolution of Barebones returned England to a situation which two parliaments had sought to change: a military rule with no legitimacy or authority other than the sword. But, in another, still more important sense, the republic had ended. For in December 1653, authority was effectively returned to a single person. The fact that, after a mere four years, government by a single person was again announced, and readily accepted as a fundamental to the constitution, sounded the death knell of a true republic. Many developments led to that outcome. Prominent among the explanations for a failure of republican government was failure to establish the legitimacy of regimes which, as a consequence, were conceived as 'expedients . . . cobbled up to fill a hiatus in legitimate government'.[67] That, in turn, amounted to a failure to devise and disseminate discourses and symbols that established legitimacy and erased the authority of monarchy. Back in 1649, *The Royal Charter Granted unto Kings* had criticized those who dismissed the outward trappings of authority as mere theatrical pomp, arguing the need for the 'signs' as well as 'the things signified'.[68] As Cromwell had so powerfully demonstrated in spurning the mace before dismissing two parliaments, the signs of authority were essential to the substance of power. As he took up the reins of single-person rule, Cromwell increasingly adopted the symbols of a king and with them many of the attributes of regal power.

PART V

REPRESENTATIONS AND REACTIONS: IMAGES OF THE CROMWELLIAN PROTECTORATE

PROLOGUE: 'BRING CROWNES AND SCEPTERS'

Dcember 1653 marked a revolutionary – or rather a counter-revolutionary – moment. Though historians have rightly cautioned against simply characterizing the shift from Commonwealth to Protectorate as a conservative reaction against radical revolution, what it did effect was the end of the fact, and even of the idea, at least in official circles, of collective rule, of an executive responsible to parliament – or a republic properly conceived.[1] Oliver Cromwell may have continued to support, even embody, the desire for social and godly reformation that many in parliament and outside had hoped for. But after December 1653 it would be *his* concept of reformation, *his* interpretation of God's will, that would shape what happened as well as what observers, both supporters and enemies, perceived to be happening. For much of the period from 1649 to 1653, Cromwell had resisted moves to highlight his person as the heroic architect of military triumph or government policies. From April 1653, still more from the moment when a majority of Barebones MPs delivered their authority to him, his person was the focus as well as locus of authority. The politics of the Protectorate is largely an account of the image, representation and reputation of Oliver Cromwell.

Indeed, the counter-revolution for which I would argue was as much a counter-revolution in representational as in constitutional forms. Few outside the ranks of students of history could recount the names of, let alone visualize, the leaders of the Rump or Barebones parliaments or their Councils of State. By contrast, Cromwell's words have echoed through the ages and few would fail to recognize his image which, of course, in the form of a statue, greets all who enter the Westminster Parliament today. Oliver may have professed reluctance to be the focus of personal attention during the Commonwealth years; but, certainly after early 1653, he made his person inseparable from his power and the representation of his authority a vital means to the establishment and maintenance of his protectoral authority.

It was this renewed focus on personality that turned attention back to kingship. The issue of Cromwell's interest in the crown has long vexed historians, but Cromwell's ambition, or lack of it, is not our principal concern here. In fact, rather than suggesting that Cromwell pursued the crown, we might posit that the demise of collective government and the creation of a protectorate turned events in a monarchical direction. Where, during the 1640s, Cromwell himself had resisted any cult of personality, Royalist satirists had devoted their attention to him, 'giving him', in Laura Knoppers's words, 'a greater role in print than he had in reality'.[2] Satirists such as John Cleveland not only represented Cromwell as military and political leader, as Machiavellian manipulator, and as ambitious to replace the king, they constructed a physical and character portrait of him as a person and set it in counterpoint to the portrayal of the virtuous Charles I.[3] In many written and visual texts, dialogues and debates, Cromwell is placed alongside, compared and contrasted with, Charles I. As the title of several pamphlets confirms, the relation between Charles and Cromwell was presented as a tragedy of the two personae who spoke for good and evil in a moral drama.[4] Though, during the 1640s, he was not even the commander of parliament's armies, let alone a leading light in civilian government, Cromwell was widely presented as a king aspirant and in waiting, or as a mock king. Even if we do not go so far as to level the charge of insincerity, we must recognize that, for all his protestations of his unimportance, Cromwell contributed to such a representation of himself. The Walker portrait we have discussed, despite its slight differences, clearly evoked Van Dyck's of Strafford, Lord-Lieutenant of Ireland, and so, at the time of Cromwell's expedition, at least directly compared him to Charles I's principal adviser and architect of personal rule.[5] Other portraits of Cromwell during the period 1649–53 also drew upon early monarchical and courtly styles. The plain 'warts and all' painting that Cromwell requested from Cooper was not typical and was arguably less a simple realist representation in the plain style than is often argued.[6]

During the republic, Royalists continued to single out Cromwell and to represent him as a grotesque, deformed counter-king. In contrast to the innumerable images of Charles I as a holy martyr who had preferred a heavenly to an earthly crown, *The Right Picture of King Oliver* presented Cromwell as disfigured, poxed, and as a knave who used force to subdue kingdoms and peoples that had been blessed under monarchy.[7] Increasingly, too, parliament joined in representing Cromwell, mounted with his martial baton, as triumphant victor and leader, in the process leading the young Marvell to take Cromwell as a figure embodying the future as much as Charles I the past, as a champion not only at arms but of a new England: one who 'cast the kingdoms old/Into another mould'.[8] If Royalist satire and Commonwealth panegyric each contributed to it, the heroicization of Cromwell had its greatest public display, as we have seen, in his triumphal entry into London after victory at the Battle of Worcester.[9] Where, in the late 1640s, he had been set in moral counterpoint to Charles I, he now rode in triumph into the city as Charles II fled and, disguised, made his escape to France. The year 1651 was not only a moment of victory, or even simple inversion; it was the beginning of a reversion to monarchical forms. It can be no accident that shortly after this the former Royalist,

Payne Fisher, became 'Cromwell's unofficial poet laureate', celebrating – in Latin – the triumph of the hero.[10] Though it has been argued that such representations dwelt more on deeds than appearances, figured Cromwell as servant of the people, and were less iconic than monarchical images, the references to 'majesty', the regal metaphors (father, helmsman, Atlas) and the comparison of him with emperors rendered Cromwell king-in-waiting.[11]

The reach of this imagery into the broader culture is fully evidenced in the reactions to the dissolution of the Rump Parliament. Several observers expected that Cromwell would assume power; one reported that men 'infer that he intends to call home the young king'.[12] One anonymous gentleman, however, a month after the dissolution, set up Cromwell's picture in the old Royal Exchange with beneath it the injunction: 'Ascend three Thrones great Captain and Divine'.[13] The verse continues:

Come Priest of God, bring Oyle, bring Robes, bring Gold
Bring Crownes and Scepters . . .

. . . Kneele and pray
To Oliver the Torch of Syon, a Starr of day.

And it ends: 'God Save the King'.

Whatever Cromwell's involvement, already before 1653 he was being written, visually represented and publicly displayed as a king. This is the subject of our next chapter: the relationship between the representation of Cromwell and the image and government of the Protectorate. Though, I shall argue, those who decried the Instrument of Government and erected the Protectorate did not seek a return to kingship, the government by a single person fostered modes of language, visual representations and public performances that made it appear quasi-monarchical. And where the constitution revived and, in some measure, re-authorized regal cultural forms, in turn those monarchical forms and images refashioned the political culture so as to make kingship once again – and not only to Royalists – acceptable; even, to many, desirable. If the origin of the Protectorate lay in the failure to construct republican discourses and images, the course and legacy of the Protectorate saw the cultural revalidation of monarchical forms and, ultimately, the reconstitution of a regal polity. Where, in the late 1640s, it was Cromwell's name that appeared alongside that of the king, by the late 1650s he was widely heralded as king in all but name.

CHAPTER 16

PROCLAIMING PROTECTORATE

I

On 16 December 1653, something happened that was (quietly) revolutionary: England had its first written constitution – or what was described as 'articles for the future government of the Commonwealth'.[1] From 1649 to 1653, as we saw, the English republic struggled to find a name and an identity or to secure allegiance. The Instrument of Government, we now know, was the creation of Major-General John Lambert, who introduced it to the Council of Officers on 13 December.[2] Though he had, as he told them, been working on it for two months, and had probably discussed it with a few officers, the meeting on the 13th was the first official presentation of the constitution; and it just may be true that Cromwell himself had not seen it in full before, the Council having concurred, it was presented to him. Whatever the extent or timing of his involvement, Cromwell did not devise the document. Moreover, a newsletter reports that in the choosing of the members of the new Council of State, there was a need 'to satisfy all parties who have had a hand in the choice'.[3] The Instrument was enacted, that is, by a small group of officers with whom Lambert had chosen to consult. During the behind-the-scenes preparations in late November there had been rumours that the Instrument would create Cromwell king – and Oliver himself later claimed that some brought the Instrument to him 'with the name of king in it'. If so, Cromwell refused it.[4] However, the Instrument, though an army document, seems to have had its origin in the recognition of a need, or widespread desire, for the return of some form of monarchical government.

When it was published to the nation on 16 December, the Instrument opened by declaring 'That the Supreme Legislative Assembly of the Commonwealth of England, Scotland and Ireland . . . shall be and reside in one person and the people assembled in parliament, the style of which person shall be the Lord Protector'.[5] Subsequent clauses specified that the Lord Protector would be 'assisted with a Council' of 13 to 21, in the presence of which every successive Protector was to swear his oath that (among other things) he would not infringe the Instrument.[6] Extensive guarantees and powers were given to parliament which ensured their calling, sitting without fear of dissolution and capacity to get bills passed into law, even without the Protector's consent.[7] But, though it was by no means unchecked, it was the authority of the single person that the Instrument emphasized: legislation, 'magistracy and administration of the government' were first and foremost vested in the Lord Protector, who was to issue all writs, grants and patents which hitherto had been issued 'in the name and style of the keepers of the liberty of England'.[8] Like a king, the Protector controlled the army and navy and conducted (with advice) diplomacy, war and peace. Unlike the earlier monarchy, he was granted a yearly revenue for the expenses of government and to maintain an army.[9] Importantly, the Lord Protector was established not only as an administrative head but as head of an honour society from whose 'name and style' all positions and honours were derived.[10] The Instrument restored not only a head of government but also a head of state.

Whatever the novelty of the new constitution and the Protectorate, Cromwell himself was well known to the people – not least through the medium of words. During the four years of the Commonwealth, parliament, as we noticed, often ordered the printing of his letters – from Dunbar, Edinburgh and Wexford – and declarations, such as that to the people of Ireland.[11] While in these accounts of campaigns and (usually) victories, Cromwell had modestly understated his own role, the parliament, which always considered him 'more worthy [of] honour', by the act of printing, presented the General to the people as a leader.[12] Cromwell's letter to the Speaker from Wexford, for example, was ordered to be copied and dispersed to all the ministers of London and the Liberties, who were required to read it to their congregations.[13] Given the tone of Cromwell's letter, the pulpit was an appropriate platform. For in missive after missive Cromwell invoked the Lord's providence, his 'unspeakable mercies', as the cause of victories which, he said, were God's alone.[14] Though the servant of the parliament, Cromwell, through these letters published by its authority, became the public spokesman of the Commonwealth, just as Milton was its penman or secretary. Ironically, it was the authority of Cromwell's rhetoric and voice that facilitated the peaceful dissolution of parliament. In his declaration of April, using the language of providence now familiar to the people, Cromwell was able to present the dissolution as another of God's mercies for his people.[15] Convinced of the importance – and effectiveness – of such utterances, Cromwell ordered copies to be widely disseminated.[16]

The major shift in power in April that gave Cromwell a new authority was – literally – a speech act. When he addressed the nominated (or Barebones) parliament on 4 July 1653, Cromwell assumed a role last exercised by Charles I: he explained why the assembly had been called and set the parameters for its action and authority.[17] Cromwell, as he observed himself, chose to explain and justify the dissolution of the Rump and the creation of Barebones by means of a speech – a medium that, despite the repeated first person plural, emphasized personal authority and restored the regal relationship between utterance and authority. Cromwell, like James I before him, joined his words with Scripture, spoke of his own 'pilgrimage' and, as it were, all but led the assembled in a service of prayer.[18] 'We shall commend you to the grace of God,' Cromwell ended his speech, 'to the guidance of His Spirit.'[19] In his long speech (of some eight thousand words), Cromwell took trouble to flatter the assembly and to depict them as a collective authority.[20] 'I think it may firmly be said,' he told them, 'that never was there a supreme authority consisting of so numerous a body as you are.'[21] The truth, however, was that the authority was Cromwell's and, as he bestowed it, so he resumed it.

Cromwell's speeches are well known and often quoted but have been little studied as strategies or representations of his novel Protectoral rule. Professor Trevor Roper powerfully argued in an influential essay that Cromwell failed to manage parliaments, and indeed paid little attention to the art of political management.[22] To this it is tempting to retort that, rather like James I, Cromwell sought to get his way by words, and especially by means of the force of his rhetoric and his self-appointed position as explicator and exegete of God's providence. It was through carefully crafted speeches that Cromwell sought to sustain his authority in parliaments and – since they were 'published by order and authority' – the nation beyond.[23] It was through speeches that Cromwell tried to make the bare outlines of the Instrument into a working constitution, through speech that he endeavoured to secure a legitimacy other than that of the sword. Through unusually long addresses to parliament and nation, the Protector began the process, little advanced since 1649, of re-establishing an authority founded on recognition and support.[24]

When he addressed his first parliament on 4 September 1654, Cromwell's use of the first person singular pronoun advertised his new, personal authority as Protector.[25] Interestingly (and not for the first time), Cromwell deployed the tactic (used in the *Eikon Basilike*) of a highly personal narrative of recent events to discredit Levellers and religious radicals whom he presented as threats to property and the ministry. Rejecting the 'pretences' of those who falsely claimed 'clear manifestations of God's presence with them', Cromwell posited the magistrate's authority (*his* authority) as a God-ordained means of saving such from error by discipline.[26] It had been to correct the errors of such men and to prevent the 'heap of confusions' that had threatened the nation, he told his auditors, that his government had been created – as a remedy.[27] While disavowing any need or desire to argue for it – 'let it speak for itself' – Cromwell proclaimed that his Protectorate had been 'calculated . . . for the interest of the people alone and for their good, without respect had to any other interest', before repeating: 'let it speak for itself'.[28] To persuade MPs that it was a government for the people, he outlined the work begun by committees to reform the Court of Chancery and the laws, initiatives and proposals that would soon be put forward as bills. Most of all, however, he flattered them, it was a government that had called a 'free parliament' – a phrase he repeated, echoing the desire articulated throughout the nation since 1649.[29] Constantly taking his theme from the sermon delivered to them in the morning, the Protector, reminding them of God's mercies, appealed to MPs to 'put the top stone to this work, and make the nation happy'; he prayed for 'the blessings of God upon your endeavours'.[30] In what was a brilliant speech, Cromwell, clever-ly renouncing 'dominion over you' and resolving 'to be a fellow servant with you', conferred on his first parliament responsibility for and authority over the 'ship of the Commonwealth'.[31] At the same time he underwrote his own (supe-rior) authority, his intimacy with God's will and ways, and prescribed the course that parliament should take. In a speech that began in the past and invoked the future, opened with 'I's' then moved to 'You's' before closing with personal valediction, Cromwell scripted the new Protectoral government as a partnership to further God's work under his authority.

Rather, however, than pursuing Cromwell's agenda, it was the nature of that partnership and the legal foundation of the Protectorate itself that consumed the opening days of the new parliament. Though Cromwell had declined the crown, debates about the relative powers of parliament and the single person replicated those of the 1640s, and before, and signalled MPs no longer ready to bow to the facts of military rule.[32] On 12 September, therefore, only eight days after he had first welcomed them, Cromwell summoned the MPs to the Painted Chamber and delivered a speech intended to end dangerous chal-lenges to the authority of the Instrument and Protector and to direct the house back on track.[33] Now, the battery of 'I's' and 'me's' with which he opened announced the personal authority that Cromwell would not allow to be ques-tioned. Moreover, he made clear that, as parliament's authority had been stated, named by him, so it would be defined by him: 'I said you were a free parliament. And so you are, whilst you own the government and authority that called you.'[34] Authority, that is to say, lay in words, in speech defined by a sovereign who, like the king, was claiming the power of definition and of signi-fication. For, Cromwell went on to explain, though he had 'called' parliament, he had not called himself to his place – 'my calling be from God' – and so was above human challenge.[35] Again, at some length, Cromwell rehearsed his efforts (alluding to his summoning Barebones) to 'be quit of the power God had most providentially put into my hand'.[36] But (he explained) Providence had led him to a government approved by the army, the city and the people, which approval was marked by public entertainments and congratulations and bore witness to God's providence. Like a monarch, in other words, albeit in the language of providence rather than divine right, Cromwell's speech claimed divine decree and popular approbation for an authority that was antecedent to the parliament and might be equated 'with any hereditary interest': 'I am deriving a title from God.'[37]

Here, then, in a speech that purported only to review recent history and explain the course of events, Cromwell constructed, or rather reconstructed, the divine right sovereignty of a single ruler. Having done so, he proceeded to lay out the famous fundamentals of the constitution, as though he were giving biblical commandments beyond dispute.[38] After a week of parliamentary debate that had raised old, as well as new, challenges to sovereign power Cromwell resolved to decree and define the 'unalterable' – to be the sovereign word and voice.[39] Henceforth, he instructed, no MP would be admitted to the house who had not first accepted its authority by subscribing to the Instrument and the 'fundamentals' he had outlined. Guards before the parliament doors ensured that his decree was enforced and subscriptions secured. Though in the matter of fundamentals Cromwell got his way, the parliament continued to scrutinize the Instrument and to attempt to modify the Protector's, and enhance its own, powers. In his final speech dissolving it, Oliver catalogued (in tedious detail) the disappointment at lost opportunities, the fomenting of divisions, the failure to settle religion, and the carping at taxes for the army that had led him to end it.[40] If in a speech that decried oratory, he no longer spoke of the divine authority he had claimed, he left none in doubt that he was resolute to sustain it.[41] Questioning his position, he told MPs, 'did look like a parricide': the death of the father – of the king.[42] And, he reminded them, 'I speak for God and not for men.'[43] Whatever his representation of the Instrument as a constitution devised 'to avoid the extremes of monarchy', Cromwell uttered his authority as inviolable sovereign.[44]

Unfortunately, as he was acutely aware, with the failure of his first parliament Cromwell's position as Protector rested more on the power of the army than on the constitutional and cultural authority which he knew were necessary for settlement. Significantly, Cromwell's speech dismissing parliament was not printed for two weeks because, it was explained, His Highness had not had 'time to peruse it . . . and correct it for the press'; and unofficial versions or extracts were banned.[45] It seems likely that Cromwell was concerned about the effect of the dissolution on public opinion and with how to put the best spin on events. If so, the delay in printing his speech only compounded his problems, for in late January MPs published vindications of their proceedings and called for the destruction of the Protectorate; placards denouncing Cromwell as a 'tyrant' were publicly posted in London.[46] At a time of Royalist conspiracy and plots among old Levellers and Fifth Monarchists, the rupture with parliament presented real dangers beyond embarrassment to the regime. In the weeks after the dissolution, the government faced a plot led by Colonel Wildman and other old republicans and a Royalist insurrection, known as Penruddock's rising after its leader, in the west.[47] The insurgency was swiftly suppressed. But the harsh measures taken against Royalists and others in the wake of it emphasized the military nature of the Protectorate and the extent of opposition to it. To that opposition the government responded with more stringent measures to censor the press and to limit the publication of news to the official *Mercurius Politicus* and *Public Intelligencer* edited by Nedham.[48] More notoriously, the Council instituted a number of Major-Generals to superintend the government of the localities and effectively bypass and subordinate the traditional government by JPs, sheriffs and constables.[49] As well as a moral police force, the Major-Generals virtually turned the nation into a military state, indeed a military dictatorship. While such measures undoubtedly increased security, they sapped popularity and undermined legitimacy.

For the next year and more, Cromwell was preoccupied with foreign affairs (especially preparation for a war with Spain) and dogged by ill health. Where the former necessitated money, the latter condition, in so far as it highlighted the uncertainty about what might follow Cromwell's death, refocused attention on the need for secure settlement. Both led the Protector, with what measure of enthusiasm or reluctance it is hard to determine, to call another parliament in July, to meet in September 1656.[50] Efforts were made to secure the election of MPs supportive of the Instrument and Cromwell, if its length alone is an indicator, carefully prepared his address to the first parliament to have assembled in two years. He opened with a plain man's denial of the arts of rhetoric.[51] Directing, as he told his auditors, their attention to things rather than words, he yet artfully endeavoured to forge unity by an appeal to dangers and old anxieties that had earlier united the enemies of Charles I. Frequently using the word 'nation', the Protector warned of the threat posed by Spain that had led him to war.[52] Enmity with Spain he presented not as a diplomatic choice or an expensive option but as 'natural', inevitable and – his favourite term – 'providential'.[53] For Spain, the spearhead of popery, had since the Reformation designed the downfall of England (which it had endeavoured with the Armada against Elizabeth) as part of a larger plan to destroy European Protestantism. Now, to effect those ends, Cromwell argued, it championed Charles Stuart – 'a captain to lead us back again into Egypt' – to subvert the Reformation and the revolution.[54] Bracketing 'papists and cavaliers' several times, and appealing to the safety of European Protestantism, Cromwell skilfully outlined threats and bogeys that might lead MPs to subordinate domestic divisions and discontents and fall in behind the government.[55] Having identified Spaniards with domestic opponents, Cromwell proceeded craftily to brand all domestic opposition as popish.[56] Exciting fear and sympathy by reminding the house of attempts on his life since the last parliament, the Protector even alluded to (while professing not to believe it) intelligence of old Commonwealth and Fifth Monarchy involvement in such plots, thereby tarring all his opponents with, as it were, the popish brush.[57]

In an admirably deft move, Cromwell proceeded to temper one of the greatest discontents with his government by presenting the hated Major-Generals as instituted to be bulwarks against all popish foes, especially (he recalled it in this speech more than once) such who had perpetrated bloody atrocities in Ireland.[58] Representing them as Protestant champions and down-playing their military role as but 'a little inspection upon the people', the Protector laid down a challenge that made any opponent appear unpatriotic and careless of his own security: 'if there be any man that hath a face looking averse to this, I dare pronounce him to be a man against the interest of England'.[59] Because they were all 'Englishmen' and 'Christian men', it was not easy to see how MPs could dissent.[60]

Having outlined the dangers to them *all*, Cromwell turned (as the good physician) to remedies that were, in fact, his programme for the parliament, so making contentious policies appear 'reformations' necessary for everyone's safety and security. For security he urged that 'we may join together' to prose-cute the war by providing supply without delay.[61] For reformation at home, he insisted on religious liberty as the best means to peace and the interest of all and the reformation of manners as the way to repair breaches among Christians.[62] Celebrating what his Protectorate had already achieved in replacing scandalous ministers, Cromwell returned to defend the Major-Generals as agents of moral and religious reformation and as custodians of peace; and, as though repetition might dispel criticism, he reiterated personal pronouns to underline his confidence in them: 'I profess I believe it', 'I will abide it notwithstanding the envy and slander of foolish men'.[63] Closing with justifications of expenditure and policies while claiming they needed no justification – 'I do not know one action, no, not one, but it hath been in order to the peace and safety of the nation' – the Protector appealed to a shared faith, Protestantism, and even a common masculinity to secure support.[64] His programmes, God's work, needed not lukewarm spirits but vigorous Christian men to stand against reprobates. Those called to the work – the MPs – were 'men of honest hearts, engaged to God, strengthened by Providence' like the Protector himself: 'it is an union between you and me . . . that must ground this work'.[65]

Calling them to action, Cromwell repeated that the work would not be effected by 'notions' or 'speeches'.[66] His own speech, however, was a brilliant effort not only to represent but to create unity and agreement out of division; to make support for him godly, patriotic, masculine, for the good of all and for each man's own interest, and to demonize all opposition as popish, reprobate, against God's will and self-destructive. Professor Abbott's different assessment, that the speech left much to be desired, is supported by the testimonies he cites of Royalists and ambassadors who heard it critically.[67] Enemies of the Protector, however, were not likely to be complimentary and it is hardly surprising that a Catholic envoy should disparage the address as adorned 'with many passages from Holy Writ'.[68] If, however, he is right and the speech impressed few and persuaded fewer, it may be that the very facts of civil war, regicide and the collapse of the republic had rendered such oratorical appeals to unity of limited effect in the face of a polarized nation. Indeed, though in this speech he contributed to alienating them, Cromwell himself came to see that any successful settlement needed to include, or at least reconcile, Royalists; and through various shifts in his own representation and style he sought to reconcile them.

For now, however, Cromwell placed his hopes in a house as carefully selected as briefed. Despite the dominance of military officers, however, the parliament proved no more pliable than its predecessor and was in no way cowed or persuaded by his injunctions.[69] Business proceeded slowly and, in defiance of his call for religious freedom, parliament arrested and indicted for blasphemy a Quaker, James Nayler, who rode into Bristol on an ass in imitation of Christ's entry into Jerusalem.[70] Just as dangerously, the house began to debate the security of the Protectorate and the issue, in the light of Cromwell's illnesses, of the succession and, in so doing, threatened to disrupt the delicate compromises that had produced the Instrument in 1653. In March, the MPs debated a remonstrance or change to the constitution that would erect Cromwell as a king against the wishes of army officers and reinstitute, in some measure, a state church.[71] Though it is unlikely that the offer of the crown displeased him, it placed Oliver in a difficult position by exposing fault lines – between army and parliament, between old republicans and new Protectorians, between radicals and conservatives – that threatened to prevent healing and settling. On the other hand, partly because the majority for it in parliament represented that in the country, it must have occurred to him that the Humble Petition and Advice might offer an alternative path to settlement. Understandably, therefore, but uncharacteristically, Cromwell had no answer but to ask for time; and he was placed in the position of responding to, not outlining, the course of events in parliament; as he put it: 'you do necessitate my answer to be categorical'.[72]

In his several, noncommittal speeches to the Commons and its committees, rather than naming the Humble Petition, Cromwell referred to the Instrument, as if to underplay the (counter) revolutionary change that parliament was proposing.[73] But what the Commons proposed was not just a name but a thing, as Cromwell had to recognize: 'not a title but an office ... interwoven with the fundamental laws of this nation' and beloved by the people.[74] While he endeavoured to make little of the name, and to present the king as laid aside by providence and rejected by the godly, the desire for kingship, for the legal security of an 'ancient constitution' would not go away.[75]

On 8 May, after weeks of evasion and probably prevarication, Cromwell summoned the Commons to give his answer. Acknowledging that he had 'been the unhappy occasion of the expense of so much time' and hinting at the struggles, personal and political, that had gone on, he sought to make refusal as palatable an answer, and as much a reinforcement of his authority, as possible.[76] Cromwell flattered them that in his mind, 'no private judgement', such as that claimed by kings, 'is to lie in balance with the judgement of parliament'.[77]

So, though he now affirmed that he could not 'undertake that government with this title of king', it was a decision made not, as he put it, in defiance of parliament, but out of respect for it, as well as in accordance with his own conscience.[78] When he succeeded in persuading an unenthusiastic house to accept his decision, and to revise the proposed constitution to retain the Protectoral title, he praised them further for their care in 'doing all those things that might truly . . . answer the ends that we have engaged for'.[79] Beseeching God to bless them all in their work of reform, Cromwell called the MPs to God's business and passed over the fundamental issue – the desire for a settlement compatible with law – as if it had been a mere interlude. On 26 June, the day on which Cromwell's investiture as hereditary Protector embraced (as we shall see) all the ceremonies of a regal coronation, the MPs departed to their localities for the summer recess.

When they reassembled in January, Cromwell, speaking more briefly than usual by reason of poor health, sought to unite the assembly (now again with an upper chamber consisting of two houses) by a reminder of the civil and religious liberties their struggles, along with God's favour, had secured and to stir them to be 'the repairers of breaches' who would continue God's work.[80] The editor of his speeches dismissed Cromwell's rhetoric as 'better suited to a conventicle than to a meeting of parliament', yet the religious tone and scriptural citations, together with the absence of a specific programme, were surely intended to temper growing divisions and, by recalling and celebrating, to realize his hope (expressed as a belief) that 'you all think the things that I speak to you'.[81] Days later, the Protector certainly had an agenda. Though denying that he had prepared any speech, and deferring to their counsel as 'the life and spirit of these nations', Cromwell outlined the very real dangers that faced them, him and the nation.[82] Unusually, he detailed the foreign threats posed by the resurgent Catholic Habsburgs which (while they were real enough), along with evocations of Queen Elizabeth, served to promote a shared Protestant patriotism that the Protector knew was vital to domestic harmony. 'We are Englishmen', he reminded them, using an inclusive term which glossed the myriad divisions of 1657, and were 'to do like Englishmen'.[83] Cromwell acknowledged the different interests – 'if they be worthy of the name' – that, but for God, might bring confusion on the nation, or even bring back the bishops and Cavaliers to destroy it.[84] More than ever, he urged, what was needed was 'consistency and agreement [within] this meeting'; agreement, that is, to uphold the settlement that he sensed could not long survive.[85] If skilful rhetoric could have secured consensus, Cromwell might have been successful. But one senses now that, as he indicated, his warning speech was crafted as much to exonerate himself as to win over others and was intended to discharge his duty to God as much as persuade men. Indeed, citing Psalm 85 – 'I will hear what the Lord will speak: he will speak peace to his people' – the Protector, like so many kings before him, melded his own words with God's, and prayed to him for them and the nation.[86]

Though it was reported, accurately, as a 'pious and eloquent speech tending to unity', the speech was – perhaps significantly – not printed.[87] Just over a week later, Cromwell, amid threats of invasion, Cavalier insurrection and army mutiny, dissolved what was to be his last parliament. Military victories secured the Protectorate from the greatest threats he had warned against, yet his speech accurately acknowledged the failure to reach a settlement that he had spoken, above all, to secure. Like so many kings before him, the Protector's rhetoric had not persuaded a divided nation to unite. But Cromwell's speeches were vital in fashioning his authority and representation, and, in large measure, his self-image as the agent of Providence. Unlike rulers such as Queen Mary, James II, or even James I, whose opponents determined for long (and still shape) the image we have of them, Cromwell, not least through powerful speeches, which many politicians have quoted since, crafted his own image.[88] As Royalists and his republican critics recognized, such authority as the Protectorate held other than that of arms was due to Cromwell's personal authority and standing. Just as the Commonwealth government had printed Cromwell's letters as the authoritative voice of the regime, so Cromwell's place as Protector was inseparable from his addresses to parliament, and in print to the nation. Shortly after Oliver's death, in a Life of the late Protector, Richard Flecknoe praised the orator as much as the military hero. Describing the 'strong and masculine eloquence' of Cromwell's speeches, 'always intermixed with sentences of Scripture', he compared the force of his godly oratory with the rhetorical skills of Cicero and Demosthenes.[89] If, since then, in the work of Carlyle and others, Cromwell's words have all but been treated as holy writ, that is an appropriate posthumous tribute to a Protector who presented himself, and was perceived by many, as a scriptural exegete.

Cromwell's declarations are far less well known than his speeches but were, in several respects, as important in the representation of the Protector and the Protectorate. While several speeches were printed and all were fairly widely reported, and Cromwell was clearly sensitive to the audience beyond Westminster, his speeches were first and foremost addresses to MPs rather than the nation. From the early seventeenth century, as we have seen, declarations became a medium through which monarchs 'spoke' directly to the people. As news organs and public debate gave platforms to critics of government, declarations became a medium through which rulers could put the royal case. They grew in importance as mounting disagreements between the early Stuarts and their parliaments produced a competition for public support; and, as the crisis of civil war loomed, they became essential in the polemical battle that preceded and continued throughout and beyond the armed conflict. During the 1650s, declarations were of particular value to Cromwell as he persistently sought a constitutional settlement. For, though several were published in his name alone, as many were published as declarations of the Protector and his Council, some even as by the Protector and parliament. Those printed with the authority of Protector and Council or parliament published to the people Cromwell as he wished to be seen to be: a servant of the commonweal, one who took counsel, a figure reluctantly brought to power who desired above all to work with parliaments. Because, however, Cromwell, no less than his regal predecessors, met with contentious parliaments as well as opposition within his own Council, declarations also enabled him to represent his case to the nation, as disgruntled MPs returned to their constituencies.

As with royal declarations, we cannot be certain, especially in the case of those issued by Protector and Council, whether more than one hand penned these words. But, as well as Cromwell's often-cited order for, or approval of, publication, the language and tone, the intense scripturalism, the mingling of personal and biblical injunctions, often echo his speeches and suggest his hand. The chronology of these addresses is also suggestive. The Protector (and Council) issued far more declarations in the first years of the new government, from 1653 to 1655, than in the later years; indeed, there are very few after 1656. While it must remain a suggestion, it may be that this chronology reflects Cromwell's early attempts to persuade parliament and people and later, not only the distractions of foreign wars, but a recognition that his government was not popular and that a permanent settlement founded on consent would not be secured without a return to the old forms. Whatever his inner feelings, throughout his Protectorate Cromwell crafted his declarations as artfully and carefully as he did all aspects of his public self-presentation.

We recall that, following the dissolution of the Long Parliament, the Council of Officers issued declarations explaining their action, which were almost certainly written by Cromwell.[90] In two declarations published in April and May, Cromwell and the officers, while effectively assuming power and indeed claiming Providence as their new authority, still denied any interest or ambition and proclaimed their devotion to lawful authority and parliaments.[91] In fact, attributing the decision to end the parliament to the (unspecified) 'honest people of this nation' who agreed it, the officers all but stated that they went along with rather than led decisions, preferring 'this cause above our names, lives, families or interests'.[92] When, in May, the second declaration argued as a just ground for the dissolution the parliament's attempt to break the army, though it defended the officers – 'God set a strong resolution upon the hearts of the officers of the army to seek after the effecting of good things' – it also insisted on their devotion to 'all lawful ways' and concern about 'doing anything against authority'.[93] Repeating the charge that parliament planned to perpetuate itself, the declaration posited the officers as the true custodians of the cause and constitution.[94] In an order and declaration of 9 June, for a continuation of the unpopular assessment, Cromwell and the Council took further pains to assure all that 'nothing is to be more wished and endeavoured next after the glory of God and securing of this great cause than the ease of the people in this particular.'[95] From the outset, Cromwell was determined to present himself not as a military leader but as the instrument of God and of the people to promote liberties and reformations.

Immediately following his investiture as Protector in December, as well as newspaper reports, a declaration concerning the new government of the three kingdoms reported the ceremonies to the people.[96] In particular, the declaration reported Oliver's speech to the mayor and judges who tendered him the oath in which he had explained that he did not desire to hold his title Protector for any longer 'than it might have a perfect dependency on the great work of the Lord, that so the gospel might flourish in its full splendour and purity; and the people enjoy their just rights and propriety [i.e. properties]'.[97] Retaining the term 'Commonwealth', the author, presumably Cromwell himself, presented the creation of the Protectorate as 'the wonder and emulation of Europe' and dismissed opponents of it as mad – 'lunatic brains'.[98] Against evidently widespread dissatisfaction with the changes, official ceremonies and representations sought to present the Protectorate as enjoying the support and acclamation of the people; that is, as a means of securing them.[99]

A major test of the support, of course, was to be Cromwell's relations with his first Protectoral parliament. During the course of its contentious life, Cromwell continued to address the people directly. As well as licensing the publication of his speeches, the Protector, as we shall see, appointed fast days by which he advertised his godliness and devotion to 'brotherly love' and unity and so implicitly figured his critics as obstacles to such good ends.[100] In what may have been intended as a show of unity, Cromwell even published, on 19 September 1654, a joint declaration with parliament denouncing those of loose opinion and murmurers against the state, and urging all rulers to work together for truth, righteousness and peace.[101] Despite such efforts, debates in parliament revealed not only differences about the means of securing such ends but fundamental challenges to the basis of the new regime itself, which led to its early dissolution in January. *A Declaration of . . . the Lord Protector*, published, with an engraved portrait, soon after the dissolution, essentially summarized the speech Cromwell had delivered to the house; but vitally it publicized to the people both the 'grounds and reasons' of his action and assurances 'touching the law of the land, the discipline of the church and their ancient rights and privileges'.[102]

If Oliver's declaration was motivated by a suspicion of how MPs might represent his actions when they returned to their constituencies, that concern proved to be more than well founded. For days after the Protector's declaration, the members of parliament 'lately dissolved' issued an alternative account of events and of Cromwell which transformed his national image.[103] Against Cromwell's assurances, the MPs claimed they were defending the 'freedom of our native country' threatened by 'the power of our mighty conqueror Oliver Cromwell' who had, they asserted, transgressed the law and subordinated all to his ambition and cruelty. Most damagingly, the MPs exposed Cromwell's protestations that he was but the people's servant, and his godly rhetoric as the Machiavellian devices of an avaricious figure who 'will do anything for his interest', including ordering the suppression of all opponents. Calling upon the people to throw him out, the MPs vowed to support the 'destruction of this devourer of all our security and happiness'. Whether it had widespread support or expressed the views mainly of Royalist enemies (the document praised the old constitution), the declaration marked a pivotal moment in both the reputation and representation of Cromwell and the Protectorate. More bitterly than ever they had against the old king, MPs were denouncing official locutions and scripts and vying for the public support which Cromwell desperately spoke and wrote to secure in order to legitimate his regime. Throughout the rest of the year, no parliament met; Cromwell faced a difficult legal challenge to his right to collect customs revenue; and plots and threats led him to institute as military rulers in the localities the Major-Generals who were to add to his unpopularity.[104] But, significantly, 1655 was the year he issued the most declarations, suggesting that, in the wake of the disastrous dissolution of parliament in January, Cromwell was acutely aware of the need to present and explain himself to the people whose support he needed if England were not to remain a military dictatorship.

In March and May, and again later in the year, Cromwell issued declarations inviting the people to days of fasting in an attempt to unite them in service to God – and to him. In two very long declarations, he also addressed the people in order to defend his actions abroad and at home. On 21 October, a declaration was published by His Highness but with 'the advice of his Council' outlining – and the possessive pronoun announcing shared responsibility is important – 'their' actions against Spain.[105] To argue for his expensive enterprise in the West Indies, Cromwell carefully evoked long-established English passions and fears. Beginning with Philip II's attempt to conquer Elizabethan England, and constantly referring to 1588, the declaration catalogued Spanish cruelties against the English in Europe and America, from stabbings of sailors in 1605 to the 'more fresh and bleeding memory' of Santa Cruce in 1651.[106] Proclaiming that 'there is not any understanding man who is not satisfied of the ... Spaniards pretensions to be sole sovereign', Cromwell – though he claimed he would 'say nothing of the bloody Spanish Inquisition' – warned of Protestantism again in danger; and, presenting it as 'founded upon clear and indisputable grounds', defended the expedition to the West Indies the principal end of which, he claimed, was the advancement of the kingdom of Christ.[107] Just five days later, another long declaration was published – again with the advice and authority of the Council, 'showing the reasons of their proceedings for securing the peace of the Commonwealth', or more particularly, defending the Major-Generals and the taxes levied to pay for them.[108] Evidently still desirous of an accommodation, Cromwell went to some lengths to demonstrate the moderation of his government and leniency to old Royalists. Recent Royalist uprisings, he explained, had necessitated a change of policy to protect the people from plots and invasions.[109] In describing – and exaggerating – the Royalist threat, the Protector again emotively pointed to 'the swarming of . . . Jesuits', and threw in old Levellers and republicans such as Wildman as agents of 'these hidden works of darkness' that God's goodness (and the Protector's watchful care) had exposed.[110] Cleverly arguing that the cause of liberty required it, Cromwell outlined the new militia instituted to ensure security.[111] And figuring the late plotters and rebels as 'other' – as, that is, men separated now from the nation – Cromwell explained that he acted for 'the good and well affected of the land' for whose sake 'we have chiefly published these things that they may know the grounds on which we do proceed towards their preservation'.[112] By casting the Royalist rebels as alien, un-English, the Protector sought to persuade the rest of the people into love and unity and support for his government. If, in the wake of Penruddock's rising, a settlement that included former Royalists appeared unlikely, Cromwell sought to use the situation to bind all others to support his government as the guarantee of their security.

From the outset, Cromwell's difficulties were evident, when over a hundred elected MPs were excluded from sitting, and he appears to have attempted to use declarations from the meeting of his second parliament, in September 1656, as symbols of unity. Days after meeting, the Protector and parliament published, by order of the house, a declaration for a day of fasting and humiliation in which blasphemers and lukewarm atheists were decried and prayers were recommended for unity, that the nation might be settled on the foundations of truth, mercy and peace.[113] A second joint declaration, printed in February, just preceded the offer to Cromwell of the crown and revealed some of the concern that led to it.[114] A proclamation of a fast, the declaration of 2 February dwelt on the continuing 'barbarous design' of the discontented and the plots, most recently Sindercombe's plot, against the life of the Protector.[115] The people were enjoined to thank God that he had frustrated all these designs – by invasion, fire and bullet – against the life of a Protector he owned as his instrument and whom he had saved 'for all the good people of this Commonwealth whose peace and comfort were designed to be taken away with the life of the Protector'.[116] The words represented more than a rhetorical show of unity. By 1656, with republicans excluded, many MPs, including some old Royalists, were ready to see Cromwell as king, if only to restore old constitutional forms and to remove the hated Major-Generals and army rule. When, for whatever reason, Cromwell declined the crown, that apparent unity, and with it the last hope of settlement, faded. Significantly, Cromwell issued no more declarations during the life of the parliament which was dissolved in January 1658. His last, published in the May and July before his final illness and death, recommended in the first case a collection for the relief of

Protestants in Poland and, in the second, a dying man's last proclamation of thanksgiving to God.[117]

It might seem straightforward to conclude that, as his speeches, though brilliant, failed to persuade parliament, Cromwell's public declarations failed to win over the people. But such a verdict would be too simple. For it seems likely that, other than hard core army and republican opponents, the nation would have accepted a monarchy in the house of Cromwell. And many, too, accepted Cromwell's self-presentation as the instrument of God's providence. While he believed in a degree of religious toleration that alienated the conservative gentry, Cromwell increasingly attempted to secure religious unity, not least through days of fast and thanksgiving that, like a monarchical Supreme Head, he regularly ordered. As we have noted in passing, many of the declarations issued by the Protector 'invited' the people to join in services which very much concerned Cromwell's own priorities and position. In 1654, for example, recommending peace in the church and 'brotherly love' among Christians, he denounced both those who claimed to be 'the only true ministry' and (as well) false prophets who pursued their own fancies and notions.[118] The next year Protectoral declarations for fast days contrasted the kind blessings of God with the blasphemies, divisions and dashed hopes of settlement that frustrated his will, as well as that of those to whom God had entrusted the affairs of the nation.[119] Further proclamations of fast days reiterated prayers for unity and criticized those who 'despise magistracy', or who 'still . . . murmur and are unquiet'.[120] In such declarations recommending prayers, as in his speeches, Cromwell liberally cited Scripture, indeed deployed it to manifest the righteousness of his own courses and the errors of his opponents. In his last order for a service of thanksgiving and atonement, issued on 3 July 1658, Oliver explicitly cast those who had ruined the chance of a settlement as enemies of God who had shown his 'good hand in our . . . deliverance' – that is the Protector's and the nation's.[121] While he acknowledged that he had not yet secured settlement, Cromwell compared the nation to the burning bush and implicitly himself to Moses whom 'God did send to be a ruler and a deliverer'.[122] Cromwell famously compared himself in a speech of April 1657 to a parish constable appointed to keep the peace.[123] In his proclamation for fasts, however, read from pulpits throughout the country, melding his own words with Scripture and interpreting God's ways, he acted the part of a priest and claimed authority as God's instrument. Cromwell, John Morrill has written, 'used the Scriptures to discern God's will'; but he also used them to advance his own.[124]

II

Cromwell was one of those early modern rulers who was very much his own best spokesman. This did not mean that he failed to exploit other official organs of communication that, as we would put it, spun the actions of his government to present it in the best light. Indeed, not long after becoming Protector Cromwell tightened the licensing laws so that, effectively, Marchamont Nedham's Monday *Public Intelligencer* and Thursday *Mercurius Politicus* became the only newspapers in existence and the official voice of the regime.[125] After his earlier support for the republican cause and a radical group led by Marten, Nedham became a powerful advocate for the Protectorate for which he also worked as an agent reporting on the activities of Fifth Monarchist opponents.[126] Nedham published a defence of the Instrument in his *True State of the Case of the Commonwealth* and became, from the establishment of the Protectorate, a spokesman for policies and values, such as religious toleration, close to Cromwell's own. Though he never ceased to champion popular sovereignty, and in 1656 was viewed by some as a critic of Cromwell, Nedham supported the Humble Petition, and the stability the Protectorate secured, and was one of the attendants in Cromwell's funeral procession in November 1658. Because little has been written about Nedham's Protectorate journalism, one best senses the service he performed by sampling his weekly newspapers. Not least important, Nedham often included the Protector's declarations, writs and statements, framed with news that placed them in a favourable explanatory context.[127] As well as reporting naval victories and honourable receptions of the Protector's agents abroad, *Politicus* relayed news of foreign events often in ways that fleshed out Cromwell's own accounts of the threats that faced the nation and that helped to justify his measures.[128] Along with frequent positive representations of the government's 'respect and care of the public good', Nedham mocked critics of the Protectorate who offered only 'fancies' and 'notions' as alternatives to the stability it preserved.[129] When Cromwell's second parliament met in September 1656, *Mercurius Politicus* made much of the occasion and proceedings that gave constitutional propriety to the Protectorate.[130] Though during the debates on the earlier Nayler's case, Nedham justified parliament's sentence for horrid blasphemy (he appears to have shared his contemporaries' loathing of Quakers) rather than followed Cromwell's inclination to lenience, he remained publicly supportive of the Protector's authority.[131] During a series of joshing (and partly ironic) exchanges with James Harrington, whose *Oceana*, published in late 1656, was taken by Cromwell as an attack on his authority and position, *Mercurius Politicus* defended the pragmatic basis of the Protectorate and Cromwell himself against scribbling carpers.[132] 'There is', Nedham countered the idealists in number 354 of *Politicus*, 'a necessity of a settlement and . . . it matters not what the form be, so we attain the ends of government.'[133] Condemning the 'Levellers' and 'enthusiasts' who wanted no law, religion or government, in the name of liberty he emphasized the need for government to secure men's rights and properties.[134] And – on more than occasion – comparing Cromwell to Basilides (Emperor of Abyssinia, who expelled the Jesuits), he praised the Protector as a saviour:

Thus while . . . the people ran out into endless factions, still further and further from a settlement, there was in conclusion no visible means left to keep the old race of kings from over-running our estates and liberties, and not the most excellent *Basilides*, that renowned prince, resolved to encounter all the monsters of scandal, prejudice, ignorance and faction at home, and the common enemy abroad.[135]

Mercurius Politicus, as its title page announced, published foreign and domestic news 'for information of the people'. But it also represented the Protectorate to them as the best government for the times and published and advertised panegyric verses on Cromwell whom Nedham presented as a truly regal figure who displayed 'majesty and authority in all his actions'.[136]

One of the signs of the Protectorate's shift to a greater emphasis on charismatic personality, if not yet the regal forms of the late 1650s, was the rise in panegyric verse lauding the leader of the state. Such verses had been, under monarchy, whether officially patronized or not, important in the representation of kings and queens but had faded during the war years and under the Commonwealth. Perhaps significantly, soon after the establishment of the Protectorate a Cambridge volume of Greek and Latin verse, of the sort regularly published to commemorate royal marriages, births and other occasions, was published *Ad illustrissimum celissimumque Oliverum . . . protectorem*.[137] Praising Cromwell as the military hero he had been, 'dux invictissime', the volume also celebrated the Protectoral peace abroad and at home and, echoing Caroline hymns to halcyon days, proclaimed: 'iam fortas dormire potest Respublica noctes'.[138] While (rhetorically) alluding to the novelty of Cromwell's position ('how should we call you?', lines asked), the poets were quick to deploy titles of honour of regal and imperial style – 'illustre caput', 'maxime' – while lauding Oliver's contempt for sceptres.[139] 'Quid superest Olivere', 'who can be greater than Oliver', a verse runs, as the panegyric volume revives a genre of poetic celebration and representation which itself bestowed, as well as lauded, majesty.[140]

The Protectorate occasioned not only the revival but a revision of panegyrical poetry praising the head of state. In 1655, three great poets turned their attention to Cromwell when it seemed that the Protectorate would be established a year after its institution. George Wither, who had penned regal panegyrics in the early seventeenth century but had captained a troop of Surrey horse for parliament in the civil war, was appointed by Cromwell in July 1655 Master of the Statute Office.[141] If Wither partly owed his place to his verse – he penned lines in 1654 celebrating the providential care of Cromwell in God's saving him from a coaching accident – on taking office he certainly lauded Oliver; and not as a king but as a Protector brought to his place by God.[142] The subtitle of Wither's 1655 *The Protector: A Poem* announces that the verse was written to 'briefly illustrate the supereminency of that dignity'.[143] Presenting

Cromwell from the opening line as he saw himself – that is as the instrument of Providence – Wither distanced his position from that of a king by explaining that God invented new titles and names for those singled out to carry on his work. 'The Subject of My Muse', Wither explained to readers, was, as well as a man, 'a TITLE', which, though as yet not well known, would soon be famous.[144] Explaining and defending how the Protectorate had come into being, Wither narrated his own biography and experience of kings, parliaments and Commonwealth.[145] The Protectorate, he posited, had been God's course to rescue the nation from confusion; therefore those who wished to restore the title of king crossed God's own wishes. More than any other title, Wither argued, that of Protector indicated a leader who sought first his people's good; and, listing the many virtues he believed the title signified, he assured the people: 'This a PROTECTOR is, or ought to be'.[146] Having in the last words given notice that Cromwell would be held, as kings had been, to the poets' account, Wither urged readers to give their obedience and support to Oliver and to his elevation to a position 'by decree from heaven'.[147] Claiming to write at a time 'when poetry itself is thought a crime', Wither added powerful poetic persuasion to the pragmatic arguments for the Protectorate and represented Cromwell not only as Christ's instrument but as 'His ways preparer', as the hope of a godly commonweal.[148]

Wither's *Poem* may have been inspired by (as well as owing a debt to) one of the great panegyrics on Cromwell, Andrew Marvell's *On the First Anniversary of the Government under His Highness the Lord Protector*.[149] Marvell had been close to the centre of government since early 1652 when Milton had recommended him as 'of singular desert for the state to make use of', and when Cromwell himself appointed him governor of William Dutton, prospective husband of his own daughter, Frances.[150] Whatever the equivocations of Marvell's earlier verse on Oliver (the *Horatian Ode*), *The First Anniversary* extolled Cromwell's virtues, position and policies. Using regal language and metaphors, Marvell succeeded in representing Cromwell as better than a king and the Protectorate settlement as a harmonious resolution of political differences. Opening with (regal) paeans to the 'Sun-like' as well as 'indefatigable' Cromwell, Marvell presents Oliver as a figure who single-handedly brought affairs to harmonious settlement.[151]

Such was that wondrous Order and Consent,
When *Cromwell* tun'd the ruling Instrument;[152]

A man singled out by Providence (Marvell also refers to his coaching accident), Oliver is represented as a Gideon, a saviour, whose virtues and chosen status matter far more than conventional titles or constitutions:[153]

For to be *Cromwell* was a greater thing,
Then ought below, or yet above a King.[154]

Though he 'seems a King by long succession born', and abroad performed better than a monarch, Cromwell disregarded the title.[155] While such lines seem written to reassure those who desired a king that, in all that mattered, they had one, Marvell also sought to reassure the Commonwealthsmen anxious about the re-establishment of the single person ruler. Echoing the language of critics of the end of the Commonwealth, he replies:

> 'Tis not a Freedome, that where All command;
> Nor Tyrannie, where One dos them withstand[156]

And, figuring Cromwell, though in a regal metaphor, as yet the perfect mean between these extremes, Marvell's lines continue:

> But who of both the Bounders [boundaries] knows to lay
> Him as their Father, must the State obey.[157]

Where earlier Marvell appeared to be torn between monarchy and republic, he here presented the Protector as a king and not a king; indeed, as (at least on the domestic front) a member of a Commonwealth of equals:

> Abroad a King he seems, and somthing more,
> At Home a Subject on the equall Floor.[158]

'A great prince', Marvell's Cromwell is yet 'the *Angell* of our Commonweal', the presidential leader of a free state.[159]

The third early poetic panegyrist of the Protectorate was Edmund Waller, whose poem was actually entitled *A Panegyric to My Lord Protector*.[160] Waller had been a central figure among the court poets of Charles I and, after the outbreak of civil war, was involved in a plot to force parliament to negotiate a settlement with the king. Fined and imprisoned, Waller was permitted to go into exile in 1644. In 1651, however, parliament revoked his banishment and Waller returned, intent on making his accommodation with Cromwell, who was his second cousin.[161] Like Wither's and Marvell's poems of the same year, Waller's 1655 *Panegyric* was written to support the legitimacy of the Protectorate. Given Waller's background and affiliations, it was probably especially valued as a poem which might encourage other former Royalists to the conformity that Cromwell desired.[162] Like Wither and Marvell, Waller praised Cromwell for restoring a divided England:

> Your drooping Countrey torn with Civil Hate,
> Restor'd by you is made a Glorious State[163]

But Waller emphasized the military victories and imperial ambitions of the Protector who recalled, he argued, Edward III and the Black Prince, as well as

Julius and Augustus Caesar.[164] Praising Cromwell's piety and personal virtues ('matchless worth'), Waller focused more closely even than his fellows on Cromwell not as servant of the Commonwealth but as an Augustus, who had brought a torn and weary England to order, peace and repose.[165] Reading Waller, we gain more of an understanding of how former Royalists could come round to accepting Cromwell as king. In David Norbrook's words, through a 'renewed form of literary Augustanism', Waller 'found an idiom for supporting the Protectorate which could appeal to a traditional political elite'.[166]

The ambiguities in poetic representation and praise of Cromwell, stemming from the need to address and persuade old Royalists on the one hand and to reassure old commonwealthsmen on the other, were more starkly revealed as MPs, from rather different motives, moved to change the Protectorate into a monarchy. Developing Waller's appropriation of regal Augustanism, a panegyric to Cromwell appended to a prose treatise (possibly Harrington's), *The Unparalleled Monarch or The Portraiture of a Matchless Prince* (1656), celebrated Oliver as 'The best of Princes in the worst of times'.[167] Though the anonymous author compared Cromwell to ancient heroes like Hercules and the biblical leaders Moses, Aaron and Joshua, and, echoing official Protectorial language, agreed 'the cause you fight is God's', the poem presented Cromwell as a king and called upon him 'T'enrich our Crown & beautifie our Throne'. A number of Latin and English poems by Payne Fisher were perhaps more successful in representing Cromwell's assumption of a distinct and different Protectorial power. Published by government printers and with dedicatory verses by other Cromwellian authors, Fisher came close to being the Protector's laureate and wrote verses to commemorate the anniversaries of his first inauguration and his second inauguration, after the Additional Petition, as hereditary Protector.[168] Fisher does deploy the metaphors associated with kings, praising Cromwell as father and prince.[169] But Cromwell was also described as a servant of the laws, as one bred to serve the state, as the 'libertatis reductor' of England.[170] Though he compared Cromwell to famous princes and (alluding to Elizabeth) described him as a phoenix, Fisher represented the Protector as another Scipio, a pious Mebellus, as one who remained a tribune of the people, even as he was led reluctantly to become ruler.[171] Throughout, Fisher presents Cromwell, as Oliver did himself in his own speeches, as one without ambition who had reluctantly taken the helm and who remained a humble servant of the state. Though called a prince, Cromwell was, as a prefatory verse to *Piscatris poemata* put it simply, 'Maxime Protector Britonum', in Fisher's words on the anniversary of his inauguration, 'magnum religionis lumen & vindex veritatis', who gloried in his title Protector.[172] Responding to attacks on Cromwell's supposed ambition from Royalists and old commonwealthsmen, Payne Fisher sustained, along with Augustan references, republican terms and images which represented the Protector and Protectorate as the best of history and as the best government for England.

The praise of the Latin poet Fisher may have earned him a pension and patronage, but vernacular support that reached a wider audience was of greater effect in winning popular support. Just after Cromwell's refusal of the crown, George Wither returned to verse with *A Sudden Flash Timely Discovering Some Reasons Wherefore the Style of Protector Should Not Be Deserted By These Nations*.[173] In a dedication to Cromwell, Wither urged readers not to assume that a leader who had refused the crown was one who aimed at even greater power.[174] Comparing it to Christ's resistance of temptation, Wither praised Oliver for carrying on with his and Christ's work for which God had raised him.[175] Assuring those who had wanted kingship that 'The *Supream Person*, always is the same/In *Soveraignty* whatever him you *name*', that the name was not material, he called upon all to support the Protector and to unite to follow him in God's service and for the public safety.[176]

While defending Cromwell's title as 'Sovereign Protector or Protector Imperial of the Commonwealth of Great Britain', Wither confessed that 'in verse it goes but lamely' and that the case for acceptance and obedience needed to be presented in prose.[177] And, despite the criticism that the dissolution of two parliaments and the establishment of the Protectorate drew, the new regime did not want for support in prose polemic from the beginning. In 1654, two panegyrics on Cromwell and his government were published in Latin, with Leyden as the stated place of publication. Written under the name of Rodrigues de Sá e Meneses, and rather doubtfully attributed to Milton, the panegyrics reached Thomason in May and thereafter probably circulated in England.[178] The treatises, presenting Cromwell as 'a sober Alexander', 'a moderate Caesar', painted the new Protector as a modest man who had eschewed honours and who 'took no thought of himself that he might attend the Commonwealth'.[179] It was, the second tract insisted, Cromwell's love of liberty that had led him to dispense with parliaments. Unlike Caesar, he did not seize the reins of power, 'but the gods assenting, the citizens calling you', effected it 'with the greatest accord of the whole people'.[180] While it is highly unlikely that he was author of these tracts, Milton's contemporary Latin *Defensio seconda* defended Cromwell's assumption of the position of Protector in some of the same terms.[181] Though indicating that he would hold Cromwell to account, Milton described him as the 'best of men and the most worthy of all applause'.[182] And clearing him of any blame for the dissolution of Barebones and of the charge of ambition, he assured readers that the new Protector was 'forced into the order for the public good' and praised Cromwell, writing that 'with a majesty far above it, you have despised the name of king'.[183]

Milton, Latin secretary to the government, addressed in his *Defensio* an international republic and the English elite. But, probably as soon as the Barebones assembly dissolved itself, Marchamont Nedham was working on a defence of the change that had taken place, aimed at all literate English subjects – and perhaps also at an audience beyond. A copy of *A True State of the Case of the Commonwealth* was acquired by Thomason on 9 February.[184] Evidently concerned to mute criticisms of change by stressing continuity, Nedham insisted that the new government corresponded with the first aims of all those who had engaged against the king in the good old cause.[185] It was Barebones, the *True State* argued, that departed from those principles by threatening to subvert liberty and property, which the change to a Protectorate was effected to preserve.[186] Nedham went to lengths to reassure those who suspected that the Protectorate had reintroduced monarchy.[187] The government, he explained, was not a monarchy but rule by a person elected and responsible to the people, who, in contrast to the royal pursuit of self-interest, held a trust for the benefit of the people.[188] Glossing the constitution so as to emphasize the separation of the executive and legislative and the guarantees it provided for parliaments, including their right in future to appoint the Council of State, Nedham defended the Protector's powers and position.[189] Though, in observing that the nation had not fought against kingship *per se* but against a tyrant, he may have intended to keep the option of the crown open for Cromwell, the thrust of the *True State* was that the Protectorate was different and better – the best synthesis of all forms which gave the Commonwealth a new face while retaining its substance.[190]

Published by Thomas Newcomb, Nedham's may have been the authorized apology for the new regime, but others preceded and rapidly followed him. Thomason acquired two defences of the Protectorate on 18 January, only four weeks after Cromwell was installed. The first under the name of Johannes Cornubiensis, appeared to echo criticism in its title *The Grand Catastrophe or The Change of Government* but, in the form of a letter to a friend, in fact set out to answer widespread objections that the government by Protector was too monarchical.[191] 'It is a gross mistake,' the tract asserted, 'to think and say that this is a monarchical or kingly government.'[192] And arguing that 'it is not a single person but a sole power which makes a monarch', the author emphasized the distinction between kingly government which was not like God's, and this new rule by one who followed the precedent of Gideon and Jepthah and the government of the Judges.[193] Admonishing Cromwell that some did suspect him of desiring hereditary succession, Cornubiensis assured readers that the Protector was not a man of ambition, that the change of regime was a mercy brought about by God, and that none had cause to doubt it.[194] John Hall's *Confusion Confounded* also reviewed recent events and defended the change of government.[195] A friend of Milton and of Nedham, who published a newsbook from 1648, Hall was a Commonwealth supporter who accommodated himself without evident difficulty to the Protectorate.[196] In *Confusion Confounded*, he was highly critical of both the recent parliaments and castigated Barebones as a group ready to destroy peace and liberty and 'raise up an insupportable tyranny.'[197] Though he acknowledged that 'some men may be unsatisfied with the present constitution', he dismissed opposition as nothing but 'spleen and ignorance' and, reminding readers that governments might be changed, suggested that this transformation was a consequence of God's will and so to be accepted.[198]

In the face of continuing opposition and unease, apologias for the Protectorate continued to argue the government's case. In April, the minister Thomas Goodwin's *Peace Protected and Discontent Disarmed*, specifically replying to recent queries raised, was published 'to allay the discontents . . . about the late revolution of government'.[199] It was God, Goodwin told readers, who had manifested his displeasure with the late parliaments and approved the present regime that 'better and more clearly asserted and secured' the 'rights, liberties and interest of the people'.[200] Similarly the Baptist Samuel Richardson came to the support of Cromwell against old allies who accused him of betraying the cause. Richardson's *Apology for the Present Government and Governor*, published in September, systematically addressed persistent objections to deny that the Protectorate was arbitrary and the Protector proud.[201] Urging that the recent change had provided the best foundation for peace, Richardson asked all to ponder whether grumbling would not undermine it.[202] An anonymous *Copy of a Letter Concerning the Election of a Lord Protector*, probably published in December, went further.[203] Written by one who professed himself as once having been against it, the author not only argued for the Protectorate as the best guarantee of security but for a hereditary Protectorate, in a moderate family such as Cromwell's, as infinitely preferable to the accident of election.[204] Reminding readers that the recent experiences of parliaments had led men to question their protection of the people's liberties, the letter was evidently intended to persuade not only the (fictional) ex-MP who was its recipient but also the nation that single-person rule was the best polity for the times.[205]

Such defences and apologies, especially those of former republicans and religious radicals, may well have converted some at least to accept the Protectorate regime. But as Cromwell strove for recognition of the legality and legitimacy of his office and government, and as former Royalists and Commonwealthsmen continued to rail against it, supporters of the regime had to sustain a polemical battle to secure public backing. Directed at different audiences, including opponents of the regime, the defences adopted different strategies of argument. One, purporting in 1655 to be printing the gist of a manuscript treatise by the Jesuit Robert Parsons, appears to have been directed at those who felt Stuart more lawful than Cromwellian rule.[206] Thomas White's *The Grounds of Obedience* argued for a similar purpose rather differently, and along Hobbesian lines dismissed Stuart pretensions and implicitly supported Cromwell.[207] Others added divine obligation to such pragmatic and utilitarian arguments. In *God's Unchangeableness*, George Smith presented to the people a Cromwell who had been singled out by Providence as England's deliverer and insisted that the authority of the Lord Protector and his Council was 'authority

. . . from God'.[208] John Moore of Dunster, Somerset in *Protection Proclaimed* advertised that in his book 'the government of the Lord Protector and his Council is proved to be of divine institution [and] . . . none other than what hath been given to those whom God hath made instrumental for his people's deliverance of old'.[209] Dedicating it to Cromwell, Moore observed that the title of Protector was given to the governors of Israel before they had a king and that it was the form of rule that most nearly approximated to that of Christ.[210] Figuring Oliver, again, as a second Moses, he urged all to rejoice in his role and damned opponents of the Protector as opponents of God.[211]

Some of the protagonists for the Protectorate published more than once in its support. John Hall of Richmond (not to be confused with the author of *Confusion Confounded*), having in 1654 published a lengthy treatise on the need for obedience, in 1656 dedicated to Cromwell *The True Cavalier*.[212] Admitting that he had been a supporter of monarchy, Hall promised Cromwell the allegiance of the Royalists to his government, to which God had ordained him, and even went so far as to say that they preferred Oliver to any other sovereign.[213] The Supreme Headship of the church, he added, belonged to the chief magistrate as much as to any monarch and therefore, he implied, Anglicans as well as Royalists supported Protectorial rule: 'I hope,' he concluded, 'none will refuse to submit to that authority'.[214] Samuel Richardson, author of the 1654 *Apology*, in his 1656 *Plain Dealing or The Unveiling of the Opposers of the Present Government* rounded on the Protector's critics.[215] Reminding Royalists that God had already passed judgment on kings, and dismissing the complaints of old Commonwealthsmen that Cromwell had broken promises, Richardson asserted that it was hardly possible to enjoy more liberty than was secured by the Protectorate.[216] Praising Cromwell and his Council, Richardson expressed his belief that God was behind the Protectorate and the Protector and prayed that he would long reign.[217]

During 1656 and early 1657, support for the Protectorate appears to have been growing among those who hoped that it might lead to a re-establishment of the old forms. Indeed, the author of *The Unparalleled Monarch or, The Portraiture of a Matchless Prince* seems to have sought to represent the Protector as a king in order to facilitate the acceptance of the crown.[218] Describing Cromwell as having a 'sovereign' countenance, 'princely eye' and 'angelical beauties', the author (interestingly again making a connection between the bodies personal and public) presented a body made for a crown and sceptre.[219] Using the language of masque, the *Portraiture* depicts him as 'enflamed with the beams of celestial and divine love', while a series of royal metaphors (the physician, the oak, the pilot, the sun) figures Cromwell as a king.[220] However, whatever the wishes of the author, *The Unparalleled Monarch* was clear: 'he is a king *and* will not put on a crown'.[221] Alongside the regal imagery, Cromwell is also portrayed in his own favoured terms: as a pious Gideon and a Joshua, with a commission from God.[222] And, in the spirit of this rather different representation, the reader is asked: 'why should we not love and embrace him though the royal blood may not . . . stream in his veins?'[223] After all, the reader is reminded, 'to be wrapt and swaddled in purple is not so much as the one half of a good prince . . . wisdom and virtue are of the perfection and essence of a regular and complete sovereignty'.[224] Though at first reading like a manifesto for Cromwell to be king, the text is ambiguous: ambiguous because, as the author acknowledges, there is opposition to kingship, not least from Cromwell himself.[225] Anxious above all for settlement, the author, presenting a king and not a king, urged in his address to the reader: 'we have no little reason to unite and stick close to our Caesar'.[226]

The Unparalleled Monarch, while appealing for unity – 'methinks we should combine like Christians and countrymen' – was written out of, and into, a culture of division.[227] Because England was divided, when he last refused parliament's offer of the crown, Cromwell, as much as he disappointed some, gained the support of others. Wither, as we saw, in *A Sudden Flash* offered reasons in verse why 'the style of Protector should not be deserted'.[228] Pamphlets publicized versions of the arguments Cromwell had used against kingship. In 1658, one T.L. in *Considerations*, as the title page has it, 'printed for the public good', defended the Protectorate and endeavoured to persuade all to submit to Richard, Cromwell's son and successor, established by the Humble Petition that followed the refusal of the crown.[229]

Oliver Cromwell, as we shall see, in death at last was given the crown that some had lobbied him to receive, that others had feared he would take.[230] The contested representations of Cromwell – king or no king, prophet or Machiavellian – continued long after his death. If, however, from 1653 to 1658 England reached some kind of peace and a settlement where most accommodated with the regime, that was due not only to the Protector himself but to the array of panegyrists and prose writers who, often but not always with official support, presented and re-presented Cromwell to the people as the best hope of stability, and who sustained hopes and countered arguments so as to keep him in office in rapidly changing circumstances. Like the course of the revolution itself, the images of Cromwell which were constructed and disseminated were always contested and changing. But from the institution in 1653 of the Protectorate as 'midway between . . . monarchical and democratical', the drift in the style and image, and in the perception of the Protector, whatever his protestations, was inexorably to the regal.[231]

CHAPTER 17

PAINTING PROTECTORAL POWER

I

One of the things best known about Oliver Cromwell's visual image is known through words: that is Oliver's supposed instruction to the artist Peter Lely, who was about to execute his portrait:

> Mr Lely I desire you would use all your skill to paint my picture truly like me & not flatter me at all. But (pointing to his own face) remark all these roughness, pimples, warts & everything as you see me. Other wise I never will pay a farthing for it.[1]

The 'warts and all' Cromwell has passed into history: as the plain man, the plain speaker and plain captain who only reluctantly took the reins of government. Recently, Laura Knoppers identified in Cromwell's portraits a 'plain style' which, she argued, was the aesthetic preference of just such a figure who resisted the crown, the champion of an aesthetic iconoclasm to match the revolutionary political and religious iconoclasm of the 1640s and 1650s.[2] Perhaps slightly contradictorily, Knoppers also observed that different artists painted Cromwell's portrait, that in writings he made no references to portraits and that he had, in contrast to monarchs, no official court painter. 'His interest in visual and verbal representations of himself,' Laura Knoppers concludes, 'was largely limited to countering the negative.'[3] The Cromwell she paints is a man who very much fits with the familiar puritan type: a figure uninterested in vanity and suspicious of the visual arts as arts of misrepresentation rather than representation.

The story, as Knoppers acknowledges, of Cromwell's injunction to Lely is not contemporary: it was first related by George Vertue about 1721 and it may be anecdotal.[4] That aside, there are difficulties with taking the injunction straightforwardly as a summation of Cromwell's attitude to his portrayal and with the interesting case that Laura Knoppers puts forward. For the danger is that one takes as Cromwell's representation, as he wished one to, his self-representation as but the commander of the 'plain russet coated captain[s]'.[5]

Surprisingly, Knoppers argues that Cromwell took little interest in 'visual *and verbal* representations of himself [my emphasis]' when, as we have seen, and most would concur, his speeches were carefully rhetorically crafted to enhance his position and authority. In those speeches, the pose of modesty, and of reluctance to govern, was coupled with endlessly rehearsed claims to be God's instrument and to an authority granted by Providence that would not brook opposition. Certainly, Oliver's critics and enemies – Royalists on the one side, old Commonwealthsmen on the other – suspected him of masking vanity and ambition in order the better to obtain dominance; and they should not be dismissed just because they were hostile. Where his portraits are concerned, Cromwell clearly took a greater interest in his image after 1653 than earlier. Where, we recall, during the 1640s, and in the particular case of the medal to commemorate the victory at Dunbar in 1650, Oliver had resisted a prominent image of himself and had advised collective representations of parliament and the army, as Protector he evidently commissioned and distributed official portraits of himself as a single, commanding figure of authority.[6] Cromwell may not have appointed an official court painter – by no means all monarchs did. But that is not to say that he was not (as the instruction to Lely itself suggests) as careful of his visual portrayal as of his verbal self-representation; nor that the so-called 'plain style' was not, in every sense, as artful as the speeches were rhetorical. The visual representations of the Protector in portraits and engravings, as on seals, medals and coins, were devised to sustain and enhance Cromwell's authority in shifting historical circumstances no less than the earlier images of kings from which they borrowed. They developed and changed with shifting circumstances and became, I shall argue, increasingly regal.

A discussion of the Protector's visual image must return us to the earlier portrait of Cromwell by Robert Walker, probably executed in 1649. David Piper, noting that Cromwell approved it, describes it as an official portrait that remained the dominant image of Cromwell until at least 1654 and one of the types which was continued to 1656.[7] There are variants as well as copies of the portrait, which was evidently hung in numerous aristocratic and gentry houses and remains one of the most frequently encountered portraits in England in replica and repetition.[8] Though all versions probably descend from one sitting, and the head remained the same, there are three-quarter-lengths and versions to the waist only, as well as one double portrait, with Major-General Lambert, which, though of uncertain date, may be connected with the institution of the Protectorate.[9] In this portrait, Cromwell, as we noted, is depicted with a baton and in armour with, behind him (on the left in most versions, but on the right in some) a page tying a silk sash around his waist. In general terms the armoured Cromwell follows a whole panoply of European representations of generals. But David Piper long ago identified a more local and topical debt to Van Dyck's portrait of Viscount Goring and Lord Newport now at Petworth;

86 *Oliver Cromwell* by Robert Walker, *c.* 1649.

more recently, I suggested the influence of the 1636 portrait of Thomas Wentworth, Earl of Stafford by Van Dyck.[10] While acknowledging these debts, Laura Knoppers interprets the portrait not as a simple replication but as an appropriation and revision of a courtly, indeed monarchical, image.[11] Though Cromwell's body is richly apparelled and elongated by the position of the page and viewer, Knoppers observes a plain head with uneven hair and suggests a contrast with the idealized version of the page, who (though she does not argue this) may stand for a courtly culture of ease in contrast to the military action Cromwell symbolizes. While, however, Knoppers is right to insist that Walker's Cromwell is not a simple reproduction of Van Dyck, the similarities remain striking. Importantly, too, at least in its signification, this is no plain – if by that is meant straightforward – record of Cromwell. Not only, as we know from the later 'warts and all' images, has Cromwell's face been cleared of blemishes, but the representation is softened and idealized.[12] The armour Cromwell wears is not that of the civil war soldier (who would have worn a cuirass with a buff coat and helmet) but of an antique, sixteenth-century style of the sort we have seen in portraits of Prince Henry and Charles I. Approving the portrait, Cromwell evidently wished to be represented in this chivalric, at least quasi-regal mode, as early as 1649 – though whether to aspire to, or erase the memory of, monarchy remains unknown. Certainly, the Walker portrait 'challenges the exclusionary claims of the Caroline court to images of power and authority'.[13] But it also sits strangely with Cromwell's reluctance to have his image on the Dunbar medal and so suggests early ambiguities about his personal position, authority and representation, perhaps even a desire to keep options open. Though proclaiming in a speech to the army in 1649 that 'it matters not who is our commander-in-chief if God be so', Cromwell's portrait by Walker positions Cromwell as just that: a commander-in-chief of the army to Ireland and perhaps potentially of the nation.[14]

It may seem ironic that while such a regal image of Cromwell circulated as portraits and engravings during the Commonwealth, after he became Protector Oliver evidently sought a less monarchical image. As David Piper has argued, a new portrait type emerged in 1654, soon after Cromwell's proclamation as Protector (in December 1653) and appears to have been a replacement official portrait.[15] Since it was in 1654 that Peter Lely began to work for Cromwell, the new image may well relate to the instruction to the painter as related by Vertue. However, it has been persuasively argued that the originator of the new style was not Lely but Samuel Cooper, the miniaturist.[16] Though his brush has been detected in the works of his uncle John Hoskins at the Caroline court, Cooper himself only became established in London after the outbreak of the civil war, during which he executed portraits of Parliamentarian generals.[17] He began to work for Cromwell in 1650, producing likenesses of Oliver and his daughter Elizabeth, and possibly other members of the Cromwell family. Cromwell's family's employment of a miniaturist suggests, John Murdoch argues, the adoption after 1653 of a French courtly practice.[18] But in Oliver's case, Cooper's first image of him, dated by Piper to 1653, was far less regal than the Walker. Indeed, Cooper's miniature, now in the Buccleuch collection, is realistic to the point of wilfully unflattering – the simple attire, receding hair and warts (one very prominent on the chin) constituting indeed a 'startlingly honest and plain depiction'.[19] Other Cooper miniatures of the Protector, including a bust facing to the right, differ but have in common the realism and plain, simple appearance of the earliest: an image that follows, in Knoppers's words, 'Cromwell's own plain-spoken Biblicism and piety'.[20]

Cooper's plain image appears to have become a model for the portraits of Cromwell which followed his appointment as Lord Protector. Lely's head and shoulders portrait in oval, now at Birmingham, follows a Cooper miniature in the pose and position of the head, though it softens the warts that were prominent in Cooper and depicts Cromwell's body in the cuirassier armour which, as we commented, was often an artistic prop signifying chivalric values and virtues.[21] As in Cooper's unfinished miniature, Lely's Cromwell does not look out to the viewer, as monarchs often did on canvas, but appears as if caught, unposed, in a moment of intense contemplation – perhaps of his duty of service to God and nation. The similarity between the two artists' portrayals suggests a new official image which can only have been commissioned by

87 *Oliver Cromwell* by Samuel Cooper, *c.* 1650.

Cromwell himself to mark his new position. Indeed, another undated portrait (attributed uncertainly to Walker), depicting Cromwell as a cavalryman, may well belong to the remaking of his image. The portrait, in the Cromwell Museum, presents the Protector in a less flamboyant manner than Walker's earlier image and contributes to the re-presentation of Oliver as the ordinary minor gentleman and soldier that the other 1654 portrayals helped to construct.

Plainness and simplicity, however, are not the only messages one takes from this canvas. The portrait owes a clear debt to Van Dyck portraits, especially the 1632 canvas of Frederick Henry, Prince of Orange who, of course, by 1640 was Charles I's son-in-law, and has some echoes of Mytens's portrait of Charles as prince.[22] Another, anonymous, painting, also in the Cromwell Museum and dated to *c.* 1654, similarly recalls earlier, regal images. Laura Knoppers

88 *Oliver Cromwell* by Peter Lely, 1654.

curiously describes the equestrian portrait of Cromwell astride a barb stallion as 'significantly non-monarchical, more like that of a Dutch burgher'.[23] In general this type of equestrian portrait, especially as here with a reproduction of Hollar's engraving of the city of London as a backdrop, was a regal, indeed a Stuart, image. And while it is true that Cromwell's velvet jacket and breeches are not especially opulent, the sugar loaf hat with feathers recalls countless engraved images of Charles I.[24] As with the Protector's speeches, new portraits of Cromwell executed after 1653, though they advertised ordinariness, yet retained distinctly recognizable monarchical forms.

The last contemporary portraits of Cromwell perpetuate that ambiguity or doubleness that was at the heart of the Protectorate as well as its representation. A recent interpretation of the portrait of Cromwell by the little-known artist Edward Mascall, acquired by the Cromwell Museum in 1966, draws attention to its simplicity. Representing Oliver as older, with no symbols of

89 *Oliver Cromwell* by an unknown artist.

office or authority, the portrait exhibits, it is argued, 'no signs of royalty nor indeed of pomp'.[25] At the time of the offer of the crown, Mascall directs the viewer not to the Protector but to the man. It may be that, as Laura Knoppers implies, Mascall's image contributed to the debate about kingship and, since he presumably sat for it, perhaps represented Cromwell's reluctance to take the crown. Yet, though plain and even austere, the portrait still evokes portraits of Charles I who tended to be depicted without the trappings of regality, representing his authority as intrinsic to his person. But most problematically, Mascall's portrait, if interpreted as a rejection of regal representation, fits uneasily with the increasingly monarchical style of Cromwell's court and with other visual images of the Protector from his last year. In 1658, for example, Oliver evidently approved the decoration of the initial letter of a charter with his portrait. Not only was this a distinctly Tudor regal form, on a charter at Chester and patent of nobility Cromwell is depicted in ermine, and in the latter

90 Anonymous equestrian painting of Cromwell, *c.* 1654.

case with a sceptre.[26] If Mascall's portrait was 'a remarkably private depiction' of Cromwell, it may be seen as a representation of one of the two bodies of a ruler who made his person the source of his authority.[27] If in that, for all their differences, he shared something with Charles I, no less than for the king were the personal and public reconciled for Cromwell in death, when the effigy of his body was represented with the regalia and the crown.

Like monarchs before him, Cromwell sent copies of his portraits to fellow rulers like Queen Christina of Sweden and the king of Denmark, gave them to Dutch and Portuguese ambassadors, presumably for presentation to their heads of state, and donated them to friends such as Colonel Robert Rich.[28] The numerous copies of Walker's and Lely's portraits and copies after Cooper's miniature in various genres (one for example in a ring, another as a jewel) indicate that there was a wide interest in the image of the Protector and that it

91 *Oliver Cromwell* by Edward Mascall, 1657.

hung as the visible face of authority in numerous gentry houses.[29] Moreover, surviving portraits of his sons, Richard and Henry, and of Cromwell's wife Elizabeth and daughters (Elizabeth, Bridget, Frances and Mary) in fashionable attire, many executed during the Protector's life, suggest that the Cromwells fostered the impression that they were, and were perceived as, a dynasty: presumably one that many thought might become the hereditary ruling family of the realm.[30] If so, Mary's marriage into a Royalist family, and Elizabeth's alleged vanity – 'she acted the part of a princess', Harrington noted – must have strengthened that perception.[31]

II

Whatever the distribution of these paintings, it was through other genres of visual representation that most Englishmen and women viewed Cromwell as

92 Letters patent for a Cromwellian hereditary peerage.

Protector from 1653 to 1658. As we have seen, the market for engravings was rapidly growing in the late sixteenth and seventeenth centuries and appears to have been stimulated by the civil war. Given that, we might expect to find more contemporary engraved portraits of Cromwell than we do. In the large English collections of prints, almost all contemporary or near-contemporary engravings of Cromwell are after Walker rather than Cooper or Lely, making the most courtly of portraits the most widely disseminated.[32] Other engravings that we can with reasonable confidence date as contemporary do nothing to qualify that regal representation. William Faithorne produced an engraved portrait of Cromwell surrounded with smaller images of the biblical kings, David and Solomon, and the imperial Alexander the Great and Caesar; and another Faithorne, perhaps anticipating a new royal dynasty, is inscribed below his portrait 'Olivarius Primus'.[33] An anonymous engraving, again of Cromwell in a plumed hat, appears to gesture to Van Dyck's *Le Roi à la chasse*, Cromwell's right hand on a cane and left arm in foreshortening being modelled on the stance of Charles I.[34] Famously – or rather infamously – an engraving executed before 1658 by Pierre Lombart of Van Dyck's canvas of a mounted Charles with Monsieur St Antoine etched Cromwell's head on to one of the most imperial images of Charles I that had conspicuously hung at the end of rows of portraits of emperors in the gallery at St James's.[35] Though in Lombart's

Olivarivs Cromwell Exercitvvm
Angliæ Reipvblicæ Dvx Generalis.
Locvm Tenens et Gvbernator Hiberniæ
Oxoniensis Academiæ Cancellarivs

93 *Olivarius Cromwell*, engraving, 1654–8.

version, the city on the hill behind may serve to represent the godly Cromwell, the image, in the most obvious material way, appropriates regal representation.

Another Faithorne engraving appears to claim, beyond that, divine, universal monarchy. A rare print in the Pepys Library and in the Richard Bull Granger at the Huntington Library, dated 1658, is titled 'The Emblem of England's Distractions as also of her attained and further expected Freedom and Happiness'.[36] In this complex image, Cromwell stands in armour between two columns, which often represented the pillars of Hercules and imperial power. The Protector crushes beneath his feet the beast of superstition and the whore of Babylon. In his right hand he bears a sword, beside which is written in Latin 'For God, the law and the people'. In his left hand he holds a book inscribed 'Tullo prolego protego' (I take up, I lead and protect). Above the Protector a dove holds an olive branch of peace beneath a Greek inscription according glory to the one God alone, inside a scroll with the legend 'I will never fail thee nor forsake thee' and 'Be still and know that I am God'. On Cromwell's right (our left), above scenes of peace and pastoral tranquillity, stands a column, topped with his initials inside a sun, moon and wreath. On the column, four tablets contain inscriptions reading 'Constancy and fortitude', 'The law is the safest pillar of state', the Roman adage 'Salvo populi suprema

94 *The Embleme of Englands Distractions*, print by William Faithorne after Francis Barlow, 1658.

lex' (the safety of the people is the supreme law) and, simply, 'Magna Carta'. Banners attached to the column are topped with one displaying Cromwell's family arms; and, above the pillar, biblical scenes of Abraham and Isaac and the ark at rest on Mount Ararat symbolize the chosen people saved. Beneath the pillar on the right (Cromwell's left) demoniac priests threaten the polity with faggots, gallows and gunpowder, the historical symbols of destructive English Catholicism. On the pillar, topped with a crenellated building symbolizing the government (with the inscription 'May the Protector and parliament of England flourish'), kneeling figures representing the three nations of England, Scotland and Ireland offer wreaths.[37] Above the pillar, the ship of state is being safely guided between the rocks of Scylla and Charybdis to safety from winds and wars. Fame with her trumpet proclaims Oliver as God's instrument who brings peace to distracted nations.

Apparently produced and sold just before Cromwell's death on 3 September, the engraving – after a drawing by Francis Barlow, who entered the Painter Stationers Company with Walker – perhaps represented Cromwell as in 1658 he wished to be seen: as the godly Protector of those nations (and Christendom) against popish plots.[38] But, for all that it celebrates Protector and parliament (and the wreaths proffered by grateful nations may symbolize the offer of a crown not taken), the image is regal and imperial. Indeed, the engraving recalls Van de Passe's 1592 plate of Elizabeth I between two crowned columns; and, interestingly, Barlow's drawing of Cromwell was reworked, with almost no change, in 1690 as a representation of William III after the Glorious Revolution.[39] Not only did he appropriate royal iconography, in revising it for Protectorial rule Cromwell bequeathed visual symbols to Protestant Whig kingship.

In Faithorne's engraving, Cromwell's family crest is permanently displayed on a banner, directly opposite the English flag, the cross of St George. In 1649, one image of regicide displayed blank escutcheons to signify the death of honour, chivalry and heraldry with the death of the king.[40] The Commonwealth took care over the devising and publicizing of new arms; but it was the return of single-person rule under Cromwell that re-established a personal and family escutcheon as the device of government. And Cromwell marked his elevation to the Protectoral office by an important revision of his arms. Cromwell's crest as Lord General had borne a demi-lion holding in its paw a halbert or pike. After he was made Lord Protector, he took away the halbert and gave the demi-lion a diamond ring in his right paw 'to signify his political marriage to the imperial crown of the three kingdoms'.[41] In 1655, the arms Cromwell approved to be worn by his bargemen re-established a recognizably royal escutcheon. The device revived the heraldic supporters of the Tudor monarchs: a lion guardant crowned and a dragon with wings, with a shield with a kingly crown and on top the royal crest of Britain, the crowned lions. To an escutcheon that was 'very much the symbol of royalty' Cromwell imported, in the midst of quarterings with symbols of the three nations, his own arms of a lion rampant, added his motto ('Pax quaeretur bello'), and replaced C.R. with his own initials O.P., for Oliver Protector.[42] In 1657 the Council ordered new coats to be issued to the watermen, in the grey cloth already worn by Cromwell's footmen and with his arms and initials, to be worn on the front and back.[43] Despite his refusal of the crown, the Protector's arms displayed on buildings, boats and the bodies of household servants signified regal – and, to English observers, specifically Tudor – authority.[44]

It is noteworthy that the establishment of the Protectorate in December 1653 was not marked by the commissioning of a new seal. While these took time to prepare and there was other pressing business, it may be that, at a time when he was anxious to convey a sense of continuity and adherence to the old cause, Cromwell chose not to, literally, stamp his image on the new government and all the documents issued by it. The Commonwealth Seal, we recall, hurriedly and poorly cast in 1649, had been remade in 1651 with, in place of the royal person and arms, the map of England on one side and, on the other, an image of a crowded House of Commons, with a legend in English 'In the third year of freedom by God's blessing restored'.[45] In the spring of 1655, after the failure and dissolution of his first parliament, Cromwell approved a new seal for the Protectorate that marked a revolution: in the seventeenth-century sense of a return to old – and again 'manifestly monarchical' – forms.[46] The obverse of the seal, in imitation of earlier royal seals, figured Cromwell armoured and mounted facing left, against a view of London, but on a pacing rather than galloping horse and with a baton of command rather than a sword. If, as has been suggested, Cromwell was keen to distance the Protectorate from its military origins, the addition of his escutcheons evidences his determination to advertise his personal authority, which is inscribed in the legend – now again in Latin: 'Olivarius dei gr[atia] rei[publicae] Angliae Scotiae et Hiberniae protector'. On the reverse, the new Protectoral arms prescribed for the watermen's badges placed Cromwell's family beast, now with a ring, at the centre of the heraldic achievements of the Tudor monarchs, with, below, Cromwell's motto repeating that peace had always been the goal, even of war. Recognition of the counter-revolution that the new seal represented comes from no less a figure than the Chief Engraver of the Mint himself. For, in submitting his account for work to the Protector, Thomas Simon itemized 'two steel seals in imitation of Charles Stuart'.[47] In some respects, the seal of Charles I, though the nearest in time, was not the closest model. As Roy Sherwood has observed, with its pacing horse and antique armour Cromwell's seal more recalls Queen Elizabeth's, and the baton lends it an imperial air.[48]

Along with the Great Seal, a new Privy Seal was ordered, on the inscription of which France was included in the Protector's (as former monarchs') fiefdoms, and a seal for the Council with Oliver's arms at the centre.[49] Not surprisingly, several observers, seeing the new seals, believed they signified a major constitutional change. The Swedish ambassador heard rumours while the seal was being made that 'it has been kept open whether he shall be designated Rex

95 Great Seal of the Cromwellian Protectorate.

or Imperator', while in May a Westminster correspondent reported that the seal 'makes people here give out generally that his Highness is to be crowned forthwith'.[50] Whatever Cromwell's speeches or protestations of humility, in a heraldic culture the display of personal arms, on badges and seals, announced not a collective but a distinctly personal authority, and not the authority of a parliament and Council but that of a sovereign monarch. And a sovereign of all three kingdoms at that. With a design similar to that for England, the Protectoral seal for Ireland had on one side an equestrian portrait of Cromwell with a view of Dublin in the background and the arms of Ireland, the harp, surmounted by an escutcheon with Cromwell's lion rampant, which was repeated on the reverse.[51] In April 1654, instructions for the new seal for a Scotland conquered and reunited with England ordered: 'And that this union may take its more full intent, be it further ordained . . . that the arms of Scotland, viz a cross commonly called St Andrews, be received into and borne from henceforth in the arms of the Commonwealth as a badge of this union.'[52] When it was finally made in 1656, the seal offered Cromwell as the sovereign of a reunited Britain, a Britain created by the succession of the Stuarts.

The shift to the representation as well as reinstitution of single-person sovereign authority is also evident in medals. Cromwell, as a commander, evidently attached importance to medals and, we recall, had strongly urged parliament to advertise its, rather than his, authority on the medal issued to celebrate the victory at Dunbar.[53] The Commons did not take his advice; and various 'reward' medals bearing Cromwell's portrait were issued during the early 1650s – along with those figuring Henry Ireton, Admiral Blake, Secretary of State John Thurloe and Bulstrode Whitelocke.[54] Yet, despite his earlier reluctance to promote his own image, Cromwell ordered a medal to commemorate his elevation as Lord Protector on 16 December 1653, and there can be no doubting that thereafter this highly personal image of authority was *the* medallic image of the new government.[55] On the obverse of the medal executed by Simon, a bust of Cromwell, after a miniature by Cooper, presented a Roman image of the Protector in decorated armour, with a plain collar and scarf looped on the left shoulder inside a Latin inscription ('Oliverus dei gra repub Angliae Sco et Hib & protector') that signalled rule over the three kingdoms and in that '&' perhaps territories beyond, as France had always been claimed in regal titles. Continuing the Roman image and the theme of peace proclaimed with the Protectorate, the reverse is engraved with a laureate lion supporting a shield displaying the crosses of St George and St Andrew, the Irish harp and the paternal coat of Cromwell, the demi-lion with the ring inside Oliver's legend 'Pax quaeritur bello'. Though officially struck in gold and silver, a copy of the medal (attributed to Simon but not by him) was also made in copper, presumably for broader distribution and sale.[56]

96 Protectorate medal.

Interestingly, though medals were struck in Holland to celebrate the Peace of Westminster signed with England on 15 April 1654, Cromwell ordered no official medal.[57] While the Dutch medals praise the Lord Protector, they also depict the cap of liberty, at a time when critics of the Protectorate accused Cromwell of surrendering it, and these official medals were answered by pro-Orangist medals figuring Charles I's daughter Princess Mary and her son William, whom Cromwell promised to exclude from power.[58] Similarly, no English medal was struck to mark the victory of the French over the Habsburgs at Dunkirk, even though Cromwell had, in accordance with his treaty obligations, sent 6,000 troops to serve under Louis XIV.[59] In fact, after the inauguration medal, no official medals of Cromwell were struck until his death, when a funeral medal was issued with Oliver's bust after Cooper, but now laureate, and, on the reverse, an olive tree and shepherds tending their flock – the symbols of peace.[60] Though Oliver died on, and the medal was issued on, 3 September, the anniversary of his great victories at Dunbar and Worcester, the death medal celebrated peace rather than war. It may be that the absence of medals marking military successes and campaigns during the period 1653–8 also reflects Cromwell's concern to portray the Protectorate as a government dedicated to peace and the return of Augustan calm and stability after a decade of turmoil and strife.

Whether by design or on account of the difficulties involved in minting a new currency, Cromwell as Protector, like several monarchs before him, continued to use the coins of the Commonwealth as ordered by parliament, with the cross, palm and laurel and the words 'The Commonwealth of England'.[61] These coins in 20, 10 and 5 shillings, half-crowns, shillings and sixpences were minted with the dates 1653, 1654, 1656 and 1657 and evidently remained in circulation to the time of Oliver's death. However, in February

1655 Cromwell appointed Thomas Simon Chief Engraver of the Mint; and it may be that he was then planning a new issue of coin to mark the Protectorate.[62] Certainly by mid-1656, about the time the rumours of his being offered the crown were mounting, Cromwell resolved on a set of new coins bearing his portrait and titles to replace the dies and he appointed Peter Blondeau, who had proposed a mint for Dublin, to strike them.[63] On 27 November, the Protector and Council approved Simon's designs and inscriptions for the new gold and silver pieces and it was probably intended that the new coins would be ready before the end of the Old Style year – that is by March (1656/7).[64] It appears, however, that though some bear the date 1656, the coins were not struck before June or July 1657, well over three years after Cromwell's investiture as Lord Protector.

The new 1656 milled coin, of fine workmanship, carried an excellent bust of Cromwell, in profile to the left and – following James I – laureate, to signify classical, imperial regimen, inside an inscription announcing Oliver as 'By the grace of God Protector of England, Scotland and Ireland &c'.[65] On the reverse, the arms of the Protector on a shield is topped with an imperial crown, almost exactly resembling that of Charles I, with Cromwell's legend inscribed around. On the edge of the 50-shilling coin is written 'Protector literis literae nummis corona et salvo', suggesting that the letters protect the coin (from clipping, for example), as the Protector did the nation. Without the inscription on the edge, this was the pattern for 20 and 10 shilling coins. For the silver half-crown, classical drapery was added to Cromwell's laureate bust, to distinguish it from the gold.[66] As well as the earliest to use milling, as opposed to the old hammer process, these coins marked an extraordinary improvement in quality, especially in the portrait of the Protector for which Cromwell may well have sat for Simon.[67] In 1656, Cromwell clearly recognized the importance of the quality of his image on the medium that most broadly represented and disseminated sovereign authority – coin.

97 Protectorate coin depicting Cromwell wearing a laurel crown.

Indeed, in 1658 Oliver instructed Blondeau to mint more coins to the value of £10,000 a week.[68] Though the production of these probably did not go on for more than weeks before Cromwell's death, coins dated 1658 are the commonest survivals of Cromwellian currency and must have circulated widely.[69] For the crown, half-crown, shilling and sixpence coins, Simon used the laureate bust of the Protector with classical drapery, similar to the 1656 half-crown; and the two highest-denomination coins were inscribed on the edge with 'Let no one take [this] from me, except on pain of death'.[70] The inscription was again a warning against clipping or other illicit use of the coin, but we may read it too, since minting coin was one of the essences of sovereign power, as an assertion of Protectoral authority. If the story is true that, finding the people still favoured the Commonwealth coin, Cromwell decided to end it and replace it with that bearing his image, the 1658 coining may be seen as an important move to erase the signs of the republic and to establish the heredi-tary Protectorate in the house of Cromwell.[71] Though formerly scholars deduced from the fine state of surviving examples that Cromwell's coins of 1656 and 1658 were patterns which never circulated as currency, the evidence points to a short period in which coins, from the largest denomination to popular pattern farthings for the poor, bore Oliver's laureate head.[72] The significance of that circulated image for contemporaries is well captured in an apologia for Cromwell published against his republican critics in 1657. In his 'answer to a treasonous pamphlet', the anonymous author of *Killing Is Murder* praising single-person rule, urged that Englishmen 'follow the possession' and obey authority.[73] Such advice, he added, had Christ given, 'commanding tribute to be paid to Caesar because the money bore his image'.[74] As well, that is, as representing authority, the image on coin endowed Caesar – and now the laureate Protector – with authority, and a prerogative that, since Bodin, early modern subjects had considered that of kings. As Bodin wrote in Book I, chapter X of the *Six Books of a Commonwealth*, the right of coining 'is of the same nature as law and only he who has the power to make law can regulate the coinage'; 'in every well-ordered state it is the sovereign prince alone who has this power'.[75] It seems therefore only appropriate that, for Cromwell's funeral, the effigy with a sceptre, globe and sword, and a crown on its head, was modelled by Oliver's medallist and Chief Engraver to the Mint – Thomas Simon.[76]

The institution of Cromwell as Lord Protector was also manifested in architec-tural changes which, increasingly, represented Oliver as a monarch. From his return from Ireland in June 1650, Cromwell and his family occupied lodgings next to the Cockpit within the precincts of the Palace of Whitehall.[77] When he was elevated to Protector, however, Whitehall Palace, along with St James's, Greenwich, Hampton Court and Windsor, were granted him 'for the mainte-nance of his . . . state and dignity'.[78] A mere week after Cromwell's investiture, an official newspaper reported that 'Whitehall is being prepared for his Highness to reside in, and the old Council Chamber is being fixed out for his honourable Council to meet in'.[79] As work commenced, government newspapers reported progress, as though a suitably good residence was felt to be essential to the image of the new regime. In the edition for 14–21 March 1654, the *Weekly Intelligencer* announced, amid the usual political news, that 'The Privy Lodgings for his Highness the Lord Protector in Whitehall are now in readiness, as also the lodgings for his Lady Protectress . . . and it is conceived the whole family will be settled there before Easter'.[80] If the language of the report suggested a return to regal arrangements, reference to the refurbished privy kitchens and the list of tables established for gentlewomen, stewards, coachmen and other servants confirmed the physical reconstitution of an earlier royal architecture. On 13 April, it was reported that the bedchambers were now ready and that Cromwell and his family would move in the next day.[81] The refurbishment was evidently considerable. During the work of 1654, John Embree, Surveyor of the Works, 'obtained warrants authorising . . . a level of expenditure unknown since the king's time'.[82] And though the Council and Treasury Commissioners urged restraint, expenditure on Whitehall and Hampton Court, to which Cromwell and his family retreated at weekends, remained high. As well as items recovered for the state's use at the time of the sale of Charles I's goods, furnishings and tapestries were purchased for the Lord Protector.[83] A new organ was installed in the Great Hall at Hampton Court and a fountain in the palace grounds.[84]

Early in 1656, John Evelyn recorded: 'I ventured to go to Whitehall, whereof for many years I had not been, and found it glorious and well furnished'.[85] Foreign observers did not doubt what it all signified. Reporting that Cromwell had had Whitehall 'done up for his own convenience', the Venetian envoy observed, 'So he will henceforth exercise regal sway under the royal roof'.[86] Not surprisingly, he had deduced that the re-equipping for Cromwell of the palaces of Tudor and Stuart kings signified the beginning of a new royal dynasty. With Mortlake tapestries, Mantegnas and Raphaels again adorning the walls, and royal furnishings and plate restored, Whitehall was reconstituted as a court and a theatre of majesty.[87] We must now turn to see how Cromwell performed in both.

CHAPTER 18

PROTECTORAL PERFORMANCES

I

Within the walls of the refurbished palaces, at Whitehall and Hampton Court, Oliver Cromwell re-established a household and court that at least imitated those of royal predecessors. The Protectoral court as re-established did not appoint a Lord Steward; but the household below stairs was run along similar lines to that of the Stuarts, with a privy kitchen and cellar, spicery and wine cellar, slaughterhouse and scullery.[1] Unlike monarchs who had been expected to 'live of their own', Cromwell was granted an annual sum to finance household expenses, in recognition, perhaps, that the court of a Protector was public as well as private and as important to the image and dignity of the government as of Oliver himself. Despite this (and even allowing for sometimes tardy payments), it appears that in Cromwell's household, as in the Stuarts', expenses exceeded revenue and that the trend was to greater extravagance. Certainly the household grew. In 1657, probably in preparation for taking the crown, the former royal posts of Comptroller and Cofferer were added to Cromwell's household and those appointed were given suites at Whitehall and Hampton Court.[2] And in 1658, it appears that the Board of Greencloth, the overseeing committee of the royal household, was reconstituted to run a growing establishment.[3]

Cromwell's household above stairs was even more obviously reconstituted along monarchical lines.[4] The Commonwealth government had, of course, necessarily maintained some of the old departments and officials of the Chamber which organized the daily activities and ceremonial rituals of the court – an Office of Works and of the Wardrobe, for example. With Cromwell's investiture as Protector, however, these officers were appointed to serve the Protector rather than the state: as we have seen, the bargemen who wore Oliver's livery very much advertised the personal allegiance that recalled feudal relations.[5] Beyond that, the Protectorate saw the revival of key royal offices, notably that of the head of the household and court, the Lord Chamberlain. The first reference to the appointment of Sir Gilbert Pickering as Lord Chamberlain occurs in August 1655; Roy Sherwood has suggested in connection with an expectation that Cromwell would take the crown.[6] Certainly little more was heard of the office until late 1657, when it even seems likely that the post was revived (along with that of Master of the Greencloth) in the reorganization along more regal lines that followed the Humble Petition and Advice.[7] Thereafter, Pickering acted as his royal predecessors and took his place directly in front of the bier at Cromwell's funeral, as previous Lord Chamberlains had for their royal masters.[8] The Protector was also served, as critics bitterly remarked, by four Gentlemen of the Bedchamber and by other gentlemen of the household who served as Gentlemen of a revived Privy Chamber and attended him on state occasions such as the reception of envoys, or the opening of parliament.[9] A guard of halberdiers attending Cromwell in state rooms and outdoors were called by some after the old name of the royal Yeomen of the Guard; and it appears that one squadron effectively acted as the former Royal Gentlemen Pensioners.[10] Oliver retained personal chaplains and, in keeping with his interests, appointed a Master and Gentlemen of His Highness's music.[11]

The very re-appearance of gentlemen, grooms, cofferers and chamberlains re-presented the Protectorate as a quasi-monarchical government, if not as a monarchy. James I had advised his son (who followed his father's advice rather than practice) that his court should be an image of his rule.[12] There can be no doubt that Cromwell's court drew the attention of contemporaries, although perceptions of it were sharply divided. Old Commonwealthsmen were predictably scornful of the Protectoral court as they were of the return to single-person rule. An anonymous treatise 'cast about the streets' in April 1656, entitled *The Picture of a New Courtier*, may stand as representative of republican criticism of the usurper's court.[13] Written in the form of an old country critique of the Stuart court, the tract condemned the pride and pomp of the Protector and the extravagance of a court that necessitated high taxes to sustain its splendour. Cataloguing the 'delight of the new rivers and ponds at Hampton Court, whose making cost vast sums of money' and the warrens enclosed for hunting, the author lamented that pay was withheld from soldiers so that the Protector could dine on sweetmeats and delicious wines and be served by 'the gentlemen ushers and gentlemen waiters, the grooms of the stool, gentlemen sewers, besides the fiddlers and others . . . which shine in their gold and silver.'[14] As a friend to the Commonwealth, the Mr Plain Heart of the pamphlet warned, he could not but remain 'an enemy to your Court.'[15] Royalists, by contrast, seem to have welcomed the restoration of a court and courtly sociability and sought, for various reasons, to downplay the distinction between the old royal court and the Protector's. In 1658, for example, *The Accomplished Courtier* presented a guide to how to live and behave at the court in the tradition of the old courtesy literature of the late sixteenth and early seventeenth centuries, while *The Mysteries of Love and Eloquence*, with a preface to the 'youthful gentry', along with advice on wooing, reprinted several Cavalier *carpe diem* songs.[16] Apologists for the Protectorate, however, endeavoured to represent Cromwell's court, like the constitution established by the Instrument, as the perfect mean between extremes. The author of *The Unparalleled Monarch* boasted that there was no lack of lustre at Cromwell's court – 'I see a kind of dawning of celestial beauty in his courts'.[17] But he contrasted its pious and sober entourage with 'these mohair linseywoolsy nits and lice gentlemen' and debauched swashbucklers who surrounded the Stuarts.[18] In a panegyric to His Highness, a verse praised:

> Your Court so modest, and so regular
> Looks like a Virgin, it is only there
> Order and State without excesse reside:
> A place of businesse; not of pomp and pride.[19]

Similarly Payne Fisher, applauding the absence of drunkenness and incontinence, celebrated in Latin a Protectoral court 'truly magnificent without being ostentatious'.[20]

The courts of kings were the stages of the ritual displays of majesty to foreign envoys and dignitaries, to the political nation and, beyond, to the people. Though there was a long 'country' suspicion of extravagant pomp, in early modern England magnificence was inseparable from government and Cromwell fully appreciated its importance in representing and validating his authority, in securing the compliance of the people without which he remained dependent on armed force. While, as we saw, the Commonwealth had not abandoned all ceremonies of state, the rituals, scripts and traditions were not easily adapted to a republic or collective rule.[21] From the outset, therefore, the Protectorate was marked by a revival of ritual forms and customs which contemporaries associated with monarchs and that shaped perceptions of the Protectoral regime.

Cromwell's investiture on 16 December 1653 was devised to be a public occasion, with some of the familiar aspects of a coronation. About one o'clock, a procession of judges, councillors, mayors and aldermen conducted Oliver in a coach, attended by his mounted guard and foot soldiers, to Westminster Hall, the place of justice and of the rituals of enthronement prior to the coronation in the abbey. Preceded by Major-General Lambert carrying the sword of state, Cromwell was led to a throne with 'rich cushions' beside which he stood while the Instrument was read and he took an oath to the Commonwealth.[22] After the oath, Oliver, now formally Protector, sat to receive as homage, as had earlier kings, a sheathed sword from Lambert, the Great Seal from the Lords Commissioners and the city sword from the mayor of London. Having taken these as symbols of his authority, Cromwell returned each of them, signifying that the recipients now acted with and by his authority. After the ceremony, 'thronged with people', four Sergeants at Arms with maces conducted Cromwell from Westminster back to Whitehall, where he and the entourage attended 'the equivalent of a coronation sermon' delivered by one of his chaplains in the Banqueting House.[23] Newsbooks reported the inauguration being publicly celebrated by a cannon salute, by 'great acclamations and shoutings all along the streets as they passed', and by big bonfires as well as bells.[24] Though the Venetian ambassador gave an alternative account – of popular murmurs of discontent – the ceremony was clearly intended to secure the people's participation in it as a legitimation of the new ruler and government.[25] It was after the ceremonies of investiture that the author of *A Declaration Concerning the Government* thought that the Commonwealth had become the wonder of Europe.[26]

Weeks after the investiture, the City of London organized a magnificent entertainment for the Protector to the end, as the *Perfect Diurnal* explicitly reported, that 'he might have the greater veneration from the people'.[27] A formal entry into the city followed by a grand dinner had formed part of the coronation ceremonies of kings and queens; and, having forgone it in 1626, Charles I had strategically made a triumphant entry into London on his return from Scotland in November 1641.[28] To demonstrate their loyalty to the new Commonwealth, the mayor and aldermen had hosted a banquet for its leaders in June 1649, among them Cromwell.[29] But it was the Lieutenant-General's elevation to Protector that saw a return to regal pomp. In his detailed description of 'The Manner of His Highness's Going to the City and Reception', Samuel Carrington described how Oliver set forth towards Grocers' Hall 'in as great a pomp and magnificence as befitted a person invested with so eminent qualities'.[30] Preceded by his lifeguard of horse, the chief officers of the army, fourteen trumpeters and attendants 'in velvet caps and grey liveries with silk and silver fringe', Cromwell rode in a chariot of state, 'the greatest part of the . . . nobility attending in their coaches and six horses'.[31] At Temple Bar, the Protector was greeted by the mayor, aldermen and Recorder who gave a welcoming speech, after which Oliver stepped down from his coach and, donning a gold-embroidered riding coat, mounted a palfrey 'richly trapped', to commence a progress through the city, behind the mayor who, riding bareheaded, carried the sword of the city before him. On both sides of the railed streets, the city companies attended in their liveries and with the banners of their crafts. At Grocers' Hall, the City Recorder addressed Cromwell in a speech which declared that his government was of divine origin and that God was the author of his power, then continued: 'My lord, there is one help more in government which God is pleased often to add to the rest which is the giving in of the affections of the people. The solemnity of this day, wherein the citizens of this great city appear in their several companies . . . speaks much to this'.[32] Observing the absence of triumphal arches, the Recorder played down the importance of 'outward pomp and glory'.[33] But, like the procession itself, the ensuing banquet was lavish, one report describing Cromwell as 'royally entertained'.[34] Comparing the grandeur and solemnity of the reception to 'such as had been at any time performed to the king', Clarendon noted that 'as like a king', the Protector 'graciously conferred the honour of knighthood upon the Lord Mayor at his departure'.[35] Whatever Cromwell's personal desires at this point, the rituals of his investiture and entertainment certainly left open the possibility of his taking the crown, and to some made it seem all the more likely.[36]

Civic entries and entertainments, though often devised in consultation with rulers, were ultimately in the control of the corporation, and Cromwell himself seemed concerned to play down his role in the ceremonial occasion.[37] However, his own orchestrations of state rituals were not marked by any less pomp or magnificence. A month after his reception at Grocers' Hall, Cromwell was presented with the occasions of giving ceremonial public audiences to envoys from the United Provinces, followed by an ambassador from France. The Commonwealth, as we saw, had (necessarily) retained the ceremonies of formal welcome, conduct and entertainment of envoys, but had pared down the royal rituals of audience and reception in the spirit of republican austerity.[38] The first embassies to the Protector saw a near-complete return to royal forms. As an account of *The Whole Manner of the Treaty* that the Dutch ambassadors had come to negotiate makes clear, from their arrival to their departure they were accorded lavish hospitality and entertainment.[39] Having been brought to London in the Protector's barge by liveried watermen, the three envoys were conducted in Cromwell's own coach, attended by the Protector's Master of the Horse and footmen and fifty coaches of the nobility and gentry, to their residence where a trumpet salute greeted them.[40] The next morning, Sir Oliver Fleming, the Protector's Master of Ceremonies, with two councillors escorted them to the Banqueting House, the site of the Stuarts' receptions which was again 'hung with extraordinary rich hangings' and filled with lords, knights, officers and what the author, surely exaggerating, counted as 'thousands of people' in the hall, galleries and surrounding courtyards.[41] As Cromwell entered with the lords of his Council, his Master of the Horse and Secretary of State, all removed their hats. When the envoys were conducted in, as they approached the chair of state they removed their hats before the Protector, who reciprocated, the familiar salute being repeated three times. After speeches, the ritual was yet again repeated before the Protector departed out of the privy door.[42]

Later in the month, on the 27th, the ambassador from France, Monseur de Bordeaux, was similarly escorted from Tower Wharf through the cities of London and Westminster 'in great state with between 50 and 60 coaches', the envoy himself riding in the Protector's coach, attended by pages wearing Cromwell's livery.[43] On 29 March, he had audience in the Banqueting House which again, it was reported, 'was richly hung with stately hangings and thousands of people present'.[44] The elaborate etiquette of 'salutings and several congies' was repeated; and Bordeaux accorded Cromwell the title 'Your most serene Highness', usually reserved for a reigning monarch.[45] It would seem that the author of *The Unparalleled Monarch* scarcely exaggerated when, describing the ritual of the Protector's giving audience to foreign envoys, he wrote of Cromwell: 'the rays of his own majesty cast over him a beautiful canopy'.[46]

The receptions of foreign ambassadors, though witnessed by thousands of Londoners, were not the only occasions of elaborate public ritual display by the Protector. Cromwell opened his first Protectoral parliament with a level of pageantry and state that emulated royal practice. On 1 September, just days before it assembled, an official newspaper reported work being done on the old House of Lords and Painted Chamber, 'where was made two steps to a throne or seat for his highness the Lord Protector', and hangings placed 'for the reception of his Highness'.[47] As the MPs gathered on Monday the 4th at Westminster to hear a sermon, Cromwell made a ceremonial journey 'in stately equipage' from Whitehall to the abbey, preceded by hundreds of gentlemen and his Life Guard.[48] Behind Cromwell's coach, attended by his liveried pages, 'richly habited', followed the Master of Horse with the Protector's horse, 'very rich', and the officers of state.[49] After the sermon, the procession went on foot, with a mace carried before the Protector, to the Painted Chamber, where monarchs had traditionally opened parliament and where Cromwell addressed them as they stood bareheaded as before a prince. For all the protestations of humility in his speech, Cromwell orchestrated a regal state opening of parliament.

As well as these formal receptions of envoys and state openings of parliament, Cromwell's government and court were marked by a new emphasis on ceremony. A petition brought by the mayor and aldermen of Guildford, for example, was received with all the trappings of state; and feasts for the dignitaries of London and army officers were frequent.[50] In the spring of 1656 Cromwell even countenanced, albeit in a private house, the first licensed dramatic performance since 1652, and its author, the former courtier Sir William Davenant, went on to perform and publish an opera which the dramatist himself described as a 'masque'.[51] A recognition of a new official acceptance of ritual surely lay behind the revival in 1655 of the Lord Mayor's shows that had lapsed just before the civil war.[52] For, though these were, first and foremost, civic occasions, they had represented royal as well as metropolitan dignity and the harmony between citizens, the corporation and the crown. The entertainment for Lord Mayor Robert Tichborn in October 1656 was no exception.[53] Flattering the Protector's government by describing such triumphant occasions as 'pleasant fruit that only springs from peace and plenty', the author of *London's Triumph* observed that they were of particular delight to princes who 'ought to be adorned to shine like the chariot of the sun'.[54] During the river procession, barges fired a salute to the Protector before the elaborate processions and pageants which symbolized the re-establishment of order and virtue.[55] When we reflect how both within the Protector's court and on the streets of London the rituals of monarchy were being restaged, the offer of the crown to Oliver Cromwell appears anything but surprising.

In a series of speeches, culminating with that of 8 May, Cromwell refused the 'title of king'. However, his ritual re-investiture as hereditary Protector represented him to the people, in most respects, as a monarch. Several contemporary accounts testify to the elaborate ceremony, as well as publicization, of Cromwell's second investiture; and the fullest, by one Mr Edmond Prestwich, 'an eye and ear witness to all that passed on this glorious occasion', provides the details of the ritual, signs and symbols carefully devised for the ceremony on 26 June.[56] At the upper end of Westminster Hall, on a raised dais, was placed under a 'prince like canopy of state' St Edward's Chair, the coronation chair of successive kings, brought from Westminster Abbey.[57] In front of it was placed a table covered with pink velvet and fringed with gold, on which lay a bible, sword and sceptre, the emblems of Protestant sovereigns. Around, in what Prestwich called a 'theatrum', MPs, aldermen and others sat on seats built 'scaffold-wise' for the occasion.[58] When all was ordered, the Protector proceeded from the Council Room into the Hall, with his gentlemen, heralds, judges, commissioners of the seal and other officers, and with the Earl of Warwick bearing the sword of the Commonwealth. Members of the revived second house (Prestwich called it the Lords) and officers of Cromwell's household followed him, together with Scottish and Irish nobles.[59] When Cromwell was stood under the cloth of state, with his son, and noble councillors behind, the Speaker of the parliament presented him with 'a rich and worthy robe of purple velvet, lined with ermine', a bible, sword and sceptre, explaining, as did the archbishop at royal coronations, what each symbolized.[60] Having delivered the regalia, the Speaker administered the oath and said a prayer, after which, as he 'sat down in the Chair of State, holding the sceptre in his hand', the heralds proclaimed Oliver Protector and required the people's obedience to him – which they answered 'with loud shouts, God save the Lord Protector'.[61] The formal ceremony over, Cromwell saluted the assembled before, 'in his princely habit', with his train borne by nobles, leading the procession out of the Hall into the New Palace Yard, where a state coach awaited to take him, with full attendance, to Whitehall.[62]

Several contemporary commentators describing the ceremony compared it to the 'solemn investiture of princes'.[63] As Edward Hyde, future Earl of Clarendon observed, it was not quite: as he put it in his *History of the Rebellion*, there was 'nothing wanting to a perfect formal coronation but a crown and an archbishop'.[64] There were, however, other elements of a traditional royal coronation missing: the sermon, the communion, most of all the anointing with holy oil that made Cromwell's investiture (curiously, given his own rhetoric of Providence) more a secular than a sacred ceremony. That said, Laura Knoppers is surely wrong in describing the ceremony of investiture as one that celebrated 'a newly recognised Commonwealth state'.[65] Many of those who orchestrated it had wanted a king and had deliberately devised a ceremony that, like the revised constitution, came as near to monarchy as was possible. Similarly, her argument that the ceremony and oath 'recognised an office . . . rather than a person' fails to persuade.[66] The whole focus of the ceremony was on Cromwell who received the emblems of sovereignty (traditionally the emblems of regality) which connected the public and private bodies of the ruler. Moreover, the hereditary, dynastic authority that the Humble Petition bestowed on the Protector was manifest in the placement at the ceremony. Directly behind Cromwell stood his son and heir, Richard, with (in the absence of his second son Henry, who was Lord-Lieutenant of Ireland) his sons-in-law Charles, Lord Fleetwood and John Claypole (who was also Master of the Horse).[67] Along with portraits and engravings of the Cromwells, the second investiture inaugurated and publicized a new dynasty.[68] And on 1 July, in another elaborate public procession that progressed from Whitehall through the city, that dynasty was proclaimed by the heralds amid acclamations and the ringing of bells.[69]

The dynastic and personal nature of Cromwell's new position were further displayed in what were effectively state marriages for his two daughters. At the marriage in November of Frances Cromwell to the grandson of the Earl of Warwick, reported in Nedham's *Mercurius Politicus*, there were several days of grand feasting, the music of forty-eight violins and fifty trumpets, dancing until dawn, and the firing of guns from the Tower that customarily announced royal nuptials.[70] Only a week later, the days of celebrations at Hampton Court of the wedding of Oliver's older daughter included a masque-like entertainment by Marvell with the bride and groom dressed as Cynthia the moon goddess and Endymion, the mythological shepherd. Fittingly, Cromwell himself, like a king in a masque, took the non-speaking role of Jove, the greatest god.[71] A new dynasty was being established, not only through marriages into the aristocratic families of England, but, as with the Tudors and Stuarts, by and through forms of ritual display.

Though rumours that Cromwell would yet agree to take the crown were not borne out by events, final rituals unequivocally presented and represented him as a monarch. The first was, on Oliver's death, the immediate proclamation of his son, Richard, as Protector. After the oath, prayers and a blessing, Richard was proclaimed 'rightful Protector of the Commonwealth of England, Scotland and Ireland and the dominions and territories thereunto belonging'. All were enjoined to serve him and to beseech God 'by whom princes rule to bless him with a long life'.[72] On the Monday next they proclaimed him in great triumph, the Councillors and great officers attending at Westminster, Temple Bar, Chancery Lane and Cheapside, with claret running from the conduits and shouts of joy.[73] The other, last ritual of the Protectorate all but surpassed any state occasion in the living memory of spectators: the funeral of Oliver, Lord Protector.

Almost from the moment of Cromwell's death on 3 September, it appears that a royal funeral was envisaged for him. On the 20th, Francesco Giavarina, the Venetian ambassador, reported: 'At Whitehall they are now preparing for the funeral . . . which will take place in four or five weeks time, with extraordinary pomp and magnificence. They are consulting ancient books to see what was done by the kings on such occasion, and say that it will be more splendid than ever before'.[74] On the same day, according to *Mercurius Politicus*, Oliver's body was removed from Whitehall and, attended by his Lord Chamberlain, Comptroller and Gentlemen of his Household, was taken to Somerset House where it was 'exposed in state to public view'.[75] In Somerset House, former residence of Queen Anne of Denmark and Henrietta Maria, the approach to the corpse followed the architecture of access to a king. The first room the people entered was formerly the Presence Chamber, and at the upper end was placed a chair and canopy of state, the symbols of a monarch's 'presence' as king, even when he was absent. A second, Privy Chamber, and a withdrawing chamber were similarly furnished and all three rooms displayed the Protector's arms 'crowned with the imperial crown' and 'upon the head of each cloth of estate . . . a large majesty escutcheon fairly painted'.[76] Around a raised and railed bed on which the effigy lay were tall candlesticks and standards displaying Cromwell's arms.[77] In a fourth room lay the body and, beneath a cloth of state of black velvet, on a bed, an effigy of Cromwell robed in purple, gold and ermine, the colours and cloths of monarchs. In the right hand of the effigy was placed a sceptre, 'representing government', in the left a globe 'representing principality', 'upon his head the cap of regality'.[78] Behind on a cushion on a chair of state lay 'the imperial crown set with stones'.[79] The effigy lay in state, and was viewed by multitudes for seven weeks before it was moved to the Hall at Westminster where, beneath four or five hundred candles reminiscent of Catholic liturgies, it was placed 'standing in an ascent' – that is in an upright position.[80] Not only was this done in imitation of the arrangements after James I's death, but the engraved frontispiece to the 1659 *Portraiture of His Royal Highness Oliver Late Lord Protector* confirms the startling description reported in *Mercurius*: that here the effigy was displayed with the royal robes and regalia and 'a crown on the head'.[81]

Cromwell was at last crowned as a king. The effigy stood for a further two weeks viewed by 'multitudes' before the elaborate preparations for the funeral were completed.[82] Finally, on 23 November, it was carried, still with the sceptre, globe and 'a crown on the head', to a hearse 'richly adorned and set forth with escutcheons' by ten gentlemen of Cromwell's household.[83] In accordance with royal precedent, a 'Knight Marshal on horseback with his black truncheon' led all the way from the Strand to Westminster a funeral procession of all Cromwell's servants, the mayor and aldermen of London, ambassadors, officers of the army and navy, judges, Privy Councillors, members of the upper house and others 'of the nobler sort' and (for the last time in a state funeral)

98 Effigy of Cromwell. Engraved frontispiece to *The Pourtraiture of his Royal Highness Oliver, Late Lord Protector &c*, 1659.

liveried paupers paid to pray for the deceased's soul.[84] With 'many thousands of people being spectators', the procession took several hours to reach the west gate of Westminster Abbey where the gentlemen took the hearse from the carriage and 'in this magnificent manner . . . carried it up to the East end of the Abbey' – to King Henry VII's chapel.[85] There, according to the author of *The Perfect Politician*, the effigy was placed 'in a most magnificent structure built in the same form as one before had been for King James but [he adds] much more stately'.[86]

All contemporary accounts testify to the opulence as well as solemnity of the funeral which Samuel Carrington described as 'managed with state and magnificence'.[87] The 'Bill of sundry particulars for the funeral of His Serene Highness' lists large payments for banners, standards, coats of arms, shields, badges, rich cloth, painting and crowns; and the cost of the funeral far exceeded that of royal obsequies.[88] It may be that the elaborate funeral liturgy was planned to counter or even efface the cult of Charles the martyr. What we cannot determine is whether such regal rites represented Cromwell's wishes: whether, though in May he declined the crown, he had hoped to leave the option open and by ritual behaviour – slowly become a king. But what is clear is that if those who orchestrated the magnificent funeral hoped not merely to honour the memory of the Protector but to erase the Stuarts and underpin the authority of his son and successor, they failed. Indeed, if Ludlow may be taken as a barometer of that party's reaction, Cromwell's funeral galvanized a newly strengthened Commonwealth movement which helped to topple Richard and the Protectorate government.[89] Cromwell's funeral was not soon forgotten, either by enemies or admirers.

II

At his speech at Cromwell's second investiture, John Widdrington, the Speaker, had told the Lord Protector in passing the civil sword to him: 'this sword is an emblem of justice' and 'justice is the proper virtue of the imperial throne'.[90] Justice, as we have seen, was the first duty of monarchs, and the theatres and performances of justice – the courts and the scaffold – were meant to represent kings to their subjects as just rulers. On some occasions, the accused turned the scripts against the king, as did Prynne, Burton and Bastwick in 1637, and in undermining the representation of a just ruler damaged royal authority, which was inextricably connected to the emblems of justice. In Cromwell's case, his self-presentation as constable, as well as his title Protector, along with his rhetoric, emphasized the safeguarding of the law and justice, the reform of which he often stated as a personal aim.[91] Yet, whatever his control of his image and representation in forms of speech, on medals and coins, or on ritual occasions, the Protector, far from succeeding in figuring himself as the fount of justice, allowed others to claim it and to represent him and his government as threats and enemies to the laws.

During the civil wars, and after, in pamphlet polemics the parties vied to be perceived as custodians of the law and to vilify opponents as the enemies to justice. The advantage the government traditionally held lay in its power to organize and manage state trials and punishments to display its just courses and the sins of traitors and plotters. While this unquestionably presented greater difficulties to Commonwealth governments operating with laws made by and for kings, the failure of the Protectorate to deploy and control the stage of justice damaged the image and perception of the regime – and perhaps not only in the eyes of implacable opponents.

From the establishment of the Protectorate, there were plots to murder Cromwell and public trials of conspirators which were meant to draw attention to the threats to the peace and stability of the country and to publicize the just authority of the government. An account, in 1654, of the trial of Colonel Ashburnham before the Council, for his role in a conspiracy to seize magazines and stir uprisings against the Protectorate, echoes Cromwell's own language in stressing the providential deliverance of a leader protected by

God.[92] But the course of public justice in the Protectorate courts did not run smoothly despite the government's efforts. At the trial in the High Court in June 1654 of John Gerhard, Peter Vowell and Somerset Fox, proceedings opened with a half-hour of prayers that signified the godliness as well as justice of the regime.[93] But if Fox's confession of his part in a design to murder the Protector and some of his councillors bode well, the others charged caused considerable embarrassment. In particular, Vowell insisted on his right by Magna Carta, and the Instrument, to trial by jury; and, even as witnesses to his plotting testified against him, insisted on his rights.[94] Though Sergeant Glyn, for the government, answered that, as well as the Protectoral ordinance against treason, 'the laws of old of treason against the king are of force . . . for it means the supreme government though it names only a king', Vowell had raised fundamental objections to the very legitimacy of Protectoral legal proceedings and ordinances.[95] They did not go away. After the insurrection at Salisbury, known as Penruddock's rising, in March 1655, an anonymous reporter, recounting the trial of some local conspirators in accordance with the late ordinance against treason, observed that the trials 'you will be pleased to note [were] not by a jury of twelve men of the county'.[96] At his own trial in May, Penruddock directly challenged the legality of the indictment against him and of the whole government: 'the law knows no such person as a Protector'.[97] Appropriating the language of the good old cause, he pressed his right as a freeborn Englishman to the law of the land, not that which 'is cut out by the point of a rebellious sword'.[98] And, he warned the jury and public, 'I observe treason in this age to be an individuum vagum, like the wind in the gospel, which bloweth where it listeth'.[99] On the scaffold (which he compared to Jacob's ladder to take him to heaven), Penruddock continued his attack on the legal foundation of the Protectorate.[100] 'The crime for which I am about to die,' he told the crowds round about, 'is loyalty (but) in this age called high treason.'[101] 'Now gentlemen,' he added, 'you may see what a condition you are in without a king; you have no law to protect you.'[102]

Penruddock and his fellow on the scaffold, Hugh Grove, were obviously Royalists who proclaimed their allegiance to Charles Stuart and the Church of England.[103] Yet their stand on the 'good old laws of the land' struck a deeper chord with radical critics of the Protectorate, such as the Levellers, and with old Parliamentarian heroes, such as Prynne.[104] Indeed, weeks after Penruddock's denunciations, in A New Discovery of Free-State Tyranny, Prynne mounted from prison a biting attack on the 'illegal, usurped and new self-created powers and jurisdictions' in England and 'the want of a true legal power, jurisdiction and courts of justice'.[105] Printing a series of his letters to Judge Bradshaw protesting against his unjust apprehension, Prynne questioned the lawfulness of the whole Protectoral establishment.

It may be that, faced with this challenge, the government made greater efforts to control the reporting of state trials. Although the fullest account of

Penruddock's trial appears to have been written from the victim's viewpoint, later accounts of proceedings against conspirators were printed by the official Protectorate printer Thomas Newcombe, and, in one case, authored by Marchamont Nedham, its official press agent.[106] *The Whole Business of Sindercome*, relating a 1657 plot to burn Whitehall and assassinate Cromwell as he came from the Abbey, details extensive testimonies against the conspirators and justifies the charge of treason not by reference to the ordinance but by the statute of 25 Edw III.[107] In this case, in which 'the prisoner seeing the evidence so clear against him had nothing material to say', the promise of a show of justice and punishment was spoiled only by Sindercombe's suicide which, as he intended, prevented the 'open shame of the world executed upon my body' – and also the process of state justice.[108]

However, if Newcombe's and Nedham's involvement was intended to improve the image of Protectoral justice, it was hardly a success. In 1658, the government succeeded in effectively trapping two Royalist conspirators, Henry Slingsby and John Hewitt, by uncovering their plans for a Royalist uprising.[109] The Secretary of State, John Thurloe, was confident that the evidence against them was unimpeachable and an official tract, *The Horrible and Bloody Conspiracy*, prepared the ground for their trial and punishment.[110] But alternative accounts were soon in print, some with elegies on 'the most pious . . . Dr John Hewitt'; and the trial itself raised far more problems than Thurloe had anticipated.[111] Like others before them, Slingsby and Hewitt requested counsel and trial by jury and rejected the validity of the court; Hewitt sat covered (wearing his hat) during the charge.[112] Though the Lord President, exasperated, insisted in the face of Hewitt's repeated objections that the court 'know themselves lawfully authorised', it was a weak response to the challenge and to Hewitt's rhetorical retort: 'I am so highly sensible of the privileges of an Englishman.'[113] In his summing up, the Lord President, invoking the Armada and Powder Plot to brand Royalist plotters as papists bent on destroying their own country, linked past Catholic conspiracies with the accused's challenge to the constitutional legitimacy of the Protectorate in a manner that might have been effective.[114] However, on the scaffold, before a 'confluence of people of all sorts . . . the like to which hath not been observed', Hewitt, cleverly presenting himself not as a Royalist but as 'a state martyr for the public good', voiced the concerns of many: 'It seems to me,' he said, after a final prayer, 'a strange thing that . . . I, pleading for the privileges, the laws, the statutes and customs of the land, . . . should die by those that should stand for the laws, the statutes and privileges of the land.'[115] Indeed, Hewitt's language, Royalist that he was, was echoed in the responses of that devoted Commonwealthsman Sir Henry Vane when he was examined before the Council for his writings, most notably *A Healing Question*.[116] In an account of *The Proceeds of the Protector (so called) and his Council against Sir Henry Vane*, the anonymous author – 'a well wisher to . . . England's liberty' – relates Vane's condemnation of the government's unlawful use of its powers and his plea to them to 'do judgement, execute justice'.[117]

For all his rhetoric, Cromwell, partly because he failed to manage the public performance of justice, failed to change his image from that of a military leader to a custodian of law and justice. A widespread and growing sense that the Protectorate was neither lawful nor just undoubtedly contributed to the demise of the regime and to a wave of support for the restoration of the monarchy as the only guarantee of the law.

CHAPTER 19

CONTESTING AND
COMMEMORATING CROMWELL

I

'The multitude', wrote Richard Flecknoe in *The Idea of His Highness Oliver, Late Lord Protector* (1659), is 'more taken with one satire than twenty elogiums' – epitaphs, or perhaps here eulogies.[1] From the creation of the Protectorate, Cromwell and the government were the targets not only of satires but of opposition writings of various genres that contested official representations. Though an apologist for the Instrument sought to disparage the 'opinionators' who protested against the new regime, far from fading with time, the attacks on Oliver personally and the regime generally increased in number and intensity.[2] Where Old Commonwealthsmen objected strongly that 'the pomp and vanity . . . is now up again', Royalists depicted the Cromwell who was the son of a brewer as an upstart with a bogus title and authority.[3] As *The Character of a Protector* versed it in 1654:

What's a Protector, tis a stately thing
That Apes it in the non-age of a King
A Tragick Actor: Caesar in the Clowne
Hee is a brasse farthing stamped with a Crowne

Fantastick shaddow of the Royal head
The Brewers with the Kinges armes quartered.[4]

On both parts, and among many not so partisan, Cromwell's new title was a 'great stumbling block' to obeying the government.[5] The collapse of the Protector's first parliament only added fuel to the opposition. The *Declaration* of the MPs lately dissolved directly accused Cromwell, 'our mighty Conqueror', of tyranny, and published that they had been purged because they had sought to restrain his avarice and ambition.[6] While the declaration praised the old balanced polity of king, Lords and Commons, its charge offered ammunition to opponents of very different sympathies. Closely following the MPs, the authors of *A Declaration to the Free-Born People of England* pilloried a man of mean estate, who, calling himself Lord Protector, aspired to tyranny; and they urged the end of such usurped powers.[7]

Rumours about Cromwell's becoming a king redoubled and sharpened opposition invective. As even the pro-Cromwellian treatise, *The Unparalleled Monarch*, acknowledged in 1656, there were swarms of malcontents and 'mountains of opposition' to Oliver which stood in the way of his taking the crown.[8] Where treatises such as *The Right of Dominion* argued strongly for the change from an artificial Protectorate to a monarchy favoured by God and Nature, others warned against an office condemned by Scripture and Providence.[9] Again, however, critics on both sides joined in accusing Cromwell of seeking an arbitrary power above that of kings. *The Picture of a New Courtier*, 'cast about the streets' for broad public consumption, described a Protector whose little finger was mightier than a king's loins, imprisoning and taxing without accountability and indulging in extravagant pomp.[10] In similar vein, the author of *The Excellency of a Free State*, making the familiar connection between luxury and tyranny, urged the end of the Protectorate, along with all traces of kingly pomp and power, and the return of the supreme power to parliament and the people.[11]

As MPs were being elected for the second Protectorate parliament during August 1656, opposition pamphlets accused Cromwell of trying to rig the election and of having 'assumed an absolute arbitrary sovereignty'.[12] Those who were excluded, in *An Appeal from the Court to the Country*, exposed, as well as the denial of their lawful places, the usurped powers of the Major-Generals and the infringement of the people's liberties, concluding that Cromwell had arrogated to himself more power without accountability than any monarch.[13] The offer of the crown to Cromwell by his second parliament arose as much from a belief that only a return to monarchy could check his power as from revived Royalism. In consequence, though his refusal may have tempered the opposition of some old Commonwealthsmen who regarded kingship as 'directly opposite to the mind and will of God' and to army engagements, it did nothing to dispel the repeated charge that Cromwell pursued tyrannical power.[14] *A Narrative of the Late Parliament*, depicting an upstart Protector whose crimes exceeded twenty-fold those of the late king, catalogued instances of bribery and corruption by means of which Oliver usurped wealth and power for himself and his family.[15] And a pseudonymous tract in Latin, directly comparing Cromwell to the historical arch-tyrant Tiberius, listed his ambition, dissimulation and pretence of justice and religion as the Machiavellian devices by which this tyrannical monster came to exercise a power far greater than regal.[16] For all the pomp of his previous re-investiture, by the summer of 1657 the voices of opposition from old republicans and Royalists, often drawing on earlier tropes of the literature attacking court favourites, seemed almost to drown the eulogies of Cromwell, leaving him to act without any obvious support or legitimacy. A final *Comment upon the Life and Actions of the Grand Tyrant . . . Oliver*, again playing with a familiar trope of the base-born upstart raised above his station, returns to poking fun at his origins as the son of a brewer and at his big nose, as well as deriding his ambition, dissimulation and arbitrariness.[17]

Presenting a critical commentary on the pomp of Cromwell's funeral, George Wither, believing that just before he died Oliver had intended to take the crown that adorned his effigy, lamented how:

> To *govern* us, we long'd for such a *Thing*
> As other Nations have; forsooth a *King*.[18]

The issue of kingship had not been resolved in 1649; the republic had collapsed partly on account of widespread distaste for non-regal government; and throughout the Protectorate the compromise of the Instrument in reinstituting a single person but not a monarch was subject to strain. Cromwell's attempt to legitimize the constitutional compromise by persistently presenting himself as a Protector failed to quieten discontents; even though he finally (and perhaps reluctantly) declined the crown, his image and style of rule became increasingly monarchical – he became king in all but name and so was widely perceived to be striving to replace one royal family with another: his own. And indeed it was not only the constitutional issue of kingship that dogged Cromwell and destabilized the Protectorate, but the Stuarts: the memory of Charles I and the presence of Charles II who, to say the least, further complicated Cromwell's position.

By the manner of his death, as we saw, Charles I erased the memory of many of his failings and, in the *Eikon Basilike*, re-presented himself as a man of conscience, devoted to the law and his subjects, who died as a martyr to the church, liberties and the people. Throughout the brief life of the Commonwealth, as even its apologists acknowledged, numerous treatises, sermons, elegies and accounts of miracles performed in his name kept the memory of Charles I powerfully alive.[19] Such textual memorials continued to be published throughout the Protectorate. As well as histories, such as the several editions of Richard Baker's *Chronicles of Kings* and prophecies regarding King Charles by Arise Evans, Anna Trapnel and William Lilly, in the first two years of the Protectorate there were published letters of Charles I, accounts of his trial, a history of *The Reign of King Charles* and verses of praise and lamentation such as *Stipendiarae Lacrymae* or *A Tribute of Tears Paid upon the Sacred Hearse of the Most Gracious and Heroic Prince, Charles I*.[20] The mounting rumours about Cromwell becoming king were accompanied by an outpouring of treatises on the Stuarts and Charles I, as many began to ask: if kingship were to be reconstituted then were not the Stuarts rightful claimants who would contest the throne? From 1656, therefore, Royalists published a series of Lives and characters of Charles I to press the virtues as well as the claim of the Stuart family. That year, for example, Peter Heylyn, former chaplain to Charles and confidant of Laud, published his *Observations on the History of the Reign of King Charles*, a highly favourable portrayal of the king.[21] The next year, as well as Richard Perrinchief's portrayal of Charles as a resolute champion of the church and man of conscience, in terms and language that echo the *Eikon Basilike*, two volumes of the king's own works were published.[22] The *Psalterium Carolinum*, a volume of devotions based on the *Eikon*, rendered into verse and set to music, was printed and freely 'sold at the Bell in St Paul's Churchyard', evidently without the obstruction of the censor.[23] And Richard Royston clandestinely published an edition of the works of Charles, with frontispiece illustrations of the royal arms and the Marshall engraving from the *Eikon*.[24] With his speeches printed as the first text in the volume, Charles's voice from the grave now competed with Cromwell's as the voice of authority. In the last year of the Protector's reign and life, Heylyn returned to print with a eulogistic *Short View of the Life and Reign of King Charles*, 'the meekest of men . . . and the best of princes . . . an example of Christian forti-tude'.[25] After his massive near-1,150-page *Compleat History of the Life and Reign of King Charles*, the Royalist historian William Sanderson urged that a king of such 'goodness and glory' deserved 'as faithful a register as earth can keep'.[26] By sheer volume of pages on the late king, the last years of the Protectorate fully bore out Heylyn's claim that Charles I 'lives in the memories of all good men'.[27] As a contemporary verse penned on Charles's anniversary in 1657 affirmed:

Though dead, thou still upon our hearts dost gain,
And so more nobly and more truly reign.[28]

Oliver's death excited both the hopes of Commonwealthsmen who, of course, desired a return to republican rule and Royalists who, throughout the confused months of 1659–60, very much kept Charles I's memory alive. Several Lives of the king were published in 1659, among them Lambert Wood's *Life and Reigne* of 'that great, though unfortunate Prince' and the anonymous *Faithful . . . Character of a Glorious King . . . His Country's & Religions Martyr*.[29] Listing his attributes and virtues of justice, mercy and patience, the *Character* depicted Charles as Christ-like, as a 'fleshly angel' who was 'of all kings of the earth the most devout'.[30] Along with other Lives and elegies, Charles's own words and works were again edited and published in two volumes totalling six hundred pages entitled *Bibliotheca Regia or the Royal Library*.[31] And it was not only words that placed the king at the centre of the nation's attention. Many of the books published during the late 1650s bore engraved images of Charles I, whether from the *Eikon Basilike*, the popular engraving of Gaywood, or new images commissioned in the hope of restored Stuart fortunes.[32] Indeed, the 1659 *Bibliotheca Regia* carried opposite an engraved title page of a ship tossed by storms an elaborate portrait of Charles I crowned and enthroned, with beneath an inscription: 'then Solomon sat on the throne of his father David and all in Israel were joyed'.[33] The reference to the Book of Chronicles had been made when Charles succeeded his father in 1603; in 1659, however, it gestured to a different succession – that of Charles I's own son and heir.

Charles II was not merely a military threat to the Protectorate regime. Since his coronation in Scotland, his supporters had represented him as the legitimate heir to all three kingdoms, and in *The Case of the Commonwealth* Nedham acknowledged that, though the Pretender (as he called him) was absent and all but a stranger to England, some still hankered after a Stuart.[34] Certainly, supporters kept Charles II in the public eye. An account of a masque

99 Charles I. Engraved frontispiece to *Bibliotheca Regia, or The Royall Library*, 1659.

in which Charles had performed in Paris was freely sold at the Anchor in the New Exchange; a 1654 anniversary ode on his birthday, purporting to be published at The Hague but probably printed and certainly circulated in England, already looked to his restoration; and a published version of a letter from Charles to his younger brother Henry advertised his constancy to his Protestant religion.[35] Amid the rumours that Cromwell might even marry his daughter Elizabeth to Charles II, one Royalist prophet foresaw Oliver furthering Stuart restoration.[36] Though Gostelo's vision was fanciful, the revived talk of kingship focused attention on Charles II: Wither was not alone in arguing (in *A Sudden Flash*) that, if Cromwell accepted the crown, it would probably ultimately bring back 'Him that's expelled'.[37] Especially from the time of Penruddock's rising, Cromwell and his supporters laboured to represent Charles as a popish threat to religion, liberties and nation.[38] But, as we have seen, in court, on the scaffold and in their published speeches, Royalist conspirators boasted their allegiance to the rightful Stuart king. In the closing months of the Protectorate, Royalists went to lengths to persuade Englishmen of Charles's solid Protestantism; and *A Character of his Most Sacred Majesty King Charles II*, supposedly provided by a bedchamberman, painted a flattering picture of Charles as a pious, virtuous and peaceful prince who alone, as God's deputy, could resettle England in peace.[39] Though, the author claimed, some who themselves desired to be king sought to stop him, God was turning the hearts of the people to his chosen deputy Charles.[40] The claim may have expressed more of hope than confidence, but like the memory of Charles I, the stock of Charles II was rising as first one Protector died, and then his son and successor's brief rule collapsed. If Oliver never finally succeeded in persuading Englishmen of the legitimacy of his title and authority, the textual memories and presence of two Stuarts undoubtedly contributed to that failure.

II

Cromwell's appointment as Protector emerged from his charisma and public profile as well as his military victories. His task was to bring to the office and constitution the support he had attracted to his person. The case of his son and heir could hardly be more different. During his father's rule, Richard had remained in obscurity. Unprepared for the responsibilities of office, he also, crucially, lacked personal authority: Cromwell had not even formally nominated him his successor.[41] One pamphleteer appears to have anticipated a struggle after Cromwell's death between his heir and Charles II, stating 'the next dispute will be whether the one family or the other has most right'.[42] Whoever had the most right, Richard was proclaimed Protector and the people, probably out of relief that peace was not disturbed, greeted his proclamation with cheers, feasts, bonfires and bells across the country.[43] From many provincial towns came addresses of congratulation to the 'rightful successor', 'prince and ruler'.[44] Though a biased Royalist source suggests that those addresses of support were 'hatched at court' and insincere, there is no reason to doubt them.[45] The people of the town of Bedford admitted to apprehensions about their safety on Cromwell's death but told Richard 'these doubts are now dispelled'.[46] From Dorset came a promise that 'they heartily own the basis on which he stands, (viz.) the form of government by a single person and two houses of parliament, according to the late Petition and Advice'.[47]

The problem for Richard was that – again from two sides – there was opposition to the compromise put in place by the constitution. During his brief tenure of office as Protector, both old republicans and Royalists waged a polemical, as well as political and military, battle to change the constitution to their favoured polity. On the one side, addresses to Fleetwood and other army officers appealed to them to restore England's lost freedom and to end the government by a single person.[48] Similarly *XXV Queries Propounded to the People* questioned Richard's right to succeed his father and advocated a Commonwealth; while the author of *Margery Good-Cow* dismissed arguments for favouring the son for the sake of the father by attacking an Oliver who had 'enthroned himself' and ruled with a rod of iron.[49] On the other side, Royalists attacked the Commonwealthsmen and called on their countrymen to return to monarchy.[50] 'Their wills are good who desire to bring in liberty,' argued the author of *A Seasonable Advertisement*, 'but their wisdom is weak'.[51] It was, the author continued, 'they who are for a prince' who are 'excellently well advised'.[52] A republic and the army needed to sustain it, the author of *Loyal Queries* pointed out, had cost over £3 million, which the rule of a prince might have saved.[53] Others, concurring that there would be no peace without the re-establishment of hereditary monarchy, represented kingship as the natural form of government and the Stuarts as England's rightful kings.[54] A treatise purporting to be the 'True Vision of England', cursing the soldiers who had made the people slaves, argued that monarchy was 'the sole government appointed by God' and assured readers that in Charles they had a tender father whom they should recall to rule over them.[55]

In the midst of the polemical exchanges, a number of pamphlets, reviving a genre first seen during the Spanish Match and revived after the execution of Strafford, staged a dialogue between the ghosts of Charles I and Oliver Cromwell, in several of which, rather than pleading his case, Oliver confesses his vices and errors, leaving Charles to argue unopposed that the English are 'wholly addicted to kingly government'.[56] In one such 'pasquil dialogue', *The Court Career*, Oliver Cromwell tells Charles I that 'your piety has seated you in a throne of glory; my tyranny has seated me in a depth of boundless infelicity'.[57] As the Protectorate collapsed, the voice of that powerful orator Oliver Cromwell was being ventriloquized and appropriated – here for monarchy, by others against it. And, as for Richard, while the noisy polemicists for republic or monarchy contended for support, he was, for the most part, silent.[58] Richard addressed parliament on 27 January 1659 in a brief speech that praised his father's legacy.[59] 'He is gone to rest,' he told them, 'and we are entered into his labours.'[60] Laying out the objectives of peace and reformation, and the dangers that loomed, Richard enjoined the MPs to 'maintain and conserve love and unity among your selves.'[61] Only three months later, the Protectorate collapsed. Richard's last statement was a letter 'showing his willingness to submit to this present government' of a revived Rump and army officers.[62] The Rump had Richard's Protectoral seal smashed and his arms removed from buildings.[63] Though he lived until 1712, from 1680 back in England from exile, little attention was paid to him and he effectively erased his own identity by using a number of pseudonyms. Mocked in 1659 as 'Queen Dick', Richard's image was dominated by critics and opponents; largely forgotten by history, when he is remembered it is as 'Tumbledown Dick'.[64]

III

Unlike his son, Oliver Cromwell did not suffer the fate of being forgotten. Rather, from the moment of his death, admirers and detractors alike represented Oliver Cromwell as the dominant force, the personification of the revolution, the figure (for better or worse) in control of events. Such representations did not entirely accurately reflect the reality of Cromwell's position or his struggle with his councillors, officers, soldiers, parliaments and erstwhile allies. What, however, this indicates, beyond a human inclination to personify great events and issues, is the extent to which Cromwell loomed large in contemporaries' perceptions and imaginations. By the time of his death, the story of the English Revolution was the story of Cromwell's life. Even before either was over, the memory of the revolution and his life was being bitterly contested in the public domain. For if Cromwell was the dominant figure of the revolution – the figure standing opposite that of Charles I in the people's imagination as well as in the many pamphlet 'dialogues' between them – then struggle over the representation, memory and impact of the revolution inevitably involved rival images of the Protector no less than of the king. Cromwell's posthumous reputation in history and memory has been the subject of some study yet is still in need of a full analysis which we cannot offer here. However, a brief survey of responses to the Protector may help to illuminate his representation as well as reputation and contribute to an assessment of how far Oliver or others determined his place in history.

Edmund Waller's *Heroic Stanzas* on Oliver's death, making an explicit comparison with Charles I, graphically recalls the frontispiece to the *Eikon Basilike*:

His *Palmes* Though under weights they did not stand,
Still thriv'd; no *Winter* could his *Laurells* fade.[65]

And the poet, in language evocative of masques, wrote of his 'calmer influence' and blend of 'Love and Majesty'.[66] Other elegies praised Cromwell's military triumphs, matching him with Caesar, Pompey and Scipio, and also compared him regally to a father, a sun, and called him a prince.[67] As well as poets, prose panegyrists bewailed the death of a 'good prince', who had been a father, husband and pilot to the nation, a second Moses and a 'beatified' person who had secured the people's safety and preservation.[68] But the opposition Oliver Cromwell faced throughout his Protectorate spilled out into denigration of him on his death. As well as the condemnatory conferences between Cromwell's and Charles I's ghosts we have glanced at, Lives and characters of Oliver in 1659 presented him as a 'grand tyrant' and a 'hammer of persecution'.[69]

The news of the Restoration, of course, launched a tide of attacks on Cromwell. Alongside the pornographic and popular squibs against the Rump, Cromwell was mocked and pilloried as hypocrite, Machiavel and devil, as a debauchee (with Mrs Lambert) and murderer.[70] Royalists, eliding the complicated politics of 1647–9, placed the blame for regicide almost entirely on Cromwell and so 'made him a more powerful and influential figure in print than he was in historical reality'.[71] Cromwell was represented as the nemesis of the martyr king Charles and, as has been observed, the disinterment, hanging, drawing and quartering of his body on the anniversary of the regicide, 30 January 1661, were intended to evoke and atone for the execution of the king. Significantly, in a satirical (and hostile) account of the meeting of the ghosts of Cromwell, Bradshaw and Ireton at Tyburn, Bradshaw, cursing Cromwell for his fate, blamed him for leading him into sinful treason with his 'alluring tongue'.[72] Not only was Cromwell being represented in print and performance as a false king and counter to the true king, his 'tongue', that is his oratory, was seen as inseparable from his 'allure' and power.

After the near-ubiquitous attacks on his memory in Restoration drama and squibs, as well as sermons and treatises, Cromwell held a less prominent place in historical memory.[73] Though he was compared with William of Orange in 1688, the house of Orange and the Whigs, anxious to stress William's legitimate claim, understandably played down such comparisons. During the 1690s, and in Queen Anne's reign, Cromwell's name was invoked by both parties at various times, to criticize military escalations; and in the eighteenth century he was summoned as a champion by dissenters.[74] But what projected him to the first rank of figures in the British public memory was the publication in October 1845 of Thomas Carlyle's edition of *The Letters and Speeches of Oliver Cromwell*. In his decision to abandon a biography to allow Cromwell to speak in his own words, Carlyle boasted: 'He who would see Oliver will find more of him here than is . . . in the history books written about him'.[75] Whatever the truth of that claim, the edition was the spur to a renewed interest in Cromwell and a new flood of biographies in which Oliver's own words took central place.

It was not only words. In the year in which Carlyle published his edition of Cromwell, the Commissioners of Fine Art appointed to recommend statues for the new Houses of Parliament nominated Cromwell.[76] Not among the sixty-three nominees proposed for statues by unanimous recommendation, but one of a second group put forward by a majority, Cromwell and his statue became the subject of contentious debate; and it was not until 1899 that Hano Thornycroft's statue of the Protector was unveiled at Westminster, on the site where it stands today. Twenty-five years earlier, the city of Bradford had honoured Oliver with a statue on the façade of its City Hall, standing between those of Charles I and Charles II; leaving the viewer, according to his preference and politics, to see the Protector as a continuation of, or disruption to, monarchical rulers.[77] Read – in the 100,000 or more copies of Carlyle's edition – or seen, Cromwell was by the end of the nineteenth century a dominant public figure, who continued to loom large in the memories of twentieth-century leaders, Italian and German as well as English.[78]

In 1935, the Cromwell Association was founded to commemorate Oliver's memory, not least with an annual memorial service by his statue on 3 September: the anniversary of his death and his great victories at Dunbar and Worcester. The Association combines academic study and research with public outreach and education, with the intention of keeping Oliver's memory alive through changing historical circumstances. Today, on its website, it points up the relevance of the Protectorate, with its united Britain and written constitution, to contemporary debates about devolution and rights and the place and power of a second chamber.[79] In keeping with modern (or possibly postmodern) times, the Cromwell Association also presents Cromwell as a key figure in the 'issue of interpretation' that the study of history raises. Seven decades after the founding of the Association, neither the memory of Cromwell nor the hotly debated interpretations of his life and legacy have abated. Voted in at number 10 in the BBC's 2002 poll to find 100 Great Britons, Cromwell shared the top honours with only one monarch – Queen Elizabeth I; but he features too, on the BBC's 'Hero or Villain' website, as 'one of English history's most controversial figures'.[80]

Where the names of those who shared the battlefields and political struggles with him – Fairfax, Manchester, Lambert, Fleetwood, to name but a few – have faded into relative obscurity, Cromwell has not only survived over 350 years in our memory; 'it is', his *ODNB* biographer rightly judges, 'doubtful if any other non-royal Englishman is so diversely commemorated'.[81] Oliver has indeed been commemorated in almost every genre of popular culture – in over 3,000 books, in film, on tankards, in folk songs and in Monty Python lyrics, not to mention the names of many streets, hotels and an apartment block in Los Angeles.[82] But most of all, he is still remembered for eminently memorable and quoted words from Carlyle's and later editions of his letters and speeches. As I write, numerous websites, such as Brainyquote, the Quotations Page, Creative Quotations, Memorable Quotations and a host of others feature a

Cromwell, some of whose words are probably familiar to most educated people. Like the queen with whom he stands in the list of Great Britons, Cromwell is there not least on account of his powerful oratory – his self-presentation in words.

The bitter contentions over him that began in life have continued ever since because Cromwell has loomed so large in the national memory, even stood, one biographer recently claimed, as 'a defining exemplar of the national character'.[83] Because from his death contemporaries reviewed the great drama of civil war, revolution and republic as one enacted by Charles I and Cromwell, Oliver has been the subject of intense controversy and 'has suffered a variety of . . . personalities at the hands of his interpreters'.[84] Few historians would expect those controversies soon to give way to consensus. But the advice on the Historical Association website that students should focus on 'what Cromwell himself said and wrote' has been echoed in the suggestion of his latest biographer that we 'allow him a final determinative word'.[85]

As the new Oxford *DNB* entry puts it, in the main 'historians have opted to take him at his own valuation'. If they have, the Protector who never finally secured the legitimacy for his position he so desired, can yet be said to have, for all the noisy opposition, imprinted his image on the national memory.

IV

'A long parenthesis of transactions': that is how one loyal preacher at Lyme described the Commonwealth and Protectorate as he awaited the return of Charles II to his throne.[86] It was not only Royalists who by 1660 had been led to conclude that 'that nation that hath formerly been ruled by a well-composed monarchical government will not, without much peril and trouble, be brought to obey a democratical government'.[87] 'Doth not Nature teach you,' a more enthusiastic Royalist asked, 'that monarchy runs in English veins?'[88] The lawyers, a pamphlet pointed out, had importuned Cromwell to take the king-ship because the title Protector had no basis in laws which were 'born . . . under that climate [of monarchy], grafted into that stock, and habituated in that air'.[89] Such natural images greeted the return of the 'old king's son' and with him the restoration of tradition and normality.

The satires and attacks on Cromwell were as necessary a part of the re-establishment of tradition and normality as Charles II's dating his reign from the day of his father's execution. Yet, as the fact of Charles's exile could not be forgotten – and was soon to be the subject of adventure stories – so the legacy of Cromwell and the Protectorate could not be easily erased.[90] Indeed, as Laura Knoppers has argued, in making Oliver the scapegoat for the sins of regicide and revolution, in staging him and publicizing him, Royalist polemic contributed to ensuring his memory and presence in the Restoration world.[91] In the 1660s, as in 1659, the memory of Cromwell stood alongside that of

Charles I; and the two not only reflected the old divisions of the country, they personified and continued those differences into the Restoration, whatever its discourse of unity and fictions of harmony.

If Commonwealth pamphlets had publicly argued that 'the quality or majesty of a king or prince is of no consideration to the steel or lead of the meanest soldier', the Protectorate had taught that 'no state can be well governed where authority is divorced from power'.[92] If such voices of cynicism were unpalatable in the euphoria of 1660, they had not gone away. The foundation of government and obedience on religion and Nature had been fundamentally disrupted. Similarly, the illusion of consensus had been exposed by bloody conflict. In 1657, amid divisive debates about the Protectorate and kingship, George Wither had urged consideration to both parties, arguing:

And that, *Truth* doth appear in her perfection
When she is polished by *Contradiction*.[93]

Two years later, in *The Idea of His Highness, Late Lord Protector*, Richard Flecknoe, foreseeing a 'war of pens' that would 'continue longer than the war of swords', recognized that in evaluating Cromwell 'everyone judges according to their own affections and inclinations'.[94] Whatever was restored in 1660, difference, division and ever-present polemical contest were to be the legacies of Cromwell's Protectorate. During the 1650s, the one through posthumous words, the other through published letters and speeches, Charles I and Cromwell had contended for support. As several were quick to warn Charles II (who did not need this admonishment), there were still many who had not been converted to restored kingship.[95] In a divided polity, one with 'the kernel, as it were, of a Commonwealth in the shell of a monarchy', argument, advocacy, image and representation were going to be all the more essential to the exercise of authority.[96] As the loyalist David Lloyd advised the new king in a work with the same title as his father's powerful last testament, 'I wish our sovereign would exercise a pen as imperial as his sceptre and write himself with the same majesty that he lives'.[97] Together with that wish, an engraving of the new king made clear Lloyd's sense that, after decades of revolution and republic, the arts of royal representation would be more important than ever.

CONCLUSION

Historians have disputed the consequences of the civil war almost as much as they have fought over the origins of the conflict. Indeed, those who prefer the term 'revolution' usually believe that the society, church and state which emerged after the period 1642–59 were fundamentally different, for all that the monarchy and indeed the Stuarts were restored. Others see the troubles of the period between the Restoration and 1688 as a continuation of pre-civil-war problems and struggles which two decades of conflict and constitutional experiment had failed to resolve.

What then, we must ask, was the legacy of the first two-thirds of the seventeenth century for the representation of authority, for the discourses and symbols of power, and for styles of kingship? Had bitter political conflict, then civil war, then republican rule, discredited the old scripts and signs of a monarchical culture; or had rule by the sword and the failure of godly revolution and republic demonstrated the power of the traditional cultural forms of power and even invested them with renewed authority and popular support?

The reigns of James and Charles I undoubtedly demonstrated that all the genres, forms and texts of royal authority were being ever more contested and how, despite royal efforts to represent it, divine authority was being challenged. However, as we have seen, the leaders of the parliamentary opposition to the Stuarts strongly voiced their criticisms of James and Charles in the languages (of Scripture, law, history and memory) used by kings themselves. Even when civil war broke out, parliament, concerned to argue that it fought not against the monarchy or even King Charles but against evil counsellors, freely deployed the portrait of Charles I and the royal arms on ordinances and declarations which defied royal prerogative. Much space in parliamentary polemics and pamphlets was given over to answering and countering royal words, mainly in recognition of the authority the royal word carried. Even as it, necessarily in order to govern and fight the war, developed its own texts and signs of power – in declarations and coins, for example – parliament yet followed, sometimes aped, regal forms, as if to advertise a continuity which it held as necessary for legitimacy. For much of its course, the civil war witnessed not so much a battle over, or between, different discourses and symbols as a continuation of the struggle to claim the same ones – and to claim to uphold them. Even after four years of fighting, the polemical battles over terms of peace and settlement were, in a measure greater than we might expect, fought in familiar and traditional terms – terms which, even though he had won neither the military nor the discursive war, yet favoured the king, and even helped him to fight the second civil war.

It was the radicals' recognition of that reality that led to the violent coup known as Pride's Purge which seized the king and took him into army custody and ultimately, when he would not submit to their terms, to the scaffold. Pride's Purge did not signal only – though that itself was a revolutionary change – a move to violence rather than normal processes of securing political ends. Since 1647, the radicals in the army had been defending their actions in the name of Providence and in terms of the rights of the soldiers and people. In petitions and agreements, rather than appropriating traditional vocabularies and scripts, they had ventured new languages to make novel, revolutionary claims: for a wide franchise, the laws in English, and religious toleration, for example. Many justified the trial and execution of the king in such terms: as the will of Providence and in the name of the people. However, whatever the new terms and arguments, the trial, as we saw, turned out to be a polemical victory for Charles. And not only for him personally but for all the traditional discourses to which he so successfully appealed and for the image of monarchy as the protector of the people. If, we might say, the old and new scripts and signs of state were on trial in 1649, the verdict was for the traditional texts and vocabularies of power, and – as importantly – was seen to be so. The *Eikon Basilike*, drafted before, and published shortly after, Charles's death, brilliantly revalidated and reclaimed for monarchy the texts and signs of Scripture and law; but it had such a popular success because Charles had already made them regal – and his personal – scripts.

It is well known that just as people dipped their handkerchiefs in the royal martyr's blood on the scaffold and the troops had to disperse them, so for the next two decades (and well beyond), subjects (not just active Royalists) collected mementoes of the king: miniatures, sometimes worn in lockets, engravings or woodcuts, tobacco boxes with his image or arms, or playing cards or counters. This souvenir industry is a powerful demonstration of how in – and through – death Charles I had succeeded both in revalidating monarchy and (as neither he nor his father had succeeded in doing before) in emulating Queen Elizabeth in making his person the affective centre of the nation. In 1649, Charles was able to do what he had probably always wished: to make a powerful case without simply entering the polemical fray as a combatant; and to combine, as had the last Tudor, mystery and popularity. His *not* answering the charge at his trial, although he spoke eloquently in defence of church, law and prerogative, demonstrated a monarch in charge of utterance, just as his demeanour and performative range (polite, calm, wry, witty) literally upstaged his judges as well as accusers. His final victory in the contest for cultural authority is evident in the fact that Charles was sentenced to death without due process and with even many on parliament's side questioning the legality and popularity of the verdict.

So, just as Elizabeth bequeathed a near-impossible legacy to the Stuarts, after years of losing the battle for image and support Charles at the end brilliantly outperformed his opponents. Though their case was far worse, their options were in many ways like those of a new dynasty: they needed either to reappropriate traditional languages and signs for their new regimen or to attempt to fashion new arguments for, and discourses of, authority. After a thousand years of monarchy, that, to say the least, presented a major challenge. As we have seen, for some time – perhaps too long – the republican apologists were more reactive than active; they concentrated on answering Charles's words as a means of undermining his hold on the people and deconstructing his authority.

Necessarily, this led many to respond in languages the king had reconstituted as regal. The more radical move was to devise new texts and new signs of a new republican regime, which some ventured to do – in poems and pamphlets, in artefacts and illustrations, in parades and processions. To observe that there was some tension between the republic's deployment of old and new arguments and languages is not to suggest the impossibility of their situation: Henry VIII, after all, had adopted different stances and styles and appealed to old and new, as it suited his polemical needs. But what was essential, if the regime was not to rely only on the power of the sword, was either to reclaim or to rewrite the scripts and signs of monarchy to legitimize the new republic.

In newspapers and pamphlets, figures such as Marchamont Nedham sought to do just that: not only to argue for republic but to fashion a republican culture. Most radically and famously, Thomas Hobbes, though he spoke for no party, rewrote the foundations of government and obedience on the basis of rational self-interest and fear. However, like Machiavelli, who was a greater influence on his thinking than has been acknowledged, Hobbes's arguments were anathema to most on both sides. The new scripts of republic were more commonly drawn from notions of popular rights or from a discourse of Providence into the workings of which, like kings who interpreted Scripture before them, the Council of State claimed special insight. Why did they fail? Why, that is, did the republic not garner public or popular support or any semblance of legitimacy beyond the people's pragmatic recognition of the need to obey a regime backed by military power? In part, as I have argued before, the answer lies in the enduring force of traditional and (after 1649 again) monarchical representations and texts.[1] But it seems evident, too, that the republic failed to form any affective bonds with subjects or, as the most successful monarchs had, to enter into the cultural imaginary, or to embody, the nation. Here the absence in England of a single figurehead, corresponding to the Doge of Venice or Stadtholder in the Netherlands, appears to have been a problem. The Commonwealth never made an impact as a collective government; it was charismatic military leaders, not least Cromwell, who were depicted and discussed.

The case of the Protectorate was very different and revealing for our wider story. For Cromwell not only established himself and his authority, he was clearly perceived as representing the government and nation, as the leaders of the Council of State and Rump had not. Cromwell was a brilliant rhetorician who made Providence appear his guide and protector as effectively as any monarch had claimed scriptural authority. He also fully understood the power of visual forms and of rituals in connecting the ruler with the people. As his words are often quoted, so his image is to this day instantly recognizable and his dramatic performances (in 1976 Michael Heseltine famously followed him in seizing the mace in the Commons) memorable. Whatever the constitutional distributions of power or behind-the-scenes manoeuvring, whatever the conflicts over toleration and the sects, the Protectorate was widely perceived as the rule of Oliver Cromwell. Cromwell, like the Elizabeth to whom he often made appeal, personalized power. And in doing so, he led even old Royalist opponents into willingness to support a Protectoral dynasty in the house of Cromwell, indeed into advocating that he take the crown.

Ironically, that offer spoke to the failure of Cromwell's position as well as his success. I do not simply mean that, as we know, Cromwell was prevented from the crown by opposition within the army. What I would suggest is that Cromwell's success in representing himself and making himself the centre of the nation had been in part founded on his appropriation of royal scripts and signs. Though his rhetoric and his image were different, Cromwell drew on the words and portraits of royal predecessors. He did so not (or not necessarily) out of ambition for a crown, but out of a recognition of the power of traditional forms and their importance for new polities. Cromwell, as a single charismatic figure (head) filled a gap, repaired a rupture, in the psyche of the nation, which was why he was addressed (as father, Sun, pilot of the ship of state) in the metaphors of kingship. Yet this presented some difficulties as well as benefits. Not only did Cromwell face opposition from within the army from old Commonwealthsmen who regrouped to bring down his son. As with Queen Elizabeth, Cromwell's intense personalizing of authority made it difficult for any to succeed him. Though Oliver established himself, he did not found a Cromwellian dynasty. The rapid fall of his son testifies not simply to his personal failings, nor even just to the revival of the Good Old Cause, but to the very force of Cromwell's person and presence, which, whatever the opposition, had held off the collapse of the regime. Today, those who imagine or fantasize about a republic think not of the Rump but of Oliver – of he whom many on both sides called King Oliver, and not without good reason.

As it had clothed republic in monarchical forms, one legacy of Cromwell's Protectorate was to make republican, constitutional, monarchy, if not republic itself, imaginable and even in some measure respectable. In the jubilation that greeted the restoration of a Stuart king, that sensibility was not what was most evident. But Cromwell had claimed back for other causes and constitutions languages and images which Charles I had re-made royal property; and Cromwell, as much as Charles I, stalked the imagination of Restoration Englishmen – not least the later Stuart monarchs.

In personalizing his authority, Cromwell had also faced the difficulties which had dogged his royal predecessors. He became, that is, the focus of opposition and his person and body the sites of lampoon and cartoon. Partly because he was not a divinely anointed king, Cromwell was mocked and pilloried for his big nose, and represented in pamphlet and woodcut as fornicating with Mrs Lambert and spiritual sisters. But as well as suffering the consequences of personalizing power, Cromwell was the first ruler to face one of the legacies of the revolution: the full emergence of the satire and abuse of figures of authority which did not, in the end, even spare kings. I have remarked before, and it remains I think striking testimony to his re-sacralization of regality, that, even after regicide, no one cartooned Charles I's body either in images or words.[2] But the civil war and Commonwealth had seen an explosion of print and a fully developed public sphere in which the principal modes of discourse had been pamphlet and woodcut animadversion, with newly sharpened polemic and new genres of satirical, sexual and pornographic invective. Whatever Charles I's reclamation of the sacred, the civil war had seen authority in general demystified and daily laid bare to forms, and to a degree, of assault hitherto unknown. Perhaps for the first time, during the civil war opposition and opposition journalism had become respectable, or at least regarded as the inevitable consequence of division and party.

Even if that divine right kingship was restored with wide popular rejoicing, and new censorship laws, these forms of opposition and animadversion could not be forgotten and became part of Restoration political culture and social life. As did divisions and parties themselves. For all the revived discourses and fictions of unity and love, the legacy of civil war to Restoration was one of permanent division which transformed the style and representation of monarchy as well as the political culture of England. Not only was the political culture marked by memories of violent conflict and the sharper divisions cemented by civil conflict. Division was, if reluctantly, recognized as part of the political culture and so as part of the exercise of kingship.[3] The Restoration may have been heralded with traditional panegyrics and signs. But, beneath the surface, people knew that the world was different and changed from that of the early Stuart years. The restored monarch did not face the challenge of establishing a new dynasty. He faced the greater challenge of re-establishing an old one after Cromwellian rule; still more difficult, of reconstituting monarchy after a decade of republic.

Throughout this study, we have seen how the greatest problem in representing authority was that of claiming and deploying traditional texts and symbols and fashioning new scripts and signs as changed circumstances and new challenges to authority demanded. In 1660 the ambiguous legacies of a revolution which had seen monarchy both destroyed and raised to its most sacred heights made the arts of representing regality, if more problematic, more vital than ever to survival. How a succession of monarchs responded to that challenge is the story of our next volume.

NOTES

Preface and Acknowledgements

1. See, for example, Roy Strong, *The Tudor and Stuart Monarchy: Pageantry, Painting, Iconography, Vol. 3: Jacobean and Caroline* (Woodbridge, Suffolk, 1997); R. Strong and S. Orgel eds, *Inigo Jones: The Theatre of the Stuart Court* (2 vols, London and Berkeley, 1973); G. Parry, *The Golden Age Restored: The Culture of the Stuart Court, 1603–42* (Manchester, 1981); R. M. Smuts, *Court Culture and the Origins of a Royalist Tradition in Early Stuart England* (Philadelphia, 1987); K. Sharpe, *The Personal Rule of Charles I* (New Haven and London, 1992); J. Peacock, *The Stage Designs of Inigo Jones: The European Context* (Cambridge, 1995); S. Kelsey, *Inventing a Republic: The Political Culture of the English Commonwealth, 1649–1653* (Manchester, 1997); L. Knoppers, *Constructing Cromwell: Ceremony, Portrait and Print, 1645–1661* (Cambridge, 2000). The best overview remains D. Howarth, *Images of Rule: Art and Politics in the English Renaissance, 1485–1649* (Basingstoke, 1997).
2. See K. Sharpe, *Selling the Tudor Monarchy: Authority and Image in Sixteenth-Century England* (New Haven and London, 2009), preface, introduction and ch. 1. Chapter 1 outlines the theoretical premises and methodological approaches that inform my whole study and readers of this volume are referred to this earlier discussion for my definitions of terms, interdisciplinary agenda and working practices.

Introduction

1. R. Morison, *An Exhortation to Styrre all Englyshe men to the Defence of Theyr Countreye. Made by Richard Morysine* (STC 18110, 1529), sigs Bi^v–ii.
2. This and what follows summarize some of my conclusions in K. Sharpe, *Selling the Tudor Monarchy: Authority and Image in Sixteenth-Century England* (New Haven and London, 2009).
3. See, for example, J. Guy ed., *The Reign of Elizabeth I: Court and Culture in the Last Decade* (Cambridge, 1995).
4. This is not to deny the importance of visual materials, especially prints, in early Protestantism (see, for example, R. W. Scribner, *For the Sake of Simple Folk: Popular Propaganda for the German Reformation*, Cambridge, 1981) but to point up the role of visuals in mystifying worship – of the sovereign as well as God.
5. Sharpe, *Selling the Tudor Monarchy*; K. Sharpe, 'Sacralization and Demystification. The Publicization of Monarchy in Early Modern England', in J. Deploige and G. Deneckere eds, *Mystifying the Monarch: Studies on Discourse, Power, and History* (Amsterdam, 2006), pp. 99–115, 255–9.
6. Sharpe, *Selling the Tudor Monarchy*, Part VI.
7. As revisionist scholars have observed, Edinburgh was by no means a cultural backwater. But debate there was more often conducted through sermons and manuscript libels than in print.

1 Writing Divine Right

1. K. Sharpe, *Selling the Tudor Monarchy: Authority and Image in Sixteenth-Century England* (New Haven and London, 2009), ch. 1.
2. Ibid., ch. 4, pp. 451–64.
3. Ibid., ch. 4 *passim* and epilogue.

4. J. A. Guy ed., *The Reign of Elizabeth I: Court and Culture in the Last Decade* (Cambridge, 1995).

5. Jean-Christophe Mayer ed., *The Struggle for the Succession in Late Elizabethan England: Politics, Polemics and Cultural Representations* (Montpellier, 2004).

6. R. C. Munden, 'James I and the "Growth of Mutual Distrust": King, Commons and Reform, 1603–1604', in K. Sharpe ed., *Faction and Parliament: Essays on Early Stuart History* (Oxford, 1978), pp. 43–72.

7. S. Daniel, *A Panegyrike Congratulatorie to the Kings Maiestie* (STC 6258, 1603), sig. B2ᵛ.

8. R. Fletcher, *A Briefe and Familiar Epistle Shewing His Maiesties Most Lawfull, Honourable and Iust Title to All His Kingdomes* (STC 11086, 1603), sig. B4ᵛ.

9. *Englands Welcome to Iames by the Grace of God, King of England, Scotland, France and Ireland, Defender of the Faith* (STC 14422, 1603), sig. A3ᵛ.

10. Sharpe, *Selling the Tudor Monarchy*, pp. 460–3.

11. See J. Bruce ed., *Letters of Queen Elizabeth and King James VI of Scotland* (Camden Society, 46, 1849); M. Vignaux, 'The Succession and Related Issues through the Correspondence of Elizabeth, James, and Robert Cecil', in Mayer, *Struggle for the Succession*, pp. 65–88.

12. J. Bruce ed., *Correspondence of King James VI of Scotland with Sir Robert Cecil and Others in England, during the Reign of Queen Elizabeth; with an Appendix Containing Papers Illustrative of Transactions between King James and Robert, Earl of Essex* (Camden Society, 78, 1861).

13. Cecil reported that Elizabeth, when asked whether she wished James to succeed her, nodded her approval, but there is no independent evidence. See W. Camden, *The Historie of the Most Renowned and Victorious Princesse Elizabeth* (STC 4500, 1630), p. 223.

14. Samuel Rowlands, *Ave Caesar: God Save the King The Ioyfull Ecchoes of Loyall English Hartes, Entertayning His Maiesties Late Ariuall in England. With an Epitaph Upon the Death of Her Maiestie Our Late Queene* (STC 21364, 1603), sig. Bii.

15. S. Daniel, *Panegyrike Congratulatorie*, sig. A6.

16. *Englands Welcome*, sig. B4ᵛ; Andrew Willet, *Ecclesia Triumphans: That Is, The Ioy of the English Church for the Happie Coronation of the Most Vertuous and Pious Prince, Iames* (STC 25676, 1603), p. 53. On Willet, see *ODNB*.

17. Especially Jenny Wormald whose biography of James we await. See Wormald, 'James VI and I: Two Kings or One?', *History*, 68 (1983), pp. 187–209.

18. *England's Welcome*, sig. B2ᵛ; Fletcher, *Briefe and Familiar Epistle*, sig. B4ᵛ.

19. G. O. Harry, *The Genealogy of the High and Mighty Monarch, Iames, by the Grace of God, King of Great Brittayne, &c. With His Lineall Descent from Noah, by Divers Direct Lynes to Brutus, First Inhabiter of this Ile of Brittayne* (STC 12872, 1604).

20. *A New Song to the Great Comfort and Reioycing of all True English Harts at our Most Gracious King Iames His Proclamation Upon the 24 of March Last Past in the Cittie of London* (STC 14426.7, 1603); Harry, *Genealogy*, p. 39; H. Petowe, *Englands Caesar His Maiesties Most Royall Coronation* (STC 19806, 1603), sig. C2.

21. Harry, *Genealogy*, p. 49; *Northerne Poems Congratulating the Kings Majesties Entrance to the Crowne* (STC 14427, 1604), p. 5.

22. J. Savile, *King Iames His Entertainment at Theobalds With His Welcome to London, Together With a Salutatorie Poeme* (STC 21784, 1603), sig. Ciii; *Post Nubila Sudum Gaudia Post Lacrymas, Sudum Post Nubila, Carmen. Gloria Res Durans Nomen* (STC 20587, 1603).

23. A. Williamson, 'Britain and the Beast: The Apocalypse and Seventeenth-century Debate about the Creation of the British State', in J. Force and R. H. Popkin eds, *Millenarianism and Modernism in Early Modern European Culture vol.III: The Millenarian Turn: Millenarian Contexts of Science, Politics, and Everyday Anglo-American Life in the Seventeenth and Eighteenth Centuries* (Dordrecht, 2001), pp. 15–28; *Northerne Poems*, p. 8.

24. W. Hubbock, *An Oration Gratulatory to the High and Mighty Iames of England, Scotland, France and Ireland, King, Defendor of the Faith, &c. On the Twelft Day of February Last Presented, When His Maiesty Entered the Tower of London* (STC 13899, 1604 sig. B3ᵛ). Hubbock was the royal chaplain of St Peter ad Vincula, within the Tower of London, *ODNB*.

25. John Gordon, *A Panegyrique of Congratulation for the Concord of the Realmes of Great Britaine in Unitie of Religion* (STC 12061, 1603); pp. 6, 23; Harry, *Genealogy*, pp. 39–40.

26. See *An Excellent New Ballad, Shewing the Petigree of Our Royall King Iames the First of That Name in England* (STC 14423, 1603).

27. Cf. A. McLaren, 'The Quest for a King: Gender, Marriage, and Succession in Elizabethan England', *Journal of British Studies*, 41 (2002), pp. 259–90.

28. J. Fenton, *King Iames His Welcome to London With Elizaes Tombe and Epitaph, and Our Kings Triumph and Epitimie* (STC 10798, 1603), sig. B4ᵛ.

29. Ibid., sig. C3ᵛ; Petowe, *Englands Caesar*, sig. C1.

30. *Englands Welcome*, sig. B2ᵛ.

31. George Marcelline, *The Triumphs of King Iames the First, of Great Brittaine, France, and Ireland, King; Defender of the Faith* (STC 17309, 1620; first published in French 1609), p. 50; Marcelline, *ODNB*. It was the extinction of the Valois dynasty that had plunged France into civil war.

32. Hubbock, *Oration Gratulatory*, sig. B2ᵛ.

33. *Englands Welcome*, sig. B4ᵛ.

34. For the poems, see J. Craigie ed., *Poems of James VI of Scotland* (2 vols, Edinburgh, 1955–8) II, 'Amatoria', pp. 69, 70.

35. Fenton, *King Iames His Welcome*, sig. B3ᵛ.

36. *Northerne Poems*, p. 11.

37. D. Bergeron, *Royal Family, Royal Lovers: King James of England and Scotland* (Columbia, Miss., 1991), p. 68; Robert Pricket, *A Souldiers Wish Unto His Soveraigne Lord King Iames* (STC 20341, 1603), sig. B3ᵛ. On Pricket, see *ODNB*.

38. Hubbock, *Oration Gratulatory*, sigs B2–2ᵛ.

39. Richard Martin, *A Speach Deliuered to the Kings Most Excellent Maiestie in the Name of the Sheriffes of London and Middlesex By Maister Richard Martin of the Middle Temple* (STC 17510, 1603), sig. B2. Martin was quoting James's *Basilikon Doron*. See C. H. McIlwain, *The Political Works of James I* (New York, 1965), p. 9.

40. Daniel, *Panegyrike Congratulatorie*, sig. A3ᵛ.

41. Ibid.

42. J. Goodare, 'Scottish Politics in the Reign of James VI', in J. Goodare and M. Lynch eds, *The Reign of James VI* (East Linton, 2000), pp. 32–54; M. Lee, *Great Britain's Solomon: James VI and I in His Three Kingdoms* (Urban, Ill., 1990); J. Wormald, *Court, Kirk and Community: Scotland, 1470–1622* (Edinburgh, 1981); I. B. Cowan, *The Scottish Reformation: Church and Society in Sixteenth-century Scotland* (1982).

43. R. Mason, 'George Buchanan, James VI and the Presbyterians', in Mason ed., *Scots and Britons: Scottish Political Thought and the Union of 1603* (Cambridge, 1994), pp. 112–38.

44. G. W. Bernard, 'The Church of England, c.1529–c.1642', *History*, 75 (1990), pp. 183–206.

45. Wormald, 'James VI and I', *passim*.

46. James VI, *Basilikon Doron Devided into Three Bookes* (STC 14348, Edinburgh, 1599); J. Craigie ed., *The Basilicon Doron of King James VI* (2 vols, Scottish Text Society, Edinburgh, 1944–50), introduction, II, pp. 4–26; J. Wormald, 'James VI and I, *Basilikon Doron* and *The Trew Law of Free Monarchies*', in L. L. Peck ed., *The Mental World of the Jacobean Court* (Cambridge, 1991), pp. 36–54.

47. James VI, *Basilikon Doron. Or His Maiesties Instructions to His Dearest Sonne, Henrie the Prince* (STC 14353, 1603).

48. S. Rypins, 'The Printing of Basilikon Doron, 1603', *Papers of the Bibliographical Society of America*, 64 (1970), pp. 393–417; Craigie, *Basilikon Doron*, II, pp. 16–23; Wormald, 'James VI and I', p. 51.

49. James VI, *Basilikon Doron* (1603 edn STC 14350), pp. 14, 60, 128.

50. For example, ibid., pp. 49, 51.

51. Ibid., sigs A1–B4; see McIlwain, *Political Works*, pp. 4–11. Henceforth, where there is no bibliographical complication, I give references to this modern edition.

52. McIlwain, *Political Works*, pp. 6–7.

53. Ibid., pp. 7–8.

54. Ibid., pp. 9, 11.

55. Ibid., pp. 10–11.

56. Wormald, 'James VI', p. 49.

57. McIlwain, *Political Works*, p. 3.

58. Ibid., p. 13.

59. Ibid.

60. Ibid., p. 15.

61. Ibid., p. 16; K. Sharpe, 'Private Conscience and Public Duty in the Writings of James VI and I', in J. Morrill, P. Slack and D. Woolf eds, *Public Duty and Private Conscience in Seventeenth-Century England* (Oxford, 1992), pp. 77–100.

62. McIlwain, *Political Works*, pp. 16–18.

63. Ibid., p. 30.

64. Ibid., p. 33.

65. Ibid., pp. 39, 40. James also recommended Lives of the virtuous Romans, p. 42.

66. Ibid., p. 43.

67. Ibid.

68. Ibid., p. 51.

69. Ibid., p. 48.

70. Ibid., p. 47.
71. James VI, *The True Lawe of Free Monarchies Or The Reciprock and Mutuall Dutie Betwixt a Free King, and His Naturall Subiects* (STC 14411, 1603). All subsequent references to the edition in McIlwain, *Political Works*.
72. Wormald, 'James VI and I', pp. 50–1.
73. McIlwain, *Political Works*, p. 60. For the international anti-Catholic context, see P. Lake, 'The King (the Queen) and the Jesuit: James Stuart's *True Law of Free Monarchies* in Context/s', *Transactions of the Royal Historical Society*, 6th ser., 14 (2004), pp. 243–60.
74. McIlwain, *Political Works*, p. 53.
75. Ibid., p. 54.
76. Ibid., p. 56.
77. Ibid., p. 58.
78. Ibid., pp. 59–60.
79. Ibid., p. 60; Acts 23: 5.
80. Ibid., pp. 55–6, 61.
81. Ibid., pp. 63–4.
82. Ibid., p. 68.
83. Ibid., p. 69.
84. Ibid., p. 70.
85. Ibid., p. 64. The phrase almost sums up James's approach to kingship.
86. In *Basilikon Doron*, ibid., p. 7.
87. Ibid., pp. 6–7.
88. K. Sharpe, *Sir Robert Cotton, 1586–1631: History and Politics in Early Modern England* (Oxford, 1979), pp. 23–4. See also Glenn Burgess, *The Politics of the Ancient Constitution: An Introduction to English Political Thought, 1603–1642* (Basingstoke, 1992).
89. McIlwain, *Political Works*, p. 63.
90. A. F. Westcott ed., *New Poems of King James I of England* (New York, 1911), p. 64.
91. Daniel, *Panegyrike Congratulatorie*, sigs A3ᵛ–A4ᵛ.
92. H. Peacham, *Minerua Britanna or A Garden of Heroical Deuises Furnished, and Adorned with Emblemes and Impresas of Sundry Natures, Newly Devised, Moralized, and Published, by Henry Peacham* (STC 19511, 1612), p. 171; G. Wither, *Prince Henries Obsequies or Mournefull Elegies Upon his Death* (STC 29515, 1612), sig. A4 mentions *Basilikon Doron*. See also J. W. Williamson, *The Myth of the Conqueror – Prince Henry Stuart: A Study of 17th Century Personation* (New York, 1978).
93. W. Pemberton, *The Charge of God and the King to Iudges and Magistrates, For Execution of Iustice In a Sermon Preached . . . at the Assises at Hartford* (STC 19568, 1619), pp. 18, 21. Pemberton quoted James's description of kingship as 'onus' not 'honos', duty more than honour (McIlwain, *Political Works*, p. 3).
94. *The Fathers Blessing: Or Counsaile to His Sonne Appropriated to the Generall, From That Particular Example of Learning and Pietie, His Maiesty Composed for the Prince His Sonne* (STC 14539, 1624). The 1624 title page announces this as the fifth edition.
95. Ibid., title page.
96. In *A Meditation Upon the Lords Prayer, Written by the Kings Maiestie* (STC 14384, 1619), sig. A4 James announces that he re-dedicated *Basilikon Doron* to Charles.
97. See D. Fischlin and M. Fortier eds, *Royal Subjects: Essays on the Writings of James VI and I* (Detroit, 2002); Jane Rickard, *Authorship and Authority: The Writings of James VI and I* (Manchester, 2007). I am grateful to Jane Rickard for permitting me to read in advance sections of her book and for discussions of James's writings.
98. James I, *Daemonologie in Forme of a Dialogue, Divided Into Three Bookes* (STC 14364, Edinburgh, 1597).
99. S. Clark, *Thinking with Demons: The Idea of Witchcraft in Early Modern Europe* (Oxford, 1997), ch. 41, especially p. 619.
100. Ibid., p. 632.
101. Ibid., p. 633.
102. James I, *Daemonologie*, p. 15.
103. Ibid., p. 21.
104. Ibid., p. 55.
105. Ibid., pp. 40, 71.
106. Ibid, p. 8; Sharpe, *Selling the Tudor Monarchy*, p. 327.
107. James I, *Daemonologie*, p. 5. The passage from I Samuel 15: 23 is interestingly translated in the King James Bible as 'For rebellion is as the sin of witchcraft'.
108. J. Craigie ed., *Minor Prose Works of King James VI and I* (Edinburgh, 1982), p. 148.
109. Ibid., pp. 149–51.

110. Ibid., p. 167 and 167–71 *passim*.
111. Ibid., p. 167.
112. *Daemonologie* (STC 14366), facing sig. A2; Craigie, *Minor Prose Works*, pp. 170–1.
113. Craigie, *Minor Prose Works*, p. 154, though see Craigie's qualifications to excessive claims for the influence of James's treatise.
114. Ibid., p. 155.
115. Clark, *Thinking with Demons*, p. 669.
116. James VI, *Ane Fruitfull Meditatioun Contening Ane Plane and Facill Expositioun of ye 7.8.9 and 10 Versis of the 20 Chap. of the Reuelatioun in Forme of Ane Sermone. Set Doun Be ye Maist Christiane King and Synceir Professour, and Cheif Defender of the Treuth, Iames the 6 King of Scottis* (STC 14376, Edinburgh, 1588); *Ane Meditatioun Upon the xxv, xxvi, xxvii, xxviii, and xxix Verses of the XV Chapt. of the First Buke of the Chronicles of the Kingis Set Doun Be the Maist Christiane King and Sincere Professour of the Treuth Iames the Sext King of Scottis* (STC 14380, Edinburgh, 1589).
117. See D. Fischlin, ' "To Eate the Flesh of Kings": James VI and I, Apocalypse, Nation and Sovereignty', in Fischlin and Fortier eds, *Royal Subjects*, pp. 388–420.
118. See title page of 1589 *Ane Meditatioun*.
119. James VI and I, *A Meditation Uppon the xxv. xxvi. xxvii. xxviii. and xxix. Verses of the xv. Chapter of the First Booke of the Chronicles of the Kings* (STC 14381, 1603), sigs A2–2^v.
120. Ibid., sig. A3.
121. Ibid., sig. A5. James may also here have been underlining his anti-Catholic credentials, especially as some had read his poem 'Lepanto' as sympathetic to papists; see below, p. 28.
122. Ibid., sig. A5^v.
123. Ibid., sig. B1^v.
124. Ibid., sig. C2. The Scottish text reads 'kirk'.
125. Ibid., sig. C2^v.
126. Ibid., sig. C4.
127. Ibid., sig. A5.
128. I am grateful to Dr Andreas Pecar for stimulating discussions of James's writings on Revelation.
129. K. Sharpe, 'Reading Revelations: Prophecy, Hermeneutics and Politics in Early Modern Britain', in K. Sharpe and S. Zwicker eds, *Reading, Society and Politics in Early Modern England* (Cambridge, 2003), pp. 122–63.
130. James VI and I, *A Fruitefull Meditation Containing A Plaine and Easie Exposition, Or Laying Open of the 7. 8. 9. and 10. Verses of the 20. Chap. of the Reuelation* (STC 14377, 1603), sig. A2.
131. Ibid., sigs A2^v A3–A4.
132. Ibid., sig. A6^v.
133. Ibid., sig. B3.
134. Ibid., sig. B4.
135. Ibid., sig. A2: 'I assure thee that before it be long by God His grace thou shalt see to thy contentment and comfort a large proof of his majesty's meaning expressed by his royal pen in that same argument.'
136. James VI, *His Maiesties Poeticall Exercises at Vacant Houres* (STC 14379, Edinburgh, 1591); James VI and I, *His Maiesties Lepanto, or Heroicall Song Being Part of his Poeticall Exercises at Vacant Houres* (STC 14379.3, 1603); Craigie, *Poems of James VI*, I, p. xlviii. See P. Herman, 'Authorship and the Royal "I": King James VI/I and the Politics of Monarchic Verse', *Renaissance Quarterly*, 54 (2001), pp. 1495–1530.
137. James, *Lepanto*, sigs A2–2^v.
138. Ibid., sig. A2^v.
139. Ibid., sig. A4.
140. Ibid., sigs B4^v, D1^v. James compares the large army to a commonweal, sig. C2.
141. Ibid., sig. E3.
142. James's treatise in verse, his *Schort Treatise Conteining Some Reulis and Cautelis To Be Observit and Eschewit in Scottis Poesie*, published in 1585, is in E. Arber ed., *The Essayes of a Prentise on the Divine Art of Poesie* (1895), pp. 53–69.
143. Several are discussed in Fischlin and Fortier eds, *Royal Subjects*.
144. *A Remonstrance for The Right of Kings*, in McIlwain, *Political Works*, p. 169.
145. James I, *The Workes of the Most High and Mightie Prince, Iames by the Grace of God, King of Great Britaine, France and Ireland, Defender of the Faith* (STC 14344, 1616).
146. *The Holy Bible Conteyning the Old Testament, and the New: Newly Translated Out of the Originall Tongues: & with the Former Translations Diligently Compared and Revised, by his Maiesties Speciall Commandement. Appointed to be Read in Churches* (STC 2216, 1611).
147. R. Carroll and S. Prickett eds, *The Bible: Authorized King James Version* (Oxford, 1997).

148. S. L. Greenslade ed., *The Cambridge History of the Bible. Vol.3: The West from the Reformation to the Present Day* (Cambridge, 1963), p. 164. See also, Adam Nicholson, *Power and Glory: Jacobean England and the Making of the King James Bible* (2003).

149. Greenslade, *The Cambridge History of the Bible*, p. 165.

150. Carroll and Prickett, *Authorized King James Version*, p. lxvii. There is a suggestion here that James got his way over the inclinations of some of the translators.

151. Ibid., pp. lv, lxii.

152. Greenslade, *Cambridge History*, p. 168.

153. Carroll and Prickett, *Authorized King James Version*, p. lxxi.

154. Ibid., p. lxxii.

155. M. Corbett and R. Lightbown, *The Comely Frontispiece: The Emblematic Title Page in England* (1979), ch. 7, pp. 107–11.

156. Ibid., ch. 11, pp. 137–42.

157. An engraving by Simon Van de Passe of James with the inscription 'Beati Pacifici' was evidently intended to face this engraved title page, so more closely yet identifying the king with the allegorical scheme. See Corbett and Lightbown, *Comely Frontispiece*, p. 141 and A. Hind, *Engraving in England in the Sixteenth and Seventeenth Centuries, II: The Reign of James I* (Cambridge, 1955), p. 259, no. 31, plate 154.

158. 'To the thrice illustrious and most excellent Prince Charles', no pagination.

159. James I, *Workes*, sig. b.

160. Ibid., sig. b2^v.

161. Ibid., sig. c4^v.

162. Ibid., sig. d4^v.

163. *Serenissimi et Potentissimi Principis Iacobi, Dei Gratia, Magnae Britanniae, Franciae, et Hiberniae Regis, Fidei Defensoris, Opera* (STC 14346, 1619 and 14346.3, 1620).

164. *The Workes of the Most High and Mightie Prince, Iames* (STC 14345, 1620). The title page has 'A Collection of His Maiesties Workes'.

165. Craigie, *Poems of James VI*, II, pp. xxii–xxiii; Westcott, *New Poems of James I*, pp. xiii–lxxi. Charles I, who annotated a manuscript of his father's poems, also published James's translations of the Psalms in 1631. See *The Psalmes of King David translated by King Iames Cum Privilegio Regiae Maiestatis* (STC 2732, 1631).

166. James I, *Two Meditations of the Kings Maiestie the One in the Yeere of Our Lord God 1618. The Other In the Yeere 1619* (STC 14412, 1620).

167. James I, *A Meditation Upon the Lords Prayer, Written by the Kings Maiestie, for the Benefit of All His Subiects, Especially of Such As Follow the Court* (STC 14384, 1618), sigs A2–A8, dedication sig. A5.

168. Ibid., pp. 11–12.

169. James I, *A Meditation Upon the 27, 28, 29 Verses of the XXVII. Chapter of St. Matthew. Or A Paterne for a Kings Inauguration. Written by the Kings Maiestie* (STC 14382, 1620).

170. See text in *Two Meditations*, title page.

171. James, *A Meditation*, sig. ¶6.

172. Ibid. ¶8^v.

173. Ibid., pp. 12, 44–6, 64.

174. Ibid., pp. 79–80.

175. Ibid., p. 126.

176. Ibid., p. 122.

177. Craigie, *Poems of James VI*, II, pp. xxii–xxiii.

178. NA SP 14/104/16; Craigie, *Poems of James VI*, II, p. 256.

179. Ibid., p. 173, no. Xb, lines 7–8.

180. Ibid., line 23.

181. Ibid., p. 177, no. XIII, line 8; cf. p. 176, no. XII.

182. Ibid., p. 179, no. XIVb, line 2. See C. Perry, ' "If Proclamations Will Not Serve": The Late Manuscript Poetry of James I and the Culture of Libel', in Fischlin and Fortier eds, *Royal Subjects*, pp. 205–32.

183. Ibid., pp. 182–3, nos XVa, b.

184. Ibid., p. 182, no. XVa, lines 7–14.

185. See A. Bellany, ' "Rayling Rhymes and Vaunting Verse": Libellous Politics in Early Stuart England', in K. Sharpe and P. Lake eds, *Culture and Politics in Early Stuart England* (Basingstoke, 1994), pp. 285–310.

186. Craigie, *Poems of James VI*, II, pp. 182, 190 no. XVa lines 23, 145–6.

187. Verse libels emerged in the 1580s when the Marprelate tracts also announced a new vitriolic mode of comment and criticism and reached their peak in the early Stuart period. Corantos and newspapers were a new Stuart genre. See J. Raymond, 'The Newspaper, Public Opinion,

and the Public Sphere in the Seventeenth Century', *Prose Studies*, 21 (1998), pp. 109–40; Raymond, *Pamphlets and Pamphleteering in Early Modern Britain* (Cambridge, 2003), ch. 4, especially pp. 128–38; A. McRae, *Literature, Satire, and the Early Stuart State* (Cambridge, 2004).

188. J. F. Larkin and P. L. Hughes, *Stuart Royal Proclamations I: Royal Proclamations of King James, 1603–1625* (Oxford, 1973), no. 35, pp. 74–7.

189. *A Fourme of Prayer with Thankesgiuing, to Be Used by All the Kings Maiesties Loving Subiects Every Yeere the Fift of August Being the Day of His Highnesse Happy Deliuerance from the Traiterous and Bloody Attempt of the Earle of Gowry and his Brother, with Their Adherents* (STC 16489, 1603). The Gowrie conspiracy was an alleged plot in 1600 to capture and murder James VI.

190. Ibid., sigs A4ᵛ, E2ᵛ–E3.

191. *A Fourme of Prayer with Thankesgiuing, to Bee Used of all the Kings Maiesties Loving Subiects Euery Yeere, the 24. of March: Being the Day of his Highnesse Entry to This Kingdome. Set Foorth by Authoritie* (STC 16483, 1604).

192. Ibid., sig. C3.

193. Ibid., sig. D4.

194. Ibid., sig. E2ᵛ.

195. Bodleian G. Pamph. 1520 (11), sig. D4ᵛ. STC shows a second edition in 1620.

196. *Prayers Appointed to be Used in the Church at Morning and Euening Prayer by Euery Minister, For the Queenes Safe Deliuerance Set Foorth and Inioyned by Authoritie* (STC 16534, 1605).

197. Ibid., sig. A2ᵛ.

198. Ibid.

199. *Prayers and Thankesgiuing to be Used by all the Kings Maiesties Louing Subiects, for the Happy Deliuerance of His Maiestie, the Queene, Prince, and States of Parliament, From the Most Traiterous and Bloody Intended Massacre by Gunpowder, the 5 of Nouember 1605. Set Foorth by Authoritie* (STC 16494, 1605), sig. A4.

200. Ibid., sigs C4–D1, E1.

201. Ibid., sigs G3–3ᵛ.

202. Some, however, clearly did; see G. P. V. Akrigg ed., *Letters of King James VI and I* (Berkeley, 1984), p. 29.

203. McIlwain, *Political Works*, p. 301.

204. Akrigg, *Letters*, pp. 24–30.

205. See also D. Bergeron, *King James and Letters of Homoerotic Desire* (Iowa, 1999).

206. W. Notestein, F. H. Relf and H. Simpson eds, *Commons Debates 1621* (7 vols, New Haven, 1935), IV, p. 71.

207. Larkin and Hughes, *Stuart Royal Proclamations*, nos 20, 30, pp. 39, 61, 63.

208. Ibid., no. 33, p. 66.

209. Ibid., no. 65, p. 136.

210. Ibid., no. 41, p. 88.

211. Ibid., no. 45, p. 95.

212. Ibid., no. 110, p. 243.

213. Ibid., nos 111, 113, 136, 140, pp. 245, 253, 303, 315.

214. Ibid., no. 145, p. 327.

215. Ibid., no. 183, p. 422 (cf. pp. 428, 432); no. 187, p. 433.

216. Ibid., nos 193, 195, pp. 450, 459.

217. Ibid., no. 208, p. 495.

218. For example, ibid., no. 217, pp. 511–19.

219. Ibid., no. 218, p. 520.

220. Ibid., no. 223, pp. 527–34, quotation, p. 532.

221. Ibid., pp. 533–4.

222. Ibid., p. 534.

223. Ibid., no. 247, pp. 583–5.

224. Perry, ' "If Proclamations Will Not Serve" ', pp. 216–17.

225. Ibid., no. 259, pp. 608–9.

226. James I, *A Declaration of His Maiesties Royall Pleasure, in What Sort He Thinketh Fit to Enlarge, or Reserue Himselfe in Matter of Bountie* (STC 9223.2, 1611).

227. Ibid., p. 3.

228. Ibid., p. 27.

229. James I, *The Kings Maiesties Declaration to his Subiects, Concerning Lawfull Sports to be Used* (STC 9238.9). There is a modern edition in Craigie, *Minor Prose Works*, pp. 101–9.

230. Craigie, *Minor Prose Works*, pp. 219–20; L. Racaut, 'The "Book of Sports" and Sabbatarian Legislation in Lancashire', *Northern History*, 33 (1997), pp. 73–87.

231. Craigie, *Minor Prose Works*, p. 107.

232. Ibid.

233. In 1624 James refused assent to a bill regulating sports on the ground that it contradicted his declaration, ibid., p. 224.

234. James I, *His Maiesties Declaration, Touching His Proceedings in the Late Assemblie and Conuention of Parliament* (STC 9241, 1621). On this parliament see C. Russell, *Parliaments and English Politics, 1621–1629* (Oxford, 1979), ch. 2.

235. Larkin and Hughes, *Stuart Royal Proclamations*, no. 223, pp. 527–34; above, p. 39.

236. James mentions that the proclamation had not given him enough space to outline his position, *His Maiesties Declaration*, p. 3.

237. Ibid., p. 2.

238. Ibid., p. 20

239. Ibid., p. 46.

240. Ibid., pp. 40, 44.

241. Fischlin and Fortier, *Royal Subjects*, p. 51.

242. *His Maiesties Declaration*, pp. 14, 19.

243. Ibid., pp. 3–4.

244. McIlwain, *Political Works*, p. 47.

245. The latest, disappointing, study asserts that 'the royal rhetoric was splendid but often vapid'. P. Croft, *King James* (Basingstoke, 2003), p. 59.

246. J. Nichols, *The Progresses, Processions and Magnificent Festivities of King James The First* (4 vols, 1828), I, pp. 530–62.

247. Anthony Nixon, *Oxfords Triumph in the Royall Entertainement of His Moste Excellent Maiestie, the Queene, and the Prince: the 27. of August Last, 1605* (STC 18589, 1605), sigs C1, C4ᵛ. On Nixon, see *ODNB*. We must, of course, allow for flattery in university praise of the king's oratory; but there is no reason to doubt that the formidable learning of a king who said that he could have enjoyed being a don impressed his Oxford auditors.

248. John Williams, *Great Britains Salomon A Sermon Preached at the Magnificent Funerall, of the Most High and Mighty King, Iames* (STC 25723, 1625), p. 40.

249. Thomas Heywood, *A Funeral Elegie, Upon the Much Lamented Death of the Trespuissant and Unmatchable King, King Iames* (STC 13324, 1625), sig. B2.

250. See the comment of Pauline Croft, above note 245; for a more favourable assessment see I. Disraeli, *An Inquiry Into the Literary and Political Character of James the First* (1816).

251. James I, *The Kings Maiesties Speech, As it Was Deliuered By Him in the Upper House of the Parliament, to the Lords Spirituall and Temporall, and to the Knights, Citizens and Burgesses There Assembled, on Munday the 19 Day of March 1603* (STC 14390, 1604); printed in McIlwain, *Political Works*, pp. 269–80.

252. Ibid., pp. 269, 278.

253. Ibid., p. 269.

254. Ibid., p. 272. He continued: 'I am the husband and all the whole isle is my lawful wife'.

255. Ibid., pp. 274–8.

256. Ibid., pp. 269, 274, 280. Malcolm Smuts has observed that these protestations of sincerity sit ill with James's European reputation for dissimulation. Though I would argue that James was being sincere in these speeches, that is not my main point, which is about his skill in oratory.

257. Ibid., p. 280.

258. See ibid., pp. 281–9.

259. For an account, see W. Notestein, *The House of Commons, 1604–1610* (New Haven and London, 1971).

260. McIlwain, *Political Works*, p. 282.

261. Ibid., p. 284.

262. Ibid., p. 281.

263. Ibid., p. 284.

264. Ibid., pp. 286–7.

265. Ibid., p. 288.

266. Ibid.

267. James I, *His Maiesties Speech to Both the Houses of Parliament, in His Highnesse Great Chamber at Whitehall, the Day of the Adiournement of the Last Session, Which Was the Last Day of March 1607* (STC 14395, 1607), printed in McIlwain, *Political Works*, pp. 290–305.

268. Ibid., pp. 298, 304.

269. James I, *The Kings Maiesties Speach to the Lords and Commons of this Present Parliament at Whitehall, On Wednesday the xxj. of March. Anno Dom. 1609* (STC 14396.3, 1610), printed in McIlwain, *Political Works*, pp. 306–25. See Notestein, *House of Commons*, pp. 278–82.

270. McIlwain, *Political Works*, p. 306.

271. Ibid., p. 325.

272. Ibid., p. 304.

273. G. R. Elton, 'Tudor Government, The Points of Contact, 1: Parliament', *Transactions of the Royal Historical Society*, 5th ser., 24 (1974), pp. 183–200.

274. See T. L. Moir, *The Addled Parliament of 1614* (Oxford, 1958); C. Russell, *The Addled Parliament of 1614: The Limits of Revision* (Reading, 1991); S. Clucas and R. Davies eds, *The Crisis of 1614 and the Addled Parliament: Literary and Historical Perspectives* (Aldershot, 2002).

275. James I, *His Maiesties Speach in the Starre Chamber, the XX of Iune, Anno 1616* (STC 14397, 1616), printed in McIlwain, *Political Works*, pp. 326–45.

276. Ibid., pp. 326–7.

277. Ibid., p. 344.

278. Ibid., p. 328.

279. Ibid., p. 330.

280. Ibid., p. 329.

281. Ibid., pp. 331, 342.

282. Ibid., pp. 332, 340.

283. Ibid., pp. 328, 343.

284. Ibid., pp. 344–5.

285. Ibid., 314; McRae, *Literature, Satire*, ch. 2; A. Bellany, *The Politics of Court Scandal in Early Modern England: News Culture and the Overbury Affair, 1603–1660* (Cambridge, 2002); below, pp. 127–8.

286. They are a notable absence in the otherwise valuable collection by G. Burgess, R. Wymer and J. Lawrence eds, *The Accession of James I: Historical and Cultural Consequences* (Basingstoke, 2006). Tim Amos is completing a Ph.D. on these panegyrics.

287. Samuel Rowlands, *Ave Caesar*, sig. Bi^v.

288. Petowe, *Englands Caesar*, sig. C2; *Post Nubila*, C2.

289. Fenton, *King Iames His Welcome*, sig. A3^v.

290. Ibid.

291. *Englands Wedding Garment Or A Preparation to King Iames His Royall Coronation* (STC 14421, 1603), sig. B1^v.

292. Thomas Rogers, *Anglorum Lacrimae In A Sad Passion Complayning the Death of our Late Soueraigne Lady Queene Elizabeth: Yet Comforted Againe by the Vertuous Hopes of Our Most Royall and Renowned King Iames* (STC 14671, 1603). Rogers was a clergyman and translator, *ODNB*.

293. Fenton, *King Iames His Welcome*, sig. C3; M. Drayton, *To the Maiestie of King Iames A Gratulatorie Poem by Michaell Drayton* (STC 7231, 1603), sig. A4.

294. *Englands Wedding Garment*, sig. A2^v.

295. Drayton, *To the Maiestie of King Iames*, sig. A4.

296. Pricket, *Souldiers Wish*, sig. B2.

297. John Lane, *An Elegie Upon the Death of the High and Renowned Princesse, Our Late Soueraigne Elizabeth* (STC 15189, 1603), sig. B3.

298. Pricket, *Souldiers Wish, passim*; William Alexander, Earl of Stirling, *A Paraenesis to the Prince by William Alexander of Menstrie* (STC 346, 1604), sig. D1.

299. *Northerne Poems*, p. 12.

300. E. C. Wilson, *Prince Henry and English Literature* (Ithaca, NY, 1946), part III; C. A. Patrides, ' "The Greatest of the Kingly Race": The Death of Henry Stuart', *Historian*, 47 (1985), pp. 402–8; Williamson, *Myth of the Conqueror*, ch. 6.

301. James Maxwell, *The Laudable Life and Deplorable Death, of our Late Peerlesse Prince Henry, Briefly Represented Together With Some Other Poemes, in Honor Both of Our Most Gracious Soueraigne King Iames . . . and Also of His Hopefull Children* (STC 17701, 1612), sig. D3^v. On Maxwell, see *ODNB*.

302. Ibid., sig. D4.

303. John Davies, *The Muses-Teares for the Losse of Their Hope; Heroick and Ne're-too-much Praised, Henry, Prince of Wales* (STC 6339, 1613), sigs B4, D2–D3^v.

304. Samuel Burton, *A Sermon Preached at the Generall Assises in Warwicke, the Third of March, Being the First Friday in Lent. 1619. By Samuel Burton, Archdeacon of Gloucester* (STC 4164, 1619), p. 17.

305. E. Welsford, *The Court Masque: A Study in the Relationship between Poetry and the Revels* (Cambridge, 1927); S. Orgel, *The Jonsonian Masque* (Cambridge, Mass., 1965); L. Barroll, 'Inventing the Stuart Masque', in D. Bevington and P. Holbrook eds, *The Politics of the Stuart Court Masque* (Cambridge, 1998), pp. 121–43.

306. J. Limon, 'The Masque of Stuart Culture', in Peck, *Mental World*, pp. 215, 221.

307. See S. Orgel, 'The Royal Theatre and the Role of King', in G. F. Lytle and S. Orgel eds, *Patronage in the Renaissance* (Princeton, 1981), pp. 261–73.

308. George Chapman, *The Memorable Maske of the Two Honorable Houses or Innes of Court; the Middle Temple, and Lyncolns Inne As it Was Performd Before the King, at White-Hall on Shroue Munday at Night; Being the 15. of February. 1613* (STC 4981, 1614), sig. D4ᵛ.

309. K. Sharpe, *Criticism and Compliment: The Politics of Literature in the England of Charles I* (Cambridge, 1987); M. Butler, 'Early Stuart Court Culture: Compliment or Criticism?', *Historical Journal*, 32 (1989), pp. 425–35; Butler, 'Ben Jonson and the Limits of Courtly Panegyric', in Sharpe and Lake, *Culture and Politics*, pp. 91–115.

310. Thomas Middleton, *A Courtly Masque* (STC 17910, 1620), sig. F2ᵛ.

311. Almost all the extensive recent work on masque has been by literary scholars and art historians.

312. S. Orgel, ed., *Ben Jonson: The Complete Masques* (New Haven, 1969), p. 76.

313. J. Gordon, *England and Scotlands Happinesse in Being Reduced to Unitie of Religion, Under Our Invincible Monarke King Iames* (STC 12062.3, 1604). Gordon was Dean of Salisbury, *ODNB*.

314. William Cornwallis, *The Miraculous and Happie Union of England and Scotland* (STC 5782.5, 1604), sigs A3, B3. Cornwallis was a Gentleman of the Privy Chamber, *ODNB*.

315. John Thornborough, *A Discourse Plainely Prouing the Euident Utilitie and Urgent Necessitie of the Desired Happie Union of the Two Famous Kingdomes of England and Scotland By Way of Answer to Certaine Obiections Against the Same* (STC 24035, 1604), pp. 34–5. Thornborough was Bishop of Bristol and Dean of York.

316. Lodovick Lloyd, *The Iubile of Britane* (STC 16623, 1607), p. 3. Lloyd was 'a notable figure at court', *ODNB*.

317. *Lucta Iacobi: Or A Bonefire for His Maiesties Double Deliuerie, from the Deluge in Perth, the 5. of August, 1600 And the Doomesday of Britaine, the 5. of Nouember. 1605* (STC 12466, 1607), pp. 3, 24 and *passim*.

318. Marcelline, *Triumphs of King Iames*, pp. 2, 64 and *passim*.

319. Ibid., p. 64.

320. Henry Peacham, *Minerua Britanna Or A Garden of Heroical Deuises Furnished, and Adorned With Emblemes and Impresas of Sundry Natures* (STC 19511, 1612), sigs A3–3ᵛ, pp. 1, 11.

321. William Leigh, *Queene Elizabeth, Paraleld in Her Princely Virtues* (STC 15426, 1612), sig. A7. Leigh was appointed tutor to Prince Henry, *ODNB*.

322. John Floyd, *God and the King Or a Dialogue Wherein is Treated of Allegiance Due to Our Most Gracious Lord, King Iames . . . By an Inuiolable Band of Loue and Duty, to their Soueraigne* (STC 11110.7, 1615), p. 79.

323. R. Eburne, *The Royal Law: Or The Rule of Equitie Prescribed Us by Our Sauiour Christ Math. 7.12.* (STC 7472, 1615), p. 22.

324. Thomas Gainsford, *The Glory of England* (STC 11517, 1618), pp. 246, 253–4. Gainsford's praise is notable coming from an ex-soldier, *ODNB*.

325. A.D.B., *The Court of the Most Illustrious and Most Magnificent Iames* (STC 1022, 1619), sigs A 3, B2, C1, p. 111.

326. Thomas Procter, *The Right of Kings Conteyning a Defence of Their Supremacy, Over All Persons and in All Causes, As Well Ecclesiasticall as Civill, Within Their Severall Dominions* (STC 20410, 1621).

327. Sharpe, *Sir Robert Cotton*; D. Woolf, *The Idea of History in Early Stuart England: Erudition, Ideology, and 'The Light of Truth' from the Accession of James I to the Civil War* (Toronto, 1990).

328. Above, pp. 14–15.

329. S. Anglo, 'The *British history* in Early Tudor Propaganda – with an Appendix of Manuscript Pedigrees of the Kings of England, Henry VI to Henry VIII', *Bulletin of the John Rylands Library, Manchester*, 44 (1961–2), pp. 17–48. Camden and some of the Elizabethan antiquaries were sceptical about the Brutus legend.

330. William Herbert, *A Prophesie of Cadwallader, Last King of the Britaines* (STC 12752, 1604), sigs G4ᵛ–H1, H4ᵛ.

331. T. Marshall, *Theatre and Empire: Great Britain on the London Stages under James VI and I* (Manchester, 2000); V. Hart, *Art and Magic in the Court of the Stuarts* (1994).

332. Thomas Heywood, *Troia Britanica: or, Great Britaines Troy* (STC 13366, 1609), p. 465; Harry, *Genealogy*, p. 1.

333. Heywood, *Troia Britanica*, p. 466.

334. T. Gainsford, *The Vision and Discourse of Henry the Seventh Concerning the Unitie of Great Brittaine* (STC 11526, 1610), pp. 20, 47, 51 and *passim*.

335. Ibid., p. 20.

336. Thomas Milles, *The Catalogue of Honour or Tresury of True Nobility Peculiar and Proper to the Isle of Great Britaine* (STC 17926, 1610), sig. A2; p. 240.

337. John Taylor, *A Briefe Remembrance of All the English Monarchs, from the Normans Conquest, Untill This Present* (STC 13736, 1618), sigs D1–2. Taylor was a professional and popular pamphleteer, ballad writer and poet, see *ODNB* and B. Capp, *The World of John Taylor the Water Poet* (Oxford, 1994).

338. Ralph Brooke, *A Catalogue and Succession of the Kings, Princes, Dukes, Marquesses, Earles, and Viscounts of This Realme of England, Since the Norman Conquest, to This Present Yeare, 1619* (STC 3832, 1619), sig.¶¶¶¶.

339. Edward Forset, *A Defence of the Right of Kings Wherein the Power of the Papacie Ouer Princes Is Refuted; and the Oath of Allegeance Iustified* (STC 11189, 1624), sig. A1ᵛ.

340. Thomas Bilson, *A Sermon Preached at Westminster Before the King and Queenes Maiesties, at Their Coronations on Saint Iames His Day, Being the 28. of Iuly. 1603* (STC 3068, 1603).

341. Ibid., sigs A6, A7–7ᵛ.

342. ibid., sigs B1ᵛ, B5.

343. Ibid., sig. B6ᵛ.

344. Ibid., sig. B8.

345. Ibid., sig. C4.

346. Anthony Rudd, *A Sermon Preached at the Court at White Hall before the Kings Maiesty, Upon Sunday Being the 13. of May 1604* (STC 21434, 1604); John King, *The Fourth Sermon Preached at Hampton Court on Tuesday the Last of Sept. 1606. By John Kinge Doctor of Divinity, and Deane of Christ-Church in Oxon* (STC 14974, 1606), p. 49. King attacked the Presbyterians as well as flattering the king.

347. John Gordon, *Enotikon or A Sermon of the Union of Great Brittannie . . . Preached by Iohn Gordoun Deane of Sarum, the 28 day of October 1604, in Presence of the Kings Maiestie at Whitehall* (STC 12059, 1604).

348. Richard Meredith, *Two Sermons Preached Before his Maiestie, in his Chappell at Whitehall the One, the xi. of Februarie, the Other the xxv. of Same Moneth. By Richard Meredeth, One of his Maiesties Chaplaines in Ordinarie* (STC 17832, 1606), pp. 8–11; William Hubbock, *Great Brittaines Resurrection* (STC 13898, 1606), sig. D4.

349. R. Wilkinson, *A Sermon Preached at North-Hampton the 21. of Iune Last Past, Before the Lord Lieutenant of the County, and the Rest of the Commissioners There Assembled Upon Occasion of the Late Rebellion and Riots in Those Parts Committed* (STC 25662, 1607), sig. F2.

350. Cf. M. Morrissey, 'Presenting James to the Public: Preaching on Political Anniversaries at Paul's Cross', in R. Houlbrooke ed., *James VI and I: Ideas, Authority, and Government* (Aldershot, 2006), pp. 107–22.

351. Daniel Price, *The Creation of the Prince: A Sermon Preached in the Colledge of Westminster, on Trinity Sunday, the Day Before the Creation of the Most Illustrious Prince of Wales* (STC 20290, 1610), sig. E4ᵛ. Price was a royal chaplain.

352. S. Benefield, *A Sermon Preached in St. Maries Church in Oxford, March xxiv. MDCX. at the Solemnizing of the Happy Inauguration of Our Gracious Soveraigne King Iames Wherein is Proved that Kings Doe Hold Their Kingdomes Immediately from God* (STC 1870, 1610), pp. 10–11 and *passim*.

353. F. Holyoake, *A Sermon of Obedience Especially Unto Authoritie Ecclesiasticall, Wherein the Principall Controuersies of Our Church are Handled, and Many of Their Obiections Which Are Refractorie to the Gouernment Established, Answered* (STC 13623, 1613), pp. 3–4, 14, 20 and *passim*.

354. Ibid., p. 31.

355. William Goodwin, *A Sermon Preached Before the Kings Most Excellent Maiestie at Woodstocke, Aug. 28. 1614. By William Goodwin, Deane of Christ's Church and Vice-Chancellor of the University of Oxon* (STC 12045, 1614), p. 2.

356. Ibid., pp. 20, 25.

357. See, for example, John Buckeridge's *Sermon Preached Before His Maiestie at Whitehall, March 22. 1617* (STC 4005, 1618) in which he preached 'neither pope nor people stand between God and the king' who received his power from God only (p. 4); Croft, *King James*, p. 101.

358. J. King, *A Sermon of Publicke Thanks-giuing for the Happie Recouerie of his Maiestie from His Late Dangerous Sicknesse Preached at Pauls-Crosse the 11. of Aprill, 1619* (STC 14983, 1619), pp. 37–8, 45–6 and *passim*.

359. On the shift in the king's policy and patronage, see K. Fincham and P. Lake, 'The Ecclesiastical Policy of King James I', *Journal of British Studies*, 24 (1985), pp. 169–207; Fincham and Lake, 'The Ecclesiastical Policies of James I and Charles I', in K. Fincham ed., *The Early Stuart Church, 1603–42* (Basingstoke, 1993), pp. 23–49.

360. W. Laud, *A Sermon Preached Before his Maiesty, on Tuesday the Nineteenth of Iune, at Wansted. Anno Dom. 1621* (STC 15301, 1621), p. 22.

361. C. Hampton, *A Sermon Preached Before the Kings Most Excellent Maiestie in the Church of Beauly in Hampshire, the Thirtieth of Iuly. M.DC.IX. By Christopher Hampton, Doctor in Diuinitie, and One of His Majesties Chapleines* (STC 12738, Dublin, 1620), p. 1.

362. Ibid., p. 20.

363. Ibid., p. 35.

364. Ibid., pp. 103–6.

365. W. Curll, *A Sermon Preached at White-Hall, on the 28. of April, 1622. By Walter Curll, D. in Diuinity and Deane of Lichfield. Published by Speciall Command* (STC 6132, 1622), pp. 10–12, 15, 18. Curll was a regular Lenten preacher; in this sermon he directly attacked the 'protestant hawks who wanted to pursue a holy war in Europe and those who caused dissension in the Church in England', *ODNB*.

366. William Loe, *The Kings Shoe Made, and Ordained to Trample On and to Treade Downe Edomites; To Teach in Briefe, What is Edoms Doome; What the Carefull Condition of the King, What the Loyall Submission of a Subiect* (STC 16686, 1623), p. 22 and *passim*. Loe had recently been reappointed a royal chaplain, *ODNB*. The kingdom of Edom was an elective monarchy with powerful chieftains (see Chronicles 36) so Loe appears to have been satirizing MPs critical of James's policies.

367. Ibid., pp. 23–7.

368. R. Willan, *Conspiracie Against Kings, Heauens Scorne: A Sermon Preached at Westminster-Abbey Before the Iudges, Upon the Fifth of Nouemb. 1622* (STC 25669, 1622), pp. 17–18.

369. Ibid., p. 41.

370. See P. McCullough, *Sermons at Court: Politics and Religion in Elizabethan and Jacobean Preaching* (Cambridge, 1998), ch. 3.

371. W. Sclater, *A Sermon Preached at the Last Generall Asise Holden for the County of Sommerset at Taunton* (STC 21843, 1616).

372. Ibid., pp. 9,17.

373. Ibid., pp. 18, 22.

374. W. Dickinson, *The Kings Right Briefely Set Downe in a Sermon Preached Before the Reuerend Iudges at the Assizes Held in Reading for the County of Berks. Iune 28. 1619* (STC 6821, 1619), sigs B1ᵛ, C4.

375. Ibid., sig. C2.

376. W. Pemberton, *The Charge of God and the King to Iudges and Magistrates . . . In a Sermon Preached . . . At the Assises at Hartford* (STC 19568, 1619), pp. 6, 20.

377. Ibid., pp. 21, 26; see above, pp. 19–21.

378. S. Burton, *A Sermon Preached at the Generall Assises in Warwicke, the Third of March . . . 1619* (STC 4164, 1619). His text was Romans 13: 4.

379. Ibid., p. 7.

380. Ibid., pp. 19–20.

2 Figuring Stuart Dynasty

1. J. Phillips, *The Reformation of Images: The Destruction of Art in England, 1535–1660* (Los Angeles, 1973); M. Aston, *England's Iconoclasts: Laws against Images* (Oxford, 1988); J. Kirk, 'Iconoclasm and Reformation', *Records of the Scottish Church History Society*, 24 (1992), pp. 366–83; C. Haigh, *English Reformations: Religion, Politics and Society under the Tudors* (Oxford, 1993), pp. 242–7; F. Heal, *Reformation in Britain and Ireland* (Oxford, 2003), pp. 262–7.

2. D. Thomson, *Painting in Scotland, 1570–1650* (Edinburgh, 1975), p. 10.

3. Ibid., p. 11–12.

4. K. Hearn, *Dynasties: Painting in Tudor and Jacobean England, 1530–1630* (1995), no. 117, p. 172; Thomson, *Painting in Scotland*, p. 28.

5. Hearn, *Dynasties*, p. 173.

6. Quoted in R. Strong, *Tudor and Jacobean Portraits* (2 vols, 1969), I, p. 178.

7. Ibid.

8. Ibid., p. 179; E. Auerbach, *Tudor Artists: A Study of Painters in the Royal Service and of Portraiture on Illuminated Documents from the Accession of Henry VIII to the Death of Elizabeth* (1954), pp. 118–19.

9. Hearn, *Dynasties*, no. 125, pp. 184–5.

10. Ibid.

11. See Leeds Barroll, 'The Court of the First Stuart Queen', in L. L. Peck ed., *The Mental World of the Jacobean Court* (Cambridge, 1991), pp. 191–208, 326–33; Barroll, *Anna of Denmark, Queen of England* (Philadelphia, 2001), ch. 3.

12. Oliver Millar, *The Tudor, Stuart and Early Georgian Pictures in the Collection of Her Majesty the Queen* (2 vols, 1963), I, pp. 80–1, II, plate 43.

13. Strong, *Tudor and Jacobean Portraits*, I, 179.

14. Millar, *Tudor, Stuart and Early Georgian Pictures*, I, no. 141, pp. 81, 93, II, plate 54.

15. Ibid., I, no. 184, p. 81, II, plate 45.

16. Strong, *Tudor and Jacobean Portraits*, I, no. 109, p. 177.
17. James Hall, *Dictionary of Subjects and Symbols in Art* (1974). On the Battle of the White Mountain, see G. Parker, *The Thirty Years War* (1997 edn), pp. 48–71.
18. T. Cogswell, *The Blessed Revolution: English Politics and the Coming of War, 1621–1624* (Cambridge, 1989).
19. Strong, *Tudor and Jacobean Portraits*, p. 180.
20. Hearn, *Dynasties*, p. 202.
21. Barroll, *Anna*, ch. 3; R. Strong, *Henry Prince of Wales and England's Lost Renaissance* (1986), pp. 86–137.
22. Barroll, *Anna*, pp. 47–58, 68–72.
23. Hearn, *Dynasties*, pp. 192–3; Strong, *Tudor and Jacobean Portraits*, II, plates 12, 13.
24. D. Scarisbrick, 'Anne of Denmark's Jewellery Inventory', *Archaeologia*, 109 (1991), pp. 193–238.
25. Millar, *Tudor, Stuart and Early Georgian Portraits*, I, no. 106, p. 81, II, plate 64.
26. Ibid., I, pp. 81–2.
27. Ibid., I, no. 405, p. 81, II, plate 42.
28. On the association with Minerva in Anna's masques, see Barroll, *Anna*, pp. 150–1.
29. Strong, *Henry Prince of Wales*, pp. 113–14.
30. Ibid., p. 114; Hearn *Dynasties*, p. 186 and fig. 49.
31. Millar, *Tudor, Stuart and Early Georgian Portraits*, I, no. 100, p. 79; II, plate 36.
32. Strong, *Henry Prince of Wales*, p. 114.
33. Hearn, *Dynasties*, no. 127, pp. 187–8.
34. Strong, *Henry Prince of Wales*, pp. 114–15.
35. Ibid., p. 115.
36. R. Strong, *The English Renaissance Miniature* (1983), p. 123.
37. Ibid., p. 126.
38. Ibid., p. 170.
39. Ibid., pp. 171–2.
40. G. Reynolds, 'Portraits by Nicholas Hilliard and his Assistants of James I and his Family' (*Walpole Society*, 34, 1958), pp. 16–22, quotation at p. 14.
41. T. T. (now identified as Thomas Talbot), *A Booke, Containing the True Portraiture of the Countenances and Attires of the Kings of England, from William Conqueror, Unto Our Soueraigne Lady Queene Elizabeth* (STC 23626, 1597); *Baziliologia a Booke of Kings Beeing the True and Liuely Effigies of All Our English Kings from the Conquest Untill This Present* (STC 13581, 1618; 13581.7, 1630).
42. National Portrait Gallery NPG D18235.
43. A. Hind, *Engraving in England in the Sixteenth and Seventeenth Centuries: Pt. II, the Reign of James I* (Cambridge, 1955), p. 163.
44. Ibid., plate 4.
45. Ibid., p. 31 and plate 5.
46. Huntington Library, Richard Bull Granger, Vol. IV, nos 3ᵛ, 7.
47. Ibid., IV, no. 7ᵛ.
48. Hind, *Engraving*, p. 35, and plate 10.
49. Ibid., pp. 39, 41, no. 1, and plate 14.
50. Ibid., pp. 56–7.
51. Ibid., no. 9, p. 291, and plate 174.
52. I Chronicles 16: 22.
53. Hind, *Engraving*, no. 4, p. 41.
54. Ibid., p. 245.
55. Ibid., p. 259, no. 31, plate 154.
56. Ibid., p. 163; see A. Griffiths, *The Print in Stuart Britain, 1603–1689* (1998), pp. 21, 26.
57. Griffiths, *Print*, p. 46.
58. Hind, *Engraving*, p. 198; above, pp. 42–3.
59. Above, p. 32.
60. Hind, *Engraving*, p. 215.
61. Griffiths, *Print*, pp. 54–6, plate 12.
62. Hind, *Engraving*, pp. 224–5, no. 18, and plate 30.
63. Indeed, in 1616 James was part of the Protestant union led by his son-in-law. I owe this observation to Malcolm Smuts.
64. Hind, *Engraving*, p. 225.
65. D. Bergeron, *Royal Family Royal Lovers: King James of England and Scotland* (Columbia, Miss., 1991), p. 64.
66. Hind, *Engraving*, pp. 181–2, no. 37; see frontispiece.

67. Ibid., p. 182, no. 38, plate 99. See too Huntington, Bull Granger, IV, no. 19.
68. Hind, *Engraving*, p. 56, no. 8, and plate 26.
69. Ibid., pp. 291–2, no. 10 and plate 176.
70. Griffiths, *Print*, pp. 65–8.
71. Ibid., p. 67; Hind, *Engraving*, pp. 295–6, no. 15.
72. Hind, *Engraving*, plate 181.
73. Jonathan Goldberg, *James I and the Politics of Literature: Jonson, Shakespeare, Donne and their Contemporaries* (Baltimore, 1983), pp. 90–1. Rather more unconvincingly, Goldberg suggests that the image may have been influenced by Venetian ideas of limited monarchy.
74. Quotations from verses below engraving.
75. J. Taylor, *A Briefe Remembrance of All the English Monarchs, From the Normans Conquest, Untill This Present* (STC 23737, 1618; 23738, 1622), image of James I [at end, not paginated].
76. J. Wickham Legg, *The Coronation Order of King James I* (1902), p. x.
77. Hind, *Engraving*, p. 50 and plate 22; J. Speed, *The Theatre of the Empire of Great Britaine* (STC 23041, 1612), opposite dedication to king.
78. Wickham Legg, *Coronation*, p. xi.
79. B. Levack, *The Formation of the British State: England, Scotland and the Union, 1603–1707* (Oxford, 1987), p. 38; J. Larkin and P. Hughes eds, *Stuart Royal Proclamations: I: Royal Proclamations of King James I, 1603–25* (Oxford, 1973), nos 9, 45, pp. 18–19, 94–7.
80. For example, *Northerne Poems Congratulating the Kings Majestie Entrance to the Crowne* (STC 14427, 1604), p. 21.
81. W. Fennor, *Fennors Descriptions, or A True Relation of Certaine and Diuers Speeches Spoken Before the King and Queenes Most Excellent Maiestie* (STC 10784, 1616), sig. F1.
82. G. Marcelline, *The Triumphs of King James the First* (STC 17309, 1610), p. 33 and pp. 30–7 *passim*.
83. A. B. Wyon, *The Great Seals of England, from the Earliest Period to the Present Time* (1877), p. 80.
84. W. de Gray Birch, *Catalogue of Seals in the Department of Manuscripts in the British Museum* (6 vols, 1887–1900), I, p. 56.
85. Before James, Ireland was not incorporated into the royal arms, even though Henry VIII was proclaimed king in 1541, Wyon, *Great Seals*, p. 79.
86. A. Franks and H. Grueber, *Medallic Illustrations of the History of Great Britain* (2 vols, 1885), I, pp. 187, no. 1, 191. no. 11; E. Hawkins, *Medallic Illustrations of the History of Great Britain* (1904–11), plate XIV, nos. 1, 11.
87. Franks and Grueber, *Medallic Illustrations*, I, p. 187, no. 2; Hawkins, *Medallic Illustrations*, plate XIV, no. 2.
88. Franks and Grueber, *Medallic Illustrations*, I, pp. 193–4, nos 14–16; Hawkins, *Medallic Illustrations*, plate XIV, nos 14–16.
89. Franks and Grueber, *Medallic Illustrations*, I, p. 194, no. 17; Hawkins, *Medallic Illustrations*, plate XIV, no. 17.
90. Franks and Grueber, *Medallic Illustrations*, I, p. 196, no. 19; Hawkins, *Medallic Illustrations*, plate XIV, no. 18.
91. Franks and Grueber, *Medallic Illustrations*, pp. 200–3 nos 29–31; Hawkins, *Medallic Illustrations*, plate XV, nos 7–8, 10. Fax means a heavenly flame.
92. Franks and Grueber, *Medallic Illustrations*, pp. 214–18, nos 61–70; Hawkins, *Medallic Illustrations*, plate XVI, nos 1–9.
93. Franks and Grueber, *Medallic Illustrations*, pp. 214–15, no. 61; Hawkins, *Medallic Illustrations*, plate XVI, no. 1; cf. Hind, *Engraving*, p. 279.
94. Franks and Grueber, *Medallic Illustrations*, pp. 226–30, nos 85–9; Hawkins, *Medallic Illustrations*, plates XVII, nos 13, 14, XVIII, nos. 1, 3.
95. Franks and Grueber, *Medallic Illustrations*, pp. 233–4, nos 95, 98; Hawkins, *Medallic Illustrations*, plates XVIII, no. 8, XIX, no. 1; see also Hind, *Engraving*, p. 281 and plate 168. Psalm 72, verse 1.
96. R. L. Kenyon, *The Gold Coins of England* (1884), pp. 135–6, 138–9.
97. Ibid. p. 146. One has the inscription associated with Tudor queens, 'Rosa sine spina', the rose without thorns.
98. Ibid., p. 136.
99. Ibid.
100. E. Hawkins, *The Silver Coins of England* (1841), p. 156.
101. Kenyon, *Gold Coins*, p. 136; C. Oman, *The Coinage of England* (Oxford, 1931), pp. 295–6.
102. Kenyon, *Gold Coins*, p. 140; J. J. North, *English Hammered Coinage, II, 1272–1661* (1991), p. 147.
103. Kenyon, *Gold Coins*, p. 141; Oman observes that the ship is a man-of-war (*Coinage of England*, p. 294).
104. Simon Thurley, *Whitehall Palace: An Architectural History of the Royal Apartments, 1240–1698* (New Haven and London, 1999), p. 68.

105. Ibid., p. 76.
106. Ibid., p. 80. Sir Dudley Carleton described James in 1607 visiting his new building to check on progress and criticizing the placement of pillars.
107. Per Palme, *Triumph of Peace: A Study of the Whitehall Banqueting House* (Stockholm and London, 1957), p. 3. Though specialized studies have refined our understanding, this still remains the best book.
108. Ibid., pp. 18–19.
109. Ibid., p. 26.
110. Above, pp. 61–3.
111. W. Dickenson, *The Kings Right Briefely Set Downe in a Sermon Preached Before the Reuerend Iudges at the Assizes Held in Reading for the County of Berks. Iune 28. 1619* (STC 6821, 1619), sig. C4. On Dickenson, see *ODNB*.
112. Per Palme, *Triumph of Peace*, p. 53.
113. Ibid., pp. 63, 68.
114. C. H. Herford, P. Simpson and E. M. Simpson eds, *Ben Jonson Works* (11 vols, Oxford, 1925–52), VII, p. 645, lines 418–23.
115. Cf. J. Charlton, *The Banqueting House Whitehall* (1964), p. 21.
116. Per Palme, *Triumph of Peace*, p. 293.
117. Thurley, *Whitehall Palace*, p. 84.
118. J. Summerson, *Inigo Jones* (Harmondsworth, 1966), p. 42.
119. Per Palme, *Triumph of Peace*, p. 174.
120. Ibid., p. 175.
121. Ibid., p. 191.
122. V. Hart, *Art and Magic in the Court of the Stuarts* (1994), pp. 145–50.
123. Ibid., pp. 145, 148.
124. R. Strong, *Britannia Triumphans: Inigo Jones, Rubens, and Whitehall Palace* (1980), pp. 17–19.
125. Ibid., *passim*; Per Palme, *Triumph of Peace*, pp. 230–48.
126. Strong, *Britannia Triumphans*, p. 10.
127. G. Martin, 'The Banqueting House Ceiling: Two Newly Discovered Projects', *Apollo*, 139 (1994), pp. 29–34, quotation, p. 30. I am grateful to Gregory Martin for discussions of this subject. See also Martin, *The Ceiling Decoration of the Banqueting Hall*, ed. Arnout Balis (Corpus Rubenianum Ludwig Burchard 2005).
128. H. M. Colvin, *The History of the King's Works, IV, 1485–1660 Part II* (1982), p. 332.
129. Quoted ibid., p. 367.
130. J. Harris, S. Orgel and R. Strong, *The King's Arcadia: Inigo Jones and the Stuart Court* (1972), p. 146.
131. Strong, *Britannia Triumphans*, pp. 62–3.
132. Ibid., p. 62. See also F. Yates, *Astraea: The Imperial Theme in the Sixteenth Century* (1975).

3 Staging Stuart Dynasty

1. Contrary to the assertion of S. J. Houston, *James I* (1973), p. 4.
2. Cf. R. M. Smuts, 'Public Ceremony and Royal Charisma: The English Royal Entry in London, 1485–1642', in A. L. Beier, D. Cannadine and J. Rosenheim eds, *The First Modern Society: Essays in English History in Honour of Lawrence Stone* (Cambridge, 1989), pp. 65–93, especially, pp. 80–2. Smuts exaggerates the decline in the visibility of the king.
3. Above, pp. 46–50.
4. T. M., *The True Narration of the Entertainment of His Royall Maiestie, From the Time of His Departure from Edenbrough Till His Receiuing at London With All or the Most Speciall Occurrences* (STC 17153, 1603), sigs B2ᵛ–3.
5. Ibid., sig. B3ᵛ.
6. Ibid., sig. B4.
7. Ibid.
8. Ibid., sig. B4ᵛ.
9. Ibid., sig. C1ᵛ.
10. Ibid., sig. C2.
11. Ibid., sigs C2–3.
12. Ibid., sig. C2ᵛ.
13. Ibid., sig. C3ᵛ.
14. Ibid., sigs C4–4ᵛ.
15. Ibid., sig. C4ᵛ.
16. Ibid., sig. D1ᵛ.

17. Ibid., sig. D2^v.
18. Ibid., sig. D3. A quotation seldom cited and one which contrasts with James's reputation for being irritated at the people's desire to see him.
19. Ibid., sig. D4.
20. Ibid., sig. E1.
21. Ibid., sig. E2.
22. Ibid., sig. E3.
23. Ibid., sigs E4–4^v.
24. John Savile, *King Iames His Entertainment at Theobalds With His Welcome to London, Together With a Salutatorie Poeme* (STC 21784, 1603), sigs A4^v, B2.
25. Ibid., sig. B1^v.
26. T. M., *The True Narration*, sig. F3^v.
27. Savile, *King Iames Entertainment*, sig. B2^v; J. Boulton, 'Wage Labour in Seventeenth Century London', *Economic History Review*, 49 (1996), pp. 268–90.
28. T. M., *The True Narration*, sig. F4^v.
29. Ibid.
30. C. H. McIlwain, *The Political Works of James I* (New York, 1965), p. 269.
31. D. H. Willson, *King James VI and I* (1956), p. 165.
32. R. Martin, *A Speach Deliuered, to the Kings Most Excellent Maiestie in the Name of the Sheriffes of London and Middlesex* (STC 17510, 1603), sig. A3^v.
33. Ibid., sigs B1–B2^v.
34. R. Dutton ed., *Jacobean Civic Pageants* (Keele, 1995), pp. 19–25.
35. J. Wickham Legg ed., *The Coronation Order of King James I* (1902), p. lxxxi.
36. Ibid., p. lxiv.
37. Ibid., pp. 18–19.
38. Ibid., p. lxxiii.
39. Ibid.
40. Ibid., p. lxxiv.
41. J. Goldberg, *James I and the Politics of Literature: Jonson, Shakespeare, Donne and the contemporaries* (Baltimore and London, 1983), p. 33.
42. J. Nichols, *The Progresses, Processions and Magnificent Festivities of King James the First* (4 vols, 1828), I, p. 325; on Hubbock, see *ODNB*.
43. W. Hubbock, *An Oration Gratulatory to the High and Mighty Iames of England, Scotland, France and Ireland, King, Defendor of the Faith, &c. On the Twelft Day of February* . . . (STC 13899, Oxford, 1604), sig. B1.
44. Ibid., sig. B2.
45. Ibid., sigs B2–3, quotation B3.
46. Ibid., sig. B4.
47. Ibid., sig. B4^v.
48. Ben Jonson, *B. Ion: His Part of King Iames His Royall and Magnificent Entertainement Through His Honorable Cittie of London, Thurseday the 15. of March. 1603* (STC 14756, 1604); Thomas Dekker, *The Magnificent Entertainment Giuen to King Iames, Queene Anne His Wife, and Henry Frederick the Prince, Uppon the Day of His Maiesties Tryumphant Passage (from the Tower) Through His Honourable Cittie* . . . *of London, Being the 15. of March. 1603* (STC 6512, 1604), printed in Dutton, *Civic Pageants*; S. Harrison, *The Arches of Triumph Erected in Honor of the High and Mighty Prince Iames. the First* . . . *King, of England. and the Sixt of Scotland At His Maiesties Entrance and Passage Through his Honorable Citty* . . . *of London Upon the 15th. Day of March 1603* (STC 12863, 1604); G. Dugdale, *The Time Triumphant Declaring in Briefe, the Ariual of Our Soueraigne Liedge Lord, King Iames into England, His Coronation at Westminster: Together With His Late Royal Progresse, from the Towre of London Through the Cittie, to His Highnes Manor of White Hall* (STC 7292, 1604). The edition by Malcolm Smuts of *The Whole Royal and Magnificent Entertainment Given to King James through the City of London* (1604) in the 2007 companion to the Oxford edition of Middleton's works appeared after I had written this chapter.
49. Harrison, *Arches of Triumph*, sig. C1.
50. Ibid.; Jonson, *King Iames Entertainement*, sigs A2–B1.
51. Dutton, *Civic Pageants*, pp. 50–1.
52. Ibid., p. 53: 'Remember James, that you have nations to govern under your command; and these shall be under your skills, to make a tradition of peace, to spare the conquered and to subdue utterly the proud.' See the reference in *Basilikon Doron* in McIlwain, *Political Works*, p. 52.
53. Dekker's description in Dutton, *Civic Pageants*, pp. 52–3; cf. Harrison, *Arches of Triumph*, sig. D1.
54. Dutton, *Civic Pageants*, p. 54.
55. Ibid., p. 56.

56. Ibid., p. 57.
57. Ibid., p. 58; *Arches of Triumph*, sig. E1.
58. Dekker, in Dutton, *Civic Pageants*, p. 65.
59. Harrison, *Arches of Triumph*, sig. E1.
60. Ibid., sig. F1; Dutton, *Civic Pageants*, pp. 66–9.
61. Ibid., p. 71.
62. Ibid., pp. 74–5.
63. Ibid., p. 85.
64. Harrison, *Arches of Triumph*, sig. H1; Dutton, *Civic Pageants*, pp. 87–91.
65. Dutton, *Civic Pageants*, p. 88.
66. Ibid., p. 92.
67. The verses refer to 'Jove's high court of Parliament', ibid., p. 94.
68. Jonson, *King Iames Entertainement*, sigs C–D3ᵛ (see Dutton, *Civic Pageants*, pp. 95–107); Harrison, *Arches of Triumph*, sig. I.
69. Dutton, *Civic Pageants*, p. 100.
70. Ibid., p. 96; Ovid, *Fasti*, I, 119.
71. Dutton, *Civic Pageants*, pp. 109–12.
72. Jonson, *King Iames Entertainement*, sig. B2ᵛ.
73. Dutton, *Civic Pageants*, pp. 23, 107.
74. Ibid., p. 20. That even the educated Dugdale misconstrued Dekker's figure of the Genius of London for a hermit suggests that the ability to read pageant was not just a matter of class or learning. I am grateful to Malcolm Smuts for this information.
75. Jonson, *King Iames Entertainement*, sig. B2ᵛ; Dekker, *Magnificent Entertainment*, sig. H3.
76. Harrison, *Arches of Triumph*, sig. B1; Cf. Dekker's comment that 'the multitude is now to be our audience', *Magnificent Entertainment*, sig. A4ᵛ.
77. Willson, *King James VI and I*, pp. 165–6.
78. F. Bamford ed., *A Royalist's Notebook: The Commonplace Book of Sir John Oglander, Kt., of Nunwell* (1936), p. 197; A. Wilson, *The History of Great Britain, Being the Life and Reign of King James The First* (Wing W2888, 1653)
79. Dutton, *Civic Pageants*, p. 22.
80. Dugdale, *The Time Triumphant*, sig. B4ᵛ.
81. Dekker, *Magnificent Entertainment*, sigs F2, H1.
82. Nichols, *Progresses*, I, pp. 414–15.
83. Ibid., p. 417; G. B. Harrison ed., *A Jacobean Journal: Being a Record of Those Things Most Talked of During the Years 1603–1606* (1941), p. 113.
84. Dugdale, *The Time Triumphant*, sig. B2ᵛ.
85. M. Drayton, *A Paean Triumphall Composed for the Societie of the Goldsmiths of London: Congratulating His Highnes Magnificent Entring the Citie* (STC 7215, 1604), sig. B1.
86. Based on Willson, *King James VI and I*, pp. 192–4.
87. H. R., *The Most Royall and Honourable Entertainement, of the Famous and Renowned King, Christiern the Fourth, King of Denmarke* (STC 21085, 1606), p. 8; Anon., *The King of Denmarkes Welcome Containing his Ariuall, Abode, and Entertainement, Both in the Citie and Other Places* (STC 5194, 1606), pp. 6–8.
88. H. R., *Royall and Honourable Entertainement*, pp. 8–10.
89. Ibid., p. 11.
90. *King of Denmarkes Welcome*, p. 11.
91. H. R., *Royall and Honourable Entertainement*, p. 12.
92. Ibid., p. 13.
93. Ibid., p. 14.
94. Ibid., p. 22.
95. Ibid., pp. 22–4; *King of Denmarkes Welcome*, p. 21.
96. Richard Davies, *Chesters Triumph in Honor of Her Prince As it Was Performed Upon S. Georges Day 1610. In the Foresaid Citie* (STC 5118, 1610), sig. A3ᵛ.
97. Ibid., sig. B4ᵛ.
98. Ibid.
99. George Chapman, *An Epicede or Funerall Song on the Most Disastrous Death, of the High-borne Prince of Men, Henry Prince of Wales, &c. With the Funeralls, and Representation of the Herse of the Same High and Mighty Prince* (STC 4974, 1613), sig. C1ᵛ; see also sigs A3–C1.
100. Ibid., sig. C3ᵛ.
101. Robert Naile, *A Relation of the Royall Magnificent, and Sumptuous Entertainement, Giuen to the High, and Mighty Princesse, Queene Anne, at the Renowned Citie of Bristoll, by the Mayor, Sheriffes, and Aldermen Thereof* (STC 18347, 1613), sigs B2–B2ᵛ, B4ᵛ.

102. Thomas Middleton, *Ciuitatis Amor: The Cities Loue, An Entertainment by Water, at Chelsey, and White-hall. At the Ioyfull Receiuing of that Illustrious Hope of Great Britaine, the High and Mighty Charles, to Bee Created Prince of Wales* (STC 17878, 1616), sig. A3.

103. Ibid., sig. B1.

104. Anon., *The Magnificent, Princely, and Most Royall Entertainments Giuen to the High and Mightie Prince, and Princesse, Frederick, Count Palatine, Palsgraue of the Rhyne: and Elizabeth, Sole Daughter to the High and Mighty King of England, Iames* (STC 11357, 1613), sig. A2.

105. Here I disagree with Roy Strong who suggested that they ceased, after Elizabeth, to praise the monarch. See R. Strong, 'Queen and City: The Elizabethan Lord Mayor's Pageant', in R. Strong, *The Tudor and Stuart Monarchy, Pageantry, Paintings, Iconography II: Elizabethan* (Woodbridge, Suffolk, 1995), pp. 17-32, especially pp. 31-2. David Bergeron's edition of many of the mayoral entertainments is forthcoming in the Oxford edition of Middleton.

106. Anthony Munday, *The Triumphes of Re-united Britania Performed at the Cost and Charges of the Right Worship: Company of the Merchant-Tayulors, in Honor of Sir Leonard Holliday Kni: to Solemnize His Entrance as Lorde Mayor of the Citty of London, on Tuesday the 29. of October. 1605* (STC 18279, 1605), sig. B2. Munday was an actor, playwright and translator, see *ODNB*. See D. Bergeron, *English Civic Pageantry, 1558-1642* (1971), pp. 141-5 and T. Hill, ' "Representing the Awefull Authoritie of Soveraigne Majestie": Monarchs and Mayors in Anthony Munday's *The Triumphes of Re-uinited Britania*', in G. Burgess, R. Wymer and J. Lawrence eds, *The Accession of James I: Historical and Cultural Consequences* (Basingstoke, 2006), pp. 15-33.

107. Ibid., sig. B4.

108. T. Dekker, *Troia-Noua Triumphans: London Triumphing, or, The Solemne, Magnificent, and Memorable Receiuing of that Worthy Gentleman, Sir Iohn Swinerton Knight, into the Citty of London* (STC 6530, 1612), sigs A3-A3ᵛ; Bergeron, *English Civic Pageantry*, pp. 164-70.

109. A. Munday, *Metropolis Coronata, the Triumphes of Ancient Drapery: or, Rich Cloathing of England, in a Second Yeeres Performance In Honour of the Aduancement of Sir Iohn Iolles, Knight, to the High Office of Lord Maior of London* (STC 18275, 1615), sig. B1ᵛ; Bergeron, *English Civic Pageantry*, pp. 152-5.

110. T. Middleton, *The Triumphs of Loue and Antiquity: An Honourable Solemnitie Performed Through the Citie, at the Confirmation and Establishment of the Right Honourable Sir William Cockayn, Knight, in the Office of His Maiesties Lieutenant, the Lord Maior of the Famous Citie of London* (STC 17902, 1619), sig. C1; Bergeron, *English Civic Pageantry*, pp. 189-91.

111. Middleton, *Triumphs*, sig. B3ᵛ.

112. T. Middleton, *The Sunne in Aries: A Noble Solemnity Performed Through the Citie ... at the Confirmation and Establishment of ... the Right Honourable, Edward Barkham, in the High Office of His Maiesties Lieutenant, the Lord Maior of the Famous Citie of London* (STC 17895, 1621), sigs B2-B2ᵛ; Bergeron, *English Civic Pageantry*, pp. 191-3.

113. John Webster, *Monuments of Honor Deriued from Remarkable Antiquity, and Celebrated in the Honorable City of London ... at the Confirmation of ... Iohn Gore in the High Office of His Maiesties Lieutenant* (STC 25175, 1624), sig. B1; Bergeron, *English Civic Pageantry*, pp. 207-11.

114. Ibid., sig. B3.

115. Ibid., sigs C1ᵛ-C2ᵛ.

116. K. Sharpe, *Selling the Tudor Monarchy: Authority and Image in Sixteenth-Century England* (New Haven and London 2009), pp. 427-9; R. Strong, 'Queen Elizabeth and the Order of the Garter', in Strong, *The Tudor and Stuart Monarchy, II: Elizabethan*, pp. 55-77.

117. See N. H. Nicolas, *A History of the Orders of Knighthood* (4 vols, 1842), I, pp. 217-20.

118. E. Ashmole, *The Institution, Laws & Ceremonies of the Most Noble Order of the Garter* (Wing A3983, 1672), p. 494.

119. Ibid.; *Cal. Stat. Pap. Venet. XII, 1610-13*, no. 236, pp. 153-4.

120. Strong, 'Elizabeth and Garter', p. 82.

121. Nichols, *Progresses*, I, pp. 193-5.

122. Ibid., II, p. 79; III, p. 480.

123. Ibid., II, p. 852.

124. Thomas Milles, *The Catalogue of Honour or Treasury of True Nobility Peculiar and Proper to the Isle of Great Britaine* (STC 17926, 1610), 'peroration' (at end, after p. 97), sig. K5.

125. William Fennor, *Fennors Descriptions, or A True Relation of Certaine and Diuers Speeches Spoken Before the King and Queenes Most Excellent Maiestie, the Prince his Highnesse, and the Lady Elizabeth's Grace* (STC 10784, 1616), sigs D4ᵛ, E1.

126. Strong, 'Elizabeth and Garter', p. 64.

127. Nichols, *Progresses*, I, p. 508.

128. R. Ashton, *James I by his Contemporaries* (1969), p. 2.

129. Nichols, *Progresses*, I, p. 164.

130. Ibid., p. 189.

131. Ibid., p. 250.
132. Ibid., p. 318.
133. Ibid., p. 427.
134. Ibid., p. 457.
135. Ibid., pp. 491, 499.
136. Ibid., pp. 521–2.
137. Ibid., II, pp. 201, 451.
138. Ibid., p. 457.
139. Ibid., p. 462.
140. Ibid., p. 180.
141. Ibid., III, p. 257.
142. Ibid., p. 264.
143. Ibid., pp. 271–4.
144. Ibid., p. 276.
145. Ibid., pp. 266, 272.
146. Ibid., p. 281.
147. Ibid., p. 317.
148. Ibid., pp. 318–19.
149. Ibid., pp. 331–4.
150. Ibid., p. 336.
151. See, for example, ibid., pp. 389–90 and 389–436 *passim*.
152. Ibid., pp. 411–12.
153. Ibid., pp. 390–4, 412.
154. Ibid., pp. 399, 424, 432.
155. Ibid., pp. 556–67 *passim*.
156. P. Harrison and M. Brayshay, 'Post-horse Routes, Royal Progresses and Government Communications in the Reign of James I', *Journal of Transport History*, 18 (1997), pp. 116–33.
157. Nichols, *Progresses*, I, p. 530.
158. Ibid., p. 538.
159. Ibid., pp. 541–3.
160. Ibid., pp. 548–50.
161. Ibid., pp. 553, 556–8.
162. Ibid., pp. 560–2.
163. Ibid., III, pp. 59, 73 and pp. 46–75 *passim*.
164. Ibid., IV, p. 837.
165. Willson, *King James VI and I*, pp. 288, 290.
166. Above, pp. 15–17.
167. William Leigh, *Queene Elizabeth Paraleld in her Princely Virtues* (STC 15426, 1612), sig. A7.
168. Cf. G. R. Elton, 'Tudor Government: The Points of Contact, III: The Court', *Transactions of the Royal Historical Society*, 26 (1976), pp. 211–28.
169. P. Hannay, *Two Elegies, on the Late Death of Our Soueraigne Queene Anne With Epitaphs* (STC 12749, 1619), sig. C2ᵛ.
170. D. Bergeron, *Shakespeare's Romances and the Royal Family* (Lawrence, Kansas, 1985), p. 47. See also D. Bergeron, *Royal Family, Royal Lovers: King James of England and Scotland* (Columbia, Miss., 1991), *passim*.
171. Above, pp. 16, 34, and 546 n. 34.
172. Bergeron, *Shakespeare's Romances*, p. 46.
173. Ibid.
174. Leeds Barroll, *Anna of Denmark, Queen of England* (Philadelphia, 2001), *passim*.
175. Thomas Campion, *A Relation of the Late Royall Entertainment Giuen by the Right Honorable the Lord Knowles, at Cawsome-House Neere Redding: To Our Most Gracious Queene, Queene Anne, in Her Progresse Toward the Bathe* (STC 4545, 1613), sig. A4; *Baziliologia: a Booke of Kings Beeing the True and Liuely Effegies of All Our English Kings from the Conquest Untill This Present* (STC 13581, 1618; 13581.7, 1630), no pagination, verse to engraving of Anne of Denmark.
176. Hannay, *Two Elegies*, sig. A4ᵛ.
177. J. Craigie ed., *Poems of James VI of Scotland* (2 vols, Edinburgh, 1955–8), II no. XI a–d, pp. 174–5.
178. Ben Jonson, *A Particular Entertainment of the Queene and Prince Their Highnesse to Althrope* (separate and second, repaginated part of Jonson, *King Iames Entertainement*), p. 13.
179. W. Alexander, *A Paraenesis to the Prince by William Alexander of Menstrie* (STC 346, 1604), sigs C3ᵛ–C4ᵛ.
180. Williamson, *Myth of the Conqueror*, pp. 22–3.
181. Ibid., pp. 27–9; above p. 68.

182. Ibid., pp. 67–9.
183. R. Strong, *Henry Prince of Wales and England's Lost Renaissance* (1980), p. 141; and pp. 141–6.
184. C. H. Herford, P. Simpson and E. M. Simpson eds, *Ben Jonson Works* (II vols, Oxford, 1925–52), VII, pp. 321–36.
185. Daniel Price, *The Creation of the Prince. A Sermon Preached in the Colledge of Westminster, on Trinity Sunday, the Day Before the Creation of the Most Illustrious Prince of Wales* (STC 20290, 1610), sig. D2. Price described himself as chaplain to the prince.
186. George Marcelline, *The Triumphs of King Iames of Great Brittaine, France, and Ireland, King; Defender of the Faith* (STC 17309, 1620; first published in French 1609).
187. Thomas Heywood, *A Funerall Elegie Upon the Death of the Late Most Hopefull and Illustrious Prince, Henry, Prince of Wales* (STC 13223, 1613), sig. B4^v.
188. John Taylor, *Great Britaine, All in Blacke For the Incomparable Losse of Henry, Our Late Worthy Prince. By Iohn Taylor* (STC 23760, 1612), sig. A1; James Maxwell, *The Laudable Life and Deplorable Death, of Our Late Peerlesse Prince Henry* (STC 17701, 1612), sig. B4; George Wither, *Prince Henries Obsequies or Mournefull Elegies Upon His Death* (STC 25915, 1612), sig. D1; John Davies, *The Muses-Teares for the Losse of Their Hope; Heroick and Ne're-too-much Praised, Henry, Prince of Wales* (STC 6339, 1613), sig. A2.
189. Anon., *The Funerals of the High and Mighty Prince Henry, Prince of Wales* (STC 13157, 1613), sig. D4.
190. Taylor, *Great Britaine, All in Blacke*, sig. A3^v.
191. Williamson, *Myth of the Conqueror*, p. 122.
192. Elizabeth, Princess and Queen of Bohemia, *ODNB*.
193. Robert Allyne, *Teares of Ioy Shed at the Happy Departure from Great Britaine, of the Two Paragons of the Christian World, Fredericke and Elizabeth, Prince, and Princesse Palatines of Rhine* (STC 385, 1613), sig. A4.
194. G. Webbe, *The Bride Royall, or The Spirituall Marriage Betweene Christ and His Church Deliuered by Way of Congratulation Upon the Happy and Hopefull Marriage Betweene the Two Incomparable Princes, the Palsegraue, and the Ladie Elizabeth* (STC 25157, 1613), p. 80.
195. A. Nixon, *Great Brittaines Generall Ioyes. Londons Glorious Triumphes Dedicated to the Immortall Memorie of the Ioyfull Mariage of the Two Famous and Illustrious Princes, Fredericke and Elizabeth* (STC 18587, 1613), sigs B3, C3^v.
196. H. Peacham, *Prince Henrie Revived Or A Poeme Upon the Birth, and in Honor of the Hopefull Yong Prince Henrie Frederick* (STC 19514, 1615), sig. B2.
197. G. Weckherlin, *Triumphall Shews Set Forth Lately at Stutgart, Written First in German, and Now in English by G. Rodolfe Weckherlin, Secretarie to the Duke of Wirtemberg* (STC 25186, 1616); Fennor, *Fennor's Descriptions*, sig. C3.
198. Taylor, *Great Britaine, All in Blacke*, sig. A3^v.
199. Wither, *Prince Henries Obsequies*, sig. E2; Maxwell, *Laudable Life*, sigs E3–3^v.
200. Maxwell, *Laudable Life*, sig. E4^v.
201. See, for example, Thomas Middleton, *Ciuitatis Amor*, sig. B4^v.
202. John Taylor, *A Briefe Remembrance of All the English Monarchs, from the Normans Conquest, Untill This Present* (STC 23736, 1618), sig. D4.
203. See, for example, Andres Almansa y Mendoza, *The Ioyfull Returne, of the Most Illustrious Prince, Charles, Prince of Great Brittaine, from the Court of Spaine* (STC 5025, 1623), pp. 3, 27, 42 and passim.
204. Webster, *Monuments of Honor*, C1^v–C2^v.
205. McIlwain, *Political Works*, p. 29.
206. Ibid., pp. 30, 33; S. Daniel, *A Panegyrike Congratulatorie to the Kings Maiestie* (STC 6258, 1603), sig. B4^v.
207. R. Lockyer, *James VI and I* (1998), p. 2.
208. Ashton, *James I*, pp. 232, 242–4.
209. Nichols, *Progresses*, I, p. 443.
210. Ashton, *James I*, pp. 238–9.
211. Thomas Gainsford, *The Glory of England* (STC 11517, 1618), p. 247.
212. Ibid., pp. 261–2.
213. See Gainsford, *ODNB* and *DNB*.
214. A.D.B., *The Court of the Most Illustrious and Most Magnificent Iames, the First King of Great-Britaine, France, and Ireland* (STC 1022, 1619), sig. A2^v.
215. Ibid., sig. A3.
216. K. Sharpe, *The Personal Rule of Charles I* (New Haven and London, 1992), pp. 216–17.
217. McIlwain, *Political Works*, pp. 37–8.
218. Above, p. 91.

219. G. Burgess, *Absolute Monarchy and the Stuart Constitution* (New Haven and London, 1996).

220. Ibid., pp. 145–7.

221. T.W., *The Arraignement and Execution of the Late Traytors with a Relation of the Other Traytors, Which Were Executed at Worcester, the 27. of Ianuary Last Past* (STC 24916, 1606), sigs B2, C3^v.

222. A. Milton, *Catholic and Reformed: The Roman and Protestant Churches in English Protestant Thought, 1600–1640* (Cambridge, 1995), pp. 57–8, 349–50.

223. McIlwain, *Political Works*, p. 311.

224. Ibid.

225. Gainsford, *The Glory of England*, p. 249.

226. J. P. Kenyon ed., *The Stuart Constitution* (2nd edn, Cambridge, 1986), p. 76.

227. John Williams, *Great Britains Salomon: A Sermon Preached at the Magnificent Funerall of the Most High and Mighty King, Iames* (STC 25723, 1625), p. 54. See also, L. Knafla, 'Britain's Solomon: King James and the Law', in D. Fischlin and M. Fortier, *Royal Subjects: Essays on the Writings of James VI and I* (Detroit, 2002), pp. 235–64.

228. Hugh Holland, *A Cypres Garland For the Sacred Forehead of Our Late Soueraigne King Iames* (STC 13591, 1625), sig. B1.

229. Andrew Willet, *King Iames his Iudgement By Way of Counsell and Advice To All His Loving Subjects, Extracted Out of His Own Speeches by Doctor Willet Concerning Politique Governement in England and Scotland* (Thomason E123/12, 1642), p. 4.

230. Ibid., p. 5.

231. W. Brown Patterson, *King James VI and I and the Reunion of Christendom* (Cambridge, 1997). My intention in the following pages is not to write a summary of Jacobean religious history but to sketch how the king's religious policy and pronouncements were part of his representation of his kingship, not least as outlined in *Basilikon Doron*.

232. John Gordon, *England and Scotlands Happinesse in Being Reduced to Unitie of Religion, Under Our Invincible Monarke King Iames* (STC 12062.3, 1604), p. 44.

233. A. Nixon, *Oxfords Triumph in the Royall Entertainement of His Moste Excellent Maiestie, the Queene, and the Prince: the 27. of August Last, 1605* (STC 18589, 1605), sig. D4^v.

234. See P. White, 'The "Via Media" in the Early Stuart Church', in K. Fincham ed., *The Early Stuart Church, 1603–1642* (Basingstoke, 1993), pp. 211–30, especially p. 217.

235. A. Milton, 'The Church of England, Rome and the True Church: The Demise of a Jacobean Consensus', in Fincham, *Early Stuart Church*, pp. 187–210; Milton, *Catholic and Reformed*, pp. 57–8, 136, 141, 276, 252, 257–8.

236. *Lucta Iacobi: Or, A Bonefire for His Maiesties Double Deliuerie, from the Deluge in Perth, the 5 of August, 1600. And the Doomesday of Britaine, the 5. of Nouember. 1605* (STC 14426, 1607), p. 58.

237. Patterson, *King James VI and I*, ch. 2 passim.

238. J. King, *The Fourth Sermon Preached at Hampton Court on Tuesday the Last of Sept. 1606* (STC 14974, 1606); A. Maxey, *The Sermon Preached Before the King, at Whitehall, on Tuesday the Eight of Ianuarie, 1604* (STC 17684, 1605), sig. G and passim.

239. A. Willet, *Ecclesia Triumphans: That Is The Ioy of the English Church for the Happie Coronation of the Most Vertuous and Pious Prince, Iames* (STC 25676, 1603), sig. ¶¶1.

240. K. Fincham and P. Lake, 'Ecclesiastical Policies of James I and Charles I', in Fincham, *Early Stuart Church*, p. 27.

241. R. Meredith, *Two Sermons Preached Before His Maiestie, in His Chappell at Whitehall* (STC 17832, 1606), p. 15.

242. Ibid., pp. 11–12; A. Foster, 'The Clerical Estate Revitalised', in Fincham, *Early Stuart Church*, pp. 139–60.

243. Meredith, *Two Sermons*, p. 9.

244. Kenyon, *Stuart Constitution*, pp. 128–30. See J. Marshall, 'Reading and Misreading King James 1622–42: Responses to the *Letter and Directions Touching Preaching and Preachers*', in Fischlin and Fortier eds, *Royal Subjects*, pp. 476–511.

245. R. Willan, *Conspiracie Against Kings, Heauens Scorne: A Sermon Preached at Westminster-Abbey Before the Iudges, Upon the Fifth of Nouemb. 1622* (STC 25669, 1622), p. 30.

246. W. Curll, *A Sermon Preached at White-Hall, on the 28. of April, 1622* (STC 6132, 1622), p. 9 and passim.

247. Milton, *Catholic and Reformed*, pp. 35–46, 503–9.

248. Abraham Browne, *A Sermon Preached at the Assises Holden at Winchester the 24. Day of Februarie Last* (STC 3906, 1623), sig. A3 and passim.

249. See, for example, Thomas Ailesbury, *A Sermon Preached at Paules-Crosse the Second Day of Iune, Being the Last Sunday in Easter Terme, 1622* (STC 1000, 1623).

250. Williams, *Great Britains Salomon*, pp. 47–9.

251. Ibid., pp. 50–1.

252. Ibid., pp. 46, 50–3.
253. G. O. Harry, *The Genealogy of the High and Mighty Monarch, Iames, by the Grace of God, King of Great Brittayne, &c. With His Lineall Descent from Noah, by Divers Direct Lynes to Brutus, First Inhabiter of this Ile of Brittayne* (STC 12872, 1604), p. 39.
254. John Thornborough, *A Discourse Plainely Prouing the Euident Utilitie and Urgent Necessitie of the Desired Happie Union of the Two Famous Kingdomes of England and Scotland* (STC 24035, 1607), p. 11.
255. L. Lloyd, *Hilaria: Or The Triumphant Feast for the Fift of August* (STC 16622, 1606), sig. B2ᵛ.
256. Rowlands, *Ave Caesar*, sig. Bii; *Englands Wedding Garment*, sig. B2ᵛ; Willet, *Ecclesia Triumphans*, p. 104.
257. Gainsford, *Vision and Discourse of Henry the Seuenth*, p. 47.
258. Davies, *Chesters Triumph*, sig. C2.
259. Middleton, *Ciuitatis Amor*, sig. B1.
260. W. Drummond, *Forth Feasting: A Panegyricke to the Kings Most Excellent Maiestie* (STC 7252, Edinburgh, 1617), sigs A4–B1ᵛ.
261. W. Laud, *A Sermon Preached Before His Maiesty, on Tuesday the Nineteenth of Iune, at Wansted. Anno Dom. 1621* (STC 15301, 1621).
262. Curll, *Sermon Preached at White-Hall*, especially pp. 18–19.
263. T. M., *The True Narration*, sig. D3ᵛ.
264. I. Disraeli, *An Inquiry into the Literary and Political Character of James the First* (1816), p. 216; above, pp. 106–7.
265. Nixon, *Oxfords Triumph*, sig. D1.
266. Disraeli, *Literary and Political Character of James*, p. 101.
267. Below, pp. 259–62.
268. M. Young, *King James and the History of Homosexuality* (New York, 2000), ch. 2.
269. Ibid., p. 42.
270. Ibid., p. 135; A. Bellany, *The Politics of Court Scandal in Early Modern England: News Culture and the Overbury Affair, 1603–1660* (Cambridge, 2002).
271. *The Answer to Tom-Tell-Troth: The Practise of Princes and the Lamentations of the Kirke* (Wing B611, 1642), p. 86; See Young, *King James*, p. 73 on the connections made between sodomy and pusillanimous effeminacy.
272. Ibid., pp. 74–5.

4 Contesting the King

1. See Sharpe, *Selling the Tudor Monarchy: Authority and Image in Sixteenth-Century England* (New Haven and London, 2009), ch. 12.; J. Guy ed., *The Reign of Elizabeth: Court and Culture in the Last Decade* (Cambridge, 1995).
2. S. Daniel, *A Panegyrike Congratulatorie to the Kings Maiestie* (STC 6258, 1603), sig. B2ᵛ.
3. Ibid., sig. A1ᵛ.
4. *Englands Welcome to Iames by the Grace of God, King of England, Scotland, France and Ireland, Defender of the Faith* (STC 14422, 1603), sig. A3ᵛ.
5. K. Sharpe, 'Private Conscience and Public Duty in the Writings of James VI and I', in J. Morrill, P. Slack and D. Woolf eds, *Public Duty and Private Conscience in Seventeenth-Century England* (Oxford, 1992), pp. 77–100.
6. T. Gainsford, *The Vision and Discourse of Henry the Seventh Concerning the Unitie of Great Brittaine* (STC 11526, 1610), p. 65.
7. Francis Mason, *Two Sermons, Preached at the Kings Court* (STC 17600, 1621), pp. 96–7. Mason was Archdeacon of Norfolk.
8. See, for example, R. W. Bushnell, *Tragedies of Tyrants: Political Thought and Theater in the English Renaissance* (Ithaca, NY, 1990).
9. A. McRae, *Literature, Satire, and the Early Stuart State* (Cambridge, 2004). See also McRae and A. Bellany, *Early Stuart Libels: An Edition of Poetry from Manuscript Sources* (AHRC Data Service, http://ahds.ac.uk/catalogue/collection.htm?uri=lll-2492–1).
10. Above, p. 35.
11. McRae, *Literature, Satire*, ch. 5; J. A. W. Bennett and H. R. Trevor-Roper eds, *The Poems of Richard Corbett* (Oxford, 1955).
12. N. E. McClure ed., *The Letters of John Chamberlain* (2 vols, Philadelphia, 1939); W. S. Powell, *John Pory, 1572–1636: The Life and Letters of a Man of Many Parts* (Chapel Hill, NC, 1977) with a microfiche of Pory's letters; BL, Harley MSS 389, 390; NA, Chancery Masters Exhibits C115.
13. R. Cust, 'News and Politics in Early Seventeenth-century England', *Past & Present*, 112 (1986), pp. 60–90, quotation at p. 90.

14. J. Raymond, *Pamphlets and Pamphleteering in Early Modern Britain* (Cambridge, 2003), pp. 100 and 130–8; Raymond ed., *News, Newspapers and Society in Early Modern Britain* (1997); Raymond, 'Irrational, Impractical and Unprofitable: Reading the News in Seventeenth-century Britain', in K. Sharpe and S. N. Zwicker eds, *Reading, Society and Politics in Early Modern England* (Cambridge, 2003), pp. 185–212.

15. Thomas Deloney, *Strange Histories, or Songes and Sonets, of Kings, Princes, Dukes, Lordes, Ladyes, Knights, and Gentlemen Very Pleasant Either to be Read or Songe: and a Most Excellent Warning for All Estates* (STC 6567, 1607).

16. Ibid., sig. F4.

17. W. Leigh, *Queene Elizabeth, Paraleld in Her Princely Vertues* (STC 15426, 1612), sig. A5.

18. Ibid., sig. A5ᵛ.

19. M. Drayton, *To the Maiestie of King Iames A Gratulatorie Poem* (STC 7231, 1603), sig. A3ᵛ.

20. A. Maxey, *Another Sermon Preached Before the King at Greenewich on Tuesday Before Easter, Being the 26. of March. 1605* (STC 17688, 1605), p. 34.

21. Richard Davies, *Chesters Triumph in Honor of Her Prince As it Was Performed Upon S. Georges Day 1610. In the Foresaid Citie* (STC 5118, 1610), sigs C2, C3, D1ᵛ.

22. Thomas Rogers, *Gloucesters Myte Deliuered With the Mournefull Records of Great Britaine, Into the Worlds Register. For the Inrolement of the Euerlasting Fame and Perpetuall Remembrance of Our Late and Most Gratious Prince Henrie* (STC 21241.5, 1612), sig. C3ᵛ.

23. For a narrative, see A. Somerset, *Unnatural Murder: Poison at the Court of James I* (1997); B. White, *Cast of Ravens: The Strange Case of Sir Thomas Overbury* (1965); see also D. Lindley, *Trials of Frances Howard: Fact and Fiction in the Court of King James* (1993). The best analysis of the consequences is A. Bellany, *The Politics of Court Scandal in Early Modern England: News Culture and the Overbury Affair, 1603–1660* (Cambridge, 2002).

24. K. Sharpe, *The Personal Rule of Charles I* (New Haven and London, 1992), p. 190. For the case, see C. Herrup, *A House in Gross Disorder: Sex, Law, and the 2nd Earl of Castlehaven* (Oxford, 1999).

25. Thomas Campion, *The Description of a Maske: Presented in the Banqueting Roome at Whitehall, on Saint Stephens Night Last at the Mariage of the Right Honourable the Earle of Somerset: and the Right Noble the Lady Frances Howard* (STC 4539, 1614).

26. Ibid., sig. B3.

27. George Chapman, *Andromeda Liberata. Or the Nuptials of Perseus and Andromeda* (STC 4964, 1614), sig. B1.

28. Bellany, *Politics of Court Scandal*; Bellany, 'Mistress Turner's Deadly Sins: Sartorial Transgression, Court Scandal, and Politics in Early Stuart England', *Huntington Library Quarterly*, 58 (1996), pp. 179–210.

29. Bellany, *Politics of Court Scandal*, p. 246.

30. Christopher Brooke, *The Ghost of Richard the Third Expressing Himselfe in These Three Parts* (STC 3830, 1614), epistle to reader; William Sclater, *A Sermon Preached at the Last Generall Asise Holden for the County of Sommerset at Taunton* (STC 21843, 1616), p. 17.

31. A.D.B., *Court of the Most Illustrious and Most Magnificent Iames* (STC 1022, 1619), epistle dedicatory.

32. Ibid., sig. B2.

33. See R. Lockyer, *Buckingham: The Life and Political Career of George Villiers, First Duke of Buckingham, 1592–1628* (1981).

34. McRae, *Literature, Satire*, pp. 75–82.

35. Ibid., pp. 79–80; Young, *King James and the History of Homosexuality*, ch. 4 (New York, 1999); T. Cogswell, 'Underground Verse and the Transformation of Early Stuart Political Culture', in S. Amussen and M. Kishlansky eds, *Political Culture and Cultural Politics in Early Modern England* (Manchester, 1995), pp. 277–300.

36. S. Burton, *A Sermon Preached at the Generall Assises in Warwicke, the Third of March, Being the First Friday in Lent. 1619* (STC 4164, 1618), pp. 3–8.

37. Ibid., pp. 16–17.

38. Ibid., p. 17.

39. Ibid., p. 20.

40. J. F. Larkin and P. L. Hughes, *Stuart Royal Proclamations I: Royal Proclamations of King James, 1603–1625* (Oxford, 1973–), no. 208, pp. 495–6.

41. A. Bellany, ' "Raylinge Rhymes and Vaunting Verse": Libellous Politics in Early Stuart England', in K. Sharpe and P. Lake eds, *Culture and Politics in Early Stuart England* (Basingstoke, 1994), p. 299.

42. R. Willan, *Conspiracie Against Kings, Heauens Scorne: A Sermon Preached at Westminster-Abbey Before the Iudges, Upon the Fifth of Nouemb. 1622* (STC 25669, 1622) pp. 17–18 and *passim*.

43. W. Curll, *A Sermon Preached at White-Hall, on the 28. of April, 1622. By Walter Curll, D. in Diuinity and Deane of Lichfield. Published by Speciall Command* (STC 6132, 1622) pp. 15, 22–3.

44. Young, *King James*, p. 62.

45. R. Zaller, *The Parliament of 1621: A Study in Constitutional Conflict* (Berkeley, 1971).

46. Young, *King James*, pp. 52–3, 62–3, 90–3.

47. Bellany, *Politics of Court Scandal*, pp. 255–8; McRae, *Literature, Satire*, pp. 77–82.

48. Helen Pierce, 'Unseemly Pictures: Political Graphic Satire in England, *c.*1600–*c.*1650' (University of York Ph.D. thesis, 2004). I am grateful to Dr Pierce, whose thesis I examined, for discussions of this subject. See now, H. Pierce, *Unseemly Pictures: Graphic Satire and Politics in Early Modern England* (New Haven and London, 2008).

49. Above, pp. 34–5.

50. A. Weldon, *The Court and Character of King James. Written and Taken by Sir A:W., Being an Eye and Eare Witness* (Wing W1273, 1650); A. Wilson, *The History of Great Britain Being the Life and Reign of King James the First, Relating to What Passed from His First Access to the Crown, Till His Death* (Wing 2888, 1653).

51. Weldon may have been dismissed from office (*ODNB*) and Wilson, who fought on the continent at Breda, was a fierce critic of James's pacifism (*ODNB*).

52. John Williams, *Great Britains Salomon A Sermon Preached at the Magnificent Funerall, of the Most High and Mighty King, Iames* (STC 25723, 1625).

53. John King, *Cenotaphium Iacobi. Sive Laudatio Funebris Piae et Foelici Memoriae Serenissimi Potentissimique Iacobi Magnae Britanniae, Franciae, & Hiberniae Monarchae Dedicata, & Publicè Recitata à Iohanne King Academiae Oxoniensis Oratore, Oxoniae* (STC 14992, 1625).

54. Phineas Hodson, *The Last Sermon Preached Before His Maiesties Funerals at Denmark House: On Tuesday the Third of May* (STC 13552, 1625), p. 21.

55. Thomas Heywood, *A Funeral Elegie, Upon the Much Lamented Death of the Trespuissant and Unmatchable King, King Iames,* (STC 13324, 1625); Hugh Holland, *A Cypres Garland For the Sacred Forehead of Our Late Soueraigne King Iames* (STC 13591, 1625).

56. F. Hamilton, *King Iames His Encomium. Or A Poeme, in Memorie and Commendation of the High and Mightie Monarch Iames* (STC 12726, Edinburgh, 1626), pp. 8–9.

57. David Primrose, *Scotlands Complaint. Upon the Death of Our Late Soveraigne King Iames of Most Happy Memorie* (STC 20386, Edinburgh, 1625), sig. A2ᵛ.

58. Holland, *A Cypres Garland*, sig. C2; Heywood, *A Funeral Elegie*, sig. B2.

59. Hamilton, *King Iames His Encomium*, pp. 3, 12.

60. John Taylor, *A Liuing Sadnes, In Duty Consecrated to the Immortal Memory of Our Late Deceased Albe-loued Soueraigne Lord, the Peereles Paragon of Princes, Iames, King of Great Brittaine* (STC 23772, 1625), p. 2.

61. Ibid., p. 4.

62. K. Sharpe, 'Private Conscience and Public Duty in the Writings of Charles I', *Historical Journal*, 40 (1997), pp. 643–6.

63. Hamilton, *King Iames His Encomium*, p. 12.

64. Anon., *Strange Apparitions, or, The Ghost of King Iames with a Late Conference Between the Ghost of That Good King, the Marquesse Hameltons, and George Eglishams, Doctor of Physick, Unto Which Appeared the Ghost of the Late Duke of Buckingham Concerning the Death and Poysoning of King Iames and the Rest* (Thomason E123/23, 1642).

65. *King Iames His Iudgement By Way of Counsell and Advice to All His Loving Subjects, Extracted Out of His Own Speeches by Doctor Willet Concerning Politique Governement in England and Scotland* (Thomason E123/12. 1642), p. 8 and *passim*.

66. Ben Agar, *King James, His Apopthegmes, or Table-talke As They Were By Him Delivered Occasionally and By the Publisher (His Quondam Servant) Carefully Received, and Now Humbly Offered to Publique View, As Not Impertinent to the Present Times* (Wing J127, 1643), preface, sig. A1ᵛ.

67. *King Iames His Iudgement*, sig. A1.

68. See *King Iames His Iudgement*.

69. D. Bergeron, 'Writing King James's Sexuality', in D. Fischlin and M. Fortier eds, *Royal Subjects: Essays on the Writings of James VI and I* (Detroit, 2002), pp. 347–51.

70. *A True and Historical Relation of the Poysoning of Sir Thomas Overbury With the Severall Arraignments and Speeches of Those That Were Executed Thereupon: Also, All the Passages Concerning the Divorce Between Robert, Late Earle of Essex, and the Lady Frances Howard* (Wing T2487, 1651).

71. *Truth Brought To Light: The Narrative History of King James, For the First Fourteen Years* (Wing S4818, 1651).

72. F. Osborne, *Historical Memoires on The Reigns of Queen Elizabeth and King James* (Wing O515, 1658); Young, *King James*, ch. 7.

73. See A. Lacey, *The Cult of King Charles the Martyr* (Woodbridge, Suffolk, 2003).

74. William Loe, *The Kings Shoe Made, and Ordained to Trample On and to Treade Downe Edomites; To Teach in Briefe, What is Edoms Doome; What the Carefull Condition of the King, What the Loyall Submission of a Subiect* (STC 16686, 1623), sig. A3.

75. William Sanderson, *Aulicus Coquinariae Or a Vindication in Answer To a Pamphlet, Entituled The Court and Character of King James* (E 1356/2, 1651), p. 205.

Part II Prologue: A Failure of Image?

1. C. S. R. Russell, *The Fall of the British Monarchies, 1637–1642* (Oxford, 1991); Russell, *The Causes of the English Civil War* (Oxford, 1990); J. Morrill, *The Nature of the English Revolution* (1993), especially ch. 15; cf. M. B. Young, *Charles I* (1997). A more balanced assessment is provided in R. Cust, *Charles I: A Political Life* (2005). It is noteworthy that the reputation of Charles I is not a subject on which historians can be persuaded by evidence. See M. Kishlansky, 'Charles I: A Case of Mistaken Identity', *Past & Present*, 189 (2005), pp. 41–80.

2. The view that Charles brought about an Arminian revolution which helped to bring down the monarchy was advanced by N. Tyacke, *Anti-Calvinists: The Rise of English Arminianism c. 1590–1640* (Oxford, 1987). This somewhat simplistic and flawed thesis was endorsed by Russell and others and became textbook orthodoxy. For criticism, see P. White, *Predestination, Policy and Polemic: Conflict and Consensus in the English Church from the Reformation to the Civil War* (Cambridge, 1993); White, 'The "Via Media" in the Early Stuart Church', in K. Fincham ed., *The Early Stuart Church, 1603–1642* (Basingstoke, 1993), pp. 211–30 and K. Sharpe, *The Personal Rule of Charles I* (New Haven and London, 1992), ch. 6. See also, J. Davies, *The Caroline Captivity of the Church: Charles I and the Remoulding of Anglicanism, 1625–1641* (Oxford, 1992); M. Questier, 'Arminianism, Catholicism, and Puritanism in England during the 1630s', *Historical Journal*, 49 (2006), pp. 53–78.

3. Russell famously charged Charles I with not being a politician (*Causes*, pp. 198–202, 205–7 and ch. 8 *passim*). We should note Kishlansky's observation that 'We must beware of the fallacies inherent in equating a seventeenth-century monarch with a twenty-first-century politician', 'Charles I', pp. 49–50.

4. K. Sharpe, *Selling the Tudor Monarchy: Authority and Image in Sixteenth-Century England* (New Haven and London, 2009) pp. 236–42, 305–16 and chs 6, 12 *passim* and above, ch. 4.

5. Below, pp. 289–90, 302.

6. Sharpe, *Personal Rule*, pp. 279–83.

7. See above pp. 40–1, S. R. Gardiner, *Constitutional Documents of the Puritan Revolution* (Oxford, 1906), pp. 99–103; below, p. 160.

8. See A. Griffiths, *The Print in Stuart Britain, 1603–1689* (1998), fig. 23 pp. 65–8; above, p. 78, fig. 16.

9. K. Sharpe, 'Private Conscience and Public Duty in the Writings of Charles I', *Historical Journal*, 40 (1997), pp. 643–65.

10. J. Brotton, *The Sale of the Late King's Goods: Charles I and his Art Collection* (2006), p. 90. I am grateful to Jerry Brotton for his kindness in letting me read this book in advance of publication and for fruitful discussions.

11. K. Sharpe, 'The Image of Virtue: The Court and Household of Charles I, 1625–1642', in D. Starkey ed., *The English Court from the Wars of the Roses to the Civil War* (1987); Sharpe, *Personal Rule*, pp. 210–12.

12. 'King Charles was much offended with King James's light and familiar way, which was the effect of hunting and drinking on which occasions he was very apt to forget his dignity', O. Airy ed., *Burnet's History of His Own Time* (2 vols, Oxford, 1897), I, p. 28.

13. K. Sharpe, *Criticism and Compliment: The Politics of Literature in the England of Charles I* (Cambridge, 1997), pp. 182–3, 187–8 and ch.5 *passim*.

14. There are remarkably few contemporary comments on Charles's stutter and few on his ability as a speaker, see Sharpe, *Personal Rule*, pp. 179–80.

15. Sharpe, *Selling the Tudor Monarchy*, pp. 336–44.

16. I first ventured this argument in K. Sharpe, 'The King's Writ: Royal Authors and Royal Authority in Early Modern England', in K. Sharpe and P. Lake eds, *Culture and Politics in Early Stuart England* (Basingstoke, 1994), pp. 131–4. The argument there was not only too brief but paid inadequate attention to the important shifts of chronology and circumstance. The detailed treatment below is intended to remedy that.

5 The Words and Silences of a King

1. *Eikon Basilike: The Pourtraicture of His Sacred Majestie in His Solitudes and Sufferings* (Wing E299A, 1649). See below, ch. 12, pp. 391–400.

2. Charles I, *Reliquiae sacrae Carolinae Or The Works of that Great Monarch and Glorious Martyr King Charls the I* (E 1220/1, 1651).
3. *Basilika: The Workes of King Charles the Martyr: With a Collection of Declarations, Treaties, and Other Papers Concerning the Differences Betwixt His Said Majesty and His Two Houses of Parliament* (Wing C2075, 1662; Wing C2076, 1687).
4. *Basilika* (1662), p. 357.
5. In 1640 Charles told his first parliament in eleven years, 'I shall not trouble you long with words; it is not my fashion', E. Cope ed., *Proceedings of the Short Parliament* (Camden Society, 4th series 19, 1977), p. 198.
6. See, for example, J. L. Larkin, *Stuart Royal Proclamations, II: Royal Proclamations of King Charles I, 1625-1646* (Oxford, 1983), no. 39, pp. 84-6; *A Shorte Forme of Thanksgiving to God for Staying the Contagious Sicknesses of the Plague: To Be Used in Common Prayer, on Sundayes, Wednesdayes, and Frydayes: Set Forth By Authority* (STC 16542, 1625). The proclamation refers to this form of service being commanded 'by his majesty's express direction' (p. 86).
7. Larkin, *Proclamations*, no. 19, p. 47.
8. *A Forme of Common Prayer, Together With an Order of Fasting: For the Auerting of Gods Heauy Visitation Upon Many Places of This Kingdome, and For the Drawing Downe of His Blessings Upon Us, and Our Armies By Sea and Land. The Prayers Are to be Read Euery Wednesday During This Visitation. Set Foorth By His Maiesties Authority* (STC 16541, 1625).
9. Ibid., sig. A4. This early invocation of the biblical and Davidic in Charles's representation has received surprisingly little attention.
10. Ibid., sigs F2, F3ᵛ, I2-I3.
11. *A Shorte Forme of Thanksgiving to God for Staying the contagious sickenesse of the Plague.*
12. Ibid., sigs A2-2ᵛ.
13. Ibid., sig. B2.
14. *A Forme of Prayer, Necessary To Bee Used In These Dangerous Times, of Warre and Pestilence, for the Safety and Preseruation of His Maiesty and His Realmes. Set Forth by Authoritie* (STC 16543, 1626).
15. Ibid., sig. E2.
16. Ibid., sigs F1, F4.
17. Ibid., sig. K2.
18. Ibid., sig. K3ᵛ.
19. Ibid., sig. L1.
20. Ibid., sig. L3.
21. *A Prayer to Bee Publiquely Used at the Going Foorth of the Fleete This Present Yeere, 1628* (STC 16546.5, 1628), broadside.
22. *A Forme of Prayer, Necessary to Bee Used in These Dangerous Times of Warre Wherein We Are Appointed to Fast According to His Maiesties Proclamation, for the Preseruation of His Maiestie, and His Realmes, and All Reformed Churches* (STC 16457.5, 1628), sig. D4ᵛ. See Larkin, *Proclamations*, II, no. 89, pp. 193-4.
23. *A Forme of Prayer* (1628), sigs D2, D4ᵛ, F1, K2; *A Prayer to Bee Publiquely Used.*
24. See K. Sharpe, *The Personal Rule of Charles I* (New Haven and London, 1992), pp. 9-23, 36-46, 65-70; C. S. R. Russell, *Parliaments and English Politics, 1621-1629* (Oxford, 1979), chs VI and VII: L. J. Reeve, *Charles I and the Road to Personal Rule* (Cambridge, 1989), ch. 3; R. Cust, *Charles I: A Political Life,* (Harlow, 2005), pp. 104-33.
25. *A Forme of Prayer, With Thanksgiuing to Bee Used of All the Kings Maiesties Louing Subiects Euery Yeere the 27. of March. Being the Day of His Highnesse Entry to This Kingdome* (STC 16485.3, 1629), sig. A2.
26. Ibid., sig. A4ᵛ.
27. Ibid., sigs C1, C3ᵛ.
28. Ibid., sig. D4ᵛ.
29. Henrietta Maria was observed performing in court entertainments while pregnant.
30. See *A Thanksgiuing and Prayer for the Safe Child-bearing of the Queenes Maiestie* (STC 16548.3, 1629). One page.
31. *A Thanksgiuing for the Safe Deliuery of the Queene, and Happy Birth of the Young Prince* (STC 16549, 1630); *A Thanksgiuing and Prayer for the Safe Child-Bearing of the Queenes Maiestie* (STC 16549.5, 1631); *A Thanksgiuing for the Safe Deliuery of the Queene, and Happy Birth of the Young Princesse* (STC 16550, 1631); *A Thanksgiuing for the Safe Deliuerie of the Queenes Maiestie, and Happy Birth of the Duke of Yorke* (STC 16550.7, 1633); *A Thanksgiuing, and Prayer for the Safe Child-bearing of the Queenes Maiestie* (STC 16552, 1635). Interestingly, it would appear that there were no services to mark royal births after 1635.

32. *A Forme of Common Prayer, Together With an Order of Fasting: For the Auerting of Gods Heauie Visitation Upon Many Places of This Kingdome, and For the Obtaining of His Blessings Upon Us. The Prayers Are to be Read Euery Wednesday During This Visitation. Set Forth by His Maiesties Authority* (STC 16553, 1636).

33. Ibid., sigs A3–A4ᵛ.

34. Ibid., sigs M2ᵛ–M3; see Sharpe, *Personal Rule*, pp. 758–60.

35. P. Donald, *An Uncounselled King: Charles I and the Scottish Troubles, 1637–1641* (Cambridge, 1990); Sharpe, *Personal Rule*, pp. 813–24; Joad Raymond, *Pamphlets and Pamphleteering in Early Modern Britain* (Cambridge, 2003), ch. 5.

36. *A Prayer for the Kings Maiestie, in His Northern Expedition to Be Said in All Churches, in the Time of Divine Service, Next After the Prayer for the Queen, and the Royall Progenie* (STC 16556, 1639), one page.

37. *A Prayer for the Kings Maiestie in His Expedition Against the Rebels of Scotland to be Said in All Churches in Time of Divine Service, Next After the Prayer for the Queen and Royall Progenie* (STC 16558, 1640), one page.

38. See *A Forme of Common Prayer: To Be Used Upon the 17th of November, and the 8th of December on Which Dayes a Fast is Appointed by His Majesties Proclamation, for the Removing of the Plague, and Other Judgements of God, from This Kingdom. Set Forth by Authority* (STC 16559, 1640); Larkin, *Proclamations*, II, no. 314, pp. 733–6. It is worthy of note that Charles chose Elizabeth's accession day as his fast day.

39. Larkin, *Proclamations*, II, pp. x–xi.

40. Ibid., p. xx.

41. Ibid., nos 7, 75, 77, pp. 13, 167–8, 171.

42. Ibid., no. 13, p. 35.

43. Ibid., no. 14, p. 37.

44. Ibid., no. 17, p. 44.

45. Ibid., no. 10, p. 28.

46. Ibid., no. 9, p. 26.

47. Ibid., nos 12, 57, pp. 32, 114.

48. Ibid., no. 103, p. 215.

49. Ibid., nos 63, 64, pp. 132, 137.

50. Ibid., no. 43, p. 92. See Sharpe, *Personal Rule*, pp. 292–8; Cust, *Charles I*, pp. 91–2.

51. Larkin, *Proclamations*, II, nos 89, 105, pp. 193, 218. Charles was paraphrasing the Book of Ephesians 4: 3.

52. Ibid., no. 53, p. 108.

53. Ibid., no. 55, pp. 110–11.

54. Ibid., p. 111.

55. Ibid., pp. 111–12.

56. Ibid., nos 89, 92, pp. 193, 198. Roger Manwaring, *Religion and Alegiance in Two Sermons Preached Before the Kings Maiestie* (STC 17751, 1627); R. Cust, *The Forced Loan and English Politics, 1626–1628* (Oxford, 1987), pp. 62–7.

57. Russell, *Parliaments and English Politics*, ch. 6; Sharpe, *Personal Rule*, p. 41.

58. Huntington Library, San Marino, Temple of Stowe MSS, Parliament Box 1, item 13; Sharpe, *Personal Rule*, pp. 42–3.

59. Temple of Stowe MS Parliament Box, 1, item 13.

60. Larkin, *Proclamations*, II, no. 97, pp. 206–7.

61. Ibid., no. 105, pp. 218–20; R. Montagu, *Appello Caesarem: A Iust Appeale from Two Uniust Informers* (STC 18031, 1625). On the controversy over Montagu's book, see Sharpe, *Personal Rule*, pp. 52, 54, 292–6; Cust, *Charles I*, pp. 85–92.

62. On the 1629 session, see Russell, *Parliaments and English Politics*, ch. 7; C. Thompson, 'The Divided Leadership of the House of Commons in 1629', in K. Sharpe ed., *Faction and Parliament: Essays on Early Stuart History* (Oxford, 1978), pp. 246–84; Sharpe, *Personal Rule*, pp. 54–6; L. J. Reeve, 'Sir Thomas Roe's Prophecy of 1629', *Bulletin of the Institute of Historical Research*, 56 (1983), pp. 120–1.

63. Larkin, *Proclamations*, II, no. 108, pp. 223–4.

64. 'A proclamation for suppressing false rumours touching parliament', ibid., no. 110, pp. 226–8.

65. Ibid., p. 227.

66. Ibid., p. 228.

67. Ibid., p. 227.

68. Ibid., p. 228.

69. *Cal. Stat. Pap. Dom, 1628–9*, pp. 550–1; NA SP 16/142/92,93.

70. For example, Larkin, *Proclamations*, II, nos 128, 230, pp. 262, 541.

71. Ibid., nos 124, 127, 141, pp. 252, 259, 298.
72. Ibid., nos 176, 185, 263, pp. 397, 427, 613–18.
73. Ibid., nos 186, 195, 196, 272, pp. 429, 450, 453, 636. On the soap patent, see Sharpe, *Personal Rule*, pp. 259–62; on saltpetre manufacture, ibid., pp. 491–2.
74. Larkin, *Proclamations*, II, no. 132, p. 273.
75. See, for example, ibid., nos 208, 210, 244, pp. 488, 495, 572.
76. Ibid., nos 241, 248, 260, pp. 565, 578, 608.
77. Ibid., no. 283, p. 674.
78. Ibid., no. 282, p. 671.
79. Ibid., no. 280, pp. 662–7; see below, pp. 161–4.
80. Ibid., no. 286, pp. 680–1.
81. Sharpe, *Personal Rule*, pp. 813–24; C. Hibbard, *Charles I and the Popish Plot* (Chapel Hill, NC, 1983).
82. Larkin, *Proclamations*, II, no. 290, pp. 688–91. On the Scottish Prayer Book crisis and Bishops' Wars, see Donald, *Uncounselled King*; Sharpe, *Personal Rule*, ch.13; C. Russell, *The Fall of The British Monarchies, 1637–1642* (Oxford, 1991), *passim*.
83. Larkin, *Proclamations*, II, no. 297, pp. 703–5.
84. Ibid., p. 704.
85. Ibid, pp. 704–5; *An Information From the States of the Kingdome of Scotland, to the Kingdome of England Shewing How They Have Bin Dealt Withall by His Maiesties Commissioner* (STC 21916.5, Amsterdam, 1640). Larkin (II, p. 704 n. 1) confuses this with *Information from the Scottish Nation, To All the True English, Concerning the Present Expedition* (STC 21917, 1640).
86. Larkin, *Proclamations*, II, p. 705.
87. Ibid., no. 310, p. 726. On the invasion, see Sharpe, *Personal Rule*, ch. 16; M. Fissel, *The Bishops' Wars: Charles I's Campaigns against Scotland, 1638–1640* (Cambridge, 1994), pp. 39–61.
88. Larkin, *Proclamations*, II, pp. 727, 728.
89. Sharpe, *Selling the Tudor Monarchy: Authority and Image in Sixteeenth-Century England*, pp. 101–3; above, pp. 40–2.
90. *By the King. A Declaration of His Maiesties Cleare Intention, in Requiring the Ayde of His Louing Subiects, in That Way of Loane Which Is Now Intended by His Highness* (STC 8843, 1626), one page. Larkin includes this as a proclamation (*Proclamations*, II, no. 55, pp. 110–12).
91. *A Declaration of the True Causes Which Moued His Maiestie to Assemble, and After Inforced Him to Dissolue the Two Last Meetings in Parliament* (STC 9246, 1626).
92. Ibid., p. 2.
93. Ibid.
94. Ibid., p. 3.
95. Ibid.
96. Ibid., pp. 6–13.
97. Ibid., pp. 19–24.
98. Ibid., pp. 27–8.
99. Ibid., p. 29.
100. Ibid., p. 3.
101. *His Maiesties Declaration to All his Louing Subiects, of the Causes Which Moued Him to Dissolue the Last Parliament Published by His Maiesties Speciall Command* (STC 9249.5, 1629). See Larkin, *Proclamations*, II, no. 108, pp. 223–4.
102. *His Maiesties Declaration*, p. 4.
103. Ibid., p. 5.
104. Ibid.
105. Ibid., p. 6.
106. Ibid., p. 10.
107. Ibid., p. 11.
108. Ibid., p. 15.
109. Ibid., p. 16; see 2 Samuel 16: 13.
110. *His Maiesties Declaration*, p. 16.
111. E. Cope, 'Public Images of Parliament during its Absence', *Legislative Studies Quarterly*, 7 (1982), pp. 221–34; J. O. Halliwell ed., *The Autobiography and Correspondence of Sir Simonds D'Ewes* (2 vols, 1845), I, p. 402; Reeve, 'Roe's Prophecy', pp. 121–2.
112. For a brief account of the writs, see Sharpe, *Personal Rule*, pp. 552–8.
113. *The Kings Maiesties Declaration to His Subiects, Concerning Lawfull Sports to Bee Used* (STC 9258, 1633).
114. *His Maiesties Commission, and Further Declaration: Concerning the Reparation of Saint Pauls Church* (STC 9256, 1633).
115. Ibid., p. 21.

116. As M. Kishlansky has observed, Sharpe's *Personal Rule* received several critical reviews but few engaged with the evidence, 'Charles I: A Case of Mistaken Identity', *Past and Present*, 189 (2005), p. 48 n. 39.

117. Edward Hyde, Earl of Clarendon, *The History of the Rebellion and Civil Wars in England*, ed. W. D. Macray (6 vols, Oxford, 1888), I, p. 25.

118. *By the King. A Proclamation and Declaration to Inform Our Loving Subjects of Our Kingdom of England of the Seditious Practices of Some in Scotland, Seeking to Overthrow Our Regall Power Under False Pretences of Religion* (STC 9135, 1639), 4 pages, unpaginated.

119. See Raymond, *Pamphlets and Pamphleteering*, ch. 5.

120. Walter Balcanquall, *A Large Declaration Concerning the Late Tumults in Scotland, From Their First Originalls Together with a Particular Deduction of the Seditious Practices of the Prime Leaders of the Covenanters: Collected Out of Their Owne Foule Acts and Writings: By Which It Doth Plainly Appeare, That Religion Was Onely Pretended By Those Leaders, But Nothing Lesse Intended By Them. By the King* (STC 21906, 1639).

121. Ibid., p. 2.

122. Ibid.

123. Ibid., pp. 3–4.

124. Ibid., pp. 6–17.

125. Ibid., pp. 19–20.

126. See, for example, ibid., pp. 39, 41, 42, 51, 54, 128, 338, 341, 343ff., 380, 382, 399.

127. Ibid., pp. 52–3, cf. p. 30.

128. Ibid., p. 66.

129. Ibid., p. 106.

130. Ibid., p. 133.

131. Ibid., p. 205.

132. Ibid., p. 220.

133. Ibid., p. 301. For the narrative, see Donald, *Uncounselled King*.

134. *A Large Declaration*, p. 308

135. Ibid., pp. 323–50 *passim*.

136. Ibid., p. 375.

137. Ibid., pp. 382, 387, 399, 413.

138. Ibid., p. 417.

139. Ibid., pp. 428–30.

140. Like so many early modern texts with which historians are familiar, it has not received, and merits, a detailed rhetorical analysis.

141. See below, pp. 173, 285–93.

142. Larkin, *Proclamations*, II, no. 297, pp. 703–5.

143. *His Majesties Declaration, Concerning His Proceedings With His Subjects of Scotland, Since the Pacification in the Camp Neere Berwick* (STC 9260, 1640). This declaration was printed by the king's printer for Scotland but authorship has been ascribed to Sir Francis Windebank.

144. Ibid., p. 3.

145. Ibid., pp. 19–23 and *passim*.

146. Ibid., p. 51.

147. Ibid., p. 56

148. Ibid., pp. 57–8. Charles had the same letter read to parliament and evidently (and not unreasonably) thought it clinched his case. See Sharpe, *Personal Rule*, pp. 862–3.

149. Sharpe, *Personal Rule*, ch. 15; Cust, *Charles I*, pp. 252–9.

150. *His Majesties Declaration*, p. 63.

151. *His Majesties Declaration to All His Loving Subjects, of the Causes Which Moved Him to Dissolve the Last Parliament. Published by His Majesties Speciall Command* (STC 9262, 1640).

152. Ibid., p. 2; above ch. 1, pp. 43–4.

153. Ibid., pp. 3–4.

154. Ibid., pp. 39–40, 41.

155. Ibid., pp. 47–8.

156. Ibid., p. 51.

157. Ibid., p. 52.

158. Ibid., pp. 53–4.

159. See E. Cope, 'The King's Declaration Concerning the Dissolution of the Short Parliament of 1640: An Unsuccessful Attempt at Public Relations', *Huntington Library Quarterly*, 40 (1977), pp. 325–31.

160. C. Dow, *Innovations Unjustly Charged Upon the Present Church and State* (STC 7090, 1637), p. 39.

161. W. Lilly, *Monarchy or No Monarchy in England: Grebner His Prophecy Concerning Charles, Son of Charles, his Greatnesse, Victories, Conquests* (Wing L2228, 1651), p. 75.

162. Sharpe, 'The King's Writ: Royal Authors and Royal Authority in Early Modern England', in K. Sharpe and P. Lake eds, *Culture and Politics in Early Stuart England* (Basingstoke, 1994), pp. 131–2; Cope, *Proceedings of the Short Parliament*, p. 198.
163. Sharpe, *Selling the Tudor Monarchy*, pp. 336–44.
164. *Cal. Stat. Pap. Venet. XXII, 1629–32*, p. 350; W. Scott and J. Bliss, *The Works of William Laud, . . . Archbishop of Canterbury* (7 vols, Oxford, 1847–60), III, p. 168; Sharpe, *Personal Rule*, pp. 179–80.
165. Lilly, *Monarchy or No Monarchy*, p. 78.
166. Bodleian Library Tanner MS 70, f. 18.
167. See *Basilika* (1662).
168. *Basilika* (1687), p. 159.
169. Ibid., p. 159.
170. Ibid.
171. Ibid.; Acts 22: 2.
172. *Basilika* (1687), p. 159.
173. See Russell, *Parliaments and English Politics*, ch. 4.
174. Ibid., pp. 269–72.
175. *Basilika* (1687), p. 160.
176. Ibid., p. 161. Charles was referring to risks from abroad but the tone of a threat remains.
177. Speech of 29 May, ibid., p. 161.
178. Ibid.
179. Ibid.
180. Above, p. 157.
181. For the narrative of this parliament, see Russell, *Parliaments and English Politics*, ch. 6.
182. *Basilika* (1687), p. 162.
183. Ibid.
184. Above, p. 153 n. 67.
185. Speech of 4 April, *Basilika* (1687), p. 162. Begin with Jove – or the king.
186. Ibid.
187. Ibid., p. 163.
188. Ibid.
189. Ibid.
190. Ibid.
191. Ibid., p. 164.
192. See C. Thompson, 'The Divided Leadership', in Sharpe, *Faction and Parliament*, pp. 246–84; Russell, *Parliaments and English Politics*, ch. 7.
193. *Cal. Stat. Pap. Venet., XXI, 1628–9*, p. 444.
194. *Basilika* (1687), p. 164.
195. Ibid., p. 165.
196. Ibid.
197. Ibid.
198. Malcolm Smuts argues for 1629 as the point when Charles moved from a rhetoric of love to one of authority, see R. M. Smuts, 'Force, Love and Authority in Caroline Political Culture', in I. Atherton and J. Sanders eds, *The 1630s: Interdisciplinary Essays on Culture and Politics in the Caroline Era* (Manchester, 2006), pp. 28–49.
199. *Cal. Stat. Pap. Venet., XXI, 1628–9*, p. 528; Sharpe, *Personal Rule*, p. 54.
200. Above, pp. 157–8.
201. G. R. Elton, 'Tudor Government: The Points of Contact, 1: Parliament', *Transactions of the Royal Historical Society*, 5th ser., 24 (1974), pp. 183–200.
202. *Cal. Stat. Pap. Dom. 1628–9*, p. 489.
203. BL Add. MS 11045, f. 109.
204. See Cope, *Proceedings of the Short Parliament*, pp. 115–21.
205. *Cal. Stat. Pap. Dom. 1640*, pp. 32–3.
206. *Basilika* (1687), p. 166; Cope, *Proceedings of the Short Parliament*, p. 115.
207. For the proceedings of the Short Parliament, see Sharpe, *Personal Rule*, ch. 15.
208. Speech of 5 May 1640, *Basilika* (1687), p. 167.
209. Sharpe, *Personal Rule*, pp. 914–21.
210. *Basilika* (1687), p. 168.
211. Ibid.
212. Sharpe, *Personal Rule*, pp. 917–18.
213. BL Harleian MS 456, f. 57.
214. See the discussion of the *Large Declaration*, above, pp. 161–4.
215. *Basilika* (1687), p. 169.

216. Ibid.
217. Ibid.
218. Below, pp. 285–9.
219. Biographies of Charles tend to pay inadequate attention to his first twenty-five years before he succeeded to the throne.
220. David Primrose, *Scotlands Complaint Upon the Death of Our Late Soveraigne King Iames of Most Happy Memorie* (STC 23086, Edinburgh, 1625), sig. A4.
221. J. Taylor, *A Liuing Sadnes, in Duty Consecrated to the Immortall Memory of Our Late Deceased Albe-loued Soueraigne Lord, the Peeereles Paragon of Princes, Iames, King of Great Brittaine* (STC 23772, 1625), pp. 10–11.
222. Francis Hamilton, *King Iames his Encomium Or A Poeme, In Memorie and Commendation of the High and Mightie Monarch Iames; King of Great Britaine. France, and Ireland* (STC 12726, Edinburgh, 1626), sig. A4.
223. Ibid., p. 13.
224. Ibid., p. 14.
225. J. Pyne, *Anagrammata Regia in Honorem Maximi et Mansuetissimi Regis Caroli Conscripta* (STC 20521.2, 1626), sigs A2–C1ᵛ, *passim*.
226. Ibid., sigs A2ᵛ, B2.
227. *Epithalamia Oxoniensia In Auspicatissimum, Potentissimi Monarchae Caroli, Magnae Britanniae, Franciae, et Hiberniae Regis, &c. Cum Henretta Maria, Aeternae Memoriae Henrici Magni Gallorum Regis Filia, Connubium* (STC 19031, Oxford, 1625), sig. H3ᵛ and *passim*.
228. Ibid., sigs A, F3, G4ᵛ.
229. Ibid., sigs G3ᵛ, K3ᵛ. One poet (K3ᵛ) speaks of the marriage leading to 'una fides', one faith, a continuation of James I's dream for a reunification of Christendom.
230. *Genethliacum Illustrissimorum Principum Caroli & Mariae a Musis Cantabrigiensibus Celebratum* (STC 4486, Cambridge 1631), p. 55 and see *passim*.
231. John Beaumont, *Bosworth-field With a Taste of the Variety of Other Poems, Left by Sir Iohn Beaumont, Baronet, Deceased: Set Forth by His Sonne, Sir Iohn Beaumont, Baronet; and Dedicated to the Kings Most Excellent Maiestie* (STC 1694, 1629), sigs A3–3ᵛ.
232. T. May, *A Continuation of Lucan's Historicall Poem Till the Death of Iulius Caesar by TM* (STC 17711, 1630), sig. A5. David Norbrook, I believe, exaggerates the republican thrust of this poem as it was published in 1630. See D. Norbrook, *Writing the English Republic: Poetry, Rhetoric and Politics, 1627–1660* (Oxford, 1999), pp. 225–6 and cf. p. 63.
233. Norbrook, *Writing the English Republic*, pp. 43–50.
234. See R. Dunlop, *The Poems of Thomas Carew* (Oxford, 1949), p. 77. See Sharpe, *Personal Rule*, pp. 608–11; R. A. Anselment, 'Clarendon and the Caroline Myth of Peace', *Journal of British Studies*, 23 (1984), pp. 37–54.
235. R. A. Anselment, *Loyalist Resolve: Patient Fortitude in the English Civil War* (Newark, Delaware, 1988), p. 46.
236. See Sharpe, *Personal Rule*, pp. 778–83.
237. *Anthologia in Regis Exanthemata: Seu Gratulatio Musarum Cantabrigiensium de Felicissimè Conservata Regis Caroli Valetudine* (STC 4475, Cambridge 1633). See J. C. T. Oates, 'Cambridge Books of Congratulatory Verses 1603–1640 and their Binders', *Transactions of the Cambridge Bibliographical Society*, I (1953), pp. 395–421. Oxford also published a volume, *Musarum Oxoniensium Pro Rege Suo Soteria Anagramma* (STC 19034, Oxford, 1633).
238. *Eisodia Musarum Edinensium in Caroli Regis, Musarum Tutani, Ingressu in Scotiam* (STC 7486, Edinburgh, 1633); *Academiae Glasguensis Charisterion ad Augustissimum Monarcham Carolum Magnae Britanniae, Franciae, et Hiberniae, Regem, Fidei Defensorem* (STC 11916, Glasgow, 1633); *Vivat Rex, Seu [prodeukòu] Pro Incolumitate Serenissimi Regis Caroli Magnae Britanniae, Franciae et Hiberniae Regis, Fidei Defensoris, Ejusque Felice in Scotiâ Inauguratione* (STC 25194, Aberdeen, 1633).
239. William Lithgow, *Scotlands Welcome to Her Native Sonne, and Soveraigne Lord, King Charles* (STC 15716, Edinburgh, 1633), sigs A1–1ᵛ.
240. Ibid., sigs B, G3.
241. Walter Forbes, *Panegyrick to the High and Mightie Monarch, Charles by the Grace of God, King of Great Britaine, France, and Ireland, Defender of the Faith* (STC 11151.5, Edinburgh, 1633), sig. A3; William Douglas, Earl of Morton, *Grampius Gratulatius to His High and Mightie Monarch, King Charles* (STC 7076, Edinburgh, 1633), no pagination.
242. D. Primrose, *Scotlands Welcome to Her Dread Sovereign King Charles*, in *Eisodia Musarum Edinensium*, sigs a–a1ᵛ; A. Ramsay, *Poemata Sacra, Andreae Ramsaei Pastoris Edinburgeni* (STC 20656, Edinburgh, 1633), sig. §4.
243. A. Boyd, *Ad Augustissimum Monarcham Carolum, Majoris Britanniae, Fran[ci]ae, et Hiberniae, Regem Potentissim[um,] Fidei Defensoris, [et]c. In Scotiam Redeuntem, Carmen Panegyricum* (STC 3443, Edinburgh, 1633), sig. A2ᵛ.

244. P.M., *King Charles His Birthright. By P.M.* (STC 17145, Edinburgh, 1633), sig. A2.

245. Ibid., sig. A3.

246. *Rex Redux, Sive Musa Cantabrigiensis Voti Damnas de Incolumitate & Felici Reditu Regis Caroli Post Receptam Coronam, Comitiáq[ue] Peracta in Scotia* (STC 4491, Cambridge, 1633). See pp. 68–9.

247. I.R, *A Poeme, On the Kings Most Excellent Maiesties Happy Progresse Into Scotland, and Much Desired Returne May. 1633* (STC 20576, 1633), p. 3 and *passim*.

248. Ibid., p. 9.

249. *Vitis Carolinae Gemma Altera Sive Auspicatissima Ducis Eboracensis Genethiliaca Decantata ad Vada Isidis* (STC 19035, Oxford, 1633), sig. I4ᵛ.

250. Ibid., sigs I1ᵛ, L1.

251. *Ducis Eboracensis Fasciae a Musis Cantabrigiensibus Raptim Contextae* (STC 4480, Cambridge, 1633).

252. *Coronae Carolinae Quadratura. Siue Perpetuandi Imperii Carolini ex Quarto Pignore Feliciter Suscepto Captatum Augurium* (STC 19036, Oxford, 1636), sig. C3. Deucalion, son of Prometheus, built an ark to save the world from a flood. He and his wife Pyrrha repopulated the world.

253. Ibid., sig. aaaa4.

254. *Synoidia, Sive Musarum Cantabrigiensium Concentus et Congratulatio, ad Serenissimum Britanniarum Regem Carolum, de Quinta Sua Sobole, Clarissima Principe, Sibi Nuper Felicisimè Nata* (STC 4492, Cambridge, 1637). These commendatory university volumes are worthy of fuller study. For a checklist, see Oates, 'Cambridge Books' and for Oxford, see F. Madan, *Oxford Books: A Bibliography of Printed Works relating to the University and City of Oxford: Oxford Literature, 1651–1680* (2 vols, 1912–31), II, pp. 98–147.

255. Above, p. 176; *Vitis Carolinae*, sig. I3; *Coronae Carolinae Quadratura*, sig. C3.

256. W. Saltonstall, *The Complaint of Time Against the Tumultuous and Rebellious Scots Sharply Inveighing Against Them (As Most Justly They Deserve) This Yeare, 1639* (STC 21643.5, 1639), sigs A1ᵛ, A4.

257. *An Exact Description of the Manner How His Maiestie and His Nobles Went to Parliament, on Munday, the Thirteenth Day of Aprill, 1640, to the Comfortable Expectation of All Loyall Subiects to the Tune of Triumph and Ioy* (STC 19230, 1640).

258. M.P., *A True Subiects Wish For the Happy Successe of Our Royall Army Preparing to Resist the Factious Rebellion of Those Insolent Covenanters (Against the Sacred Maiesty, of Our Gracious and Loving King Charles) in Scotland. To the Tune of, O How Now Mars, &c* (STC 19274, 1640).

259. Saltonstall, *Complaint of Time*, sig. A3; M.P., *Good Newes from the North, Truly Relating How About a Hundred of the Scottish Rebels, Intending to Plunder the House of M. Thomas Pudsie . . . Were Set Upon By a Troupe of Our Hoursemen* (STC 19238, 1640); L.P., *A New Spanish Tragedy* (STC 20318, 1639); *The Jew's High Commendation of the Metropolitant Cathedral Church of St Paul* (Wing J741, 1638).

260. M.P., *A True Subiects Wish.*

261. *Voces Votivae ab Academcis Cantabrigiensibus Pro Novissimo Caroli & Mariae Principe Filio Emissae* (STC 4495, Cambridge, 1640), sig. F2; *Horti Carolini Rosa Altera* (STC 19039, Oxford, 1640).

262. *Voces Votivae*, sig. b2ᵛ.

263. *Horti Carolini Rosa Altera*, sig. e4ᵛ.

264. George Marcelline, *Epithalamium Gallo-Britannicum* (STC 17038, 1625), pp. 7, 18 and *passim*.

265. Ibid., pp. 7, 33.

266. Ibid., pp. 33, 134.

267. H. Wotton, *A Panegyrick of King Charles; Being Observations Upon the Inclination, Life, and Government of Our Soveraign Lord the King* (Wing W3645), a translation of *Ad Regem è Scotia Reducem Henrici Wottonij Plausus et Vota* (STC 26010, 1633), p. 48.

268. D. Featley, *Cygnea Cantio: or, Learned Decisions, and Most Prudent and Pious Directions for Students in Divinitie; Delivered by Our Late Soveraigne of Happie Memorie, King Iames, at White Hall a Few Weekes Before His Death* (STC 10731, 1629), sigs A3–B1.

269. *Cambium Regis: or, The Office of His Maiesties Exchange Royall Declaring and Iustifying His Maiesties Right; and the Conveniencie Thereof* (STC 4471, 1628), p. 28.

270. W. Alexander, Earl of Stirling, *The Mapp and Description of New-England Together With a Discourse of Plantation, and Colonies* (STC 342, 1630), p. 46.

271. Thomas Heywood, *A True Description of His Majesties Royall Ship, Built this Yeare 1637. at Wooll-witch in Kent To the Great Glory of Our English Nation, and Not Paraleld in the Whole Christian World* (STC 13367, 1637), p. 25.

272. F. Quarles, *Emblemes by Fra. Quarles* (STC 20540, 1635), after p. 307, copy with an additional letterpress title page inserted before X1, dated 1634: *Lusus Poëticus Poëtis* 'Ad Magnae Britanniae Regem Anagramma Quadruplex'.

273. G. Wither, *A Collection of Emblemes, Ancient and Moderne Quickened With Metricall Illustrations, Both Morall and Divine* (STC 25900a, 1635), sig.∗3.

274. Ibid., sig.∗3^v.

275. Ibid.

276. Ibid., Book II, no. XVI, p. 78.

277. F. Cevoli, *An Occasionall Discourse Upon an Accident Which Befell His Maiesty in Hunting. Composed in Italian, by Francis Cevolus, and Thence Translated into English* (STC 4922, 1635), p. 6.

278. Ibid., p. 1.

279. Ibid., pp. 3–5.

280. Ibid., pp. 1, 7.

281. Ibid., pp. 6–7.

282. Ibid., p. 8.

283. See Sharpe, *Personal Rule*, chs 11, 12.

284. Thomas Morton, *New English Canaan, or New Canaan Containing an Abstract of New England, Composed in Three Bookes* (STC 18203, 1637), p. 4. Morton was in conflict with the puritans, see *ODNB*.

285. Ibid., pp. 172, 177.

286. M. de La Serre, *Histoire de L'entree de la Reyne Mere du Roy Tres Chrestien, Dans la Grande-Bretaigne Enrichie de Planches. Par le Sr. de la Serre, Historiographe de France* (STC 20488, 1639), 'Au Roy'.

287. H. Peacham, *The Duty of all True Subiects to Their King as Also to Their Native Countrey, in Time of Extremity and Danger. With Some Memorable Examples of the Miserable Ends of Perfidious Traytors* (STC 19505, 1639), pp. 6, 21.

288. Ibid., p. 22.

289. Ibid., pp. 22, 63.

290. See, for example, *The Epistle Congratulatorie of Lysimachus Nicanor of the Societie of Jesu, to the Covenanters in Scotland* (E 203/7, 1640).

291. Though rather different, this point complements David Cressy's, *England on Edge: Crisis and Revolution, 1640–1642* (Oxford, 2006), Part III. I am grateful to David Cressy for many fruitful discussions.

292. James Howell, *Dendrologia Dodona's Grove, or, the Vocall Forrest* (STC 13872, 1640), p. 57. See D. Woolf, 'Conscience, Constancy and Ambition in the Career and Writings of James Howell', in J. Morrill, P. Slack and D. Woolf eds, *Public Duty and Private Conscience in Seventeenth-Century England* (Oxford, 1992), pp. 243–78, especially pp. 256–9.

293. Howell, *Dendrologia*, pp. 178–9, 211–12.

294. Howell sounds understandably tentative: 'The thistle, I hope, will not offer to clash against the sovereign rose', ibid., p. 216.

295. Cambridge University Library MS Dd 12, 21, f. 99; Pierre Matthieu, *The Powerfull Fauorite, or, The Life of Aelius Seianus* (STC 17664, 1628); Francis Hubert, *The Deplorable Life and Death of Edward the Second, King of England Together with the Downefall of the Two Unfortunate Favorits, Gaveston and Spencer* (STC 13900, 1628).

296. John Taylor, *A Memorial of All the English Monarchs Being in Number 151, From Brute to King Charles. In Heroicall Verse by Io. Taylor* (STC 23774, 1630), sig. G4.

297. Francis Godwin, *Annales of England Containing the Reignes of Henry the Eighth, Edward the Sixt. Queene Mary* (STC 11947, 1630), sig. A1.

298. J. Weever, *Ancient Funerall Monuments Within the United Monarchie of Great Britaine* (STC 25223, 1631), dedication page.

299. Ibid., pp. 1–3.

300. P. Heylyn, *Augustus: Or An Essay of Those Meanes and Counsels, Whereby the Commonwealth of Rome was Altered, and Reduced Unto a Monarchy* (STC 13268, 1632).

301. Ibid., pp. 45, 50, 188 and *passim*.

302. T. May, *The Reigne of King Henry the Second Written in Seauen Bookes. By his Majesties Command* (STC 17715, 1633), dedication page and sig. B1^v; *The Victorious Reigne of King Edward the Third Written in Seven Bookes. By his Majesties Command* (STC 17719, 1635), sigs A3–4.

303. May was accused of deserting the Royalist cause out of pique at not attaining office, *DNB* and *ODNB*. Robert Powell, *The Life of Alfred, or, Alvred: the First Institutor of Subordinate Government in This Kingdome, and Refounder of the University of Oxford Together with a Parallell of Our Soveraigne Lord, K. Charles Untill This Yeare, 1634* (STC 20161, 1634). On the legal writer Powell, see *ODNB*.

304. Ibid., sig. a4^v.

305. Ibid., pp. 28–69.

306. Ibid., pp. 88, 104–28, 132, 139–41 and *passim*.

307. Ibid., p. 154.

308. Ibid., pp. 152–6.

309. William Habington, *The Historie of Edward the Fourth, King of England* (STC 12586, 1640). Habington was a courtier poet, see *ODNB*.

310. Ibid., sig. A2.

311. Ibid., sig. A2ᵛ.

312. Ibid.

313. Ibid.

314. K. Fincham and P. Lake, 'The Ecclesiastical Policies of James I and Charles I', in K. Fincham ed., *The Early Stuart Church 1603–42* (Basingstoke, 1993), pp. 23–49.

315. Sharpe, *Personal Rule*, pp. 308–22; A. Foster, 'The Clerical Estate Revitalised', in Fincham, *Early Stuart Church*, pp. 139–60. We await a study of Caroline court sermons along the lines of P. McCulloch, *Sermons at Court: Politics and Religion in Elizabethan and Jacobean Preaching* (Cambridge, 1998).

316. William Laud, *A Sermon Preached Before His Maiestie, on Sunday the XIX. of Iune, at White-Hall Appointed to Be Preached at the Opening of the Parliament* (STC 15302, 1625), p. 4.

317. Ibid., pp. 19, 30, 47.

318. Matthew Wren, *A Sermon Preached Before the Kings Maiestie on Sunday the Seventeenth of February Last, at White-Hall by Dor Wren, the Master of St Peters Colledge in Cambridge, and His Maiesties Chaplaine. Printed by Command* (STC 26015, Cambridge, 1628).

319. Ibid., pp. 25, 27–8, 33 and *passim*.

320. Ibid., pp. 30–3.

321. Ibid., p. 41.

322. Ibid., p. 32.

323. See above, p. 152.

324. Larkin, *Proclamations*, II, no. 92, p. 198.

325. Isaac Bargrave, *A Sermon Preached Before King Charles, March 27. 1627. Being the Anniuersary of His Maiesties Inauguration* (STC 1414, 1627), pp. 1, 2, 14, 20.

326. Ibid., p. 14.

327. Ibid., p. 18.

328. S. Denison, *The White Wolfe or, A Sermon Preached at Pauls Crosse, Feb. 11 Being the Last Sonday in Hillarie Tearme, Anno 1627 and Printed Somewhat More Largely Then the Time Would Permit at That Present to Deliuer. Wherein Faction is Unmasked, and Iustly Taxed* (STC 6607.5, 1627). For the detailed context of Denison's sermon, see P. Lake, *The Boxmaker's Revenge: Orthodoxy, Heterodoxy, and the Politics of the Parish in Early Stuart London* (Manchester, 2001).

329. Theophilus Taylor, *The Mappe of Moses: Or a Guide for Governours. Two Sermons Lately Preached Before the Iudges of Assize, and Magistrates of the Towne of Reding* (STC 23819, 1629), pp. 3, 10–11, 15, 16–18 and *passim*.

330. John Donne, *Two Sermons Preached Before King Charles, Upon the xxvi Verse of the First Chapter of Genesis. By Dr. Donne Dean of Pauls* (STC 7058, Cambridge 1634).

331. Thomas Turner, *A Sermon Preached Before the King at White-Hall, the Tenth of March. By Doctor Turner, One of His Maiesties Chaplaines* (STC 24349, 1635).

332. William Struther, *A Looking Glasse for Princes and People Delivered in a Sermon of Thanksgiving for the Birth of the Hopefull Prince Charles* (STC 23369, 1632), p. 19.

333. Ibid., pp. 102, 106.

334. Thomas Laurence, *A Sermon Preached Before the Kings Maiesty at White-Hall, the Seventh of February, 1636. By Thomas Lawrence Dr. of Divinity, and Chaplaine to His Maiestie in Ordinarie. Published by the Kings Especiall Command* (STC 15326.5, 1637), p. 12 and *passim*. On Laurence see *DNB* and *ODNB*.

335. Thomas Hurste, *The Descent of Authoritie: Or, The Magistrates Patent From Heaven Manifested in a Sermon Preached at Lincolnes Assizes, March 13. 1636. By Thomas Hurste Dr. of Divinity, and One of His Majesties Chaplains* (STC 14007, 1637), p. 5.

336. Ibid., p. 13.

337. Ibid., p. 30.

338. Ibid., p. 17.

339. Puritanism was once studied as an inherently revolutionary movement (see M. Walzer, *The Revolution of the Saints: A Study in the Origins of Radical Politics*, Cambridge, Mass., 1965, and the works of Christopher Hill). Latterly the consensus has gone with Patrick Collinson that puritanism was not a threat until Charles I and Laud made it one (e.g. P. Collinson, *The Religion of Protestants: The Church in English Society, 1559–1625* (Oxford, 1982)) – a view with which I am in complete disagreement. See Sharpe, *Personal Rule*, ch. 7.

340. See J. Morrill, 'The Church in England 1643–9', in Morrill ed., *Reactions to the English Civil War, 1642–1649* (1982), pp. 89–114; J. Maltby, *Prayer Book and People in Elizabethan and Early Stuart England* (Cambridge, 1998).

341. Thomas Morton, *A Sermon Preached Before the Kings Most Excellent Majestie, in the Cathedrall Church of Durham Upon Sunday, Being the Fifth Day of May. 1639* (STC 18196, 1639).

342. Ibid., pp. 21, 41.

343. Ibid., p. 40. Morton was one of the twelve bishops impeached in 1641.

344. Henry Valentine, *God Save the King: A Sermon Preached in St. Pauls Church the 27th. of March 1639. Being the Day of His Maiesties Most Happy Inauguration, and of His Northerne Expedition* (STC 24575, 1639).

345. Ibid., pp. 5–6.

346. Ibid., pp. 17–18.

347. Ibid., pp. 10, 15, 23, 26–7.

348. Ibid., p. 31.

349. Ibid.

350. Ibid., pp. 31–2.

351. Ibid., p. 33.

352. Ibid., pp. 35–6.

353. Henry King, *A Sermon Preached at St. Pauls March 27. 1640 Being the Anniversary of His Majesties Happy Inauguration to His Crowne. By Henry King, Deane of Rochester, and Residentiary of St. Pauls: One of His Maiesties Chaplaines in Ordinary* (STC 14970, 1640). The text was from Jeremiah 1: 10.

354. Ibid., p. 11.

355. Ibid., pp. 13–14.

356. Ibid., pp. 28–9

357. Ibid., pp. 54–7.

6 Depicting Virtue and Majesty

1. A. MacGregor ed., *The Late King's Goods: Collections, Possessions and Patronage of Charles I in the Light of Commonwealth Inventories* (Oxford, 1989), p. 53.

2. See L. Barroll, *Anna of Denmark, Queen of England: A Cultural Biography* (Philadelphia, 2001); R. Strong, *Henry, Prince of Wales and England's Lost Renaissance* (1986). Above, pp. 64–70. In the case of Thomas Howard, Earl of Arundel and his Countess, noble taste and patronage may well have influenced Anna and Henry, see D. Howarth, *Lord Arundel and his Circle* (New Haven and London, 1985).

3. J. Brotton, *The Sale of the Late King's Goods: Charles I and his Art Collection* (2006), pp. 73–5.

4. Ibid., p. 133.

5. Ibid., p. 93.

6. Ibid., pp. 93–5.

7. Ibid., p. 103.

8. Ibid., p. 146; F. Haskell, 'Charles I's Collection of Pictures', in MacGregor, *Late King's Goods*, pp. 203–31.

9. See E. Chaney ed., *The Evolution of English Collecting: Receptions of Italian Art in the Tudor and Stuart Periods* (New Haven and London, 2003), introduction, pp. 1–124 and *passim*.

10. J. Peacock, 'The Politics of Portraiture', in K. Sharpe and P. Lake eds, *Culture and Politics in Early Stuart England* (Basingstoke, 1994), pp. 199–228; P. Croft, *Patronage, Culture and Power: The Early Cecils* (New Haven and London, 2002); Chaney, *Evolution of English Collecting*, chs 4, 5, 9.

11. H. Peacham, *The Gentlemans Exercise Or an Exquisite Practise, As Well for Drawing All Manner of Beasts in Their True Portraitures: As Also the Making of all Kinds of Colours, To Be Used in Limming, Painting, Tricking, and Blaxon of Coates, and Armes, With Divers Other Most Delightfull and Pleasurable Observations, for All Young Gentlemen and Others* (STC 19509, 1634), pp. 6–7 and *passim*.

12. R. Davies, 'An Inventory of the Duke of Buckingham's Pictures at York House in 1635', *Burlington Magazine*, 10 (1907), pp. 376–82; Haskell, 'Charles I's Collection of Pictures', p. 207; P. McEvansoneya, 'Italian Paintings in the Buckingham Collection', in Chaney, *Evolution of English Collecting*, pp. 315–36; Sharpe, *The Personal Rule of Charles I* (New Haven and London, 1992), pp. 166–7; P. Shakeshaft, ' "Too Much Bewitched With Thoes Intysing Things": The Letters of James, Third Marquis of Hamilton and Basil, Viscount Fielding in Venice, 1635–1639', *Burlington Magazine*, 128 (1986), pp. 114–32; Howarth, *Lord Arundel and his Circle*; K. Sharpe, 'The Earl of Arundel, his Circle and the Opposition to the Duke of Buckingham, 1618–1628', in Sharpe ed., *Faction and Parliament: Essays on Early Stuart History* (Oxford, 1978), pp. 209–44; D. Howarth, *Images of Rule: Art and Politics in the English Renaissance, 1485–1649* (1997), pp. 191–2, 226–8.

13. Peacham, *Gentleman's Exercise*; John Bate, *The Mysteries of Nature and Art In Foure Severall Parts* (STC 1577, 1634, 2nd edn expanded, STC 1578, 1635); F. Quarles, *Emblemes by Fra. Quarles* (STC 20540, 1635); G. Wither, *A Collection of Emblemes, Ancient and Moderne Quickened With Metricall Illustrations, Both Morall and Divine* (STC 25900a, 1635), Book III, p. 137.

14. Franciscus Junius, *The Painting of the Ancients in Three Bookes: Declaring by Historicall Observations and Examples, the Beginning, Progresse, and Consummation of That Most Noble Art* (STC 7302, 1638, first published in Latin 1637).

15. See Sharpe, *Selling the Tudor Monarchy: Authority and Image in Sixteenth-Century England* (New Haven and London, 2009), pp. 389–91, 401–2.

16. G. Vertue, *A Catalogue and Description of King Charles the First's Capital Collection of Pictures, Limnings, Statues, Bronzes, Medals and Other Curiosities* (1757), pp. 41–2.

17. Ibid., p. 125.

18. See Oliver Millar, *Abraham Van der Doort's Catalogue of the Collections of Charles I* (Walpole Society, 37, 1960).

19. Wither, *Collection of Emblemes*, sig. *4.

20. Millar, *Van der Doort's Catalogue*, p. 126.

21. W. H. Carpenter ed., *Mémoires et Documents Inédits sur Antoine Van Dyck* (Anvers, 1845), p. 58.

22. Ibid., p. 33.

23. See, for example, the self-portrait of Van Dyck with a sunflower and J. Peacock, *The Look of Van Dyck: The Self-Portrait with a Sunflower and the Vision of the Painter* (Aldershot, 2006).

24. O. Millar, *The Pictures in the Collection of Her Majesty the Queen: The Tudor, Stuart and Early Georgian Pictures* (2 vols, 1963), I, p. 84.

25. Ibid.

26. Ibid., nos 115–16, 121, pp. 84–6.

27. Ibid., no. 117, p. 85; O. Millar, *The Age of Charles I* (1972), p. 24; F. M. Kelly, 'Mytens and his Portraits of Charles I', *Burlington Magazine*, 37 (1920), pp. 84–9.

28. Millar, *Tudor, Stuart and Early Georgian Pictures*, no. 118, p. 85, plate 48.

29. Millar, *Age of Charles I*, p. 25.

30. Millar, *Tudor, Stuart and Early Georgian Pictures*, no. 119, p. 86, and fig. 12.

31. Ibid., no. 120, p. 86, plate 59.

32. Ibid., p. 86.

33. Ibid., no. 113, p. 84.

34. Millar, *Age of Charles I*, no. 78, p. 54.

35. Ibid.

36. Ibid., no. 79, p. 54. Royal Collection RCIN 405746. See O. Millar, 'Charles I, Honthorst and Van Dyck', *Burlington Magazine*, 96 (1954), pp. 36–42.

37. Millar, *Age of Charles I*, p. 53.

38. Ibid., p. 22.

39. C. White, *Peter Paul Rubens: Man and Artist* (New Haven and London, 1987), p. 227. See F. Donovan, *Rubens and England* (New Haven and London, 2004).

40. M. Rooses and C. Ruelens eds, *Correspondance de Rubens et Documents Epistolaires Concernant sa Vie et Ses Oeuvres* (6 vols, Antwerp, 1887–1909), V, pp. 287–8; White, *Rubens*, pp. 228–30; Donovan, *Rubens and England*, pp. 74–5, and fig. 34; C. Brown, *Rubens: 'Peace and War': Minerva Protects Pax from Mars* (1979).

41. White, *Rubens*, p. 228; Donovan, *Rubens and England*, pp. 75–6 and fig. 35.

42. C. Brown, *Van Dyck* (Oxford, 1982), p. 137.

43. Ibid.

44. Millar, *Tudor, Stuart and Early Georgian Pictures*, p. 92; S. J. Barnes, N. De Poorter, O. Millar and H. Vey, *Van Dyck: A Complete Catalogue of the Paintings* (New Haven and London, 2004), p. 420.

45. Barnes et al., *Van Dyck*, p. 422.

46. Ibid., p. 420.

47. See K. Sharpe, *Politics and Ideas in Early Stuart England* (1989), pp. 51–2.

48. Andres Almansa de Mendoza, *Two Royall Entertainments, Lately Given to the Most Illustrious Prince Charles, Prince of Great Britaine, By the High and Mighty Philip the Fourth King of Spaine, &c. At the Feasts of Easter and Pentecost* (STC 533, 1623), p. 27.

49. H. Wotton, *A Panegyrick of King Charles* (Wing W3645, 1649), p. 2100.

50. Millar, *Tudor, Stuart and Early Georgian Pictures*, no. 144, p. 95.

51. Barnes et al., *Van Dyck*, p. 468. See also R. Strong, *Charles I on Horseback* (1972).

52. Barnes et al., *Van Dyck*, pp. 468–9.

53. Millar, *Tudor, Stuart and Early Georgian Pictures*, no. 143, pp. 93–4.

54. Ibid., pp. 462–4. See Gudrun Raatschen, 'Van Dyck's "Charles I on Horseback with M de St Antoine"', in H. Vlieghe, *Van Dyck 1559–1999: Conjectures and Refutations* (Turnhout, Belgium, 2001), pp. 139–48.

55. Speech of Wentworth in J. P. Kenyon ed., *The Stuart Constitution, 1603–1688* (Cambridge, 1969), p. 18; Sharpe, *Personal Rule*, pp. 133–5.
56. See K. Sharpe, *Criticism and Compliment: The Politics of Literature in the England of Charles I* (Cambridge, 1987), pp. 214–23.
57. Millar, *Tudor, Stuart and Early Georgian Pictures*, p. 94; Barnes et al., *Van Dyck*, p. 464.
58. M. de La Serre, *Histoire de L'entree de la Reyne Mere du Roy Tres Chrestien, Dans la Grande-Bretaigne Enrichie de Planches. Par le Sr. de la Serre, Historiographe de France* (STC 20488, 1639), sigs I2ᵛ, I4ᵛ.
59. See Brown, *Van Dyck*, ch. 3.
60. Barnes et al., *Van Dyck*, p. 468.
61. Ibid.
62. Millar, *Tudor, Stuart and Early Georgian Pictures*, no. 145, pp. 95–6.
63. C. Brown and H. Vlieghe, *Van Dyck 1599–1641* (London and Antwerp, 1999), p. 304.
64. Revelation 3: 12.
65. See Sharpe, *Selling the Tudor Monarchy*, pp. 138–40, 368–70.
66. Millar, *Tudor, Stuart and Early Georgian Pictures*, no. 119, p. 86; Vlieghe, *Van Dyck*, p. 158; Brown and Vlieghe, *Van Dyck*, pp. 241–3.
67. On the several copies of this painting, see Barnes et al., *Van Dyck*, p. 462.
68. I make this case more fully in *Personal Rule*, pp. 168–73, 183–8.
69. Millar, *Tudor, Stuart and Early Georgian Pictures*, no. 150, p. 98.
70. Barnes et al., *Van Dyck*, pp. 459–60.
71. Millar, *Tudor, Stuart and Early Georgian Pictures*, no. 151, pp. 98–9.
72. See Beverley Cuddy, *Cavalier King Charles Spaniels* (1995).
73. Millar, *Tudor, Stuart and Early Georgian Pictures*, no. 152, pp. 99–100; Barnes et al., *Van Dyck*, pp. 479–80, plate IV, 62.
74. Hermitage Museum, St Petersburg, Barnes, *Van Dyck*, no. IV, 55, p. 473.
75. Private collection, see Barnes et al., *Van Dyck*, no. IV, 64, p. 481.
76. P. Zagorin, *Court and Country* (1969); P. Thomas, 'Court and Country under Charles I', in C. Russell ed., *The Origins of the English Civil War* (1973), pp. 168–96; L. Stone, *The Causes of the English Revolution* (1972). For a critique, see Sharpe, *Criticism and Compliment*, pp. 1–22.
77. Jeremy Wood shows that Wharton, a devout puritan, owned between twenty and thirty Van Dycks, J. Wood, 'Van Dyck: A Catholic Artist in Protestant England, and the Notes on Painting Compiled by Francis Russell, Earl of Bedford', in Vlieghe, *Van Dyck*, pp. 167–98.
78. Millar rightly refers to 'a formidable number of replicas and copies', O. Millar, 'The Years in London: Problems and Reassessments', in Vlieghe, *Van Dyck*, p. 130. I am also most grateful to the late Sir Oliver Millar and the late Francis Haskell for stimulating discussions of the distribution of copies of Van Dyck paintings. The subject still requires a full investigation.
79. See, for example, the lists of copies in Barnes et al., *Van Dyck*, nos IV, 45, 46, 53, 55, pp. 460, 462, 472–3.
80. See O. Millar, *The Inventories and Valuations of the King's Goods, 1649–51* (Walpole Society, 43, 1972 for 1970–2). Though familiar evidence for the contents of the royal collection, these inventories have been little used for evidence of who purchased the king's paintings. See below, pp. 427–8.
81. A. Globe ed., *Peter Stent, London Printseller circa 1642–65: Being a Catalogue Raisonné of his Engraved Prints and Books with an Historical and Bibliographical Introduction* (Vancouver, 1985); A. M. Hind, *Engraving in England in the 16th and 17th Centuries: A Descriptive Catalogue with Introductions III: The Reign of Charles I* (1964), p. 1.
82. Bate, *Mysteries of Nature*, pp. 226–34, quotation, p. 232.
83. Vertue, *Catalogue and Description*, p. 73; Hind, *Engraving*, III, pp. 1, 175.
84. Hind, *Engraving*, p. 203, plate 99.
85. The volume was posthumous and effectively ends with the civil war. See the preface by the editors M. Corbett and N. Norton, Hind, *Engraving*, p. v.
86. I have examined collections in the Huntington Library (Richard Bull Granger), the British Museum, the Ashmolean Museum (Sutherland Collection) and Windsor Castle.
87. Hind, *Engraving*, p. 91, plate 46.
88. G. Marcelline, *Epithalamium Gallo-Britannicum* (STC 17038, 1625). The copy in the Bridgewater collection at the Huntington Library (98526) contains this large engraving. It is British Museum Image No. 1003.
89. Horace, *Odes* II, 10, 18–20.
90. See Hind, *Engraving*, p. 203; Vlieghe, *Van Dyck*, fig. 4, p. 171.
91. National Portrait Gallery NPG D16422.
92. Hind, *Engraving*, p. 225, plates 112, 113.
93. Ibid., pp. 228, 233, plates 112, 113.
94. Huntington Library, Richard Bull Granger, Vol. VI, no. 62; Hind, *Engraving*, pp. 108–9, plate 54.

95. Hind, *Engraving*, p. 102.

96. Peter Heylyn, *The Historie of that Most Famous Saint and Souldier of Christ Iesus; St. George of Cappadocia* (STC 13273, 1633).

97. Sharpe, *Personal Rule*, pp. 219-22; below, pp. 242-3.

98. Hind, *Engraving*, p. 253, plate 133.

99. Ibid., pp. 361-2, plate 205.

100. Ibid., p. 342, plates 180a, b.

101. Thomas Heywood, *The Hierarchie of the Blessed Angells Their Names, Orders and Offices the Fall of Lucifer with His Angells* (STC 13327, 1635), opposite p. 407.

102. James Yorke, *The Union of Honour Containing the Armes, Matches and Issues of the Kings, Dukes, Marquesses and Earles of England from the Conquest, Untill this Present Yeere, 1640* (STC 26103, 1640), title page and see p. 55. Hind, *Engraving* III, ch. 27b, p. 194; John Thornborough, *A Discourse Shewing the Great Hapinesse that Hath and May Still Accrue to His Majesties Kingdomes of England and Scotland by Re-uniting Them Into One Great Britain* (Wing T1042A, 1641), title page.

103. Vertue, *Catalogue and Description*, p. 57; Millar, *Abraham Van der Doort's Catalogue*, p. 124.

104. Vertue, *Catalogue and Description*, p. 28; Millar, *Abraham Van der Doort's Catalogue*, p. 97.

105. Millar, *Abraham Van der Doort's Catalogue*, pp. 137-41.

106. Ibid., pp. 134-5; R. Lightbown, 'Charles I and the Tradition of European Princely Collecting', in MacGregor, *The Late King's Goods*, p. 65.

107. H. Farquhar, 'Portraits of the Stuarts on the Royalist Badges', *British Numismatic Journal*, 2 (1906), p. 3.

108. A. Franks and H. Grueber, *Medallic Illustrations of the History of Great Britain* (2 vols, 1885), I, p. 238, no. 1; E. Hawkins, *Medallic Illustrations of the History of Great Britain* (1904-11), plate XIX, nos 7-11. For variants of this medal, see J. Peacock, 'The Visual Image of Charles I', in T. Corns ed., *The Royal Image: Representations of Charles I* (Cambridge, 1999), pp. 188-9; Farquhar, 'Portraits of the Stuarts', pp. 10-11.

109. Franks and Grueber, *Medallic Illustrations*, I, p. 243, nos. 10, 11; Hawkins, *Medallic Illustrations*, plate XX, nos. 1, 2.

110. Franks and Grueber, *Medallic Illustrations*, I, p. 252, no. 32; Hawkins, *Medallic Illustrations*, plate XX, no. 13.

111. Franks and Grueber, *Medallic Illustrations*, I, p. 250, no. 26; Hawkins, *Medallic Illustrations*, plate XX, nos 8-10

112. Franks and Grueber, *Medallic Illustrations*, I, p. 253, no. 33; Hawkins, *Medallic Illustrations*, plate XX, no. 14; see Barnes, *Van Dyck*, no. IV, 58, p. 475.

113. Franks and Grueber, *Medallic Illustrations*, I, p. 254, no. 36; Hawkins, *Medallic Illustrations*, plate XX, no. 17.

114. Franks and Grueber, *Medallic Illustrations*, I, p. 254, no. 37; Hawkins, *Medallic Illustrations*, plate XX, no. 18.

115. Franks and Grueber, *Medallic Illustrations*, I, pp. 254, 256-7, nos 37, 40-3; Hawkins, *Medallic Illustrations*, plate XXI nos 1, 2; John Selden, *Ioannis Seldeni Mare Clausum Seu De Dominio Maris Libri Duo* (STC 22175, 1635).

116. Franks and Grueber, *Medallic Illustrations*, I, pp. 265-6, no. 59; Hawkins, *Medallic Illustrations*, plate XXII, nos 1-2; Farquhar, 'Portraits of the Stuarts', p. 34.

117. Franks and Grueber, *Medallic Illustrations*, I, pp. 265-6, nos 59-61; Hawkins, *Medallic Illustrations*, plate XXII, 1, 2.

118. Franks and Grueber, *Medallic Illustrations*, I, p. 265, no. 59.

119. Ibid., I, p. 266, no. 62; Hawkins, *Medallic Illustrations*, plate XXII, no. 3. Cf. the engraving discussed above, p. 214.

120. Franks and Grueber, *Medallic Illustrations*, I, pp. 267-8, no. 64; Hawkins, *Medallic Illustrations*, plate XXII, nos 5-7.

121. Franks and Grueber, *Medallic Illustrations*, I, p. 273, no. 72; Hawkins, *Medallic Illustrations*, plate XXII, no. 13.

122. Above, pp. 196, 205.

123. Franks and Grueber, *Medallic Illustrations*, I, p. 281, no. 87; Hawkins, *Medallic Illustrations*, plate XXIII, no. 9.

124. Franks and Grueber, *Medallic Illustrations*, I, p. 281, no. 88; Hawkins, *Medallic Illustrations*, plate XXIV, no. 1.

125. Hind, *Engraving*, p. 7; above, p. 179.

126. Franks and Grueber, *Medallic Illustrations*, I, p. 282, no. 89; Hawkins, *Medallic Illustrations*, plate XXIV, no. 2.

127. Franks and Grueber, *Medallic Illustrations*, I, pp. 278-9, 285, nos 80-1, 97; Hawkins, *Medallic Illustrations*, plate XXIV, no. 10.

128. Franks and Grueber, *Medallic Illustrations*, I, p. 282, no. 90; Hawkins, *Medallic Illustrations*, plate XXIV, no. 3.
129. Franks and Grueber, *Medallic Illustrations*, I, pp. 282-3, nos 91-4; above, ch. 2, pp. 83-4.
130. Franks and Grueber, *Medallic Illustrations*, I, p. 288, no. 102; Hawkins, *Medallic Illustrations*, plate XXIV, no. 14.
131. Below, part III.
132. *Cal. Stat. Pap. Dom., 1625-6*, p. 32; D. F. Allen, 'Abraham Vandedort and the Coinage of Charles I', *Numismatic Chronicle*, 6th ser., I (1941), pp. 54-76, especially pp. 59-61.
133. Allen, 'Abraham Vandedort', pp. 65-6.
134. Ibid., p. 71; O. E. C. Theobald, *A Short Numismatic History of King Charles I* (1948), p. 2.
135. J. J. North, *English Hammered Coinage II* (1991), p. 20; Allen, 'Abraham Vandedort', pp. 57, 74-5.
136. J. J. North, *English Hammered Coinage II* (1975), pp. 129, 132, 141.
137. Ibid., pp. 134-5; J. J. North and P. J. Preston Morley, *Sylloge of Coins of the British Isles 33: The John G. Brooker Collection; Coins of Charles I* (1984), plate XX.
138. North and Preston Morley, *Coins of Charles I*, pp. xxiii, xxv.
139. North, *English Hammered Coinage*, p. 132.
140. Ibid., pp. 169-70. The inscriptions translate as 'Defender of the faith' and 'One will rule both'.
141. North and Preston Morley, *Coins of Charles I*, pp. xlvii-viii; plate cxxi.
142. Below ch. 10, pp. 361-3.
143. See Simon Thurley, *Whitehall Palace An Architectural History of the Royal Apartments, 1240-1698* (New Haven and London, 1999), p. 91 and ch. 6 *passim*.
144. John Burgh to Viscount Scudamore, 24 Feb. 1626, NA C115/N4/8606.
145. Thurley, *Whitehall*, p. 91.
146. M. Whinney, 'John Webb's Drawings for Whitehall Palace' (Walpole Society, 31, 1946), pp. 45-107; J. Harris, S. Orgel and R. Strong, *The King's Arcadia: Inigo Jones and the Stuart Court* (1973), p. 138; R. Strong, *Britannia Triumphans: Inigo Jones, Rubens and Whitehall Palace* (1980), pp. 60-1, fig. 57.
147. Sharpe, *Personal Rule*, p. 213; Thurley, *Whitehall*, p. 91.
148. For details of them, see H. M. Colvin, *The History of The King's Works Volume IV, 1485-1660 (Part II)* (1982), pp. 334-9.
149. For a full exposition, see Per Palme, *The Triumph of Peace: A Study of the Whitehall Banqueting House* (1957), pp. 248-67.
150. Robert Powell, *The Life of Alfred, or, Alvred: the First Institutor of Subordinate Government in This Kingdome, and Refounder of the University of Oxford Together with a Parallell of Our Soveraigne Lord, K. Charles Untill This Yeare, 1634* (STC 20161, 1634), p. 145.
151. J. Harris and G. Piggot, *Inigo Jones: Complete Architectural Drawings* (1989), p. 193. In a forthcoming publication Simon Thurley will demonstrate that part of the renovations included a bedchamber in the French style. I am grateful to him for this information and many helpful discussions.
152. Ibid., p. 220; Colvin, *King's Works*, pp. 216-17.
153. Colvin, *King's Works*, pp. 118-21.
154. Harris and Piggot, *Inigo Jones*, p. 226.
155. Sharpe, *Personal Rule*, pp. 322-8.
156. Harris and Piggot, *Inigo Jones*, p. 238.
157. Ibid., pp. 238-9; Sharpe, *Personal Rule*, pp. 322-4.
158. S. Orgel and R. Strong eds, *Inigo Jones: The Theatre of the Stuart Court* (2 vols, Berkeley and London, 1973), I, p. 668, fig. 334.
159. *The Jewes High Commondation of the Metropolitant Cathedrall Church of St. Paul* (Wing J741, 1638).
160. Nicola Smith, *The Royal Image and the English People* (Aldershot, 2001), p. 72.
161. See D. Howarth, 'Charles I, Sculpture and Sculptors', in MacGregor, *Late King's Goods*, pp. 73-113.
162. H. Peacham, *The Compleat Gentleman* (STC 19504, 1634), pp. 107-8.
163. Howarth, 'Charles I', p. 84.
164. Quoted in Howarth, *Images of Rule*, p. 180.
165. Howarth, 'Charles I', p. 90; Smith, *Royal Image*, p. 73.
166. Howarth, 'Charles I', p. 90; Smith, *Royal Image*, p. 141, n. 59; K. A. Esdaile, 'The Busts and Statues of Charles I', *Burlington Magazine*, 91 (1949), pp. 9-14 (see figs 12,13); K. Sharpe, 'Archbishop Laud and the University of Oxford', in H. Lloyd-Jones, V. Pearl and B. Worden eds, *History and Imagination: Essays in Honour of H. R. Trevor-Roper* (1981), pp. 146-64.
167. Howarth, 'Charles I', p. 91 and n. 105.
168. Ibid., p. 92; Smith, *Royal Image*, p. 73.
169. Howarth, 'Charles I', p. 92; Smith, *Royal Image*, p. 75.

170. Howarth, 'Charles I', p. 92.
171. Smith, *Royal Image*, p. 72.
172. Ibid.
173. Howarth, 'Charles I', p. 85; M. Whinney, *Sculpture in Britain, 1530–1830* (1988), p. 88.
174. Howarth, 'Charles I', pp. 92–3; below ch. 10, pp. 350–1; ch. 13, p. 477.

7 Performing Sacred Kingship

1. J. Richards, ' "His Nowe Majestie" and the English Monarchy : The Kingship of Charles I before 1640', *Past & Present*, 113 (1986), pp. 70–96, quotations, pp. 78, 86. The first critique of this misleading article was mounted by Mark Kishlansky, see Kishlansky, 'Charles I: A Case of Mistaken Identity', *Past & Present*, 189 (2005), pp. 41–80, an important article which has largely met with a hostile reception.
2. Richards, ' "His Nowe Majestie" ', pp. 82–3.
3. Andres Almansa y Mendoza, *The Ioyfull Returne, of the Most Illustrious Prince, Charles, Prince of Great Brittaine, from the Court of Spaine Together With a Relation of His Magnificent Entertainment in Madrid and On His Way to St. Anderas, by the King of Spaine* (STC 5025, 1623), p. 37.
4. Ibid., p. 38.
5. Ibid., p. 42.
6. J. Woodward, *The Theatre of Death: The Ritual Management of Royal Funerals in Renaissance England, 1570–1625* (Woodbridge, Suffolk, 1997).
7. Ibid., ch. 10.
8. Ibid., p. 179.
9. J. Williams, *Great Britains Salomon: A Sermon Preached at the Magnificent Funerall, of the Most High and Mighty King, Iames, the Late King of Great Britaine* (STC 25723, 1625), pp. 75–6.
10. Woodward, *Theatre of Death*, p. 187.
11. Ibid., pp. 194–5.
12. Ibid., pp. 196–8. Malcolm Smuts has informed me that the Exchequer accounts give the cost at nearer to £30,000, not including expenditures from other sources.
13. *Cal. Stat. Pap. Dom. 1625–6*, p. 19.
14. Woodward, *Theatre of Death*, p. 196.
15. *Cal. Stat. Pap. Venet. XIX, 1625–6*, no. 38, p. 30.
16. *Cal. Stat. Pap. Dom. 1625–6*, pp. 19, 22.
17. *A True Discourse of All the Royal Passages, Tryumphs and Ceremonies, Obserued at the Contract and Mariage of the High and Mighty Charles, King of Great Britaine, and the Most Excellentest of Ladies, the Lady Henrietta Maria of Burbon* (STC 5030, 1625), p. 26.
18. Ibid., pp. 28–9.
19. Ibid., pp. 29–32.
20. Ibid, p. 32.
21. Ibid., sig. C1^v (interrupted pagination).
22. Ibid., sig. C4.
23. Ibid., p. 32 (resumed but not sequential pagination).
24. Ibid., p. 31.
25. Ibid., p. 33.
26. Ibid.
27. Ibid., p. 35.
28. Ibid.
29. Richards, ' "His Nowe Majestie", p. 82; R. M. Smuts, 'Public Ceremony and Royal Charisma: The English Royal Entry in London, 1485–1642', in A. L. Beier, D. Cannadine and J. Rosenheim eds, *The First Modern Society: Essays in English History in Honour of Lawrence Stone* (Cambridge, 1989), pp. 65–93 *passim*.
30. *Cal. Stat. Pap. Dom. 1625–6*, p. 179.
31. Ibid., p. 230.
32. D. Bergeron, *English Civic Pageantry, 1558–1642* (1971), pp. 106–7.
33. Correr and Contarini reported to the Doge and Senate of Venice that 'owing to the scarcity of money the king has given up his procession through London which was arranged for his coronation', *Cal. Stat. Pap. Venet. XIX, 1625–6*, no. 640, p. 464.
34. K. Sharpe, *The Personal Rule of Charles I* (New Haven and London, 1992), p. 105.
35. See S. R. Gardiner, *History of England: From the Accession of James I to the Outbreak of the Civil War, 1603–1642* (10 vols, 1884), VI, pp. 24–58.

36. N. E. McClure ed., *The Letters of John Chamberlain* (2 vols, Philadelphia, 1939), II, p. 627.

37. Ibid.

38. *Cal. Stat. Pap. Dom. 1625–6*, p. 225.

39. M. C. Hippeau ed., *Mémoires Inédits du Comte de Tilliers* (Paris, 1892), p. 117; K. Britland, *Drama at the Courts of Queen Henrietta Maria* (Cambridge, 2006), pp. 36–7.

40. See C. Wordsworth, *The Manner of the Coronation of King Charles the First of England* (Bradshaw Society, 1892), pp. v, 6.

41. Ibid., pp. lxii, 87. For the controversy over Laud's supposed innovations to the service, see W. Scott and J. Bliss eds, *The Works of . . . William Laud, . . . Archbishop of Canterbury* (7 vols, Oxford, 1847–60), IV, pp. 211–19.

42. Below, pp. 238–9.

43. William Drummond, *The Entertainment of the High and Mighty Monarch Charles King of Great Britaine, France, and Ireland, Into His Auncient and Royall City of Edinburgh, the Fifteenth of Iune, 1633* (STC 5023, Edinburgh 1633), p. 9.

44. Ibid., pp. 3, 9, 11, 25.

45. Ibid., pp. 22, 34.

46. Ibid., p. 13.

47. Ibid., p. 35.

48. Ibid., p. 33.

49. *Cal. Stat. Pap. Venet. XXIII, 1632–6*, no. 174, p. 122.

50. Ibid., no. 184, p. 132.

51. F. Steer ed., *Orders for the Household of Charles, Prince of Wales* (Lichfield, 1959).

52. *Cal. Stat. Pap. Venet. XXIV, 1636–9*, no. 336, p. 316.

53. Ibid., no. 346, pp. 322–3; G. Glover, *The Arrivall and Intertainements of the Embassador, Alkaid Jaurar Ben Abdella, With His Associate, Mr. Robert Blake From the High and Mighty Prince, Mulley Mahamed Sheque, Emperor of Morocco* (STC 18165, 1637), p. 8.

54. T. Heywood, *A True Discription of His Majesties Royall and Most Stately Ship Called the Soverain of the Seas, Built at Wolwitch in Kent 1637* (STC 13368, 1638), p. 25.

55. Ibid., pp. 30–3.

56. Ibid., pp. 40–1; Sharpe, *Personal Rule*, pp. 717–30.

57. *Cal. Stat. Pap. Venet. XXIV, 1636–9*, no. 709, p. 577.

58. Sharpe, *Personal Rule*, p. 827 and ch. 14 *passim*.

59. M. de La Serre, *Histoire de L'entree de la Reyne Mere du Roy Tres Chrestien, Dans la Grande-Bretaigne Enrichie de Planches. Par le Sr. de la Serre, Historigraphe de France* (STC 20488, 1639) sigs B1–4. La Serre's sumptuously illustrated folio, with engravings of the Presence Chamber at St James's, was the first such lavish record of its kind and may have influenced the post-Restoration vogue for richly illustrated accounts of coronations.

60. Ibid., sigs B4^v, C2, D1.

61. Ibid., sig. F3.

62. Ibid., sigs F3, G1.

63. Ibid., sig. H1^v.

64. Ibid., sig. H4^v.

65. Ibid., sig. L2.

66. For one Robert Woodforde who was alarmed, see Sharpe, *Personal Rule*, p. 846.

67. Thomas Hurste, *The Descent of Authoritie: Or, The Magistrates Patent From Heaven Manifested in a Sermon Preached at Lincolnes Assizes, March 13. 1636. By Thomas Hurste Dr. of Divinity, and One of His Majesties Chaplains* (STC 14007, 1637), p. 15.

68. Above, pp. 161–73.

69. M. P., *An Exact Description of the Manner How His Maiestie and His Nobles Went to Parliament, on Munday, the Thirteenth Day of Aprill, 1640, To The Comfortable Expectation of All Loyall Subiects to the Tune of Triumph and Ioy* (STC 19230, 1640).

70. *Cal. Stat. Pap. Venet. XXV, 1640–2*, nos 291, 296, pp. 251, 254–5.

71. John Taylor, *Englands Comfort and Londons Ioy Expressed in the Royall Triumphant and Magnificent Entertainment of Our Dread Soveraigne Lord, King Charles* (Wing T456, 1641), p. 2.

72. *Cal. Stat. Pap. Venet. XXV, 1640–2*, p. 254 claims 600. See also *Ovatio Carolina: The Triumph of King Charles, Or the Triumphant Manner and Order, of Receiving His Maiesty into His City of London, on Thursday the 25th. Day of November, Anno Dom. 1641, Upon His Safe and Happy Return from Scotland* (Thomason E238/4, 1641), pp. 5–9.

73. Taylor, *Englands Comfort*, p. 3.

74. *Cal. Stat. Pap. Venet. XXV, 1640–2*, p. 254.

75. Ibid.

76. Ibid.; Taylor, *Englands Comfort*, p. 5.

77. Taylor, *Englands Comfort*, p. 6.
78. Ibid., p. 7.
79. *Cal. Stat. Pap. Venet. XXV, 1640–2*, p. 254.
80. See S. R. Gardiner ed., *Constitutional Documents of the Puritan Revolution* (Oxford, 1906), pp. 202–32.
81. In a depleted House, the Remonstrance passed by 158 votes to 149.
82. *Ovatio Carolina*, pp. 3, 30 and *passim*.
83. Marc Bloch, *The Royal Touch: Sacred Monarchy and Scrofula in England and France* (1973), pp. 170, 207–8.
84. Richards, ' "His Nowe Majestie" ', pp. 86–93.
85. *Cal. Stat. Pap. Dom. 1625–6*, p. 22; J. L. Larkin, *Stuart Royal Proclamations, II: Royal Proclamations of King Charles I, 1625–1646* (Oxford, 1983), no. 17, pp. 44–5.
86. Larkin, *Proclamations*, II, p. 44.
87. Ibid.
88. See Charles I to Sir William Parkhurst, Warden of the Mint, *Cal. Stat. Pap. Dom. 1635*, p. 1.
89. Larkin, *Proclamations*, II, no. 45, p. 95; cf. no. 91, p. 196, June 1628; *Cal. Stat. Pap. Dom. 1628–9*, p. 165.
90. Larkin, *Proclamations*, II, no. 116, pp. 238–9.
91. Ibid., no. 126, pp. 256–7.
92. Ibid., nos 145, 151, pp. 310–11, 330–1.
93. Ibid., no. 152, pp. 332–3.
94. Ibid., no. 158, pp. 349–50.
95. *Cal. Stat. Pap. Dom. 1631–3*, p. 347.
96. *Cal. Stat. Pap. Dom. 1634–5*, pp. 216, 357; *Cal. Stat. Pap. Dom. 1635*, pp. 35, 296.
97. Larkin, *Proclamations*, II, nos 226, 242, 245, pp. 531–2, 567, 574; cf. no. 224, pp. 528–9.
98. Ibid., II, no. 266, pp. 621–2; *Cal. Stat. Pap. Dom. 1635*, p. 1.
99. Richards, ' "His Nowe Majestie" ', p. 93.
100. On the plague, see Sharpe, *Personal Rule*, pp. 621–5.
101. *Cal. Stat. Pap. Dom.1645–7*, p. 393.
102. Larkin, *Proclamations*, II, p. 621.
103. Richards, ' "His Nowe Majestie" ', p. 92.
104. *To the Kings Most Excellent Majesty: The Humble Petition of Divers Hundreds of the Kings Poore Subjects, Afflicted with That Grievous Infirmitie, Called the Kings Evill. Of Which By His Majesties Absence They Have No Possibility of Being Cured, Wanting All Meanes to Gaine Accesse to His Majesty, By Reason of His Abode at Oxford* (Thomason E90/6, 1643); F. Madan, *Oxford Books: A Bibliography of Printed Works relating to the University and City of Oxford: Oxford Literature, 1651–1680* (2 vols, 1912–31), II, p. 219.
105. *Humble Petition*, pp. 5, 6, 8.
106. O. Millar, *Abraham Van der Doort's Catalogue of the Collections of Charles I* (Walpole Society, 37, 1960), p. 124; G. Vertue, *A Catalogue and Description of King Charles the First's Capital Collection of Pictures, Limnings, Statues, Bronzes, Medals and Other Curiosities* (1757), p. 56; A. McGregor ed., *The Late King's Goods: Collections, Possessions and Patronage of Charles I in the Light of Commonwealth Inventories* (Oxford, 1989), p. 251.
107. Andres Almansa de Mendoza, *Two Royall Entertainments, Lately Given to the Most Illustrious Prince Charles, Prince of Great Britaine, By the High and Mighty Philip the Fourth King of Spaine, &c. At the Feasts of Easter and Pentecost* (STC 533, 1623), pp. 6–7.
108. Thomas Herbert, *Memoirs of the Last Two Years of the Reign of Charles I* (1873), p. 146.
109. Elias Ashmole, *The History of the Most Noble Order of the Garter* (1715), p. 182.
110. O. Millar, *The Age of Charles I* (1972), no. 84, pp. 56–7.
111. Sharpe, *Personal Rule*, p. 219.
112. Vertue, *Catalogue and Description*, pp. 11, 22, 32; O. Millar ed., *The Inventories and Valuations of the King's Goods* (Walpole Society, 43, 1972), p. 245.
113. A. MacGregor ed., *The Late King's Goods: Collections, Possessions and Patronage of Charles I in the Light of Commonwealth Inventories* (Oxford, 1989), pp. 252–3.
114. Ashmole, *History of the Garter*, p. 148.
115. Ibid., p. 444.
116. Ibid., p. 438.
117. M. P., *A Briefe Description of the Triumphant Show Made by the Right Honourable Aulgernon Percie, Earle of Northumberland at His Installation and Intiation into the Princely Fraternitie of the Garter, Upon the 13. of May, 1635. To the Tune of Quell the Pride* (STC 19221, 1635). This broadside description clearly suggests a popular audience. W. Knowler ed., *The Earl of Strafforde's Letters and Despatches* (2 vols, 1739), I, p. 427.

118. M. P., *A Briefe Description.*
119. Ashmole, *History of the Garter,* p. 483; Sharpe, *Personal Rule,* p. 220.
120. Ashmole, *History of the Garter,* pp. 319–20.
121. Sharpe, *Personal Rule,* fig. 23, pp. 222–3.
122. *Cal. Stat. Pap. Venet. XXII, 1629–32,* no. 407, p. 331.
123. *Cal. Stat. Pap. Venet. XXIII., 1632–6,* nos 291, 452, 482, pp. 218, 355, 389.
124. Francis Malthus, *A Treatise of Artificial Fire-works Both for Warres and Recreation With Divers Pleasant Geometricall Obseruations, Fortifications, and Arithmeticall Examples* (STC 17217, 1629), sig. A4; John Babington, *Pyrotechnia or A Discourse of Artificiall Fire-works in Which the True Grounds of that Art Are Plainly and Perspicuously Laid Downe* (STC 1099, 1635); John Bate, *The Mysteries of Nature and Art In Foure Severall Parts* (STC 1577, 1634, 2nd edn expanded, 1578, 1635), Book II.
125. T. Middleton, *The Triumphs of Health and Prosperity: A Noble Solemnity Performed Through the City . . . at the Inauguration of . . . the Right Honorable, Cuthbert Hacket, Lord Major of the Famous City of London* (STC 17898, 1626), sig. A3; T. Dekker, *Brittannia's Honor Brightly Shining in Seuerall Magnificent Shewes or Pageants, to Celebrate the Solemnity of the Right Honorable Richard Deane, at His Inauguration into the Majoralty of the Honourable Citty of London, on Wednesday, October 29th. 1628* (STC 6493, 1628), sig. B3. On these entertainments, see Bergeron, *English Civic Pageantry,* pp. 171–4, 197–200.
126. John Taylor, *The Triumphs of Fame and Honour, or The Noble Accomplish'd Solemnity, Full of Cost, Art and State, at the Inauguration and Establishment of the True Worthy and Right Nobly Minded Robert Parkhurst, into the Right Honourable Office of Lord Maior of London* (STC 23808, 1634), sig. A3ᵛ; Bergeron, *English Civic Pageantry,* pp. 212–16.
127. Taylor, *Triumphs of Fame,* sigs A7ᵛ–A8.
128. T. Heywood, *Londini Artium & Scientiarum Scaturigo: Or Londons Fountaine of Arts and Sciences Exprest in Sundry Triumphs, Pageants, and Showes, at the Initiation of the Right Honorable Nicholas Raynton into the Maiorty of the Famous and Farre Renowned City London* (STC 13347, 1632), sig. B3; Bergeron, *English Civic Pageantry,* pp. 222–5.
129. Above, ch. 3, pp. 104–7.
130. Richards, ' "His Nowe Majestie" ', pp. 83–5.
131. Again, Kishlansky was the first to question them, 'Charles I', pp. 49, 61–70 *passim.*
132. *Cal. Stat. Pap. Dom. 1625–6,* pp. 23, 26; above, p. 215.
133. *Cal. Stat. Pap. Venet. XIX, 1625–6,* nos 209, 244, 246, pp. 139, 165, 169.
134. *Cal. Stat. Pap. Venet. XX, 1626–8,* nos 160, 298, pp. 137, 246.
135. *Cal. Stat. Pap. Venet. XXI, 1628–9,* nos 248, 276, 313, pp. 187, 212–13, 242.
136. *Cal. Stat. Pap. Venet. XXII, 1629–32,* nos 165, 221, 251, pp. 129, 179, 199.
137. Ibid., no. 275, p. 224.
138. Ibid., nos. 374, 376, 407, pp. 300, 303, 332.
139. Ibid., no. 465, p. 379.
140. *Cal. Stat. Pap. Dom. 1631–3,* pp. 90, 107, 119, 128, 134.
141. Bodleian Library Rawlinson MS D49; *Cal. Stat. Pap. Dom. 1633–4,* pp. 61, 83, 88, 92, 100, 122, 126, 127–8, 133, 140, 145, 152. On the progress to Scotland, see Sharpe, *Personal Rule,* pp. 778–83.
142. Sharpe, *Personal Rule,* p. 779.
143. Rawlinson MS D49 *passim.*
144. *Cal. Stat. Pap. Dom. 1633–4,* p. 176.
145. *Cal. Stat. Pap. Dom. 1634–5,* p. 149.
146. *Cal. Stat. Pap. Dom. 1635,* pp. 324, 330, 360; *Cal. Stat. Pap. Venet. XXIII, 1632–6,* no. 489, p. 393
147. *Cal. Stat. Pap. Venet. XXIII, 1632–6,* no. 491, p. 399.
148. Ibid., nos 654, 663, 667, pp. 560, 568, 570.
149. *Cal. Stat. Pap. Venet. XXIV, 1636–9,* nos 62, 65, pp. 60–1, 64; *Cal. Stat. Pap. Dom. 1636–7,* pp. 113–14; see K. Sharpe, 'Archbishop Laud and the University of Oxford', in H. Lloyd-Jones, V. Pearl and B. Worden eds, *History and Imagination: Essays in Honour of H.R. Trevor-Roper* (1981).
150. *Cal. Stat. Pap. Dom. 1636–7,* p. 91.
151. Ibid., p. 92.
152. *Cal. Stat. Pap. Venet. XXIV, 1636–9,* nos 230, 267, pp. 216, 246 and note.
153. Ibid., nos 447, 528, pp. 416, 468 and note; *Cal. Stat. Pap. Dom. 1637–8,* p. 523.
154. *Cal. Stat. Pap. Dom. 1638–9,* p. 544.
155. *Cal. Stat. Pap. Dom. 1639,* p. 421; *Cal. Stat. Pap. Venet. XXIV, 1636–9,* no. 705, p. 572.
156. *Cal. Stat. Pap. Dom. 1637–8,* p. 203.
157. Above, pp. 235–6.
158. Malcolm Smuts has observed that printed accounts of progresses fell away after 1625: I would suggest that they were less popular after Elizabeth's reign. This not only helps to explain why James's and Charles's progresses have featured much less in historical accounts, it also suggests

that the genre of the progress narrative became of less interest to contemporaries than other records of ceremonial occasions. The evidence, however, suggests that progresses themselves were still vital forms of representation and interaction with subjects.

159. H. Wotton, *Panegyrick of King Charles; Being Observations Upon the Inclination, Life, and Government of Our Soveraign Lord the King* (Wing W3645), a translation of *Ad Regem è Scotia Reducem Henrici Wottonij Plausus et Vota* (STC 26010, 1633), p. 21.

160. See K. Sharpe, 'The Image of Virtue: The Court and Household of Charles I, 1625-1642', in D. Starkey ed., *The English Court from the Wars of the Roses to the Civil War* (1987), *passim*; Sharpe, *Personal Rule*, ch. 5 *passim*.

161. On 26 April, the Venetian envoy reported that 'the king observes a rule of great decorum', *Cal. Stat. Pap. Venet. 1625-6*, XIX no. 25, p. 21.

162. William Struther, *A Looking Glasse for Princes and People Delivered in a Sermon of Thankesgiving for the Birth of the Hopefull Prince Charles* (STC 23369, 1632), p. 70.

163. Ibid.

164. Juan de Santa Maria, *Christian Policie Or The Christian Common-wealth Published for the Good of Kings and Princes, and Such as Are in Authoritie Under Them and Trusted With State Affaires . . . Written in Spanish, and Translated in English* (STC 14831, 1632), p. 371.

165. Struther, *Looking Glasse*, p. 70.

166. Sharpe, *Personal Rule*, pp. 210-19.

167. Marcelline, *Epithalamium Gallo-Britannicum* (STC 17308, 1625), p. 10.

168. F. Cevoli, *An Occasionall Discourse Upon an Accident which Befell His Maiesty in Hunting. Composed in Italian, by Francis Cevolus, and Thence Translated into English* (STC 4922, 1635), p. 8.

169. G. Wither, *A Collection of Emblemes, Ancient and Moderne Quickened With Metricall Illustrations, Both Morall and Divine* (STC 25900a, 1635), sig.*3.

170. *Horti Carolini Rosa Altera* (STC 19039, Oxford G, 1640), sig. 4.

171. 'The face of the court was much changed in the King, for King Charles was temperate, chaste and serious, so that the fools and bawds, mimics and catamites of the former court grew out of fashion', Lucy Hutchinson, *Memoirs of the Life of Colonel Hutchinson*, ed. C. H. Firth (2 vols, New York, 1885), I, pp. 119-20.

172. See Sharpe, *Personal Rule*, pp. 659-65; for an important case, compare J. A. Guy, 'The Origins of the Petition of Right Rediscovered', *Historical Journal*, 25 (1982), pp. 289-312 and M. Kishlansky, 'Tyranny Denied: Charles I, Attorney General Heath, and the Five Knights' Case', *Historical Journal*, 42 (1999), pp. 53-83.

173. Bacon, 'Of Judicature', in Bacon, *The Essayes or Counsels, Ciuill and Morall, of Francis Lo. Verulam, Viscount St. Alban* (STC 1148, 1625 edn), p. 324.

174. William Lilly, *Monarchy or No Monarchy in England. Grebner His Prophecy Concerning Charles Son of Charles, His Greatnesse, Victories, Conquests* (E638/17, 1651), p. 75.

175. Wotton, *Panegyrick*, p. 82.

176. Robert Powell, *The Life of Alfred, or, Alvred: the First Institutor of Subordinate Government in This Kingdome, and Refounder of the University of Oxford Together with a Parallell of Our Soveraigne Lord, K. Charles Untill This Yeare, 1634* (STC 20161, 1634), pp. 122, 136, 138-9.

177. Bulstrode Whitelocke, *Memorials of the English Affairs* (1682), p. 24.

178. Sharpe, *Personal Rule*, pp. 758-64.

179. H. King, *A Sermon Preached at St. Pauls March 27. 1640 Being the Anniversary of His Majesties Happy Inauguration to His Crowne* (STC 14970, 1640), p. 55.

180. Ibid., p. 57.

181. James Howell, *Dendrologia Dodona's Grove, or, The Vocall Forest* (H3061, 1649), p. 211.

182. Henry Parker, *The Case of Shipmony Briefly Discoursed* (STC 19216, 1640), p. 26. On Parker, see M. Mendle, *Henry Parker and the English Civil War: The Political Thought of the Public's 'Privado'* (Cambridge, 1995).

183. Above, ch. 3, pp. 115-18.

184. Sharpe, *Personal Rule*, pp. 275-84 and ch. 6 *passim*.

185. Thomas Laurence, *A Sermon Preached Before the Kings Maiestie at White-Hall, the VII. of February, 1636. By Thomas Lawrence D. of Divinity, and Chaplaine to His Maiestie in Ordinarie* (STC 15327, 1637), p. 12.

186. Above, p. 568, n. 2.

187. NA Signet Office SO 1/2, f. 73.

188. Larkin, *Proclamations*, nos 92, 105, pp. 197-8, 218-20.

189. *Articles Agreed Upon by the Archbishops and Bishops of Both Prouinces, and the Whole Cleargie: in the Conuocation Holden at London, in the Yeere 1562 For the Auoiding of Diuersities of Opinions, and For the Stablishing of Consent Touching True Religion* (STC 10051, 1628).

190. Ibid., pp. 1-6.

191. Henry Leslie, *A Sermon Preached Before His Maiesty at Wokin, on Tuesday the xxviij. of August. 1627. By Henry Lesly, One of His Maiesties Chaplaines in Ordinarie* (STC 15495, 1627), p. 7; on Leslie, see *ODNB*.

192. Wotton, *Panegyrick*, pp. 54-5.

193. Powell, *Life of Alfred*, pp. 103-4, 150-1.

194. H. Peacham, *The Duty of all True Subiects to Their King as Also to Their Native Countrey, in Time of Extremity and Danger. With Some Memorable Examples of the Miserable Ends of Perfidious Traytors* (STC 19505, 1639), sig.*4; Henry Valentine, *God Save the King: A Sermon Preached in St. Pauls Church the 27th. of March 1639. Being the Day of His Maiesties Most Happy Inauguration, and of His Northerne Expedition* (STC 24575, 1639), p. 32.

195. King, *Sermon*, p. 48.

196. Anthony Stafford, *The Guide of Honour* (STC 23124.5, 1634), p. 12.

197. Cf. J. Morrill, 'The Religious Context of the English Civil War', *Transactions of the Royal Historical Society*, 5th ser., 34 (1984), pp. 155-78; see also Morrill, 'The Church in England 1643-9', in Morrill ed., *Reactions to the English Civil War, 1642-1649* (1982), pp. 89-114.

198. Above, p. 234; Sharpe, *Personal Rule*, pp. 280-1.

199. As has been argued by Julian Davies in *The Caroline Captivity of the Church: Charles I and the Remoulding of Anglicanism, 1625-1641* (Oxford, 1992).

200. Sharpe, *Personal Rule*, pp. 328-33. My argument has not met with acceptance but hitherto there has been no published engagement with the evidence presented.

201. Robert Skinner, *A Sermon Preached Before the King at White-Hall, the Third of December. By Robert Skinner Chaplaine in Ordinary to His Maiestie* (STC 22628, 1634), p. 35.

202. Laurence, *Sermon*, p. 30.

203. *The Jewes High Commondation of the Metropolitant Cathedrall Church of St. Paul* (Wing J741, 1638); J. Maltby, *Prayer Book and People in Elizabethan and Early Stuart England* (Cambridge, 1998), pp. 113-24 and chs 3-5 *passim*; Morrill, 'The Church in England 1643-9'.

204. Cf. Christopher Hill, *The Economic Problems of the Church: From Archbishop Whitgift to the Long Parliament* (Oxford, 1956).

205. Larkin, *Proclamations*, no. 121, pp. 248-50.

206. Sharpe, *Personal Rule*, pp. 322-8.

207. Ibid., pp. 392-402.

208. Ibid., pp. 317-22; As well as my own researches, I am grateful to Christopher Haigh for allowing me to see unpublished papers and for discussions on early Stuart churchwardens' accounts.

209. Huntington Library Hastings MS 5537; Edward Hyde, Earl of Clarendon, *The History of the Rebellion and Civil Wars in England*, ed. W.D. Macray (6 vols, Oxford, 1888), I, p. 126.

210. Powell, *Life of Alfred*, pp. 106-9, 117-23.

211. *Jewes High Commondation*.

212. A. Foster, 'The Clerical Estate Revitalised', in K. Fincham ed., *The Early Stuart Church, 1603-1642* (Basingstoke, 1993), pp. 139-60; Sharpe, *Personal Rule*, pp. 393-9.

213. D. Cressy, *England on Edge: Crisis and Revolution, 1640-1642* (Oxford, 2006), chs 7, 8.

214. As Cressy shows, the reaction began in 1640 (ch. 11).

215. Cf. M. James, *English Politics and the Concept of Honour, 1485-1642* (*Past & Present*, Supplement, 3, 1978).

216. Above, ch. 3, pp. 109-10.

217. A. Young, *Tudor and Jacobean Tournaments* (1987), pp. 183-4.

218. T. Cogswell, *The Blessed Revolution; English Politics and the Coming of War, 1621-1624* (Cambridge, 1989).

219. J. Taylor, *A Liuing Sadnes, in Duty Consecrated to the Immortall Memory of Our Late Deceased Albe-loued Soueraigne Lord, the Peereles Paragon of Princes, Iames, King of Great Brittaine* (STC 23772, 1625), pp. 4-5; Marcelline, *Epithalamium*, pp. 7, 20: 'no man is able to perform any warlike action, either on horse or foot more strongly' (p. 20).

220. Francis Hamilton, *King Iames his Encomium. Or A Poeme, In Memorie and Commendation of the High and Mightie Monarch Iames; King of Great Britaine. France, and Ireland* (STC 12726, Edinburgh, 1626), p. 13; Abraham Holland, *Hollandi Posthuma: A Funerall Elegie of King Iames: With a Congratulatory Salve to King Charles* (STC 13579, 1626), sig. B3ᵛ.

221. K. Sharpe, *Criticism and Compliment: The Politics of Literature in the England of Charles I* (Cambridge, 1987), pp. 145-8; R. A. Anselment, 'Clarendon and the Caroline Myth of Peace', *Journal of British Studies*, 23 (1984), pp. 37-54

222. Millar, *Van der Doort's Catalogue*, p. 4.

223. Struther, *Looking Glasse*, p. 78.

224. Ibid., p. 81.

225. Sharpe, *Personal Rule*, pp. 72–3. Charles had initially supported the Earl of Hamilton's expedition to aid Gustavus though he later called him home.

226. On the reform of the militia, see ibid., pp. 487–500.

227. Wotton, *Panegyrick*, pp. 82, 100–2.

228. Powell, *Life of Alfred*, pp. 44–5, 147.

229. William Lithgow, *Scotlands Welcome to Her Native Sonne, and Soveraigne Lord, King Charles* (STC 15716, Edinburgh 1633), sig. A4ᵛ.

230. *Coronae Carolinae Quadratura. Siue Perpetuandi Imperii Carolini ex Quarto Pignore Feliciter Suscepto Captatum Augurium* (STC 19036, Oxford, 1636), sig. A2ᵛ.

231. Cevoli, *An Occasionall Discourse*, p. 2.

232. Ibid., p. 2; above, pp. 192, 205.

233. See, for example, William Davenant's *The Triumphs of the Prince d'Amour A Masque Presented by His Highnesse at His Pallace in the Middle Temple, the 24th of Februarie 1635* (STC 6308, 1635), pp. 4–8.

234. *The King and Queenes Entertainement at Richmond After Their Departure from Oxford: In a Masque, Presented By the Most Illustrious Prince, Prince Charles Sept. 1 1636* (STC 5026, Oxford, 1636), pp. 21, 26.

235. Ibid., p. 26.

236. Sharpe, *Personal Rule*, pp. 519–23; *The Manifest of the Most Illustrious, and Soveraigne Prince, Charles Lodowick, Count Palatine of the Rhine, Prince Electour of the Sacred Empire* (STC 5046, 1637).

237. Thomas Heywood, *A True Description of His Majesties Royall Ship, Built this Yeare 1637. at Wooll-witch in Kent To the Great Glory of Our English Nation, and Not Paraleld in the Whole Christian World* (STC 13367, 1637), sig. A4ᵛ.

238. Ibid., p. 24, my italics.

239. Ibid., p. 29.

240. James Loxley, *Royalism and Poetry in the English Civil Wars: The Drawn Sword* (Basingstoke, 1997), chs 1–2; R. Wilcher, *The Writing of Royalism 1628–1660* (Cambridge, 2001), ch. 6.

241. Van der Doort informs us that, when offered five limned portraits by Lady Killigew, Charles took only the portrait of his father, Millar, *Van der Doort's Catalogue*, p. 113.

242. Vertue, *Catalogue and Description*, pp. 123–5.

243. Ibid., p. 121.

244. Prince Henry, born in 1640, was, of course named to evoke Charles's great Tudor predecessor as well as his brother.

245. *Vitis Carolinae Gemma Altera* (STC 19035, Oxford, 1633), sig. I1ᵛ.

246. Ibid., sig. I3.

247. Ibid.

248. Ibid., sigs L2, L4ᵛ.

249. Powell, *Life of Alfred*, p. 156

250. *Coronae Carolinae Quadratura*, sigs A1ᵛ, A3, B2, B3.

251. Ibid., sig. C3ᵛ.

252. *Horti Carolini*, sig. b2.

253. Ibid., sigs c1, d3ᵛ.

254. *Voces Votivae ab Academcis Cantabrigiensibus Pro Novissimo Caroli & Mariae Principe Filio Emissae* (STC 4495, Cambridge, 1640), sig. a3.

255. Ibid., sig. b2ᵛ.

256. See R. Strong, *And When Did You Last See Your Father?: The Victorian Painter and British History* (1978), pp. 136–42.

257. *Horti Carolini*, sigs b4–4ᵛ.

258. K. Sharpe, ' "An Image Doting Rabble" : The Failure of Republican Culture in Seventeenth-century England', in Sharpe, *Remapping Early Modern England: the Culture of Seventeenth-Century Politics* (Cambridge, 2000), pp. 238–9; below, pp. 396–7, 453–4. For evidence of the nation feeling widowed and orphaned, see – *Jeremias Redivivus: or, An Elegiacall Lamentation on the Death of Our English Josias, Charles the First* (E556/33, 1649), p. 2; John Cleveland, *Monumentum Regale or a Tombe, Erected for that Incomparable and Glorious Monarch, Charles the First* (E1217/5, 1649); *Votivum Carolo, or A Welcome to His Sacred Majesty Charles the II. From the Master and Scholars of Woodstock-school in the County of Oxford* (Wing W3475, 1660), sig. A2; Francis Gregory, *David's Returne from His Banishment* (Wing G1888,1660), pp. 24,32, 35 and *passim*; cf. E1217/5.

259. Sharpe, *Selling the Tudor Monarchy: Authority and Image in Sixteenth-Century England* (New Haven and London, 2009), p. 336; above, p. 43.

260. *A True Discourse of All the Royal Passages*, p. 25.

261. The queen was not even permitted to bid them goodbye, Hippeau, *Mémoires Inédits*, pp. 109, 144; Sharpe, *Personal Rule*, p. 168.

262. Marcelline, *Epithalamium*, engraving folded in; *Epithalamium Illustriss. & Feliciss. Principum Caroli Regis, et H. Mariae Reginae Magnae Britanniae, &c. A Musis Cantabrigiensibus Decantatum* (STC 4484, Cambridge, 1625), p. 64.

263. Marcelline, *Epithalamium*, p. 111.

264. R. A. Anselment, *Loyalist Resolve: Patient Fortitude in the English Civil War* (Newark, Delaware, 1988), p. 27.

265. John Wing, *The Crowne Conjugall, or The Spouse Royal: A Discovery of the True Honour and Happinesse of Christian Matrimony* (STC 25845, 1632).

266. Wither, *A Collection of Emblemes*, sig.(*)3ᵛ.

267. *Coronae Carolinae Quadratura*, sig. C3.

268. Thomas Heywood, *The Royall King, and the Loyall Subject As it Hath Beene Acted With Great Applause by the Queenes Maiesties Servants. Written by Thomas Heywood* (STC 13364, 1637), sig. G1 and *passim*.

269. I have argued this case in *Criticism and Compliment*, ch. 6.

270. Marcelline, *Epithalamium*, pp. 11–12.

271. Struther, *Looking Glasse*, p. 103.

272. Above. ch. 3, pp. 108–10.

273. Sharpe, *Criticism and Compliment*, ch. 5.

274. See E. Veevers, *Images of Love and Religion: Queen Henrietta Maria and Court Entertainments* (Cambridge, 1989); Britland, *Drama at the Courts of Queen Henrietta Maria*.

275. *The Temple of Love* lines 511–13, in S. Orgel and R. Strong, eds, *Inigo Jones. The Theatre of the Stuart Court* (2 vols, Berkeley and London, 1973), II, p. 604.

276. *Coelum Britannicum*, line 279; ibid., II, p. 572. Orgel and Strong, *Inigo Jones*.

277. Ibid., lines 1100–1, p. 579.

278. For all, see Sharpe, *Criticism and Compliment*, pp. 224–56.

279. *Salmacida Spolia*, lines 471–4, Orgel and Strong, *Inigo Jones*, II, p. 734

280. Sharpe, *Criticism and Compliment*, pp. 25–7, 191–2, 216; T. Raylor, *Cavaliers, Clubs, and Literary Culture: Sir John Mennes, James Smith, and the Order of the Fancy* (Newark, Delaware, 1994), especially ch. 10.

281. See G. E. D. Bentley, *The Jacobean and Caroline Stage* (7 vols, Oxford, 1941–68), V, pp. 1156–60.

282. Ibid., p. 1162; see *Cal. Stat. Pap. Venet. XXIII 1632–6*, no. 258, p. 195.

283. Sharpe, *Personal Rule*, pp. 642, 780.

284. Newcastle invited 'all the gentry of the country' to come to the masque entertainment of the king and queen at Bolsover, Bentley, *Jacobean and Caroline Stage*, IV, p. 653.

285. Veevers, *Images of Love*, p. 75; Britland, *Drama at the Courts of Queen Henrietta Maria*, pp. 49–50.

286. Sharpe, *Personal Rule*, pp. 304–6.

287. Ibid., pp. 909–14; C. Hibbard, *Charles I and the Popish Plot* (Chapel Hill, NC, 1983).

288. Marcelline, *Epithalamium*, pp. 63, 81.

289. Ibid., pp. 83–4, 87–9.

290. Ibid., pp. 100, 112.

291. Struther, *Looking Glasse*, pp. 108–9.

292. *Epithalamia Oxoniensia In Auspicatissimum, Potentissimi Monarchae Caroli, Magnae Britanniae, Franciae, et Hiberniae Regis, &c. Cum Henretta Maria, Aeternae Memoriae Henrici Magni Gallorum Regis Filia, Connubium* (STC 19031, Oxford, 1625), sig. C2ᵛ; *Coronae Carolinae Quadratura*, sig. C3.

293. *Vitis Carolinae Gemma Altera*, sig. I2.

294. Ibid., sigs K1ᵛ–2.

295. *Horti Carolini*, sig. a4.

296. Ibid.

297. Howell, *Dendrologia Dodona's Grove*, p. 180.

298. *ODNB*.

299. Marcelline, *Epithalamium*, p. 20.

300. Ibid., pp. 22, 25.

301. Ibid., pp. 22, 33, 105; the motto was on a portrait of Charles aged eighteen, Vertue, *Catalogue and Description*, p. 78.

302. Marcelline, *Epithalamium*, p. 105.

303. Ibid., p. 29.

304. Ibid., p. 33.

305. Powell, *Life of Alfred*, p. 152.

306. See, for example, by Malachi Harris, *Brittaines Hallelujah* (STC 12807, 1639); Thomas Morton, *A Sermon Preached Before the Kings Most Excellent Majestie, in the Cathedrall Church of Durham Upon Sunday, Being the Fifth Day of May. 1639* (STC 18196, 1639) and Valentine, *God Save the King.*

307. *A Remonstrance of the State of the Kingdom. Die Mercurii 15. Decemb. 1641* (Wing E2221D, 1641), pp. 22, 24–5, 28.

8 Demystifying Majesty

1. Matthew Wren, *A Sermon Preached Before the Kings Maiestie on Sunday the Seventeenth of February Last, at White-Hall by Dor Wren, the Master of St Peters Colledge in Cambridge, and His Maiesties Chaplaine. Printed by Command* (STC 26015, Cambridge, 1628), p. 34; Isaac Bargrave, *A Sermon Preached Before King Charles, March 27. 1627. Being the Anniuersary of His Maiesties Inauguration* (STC 1414, 1627), p. 18.

2. A. Ar, *The Practise of Princes* (STC 722, 1630), sig. Aii.

3. Ibid., pp. 7,10.

4. Ibid., p. 11.

5. Ibid., p. 12, a nice example of how a metaphor or analogue with royal valence could be appropriated as criticism.

6. Thomas Beard, *The Theatre of Gods Iudgements Reuised, and Augmented* (STC 1661.5, 1631), pp. 13–17 and *passim*. The work was first published in 1597.

7. Ibid., p. 529. Though we should note that Beard was never in trouble with the authorities and was a JP in Huntingdonshire, *ODNB*.

8. P.M., *King Charles his Birthright* (STC 17145, 1633), sig. A3.

9. *The King and Queenes Entertainement at Richmond After Their Departure From Oxford: In a Masque, Presented by the Most Illustrious Prince, Prince Charles Sept. 1. 1636.* (STC 5026), p. 21.

10. Thomas Morton, *New English Canaan, or New Canaan Containing an Abstract of New England* (STC 18203, 1637), pp. 172, 177.

11. Thomas Hurste, *The Descent of Authoritie: Or, The Magistrates Patent From Heaven Manifested in a Sermon Preached at Lincolnes Assizes, March 13. 1636. By Thomas Hurste Dr. of Divinity, and One of His Majesties Chaplains* (STC 14007, 1637), pp. 5, 13.

12. Ibid., p. 32; Alexander Leighton, *An Appeal to the Parliament; Or Sions Plea Against the Prelacie* (STC 15429, 1629).

13. William Laud, *A Speech Delivered in the Starr-Chamber, on Wednesday, the XIVth of Iune, MDCXXXVII at the Censure, of Iohn Bastwick, Henry Burton, & William Prinn* (STC 15307, 1637), sig. A4.

14. R. Cust, *The Forced Loan and English Politics, 1626–1628* (Oxford, 1987); Sharpe, *The Personal Rule of Charles I* (New Haven and London, 1992), pp. 714–30 and ch. 11 *passim*.

15. Beard, *Theatre of Gods Iudgements*, ch. 38, pp. 448–9.

16. *Coronae Carolinae Quadratura. Siue Perpetuandi Imperii Carolini ex Quarto Pignore Feliciter Suscepto Captatum Augurium* (STC 19036, Oxford, 1636), sig. C3.

17. Sharpe, *Personal Rule*, p. 703; Henry Parker, *The Case of Shipmony Briefly Discoursed* (STC 19216, 1640), pp. 35, 38–9; W. Ralegh, *The Perogative of Parliaments in England* (STC 20650, 1640).

18. Above, pp. 112, 174–5.

19. Sharpe, *Personal Rule*, p. 610.

20. See *The Swedish Intelligencer Wherein … Are the Famous Actions of That Warlike Prince Historically Led Along: From His Majesties First Entring Into the Empire, Untill His Great Victory Over the Generall Tilly, at the Battell of Leipsich* (STC 23522, 1632).

21. Andreas Hildebrandt, *The Genealogie and Pedigree of the Most Illustrious and Most Mighty Kings in Sueden* (STC 13458, 1632), 'To the Reader', at end sig. a1ᵛ.

22. G. Hakewill, *A Sermon Preached at Barstaple Upon Occasion of the Late Happy Success of Gods Church in Forraine Parts* (STC 12620, 1632), p. 32; Sharpe, *Personal Rule*, pp. 646–7.

23. John Russell, *An Elegie Upon the Death of the Most Illustrious and Victorious Prince Gustavus Adolphus King of Swethland* (STC 20573, 1633), broadside.

24. *A Relation of the Funerall Pompe, in which the Body of Gustauus the Great, Late King of Sweden, Was Carryed from the Castle of Vbolgast* (STC 12537, 1633), pp. 9–10 and *passim*.

25. Ibid., p. 12.

26. 'Let Vienn's walls astonished with our cry/ Like stubble before the fire, fall downe and fly', Walter Forbes, *Panegyrick to the High and Mightie Monarch, Charles by the Grace of God, King of Great Britaine, France, and Ireland, Defender of the Faith* (STC 11151.5, Edinburgh, 1633), sig. A4.

27. *Eisodia Musarum Edinensium in Caroli Regis, Musarum Tutani, Ingressu in Scotiam* (STC 7486, Edinburgh, 1633), sig. b2.

28. Jasper Fisher, *Fuimus Troes AEneid. 2. The True Troianes, Being a Story of the Britaines Valour at the Romanes First Inuasion: Publikely Represented by the Gentlemen Students of Magdalen Colledge in Oxford* (STC 10886, 1633).

29. Robert Powell, *The Life of Alfred, or, Alvred: the First Institutor of Subordinate Government in This Kingdome, and Refounder of the University of Oxford Together with a Parallell of Our Soveraigne Lord, K. Charles Untill This Yeare, 1634* (STC 20161, 1634), p. 87.

30. Pierre Matthieu, *The Powerfull Fauorite, or, The Life of Aelius Seianus* (STC 17664, 1628).

31. Ibid., p. 12.

32. Above, p. 181 and see p. 576, n. 295.

33. Copy from Newberry Library, Chicago.

34. Matthieu, *Powerfull Fauorite*, pp. 50, 96.

35. Ibid. p. 113.

36. Hubert, *ODNB* and *DNB*.

37. Francis Hubert, *The Deplorable Life and Death of Edward the Second, King of England Together with the Downefall of the Two Unfortunate Favorits, Gavestone and Spencer* (STC 13900, 1628), p. 11.

38. Ibid., pp. 105–6, my italics.

39. Ibid., pp. 7, 10, 69.

40. D. Norbrook, *Writing the English Republic: Poetry, Rhetoric and Politics, 1627–1660* (Oxford, 1999), ch.1 *passim*.

41. T. May, *A Continuation of Lucan's Historicall Poem Till the Death of Iulius Caesar by TM* (STC 17711, 1630), sig. A7; above, p. 182.

42. D. Primrose, *A Chaine of Pearle: Or A Memoriall of the Peerles Graces, and Heroick Vertues of Queene Elizabeth, of Glorious Memory* (STC 20388, 1630).

43. Ibid., sig. A3ᵛ.

44. Ibid., pp. 3, 6, 9,11, 12 and *passim*.

45. Thomas Heywood, *Englands Elizabeth Her Life and Troubles* (STC 13313, 1631).

46. Ibid., pp. 225–8; cf. epistle to 'the generous reader'.

47. Charles Aleyn, *The Battailes of Crescey, and Poictiers Under the Leading of King Edward the Third of that Name* (STC 351, 1631), sigs A2, A7ᵛ.

48. Samuel Rowlands, *The Famous History of Guy Earle of Warwicke* (STC 21379, 1632), sigs A2–2ᵛ.

49. Ibid., sigs A3ᵛ, A4ᵛ.

50. W.H., *The True Picture and Relation of Prince Henry His Noble and Vertuous Disposition* (STC 12581, 1634), p. 46.

51. Powell, *Life of Alfred*, p. 153.

52. *The Life and Death of Queene Elizabeth from the Wombe to the Tombe, from Her Birth to Her Burial* (STC 7587, 1639), sig. A4.

53. Sharpe, *Personal Rule*, pp. 605–11.

Prologue: The Civil War and the Contest for Representation

1. See J. Raymond, *Pamphlets and Pamphleteering in Early Modern Britain* (Cambridge, 2003), pp. 27–46 and ch. 2 *passim*; Sharpe, *Selling the Tudor Monarchy: Authority and Image in Sixteenth-Century England* (New Haven and London, 2009), chs 6, 12 and pp. 236–40, 305–14 and *passim*.

2. D. Hirst, *The Representative of the People? Voters and Voting in England under the Early Stuarts* (Cambridge, 1975), ch. 9.

3. See 'The Wiper of the People's Tears', above, ch. 1, p. 35.

4. R. Cust, *Charles I: A Political Life* (2005), pp. 170–1.

5. K. Sharpe, *The Personal Rule of Charles I* (New Haven and London, 1992), pp. 644–54.

6. See C. Hill, 'Censorship and English Literature', in Hill, *Collected Essays, I: Writing and Revolution in Seventeenth-Century England* (Brighton, 1985), pp. 32–71; B. Worden, 'Literature and Political Censorship in Early Modern England', in A. C. Duke and C. Tamse eds, *Too Mighty To Be Free* (Zutfen, 1988), pp. 45–62; S. Lambert, 'The Printers and the Government, 1604–1637', in R. Myers and M. Harris eds, *Aspects of Printing from 1600* (Oxford, 1987), pp. 1–29; A. Milton, 'Licensing, Censorship, and Religious Orthodoxy in Early Stuart England', *Historical Journal*, 41 (1998), pp. 625–51.

7. Above, ch. 5, pp. 137–60.

8. Above, ch. 5, pp. 161–6.

9. See C. Russell, 'Introduction', in Russell ed., *The Origins of the English Civil War* (Basingstoke, 1973), pp. 1–31; Russell, *The Causes of the English Civil War* (Oxford, 1990), pp. 7–8.

10. B. H. G. Wormald, *Clarendon: Politics, Historiography and Religion* (Cambridge, 1989 edn), pp. 34–41, 53–4, 77–80, 83 ff. and *passim*; R. W. Harris, *Clarendon and the English Revolution*

(1983), pp. 83–4 and ch. 5 *passim*; R. Ollard, *Clarendon and his Friends* (1988), pp. 72–81; D. Smith, *Constitutional Royalism and the Search for Settlement, c.1640–1649* (Cambridge, 1994), pp. 88–90, 109–10, 152–4; Hyde, *ODNB*.

11. Above, ch. 4, pp. 125, 129–30.
12. Contemporaries referred to pamphlets as 'paper bullets', see J. Nalson, *An Impartial Collection of the Great Affairs of State* (2 vols, 1682–3), II, p. 809; see Raymond, *Pamphlets and Pamphleteering*, pp. 161–3.
13. See Adrian Johns, *The Nature of the Book: Print and Knowledge in the Making* (Chicago, 1998).
14. A. Globe ed., *Peter Stent, London Printseller circa 1642–65: Being a Catalogue Raisonné of his Engraved Prints and Books with an Historical and Bibliographical Introduction* (Vancouver, 1985), pp. 114, 115, 134, 185, plate 216; A. M. Hind, *Engraving in England in the 16th and 17th Centuries: A Descriptive Catalogue with Introductions III: The Reign of Charles I* (1964), pp. 113, 227, 341, plate 62.
15. Globe, *Peter Stent*, pp. 49–51, 61, 65, 71, 74–5, 77, 84.
16. Ibid., pp. 60–1, 63–6.
17. See below, pp. 342–8, 351–5.
18. I am most grateful to John Adamson for sending me this important chapter of his forthcoming book in advance of publication and for many stimulating discussions.

9 Wars of Words and Paper Bullets

1. *His Majesties Speech to the Committee the 9th of March 1641 When They Presented the Declaration of Both Houses of Parliament at New-market* (Wing C2801, 1642), a broadside.
2. The reference was to the so-called Army Plot, see S. R. Gardiner, *History of England: From the Accession of James I to the Outbreak of the Civil War, 1603–1642* (10 vols, 1883–4), IX, pp. 348–9, X, pp. 73–4; C. Russell, *The Fall of the British Monarchies 1637–1642* (Oxford, 1991), pp. 291–4, 330–7, 350–4.
3. *His Majesties Speech.*
4. *His Maiesties Resolution Concerning the Establishment of Religion and Church-government. Also, His Majesties Speech to the Gentry of the County of York, Attending His Majesty at the City of York, on Thursday the 12. of May. 1642* (STC 2751A, 1642).
5. *His Majesties Answer to the Nineteen Propositions of Both Houses of Parliament* (C2124A, 1642); G. Aylmer, *Rebellion or Revolution? England 1640–1660* (Oxford, 1986), p. 35.
6. *His Maiesties Speech at Leicester, to the Gentlemen, Free-holders, and Inhabitants of That County, July 20* (Wing C2781, 1642), broadside.
7. *His Maiesties Speech to the Gentlemen of Yorkshire, on Thursday the Fourth of August 1642* (C2804, 1642), pp. 2–3.
8. *His Maiesties Speech at Shrewsbury, on Michaelmas Eve Last, to the Gentry and Commons of the County of Salop, There Assembled* (C2782, 1642).
9. *His Majesties Speech to the Inhabitants of Denbigh and Flint-shire. 27. Septemb. 1642* (E200/61, 1642), p. 1.
10. Ibid., p. 4.
11. Ibid., p. 5.
12. Ibid., p. 6.
13. See Peter Young, *Edgehill, 1642: The Campaign and the Battle* (Kineton, 1968).
14. P. Young and R. Holmes, *The English Civil War: A Military History 1642–1651* (1974), pp. 80–3.
15. S. R. Gardiner, *History of the Great Civil War, 1642–1649* (4 vols, 1893), I, ch. 5 *passim*.
16. *His Maiesties Last Speech, to the Lords of His Privie Councell, and Others, at His First Notice of the Intentions of the City of London, Concerning Their Petition for Peace: Wherein Is Briefly Exprest the Royall Disposition of His Excellent Majesty Toward that Honourable City, and His Good Inclination Toward the Kingdome in Generall* (E 83/44, Oxford, 1643), published with crowned royal arms.
17. Ibid., p. 5.
18. Ibid., p. 7.
19. *His Maiesties Last Speech and Protestation which Hee Made on Sunday, the Fifth of This Instant February, in the Cathedrall Church of Oxford the Lords and the Cheife of the University Being Present Before the Receiving of the Sacrament for the Renouncing of Popery: With the Piovs Ioy of a Trve Heart Enlarged on the Contemplation and Assurance of So Great a Happinesse to the Great Comfort of All His Majestye Subjects which Will Live and Dye in the Protestant Religion and Abhorre Popery* (C 2379, Oxford, 1643); *His Majesties Speech Spoken to the Mayor, Aldermen, and Commonaltie of the Citie of Oxford, and to the High Sheriffes of the Counties of Oxford and Berks, With Divers Justices of Peace in the Said Counties, at a Generall Summons. Requesting Their Assistance by Contribution of Money, Plate, and Horses, Towards the Supportment of His Present Wars* (E 84/43, Oxford, 1643).
20. Gardiner, *History of the Great Civil War*, I, chs 8, 9, pp. 179–80.

21. Ibid., pp. 229–35.
22. *His Majesties Speech, Delivered the Twenty Second of Ianuary, 1643 [1644] to the Members of the Two Houses of Parliament at Oxford* (Wing C2785, Bristol, 1644), p. 3.
23. K. Sharpe, *The Personal Rule of Charles I* (New Haven and London, 1992), pp. 804–5.
24. *His Majesties Speech Delivered the Twenty Second of Ianuary, 1643 [1644] to the Members of the Two Houses of Parliament at Oxford* (Wing C2785, Bristol, 1644), p. 5.
25. *Two Severall Copies: The One Being His Majesties Declaration to All Forraine Protestant Churches, Both in Latine and English; the Other His Speech to the Gentry in the West, at a Place Called Kings-Moore Iuly the 23. 1644* (C2861, 1644).
26. Ibid., pp. 6–7.
27. Gardiner, *History of the Great Civil War*, II, ch. 25.
28. Ibid., IV, ch. 58.
29. *A Joyfull Message From the Kings Most Excellent Majesty; Presented to the Parliaments Commissioners on Friday Last, at Newport in the Isle of Wight: Communicating His Further Concessions for a Present Agreement* (Wing C2355, 1648); *The Kings Maiestjes Most Gracious Speech, Declaring His Desires for the Speedy Performance of a Personall Treaty With Both His Honorable Houses of Parliament, For the Establishing a True and Happy Peace* (E 453/42, 1648); *The Kings Majesties Speech Delivered to the Commissioners From the Parliament. Also Collections of Severall Papers of the Transactions of the Treaty* (E 464/28, 1648).
30. *The Last Papers Betwixt His Maiesty, and the Commissioners of Parliament, Concerning Church-government. And His Majesties Speech to the Commissioners, to Be Communicated to Both Houses of Parliament. Dated at Newport 4. Novemb. 1648* (Wing C2375, 1648), p. 6.
31. *His Maiesties Gracious Message to Both Houses of Parliament, on Munday Novemb. 27. Brought by Sir Peter Killegrey* (E 473/26, 1648), p. 5.
32. Ibid.
33. *His Majesties Farewel Speech Unto the Lords Commissioners at Newport in the Isle of Wight* (Thomason 669 f. 13/ 51, 1648), one page.
34. Ibid.
35. Above, ch. 5, pp. 161–6.
36. *His Maiesties Royall Declaration and Protestation to all His Loving Subjects in England Being a Full Satisfaction to All the Whole World Against All Aspersions Which Have Lately Been Cast Upon His Majesty, That He Is Popishly Affected, To the Great Dishonour of His Majesty and the Withdrawing His Loving Subjects From Him: Together With His Gracious Resolution for the Maintenance of the True Protestant Religion, the Laws and Liberties of the Subject with the Just Priviledges of Parliament* (Wing C2763, Oxford, 1642).
37. Ibid., sig. A2.
38. Ibid., sig. A2, my italics.
39. Ibid., sig. A2^v.
40. *Declaratio Serenissimi Potentissimique Principis Caroli Magnae Britanniae &c. Regis Ultra-marinis Protestantium Ecclesiis Transmissa* (Wing C2175, 1644); *His Majesties Declaration, Directed to All Persons of What Degree and Qualitie Soever, in the Christian World. With a Letter from Divers Godly Ministers of the Church of England, to the Assembly of the Kirk of Scotland Shewing the Cause of These Troubles* (Wing C2199, 1644). This translation undermines the king's declaration, as it reproduces it.
41. *His Majesties Declaration*, sig. A2.
42. Ibid.
43. *His Majesties Declaration to All His Loving Subjects, Concerning His Gracious Inclination for Peace* (E 404/33, 1647).
44. Ibid., p. 2.
45. Ibid., p. 3.
46. Ibid., pp. 3–4; *His Maiesties Last Speech* (E 83/44).
47. Ibid., p. 4.
48. Gardiner, *History of the Great Civil War*, III, ch. 49.
49. *A Declaration by the Kings Majestie Concerning His Majesties Going Away from Hampton-Court Written By His Own Hand and Left Upon the Table in His Majesties Bed-chamber, Dated at Hampton-Court Novemb. 11, 1647* (Wing C2189, 1647), p. 3. The title emphasizes the authenticity and sincerity of the king's words.
50. Ibid., pp. 2–3, 5.
51. *The Kings Declaration to All His Subjects of Whatsoever Nation, Quality, or Condition* (Wing C2264A, 1648).
52. Ibid., p. 1.
53. Ibid. Charles compared himself with the 'meanest of my subjects' here.
54. Ibid., p. 2.

55. Ibid., p. 5.
56. Ibid, pp. 4, 6.
57. On the second civil war, see R. Ashton, *Counter-Revolution: The Second Civil War and its Origins, 1646–8* (New Haven and London, 1994).
58. For the events, see D. Underdown, *Pride's Purge: Politics in the Puritan Revolution* (Oxford, 1971).
59. *Vindex Anglicus; Or The Perfections of the English Language Defended, and Asserted* (Wing V461, Oxford, 1644), p. 3. I owe this reference to Jerome de Groot, *Royalist Identities* (Basingstoke, 2004), p. 64.
60. *Vindex Anglicus*, p. 3.
61. J. L. Larkin ed., *Stuart Royal Proclamations, II: Royal Proclamations of King Charles I, 1625–1646* (Oxford, 1983), p. xi.
62. De Groot, *Royalist Identities*, p. 31.
63. Ibid., p. 29.
64. Ibid., p. 31.
65. Ibid., p. 32.
66. Larkin, *Proclamations*, II, no. 328, pp. 757–8.
67. Ibid., no. 337, pp. 767–9.
68. Ibid., no. 339, pp. 770–5; S. R. Gardiner, *Constitutional Documents of the Puritan Revolution, 1628–1660* (Oxford, 1889), pp. 166–8; cf. the king's proclamation condemning the ordinance, ibid., pp. 169–70.
69. Larkin, *Proclamations*, II, no. 339, pp. 771–5, quotation, p. 774; *His Majesties Answer to the Nineteen Propositions*.
70. Larkin, *Proclamations*, II, no. 341, pp. 777–81.
71. Ibid., nos 342–5, pp. 781–90.
72. Ibid., p. 789.
73. Ibid., nos 346, 348, pp. 790–4, 797–9.
74. For example, ibid., p. 797.
75. Ibid., no. 351, p. 804; cf. nos 352–63, pp. 805–17.
76. Ibid., p. 804.
77. Ibid., no. 377, pp. 830–1.
78. Ibid., no. 401, pp. 869–71.
79. Ibid., no. 409, pp. 883–6.
80. Ibid., no. 404, p. 876.
81. Ibid., nos 404, 424, pp. 876–8, 909–11.
82. Ibid., no. 416, pp. 896–8.
83. Ibid., no. 425, pp. 911–18.
84. Ibid., p. 912.
85. Ibid., p. 913.
86. Ibid., pp. 913–16.
87. Ibid., p. 917.
88. Ibid., no. 434, pp. 932–4.
89. Ibid., no. 427, pp. 920–3.
90. Ibid., no. 449, pp. 956–7.
91. Ibid., no. 465, pp. 987–90, quotation, p. 988.
92. 'Where all our good subjects shall see how willing we are to receive advice for the preservation of the religion, laws and safety of the kingdom . . . and to restore it to . . . former peace and security' (p. 988).
93. Ibid., p. 989.
94. Ibid.
95. For example, ibid., nos 482, 486, pp. 1018–20, 1025–6.
96. Ibid., no. 489, pp. 1028–30.
97. Ibid., no. 502, pp. 1044–6.
98. Ibid., no. 503, pp. 1046–9.
99. Ibid., p. 1047.
100. Ibid., p. 1048.
101. Gardiner, *History of England*, II, ch. 25.
102. Larkin, *Proclamations*, II, no. 509, pp. 1055–6.
103. Ibid., p. 1056; *A Forme of Common-prayer, To Be Used Upon the Solemne Fast, Appoynted By His Majesties Proclamation Upon the Fifth of February, Being Wednesday. For a Blessing On the Treaty Now Begunne, That the End of It May Be a Happy Peace to the King and to All His People. Set Forth by His Majesties Speciall Command to Be Used in All Churches and Chappels* (E 27/4, Oxford, 1645); below, n. 110.
104. See Gardiner, *Constitutional Documents*, pp. 205–6.

105. Larkin, *Proclamations*, II, no. 515, pp. 1063–5.
106. Ibid., p. 1064.
107. Ibid., no. 518, pp. 1068–71.
108. It was a proclamation for 'preventing of disorders in the night-time' in the garrison of Oxford, ibid., no. 519, pp. 1071–2.
109. De Groot, *Royalist Identities*, p. 30.
110. K. Sharpe, *Selling the Tudor Monarchy: Authority and Image in Sixteenth-Century England* (New Haven and London 2009), ch. 9, pp. 330–3; above, pp. 35–8, 145-50.
111. W. Shaw, *A History of the English Church during the Civil Wars and under the Commonwealth 1640–1660* (2 vols, 1900) I, ch. 1; J. Morrill, 'The Attack on the Church of England in the Long Parliament', in D. Beales and G. Best eds, *History, Society and the Churches* (Cambridge, 1985), pp. 105–24; J. Morrill, 'The Church in England,' in J. Morrill ed., *Reactions to the English Civil War* (Basingstoke, 1982), pp. 89–114; D. Cressy, *England on Edge: Crisis and Revolution 1640–1642* (Oxford, 2006), chs 8–11 *passim*.
112. *A Collection of Prayers and Thanksgivings, Used in His Majesties Chappel, and in His Armies. Upon Occasion of the Late Victories Against the Rebells, and for the Future Successe of the Forces. Published by His Maiesties Command, to Be Duly Read in all Other Churches and Chappels Within This His Kingdome, and Dominion of Wales* (E 69/6, 1643).
113. Ibid., p. 1.
114. Ibid., pp. 2–5.
115. Ibid., p. 3.
116. Ibid., pp. 5–6.
117. Ibid., p. 8.
118. Ibid., pp. 10–13.
119. *Mercurius Davidicus, or A Patterne of Loyall Devotion Wherein King David Sends His Pietie to King Charles, His Subjects. Being the Practice of the Primitive Christians, Martyrs, and Confessors, in All Ages; Very Fitting to Be Used Both Publick and Private in These Disloyall Times. Likewise Prayers and Thanksgivings Used in the Kings Army Before and After Battell. Published by His Majesties Command* (E 1144/7, 1643), pp. 2, 6 and *passim*.
120. Ibid., pp. 7, 12.
121. *The Cavaliers New Common-Prayer Booke Unclasp't It being a collection of Prayers and Thanksgivings Used in His Majesties Chappell and in His Armies* (Wing C1578, York and London 1643).
122. Ibid., p. 2.
123. Ibid.
124. Ibid., p. 3.
125. Ibid., p. 4.
126. Ibid., p. 14.
127. Ibid., pp. 7,16.
128. *Two Prayers, One for the Safety of His Majesties Person: The Other for the Preservation of This University and City of Oxford: To Be Used in All Churches and Chappells* (Wing D2667, Oxford, 1644), p. 2. Duppa had been appointed Bishop of Chichester in 1638 and wrote several prayers issued under the king's name, *ODNB*.
129. *Certain Prayers Fitted to Severall Occasions. To be Used in His Majesties Armies, and Garrisons. Published by His Highnesse Command* (E 296/25, 1645), pp. 1, 11.
130. Ibid., p. 16.
131. Ibid.,
132. *Private Formes of Prayer, Fit for These Sad Times. Also a Collection of All the Prayers Printed Since These Troubles Began* (E 1176/3, Oxford, 1645), p. 8. The volume recalls Queen Elizabeth's *Precationes Privatae*, see Sharpe, *Selling the Tudor Monarchy*, pp. 330–1.
133. *Private Formes of Prayer*, pp. 10, 25. Psalm 72: 1.
134. *Private Formes of Prayer*.
135. Ibid., p. 60.
136. Ibid., p. 61.
137. *Certain Prayers Fitted to Severall Occasions. And Are to Be Used in His Majesties Armies. Published by His Highnesse Command* (E 1146/5, 1648), p. 1.
138. Ibid., p. 5.
139. Ibid., pp. 7, 9–11.
140. Ibid., pp. 12–20.
141. The prayer is printed in *The Kings Majesties Speech Delivered to the Commissioners from the Parliament. Also Collections of Severall Papers of the Transactions of the Treaty* (E464/28, 1648), pp. 3–4.

142. *Prince Charles, His Letany and Prayers for the King of Great Britane in His Sad Condition* (Wing C3121, 1648).

143. Ibid., title page.

144. Ibid., sig. B4ᵛ.

145. Ibid., sigs A4ᵛ, B4. Psalm 55: 3.

146. E. Skerpan Wheeler, '*Eikon Basilike* and the Rhetoric of Self-Representation', in T. Corns ed., *The Royal Image: Representations of Charles I* (Cambridge, 1999), pp. 122–40; see below, ch. 12, pp. 391–400.

147. Ian Donaldson ed., *Ben Jonson Poems* (Oxford, 1974), pp. 8–9.

148. See K. Sharpe, *Criticism and Compliment: The Politics of Literature in the England of Charles I* (Cambridge, 1987), pp. 27–9 and chs 2–4, *passim*; A. Guibbory, *Ceremony and Community from Herbert to Milton: Literature, Religion, and Cultural Conflict in Seventeenth-century England* (Cambridge, 1998).

149. T. Raylor, *Cavaliers, Clubs, and Literary Culture: Sir John Mennes, James Smith, and the Order of the Fancy* (Newark, NJ, 1994); *Poems By Thomas Carew Esquire* (STC 4620, 1640); *Fragmenta Aurea: A Collection of all the Incomparable Peeces, Written by Sir John Suckling* (Wing S6126A, 1646); *Poems, &c. Written by Mr. Ed. Waller* (Wing W511, 1645); *Poems by J. C., With Aditions* (Wing C4686, 1651); *Hesperides or, The Works Both Humane & Divine of Robert Herrick, Esq* (Wing H1595, 1648); *Il Pastor Fido. The Faithfull Shepheard With an Addition of Divers Other Poems, Concluding with a Short Discourse of the Long Civill Warres of Rome ... by Richard Fanshawe, Esq* (Wing G2175, 1648); *Lucasta Epodes, Odes, Sonnets, Songs, &c. To Which Is Added Aramantha, a Pastorall. By Richard Lovelace, Esq* (Wing L3240, 1649).

150. De Groot, *Royalist Identities*, p. 69.

151. J. Loxley, *Royalism and Poetry in the English Civil Wars: The Drawn Sword* (Basingstoke, 1997) chs 2, 3; R. Wilcher, *The Writing of Royalism, 1628–1660* (Cambridge, 2001), chs. 6–9 *passim*; T. Corns, *Uncloistered Virtue: English Political Literature, 1640–1660* (Oxford, 1992), chs 4, 7. See also L. Potter, *Secret Rites and Secret Writing: Royalist Literature, 1641–1660* (Cambridge, 1989).

152. Corns, *Uncloistered Virtue*, pp. 91–128.

153. Ibid., p. 109.

154. Ibid., pp. 68–70.

155. J. Howell, *The Vote, Or A Poeme Royall Presented to His Maiestie for a New-Yeares-Gift, by Way of Discourse, 'Twixt the Poet and His Muse* (Wing H3128, 1642); above ch. 5, p. 181.

156. Ibid., pp. 1–2.

157. Ibid., p. 4.

158. Ibid., pp. 4–5.

159. Ibid., p. 9.

160. Ibid. Chief Justice Sir John Finch had referred to the prerogatives as 'the flowers of the crown' in his judgment in the ship money case of 1638. See J. W. Gough, 'Flowers of the Crown', *English Historical Review*, 77 (1962), pp. 86–93.

161. For emphasis on Royalist poetry as retreat, see Earl Miner, *The Cavalier Mode from Jonson to Cotton* (Princeton, 1971).

162. Loxley, *Royalism and Poetry*, ch. 2. See A. Rudrum, 'Royalist Lyric', in N. Keeble ed., *The Cambridge Companion to Writing of the English Revolution* (Cambridge, 2001), pp. 181–97.

163. Loxley, *Royalism and Poetry* pp. 75–6.

164. Ibid., p. 79.

165. Ibid., pp. 90, 113; de Groot, *Royalist Identities*, pp. 150–3.

166. De Groot, *Royalist Identities*, p. 112; See R. Hutton, *The Rise and Fall of Merry England: The Ritual Year, 1400–1700* (Oxford, 1994), ch. 6.

167. W. Davenant, *Gondibert: An Heroick poem* (Wing D324, 1651). Part of Cowley's poem was published in 1679, *ODNB*. See de Groot, *Royalist Identities*, pp. 121–3; Loxley, *Royalism and Poetry*, pp. 86–8.

168. John Denham, *Coopers Hill. A Poeme* (E 109/11, 1642); Henry Glapthorne, *White-hall, A Poem Written 1642* (Wing G840, 1642). Denham, the son of a judge, had been a witness for the defence at Strafford's trial, *ODNB*. Glapthorne, who dedicated verse to Strafford, was a 'noble friend' of the courtier Lovelace. His poem evoked the world of masque and the Caroline court of the personal rule, *ODNB*.

169. Glapthorne, *White-hall*, sigs A3, B4.

170. P. Hausted, *Ad Populum: Or A Lecture to the People* (E 49/2, Oxford 1644); Loxley, *Royalism and Poetry*, pp. 101–2; Hausted was a clergyman who joined the Royalists as a chaplain, *ODNB*.

171. Hausted, *Ad Populum*, p. 2.

172. Ibid., pp. 3, 6 and *passim*.

173. Ibid., p. 4.

174. Ibid., p. 6.

175. Ibid., pp. 14–16.
176. Loxley, *Royalism and Poetry*, p. 102.
177. B. Capp, *The World of John Taylor the Water Poet* (Oxford, 1994), pp. 171–82.
178. J. Taylor, *The Kings Most Excellent Majesties Welcome to His Owne House, Truly Called the Honour of Hampton Court* (E 404/31, 1647), pp. 4–6.
179. Loxley, *Royalism and Poetry*, p. 129; below, pp. 312–16.
180. Martin Lluellyn, *A Satyr, Occasioned by the Author's Survey of a Scandalous Pamphlet Intituled, The King's Cabanet Opened* (E296/1, Oxford, 1645); de Groot, *Royalist Identities*, p. 73.
181. Lluellyn, *A Satyr*, pp. 1–2.
182. Cf. Loxley, *Royalism and Poetry*, pp. 130–5.
183. Lluellyn, *A Satyr*, p. 10.
184. Ibid.
185. M. Lluellyn, *Men-Miracles. With Other Poemes* (E 1163/1, Oxford, 1646).
186. Loxley, *Royalism and Poetry*, pp. 142–5.
187. See also *His Maiesties Complaint. Occasioned by His Late Sufferings, and a Not Right Understanding Between Him and His Parliament. Commanded to be Printed and Published* (E 393/38, 1647).
188. Loxley, *Royalism and Poetry*, p. 182.
189. Milton, *Eikonoklastes*, in D. M. Wolfe ed., *Complete Prose Works of John Milton* (8 vols, New Haven and London, 1953–82), III, p. 406.
190. They were the principal sources used, for example, in the influential works of Christopher Hill.
191. De Groot rightly observes that even to this day 'there has been little sustained work on loyalism as a cultural or social phenomenon', *Royalist Identities*, p. 3.
192. *The Iust Reward of Rebels, Or The Life and Death of Iack Straw, and Wat Tyler, Who for Their Rebellion and Disobedience to Ther King and Country, Were Suddenly Slaine, and All Their Tumultuous Rout Overcome and Put to Flight* (E 136/1, 1642), sig. B4 and *passim*.
193. T.J., *A Medicine For the Times. Or, An Antidote Against Faction* (E 135/33, 1642); cf. John Taylor, *The Diseases of the Times Or, the Distempers of the Common-wealth Succinctly Describing Each Particular Disease Wherin the Kingdome Is Troubled* (E 136/6, 1642).
194. George Raleigh, *Albania or, Certaine Concernments of Great Britanny. With an Explication of the Present State Thereof; Truely Represented Under the Faigned Person of Albania* (E 179/16, 1641).
195. J. Taylor, *A Plea for Prerogative: Or, Give Caesar His Due* (E 154/22, 1642).
196. James Barlow, *A Deep Sigh Breath'd Through the Lodgings at White-hall, Deploring the Absence of the Court, and the Miseries of the Palace* (E 119/30, 1642).
197. Ibid., pp. 1,3; cf. below pp. 370–1.
198. Francis Quarles, *A Plea for the King* (E 85/29, Oxford, 1642), p. 1.
199. Ibid., pp. 2–4.
200. *Certain Considerations Upon the Duties Both of Prince and People. Written by a Gentleman of Quality, a Wel-wisher Both to the King and Parliament* (E 85/4, 1642). The tract has been attributed to Sir John Spelman.
201. Ibid., pp. 5–7 and *passim*.
202. Edward Fisher, *An Appeale to Thy Conscience: As Thou Wilt Answere It At the Great and Dreadfull Day of Christ Iesus* (E 99/4, 1643), p. 11 and *passim*. On Fisher, see *ODNB*.
203. Ibid., p. 18.
204. Ibid., p. 22.
205. Ibid., pp. 33–7.
206. Ibid., p. 38.
207. *A Rationall Discourse of the Cause of the Present War, With a Faire Paterne for a Good Peace* (E 99/9, 1643). The injunction is from 1 Peter 2: 17.
208. *To the Kings Most Excellent Majesty: The Humble Petition of Divers Hundreds of the Kings Poore Subjects, Afflicted With That Grievous Infirmitie, Called the Kings Evill. Of Which By His Majesties Absence They Have No Possibility of Being Cured, Wanting All Meanes to Gaine Accesse to his Majesty, By Reason of His Abode at Oxford* (E 90/6, 1643); see below p. 374.
209. *A Discourse, or Parly, Continued Betwixt Partricius and Peregrine (Upon Their Landing in France) Touching the Civill Wars of England and Ireland* (E 61/14, 1643), p. 4. This has been attributed to James Howell.
210. Ibid., pp. 4, 7.
211. Ibid., p. 7.
212. Ibid., p. 8.
213. Ibid., p. 12.
214. *Christus Dei, the Lords Annoynted, Or, A Theologicall Discourse Wherein Is Proved, That the Regall or Monarchicall Power of Our Soveraigne Lord King Charles Is Not of Humane, But of Divine Right,*

and That God Is the Sole Efficient Cause Thereof, and Not the People: Also That Every Monarch Is Above the Whole Common-wealth, and Is Not Onely Major Singulis, But Major Universis: Written in Answer to a Late Printed Pamphlet Intituled, Observations Upon Some of His Maiesties Late Answers and Expresses (E 92/4, Oxford 1643). Thomason's copy is illustrated with an engraving of Charles I and announces that it was printed at the king's command.

215. Ibid., p. 11.

216. *Mercurius Davidicus, or A Patterne of Loyall Devotion Wherein King David Sends His Pietie to King Charles, His Subjects* (E 1144/7, 1643), pp. 6–7.

217. Ibid., p. 8; see below pp. 395–6.

218. *The Kings Cause Rationally, Briefly, and Plainly Debated, as it Stands Defacto. Against the Irrationall, Groundlesse Misprisions of a Still Deceived Sort of People* (E 39/2, 1644). The tract has been ascribed to the clergyman John Doughty (*ODNB*).

219. Ibid., pp. 7, 30, 31.

220. Ibid., pp. 33–4.

221. Ibid., p. 45.

222. Francis Quarles, *The Shepheards Oracle: Delivered in an Eglogue* (E 52/2, 1644). See below, p. 343.

223. Ibid., sig. A1ᵛ.

224. Ibid., pp. 3–5, 8–9.

225. Ibid., pp. 11, 14.

226. Anarchus claims to 'keep the gentry down' and 'make Joan as good as my lady', ibid., p. 11.

227. *Englands Teares, For the Present Wars* (E 253/10, 1644), sigs A3–A3ᵛ, p. 1.

228. Ibid., pp. 11, 12, 14.

229. *An Orderly and Plaine Narration of the Beginnings and Causes of This Warre. Also a Conscientious Resolution Against the Warre on the Parliaments Side* (E 54/3, Oxford, 1644). The epigraph is from Proverbs 24: 21.

230. Ibid., pp. 1–6.

231. Ibid., pp. 9–14.

232. Ibid., p. 17.

233. Ibid., pp. 21–2.

234. Ibid., p. 24.

235. N.D., *Vindiciae Caroli Regis: Or, a Loyall Vindication of the King. In Answer to The Popish Royall Favourite. Wherein (As in a Christall Glasse) Is Presented the Reflection of His Majesties Actions, Since the Beginning of His Raigne* (E 257/4, 1644); W. Prynne, *The Popish Royall Favourite: Or, a Full Discovery of His Majesties Extraordinary Favours To, and Protections Of Notorious Papists, Priestes, Jesuites, Against All Prosecutions and Penalties of the Laws Enacted Against Them Notwithstanding His Many Royall Proclamations, Declarations, and Protestations to the Contrary* (E 251/6, 1643).

236. Ibid., p. 64.

237. *Transcendent and Multiplied Rebellion and Treason, Discovered, by the Lawes of the Land* (E 308/29, Oxford, 1645), p. 25. This tract has been ascribed to Edward Hyde.

238. *The Perswasion of Certaine Grave Divines, (Most of Them of the Assembly) to Such as Suffer for the King, That They Persevere in Their Sufferings* (E 26/19, Oxford, 1645), pp. 17, 19.

239. Ibid., p. 34.

240. Ibid.

241. *The Ballance Put Into the Hand of Every Rationall English-man, to Poize the State of This Kingdome; Supposed to Bee Deformed in the Yeare 1639. Cryed Up to Be Reformed in the Yeare 1646* (E 381/8, 1647).

242. Ibid., pp. 1–4.

243. Ibid., p. 5.

244. Ibid., p. 6.

245. *The Cavaliers Diurnall Written by Adventure, Most Perfectly Collected (peradventure) for Any Mans Reading, That Will Venture* (E 383/4, 1647), p. 5. The appeal was clearly intended to be broad.

246. *A Letter Really Written by a Moderate Cavallier to an Intelligent and Moderate Independent of Trust and Credit in the Now Marching Army. Occasioned by a Discourse Between Them Entertained at London, June 16th Concerning the Present Grand Affaire* (E 394/4, 1647), pp. 5–6. One notes the much more moderate and reasonable tone of this pamphlet after years of vitriolic polemic.

247. Robert Grosse, *Royalty and Loyalty or A Short Survey of the Power of Kings Over their Subjects: and the Duty of Subjects to Their Kings. Abstracted Out of Ancient and Later Writers, for the Better Composeing of These Present Distempers: and Humbly Presented to ye Consideration of His Ma.tie. and Both Howses of Parliament, For the More Speedy Effecting of a Pacification / by Ro: Grosse dd: 1647* (E 397/ 3, 1647). This is the only tract by Grosse, about whom nothing is known.

248. Ibid., p. 25.

249. Ibid., pp. 21, 62.

250. Ibid., p. 3.

251. Michael Hudson, *The Divine Right of Government: 1. Naturall, and 2. Politique. More Particularly of Monarchie; the Onely Legitimate and Natural Spece of Politique Government. Wherein the Phansyed State-principles Supereminencing Salutem Populi Above the Kings Honour: and Legitimating the Erection of Polarchies, the Popular Elections of Kings and Magistrats, and the Authoritative and Compulsive Establishment of a National Conformity in Evangelical and Christian Dutyes, Rites, and Ceremonies, Are Manifested to be Groundlesse Absurdities Both in Policy and Divinity* (E 406/24, 1647). The traditional appeal to the natural and divine (the 'sacred preroga-tives' of God and king) is here combined with arguments from 'policy'. Hudson was a clergyman and Royalist agent and pamphleteer whose writings deserve fuller study (*ODNB*).

252. *The Mirrour of Allegiance. Or A Looking-Glasse For the English, Wherein They May Reade Their Duty Towards God and Their King* (E 398/26, 1647).

253. Ibid., p. 24; Genesis 10: 1. In Book I, ch. 3 of his chronicle, Holinshed described the first kings of Britain as Samotheans after Samothes who was, in fact, the sixth son of Japheth.

254. Ibid., pp. 25 ff., 37–9, and *passim*.

255. *Anti-Machiavell. Or, Honesty Against Policy* (E 396/16, 1647). On attitudes to Machiavelli during the civil war, see Felix Rabb, *The English Face of Machiavelli* (1964), chs 4, 5.

256. *Anti-Machiavell*, p. 1.

257. Ibid., p. 16.

258. See, for example, *The Virgins Complaint for the Losse of Their Sweet-hearts, by These Present Warres, Both in City and Country* (E 351/5, 1646); *The Parliament of Women. With the Merrie Lawes of Them Newly Enacted* (E 1150/5, 1646).

259. See Alexandra Lumbers, 'The Discourses of Whoredom in 17th-century England' (Oxford University D.Phil., 2005), especially ch. 4. I am grateful to Dr Lumbers for permitting me to read her thesis and for stimulating discussions of this subject.

260. See, for example, Phyllis Mack, *Visionary Women: Ecstatic Prophecy in Seventeenth-Century England* (Berkeley, 1992), ch. 3; *A Spirit Moving in the Women-Preachers: or, Certaine Quaeres, Vented and Put Forth Unto This Affronted, Brazen-faced, Strange, New Feminine Brood. Wherein They Are Proved to Be Rash, Ignorant, Ambitious, Weake, Vaine-glorious, Prophane and Proud, Moved Onely By the Spirit of Errour* (E 324/10, 1646). See also Stevie Davies, *Unbridled Spirits: Women of the English Revolution* (1998), pp. 21–31; A. Plowden, *Our Women All On Fire: The Women of the English Civil War* (Stroud, 1998); A. McAntee, ' "The [Un]civill-Sisterhood of Oranges and Lemons" : Female Petitioners and Demonstrators, 1642–1653', in J. Holstun ed., *Pamphlet Wars: Prose in the English Revolution* (1992), pp. 92–111.

261. *The Maids Petition. To the Honourable Members of Both Houses. Or The Humble Petition of Many Thousands of the Well-affected . . . Virgins, Maids, and Other Young Women Not Married, &c. And in the Behalf of the Whole Kingdome, for Their Lawfull Dayes of Recreation. With Their Declaration, to Hold Out Stifly, and to Comply With the Apprentices or Others for their Tollerable Toleration* (E 401/26, 1647), pp. 2–5. As well as the title, the tract is littered with references to 'stiff standing' and so on.

262. Ibid., pp. 5–6.

263. G[eorge] W[harton], *Grand Pluto's Progresse Through Great Britaine, and Ireland* (E 405/16, 1647), p. 11 margin; cf. pp. 8–9. Wharton went on to edit Royalist newspapers, *ODNB*.

264. Edward Symmons, *A Vindication of King Charles: Or, A Loyal Subjects Duty. Manifested in Vindicating His Soveraigne From Those Aspersions Cast Upon Him by Certaine Persons* (E 414/17, 1647). Symmons, a loyal clergyman, was to hand the text of *Eikon Basilike* to the printer, *ODNB*.

265. 'To all that truly fear God', ibid., sigs a2–a2ᵛ.

266. Ibid., p. 67.

267. Ibid., sig. a4.

268. Ibid., p. 83.

269. Ibid., pp. 95–105 *passim*.

270. *The Royall, and the Royallist's Plea. Shewing, that the Kings Majesty Hath the Chiefe Power in This Realme, and Other His Dominions* (E 390/19, 1647), pp. 1 and *passim*. This has been ascribed to Michael Hudson, *ODNB*.

271. See, for example, Wharton, *Grand Pluto's Progresse*, p. 11; *King Charles His Royall Welcome, at His Happy and Gracious Return Towards His Parliament* (E 377/2, 1647), p. 4.

272. 'Let thy exemplary conversation convert or confound all thine enemies', ibid., p. 3.

273. John Hall, *A True Account and Character of the Times, Historically and Politically Drawn by a Gentleman to Give Satisfaction to His Friend in the Countrey* (E 401/13, 1647), p. 7.

274. Below, pp. 328–38.

275. See, for example, *An Ordinance From His Maiesty, and Both Houses of Parliament. For the Ordering of the Militia of the Kingdome of England and Dominion of Wales* (E 135/37, 1642); *A Declaration or Ordinance of the Lords and Commons Assembled in Parliament. Concerning the Taking of Horses For the Service of the Parliament* (E 101/16, 1643).

276. *All the Ordinances and Declarations of the Lords and Commons Assembled in Parliament, For the Assessing of All Such As Have Not Contributed Upon the Propositions of Both Houses of Parliament* (E 1200, 1642), p. 2; *All the Severall Ordinances and Orders Made by the Lords and Commons Assembled in Parliament, Concerning Sequestring the Estates of Delinquents, Papists, Spyes, and Intelligencers Together With Instructions For Such Persons As Are Imployed in Sequestring of Such Delinquents Estates* (E 1202, 1642). Ordinances are printed in C. H. Firth and R. S. Rait eds, *Acts and Ordinances of the Interregnum, 1642-1660* (3 vols, London, 1911), 1. In several cases, I cite the originals because I am interested in the material form and visual appearance of the ordinance to seventeenth-century readers.

277. *All the Severall Ordinances* (E1202), p. 3.

278. *An Exact Collection of all Remonstrances, Declarations, Votes, Orders, Ordinances, Proclamations, Petitions, Messages, Answers, and Other Remarkable Passages Betweene the Kings Most Excellent Majesty, and His High Court of Parliament Beginning at His Majesties Return from Scotland Being in December 1641* (E 1532, 1642).

279. Ibid., after p. 955.

280. *A Declaration of the Lords and Commons Assembled in Parliament: Concerning Coales and Salt . . . Also, Two Ordinances of Great Consequence, 1. That Whosoever Shall Assist His Majesty in This Warre, With Horse, Armes, Plate, or Money, Are Traytors to His Majesty, the Parliament, and Kingdome. 2. That the Houses of Delinquents Shall Not Bee Plundered, Pulled Downe, or Destroyed, But Reserved For the Benefit and Advantage of the Common-wealth* (E 81/29, 1643), pp. 4-5.

281. *Foure Ordinances of the Lords and Commons Assembled in Parliament Concerning the Weekly Assessment* (E 1543A, 1643), p. 1; *An Ordinance of the Lords and Commons Assembled in Parliament: To Inable the Right Honourable, Edward, Earle of Manchester, To Put in Execution All Former Ordinances For Sequestering Delinquents Estates* (E 71/26, 1643), p. 2; *Two Ordinances of the Lords and Commons Assembled in Parliament* (E 2490 A, 1643), p. 1.

282. *An Ordinance Of the Lords and Commons Assembled in Parliament, For Associating of the Counties of Pembroke, Carmarthen and Cardigan, For the Mutuall Defence and Safety of Each Other* (E 51/1, 1643), p. 3.

283. *Two Ordinances Of the Lords and Commons* (E 2424A, 1645), p. 4.

284. *A Collection Of All the Publicke Orders, Ordinances, and Declarations Of Both Houses of Parliament From the Ninth of March, 1642 Untill December, 1646* (E 878, 1646); *A Breif [sic] Collection, of Some Forgotten Votes of the Commons Alone Of the Lords and Commons Joyntly, and Ordinances of Both Houses, Reprinted To Refresh Their Memories, and Prevent All Dishonourable and Unjust Actions, Repugnant To All, Or Any Of Them* (Thomason 669 f. 11/106, 1647).

285. For example, *An Order Of the Lords and Commons Assembled in Parliament. For the Regulating of Printing, and For Suppressing the Great Late Abuses and Frequent Disorders in Printing Many False, Scandalous, Seditious, Libellous and Unlicensed Pamphlets* (E 196/15, 1643); *An Ordinance of the Lords & Commons Assembled in Parliament, Against Unlicensed or Scandalous Pamphlets, and For the Better Regulating of Printing. 28 Septembr. 1647* (E 409/20, 1647).

286. *An Ordinance*, pp. 4-5.

287. *A Declaration of the Lords and Commons Assembled in Parliament. Concerning the Particular Causes of This Division Betweene His Majestie and the Houses of Parliament. Whereunto Is Annexed the Severall Votes of Both Houses at Which His Majesty Takes Exceptions* (E 154/24, 1642); *A Declaration of the Lords and Commons in Parliament Concerning His Maiesties Late Proclamation* (E 1368, 1642).

288. *A Declaration of the Lords and Commons Assembled in Parliament Setting Forth the Grounds and Reasons that Necessitate Them at This Time To Take Up Defensive Arms For the Preservation of His Majesties Person, the Maintenance of the True Religion, the Laws and Liberties of This Kingdom, and the Power and Priviledge Of Parliament* (E 1450, 1642), p. 3.

289. Ibid., p. 5.

290. Ibid., pp. 9-10.

291. Ibid., pp. 12-15.

292. *The Parliaments Declaration Concerning the Kings Most Excellent Majesty. With the Kings Majesties Determination Concerning the Parliament* (E 2134, 1642), sigs A2^v-3; *A Declaration Of the Lords and Commons Assembled in Parliament Whereby the Good Subjects of This Kingdome May Better Discerne Their Owne Danger and Be Stirred Up With More Earnestnesse To Assist the Parliament in the Maintenance of Religion, the Common Justice and Liberty of the Kingdome* (E 1477, 1642), sigs A2-2^v.

293. *A Declaration Of the Lords and Commons Assembled in Parliament, Concerning the Publishing of Divers Proclamations, and Papers, in Forms of Proclamations in His Majesties Name* (E 1398, 1642), one page.

294. *A Declaration Of the Lords and Commons Assembled in Parliament, Concerning a Late Proclamation of His Majesties, For the Keeping of Trinity Terme at Oxford* (E 104/28, 1643).

295. *The Declaration Of the Kingdomes of England and Scotland Ioyned in Armes For the Vindication and Defence Of Their Religion, Liberties, and Lawes Against the Popish, Prelaticall, and Malignant Party / By the Honourable Houses of the Parliament* (Wing D691, 1644), especially p. 7.

296. *A Declaration Of Both Houses of Parliament Shewing the Necessity of a Present Subscription of Money and Plate, For Further Supply of the Army* (E 85/40, 1643), p. 4.

297. Ibid., pp. 4–5.

298. Ibid., p. 3; *A Declaration Of the Lords and Commons Assembled in Parliament, Concerning the Pressing Necessities of Thes Kingdome* (E 84/33, 1643), sig. A2.

299. *An Ordinance Of the Lords and Commons Assembled in Parliament With Instructions For the Taking of the League and Covenant in the Kingdom of England, and Dominion of Wales. With an Exhortation For the Taking of the Covenant* (E 2110, 1644); cf. *The Declaration of the Kingdomes of England and Scotland, Ioyned in Armes For the Vindication and Defence of their Religion, Liberties, and Lawes, Against the Popish, Prelaticall, and Malignant Party* (E 31/3, 1644) which refers to parliament's 'light of the gospel', in contrast to the apostasy, atheism and idolatry of their enemies.

300. *A Declaration of the Lords and Commons Assembled in Parliament, Concerning His Majesties Late Proclamation Threatning Fire and Sword to All Inhabitants in the County of Oxford and Berks and Parts Adjacent, That Will Not Bring in All Their Provisions For Men and Horse, to the Garrison of Oxford* (E 43/20, 1644).

301. *A Declaration . . . Concerning the Pressing Necessities of Thes Kingdome* (E 84/33), sig. A2, my italics.

302. There were only six issued in 1645.

303. *A Declaration of the Commons of England Assembled in Parliament, of Their True Intentions Concerning the Ancient and Fundamental Government of the Kingdom, the Government of the Church, the Present Peace* (E 333/19, 1646), pp. 2–4.

304. Ibid., pp. 3–4.

305. *A Declaration Of the Commons Assembled in Parliament: Against All Such Persons As Shall Take Upon Them to Preach or Expound the Scriptures in Any Church or Chappel or Any Publique Place Except They Be Ordained* (E 2554, 1647).

306. *A Declaration Of the Lords and Commons Assembled in Parliament. Die Martis, 30. Martii 1647* (E 1351, 1647), one page.

307. *A Declaration Of the Lords and Commons Assembled in Parliament Concerning the Kings Majesty and His Majesties Gracious Message and Propositions, Sent From the Isle of Wyght, For Setleing Of the Church and Kingdome, and Paying Of the Army with His Majesties Desire to Come to London to the Parliament* (E 1386A, 1647).

308. Ibid., p. 4.

309. *A Declaration Of the Lords and Commons in Parliament Assembled, Concerning a Personall Treaty With the Kings Majesty* (E 450/23, 1648); *A Declaration Of the Lords and Commons Assembled in Parliament: For, the Suppressing of All Tumultuous Assemblies, Under Pretence of Framing and Presenting Petitions to the Parliament. Die Sabbathi, 20. Maii, 1648* (E 443/24, 1648), p. 2.

310. Underdown, *Pride's Purge*.

311. *The Votes Of the Lords & Commons Assembled in Parliament Touching No Farther Address to the King With a Declaration Thereupon Published by the Commons of England in Parliament Assembled* (E 2456, 1648); *The Kingdomes Briefe Answer to the Late Declaration Of the House of Commons, Feb. 11, 1647 Touching the Reasons Of Their No Further Addresses to the King* (Wing K582, 1648), p. 2.

312. Hugh Trevor-Roper, 'The Fast Sermons of the Long Parliament', in Trevor Roper ed., *Essays in British History Presented to Sir Keith Feiling* (1964), pp. 85–138.

313. *The New Booke of Common Prayer. According to the Forme of the Kirke of Scotland, Our Brethren in Faith and Covenant* (E 89/5, 1644).

314. *A Directory For Publique Worship of God Throughout the Three Kingdoms of England, Scotland, and Ireland Together With an Ordinance of Parliament For the Taking Away of the Book of Common-prayer, and For Establishing and Observing of This Present Directory Throughout the Kingdom of England and Dominion of Wales* (Wing D 1548, 1645).

315. Ibid., sigs A1–2.

316. Ibid., pp. 1–4.

317. *A Supply of Prayer For the Ships of This Kingdom That Want Ministers to Pray with Them: Agreeable to the Directory Established by Parliament. Published by Authority* (E 284/16, 1645).

318. Ibid., pp. 9, 11.

319. *The Souldiers Catechisme: Composed For the Parliaments Army* (E 1186/1, 1644).

320. *An Ordinance of the Lords and Commons Assembled in Parliament, For the More Effectuall Puting in Execution the Directory for Publique Worship* (Wing E 1995, 1997, 1645, 1646).

321. *Two Prayers Fit to Be Used in These Times by All That Love Peace & Truth* (Wing T 3528, 1647); *A New Booke of Common-prayer, According to the Pattern of the Old; Lately Compiled For the Use Only of the Parliament, Scots Commissioners, and Assembly of Divines* (E 408/7, 1647).

322. *Victories Obtained (by Gods Blessing on the Parliaments Forces) Both by Land and Sea As Also Other Speciall Mercies to This Kingdom, Observed How They Have Been Given in Unto Us, Either a Little Before Our Monethly Fast Day, to Prevent Us: Or On the Fast to Encourage Us: Or Immediately After, As a Returne of Prayer* (Wing V343, 1647).

323. Thomas Barton, *Logos Agonios; Or, a Sermon of the Christian Race, Preached Before His Maiesty at Christ-Church in Oxford, May 9. 1643* (E 106/17, Oxford, 1643), sig. B1ᵛ. See also the 'advertisement to his countrymen who are misled', sig. D3.

324. N. Bernard, *Esoptron Tes Antimachias, Or, A Looking-Glasse For Rebellion Being a Sermon Preached Upon Sunday the 16 of Iune 1644, in Saint Maries Oxford* (Wing B2006, Oxford, 1644); James Ussher, *The Soveraignes Power, and the Subiects Duty: Delivered in a Sermon, at Christ-Church in Oxford, March 3. 1643* (E 36/13, 1644), p. 29. Manchester famously reminded his colleagues in 1644 that 'if we fight [the king] 100 times and beat him 99 he will be king still, but if he beat us but once, or the last time, we shall be hanged, we shall lose our estates, and our posterities be undone', *Cal. Stat. Pap. Dom. 1644-5*, p. 159.

325. Joseph Caryl, *Davids Prayer For Solomon, Containing the Proper Endowments and Duty Royall of a King, With the Consequent Blessings Upon a Kingdome. Delivered in a Sermon at Christ-Church London* (E 97/12, 1643). Caryl was one of the ministers most called upon to preach the fast sermons, *ODNB*.

326. John Strickland, *Gods Work of Mercy, in Sions Misery; Laid Out in a Sermon Preached Before the Honourable House of Commons at Margarets Westminster, Decemb. 27. 1643* (E 81/25, 1644), p. 33 and *passim*.

327. Obadiah Sedgwick, *A Thanksgiving-Sermon, Preached Before the Honourable House of Commons at Westminster, April 9. 1644. For the Happie and Seasonable Victory of Sir Will. Waller and Sir Will. Balfore, &c. Over Sir Ralph Hopton and His Forces Raised Against the Parliament* (E 46/10, 1644), p. 24 and *passim*. Sedgwick was another member of the Westminster Assembly, with Presbyterian sympathies, *ODNB*. Cf. John Arrowsmith, *Englands Eben-ezer Or, Stone of Help. Set Up in Thankfull Acknowledgment of the Lords Having Helped Us Hitherto. More Especially, For a Memoriall of That Help, Which the Parliaments Forces Lately Received at Shrewsbury, Weymouth, and Elsewhere. In a Sermon Preached to Both the Honorable Houses of Parliament ... at Christ-Church London, Upon the Late Solemne Day of Thanksgiving: March 12* (E 278/16, 1645). The Presbyterian Arrowsmith was another active member of the Westminster Assembly.

328. Thomas Goodwin, *The Great Interest of States & Kingdomes. A Sermon Preached Before the Honorable House of Commons, at Their Late Solemne Fast, Feb. 25. 1645* (E 325/4, 1645), p. 42. Another active member of the Assembly, Goodwin was appointed by parliament the president of Magdalen College, Oxford, *ODNB*.

329. Richard Vines, *The Hearse of the Renowned, the Right Honourable Robert Earle of Essex ... Sometime Captaine Lord Generall of the Armies Raised For the Defence of King and Parliament. As It Was Represented in a Sermon, Preached in the Abbey Church at Westminster, at the Magnificent Solemnity of His Funerall, Octob. 22, 1646* (E 359/1, 1646), p. 3 and *passim*. On Vines, see *ODNB*.

330. Sharpe, *Selling the Tudor Monarchy*, ch. 9, pp. 355-7; above, pp. 271-4.

331. F. Smith Fussner, *The Historical Revolution: English Historical Writing and Thought, 1580-1640* (1962)

332. T. Fannant, *A True Relation of That Memorable Parliament, which Wrought Wonders. Begun at Westminster, in the Tenth Yeare of the Reigne of K. Richard the Second. Whereunto Is Added an Abstract of Those Memorable Matters, Before and Since the Said Kings Reigne, Done by Parliaments* (E 157/12, 1641).

333. *Records of Things Done in Parliament (Without the Kings Consent) of Higher Consequence Then Have Yet Been Done By This Parliament* (E 55/16, 1643).

334. See, for example, *Briefe Collections Out of Magna Charta: Or, the Knowne Good Old Lawes of England· Which Sheweth; That the Law Is the Highest Inheritance the King Hath; and That if His Charter, Grant, or Pattent, Be Repugnant to the Said Lawes, and Statutes, Cannot Be Good* (E 38/12, 1643); John Vicars, *A Sight of ye Trans-actions of These Latter Yeares Emblemized with Ingraven Plats* (E 365/6, 1646). The Presbyterian Vicars went on to write eulogies on Cromwell and other Parliamentarian leaders.

335. See Larkin, *Proclamations*, II, no. 339, pp. 770-5.

336. Above, p. 314.
337. Edward Chamberlayne, *The Present Warre Parallel'd. Or A Briefe Relation of the Five Yeares Civil Warres of Henry the Third, King of England, With the Event and Issue of That Unnaturall Warre, and By What Course the Kingdome was Then Setled Againe* (E 389/11, 1647). Chamberlayne left England during the civil war.
338. Ibid., title page epigraph and pp. 6, 30.
339. Ibid., p. 4.
340. On Parker, see M. Mendle, *Henry Parker and the English Civil War : The Political Thought of the Public's 'Privado'* (Cambridge, 1995), especially ch. 4.
341. *The Game at Chesse. A Metaphoricall Discourse Shewing the Present Estate of This Kingdome* (E 88/2, 1643). This has been ascribed to William Cartwright, but his authorship seems unlikely. On Thomas Middleton's earlier play and the politics of resistance to a pro-Spanish policy, see M. Heinnemann, 'Middleton's "A Game at Chess": Parliamentary-Puritans and Opposition Drama', *English Literary Renaissance*, 5 (1975), pp. 232–50.
342. *Game at Chesse*, p. 4.
343. Ibid., pp. 5–8.
344. Ed de Claro-Vado, *The Burden of England, Scotland, & Ireland: Or, The Watchmans Alarum. In a Plain Declaration to the Kings Most Excellent Majesty, Pointing Out the Chiefe Sins, and Causes of This Civill War* (E 351/1, 1646), pp. 95–118, 181–3 and *passim*.
345. *Englands Petition to Their Soveraigne King* (E 362/22, 1646), pp. 5–6.
346. Vicars, *A Sight of ye Trans-actions*, p. 1; J. Cockayne, *Englands Troubles Anatomized* (E 12/15, 1644), sig. B1.
347. *The Battaile on Hopton-Heath in Staffordshire, Betweene His Majesties Forces Under the Right Honourable the Earle of Northampton, and Those of the Rebels, March 19* (E 99/18, 1643).
348. Ibid., p. 4.
349. Ibid., p. 8.
350. *A True Relation of the Happy Success of His Maiesties Forces in Scotland Under the Conduct of Lord Iames Marquisse of Montrose His Excellencie, Against the Rebels There* (E 269/2, 1645), pp. 7–8.
351. George Wharton, *An Astrologicall Judgement Upon His Maiesties Present Martch: Begun from Oxford May 7. 1645* (E 286/31, 1645), pp. 8–9.
352. *Most Hapy and Wellcome Newes From His Excellencie the Earle of Essex: Wherein Is Declared the True and Full Relation, of Two Famous Victories Obtained by the Parliament Forces* (E 85/30, 1643).
353. *A True Relation of a Late Skirmish at Henley Upon Thames: Wherein a Great Defeat Was Given to the Redding Cavaliers, Lately Assaulting the Aforesaid Towne of Henley* (E 86/15, 1643), p. 6.
354. *A Narration of the Great Victory, (through Gods Providence) Obtained by the Parliaments Forces Under Sir William Waller, at Alton in Surrey the 13. of this Instant December, 1643* (E 78/22, 1643), p. 7.
355. *A Perfect List of the Many Victories Obtained (through the Blessing of God) by the Parliaments Forces Under the Command of His Excellency, Robert Earl of Essex* (Thomason 669 f. 10/59, 1643).
356. I. W., *The Jubilie of England. From Nasebie to the Mount in Cornwall, and Round About: Telling of the Righteous and Glorious Acts of the Lord, Done For Us Within the Circle of the Yeere Now Past* (E 510/8, 1646), p. 6.
357. Ibid., p. 5.
358. A. Kernan, *The Cankered Muse: Satire of the English Renaissance* (New Haven, 1959); A. McRae, *Literature, Satire and the Early Stuart State* (Cambridge, 2004); N. Smith, *Literature and Revolution in England, 1640–1660* (New Haven and London, 1994), ch. 9.
359. John Taylor, *A Seasonable Lecture, or, A Most Learned Oration Disburthened from Henry Walker, a Most Judicious . . . Iron Monger* (E 143/13, 1642), p. 4. On Walker, see *ODNB*.
360. J. Taylor, *Mad Fashions, Od Fashions, All Out of Fashions, or, The Emblems of These Distracted Times* (E 138/30, 1642), sig. A2 and *passim*.
361. 'The clean contrary way' was a popular ballad refrain of the 1620s, especially in ballads against Buckingham, see A. Bellany and A. McRae eds, 'Early Stuart Libels: An Edition of Poetry from Manuscript Sources', *Early Modern Literary Studies* Text Series I (2005). See http://purl.oclc.org/emls/texts/libels/ Pi 25, n. 7.
362. J. Taylor, *The Diseases of the Times Or, the Distempers Of the Common-wealth* (E 136/6, 1642), sigs A3–3^v.
363. T. J., *A Medicine For the Times. Or, An Antidote Against Faction* (E 135/33, 1642), sig. A2^v. This is probably by Thomas Jordan, a playwright and keen supporter of the king, *ODNB*.
364. *The Dolefull Lamentation of Cheap-side Crosse: Or Old England Sick of the Staggers. The Dissenting, and Disagreeing in Matters of Opinion, Together With the Sundry Sorts of Sects Now Raving and Reigning, Being the Maine Causes of the Disturbance and Hinderance of the Common-wealth* (E 134/9, 1642).

365. *The Resolution of the Round-Heads: Being a Zealous Declaration of the Grievances Where-with Their Little Wits Are Consumed to Destruction* (E 132/39, 1642).

366. *The Bloody Game at Cards, As It Was Played Betwixt the King of Hearts. And the Rest of His Suite, Against the Residue of the Packe of Cards* (E 246/11, 1643), sig. A2, p. 2. The tract states that 'the loyal hearted subjects . . . stand for the king of hearts' who was 'not to be opposed by the common cards'. Card games were familiar ways of commenting on politics; cf. *The Knave of Clubs. Otherwise Called, A Game at Cards, and Clubs Trump* (E 245/18, 1643).

367. P. Heylyn, *The Rebells Catechisme. Composed in an Easy and Familiar Way; To Let Them See, the Hainousnesse of Their Offence, the Weaknesse of Their Strongest Subterfuges; and to Recall Them to Their Duties, Both to God and Man* (E 35/22, 1643).

368. *The Parliament of Women. With the Merrie Lawes of Them Newly Enacted. To Live in More Ease, Pompe, Pride, and Wantonnesse: But Especially That They Might Have Superiority and Domineere of Their Husbands* (E 1150/5, 1646), sigs A7, B4.

369. *Mercurius Rusticus Or, The Countries Complaint of the Barbarous Out-rages Committed by the Sectaries of This Late Flourishing Kingdome* (E 1099/1, 1646).

370. Ibid., sigs A2–7, pp. 112, 120, 130, 145 and *passim*.

371. Wharton, *Grand Pluto's Progresse*.

372. *The Resolution of the Women of London to the Parliament. Wherein They Declare Their Hot Zeale in Sending Their Husbands to the Warres* (E 114/14, 1642), sigs A2–A2ᵛ; *Nocturnall Occurrences or, Deeds of Darknesse: Committed, By the Cavaleers in Their Rendevous. Whereunto Is Conjoyned, the Severall Postures, Used with Their Whores and Pimpes* (E 117/16, 1642), sigs A3ᵛ–A4ᵛ.

373. *The Debauched Cavalleer: Or the English Midianite* (E 240/43, 1642), p. 7.

374. Above, p. 301; cf. *The Cavaliers Bible* (E 4/24, 1644); *The Souldiers Language* (E 10/10, 1644), sig. A3ᵛ; *A Charme For Canterburian Spirits* (E 269/18, 1645), p. 3.

375. Thomas May, *The Character Of a Right Malignant* (E 27/3, 1645); *The Character of a Cavaliere* (Wing C1964, 1647); John Earle, *Micro-cosmographie. Or, A Peece Of the World Discouered in Essayes and Characters* (STC 7441, 1628).

376. McRae, *Literature, Satire*, p. 219. Parliament evidently thought the attacks on Pym too damaging to leave unanswered. See *A Declaration and Vindication of Iohn Pym Esquire: Concerning the Divers Aspersions which Have Been Cast Upon Him by Sundry Base and Scandalous Pamphlets, and by Divers Malignants, and People Ill-affected to the Good of the Common-wealth* (E 91/34, 1643).

377. John Cleveland, *The Character of a London-Diurnall: With Severall Select Poems* (E 375/22, 1647), p. 6; L. Knoppers, *Constructing Cromwell : Ceremony, Portrait and Print, 1645–1661* (Cambridge, 2000), pp. 12–13, 19–20, 46–9, 67–8.

378. *The Catholikes Petition to Prince Rupert* (E4/4, 1644); I. W., *The Bloody Prince, Or, A Declaration of the Most Cruell Practices of Prince Rupert and the Rest of the Cavaliers* (Wing W38, 1643); *Englands Wolfe with Eagles Clawes or the Cruell Impieties of Bloud-thirsty Royalists, and Blasphemous Anti-Parliamentarians, Under the Command of that Inhumane Prince Rupert, Digby, and the Rest* (Thomason 669 f.10/106, 1646); Henry Neville, *An Exact Diurnall of the Parliament of Ladyes* (E 386/4, 1647); T.B., *Observations Upon Prince Rupert's White Dog, Called Boy* (E 245/33, 1643), sig. A3; McRae, *Literature, Satire*, pp. 219–20.

379. *The Last Will and Testament of P. Rupert* (E 304/4, 1645).

380. Joad Raymond, *The Invention of the Newspaper: English Newsbooks, 1641–1649* (Oxford, 1996), pp. 87–94.

381. Ibid., pp. 149–50; P. W. Thomas, *Sir John Berkenhead, 1617–1679: A Royalist Career in Politics and Polemics* (Oxford, 1969), ch. 3.

382. Raymond, *Invention*, pp. 185–8.

383. Ibid., ch. 5, *passim*; on the numbering of newsbooks, see J. Raymond ed., *Making the News: An Anthology of the Newsbooks of Revolutionary England, 1641–1660* (Moreton-in-Marsh, 1993), p. 17.

384. Raymond, *Making the News*, p. 38.

385. Ibid., p. 51.

386. Ibid., pp. 57–8.

387. Ibid., pp. 97–8.

388. De Groot, *Royalist Identities*, p. 121.

389. Raymond, *Making the News*, pp. 99, 107.

390. Ibid., p. 107.

391. Ibid., p. 105; *Mercurius Aulicus*, 25 January–3 February 1648 (E 425/8, 1648), sig. A4ᵛ; 11–18 May 1648 (E 443/20, 1648).

392. See J. Raymond, 'The Newspaper, Public Opinion, and the Public Sphere in the Seventeenth Century', in J. Raymond ed., *News, Newspapers and Society in Early Modern Britain* (1999), pp. 109–40.

393. On the emergence of a public sphere of print in the early modern period and especially the civil war, see J. Habermas, *The Structural Transformation of the Public Sphere: An Inquiry into a*

Category of Bourgeois Society (Cambridge, 1989); D. Freist, *Governed by Opinion: Politics, Religion and the Dynamics of Communication in Stuart London, 1637–1645* (1997); A. Halasz, *The Marketplace of Print: Pamphlets and the Public Sphere in Early Modern England* (Cambridge, 1997); D. Zaret, *Origins of Democratic Culture: Printing, Petitions, and the Public Sphere in Early-modern England* (Princeton, 2000); J. Raymond, *Pamphlets and Pamphleteering in Early Modern Britain* (Cambridge, 2003), ch. 6.

394. John Taylor, *Heads of All Fashions* (E 145/17, 1642), sig. A1ᵛ.
395. J. B., *The Poets Knavery Discouered, in All Their Lying Pamphlets* (E 135/11, 1642), sig. A2ᵛ; Raymond, *Pamphlets and Pamphleteering*, p. 164.
396. *A Rationall Discourse of the Cause of the Present War, with a Faire Paterne For a Good Peace* (E 99/9, 1643), sig. A2.
397. James Howell, *A Discourse, or Parly, Continued Betwixt Partricius and Peregrine*, p. 3.
398. Howell, *The Vote*, p. 5; *Britanicus His Blessing* (E 316/17, Cambridge, 1643), p. 1; Martin Lluellyn, *Men-Miracles. With Other Poemes* (E 1163/1, 1646), p. 101; *The Cavaliers Diurnall* (E 383/4, 1647), p. 7.
399. See *An Order of the Lords and Commons Assembled in Parliament. For the Regulating of Printing* (E 106/15, 1643); *An Ordinance of the Lords & Commons Assembled in Parliament, Against Unlicensed or Scandalous Pamphlets* (E 409/20, 1647).
400. Perez Zagorin, *Ways of Lying:Dissimulation, Persecution, and Conformity in Early Modern Europe* (Cambridge, Mass., 1990).
401. Above, p. 336; John Taylor, *The Liar. Or, A Contradiction to Those Who in the Titles of Their Bookes Affirmed Them To Be True, When They Were False* (E 169/8, 1641).
402. To give a few examples, see E 86/15, E115/4, E 119/25, E 150/12, E 238/21, E 34/11, E 54/3, E 108/27.
403. John Norton, *The Miseries of War* (E 85/13, 1643), p. 2; James Howell, *Englands Teares, For the Present Wars* (E 253/10, 1644), p. 6; *The Souldiers Language* (E 10/10, 1644), sig. B4ᵛ; Cleveland, *The Character of a London-Diurnall*, p. 4.
404. *The Great Assises Holden in Parnassus by Apollo and His Assesours* (E 269/11, 1645), p. 3; cf. p. 30 describing the cryer selling lies.
405. Ibid., p. 2.
406. John Gauden, *The Love of Truth and Peace* (E 204/10, 1641), p. 27.
407. *Some Observations Concerning Iealousies Betweene King and Parliament, with Their Causes and Cures* (E 110/1, 1642), p. 1.
408. *The Maids Petition* (E 401/26, 1647), p. 6.
409. H. Peacham, *The World Is Ruled and Governed By Opinion* (Wing P949.5, 1641). Cf. 'opinion is risen up to decide truth', *A Rationall Discourse of the Cause of the Present War* (E 99/9, 1643), p. 2.
410. Francis Quarles, *The Shepheards Oracles: Delivered in Certain Eglogues* (E 52/2, 1645), sig. A1ᵛ.
411. See K. Sharpe, *Reading Revolutions:The Politics of Reading in Early Modern England* (New Haven and London, 2000), pp. 53–5.
412. For example, *An Ordinance From His Maiesty, and Both Houses of Parliament* (E 135/7, 1642); *The Orders From the House of Commons for the Abolishing of Superstition* (E 171/8, 1641).
413. *A Declaration of the Lords and Commons Assembled in Parliament* (E 390/6, 1647), p. 17.

10 Visual Conflicts and Wars of Signs

1. S. R. Gardiner, *History of England: From the Accession of James I to the Outbreak of the Civil War, 1603–1642* (10 vols, 1883–4), X, p. 98.
2. Oliver Millar, *The Age of Charles I* (1972), p. 106.
3. Ibid., p. 96.
4. Ibid., p. 98.
5. Malcolm Rogers, *William Dobson 1611–1646* (1984), pp.7–14; Oliver Millar, *William Dobson, 1611–1646: An Exhibition of Paintings at the Tate Gallery* (1951), p. 3.
6. O. Millar, *The Pictures in the Collection of Her Majesty the Queen: The Tudor, Stuart and Early Georgian Pictures* (1963), no. 203, p. 113; Rogers, *Dobson*, fig. 28, pp. 64–6.
7. Rogers, *Dobson*, fig. 14, p. 36; Millar, *Tudor, Stuart and Early Georgian Pictures*, no. 204, p. 113.
8. Rogers, *Dobson*, fig. 9, pp. 35–6; Millar, *Age of Charles I*, fig. 155, pp. 97, 99–100; above p. 206.
9. Millar, *Age of Charles I*, p. 99.
10. Millar, *Tudor, Stuart and Early Georgian Pictures*, no. 205, p. 113.
11. Millar, *Age of Charles I*, no. 159, p. 102; Millar, *Dobson*, p. 18; Rogers, *Dobson*, fig. 18, p. 26.
12. Jerome De Groot, *Royalist Identities* (Basingstoke, 2004), p. 108.
13. Rogers, *Dobson*, figs 16, 30, 45, pp. 45–6, 67–8, 85–7.
14. De Groot, *Royalist Identities*, p. 108.

15. Millar, *Age of Charles I*, p. 110.
16. Jane Roberts, *The King's Head: Charles I, King and Martyr* (1999), plate 7.
17. Millar, *Age of Charles I*, p. 114.
18. Ibid., p. 123; National Portrait Gallery, NPG 1924, 6276.
19. Roberts, *King's Head*, p. 26.
20. Above, ch. 6, pp. 209–15.
21. Roberts, *King's Head*, pp. 28, 44.
22. Huntington Library, Richard Bull Granger, Vol.VI, 15; F. O'Donoghue, *Catalogue of Engraved British Portraits Preserved in the Department of Prints and Drawings in the British Museum* (4 vols, 1908), I, p. 391, no. 144.
23. For example, NPG D18213.
24. Huntington, Bull Granger VI, 10.
25. Ibid., VI, 14ᵛ; NPG D18273; see A. Globe ed., *Peter Stent, London Printseller circa 1642–65: Being a Catalogue Raisonné of his Engraved Prints and Books with an Historical and Bibliographical Introduction* (Vancouver, 1985), p. 52.
26. NPG D18293, D18296.
27. NPG D18206.
28. NPG D18217.
29. Huntington Bull Granger VI, 10; NPG D18210.
30. NPG D18203.
31. Huntington Bull Granger VI, 24c.
32. See K. Sharpe, *Remapping Early Modern England: The Culture of Seventeenth-Century Politics* (Cambridge, 2000), fig. 16. The engraving is found in editions of 1646, see Francis Quarles, *The Shepheards Oracles Delivered in Certain Eglogues* (Wing Q115B, 1646); see G. S. Haight, 'Francis Quarles in the Civil War', *Review of English Studies*, 12 (1936), p. 152 and n. 2; Huntington Bull Granger VI, 25.
33. Huntington Bull Granger, VI, 5; NPG D18217.
34. For examples, see NPG D18220, 18284, 18285, 18289.
35. Roberts, *King's Head*, fig. 33.
36. Huntington Bull Granger VI, 10, 11 carry inscriptions declaring the images to be published 'cum privilegio'.
37. *The Scourge of Civill Warre. The Blessing of Peace* (Thomason 669 f.10/27, 1645).
38. *The Kings Majesties Declaration Concerning the High and Honourable Court of Parliament* (E 405/25, 1647); *The Kings Majesties Most Gratious Message in Foure Letters* (E 414/10, 1647).
39. *Heads of His Majesties letter and Propositions Sent from the Isle of Wyght, for Setling of the Church and Kingdome* (E 416/12, 1647); *A Declaration of the Proceedings of the Kings Majesty at Carisbrooke Castle in the Isle of Wight* (E 451/8, 1648); *His Majesties Gracious Declaration to the Right Honorable the Earl of Middlesex, and the Rest of the Parliaments Commissioners, Concerning a Personall Treaty in the Isle of Wight* (E 458/13, 1648); *Die. 13. Octob. 1648. A New Remonstrance From the Kings Majesty to All His Loyall Subjects in His Three Kingdoms of England, Scotland and Ireland* (E 467/27, 1648).
40. *The Kings Majesties Last Message and Declaration to His Excellency Sir Thomas Fairfax* (E 419/7, 1647).
41. *The Kings Majesties Speech Delivered to the Commissioners from the Parliament* (E 464/28, 1648).
42. *A Declaration of the Treaty at Newport in the Isle of Wight* (E 464/35, 1648).
43. John Harvey, *Londons Lawless Liberty* (E 407/9, 1647).
44. Hudson, *Divine Right of Government*, above pp. 13, 600, n. 251; Globe, *Peter Stent*, pp. 52, 166; Edward Symmons, *A Vindication of King Charles I, or, A Loyal Subjects Duty Manifested in Vindicating His Sovereign From Those Aspersions Cast Upon Him in a Scandalous Libel Entituled The Kings Cabinet Opened* (i 414/17, 1647).
45. R. Grosse, *Royalty and Loyalty or A Short Survey of the Power of Kings over Their Subjects and the Duty, of Subjects to their King* (E 397/3, 1647); 'By me kings reign', Proverbs 8: 15.
46. *King Charles His Royall Welcome, At His Happy and Gracious Return Towards His Parliament* (E 377/2, 1647), facing p. 1.
47. See, for example, *A Remonstrance from the Army, to the Citizens of London* (E 472/13, 1648).
48. Maija Jansson, 'Remembering Marston Moor: The Politics of Culture', in S. D. Amussen and M. A. Kishlansky eds, *Political Culture and Cultural Politics in Early Modern England* (Manchester, 1995), pp. 255–76.
49. Ibid., pp. 268–9.
50. Millar, *Age of Charles I*, pp. 96, 106–7; NPG 5461.
51. D. Foskett, *Samuel Cooper and his Contemporaries* (1974), nos 27, 32, 36, 60, pp. 16, 17, 19, 27; Millar, *Age of Charles I*, nos 219, 221; NPG 1925, 2766, 3301, 5589, 5274. See D. Foskett, *Samuel Cooper, 1609–1672* (1974).

52. Millar, *Age of Charles I*, p. 96.

53. Jansson, 'Remembering Marston Moor', p. 263.

54. C. H. Firth and R. S. Rait eds, *Acts and Ordinances of the Interregnum, 1642-1660* (3 vols, London, 1911), I, pp. 265-6.

55. See T. Cooper ed., *The Journal of William Dowsing: Iconoclasm in East Anglia during the English Civil War* (Woodbridge, Suffolk, 2001); J. Morrill, 'William Dowsing, the Bureaucratic Puritan', in J. Morrill, P. Slack and D. Woolf eds, *Public Duty and Private Conscience in Seventeenth-Century England* (Oxford, 1993), pp. 173-203.

56. *Mercurius Rusticus: on The Countries Complaint of the Parlous Outrages Committed By the Sectaries* (E 1099/1, 1646), p. 32.

57. Ibid., pp. 203, 212-13.

58. Ibid., p. 212.

59. Ibid., p. 213. Interestingly, for all that he acknowledged that 'the substance of that power' had been eroded, the author still expected that 'notwithstanding', the emblems of power 'ought to have been venerable and awful to these men in respect of their *relation*' (ibid., author's italics).

60. Ibid., p. 32.

61. A. Hind, *Engraving in England in the 16th and 17th Centuries: A Descriptive Catalogue with Introductions Vol III: The Reign of Charles I* (Cambridge, 1964), p. 328, no. 1; Globe, *Peter Stent*, pp. 65-6.

62. In one version, the plate was altered to show Gustavus Adolphus, Hind, *Engraving*, p. 113, no. 35.

63. *A Perfect List of the Many Victories Obtained (through the blessing of God) by the Parliaments Forces Under the Command of His Excellency, Robert Earl of Essex* (Thomason 669 f. 10/59, 1646); Cf. Hind, *Engraving*, pp. 364-5.

64. Hind, *Engraving*, pp. 230-1; plate 188b; *A Perfect List of All the Victories Obtained (through the blessing of God) by the Parliaments Forces* (Thomason 669 f. 10/79, 1646).

65. *The Hearse of the Renowned, the Right Honourable Robert Earle of Essex* (E 359/1, 1646).

66. Globe, *Peter Stent*, pp. 8-9; Huntington Bull Granger VII, 23^v; Hind, *Engraving*, pp. 254, no. 5, 341, no. 6.

67. John Vicars, *A Sight of ye Trans-actions of These Latter Yeares Emblemized with Ingraven Plats* (E 365/6, 1646).

68. Ibid., pp. 9, 11, 23.

69. Ibid., pp. 27-8.

70. *The Sucklington Faction or (Sucklings) Roaring Boyes* (Thomason 669 f. 4/17, 1641); *The Sussex Picture, Or, An Answer to the Sea-gull* (E 3/21, 1644).

71. John Leicester, *Englands Miraculous Preservation Emblematically Described, Erected for a Perpetual Monument to Posterity* (Thomason 669 f. 10/107, 1646); Hind, *Engraving*, p. 363, no. 76, plate 207. Leicester had written *An Elegiacall Epitaph Upon the Deplored Death of that Religious and Valiant Gentlemen, Colonell Iohn Hampden Esquire* (669 f. 8/17, 1643).

72. The pun on quay and key further ties the nautical image to the divine and the ship of state to Providence.

73. Firth and Rait, *Acts and Ordinances*, I, pp. 340-2.

74. J. L. Larkin, ed., *Stuart Royal Proclamations II: Royal Proclamations of King Charles I, 1625-1646* (Oxford, 1983), p. 974; A. B. Wyon, *The Great Seals of England, from the Earliest Period to the Present Time* (1887), pp. 88-90, and plate XXIX.

75. Larkin, *Stuart Royal Proclamations*, no. 457, pp. 974-6.

76. Ibid., no. 469, pp. 996-1000.

77. Firth and Rait, *Acts and Ordinances*, I, pp. 579-80.

78. Ibid., pp. 612-13.

79. E. Hawkins, *Medallic Illustrations of the History of Great Britain and Ireland to the Death of George II (1904-11)*, plate XXIII. Above, ch. 6, pp. 215-21.

80. A. Franks and H. Grueber, *Medallic Illustrations of the History of Great Britain* (2 vols, 1885), I, pp. 270, 279, 284-5, nos 69, 85, 95; Hawkins, *Medallic Illustrations*, plate XXIII, nos 1,8, XXIV, nos 8-9.

81. Franks and Grueber, *Medallic Illustrations*, I, p. 288, no. 102; Hawkins, *Medallic Illustrations*, plate XXIV, no. 14.

82. Franks and Grueber, *Medallic Illustrations*, I, p. 292, no. 107; Hawkins, *Medallic Illustrations*, plate XXV, no. 4.

83. Franks and Grueber, *Medallic Illustrations*, I, pp. 294-5, nos 111-12; Hawkins, *Medallic Illustrations*, plate XXV, nos 8, 9.

84. Franks and Grueber, *Medallic Illustrations*, I, p. 298, no. 118; Hawkins, *Medallic Illustrations*, plate XXVI, no. 5; cf. XXVI, no. 6.

85. Franks and Grueber, *Medallic Illustrations*, I, p. 307, nos 131, 132; Hawkins, *Medallic Illustrations*, plate XXVI, nos 16, 17.

86. Franks and Grueber, *Medallic Illustrations*, I, p. 308, nos 134, 135; Hawkins, *Medallic Illustrations*, plate XXVI, nos 18–20.

87. Franks and Grueber, *Medallic Illustrations*, I, pp. 302, no. 123, p. 306, no.130; Hawkins, *Medallic Illustrations*, plate XXVI, nos 9, 15; Huntington Bull Granger VI, 29.

88. Franks and Grueber, *Medallic Illustrations*, I, pp. 301–2, nos 122–3; Hawkins, *Medallic Illustrations*, plate XXVIII, nos 8, 9.

89. Franks and Grueber, *Medallic Illustrations*, I, p. 334, no. 178; Hawkins, *Medallic Illustrations*, plate XXIX, no. 10.

90. Franks and Grueber, *Medallic Illustrations*, I, pp. 270, no. 69, pp. 275–6, nos 76–7; Hawkins, *Medallic Illustrations*, plates XXII, no. 16, XXIII, no. 1.

91. Franks and Grueber, *Medallic Illustrations*, I, p. 292, no. 108; Hawkins, *Medallic Illustrations*, plate XXV, no. 5.

92. Franks and Grueber, *Medallic Illustrations*, I, p. 293, nos 109, 110; Hawkins, *Medallic Illustrations*, plate XXV, nos 6, 7.

93. Franks and Grueber, *Medallic Illustrations*, I, p. 293, no. 110; Hawkins, *Medallic Illustrations*, plate XXV, no. 7.

94. Franks and Grueber, *Medallic Illustrations*, I, pp. 295–6, nos 113, 114; Hawkins, *Medallic Illustrations*, plate XXV, nos 10, 11.

95. Franks and Grueber, *Medallic Illustrations*, I, p. 297, no. 115, p. 298, no. 118; Hawkins, *Medallic Illustrations*, plate XXVI, nos 1, 5.

96. Franks and Grueber, *Medallic Illustrations*, I, pp. 303–4, nos 125–8; Hawkins, *Medallic Illustrations*, plate XXVI, nos 10–13.

97. Franks and Grueber, *Medallic Illustrations*, I, pp. 313–14, nos 144–5; Hawkins, *Medallic Illustrations*, plate XXVII, nos 7, 8.

98. Franks and Grueber, *Medallic Illustrations*, I, pp. 326–7, nos 164–7; Hawkins, *Medallic Illustrations*, plate XXVIII, nos 14–17.

99. Franks and Grueber, *Medallic Illustrations*, I, pp. 326–7, no. 165; Hawkins, *Medallic Illustrations*, plate XXVIII, no. 15.

100. Edward Besly, *Coins and Medals of the English Civil War* (1990), p. 1.

101. Ibid., p. 24.

102. Ibid., p. 25.

103. Ibid., pp. 29–31.

104. Ibid., p. 31, figs 35, 36.

105. *Cal. Stat. Pap. Venet. XXVI, 1642–3*, no. 168, p. 186.

106. Besly, *Coins and Medals*, p. 32.

107. Ibid., pp. 33–44; J. J. North and J. Preston-Morley, *Sylloge of Coins of the British Isles, 33: The John G. Brooker Collection: Coins of Charles I, 1625–1649* (1984), pp. xxxv–xxxvi, plates LXXIV–LXXXIX.

108. Besly, *Coins and Medals*, p. 37 and p. 42, fig. 51.

109. Ibid., pp. 44–7.

110. Ibid., p. 29; Huntington Bull Granger VI, 30–30ᵛ.

111. Besly, *Coins and Medals*, p. 91.

112. Ibid.

113. Ibid., pp. 94–5 and figs 131–2.

114. Ibid., p. 99

115. I. Gentles, 'The Iconography of Revolution: England 1642–1649', in I. Gentles, J. Morrill and B. Worden eds, *Soldiers, Writers and Statesmen of the English Revolution* (Cambridge, 1998), p. 93; pp. 91–113. I am grateful to Ian Gentles for many helpful discussions.

116. Ibid., p. 93.

117. Barbara Donagan, 'Codes and Conduct in the English Civil War', *Past & Present*, 118 (1988), pp. 65–95. See now Donagan, *War in England 1642–1649* (Oxford, 2008), which appeared after my chapter was written. I am grateful to Barbara Donagan for helpful discussions and warm hospitality in Pasadena.

118. Gentles, 'Iconography of Revolution', pp. 98, 102.

119. Ibid., p. 93. My sample is taken from the engraved banners and devices of the Royalist and Parliamentarian officers in Huntington Richard Bull Granger VIII, 1, 38. These are in turn taken from J. Cole, *A Display of the Royal Banner and Standards Bore by the Loyalists in the Grand Rebellion* (1722) and Cole, *Devices, Motto's &c Used By the Parliamentarian Officers on Standards, Banners &c in the Late Civil Wars Proper to Be Bound Up With ye Lord Clarendon's History* (1722).

120. All the following Royalist banners are reproduced in Huntington Bull Granger, VIII, 1. Several are catalogued in Henri Estienne, *The Art of Making Devises Treating of Hieroglyphicks, Symboles,*

Emblemes, Aenigma's, Reverses of Medals, Anagrams, Cyphres and Rebus. With a Catalogue of the Cornet-devises on Both Sides in the Late Warres, and Those of the Scots Taken at the Great Battails of Dunbar and Preston. The Second Edition with Additions, Embellished with Divers Brasse-Figures (translated by Thomas Blount, E 3352A, 1655). For details on many, see A. R. Young ed., *The English Emblematic Tradition 3: Emblematic Flag Devices of the English Civil Wars, 1642–1660* (Toronto, 1995). For 'Give Caesar his due', see Young, no. 0086.0, p. 46.

121. Young, *Emblematic Flag Devices*, no. 0387.0, p. 211.
122. Ibid., nos 0070.0, 0293.0, pp. 38, 160.
123. Ibid., nos 0385.0, 0438.0, 0028.0, 0266.0, pp. 210, 241, 15, 145.
124. Ibid., nos 0089.0, 0238.0, 0005.0, pp. 48, 130, 3.
125. Ibid., no. 0406.0, p. 223.
126. Ibid., no. 0430.0, p. 236.
127. Ibid., no. 0444.0, p. 244.
128. Ibid., nos 0356.0, 0005.0, pp. 193, 2.
129. All reproduced in Huntington Bull Granger VIII, 38.
130. Young, *Emblematic Flag Devices*, nos 0133.0, 0320.0, 03570, pp. 73, 174, 194.
131. Ibid., no. 0290.0, p. 159.
132. Ibid., no. 0450.0, p. 247.
133. Ibid., nos 0199.0, 0100.0, pp. 108, 54.
134. Ibid., no. 0279.0, p. 152.
135. For example, ibid., nos 0166.0, p. 90; no. 0147.0, p. 81.
136. Ibid., nos 0453.0, 1032.0, 0345.0, pp. xl–xli, 249, 72, 188; Gentles, 'Iconography of Revolution', p. 106.
137. Ibid., nos 0127.0, 0110.0, pp. 69, 59.
138. Ibid., no. 0173.0, 0047.0, pp. 94, 25.
139. *Mercurius Aulicus*, 18 June 1643, p. 323.
140. Estienne, *Art of Making Devises* (E 338/8, 1646).
141. Ibid., sigs A2–a1ᵛ.
142. Ibid., sig. A4.
143. In the Bodleian copy this passage has been underlined by a contemporary reader.
144. Estienne, *Art of Making Devises* (E 338/8, 1646), p. 21.
145. Wing E 3351, 1648; Wing E 3352, 1650; Wing E 3352A, 1655.
146. Estienne, *Art of Making Devises* (Wing E 3352A, 1655), p. 69.
147. Ibid., p. 71.
148. Young, *Emblematic Flag Devices*, pp. vii, xxxv.

11 Rival Rituals and Performances

1. Above, chs 2, 7, pp. 84–8, 261–3.
2. James Barlow, *A Deep Sigh Breath'd Through the Lodgings at White-hall, Deploring the Absence of the Court, and the Miseries of the Palace* (E 119/30, 1642).
3. Ibid., p. 1.
4. Ibid., p. 2
5. Ibid., p. 3. He compares the removal of the arras to the removal of the bishops (sig. A2ᵛ).
6. Ibid., sig. A4ᵛ.
7. Ibid., sig. A2ᵛ.
8. Ibid., sig. A3ᵛ.
9. Ibid., sig. A4ᵛ.
10. Ibid.
11. H. M. Colvin, *The History of the King's Works III, 1485–1660 (Part I)* (1975), pp. 162–3; S. Thurley, *Whitehall Palace: An Architectural History of the Royal Apartments, 1240–1698* (New Haven and London, 1999), p. 97.
12. Thurley, *Whitehall*, p. 97.
13. Colvin, *The History of the King's Works IV, 1485–1660* (Part II) (1982), p. 338.
14. Thurley, *Whitehall*, p. 98.
15. Jerome de Groot, 'Space, Patronage, Procedure: The Court at Oxford, 1642–46', *English Historical Review*, 117 (2002), pp. 1204–7.
16. Ibid., p. 1206.
17. Ibid., p. 1210.
18. Ibid., pp. 1210–11.
19. *Mercurius Rusticus*, quoted ibid., p. 1215.
20. Ibid.
21. Ibid., pp. 1218–19.

22. Ibid., p. 1223.

23. *The Kings Noble Entertainment at York With the Lord Maior of York His Worthy Speech to the King* (E 141/8, 1641); *Five Most Noble Speeches Spoken to His Majestie Returning Out of Scotland into England. The First Spoken by the Recorder of Yorke* (E 199/32, 1641); K. Sharpe, *The Personal Rule of Charles I* (New Haven and London, 1992), p. 643; above, ch. 7, p. 237–9.

24. J. H., *King Charles His Entertainment, and Londons Loyaltie. Being a True Relation, and Description, of the Manner, of the Cities Welcome, and Expression of the Subjects Love to His Royal Majestie, at His Return from Scotland* (E 177/13, 1641), p. 5 and *passim*.

25. *A True Relation of His Majesties Reception and Royall Entertainment at Lincoln, by the Knights, Esquires, Gentlemen, and Free-holders of the Said Countie* (E 108/27, 1642), p. 2.

26. Ibid., pp. 2–3.

27. Ibid., pp. 4, 6.

28. *A True and Exact Relation of the Manner of His Maiesties Setting Up of His Standard at Nottingham, on Munday the 22. of August 1642* (E 115/4, 1642).

29. Ibid., sigs A3–4.

30. Ibid., sig. A4; *A Declaration of the Lords and Commons Assembled in Parlament Whereby the Good Subjects of This Kingdome May Better Discerne Their Owne Danger and Be Stirred Up with More Earnestnesse to Assist the Parliament in the Maintenance of Religion the Common Justice and Liberty of the Kingdome* (E 1477/1642); cf. *His Majesties Gracious Message to Both Houses of Parliament, Sent from Nottingham, August 25. With the Answer of the Lords and Commons to the Said Message* (E 114/29, 1642).

31. *The Arraignment, Conviction, and Imprisoning, of Christmas: on St. Thomas Day Last. And How He Broke Out of Prison in the Holidayes and Got Away, Onely Left His Hoary Hair, and Gray Beard, Sticking Between Two Iron Bars of a Window* (E 315/12, 1646), p. 6.

32. John Taylor, *The Complaint of Christmas* (E 335/8, 1646), p. 1.

33. Ibid., pp. 4–6. To bring home the suggestion of irreligion, Taylor refers to the Koran on p. 3.

34. Ibid., p. 7.

35. Ibid., pp. 6–7.

36. Ibid., p. 8.

37. *Two Humble Petitions of the Apprentices of London and parts Adjacent, for Lawfull Recreations* (E 375/21, 1647); above, ch. 1, pp. 40–1.

38. *Joyfull Newes from the King, Being a Perfect Relation of the Proceedings of the Kings Majesty with the Commissioners, and Their Advancing from Durham, Towards the City of Yorke, and So Towards London* (E 373/17, 1647), sig. A2ᵛ.

39. *King Charles His Royall Welcome, at His Happy and Gracious Return Towards His Parliament; Who Came on Munday Feb. 15. to Holmby in Northhamptonshire in Peace* (E 377/2, 1647), p. 2.

40. *Gallant Newes for London. From His Majesties Royall Court at Holmby* (E 377/19, 1647), sig. A3.

41. Ibid., sig. A3ᵛ.

42. *A Joyfull Message for All Loyall Subjects: Sent from the Kings Majesties Royall Court at Causam* (E 398/15, 1647), sig. A3.

43. John Cleveland, *The Kings Disguise* (E 372/2, 1647), p. 6; J. Loxley, *Royalism and Poetry in the English Civil Wars: The Drawn Sword* (Basingstoke, 1997), pp. 138–47.

44. *Londons Love, Or, the Entertainment of the Parliament* (E 132/1, 1642).

45. Ibid., sig. A3ᵛ.

46. Ibid., sig. A4.

47. John Vicars, *A Sight of ye Trans-actions of These Latter Yeares Emblemized with Ingraven Plats* (E 365/6, 1646), p. 21.

48. John Vicars, *England's Parliamentary Chronicle*, part 2, pp. 326–7, quoted in J. Spraggon, *Puritan Iconoclasm during the English Civil War* (Woodbridge, Suffolk, 2003), p. 159.

49. Vicars, *A Sight of ye Trans-actions*, p. 21.

50. Ibid.

51. *Mercurius Rusticus*, p. 33.

52. Ibid., p. 112.

53. Ibid., p. 213.

54. This analysis very much complements John Adamson's observation that 'during the autumn of 1646, the control of ritual and of the traditional values that it could be made to confirm, assumed an unprecedented prominence in parliamentary political culture', Adamson, *The War of the Realms* (forthcoming). I am grateful to John Adamson for his kindness in sending me a section of his book in advance of publication and for many helpful discussions.

55. J. W., *The Royall Entertainment of the King, by the Royalists of Huntington* (E 298/26, 1645), p. 7.

56. The foregrounding of Essex also connected the parliamentary resistance to Charles to a history of nobles standing up against wayward kings and so lent legitimacy to novel courses.

57. *The Resolution of the Right Honourable the Earl of Essex, Lord Generall of All His Forces for the Preservation of His Majesty and Parliament with a Speech Made by the Lord Roberts to His Excellence: Also the Manner of His Setting Forward and His Passing Through the City* (Wing R1155, 1642); J. Adamson, 'Chivalry and Political Culture in Caroline England', in K. Sharpe and P. Lake eds, *Culture and Politics in Early Stuart England* (Basingstoke, 1994), p. 187 and pp. 161–97 *passim*.

58. For example, *The True Character of a Noble Gennerall: Seen and Allowed of By His Excellencie, the Earl of Essex. Written in Prose and Verse* (E 52/4, 1644); Stephen Marshall, *A Sacred Panegyrick, or, A Sermon of Thanks-giving, Preached to the Two Houses of Parliament, His Excellency the Earl of Essex, the Lord Mayor* (Wing M772, 1644).

59. *A Funeral Monument or the Manner of the Herse of the Most Renowned Robert Devereux, Earl of Essex* (Thomason 669 f. 10/89, 1646); *Cal. Stat. Pap. Dom. 1645–7*, pp. 468–9.

60. Adamson, 'Chivalry and Political Culture', p. 191; Adamson, *War of the Realms*.

61. Gardiner's view of the civil war as a 'puritan revolution', which went out of fashion in the historiography of the early twentieth century, has regained currency (see J. Morrill, 'The Religious Context of the English Civil War', *Transactions of the Royal Historical Society*, 5th ser., 34 (1984), pp. 155–78); Morrill, 'Introduction: England's Wars of Religion', in Morrill, *The Nature of the English Revolution* (1993), pp. 33–44). Morrill, however, underestimates the revolutionary nature of puritanism.

62. *A Rationall Discourse of the Cause of the Present War* (E 99/9, 1643), sig. A3.

63. *A Puritane Set Forth in His Lively Colours: Or K. James His Description of a Puritan* (E 113/11, 1642), p. 1 and *passim*; *An Orderly and Plaine Narration of the Beginnings and Causes of This Warre* (E 54/3, 1644).

64. See, for example, Judith Maltby, 'Petitions for Episcopacy on the Eve of the Civil War, 1641–2', in S. Taylor ed., *From Cranmer to Davidson: A Church of England Miscellany* (Woodbridge, Suffolk, 1999), pp. 103–67; Morrill, 'The Church in England', in J. Morrill ed., *Reactions to the English Civil War* (Basingstoke, 1982), pp. 89–114.

65. John Taylor, *A Swarme of Sectaries, and Schismatiques: Wherein Is Discovered the Strange Preaching (or prating) of Such As Are by Their Trades Coblers, Tinkers, Pedlers, Weavers, Sowgelders, and Chymney-Sweepers* (E 158/1, 1642), p. 7 and *passim*.

66. *A Puritane Set Forth*, p. 6. Cf. *A Spirit Moving in the Women-Preachers: Or, Certaine Quaeres Vented and Put Forth Unto This Affronted, Brazen-faced, Strange, New Feminine Brood* (E 324/10, 1646).

67. James Howell, *Englands Teares, for the Present Wars* (E 253/10, 1644), p. 11.

68. *Mercurius Rusticus*, pp. 1, 22–3, 25, 27, 49, 77, 80.

69. See John Hall, *A True Account and Character of the Times, Historically and Politically Drawn by a Gentleman to Give Satisfaction to His Friend in the Countrey* (E 401/13, 1647), pp. 3–7 and *passim*.

70. *The Ballance Put Into the Hand of Every Rationall English-man, to Poize the State of This Kingdome* (E 381/8, 1647), p. 5.

71. R. H. Nichols, 'The Tercentenary of the Westminster Assembly', *Church History*, 13 (1944), pp. 25–41.

72. R. D. Bradley, 'The Failure of Accommodation: Religious Conflict between Presbyterians and Independents in the Westminster Assembly 1643–1646', *Journal of Religious History*, 12 (1982), pp. 23–47.

73. *The Cavaliers Bible, or a Squadron of XXXVI. Several Religions By Them Held and Maintained* (E 4/24, 1644).

74. Ibid., sig. A4ᵛ.

75. *A Charme for Canterburian Spirits* (E 269/18, 1645); Thomas Elyson, *The Shepherds Letters* (E 319/3, 1646), pp. 2–3.

76. Henry Robinson, *Liberty of Conscience: Or The Sole Means to Obtaine Peace and Truth* (E 39/1, 1643).

77. Ibid., pp. 27, 40.

78. The classic statement of this thesis is G. R. Abernathy, 'The English Presbyterians and the Stuart Restoration, 1648–63', *Proceedings of the American Philosophical Society*, 55 (1965), pp. 5–101. See my study of images of monarchy in England, 1660–1714 (forthcoming).

79. Sharpe, *Personal Rule*, pp. 758–65; above ch. 7, pp. 249–50.

80. J. H. Timmis, *Thine is the Kingdom: The Trial for Treason of Thomas Wentworth, Earl of Strafford, First Minister to King Charles I, and Last Hope of the English Crown* (Tuscaloosa, Ala., 1975); Timmis 'The Basis of the Lords' Decision in the Trial of Strafford: Contravention of the Two-witness Rule', *Albion*, 8 (1976), pp. 311–19; T. Kilburn and A. Milton, 'The Public Context of the

Trial and Execution of Strafford', in J. Merritt ed., *The Political World of Thomas Wentworth Earl of Strafford, 1621–1641* (Cambridge, 1996), pp. 230–51.

81. *The Confession, Obstinacy, and Ignorance, of Father Bell, a Romish Priest* (Wing B1799A, 1643), p. 5.

82. *The Whole Confession and Speech of Mr. Nathaniel Tompkins, Made Upon the Ladder at the Time of His Execution, on Wednesday the Fifth of July, 1643* (E 59/9, 1643); *Mr. Challenor His Confession and Speech Made Upon the Ladder Before His Execution on Wednesday the Fifth of July 1643* (E 59/7, 1643). See A. Hast, 'State Treason Trials during the Puritan Revolution, 1640–1660', *Historical Journal*, 15 (1972), pp. 37–53, especially p. 45.

83. Ithiel Smart, *A More Exact and Perfect Relation of the Treachery, Apprehension, Conviction, Condemnation, Confession, and Execution, of Francis Pitt, Aged 65. Who Was Executed in Smithfield on Saturday, October the 12. 1644. for Endeavouring to Betray the Garrison of Rushall-Hall in the County of Stafford, to the Enemy* (E 13/8, 1644), pp. 6, 8–9; see also the postscript to the reader, pp. 14–17.

84. The full proceedings of the trial are printed in W. Scott and J. Bliss eds, *The Works of William Laud* (7 vols in 9, Oxford, 1847–60), IV.

85. *The Archbishop of Canterbury's Speech: Or His Funerall Sermon, Preacht by Himself on the Scaffold on Tower-Hill, on Friday the 10. of Ianuary, 1644. Upon Hebrews 12. 1,2* (E 24/15, 1645), p. 9.

86. Ibid., pp. 9, 11, 13–14.

87. J. A. Sharpe, ' "Last Dying Speeches": Religion, Ideology and Public Execution in Seventeenth-Century England', *Past & Present*, 107 (1985), pp. 144–67; K. Royer, 'Dead Men Talking: Truth, Texts and the Scaffold in Early Modern England', in S. Devereaux and P. Griffiths eds, *Penal Practice and Culture, 1500–1900: Punishing the English* (Basingstoke, 2004), pp. 63–84.

88. *Foure Queries Resolved for the Satisfaction of All Men, Who Are Not Willingly Ignorant, Touching the Late Arch-bishop* (E 271/7, 1645), p. 4.

89. W. Starbuck, *A Briefe Exposition, Paraphrase, or Interpretation, Upon the Lord of Canterburies Sermon or Speech, Upon the Last Pulpit That Ever He Preached, Which Was the Scaffold on Tower-Hill* (E 26/1, 1645), p. 14.

90. Ibid., pp. 10, 15 and *passim*.

91. Ezekias Woodward, *The Life and Death of William Lawd, Late Archbishop of Canterburie: Beheaded on Tower-Hill, Friday the 10. of January. 1644* (E 26/17, 1645), sig. A2, pp. 9, 34.

92. Henry Burton, *The Grand Impostor Unmasked, Or, A Detection of the Notorious Hypocrisie, and Desperate Impiety of the Late Archbishop (so styled) of Canterbury, Cunningly Couched in that Written Copy, which he Read on the Scaffold at His Execution* (E 26/4, 1645), pp. 5, 7–8, 12 and *passim*.

93. Ibid., pp. 12, 14.

94. David Lagomarsino and Charles T. Wood eds, *The Trial of Charles I: A Documentary History* (Hanover, NH, 1989), p. 17.

95. S. Kelsey, 'Staging the Trial of Charles I', in J. Peacey ed., *The Regicides and the Execution of Charles I* (Basingstoke, 2001), p. 72.

96. Lagomarsino and Wood, *The Trial of Charles I*, p. 24; Kelsey, 'Staging the Trial', p. 79.

97. Kelsey, 'Staging the Trial', p. 80.

98. Ibid., p. 81. Evidently over £1,000 was spent on the constructions, Lagomarsino and Wood, *The Trial of Charles I*, p. 40.

99. Lagomarsino and Wood, *The Trial of Charles I*, pp. 43, 57.

100. Kelsey, 'Staging the Trial', p. 84.

101. Ibid.; Lagomarsino and Wood, *The Trial of Charles I*, p. 59.

102. Kelsey, 'Staging the Trial', p. 77.

103. Lagomarsino and Wood, *The Trial of Charles I*, p. 64.

104. Ibid.

105. Ibid., pp. 64–5.

106. Ibid.

107. Ibid., p. 67.

108. Ibid., pp. 67–9.

109. Ibid., pp. 71–3.

110. Ibid., p. 75; see D. P. Klein, 'The Trial of Charles I', *Journal of Legal History*, 18 (1997), pp. 1–25; S. Kelsey, 'The Trial of Charles I', *English Historical Review*, 118 (2003), pp. 583–616

111. Charles planned a full speech, see Lagomarsino and Wood, *The Trial of Charles I*, pp. 79–82.

112. Ibid., p. 85.

113. Ibid., p. 86.

114. Klein, 'Trial of Charles I', p. 16.

115. Lagomarsino and Wood, *The Trial of Charles I*, p. 89.

116. Ibid., p. 99.
117. Ibid., p. 103.
118. Ibid., p. 104.
119. Ibid., p. 105.
120. Ibid., p. 110; Peacey, *The Regicides*, p. 167.
121. Lagomarsino and Wood, *The Trial of Charles I*, pp. 111, 114.
122. Ibid., p. 117; cf. p. 128.
123. Ibid., pp. 121-8.
124. Kelsey, 'Staging the Trial of Charles I', p. 71.
125. Klein, 'Trial of Charles I', p. 3.
126. Jason Peacey, 'Reporting a Revolution: A Failed Propaganda Campaign', in Peacey, *The Regicides*, pp. 161-80.
127. Ibid., p. 173.
128. Lagomarsino and Wood, *The Trial of Charles I*, p. 64.
129. Ibid., p. 80; Ecclesiastes 8:4.

Prologue: Representing Republic

1. K. Sharpe, ' "An Image Doting Rabble": The Failure of Republican Culture in Seventeenth-Century England', in K. Sharpe and S. N. Zwicker eds, *Refiguring Revolutions: Aesthetics and Politics from the English Revolution to the Romantic Revolution* (Berkeley, 1998), pp. 25-56, 302-11.
2. See Sean Kelsey, *Inventing a Republic: The Political Culture of the English Commonwealth, 1649-1653* (Manchester, 1997); David Norbrook, *Writing the English Republic: Poetry, Rhetoric and Politics, 1627-1660* (Cambridge, 1999).
3. P. Collinson, 'The Monarchical Republic of Queen Elizabeth I', *Bulletin of the John Rylands University Library of Manchester*, 69 (1987), pp. 394-424; M. Peltonen, *Classical Humanism and Republicanism in English Political Thought, 1570-1640* (Cambridge, 1995); Peltonen, 'Citizenship and Republicanism in Elizabethan England', in M. van Gelderen and Q. Skinner eds, *Republicanism: A Shared European Heritage Vol.I: Republicanism and Constitutionalism in Early Modern Europe* (Cambridge 2002), pp. 85-106.
4. In *The History of Britain*, Milton argued that 'many civil virtues must be imported into our minds from foreign writings and examples of best ages, we shall else miscarry', Milton, *History of Britain*, in D. Wolfe et al. eds, *Complete Prose Works of John Milton*, V (New Haven and London, 1971), p. 450. See also, S. Achinstein, *Milton and the Revolutionary Reader* (Princeton, 1994).
5. Above, chs 5, 7, pp. 161-7, 238-9.
6. See D. Underdown, *Pride's Purge: Politics in the Puritan Revolution* (Oxford, 1971).
7. J. Peacey, 'Reporting a Revolution: A Failed Propaganda Campaign', in J. Peacey ed., *The Regicides and the Execution of Charles I* (Basingstoke, 2001), pp. 161-80.
8. Graham Edwards, *The Last Days of Charles I* (Stroud, 2001), p. 169 and ch. 14 *passim*; cf. R. Lockyer, *The Trial of Charles I: A Contemporary Account Taken from the Memoirs of Sir Thomas Herbert and John Rushworth* (1959).
9. Ibid., pp. 172-3.
10. Ibid., p. 179.
11. Ibid., pp. 180-1.
12. S. R. Gardiner, *History of the Great Civil War, 1642-1649* (4 vols, 1893), IV, p. 323; C. V. Wedgwood, *The Trial of Charles I* (1964), pp. 185-97.
13. Lockyer ed., *The Trial of Charles I*, p. 141.
14. Gardiner, *History of the Great Civil War*, IV, p. 325 notes that the bookseller, publisher and collector George Thomason dated his copy 9 February. It may have been published earlier and it has even been suggested that it was published the very day of the king's death, F. F. Madan, *A New Bibliography of the Eikon Basilike of King Charles the First* (Oxford, 1950), pp. 1-5; J. Gardner-Flint, 'The King's Book: The Puzzle of the *Eikon Basilike*', *University of Rochester Library Bulletin*, 34 (1981).

12 Writing Republic

1. See F. F. Madan, *A New Bibliography of the Eikon Basilike of King Charles the First; With a Note on the Authorship* (Oxford, 1950). See below, pp. 400-3. Controversy over authorship flared up again in 1692 with the publication of the Anglesey memorandum. I will be dealing with this in my study of images of late seventeenth-century monarchy.
2. Madan, *Bibliography*; E. Skerpan Wheeler, '*Eikon Basilike* and the Rhetoric of Self-Representation', in T. Corns ed., *The Royal Image: Representations of Charles I* (Cambridge, 1999), pp. 122-40; A.

Lacey, *The Cult of King Charles the Martyr* (Woodbridge, Suffolk, 2003), ch. 4; L. B. McKnight, 'Crucifixion or Apocalypse? Refiguring the *Eikon Basilike*', in D. Hamilton and R. Strier eds, *Religion, Literature and Politics in Post-Reformation England, 1540–1688* (Cambridge, 1996), pp. 138–60; L. Potter, 'Royal Actor as Royal Martyr: The *Eikon Basilike* and the Literary Scene in 1649', in G. Schochet, P. E. Tatspaugh and C. Brobeck eds, *Restoration, Ideology and Revolution* (Washington, DC, 1990), pp. 217–40.

3. *Eikon Basilike* (1879 edn), pp. 11, 52, 75, 106–7.
4. Ibid., pp. 45, 48, 74, 118, 153.
5. Ibid., p. 138.
6. Ibid., for example, pp. 21, 41, 58, 70, 80, 110.
7. Ibid., p. 1.
8. For example, ibid., pp. 35, 38, 77, 129, 152.
9. Ibid., pp. 2, 41, 187.
10. Ibid., p. 187.
11. Ibid., p. 189.
12. Ibid., pp. 29, 33, 44, 132, 164,
13. K. Sharpe, *Criticism and Compliment: The Politics of Literature in the England of Charles I* (Cambridge, 1987), chs 5, 6; K. Sharpe, *The Personal Rule of Charles I* (New Haven and London, 1992), pp. 222–35.
14. *Eikon*, p. 31; cf. p. 44.
15. John Milton, *Eikonoklastes*, in D. Wolfe et al. eds, *The Complete Prose Works of John Milton*, III, ed. M. Hughes (New Haven, 1962), p. 403.
16. *Eikon*, pp. 29, 70, 132.
17. Ibid., p. 164
18. K. Sharpe, 'Private Conscience and Public Duty in the Writings of James VI and I', in J. Morrill, P. Slack and D. Woolf eds, *Public Duty and Private Conscience in Seventeenth-Century England* (Oxford, 1992), pp. 77–100.
19. K. Sharpe, 'Private Conscience and Public Duty in the Writings of Charles I', *Historical Journal*, 40 (1997), pp. 643–65.
20. See Blair Worden, 'Providence and Politics in Cromwellian England', *Past & Present*, 109 (1985), pp. 55–99; below ch. 16, pp. 470–7.
21. *Eikon*, pp. 78, 109.
22. Ibid., p. 80.
23. Ibid., pp. 88, 91, 100, 153; Sharpe, 'Private Conscience and Public Duty in the Writings of Charles I'.
24. *Eikon*, p. 88.
25. Ibid., p. 89.
26. Ibid., ch. 17 *passim*.
27. Ibid., p. 125.
28. Ibid., p. 174.
29. Above, ch. 5, pp. 145–50.
30. Above, ch. 9, pp. 325–6.
31. For example, *Eikon*, p. 174.
32. Ibid., pp. 25, 165.
33. Skerpan Wheeler, '*Eikon Basilike*'; cf. E. Skerpan, *The Rhetoric of Politics in the English Revolution, 1642–1660* (1992), ch. 5, especially pp. 103–4; McKnight, 'Crucifixion or Apocalypse?'
34. *Eikon*, pp. 32, 190.
35. Ibid., p. 214.
36. Ibid., p. 217.
37. Above, ch. 9, pp. 323–6.
38. *Eikon*, p. 25.
39. Ibid., p. 34.
40. Ibid., p. 35.
41. Ibid., p. 36.
42. In ibid., ch. 7 Charles compares his constancy to his wife with that to his cause, his faith and the law.
43. Ibid., p. 191.
44. Ibid., p. 55.
45. J. Roberts, *The King's Head: Charles I, King and Martyr* (1999), pp. 30–4; Madan, *Bibilography*, pp. 1–5.
46. Skerpan, *Rhetoric of Politics*, p. 113.
47. *Eikon Alethine. The Pourtraiture of Truths Most Sacred Majesty Truly Suffering, Though Not Solely. Wherein the False Colours Are Washed Off, Wherewith the Painter-steiner Had Bedawbed Truth,*

the Late King and the Parliament, in His Counterfeit Piece Entituled Eikon Basilike (Thomason E 569/16, 1649), sigs A–A2ᵛ.

48. Ibid., sig. A1ᵛ.
49. Ibid., sig. A3.
50. Ibid., sigs A3ᵛ–A4, p. 51.
51. Ibid., p. 6.
52. Skerpan, *Rhetoric of Politics*, p. 113.
53. Milton, *Eikonoklastes*, III, p. 337.
54. Ibid., pp. 360–3. Milton uses the word 'plagiarie', p. 547.
55. Ibid., p. 365.
56. Ibid., pp. 423–32.
57. Ibid., p. 497.
58. Ibid., p. 342.
59. Ibid., p. 403.
60. Ibid., p. 418.
61. Ibid., p. 564.
62. Ibid., pp. 420–1.
63. Ibid., p. 421.
64. Ibid., pp. 406, 421.
65. Ibid., p. 585.
66. Ibid., p. 433.
67. Ibid., pp. 493, 533.
68. Ibid., p. 382.
69. Ibid., p. 405.
70. Ibid., p. 531.
71. Ibid., p. 530.
72. Ibid., p. 377.
73. Ibid., p. 342.
74. Ibid., pp. 498, 530.
75. Ibid., p. 601.
76. Ibid.
77. Below pp. 438, 453–5; Roberts, *King's Head*, pp. 19–35; H. Farquhar, 'Portraits of the Stuarts on the Royalist Badges', *British Numismatic Journal*, 2 (1906), pp. 23–30.
78. *Eikonoklastes* (Wing M2114,1650); *Eikonoklastes* (Wing M2115, 1690).
79. Sean Kelsey, *Inventing a Republic: The Political Culture of the English Commonwealth, 1649–1653* (Manchester, 1997), p. 1.
80. *A Declaration of the Lords and Commons Assembled in Parliament, Concerning the Tryall of the King* (E 536/36, 1649); *A Declaration of the Commons of England Assembled in Parliament, Expressing Their Reasons for the Adnulling and Vacating of These Ensuing Votes* (E 538/23, 1649).
81. C. H. Firth and R. S. Rait, *Acts and Ordinances of the Interregnum, 1642–1660* (3 vols, London, 1911), II, pp. 24, 6–9; *The Declaration and Resolution of His Highnesse the Prince of Wales, Upon the Death of His Royall Father* (Wing C2956, Edinburgh 1649); *A Declaration from His Hignesse the Prince of Wales: Concerning the Illegall Proceeding of the Commons of England* (E 542/15, 1649); *The Declaration and Resolution of the King of Scotland to All His Loving Subjects Within the Territories of That Kingdome* (E 554/9, 1649).
82. *A Declaration of the Parliament of England, for Maintaining the Fundamental Laws of This Nation* (E 1060/4, 1649).
83. Firth and Rait eds, *Acts and Ordinances*, II, pp. 18–20.
84. Ibid., p. 19.
85. Ibid., pp. 19–20.
86. *A Declaration of the Parliament of England, Expressing the Grounds of Their Late Proceedings, and of Setling the Present Government in a Way of a Free State* (E 548/12, 1649).
87. Thomason did not annotate this document, as he did many, with the date he acquired it.
88. *A Declaration of the Parliament*, pp. 5–6.
89. Ibid., p. 6.
90. Ibid.
91. Ibid., pp. 6–8, 17–18. Scandalous opposition pamphlets had accused Charles and Buckingham of poisoning King James.
92. Ibid., p. 10.
93. Ibid., p. 11.
94. Ibid., p. 13.
95. Ibid., p. 14.

96. Ibid.
97. Ibid., p. 15.
98. Ibid., p. 16.
99. Ibid.
100. Ibid.
101. Ibid., p. 17.
102. Ibid., p. 19.
103. Ibid., pp. 20–1.
104. *A Declaration of the Commons of England Assembled in Parliament, of Their True Intentions Concerning the Ancient and Fundamental Government of the Kingdom* (E 333/19, 1646).
105. *Declaration* (E 548/12, 1649), p. 21.
106. Ibid., pp. 22–3.
107. Ibid., p. 24.
108. Ibid., pp. 25–7.
109. Ibid., p. 27.
110. See *A Letter from the Commissioners of the Kingdome of Scotland Residing Here at London, to William Lenthal Esquire, Speaker to the House of Commons. Concerning the Present Proceedings in This Kingdome, Against Religion, the King, and Government: Together With Their Declaration and Protestation, Against the Taking Away of His Majesties Life* (E 539/11, 1649).
111. *A Declaration of the Parliament of England, in Answer to the Late Letters Sent to Them from the Commissioners of Scotland* (E 544/17, 1649).
112. Ibid., p. 28.
113. Ibid., pp. 35–7.
114. *A Declaration of the Proceedings of the Parliament of Scotland and Their Message and Proposals to Their New King in Holland; Declaring Their Full Resolution and Desires, Touching the English Army; As Also, Their Further Resolution for the Raising a Great Army . . . to Engage Against England* (E 545/1, 1649); *The Desires of the Commissioners of the Kingdom of Scotland: That Both Houses of Parliament May Sit in Freedom for Setling of Religion According to the Covenant. That King Charls the Second (Upon Just Satisfaction Given) May Be Admitted to the Government of These Kingdomes. Together with Their Protestation Against Their Proceedings to the Contrary* (E 545/28, 1649); *A Declaration of the Parliament of Scotland for Rerigion [sic], Crown, and Covenant, and Their Resolution to Adhere Thereunto, and to Preserve and Maintain Their Ancient Government, by a Mixt Monarchy of King, Lords, and Commons, and Their Further Proceedings Thereupon, in Relation to Their Young King, and the Parliament of England* (E 563/4, 1649). Quotation from *A Message Sent from the Parliament of Scotland to the Queen of Sweden and Their Desires Touching Prince Charles, and the Parliament of England; With a Narrative of Their Falling Off, and Detesting Against the Late Proceedings, in Reference to Charles the I* (E 563/5, 1649).
115. *A Declaration of the Parliament of England Concerning Their Late Endeavors, in a Peaceable Way, to Remove All Misunderstandings, and Differences Between the Common-wealth of England, and the Kingdome of Scotland* (E 565/17, 1649).
116. Ibid., p. 4.
117. Ibid., p. 5.
118. Ibid., pp. 6–7.
119. See ibid., p. 9.
120. Ibid., p. 10.
121. Isaac Dorislaus, *ODNB*.
122. *A Declaration of the Parliament of England, of Their Just Resentment of the Horrid Murther Perpetrated on the Body of Isaac Dorislaus, Doctor of the Laws, Their Resident at the Hague, on the 12th of May, 1649* (E 1060/28, 1649), p. 246.
123. Ibid., p. 246.
124. Ibid., p. 247.
125. Firth and Rait eds, *Acts and Ordinances*, II, pp.20–2, 24–57, 63–5.
126. Ibid., pp. 152–4, 155–6, 160–91. See below, pp. 427–8.
127. Ibid., pp. 193–4.
128. Ibid., pp. 245–54.
129. Ibid., p. 245.
130. Ibid., p. 245, my italics.
131. Ibid.
132. *A Declaration of the Parliament of England, in Vindication of Their Proceedings, and Discovering the Dangerous Practices of Several Interests, Against the Present Government, and Peace of the Commonwealth* (E 575/9, 1649).
133. Ibid., p. 6.

134. Ibid., p. 8.
135. Ibid., p. 9.
136. Ibid.
137. Ibid., pp. 10–12.
138. Ibid., p. 13.
139. Ibid., p. 14.
140. Ibid., pp. 14–19.
141. Ibid., p. 18.
142. Ibid., pp. 18, 21.
143. Ibid., pp. 22, 25.
144. Ibid., p. 20.
145. Ibid., p. 28.
146. Ibid., p. 29.
147. Ibid., p. 30.
148. Firth and Rait eds, *Acts and Ordinances*, II, pp. 325–9.
149. On the engagement, see Blair Worden, *The Rump Parliament, 1648–1653* (Cambridge, 1974), pp. 226–30; Quentin Skinner, 'Conquest and Consent: Thomas Hobbes and the Engagement Controversy', in G. E. Aylmer ed., *The Interregnum: The Quest for Settlement, 1646–60* (1972), pp. 79–98.
150. Firth and Rait eds, *Acts and Ordinances*, II, p. 325.
151. Worden, *Rump Parliament*, p. 227.
152. S. R. Gardiner, *History of the Commonwealth and Protectorate, 1649–1656* (4 vols, 1903), I, pp. 240–1.
153. Ibid., p. 248; Worden, *Rump Parliament*, pp. 231–2. *Mercurius Pragmaticus* (E 600/6, 30 April–7 May), p. 6 reported that 'the great work of engagement is not so eagerly followed now the saints have other fish to fry'.
154. *A Declaration of the Parlament of England, Upon the Marching of the Armie into Scotland. Die Mercurii Junii 26. 1650* (E 604/6, 1650).
155. Ibid., pp. 2–3.
156. Ibid., p. 7.
157. Ibid., p. 9.
158. *A Declaration of the Army of England, Upon Their March into Scotland. Signed in the Name, and by the Appointment of His Excellency the Lord General Cromwel, and His Councel of Officers. Jo: Rushworth Secr' Die Veneris, 19 Julii, 1650. Resolved by the Parliament, That This Declaration Be Forthwith Printed and Published. Hen: Scobell, Cleric. Parliamenti* (E 607/20, 1650).
159. Ibid., p. 3.
160. Ibid., p. 6.
161. Ibid., pp. 7, 9.
162. Ibid., pp. 9–10, 15.
163. Ibid., pp. 2–3, 14 and *passim*.
164. Gardiner, *History of the Commonwealth and Protectorate*, I, pp. 276–9; *A Declaration by the Kings Majesty, to His Subjects of the Kingdomes of Scotland, England, and Ireland* (Wing C2959, Edinburgh, 1650).
165. *An Act and Declaration of the Parliament of England Touching a Pamphlet, Entituled, A Declaration by the Kings Majesty, to His Subjects of the Kingdoms of Scotland, England and Ireland. Printed at Edinburgh, 1650* (669 f. 15/51), one page.
166. *The Answer of the Parliament of England, to a Paper, Entituled, A Declaration by the Kings Majesty, to His Subjects of the Kingdoms of Scotland, England and Ireland. Printed at Edinburgh, 1650* (E 613/2, 1650).
167. Ibid., pp. 5–6.
168. Ibid., p. 7.
169. Ibid., pp. 7, 19.
170. Ibid., pp. 20, 30–1.
171. Ibid., pp. 35–6.
172. Firth and Rait eds, *Acts and Ordinances*, II, pp. 369–78, 387–9, 409–12, 455–6.
173. *A Declaration by the Kings Majesty to His Subjects of the Kingdomes of Scotland, England, and Ireland* (C 2960A, 1650).
174. Gardiner, *History of the Commonwealth and Protectorate*, II, pp. 8–9; *A Declaration Conteynyng the Iust Causes and Consyderations of This Present Warre With the Scottis Wherin Alsoo Appereth the Trewe & Right Title, That the Kinges Most Royall Maiesty Hath to the Souerayntie of Scotlande* (H 1470, 1651), originally printed by Thomas Berthelet in 1542.
175. *Resolved by the Parliament That Whatsoever Person or Persons Have, Or Shall Have in Their Custody Any of the Printed Papers (Entituled, His Majesties Declaration to All His Loving Subjects*

of the Kingdom of England and Dominion of Wales) Be Injoyned Forthwith to Bring the Same in to the Councel of State (Wing E 2248, 1651).

176. *A Proclamation of the Parliament of the Commonwealth of England Declaring Charls Stuart and His Abettors, Agents and Complices, to be Traytors, Rebels and Publique Enemies* (669 f. 16/21, 1651).

177. See Gardiner, *History of the Commonwealth and Protectorate*, II, ch. 16.

178. *A Declaration of the Parliament of the Commonwealth of England Concerning the Settlement of Scotland* (E 655/11, 1652). Thomason's copy is dated 23 February.

179. Gardiner, *History of the Commonwealth and Protectorate*, II, pp. 145–6.

180. Ibid., II, ch. 24.

181. See Worden, *Rump Parliament*, chs 13–15 *passim*.

182. *A Great and Bloudy Fight at Sea: Between Five Men of War Belonging to the Parliament of England, and a Squadron of the Irish Fleet* (E 542/6, 1649).

183. Ibid., pp. 4–5.

184. *The Lord Gen. Cromwel's Letter: With a Narrative of the Proceedings of the English Army in Scotland* (E 610/4, 1650).

185. *A True Relation of the Routing the Scotish Army Near Dunbar, Sept. 3. Instant: The Particulars of the Fight, Numbers Slain, and Prize Taken* (E 612/9, 1650).

186. Ibid., pp. 4–5.

187. *A Letter from the Lord Generall Cromwell to the Parliament of England, Concerning His Proceedings with Their Army in Scotland and the Late Victory God Hath Given Them Over the Scottish Army There Together with an Act of Parliament for Publique Thanksgiving in England Thereupon* (C7104, 1650).

188. Ibid., sigs A2–3ᵛ.

189. Ibid., sig. A3ᵛ.

190. Ibid.

191. *A Great Victory by the Blessing of God, Obtained by the Parliaments Forces, Against the Scots Forces. Commanded by the Earl of Derby, on the 25 of August 1651* (E 640/27, 1651).

192. See, for example, above, ch. 9, pp. 323–5.

193. *An Act for Setting Apart a Day of Publique Thanksgiving, and Declaring the Reasons and Grounds Thereof. Die Veneris, 1 Junii, 1649. Ordered by the Commons Assembled in Parliament, That This Act be Forthwith Printed and Published* (E 1060/34, 1649). See also, *A Form of Prayer: to be Used for Both the Days of Publique Thanksgiving for the Seasonable and Happy Reducing of the Levellers, being Thursday June 7. and All England Over on Thursday June 28. 1649* (E 558/22, 1649).

194. *Act for Day of Publique Thanksgiving*, p. 277.

195. *An Act for Setting Apart a Day of Publique Thanksgiving, to be Kept on Wednesday the 29th of August, 1649* (E 1060/55, 1649), p. 451.

196. Ibid., pp. 452, 454–5.

197. Ibid., p. 456.

198. *An Act for a Day of Publique Thanksgiving to be Observed Throughout England and Wales, on Thursday on the First of November, 1649 Together with a Declaration of the Grounds Thereof* (669 f. 14/80, 1649), a broadside.

199. Ibid.

200. For example, *An Act for the Setting Apart a Day of Publique Thanks-giving, to be Kept on Friday the Twenty Sixth of This Instant July. Together with a Declaration & Narrative, Expressing the Grounds and Reasons Thereof. Die Jovis, 11 Julii, 1650. Ordered by the Parliament, That This Act, Together with the List of the Officers and Soldiers Slain and Taken . . . be Forthwith Printed and Published* (E 1061/7, 1650).

201. *An Act for Setting Apart Tuesday the Eighth of October Next, for a Day of Publique Thanks-giving* (E 1061/17, 1650), p. 1002.

202. Ibid., p. 1003.

203. *An Act for Setting Apart Thursday the Thirtieth Day of January, 1650. for a Day of Publique Thanksgiving: Together with a Declaration of the Grounds and Reasons Thereof. Die Martis, 3 Januarii, 1650* (E 1061/33, 1651), p. 1270.

204. Ibid., p. 1272.

205. *An Act for Setting Apart a Day of Publique Fasting and Humiliation to be Observed on Thursday the Thirteenth Day of March, 1650. Within the Cities of London and Westminster; and on the Second Day of April, 1651. In All Other Places Within This Commonwealth* (E 1061/42, 1650), p. 1315.

206. Ibid., pp. 1317–19.

207. *An Act for Setting Apart Friday the Four and Twentieth Day of October, One Thousand Six Hundred Fifty One, for a Day of Publique Thanksgiving* (E 1061/57, 1651), p. 1433.

208. Ibid., p. 1440.

209. H. R. Trevor-Roper, *Religion, the Reformation and Social Change* (1984), ch. 6.
210. Ibid., pp. 325–9.
211. John Owen, *A Sermon Preached to the Honourable House of Commons, in Parliament Assembled: On January 31* (E 549/1, 1649).The Clerk of the Parliament's order to publish is printed opposite the title page.
212. See, for example, Owen, *Ouranon Ourania· The Shaking and Translating of Heaven and Earth. A Sermon Preached to the Honourable House of Commons in Parliament Assembled: On April 19. a Day Set Apart for Extraordinary Humiliation* (E 551/4, 1649); Owen, *ODNB*.
213. John Owen, *The Stedfastness of Promises, and the Sinfulness of Staggering: Opened in a Sermon Preached at Margarets in Westminster Before the Parliament Febr. 28. 1649* (E 599/9, 1649).
214. Thomas Watson, *Gods Anatomy Upon Mans Heart. Or, A Sermon Preached by Order of the Honorable House of Commons, at Margarets Westminster, Decemb. 27. Being a Day of Publique Humiliation* (E 536/7, 1649), p. 2 (Watson was pastor of Stephen's Walbrook, London); John Warren, *The Potent Potter: Or, A Sermon Preached Before the Honourable, the Commons of England Assembled in Parliament; on Thursday the 19. of April 1649. Being a Day Set Apart for Solemne Humiliation at Margaret's Westminster* (E 551/5, 1649), p. 12. Warren was minister of Hatfield Broad Oak, Essex.
215. Warren, *Potent Potter*, pp. 14–15.
216. Thomas Brooks, *The Hypocrite Detected, Anatomized, Impeached, Arraigned, and Condemned Before the Parliament of England* (E 614/3, 1650), p. 22. On Brooks, a steady supporter of the army later, see *ODNB*.
217. Vavasour Powell, *Christ Exalted Above All Creatures by God His Father or A Sermon Preached Before the Right Honourable, the Parliament of the Commonwealth of England. (At Their Solemne Fast, Observed the Last Day of the Last Month Called February 1649.)* (E 1332/4, 1651), p. 87. Powell was a Welsh Fifth Monarchist.
218. See John Owen, *The Labouring Saints Dismission to Rest. A Sermon Preached at the Funeral of the Right Honourable Henry Ireton Lord Deputy of Ireland: in the Abbey Church at Westminster, the 6th. Day of February 1651* (E 654/3, 1652).
219. J. Owen, *The Advantage of the Kingdom of Christ, in the Shaking of the Kingdoms of the World: Or Providential Alterations in Their Subserviencie to Christ's Exaltation Opened, in a Sermon Preached to the Parliament, Octob. 24. 1651* (Wing 0711A), sig. A1^v.
220. Ibid., sig. A4^v.
221. Owen nominated members to the Barebones Assembly, *ODNB*.
222. Joad Raymond, *Pamphlets and Pamphleteering in Early Modern Britain* (Cambridge, 2003), p. 154. On Nedham see also Raymond, *Making the News: An Anthology of the Newsbooks of Revolutionary England, 1641-1660* (Moreton in Marsh, 1993), ch. 8; B. Worden, ' "Wit in a Roundhead": The Dilemma of Marchamont Nedham', in S. Amussen and M. Kishlansky eds, *Political Culture and Cultural Politics in Early Modern England* (Manchester, 1995), pp. 301–37; Worden, *Literature and Politics in Cromwellian England: John Milton, Andrew Marvell, Marchamont Nedham* (Oxford, 2007) chs 1–3.
223. Raymond, *Pamphlets*, p. 155; *Mercurius Politicus* 4–11 July 1650 (E 607/12), p. 65.
224. D. Norbrook, *Writing the English Republic: Poetry, Rhetoric and Politics, 1627–1660* (Cambridge, 1999), p. 223.
225. *Mercurius Politicus* 4–11 July 1650 (E 607/12), p. 65.
226. Ibid., pp. 65–6.
227. Raymond, *Making the News*, p. 365.
228. Ibid., pp. 365–6.
229. Ibid., p. 366.
230. Ibid., p. 367. See *Mercurius Politicus* 9–16 January 1651 for a succinct pre-formulation of the argument of Hobbes's *Leviathan*.
231. Raymond, *Making the News*, pp. 368–9.
232. Ibid., pp. 367–9.
233. Worden, ' "Wit in a Roundhead" ', p. 326.
234. Norbrook, *Writing the English Republic*, pp. 225, 328; Raymond, *Making the News*, p. 336; Worden, ' "Wit in a Roundhead" '.
235. Norbrook, *Writing the English Republic*, p. 203.
236. Ibid., ch. 5 *passim*.
237. Ibid., p. 216; John Hall, *An Humble Motion to the Parliament of England Concerning the Advancement of Learning, and Reformation of the Universities* (Wing H350, 1649).
238. Norbrook, *Writing the English Republic*, pp. 225–8; Thomas May, *Lucans Pharsalia, or, The Civil-Wars of Rome, between Pompey the Great, and Julius Caesar the Whole Ten Books Englished by Thomas May, Esquire* (Wing L3387, 1650).

239. John Warr, *The Priviledges of the People, or, Principles of Common Right and Freedome, Briefely Laid Open and Asserted in Two Chapters* (E 541/12, 1649), see Warr, *ODNB*; Robert Wharton, *A Declaration to Great Britain and Ireland, Shewing the Downfall of Their Princes, and Wherefore It Is Come Upon Them* (E 555/35, 1649).

240. Robert Bennet, *King Charle's Triall Justified: Or, Eight Objections Against the Same Fully Answered and Cleared, by Scripture, Law, History and Reason* (E 554/21, 1649), p. 3 and *passim*.

241. John Goodwin, *Hybristodikai. The Obstructours of Justice. Or a Defence of the Honourable Sentence Passed Upon the Late King, by the High Court of Justice* (E 557/2, 1649), sig. A3.

242. Ibid., sigs A3–3ᵛ and *passim*.

243. *A Short Discourse Between Monarchical and Aristocratical Government. Or a Sober Perswasive of All True-Hearted Englishmen, to a Willing Conjunction with the Parliament of England in Setting Up the Government of a Common-Wealth* (E 575/31, 1649), pp. 4–7.

244. Ibid., pp. 8, 11.

245. Ibid., p. 19.

246. Ibid., p. 12.

247. *The Lawfulnes of Obeying the Present Government* (E 551/22, 1649). The pamphlet has been ascribed to Francis Rous.

248. *The Bounds & Bonds of Publique Obedience. Or, A Vindication of Our Lawfull Submission to the Present Government, Or To a Government Supposed Unlawfull, But Commanding Lawfull Things* (E 571/26, 1649), pp. 30–1. This has been attributed to Antony Ascham.

249. Albertus Warren, *The Royalist Reform'd or Considerations of Advice, to Gentlemen, Divines, Lawyers. Digested into Three Chapters. Wherein Their Former Mistakes Are Examined, and Their Duties of Obedience, Unto the Present Authority, Succinctly Held Forth as Rationall, and Necessary* (E 582/4, 1649), p. 20 and *passim*.

250. S. Barber, 'The Engagement for the Council of State and the Establishment of the Commonwealth Government', *Historical Research*, 63 (1990), pp. 44–57.

251. *A Logical Demonstration of the Lawfulness of Subscribing the New Engagement. Or, Promise to be True and Faithful to the Common-Weal As It Is Now Established: in Four Arguments* (E 590/11, 1649). The author endeavoured to reinterpret Romans 13 as an argument for the Commonwealth (pp. 1–2).

252. Ibid., p. 5.

253. M. Nedham, *The Case of the Common-Wealth of England, Stated: Or, The Equity, Utility, and Necessity, of a Submission to the Present Government; Cleared Out of Monuments Both Sacred and Civill, Against All the Scruples and Pretences of the Opposite Parties* (E 600/7, 1650).

254. Ibid., sig. A2.

255. Ibid., pp. 1–5.

256. Ibid., pp. 6–17.

257. Ibid., pp. 17–18.

258. Ibid., pp. 23, 25.

259. Ibid., p. 31.

260. Ibid., p. 92.

261. Ibid., p. 93.

262. *A Word of Councel to the Disaffected* (Thomason 669 f. 15/74, 1650), broadside.

263. See, for example, John Parker, *The Government of the People of England Precedent and Present the Same* (E 594/19, 1650).

264. Henry Parker, *The True Portraiture of the Kings of England; Drawn From Their Titles, Successions, Raigns and Ends* (E 609/2, 1650), p. 15.

265. Nathaniel Bacon, *The Continuation of An Historicall Discourse, of the Government of England, Untill the End of the Reigne of Queene Elizabeth. With a Preface, Being a Vindication of the Ancient Way of Parliaments in England* (E 624/1, 1651), p. 307.

266. *Anglia Liberata, Or, The Rights of the People of England, Maintained Against the Pretences of the Scotish King* (E 643/7, 1651), p. 43 and *passim*.

267. Ibid., pp. 49–59, 63, 67–8.

268. William Lilly, *Monarchy or No Monarchy in England. Grebner His Prophecy Concerning Charles Son of Charles, His Greatnesse, Victories, Conquests* (E 638/17, 1651), p. 54.

269. John Cook, *Monarchy No Creature of Gods Making, &c. Wherein Is Proved by Scripture and Reason, that Monarchial Government Is Against the Mind of God* (E 1238/1, 1652), sig. a1, pp. 3, 44, 80, 116 and *passim*. Cook was Chief Justice of Munster.

270. As he was called in several tracts, for example *Anglia Liberata*, p. 49.

271. Lilly, *Monarchy or No Monarchy*, pp. 74 ff.

272. Ibid., p. 81.

273. Balthazar Gerbier, *The None-Such Charles His Character Extracted, Out of Divers Originall Transactions, Dispatches and the Notes of Severall Publick Ministers, and Councellours of State as*

Wel at Home as Abroad. Published by Authority (E 1345/2, 1651). On Gerbier, a former agent for Charles I in collecting pictures turned Commonwealth apologist, see *ODNB*.

274. *The Life and Reigne of King Charls or, the Pseudo-Martyr Discovered. With a Late Reply to an Invective Remonstrance Against the Parliament and Present Government* (E 1338/2, 1652), sig. A3ᵛ. This work is almost certainly by, or partly by, John Milton.

275. Ibid., sigs * A8–*a¹. The language closely follows Milton's *Eikonoklastes*.

276. Ibid., p. 178.

277. William Ball, *A Briefe Treatise Concerning the Regulating of Printing. Humbly Presented to the Parliament of England* (E 1295/3, 1651).

278. Robert Spry, *Rules of Civil Goverment Drawn from the Best Examples of Forreign Nations, and Common-Wealths Briefely Discovering the Excellency and Benefit of Good Governors, and the Dangerous Consequence of Corrupt Self-Seekers* (E 1484/3, 1653), sig. A3.

279. Ibid., 'Postscript' after p. 55.

280. A. Woolrych, *Commonwealth to Protectorate* (Oxford, 1982), p. 144.

281. *A Declaration of the Parliament of the Commonwealth of England* (E 1062/5, 1653).

282. Ibid., p. 2.

283. Ibid., pp. 3, 6.

284. Ibid., p. 5.

285. Woolrych, *Commonwealth to Protectorate*, pp. 157 ff.

286. Gardiner, *History of the Commonwealth and Protectorate*, II, p. 290.

287. Woolrych, *Commonwealth to Protectorate*, ch. 9 *passim*; Firth and Rait, *Acts and Ordinances*, II, pp. 753–68.

288. Woolrych, *Commonwealth to Protectorate*, p. 165 and ch. 6 *passim*.

289. Ibid., pp. 326–7.

290. A. Woolrych, *Britain in Revolution, 1625–1660* (Oxford, 2002), p. 538.

13 A Republican Brand?

1. C. H. Firth and R. S. Rait eds, *Acts and Ordinances of the Interregnum, 1642–1660* (3 vols, 1911), II, pp. 160–8.

2. Ibid., p. 160.

3. Ibid., p. 167.

4. Ibid., pp. 165–6.

5. A. MacGregor, 'The King's Goods and the Commonwealth Sale. Materials and Context', in A. MacGregor ed., *The Late King's Goods: Collections, Possessions, and Patronage of Charles I in the Light of the Commonwealth Sale Inventories* (Oxford, 1989), pp. 16 and 13–52 *passim*. See also Jerry Brotton, *The Sale of the Late King's Goods: Charles I and his Art Collection* (Basingstoke, 2006).

6. Firth and Rait, *Acts and Ordinances*, II, p. 162.

7. F. Haskell, 'Charles I's Collection of Pictures', in MacGregor, *Late King's Goods*, p. 227.

8. See Oliver Millar ed., *The Inventories and Valuations of the King's Goods, 1649–51* (Walpole Society, 43, 1972 for 1970–2), pp. 63–4, 121, 161–2, 165, 189, 205, 256–8, 260, 272, 299, 302, 305, 310, 313–15, 318, 325, 338

9. Ibid. See index for former royal jewellers, tailors, grooms, gardeners, plumbers and merchants, army officers and soldiers who acquired formerly royal artefacts. Most of what was purchased were household artefacts but we should not underestimate the number of portraits that were sold. Along with scores of portraits of Tudor and contemporary European kings, queens, princes and princesses, and many of members of the Stuart royal family (James I, Anne, Prince Henry and Princess Elizabeth, the Prince of Orange), I counted two dozen paintings of Charles I, Henrietta Maria and their children sold.

10. Maija Jansson, 'Remembering Marston Moor: The Politics of Culture', in S. Amussen and M. Kishlansky eds, *Political Culture and Cultural Politics in Early Modern England* (Manchester, 1995), p. 255.

11. Ibid., p .256.

12. Ibid., pp. 256–9; D. Cressy, *Bonfires and Bells: National Memory and the Protestant Calendar in Elizabethan and Stuart England* (1989), ch. 7.

13. Jansson, 'Remembering Marston Moor', p. 257.

14. Ibid., p. 258. Such a canvas would indeed have been an innovation to England but, for the fledgling republic, an important one.

15. Gerbier, *ODNB*; above, p. 424.

16. Above, pp. 339, 349–50; O. Millar, *Sir Peter Lely, 1618–80* (1978) no. 22, pp. 46–7.

17. George Geldorp, *ODNB*.

18. Jansson, 'Remembering Marston Moor', p. 258. Joint financing would also have been in the Commonwealth spirit of community and co-operative action.

19. Ibid., p. 268.

20. Ibid., p. 269.

21. K. Sharpe, ' "An Image Doting Rabble": The Failure of Republican Culture in Seventeenth-century England', in K. Sharpe and S. Zwicker eds, *Refiguring Revolutions: Aesthetics and Politics from the English Revolution to the Romantic Revolution* (Berkeley and London, 1998), pp. 25–56, 302–11.

22. Again my sample of engravings is from the Huntington Bull Granger, Ashmolean Sutherland and British Museum collections. Illustrations to Thomason tracts are easily located via the *Catalogue of the Pamphlets, Newspapers and Manuscripts Relating to the Civil War, the Commonwealth, and Restoration, Collected by George Thomason, 1640–1661* (2 vols, 1908) and Early English Books Online.

23. John Parker, *The Government of the People of England Precedent and Present the Same* (E 594/19, 1650).

24. Ibid., p. 1.

25. *The Articles of Agreement, for the Surrender of the Strong & Invincible Castle of Edinborough* (E 620/15, 1651).

26. *A List of the Princes, Dukes, Earls, Lords, Knights, Generals, Maior Generalls, &c. and Colonells, of the Scots Kings Party Slaine and Taken Prisoners* (Thomason 669 f. 16/29, 1651).

27. *A Narration of the Most Material Parliamentary Proceedings of This Present Parliament and Their Armies in Their Civil and Martial Affairs which Parliament Began the Third of November 1640, and the Remarkable Transactions Are Continued Until This Year* (Wing N161, 1651)

28. See part II (repaginated), p. 17.

29. *The Maner of Siting of the Parliament of the Commonwealth of England* (Thomason 669 f. 17/37, 1653).

30. Above, ch. 10, pp. 351–4.

31. National Portrait Gallery NPG D2347, 3301, D10580; F. O'Donoghue, *Catalogue of Engraved British Portraits* (6 vols, 1908–25), II, pp. 224, 605, III, p. 456; *ODNB*; A. Globe ed., *Peter Stent, London Printseller circa 1642–65: Being a Catalogue Raisonné of his Engraved Prints and Books with an Historical and Bibliographical Introduction* (Vancouver, 1985), pp. 8–9, 61; *An Elegy (sacred) to the Immortal Memory of that Most Renowned, Religious, Prudent, and Victorious Commander, Henry Ireton Late Lord Deputy of Ireland* (E 445A, 1652), illustrated broadside.

32. See, for example, NPG D16565, D16572, D16574, D16575.

33. *A Perfect Table of One Hundred Forty and Five Victories Obtained by the Lord Lieutenant of Ireland, and the Parliaments Forces Under His Command, Since His Excellency Was Made Governor Generall by the Parliament of England from Wednesday August i. 1649. to March the Last, 1650* (Thomason 669 f. 15/26, 1651).

34. See J. R. Paas, 'The Changing Image of Gustavus Adolphus on German Broadsheets 1630–3', *Journal of the Warburg and Courtauld Institutes*, 59 (1996), pp. 205–44, illustration p. 213; below ch. 17, pp. 497–50.

35. *A Perfect List of All the Victories Obtained by the Lord General Cromwel From the Time that His Excellency Was Made Captain General and Commander in Cheif of the Parliament Forces in England, Ireland, and Scotland* (Thomason 669 f. 16/27, 1651). See below, p. 435, fig. 77.

36. See S. J. Barnes, N. De Poorter, O. Millar and H. Vey, *Van Dyck: A Complete Catalogue of the Paintings* (New Haven and London, 2004), fig. IV.215, pp. 598–9. I discuss this image of Cromwell below pp. 494–5.

37. Laura Knoppers, *Constructing Cromwell: Ceremony, Portrait and Print, 1645–1661* (Cambridge, 2000), p. 58. I am grateful to Laura Knoppers for many stimulating and helpful discussions.

38. Payne Fisher, *Veni; Vidi; Vici. The Triumphs of the Most Excellent & Illustrious, Oliver Cromwell, &c., Set Forth in a Panegyricke* (E 1298/1, 1652).

39. Payne Fisher, *Irenodia Gratulatoria, Sive Illustrissimi Amplissimiq[ue] Viri Oliveri Cromwelli, &c. Epinicion* (E 796/30, 1652).

40. H. W. Henfrey, *Numismata Cromwelliana: Coins, Medals and Seals of Oliver Cromwell* (1877), p. 3; below p. 440. It has been pointed out to me that it is not surprising that images of Cromwell were favoured. I agree; but, as Oliver intuited, this was not the best way to represent or establish a Commonwealth.

41. L. Knoppers, 'The Politics of Portraiture: Oliver Cromwell and the Plain Style', *Renaissance Quarterly*, 51 (1998), pp. 1283–319.

42. See below ch. 17, pp. 493–511.

43. On satires of Cromwell as general, see Knoppers, *Constructing Cromwell*, pp. 17–19.

44. S. Sean Kelsey, *Inventing a Republic: The Political Culture of the English Commonwealth, 1649–1653* (Manchester, 1997), p. 85.

45. Ibid., p. 86.
46. Ibid.
47. Ibid., pp. 87–8.
48. Ibid., p. 89.
49. Ibid., pp. 90–1; Firth and Rait, *Acts and Ordinances*, II, p. 17.
50. The oak was sacred to Jupiter, chief of the classical gods, and to the Druids, founders of Britain.
51. Kelsey, *Inventing a Republic*, pp. 91–2.
52. Above, ch. 10, p. 355–7.
53. Kelsey, *Inventing a Republic*, p. 94; A. B. Wyon and A. Wyon, *The Great Seals of England, from the Earliest Period to the Present Time* (1887), pp. 90–2.
54. Wyon and Wyon, *The Great Seals of England*, pp. 93–4, plate XXXI; *An Act for a Seal of the Parliament of the Commonwealth of England* (Thomason 669 f. 15/76, 1651).
55. See E. Hawkins, *Medallic Illustrations of the History of Great Britain and Ireland to the Death of George II* (1904–11), plates XXIX, nos 19–20, XXX, nos 1–9, XXXI, nos 1–2, XXXII, nos 5–26, XXXIII, nos 1–11; A. Franks and H. Grueber, *Medallic Illustrations of the History of Great Britain* (2 vols, 1885), I, pp. 341–52, nos 188–211, 359–66, nos 229–49, 367–71, nos 250–6; J. Roberts, *The King's Head: Charles I, King and Martyr* (1999), pp. 30–4.
56. Franks and Grueber, *Medallic Illustrations*, I, p. 349, no. 208; Hawkins, *Medallic Illustrations*, plate XXX, no. 18.
57. Franks and Grueber, *Medallic Illustrations*, I, p. 384, no. 1; Hawkins, *Medallic Illustrations*, plate XXXIV, no. 10.
58. Franks and Grueber, *Medallic Illustrations*, I, p. 384, no. 204; Hawkins, *Medallic Illustrations*, plate XXXIV, nos 20–2.
59. Franks and Grueber, *Medallic Illustrations*, I, pp. 386–7, nos 5–6; Hawkins, *Medallic Illustrations*, plate XXXIV, nos 23–4. The verse on the medal for Montrose ran: 'Treu pelican who / Shlit his blood/ To Save his King/ do's Country good'.
60. Franks and Grueber, *Medallic Illustrations*, I, pp. 388–9, nos 7–10; Hawkins, *Medallic Illustrations*, plate XXXIV, nos 25–7, XXXV, no. 1. Henfrey has questioned the dating and suggested that these medals were struck after Dunbar. However, the evidence is unclear and it seems likely that Cromwell's succession to Fairfax would have been so commemorated. The satirical medals indeed suggest a Machiavellian Cromwell who had deceived Fairfax into surrendering office to gain his place.
61. Franks and Grueber, *Medallic Illustrations*, I, p. 390, no. 12; Hawkins, *Medallic Illustrations*, plate XXXV, nos 2, 3.
62. Franks and Grueber, *Medallic Illustrations*, I, pp. 390–2, nos 12–14; Hawkins, *Medallic Illustrations*, plate XXXV, nos 4–5.
63. Henfrey, *Numismata Cromwelliana*, p. 3.
64. Ibid., pp. 1–9; Franks and Grueber, *Medallic Illustrations*, I, p. 391, no. 13; Hawkins, *Medallic Illustrations*, plate XXXV, no. 4.
65. Henfrey, *Numismata Cromwelliana*, p. 3.
66. Ibid.
67. Franks and Grueber, *Medallic Illustrations*, I, p. 391, no. 13; Hawkins, *Medallic Illustrations*, plate XXXV, nos 4, 5. It was also issued in copper and lead, presumably for distribution to the people, Henfrey *Numismata Cromwelliana*, p. 5.
68. Franks and Grueber, *Medallic Illustrations*, pp. 393–4, no. 17; Hawkins, *Medallic Illustrations*, plate XXXV, no. 7.
69. Franks and Grueber, *Medallic Illustrations*, I, p. 394, no. 18; Hawkins, *Medallic Illustrations*, plate XXXV, no. 8.
70. For the narrative of these events, see Richard Ollard, *The Escape of Charles II after the Battle of Worcester* (1966); Brian Weiser, 'Owning the King's Story: The Escape from Worcester', *Seventeenth Century*, 14 (1999), pp. 43–62. I analyze these narratives as a representation of Charles in my study of images of monarchy in late seventeenth-century England (forthcoming).
71. Franks and Grueber, *Medallic Illustrations*, I, p. 394, nos. 19, 20; Hawkins, *Medallic Illustrations*, plate XXXV, nos 9, 10.
72. Franks and Grueber, *Medallic Illustrations*, I, pp. 398–400, nos 26–9; Hawkins, *Medallic Illustrations*, plate XXXV, nos 14–16.
73. Franks and Grueber, *Medallic Illustrations*, I, p. 398, no. 26; Hawkins, *Medallic Illustrations*, plate XXXV, no. 14.
74. *The Life and Reigne of King Charls or, the Pseudo-Martyr Discovered. With a Late Reply to an Invective Remonstrance Against the Parliament and Present Government* (E 1338/2, 1652), p. 57. The text has been attributed to Milton.
75. Firth and Rait, *Acts and Ordinances*, II, pp. 191–2.
76. Ibid., p. 191.

77. P. Seaby, *The Story of British Coinage* (1985), pp. 115–16; R. Ruding, *Annals of the Coinage of Great Britain* (3 vols, 1840), I, pp. 407–18; G. C. Brooke, *English Coins* (1932), plate LIX.
78. Firth and Rait, *Acts and Ordinances*, II, p. 192.
79. Kelsey, *Inventing a Republic*, p. 87.
80. Henfrey, *Numismata Cromwelliana*, p. 29.
81. Ibid., pp. 29–31: H. Grueber, *Handbook of the Coins of Great Britain and Ireland* (1899), pp. 125–6.
82. Above, ch. 6, pp. 223–4.
83. Firth and Rait eds, *Acts and Ordinances*, II, pp. 168–91.
84. H. M. Colvin, D. R. Ransome and J. Summerson, *The History of the King's Works Vol. III, 1485–1660*, part I (1975), p. 164.
85. Ibid., p. 165.
86. S. Thurley, *Whitehall Palace: An Architectural History of the Royal Apartments, 1240–1698* (New Haven and London, 1999), p. 98.
87. Ibid.
88. Milton, of course, had condemned lofty ceremonialism and Marvell praises the modesty of Fairfax's Appleton House. But regal grandeur was not the only way that a building might signify authority. In continuing to use royal palaces but not alter their public signification, the Commonwealth arguably had the worst of both worlds. I am grateful to Malcolm Smuts for a discussion of this subject, even if I depart from his conclusions.
89. Ibid., p. 98. J. S. Wheeler, *The Irish and British Wars, 1637–1654: Triumph, Tragedy, and Failure* (2002), p. 220.
90. Interestingly, Timothy Mowl has argued quite persuasively for a new style of republican domestic architecture which leaves the failure of the government to represent itself in stone all the more puzzling, see T. Mowl, *Architecture without Kings: The Rise of Puritan Classicism under Cromwell* (Manchester, 1995), pp. 100–17, 137–9 and *passim*.

14 Staging Republic

1. See K. Sharpe, *Selling the Tudor Monarchy: Authority and Image in Sixteenth-Century England* (New Haven and London 2009), pp. 157–76, 219–27, 204–305, 417–50.
2. See my review of some of the recent discussions of this ibid., pp. 48–52.
3. Above, ch. 11, pp. 373–4.
4. *Mercurius Impartialis*, 5–12 December 1648 (E 476/3) p. 5. I owe this reference to Sean Kelsey, *Inventing a Republic: The Political Culture of the English Commonwealth, 1649–1653* (Manchester, 1997), p. 58.
5. M. Nedham, *The Case of the Common-Wealth of England, Stated: Or, The Equity, Utility, and Necessity, of a Submission to the Present Government; Cleared Out of Monuments Both Sacred and Civill, Against All the Scruples and Pretences of the Opposite Parties* (E 600/7, 1650), pp. 82–3.
6. Henry Parker, *The True Portraiture of the Kings of England; Drawn From Their Titles, Successions, Raigns and Ends* (E 609/2, 1650), p. 1.
7. Kelsey, *Inventing a Republic*, p. 58.
8. Ibid., pp. 59–60. Fleming's report is in NA SP 18/1, 73.
9. Kelsey, *Inventing a Republic*, p. 60.
10. *Cal. Stat. Pap. Venet. XXVIII, 1647–52*, no. 490, pp. 182–3; Kelsey, *Inventing a Republic*, p. 61.
11. Kelsey, *Inventing a Republic*, p. 61; *Several Proceedings in Parliament*, 26 December 1650–2 January 1651 (E 781/20), p. 987.
12. *Several Proceedings*, p. 988.
13. Ibid.
14. *Several Proceedings in Parliament*, 11–18 December 1651 (E 791/28), p. 1801.
15. *The Faithful Scout Impartially Communicating the Most Remarkable Passages of the Armies, in England, Scotland, and Ireland*, 12–19 December 1651 (E 791/30), p. 375.
16. *A Perfect Diurnall*, 15–22 December 1651 (E 791/31), pp. 1540, 1546, 1550.
17. *A Perfect Diurnall*, 27 September–4 October (E 799/7), p. 2157 (erratic and erroneous pagination).
18. Ibid., p. 2195; cf. *Weekly Intelligencer*, 28 September–5 October 1652 (E 676/3), p. 613; *Cal. Stat. Pap. Venet.*, XXVIII, 1647–52, nos 662, 676, pp. 284, 295.
19. *Weekly Intelligencer*, p. 613.
20. Kelsey, *Inventing a Republic*, pp. 62–3.
21. Ibid., pp. 56, 62–3
22. *Mercurius Politicus*, 27 March–3 April–10 April 1651 (E 626/17, 22).
23. *Joyful Newes from Holland: Shewing, the Royall Entertainment Given by the States of the United Provinces, to the Lords Embassadours of the Common-wealth of England* (E 626/18, 1651), p. 2 and *passim*.

24. Ibid., p. 5.
25. Ibid., full title.
26. Above, ch. 7, pp. 235–6; Kelsey, *Inventing a Republic*, pp. 71–2.
27. Ibid., p. 72.
28. Ibid., p. 73.
29. G. E. Aylmer, *The State's Servants: The Civil Service of the English Republic, 1649–60* (1973), pp. 41–2; S. Thurley, *Whitehall Palace: An Architectural History of the Royal Apartments, 1240–1698* (New Haven and London, 1999), p. 98; Kelsey, *Inventing a Republic*, p. 45.
30. Aylmer, *State's Servants*, p. 38 and ch. 2 *passim*.
31. Ibid., p. 100 and ch. 3 *passim*.
32. On Marten, see S. Wiseman, ' "Adam, the Father of All Flesh": Porno-Political Rhetoric and Political Theory in and after the English Civil War', in J. Holstun ed., *Pamphlet Wars: Prose in the English Revolution* (1992), pp. 134–57.
33. Cf. Kelsey, *Inventing a Republic*, pp. 154–65.
34. See, for example, R. Latham and W. Matthews eds, *The Diary of Samuel Pepys* (11 vols, 1970–83), III, p. 90, VIII, pp. 250, 377–8, 390–1.
35. Aylmer, *State's Servants*, p. 284.
36. Cf. Blair Worden, *The Rump Parliament, 1648–1653* (Cambridge, 1974), ch. 5.
37. S. R. Gardiner, *History of the Commonwealth and Protectorate, 1649–1656* (4 vols, 1903), II, pp. 4, 82.
38. Ibid., pp. 97–8; C. H. Firth and R. S Rait eds, *Acts and Ordinances of the Interregnum, 1642–1660* (3 vols, 1911), II, pp. 409–12.
39. Gardiner, *History of the Commonwealth and Protectorate* I, p. 34.
40. Ibid., p. 42.
41. Ibid., pp. 161–4; J. Lilburne, *An Impeachment of High Treason Against Oliver Cromwel, and His Son in Law Henry Ireton* (E 568/20, 1649).
42. *The Triall, of Lieut. Collonell John Lilburne, By an Extraordinary or Special Commission, of Oyear and Terminer at the Guild-Hall of London, the 24, 25, 26. of Octob. 1649* (E 584/9, 1649), p. 151; Gardiner, *History of the Commonwealth and Protectorate*, I, p. 169.
43. *Trial of Lilburne*, pp. 151, 153; John Lilburne, *Truths Victory Over Tyrants and Tyranny. Being the Tryall of That Worthy Assertor of His Countreys Freedoms, Lieftenant Colonell John Lilburne, Defender of the Ancient and Known Laws of England, Against Men and Devills, Whether in King, Parliament, Army, or Councell of State* (E 579/12, 1649), pp. 6–7.
44. *Truths Victory*, p. 7.
45. Ibid.; cf. *Certaine Observations Upon the Tryall of Leiut. Col. John Lilburne* (Wing C1715, 1649), p. 3.
46. Christopher Love, *A Modest and Clear Vindication of the Serious Representation, and Late Vindication of the Ministers of London, from the Scandalous Aspersions of John Price . . . By a Friend to a Regulated Monarchy, a Free Parliament, an Obedient Army, and a Godly Ministry* (E 549/10, 1649); Love, *ODNB*.
47. *The Perfect Weekly Account*, 5–13 September 1649 (E 573/20), p. 6.
48. *ODNB*.
49. Gardiner, *History of the Commonwealth and Protectorate*, II, pp. 16–17, 20.
50. C. Love, *A Cleare and Necessary Vindication of the Principles and Practices of Me Christopher Love, Since My Tryall Before, and Condemnation By, the High Court of Justice* (E 790/5, 1651), p. 9.
51. Ibid., pp. 4, 7, 41–2.
52. *Mr. Love's Speech Made on the Scaffold on Tower-Hill, August 22. 1651. With His Proposals to the Citizens of London; His Desires Touching Religion, and His Judgment Concerning the Presbyterian-Government; as Also, His Perfect Prayer Immediately Before His Head Was Severed from His Body* (E 641/8, 1651), p. 7 and *passim*.
53. Ibid., pp. 6, 9–10.
54. *Mr. Love's Case: Wherein Is Published, First, His Several Petitions to the Parliament. Secondly, a Full Narrative of the Late Dangerous Design Against the State* (E 790/1, 1651), pp. 31–54. See *A Just Balance: Or, Some Considerable Querees About Mr Love's Case, Tryal, & Sentence . . .* (E 638/6, 1651).
55. *Mr. Love's Case*, p. 32 and pp. 31–66 *passim*.

15 Subverting the Commonwealth

1. *Eikon e Piste. Or, the Faithfull Pourtraicture of a Loyall Subject, in Vindication of Eikon Basilike* (E 573/11, 1649); *The Subjects Sorrow: or, Lamentations Upon the Death of Britaines Iosiah, King Charles, Most Unjustly and Cruelly Put to Death by His Owne People, Before His Royall Palace White-Hall, January the 30. 1648* (E 546/16, 1649) p. 19 and see the homage to Marshall's engraving in the frontispiece; *An Elegie on the Meekest of Men, the Most Glorious of Princes* (E

553/1, 1649), p. 14; *An Elegie Upon the Death of Our Dread Soveraign Lord King Charls the Martyr* (Thomason 669 f. 14/42, 1649).

2. *An Elegie on the Meekest of Men, the Most Glorious of Princes, the Most Constant of Martyrs, Charles the I* (E 553/1, 1649), pp. 2, 5; *His Majesties Prayers Which He Used in Time of His Sufferings* (E 1317/2, 1649); *An Elogie, and Epitaph, Consecrated to the Ever Sacred Memory of that Most Illustrious, and Incomparable Monarch, Charles* (E 554/1, 1649), p. 4. See A. Lacey, 'Elegies and Commemorative Verse in Honour of Charles the Martyr, 1649–60', in J. Peacey ed., *The Regicides and the Execution of Charles I* (Basingstoke, 2001), pp. 225–46.

3. *A Deep Groane, Fetch'd at the Funerall of that Incomparable and Glorious Monarch, Charles the First* (E 555/19, 1649), p. 6; *Jeremias Redivivus: Or, An Elegiacall Lamentation on the Death of Our English Josias, Charles the First, King of Great Britaine* (E 556/33, 1649), p. 2.

4. See, for example, the frontispieces to *The Kingly Myrrour, or King Charles His Last Legacy to the Prince His Son* (E1317/2, 1649); *Regale Lectum Miseriae Or, a Kingly Bed of Miserie* (E 1345/1, 1649), see also portrait at end; *The Mounument of Charles the First, King of England* (Thomason 669 f. 14/36, 1649).

5. *The Royall Legacies of Charles the First of that Name, of Great Britaine, France, and Ireland, King and Martyr* (E 557/1, 1649), p. 3; *Regale Lectum Miseriae*, sigs A2–3.

6. *A Miracle of Miracles: Wrought by the Blood of King Charles the First, of Happy Memory, Upon a Mayd at Detford Foure Miles from London* (E 563/2, 1649); *The Confession of Richard Brandon the Hangman (upon his death bed) Concerning His Beheading His Late Majesty, Charles the First, King of Great Brittain* (E 561/14, 1649).

7. *The Right Picture of King Oliure, From Top to Toe* (E 587/9, 1650), pp. 6–7 and *passim.*

8. *A Coffin for King Charles a Crowne for Cromwell* (Thomason 669 f. 14/22, 1649).

9. *A Letter from Scotland: and the Votes of the Parliament for Proclaiming Charles the Second, King of Great Britain, France & Ireland* (E 554/12, 1649).

10. *Vox Veritatis* (E 616/6, 1649), p. 26.

11. *Anglia Liberata, or, The Rights of the People of England Maintained Against the Pretences of the Scotish King As they Are Set Forth in an Answer to the Lords Ambassadors Propositions of England* (E 643/7, 1651), p. 49. See *The True Manner of the Crowning of Charles the Second King of Scotland, on the First Day of January, 1650* (Thomason 669 f. 15/81, 1651). We note that the engraving emulates not only previous royal images but the engravings of Essex and Cromwell in a visual act of reappropriation.

12. *The True Manner of the Crowning of Charles II, King of Scotland* (Thomason 669 f. 15/81, 1657), broadside.

13. *The Queen of England's Prophecie Concerning Prince Charles* (E 552/13, 1649?), p. 3.

14. *A Religious Demurrer, Concerning Submission to the Present Power* (E 530/19, 1649), p. 2.

15. T.B., *The Royal Charter Granted Unto Kings, by God Himself and Collected Out of His Holy Word, in Both Testaments* (E 1356/1, 1649), p. 7.

16. *Ibid.*, p. 85.

17. *The Rebels Looking-Glasse: Or, The Traytors Doome. Wherein Is Discovered the Judgements of God Upon the Rebels and Traytors in All Ages* (E 554/23, 1649), p. 16.

18. T.B., *The Royal Charter*, p. 33. Cf. *The Royall Legacies of Charles the First*, pp. 36–7.

19. *A Religious Demurrer*, p. 5.

20. *Monarchia Transformata in Respublicam Deformatam* (Thomason 669 f. 14/75, 1649); *Regale Lectum Miseriae*, p. 4.

21. *A Religious Demurrer*, p. 7.

22. *The Life and Death of King Charles the Martyr Parallel'd with Our Saviour In All His Sufferings* (E 571/2, 1649), p. 2.

23. *The Subjects Sorrow*, p. 46.

24. *A Second Part of the Religious Demurrer; By Another Hand. Or, an Answer to a Tract Called The Lawfullnesse of Obeying the Present Government* (E 530/31, 1649), p. 7.

25. *Majestas Intemerata Or the Immortality of the King* (E 1347/1, 1649), title page epigraph.

26. *God and the King: Or, The Divine Constitution of the Supreme Magistrate; Especially in the Kingdome of England: Against All Popular Pretenders Whomsoever. Published for the Satisfaction of the Weake: Being a Private Discourse of a Reverend Judge, With Some Commanders of the Army* (E 550/2, 1649), pp. 1, 4 and *passim.*

27. *King Charles the First, No Man of Blood: But a Martyr for His People* (E 531/3, 1649), p. 57.

28. *The English Tyrants. Or, A Brief Historie of the Lives and Actions of the High and Mighty States, the Lords of Westminster, and Now (by usurpation) Kings of England* (E 569/4, 1649).

29. R. W. K. Hinton ed., *A Serious and Faithful Representation of . . . Ministers of the Gospel within the Province of London Contained in a Letter from them to the General and His Council of War . . . 18 Jan., 1648/9* (Reading, 1950).

30. *Ibid.*, p. 17.

31. *The Rebels Looking-Glasse*, sigs A2–3; *A Religious Demurrer*, p. 7.

32. *An Exercitation Concerning Usurped Powers: Wherein the Difference Betwixt Civill Authority and Usurpation Is Stated* (E 585/2, 1650), p. 13.

33. *The Vindication of Abraham Reinaldson, Late Lord Major of the City of London. With Certaine Queryes of Conscience Resolved, Concerning His Refusing to Obey a Late Order of Parliament, for the Proclaiming an Unjust Act for Abolishing the Kingly Office in England and Ireland* (E. 550/9, 1649), pp. 3–6.

34. *To the Present Visible Supreame Power, Assembled at Westminster The Humble Petition, and Desires of Many Thousand Well-Affected Persons, In, and About the City of London* (Thomason 669 f. 13/75, 1649).

35. *A Curse Against Parliament-Ale* (E 575/33, 1649), p. 3; *The Royall Legacies*, p. 49.

36. *The Rebels Looking-Glasse*, sig. A2; cf. the address to 'those few commoners who now call themselves a parliament', William Prynne, *The First Part of an Historical Collection of the Ancient Parliaments of England, from the Yeer of Our Lord 673, Till the End of King John's Reign, Anno 1216* (E 569/23, 1649), title page.

37. *A Religious Demurrer*, p. 6.

38. Ibid., p. 3.

39. *An Elegie on the Meekest of Men*, p. 1.

40. *A Religious Demurrer*, p. 6; *The Rebels Looking-Glasse*, p. 13; *The Royall Legacies*, p. 30.

41. *Curse Against Parliament-Ale*, p. 4.

42. *The Earl of Pembrookes Speech to Nol-Cromwell, Lord Deputy of Ireland* (E 566/9, 1649); *The Right Picture of King Oliure*. See Laura Knoppers, *Constructing Cromwell: Ceremony, Portrait and Print, 1645–1661* (Cambridge, 2000), pp. 11–20.

43. *Two Treatises Concerning the Matter of the Engagement* (E 615/12, 1650), p. 17.

44. *Vox Veritatis*, p. 31.

45. *Observations Upon Aristotles Politiques, Touching Forms of Government. Together With Directions for Obedience to Governours* (E 665/8, 1652), p. 36. This treatise has been ascribed to Sir Robert Filmer, author of *Patriarcha*.

46. *Modern Policies, Taken from Machiavel, Borgia, and Other Choise Authors, By an Eye-Witnesse* (E 1399/3, 1652), unpaginated, see Principle VIII.

47. Robert Spry, *Rules of Civil Goverment, Drawn from the Best Examples of Forreign Nations, and Common-wealths* (E 1484/3, 1653), sig. A3.

48. S. R. Gardiner, *History of The Commonwealth and Protectorate, 1649–1656* (4 vols, 1903), II, p. 245.

49. For the background, see ibid., ch. 25 and Blair Worden, *The Rump Parliament 1648–1653*, (Cambridge,1974), ch. 16.

50. W. C. Abbott ed., *The Writings and Speeches of Oliver Cromwell* (4 vols, Cambridge, Mass., 1937–47) II, pp. 641–3.

51. Ibid., p. 642.

52. Ibid., p. 643.

53. Ibid. An incident often recalled, recently in a *Times* leader of 4 February 2006.

54. Worden, *Rump Parliament*, pp. 345–8.

55. Ibid., p. 352.

56. Sean Kelsey, *Inventing a Republic: The Political Culture of the English Commonwealth, 1649–1653* (Manchester, 1997), p. 166.

57. Ibid., p. 2.

58. Ibid., pp. 169–70.

59. A. Woolrych, *Commonwealth to Protectorate* (Oxford, 1982), pp. 144–5, 151–2 and ch. 5 *passim*; p. 171; Kelsey, *Inventing a Republic*, p. 171.

60. *A Declaration of the Parliament of the Commonwealth of England* (E 1508, 1653).

61. Ibid., pp. 2–3, 6.

62. Woolrych's observation that the declaration is strange misses the crucial point about legitimacy, *Commonwealth to Protectorate*, p. 155.

63. Ibid., p. 164. Woolrych corrects some of the myths about the low status of the members in ch. 6.

64. Ibid., p. 235.

65. Ibid., pp. 320, 325.

66. Ibid., p. 345.

67. Ibid., p. 391.

68. *The Royal Charter Granted Unto Kings*, p. 18.

Prologue: 'Bring Crownes and Scepters'

1. A. Woolrych, *Commonwealth to Protectorate* (Oxford, 1982), ch. 1.

2. Laura Knoppers, *Constructing Cromwell: Ceremony, Portrait and Print, 1645–1661* (Cambridge, 2000), p. 11.

3.   Ibid., pp. 11–12; John Cleveland, *The Character of a London Diurnall* (E 268/6, Oxford, 1645).
4.   See, for example, *A Coffin for King Charles a Crowne for Cromwell: a Pit for the People* (Thomason 669 f. 14/22, 1649); *The Famous Tragedie of King Charles I* (Wing F 384, 1649); *A New Conference Between the Ghosts of King Charles and Oliver Cromwell* (E 988/28, 1659). See below, pp. 532–3.
5.   Above, ch. 13, pp. 434–5.
6.   Knoppers, *Constructing Cromwell*, p. 43; L. Knoppers, 'The Politics of Portraiture: Oliver Cromwell and the Plain Style', *Renaissance Quarterly*, 51 (1998), pp. 1283–1319. Knoppers's valuable discussion exaggerates the differences. Horace Walpole for one wrote of Cooper's portrait of Cromwell, 'if his portrait of Cromwell could be enlarged, I don't know but Van Dyck would appear less great by the comparison'. The emulation of regal forms is what remains to me most striking.
7.   *The Right Picture of King Olivre, From Top to Toe* (E 587/9, 1650).
8.   Marvell, 'An Horation Ode Upon Cromwell's Return from Ireland', in N. Smith ed., *The Poems of Andrew Marvell* (2003), p. 275.
9.   Above ch. 14, pp. 440, 455–9.
10. Knoppers, *Constructing Cromwell*, p. 58; Payne Fisher, *Irenodia Gratulatoria, Sive Illustrissimi Amplissimiq[ue] Viri Oliveri Cromwelli, &c. Epinicion* (E 796/30, 1652). See D. Norbrook, *Writing the English Republic: Poetry, Rhetoric and Politics, 1627–1660* (Cambridge, 1999), pp. 233–8, 256–7.
11. Fisher, *Irenodia Gratulatoria*, sigs B1ᵛ, B2, B3ᵛ, B4ᵛ, C4, E1, H1, and *passim*.
12. Sean Kelsey, *Inventing a Republic: The Political Culture of the English Commonwealth, 1649–1653* (Manchester, 1997), p. 169.
13. Bodleian Library Clarendon MS 47, f. 207, quoted in Knoppers, *Constructing Cromwell*, p. 67.

16 Proclaiming Protectorate

1.   C. H. Firth and R. S. Rait eds, *Acts and Ordinances of the Interregnum, 1642–1660* (3 vols, London, 1911), II, p. 813 and pp. 813–22 *passim*.
2.   A. Woolrych, *Commonwealth to Protectorate* (Oxford, 1982), p. 353.
3.   Ibid., p. 359.
4.   Ibid., pp. 354–5.
5.   Firth and Rait eds, *Acts and Ordinances*, II, p. 813.
6.   Ibid., clause II.
7.   Ibid., pp. 814–19, clauses VII–XXIV.
8.   Ibid., p. 813, clauses II, III.
9.   Ibid., p. 820, clause XXVII.
10. Ibid., p. 813, clause III.
11. For a few examples, see *A Letter from the Lord Lieutenant of Ireland, to the Honorable William Lenthal Esq; Speaker of the Parliament of England Giving an Account of the Proceedings of the Army There Under His Lordships Command; and Several Transactions Between His Lordship and the Governor of Wexford* (E 576/2, 1649); *A Letter from the Lord General Cromwel from Dunbar* (E 612/11, 1650); *A Letter from the Lord General Cromwel, Concerning the Rendition of the Castle of Edinburgh to his Excellency* (E 621/2, 1650); *A Letter From the Lord General Cromwell, Touching the Great Victory Obtained Neer Worcester* (E 641/5, 1651); *A Declaration of the Lord Lieutenant of Ireland. For the Undeceiving of Deluded and Seduced people* (E 596/6, 1650); *A Declaration of Oliver Cromwell, Captain General of All the Forces of This Common-Wealth* (Thomason 669 f. 17/6, 1653).
12. Richard Flecknoe, *The Idea of His Highness Oliver, Late Lord Protector, &c. With Certain Brief Reflexions on His Life* (Wing F1226, 1659), p. 29.
13. *A Letter from the Lord Lieutenant of Ireland*, sig. A1ᵛ.
14. *A letter from the Right Honorable, the Lord Lieutenant of Ireland, to the Honorable William Lenthall Esq; Speaker of the Parliament of England, Concerning the Taking In and Surrendring of Enistery. Carrick Town and Castle* (E 584/6, 1649), p. 7.
15. W. C. Abbott ed., *The Writings and Speeches of Oliver Cromwell* (4 vols, Cambridge, Mass., 1937–47), III, pp. 5–8.
16. See Cromwell's letter to the sheriff of Carmarthen, ibid., pp. 8–9.
17. Ibid., pp. 60–1.
18. Ibid., p. 62.
19. Ibid., p. 65.
20. Ibid., pp. 52–66.
21. Ibid., p. 64.
22. H. R. Trevor-Roper, 'Oliver Cromwell and his Parliaments', in R. Pares and A. J. P. Taylor eds, *Essays Presented to Sir Lewis Namier* (1956), pp. 1–48.

23. For example, *The Speech of His Highnesse the Lord Protector to the Parliament in the Painted Chamber at Westminster, on Munday Last, Being the Fourth of This Instant September, 1654. Examined by the Original Copy; Published by Order and Authority* (Wing 7170A, 1654). There are several copies of Cromwell's speeches of 4 and 12 September 1654.

24. Cromwell spoke customarily at far greater length than his royal predecessors.

25. Abbott, *Writings and Speeches*, III, p. 434.

26. Ibid., pp. 437-8.

27. Ibid., p. 439. The use of the metaphor of healing was itself an appropriation of a familiar regal trope of the king as good physician.

28. Ibid., p. 439.

29. Ibid., p. 440. The repetition 'a free parliament . . . I say a free parliament' was a Cromwellian rhetorical stock in trade.

30. Ibid., p. 442. The sermon preached by Godwin concerning a people brought out of Egypt was apparently not published.

31. Ibid.

32. Ibid., ch. 10 *passim*; J. T. Rutt ed., *Diary of Thomas Burton Esquire, Member in the Parliaments of Oliver and Richard Cromwell . . . With an Introduction Containing an Account of the Parliament of 1654* (4 vols, 1828), I, pp. i–cxxxiii.

33. Abbott, *Writings and Speeches*, III, pp. 445-52.

34. Ibid., pp. 451-2.

35. Cromwell repeated 'I called not myself to this place', ibid., p. 452.

36. Ibid., pp. 453-4.

37. Ibid., p. 458. The Commonwealth had, as any authority in early modern England had to, claimed divine authority; what is different with Cromwell is that – and how – he translated providential authority from the collective, and the people, to an individual ruler: himself.

38. 'Some things are fundamentals . . . they may not be parted with, but will (I trust) be delivered over to posterity, as being the fruits of our blood and travail', ibid. The biblical tone, with allusions to Moses and the Commandments, is reinforced by the reference to the exodus to New England (p. 459).

39. Ibid., p. 460.

40. Ibid., pp. 579-93.

41. Ibid., p. 580: 'If I had purposed to play the orator' . . .!

42. Ibid.

43. Ibid., p. 591.

44. Ibid., p. 587.

45. Ibid., p. 594.

46. Ibid., pp. 595, 608. See, for example, *A Declaration of the Members of Parliament, Lately Dissolved by Oliver Cromwell, Esquire* (669 f. 19/67, 1655). See also W. C. Abbott, *A Bibliography of Oliver Cromwell* (New York, 1969), p. 77, no. 617. I have not traced this pamphlet and believe Abbott may have confused it with a treatise of 1659 (E 1013/18).

47. S. R. Gardiner, *A History of the Commonwealth and Protectorate, 1649–1656* (4 vols, 1903), III, chs 38 and 39 *passim*.

48. Abbott, *Writings and Speeches*, III, p. 837.

49. Instructions to them are ibid., pp. 844-8. See C. Durston, *Cromwell's Major Generals: Godly Government during the English Revolution* (Manchester, 2001).

50. Abbott, *Writings and Speeches*, IV, p. 198.

51. Ibid., p. 260.

52. Ibid., pp. 260-1 and 260-80 *passim*.

53. Ibid., p. 262.

54. Ibid., p. 263.

55. Ibid., pp. 263-4.

56. Ibid., pp. 266-8.

57. Ibid., p. 268.

58. Ibid., p. 269.

59. Ibid.

60. Ibid., p. 270.

61. Ibid., pp. 270-1.

62. Ibid., pp. 271, 273.

63. Ibid., p. 274.

64. Ibid., pp. 275-6: 'show yourselves to be men, quit yourselves like men'.

65. Ibid., p. 277.

66. Ibid.

67. Ibid., p. 280.
68. Antoine de Bordeaux Neufville to Henri, comte de Brienne, quoted ibid.
69. Ibid., pp. 282-3.
70. Ibid., pp. 349-50, 356-9; see T. A. Wilson and F. J. Merli, 'Naylor's Case and the Dilemma of the Protectorate', *University of Birmingham Historical Journal*, 10 (1965-6), pp. 44-59.
71. Abbott, *Writings and Speeches*, IV, pp. 377-81, 433-41 and ch. 8 *passim*.
72. Ibid., p. 445. Laura Knoppers observes that in his speeches during the kingship negotiations Cromwell had diminished agency, Laura Knoppers, *Constructing Cromwell: Ceremony, Portrait and Print, 1645-1661* (Cambridge, 2000), p. 120.
73. Cromwell only spoke of 'this paper', but named the Instrument, Abbott, *Writings and Speeches*, IV, p. 446; cf. pp. 467, 483.
74. Ibid., p. 467.
75. Ibid., See R. Sherwood, *Oliver Cromwell: King in All but Name* (Stroud, 1997), ch. 7, pp. 80-90.
76. Abbott, *Writings and Speeches*, IV, p. 512.
77. Ibid., p. 513.
78. Ibid., pp. 513-14.
79. The speech of 25 May 1657 was unusually brief – 'but a word', as Cromwell put it, ibid., pp. 535-6.
80. Ibid., pp. 705-8.
81. Ibid., pp. 707, 708. There was a recent use of the same tactic by Michael Howard and the UK Conservative Party in the election of 2005 where the party adopted, often below a list of policies it advocated, the slogan: 'Are you thinking what we're thinking?'
82. Ibid., p. 712, 25 January 1658.
83. Ibid., p. 716.
84. Ibid., pp. 716-17.
85. Ibid., p. 718.
86. Ibid., p. 720; Psalms 85: 8.
87. Ibid., pp. 721-2.
88. See ibid., p. 893. On the influence of Carlyle's edition of Cromwell's speeches, see I. Roots, 'Carlyle's Cromwell', in R. C. Richardson ed., *Images of Oliver Cromwell* (Manchester, 1993), pp. 74-95; Blair Worden, 'Thomas Carlyle and Oliver Cromwell', *Proceedings of the British Academy*, 105 (2000), pp. 131-70; Blair Worden, *Roundhead Reputations: The English Civil War and the Passions of Posterity* (2001), pp. 264-95. While Cromwell has undoubtedly benefited from sympathetic nineteenth- and twentieth-century editors, it is because the speeches are so quotable and memorable that they are quoted and remembered.
89. Flecknoe, *The Idea of His Highness Oliver*, p. 14.
90. See above, chs 12, 16, pp. 414-15, 465, 469.
91. *A Declaration of the Lord Generall and His Councel of Officers; Shewing the Grounds and Reasons for the Dissolution of the Late Parliament* (E 692/6, 1653); *Friday, April 22. 1653. The Declaration of the Lord Generall, and His Councell of Officers, Shewing the Grounds and Reasons for the Dissolution of the Parliament, April 20. 1653* (E 693/3, 1653); *Another Declaration: Wherein Is Rendred, a Further Account of the Just Grounds and Reasons of the Dissolving the Parliament; by the Lord Generall and His Council of Officers* (E 693/17, 1653).
92. *A Declaration* (E 692/6), pp. 1, 4, 6, 8.
93. *Another Declaration*, p. 3.
94. Ibid., pp. 5-7 (erratic pagination).
95. *A Declaration and Order of His Excellency the Lord Generall Cromwell, and His Councill of Officers for the Continuance of the Assesment for Six Moneths, from the 24th. of June 1653. to the 25th. of December Following* (E 1062/2, 1653), pp. 1-2.
96. Knoppers, *Constructing Cromwell*, pp. 70-1; *A Declaration Concerning the Government of the Three Nations of England, Scotland, and Ireland, by His Highness the Lord Protector Cromwel* (E 725/2, 1653).
97. *A Declaration*, p. 5.
98. Ibid., pp. 6-7.
99. Thurloe, Cromwell's Secretary of State, intercepted a letter of 22 December 1653 in which it was said that the new Protector 'hath lost much of the affections of the people since he took the government upon himself', *A Collection of the State Papers of John Thurloe* (7 vols, 1742), I, p. 641.
100. *A Declaration of His Highness the Lord Protector, Inviting the People of England and Wales, to a Day of Solemn Fasting and Humiliation* (669 f. 17/79, 1654); below, p. 480.
101. *A Declaration of His Highness the Lord Protector and the Parlament of the Common-wealth of England, Scotland, & Ireland, For a Day of Solemn Fasting & Humiliation in the Three Nations* (Wing C 7068A, 1654), p. 3 and *passim*.

102. *A Declaration of His Highness the Lord Protector, Upon His Actual Dissolution of the Parliament of England, on Munday the 22th of January, 1654* (E 826/13, 1655), title page.
103. *A Declaration of the Members of Parliament, Lately Dissolved by Oliver Cromwell, Esquire* (Thomson 669 f. 19/67, 1655), a broadside.
104. See Gardiner, *History of the Commonwealth and Protectorate*, III, pp. 299–300.
105. *A Declaration of His Highnes, By the Advice of His Council Setting Forth, on the Behalf of This Commonwealth, the Justice of Their Cause Against Spain. Friday the 26. of October, 1655. Ordered by His Highness the Lord Protector, and the Council, That This Declaration Be Forthwith Printed and Published* (Wing C 7081A, 1655).
106. Ibid., pp. 5, 14, 18–19; Gardiner, *History of the Commonwealth and Protectorate*, III, ch. 34.
107. *Declaration of His Highnes* (C 7081A), pp. 7, 18–19.
108. *A Declaration of His Highnes, By the Advice of His Council, Shewing the Reasons of Their Proceedings for Securing the Peace of the Commonwealth, Upon Occasion of the Late Insurrection and Rebellion. Wednesday, October, 31. 1655* (E 857/3, 1655).
109. Ibid., p. 11.
110. Ibid., pp. 15–23, 28, 31.
111. Ibid., pp. 33–4, 36.
112. Ibid., pp. 38–9.
113. *A Declaration of His Highnes the Lord Protector and the Parliament of the Commonwealth of England, Scotland, and Ireland, For a Day of Solemn Fasting and Humiliation in the Three Nations. Tuesday the 23th of September, 1656. Ordered by the Parliament, That This Declaration be Forthwith Printed and Published* (E 1065/10, 1656).
114. *A Declaration of His Highness the Lord Protector and the Parliament, for a Day of Publique Thanksgiving on Friday the Twentieth of February, 1656* (E 1065/12, 1656).
115. Ibid., pp. 1–5; C. H. Firth, *The Last Years of the Protectorate* (2 vols, 1909), I, pp. 35–8.
116. *Declaration of His Highness* (E 1065/12), p. 5.
117. *A Declaration of His Highness, for a Collection Towards the Relief of Divers Protestant Churches Driven Out of Poland; and of Twenty Protestant Families Driven Out of the Confines of Bohemia* (E 1073/1, 1658); *A Declaration of His Highnesse the Lord Protector for a Day of Publick Thanksgiving* (E 1075/5, 1658).
118. *A Declaration of His Highness the Lord Protector, Inviting the People of England and Wales, to a Day of Solemn Fasting and Humiliation* (Wing C 70681H 1654).
119. *A Declaration of His Highness, With the Advice of His Council Inviting the People of This Commonwealth to a Day of Solemn Fasting and Humiliation* (Thomason 669 f. 20/19, 1655).
120. *A Declaration of His Highness, Inviting the People of England and Wales to a Day of Solemn Fasting and Humiliation* (Wing C 7079, 1656).
121. *A Declaration of His Highnesse the Lord Protector For a Day of Publick Thanksgiving* (E 1073/5, 1658).
122. Ibid.; see Exodus 3: 2–4, Acts 7: 35.
123. Abbott, *Writings and Speeches*, IV, p. 470. John Morrill has observed that, though he was of a 'type with Moses', Cromwell 'never hailed himself as Moses', J. Morrill ed., *Oliver Cromwell and the English Revolution* (1990), ch. 10, p. 271. The distinction is a fine one here.
124. J. Morrill, Cromwell, *ODNB*.
125. J. Raymond, *Making the News: An Anthology of the Newsbooks of Revolutionary England, 1641–1660* (Moreton in Marsh, 1993), p. 336.
126. Raymond, 'Marchamont Nedham', *ODNB*; B. Worden, ' "Wit in a Roundhead": The Dilemma of Marchamont Nedham', in S. Amussen and M. Kishlansky eds, *Political Culture and Cultural Politics in Early Modern England* (Manchester, 1995), pp. 301–37; Worden, *Literature and Politics in Cromwellian England: John Milton, Andrew Marvell, Marchamont Nedham* (Oxford, 2007) chs 2, 3.
127. For example, *Mercurius Politicus* 22, 29 November 1655 (E 489/18, 1655), pp. 3774–6; 26 June–3 July 1656 (E 494/8, 1656), p. 7076.
128. *Mercurius Politicus*, 24–31 January 1656 (E 491/19, 1656), pp. 5917–18, 5920–7; 6–13 March 1656 (E 492/14, 1656), pp. 6022–3.
129. *Mercurius Politicus*, 17–24 April 1656 (E 493/8, 1656) pp. 5917–18, 5920–7, p. 6916; Raymond, *Making the News*, p. 372.
130. *Mercurius Politicus*, 11–18 September 1656 (E 497/20, 1656), p. 7254; 18–25 September 1656 (E 492/22, 1656), p. 841.
131. Ibid., 11–18 December 1656 (E 500/7, 1656), p. 7453; *Publick Intelligencer*, 15–22 December 1656 (E 500/9, 1656), p. 1059; ibid., 2–10 March 1657 (E 502/10, 1657), p. 1235.
132. Raymond, *Making the News*, pp. 369–79; J. Harrington, *The Common-Wealth of Oceana* (Wing H 809, 1656). Nedham edited some of his newspapers of that year 'From Oceana' and 'from Utopia'.
133. Raymond, *Making the News*, p. 373.
134. *Mercurius Politicus*, 19–26 March 1657 (E 502/15, 1657).

135. Ibid., pp. 7674–5.
136. Ibid., 9–16 February 1654 (E 729/14, 1654), p. 3270; Knoppers, *Constructing Cromwell*, p. 98; *Public Intelligencer*, 30 March–6 April 1657 (E 502/18, 1657), p. 1069.
137. *Oliva Pacis. Ad Illustrissimum Celsissimumq; Oliverum, Reipub. Angliae, Scotiae, & Hiberniae Dominum Protectorem; De Pace cum Foederatis Belgis Feliciter Sancita, Carmen Cantabrigiense* (E 740/2, 1654).
138. Ibid., sigs ¶2, C2. Now the republic can sleep securely at night.
139. Ibid., sigs D1, F1ᵛ, G3, H1ᵛ.
140. Ibid., sig. E4ᵛ.
141. Wither, *ODNB*. Since this chapter was written, Edward Holberton has published a rather limited but worthy study of *Poetry and the Cromwellian Protectorate: Culture, Politics, and Institutions* (Oxford, 2008).
142. George Wither, *Vaticinium Causuale. A Rapture Occasioned by the Late Miraculous Deliverance of His Highnesse the Lord Protector, from a Desperate Danger. With, a Noverint Universi, in the Close* (E 813/14, 1654); David Norbrook, *Writing the English Republic: Poetry, Rhetoric and Politics, 1627–1660* (Cambridge, 1999), pp. 352–3.
143. *The Protector. A Poem Briefly Illustrating the Supereminency of that Dignity; and, Rationally Demonstrating, that the Title of Protector, Providentially Conferred Upon the Supreme Governour of the British Republike, Is the Most Honorable of all Titles, and, That, which, Probably, Promiseth Most Propitiousness to These Nations; If Our Sins and Divisions Prevent it Not* (E 1565/2, 1655).
144. Ibid., sig. B1.
145. Ibid., pp. 1–14 *passim*.
146. Ibid., p. 17.
147. Ibid., p. 33.
148. Ibid., pp. 28, 47.
149. Andrew Marvell, *The First Anniversary of the Government Under His Highness the Lord Protector* (E 480/1, 1655): see Worden, *Literature and Politics*, ch. 6, pp. 137–53.
150. Marvell, *ODNB*.
151. Marvell, *First Anniversary*, pp. 1, 3.
152. Ibid., p. 4.
153. Ibid., pp. 10, 13.
154. Ibid., p. 12.
155. Ibid., p. 20.
156. Ibid., p. 15.
157. Ibid.
158. Ibid., p. 20.
159. Ibid., p. 21.
160. Edmund Waller, *A Panegyrick to My Lord Protector, of the Present Greatness and Joynt Interest of His Highness, and This Nation* (E 841/2, 1655).
161. Waller, *ODNB*.
162. Cf. Norbrook, *Writing the English Republic*, p. 307.
163. Waller, *Panegyrick*, p. 2.
164. Ibid., pp. 5, 9, 10.
165. Ibid., pp. 8, 10:
As the vext world to find repose at last
It self into *Augustus* Arms did cast:
So *England* now, doth with like toyle opprest,
Her weary head upon your bosome rest.
166. Norbrook, *Writing the English Republic*, pp. 302, 307.
167. *The Unparalleld Monarch. Or, The Portraiture of a Matchless Prince, Exprest in Some Shadows of His Highness My Lord Protector* (E 1675/1, 1656), 'A Panegyric to His Highness my Lord Protector', at end, unpaginated.
168. See Knoppers, *Constructing Cromwell*, pp. 115–18; Norbrook, *Writing the English Republic*, pp. 228–38, 256–7.
169. Payne Fisher, *Piscatoris Poemata vel Panegyricum Carmen in Diem Inaugurationis Olivari* (Wing F1034, 1656) sigs C1, C1ᵛ.
170. Ibid., sigs A3, D1, Aa2.
171. Ibid., sigs A3, Bb1, Cc3.
172. Ibid., sig. b; in Huntington copy (HL 430967) bound in Fisher, *Oratio Anniversaria* (Wing F1301, 1655), sig. B3ᵛ.
173. G. Wither, *A Suddain Flash Timely Discovering Some Reasons Wherefore, the Stile of Protector Should Not be Deserted by these Nations* (E 1584/3, 1657).

174. Ibid., pp. 2–4.
175. Ibid., pp. 5–6.
176. Ibid., pp. 36, 43, 54.
177. Ibid., pp. 41–2.
178. F. Peck, *Memoirs of the Life and Actions of Oliver Cromwell: As Delivered in Three Panegyrics of Him, Written in Latin* (1740); João Rodrigues de Sá e Meneses, *Dvo Panegyrici Cromwello Scripti Londini* (Wing D2635A, 1654); idem, *Panegyrici Cromwello Scripti. Vnus à Legato Portugallici Regis. Alter à Quodam Iesuita* (E 1069/3, 1654). I quote from the translation by Peck.
179. Peck, *Memoirs*, pp. 51, 67.
180. Ibid., p. 110.
181. Knoppers, *Constructing Cromwell*, pp. 93–5; John Milton, *Joannis MiltonI Angli Pro Populo Anglicano Defensio Secunda* (E 1487/3, 1654).
182. Peck, *Memoirs*, p. 118. Peck's third panegyric is extracted from *Defensio Secunda*. See Milton, *A Second Defence of the English People*, in D. Wolfe et al. eds, *Complete Prose Works of John Milton* (8 vols, New Haven, 1953–82), IV (part I), p. 666 and pp. 662–86 *passim*. For a discussion, see Norbrook, *Writing the English Republic*, pp. 331–7.
183. Peck, *Memoirs*, p. 123; Milton, *Second Defence*, p. 672.
184. *A True State of the Case of the Commonwealth of England, Scotland, and Ireland, and the Dominions Thereto Belonging* (E 728/5, 1654).
185. Ibid., p. 3.
186. Ibid., pp. 13, 28.
187. Ibid., pp. 28–9.
188. Ibid., p. 29.
189. Ibid., p. 46.
190. Ibid., p. 5; cf. Norbrook, *Writing the English Republic*, p. 328.
191. Johannes Cornubiensis, *The Grand Catastrophe, Or The Change of Government: Being a Word About the Last Turn of These Times Written in a Letter to a Friend, As an Essay, Either to Give, or to Receive Satisfaction in the Dispute of the Last Change* (E 726/12, 1654).
192. Ibid., p. 11.
193. Ibid., pp. 7–8, 12.
194. Ibid., pp. 10, 13, 15. 'Let him be the shame of men . . . if he make his Protectorship a step to king-ship' (p. 13).
195. J. Hall, *Confusion Confounded: Or, A Firm Way of Settlement Settled and Confirmed. Wherein Is Considered the Reasons of the Resignation of the Late Parlament, and the Establishment of a Lord Protector* (E 726/11, 1654).
196. Hall, *ODNB*.
197. Hall, *Confusion Confounded*, pp. 5, 8.
198. Ibid., pp. 20–1.
199. John Goodwin, *Peace Protected, and Discontent Dis-armed. Wherein the Seventeen Queries . . . Lately Published, Partly to Allay the Discontents of Some About the Late Revolution of Government, But More Especially to Guide Every Mans Feet into the Way of Peace* (E 732/27, 1654).
200. Ibid., sig. A3, p. 75.
201. Samuel Richardson, *An Apology for the Present Government, and Governour: With an Answer to Severall Objections Against Them* (E 812/18, 1654).
202. Ibid., pp. 11, 14.
203. *A Copy of a Letter Concerning the Election of a Lord Protector. Written to a Member of Parliament* (E 818/20, 1654).
204. Ibid., pp. 13, 20–5, 27 and *passim*.
205. Ibid., p. 36.
206. *A Treatise Concerning the Broken Succession of the Crown of England: Inculcated, About the Later End of the Reign of Queen Elisabeth* (E 481/2, 1655).
207. Thomas White, *The Grounds of Obedience and Government. By Thomas White, Gentleman* (E 1711/2, 1655); see pp. 142, 180–1. See Thomas White (1593–1676), *ODNB*.
208. George Smith, *Gods Unchangeableness: or Gods Continued Providence* (E.824[4], 1654), sig. A2ᵛ, pp. 17, 52.
209. John Moore, *Protection Proclaimed (Through the Loving Kindness of God in the Present Government) to the Three Nations of England, Scotland, and Ireland* (E 860/5, 1655), full title.
210. Ibid., sigs A2–A3ᵛ.
211. Ibid., pp. 6, 10 and *passim*.
212. J. Hall, *Of Government and Obedience As They Stand Directed and Determined by Scripture and Reason Four Books* (Wing H 360, 1654); Hall, *The True Cavalier Examined By His Principles* (E 885/10, 1656).

213. *True Cavalier*, sigs A3–A4ᵛ, pp. 58, 101–2, 116, 123, 134, and *passim.*
214. Ibid., p. 134.
215. S. Richardson, *Plain Dealing: Or the Unvailing of the Opposers of the Present Government and Governors* (E 865/3, 1656).
216. Ibid., pp. 4, 7, 19, 21–3.
217. Ibid., pp. 11, 21–2, 24.
218. *The Unparalleld Monarch. Or, The Portraiture of a Matchless Prince, Exprest in Some Shadows of His Highness My Lord Protector* (E 1675/1, 1656).
219. Ibid., 'To the Reader' (erratic signification).
220. Ibid., 'To the Reader' and pp. 12, 51, 103.
221. Ibid., p. 13.
222. Ibid., p. 9.
223. Ibid., p. 65.
224. Ibid., 'To the Reader'.
225. Ibid., pp. 13, 23, 27, 45, 50, 75, 84.
226. Ibid., 'To the Reader'.
227. Ibid., sig. A6.
228. Above n. 173.
229. T.L., *Considerations Humbly Proposed As Well to the Officers and Souldiers of the Army, as to Others in Order to a Quiet and Christian Submission to His Highness the Lord Protector* (Wing L 71, 1658).
230. Below, pp. 519–22.
231. S. Carrington, *The History of the Life and Death of His Most Serene Highness, Oliver, Late Lord Protector* (Wing C 643, 1659), pp. 164–5.

17 Painting Protectoral Power

1. D. Piper, 'The Contemporary Portraits of Oliver Cromwell' (Walpole Society, 34, 1958), p. 31.
2. L. Knoppers, 'The Politics of Portraiture: Oliver Cromwell and the Plain Style', *Renaissance Quarterly*, 51 (1998), pp. 1283–319, *passim.*
3. Ibid., p. 1295.
4. Piper, 'Portraits of Cromwell', p. 31.
5. Cromwell to Sir William Spring, 1643, T. Carlyle, *Oliver Cromwell's Letters and Speeches* (1849), pp. 134–5.
6. Above, p. 440.
7. Piper, 'Portraits of Cromwell', pp. 31–2.
8. Ibid., p. 30.
9. Ibid., pp. 38–9 (see 1d).
10. Ibid., p. 38; S. Barnes et. al, *Van Dyck: A Complete Catalogue of the Paintings* (New Haven and London, 2004), IV, p. 598, no. 216; above, pp. 434–5.
11. Knoppers, 'The Politics of Portraiture', pp. 1298–9; L. Knoppers, *Constructing Cromwell: Ceremony, Portrait and Print, 1645–1661* (Cambridge, 2000), pp. 32–4.
12. Piper compares its execution to 'the manner of many society photographers', 'Portraits of Cromwell', p. 30.
13. Knoppers, 'The Politics of Portraiture', p. 1299.
14. W. C. Abbott ed., *The Writings and Speeches of Oliver Cromwell* (4 vols, Cambridge, Mass., 1937–47), II, p. 37.
15. Piper, 'Portraits of Cromwell', p. 31.
16. Ibid.
17. Cooper, *ODNB*. D. Foskett, *Samuel Cooper, 1609–72* (1974).
18. Murdoch 'Cooper', *ODNB*.
19. Knoppers, 'The Politics of Portraiture', p. 1303.
20. Knoppers, *Constructing Cromwell*, p. 43; K. Pearson and G. M. Morant, *The Portraiture of Oliver Cromwell with Special Reference to the Wilkinson Head* (1935), p. 1 identifies at least ten of these miniatures.
21. Piper, 'Portraits of Cromwell', pp. 39–40, no. 5.
22. Knoppers, *Constructing Cromwell*, p. 43; O. Millar, *The Age of Charles I* (1972), p. 24, no. 18.
23. Knoppers, *Constructing Cromwell*, p. 82.
24. On this canvas, Cromwell's features even bear a passing resemblance to Charles I.
25. Knoppers, 'The Politics of Portraiture', p. 1307.
26. Piper, 'Portraits of Cromwell', p. 36 and plate XIVA; R. Sherwood, *Oliver Cromwell: King In All But Name* (Stroud, 1997), pp. 105–6.
27. Knoppers, 'The Politics of Portraiture', p. 1307.

28. Pearson and Morant, *Portraiture of Oliver Cromwell*, pp. 76–80; Piper, 'Portraits of Cromwell', pp. 38–40, nos 1a, 1e, 5, 6.

29. Sherwood, *Oliver Cromwell*, p. 60; Huntington Art Library photo archive.

30. Sherwood, *Oliver Cromwell*, pp. 5, 108, 127, 133; National Portrait Gallery NPG 4350. One notes in the double portrait of Cromwell and his wife the debt to Mytens's portrait of Charles I and Henrietta Maria.

31. Harrington Sherwood, *Oliver Cromwell*, pp. 108–19; J. Toland ed., *The Oceana of James Harrington, and His Other Works* (Wing H 816, 1700) p. xix; Elizabeth Claypole [née Cromwell], *ODNB*.

32. W. C. Abbott, *A Bibliography of Oliver Cromwell* (New York, 1969), pp. 383–424.

33. Huntington Library, Richard Bull Granger, Vol. X, nos 14, 17.

34. See Knoppers, *Constructing Cromwell*, pp. 83–5, fig.18.

35. O. Millar, *The Pictures in the Collection of Her Majesty the Queen: The Tudor, Stuart and Early Georgian Pictures* (2 vols, 1963), I, no. 143, pp. 93–4 and fig. 32; A. Griffiths, *The Print in Stuart Britain, 1603–1689* (1998), pp. 180–1, fig. 117; G. S. Layard, *The Headless Horseman* (1922).

36. Griffiths, *Print*, pp. 176–7, no. 115; R. R. Wark, *Early British Drawings in the Huntington Collection, 1600–1750* (San Marino, 1969), pp. 15–17; M. Lenihan, 'Curious Engraving of Oliver Cromwell', *Notes and Queries*, ser. IV, 6 (1870), pp. 345–6; See website catalogue, British Printed Images to 1700 (http://www.bpi1700.org.uk/printsMonths/august2006.html).

37. Not, as Griffiths, *Print* (p. 176), crowns.

38. Griffiths, *Print*, p. 141.

39. Huntington Bull Granger, XX, no. 22; Griffiths, *Print*, pp. 176–8, fig. 115. The William III version is the fifth state of the plate.

40. *The Kings Last Farewell to the World* (Thomason 669 f. 13/77, 1649).

41. F. Peck, *Memoirs of the Life and Actions of Oliver Cromwell: As Delivered in Three Panegyrics of Him, Written in Latin* (1740), p. 130.

42. R. Sherwood, *The Court of Oliver Cromwell* (1977), pp. 65, 97.

43. Sherwood, *Oliver Cromwell*, pp. 106–7.

44. Ibid., p. 46.

45. Above, ch. 13, p. 437–8.

46. Sherwood, *Oliver Cromwell*, pp. 43–8 and illustration p. 44.

47. H. W. Henfrey, *Numismata Cromwelliana: Coins, Medals and Seals of Oliver Cromwell* (1877), p. 219.

48. Sherwood, *Oliver Cromwell*, p. 44.

49. Ibid., p. 48.

50. Ibid., pp. 48–9.

51. Henfrey, *Numismata Cromwelliana*, p. 214.

52. Ibid., p. 209.

53. Above, ch. 13, p. 440–1.

54. See A. Franks and H. Grueber, *Medallic Illustrations of the History of Great Britain* (2 vols, 1885), I, pp. 387–8, nos 6–8, 401, no. 30, 406–7, nos 40–1; E. Hawkins, *Medallic Illustrations of the History of Great Britain and Ireland to the Death of George II* (1904–11), plate XXXIV, nos 24, 25, 26, XXXVI, no. 2, XXXVII, nos 4, 5.

55. Henfrey, *Numismata Cromwelliana*, p. 18; Franks and Grueber, *Medallic Illustrations*, I, p. 409, no. 45; Hawkins, *Medallic Illustrations*, plate XXXVII, no. 8.

56. Franks and Grueber, *Medallic Illustrations*, I, p. 410, no. 46; Hawkins, *Medallic Illustrations*, plate XXXVII, no. 9.

57. Franks and Grueber, *Medallic Illustrations*, I, pp. 413–14, nos 50–1, 415, no. 52, 416–17, nos 53–4; Hawkins, *Medallic Illustrations*, plate XXXVII, no. 18, XXXVIII, nos 1–5.

58. Franks and Grueber, *Medallic Illustrations*, I, pp. 417–18, nos 55–6; Hawkins, *Medallic Illustrations*, plate XXXVIII, no. 5.

59. Franks and Grueber, *Medallic Illustrations*, I, pp. 425, 427, nos 67, 70; Hawkins, *Medallic Illustrations*, plate XXXIX, nos 6, 7.

60. Henfrey, *Numismata Cromwelliana*, p. 164; Franks and Grueber, *Medallic Illustrations*, I, pp. 433–5, nos 82, 84, 85; Hawkins, *Medallic Illustrations*, plate XL, nos 3–5.

61. Henfrey, *Numismata Cromwelliana*, p. 29.

62. Ibid., p. 35.

63. Ibid., p. 93; P. Seaby, *The Story of British Coinage* (1985), pp. 116–17.

64. Ibid., p. 97.

65. Ibid., p. 102 and plate III.

66. Ibid., p. 108; Sherwood, *Oliver Cromwell*, pp. 94–5.

67. Henfrey, *Numismata Cromwelliana*, pp. 112–13; Sherwood, *Oliver Cromwell*, p. 95.

68. Henfrey, *Numismata Cromwelliana*, p. 128.

69. The dies in the British Museum examples show signs of wear, ibid., pp. 131, 134.
70. Ibid., p. 129.
71. Ibid., p. 130.
72. Ibid., pp. 154–8.
73. *Killing Is Murder: Or, An Answer to a Treasonous Pamphlet Entituled, Killing Is No Murder* (E 925/12, 1657), p. 10.
74. Ibid.
75. Translation from J. H. Franklin, *Bodin: On Sovereignty* (Cambridge, 1992), p. 78.
76. Henfrey, *Numismata Cromwelliana*, p. 165.
77. Sherwood, *Oliver Cromwell*, p. 26.
78. Sherwood, *Court of Cromwell*, p. 15; Knoppers, *Constructing Cromwell*, p. 110.
79. Sherwood, *Oliver Cromwell*, p. 26.
80. *Weekly Intelligencer* (E 732/5, 1654), p. 179.
81. *Severall Proceedings of State Affaires in England, Ireland and Scotland, With the Transactions of the Affaires in Other Nations* (E 227/21, 1654), p. 3771.
82. H. Colvin, *The History of the King's Works, Vol.3, 1485–1660, pt.1* (1975), p. 165.
83. Sherwood, *Oliver Cromwell*, p. 33; Sherwood, *Court of Cromwell*, p. 27.
84. Sherwood, *Oliver Cromwell*, p. 57.
85. E. S. de Beer ed., *The Diary of John Evelyn* (6 vols, Oxford, 1955), III, p. 166. Evelyn noted the Holbein Privy Chamber mural and was 'glad to find they had not much defaced it'.
86. *Cal. Stat. Pap. Venet. XIX, 1653–4*, no. 235, p. 196.
87. Sherwood, *Court of Cromwell*, p. 28.

18 Protectoral Performances

1. R. Sherwood, *The Court of Oliver Cromwell* (1977), ch. 2 *passim*.
2. Ibid., pp. 41–4.
3. Ibid., p. 45.
4. Ibid., ch. 4 *passim*.
5. Above, p. 505.
6. Sherwood, *Court of Cromwell*, p. 65.
7. Ibid., pp. 65–6.
8. Ibid., pp. 67–8.
9. Ibid., pp. 71, 73.
10. Ibid., pp. 77, 83.
11. Ibid., pp. 84, 136–7.
12. Above, ch. 1, p. 21.
13. I.S., *The Picture of a New Courtier Drawn in Conference, Between Mr. Timeserver, and Mr. Plain-Heart* (E 875/6, 1656). Thomason wrote 'April 18. cast about the streets' on the title page of his copy.
14. Ibid., pp. 11, 13–14.
15. Ibid., p. 15.
16. H. W., *The Accomplish'd Courtier. Consisting of Institutions and Examples By Which Courtiers and Officers of State May Square their Transactions Prudently and in Good Order and Method* (E 1824/1, 1658); *The Mysteries of Love & Eloquence, Or the Arts of Wooing and Complementing; As They Are Manag'd in the Spring Garden, Hide Park; the New Exchange, and Other Eminent Places* (E 1735/1, 1658), sigs A3–A6 and *passim*.
17. *The Unparalleld Monarch. Or, The Portraiture of a Matchless Prince, Exprest in Some Shadows of His Highness My Lord Protector* (E 1675/1, 1656), p. 42.
18. Ibid., pp. 70–1.
19. Ibid., panegyric at end, sig. I7.
20. 'Vere magnificus sine ostentatione', Payne Fisher, *Piscatoris Poemata vel Panegyricum Carmen in Diem Inaugurationis Olivari* (Wing F1034, 1656), sig. C1.
21. Above, ch. 14, pp. 445–9. Even the republics of Venice and the Netherlands developed quasi-monarchical forms for the receptions of ambassadors and envoys.
22. *Severall Proceedings of State Affaires*, 15–22 December 1653 (E 222/29, 1653), pp. 3498–9; R. Sherwood, *Oliver Cromwell: King in All But Name* (Stroud, 1997), pp. 7–9.
23. Ibid., p. 11.
24. *Severall Proceedings of State Affaires*, 15–22 December 1653, p. 3500.
25. *Cal. Stat. Pap. Venet. XXIX 1653–4*, no. 198, pp. 164–6.
26. *A Declaration Concerning the Government of the Three Nations* (E 725/2, 1653), p. 6.
27. *A Perfect Diurnall*, 6–13 February 1654 (E 225/1, 1654), pp. 3093 ff., erratic pagination; Sherwood, *Oliver Cromwell*, p. 16.

28. Above ch. 7, pp. 238–9.
29. Sherwood, *Oliver Cromwell*, pp. 16–17.
30. Carrington, *History of the Life and Death of … Oliver Late Lord Protector* (Wing C 643), pp. 167–70.
31. Ibid., p. 168.
32. *Mr. Recorders Speech to the Lord Protector Upon Wednesday the Eighth of Febru. 1653. Being the Day of His Highnesse Entertainment in London* (E 729/2, 1654), p. 4.
33. Ibid.
34. Sherwood, *Oliver Cromwell*, p. 18.
35. Edward Hyde, Earl of Clarendon, *The History of the Rebellion and Civil Wars in England*, ed. W. D. Macray (6 vols, Oxford, 1888), V, p. 287.
36. Knoppers, I think, exaggerates the differences between the investiture and royal ceremony, L. Knoppers, *Constructing Cromwell: Ceremony, Portrait and Print, 1645–1661* (Cambridge, 2000), pp. 76–8.
37. W. C. Abbott ed., *The Writings and Speeches of Oliver Cromwell* (4 vols, Cambridge, Mass., 1937–47), III, p. 456.
38. Above, ch. 14, pp. 446–8.
39. *The Whole Manner of the Treaty, with the Several Speches that Passed in the Banqueting-House at White-hall, Between His Highness the Lord Protector, and the Lords Embassadors of the United Provinces of Holland* (E 731/14, 1654).
40. Ibid., pp. 3–5.
41. Ibid., p. 4.
42. Ibid., pp. 5–6.
43. *Severall Proceedings*, 23–30 March 1654 (E 227/3, 1654), pp. 3729, 3731.
44. Ibid., p. 3737.
45. Ibid.; Sherwood, *Oliver Cromwell*, p. 23.
46. *Unparalleld Monarch*, p. 93.
47. *Severall Proceedings*, 31 August–7 September 1654 (E 233/22, 1654), p. 4085.
48. Ibid., p. 4089.
49. Ibid.; *Mercurius Politicus*, 31 August–7 September 1654 (E 809/24, 1654), p. 3743.
50. Sherwood, *Oliver Cromwell*, p. 30; *Enthusiasm Display'd* (1743), p. 21.
51. Sir William Davenant, *The First Days Entertainment at Rutland-House, by Declamations and Musick: After the Manner of the Ancients* (E 1648/2, 1656); J. Clare, *Drama of the English Republic, 1649–1660* (Manchester, 2002), pp. 181–91.
52. Edmund Gayton, *Charity Triumphant, or, The Virgin-Shew Exhibited on the 29th of October, 1655, Being the Lord Mayor Day* (Wing G 407, 1656).
53. John Bulteel, *Londons Triumph: or, The Solemn and Magnificent Reception of that Honourable Gentleman, Robert Tichborn, Lord Major After His Return from Taking His Oath at Westminster, the Morrow After Simon and Jude Day, Being October 29. 1656* (E 892/7, 1656).
54. Ibid., pp. 8–9.
55. Ibid., pp. 11–15.
56. *Mercurius Politicus*, 25 June–2 July 1657 (E 505/1, 1657), p. 7883; J. Prestwich, *Prestwich's Respublica; Or a Display of the Honors, Ceremonies & Ensigns of the Common-Wealth, Under the Protectorship of Oliver Cromwell* (1743), pp. 2–85 passim.
57. Prestwich, *Prestwich's Respublica*, p. 3; Sherwood, *Oliver Cromwell*, p. 96.
58. Prestwich, *Prestwich's Respublica*, p. 3.
59. Ibid., pp. 4–7.
60. Ibid., pp. 16–18
61. Ibid., pp. 18–19; *Mercurius Politicus*, p. 7883.
62. *Mercurius Politicus*, p. 7884; Prestwich, *Prestwich's Respublica*, p. 19.
63. Carrington, *History of the Life and Death of … Oliver Late Lord Protector* (Wing C643, 1659), p. 203; Prestwich, *Prestwich's Respublica*, p. 17.
64. Clarendon, *History of the Rebellion*, VI, p. 32.
65. Knoppers, *Constructing Cromwell*, p. 123.
66. Ibid., p. 124.
67. Prestwich, *Prestwich's Respublica*, p. 16.
68. Huntington Library, Richard Bull Granger, Vol. X, 32, 38, XI, 89; Sherwood, *Oliver Cromwell*, pp. 54, 108, 127, 133; National Portrait Gallery NPG 952, 4350, D21358, D21362.
69. Sherwood, *Oliver Cromwell*, p. 104.
70. *Mercurius Politicus*, 5–12 November 1657 (E 747/4, 1657), p. 96; Sherwood, *Oliver Cromwell*, pp. 112–14.
71. *Mercurius Politicus*, 5–12 November 1657 (E 747/8, 1657), p. 117; for a full account, see Sherwood, *Oliver Cromwell*, pp. 115–17.

72. Prestwich, *Prestwich's Respublica*, pp. 204–5; *A True Catalogue, or, An Account of the Several Places and Most Eminent Persons in the Three Nations, and Elsewhere, Where, and by Whom Richard Cromwell Was Proclaimed Lord Protector of the Commonwealth of England, Scotland, and Ireland* (Wing T 2593, 1659), pp. 15–16.

73. *A True Catalogue*, pp. 16–17.

74. *Cal. Stat. Pap. Venet. XXXI, 1657–9*, no. 217, p. 243.

75. *Mercurius Politicus*, 16–23 September 1658 (E 756/19), p. 875; 14–21 October 1658 (E 760/6, 1658), pp. 927–8; Sherwood, *Oliver Cromwell*, pp. 145–6. Sherwood mistakenly refers to *Mercurius Politicus* for 18–25 November.

76. E 760/6, p. 927.

77. K. Pearson and G. M. Morant, *The Portraiture of Oliver Cromwell with Special Reference to the Wilkinson Head* (1935), p. 33.

78. E 760/6, pp. 927–8; *The True Manner of the Most Magnificent Conveyance of His Highnesse Effigies from Sommerset-House to Westminster on Tuesday November 23, 1658* (E 1866/2, 1658), pp. 1–10.

79. Ibid., p. 928.

80. *Enthusiasm Display'd*, p. 28; *The True Manner*, pp. 11–12.

81. *The True Manner*, p. 12; H. D., *The Pourtraiture of His Royal Highness, Oliver Late Lord Protector &c. in His Life and Death With a Short View of His Government, as Also a Description of His Standing and Lying in State at Sommerset-House, and the Manner of His Funeral Solemnity on Tuesday November 23* (Wing D448A); *Mercurius Politicus*, 18–25 November 1658 (E 760/16, 1658), pp. 30–2; Carrington, *History of the Life and Death of … Oliver Late Lord Protector*, p. 235. Prestwich observed that 'his purple velvet was changed for a crown', *Prestwich's Respublica*, p. 175.

82. The funeral was twice postponed, see *Cal. Stat. Pap. Dom. 1658–9*, p. 152; Pearson and Morant, *Portraiture of Oliver Cromwell*, p. 35.

83. E 760/16, pp. 30–2.

84. I owe this last information to the kindness of Malcolm Smuts.

85. E 760/16 pp. 31–2.

86. Henry Fletcher, *The Perfect Politician: Or, A Full View of the Life and Actions (Military and Civil) of O. Cromwel* (E 1869/1, 1660), p. 346.

87. Carrington, *History of the Life and Death of … Oliver Late Lord Protector*, p. 204.

88. Prestwich, *Prestwich's Respublica*, pp. 193–8; Sherwood, *Oliver Cromwell*, p. 164.

89. C. H. Firth ed., *The Memoirs of Edmund Ludlow, Lieutenant-General of the Horse in the Army of the Commonwealth of England, 1625–1672* (2 vols, Oxford, 1894), II, pp. 47–8.

90. *A Further Narrative of the Passages of These Times in the Common-wealth of England* (Wing F 2560A, 1658), p. 33.

91. Abbott, *Writings and Speeches*, III, p. 470; N. L. Matthews, *William Sheppard, Cromwell's Law Reformer* (Cambridge, 1985), ch. 3.

92. *The Tryal of Col. Ashburnham, (Prisoner in the Tower of London) Before His Highness the Lord Protectors Council at White-hall* (E 738/17, 1654).

93. *The Triall of Mr. John Gerhard, Mr. Peter Vowell, and Sommerset Fox, by the High Court of Justice Sitting in Westminster Hall on Friday 30 June, 1654. With Their Charge, and a Declaration of the Particulars of the Whole Plot to Have Murthered His Highnesse the Lord Protector* (E 231/4, 1654), p. 1.

94. Ibid., p. 12.

95. Ibid.; C. H. Firth and R. S. Rait, *Acts and Ordinances of the Interregnum, 1642–1660* (3 vols, London, 1911), II, pp. 831–5.

96. *The Tryal and Sentence of Death … Pronounced Against Mr. Mack an Apothecary of Salisbury, Mr. John Thorp an Inn-Keeper of the Same Town, Mr. Kensey a Chyrurgeon of Newbery, and Mr. Dean, and Mr Lakes of Hungerfo[r]d. Upon a Charge of High Treason, for Conspiring Together, to Take Up Arms, and Raise New Forces for the King of Scots* (E 833/3, 1655), p. 8.

97. *The Triall of the Honourable Colonel Iohn Penruddock of Compton in Wiltshire, and His Speech* (E 845/7, 1655), p. 5 and *passim*.

98. Ibid., p. 5.

99. Ibid., p. 6.

100. Ibid., p. 11.

101. Ibid.

102. Ibid., p. 15.

103. *The True Speeches of Collonel John Penruddock, and Hugh Grove Delivered on the Scaffold at Exeter Castle, May the 17th, 1655* (P 1431A, 1655).

104. Ibid., p. 18, scaffold speech of Grove.

105. W. Prynne, *A New Discovery of Free-State Tyranny: Containing Four Letters, Together with a Subsequent Remonstrance of Several Grievances and Demand of Common Right* (E 488/2, 1655), sig. B2ᵛ.

106. *The Triall of the Honourable Colonel Iohn Penruddock*, p. 1 indicates that the account was Penruddock's own. Nedham dedicated to Cromwell *The Great Accuser Cast Down; Or, A Publick Trial of Mr. John Goodwin of Coleman-street, London, at the Bar of Religion & Right Reason* (E 920/1, 1657), sigs A2–A4.
107. *The Whole Business of Sindercome, From First to Last* (E 903/7, 1657), p. 9.
108. Ibid., pp. 8, 14.
109. Hewitt, *ODNB*; Slingsby, *ODNB*.
110. *The Horrible and Bloody Conspiracy Undertaken by Many Desperate Persons Who Cry Up and Introduce the Interests of Charles Stewart* (E 1881/1, 1658).
111. *The Speech and Deportment of John Hewit, D. D., Late of St. Gregories London at the Place of Execution on Tower Hill, June 8, 1658 Taken By an Impartial Hand; and the Substance of His Triall Before the High Court of Justice, His Letter to Dr. Wilde After Sentence, His Discourses and Demeanor on the Scaffold; With an Elegie on the Said Dr.; Published for the Satisfaction of His Friends* (Wing H 1638, 1658).
112. Ibid., pp. 4, 9 and *passim*; *The Tryals of Sir Henry Slingsby Kt. and John Hewet D. D. for High Treason, in Westminster-Hall* (E 753/5, 1658), pp. 9–10.
113. Ibid., p. 11.
114. Ibid., pp. 16–17.
115. Ibid., p. 20; *Speech and Deportment of John Hewit*, pp. 8–9.
116. *The Proceeds of the Protector (so called) and His Councill Against Sir Henry Vane, Knight* (E 937/2, 1656); Vane, *A Healing Question Propounded and Resolved* (E 879/5, 1656).
117. *Proceeds of the Protector*, pp. 7, 9.

19 Contesting and Commemorating Cromwell

1. Richard Flecknoe, *The Idea of His Highness Oliver, Late Lord Protector, &c. With Certain Brief Reflexions on His Life* (Wing F1226, 1659), sig. B1ᵛ.
2. *A Declaration Concerning the Government of the Three Nations* (E 725/2, 1653), p. 6.
3. Samuel Richardson, *An Apology for the Present Government, and Governour* (E 812/18, 1654), p. 10.
4. *The Character of a Protector* (E 743/2, 1654), a broadside.
5. John Moore, *Protection Proclaimed . . . to the Three Nations of England, Scotland, and Ireland: Wherein the Government Established, in the Lord Protector and His Council, is Proved to Be of Divine Institution; and the Great Stumbling-Block of Thousands of Christians (in Regard of His Title) Removed* (E 860/5, 1654).
6. *A Declaration of the Members of Parliament, Lately Dissolved by Oliver Cromwell* (Thomason 669 f. 19/67, 1654).
7. *A Declaration to the Free-Born People of England Now in Arms Against the Tyrannie and Oppression of Oliver Cromwell esq.* (Thomason 669 f. 19/70, 1654).
8. *The Unparalleld Monarch. Or, The Portraiture of a Matchless Prince, Exprest in Some Shadows of His Highness My Lord Protector* (E 1675/1, 1656), sigs A5ᵛ–A6, p. 37.
9. M.H., *The Right of Dominion, and Property of Liberty, Whether Natural, Civil, or Religious* (E 1636/1, 1656), pp. 53, 70, 93, 96, 106, 150 and *passim*.
10. I.S., *The Picture of a New Courtier Drawn in Conference, Between Mr. Timeserver, and Mr. Plain-heart* (E.875/6, 1656), p. 4; above, p. 513.
11. *The Excellencie of a Free-State: Or, The Right Constitution of a Common-Wealth* (E 1676/1, 1656), p. 49.
12. *To All the Worthy Gentlemen Who Are Duely Chosen for the Parliament, Which Intended to Meet at Westminster the 17 of September 1656. And to All the Good People of the Common-wealth of England* (E 898/8, 1656), no pagination.
13. *An Appeale from the Court to the Country. Made by a Member of Parliament Lawfully Chosen, But Secluded Illegally by My L. Protector* (E 891/3, 1656), pp. 2–4.
14. *English Liberty and Property Asserted in Pursuance of the Statute Laws of This Common-Wealth. Discovering Israels Sin in Chusing a King, By Several Questions Humbly Propounded to the Grave Senators at Westminster* (E 905/2, 1657), p. 6; cf. *To the Parliament of the Commonwealth of England* (E 905/3, 1657).
15. *A Narrative of the Late Parliament, (so called) Their Election and Appearing, the Seclusion of a Great Part of Them* (E 935/5, 1657), pp. 5, 8–9, 16, 28 and *passim*.
16. *Comparatio Inter Claudium Tiberium Principem, et Olivarium Cromwellium Protectorem* (1657, Huntington Library, 426690), pp. 5–9, 26–8. I have not found this work in Wing.
17. *A Copie of Quaeries, Or A Comment Upon the Life, and Actions of the Grand Tyrant and His Complices; Oliver the First and Last of That Name, Not Unfit, Nor Unworthy of Thy Perusall* (E 988/10, 1659), pp. 4, 8 and *passim*.

NOTES to pp. 528–31   **641**

18. George Wither, *Salt Upon Salt: Made Out of Certain Ingenious Verses Upon the Late Storm and the Death of His Highness Ensuing* (E 1827/2, 1658), p. 30.

19. M. Nedham, *The Case of the Common-Wealth of England, Stated: Or, The Equity, Utility, and Necessity, of a Submission to the Present Government; Cleared Out of Monuments Both Sacred and Civill, Against All the Scruples and Pretences of the Opposite Parties* (E 600/7, 1650), pp. 82–3.

20. R. Baker, *A Chronicle of Kings of England from the Time of the Romans Government Unto the Reign of King Charles Containing All Passages of State and Church, With All Other Observations Proper for a Chronicle* (Wing B 503A, 1653); A. Evans, *The Bloudy Vision of John Farly, Interpreted by Arise Evans* (E 1498/1, 1653); *Strange and Wonderful Newes from White-Hall: Or, The Mighty Visions Proceeding From Mistris Anna Trapnel* (E 224/3, 1654); W. Lilly, *Monarchy or No Monarchy in England. Grebner His Prophecy Concerning Charles Son of Charles, His Greatness, Victories, Conquests* (Wing L 2228 A, 1655); *Cabala, Mysteries of State, in Letters of the Great Ministers of K. James and K. Charles* (E 221/3, 1653; C183, 1654); *The Full Proceedings of the High Court of Iustice Against King Charles* (Wing F 2353, 1654, F2353, 1655); *The Reign of King Charles an History Faithfully and Impartially Delivered and Disposed into Annals* (L 1189, 1655); *Verses in Praise of Charles* (Thomason 669 f. 17/4, 1653); *Stipendariae Lacrymae, Or, A Tribute of Teares. Paid Upon the Sacred Herse of the Most Gracious and Heroick Prince, Charles I Late King of Great Brittaine, France, and Ireland, Murdered at Westminster, By His Own (regicide) Subjects, on Jan. 30. 1648* (E 745/23, ? The Hague, 1654).

21. P. Heylyn, *Observations on the Historie of The Reign of King Charles* (Wing H 1727, 1656).

22. R. Perrinchief, *Nuntius a Mortuis: Or, a Messenger from the Dead. That Is, a Stupendous and Dreadfull Colloquie, Distinctly and Alternately Heard by Divers, Betwixt the Ghosts of Henry the Eight, and Charles the First* (Wing P 1599A, 1657).

23. John Wilson, *Psalterium Carolinum. The Devotions of His Sacred Majestie in His Solitudes and Sufferings, Rendred in Verse* (E 1076, 1657).

24. *Reliquiae Sacrae Carolinae. Or the Works of That Great Monarch and Glorious Martyr King Charles the I* (Wing C 2074, 1657).

25. P. Heylyn, *A Short View of the Life and Reign of King Charles* (Wing H 1735A, 1658), p. 161.

26. W. Sanderson, *A Compleat History of the Life and Raigne of King Charles from His Cradle to His Grave Collected and Written by William Sanderson, Esq* (Wing S 646, 1658), p. 1149.

27. Heylyn, *Short View of the Life*, p. 162.

28. Thomas Forde, *Virtus Rediviva A Panegyrick On Our Late King Charles the I. &c. of Ever Blessed Memory* (E 1806/1, 1660), sig. C5ᵛ.

29. Lambert Wood, *The Life and Raigne of King Charles, from His Birth to His Death. Faithfully and Impartially Performed by Lambert Wood Gent* (E 1760/2, 1659); *The Faithful, Yet Imperfect, Character of a Glorious King, King Charles I, His Country's & Religions Martyr* (E 1799/1, 1660).

30. *The Faithful, Yet Imperfect, Character*, pp. 4, 23.

31. *An Elegy, Consecrated to the Inestimable Memory of Our Late Most Famous Monarch, Charles the First* (669 f. 24/68, 1660); *Bibliotheca Regia, Or, The Royall Library* (E 1718/1, 1659).

32. There are engraved portraits of Charles I in Wood's *Life and Raigne* and *The Faithful, Yet Imperfect, Character*.

33. The frontispiece engraving is explicated by verses defending divine right. The scriptural reference is to 1 Chronicles 29: 23.

34. Nedham, *Case of the Common-wealth*, pp. 47–8.

35. *The Nuptialls of Peleus and Thetis. Consisting of a Mask and a Comedy, or The Great Royall Ball, Acted Lately in Paris Six Times by the King in Person* (E 228/3, 1654); *An Anniversary Ode, Upon the Kings Birth day. May 29. Written for This Yeare 1654* (E 745/24, Hague, 1654); *A Letter Sent from the King att Collen to His Brother Henry Duke of Gloucester att Paris. Novemb: 10 1654* (E 816/11, 1654).

36. Walter Gostelo, *Charls Stuart and Oliver Cromwel United, Or, Glad Tidings of Peace to All Christendom, to the Jews and Heathen* (E 1503/3, 1655). On the Royalist prophet Gostelo, see ODNB.

37. George Wither, *A Suddain Flash Timely Discovering, Some Reasons Wherefore, the Stile of Protector, Should Not Be Deserted by These Nations* (E 1584/3, 1657), p. 11.

38. See, for example, *A Discovery Made by His Highnesse the Lord Protector, to the Lord Mayor, Aldermen, and Common-Councell of the City of London, on Friday, March the 12. 1657. Concerning the New Attempts and Designs of Charles Stewart and His Party, Both at Home and Abroad, to Imbroile This Nation Againe in a New War* (E 1644/2, 1658).

39. *Certamen Brittanicum, Gallico Hispanicum, A True Relation of a Conference Holden Between Charles Stuart King of Scots, Don Lewis de Haro, and the Cardinall Mazarine . . . Wherein Is Touched Something of the Interests of the Said States One to the Other, and of Both in Relation to the Said King of Scots. As Also How Much It Hath Been Endeavoured to Make Him Turn Catholike,*

With His Constant Resolution to Live and Dye in the True Protestant Religion (E 1005, 1659); *A Character of His Most Sacred Majesty King Charles the IId* (E 1836/3, 1660).

40. *Character*, p. 34.
41. R. Hutton, *The Restoration: A Political and Religious History of England and Wales, 1658–1667* (Oxford, 1985), p. 18. I would like to express my thanks to (as well as admiration of) Ronald Hutton for all the helpful discussions we have had over twenty-five years and for his friendship.
42. *A Brief Relation Containing an Abreviation of the Arguments Urged by the Late Protector Against the Government of This Nation by a King or a Single Person* (E 965/4, 1659), p. 7.
43. *A True Catalogue, Or, An Account of the Several Places and Most Eminent Persons in the Three Nations, and Elsewhere, Where, and by Whom Richard Cromwell was Proclaimed Lord Protector of the Commonwealth of England, Scotland, and Ireland* (E 999/12, 1659).
44. Ibid., pp. 33, 35.
45. Ibid., p. 53; cf. sigs A2–3.
46. Ibid., p. 31.
47. Ibid., p. 35.
48. *An Invocation to the Officers of the Army, for Preventing Their Own, and the Ruine of the Good Old Cause At the Very Door of Destruction* (E 979/1, 1659); *To the Right Honourable the Ld. Fleetwood, to Be Communicated to the Officers of the Army, the Humble Representation of Divers Well-Affected Persons of the City of Westminster and Parts Adjacent* (E 979/5, 1659); *To His Excellency the Lord Fleetwood, and the General Council of Officers of the Armies of England, Scotland, and Ireland. The Humble Address of the Inferiour Officers and Souldiers of the Late Lord Pride's regiment* (E 974/5, 1659).
49. *XXV Queries: Modestly and Humbly, And Yet Sadly and Seriously Propounded, to the People of England, and Their Representatives: and Likewise to the Army in This Juncture of Affairs* (E 968/5, 1660), pp. 5, 8, 13 and *passim*; *Margery Good-Cow* (E 984/9, 1659), p. 1.
50. See, for example, William Prynne, *The Re-publicans and Others Spurious Good Old Cause, Briefly and Truly Anatomized* (E 983/6, 1659).
51. *A Seasonable Advertisement to the People of England. Whether a Monarchy, or Free State, Be Better; in This Juncture of Time* (E 988/30, 1659), pp. 6–7.
52. Ibid., p. 7.
53. *Loyal Queries, Humbly Tendred to the Serious Consideration of the Parliament, and Army, by a Peaceable-Minded Man, and a True Lover of His Country* (E 986/15, 1659), p. 7.
54. See, for instance, *Three Propositions from the Case of Our Three Nations: viz. I. That Monarchie, or Regal Government by One Person, Is the Best Way of Government* (E 985/17, 1659).
55. *Vox Verè Anglorum: Or Englands Loud Cry for Their King. Written by a Hearty Well-Willer to the Common-weale, and the Flourishing of Our Nations* (E 763/3, 1659), p. 6.
56. *A Dialogue Betwixt the Ghosts of Charls the I, Late King of England: and Oliver the Late Usurping Protector* (E 985/24, 1659), p. 7; cf. A. Wood, *A New Conference Between the Ghosts of King Charles and Oliver Cromwell. Faithfully Communicated by Adam Wood* (E 988/28, 1659). For earlier examples of the ghost pamphlet as an opposition genre, see Thomas Scott, *Robert Earle of Essex His Ghost, Sent from Elizian to the Nobility, Gentry, and Communaltie of England* (STC 22084, 1624); Scott, *Sir Walter Rawleighs Ghost, or Englands Forewarner Discouering a Secret Consultation, Newly Holden in the Court of Spaine* (STC 22085, 1626); *The Deputies Ghost, or, An Apparition to the Lord of Canterbury in the Tower* (STC D1084, 1641).
57. *The Court Career Death Shaddow'd to Life. Or Shadowes of Life and Death. A Pasquil Dialogue Seriously Perused and Highly Approved by the Clearest Judgments* (E 989/26, 1659), p. 4.
58. It is not known whether the Protector was behind the pamphlet *A Brief Relation Containing an Abreviation of the Arguments Urged by the Late Protector Against the Government of This Nation by a King or a Single Person. To Convince Men of the Danger and Inconveniency Thereof* (E 965/4, 1659).
59. It was said to last only fifteen minutes, Richard Cromwell, *ODNB*.
60. *The Speech of His Highness the Lord Protector, Made to Both Houses of Parliament at Their First Meeting, on Thursday the 27th of January* (E 968/1, 1659), p. 3.
61. Ibid., p. 9.
62. *His Late Highness's Letter to the Parliament of England. Shewing His Willingness to Submit to This Present Government* (Wing C7185, 1659).
63. *ODNB*.
64. See *Fourty Four Queries to the Life of Queen Dick* (E 986/18, 1659).
65. *Three Poems Upon the Death of His Late Highnesse Oliver Lord Protector of England* (Wing W 526, 1659), p. 4.
66. Ibid., p. 5
67. Ibid., pp. 8, 21; *Musarum Cantabrigiensium Luctus & Gratulatio Ille in Funere Oliveri Angliae, Scotiae, & Hiberniae Protectoris* (Wing C345, 1658), ff. 1, 3, 4, 4ᵛ, sigs A1ᵛ, A3ᵛ, C2ᵛ, C3, G4ᵛ, H1, H3.

68. George Lawrence, *Peplum Olivarii, or A Good Prince Bewailed by a Good People* (E 959/4, 1658), pp. 12, 33 and *passim*; H. D., *Historie & Policie Re-viewed, in the Heroick Transactions of His Most Serene Highnesse, Oliver, Late Lord Protector* (E 1799/2, 1659) title page; *An Account of the Last Houres of the Late Renowned Oliver Lord Protector* (Wing W 367A, 1659), p. 1.

69. *A Copie of Quaeries, Or A Comment Upon the Life, and Actions of the Grand Tyrant and His Complices*; Robert Pittilloh, *The Hammer of Persecution: Or, The Mystery of Iniquity, in the Persecution of Many Good People in Scotland, Under the Government of Oliver Late Lord Protector* (E 993/4, 1659). See also L. Knoppers, *Constructing Cromwell: Ceremony, Portrait and Print 1645-1661* (Cambridge, 2000), pp. 158-66.

70. See the excellent article by Mark Jenner, 'The Roasting of the Rump: Scatology and the Body Politic in Restoration England', *Past & Present*, 177 (2002), pp. 84-120; Knoppers, *Constructing Cromwell*, p. 176.

71. Knoppers, *Constructing Cromwell*, p. 191.

72. Ibid., pp. 186-7.

73. See R. Howell, ' "That Imp of Satan": The Restoration Image of Cromwell', in R. C. Richardson ed., *Images of Oliver Cromwell* (Manchester, 1993), ch. 2. On Cromwell's historical reputation, see also Blair Worden, *Roundhead Reputations: The English Civil Wars and the Passions of Posterity* (London, 2001), ch. 8, pp. 215-42.

74. W. A. Speck, 'Cromwell and the Glorious Revolution', Richardson, *Images of Oliver Cromwell*, ch. 3, pp. 56-8; ibid., ch. 4, p. 70.

75. Ibid., p. 90; see also B. Worden, 'Thomas Carlyle and Oliver Cromwell', *Proceedings of the British Academy*, 105 (2000), pp. 131-70; Worden, *Roundhead Reputations*, pp. 264-95.

76. Nicola Smith, *The Royal Image and the English People* (Aldershot, 2001), p. 189. See also, Worden, *Roundhead Reputations*, pp. 296-315.

77. Ibid., p. 192.

78. R. C. Richardson, 'Cromwell and the Inter-war European Dictators', in Richardson, *Images of Cromwell*, ch. 7.; Cromwell, *ODNB*; Carlyle's Cromwell was one of the ten bestsellers of the Victorian era (http://www.lib.cam.ac.uk/Exhibitions/Cromwell/ cromwell.htm).

79. http://www.lib.cam.ac.uk/exhibitions/Cromwell/assoc.htm

80. http://news.bbc.co.uk/1/hi/entertainment/tv_and_radio/2341661.stm; (cf. Wikipedia 100 Greatest Britons); http://news.bbc.co.uk/1/hi/uk/326121.stm

81. John Morrill, 'Cromwell', *ODNB*. Several of Cromwell's fellow generals await a first historical biography.

82. Oliver Cromwell, Wikipedia.The apartments are 418, S. Normandie Ave, LA.

83. J. C. Davis, *Oliver Cromwell* (2001), p. 1.

84. BBC 'Oliver Cromwell: Hero or Villain?', http://news.bbc.co.uk/1/hi/uk/326121.stm

85. HistoricalAssociation http://www.hamessageboards.org.uk/noticeboard/index.php?s=973b8a133e 00a779677981a26bed3874&showtopic=3; Davis, *Cromwell*, p. 196.

86. Ames Short, *God Save the King: or, A Sermon Preach'd at Lyme-Regis May 18. 1660. At the Solemn Proclamation of His Most Excellent Majesty* (E 1919/2, 1660), sig. A4.

87. *Three Propositions from the Case of Our Three Nations*, p. 4.

88. *Englands Faiths Defender Vindicated: Or, A Word to Clear a Most Foul, Damnable and Scandalous Aspersion, Which Hath Been Cast Upon That Patient and Suffering Prince, Charles II* (E 1017/17, 1660), p. 7.

89. *No King But the Old Kings Son. Or, a Vindication of Limited Monarchy, as it Was Established in this Nation, Before the Late War Between the King and Parliament* (Thomason 669 f. 24/30, 1660), broadside.

90. On the stories of Charles's escape from Worcester, see my study of representations of late seventeenth-century monarchs (forthcoming).

91. Knoppers, *Constructing Cromwell*, ch. 6.

92. *Anglia Liberata, Or, The Rights of the People of England, Maintained Against the Pretences of the Scotish King* (E 643/7, 1651), p. 28; *Reasons Why the Supreme Authority of the Three Nations (for the time) Is Not in the Parliament, but in the New-Established Councel of State* (E 697/19, 1653), p. 6.

93. Wither, *A Suddain Flash*, p. 53.

94. Flecknoe, *Idea of His Highness*, sigs A2ᵛ–A3.

95. For example, Fabian Phillips, *Veritas Inconcussa Or, a Most Certain Truth Asserted, that King Charles the First, Was No Man of Blood, But a Martyr for His People* (E 1925/2, 1660), sigs a3–a8, especially a7.

96. *A Plea for Limited Monarchy, as It Was Established in This Nation, Before the Late War* (E 765/3, 1660), p. 5.

97. David Lloyd, *Eikon Basilike Or, The True Pourtraicture of His Sacred Majesty Charls the II in Three Books* (E 1922/2, 1660), p. 3.

Conclusion

1. K. Sharpe, ' "An Image Doting Rabble": The Failure of Republican Culture in Seventeenth-Century England', in K. Sharpe and S. N. Zwicker eds, *Refiguring Revolutions: Aesthetics and Politics from the English Revolution to the Romantic Revolution* (Berkeley, 1998), pp. 25–56, 302–11.
2. Ibid.
3. Cf. Sharpe and Zwicker, *Refiguring Revolutions*, introduction, pp. 1–21.

INDEX

Page numbers in italics refer to illustrations. Where two sequences of notes occur on one page, notes are distinguished in the index by the addition of a or b.